KT-379-814

FACT OR FANTASY

Compelling Collection of Awe-inspiring Tales

CAXTON

Material in this book previously appeared in the partwork
The Unexplained

This edition specially produced for CEEPI Ltd/Dealerfield Ltd
in 1990

ISBN 0 907 305 44 X

Consultants to *The Unexplained*
Professor A. J. Ellison
Dr J. Allen Hynek
Brian Inglis
Colin Wilson

Printed and bound in Hungary by Novotrade Co Ltd—Egyetemi Press

Contents

PART 1

THE ALIEN WORLD

THE ALIEN WORLD

Contents

Introduction

IT IS A CURIOSITY of the history of unidentified flying objects that most writers on the subject state that the phenomenon started in 1947, with Kenneth Arnold's legendary sighting of a number of airborn discs while he was flying across the state of Washington. In fact, UFOs have disturbed or astonished the world's populace for hundreds, if not thousands, of years. What really started in 1947 was the systematic *study* of the phenomenon – and for one very good reason which we will return to later.

Today, attitudes to UFOs are much more complex than the belief – or hope or fear – that little green men are skimming about our skies in solid, 'nuts-and-bolts' machines. In Britain and in the United States a loose movement of researchers has come together under headings such as 'the new ufology', and, roughly speaking, they are suggesting that the phenomenon is indeed paranormal – inexplicable by normal logic – but that it is essentially Earthbound, possibly even the product of the human mind in some way. The new ufology occupies the middle ground between the nuts-and-bolts school who believe in the extra-terrestrial hypothesis (ETH) and those who suggest that the UFO experience is only another form of delusion, a sophisticated form of hallucination.

Even that is a simplification however, for there are ufologists who fully believe in the nuts-and-bolts interpretation, yet who refuse to believe the extra-terrestrial hypothesis and speak darkly of government conspiracies and secret military hardware. At the other end of this scale are those who are perfectly prepared to agree that the UFO experience – especially the kind that includes apparent contact with aliens – is 'all in the mind': but, they say, someone or something *out there* is feeding this information to selected individuals for purposes that we can only guess at.

A variety of such interpretations of the UFO data is presented here. What perhaps needs to be said, given the differing analyses existing, is that in fact one person's UFO experience may be entirely different from another's – one person may report a sighting of a nuts-and-bolts craft that doesn't conform to 'normal' specifications on the same night and at the same hour that another has an inexplicable hallucination of being taken aboard an enormous UFO and meeting tall, benign blond strangers. Both these people have become 'UFO cases'. Both have undergone experiences that were completely real to them at the time, but each has been through something completely different from the other. The questions that remain are: Do their different experiences have anything in common? and: What do these experiences mean – if anything?

What is perhaps the next most obvious question to ask is why anyone should assume that extra-terrestrials are involved in the first place. Among ufologists there are a number of astronomers, and almost all of them are mildly embarrassed by the extra-terrestrial hypothesis. After all, they reason, the conditions under which life is likely to arise elsewhere are very narrow. They involve the formation of a star that will be curiously like our own Sun – one that will be neither too large and bright (and so burn itself out quickly) nor too small and weak (and so be too feeble to warm its planets to the proper temperature). Stars of the right size will last the appropriate length of time, but they may be part of a planetless double-sun system as opposed to a star-and-planets arrangement. Always supposing that these conditions are met, primitive life has to have time to evolve in to *intelligent* life. It then has to undergo a transformation no less radical than our own Renaissance in order to acquire the necessary desires, riches and technological means to reach out to other stars, other peoples.

The odds against this happening are, it will surely be obvious, enormous. It is even less likely that such a civilisation will have developed to this state at a time when their technology and awareness matches or surpasses our own – even supposing that they had the resources to mount such expeditions in the first place. After all, it is within the technical capability of Earth to explore space, even to communicate with possible other races by radio, but by and large we choose to spend our money on other projects. Anyone 'out there' who chances to come across the remains of our deep-space probes will not do so for hundreds or even thousands of years and, unless they have solved the problem of beating the time barrier, any reply they may send could similarly take centuries to reach us.

Put these rather bald and grim facts against the sheer variety of seemingly alien contacts that people have had on Earth, and we are clearly in difficulties at once; the idea that vast numbers of different civilisations are (more or less quietly) getting in touch with us simply doesn't stand up to common sense. A single civilisation may have done so by a massively remote chance; perhaps they have been keeping an eye on us for thousands of years before trying to announce their presence. But 'contactees' tell such different stories, describe such different entities and offer so many conflicting opinions that one rapidly finds the whole proposition untenable, or at least highly unlikely – since the possibility remains that somewhere in this mass of data and experience there is a kernel of truth, could we but discern it.

Still, *why* should people want to believe that aliens are out there watching us? The answer may lie in the fact that the flying saucers seen by Kenneth Arnold caught public attention just as governments were seriously thinking about space exploration for the first time. But that was also a time when the cold war was at its height, only just after the most appalling destruction had been let loose in the shape of the atomic bomb, and when a large number of people suddenly felt deeply insecure about their own futures and the future of humanity. It was comforting to many to believe that another race, either by example or by positive guidance, might solve the perennial and very frightening problems that humanity had made for itself. Perhaps it is no accident that much of what is supposed to be alien philosophy concerns itself with living in peace and brotherhood.

One more point leads us to suspect the validity of the case for the ETH, and that is the way in which so-called alien technology is never more than a step in front of our own. This suggests that a purely human imagination is at work, elaborating on facts that have already become common knowledge. (The counter, and perfectly logical, argument is that the space people, being excellent anthropologists, do not want to upset us by pushing us too far, and carefully refrain from introducing us to ideas or achievements that are not already familiar to us.)

However unassailable the logic is, however, the evidence for the ETH is not very convincing. One of the most grandiose claims for contact with space beings has been that put forward by the Swiss farmer Billy Meier, who supplied not only large numbers of very elegant photographs of the craft they arrived in, but thousands of pages of communications. Unfortunately the photographs included very few of the space people themselves, and those that did surface were of ladies strangely reminiscent of Herr Meier's girlfriends. Not only that, but the pictures of the 'spaceships' involved do not stand up to rigorous analysis, despite the vehement claims of the photographer's supporters. No less problematic is the famous French case from Cergy-Pontoise, which made the front page of no less a paper than the London *Times* when the story first broke. On close inspection, large holes appear in the tale that are none too credibly papered over by the embarrassed mutterings of those concerned.

Even so, there is clear evidence that people have experienced something very strange indeed – and not only in our own time. The 'scareship invasion' of monstrous airships over the British isles just before the First World War is a case in point. And it is made scarcely less interesting by the fact that a similar wave of sightings was made in the United States – particularly in the wide-open spaces of the prairie states such as Nebraska and Iowa – during 1896 and 1897. The American sightings are fascinating because they illustrate the point about 'alien' technology being only a step ahead of *existing* knowledge – since the airship at that time was a very new and crude vehicle. The British, on the other hand, were well aware of German developments in airship design by 1913 and were besides engaged in a massive arms race with their continental rivals. Was some form of mass hysteria or mass illusion at work in both the United States and Britain at the time? And if so, what would have caused such a psychological phenomenon in America? Or was some more bizarre form of paranormal manifestation going on – some type of mass precognition?

We are now edging into the territory of the 'new ufology'. A classic case that has caught the attention of this movement is the lights produced by Mrs Mary Jones during her part in a religious revival in rural Wales in 1905. To say 'produced' of course presumes that somehow she was in control of them, whereas there are no real grounds for supposing that they did not appear because of forces – divine or otherwise – that as much as anything were also in control of her.

The new ufology has even gone as far as to suggest that some cases of UFO sighting are a peculiar combination of psychic and material forms. This theory says that the belief in UFOs can become so strong – whatever the original stimulus may be (and it may be something as banal as an aircraft mistaken for a UFO, or as actual as a dream about UFOs) – that the thought takes on a material reality. This virtually solid 'thing' may then be witnessed by people who are quite independent of the original source. This is a mind-boggling idea, but given what we know about poltergeists and other spontaneous psychic phenomena, it may not be as far-fetched as it seems at first. Quite how it can be researched and verified however, is an altogether different matter.

Perhaps the creepiest of UFO-related experiences is the encounter with the Men in Black (or MIB) who appear to UFO witnesses after the event. Once more the interpretation will depend on the predilections of the analyst or ufologist involved, but the characteristics of these shadowy figures are unnerving, to say the least. It is precisely because they are so weird that they raise all the questions we have been asking about the true nature of the UFO phenomenon. Men in Black call on UFO witnesses and tell them to remain silent (often the witnesses don't otherwise we'd never know about MIBs). They behave like stereotype G-men out of bad B-movies, and dress in outdated clothes into the bargain. They make threats they cannot, or do not, fulfil. Yet they know things that only the witness could know. On the other hand, they don't quite look human and in some cases seem to have no idea of what is acceptable behaviour in polite society. Are they then, even if only occasionally, actual government representatives (behaving with deliberate strangeness for some reason of their own)? Are they part of some enormous hoax – or even practical joke? Are they an hallucinatory reaction to an unreal but deeply disturbing event? Or are they none, or part of these things.

It is this very range of possibilities that makes ufology so fascinating: in it, all shades of the paranormal are present.

PETER BROOKESMITH

The story of the 'Welsh triangle'

The astonishing series of events in Dyfed in 1977 drew UFO enthusiasts and investigators from all over the country. But, says HILARY EVANS, the west Wales flap was not quite what it seemed

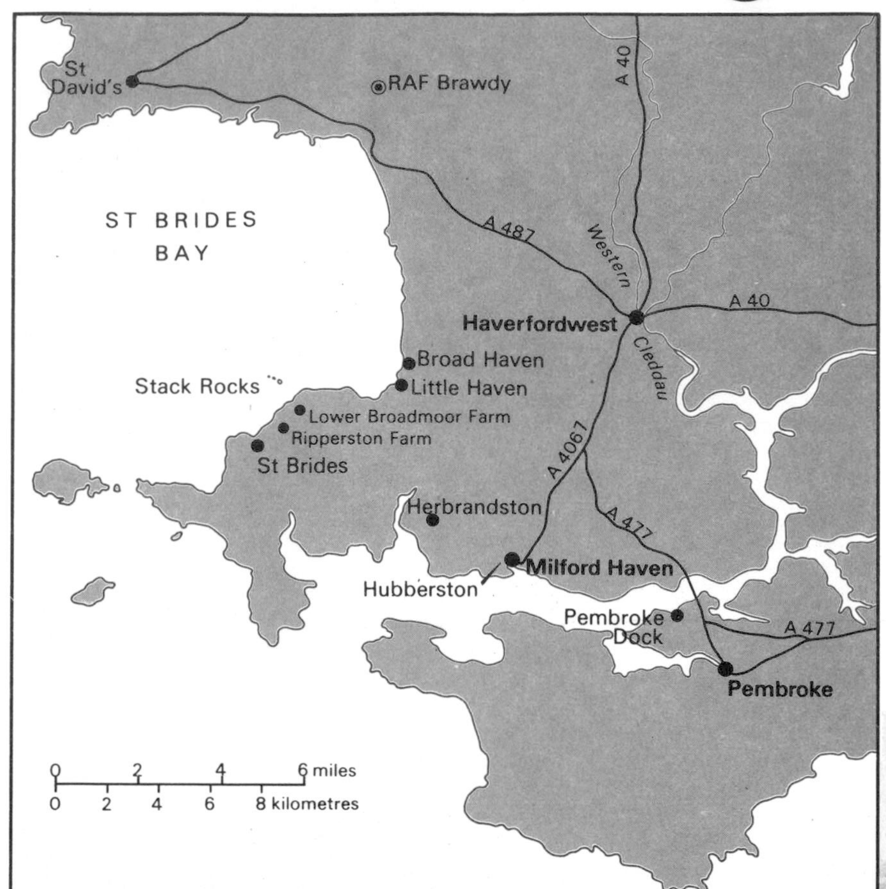

UFOS IN THE SKY and on the ground. Cars pursued by orange footballs. Glowing cigars hovering over schools. Discs flying into solid rock and vanishing between sliding doors. Silver-suited entities with no faces stalking across fields and peering through cottage windows. Mysteriously malfunctioning cars, television and radio sets. Visits from sinister aliens with psychic powers. The teleportations of entire herds of cattle. Such, if the reports are to be believed, are just some of the extraordinary events that occurred not in some far-off land but in peaceful, homely Wales, and not at some distant time but as recently as the spring of 1977.

Are these astonishing reports to be believed?

In so accessible a region, and at so recent a date, there should be no problem about ascertaining the facts. Yet already discrepancies are apparent that may never now be resolved. The local paper, the *Western Telegraph*, did an excellent job of reporting the events as they occurred, but the affair attracted wider attention. It brought into west Wales reporters from the national press and television; it lured investigators, some competent and some not; it enticed unscrupulous authors. Between them they created a confusion that is well-nigh impossible to disentangle. Accounts vary from one version to another; dates are incorrectly stated; the order of events is confused. And, as we shall see, the personal bias of some investigators, the desire of certain reporters for a 'good story' regardless of truth, the gullibility of some witnesses and the suggestibility of others – all these have combined to add distortion to confusion. Does this mean that the west Wales 'flap' doesn't deserve our attention? On the contrary, it remains a classic case – but not quite in the way it has been made out to be.

The build-up to the events of 1977 had begun before the close of the previous year. Already residents of this remote corner of Wales were reporting UFO sightings on a scale that led Randall Jones Pugh, a local British UFO Research Association investigator who was interviewed by a journalist on 13 January, to forecast: 'The country is in for a spate of such incidents.'

His prediction was confirmed on the afternoon of 4 February, when he received a telephone call from the mother of a pupil at

Left: the area of Dyfed in west Wales where a wave of UFO activity was reported over a period of several months in 1977

Below: the primary school at the village of Broad Haven in Dyfed where 15 children claimed to have seen a UFO on 4 February 1977. The object was first seen at lunchtime in a nearby field; when the children came out of school at 3.30 p.m. it seemed to have disappeared, but then it rose into the air from behind a bush. However, when the field was examined later no traces of a landing could be found

nearby Broad Haven primary school, saying that her son, along with a dozen other children, had seen a UFO that afternoon, over a period of some hours, on the ground close to the school.

Although, the Broad Haven school incidents were not the most sensational events of the west Wales flap, they were the first to alert the general public to the fact that something extraordinary was taking place in the locality. And, unlike some of the later occurrences, the facts – if not the explanations for them – are reasonably well-established.

The first sighting took place during the lunch break, when a group of boys aged between 9 and 11, who were playing football in a field beside the school, noticed an unfamiliar object in another field close by. It was apparently at ground level and was partly obscured by trees and bushes, so that they could discern only its upper portions; they could see enough, however, to feel sure that it was a UFO. Some of the boys rushed into the school with the news; others came out to see what it was. Eventually there were 15 children who saw the object.

They described it as being 'as long as a coach or maybe a bit longer'. One description

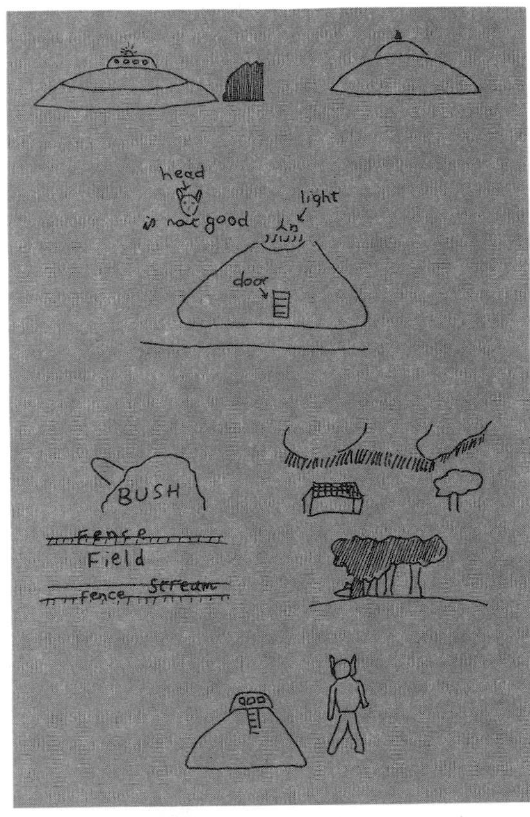

Above: some of the drawings made by Broad Haven schoolchildren to illustrate what they had seen. Many of the witnesses described a silver, cigar-shaped object with a dome on top; some reported a flashing light on the dome, and that the object seemed to be humming. Six of the children said they saw one or two beings near the UFO and described a small, silver-suited man with long, pointed ears was of two saucers stacked one against the other to make a sort of dome, with a round 'ashtray' added to make a smaller dome on top. One boy saw three or four windows around the edge, on top of the dome; others thought they saw 10 or 11. Several thought they saw a light flashing on top, and one witness claimed that it was red. One saw a door in the side, with a runway leading down from it. Some, but not all, heard a humming sound. In addition, six of the witnesses reckoned that they saw one or two entities near the object. 'We saw something come out of it. It had a helmet,' said one. A second described 'a silver man with spiked ears', while a third added, 'He wasn't a very tall person, and he didn't look very nice either.'

The children watched the object for some 20 minutes. Two of them went to tell the headmaster, but he does not seem to have been sufficiently convinced to come to see for himself, though one boy 'was nearly crying because he was scared that he was going to be disintegrated or something'.

At 2 p.m. they went back into class, to re-emerge at 3.30. Naturally, they returned to the field at once to see if their UFO was still there. At first they couldn't see it and tried to get closer, though this meant crossing a fence and a stream. But just then the UFO popped up again from behind a bush, and they all took to their heels. This time they reported, 'The cigar object seemed to be tugging an object which was silver.' Again it disappeared behind a bush.

Many of the children told their parents about the incident when they got home. Randall Jones Pugh's name was familiar in the region as that of the local UFO specialist, so it was natural that he should be the first to be contacted. At 6 p.m. he visited the site with one of the boys. By now, however, it was raining heavily, and the light was fading fast, so he returned next morning, with a reporter from the *Western Telegraph*. However, no traces of the landing were to be seen.

News of the occurrence spread rapidly, and the tiny seaside village immediately found itself the centre of intense interest. On Monday the headmaster overcame his initial scepticism and asked the witnesses to draw what they had seen. By this time the children had had plenty of opportunity to discuss the matter both among themselves and with enquirers and reporters: the consensus was that they had seen a silver, cigar-shaped object with a dome and possibly a light.

It was in much the same terms that, two weeks later, one of the teachers described a large object that she had seen on the same spot, though she glimpsed it only for four or five seconds and in pouring rain. She was about to call others when it glided away with a humming sound. Later that day two other adults, canteen workers at the school, noticed an object in the same place, saw a figure climb into it and watched it move up a slope. They did not think for one moment that they were watching a UFO but considered that it was a vehicle associated with the sewage works close by. Even when it was pointed out that it would have been very difficult for any type of vehicle to get to that location, they refused to accept that they had seen a UFO.

Despite their scepticism, the Broad Haven school sighting, taken at face value, appears to be quite convincing. There are, however, some additional factors that investigators at the time failed to take into account: these we shall consider when we have looked at some of the other sightings reported from the area. For from then until the late summer hardly a week was to go by

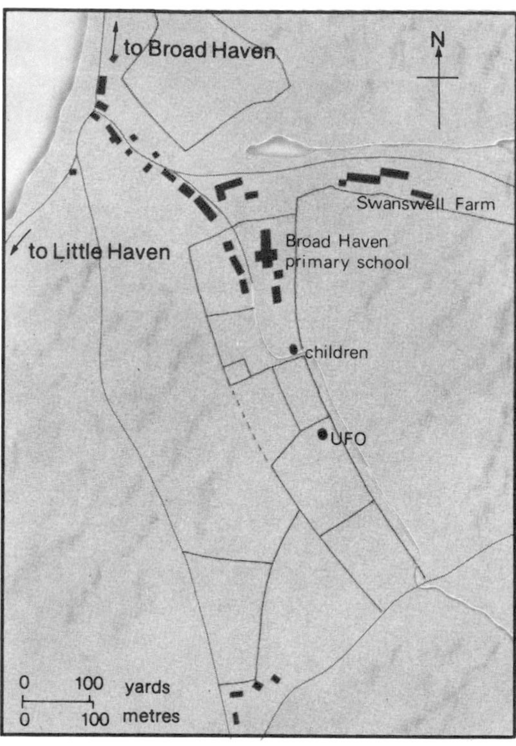

Below: witnesses point out the site of the alleged UFO landing (right) for newspaper reporters. About two weeks after the first sighting, a teacher watched a large silvery object glide away from the same spot, and a couple of hours later two canteen workers at the school saw a strange object in the field. The canteen ladies, however, firmly believed that what they had seen was a tanker from the nearby sewage works; they visited the site with their husbands the next day to look for tyre marks, but found none

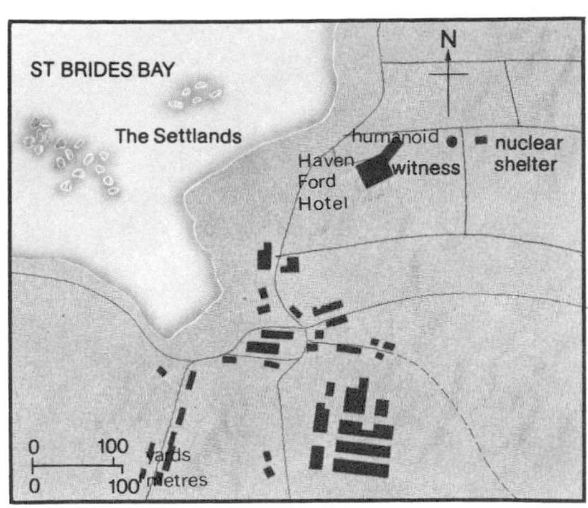

Left: the site of a UFO landing reported by Mrs Rose Granville, proprietor of the Haven Fort Hotel (below), on 19 April 1977. The witness claimed to have seen two humanoids apparently examining something close to their craft. Local BUFORA investigator Randall Jones Pugh has pointed out that there is a nuclear shelter at the site for the use of the Royal Observer Corps. Did this attract the ufonauts?

without some fresh incident being reported in the neighbourhood. Public interest was kept simmering not only by newspaper reports but also by widespread discussion, by visiting reporters for press and television and by investigators from UFO organisations. For the next six months or more, UFOs were to be front-page news in the area.

Here, taken from among 45 cases described in minute detail in reports and interviews, not to mention others reported in less detail, are a handful of selected incidents.

On 10 February two 12-year-old boys saw a UFO in a field near Haverfordwest grammar school. It was a blue flashing light, seen at a distance of about 130 yards (40 metres). One boy threw a stone at it, whereupon it took off; as it did so, an orange cigar shape about 16 feet (5 metres) long materialised beneath it. It hovered for a while, then vanished.

On 16 February Graham Howells, a 13-year-old schoolboy of Pembroke Dock, saw a bright, metallic object hovering over Pembroke school as he arrived in the morning. Although the weather was misty, he claimed a clear view of the object, which had

> a dome in the middle which was dark grey most of the time, but flashed to a dazzling white about every five seconds. It resembled a plate with a burnt fried egg on it. Around the rim of the 'plate' it had greeny-yellowish lights and what seemed to me to be retro-rockets. The 'plate' seemed to be revolving as well. . . . I'm sure it wasn't a helicopter or a weather balloon.

On 13 March Stephen Taylor, aged 17, saw a UFO at about 9 p.m. It was a glowing light with an orange halo around it. He went to the house of some friends to tell them about it, but they did not believe him. About half an hour later, in a field, he saw a dome-shaped UFO about 20 feet (6 metres) high and stopped to look at it. Then a figure like a tall man approached, wearing a semi-transparent suit and a kind of spaceman's helmet. 'I was so frightened,' Stephen said, 'that I just took a swing at it and ran.'

On 7 April, Cyril John, aged 64, woke at about 4.45 a.m., disturbed by a strange orange light pulsating in his bedroom. It came from outside and was reflected off the walls. He got up, looked out of the window and saw that the sky was orange.

> Immediately outside here I saw two silvery-coloured objects. The first was like a very large Easter egg, about 4 feet [1.2 metres] in diameter, and it was swinging back and forth a little above and behind the chimneys of the house opposite. I then saw an object like a man in a silvery boiler suit about 40 feet [12 metres] above my window. It was at least 7 feet [2 metres] tall, and it hung stationary, on a level with the 'Easter egg'. Its attitude was in the position of a free-fall parachute jumper. . . . It hung motionless in the sky, face-downwards, for about 25 minutes. The 'egg' then moved up above roof-level and glided away sideways, as did the figure.

On 19 April Mrs Rose Granville, proprietor of the Haven Fort Hotel, was just going to bed, at about 2 a.m., when she was disturbed by a strange humming sound. At first she took it for the central heating, but then she realised that it was something unfamiliar. A flash outside her window caused her to look out: she saw a bluish light circling around, pulsating as it went. She got her binoculars and saw an oval object resting on the ground and, near it, two figures in 'whitish, plasticated' clothing like boiler suits; they had no faces. When the local newspaper printed a picture of a hoax spaceman and suggested that this was what she had seen, she wrote an indignant denial.

With cases such as these being reported almost every week, it is not surprising that as early as 17 February investigator Randall Jones Pugh commented to a local reporter: 'There's certainly a minor flap down here.' On 28 April he told the same paper that he was planning a book on the sightings. No doubt he was encouraged in this venture by a further series of events, which were even more extraordinary: the astonishing incidents reported by the inhabitants of Ripperston Farm, just south of Broad Haven.

Four remarkably similar versions of the Broad Haven UFO, drawn by children from the school. The witnesses made the drawings independently, but not until three days after the sighting, so they would have had plenty of time to discuss what they had seen

A giant, faceless humanoid, the strange teleportation of cattle, and a car-chasing UFO – just some of the many phenomena allegedly experienced by the Coombs family at Ripperston Farm. But how much of what was reported actually took place?

DURING THE AUTUMN OF 1977 an enterprising hotelier in west Wales was offering special weekend breaks for UFO investigators. Enthusiasts would be free to use the hotel facilities all night long, and an expert would guide them to the most favourable locations for UFO spotting, though sighting was not guaranteed. 'Pembrokeshire is quite a way ahead in this sort of thing,' the hotelier observed, and she professed herself 'flabbergasted at the number of people who have written or telephoned'.

What was drawing the attention of UFO enthusiasts, not only from Britain but also from abroad, was the continuous flow of remarkable reports from what the newspapers were naming 'the Broad Haven triangle'. Serious ufologists have learned to be cautious about 'flaps'. Periods when more

The Ripperston Farm riddle

than the usual number of reports come in may genuinely represent an increased level of activity, but it may simply be that the publication of reports encourages witnesses to come forward who would otherwise have kept their experiences quiet. No more incidents occur; it is just that more are disclosed. And there is the further possibility that news about sightings may stimulate some people to have imaginary experiences.

Such possibilities are anathema to those ufologists who are convinced that all UFO sightings are grounded in physical fact and deny that there may be a psychological aspect to such experiences. But that some kind of 'contagion of ideas' was operating in west Wales during the spring and summer of 1977 is suggested by many of the reports – most of all by the series of astonishing events that were alleged to have taken place at Ripperston Farm, focusing on the Coombs family. So completely did these events capture the public imagination that three books were wholly or in large part devoted to them, as well as extensive coverage by press and television. Unfortunately, this resulted in so much contradiction and confusion that the true facts are often impossible to establish. In what follows the most probable version of the truth has been selected, but frequently it has been a matter of choosing between contradictory accounts, and absolute accuracy cannot be guaranteed.

Billie Coombs was a herdsman, one of three men responsible for looking after the dairy herd at Ripperston Farm on behalf of the farm manager, Richard Hewison, who lived at neighbouring Lower Broadmoor

Left: Ripperston Farm, near St Brides Bay in west Wales, home of the Coombs family who reported many seemingly paranormal events in the spring and summer of 1977. One of the striking aspects of this case is that Brian and Caroline Klass, whose cottage adjoined that of the Coombs, did not see or hear anything unusual at this time – or at least chose not to publicise their experiences

Farm and was in turn responsible to the company that owned both farms. Mr Coombs and his wife Pauline lived with their five children in a cottage on Ripperston Farm. Immediately next door was another cottage, where Brian Klass, also a Ripperston employee, lived with his wife Caroline.

Although Pauline Coombs reported some earlier UFO experiences, the first major event occurred on 16 April. She was driving home one evening after dark, with three of her children, when her 10-year-old son Keiron, who was in the back seat, reported a strange light in the sky. It was about the shape and size of a rugby ball, luminous, yellowish, with a hazy, greyish light underneath and a torch-like beam shining down from it. Keiron told his mother that the light had U-turned and was following them. The object caught up with the car and travelled along beside it, at which point the car lights started to fade. Near the house the engine cut out altogether, so that Mrs Coombs had to coast the rest of the way. She ran in to call her husband. He and their eldest son, Clinton, came out just in time to see the UFO heading out to sea. When Mr Coombs tried to start the car, it functioned perfectly.

A few weeks later Mrs Coombs reported seeing another UFO from her kitchen window. It was about 20 feet (6 metres) in diameter and rested about 3 feet (1 metre) off the ground. Silvery in colour, it had antennae and a tripod undercarriage. It took off towards the sea, leaving a circular 'burn mark'. On another occasion two of the younger children claimed to have seen three UFOs in the sky, circular in shape and with domes. One was only about 50 feet (15 metres) above the ground, and from it a ladder was lowered, down which the children saw a silver-suited figure climb. The UFO also dropped a bright red, fluorescent box-like object into the grass of the field: later the children looked for the box but it had apparently disappeared.

Above: the road leading to Ripperston Farm along which Pauline Coombs was driving on the evening of 16 April 1977 when, she claimed, the car was chased by a UFO (left). She and the children were terrified, and their fear increased when, as they approached the house, the car engine and lights cut out completely so that they had to coast the rest of the way home

On 22 April Mr and Mrs Coombs were watching a late-night film on television, despite interference, which was particularly bad that evening. At about 11.30 p.m. Mrs Coombs became aware of a glow outside the uncurtained sitting-room window. An hour or so later her husband saw a face at the window. 'It was a man – but a terrible size,' he later reported, estimating the height of the figure at nearly 7 feet (2 metres). The creature was wearing a white suit. Its face – if it had one – was concealed behind a kind of black visor.

Terrified, Mr Coombs telephoned first the farm manager, Richard Hewison, and then Randall Jones Pugh, the local British UFO Research Association investigator. Pugh advised him to inform the police. Hewison came round at once, followed by the police, but they found no trace of the intruder. About three weeks later a similar figure was sighted by the eight-year-old twins. They were out in the fields, 'playing roly-poly in the grass', when they saw an entity that they described in almost the same terms as their parents had – it was dressed in silver, with a black head. It walked past them, about 50 feet (15 metres) away, then it disappeared, apparently having walked through a barbed-wire fence.

A strange disappearance

Of all the events that were reported from Ripperston Farm, the most bizarre was the seemingly supernatural movement of cattle. On several occasions, Billie Coombs found that the cattle – sometimes only one or two animals, but frequently the entire herd – had disappeared from the yard. On at least one occasion he received an angry telephone call from a neighbouring farmer asking him to come to collect his herd. Mr Coombs insisted that the animals had been properly fastened in, adding that he had secured the bolt with binder twine as an extra precaution. To escape in the way indicated the herd would have had to move past the cottage: yet neither he nor his wife had heard a sound. On one occasion, he reported, there simply had not been enough time between the moment at which the cattle had last been seen and the moment when they were reported at another farm for them to have traversed the distance in any natural way. The implication had to be that they had somehow been spirited from one place to the other. The cattle were badly frightened, and the milk yield was down.

This extraordinary movement of cattle presents the toughest challenge to our credulity. The UFO and entity sightings, remarkable as they are, fall within a commonly accepted range of phenomena, but this movement of animals seems to belong to a different class.

It is not, however, entirely without precedent. In his book *Haunted houses* (1897),

animals. Bricks and stones fell in the rooms, although the windows were closed. There was spontaneous displacement of objects. A pair of oxen were even found to have been carried from one stall to another without human agency. . . . A doctor and psychical researcher found a 16-year-old girl with strong mediumistic faculties who was the involuntary means of the striking phenomena.

This last case indicates that poltergeist activity was diagnosed, which raises the question of whether a similar agency was at work at Ripperston. If so, it was a particularly powerful one: the teleportation of an entire herd of cattle transcends any poltergeist phenomenon ever reported. Nonetheless, other events reported from Ripperston might be seen as supporting the poltergeist hypothesis. It is noteworthy, for example, that the place seemed to exert a highly malevolent influence on mechanical objects. Apart from the alarming failure of Pauline Coombs's car at the climax of her frightening UFO chase, Billie Coombs reported that he

John Ingrams describes a strange report from Birchen Bower, near Oldham in Lancashire. At this house a macabre custom was observed. A former owner, terrified of being buried alive, had refused to allow her body to be buried. Instead she left instructions that it should be embalmed and brought to the house every 21 years, where it was left in a granary for a week. This had an extraordinary effect on the livestock:

> In the morning, when the corpse was fetched, the horses and cows were always found let loose, and sometimes a cow would be found up in the hay-loft, although how it came there was, indeed, a mystery, as there was no passage large enough to admit a beast of such magnitude. . . . A few years ago, when a cow belonging to the farmer then tenanting the place was found in the hay-loft, it was the firm belief of many thereabouts that supernatural agency had been employed to place it there. . . . How the cow was got up was a mystery to everyone, whilst that blocks had to be borrowed from Bower Mill to let it down through the hay-hole outside the barn was an equally well-known fact.

The *Daily Mail* of 18 May 1906 noted, in the course of a report on a disturbed house: 'A horse vanished from the barn and was found in the hay room. A partition had to be knocked down to get him out.' And in April 1936 the Italian journal *Ali del Pensiero* reported:

> Phenomena of incendiary infestation have been recently established on a farm in Prignano (Salerno); fires broke out spontaneously, destroyed household objects, and burned persons and

Above: from her kitchen window Pauline Coombs saw a UFO flying towards the sea

Right: map showing the position of Ripperston Farm in relation to that of Lower Broadmoor Farm. On several occasions Billie Coombs reported that cattle had mysteriously disappeared from his yard – even though he had secured the gate – only to turn up at Broadmoor Farm a half-mile (800 metres) away. Local BUFORA investigator Randall Jones Pugh (below) visited the farm but could find no explanation for the mystery

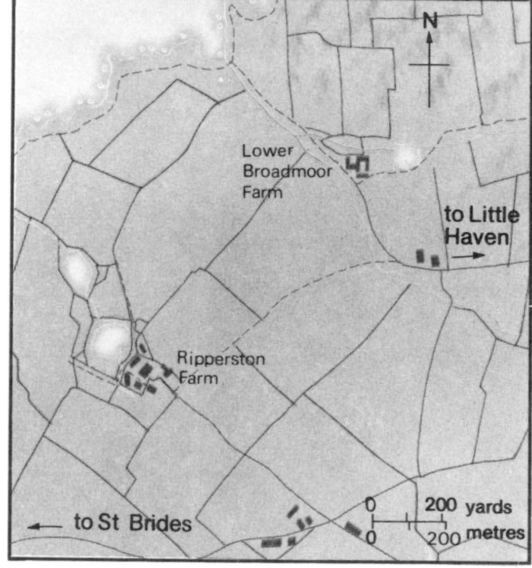

had to replace his car five times during 1977 and that they suffered an even higher accident rate with television sets. Again, the family's electricity bill was so high that they asked the Electricity Board to inspect the meters. No fault was found.

The suggestion that psychic forces may have been at work is supported by the earlier history of Pauline Coombs, who was by faith a Roman Catholic. Some time before coming to Ripperston, the Coombs family had been living in a caravan at nearby Pembroke Dock. Strange manifestations began to occur. Every evening, from the inside of the caravan, Mrs Coombs could see a life-size apparition of the Virgin, who was wearing a white dress. She had a rosary tied round her waist and was holding the child Jesus. Later the figure became that of Jesus on his own. The figure remained for half an hour. Word got around, and soon every evening there was a crowd of sightseers hoping to catch sight of the phenomenon. Eventually, the owner of the caravan had it destroyed because he was annoyed by the flow of visitors. As reported, this incident is very unsatisfactory. Caravan owners do not usually resort to destroying their own property, even for such a reason. However, for our purpose, the suggestion is clear that there was already some quality about Pauline Coombs that might make her prone to strange experiences.

The proliferation of incidents at Ripperston Farm made it a focus of interest for reporters and investigators on and off throughout the spring and summer of 1977. And perhaps it was only to be expected that sooner or later those ubiquitous figures, the sinister men in black (see page 30), should be reported as turning up at the farm. One day, so the account alleges, an unusual car drove up, but silently, so that no one heard it. It contained two men who were remarkably similar in appearance. One of them got out, immaculately dressed in a neat grey suit and gleaming shoes. He was inspecting the cattle yard when Caroline Klass first saw him from her cottage next door, yet in some uncanny way he was instantly beside her, asking where Pauline Coombs was, somehow knowing that Mrs Klass was not her. He is described as speaking with a foreign accent and as having something alien about him. He possessed 'large, penetrating blue eyes which seemed to go right through her and examine her thoughts'.

The report alleges that the Coombs's eldest son, Clinton, was in the neighbouring cottage at the time but was too frightened by the visitors to open the door to them; instead, he bolted it and hid upstairs. Failing to get an

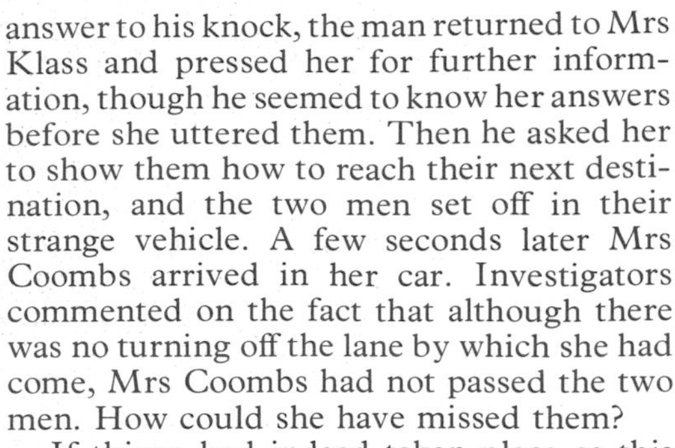

answer to his knock, the man returned to Mrs Klass and pressed her for further information, though he seemed to know her answers before she uttered them. Then he asked her to show them how to reach their next destination, and the two men set off in their strange vehicle. A few seconds later Mrs Coombs arrived in her car. Investigators commented on the fact that although there was no turning off the lane by which she had come, Mrs Coombs had not passed the two men. How could she have missed them?

If things had indeed taken place as this report suggests, we would have good reason to believe that something genuinely uncanny had occurred at Ripperston that day. However, more objective investigation reveals the

Above: Pauline Coombs at the window through which she and her husband saw a humanoid at about 1 a.m. on 23 April 1977. Mrs Coombs had noticed a 'glow' at the window an hour or so before, but decided not to mention it to her husband because she believed he would think she was 'suffering from nerves'. But then Mr Coombs saw a creature, a silver-suited man of 'a terrible size', pressed right up against the window (right). The police were called, but they found no signs of the intruder

Below: a silver-suited entity was seen by two of the Coombs children

'evidence' to be a hotch-potch of misleading statements and mischievous inventions. The two men were not foreigners. They were not uncannily identical. Their questions were perfectly natural. Moreover, far from knowing that Caroline Klass was not Pauline Coombs, their first action was specifically to ask if she *was*. Clinton was not hiding in the house, terrified. And as for the question of why Mrs Coombs had not passed their car as she drove up, the explanation is perfectly simple – Mrs Klass had indicated to them a short cut that would enable them to reach their destination more quickly, and it led away from the farm by a different road.

In short, the whole episode, as it has been reported, is an irresponsible distortion designed to create a sensational story out of a simple and perfectly natural incident. And this was far from being the only incident in the west Wales sightings in which the true facts were somewhat different from those that were reported.

The west Wales sightings form one of the most complex and richly documented UFO cases on record. But the facts were often markedly different from those that were reported

The truth about the Welsh triangle

THE REPORTS OF UFO activity in Dyfed in 1977 provide a dazzling variety of incidents and a small army of witnesses, as well as phenomena ranging from distant sightings to close encounters, with all manner of picturesque happenings on the side. Small wonder that the media moved into the area in force, and that innumerable newspaper and magazine articles and television programmes should by devoted to the astonishing events in this one small corner of Britain.

But in the end it was the sheer scale of this blaze of publicity that revealed the weaknesses of the accounts offered to the public. Had there been but one version, it might have been accepted as gospel, but there were several, and they all differed in detail and contradicted one another in interpretation. No reader with his wits about him can fail to notice the number of discrepancies and, once alerted, he starts to notice other defects – assumptions too easily made, questions not asked, awkward facts lightly passed over. Finally he realises that in some respects the investigation has been woefully incomplete, while in others the facts have been distorted or exaggerated almost beyond recognition.

In the light of more objective investigation into the west Wales sightings it is possible to see just how much truth subsists in the accounts given to the public, and to reassess some of the events outlined in preceding articles.

The Pembrokeshire UFO 'flap' may be said to have started at Broad Haven primary school, and it is appropriate that reassessment should start with a visit to the site of the alleged sighting. Straight away we are in for a surprise. The reports hardly emphasise how densely the site is covered with bushes and trees, so that any sighting must have been largely screened. It would have been impossible for the children to have seen the UFO in its entirety, so the sketches that they drew the following Monday must be regarded as largely make-believe. Again, we find that the field is in a narrow valley, overlooked by a number of houses. It has always seemed improbable that a UFO should remain in a field in broad daylight for three hours and more – there is no precedent for such a sighting. The proposition becomes even more improbable in the light of the fact that its alleged location was within constant sight of a semi-circle of houses. It should also be recalled that the events all took place on a winter afternoon: 'It was a very dull day, but I did see something,' said one witness, which suggests an uncertain, indistinct sighting that would hardly permit the precise pinpointing of the landing site.

However, it does not seem justifiable to accuse the children of deliberate hoaxing. The fact that, when their teachers did not believe them, they took the brave step of handing in a petition at the police station speaks well for their sincerity. Undoubtedly, they saw something that they could not identify. What that something was we may never know for certain, but it seems probable that the suggestion of the two canteen workers who saw an object at the same spot, that it was a vehicle associated with the sewage works located close by, is the correct one.

Why, then, did the children suppose that they were seeing a UFO? Here we move from physical to sociological considerations. Two days before, several schoolboys at Penarth, Cardiff, claimed to have seen a cigar-shaped UFO. The following day – the day before the Broad Haven sighting – the *Western Telegraph* reported that another cigar-shaped UFO had been seen at nearby Hubberston primary school, for between 10 and 15 minutes, by children playing football. There is no need to suppose that the Broad Haven children were consciously seeking to emulate

One of the many reports of UFOs in Dyfed in 1977 was made by 13-year-old Deborah Swan, who claimed that while she and some friends were on a UFO hunt they were terrified by a 'brilliant gleaming silver' object, the size of a football, that was hovering in a field close by. But did the children really see a UFO? Or did they simply want to believe they had seen one because so many others seemed to have done so?

the others, but it is evident that the idea of UFOs was very much in the air at the time and might have come naturally to the minds of schoolchildren confronted with an unfamiliar object. The boy who was scared that he might be 'disintegrated' by UFO entities – like the other witness who thought he could distinguish 'retro-rockets' on the side of a UFO – already had in his mind the raw materials from which an imaginary UFO could be constructed.

The Broad Haven story immediately stimulated the public imagination. The next week's *Western Telegraph* noted: 'Reporters, photographers and television cameramen arrived in a two-day procession to see the starstruck youngsters, who were only too willing to repeat their fantastic story.' Even those who did not believe that story were made aware that curious things were going on; while those who *were* ready to believe drew fresh encouragement from this flare-up of interest. Soon local investigator Randall Jones Pugh was telling reporters, 'The phone hasn't stopped ringing since the Broad Haven sightings. People are beginning to come forward now that they realise nobody is going to take the mickey out of them.'

How many of the sightings reported to Pugh and others in this way have any basis in fact it is probably now impossible to ascertain. But as one leafs through the files of the local newspaper, presumably read by a high proportion of the local populace, one is struck by the way in which the subject was kept simmering throughout the spring and summer of 1977. Week after week the correspondence columns included letters presenting views for or against. The reports were both serious and objective, never sensational and at the same time never mocking. This fact in itself would have been sufficient to create a favourable soil in which the false could be nurtured along with the true.

With the national media, on the other hand, it was a different matter. Absurd tales, heavy with exaggeration, were concocted by journalists who dropped in for brief visits, then returned to London to write about the terrified locals who dwelt in the 'terror triangle', as the *Sun* named it. It is in the light of this emotional climate that cases such as the following must be evaluated.

On 14 April 13-year-old Deborah Swan of Herbrandston was playing with friends in the park at about 6.30 p.m. Since there had been so many reports of weird happenings, they decided to see if they could find this 'outer space thing', but having gone a little way from the park, two of them turned back because 'it began to get scary.' The others went on, under fences, across a potato field, down a bank – and then, as Deborah later reported:

> There was something in the field opposite out of the ordinary. I have never seen anything like it before in my life. . . . I thought it was my eyes playing a trick – but it wasn't. The most astonishing thing about it was the colour, which was a brilliant gleaming silver. The shape was like a round football, and also the movements. . . . It moved at all angles – backwards, frontwards, left to right . . . as we moved, it moved as well. We then ran back as fast as we could. . . . We didn't hesitate to look back, but just kept running.

What did Deborah and her companions see? Was it really a UFO or just an hallucination? Was it a misperception? Was it pure imagination or deliberate fiction? One thing is certain: it is altogether without precedent for anyone to go looking for UFOs and to run across one within a few minutes. And yet Deborah's story was accepted literally at the time by all those who were supposed to be conducting an objective investigation into the facts.

It was the happenings at Ripperston Farm that were the most widely publicised of the west Wales sightings. How do they stand up to objective investigation? Right away, one is struck by the fact that the Coombs family had neighbours who lived not simply nearby but in a cottage that was actually joined to their own. Throughout the period of the alleged incidents Brian and Caroline Klass were living right next door, working alongside Billie Coombs. Yet it is a fact, however hard to believe, that not one single reporter or investigator bothered to ask the Klasses for their view of the matter. On the occasion of the only event in which they were directly involved, the sinister visit of the two 'foreigners', false statements were put into Mrs Klass's mouth to give the incident a totally misleading slant.

Invention clearly embroidered the matter of the 'miraculously' transported cattle. Both the farm manager and Billie Coombs's fellow

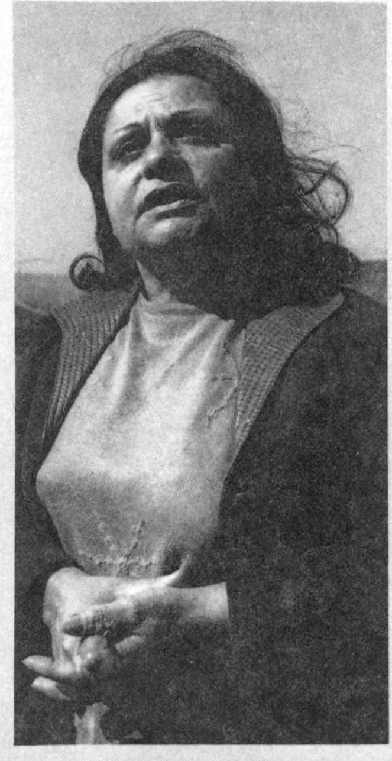

Stack Rocks in St Bride's Bay, which allegedly attracted the attention of 'silvery' humanoids in October 1977. The figures were seen climbing on the rocks by Mrs Rose Granville (above), who claimed to have observed them through binoculars from the Haven Fort Hotel. However, the hotel is about 3 miles (5 kilometres) from the rocks and it is unlikely that she would have been able to make out much detail at this distance worker testify that the Ripperston cattle were continually getting loose and finding their way on to neighbouring farms. Could they get past the cottages without anyone hearing? Certainly, declares Billie Coombs's neighbour. When there was a wind blowing they wouldn't hear a thing, particularly if the television or radio were on.

And there are other happenings at Ripperston that, looked at objectively, turn out to be less than inexplicable. There is the mysterious force that allegedly acted on mechanical objects, destroying five cars in the course of a year. Those who knew Mr Coombs have pointed out that a cowman doesn't have the resources to buy that many new cars. What he did was to purchase more or less condemned cars from a scrap yard, get them working as best he could and drive them until they finally fell to pieces. A similar explanation accounts for the high accident rate among the family's television sets. As for the abnormally high electricity bill, a neighbour alleges that the Coombs family were forever leaving the central heating fully on while doors and windows were open.

One of the most sensational incidents was the appearance, on the night of 22 April, of a mysterious entity at the Coombs's sitting-room window. On this occasion there is no doubt that something really did happen; the farm manager whom Mr Coombs telephoned in the middle of the night was convinced that he was genuinely frightened. But by what?

Some time earlier two local men were passing the Haven Fort Hotel, in whose grounds the proprietor had recently reported seeing a UFO and a couple of entities. On an impulse, they decided to play a trick on her. They proceeded to tramp around the building in a sinister fashion, using a torch to enhance the effect. It seems probable that it was these same jokers who were later responsible for the Coombs 'entity'. Although the identity of the jokers is widely suspected, they have not openly admitted their complicity, so the explanation must remain conjecture only. However, the hoax explanation is generally accepted in the area today.

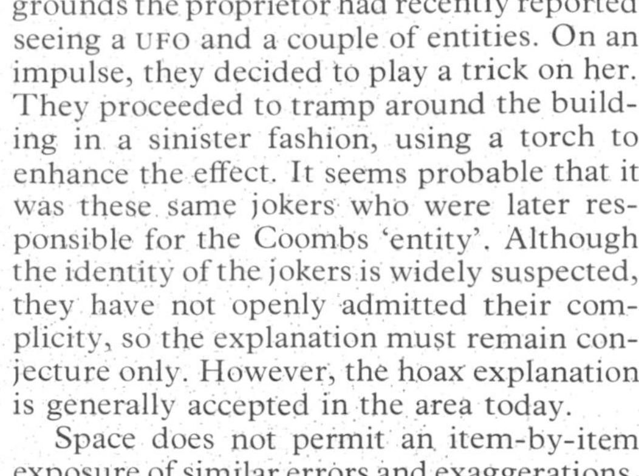

Space does not permit an item-by-item exposure of similar errors and exaggerations, but the sensational Stack Rocks sighting must be mentioned. Unfortunately, the discrepancies between the various reported accounts of this incident are even more glaring than usual, so it is impossible to say quite what happened or in what sequence. What is supposed to have occurred is roughly as follows.

A flash in the sky

Early one evening in October Pauline Coombs was driving to Ripperston with her mother and some of the children when her mother saw a disc-shaped UFO fly overhead towards Stack Rocks, which stand out at sea some distance from the mainland. The UFO circled the rocks, then dived into them through what appeared to be sliding doors.

Alarmed, they continued on their way. Hardly had they arrived home when the telephone rang. Mrs Granville, of the Haven Fort Hotel, had seen a flash in the sky, which had prompted her to fetch her binoculars to examine Stack Rocks (which, incidentally, were her property). She had seen figures climbing about on the rocks, and wondered if Mrs Coombs had seen any such thing? Mrs Coombs immediately set off from the farm towards the cliff, accompanied by some of the children, to obtain a better view.

According to the reports, they came back confirming Mrs Granville's sighting. However, closer investigation reveals that what happened was that on their return from the cliffs some of the children ran on ahead of their mother. Caroline Klass, their neighbour, asked the boy Keiron if they had seen anything, to which he replied, no, of course they hadn't. But when Mrs Coombs arrived she insisted that they had indeed seen entities clambering about the rocks on what appeared to be stairs.

What are we to make of this? Again, a visit to the site certainly helps. The Haven Fort Hotel is some 3 miles (5 kilometres) from Stack Rocks, which makes it improbable that any movement could be seen in detail, particularly as it was evening, and the side of the rocks facing the mainland was in shadow. Additionally, the side facing the hotel is at an angle of 90° from Mrs Coombs's viewpoint, so it is unlikely that she would be able to see the same thing. Mrs Granville's explanation

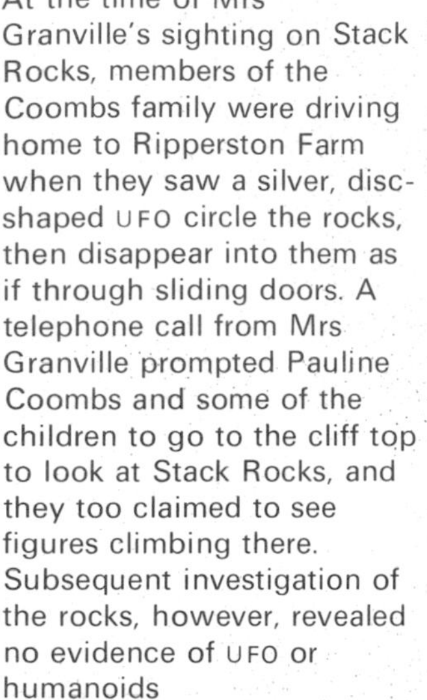

At the time of Mrs Granville's sighting on Stack Rocks, members of the Coombs family were driving home to Ripperston Farm when they saw a silver, disc-shaped UFO circle the rocks, then disappear into them as if through sliding doors. A telephone call from Mrs Granville prompted Pauline Coombs and some of the children to go to the cliff top to look at Stack Rocks, and they too claimed to see figures climbing there. Subsequent investigation of the rocks, however, revealed no evidence of UFO or humanoids

for her alarm at the flash and her subsequent inspection of the rocks is not convincing, for the sky above St Bride's Bay is continually flown over by jets from the RAF base at nearby Brawdy, Stack Rocks being a mark in the flight path of aircraft approaching the airfield. Flashes in the sky over Stack Rocks must occur many times every day.

One notes, too, that the Coombs's first sighting must have been made from a moving car that was travelling along a bumpy, unsurfaced road, from which the rocks can be glimpsed only intermittently. At that point they must have been about 2 miles (3 kilometres) away. A BBC investigator visited the rocks to see if there was anything that might have given rise to the sighting. He found nothing. It is noteworthy, though, that from the approximate angle at which the Coombs family must have seen the disc dive into the rocks, there are two large rock slabs, separated by a darker area, that could conceivably lend themselves to interpretation as a pair of sliding doors.

Finally, what value can be placed on Pauline Coombs as a witness? It has been suggested that she might have been a natural psychic, but it is also possible that she was either very suggestible or highly imaginative. Some time after the events of 1977, and shortly after a television programme featuring a notable UFO contactee, Mrs Coombs confided to Caroline Klass that she, too, had been taken for a trip in an alien spaceship.

The investigation that has led to the disclosures made here was undertaken specifically for *The Unexplained*, not with the intention of debunking the reports but simply in order to establish the real facts. The unearthing of such a farrago of exaggeration and omission, of gratuitous distortion and outright falsehood, was as unexpected as it was dismaying. Inevitably, one is forced to ask whether there is any substance whatever in the west Wales flap of 1977.

Above: Josephine Hewison, who reported seeing a huge object 'like a squashed jelly mould' in a field at Lower Broadmoor Farm (top). Researchers were convinced by her straightforward and objective account of the sighting, and there seems to be little reason to doubt that she did indeed see something paranormal

Fortunately, not all the findings were as disillusioning. There seems no reason to doubt that a good many of the witnesses who submitted their experiences to the press or to the British UFO Research Association representative, Randall Jones Pugh, did so in good faith and were reporting events that may well have been genuine UFO sightings. Of all these cases, one must stand for the rest.

A little before 8 a.m. on Saturday, 26 March, Josephine Hewison of Lower Broadmoor Farm, whose husband Richard manages the farm that includes Ripperston, was standing at her bedroom window. In a field just beyond the drive that circles around the front of the house she saw a massive object some 50 feet (15 metres) wide, large enough to hide, almost completely, a greenhouse that stood behind it. It had a round, three-tiered shape – a broad base, then a rounded ridge with a dome above. The whole thing, in Mrs Hewison's words, was 'rather like a squashed jelly mould'. It was smooth, bulbous, aluminium-coloured. There was no sound, no indication of activity. It was full daylight but overcast, which invalidates the theory that she might have been dazzled by sunlight reflected from the greenhouse.

She gazed at it for about two minutes, then realised that she ought to tell somebody else. She went to wake up her children, but when she looked out of the window again, the object had vanished.

Curious and unforgettable

There is no way to confirm or refute Josephine Hewison's testimony. But a visit to the site makes it clear that there is nothing there that she could have misinterpreted. Either she saw something real or she was hallucinating – and there seems no reason to suppose that she was hallucinating. Today her view of the incident is a measured, objective one. She knows that she saw something that morning, and she continues to think it likely that she saw something 'real'. Though some reporters described her as 'terrified', what she saw didn't frighten her at all. It was simply a curious and an unforgettable experience.

The story of the west Wales flap is a sad revelation of human nature. Some of those involved emerge as simple-minded, only too ready to believe what they are told without questioning. Others, though claiming to be objective investigators, have shown themselves to be incompetent or prejudiced. Some who have proffered evidence are to be seen as simply unreliable, others may be considered fraudulent. Just a few people, like Josephine Hewison, seem to have had genuinely paranormal experiences. But because of the way in which the affair was treated, the truth has been buried beneath every kind of error and evasion, fiction and fraud.

Of the many Welsh religious revivals, that of 1905 was unique. For at its heart was the preacher Mrs Mary Jones who, as KEVIN MCCLURE describes, could summon up miraculous lights over the Welsh countryside

PROBABLY THE MOST remarkable series of phenomena ever reported in Wales were the mysterious Egryn lights. Yet few people today (even among those interested in paranormal happenings) have heard of them or of their apparent inspiration, the visionary preacher Mrs Mary Jones. The background to the appearance of inexplicable lights seen around Mrs Jones was the Welsh Methodist revival of 1905, which was led by the young evangelist, Evan Roberts.

Wales had long been the home of such intense and emotional revivals, involving large numbers of converts who experienced drastic, if temporary, changes in their way of life as a result. By September 1904, when the latest revival began, a traditional pattern was already well-established. Since the Great Revival of 1859 – when a staggering 110,000 converts were claimed – there had been important local revivals in 1866, 1871, 1882–83, 1887, 1892 and 1893.

A study of the 1905 revival describes the 'mystic doctrine of salvation by personal experience, in which realisation of sin led to an emotional crisis which convinced them [the converts] that they had been saved.' Preachers denounced sinners from the pulpit, cajoled and promised the glories of heaven for those who repented. Packed services ran for hours at a time.

But this particular revival quickly showed unusual features. Evan Roberts based his personal 'testimony' on his alleged visions from angels and from Christ himself. Methodism is not a faith that takes kindly to mysticism or other 'Popish' traits and Roberts was severely criticised for his emphasis

Above: Mrs Mary Jones, focus of the miraculous lights

Right: a sketch of the scene at Pensarn where a train driver saw a light shoot in 10 directions while Mrs Jones preached nearby

Below: the modest little chapel at Egryn as it was during the revival of 1905. One well-attested event was the coming of a 'star' from over the sea to flood the chapel with light

Fire within and without

Right: map of the Egryn district, where Mrs Jones's phenomena occurred during the peak of her ministry in 1905

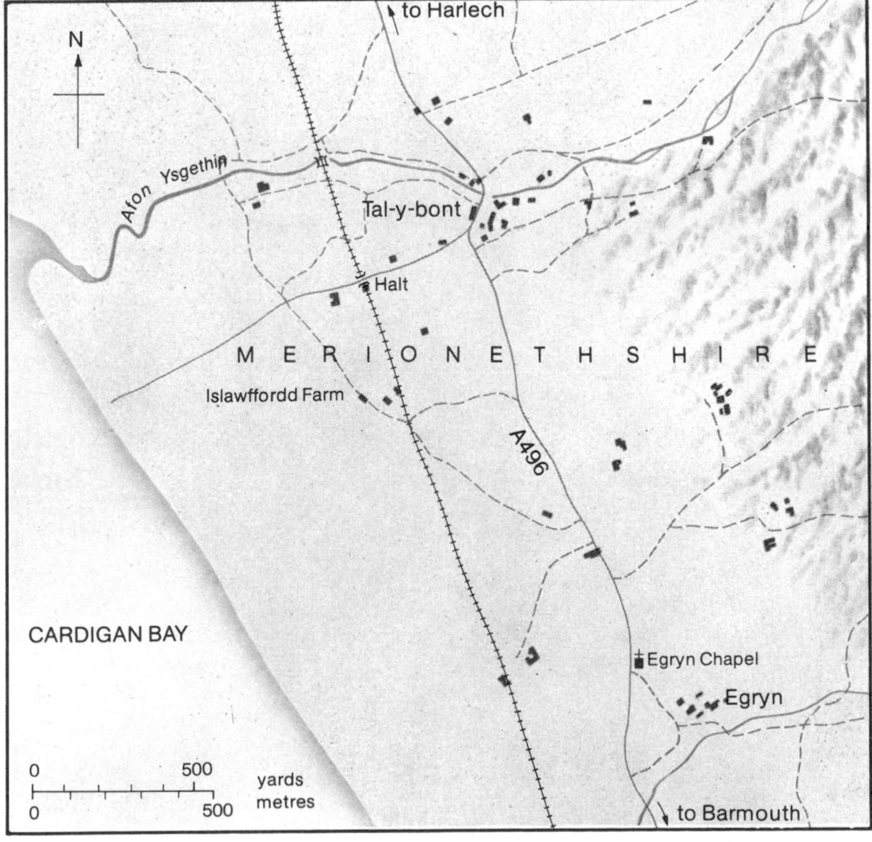

on personal revelation of this literal kind. Perhaps this censure explains partly why few chose to remember the revival in later years; after all, claims of visitations from holy persona are not uncommon in Catholic centres such as Lourdes in France or Fatima in Portugal. The good Methodists of Merionethshire had no taste for pilgrimages and shrines.

Yet the controversial activities of Evan Roberts paled into relative insignificance beside the wonders that came to be associated with Mrs Mary Jones, a 35-year-old farmer's wife from Egryn, a hamlet between Barmouth and Harlech in Merionethshire (now Gwynedd).

Seeing is believing

Experiences such as Evan Roberts's visions are often subjective, only experienced by one person. Consequently it is hard to prove whether or not they really happened. But Mary Jones did more – she inspired phenomena that others could see. She experienced visions, found herself surrounded by moving lights, received messages from 'The Saviour in bodily form'. She firmly believed herself to have been chosen to be 'the accepted medium for the spreading of the Revival throughout Merionethshire.' These experiences led her to commence a nightly mission in her local chapel and soon others also began to witness lights, to see visions – and they were converted.

The first of many independent reports comes from the *Cambrian News* of 13 January 1905. Reporting her successful conversion work, it mentions that until recently the lights she has claimed to have seen had been regarded 'as one of her own inspiring thoughts', but that they have now been seen by others.

> Last week Mrs. Jones attended a meeting at Pensarn, where hundreds of people congregated. The chapel can be seen from the railway and as a train, driven by a Machynlleth man, was passing, a strange light was seen shooting out of ten different directions, and then coming together with a loud clap. 'Never do I wish to see anything like it again', said the driver in relating his experience. Both he and his mate saw the light.

Clearly Mrs Jones and her lights were by now well-known along the Cambrian coast, and the appearance of independent testimony attracted several journalists from respectable newspapers to the little Islawrffordd farmhouse that lies between the sea and Tal-y-bont halt on the railway. Once there, they attempted to establish the background of this seemingly ordinary country woman.

They found that, like so many others who are the centre of psychic or paranormal phenomena, she had been far from happy in her childhood and adolescence. Orphaned at

an early age, she was cared for by her sister. Then her sister died, too, and Mary lost her lifelong faith in God.

But during the first stirrings of the revival in South Wales she underwent a dramatic, though solitary, conversion experience and returned to regular attendance at the Egryn chapel. Gradually she became more involved; then her visions began, and she decided to start her own daily meetings at the tiny chapel. She told Beriah Evans, a Caernarvon journalist, of her experiences at this time, and accounts appeared in the *Manchester Guardian* and the *Barmouth Advertiser*:

> The first night's mission was marked by the appearance for the first time of Mrs. Jones' 'Star' and 'Lights'. The star was heralded by a luminous arch, of the character of the 'Aurora Borealis', one end resting on the sea, the other on the hill-top – a distance of well over a mile [1.6 kilometres] – bathing the little chapel in a flood of soft effulgence. The star soon after appeared, its light flooding the chapel itself.

In the same articles, Evans wrote of the apparent 'intelligence' of the star or lights, which seemed to respond to both individuals and situations.

> The star has seemed to rest above particular houses, whose roofs are thrown out in bold relief amid the surrounding darkness. When this occurs in the Egryn district a convert or converts invariably turn up at the next meeting from that particular house. . . . It [the star] glows placidly on the roof of the chapel where her service is held, and when it does so the spiritual character of the meeting is very marked.

The Reverend Elvet Lewis, writing for the Christian *British Weekly*, records similar events of lights appearing over the houses of those who were to be converted. He stated that a Wesleyan minister in Barmouth could confirm them and, therefore, everyone else should take the reports seriously.

As the journalists arrived, many of them became witnesses to the lights, and were able to publish the names and addresses of other responsible witnesses. Perhaps because he was a local man, Beriah Evans was the first into print. On 9 February 1905 this account appeared in the *Daily News*:

> After tea, we had two miles [3 kilometres] walk to the chapel. Besides myself, there were present the Rev. Llewelyn Morgan, Harlech, the Rev. Roger Williams, Dyffryn, and one other – Mrs.

Above: artist's impression of the strange phenomena surrounding Mrs Jones's first night as an evangelist. While she was preaching inside Egryn chapel a luminous arch, something like the *aurora borealis*, began to take shape with one end resting on the sea and the other on a hilltop a mile (1.6 kilometres) away. Soon afterwards a 'star' appeared, filling the chapel with soft light

Above right: journalists witnessed an intense, sparkling 'star' flash over a nearby railway crossing, apparently caused by Mrs Jones's presence

Right: Mrs Jones's 'star' was frequently seen to hover over a specific house, and invariably this preceded the conversion of one or more of the inhabitants, usually the following day

Jones came in dressed for her journey. Going outside, she immediately returned, remarking: 'We cannot start yet, the Light has not come.'

Five minutes later she went out, returning promptly to say: 'Now we can go, the light has come.'

The announcement was received with a perceptible tremor by the only unbelieving member of our company. We had just passed the level-crossing of the Cambrian railway when Mrs. Jones directed our attention to the southern sky. While she spoke, between us and the hills, apparently two miles [3 kilometres] away, there suddenly flashed forth an enormous luminous star, an intensely brilliant white light, emitting from its whole circumference dazzling sparklets like flashing rays from a diamond.

'It may be the head light of a train?' suggested our doubting Thomas.

'No,' was Mrs. Jones's reply; 'it is too high for that.'

As though in corroboration, the star made a sudden jump towards the mountains, returning almost immediately to its old position, and then rushing at an immense speed straight for us. Then came the unmistakeable rumbling of the train approaching from the direction of Barmouth.

'I thought it was the train,' came with a sigh of relief from our unbeliever. False hope!

'No', was Mrs. Jones's confident contradiction. 'The train light has yet to come.'

And a second light, very different in character from the first, became perceptible some distance below the star, both obviously rushing towards us. As the train drew near the 'star' disappeared. With a rush and a roar the train was past. But before our Thomas's sigh of thanks at the disappearance of the star was well out, the . . . star reappeared nearer, and if possible more brilliant than ever. Then it vanished . . .

'Wait', said Mrs. Jones. In a moment, high up on the hillside, quite two miles [3 kilometres] away from where the 'star' had been a moment previously, a 'Light' again flashed out, illuminating the heather as if bathed in brilliant sunshine. Again it vanished – only again to reappear a mile [1.6 kilometres] further north, evidently circling the valley, and in the direction for which we were bound.

And Mary Jones's lights were to assume many different forms and elude rational explanation for some time to come.

'Lighten our darkness'

What were the mysterious lights that accompanied Mary Jones's 1905 Welsh ministry? This chapter continues the bizarre tale of religious fervour and its 'UFO' connection – and considers contemporary allegations that the lights were hoaxes

MOST OF THE EYEWITNESS REPORTS we have of Mary Jones of Egryn, the 'Merionethshire Seeress' as she became known, come from local and national newspapers, and articles in the *Occult Review*. The Society for Psychical Research (SPR) produced a long and detailed report in its *Proceedings* for 1905, but conducted its investigation by postal questionnaire. However, it is hard to see what the most experienced psychical researcher, more accustomed to seances and hauntings, would have made of the following account, from the correspondent of the *Daily Mirror*. He tells of the journey back from a revival meeting:

> In the first carriage were Mrs. Jones and three ladies; in my own with me, the 'Daily Mirror' photographer, a keen-witted, hard-headed Londoner. The weirdness of that drive in semi-darkness at breakneck speed by river and mountain round deadly corners and down precipitous hills, I shall never forget. For three miles [5 kilometres] we had driven in silence, and I had given up hope. It was close on midnight, and we were nearing Barmouth when suddenly, without the faintest warning, a soft shimmering radiance flooded the road at our feet. Immediately it spread around us, and every stick and stone within twenty yards [18 metres] was visible, as if under the influence of the softest limelight. It seemed as though some large body between earth and sky had suddenly opened and emitted a flood of light from within itself. It was a little suggestive of the bursting of a firework bomb – and yet wonderfully different. Quickly as I looked up, the light was even then fading away from the sky overhead. I seemed to see an oval mass of grey, half-open, disclosing within a kernel of white light. As I looked it closed, and everything was once again in darkness.

Who knew anything about UFOs in 1905?

The same team also witnessed another form of the phenomenon – one also described by Beriah Evans, and the Dyffryn police-constable. It seems that each night in the early part of 1905 there was a regular gathering of intrigued observers along the road by the chapel, all hoping for the lights to appear. The *Daily Mirror* reporter saw:

> A bar of light quite four feet [1 metre] wide, and of the most brilliant blue. It blazed out at me from the roadway, a few yards from the chapel. For half a moment it lay across the road, and then extended itself up the wall on either side. It did not rise above the walls. As I stared, fascinated, a kind of quivering radiance flashed with lightning speed from one end of the bar to the other, and the whole thing disappeared.

Meanwhile, the reporter from the *Daily Mail*, having walked several miles from Barmouth station, saw:

> A ball of fire above the roof of the chapel. It came from nowhere, and sprang into existence instantaneously. It had a steady, intense, yellow brilliance, and did not move. It seemed to me to be at twice the height of the chapel, say fifty feet [15 metres]. Suddenly it disappeared, having lasted about a minute and a half. . . . The minutes crept by, then two lights flashed out, one on each side of the chapel. They seemed about 100 yards [90 metres] apart, and about 100 feet [30 metres] above the roof of the chapel. They shone out brilliantly and steadily

The 'soft, shimmering radiance' that illuminated the countryside as described by the *Daily Mirror* reporter who had gone to investigate Mrs Jones and her lights. It was on the way back from a prayer meeting that the mysterious light suddenly flooded the road around them. Although it was nearly midnight the strange light picked out the detail of 'every stick and stone' within 20 yards (18 metres). The reporter and his colleague had just time to notice an oval mass of greyish light with a brilliant white kernel overhead when they were all suddenly plunged back into darkness for a space of 30 seconds. Then they both began to flicker while one could count ten. Then they became steady again. In the distance they looked like large and brilliant motor-car lights.

Many reports such as these could be quoted. But are there any real clues as to the nature of the phenomena described as 'stars' and 'lights'? How can we begin to track down their source? Were there real, physical lights, or were they illusions experienced by the followers of Mary Jones through the power of suggestion, when she told them that she could see lights? Were they seen only when she was present? Did they occur only in one small area? And if so, could an explanation lie in the fact that there is marshland near the chapel – might the lights have been marsh gas spontaneously igniting?

Unlikely explanations

If the phenomena had in fact occurred only around the Egryn chapel, a number of possible explanations for what was seen and reported could have been found. For example, hoaxers carrying lanterns on the hills behind the chapel would certainly have been high on the list of possibilities. So too would misapprehension of the lights of the chapel itself, or those of the scattered farmhouses in the district, or of the distant St Tudwal lighthouse. Few of the conventional sources of light encountered by UFO investigators in the 1980s would have occurred then: car lights were rare, train lights unmistakable – due to the accompanying steam engine noise – and aeroplanes (particularly flying at night) almost unheard of.

Right: the ball of fire that appeared before a reporter's startled gaze. It hovered motionless above Egryn chapel, brilliantly illuminating the roof, then abruptly disappeared. Even if this particular version of the Egryn lights could be explained away as ball lightning, Mrs Jones's other phenomena remain mysterious

Below: the electric blue bar of light witnessed by, among others, the *Daily Mirror* reporter and a local policeman. As Mary Jones preached, this strip of light appeared across the wall by the chapel. It quivered violently – then vanished

However, the problems in analysing the Welsh lights are not easily resolved. While the appearance of the stars and lights and, later, of other extraordinary phenomena, do seem to have been related to the presence of Mary Jones, there appears to have been no geographical limit to where they could be seen. The *Barmouth Advertiser* of 20 April 1905 reported:

> This week Mrs. Mary Jones of Egryn, the 'Merionethshire Seeress' is conducting revival meetings in the Wrexham district. Some of the women present at the afternoon meeting on Monday declare that they saw a light hovering over the head of Mrs. Jones while she was speaking and praying.
>
> At the evening meeting, as she delivered a very powerful address, and offered a most earnest prayer, the 'lights' were seen by a large number of people in the chapel. The first was a flash like lightning while she delivered the first part of her address; a second flash appeared when she began in her address to describe the 'lights' in the Egryn district, and a third flash was seen when she was praying. She said in the course of her address that the

Above: the interior of the unassuming Egryn chapel as it was in 1905. During a meeting in April many witnesses saw strange lights flash around Mary Jones's head. And on several occasions the lights hovering outside the chapel flooded it with an unearthly glow

Below right: on 23 July 1905 a group of young Methodists returning from one of Mary Jones's Glamorganshire meetings witnessed one of the more spectacular phenomena associated with her. A 'ball of fire' appeared in the sky with two brilliant 'arms' reaching to the ground. Between them was a host of twinkling stars. They watched this 'display' for about 10 minutes, then suddenly the sky returned to normal

> 'lights' had appeared wherever she had visited, with two exceptions, and now she knew that she had not been divinely guided to go to those places where the lights did not follow her. The visit of Mrs. Jones, followed by the lights, has created quite a sensation in the district.

Wrexham (in what is now Clwyd) is on the other side of Wales from Egryn.

Two fiery arms

On 23 July 1905, about three weeks after Mrs Jones had held a mission nearby, a group of young people returning from a prayer meeting at Ynysybwl, near Pontypridd, Glamorgan, had a remarkable experience. They told local reporters: 'There appeared in the heavens a very large and bright ball of fire. It had two brilliant arms which protruded towards the earth. Between these arms appeared lights resembling a cluster of stars, quivering with varying brightness. It lasted for ten minutes. . . .'

A doctor from Tylorstown recounted for the SPR enquiry an incident that occurred on 27 May 1905.

> About 10 p.m. on Saturday night I was coming home with my wife, when she drew my attention to a bright light over the Libanus Chapel, towards the side of the mountain. It appeared as a ball of fire about the size of a cheese-plate; it was perfectly fixed. As soon as I saw it I marked its position, in order to be sure that it could not be some one with a light on the road which passes over the mountain, but its position was far enough away from the road.

Meanwhile, in April 1905, three clergymen from the Llangollen area gave the *Barmouth Advertiser* the results of their own investigations. The three had watched the part of the Dee Valley where Mary Jones claimed lights had appeared over the homes of those who were 'spiritually troubled'. They saw 'two large balls of fire rise from the earth and suddenly burst luridly. On the third occasion . . . a similar light travelling towards Vroncysyllte.' All were satisfied that, 'Some mysterious phenomenon had appeared in their midst simultaneously with the visit of the seeress.' Together with the many other calm and responsible reports from witnesses all over Wales, it makes a solid case for a genuine mystery. Hoax, misapprehension, illusion, or natural explanations seem particularly unlikely here.

Newspapers have hinted that there was a UFO connection, and the links between the revival phenomena and other well-established paranormal events seem clear enough. The following piece from the *Occult Review* hints at the scope of what is involved:

> The bedroom of an exceptionally intelligent young woman in the neighbourhood has been visited three times in succession by a man dressed in black, whose appearance corresponds with that of the 'Devil' seen by Mrs. Jones. This figure has delivered a message to the girl which, however, she is forbidden to relate. In Bryncrug, a similar apparition was seen simultaneously from different standpoints. A local professional man, startled, uttered an involuntary prayer. Immediately, one of Mrs. Jones's mysterious 'lights' appeared above, a white ray darting from it which pierced the figure, which thereupon vanished. An apparition, appearing first as a man, then transforming itself into a large black dog, was seen at Abergynolwyn, a mining centre not far distant.

Above: Welsh converts during the revival of 1904 to 1905 queue to be baptised

A fading star

While mysterious lights flashed and hovered around Mary Jones, other strange events were reported in the Egryn area. Coincidence? Or were all the phenomena projections from Mrs Jones?

THE LIGHTS ASSOCIATED with Mary Jones in 1905 were not the first to be seen in the north-western part of Wales. The *Barmouth Advertiser* found this account in a geography of Wales published in about 1800:

> 'Tis creditably reported that in the year 1692 a fiery exhalation was seen to cross the sea, and set fire to the ricks of hay, corn and barns near Harlech, and to infect the grass, but was not mischievous to men, though they were in the midst of it. It proceeded in the night from the same place for some months, commonly on Saturdays or Sundays. The only remedy to extinguish or drive it away was to sound horns or trumpets, or to discharge guns.

The Reverend Fryer, who conducted the enquiry for the Society for Psychical Research (SPR), found similar – though less dramatic – reports of blue or white lights in 1869, 1875 and 1877, at points along the Cambrian coast.

Perhaps if the contemporary investigations into the lights had been more thorough, we might now be able to say what really happened in 1905. The investigations that did take place were far from adequate, though the problems that the phenomena presented were many. How do you catch, or measure, or analyse a flying light? As it is, we can only consider how trustworthy the witnesses were, and look for common features in their reports.

The *Daily Mail* sent a Mr Redwood, the son of a famous scientist, to investigate. He set up some sort of 'instruments capable of being influenced by any extraordinary electrical condition of the atmosphere', about a mile (1.6 kilometres) from the Egryn chapel. Unfortunately, despite several hours' waiting in heavy rain, he recorded no positive results save for a sudden onslaught by two other observers who, believing the light from his lantern to be miraculous, rushed up and took a photograph of it. But a local man had warned him before his experiment: 'Ah, you won't see the light tonight, for Mrs Mary Jones has gone away.'

Of the British newspapers, only the *Manchester Guardian* seems to have sent someone to talk to the actual witnesses to find out what was really happening. The article, credited to 'A visitor', appeared on 14 February 1905 and was entitled 'Fire without and within'. After a discussion of the place of the lights in the current religious revival, it concluded:

> While everybody speaks of Mrs. Jones with great respect, a good many of her neighbours smile when the lights are mentioned. They have not seen them, though they are always sweeping the heavens with their eyes. One man saw two arc-like lights one night which were neither stars nor lamp-lights but may, he thinks, have been produced in some oblique way by the rays of the moon. 'I have often seen Mrs. Jones driving to Revival meetings,' said the same man, 'but I have never seen any lights attending her. . . .'
>
> A woman who thoroughly believes in the lights says she saw a large star one evening as she was going into Chapel. 'Nearly as big as the moon – well, not

Below: Denbigh Asylum, last earthly home of some who suffered religious mania

The Times had reported: 'Ten patients suffering from religious mania are already in the Joint Counties Asylum at Denbigh. One or two show signs of improvement, but the general condition of the others is stated to be very bad.'

Paranormal events are always being reported, regardless of revivals, evangelists, or enquiring journalists. Generally, only a small proportion of those people who have such experiences make them public, and it must be assumed that in 1905 a higher proportion than usual were persuaded, due to press interest and revival enthusiasm, to do so. Many other accounts of unusual events did reach investigators. The SPR enquiry discovered a clergyman who heard a choir of voices singing a previously undocumented Welsh hymn in the middle of a deserted hillside. Various men in Montgomeryshire heard bells in a church service, the sound of singing along an empty road, and an unexplained thunderclap. A minister from Maesteg told of how a young parishioner suddenly 'knew', while praying in church, of the death of his absent father. An unnamed woman, probably in early 1905, is rumoured to have seen a column of fire below which appeared the Egryn chapel, apparently in mid-flight; it later turned into an 'eye', split into two parts, fell, and re-formed

> quite so big – and a bluish colour.' It had disappeared when she came out of the chapel two hours later. . . .
>
> Taking the existence of the 'lights' to be admitted – and there seems to be abundant evidence – it may be hoped that some competent enquiry will be directed as to their cause. . . . As against the purely physical character of the 'lights', they are said at the same time to be visible to some and invisible to others.

Certainly, local feelings about the lights did seem to be mixed, and some who had at first been enthusiastic about the phenomena later saw them as a liability, and an embarrassment bringing ridicule upon local people. The *Cambrian News*, published in Aberystwyth, came to be of this opinion. On 24 February 1905, after reporting lights at Tre'rddol, it commented:

> When a person sees flashing lights he may take it for granted that he has jim-jams. Jim-jams are really dangerous, and when he hears knockings as well he is in a fair way to find himself locked up in a padded room. . . .

Over the next few weeks it continued with its criticism, crowning its efforts in verse:

> If these things you see and hear,
> Sometimes distant, sometimes near
> Don't you seek to reconcile 'em,
> They'll do that in the Asylum!

It must be admitted that on 10 January 1905

Above: during Mrs Jones's ministry it was rumoured that an unnamed woman had a vision of a flying Egryn chapel surrounded by a pillar of fire. This was only one of the many reported paranormal events associated with the Welsh revival

Right: St Elmo's fire, a natural phenomenon akin to that of ball lightning – one of the alternative explanations to Mrs Jones's lights

Below: St Tudwal's lighthouse, whose flashing light could have been taken as miraculous

into what appeared to be the shape of a man.

A similar experience was had by 'an aged Welsh bard of some repute', who had been unable 'to forgo the temptations of the tavern'. He found himself in a 'strange land', being threatened by 'ravening beasts'. Rescued by a mysterious figure from this predicament, he said: 'I realised I had seen my Saviour.' He gave up drinking, took up missionary work during the revival, and 'influenced for good many of his old boon companions'.

Though the visions of the converts happened in the same country as the lights, amid the same religious fervour (and were reported in the same magazines and newspapers), they are probably entirely different phenomena, although no one today can be sure.

A matter of history

There are many problems to be overcome in attempting any assessment of the lights associated with Mary Jones. It is now many years since the phenomena occurred. Though there are many cases, most are undated, and those reported to the SPR are often anonymous; it is difficult to assess their worth. We know little of weather conditions and other vital factors at the times the lights were seen. Faced with possible explanations as varied as sightings of Venus, of St Elmo's fire, of marsh gas, ball lightning, phosphorescence, fireflies, and the lights of St Tudwal's lighthouse, it is impossible to investigate further. Any of these might or might not have caused any particular incident. A holiday the author took at Tal-y-Bont (a village near Egryn) revealed few local memories of either Mrs Jones or her phenomena. Local explanations related to 'men carrying lanterns in the fields' and 'moonlight shining on broken glass'.

The key to any objective assessment of the phenomena lies in the independent testimony from journalists and clergymen. This does seem strong enough to support the view that genuinely paranormal events did take place. Most of them took the form of varying shapes of bright white or coloured light, behaving in an entirely mysterious manner. That the lights were seen, and that they were seen to move in an apparently purposeful manner, appears certain. As *The Guardian* said of them, 'There seems to be abundant evidence.'

So, if the lights, with their paranormal behaviour, did occur, or were seen to occur, how and why did they do so? Where did they come from, what directed their behaviour, and where did they go?

There are no firm answers to these questions, but perhaps the best clue lies in what the lights, by their appearance and behaviour, achieved. That was, simply, Mrs Jones's own ambitions: to be the 'accepted medium for the spreading of the Revival in Merionethshire', and to run a successful mission in her own local chapel. The lights were the means of her fame, and the basis of the remarkable extent of her missionary work. She believed her faith created the lights and this gave her the power to convert.

But if the evidence does argue for the physical, though paranormal, reality of the lights, then there seem to be only two possible explanations. Either God was demonstrating his power to convert sinners – or some equally extraordinary, but more natural, factor was responsible. In short, the production of visible, controllable phenomena, perhaps constructed of some form of electrical energy, by an act of conscious or unconscious will; and there we find ourselves in the area of poltergeists (which seem to occur in the vicinity of the emotionally troubled), and the physical phenomena of Spiritualism.

Whether or not the will of Mary Jones could conjure up lights that would do her bidding, we are unlikely ever to know. Although she continued her mission until the revival finally lost its force in 1906, there is no known report of the lights after July 1905.

Of Mary Jones's later life we know little, but it seems she never found domestic happiness. Her husband – of whom we know nothing – died in 1909, and both her daughter and her son died young. She continued to teach at Egryn chapel Sunday school, and occasionally took part in prayer meetings. She lived on alone, near the chapel, until her death in 1936, and she was buried in the Horeb cemetery at Dyffryn, where the grave can still be seen. After her hard life, with its brief, yet remarkable, interlude of fame, perhaps it is as well that her achievements are not entirely forgotten.

Right: Mary Jones's tombstone in the Horeb cemetery at Dyffryn in north Wales. She died lonely and forgotten in 1936. The lights had long since abandoned her

became almost unbearable. It was then I sensed that they were conveying a message to me by telepathy.'

His visitors confirmed that Bender was right in his speculations as to the true nature of UFOs – one of them was carrying Bender's report – and provided additional information. This so terrified him that he was only too willing to go along with their demand that he close down his organisation and cease publication of his journal. He was instructed not to tell the truth to anyone 'on his honour as an American citizen'.

Did Bender expect anyone to believe his story? His friends and colleagues were baffled by it – one of them, Gray Barker, published a sensational book, *They knew too much about flying saucers*, and Bender himself supplied an even stranger account in his *Flying saucers and the three men* some years later, in response to persistent demands for an explanation from former colleagues. He told an extraordinary story involving extraterrestrial spaceships with bases in Antarctica that reads like the most far-fetched contactee dreamstuff; it has been suggested that the implausibility of Bender's story is

Who are t

As UFO sightings increase so, allegedly, does the harassment of the witnesses – by the sinister Men In Black. HILARY EVANS discusses these frightening and bizarre encounters

'I WENT INTO THE FANTASTIC and came up with the answer,' declared Albert Bender, director of the International Flying Saucer Bureau, an amateur UFO organisation based in Connecticut, USA. 'I know what the saucers are.' Unfortunately, the rest of the world is still none the wiser – for Bender was prevented from passing on his discovery to the world by three sinister visitors: three men dressed in black, known as 'the silencers'.

It had been Bender's intention to publish his momentous findings in his own journal, *Space Review*. But before committing himself finally, he felt he ought to try his ideas out on a colleague. He mailed his report – and a few days later, the men came.

Bender was lying down in his bedroom, having been overtaken by a spell of dizziness, when he noticed 'three shadowy figures in the room. The figures became clearer. All of them were dressed in black clothes. They looked like clergymen, but wore hats similar to Homburg style. The faces were not clearly discernible, for the hats partly hid and shaded them. Feelings of fear left me. . . . The eyes of all three figures suddenly lit up like flashlight bulbs, and all these were focussed upon me. They seemed to burn into my very soul as the pains above my eyes

Above: most accounts of MIBs describe them as wearing conventional black suits, white shirts and black ties. Often they are said to look strangely uncomfortable as if unused to wearing such clothes. The clothes themselves seem brand-new – yet oddly old-fashioned

Right: the MIBs have a surreal quality, like people in a nightmare. Even their cars are disconcertingly new – smelling of 'new leather' – yet the models are dated and the number plates, when checked, are frequently discovered never to have been issued

designed to throw serious UFO investigators off the track.

Believable or not, Bender's original account of the visit of the three strangers is of crucial interest to UFO investigators. For the story has been paralleled by many similar reports, frequently from people unlikely to have so much as heard of Bender and his experiences. UFO percipients and investigators are equally liable to be visited by men in black (MIBs); and, although the majority of reports are from the United States, similar claims have come from Sweden and Italy, Britain and Mexico. And like the UFO phenomenon, MIBs span three decades, and may well have had precursors in earlier centuries.

Like Bender's story, most of the later reports not only contain implausible details, but are also inherently illogical; in virtually every case, there seems on the face of it more reason to disbelieve than to believe. But this does not eliminate the mystery – it simply requires us to study it in a different light. For, whether or not these things actually happened, the fact remains that they were reported; and why should so many people, independently and often reluctantly, report these strange and sinister visitations? And why is it that these accounts are so similar, echoing and in turn helping to confirm a persistent pattern that, if nothing else, is one of the most powerful folk myths of our time?

The archetypal MIB report runs something like this: shortly after a UFO sighting, the subject – he may be a witness, he may be an investigator on the case – receives a visit. Often it occurs so soon after the incident itself that no official report or media publication has taken place: in short, the visitors should not, by any normal channels, have gained access to the information they clearly possess – names, addresses, details of the incident and about the people involved.

Right: Albert Bender, American UFO investigator, with one of his many representations of a UFO landing. Bender is an eccentric occult and horror enthusiast who claims that he was prevented from making public his insights into the nature of UFOs by the threats of three MIBs

e Men In Black?

The victim is nearly always alone at the time of the visit, usually in his own home. His visitors, usually three in number, arrive in a large black car. In America it is most often a prestigious Cadillac, but seldom a recent model. At the same time, though old in date, it is likely to be new and immaculate in appearance and condition, inside and out, even having that unmistakable 'new car' smell. If the subject notes the registration number and checks it, it is invariably found to be a non-existent number.

The visitors themselves are almost always men: only very rarely is one a woman, and never more than one. In appearance they conform pretty closely to the stereotyped image of a CIA or secret service man. They wear dark suits, dark hats, dark ties, dark shoes and socks, but white shirts: witnesses very often remark on their clean, immaculate turn-out – all the clothes looking as though just purchased.

The visitors' faces are frequently described as vaguely foreign, most often 'oriental': slant eyes have been specified in many accounts. If not dark skinned, the men are likely to be very heavily tanned. Sometimes there are bizarre touches; in the case of Dr Hopkins, which we shall look at more closely later, the man in black appeared to be wearing bright lipstick! The MIBs are generally unsmiling and expressionless, their

The man who shot a humanoid

One inclement evening in November 1961 Paul Miller and three companions were returning home to Minot, North Dakota, after a hunting trip. What they could only describe as 'a luminous silo' landed in a nearby field. At first they thought it was a plane crashing – but had to revise their opinion when the 'plane' abruptly vanished. But as the hunters drove off the object reappeared and two humanoids emerged from it. Miller panicked and fired at one of the creatures, apparently wounding it. The other hunters fled.

On their way back to Minot all of them experienced a blackout and 'lost' three hours. Terrified, they decided not to report the incident to anyone.

Yet the next morning, when Miller reported to work (in an Air Force office) three men in black arrived. They said they were government officials – but showed no credentials – and remarked unpleasantly that they hoped Miller was 'telling the truth' about the UFO. How did they know about it? 'We have a report,' they said vaguely.

'They seemed to know everything about me, where I worked, my name, everything else,' Miller said. They asked questions about his experience as if they already knew the answers, yet oddly they said nothing about the wounding of the humanoid. They seemed instead to be fascinated by the clothes Miller had worn when he saw the UFO, even going to his house to inspect them. They left such a lasting impression of menace that Miller did not dare to tell his story for several years.

movements stiff and awkward. Their general demeanour is formal, cold, sinister, even menacing: there is no warmth or friendliness shown, even if there is no outright hostility either. Witnesses often hint that they felt their visitors were not human at all.

Some MIBs proffer evidence of identity; indeed, they sometimes appear in US Air Force or other uniforms. They may produce identity cards, but since most people would not know a genuine CIA or other 'secret' service identity card if they saw one, this proves nothing. If they give their names, and the witness subsequently checks them, they are invariably found to be false.

The interview is sometimes an interrogation, sometimes simply a warning. Either way, the visitors, even though they are asking questions, are clearly very well-informed, with access to restricted information. They speak with perfect, sometimes too perfect, intonation and phrasing, and their language is apt to be reminiscent of the conventional villains of crime films – 'Again, Mr Stiff, I fear you are not being honest!', 'Mr Veich, it would be unwise of you to mail that report' – immediately suggesting the unctuous threatener beloved of Hollywood writers.

The visit almost invariably concludes with a warning not to tell anybody about the incident, if the subject is a UFO percipient, or to abandon the investigation, if he is an investigator. Violence is often threatened. And the MIBs depart as suddenly as they came.

Most well-informed UFO enthusiasts, if asked to describe a typical MIB visit, would give some such account as the foregoing. However, a comparative examination indicates that such 'perfect' MIB visits seldom occur in practice. Study of 32 of the more detailed and reliable cases reveals that many details diverge from the archetypal story: there were no visitors at all in four cases, only telephone calls and, of the remainder, only five involved three men, two involved four, five involved two, while in the rest there was only a single visitor.

Although the appearance and behaviour of the visitors does seem generally to conform to the prototype, it ranges from the entirely natural to the totally bizarre. The car, despite the fact that in America it is by far the commonest means of transportation, is in fact mentioned in only one third of the reports; as for the picturesque details – the Cadillac, the antiquated model, the immaculate condition – these are in practice very much the exception. Of 22 American reports, only nine mention a car; of these only three were Cadillacs, only two were specified as black and only two as out-of-date models.

On the other hand, these archetypal

details tend to be more conspicuous in less reliable cases, particularly those in which investigators, rather than UFO percipients, are involved. This will be relevant when we come to consider possible explanations for the MIB phenomenon.

However, although the 'ideal' MIB case is far from being universal in practice, it has value as a kind of composite picture, embodying all the various features that have been reported. Perhaps the case that comes closest to the archetype is that of Robert Richardson, of Toledo, Ohio, who in July 1967 informed the Aerial Phenomena Research Organization (APRO) that he had collided with a UFO while driving at night. Coming round a bend, he had been confronted with a strange object blocking the road: unable to halt in time, he had hit it, though not very hard. Immediately on impact, the UFO vanished. Police who accompanied Richardson to the scene could find only his own skid marks, but on a later visit, he found a small lump of metal which he thought might have come from the UFO.

Three days later, at 11 p.m., two men in their twenties appeared at Richardson's home and questioned him for about 10 minutes. They did not identify themselves, and Richardson – to his own later surprise – did not ask who they were. They were not unfriendly, gave no warnings, just asked questions. He noted that they left in a black 1953 Cadillac – that is, a 14-year-old model: the number, when checked, was found not yet to have been issued, proving that, whoever his visitors were, they were undoubtedly impostors of some sort.

MIBs seem to model their behaviour on that of 'B-movie' heavies, such as Dennis O'Keefe in the 1947 film *T-men* (left). Not only do the MIBs resemble the 'tough guys' of the early cinema in dress (above) but they also use cliché threats that could have been inspired by the scripts of countless indifferent gangster movies

A week later, Richardson received a second visit, from two *different* men, who arrived in a current model Dodge. They wore black suits and were dark complexioned: although one spoke perfect English, the second had an accent, and Richardson felt there was something vaguely foreign about them. At first they seemed to be trying to persuade him that he had not in fact hit anything at all, but then they asked for the piece of metal. When he told them it had been passed to APRO for analysis, they threatened, 'If you want your wife to stay as pretty as she is, then you'd better get the metal back.'

The existence of the metal was known only to Richardson and his wife, and to two senior members of APRO; seemingly the only way the strangers could have learned of its existence would be by tapping either his or APRO's telephone. There was no clear connection between the two pairs of visitors: but what both had in common was access to information that was not freely and publicly available. And it may be this that is the key to the MIB mystery.

Agents of the dark

Rarely – if ever – do the threats of the mysterious men in black come to anything. So what is the purpose behind their visits?

IN SEPTEMBER 1976 Dr Herbert Hopkins, a 58-year-old doctor and hypnotist, was acting as consultant on an alleged UFO teleportation case in Maine, USA. One evening, when his wife and children had gone out leaving him alone, the telephone rang and a man identifying himself as vice-president of the New Jersey UFO Research Organisation asked if he might visit Dr Hopkins to discuss the case. Dr Hopkins agreed – at the time it seemed the natural thing to do. He went to the back door to switch on the light so that his visitor could find his way from the parking lot, and saw the man already climbing the porch steps. 'I saw no car, and even if he did have a car, he could not have possibly gotten to my house that quickly from *any* phone,' he later commented in astonishment.

But at the time Dr Hopkins felt no particular surprise as he admitted his visitor. The man was dressed in a black suit, with black hat, tie and shoes, and a white shirt: 'I thought, he looks like an undertaker.' His clothes were immaculate: suit unwrinkled, trousers sharply creased. When he took off his hat he revealed himself as completely hairless, not only bald but without eyebrows or eyelashes. His skin was dead white, his lips bright red: in the course of their conversation he brushed his lips with his grey suede gloves, and the doctor was astonished to see that his lips were smeared and the gloves stained with lipstick!

Visitor from another dimension?

It was only afterwards, however, that Dr Hopkins reflected on the strangeness of his visitor's appearance and behaviour. At the time he sat discussing the case in a normal manner. When he had given his account, his visitor stated that his host had two coins in his pocket, which was indeed the case. He asked the doctor to put one of the coins in his hand: he did so. The stranger asked Dr Hopkins to watch the coin, not himself: as he watched, the coin seemed to go out of focus, and then gradually vanished. 'Neither you nor anyone else on this plane will ever see that coin again,' the visitor told him.

After talking a little while longer on UFO topics, Dr Hopkins noticed that the visitor's speech was slowing down. The man rose unsteadily to his feet and said, very slowly, 'My energy is running low – must go now – goodbye.' He walked falteringly to the door, and descended the outside steps uncertainly, one at a time. Dr Hopkins saw a bright light shining in the driveway, bluish-white and distinctly brighter than a normal car lamp; at the time, however, he assumed it must be the stranger's car although he neither saw nor heard it.

An MIB visited Dr Herbert Hopkins and told him to discontinue his investigations into an alleged UFO teleportation case on which he was working at the time. Taking a coin from Dr Hopkins, the MIB made it disappear – remarking that 'Neither you nor anyone else on this plane will ever see that coin again'

Later, When Dr Hopkins's family had

returned, they examined the driveway and found marks that could not have been made by a car because they were in the centre of the driveway, where the wheels could not have been. By next day, although the driveway had not been used in the meantime, the marks had vanished.

Dr Hopkins was very much shaken by his visit, particularly when he reflected on the extraordinary character of the stranger's conduct. Not surprisingly, he was so scared that he willingly complied with his visitor's instruction to erase the tapes of the hypnotic sessions he was conducting with regard to his current case, and to have nothing further to do with the case.

Curious incidents continued to occur both in Dr Hopkins's household and in that of his eldest son. He presumed that there was some link with the extraordinary visit, but he never heard from his visitor again. As for the New Jersey UFO Research Organisation, no such institution exists.

Dr Hopkins's account is probably the most detailed we have of an MIB visit, and confronts us with the problem at its most bizarre. First we must ask ourselves if a trained and respected doctor would invent so strange a tale, and if so, with what conceivable motive? Alternatively, could the entire episode have been a delusion, despite the tracks seen by other members of his family? Could the truth lie somewhere between reality and imagination: that is to say, could there have been a real visitor, albeit an impostor making a false identity claim, visiting the doctor for some unknown reason of his own, and somehow acting as a trigger for the doctor to invent a whole set of weird features that to a third party might have had some quite natural explanation?

Frightening aftermath

What seems the *least* likely explanation is that the whole incident took place in the doctor's imagination. When his wife and children came home, they found him severely shaken, with the house lights blazing, seated at a table on which lay a gun. They confirmed the marks on the driveway, and a

The odd couple

On 24 September 1976 – only a few days after Dr Hopkins's terrifying visit from an MIB – his daughter-in-law Maureen received a telephone call from a man who claimed to know her husband John, and asked if he and a companion could come and visit them.

John met the man at a local fast-food restaurant, and brought him home with his companion, a woman. Both appeared to be in their mid-thirties; they wore curiously old-fashioned clothes. The woman looked particularly odd: her breasts were set very low, and when she stood up, it seemed that there was something wrong with the way that her legs joined onto her hips. Both strangers walked with very short steps, leaning forward as though frightened of falling.

They accepted Coca-Colas, but did not so much as taste them. The strangers sat awkwardly together on a sofa while the man asked a number of detailed personal questions: Did John and Maureen watch television much? What did they read? And what did they talk about? All the while, the man was pawing and fondling his female companion, asking John if this was all right and whether he was doing it correctly.

John left the room for a moment, and the man tried to persuade Maureen to sit next to him on the couch. He also asked her 'how she was made' – and whether she had any nude photographs of herself.

Shortly afterwards, the woman stood up and announced that she wanted to leave. The man also stood, but made no move to go. He was between the woman and the door, and it seemed that the only way she could get to the door was by walking in a straight line, directly through him. Finally the woman turned to John and asked, 'Please move him; I can't move him myself.' Then, suddenly, the man left, followed by the woman, both walking in straight lines. They did not even say goodbye.

Towards the end of Dr Hopkins's MIB visit, he noticed that the man's speech and movements seemed to be slowing down. The MIB got up unsteadily and left, walking very shakily; Dr Hopkins watched him walk down the front steps of his house and into the driveway, and saw a bright, bluish-white light – far too intense for car headlights – but failed to see, or hear, anything else as the stranger departed

series of disturbances on the telephone that seemed to commence immediately after the visit. So it would seem that some real event occurred, although its nature remains mystifyingly uncertain.

The concrete nature of the phenomenon was accepted by the United States Air Force, who were concerned that persons passing themselves off as USAF personnel should be visiting UFO witnesses. In February 1967 Colonel George P. Freeman, Pentagon spokesman for the USAF's Project Blue Book, told UFO investigator John Keel in the course of an interview:

'Mysterious men dressed in Air Force uniforms or bearing impressive credentials from government agencies have been "silencing" UFO witnesses. We have checked a number of these cases, and these men are not connected with the Air Force in any way. We haven't been able to find out anything about these men. By posing as Air Force officers and government agents they are committing a federal offence. We would sure like to catch one. Unfortunately the trail is always too cold by the time we hear about these cases. But we're still trying.'

A question remains: were the impostors referred to by Colonel Freeman and Dr Hopkins's strange visitor similar in kind? UFO sightings, like sensational crimes, attract a number of mentally unstable persons, who are quite capable of posing as authorised officials in order to gain access to the witnesses; it is likely that some supposed MIBs are simply pseudo-investigators of this sort.

One curious recurrent feature of MIB reports is the ineptitude of the visitors. Time and again they are described as incompetent: if they *are* impersonating human beings, they don't do it very well; they arouse their victim's suspicions by improbable behaviour, by the way they look or talk, by their ignorance as much as by their knowledge. Of course it could be that the only ones who are spotted as impostors are those who are not good at their job: and so there may be many more MIB cases that we never learn about simply because the visitors successfully convince their victims that there is nothing suspicious about the visit, or that they will do best to keep quiet about it.

A feature of a great many MIB visits is the instruction to the witness not to say anything about the visit, and to cease all activity concerning the case: clearly, we know of these cases only because such instructions have been disobeyed. Curiously, however, no terrible retribution follows, although violence is frequently threatened if the witness does not comply with instructions. Canadian UFO witness Carmen Cuneo, in 1976, was told by a mysterious visitor to stop repeating his story and going further into his case, or he would be visited by three men in black. 'I said, "What's that supposed to mean?" "Well," he said, "I could make it hot for you . . . It might cost you certain injury."' A year earlier, Mexican witness Carlos de Los Santos was stopped on his way to a television interview by not one but two large black limousines, and one of the occupants – dressed in a black suit and 'Scandinavian' in appearance – told him, 'Look, boy, if you value your life and your family's too, don't talk any more about this sighting of yours.'

However, there is no reliable instance of such threats ever having been carried out, though a good many witnesses have defied their warnings. Indeed, sinister though the MIBs may be, they are notable for the lack of violence associated with them: the worst that can be said of them is that they harass the witnesses with their untimely visits and telephone calls, or simply disturb them with their very presence.

David Tansley, a UFO theorist who has suggested that MIBs are some kind of demonic psychic entity

Threats of violence

While for the victim it is just as well that the threats of violence are not followed through, this is for the investigator one more disconcerting aspect of the phenomenon. For violence, if it resulted in physical action, would at least help to establish the reality of the phenomenon. For it remains a fact that most of the evidence is purely hearsay in character, and not often of the highest quality: cases as well-attested as those of Mr Richardson and Dr Hopkins are unfortunately in the minority. There is a dismaying lack of precision about too many of the reports. Popular American writer Brad Steiger alleges that '*hundreds* of ufologists, contactees and chance percipients of UFOs claimed to have been visited by ominous strangers – usually three, usually dressed in black'; but he cites only a few anecdotal instances. Similarly, John Keel, an expert on unexplained phenomena, claims 'on a number of occasions I actually saw the phantom Cadillacs as advertised, complete with sinister-looking Oriental-like passengers in black suits', but for a trained reporter he shows a curious reluctance to pursue these sightings or to give us chapter and verse in such an important matter. Such loose assertions are valueless as evidence: all they do is contribute to the myth.

And so we come back once again to the MIB myth, and the possibility that there is nothing more to the phenomenon than the myth itself. Can we not write off the whole business as delusion, the creation of imaginative folk whose personal obsessions take on this particular shape because it reflects one or other of the prevalent cultural preoccupations of our time? At one extreme we find contactee Woodrow Derenberger insisting that the 'two men dressed entirely in black' who tried to silence him were emissaries of the Mafia: at the other, theorist David Tansley suggests that they are psychic entities, representatives of the dark forces, seeking to prevent the spread of true knowledge. More matter-of-factly Dominick Lucchesi, one of Albert Bender's friends, held that they emanated from some unknown civilisation, possibly underground, in a remote area of Earth – the Amazon, the Gobi Desert or the Himalayas.

A Mexican UFO witness, Carlos de los Santos, was stopped by MIBs travelling in two large black limousines on his way to a television interview about his UFO sighting. The MIBs warned him to keep silent, and he cancelled the interview. Two weeks later, however, he changed his mind and made the broadcast – and not a word was heard from the MIBs, despite their threats

But there is one feature that is common to virtually all MIB reports, that any theory must account for, and that perhaps contains the key to the problem. This is the possession, by the MIBs, of information that they should not have been able to come by – information that was restricted, not released to the press, known perhaps to a few investigators and officials but not to the public, and sometimes not even to them. The one person who *does* possess that knowledge is the person visited. In other words, the MIBs and their victim share knowledge that perhaps nobody else possesses. Add to this the fact that in almost every case the MIBs appear to the witness when he or she is alone – in Dr Hopkins's case, for example, the visitor took care to call when the wife and children were away from home, and established this fact by telephone beforehand. The implication has to be that some kind of paranormal link connects the MIBs and the persons they visit.

Truth – or paranoia?

To this must be added other features of the phenomenon that are not easily reconciled with everyday reality. These notorious black cars, for instance: where are they, when they are not visiting witnesses? Where are they garaged, serviced? Do they never get involved in breakdowns or accidents? Can it be that they materialise from some other plane of existence when they are needed?

These are only a few of the questions raised by the MIB phenomenon. What complicates the matter is that MIB cases lie along a continuous spectrum ranging from the easily believable to the totally incredible. At one extreme are visits during which nothing really bizarre occurs, the only anomalous feature being, perhaps, that the visitor makes a false identity claim, or has unaccountable access to private information. But at the other extreme are cases in which the only explanation would seem to be that the witness has succumbed to paranoia. In *The truth about the men in black*, UFO investigator Ramona Clark tells of an unnamed investigator who was confronted by three MIBs on 3 July 1969. 'On the window of the car in which they were riding was the symbol connected with them and their visitations. This symbol had a profound psychological impact upon this man. I have never encountered such absolute fear in a human being.'

That first meeting was followed by continual harassment. There were mysterious telephone calls; the man's house was searched. He began to hear voices and see strange shapes. 'Black Cadillacs roamed the street in front of his home, and followed him everywhere he went. Once he and his family were almost forced into an accident by an oncoming Cadillac. Nightmares concerning MIBs plagued his sleep. It became impossible for him to rest, his work suffered and he was scared of losing his job.'

Was it all in his mind? One is tempted to think so. But a friend confirmed that, while they talked, there was a strange-looking man walking back and forth in front of the house. The man was tall, seemed about 55 years old – and was dressed entirely in black.

The long shadow of fear

Men in black excited a great deal of attention when they began to threaten UFO witnesses in the 1950s. But the powerful symbol of the sinister black-clad figure is centuries old

UFO PERCIPIENTS AND INVESTIGATORS are by no means the only people to receive visits from men in black. Researchers Kevin and Sue McClure, investigating the North Wales religious revival of 1905, found accounts that bear at least a *prima facie* similarity to the current MIB phenomenon:

> In the neighbourhood dwells an exceptionally intelligent young woman of the peasant class, whose bedroom has been visited three nights in succession at midnight by a man dressed in black. This figure has delivered a message to the girl which, however, she is forbidden to relate.

The young woman in question, farmer's wife-turned-preacher Mary Jones – one of the leading figures of the revival – was well known for the mysterious lights that appeared as she pursued her mission. On one occasion when she encountered her sinister visitor at night, Mary was 'rescued' by one of her lights, which darted a white ray at the apparition. The MIB promptly vanished.

Above: Montague Summers (1880–1948), a writer who found a number of historical MIB cases – years before the first modern, UFO-related MIB encounter in 1953

Below: the Last Judgement, by Fra Angelico (*c.*1400–1455): the damned (right) are being dragged off to hell by black demons. Some modern writers have gone as far as to suggest an identification between these sinister figures and MIBs

It all sounds like the wildest fantasy – except that there is substantial evidence for some of the phenomena reported, many of which were seen by several independent witnesses, some of them avowedly sceptical. Does this mean that the MIBs *really* existed, *really* appeared in the bedroom of that 'intelligent young woman of the peasant class'? What we are learning about the current wave of MIBs may help us to understand similar cases reported in earlier periods.

Men in black turn up, in one form or another, in the folklore of every country, and periodically they emerge from legend into everyday life. On 2 June 1603, a young country lad confessed before a court in south-west France to several acts of werewolfery, culminating in kidnapping and eating a child. He stated that he was acting under the orders of the Lord of the Forest, to whom he was bond-slave. The Lord of the Forest he described as a tall dark man, dressed all in black, and riding a black horse.

Under the cover of darkness . . .

Montague Summers, who reports the case in his book *The werewolf* (1933), has no hesitation in identifying this and all other MIBs with the Devil of Christian teaching, and this continues to be a widespread interpretation: even today there are theorists who claim that UFOs are diabolical in origin, and the MIBs consequently must be Satan's agents. In the parts of the world where the prevailing religious doctrine presupposes two warring factions of good and evil, good is equated with light and evil with darkness, the agents of good tend to be blond and dressed in white, while the agents of evil have dark hair and are dressed in black. Other connotations follow naturally. Under cover of darkness, all kinds of tricks can be carried out and crimes committed. Darkness is also associated with winter, and so with death: in almost all parts of the world, death rites and customs are associated with the colour black.

So, whatever his specific role, the MIB is a distinctly sinister figure. He is a trickster, not working openly; he stands for lies rather than truth, death rather than life.

Because of the obviously symbolic elements involved, many theorists speculate that MIBs are not flesh-and-blood creatures at all, but mental constructs projected from the imagination of the percipient, and taking on a form that blends traditional legend with contemporary imagery. But it can't be quite that simple: too many of the accounts show evidence of relating to physical creatures moving in the real, physical world.

To those who report MIB encounters, there are several possible origins. At his most concrete, the MIB is supposed to be the representative of an official department; sometimes as straightforward and above-board as the Air Force, sometimes a more covert organisation such as the CIA or FBI. The average American, in particular, seems far from convinced that investigative bodies such as the CIA are necessarily working in the public interest, and the same attitude of mind as has evolved the conspiracy theories about UFOs, that a gigantic cover-up is being mounted by the government, suggests that the MIBs are part of this operation, their sole object being to conceal the facts by silencing witnesses and purloining photographs and other evidence.

The fact that the identities of a great many MIBs have been checked, and they have invariably been found not to be the persons they purport to be, lends strength to this suspicion, which can amount to virtual paranoia. Thus in 1970 an American theorist, Tony Kimery, wrote in all seriousness:

> The mysterious MIB and the entire collection of their thugs, henchmen, and highly trained intelligence officers, are a big part of the complex UFO phenomena which is in turn part of another big and complex phenomena (*sic*). It is known that projects by them are now under way for the complete control of . . . political, financial, religious and scientific institutions. They – the MIB – have a very long background and history that stretches back for centuries, indicating a massive build-up of concentration to where it is today.

Below: a representation of the demon god Kal Bahairab from the Hanuman Doka temple in Nepal. The god was always shown with a hideous face, four arms and – significantly – black skin. Human beings were, in former times, sacrificed to it to satisfy its lust for blood

Below: Richard Baxter, a 17th-century writer, who recounted the tale of a London woman of the time – a 'pious, credible woman' – who was encouraged to hang herself by the Devil in the shape of a big black man. The archetype of black as a symbol of evil reappears in the MIB myth

MIBs are often reported as dark skinned, as having either defective command of English, or conversely an over-precise, over-meticulous way of speaking that suggests that they are not speaking a tongue natural to them. Mary Hyre, a West Virginia journalist, noted that a strange visitor picked up a ball-point pen from her desk and examined it with amazement, as if he had never seen anything like it before. And UFO percipient Mrs Ralph Butler, who received a visit from a man who claimed to be an Air Force major, was astonished to find that he was so unfamiliar with American food that he had to be shown how to eat it. The implication is that they are foreigners, an attitude encouraged by American xenophobia. Curiously, though, no witness appears to have suggested that the MIBs are of Russian origin: where specific details are mentioned, it is always implied that they are vaguely 'oriental'. Slanting eyes are frequently reported; the deadpan faces suggest the inscrutable Asiatic; sometimes heads are totally bald. (By linking 'the yellow peril' with the 'man in black', of course, it is possible to frighten oneself with two bogeymen for the price of one!)

Although witnesses rarely state openly that they believe their visitors to come from beyond Earth, this is often clearly implied. Bender's three men were clearly of alien origin. Other MIBs have displayed behaviour traits that seem to suggest that they are able to function only for a limited time-span: after a while they insist that they have to leave, or take pills, or ask for water, and sometimes show signs of losing strength.

A further possibility remains: that the MIBs are neither flesh-and-blood (even extra-terrestrial flesh-and-blood) on the one hand, nor pure hallucination/illusion on the other, but something in between. The entities encountered in a recent French case seem to have existed, if existed is the word, on some alternative plane of being.

Abduction and threats

The alleged abduction, in December 1979, of Franck Fontaine for seven days on board a UFO was one of the rare French cases to have attracted worldwide attention. The abduction itself was of course the central event of the case, but it was only the start of a series of incidents: one of these, involving MIBs, concerned another member of the trio, Jean-Pierre Prévost, who told this story:

'The night of Friday the seventh to Saturday the eighth of December 1979, Franck, Salomon and I had sat up talking for a long time, and went to bed sometime around 5 to 5.30 in the morning. At 7 there was a ring at the door: Salomon and Franck didn't hear it, so I went to open the door. I found myself in the presence of three fellows. One was of average height, very well dressed in dark green, almost black, black tie, white shirt, and waistcoat to match his suit; he had a fringe of beard, black like his hair, and a moustache. His general appearance was pretty good. The others were bigger than him, taller and more heavily built.

'What follows, I haven't told the police – I reported the visit itself to them – because we've already had enough of being taken for crackpots! But these two types, with the bearded man, didn't really exist, that I'm certain of! In the first place, they had no sight. That's hard to explain: they fixed me with their eyes, but those eyes were nothing but a white mass, all over. They were terrifying!

'The bearded fellow asked me, Are you one of the three?, by which obviously he meant, was I one of the three people concerned in the Cergy-Pontoise case? I said yes, and he went on, Good, in that case, you can pass the word to your companions: you've already said too much. An accident will happen to you. And if you say any more, it will be more serious than that . . .

'And with that they vanished; but how, that's something I can't begin to explain. They didn't take the lift, I'd have heard it if they did; and even more so if they'd used the stairs, the door makes a deafening row! I went to the window that overlooks the parking lot. I can tell you definitely that all night, at least until 5 a.m. or later, we'd noticed a Ford Capri in metallic green standing beneath our window, a Ford that we didn't recognise. Well, when I looked down, there was this Ford, just starting up. How had they managed to get to it without using the stairs or the lift? Complete mystery.

'I woke up Franck and Salomon and we went to the police, without giving them the unbelievable details about the two toughs. The police said, So long as they didn't actually attack or wound you, there's nothing we can do, so get back home. And that was that.'

Forces of evil

Jean-Pierre told investigators that he had seen the three men on several subsequent occasions. Generally, it was simply a matter of seeing them across the street or at a market, but on one occasion he received another warning while he was in a tobacco store buying cigarettes, telling him to keep quiet about their experiences and making threats. Subsequently, under hypnosis, Jean-Pierre indicated that the entities were not extra-terrestrials but *intra*-terrestrials, forces of evil from inside the Earth. He also added – intriguingly – that the bearded man had been real but that his two henchmen had been unreal.

Cases such as this are made baffling by their inconsequentiality. But one thing seems certain: just as the MIB visits seem to originate from some psychic or mental link between the MIBs and the witness, so the consequences of the visit depend less on the MIBs than on the attitude adopted by the witness. If he takes the MIBs at their face value, if he believes their threats, he is liable to find himself heading for a breakdown: paranoia may develop, and he may believe himself followed everywhere, harassed by paranormal happenings such as strange telephone calls and poltergeist phenomena. It is even possible that these second-stage phenomena are genuine as far as the victim himself is concerned: they are manifestations of his fears – but none the less real for that – and will not disappear until he capitulates and gives up his UFO studies, if he is an investigator, or keeps quiet about his experiences if he is a witness.

Salomon N'Diaye, Jean-Pierre Prévost and Franck Fontaine (above, left to right) were involved in a famous case of alleged abduction by the UFO shown in the sketch (inset). Prévost was later the victim of a threatening visit from MIBs

If, on the other hand, he braves the matter out – if he refuses to abandon his investigation, continues to tell the world of his experiences – it seems the MIBs are powerless against him. Carlos de los Santos, stopped on his way to a television interview by a gang of tough, threatening characters, was momentarily scared; he turned his car round, went home and cancelled the interview. But a friend reassured him and persuaded him not to let himself be intimidated: a fortnight later he gave the interview – and there wasn't a squeak from the MIBs!

The MIB phenomenon is clearly worth studying carefully. Whatever the nature of the MIBs – whether they are wholly illusory, or whether there is a measure of reality in them – they exert a great deal of power over the minds of their victims. The better we understand them, the more we may learn about how such power may be deployed. And, if for no other reason, the MIB phenomenon is important because it gives the sociologist a chance to study a legend in the making. The sinister MIB masquerade provides us with contemporary phenomena that rank with the witch, the vampire and the werewolf of times past.

The farmer and the cosmonauts

Cousins of the human race dwell in the Pleiades star cluster – and a Swiss farmer is their confidant on Earth. PETER BROOKESMITH analyses his claims, and the remarkably detailed photographs that back them up

EARLY ONE JANUARY AFTERNOON in 1975, a Swiss farmer, Billy Meier, was out walking near his home at Hinwel, in Zurich canton. He looked across the empty road to the meadow opposite and reflected on how remote this stretch of countryside was. Just then, however, he realised that he was not alone: a peculiar hum filled the air. He looked up and saw a classic UFO – a silver disc-shaped craft – circling slowly above him.

By unusual good fortune Billy Meier was carrying a camera. He managed to take a number of pictures of the craft before it 'swooped down' and landed about 300 feet (100 metres) away from him. He judged it to be about 23 feet (7 metres) in diameter. He began to run towards it, but was stopped by 'an unknown force' some 150 feet (50 metres) from the craft. Then, as Meier looked on amazed, a figure appeared from behind the grounded disc and approached him.

So began the first of more than 100 meetings with cosmonauts from the Pleiades star cluster. In the course of them Meier took some 3000 pages of notes and hundreds of photographs. From his experience came a book: *UFO . . . contact from the Pleiades.* And the whole strange business set off a major controversy among ufologists.

Three 'Pleiadean spacecraft' hover above the Swiss countryside in one of the innumerable sightings claimed by Billy Meier. They have supposedly travelled more than 400 light years to reach the Earth. But they employ a technology so advanced that 'fractions of seconds are sufficient to accomplish light years . . .

Meier's story was first investigated – and publicised – by Wendelle Stevens, a retired USAF colonel living in Tucson, Arizona. According to Stevens he first heard of the Meier contacts through a niece of the psychologist C. G. Jung, with whom he had been swapping pictures of UFOs for some years. (Stevens is said to have one of the largest collections of UFO photographs in the world.) In 1975 she learned about Meier's pictures, taken only some 35 miles (55 kilometres) from her home, and went to visit Meier. Stevens says that she met eight other witnesses to the Pleiadean contacts during her two-day stay and collected more pictures. Copies of these were sent to Stevens, and in due course the lady arrived in Tucson to see him, bringing some 16 more photographs with her. 'The pictures were super fantastic. I had never seen anything like them before,' said Stevens.

A correspondence then grew up between Stevens and Meier, with Jung's niece acting as courier and translator. 'This went on for eight or nine months before I decided I'd better go and look this guy in the eye. He was taking more and more pictures and they all looked really good.'

Not everyone who looks at Billy Meier's

photographs is as impressed by them, but Stevens duly flew to London and went on to Switzerland by train. There he learned that Meier had begun having unusual and anomalous experiences at the age of five, when he saw a 'large circular craft' fly over the local church. From about that time until the age of eight he heard voices in his head. Then a new voice took over and apparently acted as a guide – 'tutoring' him, according to Stevens. Which was perhaps just as well, for Meier left school at the age of 12 to begin a life of odd-jobbing and oddity, which included car-racing, a short period in jail for thieving, a spell of service with the French Foreign Legion and a couple of years in an Indian ashram – followed by gainful employment in an Indian village as official snake catcher. He worked his way to Turkey, where he claimed to have acted as an informer for US drug-smuggling investigators and so paid his way back to Switzerland.

Right: Billy Meier had a chequered history even before the Pleiadeans made their alleged contacts with him. It included periods in jail, in the French Foreign Legion and in an Indian ashram. In a former life, he was told, he was a Pleiadean

Exodus in space

While at the ashram, Meier had started to hear voices again. This time they were female and said they were from 'the Dal universe'. While in India he also saw 'spacecraft' once again and took photographs of them – as he also did, apparently, of his female 'Dal' contact. These experiences with the Dals lasted some two years – until, Meier says, their mission to Earth was complete. Then, until 1975, there was silence.

When the Pleiadeans came, there were three of them – Semjase, Ptaah and Asket – and two of them were distinctly female. They had much to tell him. Their home planet is called Erra, and it circles a small sun 'in the system of Taygeta' in the Pleiades cluster. However, this was not their original home: their civilisation had reached great heights on a planet of a star in the constellation of Lyra millions of years previously, but had been unable to cope with its own technological prowess. Before this society finally tore itself apart in a thermonuclear war, a Lyran named Pleione led a mass exodus into space to colonise planets in the Pleiades, in the Hyades cluster and on a planet of the star Vega. Once the colonists were safely established, space exploration was renewed – bringing the Pleiadeans in due course to our own solar system, which they first reached some thousands of years ago. The cosmonauts told Meier that they reckoned their civilisation was 3000 years in advance of ours on Earth and that 'our sector' of the Universe is governed by the 'Andromeda Council'. The Pleiadeans are also members of a union of planets whose inhabitants number 127 billion people – not superhumans 'but men, like us, benefiting from greater time, and greater knowledge'.

The Pleiades is a group of stars in the constellation of Taurus. To the naked eye it appears to be made up of six or seven stars.

Above: this is one of the Pleiadean spacecraft types that are capable of interstellar flight, according to Meier. This photograph, lacking ground features or other context, offers few clues to the sceptical analyst trying to judge its authenticity

Left: a Pleiadean spacecraft is just visible beyond Meier's moped in this shot. Time and again he would tour the countryside on the moped in response to strange impulses that were reliable signs of an imminent encounter with the Pleiadeans

Below: Semjase, the lovely Pleiadean cosmonaut, had no difficulty, apparently, in communicating with Meier. She and her fellow space travellers were telepathic, and understood his questions before he spoke. Nevertheless, their replies to him were spoken, and were in an oddly accented dialect of Swiss-German

The telescope reveals that these are part of a cluster of many hundreds of stars, 430 light years distant from the Earth. How then, did the cosmonauts ever reach us?

According to them, the journey takes about seven hours and is made in a variety of craft. The barrier posed by the speed of light is broken by a 'hyper-space drive system', and the ships equipped with it are known as 'beamships'. The hyper-space drive apparently works on a 'tachyon system' (tachyons are hypothetical faster-than-light particles). Propulsion below the speed of light is effected by a light-emitting drive. When pressed for more details the cosmonauts told Meier that terrestrial scientists were working on similar systems, known by other names but using the same principles. Five types of craft are used by the Pleiadeans, four of which have an interplanetary capacity – and one of these also has a time-travel mode. The fifth type of craft is used solely for sub-atmospheric reconnaissance.

So, what are the Pleiadeans doing here? And, perhaps a more intriguing question, why was it Billy Meier, a small-time farmer and one-time thief, that they chose to contact?

According to the cosmonauts, their purpose was quite simply to make us aware of the existence of extra-terrestrial life – which was both good and bad by earthly standards, and both human and non-human. Semjase, the elegant lady Pleiadean, put it like this in an early encounter: 'We, too, are still far removed from perfection and have to evolve constantly, just like yourselves. We are neither superior nor superhuman, nor are we missionaries. . . . We feel duty-bound to the citizens of Earth, because our forefathers were your forefathers.' Semjase did not reveal who those common ancestors were, nor was she entirely clear about the nature of the Pleiadean mission:

> We have taken on certain tasks, such as, for example, the supervision of developing life in space, particularly human, and to ensure a certain measure of order. In the course of these duties we do here and there approach the denizens of various worlds, select some individuals and instruct them. This we

The Pleiadean spacecraft

Billy Meier's photographs show five different types of alleged spacecraft, the functions of which were described to him by Semjase. The first four can travel across interstellar distances by means of a device that transports ship and crew 'in a twinkling of an eye through uncounted light years of distance as we understand it'. A second propulsion system permits travel below the speed of light in the neighbourhood of planets. Artificial gravity can be provided. These craft are 23 feet (7 metres) in diameter, and can be crewed by up to seven cosmonauts, though the usual number is three. Semjase explained that 'our spaceships are protected by a screen of energy which automatically rejects any kind of resistance and every bit of matter. . . .' Interstellar flight calls for transitions through higher dimensions: 'If a spaceship breaks through the barrier of light velocity without reaching hyper-space instantly, a catastrophe is due for ship and crew.'

The fifth type of craft is made in two versions, 12 feet (3.5 metres) and 16 feet (5 metres) in diameter respectively. Used to gather data, they are normally remotely controlled, though the larger models can carry one person. They can be used only in planetary atmospheres.

Pleiadean spacecraft are constantly being developed and improved. Type 1 was superseded after centuries of use because of 'radiation leakage problems'.

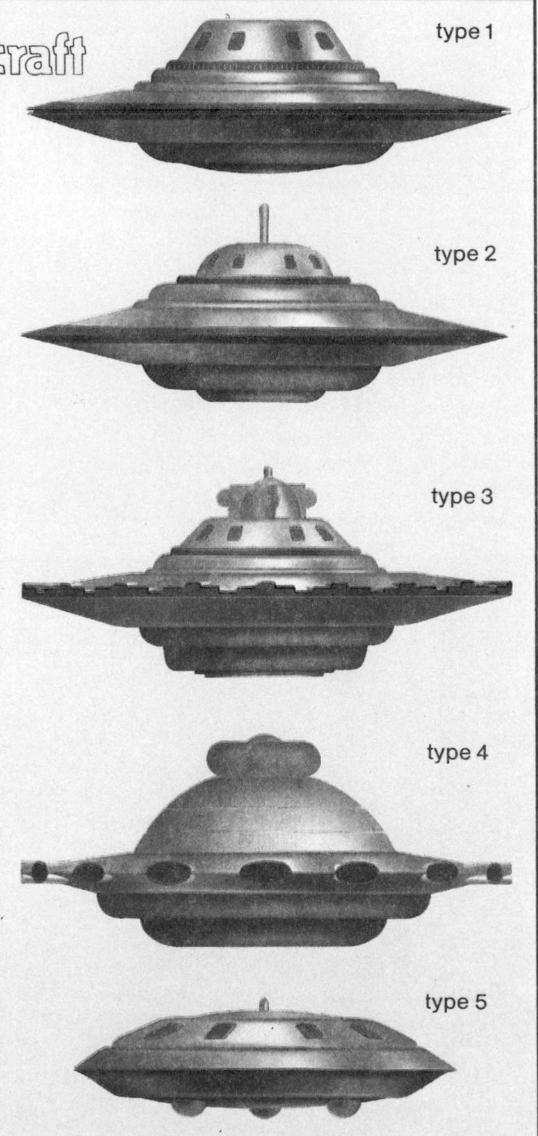

> do only when a race is in a stage of higher evolution. Then we explain (and prove) to them that they are not the only thinking beings in the universe.

The Pleiadeans, however, in common with other aliens who have purportedly communicated with people on Earth, are not greatly impressed with the way we are managing our affairs. In the course of their contacts they let it be known to Meier that

> in their opinion, we terrestrials were not capable of changing mass consciousness, that we were an insane society rushing headlong to our own destruction, that we were not only content with exterminating each other, but we now are bent on destroying all forms of life on this planet as well as the critical life support systems.

Such a state of affairs once pertained when the Pleiadeans inhabited their home system in Lyra, of course: but unlike them, we do not take our world crisis seriously, and no one has made suitable preparations for escape from our doomed planet. Even so, the Pleiadeans refuse to interfere with our way of life or our power structure. We, and we alone, are responsible for our own destiny.

This Zen-like combination of fierce moral comment and studied indifference is driven home by various quasi-mystical utterances by the cosmonauts. Some examples:

> Man should know that the God force is quite simply that of creation, and that man also . . . is subject to creation and respectively complementary to it.
>
> Material life on Earth is only a passing event, a phenomenon vanishing after a time. However, before him and after him there continues to exist the creative presence of the universe.
>
> When the spirit, this universal self, manifests itself in the human being through constant love, wisdom and

Above: a fleet of spaceships photographed by Meier in February 1975. He claims to have witnessed them making occasional instantaneous 'jumps' from place to place

Below: a swirl of grass said to have been formed by a spacecraft's landing gear

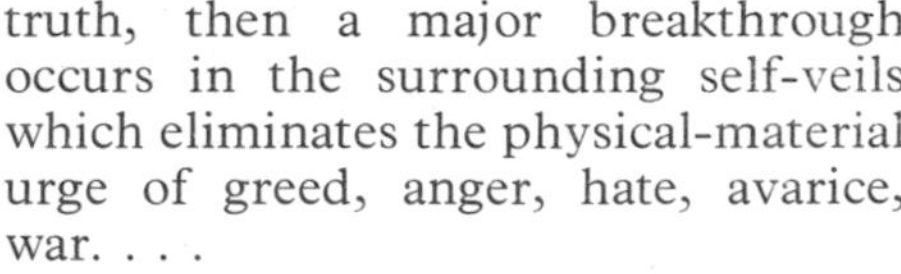

> truth, then a major breakthrough occurs in the surrounding self-veils which eliminates the physical-material urge of greed, anger, hate, avarice, war. . . .
>
> And neither is it consistent with the truth that our brothers and sisters come from other parts of space on behalf of a God to bring to the world the long-awaited peace. In no case do we come on behalf of anybody, since creation, by itself, confers no obligation. It is a law unto itself, and every form of life must conform with it and become a part of it.

Thus spoke Semjase, Pleiadean cosmonaut, to Billy Meier during 1975.

But why was it Meier that was chosen? Wendelle Stevens believes he knows the answer: 'They told him that they had been in contact with him before in other lifetimes.' Such an idea might, of course, occur to someone who had spent two years listening to the kind of conversation that takes place daily in an ashram. But Meier's belief is a little more elaborate, according to Stevens's testimony:

> They said that their ancestors had contacted him during prior incarnations on Earth. They told him that he was one of them who had been caught in an Earth evolution by his own choice several thousand years ago. Since his

soul patterns were more akin to them it was registered in their computers. Supposedly, they could find him wherever he was. As he was one of them and familiar with their mission, his soul could understand ideas communicated to him better than our souls could.

The Pleiadean computer, it will be noted, is obviously a remarkable piece of machinery, able to record 'soul patterns'. But then, it is not clear how material the cosmonauts are themselves. The delectable Semjase told Meier that when coming to Earth the Pleiadeans 'are forced into making a "slight adjustment" which allows us to function properly within your dimensional world'. Without such an 'adjustment', no extraterrestrial could make contact with people on Earth. It ensures 'a correct state of mind and corresponds with the human vibrational pattern'.

This may (or may not) have something to do with the high level of spiritual development claimed by the Pleiadeans. Using their telepathic powers, they are apparently able to think in concert, 'exercising their astute powers of purity of thought' to control their tendencies to discord and strife. Thus freed from bickering, their technology has flourished and so has their medicine, giving the Pleiadeans an average life expectancy of 1000 years.

Despite these talents, Meier observed, the cosmonauts spoke in an oddly accented form of Swiss-German. The remarkable nature of the Pleiadean computer is seemingly responsible, as Semjase explained:

> We are in possession of all Earth languages which are spoken at the moment or have ever been spoken in past ages. We have exact data on them from which we have developed language courses. This happens through computer-like apparatus under the supervision of language experts. . . . Other types of apparatus may serve to connect us to the 'computer' in such a way to make it virtually possible for the languages to be inspired into us. . . .

Such a process, it seems, is still unable to induce a perfect accent.

And the question is still unresolved as to quite what the Pleiadeans expected Meier to *do* with all this information – unless they foresaw his contact with Colonel Stevens and the resulting publicity. Once familiar with the outlines of the case, Stevens certainly lost no time in gathering the evidence: photographs, metal samples given Meier by the cosmonauts, physical traces of the landings, film, tape recordings, computer analysis of pictures, statements from other witnesses, all gathered in a total of 62 days spent with Meier in Switzerland. But what is the significance of that investigation?

UFOS in the sunset. Two photographs taken within a short time of each other, showing 'spacecraft' of two different types manoeuvring over Meier's farm, visible in the background (below left). To seasoned ufologists, pictures as spectacular as this seem 'too good to be true', but Colonel Wendelle Stevens rapidly became convinced of their authenticity and has staunchly defended them

Billy Meier's tales of meetings with space people are not marked by restraint. This chapter recounts more of these amazing claims – and describes the intellectual contortions of Meier's supporters

A mass of contradictions

SWISS FARMER BILLY MEIER'S claim to have had over 130 meetings with cosmonauts from the Pleiades star cluster between 1975 and 1978 is perhaps the most elaborately documented contactee case in the literature of ufology. For Meier supported his story not only with a mass of photographs but with samples of metal allegedly given him by the Pleiadeans, with tape recordings of their craft in flight, and, according to Colonel Wendelle Stevens (who first investigated the affair), produced other witnesses to the remarkable events that he described. All this evidence was, Stevens says, subjected to rigorous scientific testing – and was passed as authentic. The results of Stevens's investigation were published in the United States in 1979 in a lavish book called *UFO . . . contact from the Pleiades.*

Material that has surfaced since then, together with further revelations by the seemingly irrepressible Billy Meier, may lead one to wonder just what Meier's purpose is in all this. For his story has now become so bizarre that even the most gullible devotee of the extra-terrestrial hypothesis ought to be feeling just the teeniest twinges of doubt. And that is without knowing the results of the independent scientific tests of the evidence that have been carried out.

Right: a Pleiadean craft, enabled to make its rendezvous with Meier by detecting his 'brain wave patterns'. According to the Pleiadeans, this process 'normally enables our computer/auto-pilot to direct our beam ship to the exact location without interference'

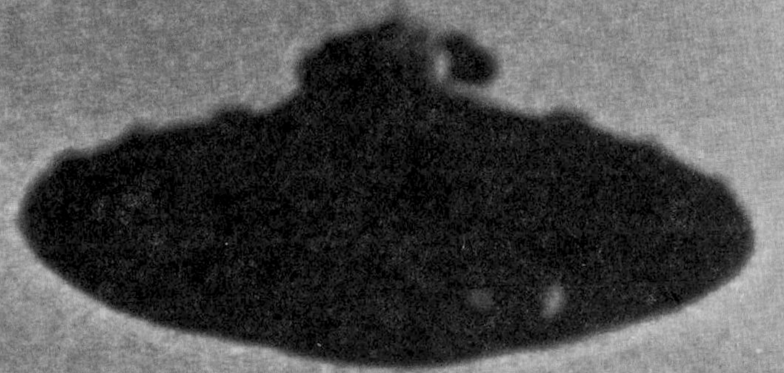

Below: one of the outmoded Variation Type-1 spacecraft

The most startling of Meier's later claims is to have been taken in one of the Pleiadean spacecraft (known as Variation Type-4, apparently) on a journey through time. On this trip, says Meier, he went back to the age of the dinosaurs and photographed them; he also visited Jesus Christ, who was so impressed with Meier that he appointed him a disciple. Meier says he returned to this day and age in order to avoid being crucified. He also claims to have visited other planets, to have photographed the link-up between the Apollo and Soyuz spacecraft as he flew by (odd that neither NASA nor the Russians seemed aware of the Pleiadeans flitting past), and, most extravagant of all, to have taken a photograph of the eye of God. Meier also was taken into the future by the Pleiadeans to see San Francisco come to a sticky end, sinking into the bay as the San Andreas fault at last produced its much-heralded catastrophe.

These tales have naturally attracted some laughter, and Meier's responses to his critics have scarcely helped his case. When asked why he failed to photograph both eyes of God, for example, he replied that the other was closed: the Lord was winking at his companion (who was, needless to say, the shapely Pleiadean Semjase). Other 'evidence' is so peculiar as to need no comment – such as the photograph of a pterodactyl that shows a pyramid in the background!

As Meier's defenders – mainly the group known as Genesis III, who published Colonel Stevens's book on the Meier case – have attempted to come to the rescue, they too have fallen into confusion and contradiction. Or perhaps worse. The chief critic of the Meier case has been Kal Korff, and the title of his book on the subject sums up his attitude more than adequately: *The most infamous hoax in ufology*.

One instance of self-contradiction on the part of Meier and his defenders concerns a sequence of photographs purporting to show a Pleiadean spacecraft circling a tree. An

unfortunate aspect of this series is that when independent investigators visited the site, no tree was to be found. Meier's explanation for this was that the spacecraft had subsequently disintegrated the hapless arboreal specimen. When taxed with the same question, Wendelle Stevens told Korff that the tree vanished because it had been teleported into 'another time frame'. Kal Korff's suspicion is that neither of these things happened, since a close look at the pictures – reputedly taken within a few seconds of one another – reveals markedly different cloud patterns from frame to frame. Genesis III's claim that the day in question was particularly windy is not borne out by the weather record, which shows wind speeds reaching a maximum of 15 miles per hour (25 km/h). Korff reasons that a model UFO and model tree were superimposed on pictures of the site. And indeed models of the Pleiadean craft have been found on the Meier farm – though Meier says that they were inspired by his actual encounters.

Above: a spacecraft circles a tree in this sequence shot by Meier. In other frames, the tree's top is alleged to move, owing to the 'force' of the craft. But according to hostile photographic analysts, the pictures are the result of superimposing the UFO and tree images onto the background sequence. The cloud patterns could not have changed so much, they say, in the short time that the UFO was allegedly circling the tree

Possibly the least plausible of Meier's defenders is Jim Dilettoso, of Genesis III. Kal Korff prints a long interview with him (and dismantles most of his statements) in which he says that in the 1950s Wendelle Stevens and another ufologist, Richard Miller, performed something called 'transchannelling' on aliens for the US Air Force:

> They would fly up to Alaska because they were told that the magnetic fields there were proper for resonance induction, and we have hundreds and hundreds of audio recordings of Richard and other CIA officers doing transchannelings of aliens. . . . Two of those CIA officers . . . have developed serious personality aberrations.

Asked why, Dilettoso replied:

> . . . it seems like something consistent in people that do channeling . . . that their cell-salt structures change, and they develop diabetes.
>
> There's also studies done that the last two Popes developed diabetes, as do a lot of Eastern gurus. So what's the correlation between transchanneling

> and cell-salts and diabetes, then diabetes going unchecked, developing into other neurotic and schizophrenic . . . behaviors that usually show up as olfactory and motor sense disturbances like Parkinson's disease. It's not where they become schizophrenic where their thinking is impaired, but where their body reactions are affected, and Billy [Meier] shows signs of that also. . . .
>
> But that seems consistent in the, oh . . . some thousand contactee cases that are being studied. In that the vibrating field put out by the ship and by the beings themselves *dominates* the aura, the magnetic field that can be kirlian photographed, dominates it so much, that it appears to even get down and start reprogramming the DNA.

One may be forgiven for suspecting that Stevens, and his associates who make up Genesis III, did start by believing Meier and accepting his evidence at face value. Then, embarrassed by the jeers, laughter and protests of more painstaking ufologists, they were forced into defending their lost cause. Meier, however, has simply continued to make ever more extravagant comments – not, perhaps, without a certain impish humour – which Genesis III have tumbled over themselves to make respectable. The results, after the fashion of tumbling, bear a close resemblance to slapstick, however. The paucity of photographs of the Pleiadeans themselves is explained by Wendelle Stevens thus: 'They are afraid of being hurt . . . they do not want to be recognised. Supposedly, they do walk the streets in Europe and don't wish to be compromised.' Billy Meier, on the other hand, has happily admitted the strong resemblance between Semjase and his own girlfriend – so who is really worried about being recognised on the streets of Europe?

A spacecraft hovers in the distant sky beyond the tripod-mounted camera. The telepathic promptings that Meier received before each encounter enabled him to come to it well-prepared with such photographic equipment as he possessed – which, however, was somewhat inadequate to the world-shaking nature of these events

Less edifying are the claims made by Meier and Genesis III concerning the samples of metal and crystal given Meier by the Pleiadeans as examples of their technological wizardry. Meier actually produced these while Stevens and his team were in Switzerland. They called on him one morning and were told that he had had his 105th contact during the night and 'had a surprise' for the investigators. This turned out to be a package, handed over by the cosmonaut Quetzal, of four metal, one biological and nine mineral and crystal specimens. According to the book, the scientists who conducted 'in-depth, highly sophisticated examination' of these samples found them to have unique qualities and said they had 'never seen anything like it before'. The level of purity in the metal was 'not immediately explainable' while the general characteristics 'seemed to indicate a non-electrolytic, cold fusion synthesis process not generally known to earth technology'.

Kal Korff found rather less to be excited about. He interviewed Dr Marcel Vogel, who had analysed the samples for Genesis III – and had drawn rather different conclusions

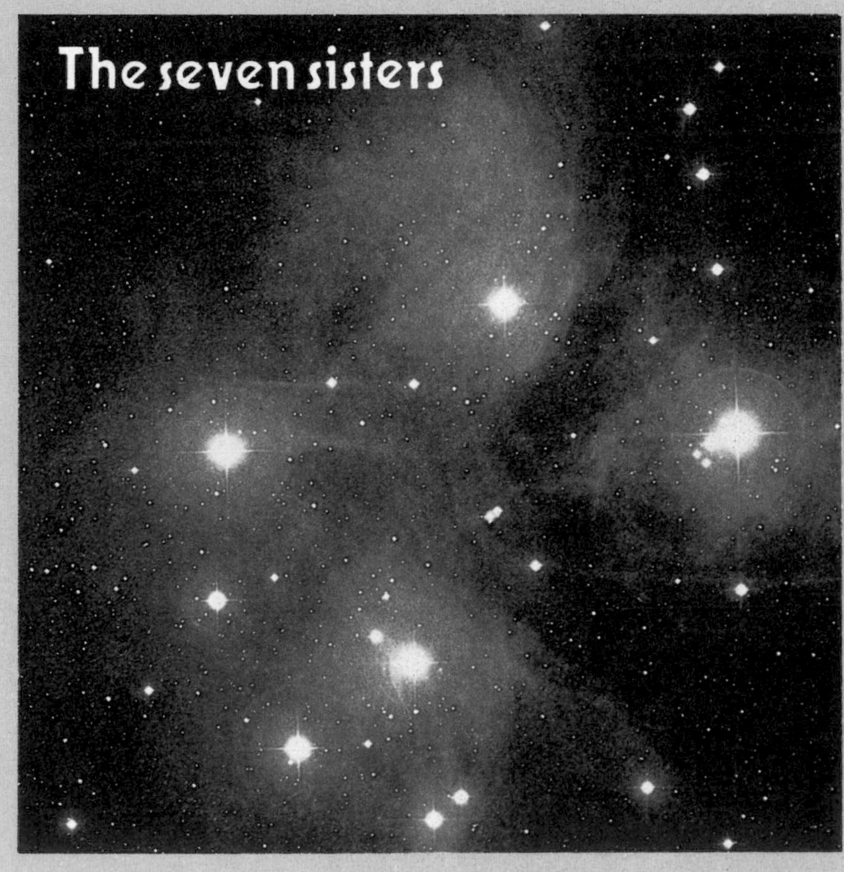

The seven sisters

The Pleiades (left), the star cluster that is the home of the space people with whom Billy Meier claims to meet so regularly. The haze of gas and dust indicates the comparative youth of the cluster, for as the group matures the interstellar matter will disperse. The few hundred stars of the cluster were born together a mere 60 million years ago – by contrast with the 5000 million years of the Sun's existence to date. This time is too short to have permitted the formation of any planets, or the appearance of indigenous life. According to Meier, the space people migrated to the Pleiades from their original home in the constellation of Lyra. But how do they survive there? Is Erra, their supposed home, an artificial planet constructed by the migrants?

The Pleiades of Greek myth were seven sisters, named Alcyone, Asterope, Electra, Celaeno, Maia, Merope and Taygeta. They were daughters of Atlas and Pleione. As it happens, the leader of the migration from Lyra was called Pleione, according to Meier. Was the mythical name a faint memory of the space traveller? Or was the space traveller's name suggested to Meier by the half-remembered mythical name?

from those published in the book. Only the first sample was unique, said Dr Vogel, consisting of aluminium, silver and thulium, each having a high degree of purity. The other samples were ordinary crystals of quartz, citrine, amethyst and silver solder, and there is no reason to believe they are of extra-terrestrial origin. Jim Dilettoso characteristically failed to further the cause by claiming that Genesis III hold a 10-hour videotape of 'the entire lab proceedings' (which Dr Vogel denies having made). 'And,' Dilettoso incautiously persisted, 'we have about an hour of him discussing why the metal samples are not possible in earth technology, going into intrinsic detail of why it is not done anywhere on earth, that type of chemistry.' Of course, Dr Vogel may not be the only scientist to have analysed the samples (no mention is made by either party of the biological specimen), but then Genesis III are notably coy about naming any of the 200 scientists they say have verified Meier's remarkable story.

They are no less reticent about the numerous other witnesses who, they say, saw – and in some cases photographed – the Pleiadean craft skimming around the Swiss valleys. No other photographs have surfaced, none are printed in the book, and none of these other witnesses are named. The best the book offers is a number of photographs of unidentified people sitting around Billy Meier's dining table and the assertion that tapes of conversations with the witnesses were subjected to psychological stress evaluation (PSE). The pictures by themselves prove absolutely nothing, while PSE is a notoriously unreliable method of lie detection, despite Genesis III's talk of 'special computers standing by in northern California' to perform the analysis.

Genesis III do not mention any analysis of the notes made by Meier of his contacts with the Pleiadeans. But Jim Lorenzen of APRO quotes Dr James Hurtak, a language specialist who has taken the opportunity to read most of the 3000 pages of the 'Semjase correspondence' in the original German. 'The linguistic use of Egyptian-Aramaic and Egyptian-Hebrew names . . . is "latterday patchwork",' he says. 'All this shifting play of correspondences by which everything . . . is cheated of its individual logic creates a mood of pensive jesting . . . and even sublime travesty. By all the standards of genuine "ancient knowledge" . . . this civilisation which lays claim to being 3000 years into the future has not offered much in the way of a quantum jump over what our ancestors had 5000 years ago (in the way of intellectual transformation).'

'The aliens gave Meier the most sought after prize of all – wisdom,' remarks Kal Korff, adding: 'It was very basic wisdom indeed.' Certainly, reading through the pronouncements on life, the Universe and everything that Semjase condescended to give Meier (see page 43), one is embarrassed by their halt-familier triviality.

But of all the evidence produced by Meier, none is as controversial as his photographs of Pleiadean spacecraft.

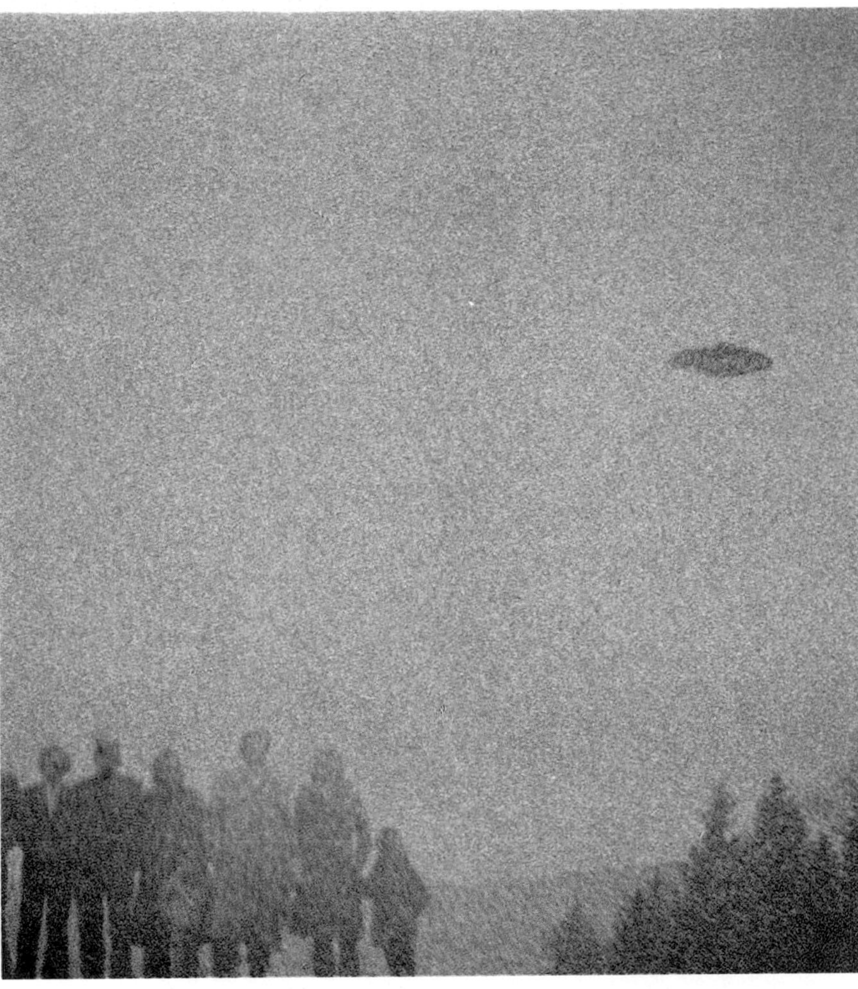

Above: witnesses pose for Meier's camera – seemingly too blasé about spacecraft to heed the hovering disc

Below: the fortunate Meier merits visits by whole squadrons of spacecraft

The camera never lies?

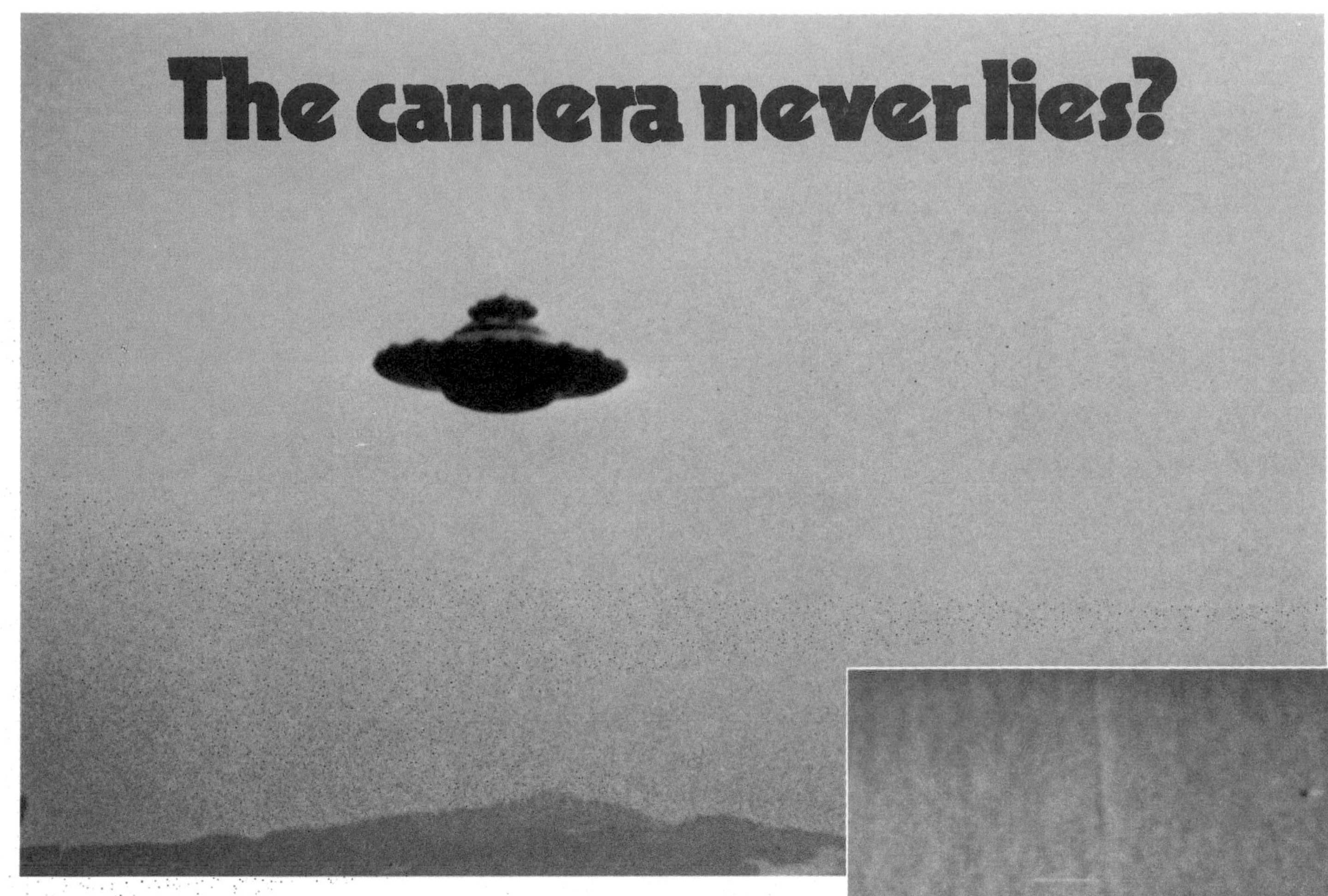

Massive scientific expertise has vindicated Billy Meier's spacecraft photographs, according to his supporters. These claims however should be pitted against the rather different conclusions of skilled ufologists

A Type-4 spacecraft over Mount Auruti, Switzerland, photographed by Billy Meier on 29 March 1976 (above). Two computer-enhanced images made from this photograph (above right) reveal a great deal about this picture. The left-hand image shows, in the words of Ground Saucer Watch who made the computer analyses, 'evidence of a linear structure' above the craft – in plain English, a string or a thin rod supporting the object. The structure is equally clear in the computerised enlargement in the second image. In addition, study of the focus in this picture indicates that the object is close to the camera and is therefore small – about 8 inches (20 centimetres) across, not 23 feet (7 metres) as claimed

THE PHOTOGRAPHS TAKEN by 'Billy' Meier of Pleiadean spacecraft as they flew around the valleys near Hinwel, Switzerland, are among the most striking UFO pictures ever published. They are so striking that they evoke that paradoxical response: *too* good to be true. But after a while one realises, looking at these elegant productions, that one's instinct has backed away from them for a less cynical reason: the pictures simply don't *fit* with one's sense of light and shade as seen in the real world. They are visually disjointed, offending one's sense of balance, clashing with one's memory of how things look. Then, on a closer look, certain patterns in the pictures emerge – and certain suspicions are aroused.

Is it coincidence, for example, that so many pictures of the same craft seem to show the flying disc at exactly the same angle to the camera, despite the very different locations and times of day at which the pictures were supposedly taken? Why do the reflections and shadows on the Pleiadean spaceships appear the same, too, despite the various backgrounds? Why are the undersides of the craft always so dark – as they would be if they were models, say, close to the camera? Why does only one picture, of extremely low quality, exist of a landed disc? Is there any significance in the massive preponderance of shots in which the craft are shown against a clear, light sky – the best type of background on which to superimpose a UFO image?

Wendelle Stevens and Genesis III – whom it seems fair to call both investigators and publicists of the Meier case – have their own answers to some of these questions. In an interview with the ufologist Timothy Green Beckley, Wendelle Stevens rather disarmingly remarked:

> First of all, photographs are poor evidence because there are so many things that we can do technically to produce images. However, there are also so many ways we can detect a hoax. We can tell if we are dealing with superimposed overlays, reflected images,

> double exposures. We can tell by looking through special microscopes and searching for grain density and grain patterns. We can pretty much tell if an object has been thrown into the air or suspended by something in the air.

And in keeping with that scepticism, the book published by Genesis III, *UFO . . . contact from the Pleiades*, shows computer-processed versions of the photographs that appear to validate their authenticity. It is when Wendelle Stevens starts to explain some of the computer enhancements that the reader's credulity is stretched. Says the colonel:

> We can [analyse photographs] with a computer by studying the edges around any given object. In high magnification an edge is seen as a series of shock waves. There is a special formula for the spacing of these shock waves that make up the edge. How strong they are, how far apart they are, will tell you how far apart that edge of the object is from the camera. If the body is in motion, the shock waves are compressed on the leading edge, and expand on the trailing edge.

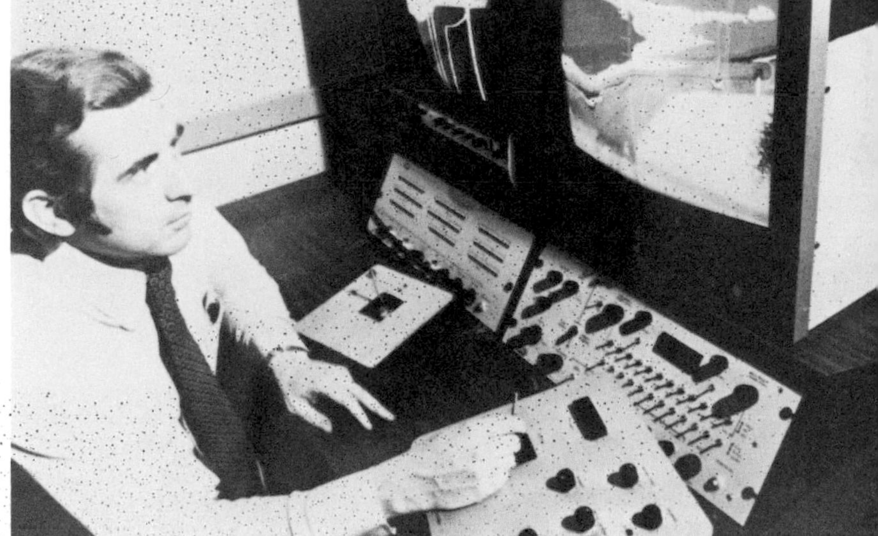

William H. Spaulding, Director of the Western Division of Ground Saucer Watch (GSW), at the console of the image-processing computer with which GSW analyse UFO photographs. GSW's verdict on the Meier pictures that they studied: 'total hoaxes'

In fact, nothing of the kind happens. What this particular computer process does is enhance the picture contrast in areas where the image brightness varies – especially at the edges of features, making it possible to make judgements about how far the object photographed is from the camera. In some cases, it is possible to intensify otherwise hard-to-detect strings or supports attached to the object. This has nothing whatever to do with shock waves, though Stevens has repeated the idea more than once.

In Genesis III's book, the 12 or so pictures purporting to show analytic enhancements of Meier's pictures are accompanied by details of the various tests to which the photographs were subjected. It is claimed that the computer enhancements showed how the light values of the landscape are consistent with those on the bottom of the craft. Supposedly, the test eliminates double exposures or 'paste-ups' – splicing images from two different transparencies together. So far, perhaps, so good. The name of a reputable computer systems company, De Anza Systems, appears on the edge of one frame.

Kal Korff took the simple step of asking Mr Wayne Heppler, manager of De Anza Systems, if an analysis had been performed for Genesis III. Replied the honest Mr Heppler:

> What these guys did was come down to De Anza Systems claiming that they wanted to *buy* a computer from us. So we took one of their pictures, one showing the UFO, and enhanced it to make certain parts of the picture stand out. Then they took pictures of it, left, and stated they would get back in touch with us. And we haven't heard from them since.

Korff then asked if De Anza had the technical capability to analyse the pictures. The answer: 'No. We are in no position to do an analysis.'

At a lecture at the UFO '80 Symposium held in Oakland, California, in August 1980, Jim Dilettoso of Genesis III said that 'z-scale contouring' and 'edge identification' tests were run on the pictures. The only drawback to this is that these are simply colour contouring techniques (and can be used to analyse the 'density' at each point of an image – its lightness or darkness). They are *not* light distortion tests, such as edge enhancement, which might reveal the information Genesis III claim to have gained by the techniques.

Dilettoso also (perhaps rather rashly) took exception to a Ground Saucer Watch (GSW) colour contouring of one of the Meier pictures. This shows a similar level of light reflectivity on both the ground and the Pleiadean spacecraft – indicating that *something* is wrong with the photograph, since the

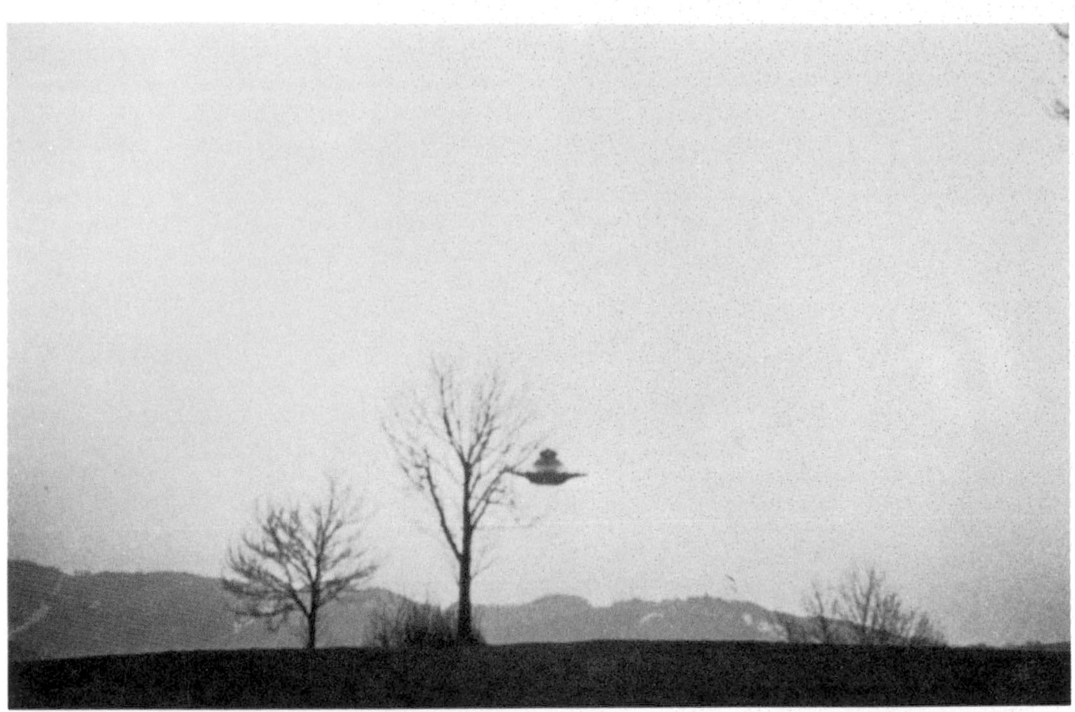

This photograph (left) was taken within a few minutes of the one on the previous page. The craft is said to be hovering beyond the tree, which is about 165 feet (50 metres) away. Two computer-processed versions appear opposite. The edge enhancement on the left revealed, according to GSW, inconsistencies between the shadows on the disc and on the tree. This suggests that the UFO and landscape images have been superimposed. The colour-contoured image on the right suggested to GSW that the UFO image was actually superimposed *on top* of the tree image, as if the UFO were closer than the tree – 'indicating very sloppy work', in Kal Korff's words

materials, at the claimed distances, should reflect (and so colour contour) differently. Dilettoso's objection was unfortunate, since even Genesis III's computer-generated picture shows both the craft and its background in the same colour contour.

It did so, Kal Korff discovered, for reasons that could prove nothing about the authenticity of Billy Meier's photographs. According to Ken Dimwiddie, one of the technicians at De Anza Systems, who was present when Dilettoso appeared in the guise of a prospective customer, it was Dilettoso himself who assigned the colours on the computer's read-out screen. In other words, the colours may indicate almost anything about the actual qualities of the original photograph. They have little value except to satisfy Jim Dilettoso's aesthetic fancy.

Computer-aided analyses of the Meier pictures by Ground Saucer Watch, however, are devastating by comparison. They inspired two GSW researchers, Fred Adrian and William Spaulding, to describe them as 'hoaxes, both crude and grandiose'.

Even without the aid of computer enhancement the photographs are dubious. Shadows on the Pleiadean craft do not conform to the light in the landscape, and the sharpness of the UFO images indicates that the object shown is extremely close to the camera – as a model would be. (GSW's estimate is that the various 'spaceships' are, in fact, between 8 and 12 inches [20 and 30 centimetres] in diameter.) Fuzziness that would result from atmospheric effects is often lacking.

Where the images are more consistent with expectations, one is still left baffled by the testimony of Meier himself. Despite his

Below: this picture, from a scorched negative found in Meier's barn, was never intended by him to be published. It shows, unmistakably, a model spacecraft on a table-top. Meier admitted that he possessed models of the Pleiadean craft – made by his children from his descriptions, he insisted

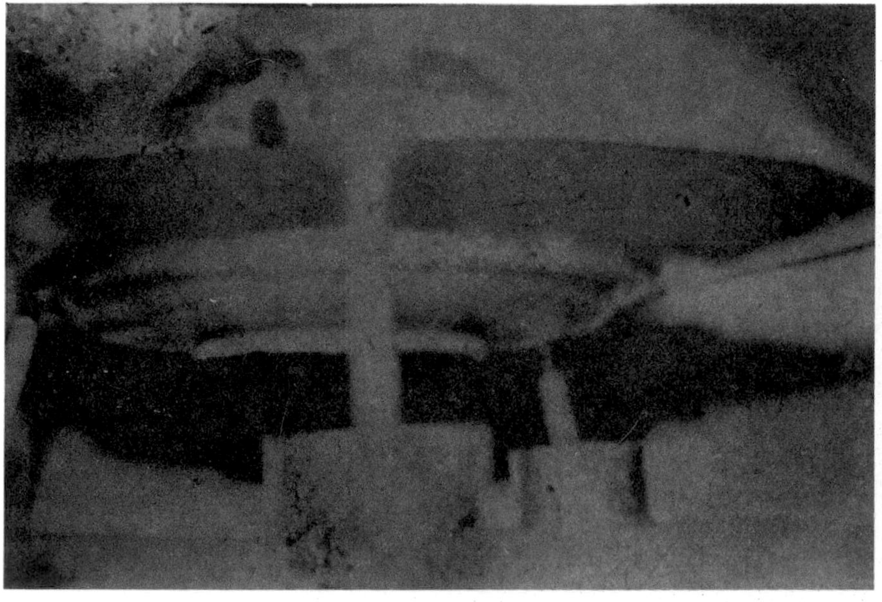

Below right: Billy Meier kneels between Wendelle Stevens (writing) and Lee Elders, co-author of *UFO . . . contact from the Pleiades*. The child is Meier's youngest son

constant contacts and the priceless photographic evidence he was gathering on behalf of mankind, Meier never bothered to repair or replace his allegedly broken camera, whose lens was stuck, focused at infinity. Yet different focusings *do* seem to have been achieved – resulting in 'distant' objects coming out as suitably fuzzy.

But then the testimony concerning Meier and his photographic techniques occasionally leaves the disinterested enquirer gasping. It should be pointed out that Billy Meier lost his left arm in an accident, which one would expect to make for difficulties with a camera. Wendelle Stevens nevertheless has made the startling claim that Meier shot all his pictures from the hip, because the mirror in his camera had 'jammed closed' as well. And yet he manages to centre his UFOs in every frame with amazing precision.

Jim Dilettoso also says that a professional photographic expert claimed he would need 'a million dollars' to duplicate the Meier pictures. Less excitably, Wendelle Stevens attempts to debunk the claims that the UFOs are models by asking: 'How many models can a one-armed man carry on a moped when he is driving with the only arm he's got?' One might reply: 'As many as will fit in a bag.'

So, what is one to make of the Meier case?

Certainly, the material evidence is anything but convincing, and the tales told by Meier have (as GSW have pointed out) all the hallmarks of American George Adamski's extravaganzas, updated and technically sophisticated for a more demanding age.

It is disheartening to learn that Stevens received an invitation to present his case to the House of Lords UFO Committee, who should have known better than to invite him in the first place.

Genesis III come out of the affair in greater embarrassment than Meier, who, after all, is apparently renowned for being 'a sort of person who gets great satisfaction out of fooling the authorities'. Genesis III have published some remarkable claims on behalf of Meier, yet none of those claims has been validated by independent research. Wendelle Stevens may attempt to disarm the ufologist Jim Lorenzen by saying, 'As you well know, Jim, the book was never designed to present any hard facts,' yet it gives every impression of doing just that.

Left: Meier reported that these discs were photographed about 1½ hours after the one seen above and on the previous pages. GSW found that the focus on the discs is much sharper than on the trees, showing that the discs are much closer. Again, there is evidence that the UFO images were superimposed on the landscape picture

As for Meier himself, it is possible that some *subjective* experience lies behind the discredited material evidence. If the stories of voices in the head, going for rides in 'pear-shaped UFOs' with 'a very old man' at the age of five, and the sightings he had from a very early age are anything to go by, this may be the best explanation. In which case, the model spacecraft (whose existence Meier doesn't deny) may well have been constructed as a result of an actual series of contactee experiences, however unlikely it is that these represent an attempt by any Pleiadeans to get in touch with us on Earth. If so, then Billy Meier has unfortunately allowed his experience to be turned by others into something like an industry.

The British scareship invasion

A policeman's sighting of a huge and mysterious airship early in 1909 started a spate of reports of similar terrifying craft. Were they, asks NIGEL WATSON, German Zeppelins – or were they something much stranger?

IN THE EARLY MONTHS of 1909 an aerial horror began to haunt the imaginations of the British people. The first sighting of a phantom airship to have a major impact on the public consciousness was made by a Cambridgeshire policeman, PC Kettle. He was patrolling Cromwell Road in Peterborough on the morning of 23 March when he heard the sound of a distant motor car. As he continued to 'hear the steady buzz of a high power engine' he suddenly realised that the noise was coming from above. On looking up he saw a bright light attached to a long oblong body outlined against the stars. This strange aerial object crossed the sky at a high speed, and was soon lost from sight.

News of this sighting was met with a certain amount of scepticism. Nevertheless, it set the pattern for future 'airship' watchers: reports from people who had seen bright, powerful lamps or searchlights attached to dark bodies making a noisy passage across the night sky soon became numerous. Another common feature of such stories was the happy habit of many self-proclaimed experts of submitting explanations for such marvellous visions. In the case of PC Kettle's sighting, a Peterborough police officer announced to the press that a 'very fine kite flying over the neighbourhood of Cobden Street' had been the cause. The bright light was easily explained as a Chinese lantern that had been attached to the kite.

'But how about the matter of the airship going at a tremendous pace?' asked a reporter.

'Oh, that was a little poetic touch on Kettle's part for the benefit of you interviewers. He did not officially report that, and the wind driving the kite would give the impression of movement,' replied the officer.

'But how do you get over the whirring and beating of engines?' asked the still puzzled reporter.

'Oh, that,' responded the officer, as he went to take his leave, 'was the motor which goes all night in the Co-operative Bakery in Cobden Street!'

This bland dismissal of PC Kettle's observation might have carried more weight if it had been released soon after the sighting.

Above: an early dirigible, the Zeppelin Mark 2, in flight over Lake Constance in April 1909. The same year, there was a spate of mystery airship sightings throughout Britain. Many people believed that the aircraft were German Zeppelins making reconnaissance flights in preparation for an invasion of Britain – but German airships were far too unreliable for it to be possible to employ them on such a dangerous mission

Below: Cromwell Road, Peterborough, the site of the first 'scareship' sighting

Instead, it took the Peterborough police at least six weeks to arrive at this simple answer to the mystery of the airship. It seems they preferred to imply that PC Kettle was a simpleton who could not distinguish between a kite and an airship, rather than to see the Peterborough police force implicated in giving credence to such an unlikely story.

At first PC Kettle's observation seemed an isolated occurrence. But around the beginning of May sightings began to be reported daily throughout south-east England. A typical report was made by a Mr C. W. Allen. As he and some friends were driving through the village of Kelmarsh, Northamptonshire, on 13 May, they heard a loud bang. Then above them they heard the 'tock-tock-tock' sound of a motor engine. Although the sky was dark they were able to see a 100-foot (30-metre) long torpedo-shaped airship that carried lights fore and aft. It was moving swiftly, but this did not prevent the witnesses seeing a platform suspended beneath the craft, which appeared to contain its crew. The airship disappeared in the direction of Peterborough.

There were many more such reports. But what were the aircraft? The fact that the exploits of Count Zeppelin were well-known in Britain (see box), combined with the antagonism between Germany and Britain, soon led people to believe that German airships were making a reconnaissance in preparation for a future invasion.

Right: a clipping from the Cardiff *Evening Express and Evening Mail* of Wednesday, 19 May 1909 describes a sighting of the mystery airship made by Mr C. Lethbridge on 18 May on Caerphilly Mountain. Mr Lethbridge saw a huge 'long, tube-shaped object' lying on the grass at the side of the road. Newspaper cuttings relating to airship sightings and to German military matters were later found scattered over the area

Below: the Wellman airship at the Aero Show of 1909. Prior to the First World War, Britain devoted very little research to airships; government construction was begun in 1907, but at the outbreak of war in 1914 only five British ships had been built

The major flaw in the hypothesis, however, was the sheer number of airship sighting reports, which came from all regions of Britain. At the time, Germany barely had the resources to make even one or two reconnaissance flights over Britain. For this reason, a few newspapers were prepared to discount the entire phenomenon as imaginary, and sent readers who had reported airship sightings to what they picturesquely called 'lunacy experts'. From one expert, they received this diagnosis:

> In every thousand men there are always two every night who see strange matters – chromatic rats, luminous owls, moving lights, fiery comets, and things like those. So you can always get plenty of evidence of this sort, particularly when you suggest it to the patient first.

The most puzzling and sensational sighting was made by an elderly Punch and Judy showman, Mr C. Lethbridge. With this report, made on 18 May, the focus for the airship's activities shifted from the east coast to mid Glamorgan, Wales. By now there were well-attested reports of a 'long-shaped

A phantom fleet?

Could the mysterious airships seen over Britain during 1909 have been German Zeppelins? It seems unlikely.

The pioneer of German airship research was Count Ferdinand von Zeppelin (right), who launched his first dirigible, the *Luftschiff Zeppelin 1* – or *LZ1* – over Lake Constance in July 1900, shortly before his sixty-second birthday. *LZ1*, simply an enormous bag filled with gas and propelled by an engine, remained in the air for just over 17 minutes – but its short flight was impressive, and the future of airships seemed bright.

Count Zeppelin set in motion an ambitious airship-building programme, but by 1909, owing to a number of crashes and shortage of money, there were only three working Zeppelins in existence – the *LZ3*, rebuilt from an earlier airship that had crashed, the *LZ5* and the *LZ6*. Of these, only two, the *LZ3* and the *LZ5*, were in the hands of the army – and they were very much in their experimental stages, and certainly not capable of long and hazardous journeys, or of carrying out the high-speed manoeuvres reported by the witnesses of the British 'scareships'.

object' with red flashing lights seen over Belfast, Ireland, on 17 May, and there seemed to be no area of Britain left unaffected by the scare. A few hours after his sighting – which amounted to a close encounter – Mr Lethbridge told inquisitive reporters:

> Yesterday I went to Senghenydd and proceeded to walk home over Caerphilly Mountain. You know that the top of the mountain is a very lonely spot. I reached it about 11 p.m., and when turning the bend at the summit I was surprised to see a long, tube-shaped affair lying on the grass at the roadside, with two men busily engaged with something nearby. They attracted my close attention because of their peculiar get-up; they appeared to have big, heavy fur coats and fur caps fitting tightly over their heads. I was rather frightened, but I continued to go on until I was within twenty yards [18 metres] of them and then my idea as to their clothing was confirmed. The noise of my little spring-cart seemed to attract them and when they saw me they jumped up and jabbered furiously to each other in a strange lingo – Welsh or something else; it was certainly not English. They hurriedly collected something from the ground, and then I was really frightened. The long thing on the ground rose up slowly. I was standing still all the time, quite amazed, and when it was hanging a few feet off the ground the men jumped into

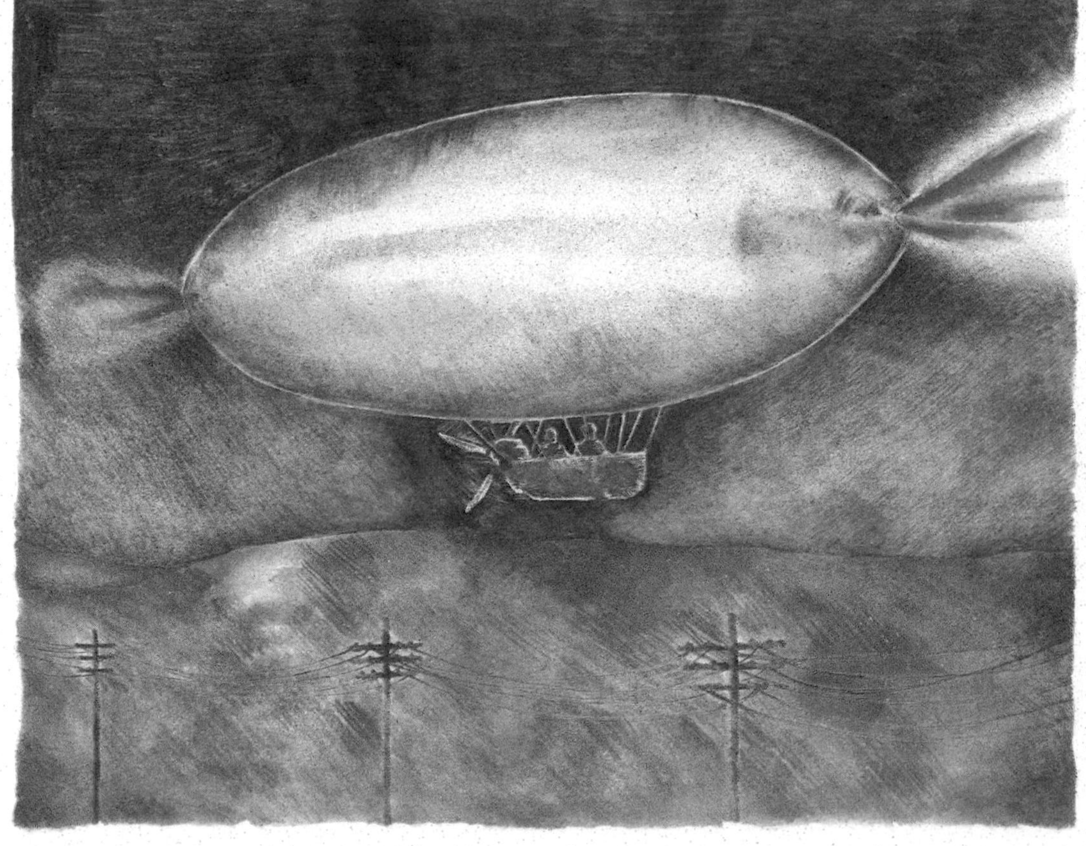

Left: the 'scareship' seen by Mr C. Lethbridge on Caerphilly Mountain on 18 May 1909 'rose in the air in a zig-zag fashion' and sailed away towards Cardiff

Right: Ham Common, on the outskirts of London. Here, on the night of 13 May 1909, a Mr Grahame and a Mr Bond saw a remarkable airship whose pilots, whom they described as a Yankee and a German, apparently steered their craft by pulling beer handles

Right: the village of Kelmarsh, Northamptonshire where, on 13 May 1909, a Mr C. W. Allen saw a 100-foot (30-metre) airship moving swiftly north-eastwards

Below: a cartoon published in *Punch* of 26 May 1909. The cartoon shows a sea serpent staring glumly at a headline in the *Daily Scare*: 'Mysterious air-ship seen everywhere by night' – and commenting, 'Well, if this sort of thing keeps on, it'll mean a dull August for me'

a kind of little carriage suspended from it, and gradually the whole affair and the men rose in the air in a zig-zag fashion. When they had cleared the telegraph wires that pass over the mountain, two lights like electric lamps shone out, and the thing went higher into the air and sailed away towards Cardiff.

When Mr Lethbridge, accompanied by reporters, returned to the site where he had his encounter, they found several traces of the airship's presence. The ground where the 45-foot (14-metre) long object had been seen was churned up as though by a plough-share. All over the area they discovered a quantity of newspaper cuttings of accounts of airship sightings and references to the German emperor and army. Along with these items they found a large quantity of papier-mâché packing material, a lid from a tin of metal polish, a few dozen pieces of blue paper bearing strange writing, and a metal pin with a red label attached to it. The label of the pin carried instructions in French and excited attention when some commentators thought that it was part of an explosive device, but further enquiry showed it probably to have been a valve plunger for a motor car tyre.

Several witnesses came forward to support Lethbridge's story. In Salisbury Road, Cathays, Cardiff, residents said that on the same evening, between 10.40 and 10.50 p.m., they saw an airship-like object in the air.

Cigar-shaped 'boat'

Additional testimony came from workers on Cardiff docks who, two hours after Lethbridge's encounter, saw a fast moving 'boat of cigar shape' flying from the direction of Newport, and going eastwards. The airship carried two lights, and its engines made a loud whirring noise. One witness said, 'We could not see those on board. The airship was too high up for that at night, but it was plain that it was a big airship.'

Two gentlemen, a Mr Grahame and a Mr Bond, made some even more extravagant claims, to the effect that they had seen a 200- to 230-foot (60- to 70-metre) long airship 'like a collection of big cigar boxes with the ends out' on Ham Common, London. The occupants of the craft, whom they met on the night of 13 May, they described as a clean-shaven Yankee and a German who smoked a calabash pipe. The German asked for some tobacco, which Mr Grahame supplied out of his own pouch. Although they were blinded by a searchlight that played on their faces, the witnesses were able to see that the 'Yankee' was positioned in a kind of wire cage, and in front of him he had a row of levers similar to draught beer pump handles. In front of the German was positioned a map with pins dotted all over it. The encounter apparently came to an abrupt end when the 'Yankee' pulled one of the levers down, 'and then he switched the light off, and the aeroplane went without either of the men saying good-bye.'

With such a variety of bizarre reports, it is hardly surprising that the mystery of the phantom scareship that plagued Britain in 1909 has proved difficult to solve.

Who sent the scareships?

When the 1909 epidemic of 'scareship' sightings died down, it seemed to be the end of the story – until, in 1912, new and more mysterious sightings began to be reported

RUMOURS OF A FLIGHT by a Zeppelin airship over Sheerness, Kent, on the evening of 14 October 1912 caused questions to be asked in the House of Commons. On 27 November 1912, opposition MP Mr William Joynson-Hicks asked the First Lord of the Admiralty, Mr Winston Churchill, if he knew anything about this matter. Mr Churchill affirmed that an unidentified aircraft had been reported on that date. It was heard flying over the district at 7 p.m., and caused flares to be lit at nearby Eastchurch in anticipation of a landing by the craft. However, nothing descended from the night sky, and the nationality and origin of the craft, Mr Churchill had to admit, remained a mystery.

Enquiries by the press in Eastchurch revealed that the townspeople had heard a buzzing noise between 6.30 and 7 p.m. on 14 October. But at the time it was assumed to be the sound of an airship or aeroplane making its way to the naval aviation school at Eastchurch. This was not the case, however, for no aircraft made any night flight on the date in question, from or to that base.

The public discussion that followed in the wake of the exchange between Mr Joynson-Hicks and Mr Churchill had many unforeseen consequences.

Almost immediately the German *L1* Zeppelin, which had started a 30-hour proving flight on 13 October, was blamed as the cause of the Sheerness incident. Whether or not the *L1*, or any other of Germany's airships, visited Sheerness in 1912 is still a matter for debate. Whatever the reason for the incident, the British government decided to strengthen the Aerial Navigation Act of 1911, in order to pacify public and official disquiet. The bill was quickly passed through parliamentary channels and was given the royal assent on 14 February 1913. It gave the Home Secretary the power to prohibit aerial traffic over areas of the United Kingdom and its territorial waters. It also meant that if an aerial vehicle failed to respond to ground signals, or violated the prohibited areas, it was liable to be fired at.

Not everybody was pleased with the amended act. Feverish efforts were made to construct an efficient sky gun – but while the project remained in its experimental stages,

The state of the art

The government of the day claimed it knew nothing of the 'scareships' of 1913. Could this really have been the case? The first two army airships, the *Nulli Secundus* I and II, had been dismantled by 1909; the first of the smaller airships that followed them, the *Beta*, made its maiden flight in 1910. Clearly whatever caused the 1909 sightings could not have been an army machine. The same applies to the 1913 sightings. The successors of the *Beta* – the *Gamma* and *Delta* – were too small to be mistaken for 'scareships', and two airships ordered from France, and one made in Britain by Vickers, had met with disaster.

There remains the possibility that some of the Welsh sightings may be explained as misidentifications of airships built by the only private manufacturer of note, E.T. Willows of Cardiff. But these ships were familiar to local people; Captain Lindsay, for example, actually compared the 'scareship' he saw over Cardiff on 17 January 1913 with the Willows airship. The mystery remains.

Left: the Krupp 6.5-centimetre gun, designed in Germany in 1909 for shooting down airships, shown with an artist's impression of a Zeppelin. Sightings of an unidentified airship over Kent in October 1912 led opposition MP Mr William Joynson-Hicks (inset) to ask questions in the House of Commons; and in 1913 parliament passed a bill that meant that any unauthorised foreign aircraft found in Britain's airspace was liable to be fired at. Unlike Germany, however, Britain lacked an effective long-range anti-airship gun

Below: Clyne Woods, Swansea, scene of an impressive scareship sighting in January 1913

many argued that the act was like a dog with a loud bark, but with no teeth to bite with. It was against this background of events that a new wave of phantom airship sightings began in January 1913.

Early in the morning of 4 January three witnesses, including a police constable, saw and heard an airship flying over Dover. It came from the direction of the sea and disappeared from sight to the north east. Despite a strong westerly wind, the craft, which displayed a light and made a distinct droning sound, flew at a great speed. In this case it was alleged that a French airship from a base at Verdun, 120 miles (200 kilometres) away, had been the culprit, though it is hard to imagine why the craft would have made such a perilous journey at such an early hour in poor weather conditions.

Another significant sighting was made by Captain Lionel Lindsay, Chief Constable of Glamorganshire, on 17 January. At 4.45 p.m. he saw an airship pass over Cardiff. He said:

> It was much bigger and moved faster than the Willows airship and left in its trail a dense volume of smoke. I called the attention of a bystander to the object, and he agreed with me that it was some large aircraft. It disappeared quickly so giving evidence of speedy movement.

Steven Morgan, of Merthyr, saw a similar object from his bedroom window, half an hour after Captain Lindsay. He was also impressed by the trail of smoke the airship left behind it. Before he could obtain the use of a powerful telescope the craft went out of view over the Aberdare Valley.

These sightings encouraged more witnesses to come forward. One such observer was a postman from Sketty, Swansea, who saw what looked like a very bright light hovering over Clyne Woods on 21 January at 7 p.m. Four days later, a mysterious aircraft going at a speed of 25 miles per hour (40 km/h) was seen by several people in Liverpool. Although members of a local flying club had been in the air earlier in the day, they said that at the time of the sighting it had been too windy for an extended flight. On several nights at the end of January many witnesses reported seeing a bright light moving over Manchester, which puzzled them.

Epidemic 'airshipitis'

The sightings of the airship, or airships, spread throughout the land to such an extent that a newspaper nicknamed the epidemic of reports 'airshipitis'.

When MP Mr Joynson-Hicks was asked about Captain Lindsay's sighting, he replied:

> I don't doubt the report at all, for though our own aircraft can only do thirty or forty miles [50 or 65 kilometres], the Zeppelin vessels can cross the Channel. I believe, in fact, that foreign dirigibles are crossing the English Channel at will. It is a very serious matter.

Yorkshire became a new focal point for the sightings in February. Two young people in Scarborough were the first to see anything unusual in the night sky. At some time early in the month, Mr Taylor and Miss Hollings saw a light hovering over Scarborough racecourse. They were attracted by the sound of

A spectacular airship was seen by two men who were dredging the river Ouse at Beningborough, Yorkshire, between 9.00 and 9.30 p.m. on 21 February 1913. The men saw the same airship again close by at 4 a.m. the next day, and kept it under observation for around an hour and a half

machinery, which they attributed to the light. After a few minutes a conical beam of white light descended from the craft and was played upon the racecourse for six or seven minutes. The beam of light vanished and then reappeared briefly before the thing flew away towards Selby.

Another Yorkshire sighting occurred on 21 February, between 9 and 9.30 p.m., when two men on the sand barge *Star* were dredging the river Ouse at Beningborough, and saw a light in the sky. One of the witnesses, Mr Riply, said: 'It went round and round and then stopped. It stood stationary for a short time, and then went over Billington Locks. It stood there again for some time, and then went round and round as if surveying the country.' It repeated this activity several times before finally disappearing.

At the same time in Selby, a solicitor named Mr March saw from his home a bright star over Hambleton. The star moved up and down, and backwards and forwards, as if surveying the area, or looking for something. After 45 minutes it rapidly sailed towards Leeds.

It seems that 21 February must have been a busy night for the crew of the airship – if there was, indeed, only one – for not only did many people throughout Yorkshire report seeing its lights and hearing its motors, but it was also seen over Exhall, Warwickshire and Hunstanton, Norfolk.

It was at this stage in the proceedings that the War Office began to take an interest in the sighting reports, and efforts were made to discover the identity of the mystery airship; the results of their investigations were, however, never disclosed.

Hundreds of sightings were made at the end of February by people throughout the United Kingdom. Many of these observations were, however, explained as visions of Venus, or balloons sent up by jokers. This was, indeed, true in many instances.

An impressive sighting that was not so easily explained was made by Captain Lundie and his crew aboard the *City of Leeds* steamer on 22 February at 9.15 p.m. As they were leaving the mouth of the Humber they saw high over the Yorkshire coast something that 'resembled a shark in appearance', said the captain. 'It had wings on either side, and we saw the tail of the machine. No lights were visible, but owing to the rays of the moon these were not necessary. . . . We had it under observation for about five minutes. It maintained a high altitude all the time, and finally disappeared over Grimsby.'

Mystery biplane

An intriguing sighting, possibly connected with the 'scareship' incidents, was made by a Mr Collins on board his yacht in Killary Harbour, Ireland. In late February he heard a droning sound above the bay, and saw an aeroplane coming from the direction of the sea. Suddenly it descended and landed inland. Mr Collins said:

> I ran to shore thinking they might want help or information, as it might be a breakdown. I saw it was of the bi-plane type. The occupants were three in number, and one apparently a mechanic whom I could not see, tinkering at the engines. the other two were foreigners pretty stout, with florid complexions, and very intelligent foreheads, apparently Germans.

When he asked them, in German, if he could help them, one of the men answered him in French saying he did not understand, and then brusquely told him to go away as they had everything under control. Mr Collins did not see the aircraft take off again, but he did see a steamer on the horizon, which appeared to be waiting for the return of the aircraft and its impolite aeronauts.

The sheer number of sightings made in the beginning of 1913 makes this wave difficult to research and analyse, especially since there are nearly as many explanations put forward by the pundits of the period. However, mystery still shrouds many of these sightings, though UFO researchers have made a determined effort to come to terms with this material. The result of these researches should have interesting implications for modern-day UFO studies, when the data is finally collated.

UFOs and the digital computer

Computer processing of photographs of UFOs creates striking and bizarre images, while revealing subtleties that are difficult to discern in the originals. WILLIAM H. SPAULDING, director of Ground Saucer Watch, explains this new research technique

Top: a swirl of vivid hues is a 'computer eye view' of a glowing disc seen over Colorado, USA (inset). The colours represent different brightness levels in the original image and forcefully portray detailed structure in the UFO and surrounding sky. The lines on the coloured image are 'drawn' by the computer as it makes measurements on the picture

MOST PHOTOGRAPHS of unidentified flying objects are disappointing. They are blurred, lacking in detail and uninformative at a casual glance. Often they lack the context of landscape or everyday objects that would enable one to judge the size and distance of the UFOs. The few that are sharp and clear usually turn out to be fakes.

It is the task of the UFO photo analyst to sift through this mass of low-grade material, weed out the frauds and the misidentified aircraft, birds and astronomical objects, and call attention to the small residue of photographs that resist all attempts at being explained away.

Traditionally, UFO photo analysts have been limited to a few techniques of study. By measuring shadows they may be able to show that the picture consists of a landscape shot combined with a picture of a model taken under totally different lighting conditions. By studying the focus on the UFO they may be able to show that it is much closer to the camera than the witness claimed, and is therefore much smaller than it appears. By enlarging details they may be able to reveal the presence of a tell-tale 'Frisbee' trade mark. More frequently they can identify the shot as showing some natural object – even that sceptics' favourite, the planet Venus, seen under unusual atmospheric conditions.

But all too often the label 'unidentified' has remained on the photograph because there was apparently too little information to resolve the question 'What is this mysterious object in the sky?' Yet even in the fuzziest photograph there are many subtle clues hidden away. Now a powerful new tool, the computer, promises to disclose them.

One UFO investigation group, Ground Saucer Watch, has applied the computer to the analysis of UFO photographs on a large scale. Ground Saucer Watch was founded in Cleveland, Ohio, USA, in 1957 in order to bring a high level of technical expertise to the study of UFO reports. The group wanted, in the words of a statement made then, to 'see positive scientific action taken to end the elements of foul-up and cover-up in UFO research'. A network of 500 scientific and engineering consultants assists it in this task.

Now the computer is available as an aid. It enabled Ground Saucer Watch, in a study of 1000 photographs that had *prima facie* plausibility, to reject all but 45 as misidentifications or hoaxes. Here are some of the techniques that are used to sift such quantities of material.

The pictures were analysed with a Computer Eye, manufactured by Spatial Data Systems, Inc. It uses a television-type camera that scans a picture and breaks it down into nearly a quarter of a million tiny 'pixels' (picture cells), in an array consisting of 512 columns and 480 rows.

Although the colours of the photographs provide important information, they do not come into our computer analyses. The scanner 'sees' only a black and white picture. The scanner measures the brightness of each pixel and assigns it a rating on a 'grey scale' from 0 (completely dark) to 31 (bright white). So the whole picture is reduced to a quarter of a million numbers, which are stored in the computer's memory. They can be recalled and used to build up a black and white image, a direct copy of the original, on a television screen linked to the computer. But they can also be manipulated in countless different ways to generate new images, which reveal unsuspected information in the original picture, or display it in unfamiliar and striking ways.

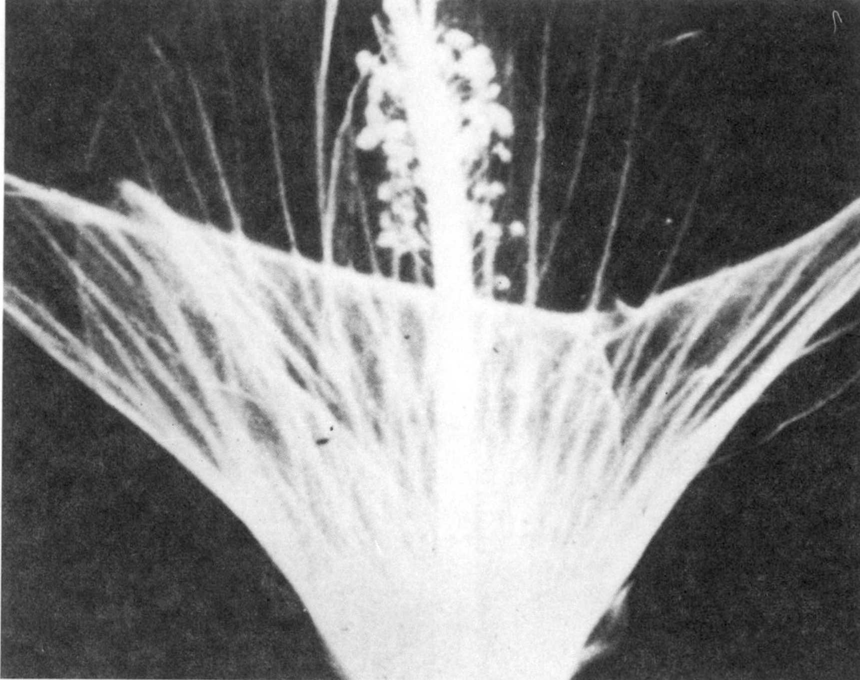

Above: an X-ray photograph of a flower. Lighter areas represent thicker tissues, which absorb X-rays more strongly than the thinner areas. Careful study is needed to see the details

Below: a computer-processed version of the picture above, in which edges separating light and dark areas have been enhanced. Some UFO pictures can be similarly clarified

At the touch of a button the computer operator can do most of the things that the photo technician can do only at the cost of several hours' work in his laboratory.

The computer can instantly enlarge any selected detail of the picture to full-screen size. There are limits to the degree to which this can usefully be done. The picture becomes coarser as the mosaic of pixels becomes more evident. This begins to happen when the picture has been enlarged by about four times, in height and breadth.

The computer can 'stretch' the contrast, brightening the light areas and darkening the shadows, so emphasising the detail in a murky original. (This is what you do to your television picture when you turn up the contrast control.)

Enhancing the image

Measurements of distances and angles on the image become extremely easy. Crossed lines can be superimposed on the picture and moved at will, to identify points of interest. The computer can measure the positions of those points and instantly calculate distances and angles.

All this makes life easier for photo analysts, and enables them to plough through much more material than before. But the computer can also easily accomplish a number of feats that are impracticable, or even impossible, for the photo technician to perform.

For example, the computer can enhance the edges of the features seen in a photo. The effect of edge enhancement is illustrated here with a picture that is a little more conventional than a UFO photo. The X-ray picture of a flower is in black and white. Each shade of grey carries information about the flower – its thickness, and hence ability to absorb X-rays, at that point. In this negative image, the brighter areas correspond to thicker areas of plant tissue. There is a great deal of delicate structure to be seen in the petals and the central pistil.

But the eye's ability to distinguish shades of grey is limited. The result obtained when the edges are enhanced is also shown opposite. Areas of uniform shade in the original are represented as a medium grey in the computer-processed picture. Wherever the original increases in lightness (from left to right) the computer draws a bright line, while where there is a transition from light to dark it draws a dark line. The result is arresting. The flower's structure, which was lost in the subtle, veil-like X-ray image, is now laid bare in a tracery of metallic clarity.

Edge enhancement has little relevance to the indistinct forms visible in many UFO pictures. However, it is revealing when applied to UFO images showing faint detail; these are generally dark objects seen against the daytime sky (see page 66). But another technique, colour coding, can extract information from the brightness pattern in the original pictures. It exploits the fact that the eye can distinguish colours far more readily than it can distinguish shades of grey.

Like an artist with a taste for poster paints, the computer has transformed the X-ray flower picture on the opposite page into a bold pattern of colours. All the detail below is present in the original picture, but is now presented in a form that is more easily 'read' by the human eye and brain

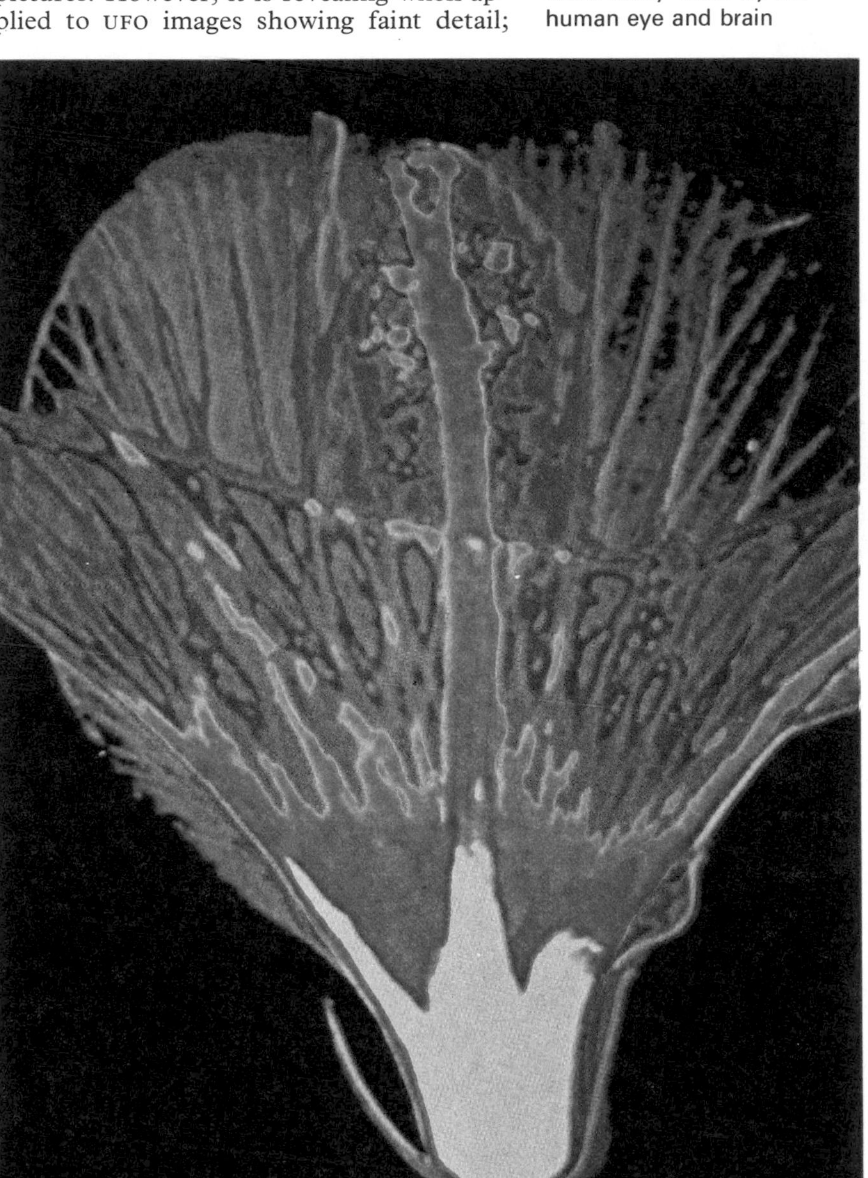

To colour-code a picture, the computer is linked to a colour television set. Each pixel is assigned a colour according to its brightness. Thus, in the X-ray picture of the flower, the darkest areas are shown as black. The darkest shades of grey (the thinnest parts of the flower) are rendered as shades of violet and red. Increasingly light areas are shown as shades of yellow, green and blue. The lightest areas (the thickest parts of the plant) are rendered as white.

The result is a gaudier flower than nature has ever created, with all the details of structure leaping out at the eye. Radiographers use this type of colour coding on X-ray pictures to improve their view of the interior of the human body.

Astronomers and space engineers apply the same techniques to the photos they take with ground-based telescopes, and to the television images sent back from space satellites and probes. In the original picture, brightness levels may represent the actual brightness of a planet's surface, or the temperature of a gas cloud in space, or the intensity of radio waves from distant galaxies. The patterns in the computer-generated image will represent this information in terms of colour. So, though there is a superficial resemblance in these different types of picture, the information they give is totally different in nature.

An ambiguous message

What does the procedure reveal specifically about UFOs? The brightness pattern of light and dark in the photo image of a UFO is a complex and ambiguous 'message', involving the shape of the object, the amount of light it may be emitting at each point, its intrinsic lightness or darkness if it is being seen by reflected light, the effects of glare and atmospheric haze, and so on. Emphasising the pattern by the colour-coding technique often reveals the true form of the object immediately. A broken, uneven density may indicate a cloud. A cylindrical shape with protruberances may appear, indicating an aircraft body and wings partly hidden by glare. The contours of a 'daylight disc' (meaning any daytime UFO) are revealed, and often turn out to be suspiciously like those of a camera lens cap, a pie plate, or a hub cap.

Ground Saucer Watch has employed these techniques on thousands of photographs. Take as an example the two famous 'Colorado pictures' overleaf. They show a single UFO sighted and photographed at precisely 6.20 a.m. local time on 28 August 1969 by Mr Norman Vedaa and his passenger while driving north-east on State

Route 80s, approximately 70 miles (110 kilometres) east of Denver, Colorado. Mr Vedaa described the object as yellow-gold, tremendously brilliant, oval in shape, and soundless. He said: 'The object was bright, hard to look at – and appeared to hover momentarily. The object's glow . . . was producing a reflective light on the clouds below. . . .' Two colour transparencies were taken and do indeed show a bright yellowish glow with well-defined edges, back-lighting the clouds.

The colour-coding technique was used on the Colorado photographs, and the result is reproduced on page 61. Again, lighter parts of the original are represented by white, blue and yellow, while darker parts are represented by red, violet and black.

The light vertical lines in that picture and in the one below are just a different way of showing brightness information. The computer has taken a 'slice' down the picture along the left-hand line. At the right, it has plotted a graph of the brightness of the scene along that line, shown by the fluctuating line. Thus the 'bump' in the wavy line represents the bright centre of the object.

The computer also speeds up the detailed study of light and shadow at any selected region of the picture. Ground Saucer Watch has a 'library' of data on the proportion of light that is reflected by each of a large range of materials. In some photographs of UFOs seen by reflected daylight, everyday objects, such as trees or houses, are visible, with which the UFO image can be compared. This

Top: a tantalising glimpse of a UFO. An American motorist, Norman Vedaa, saw a brilliant disc and stopped his car to photograph it. It is visible near the top centre. The second picture (above) was taken within a few seconds, and was the original of the processed UFO images elsewhere in this article. The disc flew off at high speed

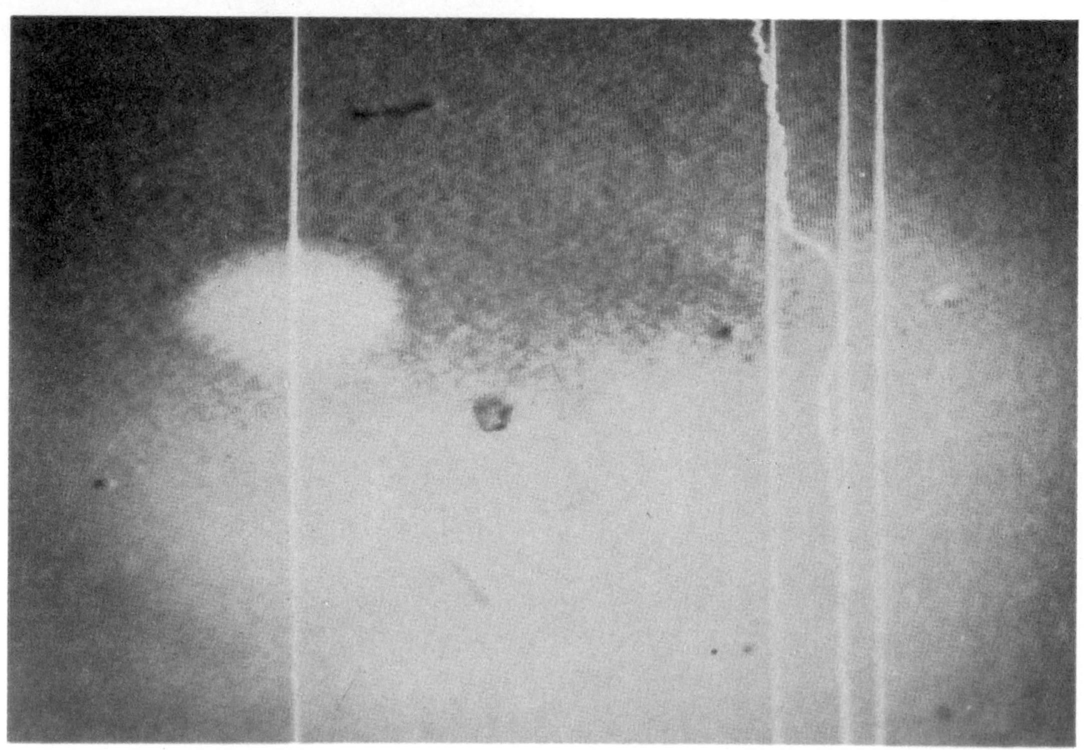

Right: measurements of image brightness made by the computer. The measurements are made along the left-hand line. The fluctuating line at the right shows the brightness: it curves to the right where the photograph is brightest. The curve helped to prove the disc was not a lens flare, weather balloon or aircraft

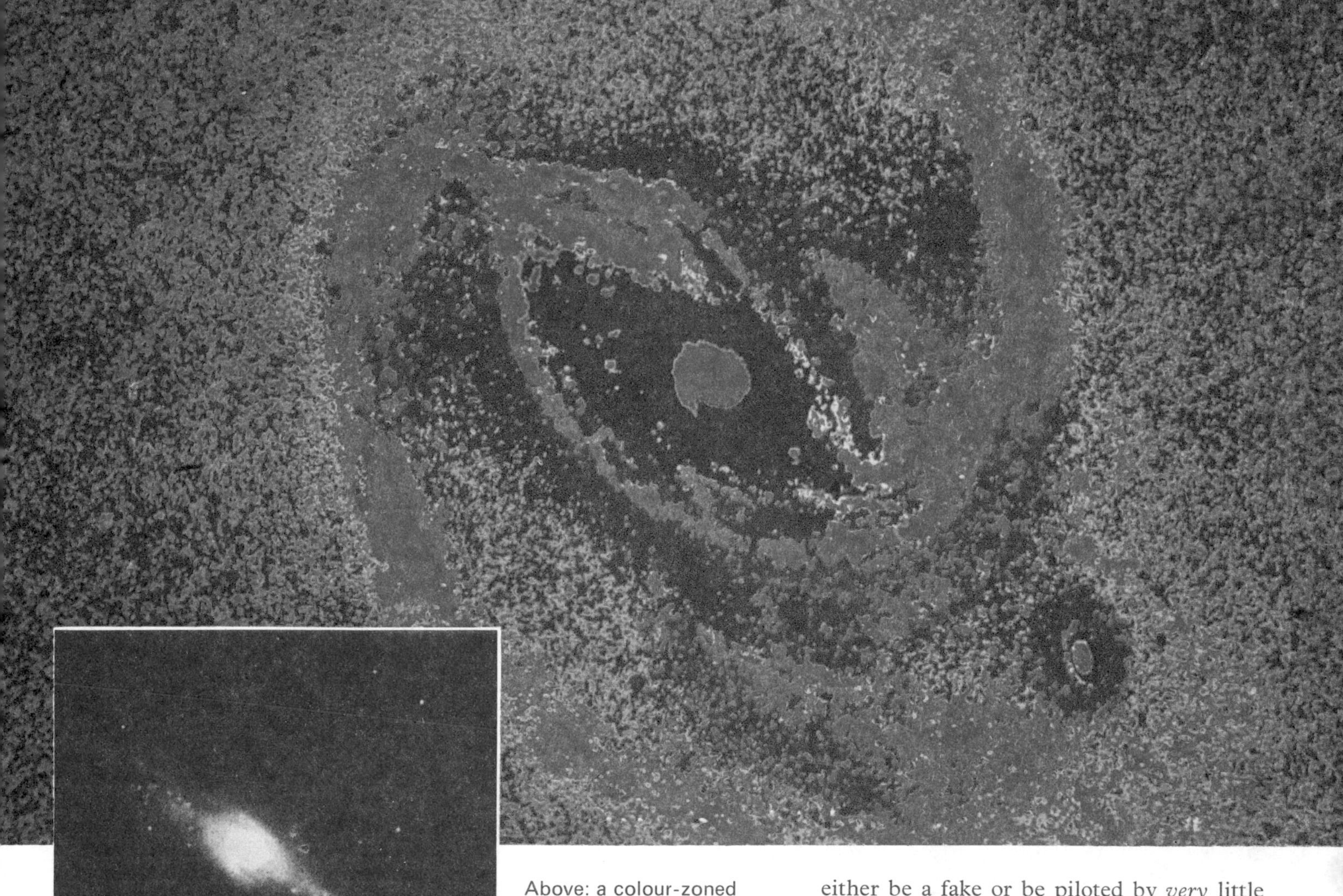

Above: a colour-zoned image of a giant star system reveals the detail latent in a black and white picture (left), itself the computerised average of five photographs. The galaxy, a mass of billions of stars and vast quantities of gas and dust swirling in a spiral, is 40 million light years from us. The coloured image shows its spiral arms extending as far as its companion elliptical galaxy at lower right. Further image processing revealed extraordinary ray-like structures surrounding the spiral galaxy. Astronomers realise the value of the computer in extracting information from their photographs. Scientific UFO study may benefit equally

may enable the analyst to make a tentative judgement about the composition of the UFO.

We can compare the contrast in the light and shadowed areas of the UFO image and in landscape features: if there is a serious discrepancy, a composite picture or a model close to the camera is indicated. Essentially the same method can be used to estimate the degree to which atmospheric haze veils the UFO image. The more distant the object is, the lighter and less contrasty it will appear because of light scattered by air molecules, dust and water vapour. This often allows us to make an estimate of the distance of the UFO from the witness.

Careful measurements on the sharpness of various features in the picture are also a valuable indicator of distance. In fact, the annoying fuzziness of most UFO pictures – which are no worse than most holiday snaps in this respect – can be turned to advantage.

Sometimes the image of a UFO in the sky is beautifully sharp, while all ground features more than 50 feet (15 metres) away are slightly out of focus. This shows that the object is close to the camera – and so must either be a fake or be piloted by *very* little green men. Making comparisons of focus is a traditional part of UFO photo analysis, now greatly facilitated by the computer.

In its study of the Vedaa pictures, Ground Saucer Watch was able to rule out more and more explanations that seek to reduce the sightings to causes that are well-known and understood. This was no weather balloon, flock of birds or daylight meteor – the brightness distribution was that of a disc. It was not an aircraft hidden in the glare of reflected sunlight – it was too bright for that, and not a trace of tail or wings could be found. Lens flares, reflections from clouds, mirages and other atmospheric effects are all ruled out: the Sun is in the wrong position for them. The object was three-dimensional in form, and it was certainly a long way from the camera.

Objective research will progress with the aid of modern technology, of which the computer is an important component. In the near future photo analysis will be carried out by more sophisticated computer programming, in conjunction with more powerful 'hardware' – faster computers with bigger memory capacity, working with scanners that can break the original image down into yet finer detail. Soon it will become virtually impossible to fake a UFO photograph. Then, perhaps, the UFO mystery will be solved.

Analysing the Trent photos

Computer analysis lends support to two of the best known UFO photographs. This chapter describes the studies carried out on these classic pictures – and suggests that the US government has for years sown confusion about UFOs

Above: a huge disc glides silently across the sky over the small Trent farm in Oregon, USA, and is captured in one of the most famous UFO photographs

Above: one of the Trents' pictures of the mysterious object shows its disc-shaped outline. In the Trents' words: 'The object was coming in toward us and seemed to be tipped up a little bit. It was very bright – almost silvery – and there was no noise or smoke'

THE COMPUTER HAS BEEN USED to analyse two of the most impressive UFO photographs to date, taken by an American couple, Mr and Mrs Trent, near McMinnville, Oregon, USA. The computer study has endorsed and extended the findings of the expert appointed by the University of Colorado's Condon Committee – that the pictures show an object that is not explicable as any known phenomenon, natural or artificial.

By the Trents' own account, the object appeared over their small farm in the early part of the evening on 11 May 1950. It was seen by Mrs Trent as she fed the farm's rabbits, and she called her husband. The family camera was found, and Mrs Trent took two photographs from positions a few feet apart. There was no sound as the disc glided from the north-eastern part of the sky across to the north-west.

There were a few unused frames left on the roll of film. The Trents attached so little importance to the pictures that they waited a few days, until they had used up the rest of the film, before they had the roll developed. They then ignored the photographs and it was only by chance that the local newspaper heard about them. When they did, however, the pictures caused a sensation, finally being featured in *Life* magazine. They were the only photographs that were not dismissed by the US Air Force's highly sceptical Condon report of 1967, which was scathing about the mass of evidence presented to it. Their investigator, William K. Hartmann, concluded that all the factors he had investigated, both in the photographs and at the scene of the sighting, were consistent with the assertion 'that an extraordinary flying object, silvery, metallic, disc-shaped, tens of metres in diameter, and evidently artificial, flew within sight of two witnesses'. The evidence, he said, did not positively rule out a hoax – which, coming from a member of the Condon team, almost rates as an endorsement of authenticity.

Controversy blew up around these photos, however, as it does around all UFO pictures that stand up to scrutiny (see box). The advent of the computer afforded an opportunity to review the Trent photographs in order to discover more than the human eye can see, even when it is aided by the microscope.

The principles involved in the computer study techniques used to analyse the photographs have already been described (see page 61). A television camera scans the picture, breaking it down into nearly a quarter of a million pixels (picture cells) and recording the lightness or darkness of each pixel as a number stored in its memory. The computer can process these numbers in countless different ways to create new images, which it displays on a television screen. Each such picture has something new to say about the information contained in the original photographic negative.

Colour-contouring the image

The first thing that Ground Saucer Watch, the investigating organisation, did with the Trent photos was to colour-contour the image, converting each shade of grey in the original picture into a different bright colour. The result was to make the distribution of light and shade over the object far easier to 'read'.

The lower surface of the disc shows only a few different shades, confirming an evenly lit, flat lower surface. The second photograph, showing the edge-on disc, disclosed a darker shade in the centre of the object than at the extreme edges, which indicates a circular shape and bevelled disc profile.

The colour-coding technique makes the light-and-shade pattern of the image plainly visible to the eye. Detailed calculations by the computer provide a more sophisticated judgement confirming the detailed shape of the object shown.

Hoax photographs generally show such items as hub caps or dishes, but the obvious shapes of such objects would be resolved by the colour-contouring technique applied to the magnified image.

The computer technicians measured the lightness of the UFO image and compared it with the shadows that can be seen on the nearby garage. The UFO turned out to be much lighter. The most straightforward explanation of this effect is that the object is at a great distance from the camera. Atmospheric haze over that distance would veil the disc – just as an observer, looking at the distant horizon, finds that it looks paler than nearby foreground objects, even on days when the air is at its clearest. However, other possible factors, including reflected ground light and grease on the camera lens, have been brought into the controversy. But this objection cannot be brought against the estimation of the object's distance by means of the sharpness of the UFO image. The foreground objects, such as the telephone wires and the building, are sharper than the UFO and distant objects on the ground.

The next step in the analysis was to search for wires suspending or supporting the disc, which would imply that the object was a small model, comparatively close to the camera. To

Below: a computerised view of the disc seen in the Trent photographs. Each shade of grey in the original has been turned into a particular colour, making the details in the picture easier to 'read'. The object is seen to have a flat, evenly lit underside

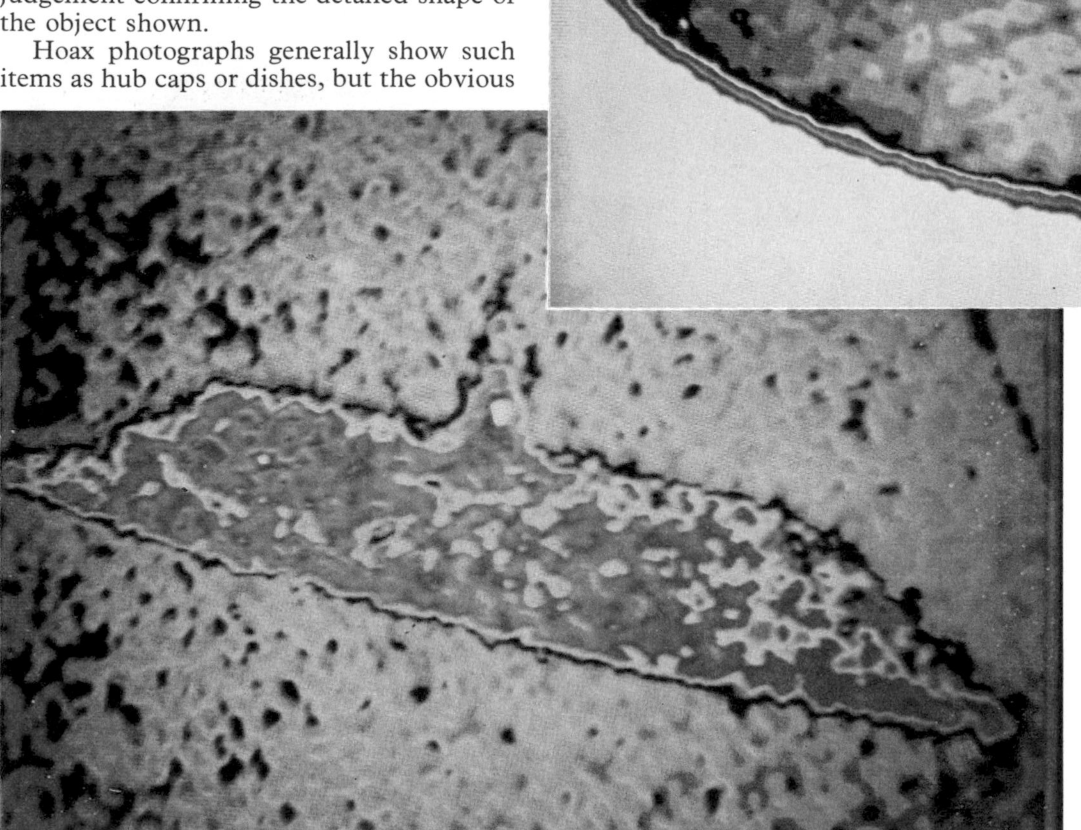

Left: colour-coding emphasises the form shown in the side-on view of the object. This wingless disc, with its curious off-centre tower, is unlike any known man-made aircraft

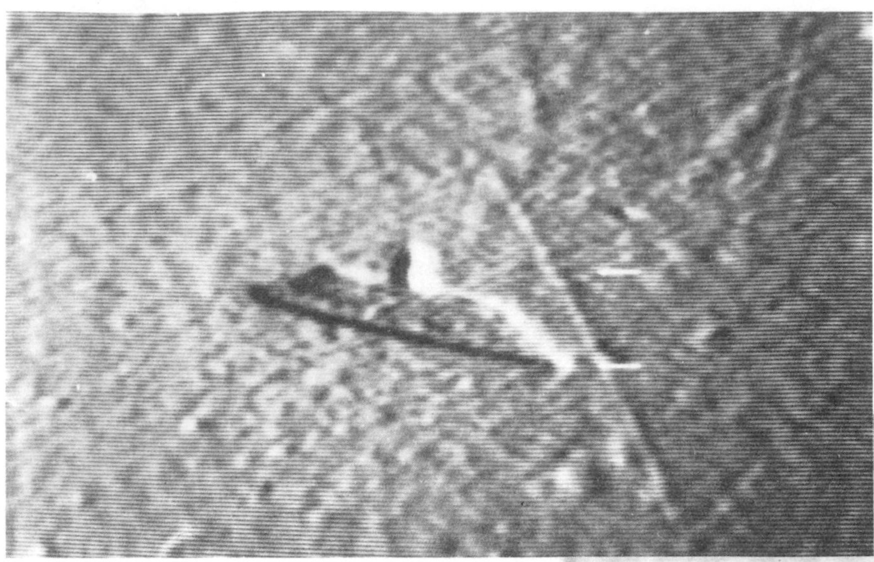

do this, the group took advantage of the edge-enhancement facility of the computer.

The resulting pictures have something of the look of a bas-relief carved in rough stone and lit at a low angle. Bright and dark lines now mark the edges of features on the object, and even small flaws in the negatives. The edge-enhancement technique can reveal, under typical conditions, the presence of a wire less than one hundredth of an inch (a quarter of a millimetre) thick, at a distance of 10 feet (3 metres). There is definitely no evidence of such a supporting wire or string in the area around the object.

The edge-enhancement technique not only ruled out the theory of a suspended model: it made it easy for Ground Saucer Watch to make measurements of the size of the image, which, when coupled with the analysts' assessment of the distance of the object, enabled them to draw conclusions about its true size.

Results of the analysis

The accumulated evidence gleaned from the several lines of attack that Ground Saucer Watch followed in its computer study led the organisation to the sober conclusion that the picture shows a flying disc, between 65 and 100 feet (20 and 30 metres) in diameter, and probably made of polished metal (since its light reflection was consistent with laboratory specimens of metal).

The entire UFO phenomenon deserves a properly conducted scientific investigation, undistorted by preconceived opinions. Modern technology has the means to make progress on the subject. However, there is a factor that impedes serious UFO research. Most governments have preferred to conceal the full extent of their own evidence from their citizens. The United States government probably has available to it the largest pool of data that exists anywhere in the world – data that have come from its own employees, military personnel, policemen and ordinary citizens. Civilian UFO researchers have long asserted that the United States intelligence agencies are aware of the existence and origins of UFOs. For more than 25 years they have maintained that the government knew more than it was telling. On numerous occasions when the government became involved in the investigation of a sighting, evidence would mysteriously disappear or be destroyed. The computer and other modern aids to analysis cannot demonstrate their full potential while vital evidence is withheld.

However, the Freedom of Information Act now gives American citizens powers to

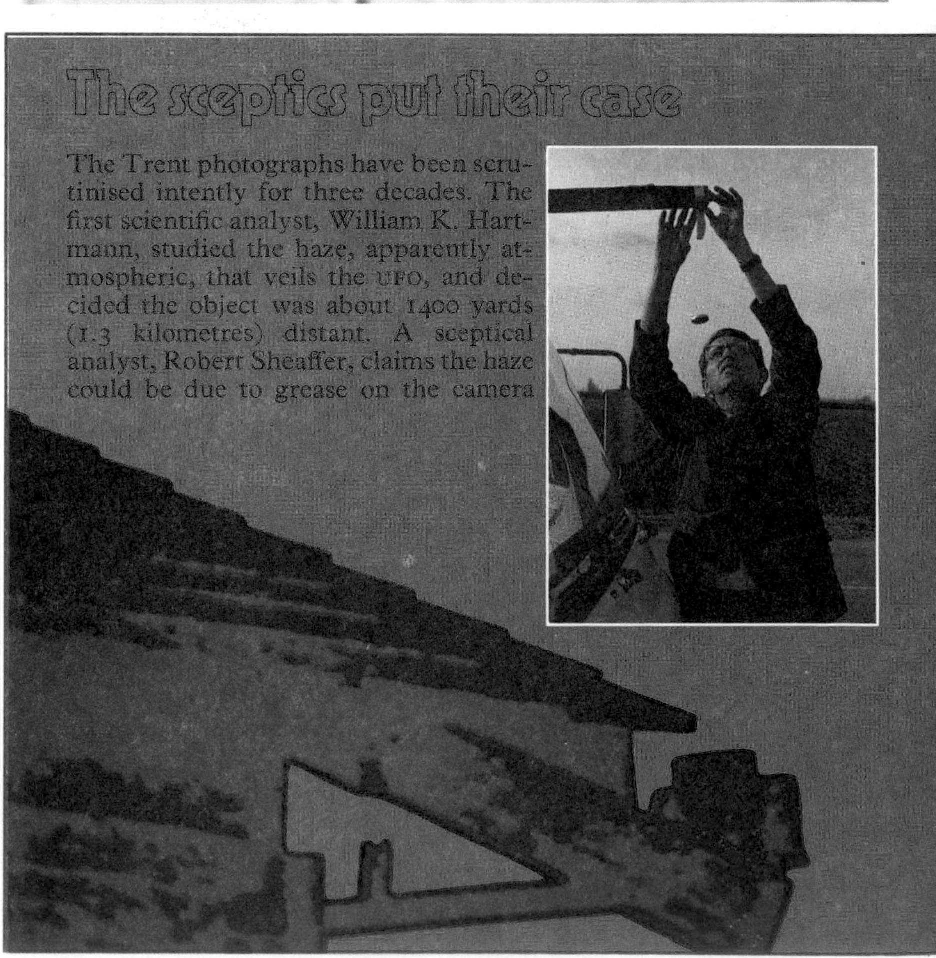

The sceptics put their case

The Trent photographs have been scrutinised intently for three decades. The first scientific analyst, William K. Hartmann, studied the haze, apparently atmospheric, that veils the UFO, and decided the object was about 1400 yards (1.3 kilometres) distant. A sceptical analyst, Robert Sheaffer, claims the haze could be due to grease on the camera

Left: the edges of the features visible in the two Trent photographs are enhanced in these two computer-generated images. Scratches and other blemishes on the ill-treated negatives are clearly brought out – but there is no trace of the wire that would be expected if the object were a model suspended from the telephone wires overhead

Right: colour-coded detail from one of the Trent photographs. The focus of the telephone pole seen here, and of other objects in the pictures, was studied and compared with the focus of the disc images. The comparison indicated that the disc was too far from the camera to be a model

compel their government to disclose the information that its agencies hold on file. The first legal skirmishes have taken place and documents that the CIA would have preferred to keep to itself have been made available to ufologists.

It may prove, as more information is prised from unwilling hands, that the role of the US government has been more active than previously suspected – that the clouding of UFO investigation they have brought about is due to more than the usual torpor, confusion and conservatism of government departments. On the contrary, some small and as yet unidentified group within the government machine may have been manipulating public opinion and the work of ufologists. They could have done this by familiar techniques of 'disinformation' – releasing distorted reports and data, starting rumours, feeding ufologists with 'confidential' but misleading stories – even setting up the occasional spurious sighting. They would have done this to set up a background of widespread UFO belief – at the same time that other government agencies were busily debunking UFOs.

There could be several motives for such a devious strategy. Public attention has occasionally been distracted from other issues by well-timed 'saucer flaps'. For example, a wave of sightings over Texas and New Mexico occurred within hours of the news of the Soviet Union's launching of a second Sputnik in November 1957, at a time when America's Vanguard rockets were failing to get off the launch pad.

The long-running UFO story could also provide vast quantities of data on the psychology of individuals and groups as they found themselves under supposed surveillance by unknown and possibly threatening forces. The official interest in the psychological warfare aspects of UFO scares is documented in secret memoranda only now becoming available.

The plethora of sightings that has grown up during the last 30 years could also serve to bury the occasional sighting of advanced types of aircraft by citizens or unauthorised service personnel.

A UFO tradition

An agency wishing to foment a UFO tradition and the occasional outbreak of UFO hysteria would not need to do a great deal. The enthusiasts and the general public would do it for them, at the stimulus of a few hints, added to the UFO reports made in good faith. Better analysis of UFO data of all kinds, in which computerised image-processing has a large part to play, can improve the situation by countering such a campaign and combatting the extremes of credulity and scepticism. But for this all the evidence hidden in government files is needed.

So, while Ground Saucer Watch adheres firmly to its judgement that remarkable physical phenomena lie behind many of the UFO photographs, it believes that the battle to discover the true nature and origin of those phenomena may be fought out in the courtroom before it can be taken up in the photo analyst's laboratory.

Below left: the puzzling garage shadows, clarified by colour-contouring

Left: during an investigation, William K. Hartmann tries to fake a UFO by a means of a small suspended model

Below: Philip J. Klass, who attacks the authenticity of the Trent photographs

lens, and the object could be close to the camera. He also points out that shadows of the garage eaves appear on the wall in the picture; but this wall faces east, suggesting the photograph was taken in the early morning, not the evening as the Trents claimed. The UFO sceptic Philip J. Klass suggests a motive for falsifying the time of the event: a morning sighting would be implausible since local farmers would be in the fields and it would be surprising that none of them had seen the UFO. Another investigator, Bruce Maccabee, replies that the garage shadows indicate a diffuse light source, probably a bright cloud illuminated by the evening Sun. He has calculated the UFO to be over 1000 yards (1 kilometre) away, even allowing for lens grease. Klass also asserts that the shift in UFO direction between the pictures exactly equals what would be expected if it were a stationary model suspended close to the camera. While Klass points out that the Trents have shown reluctance to take lie-detector tests, Maccabee and other investigators insist on the transparent sincerity of the couple in all interviews. The experts seem unable to dispel the dust they themselves have raised, and the controversy will continue.

UFO photos: facts and frauds

Nine out of ten photographs of alleged UFOs are misinterpreted pictures of everyday events or are the work of hoaxers. ROBERT S. DIGBY, of the British UFO Research Association, and CHRIS COOPER describe the gauntlet of tests that such photos must run

WELL-TRIED METHODS of analysing and evaluating UFO photographs will be supplemented, but not superseded, by newer methods of image-processing by computer. In fact the more sophisticated and expensive techniques of analysis are generally reserved for photographs that have survived the more traditional examination. These are a small minority of all claimed UFO pictures. At most, 10 per cent of the photographs that analysts study still seem convincing after they have been exposed to a battery of tests.

A UFO photograph is a report like any other, and requires to be supported in the same way. Many pictures that seem to be authentic cannot be used as evidence for the occurrence of some inexplicable phenomenon simply because of the unsatisfactory circumstances of the sighting. The photographer may have been alone at the time, for example; however strongly a researcher might be convinced of the sincerity of the witness, sceptics can hardly be blamed for insisting on the possibility of a hoax.

Inducements for hoaxers

Financial motives for creating a successful hoax photograph are very strong. One person who took photographs allegedly showing the Loch Ness monster refused to release the negatives for study by experts. Despite this and the fact that there are inconsistencies in his account of the sighting, his photographs were prominently featured in the British press and continue to be used. He has commented that the use of the pictures by the media all over the world would fetch something like £200,000 over the first six months. Income would continue long after that, of course, and there would also be fees for lectures and personal appearances. There are great incentives for providing what the public wants to see.

Among some people, especially bright schoolchildren, it has become a hobby to fake 'flying saucer' photographs. One of the best-known cases is that of Alex Birch, which took place in Britain. In 1962, when Alex was a 14-year-old schoolboy, he produced a photograph of a group of five saucer-like objects. He was interviewed on radio and television and by the Air Ministry. He appeared before the inaugural meeting of the British UFO

Above: UFO hoaxster Alex Birch revealing how he faked a picture of 'flying saucers' that had been accepted as real ever since he took it, 10 years before he made his confession

Above right: the 'daylight discs' that Alex Birch, then 14 years old, claimed to have photographed as they passed over Sheffield, in northern England, in 1962. The shapes were actually painted on the windowpane through which he took the photograph

Right: one of many pictures of flying discs taken in New Mexico by Paul Villa, who claimed to have talked with their crews. Computer studies indicated that the pictures showed small models

Research Association to explain the circumstances of his sighting. It was only 10 years later that his plausible, tenaciously defended and apparently sincere story was admitted to be a hoax.

Hence the vital importance of having independent witnesses to a sighting. The ideal case, from the investigator's viewpoint, is one in which the witnesses are neither friends nor relatives of the photographer, and make full statements of the circumstances of the sighting before the film has been processed. Hoaxers are rarely bold enough to announce their 'sightings' before they have made quite sure that their pictures are sufficiently convincing.

Hard evidence

So the first requirement for a photograph if it is to provide 'hard' scientific evidence is that there should be at least one other witness, who is independent of the photographer. The second requirement is that the original film – whether it is a black and white negative, a colour negative or a colour transparency – be submitted to qualified analysts for examination and evaluation. The whole film roll should be provided, even if only one or two frames show the UFO image. The other pictures may provide valuable evidence about the weather conditions, whether there was grease or dirt on the lens, whether there was stray light in the camera, the characteristics of that particular sample of film, and much else besides.

The third requirement is that there should be reference points in the picture. If it shows an object against a blank sky and nothing more, distance and size cannot be calculated.

The fourth requirement is not obligatory, but it is highly desirable: that there should be a sequence of pictures. A series of still photographs provides more information than a single one could; and a movie sequence is still more valuable. A movie film is harder to fake than a still photograph, and it provides information about the time elapsed during the sighting. (On some cameras the speed of the film can be varied from the normal 24 frames per second. It is essential that the witness report should specify what speed was used during the filming of the UFO.)

The UFO investigator presented with a photograph will also want to know full details of the camera and film used, the distance, aperture and speed settings, whether there was a filter over the lens and if so, of what type it was, whether the camera was hand-held or tripod-mounted, and any other information that might be relevant.

So a great deal of the investigator's work is done before he or she gets down to a detailed study of the picture. What needs to be done when that analysis at last begins?

The University of Colorado was given a contract in 1966 to study UFOs on behalf of the US Air Force. Many UFO investigators have been sceptical of the value of the report that was finally published under the title *The scientific study of unidentified flying objects*;

Below: a small, near object can produce a photographic image of the same size as a large object farther away. The true size can be calculated if its distance can be determined – for example, by analysis of its sharpness of focus

Bottom: an orbiting 'saucer' photographed from the spacecraft *Aurora 7* in May 1962. This ambiguous image could have fuelled endless speculation about alien observation of human space activity if Scott Carpenter, who took the picture, had not known its true nature: a small clump of ice crystals that had detached themselves when he knocked the side of the craft

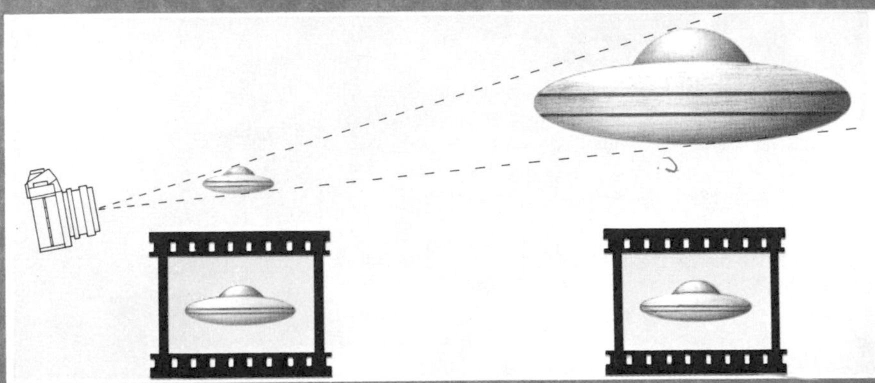

however, the approach that photographic evidence requires was clearly outlined by the Colorado investigators, and can provide a good guide to other analysts. This approach falls into several phases:

Firstly there is a subjective evaluation. Do various photographic factors such as clarity and contrast, combined with the witnesses' testimony, make the picture appear both plausible and informative about a potentially unusual phenomenon?

If a photograph passes this initial qualitative assessment, the second phase of investigation asks whether there is any rational explanation for what is shown in the picture. This question can be tackled only by someone who has wide experience with astronomical, meteorological, optical and photographic effects. Only such a person is equipped to know the surprising forms that can be assumed by aircraft vapour trails, stars and planets seen under unusual atmospheric conditions, lens flares, faulty film processing and countless other straightforward but poorly appreciated effects. Yet such possible causes of a 'UFO' image are so infinitely diverse that even the expert will be fooled on occasion. Nevertheless many photographs will be rejected at this stage of examination as cases of mistaken interpretation.

In the third phase of investigation the possibility of a fake is examined. Even with the best credentials concerning the sincerity of the report, this possibility remains and must be tested by the investigator. Are there any signs of tampering with the original film? Such interference can usually be detected. An elementary question to ask is: do the frames represent a continuous sequence? If the manufacturer's frame numbers reveal that the available pictures are separated by others, which the witness cannot or will not make available, the suspicion arises that the shots do not belong to a single sighting but were 'set up' on separate occasions – or else that obviously unconvincing shots have been deliberately withheld.

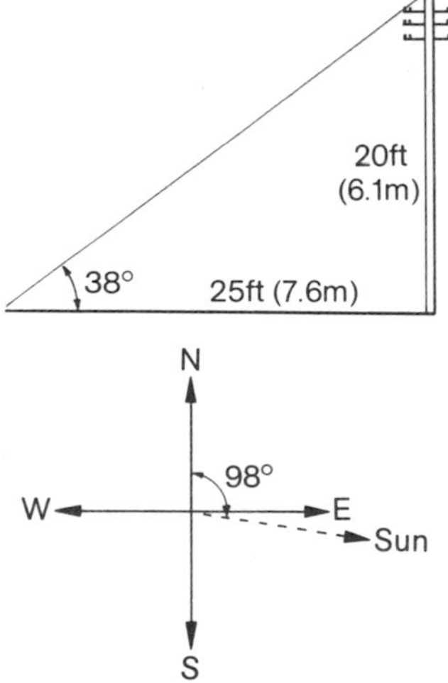

Top: when was the UFO photographed? A hypothetical picture like this has many clues for the analyst. The relation between the height of the telephone poles and the length of their shadows shows that the elevation of the Sun is 38° (centre). An on-the-spot study of the direction of the shadows in relation to landmarks reveals the direction of the Sun (above) as 8° south of east. From this, and the latitude of the site, the date and time at which the picture was taken can be calculated

Are the focus, sharpness and contrast in accord with the description by the photographer and others? If the object is alleged to have sped across the sky there should be some corresponding degree of blurring in the UFO image – or, if the photographer panned while taking the shot, there should be some blurring of the landscape.

The focus of the image can provide an accurate estimate of the distance of the object. This is crucial to a judgement of the authenticity of a photograph, since most hoaxes involve small objects positioned close to the camera. Nevertheless, even if the UFO image is judged to be distant from the camera, the possibility remains that the witness knows it to be an everyday object, such as an aeroplane at an unusual angle, but has decided to cash in on the peculiarity of its appearance in the picture.

Clues from lighting conditions

Further tests of consistency between the pictures and the witnesses' testimony can be made. In daytime photographs, angles of sunlight and weather conditions can be checked to see whether they agree with the stated time and date of occurrence of the sighting. If the height of an object appearing in the picture and the length of its shadow can both be measured, the height of the Sun can immediately be calculated, and by the use of an astronomical *ephemeris* or nautical almanac the time of day can be found. The local weather office will have detailed records of the weather on that day. Not only might they confirm or contradict the time of the alleged sighting, but such information as the height of the cloud base can, in some circumstances, give information about the height of the object photographed.

Study of the lighting conditions may also show whether the photographs in a sequence have been taken within a short period of each other. If a sighting is described as having lasted a few seconds, and the Sun is found to have moved through, say, 10 degrees between one shot and another – corresponding to 40 minutes – then the credibility of the witnesses is destroyed.

This investigation may very well be carried on to an examination of the camera itself, if this is available. The true shutter speeds and apertures of most cameras can be substantially different from their nominal values and it can be vital to obtain an accurate value.

It is also highly desirable to visit the scene of the sighting. The purpose of this is generally not to look for physical traces of the UFO – though such evidence, if available, is invaluable – but to make measurements to determine the sizes and directions of objects

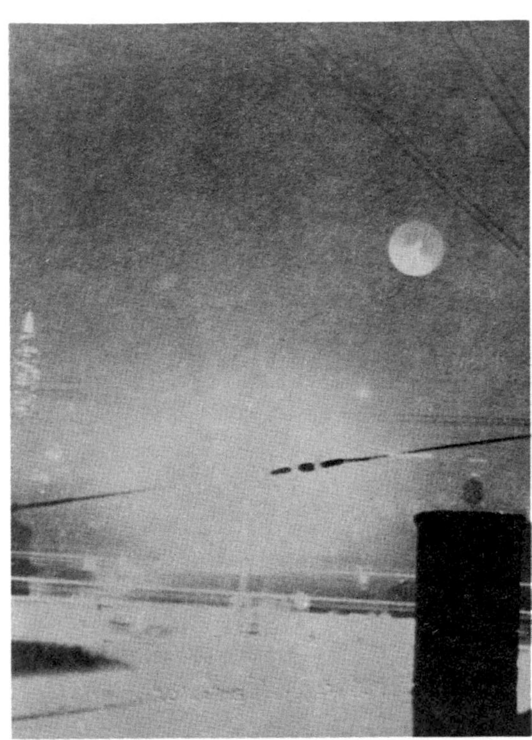

Left: a spherical UFO hovers over the city of New York – or so it seems. The picture was taken by civil defence observers as they watched a 'round orange light' drift over the city. But the 'globe' has been judged to be a lens flare, formed coincidentally

Below: a large domed disc flew over the home of Ralph Ditter in Ohio, USA, in November 1966, according to his account. He took three Polaroid pictures during the $1\frac{1}{2}$ minutes of the sighting. Two came out – but the print allegedly taken first was actually taken later, according to the maker's numbers. And the interval between the pictures, as indicated by the shadows, was much greater than the reported $1\frac{1}{2}$ minutes

that are visible in the picture.

Of the photographs that run this gauntlet of tests, few survive with their credibility intact. But when they do, the final classification is essentially of a negative kind – the object shown is not a nearby object, not a plane, not a meteor. Unfortunately the ideas often associated with the term 'UFO' – ideas of extra-terrestrial craft – cause misunderstanding between the public and serious-minded researchers. People ask, in all seriousness: 'Do UFOs exist?'. This is tantamount to asking whether anything has ever been seen in the skies that remains unidentified – and this is obviously so. The question that such enquirers really have in mind is: do alien spaceships visit the Earth? And to this we do not have an answer. No firm evidence exists that unambiguously shows the phenomena to be due to this cause.

We might ask, less ambitiously: are there any photographs that have resisted all attempts to discredit them? There are many candidates – though it seems that controversy concerning such pictures never quite dies down. Some of the most convincing photographs are the stills taken aboard a Brazilian naval ship participating in scientific studies as part of the International Geophysical Year. At 12.15 p.m. on 16 January 1958, while the ship was off Trindade Island in the South Atlantic, large numbers of personnel on the deck of the ship saw a strange object approach the island at high speed, hover over it for a while, disappear behind a peak, reappear and head out to sea. Four photographs taken by Almiro Barauna, a civilian photographer on board at the time, show an object resembling two dishes face-to-face surrounded by a vapour or mist.

In many respects this was a near-perfect sighting. There were many witnesses and the negatives were developed immediately, virtually ruling out a fake.

The US Air Force later claimed they had made a detailed investigation and concluded that the affair was a hoax. However, their publicly available file does not contain any evaluation of the case. If they have any

information throwing doubt on the pictures, they have kept it to themselves. There is no publicly available evidence against the authenticity of the Trindade Island photographs. The Brazilian investigators decided that the object seen in the pictures was 120 feet (36 metres) across and flying at 560 to 620 miles per hour (900 to 1000 km/h).

Equally remarkable objects are shown in many other photographs (see pages 61 and 66). But whether they are space visitors or something even more exotic, such as thought projections, cannot be discovered by photographic analysis alone.

Scientific attempts to make contact with intelligent life on other planets have so far been unsuccessful. But what of the evidence from people who claim to have met aliens? JENNY RANDLES examines their reports

Encounters of the fourth kind

ON A WET AND WINDY NIGHT in November 1980, Mario Luisi was walking through sodden meadows by a river outside his home village of Burneside in the English Lake District. In the darkness he saw what he took to be a cow. Then he thought it might be a crudely constructed sheep shelter. But then he saw that the object was hovering 3 feet (1 metre) above the ground and looked like nothing so much as a distorted aeroplane. It was about the size of a helicopter and had what seemed to be a tailplane, but no wings. It bore strange symbols, the like of which Luisi had never seen before.

As he stared at the weird object glinting in the beam of his lantern, he became aware of a squelching sound. He realised that someone was approaching him across the soggy ground and turned the beam of the lantern in the direction of the sound. He saw two figures, apparently human, about 6 feet (2 metres) away, beside an old oak tree. They were wearing dark, skin-tight suits. At that instant one of them, apparently female, raised a small pencil-shaped object in her hand. A bright light shot out from it, striking the face of Luisi's lantern. The glass front shattered and, as Luisi watched, the metal reflector became warped and twisted.

The remainder of Mario Luisi's encounter took place by the light from a paper mill on the other side of the river. The female figure spoke to him, telling him that she and her companion meant no harm and had come to the Earth in peace. (Presumably, then, their 'attack' was a defensive measure against what they had taken to be a weapon – the lantern.) Luisi was told that he must not reveal the strange symbols on the ship, nor those on the lapel badges worn by both figures. He could only stare, his legs shaking, as the two beings, who were fair-skinned, entered their craft by means of a ladder that descended from it. Presently the object shot upwards, leaving a glow in the sky.

The encounter left Mario Luisi with a memory that would change his outlook on life. For him, at least, there was no longer any doubt – no need to question whether the human race is alone in the Universe. He 'knew' that we are not.

This problem has fascinated mankind ever since it was realised, in the 16th century, that the planets are other worlds, and the stars are other suns, possibly possessing their own planets. The human race seems to abhor the idea of being alone in an immeasurably vast Universe. This sentiment was exploited to great effect by Steven Spielberg's epic film *Close encounters of the third kind*, which was released in 1977. Spielberg brought the idea vividly to life. He himself is keenly interested in UFOs and is associated with the Center for UFO Studies, in Evanston, Illinois, USA, which is run by J. Allen Hynek, a consultant to *The Unexplained*.

The most fantastic type of evidence on the question consists of the numerous accounts of close encounters of the fourth kind – of which Mario Luisi's is one. These go beyond close encounters of the third kind, in which aliens are merely seen: witnesses claim to

In this scene from Steven Spielberg's film *Close encounters of the third kind*, the protagonist enters a space-ship, surrounded by aliens who, although their only means of communication with human beings appears to be the repetition of a tune of five notes, are obviously benevolent. Despite its title, Spielberg's film deals with what UFO experts have labelled close encounters of the fourth kind – those in which there is intelligent contact with aliens have met, talked to, travelled in company with, or even been abducted by creatures not of this world.

Four varieties of close encounters of the fourth kind have been distinguished. Mario Luisi's experience is typical of type A, which embraces straightforward encounters where the witness fully remembers what took place. There are no memory blocks, no intervals of time that the subject is unable to recall, no obvious reason to doubt that the experience was of something completely real. It is just as much a part of the sequence of events as getting up that morning.

These type A events are the most sober evidence for the reality of aliens. And they are by no means rare. Although close encounters of the fourth kind as a whole make up no more than about 1 or 2 per cent of the total number of UFO reports made each year, this still amounts to many hundreds of cases since the Second World War. They come from almost every country and all social groups. And over half of these encounters are of type A. It is thought that they could be even more common than the figures suggest, for there is evidence that witnesses are unwilling to talk about this kind of experience.

Seeing an unidentified light in the sky is almost commonplace these days, and people are more willing to report it than they once were. But talking to a creature from another world is, for many people, something to keep quiet about. This is unfortunate, since it means that researchers are unsure of the true scale of the phenomenon. But the information supplied by courageous witnesses is sufficient to indicate that something truly extraordinary is going on.

But serious problems arise, even in these seemingly rational type A accounts. The Mario Luisi case is typical in this respect. He volunteered the lantern for scientific study. The results of two independent analyses were identical: in the opinion of experts the damage was done by ordinary means, probably by a blow-torch. Had Luisi concocted his story and damaged the lantern himself, it would have been odd for him to be so cooperative. And it is not possible to disprove his claim, by which he stands, that the lantern was struck by a beam from an alien weapon.

Certain other points in Mario Luisi's story support his claims. But support is not proof: and we never do get proof in cases of close encounters of the fourth kind that a witness is not lying. The difficulty, of course, is that even if the witness is telling the truth, there is no guarantee that his alien contacts are not using materials and technology indistinguishable from our own. Nevertheless, when what is presented as evidence could perfectly well be of earthly origin, one is bound to become suspicious.

Science and the aliens

A number of researchers have been conducting studies into close encounters of the fourth kind, analysing the features of the stories in detail. Type A cases stand out from the other reports in many ways. They tend to occur outside the usual surroundings of the witness – in the open, perhaps in a field, and so on. They happen at any time of the day, even though UFOs are predominantly nocturnal. The average number of witnesses per case is well below the average for all UFO cases, but close to the average for all close encounters of the fourth kind.

Photographs purporting to show alien beings are, disappointingly, rare. This seems highly significant when it is remembered that UFO photographs are very numerous. If the

Previous page: two aliens allegedly visited a Lake District village one stormy November night in 1980. Disturbed by Mario Luisi on a night-time stroll, they apparently mistook his lamp for some kind of weapon, and destroyed it with a ray gun. Luisi later produced the damaged lamp as evidence (below) but expert analyses established that the damage could have been done with an ordinary blow-torch. On the other hand, there is no reason why an alien weapon should *not* have the same effect as a blow-torch!

number of pictures of aliens were in the same proportion as the number of contact cases – 1 or 2 per cent – then we would have a great deal of material to work on. In fact there are no more than two or three photographs and none that, beyond reasonable doubt, link an alien being with a UFO.

Yet we cannot complacently dismiss the phenomenon as unreal. For there are cases in which several witnesses see aliens. One example occurred on 3 March 1980, at Rio Pièdras, Puerto Rico. Two teenage children, Vivian and José Rodriguez, were woken at 3.30 a.m. by a barking dog. They looked through the window of their farm to see five strange creatures, with pointed ears and webbed feet, wearing tight-fitting clothes. The aliens seemed interested in the family's chickens. No UFO was observed by the children.

Next day it was discovered that at the same time of night two men nearby had seen the same creatures. The witnesses had been sleeping in a parked car, resting during a long journey. They had woken up and had seen a large domed object on the ground. Beings fitting the description given by the children had emerged from the object and headed in the direction of the Rodriguez farm.

Such a story, if true, is very hard to explain as anything other than a real, physical event. The apparent subjectivity of these type A cases should not be overstressed.

The second group of contact cases, type B, is quite different. The aliens involved are often called 'bedroom visitors' because so many of them make their appearance in the bedroom; the witnesses usually claim to have experienced the encounter while wide awake. These encounters have a good deal in common with ghost sightings that happen in the bedroom.

What distinguishes these events from type A cases is that they possess obvious distortions of reality – parts of the sequence of events are completely forgotten, there are jumps in the story from one scene of action to another, as in a film or a dream. The reality of the events is much more doubtful than that of the type A cases.

For example, on 5 January 1980 a 33-year-old house-painter awoke at 5 a.m. in his bedroom at Trowbridge, Wiltshire, in southern England. He saw a glowing green figure, 7 feet (2.1 metres) tall, at the foot of his bed. It looked more like a projected image

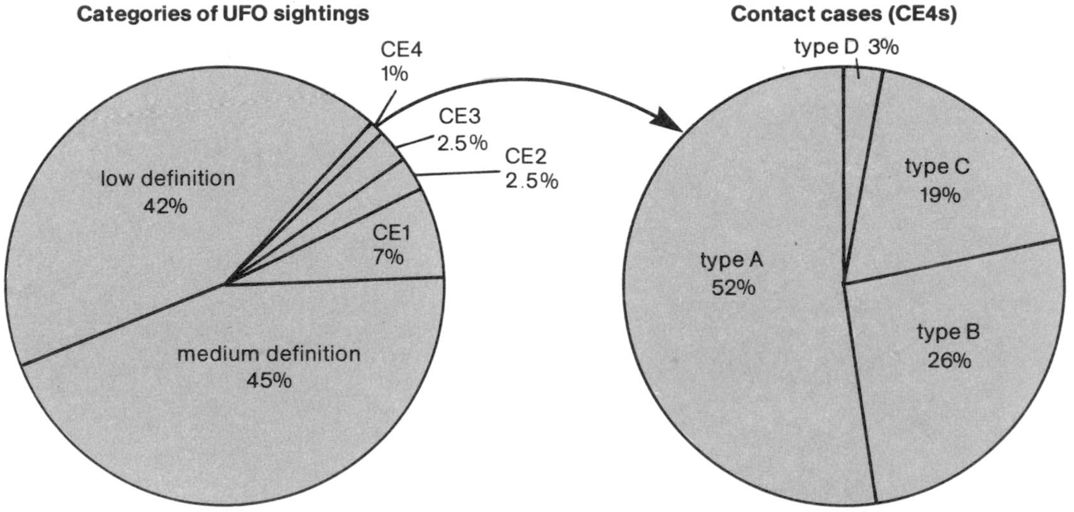

Right: an analysis of UFO reports from the United Kingdom over the period from 1975 to 1979. Low definition cases are reports whose details are sparse, with only brightness, colour and movement clearly describable. Medium definition cases are those in which the object has a definite physical substance and shape. The remainder of cases are classified as close encounters (CEs). Close encounters of the fourth kind are, in turn, divided into four categories (far right)

	non-contact UFO sightings	contact cases (CE4s)		
		type A	type B	type C
average number of witnesses	2.19	1.28	1.16	1.62
sex of witnesses	68% male	75% male	51% male	60% male
most common place of occurrence	home environment	in the open	room inside a building	in a car on a country road
most common time of occurrence	peak at about 9 p.m.	all times of day and night	peak at about 3 a.m.	peak at about 11 p.m.

This seems to suggest that the two types of contact are different in nature: type A sound like real contacts with something physical; type B sound like some kind of hallucination. It seems a plausible working hypothesis, though there are cases in which it is hard to decide whether a case belongs to type A or type B.

The third category of contact report, type C, involves an experience that is not immediately remembered. The experience of an English family, the Days, will illustrate how disturbing this can be.

Late-night encounter

One evening in October 1974, John and Sue Day were driving to their home at Aveley, in Essex. They had been visiting relatives and were now hurrying, hoping to catch a late-night television play. Their three children were with them and fell asleep during the journey. Then their parents saw a blue light pacing the car. They watched it for some time but were unable to identify what it could be.

Then the light disappeared – and the car turned a corner and ran into a well-defined bank of eerie green mist. The Days were in the mist for only a few seconds, but the car radio sparked and crackled. John instantly yanked out its wires to prevent a fire hazard. After recovering their composure the family drove the few hundred yards to their home.

When they got home they switched on their television set, but the screen remained blank. It was two hours later than they had

than a solid figure. The alien told the witness that the people to whom he belonged regularly shipped human beings off to other worlds in order to colonise them. When a planet became overcrowded they started a war in order to reduce the population. This behaviour seemed to be in conflict with other efforts that they were making to protect us: it seemed that our planet was liable to split in half and the alien visitors were desperately trying to plug the cracks by injecting a liquid cement from their remotely controlled space vehicles!

Interestingly, the witness's wife was in bed beside him all this time, yet she did not awaken, nor did it occur to him to disturb her. It seems most unlikely that anyone would make up such a story and expect anyone to believe it. It is not necessary to doubt the witness's sincerity – but neither is it necessary to take this weird story at all seriously.

Type B cases are rarer than type A – they form about a quarter of all contact reports. They are far more subjective, since they are almost exclusively single-witness encounters. By far the majority of them occur in the home or its immediate surroundings – fully two thirds of the cases occur in the bedroom. And most of them happen in the early hours of the morning.

Strange creatures with pointed ears and webbed feet seen examining chickens on a Puerto Rican farm on 3 March 1980 were also observed near their spacecraft (above). Although their purpose is mystifying, the account of the event itself is straightforward – putting it in the category of close encounter of the fourth kind known as 'type A'

Right: a Trowbridge man claimed he was awoken by a tall, greenish alien in the early hours of 5 January 1980. The creature said he came from a planet where war is used to control the population level, and that he was trying to prevent the Earth splitting in half by injecting it with cement! This kind of close encounter of the fourth kind, with its obvious conflict with reality, belongs to the category labelled 'type B'

thought, and the station had closed down. Someone or something had stolen a piece of their lives.

The family were naturally perturbed by this mysterious time lapse. Over the next few months they had several dreams about it – fleeting visions of weird faces, occasional strange impulses to refrain from eating meat or drinking alcohol. Eventually two UFO investigators, Andy Collins and Barry King, heard of the event. They brought in the help of a medical hypnotist – Leonard Wilder, a London dentist. The Days underwent regression hypnosis in the hope of retrieving memories of that missing time. And the memories came.

Under hypnosis John and Sue told stories that were in close agreement. However, there were some differences, and they did indeed claim to have been separated for much of the 'missing' time. The children also seemed to recall the experience in subsequent dreams.

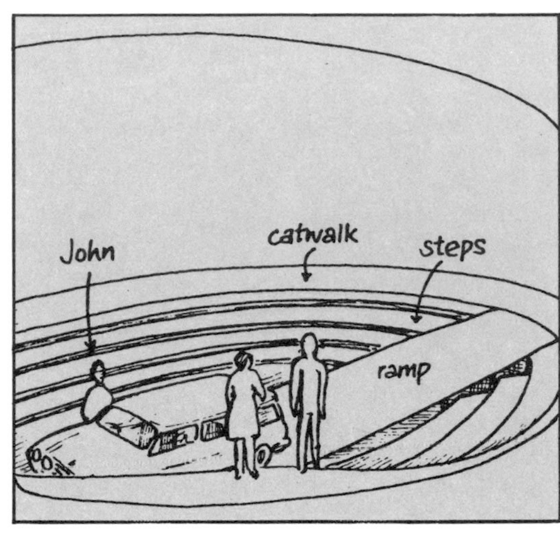

Perhaps the strangest category of close encounter of the fourth kind is that known as 'type C' – where the witnesses are subject to loss of memory following their experience. The Day family of Aveley, Essex, England, underwent this after the events of one October night in 1974. They were driving home when, they claimed, they encountered a UFO (left) that interfered with their car radio – so much, at least, they remembered afterwards. But when they arrived home, they found it was two hours later than they thought – and it subsequently emerged under hypnosis that they believed that they had been taken aboard a UFO by aliens (below) and subjected to medical examinations

A UFO had landed and the family had been taken on board. They were given medical examinations and shown around the craft. They were informed about its propulsion system and the way of life and intentions of the alien visitors. Eventually they were returned to their car by a process akin to astral projection, and they continued their journey. But their lives could never be the same again.

To those who interviewed them, the Day family seemed a group of pleasant and sincere people who had never tried to force their story onto anyone, or to make money from it. Something quite certainly happened to them that night . . . but what?

In type C contacts, something blocks the witnesses' memory. Occasionally recall of the 'missing' events is triggered by normal events. Not infrequently the subject has dreams that hint at what took place during the missing minutes, hours – or even, in a very few instances, days. But the most common means by which the floodgates of memory are opened is regression hypnosis.

Type C abductions are remarkably consistent. One in five stories of alien contact involves amnesia and alleged abduction. Type C cases are more subjective than ordinary UFO sightings, since they tend to involve fewer witnesses; but they have a higher number of witnesses per case than type B or, surprisingly, type A cases. The aliens involved usually resemble human beings and are usually the normal human size, or larger; there are very few entities of small stature, unlike those featured in type A cases. The most common time for type C incidents to occur is between about 10 p.m. and midnight. And a very large proportion of them involve young couples driving cars along quiet roads (quite often carrying children with them). It is also common for one or more of the witnesses to have a history of strange experiences – witnessing ghosts or poltergeists, for example. And the way of life of the subjects may undergo drastic changes, even before the memory of an apparent abduction is at last retrieved and the cause of the changes made apparent.

The fourth group of close encounters of the fourth kind comprises very few cases. It consists of those experiences in which the encounter does not seem to involve physical contact: communication is by means of telepathy, automatic writing, or something of the kind. We shall not discuss these in this series of chapters. We shall try instead to see whether among all the details of the cases of types A, B and C there is a clue to the reasons why such experiences occur.

Creatures from inner space?

Have beings from other worlds met and talked with people of Earth – or are they creations of the subconscious mind?

Above: life on Jupiter, as imagined by the astronomer Carl Sagan. Herds of floating creatures, little more than living gas-bags, drift above the towering clouds of frozen ammonia crystals in the planet's atmosphere. Some of these beings are visible in the foreground and at the left. It is possible that living creatures have evolved to this level on many planets, but beings capable of building spaceships are much less probable

HYPNOSIS IS STILL A CONTROVERSIAL subject. Its significance becomes even more obscure when it is used to recover the blocked memories of a witness in a UFO contact case. Experts dispute the origin of the images that come to the mind of such a person in a hypnotic trance. Is the subject's psychic potential boosted? Does he become able to dredge information from the collective unconscious, potentially becoming aware of everything that has ever happened anywhere at all? Or is the abduction memory that comes to the witness simply a respinning by his mind of a story once read and now forgotten – the re-creation of a modern myth? For certainly alien beings and their spacecraft have attained the commanding status of myths of our time, whatever the reality that lies behind them (see page 426). Or does regression hypnosis simply free the memory so that the barriers to recall can be hurdled and the 'missing' period relived? There is a very difficult problem of assessment whenever a witness in a type C case retrieves a 'memory'. What is its true significance?

A case similar to that of the Day family (see page 74) occurred in June 1978, again in England. A young couple, their children and another adult were involved. The alleged abduction took place during a car journey in Oxfordshire; again there were many similarities with other abduction stories: for example, three-dimensional ('holographic') shows were displayed to the witnesses. But the story as a whole was quite unlike any of the 100 or more other type C cases that have been documented by ufologists. The aliens looked humanoid – indeed, very like those seen by John and Sue Day – and they told of the origin of their race on Earth and their emigration to the planet Janos. Now a horrific natural disaster had precipitated their flight back to Earth. They wish to move in with us . . . a million or so refugees from this cosmic catastrophe.

What is interesting about this case is, partly, how it resembles in outline other incidents, such as the Day case (which had received publicity in the British press). But

Overleaf: Gaynor Sunderland, a Welsh girl who has reported numerous encounters with aliens. On one occasion two strange beings allegedly from another planet, visited her and told her that they were products of her own subconscious mind. Other members of Gaynor's family have reported alien contacts more importantly, the interests, attitudes and manner of questioning of the investigators found their way into the story that was told – as if the hypnotised witnesses were picking up 'cues' from the investigators and fitting them into their accounts as they told them. This is rather like the game in which you are given a series of objects – say, a book, a pen, a candlestick and a toy balloon – and are asked to use your imagination to weave a story in which they all figure.

This curious problem is further illustrated by the experiences of young Gaynor Sunderland, from Oakenholt in North Wales. She and her family had many weird encounters, including contacts with aliens who, again, looked rather like the ones met by others who reported similar experiences.

On one occasion Gaynor was having trouble sleeping because she kept seeing two aliens – one male, one female. (Later she found that they were named Pars and Arna.) I was then investigating the case and I suggested to her mother, Marion Sunderland, that she could tell Gaynor a white lie. Gaynor was told: 'If you put a loaded camera in the bedroom the aliens will not come because they do not like having their pictures taken.' A couple of nights later Gaynor was allegedly abducted to another world and taken on a tour of a city there by Arna and Pars. She was told that she was not really there: the experience was in her subconscious mind, a kind of dream. Yet the aliens maintained: 'We did not come to you because of the camera.'

It is highly paradoxical that an alien entity should first admit to being a product of the unconscious mind and then claim to dislike being photographed. It seems that Gaynor's mind somehow wove the idea concerning the camera into her experience of the trip to another world. But she remained convinced of the reality of her experience and said it was far more vivid than a typical dream.

We sometimes find that the initial stimulus for an abduction experience is an event that can be explained straightforwardly. This casts doubt on the remainder of the account provided by the witnesses. One of the most famous type C cases involved an American couple, Betty and Barney Hill, who were returning from holiday across the mountains of New England during September 1961. A mysterious 'craft' followed them and then came down nearby; Barney Hill watched it through binoculars before driving away in panic. All the classic features of such incidents were there: a psychic witness (Betty had experienced many types of weird phenomena throughout her life); a blank in their memory of events; strange dreams afterwards; and finally, under hypnosis, memories of abduction and medical examination on board the UFO. Yet it has been argued very convincingly that the light in the sky that marked the beginning of the whole train of events was nothing more than the planet Jupiter.

This does not in itself tell us anything about the reality of the experience; witnesses often link completely unassociated events in their recollections of some incident, simply because those events happened to occur at roughly the same time. But it is just part of the process by which human beings misperceive events, distort their memories of them, and come to mistaken conclusions

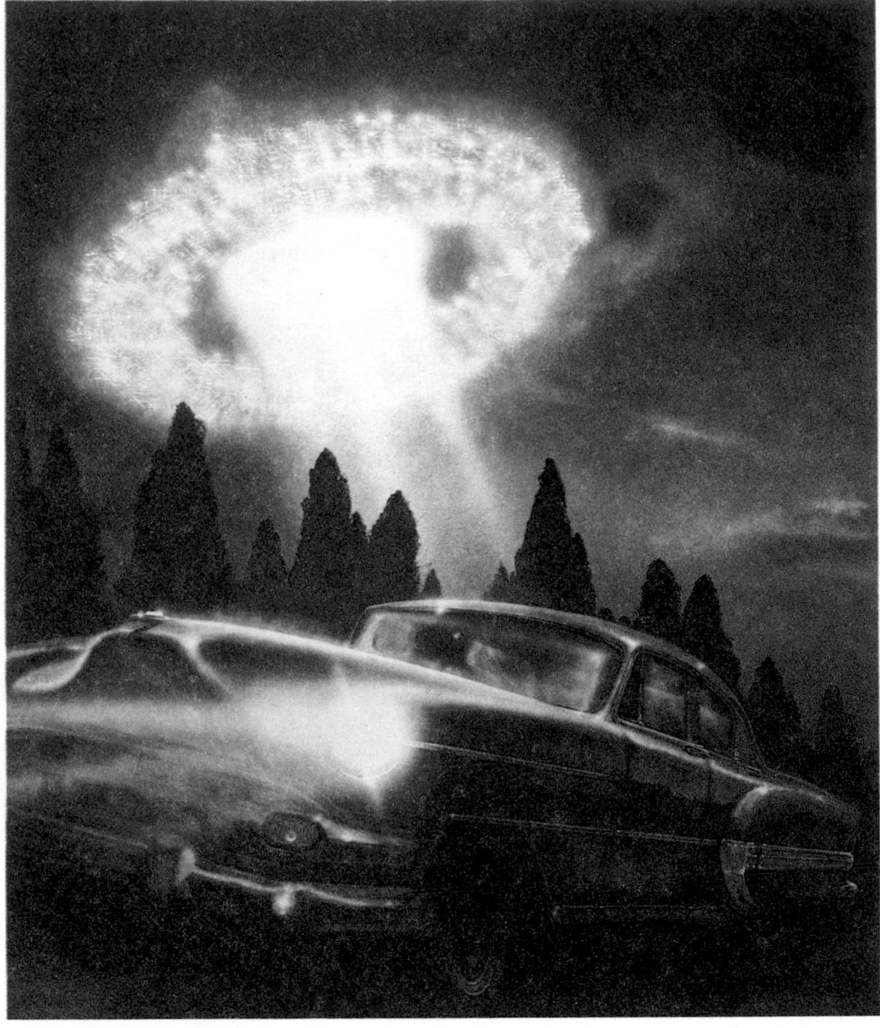

Above: the encounter of Betty and Barney Hill with a mysterious craft in September 1961 is a classic contact case. The Hills' recollections of being taken on board the craft emerged later, first in dreams and subsequently in regression hypnosis

about them later. We should bear this complex process of interpretation and misinterpretation in mind as we consider the appearance presented by aliens and their craft in contact reports.

What should we expect extra-terrestrial life forms to look like? This is a very hard question to answer, since our only examples of life come from one planet – the Earth. Yet when we see the amazing range of species hosted by our environment and recognise that mankind is just a link in a long evolutionary chain in which an even greater diversity of forms has existed, we find little reason to suppose that alien beings should look like us. Admittedly the humanoid form is well-adapted to a wide range of environments on the Earth's surface, and it may well be common on other Earth-like planets throughout the Galaxy; but the human form is presumably not a necessary condition for dominance. Since other worlds would have a great range of habitats, and local conditions would vary greatly, life there would undoubtedly be equally diverse. Carl Sagan, the eminent astronomer, has even proposed possible life forms capable of surviving on Jupiter: such as living balloons in the oceans of water that may exist in the warm depths of the planet, below the perpetually frozen clouds that we see.

The last thing we would expect is a menagerie of alien races looking more or less like us – and yet, according to contactees, this is precisely what we do find.

Only 7 per cent of contact cases involve creatures that are not humanoid. Such beings as the giant white maggots that crawled across a road in Yssandon, France, in 1960, during a UFO sighting, are rare.

There are three distinct groupings among the humanoids that form the bulk of the data: small – below 5 feet (1.5 metres) tall, and usually about $3\frac{1}{2}$ feet (1 metre); medium – 5 to 6 feet (1.5 to 1.8 metres); and large – up to about 7 or 8 feet (2.1 to 2.4 metres). In type B ('bedroom visitors') encounters, the entities witnessed are fairly normal, with a slight tendency to larger sizes. In no fewer than 41 per cent of type A cases, on the other hand, the entities seen are small. There are other fairly common features, such as large eyes, fair skins, and angular features. But other factors, such as clothes, show great diversity.

One might not consider this to be a problem. After all, people on Earth wear a wide variety of clothes, and human beings of different ages, races and sexes are extraordinarily diverse. But the difficulty with contact cases is more fundamental: the aliens as described are just too much like us. They usually speak the language of the contactee, whether it be English or Serbo-Croat. Nearly always they speak it faultlessly, and without any noticeable accent. This means, of course, that they are speaking in the same accent as the contactee himself (a vital, but usually overlooked, point).

Their fashions, too, are far too similar to those on Earth. It seems nonsensical to imagine that an alien from a planet light years away should wear a cloak buttoned at the neck and sport a badge on the breast of a jumpsuit-style garment. Yet this is what contactees claim, and it is all too reminiscent of the limited imaginations (or wardrobe budgets) of science-fiction film-makers.

If a witness asks for the origins of an alien, he is almost invariably told that the entity comes from space. In the earliest contacts the aliens' home planets belonged to our solar system – Mars, Venus, Saturn and so on. Now we know that humanoid life on these worlds is impossible, and present-day contactees are told the aliens come from planets circling distant stars. As yet, of course, science knows little about the very existence of such planets, let alone their suitability for life.

What is it like inside an alien craft? The witnesses' answers to this question also raise

Six types of alien being reported by contact case witnesses. These pictures should be viewed as symbolising the various categories, not as accurately portraying any particular entity encountered by a witness. The majority of beings reported are human or humanoid in form – and also remarkably human in their clothing and technology. 'Monsters' are rare. (The 'apparitional' entities come under the heading of type D – 'psychic' – encounters.) Images such as these are firmly stamped into popular consciousness by science fiction films and comics, which may thereby influence perceptions during contact experiences

grave questions about the nature of their experience. Imagine a Stone Age man transported through time and taken onto the flight deck of a Concorde airliner. The instruments and controls would be quite incomprehensible to him. How could he possibly describe what he saw in any intelligible way, knowing nothing of the purpose and importance of what he was seeing? This would be the predicament of any Earth-dweller taken inside an alien starship.

Yet these amazingly advanced visitors, who traverse interstellar space at a whim, apparently do so in spaceships that would not look out of place in one of our engineering museums. They use levers and valves, wires, and old-fashioned bulky computers. They have flashing lights, in the manner of *Star Trek* and *Doctor Who*. They are slow in catching up with our primitive technology. They are just getting round to using lasers and holograms (which they did not have before we did), and they do not as yet have the liquid crystal displays that are now standard on our watches and calculators. What is more, their spaceships are always breaking down. . . .

Not infrequently the aliens enlist the help of Earth-dwellers to sort out their problems. Once they asked an eight-year-old boy to fix their propulsion unit. Evidently the origin of all this is not the face-value explanation beloved of the alien spacecraft theorists.

Under alien eyes

Once the contactees are aboard, the aliens usually carry out a medical examination. Taking blood samples is an integral part of this. The Irish ufologist John Hind points out that the doctor is the symbol of authority who plays the greatest role in the lives of many people. There seem to be significant resemblances between these examinations by aliens and the contactees' previous experience of medical treatment. One Canadian abduction appeared to feature a replay of an appendicectomy that the witness had earlier undergone.

The memory blocks in type C cases present an interesting problem. If aliens can suppress memories, why do they do it in such an ineffective way? The memories usually filter through spontaneously and are easily retrievable in full by hypnosis. Why block them at all? Unless the memory block in fact works successfully in most cases – implying that there are thousands of people who are abducted and have no inkling of the fact afterwards.

Whatever the reason for these memory blocks, the lapse of time between the original occurrence and its subsequent recall severely impedes the investigation of the case. And this, of course, may be the most significant function that the memory loss serves.

When aliens give us messages they are almost always of one form: warnings about the future of the Earth, with hints of nuclear war and impending doom. If only we were sometimes given something startling and original – a new scientific theory, a helpful invention, a cure for cancer. But no; we are told that, because of our nuclear tests, 'the balance of the Universe is being disturbed.'

Occasionally there is some light relief. In spring 1978 a Red Army officer was abducted by the shores of the Pyrogovskoye Lake in Russia. Once he had got used to his humanoid hosts, he suggested they ought to toast this cross-cultural contact with a suitable drink. They did not understand. So he sketched out the chemical structure of alcohol, and the aliens retired and immediately made some. 'How is it that such a highly developed civilisation does not use something like this?' the Russian asked. 'Maybe if we had used it we would not be so highly developed,' was the response.

A teetotal message in the form of a joke makes a welcome change from the usual run of communications from other worlds.

In a spaceship from a distant star system, a gigantic robot towers over a prone human form. In this scene from the 1951 film *The day the Earth stood still* the robot, Gort, is bringing its dead master, Klaatu, back to life – but this powerful image epitomises, and may have done much to influence, a whole class of contact case reports: the medical examination of abducted witnesses on board alien craft

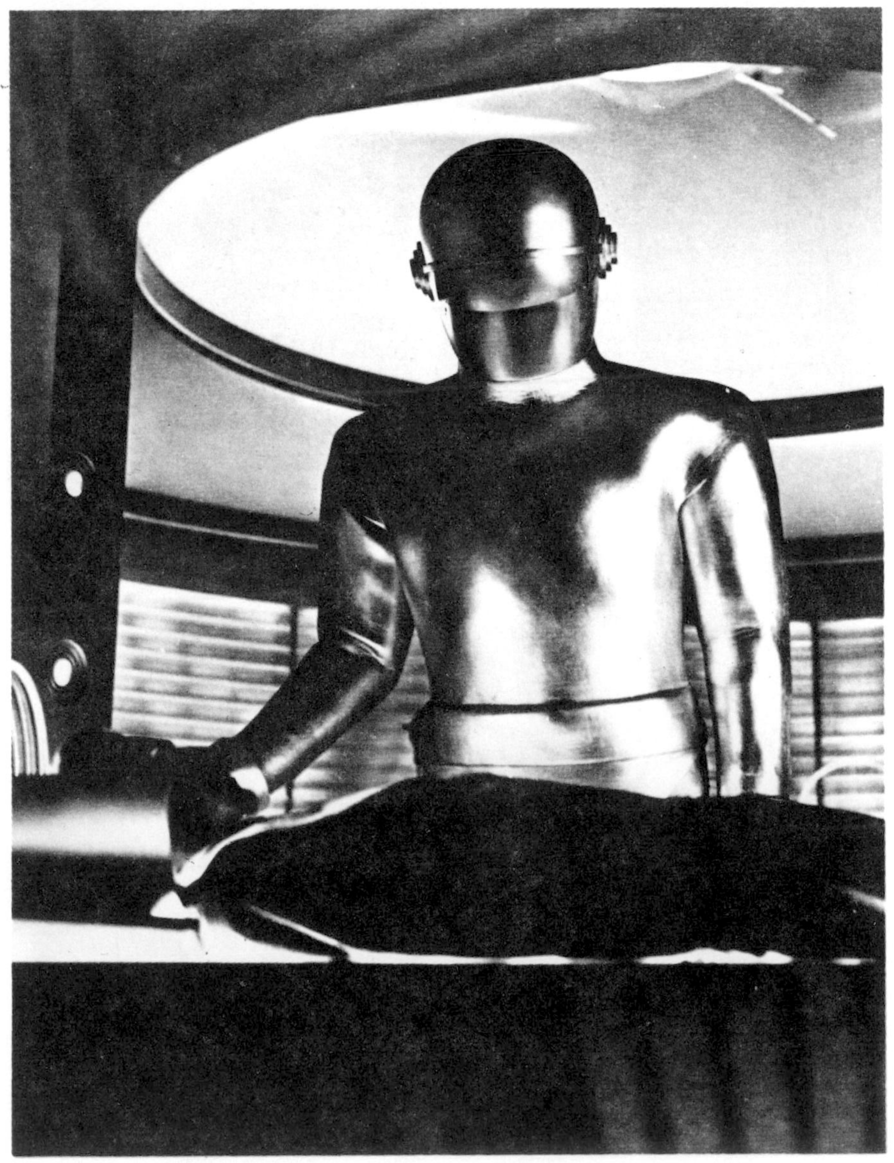

Alien spacecraft, hallucinations or fraud? The theories about UFO contact cases are legion. This chapter assesses each explanation and concludes that the phenomenon lies outside our usual categories of thought

Stranger than fiction

ALIENS BEINGS MUST EXIST – somewhere in the Universe, in some form or other. Of this there is little doubt. The problem confronting us is whether the evidence we possess proves that some of these aliens are visiting the Earth now. If this is so, then proving the fact would be of the utmost significance. It would be perhaps the most momentous occasion in the history of the world.

But we do not possess photographs, movie films or tape recordings of aliens, or artefacts manufactured on another world . . . anything that goes beyond mere testimony. In view of this paucity of hard evidence we can hardly say, with any definiteness, whether aliens are or are not visiting us. We can only make a reasoned assessment of the facts.

The dilemmas posed by close encounters of the fourth kind are starkly illustrated by a case that occurred in the north of England on 28 November 1980. Police Constable Alan Godfrey had been called out to pursue some cows that were allegedly roaming a housing estate. By 5.15 a.m., still not having found them, he was ready to give up the search. While making one last trip in his patrol car before coming off duty, he saw a glow on the road ahead. He instantly thought of a works bus that regularly travelled the route and idly wondered why it was a little early. Then, as he approached the glow, it became obvious that he had been wrong.

The object that confronted PC Godfrey was like a spinning top with windows. It was hovering just above the road surface, spanning the gap between two lamp posts, and it was rotating. He could see his headlights reflected in the metallic surface of the object. He could see leaves on the roadside bushes moving in the vortex created by its rotation. The road surface, soaking wet in other places, was dry in blotchy patches directly beneath the object. There was no doubt in his mind that the object was real.

Maintaining the traditional calm of the British 'bobby', the officer propped his clipboard on the windscreen and carefully sketched the object. But then something inexplicable happened. He suddenly found himself further down the road, driving the car away from the scene. Nonplussed, he turned the car round and drove past the spot, now deserted, where the object had been. He carried on the short distance into town and collected a colleague. Only at this point did he notice the time. Somewhere, since the moment he first saw the UFO, 10 minutes had disappeared.

Constable Godfrey had a dim memory, however – of a strange voice saying: 'This is not for your eyes. You will forget it.' Additional fragmentary recollections gradually

Previous page, top: in the north of England a craft resembling a spinning top hovers above a road. The witness – a police constable. Later he recalled an experience of being taken aboard the craft and examined by terrifying creatures

Previous page, bottom: Alan Godfrey, the police constable who believes he was taken aboard an alien craft in November 1980, standing at the scene of the incident. The ufonauts who abducted him included, he said, eight small 'robots'

filtered back to him until, nine months after the incident, and with the help of ufologists, he underwent regression hypnosis. This was conducted by an eminently qualified and rather sceptical psychiatrist, and what appeared to be a coherent memory of the incident emerged.

The story was of the usual type: the officer had been taken on board the UFO and given a medical examination by two distinct types of humanoid creature – one tall, the other small and somewhat ugly. Remarkably, this is almost exactly what the Day family claimed happened to them during their abduction at Aveley in Essex (see page 74). In fact, contact cases reported from Britain share such similarities in many features. Cases reported from other countries, on the other hand, show different similarities among themselves.

What happened to the police constable? Is he lying to us? If not, did he have an hallucination or did he undergo the events he described? Or was it something between hallucination and straightforward experience – a distortion or misinterpretation of some extraordinary events?

There happens to be unusual and powerful support for the 'face-value' interpretation of the story. Four police officers on patrol 8 miles (13 kilometres) away had to duck as a UFO streaked low over their heads, moving directly towards the town near which the encounter took place. And a caretaker lighting a school's boilers saw in the direction of the town an object that fitted PC Godfrey's description, climbing into the sky. These stories were reported independently while the police officer was still reporting what he had just observed.

When faced with an issue like this, most people take sharply contrasting attitudes. Some would want to believe that aliens were involved. Others would deny that this was possible, and would cling to the hallucination theory. Unfortunately these two hypotheses have points both in their favour and against them. So let us survey some of the difficulties that the various answers face.

Why do aliens look like us? Why do they behave like us? Why do they mirror our social and scientific developments? Why do they never tell us anything valuable to which we do not already have access? These problems are curiously like those involved in alleged memories of past lives, spirit messages and other demonstrations of survival of death. It is surely not without significance that the common factor in these cases is the frequent use of regression hypnosis and the role of the human mind. Taken together, these facts suggest a mental origin for these strange experiences.

Between waking and sleep

To this type of evidence we should add research into lucid dreams. These are dreams in which the dreamer is fully aware that he is dreaming. Often the course of the dream can be controlled by conscious effort. Such dreams are rare and seem to overlap with such phenomena as hypnagogic imagery (the images, often compellingly 'real', that come when we are between waking and sleep).

Although they seem so real at the time, lucid dreams and hypnagogic images give away their 'unreal' nature in various subtle hints. For example, the subject does not react with normal responses. He may feel no fear, despite the weirdness of the experience. He will not wake up a sleeping bed partner to witness the events. In one case a person had such an experience, in which he thought an atomic bomb had just exploded in his garden. His response was to yawn and fall asleep. The behaviour of contact case witnesses is often like this.

Interestingly, such symptoms also occur in hallucinations that follow long periods of sensory deprivation. When a person is kept in darkness and silence, and even his sense of touch is deprived of its normal stimulation because his hands are enveloped in special gloves, his mind starts to manufacture its own 'perceptions' – hallucinations of sound, sight and touch. When we consider the usual setting of a type C contact – night-time, a tired driver, a lonely country road, and the sudden appearance of a slightly unusual sight, such as a bright light in the sky – it does not stretch credulity very far to suggest that these could be hallucinations brought about by the lack of sensory stimulation.

In the USA Dr Alvin Lawson, a professor of

Words of wisdom

Surveying 16 years of editing *Flying Saucer Review*, Charles Bowen, a contributor to *The Unexplained*, commented on the rich absurdities of the UFO occupants' messages. In 1968 in Argentina two 'men' with transparent legs gave a farmer's son a written message that may be rendered as: 'You shall know the world. F. Saucer.' In 1965 in Venezuela two beings 7 to 8 feet (2.1 to 2.4 metres) tall, with long yellow hair and protruding eyes, were asked whether there were 'any human beings like you living among us?' The answer was: 'Yes. 2,417,805.' (Surely one of them will be spotted soon!) During the 1954 'flap' a French witness encountered a small being standing before a glowing disc-shaped craft. The alien repeated several times in a 'mechanical' voice: '*La veritée est refusée aux constipés,*' and: '*Ce que vous appelez cancer vient des dents.*' Translated, these messages from another civilisation read: 'Truth is denied to the constipated' (or: 'to the ill at ease'), and: 'That which is known as cancer comes from the teeth' (or: 'through what you eat').

We can't say we weren't warned.

The trouble with hypnosis

In 1977 Professor Alvin Lawson began to investigate the validity of UFO abduction reports obtained under hypnosis. He hypnotised a total of 16 volunteers who knew very little about UFOs. Once in trance, they were asked to imagine a series of events – seeing a UFO, being taken on board, given an examination and so on. Lawson hoped to find differences between their imaginary accounts and those given by alleged UFO contactees. Such differences would enhance the credibility of the 'real' reports.

To his surprise, it was the similarities that were most striking. For example, among his test subjects' narratives were descriptions of 'tubes of light', which extended from UFOs or retracted into them, perhaps 'levitating' the subject aboard. Sometimes the subject described the UFO as 'getting bigger and smaller'. And patterns of pulsating colours, rotating spirals and geometric patterns were often reported. All these features are common in 'real' UFO reports, but they are rare in science fiction stories and films, a likely source of UFO imagery.

The experiments showed that authentic-sounding reports could be produced in abundance by subjects who have never claimed to have been abducted by a UFO. Dr Lawson concluded that contact case witnesses were not lying – but he could offer no hypothesis as to the nature of the stimulus causing their experience.

English at the University of California, has conducted experiments that are relevant to the hallucination theory. He advertised for people of a 'creative' turn of mind to take part in an unspecified experiment. He screened out all those who seemed to have a knowledge of, or interest in, UFOs. The rest were asked to imagine, under hypnosis, that they were being abducted by aliens. They were led on with certain key questions, and the results, he claimed, were so closely akin to the stories told of allegedly real abductions that it was likely that these also were, wholly or in part, subconscious fantasies.

These different types of evidence constitute impressive support for the contention that alien contacts are hallucinatory. But unfortunately there is a fair amount of negative evidence too. Some contact experiences are shared; while collective hallucinations can occur, they are not well-understood, and some encounters stretch this hypothesis to breaking point. One Italian type A case involved seven witnesses; one British type A involved four. In some cases, such as those in Puerto Rico and that involving the English police officer, there is at least some degree of *independent* corroboration.

Alvin Lawson's work, as he himself recognised, showed major differences between allegedly real abductions and imagined ones, as well as similarities. When, in a UFO contact case, memories emerge by way of hypnosis, they are almost invariably associated with very strong emotions, more consistent with the memory of a real event than a fantasy. The 'abductions' imagined in the laboratory did not display this effect, and in general those who took part in the experiment knew afterwards that they had been fantasising. Contact witnesses are never in any doubt that their regression memory is of a real event. It can still be argued, of course, that the remembered event, though real, is purely 'mental' – an hallucination or dream.

We must also consider the frequent reports of physical effects on a witness's body,

Right: more outlandish than most descriptions of aliens provided by UFO contactees: Alpha Centauri, a well-dressed science fiction monster from the television series *Dr Who*. 'Real' ufonauts are far more similar to human beings – or to gnomes, giants, dwarves and other 'traditional' mythical creatures

Left: two high officials of the Draconian race – another instance of the television designer's imagination outstripping the diversity of reported aliens. Animal forms, or hybrid animal-human forms like these, might be expected among ufonauts – whether they were genuinely extra-terrestrial or the products of the human imagination. In fact, both 'real' accounts and 'imaginary' ones produced under laboratory conditions are seldom of this type such as burns on the skin. Marks on the ground sometimes accompany these cases as well. But, on the other hand, there is almost no photographic support for the contact witnesses' stories – and physical effects can be produced psychosomatically.

Looking at more subtle features of the accounts, considerable consistency and a kind of lucid cohesiveness appear in all but the type B 'bedroom visitor' cases. This tends to make the UFO investigator doubt that he is dealing with experiences more akin to dreams than reality.

It is very difficult to sort out these contradictory elements. Perhaps the fairest judgement we can make at present is to say that type B experiences *seem* more like vivid hallucinations than reality. Type C ('memory block') cases have elements suggesting hallucinations but, unlike type B experiences, offer some data that cast doubt on this assumption. If type C cases are indeed hallucinations, they seem to be of a unique type – almost a hybrid between dream and reality. As for the most common contact cases, type A, they are the least like hallucinations. While they are full of problems, we cannot explain them as hallucinations with any degree of confidence.

What of the other extreme? Are these contacts extra-terrestrial in nature? This, the 'face-value' hypothesis, implies that hundreds of different races (most of them not very imaginative variants on ourselves), from many different worlds, are taking a great deal of interest in the Earth. They perform medical examinations interminably, and gather up endless cargoes of soil and rock samples. For no apparent reason the Earth is the Galaxy's Grand Central Station.

The sceptics invariably ask why the aliens don't contact someone important. Why not land on the White House lawn and thus dispel all doubts?

Gaynor Sunderland (see page 80) asked Arna, one of the aliens she claimed to have met, this very question. She was told that people in authority had so much credibility to lose that there was no point in contacting them, although this had been tried on a few occasions. Fear of the consequences kept such people silent. Instead the aliens pursue a policy of contacting children or simple folk, knowing that some of these will brave the ridicule and speak out.

This argument makes an intriguing amount of sense. Widespread belief in the existence of alien life is the only tangible result of decades of UFO stories. A slow, covert process of conditioning world opinion to the idea of extra-terrestrial visitors fits well with the 'provocative but not probative' evidence that we possess. Solid proof would be detrimental to such a policy: it would be impounded, or hidden, or denied outright. Suggestive indications, on the other hand, avoid the unwelcome attention of authority while providing a stimulus to continued interest and promoting the long, slow build-up of belief. Even the confusing and ridiculous behaviour of the aliens would fit this theory. In the end the only people who will not be convinced that aliens come from space will be the UFO investigators themselves!

A great deal of fascinating work remains before we can hope to know the truth. There is no hard evidence that a superior intelligence has made contact with the Earth – but we do have suggestive hints that this *might* be true. And, since most of us would wish UFOs to come from space, our judgement is clouded by an enormous emotional bias.

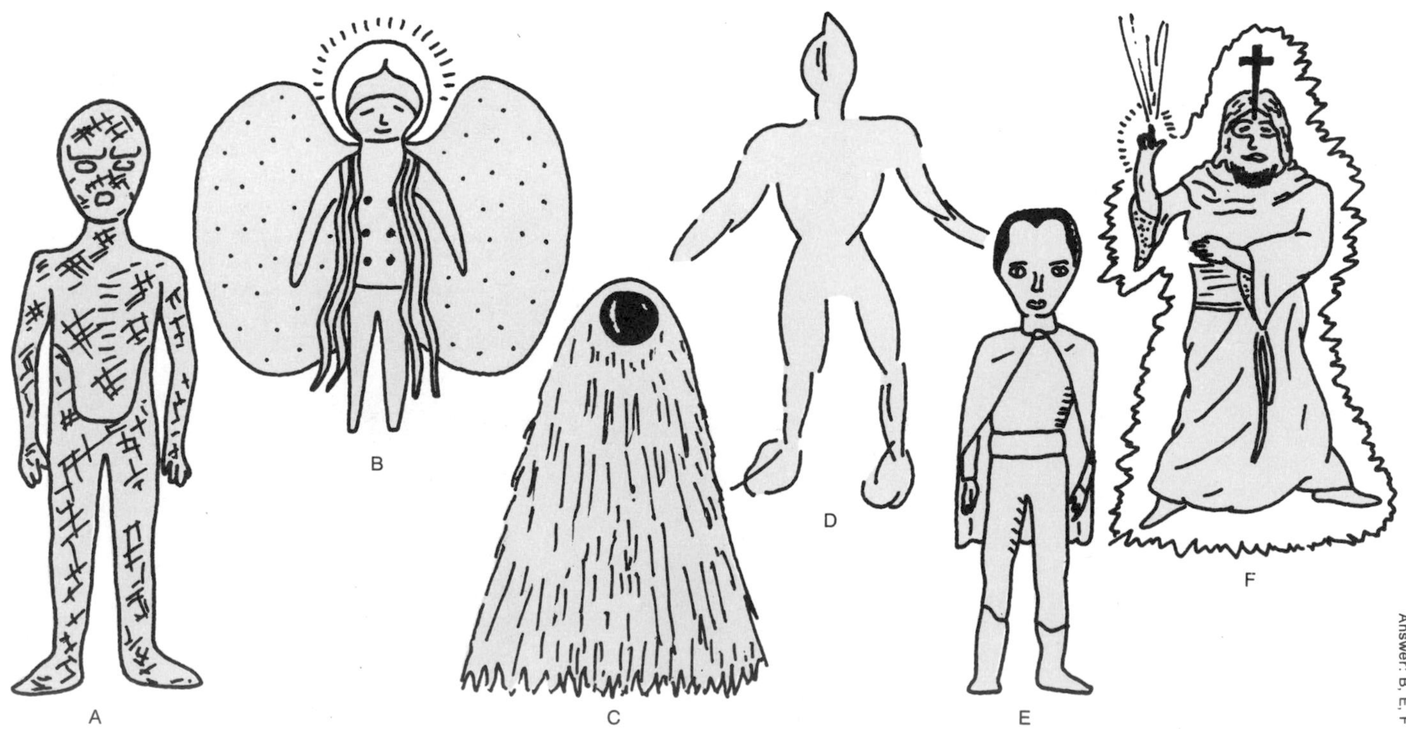

Of the six drawings below, three were made by witnesses in UFO contact cases, and were offered as *bona fide* representations of alien beings. The others were made by participants in Alvin Lawson's 'simulated abduction' experiments. These subjects, though they produced their accounts under hypnosis, were never in doubt about the imaginary nature of their experiences. Is there a different 'feel' about the two types of drawing? Can you pick out the three 'real' contact witness drawings? The answer is printed at the lower right

Three young Frenchmen hit the news headlines in early December 1979 with a tale about a UFO abduction at Cergy-Pontoise. But was their amazing story a fabrication? HILARY EVANS sorts out the facts from the fiction

Mystery of the lost week

'FRENCHMAN BACK TO EARTH with a bump' was the headline in the London *Times* – and across the world the media reported the news with the same uncertainty whether to take it seriously or not. But this much was certain: Franck Fontaine, who had allegedly been kidnapped by a UFO a week before, had been restored to friends, family, and a wondering world in the early hours of Monday, 3 December 1979.

Where had he spent those seven days? The world, hoping for a story that would make the Moon landing seem tame, was disappointed. Fontaine's recollections were few and confused. It seemed to him he had simply dropped off to sleep for half an hour: he was astonished and dismayed to find he had been away for a week. He attributed the strange images in his mind to dreams: he was bewildered to learn that he might have been abducted by extra-terrestrial aliens and carried to their distant world.

Police search a field in Cergy-Pontoise, France, for clues to the disappearance of Franck Fontaine, reported as having been abducted by a UFO. Fontaine's two friends, Jean-Pierre Prévost and Salomon N'Diaye, said they had witnessed the kidnapping early one morning in late November 1979. In the background is the block of flats in which Prévost and N'Diaye lived and near which the event occurred

Fontaine was no less dismayed to find himself the focus of the world's attention. During his seven-day absence, it had been his friends Salomon N'Diaye and Jean-Pierre Prévost, witnesses of his abduction, who had been the objects of attention. Ever since their first startling telephone call to the police – 'A friend of mine's just been carried off by a UFO!' – they had been subjected to interrogation by the police, by the press, and by UFO investigative groups ranging from the scientific to the bizarre. If Fontaine's return brought renewed publicity and fresh problems, at least it cleared them of the suspicion that they were responsible for their friend's disappearance – perhaps even his death.

The life-style of the three young men was not of a sort to dispel suspicion. All three – Prévost, aged 26, N'Diaye, 25, Fontaine, 18 – scraped an uncertain living by selling jeans in street markets. They drove an old car that was unlicensed and uninsured, none of them having a driving licence. Prévost was a self-declared anarchist. He and N'Diaye lived next door to each other in a modern block at Cergy-Pontoise on the outskirts of Paris. Fontaine lived 2 miles (3 kilometres) away.

According to their account, Fontaine had

spent Sunday evening in Prévost's flat because they wanted to be up by 3.30 a.m. to travel the 35 miles (60 kilometres) to the street market at Gisors. The market didn't start until 8 a.m. but they wanted a good place. Besides, their Taunus estate car had been acting up lately, so they thought it prudent to allow extra time. At 3.30, after only about four hours' sleep, they were up and ready to load the car with clothes.

First, though, they gave the car a push-start to make sure the engine would function. Having got it going, they decided that Fontaine should stay in the car to make sure it didn't stop again while the other two got on with the loading. Fontaine had leisure to look about him, and so it was that he noticed a brilliant light in the sky some distance away. When his companions arrived with their next load, he pointed the object out. It was cylindrical in shape, but otherwise unidentifiable. When it moved behind the block of flats, N'Diaye rushed upstairs to fetch a camera, thinking he might take a photograph of the object to sell to the newspapers. Prévost went in to get another load of clothing while Fontaine, hoping for another view of the mysterious object, drove up onto the main road that ran close by the flats.

Hearing the sound of the moving vehicle, his companions looked out of the windows of their respective flats. Both saw that Fontaine had stopped the car on the main road and noted that the engine was no longer running. Prévost, angry because they would probably have to push-start the car a second time, rushed downstairs again. He called to N'Diaye to forget about his camera because the UFO had vanished. N'Diaye came after him saying that in any case he had no film in his camera, and adding that from his window it had looked as though the car was surrounded by a great ball of light.

Outdoors again, the two young men stopped in amazement: the rear of their car was enveloped in a sharply defined sphere of glowing mist, near which a number of smaller balls of light were moving about. While they stood watching, they saw the larger globe absorb all but one of the smaller ones. Then a beam of light emerged, which grew in size until it was like the cylindrical shape they had seen earlier. The large sphere seemed to enter this cylinder, which shot up into the sky and disappeared from sight.

The two hurried to the car, but found no sign of Fontaine. He was not in the car, in the road, or in the cabbage field beside the road. Prévost insisted on calling the police immediately and N'Diaye went off to do so. Prévost, remaining near the car, was the only witness to the last phase of the incident: a ball of light, like those previously moving about

Top: Franck Fontaine leaving the police station after being questioned upon his safe return. He said that his 'missing week' was a blank in his mind

Salomon N'Diaye (above) and Jean-Pierre Prévost (right) reported the UFO incident to the police at once – a fact that convinced many they were telling the truth the car, seemed to push the car door shut. Then it too vanished.

Such was the account that the two young men gave to the police on their arrival a few minutes later. Because UFO sightings are a military matter in France, the police instructed Prévost and N'Diaye to inform the gendarmerie, which comes under the Ministry of National Defence. The two spent most of the day with the gendarmes, telling and retelling the story. The interrogators stopped for lunch, during which time the witnesses telephoned the press with their story. Later, Commandant Courcoux of the Cergy gendarmerie told the press that there were no grounds for disbelieving the young men's story, that he had no doubt 'something' had occurred, and that he could give no indication of what that 'something' might be. In a later interview he admitted, 'We are swimming in fantasy.'

For a week, that was all the world knew. During that week, the young men were questioned over and over again. Some people accepted the UFO story as it stood. Others suspected it to be a smokescreen, perhaps a cunning plan to help Fontaine avoid doing his military service, perhaps something more sinister. But one fact stood out clearly: Prévost and N'Diaye had informed the police promptly and voluntarily. Given their backgrounds, wasn't this convincing proof of their sincerity?

When Fontaine gave his version of the story, there seemed no reason to question his sincerity either. He told how he had woken to find himself lying in the cabbage field. Getting to his feet, he realised he was just across the main road from the flats, close to where he had stopped the car to watch the UFO. But the car was no longer there. His first thought, as he hurried towards the still-darkened building, was that somebody had stolen their car and its valuable load of clothing. Neither Prévost nor N'Diaye was to be seen, so he rushed upstairs and rang the bell of Prévost's flat. When there was no reply, he went to N'Diaye's. A sleepy N'Diaye appeared, gawped at him in amazement, then flung his arms round him in delighted welcome. Fontaine, already surprised to find his friend in his night clothes, was even more amazed to learn that an entire week had gone by since the morning of the Gisors market.

Jimmy Guieu, well-known science fiction writer and founder of a UFO group. The trio put themselves into his hands exclusively; other UFO investigators found them to be very unco-operative

He had little to tell the press or the police. The world's media reported his return but reserved judgement till they heard what the authorities had to say. But the police declared it was no longer their business: no crime had been committed. Apart from the inherent improbability of Fontaine's story, they had no reason to doubt his word or that of his friends.

Besieged by ufologists

So now it was up to the UFO organisations to see what further light could be thrown on the case. From the start, the witnesses had been besieged by the various French groups; there are dozens of these, most of them fiercely independent and reluctant to co-operate with the others. One of the most reputable of all is Control, to whom we owe most of what we now know of the inside story of the Cergy-Pontoise case.

But another group declared its interest before Control, while Fontaine was still missing: the *Institut Mondial des Sciences Avancés* (World Institute of Advanced Sciences). Its co-founder and spokesman was the well-known science fiction writer and author of two books about UFOs, Jimmy

Right: the cylinder-shaped UFO seen by the three friends appeared to have a diameter larger than that of the full Moon that night. It had a rounded front end and a tail that trailed off into a hazy cloud. It was when Fontaine went closer to the UFO – alone – that he disappeared

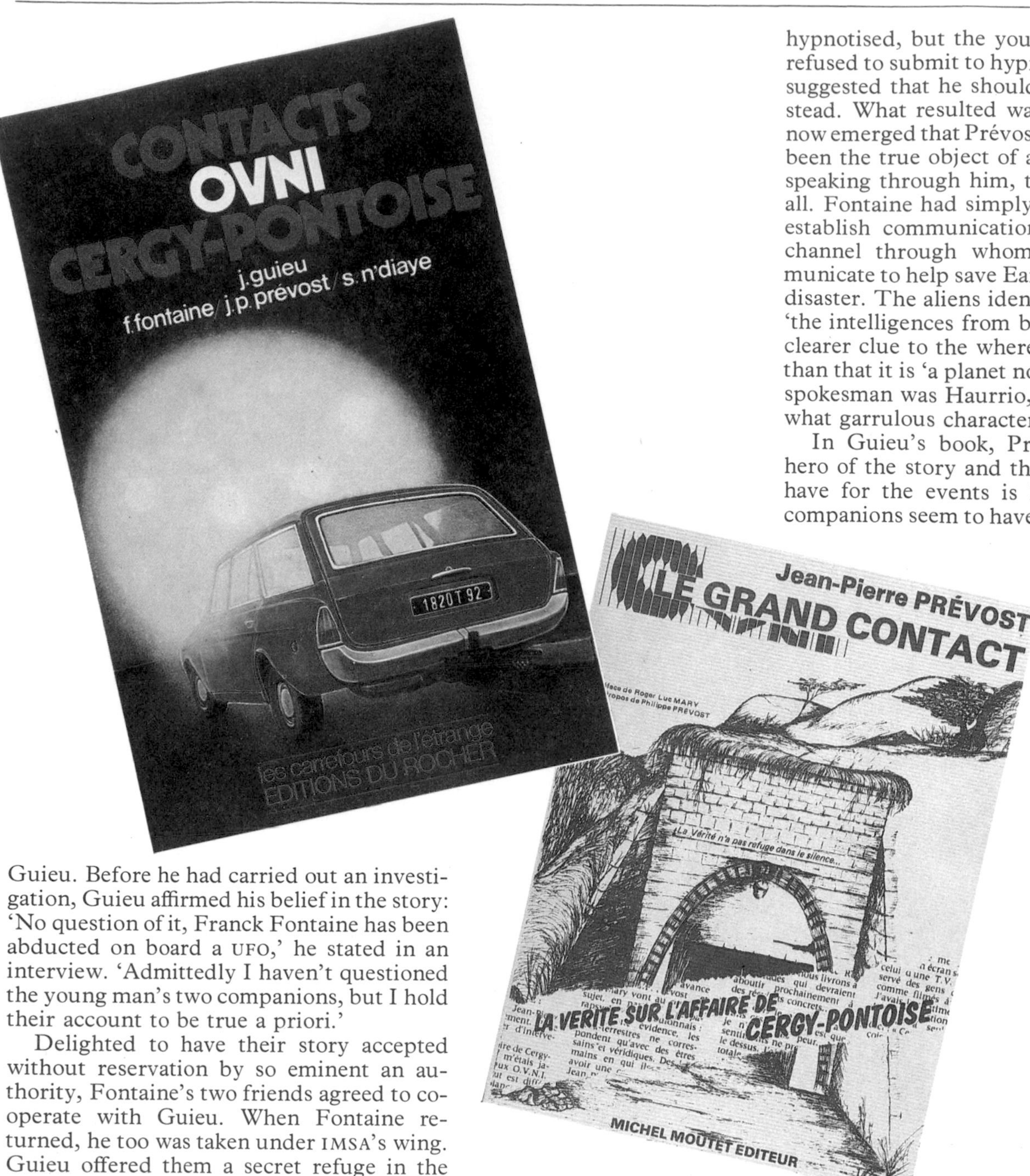

Jimmy Guieu's book *Cergy-Pontoise* UFO *contacts* (top) and Jean-Pierre Prévost's book *The truth about the Cergy-Pontoise affair* (above). Both were published speedily after the alleged kidnapping of Franck Fontaine. Both were long on fantasy and short on facts, disappointing all who hoped for some clarification of what had really happened

Guieu. Before he had carried out an investigation, Guieu affirmed his belief in the story: 'No question of it, Franck Fontaine has been abducted on board a UFO,' he stated in an interview. 'Admittedly I haven't questioned the young man's two companions, but I hold their account to be true a priori.'

Delighted to have their story accepted without reservation by so eminent an authority, Fontaine's two friends agreed to cooperate with Guieu. When Fontaine returned, he too was taken under IMSA's wing. Guieu offered them a secret refuge in the south of France where they could work on a book together, Guieu writing it and all sharing the proceeds.

Guieu's book, *Cergy-Pontoise UFO contacts*, was rushed into print with astonishing speed, appearing a bare four months after Fontaine's return. Thanks to the combination of Guieu's name and the intense interest in the case, it was an instant bestseller. But readers hoping for a conclusive verdict were disappointed. The book was padded out by Guieu's journalistic style and digressive accounts of other cases, and there was an almost total absence of first-hand testimony from the principal witness – the abducted Fontaine – whose story the world wanted to hear. Such revelations as the book contained were of quite another nature.

Guieu had hoped that Fontaine would be able to recall more of his adventure if he were hypnotised, but the young man obstinately refused to submit to hypnosis. Then Prévost suggested that he should be hypnotised instead. What resulted was truly amazing. It now emerged that Prévost, not Fontaine, had been the true object of alien interest. Now, speaking through him, the aliens explained all. Fontaine had simply been the means to establish communication: Prévost was the channel through whom they could communicate to help save Earth from impending disaster. The aliens identified themselves as 'the intelligences from beyond' but gave no clearer clue to the whereabouts of 'beyond' than that it is 'a planet not like yours'. Their spokesman was Haurrio, a friendly if somewhat garrulous character.

In Guieu's book, Prévost becomes the hero of the story and the only evidence we have for the events is his word. His two companions seem to have become irrelevant.

This book having raised more questions than it answered, much was hoped for when Prévost announced that he was writing his own account of the event. But *The truth about the Cergy-Pontoise affair*, published later that same year, was even less satisfactory. It was a rambling, incoherent farrago in which great doses of alien 'philosophy' – transmitted by Prévost – show that pious platitudes about the need for more love and less science are not confined to planet Earth.

There is virtually no mention of Franck Fontaine's abduction: indeed, he and Salomon N'Diaye are scarcely referred to. But Prévost's visit to a secret alien base is described in some detail, and this gives us a good yardstick for evaluating the rest of the material. It seems that one morning soon

Above: a group of people anticipate a close encounter with aliens at Cergy-Pontoise on 15 August 1980. They gathered there when Fontaine revealed that he had made an arrangement to meet on that day with his abductors of the previous December

Left: a being named Haurrio allegedly contacted Prévost on behalf of the 'intelligences from beyond'. On one occasion Haurrio was dressed in a one-piece silver garment, looking decidedly 'like an alien'. On another he had long blond hair and looked like a masculine woman in a suit. He was said to be friendly and very talkative

after Fontaine's return, there was a ring at Prévost's door. The caller was a travelling salesman, a total stranger who said he had to make a trip to Bourg-de-Sirod and invited Prévost to come along. Now, Bourg-de-Sirod is a small village near the Swiss border some 225 miles (360 kilometres) from Cergy. On the face of it, there is no conceivable reason why a salesman should go there, nor why he should think that Prévost might wish to go there given that they were strangers in the first place.

However, there was a reason for interest by Prévost. Bourg-de-Sirod was a specially significant place for him because as a child he had gone to a summer camp nearby and had later worked there. More recently still, he and Fontaine had spent a camping holiday there. So Prévost, though surprised at the stranger's offer, cheerfully accepted it. The salesman dropped him off at the village and he set off up the hill towards a particular site that had always fascinated him – a railway tunnel containing an abandoned train carriage from the Second World War.

Arriving at the tunnel in late evening, Prévost found that other people were there before him: a group of young men gathered round a fire in the open. One of them called out his name; he was from the Sahara and had recently written to Prévost. It turned out that he and the others had come there from many parts of the world, thanks to the 'intelligences from beyond'. Each spoke his own language – but was understood by the rest.

When Haurrio, the alien representative, arrived, he informed them that they had been chosen to spread the philosophy of the 'intelligences' on Earth. A beautiful female alien then took them on a tour of the tunnel, now being used as a UFO base. They saw several spacecraft, similar to ones that Prévost had seen as a child. After their tour, the young men returned to their camp fire and went to sleep on the ground – which, on a December night in the mountains, must have been less than comfortable. Next morning Prévost found his friendly salesman waiting to chauffeur him back to Cergy.

Whether Jimmy Guieu and Jean-Pierre Prévost seriously expected their accounts to be believed, we may never know. But the more they provided in the way of checkable statements, the harder it became to accept the original account of the alleged abduction. Doubts grew even more when an investigative team from Control persisted in taking up the case without the co-operation of the witnesses – checking all the conflicting statements and fragmented testimony as best they could.

Long after the much-publicised disappearance of Franck Fontaine from Cergy-Pontoise, confusion still reigns over whether he was abducted by a UFO. Was it all a put-up job by him and his two friends? Or did it really happen?

THE ABDUCTION OF Franck Fontaine by a UFO, though unsubstantiated by scientific evidence, seemed a plausible story on first hearing. Had he and his friends Jean-Pierre Prévost and Salomon N'Diaye been content to tell that story and nothing else, they might have convinced an interested world of its truth. But the two books on the case – one by the well-known science fiction writer Jimmy Guieu and one by Prévost himself – raised questions that cast suspicion on the entire affair. Moreover, there were many interviews and conferences in which widely divergent material was put forward. And Prévost, who had pre-empted Fontaine as the hero of the Cergy-Pontoise UFO affair, even published a short-lived journal in which he kept the public informed of his continuing dialogue with the 'intelligences from beyond' who he claimed had contacted him.

All this increased the doubts of the sceptics. Michel Piccin and his colleagues of the Control organisation had detected inconsistencies and contradictions in the witnesses' statements from the start. And the more they probed, the more discrepancies they found.

It began with trivial, marginal matters, like Prévost's insistence that before the encounter he had no interest in or knowledge of UFOs. The Control investigators found that his brother was a French representative of the American UFO organisation APRO. Even if Prévost did not share his brother's interest in UFOs, he could hardly have been unaware of them. Besides, in his own book, Prévost had said that he saw several spacecraft similar to ones he had 'seen as a child' when the 'intelligences' took him to their UFO base. He also denied seeing a magazine in which a UFO abduction story, very like Fontaine's, was being serialised. Yet Control established that this very magazine was in Prévost's flat at the time of the Cergy-Pontoise abduction.

The events of the night before the abduction became more confused the more they were investigated. Control discovered that there were five people – not three – in

Fact, fraud or fantasy?

Above: Franck Fontaine, whose disappearance for a week – allegedly as an abductee of aliens – stirred worldwide interest. He was never very forthcoming about what had happened to him

Left: the cabbage field in which Fontaine awoke on his return to Cergy-Pontoise

Prévost's flat that night. Why had the published accounts almost completely failed to mention the presence of Corinne, Prévost's girlfriend, and Fabrice Joly? One reason suggested itself: knowledge of the presence of the fourth young man, Joly, might throw doubt on one of the facts most favourable to Prévost and N'Diaye. They had claimed that they had gone straight to the police when Fontaine vanished from their car, even though they knew they might get into trouble because they were driving without a licence. But Joly was there because he had a valid licence and had agreed to drive the three friends to the market at Gisors.

Discrepancies abound

Why were Corinne and Joly never questioned about what happened? Did they see and hear nothing? They could certainly have straightened out some of the contradictions, for Fontaine, Prévost and N'Diaye could not even agree on who had been at the flat on the night before the abduction – surely one of the most memorable of their lives. First the three had said they spent the night together. Then Prévost recollected that he had watched a television film with friends elsewhere.

Other discrepancies force us to ask how far we can trust their account. They said that they were dubious about their car's ability to start and pushed it to get the motor running, then left Fontaine in the car to make sure it didn't stop. Why didn't Joly, the only licensed driver, do this so that Fontaine could lend a hand with loading the jeans for the market? Did they really sit outside the block of flats at 4 a.m. with the motor running without any complaint from the neighbours? None of the other residents seem even to have heard the sound. What about N'Diaye's completely opposing statement that they loaded the car first and only then started the motor? Whom should we believe?

The account of the one neighbour who did witness anything only makes matters more confused. Returning home at the time the young men were supposedly loading the car, he said he saw two people get into the Taunus estate car and drive away. Yet the three involved said that Fontaine was alone when he drove up onto the road to get a better view of the UFO they had spotted.

Even though UFOs are notoriously difficult to describe, the three accounts of the one at Cergy-Pontoise are particularly far apart. One saw 'a huge beam', another 'a ball', the third 'a flash'. One said it was moving fairly slowly, taking two minutes to cross the sky; the others said it was moving fast, gone in a matter of seconds. There was further disagreement about the direction in which it was moving.

The circumstances of Fontaine's return a week after his supposed abduction are no less confused as several stories emerged. One of the journalists covering the case was Iris Billon-Duplan, who worked for a local newspaper and lived close by. Apart from the special interest of a case that had occurred almost on her doorstep, the fact that she lived nearby meant she could follow it personally. As a result, she became closely involved with the witnesses. Indeed, she spent the night before Fontaine's return with Prévost, preparing a definitive account of the case.

According to the journalist's published account, N'Diaye went off to bed shortly after midnight, leaving her with Prévost. He told her that he had no food or money because his involvement in the UFO affair was keeping him from working. So she suggested that they go to her flat where she could give him a meal while they continued to work on

Space briefing

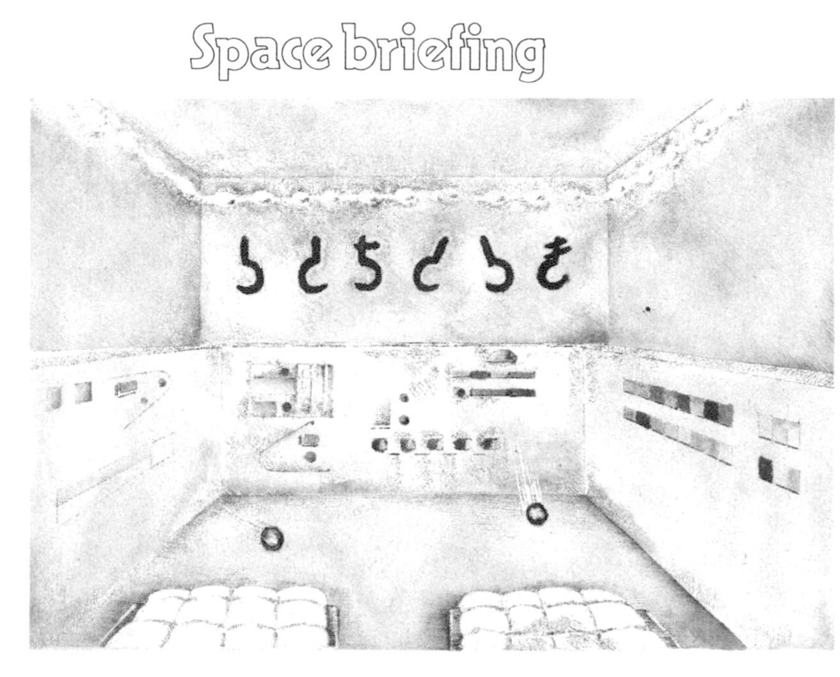

Franck Fontaine remembered things that had happened to him during his week 'out of this world' only slowly and bit by bit, but refused to undergo hypnosis to speed the process. However, strange – and sometimes very disturbing – dreams helped him to recall his experiences, he said.

In one instance that he recalled, he was in a large white room with machines that went all round the walls. They were all the same height and had opaque white glass fronts that lit up and went out almost simultaneously. He was lying on a sort of couch and two small luminous spheres – the extra-terrestrials – were talking to him about problems on Earth and how to solve them.

His abductors, who were always kind, told him that he would be the sole judge of what to reveal of his adventure. He seems to have decided to say as little as possible.

the article. This explains why Fontaine did not find Prévost in when he returned and went to Prévost's flat. We know that Fontaine then went to N'Diaye's flat and succeeded in rousing him. But according to the journalist's account, N'Diaye then left Fontaine and hurried round to her flat to tell her and Prévost the news.

Should we believe Iris Billon-Duplan or Salomon N'Diaye? For his statement, made to the police, flatly contradicts hers.

His story was that he happened to wake up at about 4.30 a.m., looked out of his window and saw a ball of light on the main road. When he saw a silhouetted figure emerge from it, he recognised his friend Franck Fontaine. He then hurried to a telephone to report the return to Radio Luxembourg, believing he would get a reward for information about Fontaine's whereabouts. (In this he was mistaken; it was Europe Numéro 1 that had offered a reward.)

Radio Luxembourg later confirmed that such a call had been made, but not at 4.30 a.m. because there was nobody on duty at that hour. The implication is that N'Diaye telephoned later than 4.30 a.m. and that he waited to inform the police until he had attempted to claim the reward money – not saying much for his concern about his friend. In the event, it was Radio Luxembourg staff who told the police that Franck Fontaine had returned. According to them, they had received an *anonymous* call from a man who, just as he was going to work, saw Fontaine coming back. Surely N'Diaye would not have made an anonymous call if he wanted to collect the reward.

These contradictions are just a sample from Control's 50-page report. There is confusion, if not outright deception, at every stage of the affair. Some of the discrepancies can be attributed to faulty memory, but such an explanation can hardly be stretched to account for Prévost's extraordinary visit to the tunnel. As a case history, Cergy-Pontoise is so ambiguous that few will be ready to give it serious credence. Yet it caused such a sensation that it is still worth asking what really happened. If the abduction was not genuine, was it a put-up job from the outset? Or did the witnesses gradually distort what was fundamentally a true UFO experience? If so, at what point did deceit and contrivance begin? There are several ways to answer these questions.

An elaborate tale

We may believe that Franck Fontaine was abducted as claimed, that all the witnesses were doing their best to tell the truth and that contradictions crept in because of defective memory. However, the extent of the discrepancies makes it easier to believe that the trio elaborated the story for their own purposes, adding sensational details that they may or may not have believed actually happened.

Alternatively, we may surmise that Franck Fontaine was not in fact abducted, but that he sincerely believed he was. He may have been in, or put into, some altered state of consciousness in which he experienced the illusion of the abduction. That this can happen is an established psychological phenomenon, so we cannot rule it out altogether. But it does raise questions about Fontaine's two friends. If he was deluded,

Top: Jean-Pierre Prévost with Patrick Pottier of the Control group. Control carried out as thorough an investigation as they could without the active co-operation of Prévost and the other two involved

Above: Saloman N'Diaye in front of the Taunus estate car which, he said, he and Prévost saw enveloped by a UFO just before their friend Fontaine disappeared

where do they stand? Were they also in an altered state of consciousness, experiencing or being made to believe in the same illusion? And does this explain the contradictions? If so, who fed them the illusion and made them believe in its reality?

While neither of these explanations can be ruled out entirely, we may consider it most plausible that the whole affair was a fabrication from the start – that there never was any abduction and that the three young men put the story together for fun, for gain or for some undiscovered ideological motive. We know that the trio immediately co-operated with Jimmy Guieu in a commercial enterprise. We learn from Control that Prévost, clearly the dominant one of the three, was noted for practical joking at school. Indeed he told the Control investigators, 'You bet I'm a clown!'

More questions than answers

The reports are consistent with the hypothesis that Prévost persuaded his two companions to stage a hoax, but that Corinne and Fabrice Joly refused to go along. Perhaps none of them expected their story to attract so much attention and they were forced to improvise beyond their prepared narrative. This could explain such muddles as the contradictory accounts of Fontaine's return.

Another question then arises: was Guieu a party to the deception? Did he suspect the story from the start but, as a professional writer, recognise its money-making potential? Did he start by believing them, as he claimed to do, then discover the hoax but decide to go along with it – perhaps because he was already committed? Or did he believe that the affair was genuine? The last supposition seems unlikely in the light of Guieu's long involvement with ufology, unless he was unusually gullible. On the other hand, it is hard to believe that he would risk his reputation by endorsing a case that he knew to be a fake. We are probably left with the surmise that he discovered a hoax but decided not to reveal it for reasons of his own.

If the Cergy-Pontoise contact was indeed all a hoax, it would explain why the trio committed themselves to the uncritical Guieu and his *Institut Mondial des Sciences Avancès* (World Institue of Advanced Sciences). IMSA has little following or reputation, but Guieu offered the backing of a big name, sympathetic support and the chance to make a substantial profit from a book bearing his name. And other UFO organisations might have uncovered the deceit in a short time, if deceit it was.

In the absence of any definite proof, all this is merely speculative. Will the truth ever be established? There are hopes that it may be. During their researches, Control came across a tantalising clue that they were unable to follow up. It seems that during Fontaine's disappearance, a school in Cergy-Pontoise was working on a project about it with the local newspaper – the one that was later to carry Iris Billon-Duplan's version of Fontaine's return. Some of the children learned that one of the school workers was an aunt of Fontaine and interviewed her as part of their project in the presence of one of the teachers and one of Iris Billon-Duplan's colleagues from the paper. During the interview, Fontaine's aunt said angrily that she knew perfectly well where her nephew was. He was, she said, staying with a friend.

Was she stating a fact or simply saying what she thought to be true? Who was the friend and where did he or she live? The answers to these questions could settle the Cergy-Pontoise mystery. But until we learn if someone knew where Fontaine was all the time, the case must remain open.

Right: a UFO base in a disused railway tunnel, as described by Jean-Pierre Prévost in his book on the Cergy-Pontoise affair. The tunnel also contained an abandoned Nazi train carriage left over from the Second World War. Prévost, always the dominant member of the trio of witnesses, quickly became the 'star of the show' and the other two receded into the background – for, said Prévost, the aliens had simply used Fontaine to establish contact with himself

PART 2

GREAT HAUNTINGS

GREAT HAUNTINGS

Contents

Introduction

ON THE VERY LAST DAY of the Second World War in Europe, when the shooting and bombing and carnage had ceased, my uncle Edward, serving in the Coldstream Guards, was killed in a minor railway accident near Berlin. He had survived almost five years of bloodshed and unparalleled violence and yet there he was at the end, dead not through human malice but the malfunction of machinery.

His mother, my grandmother, was very old and living in Yorkshire. She was senile and rarely left her fireside chair, but on that particular morning she grasped the head of her walking stick and rose to her feet when my mother entered.

'Teddy is dead,' she said. 'I've just seen him in his altar boy clothes.'

As far as my mother could make out, the vision had been that of her brother when he was about ten years old, a time when he had served at Mass wearing his white cotta and red cassock. When he died he was in his early twenties, wearing his khaki 'walking-out' dress uniform, complete with Sam Browne belt. Two days later a War Office telegram confirmed the news that the accident had happened at the time my grandmother had seen the 'ghost' of her son.

Such stories are commonplace in the annals of psychical research and even have a name: 'crisis apparitions.' But are they 'ghosts' in the sense of revenant spirits? The general theory is that at the emotionally supercharged moment of death the spirit projects itself onto the consciousness of those nearest to it in life; but this theory, as we shall see on later pages, has a drawback. On many occasions, the 'vision' seen has been that of a live person, going through a moment of intense happiness, relief, or fear. Many well attested wartime 'crisis apparitions' later turned out to have occurred at a moment when the subject was wounded or in grave danger, even though he or she eventually survived.

Indeed, the majority of true life 'ghosts' seem to have relevance not to the dead but to the living. Most poltergeist phenomena appear to centre around pre-pubescent or disturbed persons, though the celebrated 18th century Cock Lane ghost recalled in this book may be said to fit into the 'returned spirit' category of hauntings. Other hauntings could well be the result of wishful thinking, of people wanting to believe in a life beyond our own.

I am convinced that the famous haunting at Borley Rectory, Suffolk, was one of these examples. A 19th century incumbent liked to tell his daughters and parishoners that his house and garden were haunted; later his daughters fostered the rumour. Still later, the neurotic wife of another rector appears to have 'staged' incidents at the house, as a result of which the popular press became interested and asked the late Harry Price, who had made his name as a ghost hunter, to investigate. There seems little doubt today that Price was not a man of great integrity when it came to solid facts; his books and articles on the subject of Borley promoted the ugly building as 'the most haunted house in England', yet a closely analysed examination of the events he described, produced by three prominent members of the Society for Psychical Research in the 1950s, showed little evidence of anything but sheer chicanery on Price's part.

Nevertheless the site of Borley Rectory is still the object of pilgrimages by amateur ghost hunters from all over the world. Though the house itself burned down some years before Price's death in 1948, reports still surface of phantom nuns walking in what was once the garden, and a ghostly carriage and horses thundering down the hill towards the nearby town of Long Melford. In the 1970's, attention shifted to the parish church itself, and reliable investigators – including a team from the BBC – have recorded what appear to be inexplicable noises: grunts, heavy sighs, the sound of metallic objects being thrown down the aisle, and ponderous footsteps in the ancient church. Apparently, all precautions were taken to preclude any natural or fraudulent effects finding their way onto the tapes, and the results are impressive. But in the subjective, empirical world of paranormal theory, who can say exactly what the cause was? Experiments seem to show that the mind can have power over matter; perhaps the years of obsession with Borley as a haunted spot have finally impinged themselves onto it, producing 'genuine' as opposed to Harry Price's 'fake' phenomena.

The integrity of witnesses and researchers is, of course, vital in any attempt to assimilate the paranormal into a universal scheme of things. Many a good chilling ghost story must have its origin in, say, a drunken farmer stumbling home from the village pub, mistaking a sheep for an ethereal presence in the darkness, retailing his experience and laying the foundations of a piece of folk lore.

Some years ago, while writing on the supernatural for a magazine named *Man, Myth and Magic* I found so many examples of such unreliable stories that I decided to 'plant' one of my own. As outlined on page 74 of the present book, I invented the 'Phantom Vicar of Ratcliffe Dock,' and wrote about my creation in the magazine.

I determined, however, that if any researcher approached me for information on the subject, I would confess to my fakery; only one journalist, Bill Grundy who was then with Thames Television and has always been a paragon of professionalism, did so. When I eventually 'confessed' in the *Sunday Times* and later on BBC-2's *A leap in the dark* series, there was an outcry from the motley crew of popular ghost hunters who carry on the traditions of Harry Price. One claimed that the 'phantom vicar' had been a real ghost, who had somehow influenced me into making him 'come true.' Another, who had inherited Price's seat as secretary of a rather whimsical ghost club, described me in his autobiography as 'unscrupulous'; the truth is that both persons had

Tens of thousands of people were burned at the stake in Europe during the late medieval period. Some of these unfortunates had committed no greater sin than believing they had heard or seen a spirit been caught out by a deliberate fraud which they made no effort to detect.

Oddly enough, despite newspaper and television articles relating what I had done, the 'phantom vicar' continues to thrive, and I was assured by the landlord of a local pub that my story of the *fake* had been an invention; the ghostly vicar himself had been well known in the area for years.

The whole world of the paranormal lends itself to fraud, both deliberate and accidental, but there are many cases on record which are not easily dismissed. The case of Frendraught House in Aberdeenshire, told on page 56, is a case in point. Here we have an historical record of events which happened in 1630, and a long tradition of sightings. Mrs Yvonne Morison, the owner's wife, is a person of the utmost integrity and common sense, who had nothing to lose or gain by claiming to have heard ghostly footsteps in the house; nor had her guests – who fled Frendraught in terror after hearing bumps and crashes in the night. Again in Scotland, Glamis Castle, the childhood home of the Queen Mother, has a centuries old reputation for being inhabited by a creature or creatures not of this world, and far from being glamorous the stories have been a source of annoyance and even trepidation to successive Earls of Strathmore.

Most students of the paranormal would put down the haunting of places like Frendraught and Glamis to the 'psychic recording' catalogue of such events (violence or tumultuous emotion which impregnates the site on which it has occurred by a sort of preternatural osmosis), a chronic form of the 'crisis apparitions' mentioned earlier. The Dower House at Killakee in Ireland has a history of such violence ranging from the early eighteenth century, when it was the haunt of 'Hellfire Club' rakes, to the twentieth century, when IRA gunmen shot each other to death there. Almost everyone has experienced a building which exudes a feeling of tranquility, of having been loved; perhaps extremes of anger and hatred leave behind a stronger residue.

The battlefield hauntings recalled by Joan Forman seem to reflect this, particularly in the impressive case of Edgehill, when that English Civil War battle was re-enacted on at least two occasions in front of witnesses who had been present at the original fight, and who recognised in the midst of the ghostly melée not only men who had died, but some who were still very much alive. In the case of Edgehill there appears to be no case of revenant spirits; more of an 'action replay' on some supernatural three-dimensional television screen.

Once having become part of legend, a ghost story is notoriously difficult to lay; classic cases in point are the 'screaming skull' legends retold here. In the case of 'Owd Nance' of Burton Agnes Hall, Yorkshire, we have an historic record to work on, the head of a former occupant having been kept in the hall at his sentimental if gruesome last request. But the screaming skull of Bettiscombe in Dorset, the basis for a ghostly tale by that master of spirit fiction Montague Rhodes James, is of much greater antiquity. Despite legends that the skull is that of a Negro slave, or of a woman mysteriously kept locked up in the house many years ago, fairly recent research seems to show that it is the cranium of a prehistoric woman: perhaps a 'foundation sacrifice' laid down to protect the original building on the site whose memory has been kept alive by that tenuous but enduring process 'folk tradition.'

What, however, are we to make of 'soulless ghosts' – the ships, coaches, and latterly aeroplanes and at least one red London bus? We might, to paraphrase one writer, be prepared to believe in the spirits of people and animals, but what of phantom shoes, shirts, and hats – for few ghosts ever seem to appear naked. Do modesty and decorum play a part in the afterlife?

Despite years of writing and broadcasting on the subject of apparitions, the 'family ghost' of my uncle is the nearest I have ever consciously come to experiencing one. I say consciously, because 'real life' spooks, as opposed to those of fiction, invariably appear as solid, lifelike figures; only when they suddenly walk through a wall or disappear are their observers filled with alarm and sometimes despondency. Undoubtedly the hundreds of people who have such psychic experiences cannot all be frauds, liars, or lunatics; *something* happens – but what?

The truth is that ghosts resolutely avoid being tested under laboratory conditions, thus putting them beyond the pale as far as orthodox science is concerned. They obey no one set of rules, and cannot be any more than loosely catagorised. In short they are a chilling but fascinating enigma: long may they remain so!

FRANK SMYTH

Was Borley Rectory really 'the most haunted house in England' – or was its fame built on a great publicity stunt by ghost hunter Harry Price? Indeed, was Price a headline-seeking fraud? FRANK SMYTH **investigates**

Borley: a haunting tale

BORLEY PARISH CHURCH stands on a hillside overlooking the valley of the river Stour, which marks the boundary between the counties of Essex and Suffolk in England. Borley can hardly even be called a village: the hundred or so inhabitants of this Essex parish, mainly agricultural workers and weekend cottagers, do their shopping and socialising in Long Melford or Sudbury, the two nearest small towns on the Suffolk side; for more important business they travel from Borley Green to Bury St Edmunds, about 25 miles (40 kilometres) away.

But in 1940 the publication of a book entitled *The most haunted house in England* made the community world famous, and in 1946 a further volume, *The end of Borley Rectory*, set the seal on its fame. Both were written by the flamboyant ghost hunter Harry Price, who made psychical research headlines in his day. The two books claimed that Borley Rectory, a gloomy Victorian house that had burned down in 1939, was the centre of remarkably varied paranormal phenomena. These included a phantom coach, a headless monk, a ghostly nun who may or may not have been the monk's lover, the spirit of a former vicar, eerie lights, water that turned into ink, mysterious bells, and a multifarious cascade of things that went bump in the night.

'One of the events of the year 1940' was how the first book was described by *Time and Tide* in its glowing review, while the *Church Times* said that it would 'remain among the most remarkable contributions ever made to the study of the paranormal'. Price, who professed to have devoted 10 years to his study of Borley's ghosts, continued to lecture, broadcast and write on the subject until his death on 29 March 1948. An obituary in *The Times* the following day summed him up as a psychical researcher with 'a singularly honest and clear mind on a subject that by its very nature lends itself to all manner of trickery and chicanery'.

Not everyone who knew or worked with Price agreed with this glowing testimonial, however. Some months after his death, and with the danger of libel safely out of the way, an article by Charles Sutton of the *Daily Mail* appeared in the *Inky way annual*, a World's Press News publication. Writing of a visit he had paid to Borley in 1929, in the

Borley Church, whose vicars lived in the reputedly haunted Borley Rectory not far away. Harry Price, ghost hunter, psychical researcher and author, put the parish of Borley 'on the map' when he wrote a book about the rectory hauntings in 1940

middle of Price's first investigation with another colleague, Sutton said that he had discovered what might be fraud on Price's part. After a large pebble had hit Sutton on the head, he found that Price had 'bricks and pebbles' in his pockets.

On a more careful investigation, two members of the Society for Psychical Research (SPR) – Lord Charles Hope and Major the Hon. Henry Douglas-Home – had had serious doubts about 'phenomena' they had witnessed at the rectory in the late 1920s. Both of them filed testimony with the SPR stating that they had grave suspicions. Douglas-Home went as far as to accuse Price of having a 'complete disregard for the truth in this matter'. He told how, on one occasion, he was accompanying Price around the rectory in the darkness when they heard a rustling that reminded him of cellophane being crumpled. Later, he sneaked a look into Price's suitcase and found a roll of cellophane with a torn edge.

It was as a result of this testimony that the Council of the SPR invited three of their members, Dr Eric J. Dingwall, Mrs K. M. Goldney and Mr Trevor H. Hall, to undertake a new survey of the evidence. The three were given access to Price's private papers and correspondence by his literary executor, Dr Paul Tabori. They also had access to documents in the Harry Price Collection, which Price had placed on permanent loan to the University of London in 1938 and bequeathed to that institution on his death. This survey took five years to prepare and was published in 1956 under the title *The haunting of Borley rectory*.

The reviews of this book were as enthusiastic as those of Price's two volumes in the 1940s, although for diametrically different reasons. The *Sunday Times* said that the Borley legend had been demolished 'with clinical thoroughness and aseptic objectivity', while Professor A.G.N. Flew in the *Spectator* commented that the 'shattering and fascinating document' had proved that Borley had been 'a house of cards built by the late Harry Price out of little more than a pack of lies'.

Price in action: on the radio direct from a haunted house in Meopham, Kent, in 1936 (above) and on a much-publicised trip to Germany with C.E.M. Joad to re-create a magical scene on the Brocken in the Harz mountains in 1932 (below)

There, perhaps, the matter should have rested, but due to a combination of factors it did not. The principal reason may have been that Borley had made sensational copy for the world's popular newspapers for over a quarter of a century, and even the most objective of reporters dislikes seeing a good source dry up. Newspapers and television programmes glossed over the painstaking evidence of Dingwall, Goldney and Hall, one referring to them as 'the scoffers who accused Harry Price, the greatest of ghost seekers, of rigging the whole legend'. And once more, the events described by Price were said to be 'puzzling, frightening, and inexplicable'. Peter Underwood, the president of the Ghost Club, and the late Dr Tabori returned to Price's defence in 1973 with a book entitled *The ghosts of Borley: annals of the haunted rectory*. They dedicated it to 'the memory of Harry Price, the man who put Borley on the map'.

In his book *The occult*, published in 1971, Colin Wilson made a fair and scrupulously unbiased summing up of the evidence for and against the Borley case. His conclusion was that 'a hundred other similar cases could be extracted [from SPR records]. . . . Unless someone can produce a book proving that Price was a pathological liar with a craving for publicity, it is necessary to suspend judgement.'

And, indeed, in 1978 SPR investigator Trevor H. Hall set out to prove Price 'a pathological liar with a craving for publicity'. The title of his book, *Search for Harry Price*, was a pun based on Price's own autobiography *Search for truth* (1942).

Had it been less carefully documented, Hall's book could have been fairly described as a piece of muckraking. He revealed, for instance, that Price's father was a London grocer who had seduced and married Price's mother when she was 14 and he was over 40. Price himself, in his autobiography, had claimed to be the son of a wealthy paper manufacturer who came of 'an old Shropshire family'.

Price stated that his childhood had been spent between the London stockbroker suburb of Brockley and the family's country home in an unnamed part of Shropshire. He said that he usually 'broke his journey' there on the way to and from school, implying that he was educated at a boarding school in the country. Hall's researches clearly showed the family home to have been in New Cross, not far from, but far less salubrious than, Brockley. Price, said Hall, attended a local secondary school, Haberdasher's Aske's Hatcham Boys' School, a perfectly respectable lower middle class establishment, but not a public boarding school. The only family connection

Above: Peter Underwood, the president of the Ghost Club, who came down on the side of Price in the controversy over the latter's integrity

Below: the ruins of Borley Rectory four years after it was completely destroyed by a mysterious fire. This did not end the speculation over its haunting

with Shropshire was that Price's grandfather had once been landlord of the Bull's Head at Rodington.

According to Price, he had held a directorship in his father's paper manufacturing company after leaving school, spending the 10 years between the end of his schooldays and his marriage in 1908 pleasantly as an amateur coin collector and archaeologist. In fact, according to Hall, Price earned his living in New Cross in a variety of odd ways. He took photographs of local shopfronts for advertising purposes; hired out his portable gramophone and records for dances, parties and other functions; performed conjuring tricks at concerts – a skill that he was later accused of using during his Borley investigation – and peddled glue, paste and a cure for footrot in sheep from door to door in the Kent countryside. Price had an indubitable flair for writing, as the impressive sales of his books – some 17 in all – testify.

In 1902 Price wrote an article for his old school magazine, *The Askean*, about the excavation of a Roman villa in Greenwich Park, quoting as his source a book written by the director of the project. By 1942, in *Search for truth*, he was claiming that he had actually helped to excavate the site. He also contributed a series of articles to the *Kentish Mercury* on coins and tokens of the county, following this up with another series for Shropshire's *Wellington Journal* on 'Shropshire tokens and mints'.

Hall asked the Reverend Charles Ellison, Archdeacon of Leeds and a leading authority

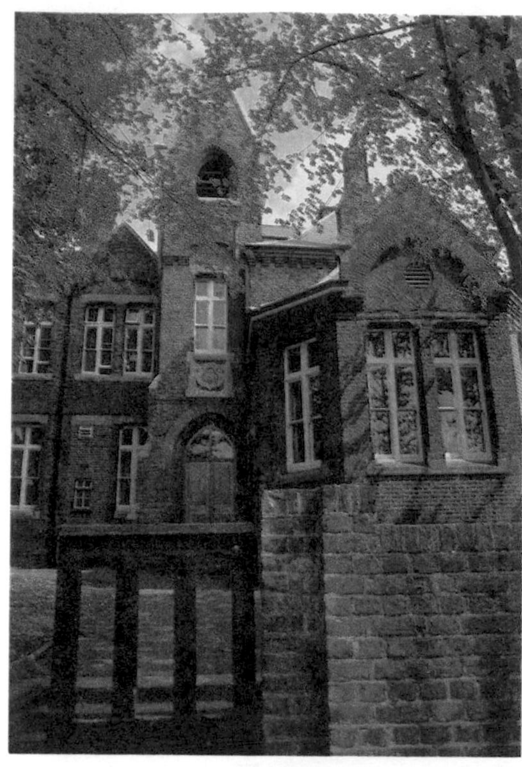

Left: Haberdasher's Aske's Hatcham Boys School, where Price had his education, as it looks today. According to Price's detractor, Trevor H. Hall, Price hinted in his autobiography that he had attended a public school

Below: the Harry Price Library in the Senate House at London University. Price bequeathed to the university his outstanding collection of thousands of books on magic and the occult – which Hall characterises as Price's 'most useful achievement'. Price also tried to get the university to establish a psychical research department, but failed. Some say that the institution was scared off by his flamboyant approach to scientific investigation

on numismatics, to examine Price's writings on coins. The archdeacon found them to be straight plagiarisms from two obscure works on the subject. 'It is unsafe to rely on any statement made by Harry Price which lacks independent confirmation,' he concluded.

Hall reported that Price's financial independence came from his marriage to Constance Knight, who inherited a comfortable fortune from her father. It was her means, and not family wealth as claimed, that gave him the leisure to put his days of door-to-door peddling behind him and embark on his career as psychical researcher and book collector. The assembling of a library of occult and magical books running into several thousand volumes was, said Hall, 'Price's most useful achievement during his life'.

Even the library seemed to offer opportunities for chicanery, however. In the collection Hall found several valuable books clearly marked with the imprint of the SPR. Price had catalogued them as his own, even attaching his own book plate.

Price's book plates were a source of interest and amusement for Hall, as well as another example of Price's covertness. Price used two crested plates. One featured a lion rampant and proved on investigation to be the family crest of Sir Charles Rugge-Price of Richmond, with whom Harry Price had no connection. The other, bearing a crest and coat of arms, carried the name 'Robert Ditcher-Price' and the address 'Norton Manor, Radnor'. Hall's investigations revealed that the crest and arms were those of Parr of Parr, Lancashire, and that Norton Manor belonged to Sir Robert Green-Price, Baronet, whose family had lived there since the 17th century. A letter from Lady Jean Green-Price unequivocally stated that she had never heard of Robert Ditcher-Price and that she was 'quite certain that he never resided at Norton Manor'.

In his first book on Borley Rectory in 1940 Price used a version of the 'nun's tale' supplied by the Glanville family – father Sydney, son Roger and daughter Helen. While holding a seance with a planchette at their home, Helen Glanville elicited the information that a nun had indeed been murdered at Borley and that she was a Frenchwoman called Marie Lairre. On the subject of this and subsequent seances he held, Sydney Glanville was almost apologetic to SPR researchers Dingwall, Goldney and Hall, admitting that suggestion had played a part: all three Glanvilles had studied the history of the Borley hauntings.

After the story of the French nun's ghost appeared in *The most haunted house in England*, Price received an elaborate theory from Dr W. J. Phythian-Adams, Canon of Carlisle, to the effect that Marie Lairre had been induced to leave her convent and marry one of the local landowners. She had been strangled by her husband and buried in a

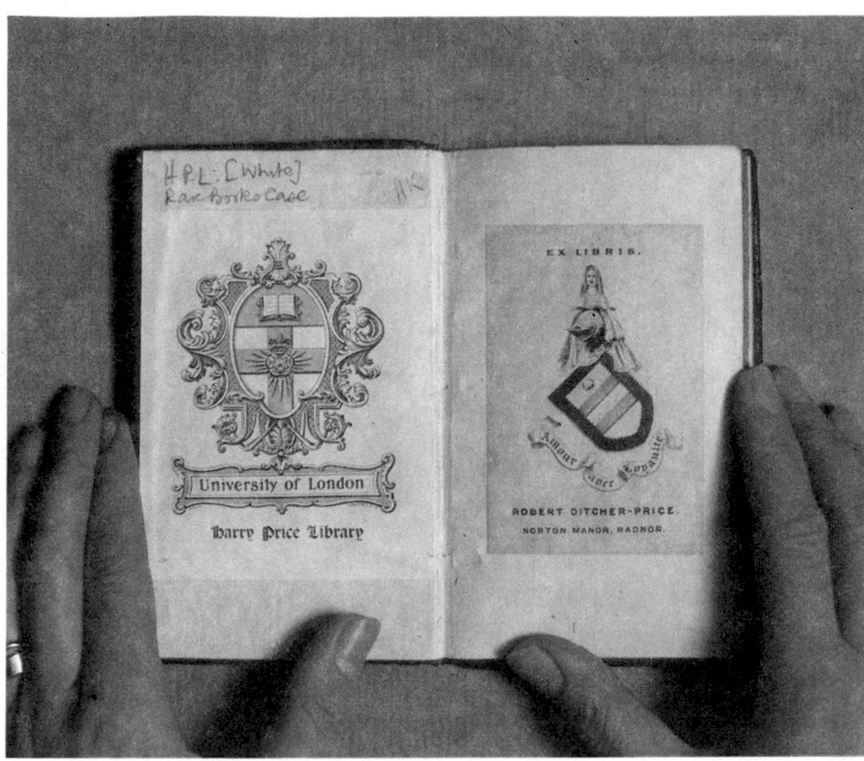

Three of Harry Price's book plates. The one on the far right, bearing the name of 'Robert Ditcher-Price' and the address 'Norton Manor, Radnor', was investigated by Hall. He says that the titled family residing at Norton Hall, the Green-Prices, had never heard of a Robert Ditcher-Price

well on the site of the rectory. The canon suggested that the ghost of the former nun stole a French dictionary from the residents of Borley Rectory in the 19th century so that she could brush up on her English in order to communicate with them.

Despite some other preposterous twists in the canon's theory, Price seized on it eagerly. Hall accuses him of manufacturing and planting evidence to back it up. Part of this evidence was two French medals that Price claimed had appeared as 'apports' during his first visit to the rectory in 1929. One was a Roman Catholic confirmation medal and the other a badge or pass issued to members of the National Assembly after the revolution. Yet previously, Price had said that there was one apported medal and that it was a 'Loyola' medal. Price's faithful secretary stated that the Loyola medal was the only one she had ever seen.

Puzzling finds

Further to this case, Hall recounts how Price had excavated what he called a well in the ruined cellars of Borley Rectory in 1943, discovering a human jawbone in the soft earth. The excavation was made by lamp-light. The well turned out to be a modern concrete basin. And during the demolition of the ruins, a switch and lengths of wire were found in the cellar, though the house had never been supplied with electricity. Had Price used this equipment with a portable battery to light the cellars as he secretly buried the jawbone for later discovery?

And so Trevor Hall's book goes on, each damning fact backed by documentary evidence, much of which is from Price's own unpublished notes and correspondence. Price's accounts of psychical research projects are shown time and again to be inaccurate, or almost entirely invented, or presented over the years in different versions with contradictory details. *Search for Harry Price* certainly fulfills Colin Wilson's criterion: it shows Price as a confirmed liar and publicity seeker. The absurd experiment in which Price and Professor C. E. M. Joad conducted a magical ceremony in the Harz mountains in Germany for a regiment of press photographers more than proves the latter. But even more, the revelations indicate that he was a fraud.

But does the tarnishing of Price's character necessarily mean that the haunting of Borley Rectory was fraudulent? From the year the rectory was built in 1863 until 1929, when Price first became interested in it, stories circulating in the area had seemed to suggest paranormal happenings. Furthermore, from 1930 to 1937 Price visited Borley only once, and yet at least 2000 allegedly paranormal incidents were recorded during that time. In a year straddling 1937 and 1938, when Price rented the empty rectory and recruited a team of independent witnesses through an advertisement in *The Times* to live there with him, several incidents were reported in Price's absence. Finally, between Price's residency and 27 February 1939, when the rectory was 'mysteriously' destroyed by fire at midnight, odd events occurred.

So, regardless of Price's role, was Borley Rectory in fact the 'most haunted house in England?'

Borley: the tension mounts

Large, dark and ugly, Borley Rectory seemed to invite haunting. And with the arrival of ghost hunter Harry Price, it became a hive of paranormal activity. New discoveries began to emerge or was someone helping things along?

ALTHOUGH IT SERVED as rectory to the 12th-century Borley church, which stood amid ancient gravestones on the opposite side of the Sudbury road, the ' most haunted house in England' was only 76 years old when it burned to the ground in the winter of 1939. Borley Rectory was an ugly two-storey building of red brick, its grounds dotted with tall trees that cast gloom on many of its 23 rooms. It was built in 1863 by the Reverend Henry D. E. Bull, who was both a local landowner and rector of Borley church, to house his wife and 14 children.

Immediately behind and to one side of the house lay a farmyard bounded by a cottage, stabling and farm buildings. When an extra wing was added to the house in 1875, a small central courtyard resulted. The dining-room fireplace was carved with figures of monks, a decoration suggesting that the Rev. Bull may have believed a local legend that a 13th-century monastery had once occupied the spot. One of the monks from this monastery gave rise to the first ghost story about the site. He was said to have eloped with a nun from a convent at Bures, some 8 miles (13 kilometres) away. But the couple were caught and executed, he being beheaded and she walled up in the convent. And their ghosts haunted the area. The roots of this picturesque tale were cut away in 1938 by a letter from the Essex Archaeological Society to Sidney Glanville, one of the most diligent and

Presented to The Revd Henry Foster Bull
Choir and Organist of Borley Church. September

Above: the Reverend Henry (Harry) Bull and the choir of Borley church. Like his father before him, Harry Bull perpetuated the story of the haunting of the rectory by a nun

Below: the gloomy 23-room rectory as seen from the tower of the church honest volunteer investigators for the ghost hunter and author Harry Price. It stated that neither the monastery nor the nunnery had ever existed.

However, there is evidence that both the Rev. Henry Bull and his son and successor as rector, the Rev. Harry Bull, enjoyed telling the story. It gained currency particularly among Sunday school children, many of whom presumably grew up believing it – in view of its source – to be 'gospel'.

Before this first 'nun's tale' was replaced by a later version, reports grew that various members of the Bull family – notably two of the sisters, Millie and Ethel – had seen a shadowy figure in the long rectory garden moving across what then became known as the 'nun's walk'. This route followed the path of an underground stream, along which clouds of gnats were inclined to drift on warm summer evenings. The two sisters told Price that they had seen the nun in July 1900, adding only that it was 'evening' and 'sunlit' – so no one can be sure it was not a formation of gnats. A later rector, the Rev. G. Eric Smith, told of being startled by a 'white figure' that turned out to be the smoke from a bonfire, while V. C. Wall, a *Daily Mirror* reporter, saw a similar apparition that proved to be the maid.

The Bull family lived at Borley Rectory in basic discomfort – without gas, electricity or mains water – for almost 65 years. When his father died in 1892, Harry took over as rector and continued to live in the house with his numerous siblings. At least three of the family remained in occupation until Harry's death in June 1927. He himself moved across the road to Borley Place when he married in 1911, but returned to the rectory in 1920, presumably after his wife's death.

Above: the summerhouse in which Harry Bull dozed away his last years. He claimed that he saw the ghostly nun and other apparitions while he rested here

Below: the place where the ghost of the nun disappears after her walk in the rectory garden. Up to this point – and where she walks – the stream is underground

Despite the architectural gloom of their surroundings, the younger Bulls seem to have been a lively crowd, according to the testimony of friends and acquaintances who contacted researchers in the late 1940s and early 1950s. The house had curious acoustics that lent themselves to practical jokes. According to Major the Hon. Henry Douglas-Home of the Society for Psychical Research, footsteps in the courtyard at the rear of the house and voices in the adjoining cottage could clearly be heard in the rectory, along with the noise made by the hand pump in the stable yard. These provided plenty of thumps and groans, he said. Another source told researchers that the young Bull sisters took a delight in telling maids that the house was 'haunted', and one old servant mentioned that after being primed in this way by Edith Bull, she had heard 'shuffling' noises outside her room.

As he grew older, Harry Bull added his own contributions to the village gossip. He appears to have had narcolepsy, a condition in which the sufferer is always drowsy, and took to sleeping for most of the day in a summerhouse. After his snoozes, he claimed he had seen the nun, heard the phantom coach in which she had eloped with the monk, and spoken to an old family retainer named Amos, who had been dead for years. By 1927, when Bull died and the family finally left the rectory, it had become a 'haunted house' in local imagination. This reputation was probably enhanced as the house lay empty and dilapidated for over a year.

On 2 October 1928, the new rector of Borley arrived with his wife. The Rev. G. Eric Smith had spent his early married life in India, but following his wife's serious illness there, he decided to return home, take holy orders, and seek a living. Desperation may have been setting in when he accepted Borley, for he took it on trust and both he and his wife were dismayed when they discovered the condition of the rectory.

To add to their troubles during the first winter, the Smiths soon heard that the house was 'haunted'. The 'ghosts' themselves did not trouble them, however. As Mrs Smith was to write in a letter to the *Church Times* in 1945, neither of them thought the house haunted by anything but 'rats and local superstition'.

Smith's main worry was that the more nervous of his parishioners were unwilling to come to the rectory for evening meetings. When he failed to talk them out of their fears, he took what was perhaps the fatal step of writing to the editor of the *Daily Mirror* to ask for the address of a psychical research society. He hoped that trained investigators could solve the mystery in a rational way and allay the fears of the locals.

Instead, the editor sent a reporter, V. C. Wall, and on Monday, 10 June 1929, he filed the first sensational newspaper account about Borley Rectory. His story talked of 'Ghostly figures of headless coachmen and a nun, an old-time coach, drawn by two bay horses, which appears and vanishes mysteriously, and dragging footsteps in empty rooms. . . .'

The *Mirror* editor also telephoned Price, who made his first visit two days later. With Price's arrival, 'objective phenomena' began for the first time. Almost as soon as he set foot on the premises, a flying stone smashed a window, an ornament shattered in the hallway, showers of apports – pebbles, coins, a medal and a slate – rattled down the main stairs. The servants' bells jangled of their own accord and keys flew out of their locks. During a seance held in the Blue Room – a bedroom overlooking the garden with its 'nun's walk' – rappings on a wall mirror supposedly made by the late Harry Bull were heard by Price and his secretary, Wall, the Smiths, and two of the Bull sisters who were visiting the house.

Price made several trips to the house during the weeks that followed, each visit being accompanied by strange phenomena that were duly reported in the *Daily Mirror* by Wall.

The results were predictable: far from quelling his parishioners' fears, the Rev. Smith had not only unwittingly increased them but added another dimension to his catalogue of woes. The district was invaded by sightseers night and day. Coach parties were organised by commercial companies and the Smiths found themselves virtually under siege. On 14 July, distressed by the ramshackle house and its unwelcome visitors, they moved to Long Melford. Smith ran the parish from there before taking another living in Norfolk in April 1930.

Price must have been made uneasy on at least two occasions at Borley. One of these was when some coins and a Roman Catholic medallion featuring St Ignatius Loyola 'materialised' and fell to the ground at about the same time as some sugar lumps flew through

Below: the spectral nun and the phantom coach haunting the site of Borley Rectory (seen on the left). In some versions of the story, the drivers of the coach were beheaded – which accounts for the headless figures in this picture. The nun was eloping with a monk, who was hanged when the two were caught. She was bricked up into a wall, we are told

Bottom: pointing out the place where the apparitional coach vanishes

the air. When they were picked up, they were, recalled Mrs Smith, strangely warm to the touch, as if from a human hand. Her maid Mary Pearson, a known prankster, gave her the solution: 'That man threw that coin,' she explained, 'so I threw some sugar.' An even more farcical incident marked the second near-miss for Price during a further seance in the Blue Room. Heavy footsteps were heard outside, accompanied by the slow rumble of shutters being drawn back. In the doubtless stunned hush that followed, Price asked aloud if it were the spirit of the Rev. Harry Bull. A guttural voice, clearly recognisable as that of a local handyman, replied: 'He's dead, and you're daft.'

Rats, Mrs Smith later averred, lay behind the bell ringing – the bell wires ran along rafters under the roof. As for a mysterious light that 'appeared' in an upstairs window, it was well-known locally as a trick reflection of light from the railway carriages that passed along the valley.

For six months after the Smiths left Borley parish, the rectory was unoccupied once more. Then on 16 October 1930 the Rev. Harry Bull's cousin, Lionel A. Foyster, moved in as the new rector. The Rev. Foyster, a man in his early fifties, had moved back home from his previous post as rector of Sackville, Nova Scotia, which he had held between 1928 and 1930. He suffered from rheumatism but, despite his painful illness, he was a kindly and well-liked man. He was deeply devoted to his attractive wife Marianne, who was 31, and their adopted daughter Adelaide, a child of about two and a half.

During the five years that the Foysters lived at Borley, an estimated 2000 separate 'incidents' occurred, most of them within a period of about 14 months. These included voices, footsteps, objects being thrown, apparitions and messages scribbled in pencil on walls. It is probably true to say that with one possible exception, none of these could be attributable to Harry Price, who visited the rectory only once while the Foysters were there. The day after his visit, on 15 October 1931, he wrote one of the few straightforward statements he was ever to make on the Borley mystery in a letter to a colleague: '... although psychologically, the case is of great value, psychically speaking there is nothing in it.'

Six months had elapsed since the Smiths' departure and the Foysters' arrival, and in that time Borley Rectory had become more dilapidated than ever. According to her husband's cousins, the Bulls, Mrs Foyster hated the place from the moment she saw it. She made no friends locally, and her only companion, apart from Lionel, was a family friend, François D'Arles, a French-Canadian much nearer her own age. He rented the cottage at the rear of the house, and SPR investigators got the impression that he dominated the household. By 1932 Marianne Foyster and D'Arles had opened a flower shop together in London and returned to Borley only at weekends, the implication being that they had become lovers. Mrs Foyster often behaved oddly, if not hysterically, fainting when frustrated. Once she flung herself on her knees before assembled investigators to pray to St Anthony for 'vindication' when no manifestations were forthcoming – as though she expected to be able to produce them.

When the 'hauntings' of Borley Rectory began again shortly after the Foysters' arrival, the villagers accused Marianne Foyster – to her face – of being behind them.

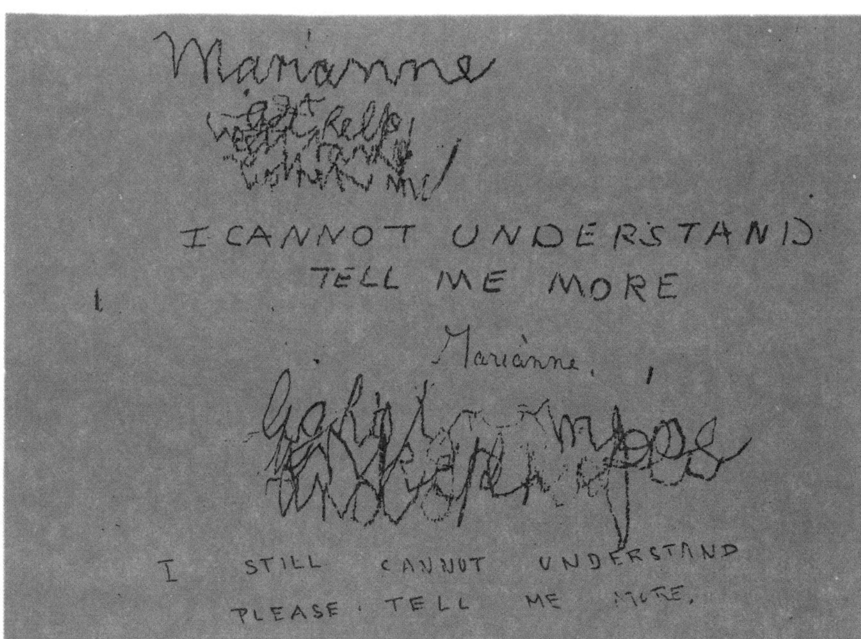

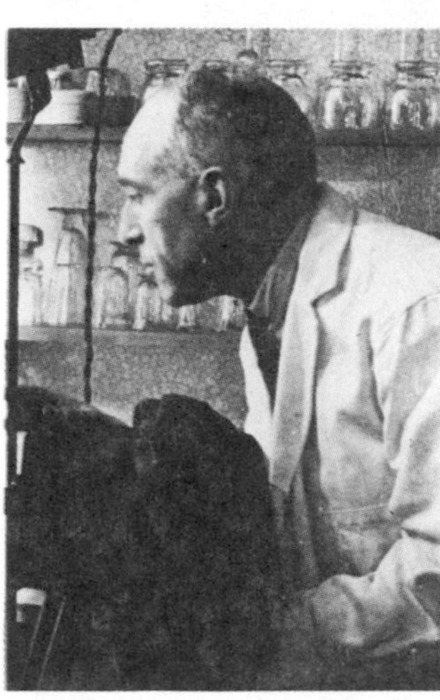

Top: an example of the 'spirit' writing on the wall of the rectory, addressed to Marianne Foyster. Paranormal phenomena increased when the Foysters came to live at Borley

Above: Harry Price at work in his own laboratory. His investigation of the Borley haunting is one of the most controversial of his career

Left: the foot of the main stairs of the rectory, scene of a rain of apports – coins, pebbles and other materialised objects. This happened almost immediately after Price arrived

Writing on the walls, bells that ring themselves, apparitions and mysterious fires – such were the non-stop paranormal phenomena that occurred after the Foyster family moved into Borley Rectory. The question was, were they real?

IN 1878 A YOUNG WOMAN named Esther Cox became the centre of 'mysterious manifestations' at her sister's home in Amherst, Nova Scotia. Esther saw apparitions visible to no one else. Objects were thrown, furniture was upset, small fires broke out in the house and messages addressed to the girl were found scribbled on the walls. The 'hauntings' became the subject of a book, *The haunted house: a true ghost story . . . the great Amherst mystery* (1879) by Walter Hubbell. The book was a huge success, running through 10 editions and selling over 55,000 copies. But in 1919 the American Society for Psychical Research printed a 'critical study' by Dr Walter F. Prince, suggesting that the Amherst case was not in fact a poltergeist manifestation. Prince said it was all trickery by Esther Cox while in a state of dissociation, or conversion hysteria.

The township of Amherst is about 5 miles (8 kilometres) from the equally small community of Sackville, where another of Esther Cox's married sisters lived and where, 50 years afterwards, the Reverend Lionel Foyster and his wife Marianne lived. The Foysters would have heard of the Amherst case as surely as anyone living in, say, Sudbury today would have heard of the Borley mystery. The fact that Foyster used the pseudonym 'Teed' when writing of the happenings at Borley Rectory during his stay there offers what is tantamount to proof that he not only knew of the Amherst case but was familiar with its details: the unusual name 'Teed' was the married name of Esther Cox's sister. It seems likely, therefore, that his wife also knew of the case, though whether she made deliberate – if unconscious – use of it for her own behaviour is a matter for conjecture. The resemblance between both cases is, in fact, striking; Dingwall, Goldney and Hall in *The haunting of Borley Rectory* offer no less than 19 points of general concurrence, including the ringing of bells, throwing of objects, setting of small fires, and mysterious messages written on walls.

For example, a short time after Marianne Foyster arrived at Borley and took such a dislike to the place, she began to 'see apparitions'. No one else did. Shortly afterwards

Above: Borley Rectory, which seemed to reach the peak of its haunting when Marianne Foyster lived there. It is still an open question as to whether she created the events herself. If so, was it because she suffered from an hysteric disorder she could not control – like Esther Cox in the similar Amherst case? Or did she produce the phenomena through PK?

Below: the cottage that was once part of the Borley Rectory property and in which François D'Arles lived

Borley in ruins?

the manifestations, so similar to the Amherst case, began. Her husband, loyal and devoted, answered villagers who accused her of faking that he could not see the visions because 'he wasn't psychic', but in her 'defence' he began to keep a rough record of events. This was not perhaps as helpful as he hoped it might be because, as he admitted, much of it was written later and many things were confused.

In October 1931, in answer to a plea from the Bull sisters, Harry Price returned to Borley once more. It is interesting to speculate on the motives behind the Bulls' concern: perhaps because they knew the source of the pranks and hoaxes during their own tenancy, they suspected the genuineness of the new 'haunting'. The same could be said of Harry Price, for he returned from his visit convinced that Mrs Foyster was directly responsible for fraud.

In their examination of the alleged phenomena, Dingwall, Goldney and Hall analysed the incidents described in Foyster's first record, which he later elaborated upon. Treating the constant bell ringing as a single phenomenon, they isolated 103 different instances. Of these, 99 depended totally on Mrs Foyster's sincerity, three were readily attributable to natural causes, and only one was in any way 'inexplicable'.

Among the most suspicious incidents was the appearance of pencilled writings on the walls. About seven messages appeared during the Foysters' tenancy, most of them addressed to Marianne and appealing for 'light, mass, prayers'. Another, not noted by Price in his Borley books, spelled 'Adelaide', the name of the Foysters' adopted daughter. All the messages were in a childish scribble. Little Adelaide may have been responsible for one or both of the 'mysterious' small fires that broke out in the rectory, for she was caught on at least one occasion trying to set fire to bedclothes.

In 1933 when the Foysters went on leave for six months, they left Canon H. Lawton as locum. Nothing untoward happened though the canon, like Major Douglas-Home of the Society for Psychical Research, noted the curious acoustics of the house and surroundings. In any case, by that time Mrs Foyster was spending most of her time in London with François D'Arles at their flower shop. An exorcism by a group of Spiritualists the previous year, when Marianne and François first left to open their shop, seemed to have put paid to what the Foysters cosily called 'the goblins'. Or was it that Marianne Foyster was no longer on the premises?

In October 1935 the Foysters left Borley. When the Reverend A.C. Henning was appointed five months later, he chose to live elsewhere, and since his time the rectors of Borley have lived at Liston or Foxearth

Below: the ghost hunter Harry Price (left) and Mrs K. M. Goldney of the Society for Psychical Research (right) pose with the Foyster family at Borley Rectory. The Foysters' adopted child Adelaide and an unidentified playmate complete the picture

Bottom: one of several messages that appeared on the walls of the rectory. All of them were scribbled in pencil in a childish hand and were mostly addressed to Marianne Foyster

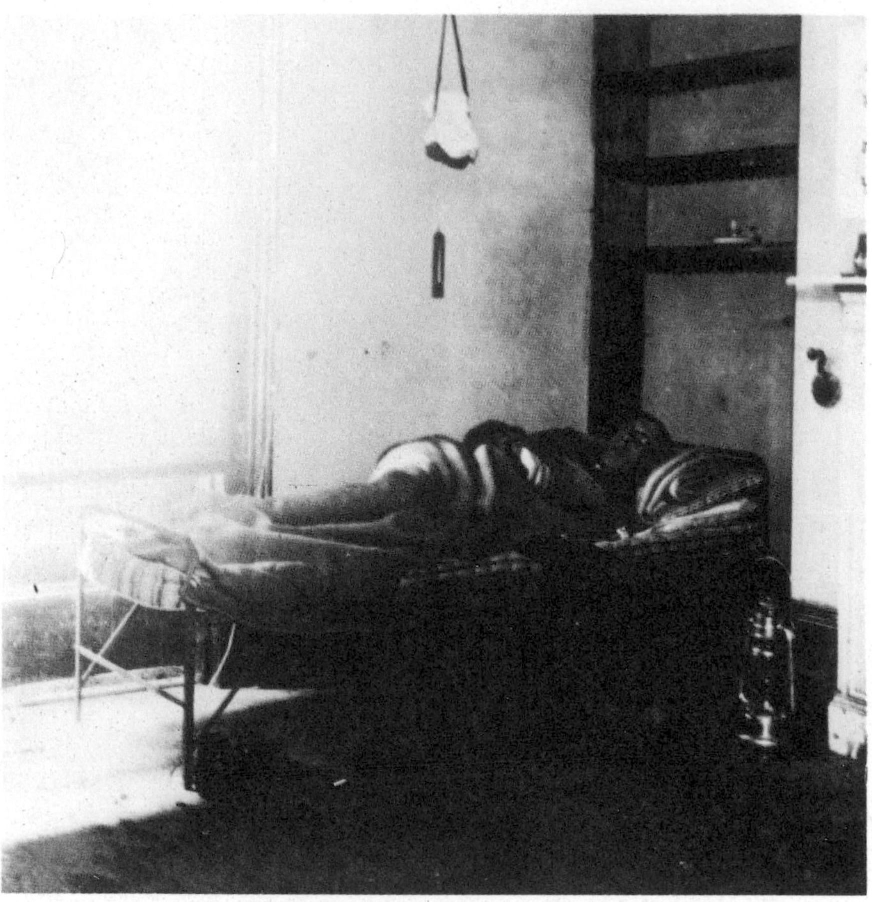

One of Price's 48 volunteer investigators takes a break from his duties at the rectory. Price rented Borley for a year and gathered a team of 'observers' through an advertisement in *The Times* to work with him there. He did not ask for experience in psychical research, but required his volunteers to have 'leisure and intelligence' and to be 'critical and unbiased'

rectories, parishes amalgamated with Borley since the 1930s.

But the battered, drama-ridden old house had still another four years of life to run. On 19 May 1937 Harry Price rented the rectory, and a week later inserted an advertisement in *The Times* asking for 'responsible persons of leisure and intelligence, intrepid, critical and unbiased' to form a rota of observers at the house. If, he later stated, they 'knew nothing about psychical research, so much the better'.

As has been pointed out by Price's critics, ignorance of psychical research is a curious requirement for a team of ghost hunters, but could make it easier to use their 'experiences' to build a good story.

If Harry Price and Marianne Foyster had used fraud for their own personal ends, another trickster who came on the scene in November 1938 was working for purely financial gain. He was Captain William Hart Gregson, who bought Borley Rectory six months after Price's tenancy expired. He immediately asked Price's advice about organising coach trips to see his new property and broadcast on the radio, recounting several minor 'phenomena'. But his coach tour plans were brought to an abrupt end at midnight on 27 February 1939 when fire gutted the building, leaving only a few walls, charred beams, and chimney stacks standing.

Sidney Glanville, one of Price's volunteer researchers of impeccable reputation, said that at a seance at the Glanville home, an entity named 'Sunex Amures' had threatened to burn down Borley Rectory. But the real cause was flatly stated by Sir William Crocker in his autobiography *Far from humdrum: a lawyer's life* (1967). Crocker, a distinguished barrister, and Colonel Cuthbert Buckle, an insurance adjuster, investigated the claim made by Gregson on behalf of the insurers. Crocker states: 'We repudiated his impudent claim for "accidental loss by fire" . . . pleading that he had fired the place himself.'

'Bare-faced hocus pocus'

The ruins of Borley Rectory were finally demolished in the spring of 1944 and the site levelled. An orchard and three modern bungalows now occupy the spot. During the demolition, Price took a *Life* magazine photographer and researcher Cynthia Ledsham to Borley, and by sheer fluke, the photographer captured on film a brick that was apparently 'levitated' by unseen forces – but was in fact thrown by a worker. *Life* published the photograph over a jokey caption, but Price, in his book *The end of Borley Rectory* (1946), claimed it as a final 'phenomenon'. Cynthia Ledsham was astounded, calling it 'the most bare-faced hocus pocus on the part of . . . Harry Price.'

The truth is that the haunting of Borley Rectory was the most bare-faced hocus pocus from start to finish, with Price feeding his craving for personal publicity from it in the most short sighted way. For, as was shown after his death, his shallow frauds could not hope to withstand investigation.

In a letter to Mr C.G. Glover in 1938, Price wrote: 'As regards your various criticisms, the alleged haunting of the rectory stands or falls not by the reports of our recent observers, but by the extraordinary happenings there of the last 50 years.'

But he wrote to Dr Dingwall in 1946 in reference to the occasion when a glass of water was 'changed' into ink: 'I agree that Mrs Foyster's wine [*sic*] trick was rather crude, but if you cut out the Foysters, the Bulls, the Smiths, etc., something still remains.' It is then logically left that the 'something' is the 'reports of our recent observers'.

As Dingwall, Goldney and Hall said: 'If one wished to dispose of the Borley hauntings on one small piece of paper merely by reference to Price's privately expressed opinions of the evidence', it would be necessary only to quote the two letter extracts in juxtaposition. However, one great irony remains. Despite the demolition of Price's pack of lies, ghost hunters of the 1960s and 1970s doggedly persisted in investigating the area. And they may just have stumbled on something truly paranormal – not at the rectory site, but in Borley church itself.

No end to Borley

Were Harry Price, his detractors and his defenders, chasing ghosts in the wrong place by concentrating on Borley Rectory? This chapter examines a case for a genuine haunting across the road at Borley church, under investigation since the 1970s

IN ALL HIS BORLEY investigations and writings, Harry Price paid scant attention to the 12th-century church itself. He was aware of a story, told to him by Ethel Bull in 1929, that coffins in the Waldegrave family vault under the church had been mysteriously moved at some time during the 19th century, but he made little attempt to follow up the matter. Price may have missed his real chance to confront the paranormal. For, since the early 1970s, unexplained events in and around the church – many of them recorded on tape – have proved to be far more baffling than anything that happened in the old rectory.

The manor of 'Barlea' – the Anglo-Saxon for 'boar's pasture' – was mentioned in Domesday Book, when a wooden church served the locality. The south wall of the present church contains remnants of the flint and rubble building erected in the 12th century. The chancel, the north wall of the nave, and the west tower were added in the 15th century, followed a hundred years later by the red brick south porch.

In the little churchyard itself, planted around with clipped yews and horse chestnut trees, lie the graves of the Bull family. Vandals have broken the stone cross on that of the Rev. Harry Bull, the Victorian rector who drowsed away his last days in the

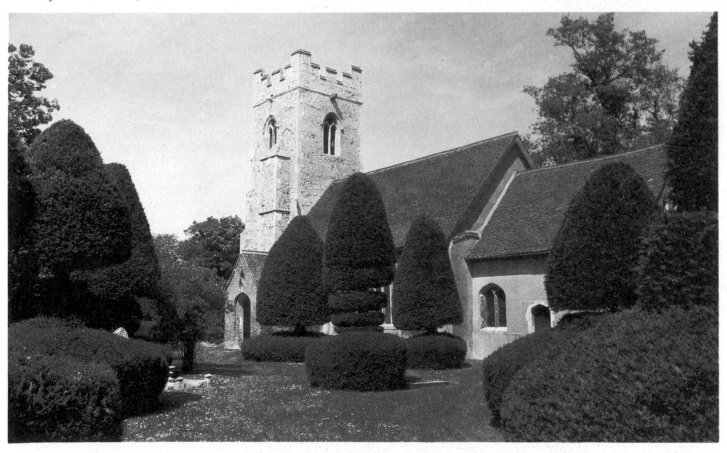

Below: Borley church, the major part of which was constructed in the 15th century. Should the many who investigated the Borley Rectory hauntings have looked here instead?

summerhouse and reported seeing a ghostly nun and phantom coach. Geoffrey Croom-Hollingsworth, who runs a small psychical research group at Harlow, Essex, believes from his investigations that the cause of the rector's death in 1927 was syphilis. Advanced syphilis is accompanied by narcolepsy, a constant drowsiness, during which the sufferer hallucinates – a fact that would seem to explain the rector's 'visions' neatly. But Croom-Hollingsworth does not think this is the whole answer, for he and an assistant, Roy Potter, claim to have observed the phantom nun themselves for a period of about 12 minutes.

Croom-Hollingsworth came upon the Borley controversy in the 1960s and decided to examine the facts himself. He and his group began a series of vigils at Borley. Like subsequent investigators, they chose to keep watch at night to avoid interruption. Over a period of years, in differing weather conditions and at different times of year, they heard an assortment of noises: raps, heavy panting and the sound of furniture being moved. On one occasion while in the orchard, something huge and dark, 'like an animal', approached them between the fruit trees and banged loudly on the fence.

On another night, at about 3 a.m., the group heard 'laughter and merriment . . . which seemed to be coming up the road towards Borley church'. The night was misty, but there was sufficient light to see that nobody was in the roadway. Assuming that the voices were those of late-night revellers, but puzzled by the direction of the sound, Roy Potter got into his car and coasted down the road towards Long Melford with his engine off. He met nobody. Using his walkie-talkie link with Croom-Hollingsworth, he arranged the experiment of shouting at various points along the Long Melford road to see if the sound carried. The listeners in the churchyard heard nothing. In an attempt to record similar noises, a tape recorder was set up in the porch of the church, while the group kept watch from a distance. Nobody was seen to enter the porch, but the group heard a loud crash and found the tape recorder 'pretty well battered'. The tape had been torn from its reels and lay in a tangle.

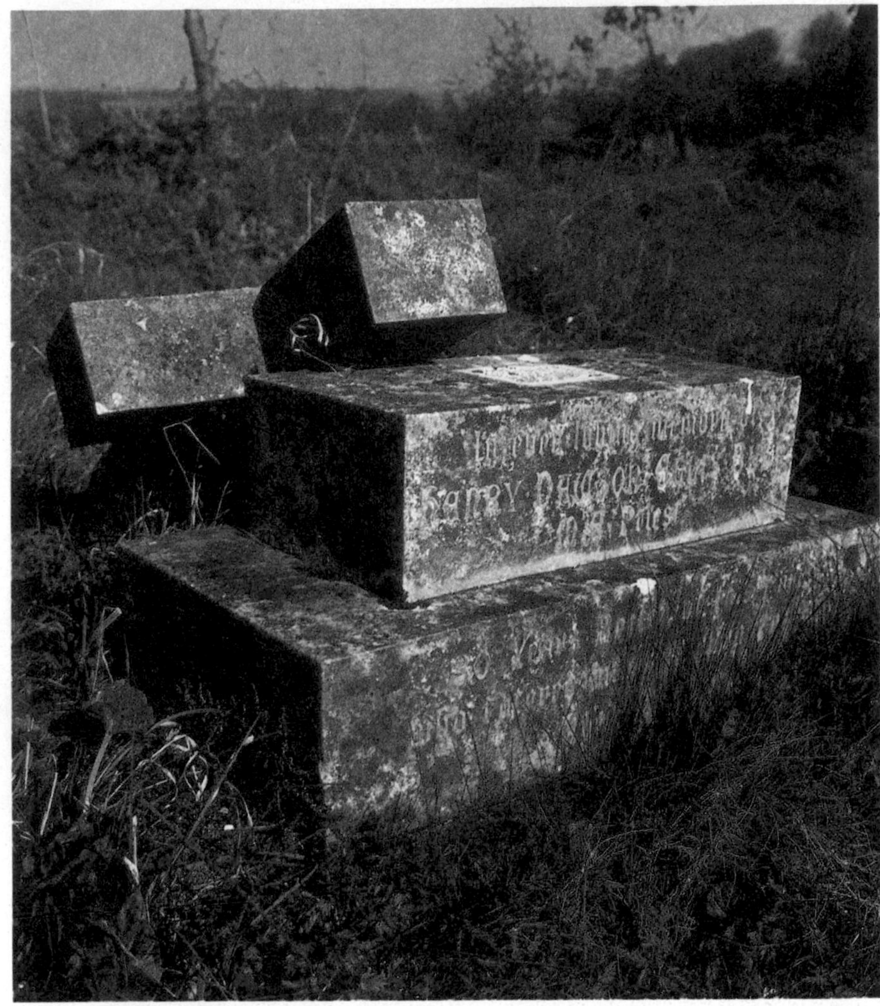

Previous page: the Enfield Parapsychical Research Group at Borley church. Ronald R. Russell (far right), a founding member, leans towards Price's side in the controversy over Borley's hauntings. But the group have found the church itself of most interest and have done many tests with cameras and sound equipment (right)

Above right: the vandalised grave of the Reverend Harry Bull in Borley churchyard. Harry's father built the nearby rectory that became famous as 'the most haunted house in England', so drawing attention away from the church

But it was the sighting of the nun that convinced the Harlow group that something was indeed strange about Borley. One clear night, Croom-Hollingsworth was standing in the orchard, looking towards the 'nun's walk':

> Suddenly I saw her quite clearly, in a grey habit and cowl as she moved across the garden and through a hedge. I thought 'is somebody pulling my leg?' Roy was out in the roadway, the nearest of the group, and I shouted to him. The figure had disappeared into a modern garage, and I thought that was that, but

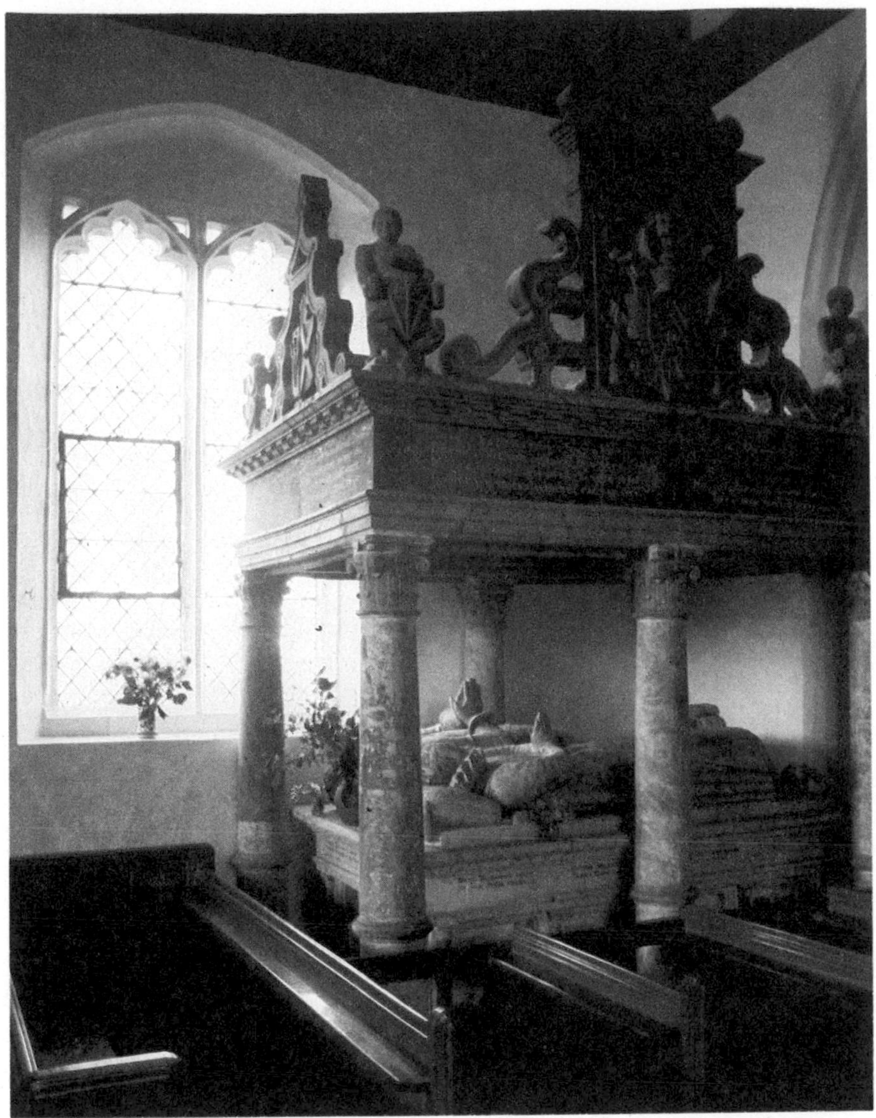

BBC as a basis for a television programme, are, Densham says, 'quite baffling'.

The first taping began at midnight during the winter months. After the church was carefully examined and searched, a cassette player was placed by the altar and the investigators sat at the other end of the church. The tape picked up a series of bumps and raps. Next, two tape recorders were locked up in the church, one by the altar and the other halfway down the aisle. Both picked up the unmistakable sound of a heavy door being opened and slammed shut, complete with the squeaking of a bolt. Neither the porch door nor the smaller chancel door had been opened – the researchers had kept watch on the church from outside – and examination showed that the chancel door bolt did not squeak.

The following week Densham and his team started their vigil at 12.30 a.m. They set up a sophisticated stereo tape with two high quality microphones, again placing one near the altar and the other halfway down the aisle; an additional cassette machine was positioned in front of the altar. Then half the team were locked into the church and the other half kept watch in the churchyard.

'Suddenly there was a curious change in the atmosphere,' said Densham. 'One of the team felt as if he was being watched, and we all felt very cold.' During the next few minutes the tapes picked up a clatter, as if something had been thrown down the aisle. There were also knockings, rappings, the sound of the door opening again – although both doors remained locked and bolted – and, chillingly, the sound of a human sigh. Afterwards, the team found that the small cassette recorder had jammed, and the tape

> as Roy joined me we both saw her come out of the other side. She approached to about 12 feet [3 metres] from us, and we both saw her face, that of an elderly woman in her sixties, perhaps. We followed her as she seemed to glide over a dry ditch as if it wasn't there, before she disappeared into a pile of building bricks. Neither of us was frightened. It was an odd sensation, but peaceful and tranquil.

Not surprisingly in view of his experiences, Croom-Hollingsworth has little time for the critics who point to the discrepancies in Price's account of the haunting. On the other hand, he says,

> I don't give a damn if Price invented things or not. The basic question is – is the place haunted? And you can take it from me it is. I have invented nothing. Roy and I saw the nun quite clearly for a period of about 12 minutes. . . .

Croom-Hollingsworth's determination impressed Denny Densham, a film director and cameraman. In 1974 he got permission to experiment with tape recorders in the church. The results, which were used by the

Above: the Waldegrave tomb, memorial to an old and influential Borley family. Local gossip had it that the Waldegrave coffins in the vault under the church were 'mysteriously moved' in the 19th century

Right: one of the stained glass windows of the church, dedicated to the Reverend Henry Bull. His retelling of the story of the ghostly nun of Borley Rectory gave a boost to the reputation of his family home as a haunted house

had been extracted and tangled up, as the Croom-Hollingsworth tape had been.

In July, the party visited Borley again. At 1.45 a.m., they felt a change in the atmosphere.

> We all felt watched, and a curious tingling sensation was felt; oddly enough the machines seemed to pick up a lot of static at this point. We recorded stealthy sounds near the altar, the sound of the door shutting again, a crash as of something being knocked over, and then the sound of hollow, heavy footsteps, like those of a very large man walking by the altar rail. We could not reproduce them normally: the floor there is of stone, heavily carpeted.

The observers then saw a glow of light near the chancel door, followed by a terrifying grunt. On this, their final visit, the team saw pinpoints of light in the curtains by one door, and heard the sound of a heavy crash. Densham said:

> Frankly, I am at a loss to explain what goes on at Borley. We made every effort to ensure that our legs weren't being pulled, and the tapes were new and untampered with. No theory I have tried to put forward seems to pan out. We tried leaving pencil and paper in the church, asked the thing to rap and so on, but it doesn't seem to be trying to communicate, unless the damage to the tapes and the throwing of invisible objects in our direction meant that it resented our presence. One's left with the feeling that whatever causes the phenomena is indifferent to or perhaps unaware of observers.

'Ectoplasm' in the churchyard

Since that summer of 1974, one of the most regular researchers at Borley has been Ronald R. Russell, a member of the Enfield Parapsychical Research Group and professional photographer. Frank Parry, an electrical engineer, and John Fay, a mechanical engineer, usually work with him. Russell has achieved odd results while taking photographs of the area with an Agfa CC21 camera, in which the film is contained in a cassette and processed in the Agfa laboratory.

> Sandwiched between perfectly normal frames we got 'ectoplasmic' stuff in the churchyard, shadows where no shadows should be, and a thin light near the north door. As a photographer I'm at a loss to explain this as camera or film malfunction.

Parry has used a graphic analyser, an eight-channel recording machine with slider controls that adjust pitch and level, cut out interference, and enable its operator to 'pinpoint' sounds. As Russell said:

> We have recorded hundreds of extraordinary noises, footsteps, crashes and so on. On one occasion we located a centre of disturbance near the Waldegrave tomb; it was tangible, like a swirling column of energy. When you passed your hand through it you felt a sort of crackle, like static electricity. On another occasion we heard a deep, grunting voice, which reminded me irresistibly of Lee Marvin singing *Wandering Star*.

The altar in Borley church. In 1974 some strange sounds – including raps, crashes and mysterious footsteps – were picked up here on a cassette recorder

Russell is inclined to side with the Price faction on Borley, though he concedes that Price may have embellished facts.

> I think there may be three basic factors at work here. First, the nun. There would be nothing odd about a nun in the household of a Catholic family like the Waldegraves. Perhaps the apparition which Mr Croom-Hollingsworth saw is simply a psychic record of some such person. Secondly, there seems to be some sort of power concentrated in the church itself. It is on the intersection of two ley lines, and when you try dowsing in the church the rod practically twists from your hands. Thirdly, I would suggest that the power is boosted by the presence of observers, and also that it waxes and wanes with the seasons; in January phenomena are sporadic, while in August they seem to be at full flood.

The church authorities are non-committal, preferring to avoid discussion of the topic. But in the parish guidebook, under the heading 'ghosts', is a footnote:

> There are, of course, those who suggest the church itself is haunted. Many old churches and buildings have noises and chill areas which some would classify as ghostly, but those who have lived long in the village and we who worship in the church have not experienced anything which would support such thoughts. . . . Visitors should please remember that this is God's house and treat it with reverence.

Beware – PK at work

When a Bavarian lawyer started to have trouble with his telephone, he little suspected that his quiet office was about to be plagued by a massive poltergeist attack, resulting in one of the most startling cases of psychokinesis ever reported

A LAWYER'S OFFICE IN ROSENHEIM, Bavaria, was the unlikely setting for a poltergeist case that completely altered public opinion on the subject of poltergeists in Germany.

Armed with introductions from Hans Bender, director of the Freiburg Institute of Parapsychology, the authors travelled with a camera team to Rosenheim in the spring of 1975 to make a television documentary on the case for BBC television. Arriving at the centre of town, we sought out Königstrasse 13, a tall building in which various professional men had their consulting rooms, and which had been the scene of the notorious poltergeist activities we had come to investigate. They had centred on the office of a lawyer named Adam.

Top: the entrance to lawyer Adam's office at Königstrasse 13 in the quiet Bavarian town of Rosenheim (above). 'No 13' was to prove an unlucky address for Herr Adam as the increasing ferocity of the poltergeist there made work almost impossible

Herr Adam told us that the events that were to become so famous began quietly enough in the summer of 1967, when telephone malfunctions were reported by office staff. Calls to the office on Rosenheim 1233 had been interrupted by clicks or cut off, and sometimes all four receivers would ring at once although the line was dead. The malfunctions had become too frequent to overlook, and the office manager, Johannes Engelhard, called in repair men from Siemens, the company that had installed the equipment – a junction box and four telephones.

The Siemens engineers worked in the

office for several weeks, testing wiring and equipment. Although they found no faults, they replaced the receivers and junction box – but, as this did not improve matters, they called in the post office.

Early in October, the post office replaced the Siemens equipment with official post office telephones. They installed a meter so that, as they were made, calls could be recorded visibly in the office on a counter, with a similar meter at the telephone exchange to provide an official record. At the same time, Herr Adam asked his staff, the office manager Johannes Engelhard, two office clerks and a part-time worker, to make a note of their calls.

On 5 October 1967, Adam and Engelhard were amazed to see the meter register a call although no one in the office was using the telephone. On 19 October, the same thing happened while Adam was with accountant Dr Schmidt, who produced an affidavit for Adam to show the post office. Comparing the records from his own meter, the meter at the exchange and the notes of his staff, Adam realised that these two incidents were by no means isolated. Dozens of undialled calls had been registered. The post office insisted that all the calls had been made in the normal way and, even more peculiar, they had all been made to the speaking clock.

A row broke out between the post office and Herr Adam. Adam pointed out that all his staff had watches and could hear the chimes of at least two church clocks, and could therefore keep a record of the timing of their telephone calls. Furthermore, no one was ever alone in the office, and it was ridiculous to suppose that so many calls could have been made unnoticed by anyone.

Below: trouble with the telephone was the first sign of poltergeist activity in Herr Adam's office. No mechanical or electrical fault could be found with the instrument, but massive bills were run up – and not, it seemed, by any of the employees. When records of the calls made were checked (bottom) it was discovered that someone – or *something* – had been making persistent calls to the speaking clock. The odd thing was that more calls were made than it was physically possible to dial in the time available. What could be making them?

Between 7.42 and 7.57 a.m. on 20 October 1967, 46 telephone calls were registered to the speaking clock. Adam further pointed out that although at least 17 seconds are needed to dial and connect with the speaking clock, even if one does not wait to hear the time, the post office claimed that as many as six calls a minute had been made, and continued to send enormous bills. Nevertheless, on 31 October, they replaced the telephones again. This time, the dials were locked and only Herr Adam had a key.

This step made no difference, and on 8 November Herr Adam was extremely angry to receive another huge bill that did not correspond with the records at all. He issued an accusation – against person or persons unknown – of fraud or embezzlement; it began: 'For several months my telephone installation has been so disturbed that a regular telephone call is impossible.'

Addicted to the time

In the spring of 1975, Adam showed us a sheaf of statements from the post office in which 0119, the number of the speaking clock, appeared over and over again. 'In five weeks,' he said, 'the speaking clock has been connected between 500 and 600 times. In one day, 80 times. I was very angry with the post office; I even wanted to found an association for the protection of the subscriber.' However, Adam soon had disturbances of a different nature to deal with.

On 20 October 1967, the office lights suddenly went out with a bang. Herr Bauer, an electrician from Stern's, a local firm, was called in to repair them. He examined the lights and found that each fluorescent tube had been turned 90° in its socket and disconnected. He had finished replacing the tubes and put away his ladder when there was

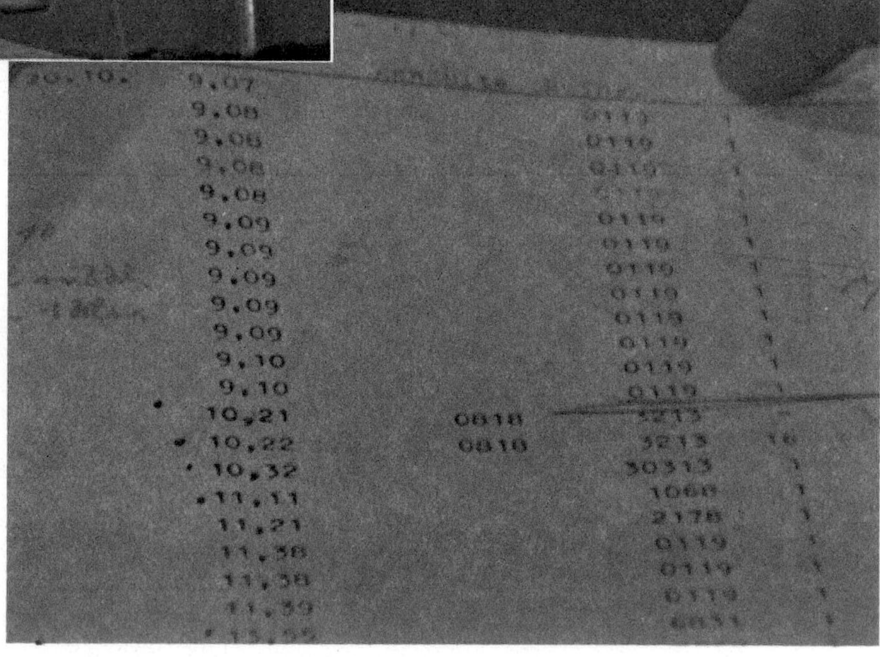

20.10.	9,07			
	9,08		0119	1
	9,08		0119	1
	9,08		0119	1
	9,08		[illegible]	1
	9,09		0119	1
	9,09		0119	1
	9,09		0119	1
	9,09		0119	1
	9,09		0119	1
	9,10		0119	1
	9,10		0119	1
	10,21	0818	3213	[illegible]
	10,22	0818	3213	16
	10,32		30313	1
	11,11		1068	1
	11,21		2178	1
	11,38		0119	1
	11,38		0119	1
	11,39		0119	1
	[illegible]		[illegible]	1

another bang. The tubes had twisted and disconnected themselves again. He was even more puzzled when the office staff told him that the automatic fuses in the office ejected themselves for no apparent reason, sometimes on all four circuits at once. Bauer began a full investigation of the office wiring and equipment, all of which he found in excellent order. He confessed to Adam: 'I was faced with a puzzle and called it "witchcraft".'

Since no fault could be found in the office, he concluded that something must be wrong with the electricity supply itself. The *Elektrizitätswerk* – German electricity board – was asked to take over the investigation. Accordingly, Paul Brunner, Auxiliary Works Manager, arrived at Adam's office on 15 November 1967.

Brunner is a small, dynamic man who impressed us with his authority and his efficiency. He was born in Rosenheim and belonged to the second generation of his family to work at the electricity board. He told us that he had had no interest in the occult, but approached Adam's office with curiosity because of its scientific challenge – yet, ironically, the official report he prepared became one of the most significant documents in paranormal research.

Right: Paul Brunner, the auxilliary works manager for the German electricity board

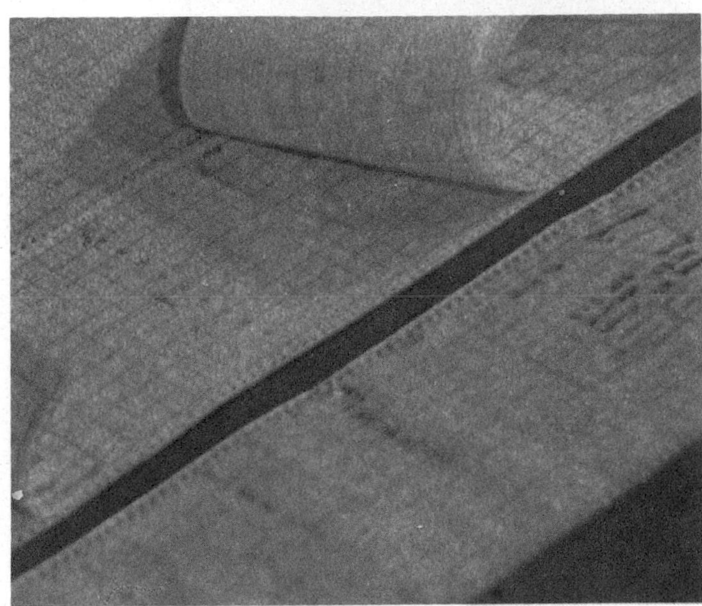

Below: the Unireg recorder (left) on which abnormalities in the electricity supply were detected and traced on a graph (right). At first the investigators thought that these were caused by the local electricity substation – but they found absolutely no faults there

The escalation of the Rosenheim phenomena can be seen when viewed chronologically. On Wednesday, 15 November 1967, extensive checks were run on the wiring and appliances at 13 Königstrasse, especially in Adam's flat. Everything was found to be satisfactory and short circuits were ruled out as a possible cause of the phenomena.

On Thursday, 16 November, a Siemans Unireg – an electrical instrument that shows voltage fluctuations on a single-track pen recorder – was installed at the office. Later a Tektronix plug-in unit with a storage oscilloscope was added, giving two more pen traces that showed fluctuations in the magnetic field and the noise level. A pen recorder gave a continuous read-out of current and voltage variations at selected points in the office circuitry, and the times at which they happened. The machine was sealed to prevent tampering. Over the next few weeks, it was established that abnormal deflections on the paper record occurred, but only in office hours and never at weekends. The automatic fuses were replaced with screw-in types and, to rule out trickery, these were also sealed.

On Monday, 20 November, after a 'normal' morning of twisting tubes, inexplicable voltage variations and bangs, a fluorescent tube in Adam's private office fell to the floor and shattered. At the same moment, a huge surge in the electric current – 50 amps – was registered, yet the safety fuses did not blow. On examining the read-out, Brunner was puzzled to see loops instead of the expected straight lines. Other tubes fell as the day wore on.

On Tuesday, 21 November, as a safety measure, all the fluorescent tubes in the office were replaced by normal light bulbs. More loud bangs were heard, and the photocopier

Above: Herr Adam inspects one of the lamps that began to swing wildly on 27 November 1967. The lamp on the office landing moved as much as 22 inches (55 centimetres) from its normal position

Above right: one of the more violent deflections of the trace on the Unireg recorder. No physical reason could be found for the disturbances in the electricity supply – though they did occur only during office hours, suggesting that someone on the staff was somehow responsible

began leaking chemicals. It was plugged in but not switched on. Brunner wondered if electricity were being conducted into the building through gas and water mains. The team ran a number of tests – and this possibility, too, was ruled out.

On Wednesday, 22 November, the light bulbs began to explode. The neighbourhood was searched for freak power sources. None was found.

On Thursday, 23 November, the office apartment was disconnected from the electricity mains and was connected directly by cable to the transformer, High Tension Station K11 in Königstrasse.

On Friday, 24 November, Brunner thought the mystery was over. He found full deflections on the paper record, some so savage that the paper had been torn by the pen. As the meter was connected directly to K11, he thought the fault had to be there in the supply itself, and that his team had been correct in pronouncing all the electrical equipment in the office satisfactory. With relief, engineers, equipment and cable were evacuated from the office and camp was set up at K11, to pinpoint the fault. But no fault was found. Camp was reinstated at the office.

The entire supply grid of Rosenheim was checked and pronounced sound.

On Monday, 27 November, a girl was cut by flying glass from an exploding light bulb. All remaining bulbs were covered by nylon bags to prevent further accidents. Four more exploded that afternoon. Between five and six o'clock, an alarming new development forced Brunner to admit that he was dealing with something outside his experience: the lights began to swing.

The next few days were spent observing swinging lamps and trying to find an explanation for their movement: 'We leapt repeatedly up and down the floor overhead to try to make the lamps swing – without success. The traffic outside was also watched carefully, and tests were made for electrostatic charges, but none was found.'

On Thursday, 30 November, the office was severed from the mains, and power supplied instead by a 7-kilowatt generator-truck parked outside. The generator's meter showed a steady 220-volt output, yet inside the office deflections and crashes continued, lamps swung, bulbs exploded and fuses were ejected erratically.

On Thursday, 7 December, over 90 deflections were registered during the morning. Lamps swung so violently that they smashed against the ceiling, denting the plaster.

Paintings begin to twirl

To vindicate his methods and results, and to safeguard his reputation, Brunner asked the advice of Dr Karger of the Max Planck Institute of Plasma Physics, and Dr Zicha of Munich University, two of Germany's most eminent physicists. Following a suggestion from Karger, Brunner disconnected the office supply from the Unireg and placed an ordinary 1.5-volt battery across the Unireg terminals. To the astonishment of everyone, instead of registering 1.5 volts until the battery exhausted its charge, the pen began its trace at 3 volts and then zig-zagged wildly across the paper. The Unireg (which was in perfect working order) could not be monitoring the battery to which it was connected.

On Monday, 11 December, at 8.45 a.m., Brunner and his assistant, Mayr, were chatting together in the typists' office, when suddenly a painting twisted on its hook. Surprised, Brunner stretched out his hand to straighten the picture. Other paintings in the room started to rotate, some falling to the floor. The typists, who later said they had felt unusually tense that morning, were rooted to their desks with fear, but Mayr and Brunner stationed themselves at vantage points to observe this new phenomenon. They saw the first painting to move turn through 320°, its string wrapping itself round its hook.

At this point, Brunner, realising that he was out of his depth, prepared to wind up the experiments and wrote his official report. In it, he was relieved to point out the excellent state of Rosenheim's electricity supply, which had been thoroughly checked – to even Herr Adam's satisfaction; yet inexplicable voltage deflections still occurred in the office:

> It became necessary to postulate the existence of a power hitherto unknown to technology, of which neither the nature nor strength nor direction could be defined. It is an energy quite beyond our comprehension.

Alarmed by the thought that there was no apparent way of controlling this mysterious and often harmful energy, Brunner handed over the investigations to the physicists who had been monitoring the experiments.

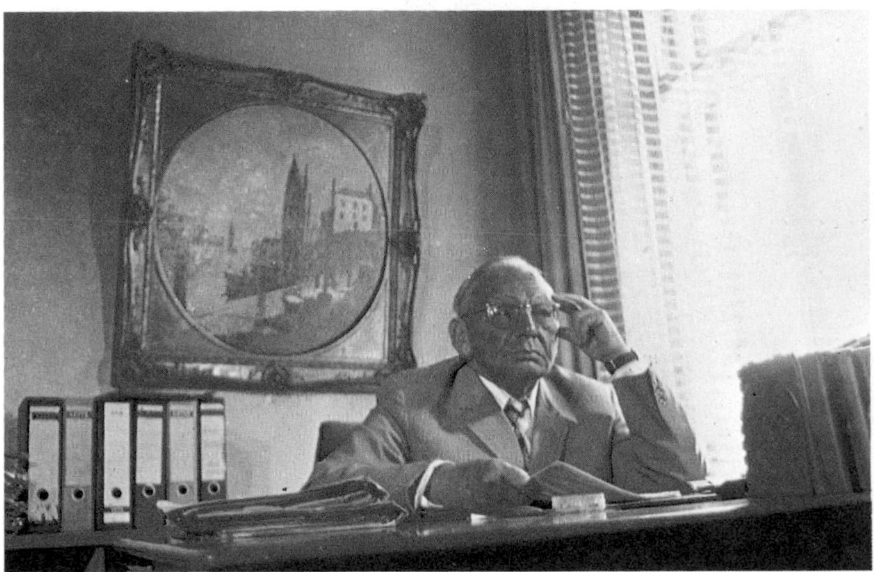

Herr Adam sits pensively in front of the painting that turned, by itself, through almost a complete circle – to the terror of the watching office staff

Like Brunner, Dr Karger and Dr Zicha were fascinated by the scientific challenge of explaining the electrical disturbances in Adam's office, and they carried out an independent investigation using the most sophisticated equipment. They concentrated on finding the cause of the deflections on the meter, installing probes to examine voltage levels, magnetic fields and sound levels. Their questions and answers can be summarised as follows.

1. Were the deflections accompanied by voltage surges? *No, voltage remained constant.*

2. Were the disturbances caused by high-frequency voltage transmission from outside the office? *None measured and none found.*

3. An electrostatic charge? *No.*

4. A static magnetic field? *None detected.*

5. Loose contact in the measuring equipment's amplifier? *None found. A second machine also showed the same anomalies.*

6. Ultrasonic or infrasonic vibrations? *None found.*

7. Manual interference? *Fraud and trickery impossible.*

While measuring sound levels, they noticed that, although no sound was heard, their monitor showed a huge deflection, so they concluded that there must have been direct pressure on the crystal in the microphone. They speculated that a similar invisible force could be acting on the pen of the Unireg itself, causing the unnatural loops directly, independently of the electric current. They speculated further: the same force could be acting on the tiny springs inside the telephone, bypassing the dial. It was active only for short periods, its nature was complex and it was not electrodynamic. Known physics could not explain it.

A fugitive intelligence

Karger and Zicha also felt that the telephone anomalies suggested that an intelligent force was at work, because it had 'chosen' to focus its attention on the speaking clock. It was clear that the force resisted investigation, and this was another reason to speculate on the existence of an intelligence avoiding scrutiny. They prepared their report and left.

As the physicists left Adam's office, teams of investigators from other scientific fields were eager to take their place, including Professor Hans Bender from the Freiburg Institute, who began his experiments in mid December. He was joined by several policemen who had come as a result of Adam's exasperated accusation 'Against person or persons unknown', and independently these new investigators began gathering evidence. The physicists had left two important clues. First, they had suspected that a rational being was behind the phenomena and second, they confirmed that the 'poltergeist' was active in office hours only. Investigations were now centred on the office staff, Johannes Engelhard, Frau Bielmeier (the part-time assistant) and the two clerks, 17-year-old Gustel Huber and 18-year-old Annemarie Schneider.

A spirit of anger

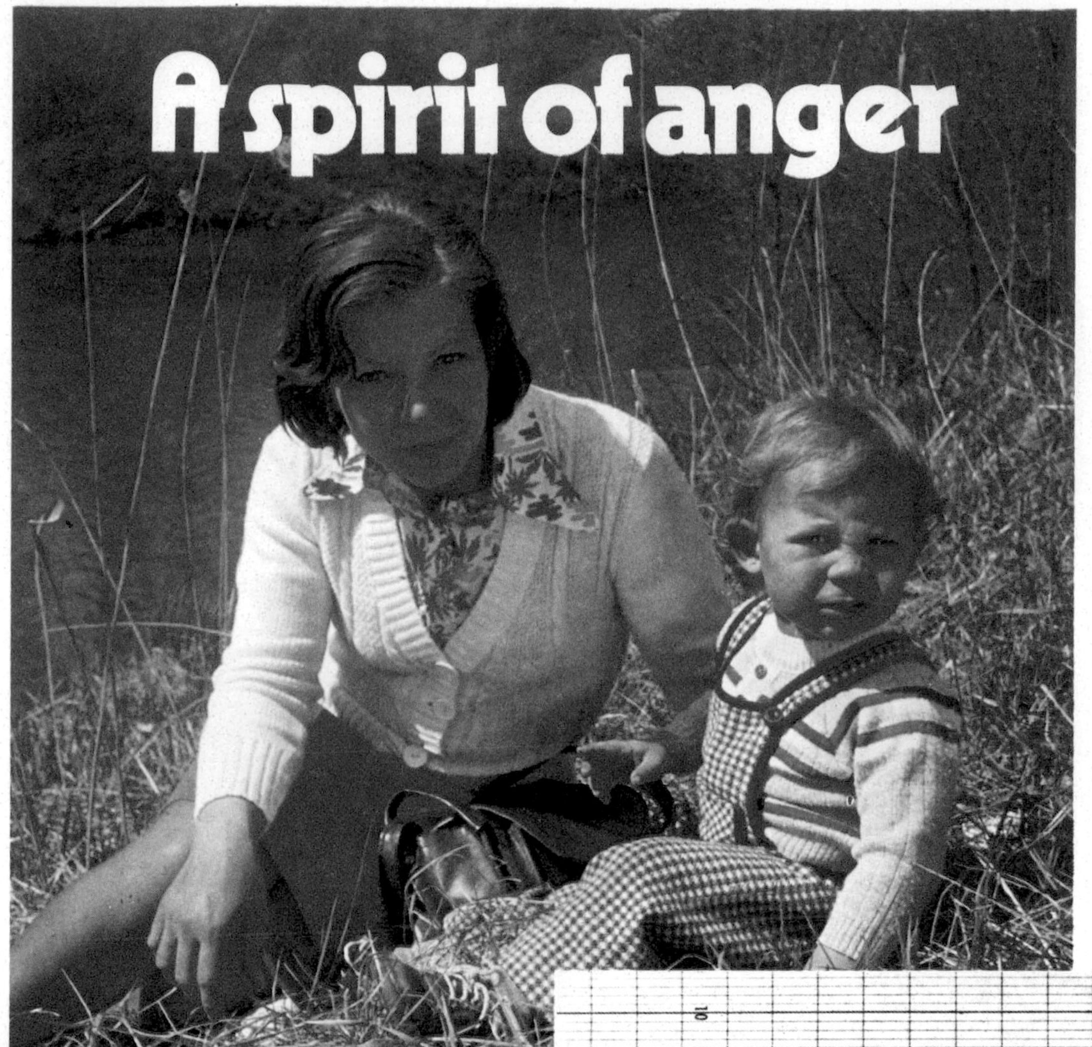

Left: Annemarie Schneider, centre of the Rosenheim poltergeist phenomenon, photographed with her young son in April 1975

Below: a portion of the Unireg pen trace showing violent deflections beginning around 7.30 a.m. – the hour when Annemarie reported for work

Teams of investigators were mystified by the weird events at the Rosenheim lawyer's office. At length they began to suspect that the happenings were centred on a member of the office staff. The search began to discover who it was and why

AS THE PARANORMAL EVENTS in Herr Adam's office continued, work became increasingly difficult. The army of investigators and reporters who were constantly present did not make things any better, and the staff, who felt they were under continuous scrutiny, became tense and nervous. It was bad enough to have to cope with the poltergeist phenomena that continually interrupted their work, but they also had to cope with mutual suspicion each time something happened. A typical event occurred on 12 December, when Johannes Engelhard, the office manager, was opening the morning post with a knife. Frau Adam called to him from the next room, and, as he walked to the door, he heard a picture fall somewhere behind him. He spun round to see the painting lying on the floor. But that was not all. Neatly stacked on it were the letters he had been opening, together with the knife. Although the two clerks were in the office, they could not have touched the letters or the picture in the moment it took for Engelhard to turn round. All the same, he could not help suspecting that they had played a trick on him.

Soon, however, suspicion began to centre on Annemarie Schneider. She appeared to be the most tense of the office staff, and she twitched strangely whenever poltergeist activity took place. The Unireg record, which

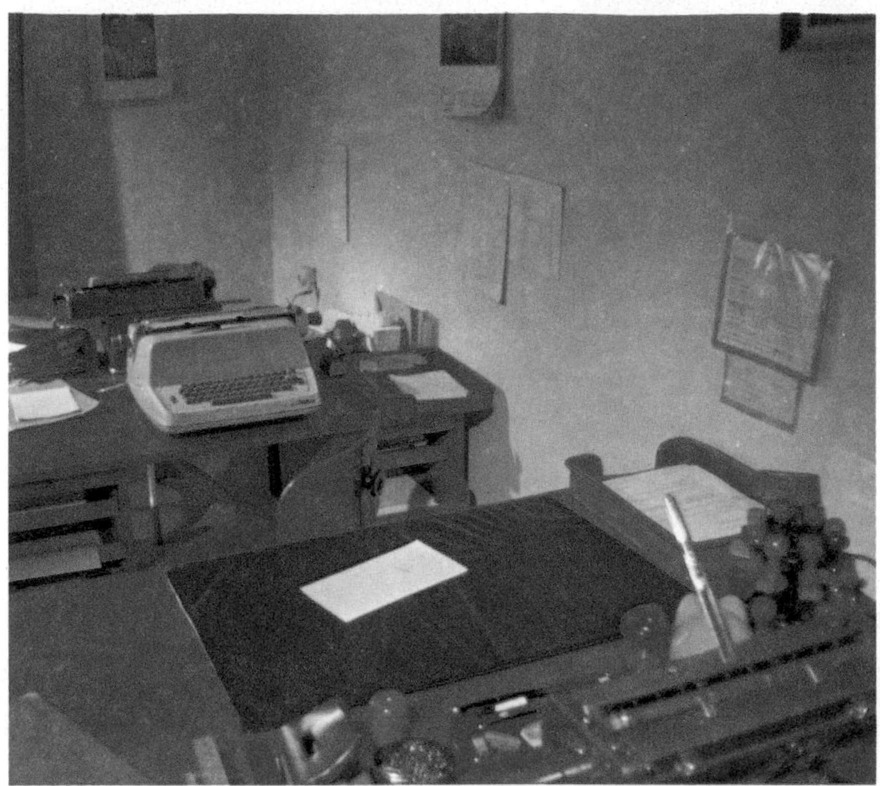

Above: the desks at which the two girl clerks in Herr Adam's office, Gustel Huber and Annemarie Schneider, worked

had shown deflections only in office hours, was checked closely, and it was found that events began at 7.30 a.m. – the time that Annemarie reported for work. Hans Bender's team from the Freiburg Institute had discreetly centred investigations on her for some time. One day, one of Bender's assistants noticed a lamp swinging strangely as Annemarie walked along the corridor underneath it. It had already been decided that each of the office staff would take a short holiday, since things had been so trying. This would also enable the research team to check who, if anyone, was responsible for the phenomena. Annemarie was given first leave – and, sure enough, the office was peaceful again.

Screaming and sobbing

When Annemarie returned to work on 18 December, she seemed even more tense than before, and screamed out when a lamp began to swing. The phenomena had returned with her – and with renewed intensity. Pictures swung merrily, dropping to the floor with a force that dismantled their frames, but left their glass intact. Pages flew off the calendar, and light bulbs exploded. Drawers slid out of desks, and Frau Bielmeier had to wedge one shut with a stool weighted by a typewriter. Annemarie grew more tense every day, screaming and sobbing when phenomena occurred close to her. Fortunately, the Christmas holidays arrived.

Work at the office recommenced on 1 January 1968. When everything had been normal for over a week, Adam began to hope that he was no longer Rosenheim's principal consumer of light bulbs and fluorescent tubes – until 10.30 a.m. on 9 January, when Annemarie returned.

As before, the phenomena returned with Annemarie, and as before, they had grown still more violent. Annemarie received an electric shock in her leg as she picked a picture up off the floor, and Frau Bielmeier had a cracking sensation in her ear.

The climax was reached on 17 January. With only Annemarie and Frau Adam in the office, a number of light bulbs exploded. Annemarie was so frightened that she ran upstairs to the dental surgery, where Herr Geistaller, the dentist, managed to calm her down. Later, the police came to photograph the damage. Annemarie was back at her desk, typing, when the calendar fell from the wall and desk drawers slid out. Suddenly, a metal cash box jumped out of a drawer and clattered to the floor, spilling coins and stamps everywhere. The police, who also believed Annemarie was somehow at the centre of the phenomena, began to keep a closer watch on her.

Officer Wendl was in charge of the police investigation, and he was eager to solve the case. His belief that he would eventually catch Annemarie moving objects physically was shaken that afternoon when a heavy oak cabinet moved a foot (30 centimetres). The cabinet weighed over 400 pounds (180 kilograms), and Wendl realised that, even using levers or with the help of Fräulein Huber, Annemarie could not have moved it. It had been lifted clear over the edge of the linoleum, which would have puckered had the cabinet been shoved, and it took the efforts of two burly policemen to restore it to its place. Had the cabinet episode not occurred, Wendl would have felt sure that he had proved his case, but now he doubted it. He

Below: on the afternoon of 17 January 1967 this oak cabinet, which weighs over 400 pounds (180 kilograms), moved a distance of more than a foot (30 centimetres)

strange red patches appeared on her skin. That day, she was given further leave of absence. As she left, she noted sadly in a diary she had been asked to keep by Hans Bender: '18 January. As from today, I am on the sicklist. . . . I hope everything will proceed quickly so I can have my rest at last.'

Herr Adam lost no time. Annemarie was dismissed, and never returned to the Königstrasse office – and neither did the strange phenomena. During the poltergeist activity, the cost of the damage had amounted to 15,000 Deutschmarks, which the unfortunate Adam was obliged to pay.

Hans Bender took the opportunity of asking Annemarie to visit his Freiburg Institute so that he could do some laboratory tests and, after initial reluctance to leave home, she agreed to spend from 21 to 26 January 1968 there. A team of scientists duplicated the circuits and equipment of Adam's office, hoping to reproduce the poltergeist effects, but none of the deflections or other phenomena occurred. It seems that Annemarie could produce paranormal events only in certain specific circumstances.

Abandoning the attempt to reproduce psychokinesis, Bender tried testing Annemarie's ESP abilities. Again, nothing significant was discovered – except momentarily, when Annemarie scored highly while upset by an unpleasant memory. This seemed to confirm that stress encouraged paranormal events in her case.

Stress and frustration were seen to play a major role in Annemarie's personality. During her stay at Freiburg, she underwent extensive psychological assessment by a psychologist colleague of Bender, John Mischo. He concluded that she was unstable, irritable and suffering from frustrated rages.

was beginning to think, along with the scientists, that the ordinary laws of physics did not apply in the office, but as an extra check he organised a search for tools. None was found.

At 4.30 the same afternoon, Frau Adam arrived at the police station to inform Wendl that the cabinet had moved again. He and Officer Tischler accompanied her back to the office, which they found in chaos. The girls were almost hysterical because they had been getting electric shocks in their arms and legs all day, and before the second movement of the cabinet, tables and chairs had moved. One table had jerked along with a horrified visitor perched on it. When Frau Bielmeier left the typing room, her chair had risen, and Annemarie and Fräulein Huber's chairs both sunk. The height of the typing chairs is adjusted with a ratchet that, to prevent accidents, cannot be altered when any weight is on the seat – yet that afternoon, Professor Büchel of the Physics Institute at Pulach, near Munich, had watched Annemarie's chair descend while she was still sitting on it. She was shocked; her face blanched, then

She was unable to tolerate denial and was aggressive, although she suppressed her aggression. He believed that her constant frustrations discharged themselves through psychokinesis, via a process yet to be explained. Her own doctor had remarked on the severity of her nervous symptoms, which included hyperaemia (an excess of blood gathering in one place) and cramps. Her cramp attacks always followed the same pattern: she would cry out, and her eyes would glaze as the cramp spread. Her hands and feet would be worst affected, fingers and toes stretched painfully rigid. Muscles in her knees and hips would also flex agonisingly.

Professor Bender looked for psychological motives for the phenomena. He felt that the speaking clock was contacted as a result of Annemarie's constant desire to know when she could leave the office. Furthermore, it seems as if the damage in the office could have been prompted by aggression towards Herr Adam, as Annemarie had felt particularly tense in his office and had disliked being in his employment. Apparently, early on in the sequence of phenomena, Adam had sarcastically said: 'All we want now is for the paintings to start moving.' Annemarie was within earshot – and, moments later, the first painting started to move.

A subsequent incident confirmed, according to Bender, that Annemarie seemed to instigate psychokinesis in response to emotional problems. She seemed to Bender to be subconsciously trying to rid herself of her fiancé who, appropriately enough, was an electrical engineer. They used to go bowling together in a small alley in Raubling, a suburb on the outskirts of Rosenheim. Bowls are returned automatically, and the pins are attached to cords controlled by a system of relays that replaces them when they are knocked over. Scores are displayed on an illuminated score board.

Annemarie continues the story:

> We had been engaged for three years and once a week we went bowling. On one occasion, the relays behaved in an eccentric way and the bowling was spoiled. I was told the relays had been put out of action, I don't know what they were talking about. My fiancé took the whole thing much too seriously and said that under the circumstances, marriage would be quite impossible.

This happened in the summer of 1969. Whatever the scientists' belief about Annemarie's subconscious wishes, she took several years to get over her broken engagement. She felt victimised, since there had been nothing to prove that the failure of the bowling mechanism was anything whatsoever to do with her.

Below: the bowling alley in Raubling, on the outskirts of Rosenheim. Annemarie used to go bowling here with her fiancé – but, after an incident in the summer of 1969 in which she apparently disrupted the electronically controlled bowling system, her fiancé broke off the engagement

Above left: Hans Bender and a colleague inspect the fluorescent light fittings that spontaneously unscrewed themselves while Annemarie Schneider was present in the office

Left: Annemarie inspects a pen trace during tests conducted by Hans Bender at the Freiburg Institute in January 1968. The results of the tests, in the sympathetic surroundings of the Institute, were disappointing: it seems that, to produce paranormal events, Annemarie had to be in a condition of stress

Blamed for a death

Finally, a team of investigators went to talk directly to Annemarie. They met with her in April 1975. She turned out to be a stout, plain girl with a sad, prematurely aged face. She told them that after leaving Adam's office, she had been employed by another solicitor, Weinzier. Stories of her ability to move lamps and produce other phenomena followed her. This was the first in a long series of jobs, since the unfortunate Annemarie would always be dismissed if anything odd occurred. 'I never had influence over anything. I was very hurt indeed.' Her Bavarian colleagues still had medieval superstitions and apparently whispered that she was a witch.

She went on: 'I worked in Regenfelchen in a paper factory, and there was an accident there when a man was killed. The workers who knew who I was said, "That woman is responsible for the man's death." They didn't give me the sack from the factory immediately, they just dropped hints, so I left on my own accord. I wasn't even in the factory when it happened.'

Since that highly dubious case, there have been no new reports of paranormal happenings associated with Annemarie. She has moved to Munich where, in the anonymous surroundings of a big city, her reputation for producing psychokinetic effects has not been able to catch up with her to plague her. And perhaps this has something to do with the fact that she apparently no longer produces these effects: for, unlike most paranormal phenomena, these seemed actually to be encouraged by attention from scientists and the media. Hans Bender has pointed out that this most remarkable of cases was observed over a period of several months by more than 40 witnesses from widely ranging walks of life – office workers, electrical engineers, lawyers, scientists, psychologists and the police. For all the documentary evidence, however, *how* Annemarie produced the phenomena remains as much a mystery to scientists as ever it was.

Spook lights over America

Pale, silent, flame-like lights sometimes appear in the night in country districts and to sailors at sea. Their cause has baffled many investigators. Frank Smyth begins a series of chapters on spine-chilling hauntings with these strange tales of spook lights

THE 'WILL O' THE WISP' or 'Jack O' Lantern' was part of European ghostly lore right up until the advent of gas lighting simply because he indubitably existed. Some said he was a lost soul, treacherously leading travellers onto lonely moorland or dangerous swampland. Others said that he was an essentially benign spirit, and that if you had the courage to dig at the spot indicated by his flickering blue light on Walpurgis Night you would discover buried treasure.

But bad, good or indifferent, he was not, like some ghosts, the product of an overheated imagination: anyone who cared or dared to venture out into certain parts of the countryside after dusk could observe his eerie glow for themselves. With the coming of gas light, even country folk learned the true nature of 'Will' or 'Jack': he was simply iridescent marsh gas, similar to the stuff they now used to light their homes and streets. His mystery, if not his beauty, had vanished.

Over the years science, to the disappointment of romantics, has explained away most of the 'mystery lights' that appear in records down the centuries: airplane headlights or UFOs, shooting stars or ball lightning, reflections and refractions from the atmosphere or the surface of the sea. But not all these mysterious phenomena have succumbed to explanation so readily: some refuse to fit neatly into known patterns. Many of these seem peculiar to the United States, and American psychical researchers have jauntily dubbed them 'spook lights' – a tag that is as good as any.

One of the classic American spook light stories has its roots firmly in supernatural tradition. If any completely rational explanation exists, it has yet to be put forward, although several interesting theories have appeared over the years. The story begins in a strictly factual manner with the voyage of the *Palatine*, an elderly ship that set out from Holland in the autumn of 1752 crammed with Dutch families determined to make a

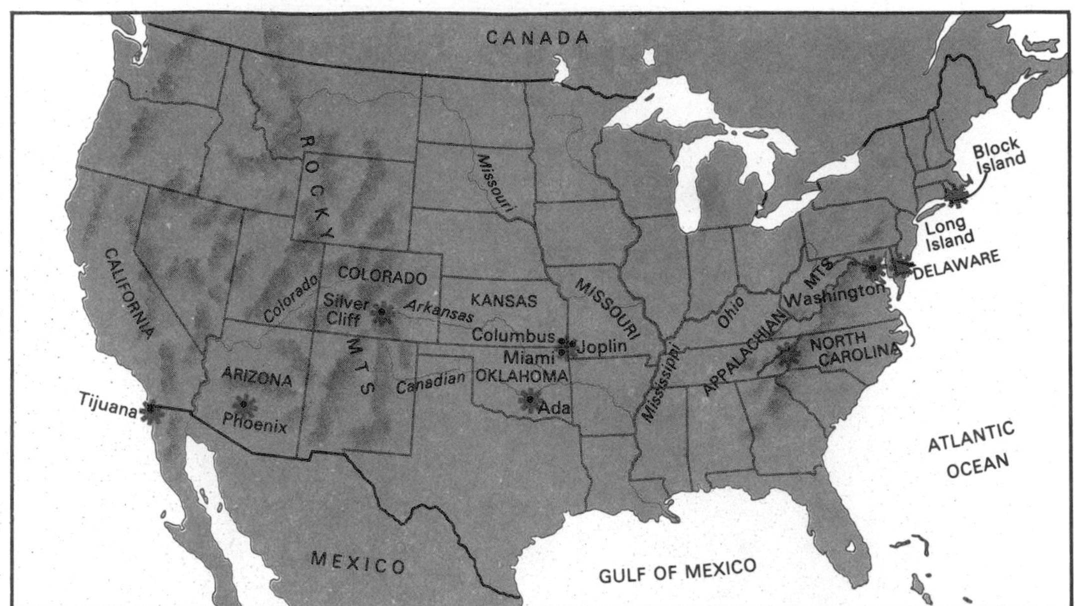

Right: some of the places in the United States where spook lights have been seen repeatedly. Many sightings are associated with rivers or bodies of water, but one is in the Arizona desert

Left: a will o' the wisp glows over the stagnant waters of a marsh, 'like a taper gleaming from some cottage window', in the words of one 19th-century account. The will o' the wisp often led the unwary onto dangerous ground

Below: terrified seamen witness the Flying Dutchman's ship, harbinger of doom. Could ghost ships and spook lights have the same natural explanation?

new life for themselves in the New World.

The vessel's scheduled destination was Philadelphia, but several factors combined to prevent it reaching its port – among them a drunken captain, a surly crew and persistent foul weather, all of which helped to keep the *Palatine* at sea for over two months. As the ship neared the New England coast, there was an argument between the officers as to the ship's exact position, and during the ensuing row the captain either fell or was thrown over the side. Heartlessly, the crew opted to save their own necks and, after robbing the passengers of what cash they could find, they put to sea in the only two lifeboats, leaving the colonists to their fate.

One morning between Christmas and New Year the *Palatine*, with its hapless passengers, grounded on the desolate coast of Block Island, about 11 miles (18 kilometres) off Long Island between Montauk and Gay Head. The local community of fishermen, accustomed to supplementing their poor livings by wrecking, evacuated the passengers but afterwards looted the ship and then set it on fire, allowing it to drift out to sea and sink. This is the story, and tradition adds that one terrified woman had hidden herself below decks. As the burning hulk was swept seaward by the tide, onlookers were horrified to see her standing at the rails screaming for help, but by that time there was nothing they could do.

Ever since then people living on the Rhode Island coast opposite Block Island have sporadically reported seeing the blazing outline of a ship during Christmas week; sometimes it appears luminous white, although in 1969 several people reported to the local newspaper, the *Westerly Sun*, that it was 'a great red fireball on the ocean.'

One of the best reports of a sighting was given by a Long Island fishing-boat owner in *Scientific American* in 1882, though he was hard-headed enough to offer an explanation that was satisfactory – and he was able to use the incident to his own profit. His boat was out after menhaden – a particularly oily fish related to the herring – with himself on board, when one of the mates said that 'he hoped we were not going off the Point, meaning Montauk. I asked him why. He seemed kind of offish, but at last let out that he had seen sailing ships sailing about in the dead of night in a dead calm.'

The mate was laughed to scorn and the fishing boat eventually made anchor in Gardiner's Bay, a few miles to the west of Block Island. That night the owner was shaken awake by the mate, who pointed anxiously out to sea.

A coaster in the spirit trade

'Sure enough, there was a big schooner about an eighth of a mile [200 metres] away, bearing down on us. There wasn't a breath of wind in the bay, but on she came at a ten-knot [18-km/h] rate, headed right for us. . . . I swung into the rigging and yelled "Schooner ahoy" and shouted to her to bear away, but in a second the white sails were right aboard of us. I shouted to the hands and made ready to jump, when, like a flash, she disappeared, and the skipper came on deck with all hands and wanted to know if we had the jimjams.'

He would have sworn, said the owner, that he had seen the Flying Dutchman's ship but a week later saw the thing again, passing round them and heading back up the bay. Apparently acting on impulse, the owner ordered the skipper to take the fishing boat after the 'phantom', at the same time setting his seine net.

'As sure as you are alive we made the biggest single haul of menhaden on record. The light to my mind was nothing more or less than the phosphorescence that hovered over the big shoal. The oil from so many millions of fish moving along was enough to produce a light; but you will find men all

The northern lights, or *aurora borealis*, glow over a lake in Manitoba, Canada. The aurora is caused by electrically charged particles from space, which collide with atoms in the atmosphere high above the Earth and make them glow. The eerie spectacle is seen regularly in the northern latitudes but has often been misinterpreted on its occasional appearances farther south. It may have been responsible for some of the stories of angelic hosts and ghostly armies seen in the sky. Seen low over the horizon, the aurora can look like lights on the ground in the distance, and could have given rise to stories of ghostly activity

along the shores of Long Island that believe there is a regular phantom craft that comes in on and off – sort of a coaster in the spirit trade.'

This belief was first investigated in some depth by Professor W. F. Ganong at the turn of the century and his findings were published by the *Bulletin* of the National Historical Society of New Brunswick. After interviewing numerous witnesses and examining all the evidence, he made four positive points on what he called 'The fact basis of the fire (or phantom) ship':

> It appears to the author plain that (1) a physical light is frequently seen over the waters, (2) that it appears at all seasons, or at least in winter and summer, (3) that it usually precedes a storm, (4) that its actual form is roughly hemispherical with the flat side to the water, and that at times it simply glows without much change of form, but that at other times it rises into slender moving columns, giving rise to an appearance capable of interpretation as the flaming rigging of a ship.

Professor Ganong inclined to the opinion that the 'phantom' was due to St Elmo's fire, but cautiously added that he was 'not aware of any reports of similar phenomena, of such frequency in one locality, and of such considerable development.'

Only a decade afterwards, however, very similar spook lights were the subject of a Government enquiry. Since about 1850 the people of the Rattlesnake Knob area of North Carolina had observed lights, sometimes red, sometimes yellowish white, appearing over the 2500-foot (760-metre) plateau of Brown Mountain, a blunt outcrop of the Appalachians. Stories grew of spirits on the mountain, though some citizens went in search of brush fires – to no avail.

The Brown Mountain lights continued to be seen for over 60 years, until finally a North Carolina Congressman mentioned the curiosity in Washington, and in 1913 an investigator from the United States Geological Survey was sent down to view it. Examining the mountain, he found that it consisted of ordinary Cranberry granite, which is widespread in the area. There was no marshland on the mountain's slopes, so the 'will o' the wisp' theory was ruled out. Witnesses said that the lights usually appeared at about seven in the evening, stayed for about 30 seconds, and then vanished, often to reappear 'four or five times' before dying out for the night. Others reported a single light that rose from the slopes of the mountain, hovered and then disappeared 'like a bursting skyrocket'.

Investigation renewed

The geologist was perfunctory in his report, ascribing all the lights to locomotive headlights. The Congressman who had instigated the enquiry in the first place was annoyed, and insisted that a second man be sent. The new investigator was more thorough but, after studying maps and geological details of the area, claimed that 47 per cent of the phenomena originated in locomotive headlights, 33 per cent in those of cars, and the remaining 20 per cent in fixed lights and bush fires equally. He added that the countryside at the foot of Brown Mountain was alternately dusty and misty, a combination of conditions that made the air very refractive.

However, a further report in 1925 pointed out several fairly obvious faults in the refraction theory, not the least of which was that the lights had been faithfully recorded for over 70 years – several decades before railroads were built in the area and half a century before the first automobile made its appearance. Furthermore, a season of floods in 1916 had put both railroads and highways out of action for some time, and still the 'phantom' lights appeared. One perhaps significant pointer was given: the lights disappear for long stretches during and for some time after a protracted drought. It may be that water – either the ocean or a river – is in cases such as this conducive to the appearance of ghost lights. (The John River runs by Brown Mountain.) Since 1925, no one has offered any further explanation – but the lights shine on.

In the 'tri-state' area where Kansas, Missouri and Oklahoma meet, spook lights appear so regularly that they have become a tourist industry. This area forms a triangle, the points of which are the towns of Columbus, Joplin, and Miami, about 20 miles (30 kilometres) from each other. Again a river, the Spring, cuts through this triangle, and the nearby US Highway 66 has given rise to the theory that the lights are those of automobiles, refracted by mist rising from the river. In favour of this is that fact that, viewed through binoculars, some of the lights appear in parallel pairs, with both members of each pair either white or red – like the head and tail lights of cars on a motorway.

Against the theory is the objection posed at Brown Mountain – that the lights have a venerable history dating far back beyond the automobile. And, like those of Ada, they occasionally bound up to onlookers; one farmer, ploughing by lamplight, abandoned his tractor and fled in terror when a red globe zoomed at him. So far, however, the lights have done no more than frighten and fascinate – so much so that for the past decade the hoteliers and bar-owners of the three towns have advertised the attractions of 'Spooksville', as they call it, in tourist brochures that they have distributed throughout the country.

There are a number of other 'spook light' sites in the United States. One of the best documented and most intriguing must be that on a hill in the Wet Mountain Valley area of Colorado, not only because the lights have appeared almost every night for just over 100 years, but also because they focus on that favourite scene of traditional hauntings – a disused cemetery.

In 1880, the township of Silver Cliff grew up in the wake of a sudden 'silver rush' and by the end of its first year's existence the population topped 5000. Due to the usual deaths by violence and mining incidents, a 'Boot Hill' cemetery grew at the same time on the foothills of Wet Mountain. The boom faded as quickly as it came, however, and today only about 100 prospectors live among the dilapidated buildings.

The strange phenomena that haunt the Silver Cliff graveyard were first reported shortly after its foundation, when a group of drunken miners returning to their diggings reported seeing eerie blue lights hovering over each grave. Nor were these lights just a by-product of whiskey – they appeared on other nights to sober observers. In 1956 an article about the lights in the *Wet Mountain Tribune* excited some comment in the Western United States, but it was not until 1967 that the *New York Times* sent a reporter to Silver Cliff to make an investigation.

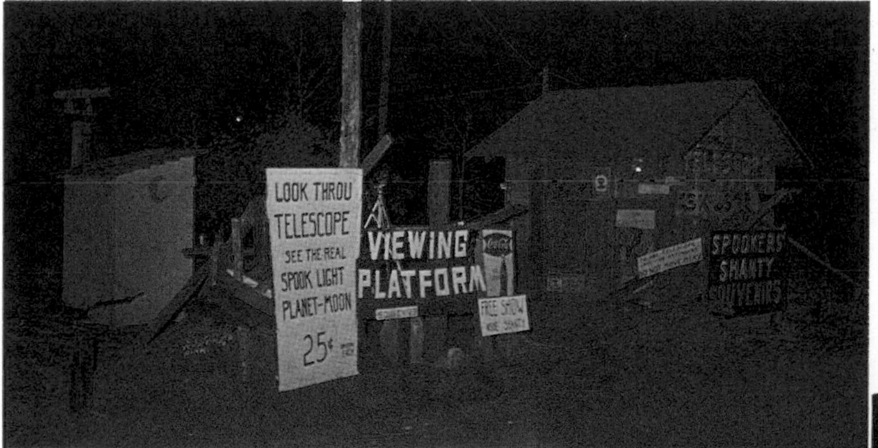

Below: the proprietor of 'Spookers' Shanty', near Joplin, Missouri, has managed to make a profit out of the local mystery lights. The lights are visible here beyond the bushes. As the sign indicates, the Moon and planets are alternative attractions when the spook lights do not appear

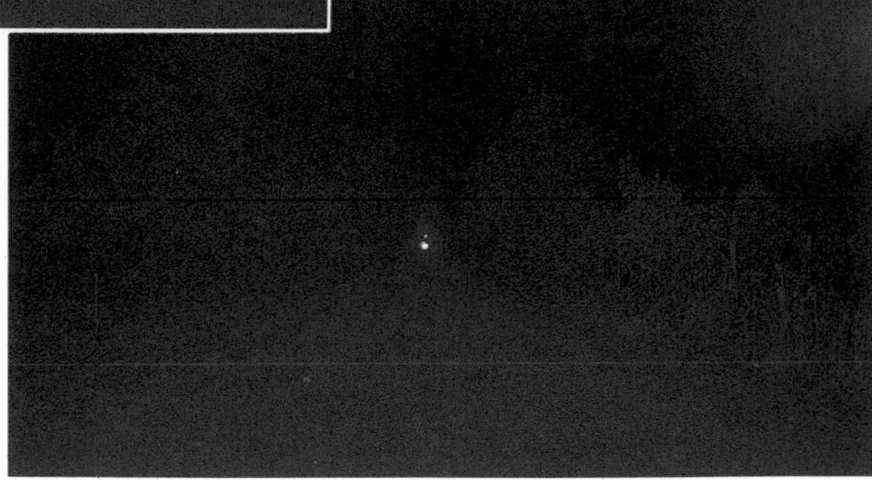

Bottom: a group of the Joplin spook lights in the far distance, captured in a prize-winning photograph. Spook lights at other locations appear in conditions remarkably similar to these: down tree-lined highways or along railway tracks

Two years later, in an article about Colorado in the *National Geographic*, assistant editor Edward J. Linehan described how he viewed the lights in the company of Westcliffe resident Bill Kleine. It was dark when the two reached the graveyard, and Linehan switched off his headlights. They got out of the car, and Kleine pointed: 'There! See them? And over there!'

Linehan saw them, '. . . dim round spots of blue white light' glowing above each grave. He stepped forward for a better look at one but it vanished, then slowly reappeared. He switched on his flashlight and aimed it at one of the lights. The beam revealed only a headstone. For 15 minutes the men pursued the elusive ghost lights among the graves.

Most people, said Kleine, reckoned that the lights were 'reflections' of the town lights of Westcliffe. Looking back at the tiny cluster far below, Linehan found this impossible to believe, particularly as Kleine went on: 'Both me and my wife have seen them when the fog was so thick you couldn't see the town at all.'

Other theories recounted and discounted by Linehan were that the lights were caused by radioactive ore – but a Geiger counter test of the whole area revealed no trace of radioactivity; that the ghost lights were luminous paint, daubed on the tombs by hoaxers – but no evidence has ever been found to support this charge. Gas from decaying bodies seemed a far-fetched idea, as the last burial took place around the turn of the century. The mercury vapour lights of Westcliffe might, it was suggested, have caused 'special effects' on the hill side; but not only were they a late installation but on several occasions when power cuts had blacked out every township for miles around, the graveyard illuminations still shone.

Among the old-timers of Silver Cliff only one explanation holds good, said Linehan: the blue-white spots are the helmet lamps of long-dead miners, still seeking on the deserted hillside for traces of silver.

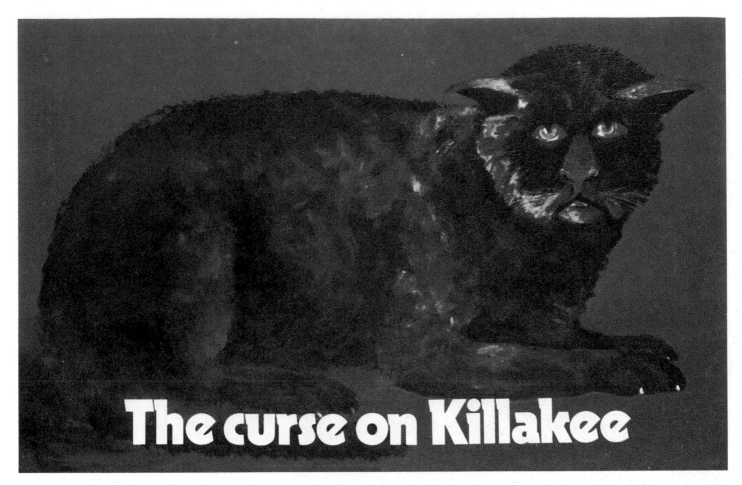

The curse on Killakee

From the days of the Dublin Hell Fire Club to the times of the Troubles, the history of Killakee House was stained by violence and bloodshed. This chapter tells the story of a disturbed past and its modern legacy: hauntings by a frightening supernatural beast

THE VICTORIAN WRITER E. Bulwer-Lytton used the phrase *Haunters and haunted* as a title for a celebrated story. He implied by the phrase that there was a definite relationship between the phenomena witnessed at a haunted house and the people who witnessed them – it was not a matter of chance that one person should see a ghost while another did not do so.

This certainly seems to be true in many well-attested poltergeist cases. These disturbances frequently centre on adolescents, and several researchers go so far as to claim that in such cases the 'haunters' emanate from the minds of the 'haunted' themselves, and are simply physical manifestations of teenage traumas. In other cases the person most closely involved in the phenomena appears to act as a catalyst for an already well-established haunting, fanning its embers into flame by his mere presence.

A combination of these factors may have been present when Killakee House in County Dublin became the centre of a veritable storm of psychic activity in the late 1960s and early 1970s. The onset of the phenomena occurred when new residents moved in, and ended when they left.

A story by Edward Bulwer-Lytton (below) suggests that hauntings can be caused by their 'victims'. Did something like this happen at Killakee House?

Killakee lies in the foothills of the Wicklow Mountains, overlooking the city of Dublin. Killakee House, built in the early 18th century as the dower house of the Massey family, is a robust stone building with a small tower. Behind the house rises the steep slope of Montpellier Hill, its scrubby grass worn bare by the feet of tourists hardy enough to make the ascent to the top. On the summit stands the stone shell of a fire-ravaged hunting lodge, constructed by the Earl of Rosse in the 18th century. It was used by him and such 'bucks' as Harry Barry, first Lord Santry, and Richard 'Burnchapel' Whaley as the headquarters of the Dublin Hell Fire Club – a close imitation of the contemporary English version founded by Sir Francis Dashwood.

Rosse had a cruel sense of humour and a hatred of black cats. He used to hold court at the Eagle Tavern on Cork Hill in Dublin. On one occasion, to frighten the local inhabitants, he doused a black cat in spirits, set it alight and watched it run screaming down the hill. Dubliners swore that it was the Devil himself.

There is strong evidence that Rosse's brutal and puerile humour was given play at the hunting lodge on Montpellier Hill. On one occasion, after a black mass, he put a black cat in the seat of honour when Satan failed to turn up in person. It was also said that a half-witted dwarf with a twisted body and unnaturally large head was beaten to death by Rosse and his cronies, shortly before the lodge burned down in the 1750s.

Rosse's friends often lodged with him in Killakee House and violent scenes often took place there. The Irish rakes were addicted to pistol duelling (one of the first questions asked by a prospective father-in-law of a noble suitor was 'do you blaze?', meaning 'do you fight duels?'). At least three deaths from duelling took place in the grounds.

Violence renewed

After a long interval that was relatively untroubled, there was again bloodshed at the house in the early 20th century. The house was then occupied by Countess Constance Markievicz, the 'Red Countess'. A friend of the mystical poet William Butler Yeats, she was the first woman to be elected to the House of Commons, although she never took her seat. The Countess participated in the 1916 rebellion, and five IRA men died in a gun battle at the house during her tenancy. All in all, Killakee House and the surrounding area were imbued with more violence and savagery than most haunted places.

Killakee House lay empty and derelict for some years after the Second World War. In the late 1960s it was bought by Mrs Margaret O'Brien, who wanted a centre in which Irish artists and sculptors could work and exhibit their art. When she moved into the place in 1968, she heard stories from locals that its grounds were haunted by a black cat the size of an Airedale dog. 'Haunted' was an appropriate term because the stories covered a period of over 50 years – much longer than the life-span of a normal cat.

Mrs O'Brien knew some of the tales related about her new property and its environs, and was rather shaken when she caught glimpses of a 'big black animal' disappearing into the thick shrubbery of her garden. She thought no more about it, however, until her friend Tom McAssey, a Dublin artist, and two colleagues had a terrifying experience one night while redecorating Killakee House in March 1968. They were working on the stone-flagged front hall, which opened onto what had been a ballroom. McAssey told a radio reporter:

> I had just locked the heavy front door, pushing a 6-inch [15-centimetre] bolt into its socket. Suddenly one of the two men with me said that the door had opened again. We turned, startled. The lock was good and the bolt was strong, and both fastened on the inside.
>
> We peered into the shadowed hallway, and then I walked forward, and sure enough the door stood wide open, letting in a cold breeze. Outside in the darkness I could just discern a black-draped figure, but could not see its face. I thought someone was playing a trick

Left: Tom McAssey's painting of the Black Cat of Killakee, which scared him and two companions one night in 1968. The picture now hangs in the house, which is an art centre

Below: the long low bulk of Killakee House stands beneath the hill on which the burnt-out ruin of the Hell Fire Club stands. A prehistoric cairn and a standing stone existed on the hill's summit before these buildings were put up

Left: Countess Markievicz, who occupied Killakee House for a period. She was sentenced to death for her part in the 1916 uprising, but this was commuted to penal servitude for life. She was actually released in 1917 and became a noted Irish politician

and said: 'Come in. I see you.' A low, guttural voice answered: 'You can't see me. Leave this door open.'

The men standing behind me both heard the voice, but thought it spoke in a foreign language. They ran. A long-drawn-out snore came from the shadow, and in panic I slammed the heavy door and ran too. Halfway across the gallery I turned and looked back. The door was again open and a monstrous black cat crouched in the hall, its red-flecked amber eyes fixed on me.

Beside Killakee House in a trailer in the wooded grounds lived Val McGann, a former Irish pole-vault champion who painted and showed his work at the gallery. He evinced no surprise at McAssey's story, because he had seen the huge cat on several occasions, lurking in the scraggling undergrowth of the overgrown garden.

'The first time I saw it, it frightened me stiff,' he said, 'but on subsequent occasions I have been more interested and amazed at the size of the beast. It is about the size of a biggish dog, with terrible eyes. I've even stalked it with my shotgun, but have never been able to corner it.'

For some months after McAssey's vision, apparitions were seen by workmen and artists at Killakee. They usually appeared at night, although two men saw what they thought was a nun, with her back to them, at midday in the old ballroom. When they approached her she disappeared, and a subsequent search of the house and garden failed to turn up any evidence of a real figure.

Following reports in the Dublin press and on television of the strange hauntings, a group of Irish show-business personalities persuaded Mrs O'Brien to let them try a seance in Killakee House. They included a stage conjurer who was an expert on illusions and who believed that he could rule out any 'fakery' on the part of residents.

The group arranged cards carrying the letters of the alphabet in a circle on a table and placed an upturned glass in the centre. Each participant rested one finger lightly on the glass. Those who have tried this well-known technique will know that the glass will slide around the table, from letter to letter, apparently spontaneously, with no one present applying any pressure to it – consciously, at any rate.

The group at Killakee asked any 'spirits' present to manifest themselves – but the 'replies' were gibberish. However, on two occasions the lights failed, although a subsequent check of the fuses revealed no fault, and the light bulbs and wiring appeared to be completely normal.

Two days later, however, events began to take a more frightening turn. First there were bumps and knockings in the night. Lights were switched rapidly on and off.

Bells in the night

Throughout the whole of one night the sound of door bells, in the front and back halls, could be heard. Yet those bells had been removed many years before.

A minor but curious manifestation was the fact that none of the residents – five or six in all – was able to sleep even on 'calm' nights; after retiring to bed exhausted from a heavy day's work, they reported lying awake, tossing and turning and managing to sleep only after sunrise.

About four days after the seance, everyone in the house heard heavy crashes and went to investigate. They found large pieces of furniture – some stored in locked rooms – thrown 'like matchboxes', some upside down, some pushed into corners. One oak medieval chair had been carefully pulled apart, joint from joint; even the brass tacks holding its tapestry in place had been pulled out and placed in neat rows. On the other hand, another similar chair had been smashed into tiny slivers.

After this outbreak, peace descended again for a matter of weeks. Then the 'haunters' turned their attention to exhibits on show in the house: a potter's works were hurled all over the room and smashed, while oil paintings were torn into long narrow strips.

At this point Margaret O'Brien sought the assistance of a priest, who, after obtaining permission from his superiors, performed a Roman Catholic rite of exorcism on Killakee House. The violent outbreaks stopped, but even more bizarre incidents began to occur in their place.

Mrs O'Brien had still not completed furnishing her house, and she lacked a refrigerator. She had asked the milkman to leave the milk in a pool in a cool stream that ran

Below: the building used by the Hell Fire Club as it was at the height of the society's infamy. It was built about 1725 as a hunting lodge, and commanded magnificent views of the mountains and forests of the surrounding countryside. It was burned down in mysterious circumstances – supposedly during one of the club's orgies of violence

Above: duelling, then a legal activity, claimed the lives of several noblemen at Killakee House during the 18th century. A duel could be substituted for a trial: the defendant had the right to challenge his accuser. Even after the abolition of such 'judicial' duels, personal combat, regulated by strict rules, remained legal between military men until it was finally outlawed in the mid 19th century

through the grounds. After the exorcism, Mrs O'Brien found that all the tinfoil tops had been removed from the bottles, although the milk was undisturbed.

Furthermore, no trace of the foil could be found. Mrs O'Brien assumed that it had been carried off by birds, possibly magpies or jackdaws. To stop the nuisance, she had a heavy four-sided box of stone built in the stream, with a large slate lid. Nevertheless, the caps continued to disappear.

The humour of the haunters

At this juncture, the 'haunters' showed a trace of humour as well as causing a rare psychic manifestation called an 'apport' – the sudden appearance of objects through apparently preternatural means. Following the disappearance of the caps from the bottles, 'caps' began to appear in the house itself – but these caps were types of headgear.

After the manifestations, Mrs O'Brien had made a practice of locking and checking all the doors before retiring. Despite this, a profusion of small caps began to appear all over the house. They would appear in odd places – on picture hooks or behind doors. Sometimes, rosary beads would be found, equally inexplicably.

At the end of 1970 the caps ceased to appear, although spasmodic knockings in the night continued to be heard. Then, a few months later, came a discovery that might have had a grim bearing on the whole strange series of incidents. While structural alterations to the kitchen were being made, an excavation for new plumbing was carried out. In a shallow grave a few feet under the surface was found the skeleton of a dwarf, with a skull too large for its small frame – a sinister echo of the legend told of the Hell Fire Club for so many years. In the grave, too, was a brass figurine, depicting a horned and tailed devil thumbing its nose.

Once again the priest was called, this time to conduct a proper burial service on the unknown unfortunate, and after that the manifestations ceased. Mrs O'Brien sold the premises six years later.

Was the Black Cat of Killakee – later portrayed in oils by Tom McAssey as he had seen it on that frightening night – a manifestation that was attached to the house, or had it somehow been conjured into existence by the new occupants? Were the voices, the bells and the broken furniture results of the seance, which somehow provided a focus for them? Or was the whole series of hauntings provoked by the unhappy ghost of the dwarf, brutally murdered, according to legend, by the drunken bucks of the Hell Fire Club?

It is unlikely that the answer will ever be known for sure, but we do know that all psychical phenomena ceased in 1977, when Joseph Frei took over the unfortunate house and added a restaurant to the art centre's facilities.

'Perhaps the previous owners were, shall we say, unlucky with the place,' he said. 'I and my family have been very happy here – I know about the history of it, but we have only experienced a feeling of warmth and comfort. Perhaps the "haunters" like what we are doing with their "haunt".'

The horror of Glamis

For centuries Glamis Castle has had a reputation as a place of strange and awful happenings – events that strike terror at the hearts of all who witness them. So what truth lies behind this ancient haunting?

GLAMIS CASTLE stands in the great vale of Strathmore in Tayside, Scotland. For hundreds of years the vast fortified house with its battlements and pointed towers – looking like the setting for a fairy tale – has been the ancestral home of the Earls of Strathmore. Their family secret is reputedly hidden within the walls of Glamis, famous as one of the most haunted houses on earth.

That there was unpleasantness within the castle's walls is an undoubted historical fact. And that the castle is today the centre of a triangle formed by three biblically named villages – Jericho, Zoar, and Pandanaram – may indicate the terror felt by its minions, for, according to a Scottish National Trust guidebook, the men who built and named them 'had at least some knowledge of the Scriptures and regard for the wrath of God'. That wrath, claim locals even today, was called down on Glamis for the sins of the first dozen or so Lairds. The present, 17th Earl of Strathmore, Fergus Michael Claude Bowes-Lyon, is well-liked by his tenants, and there is no evidence that his immediate forbears

Below: Glamis Castle, picturesque home of the Earl of Strathmore and Kinghorne, was a wedding gift from King Robert II upon the marriage of his daughter to Sir John Lyon in the 14th century. From the time Sir John moved to Glamis, the family seemed to be dogged by misfortune

Right: the painting of the third Earl, Patrick, with his children and greyhounds dominates the far wall of the drawing room at Glamis. It is around Patrick that two of the strangest stories revolve

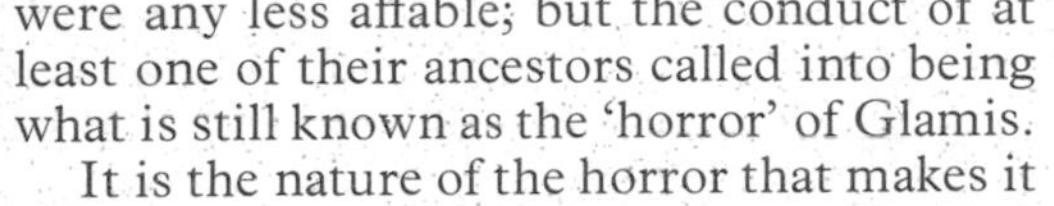

Above: Malcolm II, who reigned as King of Scotland from 1005 until his death at Glamis in 1034 at the hands of an army of rebels. Tradition holds that he was slain in what is now known as King Malcolm's Room (top right), and that his brutal murder saw the start of the 'horror' at the castle

were any less affable; but the conduct of at least one of their ancestors called into being what is still known as the 'horror' of Glamis.

It is the nature of the horror that makes it one of the great mysteries. No recent Earl has ever spoken of it to an outsider, except in enigmatic terms. No woman has ever been let in on the secret. It is passed on only to the Strathmore heir on his 21st birthday.

The historical record of horror at Glamis Castle goes back to 1034, when King Malcolm II was cut down by a gang of rebellious subjects armed with claymores, the large broadswords peculiar to Scotland. It was said that every drop of Malcolm's blood seeped from his body into the floorboards, causing a stain that is still pointed out today, in what is called King Malcolm's Room. That the stain was made by Malcolm's blood is disputable, however, for records seem to show that the flooring has since been replaced. Nevertheless, Malcolm's killers added to the death toll of Glamis by trying to escape across a frozen loch, but the ice cracked and they were drowned.

Curse of the chalice

The Lyon family inherited Glamis from King Robert II, who gave it to his son-in-law, Sir John Lyon, in 1372. Until then the Lyon family home had been at Forteviot, where a great chalice, the family 'luck', was kept. Tradition held that if the chalice were removed from Forteviot House a curse would fall on the family; despite this, Sir John took the cup with him to Glamis. The curse seemed to have a time lapse, for though Sir John was killed in a duel, this did not occur until 1383; nevertheless, the family misfortunes are usually dated from this time.

The 'poisoned' chalice may well have influenced events 150 years later when James V had Janet Douglas, Lady Glamis, burned at the stake in Edinburgh on a charge of witchcraft. The castle reverted to the Crown, but after the falsity of the charge was proved, it was restored to her son. The spectre of Lady Glamis – the 'Grey Lady' as she is known – is said to walk the long corridors even today.

It was Patrick, the third Earl of Strathmore, who made the idea of a Glamis 'curse' widespread in the late 17th century; indeed, to many people he seemed the very embodiment of it. A notorious rake and gambler, his drunken debauches were well-known in London and Edinburgh as well as throughout his home territory. The facts of his career and his character are festooned with folklore, but he must have been something of an enigma, for despite his wild ways he was philanthropic towards his tenants at least. The Glamis Book of Record, for instance, details his plans for building a group of lodges on the estate for the use of retired workers. Now known as Kirkwynd Cottages, they were given to the Scottish National Trust by the 16th Earl of Strathmore in 1957 to house the Angus Folk Collection.

Two principal stories endure about Patrick. The first is that he was the father of a deformed child who was kept hidden somewhere in the castle, out of sight of prying eyes. The second is that he played cards with the Devil for his soul – and lost.

The first is fed by a picture of the third Earl that now hangs in the drawing room. It shows Patrick seated, wearing a classical bronze breastplate, and pointing with his left hand towards a distant, romanticised vista of Glamis. Standing at his left knee is a small, strange-looking green-clad child; to the child's left is an upright young man in scarlet doublet and hose. The three main figures are placed centrally, but two greyhounds in the picture are shown staring steadfastly at a figure, positioned at the Earl's right elbow. Like the Earl this figure wears a classical breastplate apparently shaped to the muscles of the torso – but if it is a human torso it is definitely deformed. The left arm is strangely foreshortened. Did the artist paint from life – and if so does the picture show the real horror of Glamis?

The second story goes like this. Patrick and his friend the Earl of Crawford were playing cards together one Saturday night. A servant reminded them that the Sabbath was approaching, to which Patrick replied that he would play on, Sabbath or no Sabbath, and that the Devil himself might join them for a hand if he so wished. At midnight, accompanied by a roll of thunder, the Devil appeared and told the card-playing Earls that they had forfeited their souls and were doomed to play cards in that room until Judgement Day.

The pact presumably came into operation only after Patrick's death, for there is some evidence that he revelled in the tale: but did he tell it merely as a joke or as some sort of elaborate cover up, to scare intruders forever from the castle? If the latter was his intention, it was strikingly successful. In 1957 a servant at the castle, Florence Foster, complained in a newspaper article that she had heard the Earls at their play in the dead of night, 'rattling dice, stamping and swearing. Often I lay in bed and shook with fright,' she said. She resigned rather than risk hearing the phantom gamblers again. The story persists of a 'secret room' known only to the Earls themselves, and it is true that no one knows for certain which of the hundred-odd rooms at Glamis was used by Patrick for his diabolical game of cards.

Grisly tales

One story tells – with curious precision – of a grey-bearded man, shackled and left to starve in 1486. A later one, which probably dates from before Patrick's time also, is gruesome in the extreme. A party of Ogilvies from a neighbouring district came to Glamis and begged protection from their enemies the Lindsays, who were pursuing them. The Earl of Strathmore led them into a chamber deep in the castle and left them there to starve. Unlike the unfortunate grey-bearded man, however, they had each other to eat and began to turn cannibal, some, according to legend, even gnawing the flesh from their own arms.

One or other of these tales may account for the ghost of a skeletally thin spectre known as Jack the Runner. And the ghost of a Negro pageboy, also seen in the castle, would seem to date from the 17th or 18th century, when young slaves were imported from the West Indies. A 'white' lady haunts the castle clock tower, while the grey-bearded man of 1486 appeared, at least once, to two guests simultaneously, one of whom was Mrs MacLagan, wife of the Archbishop of York at the turn of the 20th century. Mrs MacLagan told how, during her stay at the castle, one of the guests came down to breakfast and mentioned casually that she had been awakened by the banging and hammering of carpenters at 4 a.m. A brief silence followed her remarks, and then Lord Strathmore spoke and assured her that there were no workmen in the castle. According to another story, as a young girl Queen Elizabeth the Queen Mother (daughter of the 14th Earl, Claude George Bowes-Lyon) once had to move out of the Blue Room because her sleep was being disturbed by rappings, thumps, and footsteps.

Fascinating as all these run-of-the-mill ghosts and their distinguished observers are, however, it is the horror that remains the great mystery of Glamis. All the principal rumours – cannibal Ogilvies notwithstanding – involve a deformed child born to the

Below: Lady Elizabeth Bowes-Lyon, the future Queen Mother, grew up at Glamis. She is said to have felt the presence of the horror in the Blue Room

The 13th Earl of Strathmore, Claude Bowes-Lyon (left), was deeply troubled by the tales of strange events at Glamis. The wife of the Archbishop of York wrote that 'for many years, after the revelation of the secret, Claude was quite a changed man, silent and moody, with an anxious scared look on his face. So evident was the effect on him that his son, Glamis, when he came of age in 1876, absolutely refused to be enlightened'

The 14th Earl (below) and Mr Gavin Ralston, the estate factor (below right). When told the secret by the Earl, Mr Ralston was so appalled he vowed never to sleep at the castle again

family and kept in a secret chamber who lived, according to 19th-century versions of the story, to a preternaturally old age. In view of the portrait openly displayed in the Glamis drawing room, and always supposing that the mysterious child is actually portrayed, the subsequent secrecy seems rather pointless. If Patrick himself was prepared to have his 'secret' portrayed in oils, why should his successors have discouraged open discussion of the matter?

An unmentionable horror

Despite the secrecy, at the turn of the 19th century the stories were still flying thick and fast. Claude Bowes-Lyon, the 13th Earl who died in 1904 in his 80th year, seems to have been positively obsessed by the horror, and it is around him that most of the 19th-century stories revolved. It was he, for instance, who told an inquisitive friend: 'If you could guess the nature of the secret, you would go down on your knees and thank God it were not yours.' Claude, too, it was who paid the passage of a workman and his family to Australia, after the workman had inadvertently stumbled upon a 'secret room' at Glamis and been overcome with horror. Claude questioned him, swore the man to secrecy, and bundled him off to the colonies shortly afterwards. To a great extent the obsession seems to have visited itself upon his son, Claude George, the 14th Earl, who died in 1944.

In the 1920s, a party of 'gay young things' staying at Glamis decided to track down the 'secret chamber' by hanging a piece of linen out of every window they could find. When they finished they saw there were several windows they had not been able to locate. When the Earl learned what they had done he flew into an uncharacteristic fury. Unlike his forbears, however, Claude George broke the embargo on the secret by telling it to his estate factor, Mr Gavin Ralston, who subsequently refused to stay overnight at the castle again.

When the 14th Earl's daughter-in-law, the next Lady Strathmore, asked Ralston the secret, Ralston is said to have replied: 'It is lucky that you do not know and can never know it, for if you did you would not be a happy woman.'

That statement, surely, is the clue to the horror of Glamis. Old Patrick's deformed offspring did not alarm the father because nothing like it had been seen in the family before. Possibly the 'wicked' Earl rather delighted in him. But if the same deformity appeared even once in a later generation, the head of an ancient, noble and hereditary house would certainly have been reluctant to broadcast the fact. Perhaps Claude, 13th Earl of Strathmore, knew of such a second, deformed child in the Bowes-Lyon line, and passed the secret and the fear of its recurrence on to his successors?

Left: the chapel at Glamis where a secret room was discovered in the late 19th century. A workman came upon the door by chance and, finding that it led into a long passage, decided to investigate – but he emerged soon after, shaking with fright. He reported his experience to the Earl who, anxious to preserve the family secret, persuaded the man to emigrate

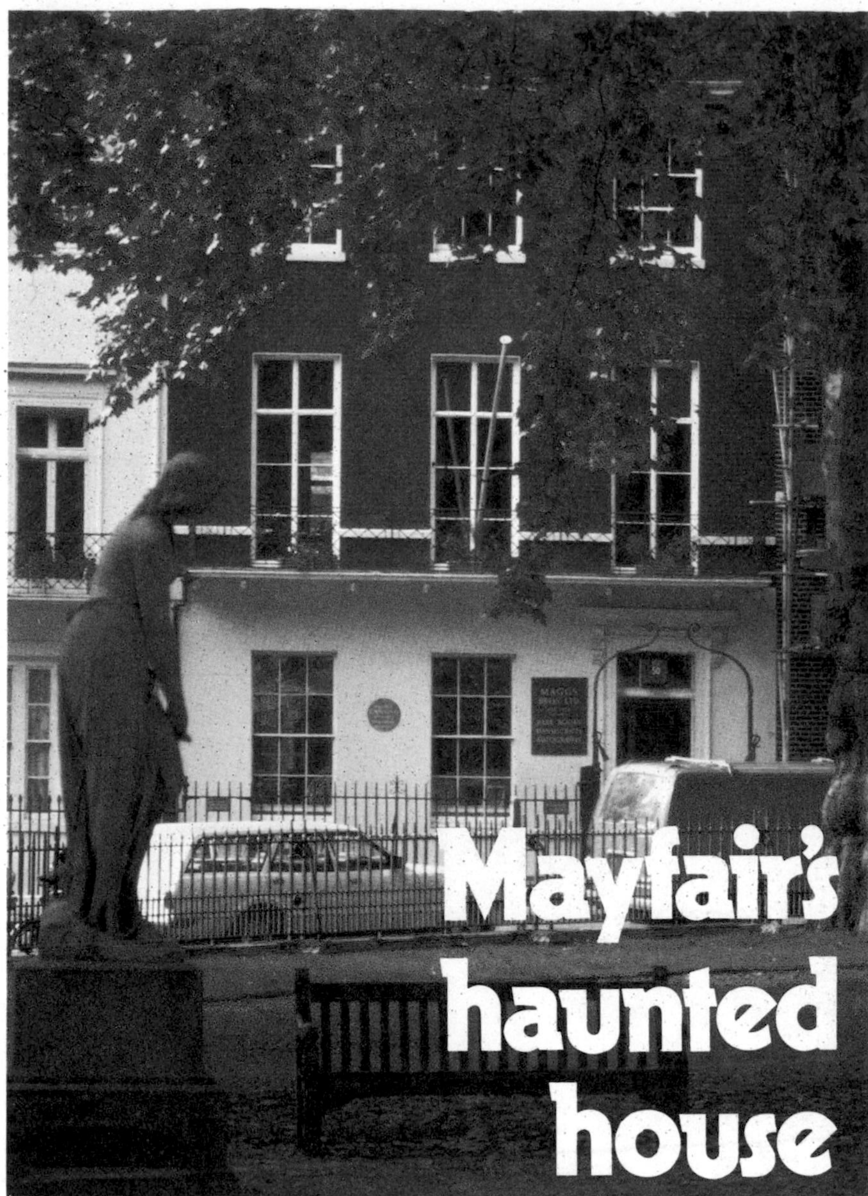

Mayfair's haunted house

For decades the elegant house in the heart of London's West End was plagued by ghosts, but each haunting seemed to take a new and different form. Experts may now have some explanations

IN 1884 the *National Observer* magazine published a poem by Rudyard Kipling. Entitled *Tomlinson*, it told the story of a London society 'waster' whose soul was rejected by the Devil on the grounds of mediocrity. But it was the setting of the poem that was calculated to interest the general public. It began:

Now Tomlinson gave up the ghost in
  his house in Berkeley Square,
And a spirit came to his bedside and
  gripped him by the hair . . .

For the previous four decades, Berkeley Square had been synonymous with ghosts (as it was with nightingales 60 years later).

According to popular rumour the focus of the trouble was No 50, a four-storey town house of brick and stone, built in the mid 18th century. For some years it had been the London home of Prime Minister George Canning (1770–1827), but it seemed unlikely that the supernatural disturbances in the house had any connection with his restless spirit. Canning was not particularly ethereal in life and in any case had breathed his last at Chiswick, some miles away.

The general consensus seemed to be that the 'thing' that haunted No 50 was 'too horrible to describe' – it seemed to be more a demon or terrible elemental than an ordinary ghost. Even before Bulwer Lytton used the house as a setting for his famous ghost story *The haunters and the haunted*, stories abounded of a 'nameless, slimy thing' that slithered up and down the stairs, leaving a foul-smelling, snail-like trail in its wake.

One tale, not unlike Bulwer Lytton's, told of two sailors who had broken into the empty house to shelter for the night. On the morrow, one was found dead, impaled on the railings in the street below, having leapt from the top storey in a frenzy of fear, while his companion was discovered white-haired and mad in the house itself.

No matter that no documentary evidence for such a remarkable incident existed. The story was firmly believed by society dandies and East End costermongers alike, and for several decades was kept alive by poems, newspapers and music hall songs.

Charles Harper, writing in 1907, remarked that 'the famous "haunted house" in Berkeley Square was long one of those things that no country cousin coming up from the provinces to London on sightseeing bent ever willingly missed.'

Harry Price investigated the mystery in the 1920s, two decades before his mishandling – or worse – of the Borley Rectory case made him an object of suspicion in psychical research circles. In the Berkeley Square investigation he seems to have done a

Above: 50 Berkeley Square as it appears today

Right: the front door, from behind which startled neighbours heard curious thumps, bumps and the ringing of bells reasonably objective job: without, however, reaching any firm conclusions. On the one hand, he said, he had discovered some evidence that in the late 18th century – presumably before Prime Minister Canning's tenancy – the house had been the headquarters of a gang of forgers and coin clippers, who actively encouraged tales of the supernatural in order to disguise the true nature of the 'bumps in the night' that neighbours heard from time to time.

On the other hand he pointed out that the house had been empty for remarkably long periods and, while empty houses often tend to father ghost stories around themselves, 50 Berkeley Square was one of the most desirable addresses in London – so why had it been deserted for so long? Perhaps the rumours had some truth after all?

Left: Rudyard Kipling, from a portrait by Burne-Jones. Kipling's poem *Tomlinson* exploited the notoriety of the house in Berkeley Square – and helped sell out the magazine in which it appeared

Price's final surmise was that No 50 may well have been a target for poltergeist activity. In 1840, he discovered that several of the neighbours had heard a variety of noises coming from the empty premises, including bumps on the stairs, dragging noises as if heavy furniture were being moved about, tramping footsteps and, fairly regularly, the jangling of the signal bells below stairs.

One of the more headstrong neighbours, weary of the commotion, obtained a key and, as soon as he heard the bells tinkling, dashed into the house and down to the kitchen. He found the bells still bouncing on their curled springs, but no other sign of life in the locked house. All this, pointed out Price, fitted exactly with the type of phenomenon described by the Society for Psychical Research as poltergeist activity: the one difference being that poltergeists – in practically all known cases – centre themselves on people.

In the course of his investigation Price had had to wade through a great deal of speculative data that rarely gave dates or names. For instance, in the 1870s the magazine *Notes and Queries* had launched an investigation into the case, culminating in a long series by the writer W. E. Howlett.

> The mystery of Berkeley Square still remains a mystery [he wrote]. We are in hopes that during the last fortnight a full, final, and satisfactory answer would have been given to our questions: but we have been disappointed. The story of the haunted house in the heart of Mayfair can be recapitulated in a few words. . . . The house in Berkeley Square contains at least one room of which the atmosphere is supernaturally fatal to body and mind. A girl saw, heard, or felt such horror in it that she went mad, and never recovered sanity enough to tell how or why.
>
> A gentleman, a disbeliever in ghosts, dared to sleep in it and was found a corpse in the middle of the floor after frantically ringing for help in vain. Rumour suggests other cases of the same kind, all ending in death, madness or both as a result of sleeping, or trying to sleep in that room. The very party walls of the house, when touched, are found saturated with electric horror. It is uninhabited save by an elderly man and his wife who act as caretakers; but even these have no access to *the* room. This is kept locked, the key being in the hands of a mysterious and seemingly nameless person who comes to the house once every six months, locks up the elderly couple in the basement, and then unlocks *the* room and occupies himself in it for hours.

In 1881, an anonymous writer, again in *Notes and Queries*, testified to the truth of the

Right: Edward Bulwer Lytton, who used 50 Berkeley Square as a setting for a gruesome short story

'electric party walls' story, though he too failed to name names, possibly because the witnesses were 'society people'.

The incident in question had taken place at a ball given in 49 Berkeley Square early in the season of 1880. 'A lady and her partner,' said the writer, 'were sitting against the party wall of number fifty when on a sudden she moved from her place and looked around. The gentleman was just going to ask the reason when he felt impelled to do the same. On comparing their impressions, both had felt very cold and had fancied that someone was looking over their shoulders from the wall behind! From this it would appear that "stone walls do not a prison make" for these uncomfortable ghosts, who can project themselves right through them to the great discomfort of the next door neighbours.'

The most likely explanation of the origins of No 50's sinister reputation was printed shortly after this account appeared, and differed from most in that it could be verified, at least in part: doubtless because the parties mentioned were dead. According to the writer, in *Pall Mall* magazine, the house had been bought after George Canning's death by an Hon. Miss Curzon, who lived there from time to time until her death in 1859 at the age of 90. It was then leased by her executors to a Mr Myers, a well-to-do man about town who was engaged to be married and who spent the next few months of his tenancy redecorating and furnishing, only to have his bride jilt him on the eve of her wedding day. The unfortunate Myers became a recluse in his new home, developing a curiously Dickensian character, part Scrooge, part Miss Havisham.

In 1873 he was prosecuted by Westminster council for non-payment of rates, and refused to answer the summons in person. Despite this, the magistrate gave him time to pay, and was surprisingly lenient with him in his summing up: 'The house in question is known as "the haunted house" and has occasioned a good deal of speculation among the neighbours. Mr Myers' failure to pay his rates had arisen from eccentricity.'

The *Pall Mall* author went on: 'The disappointment [of his rejection] is said to have broken his heart and turned his brain. He became morose and solitary, and would never allow a woman to come near him. The miserable man locked himself away in the ill-fated top room of the house, only opening the door for meals to be brought to him occasionally by a manservant. Generally speaking he slept during the day and, at night, would emerge from his self-imposed exile to wander, candle in hand, around the house that was to have been the scene of his happiness.'

Possibly Myers was the 'mysterious and nameless person' alluded to by W. E. Howlett, for he died, apparently, towards the end of the 1870s.

'Thus,' said the writer in *Pall Mall*, 'upon the melancholy wanderings of this poor lunatic, was founded that story of the

Below: Berkeley Square in the 1860s. The macabre goings-on at No 50 sorted ill with its gentility and refinement

ghost . . . those whom so many persons insist on calling "mad doctors" could tell of hundreds of cases of minds diseased and conduct similar to that of poor Myers. His sister was, it was said, his only relative, and she was too old or great an invalid to interfere.'

New twists to the tale

There the story should have ended, but did not. In 1912, Jessie A. Middleton, a popular author on the occult, wrote in her *Grey ghost book* that her own research had shown that the ghost was that of a little girl in a Scots kilt. She claimed that the child had been either frightened or starved to death in the fourth-floor room and had been seen there from time to time ever since, weeping and wringing her hands in dismay. But Miss Middleton added that another version of the story – echoing the 'falling sailor' tale – held that the girl had not been so young, that her name was Adeline, and that rather than submit to a 'fate worse than death' at the hands of her wicked guardian, she had leapt from the window and been spiked to death on the area railings.

As late as 1969 another strand was added to the already tangled skein of the Berkeley Square affair. Mrs Mary Balfour, an octogenarian lady of noble Scottish family, whose letters from society names attested to her apparently remarkable powers of clairvoyance, told a reporter of the only actual ghost that she had seen. Early in 1937 she had moved with her maid into a flat in Charles Street, which is adjacent to Berkeley Square, having lived previously in the Highlands of Scotland.

'It was about the time of New Year,' she recalled, 'and I had come in late when my maid summoned me to the kitchen at the back of the flat. We could see into the back windows of a house diagonally opposite and in one of them stood a man in a silver-coloured coat and breeches of eighteenth-century cut, wearing a periwig and with a drawn, pale face. He was looking out sadly, not moving. I thought perhaps that he had been to some New Year party in fancy dress, and either had a hangover or some personal trouble, I rebuked the girl for staring at him so. It was only afterwards that I discovered that the house was number fifty. Believe it or not, I had not until that time heard of the reputation of the house.'

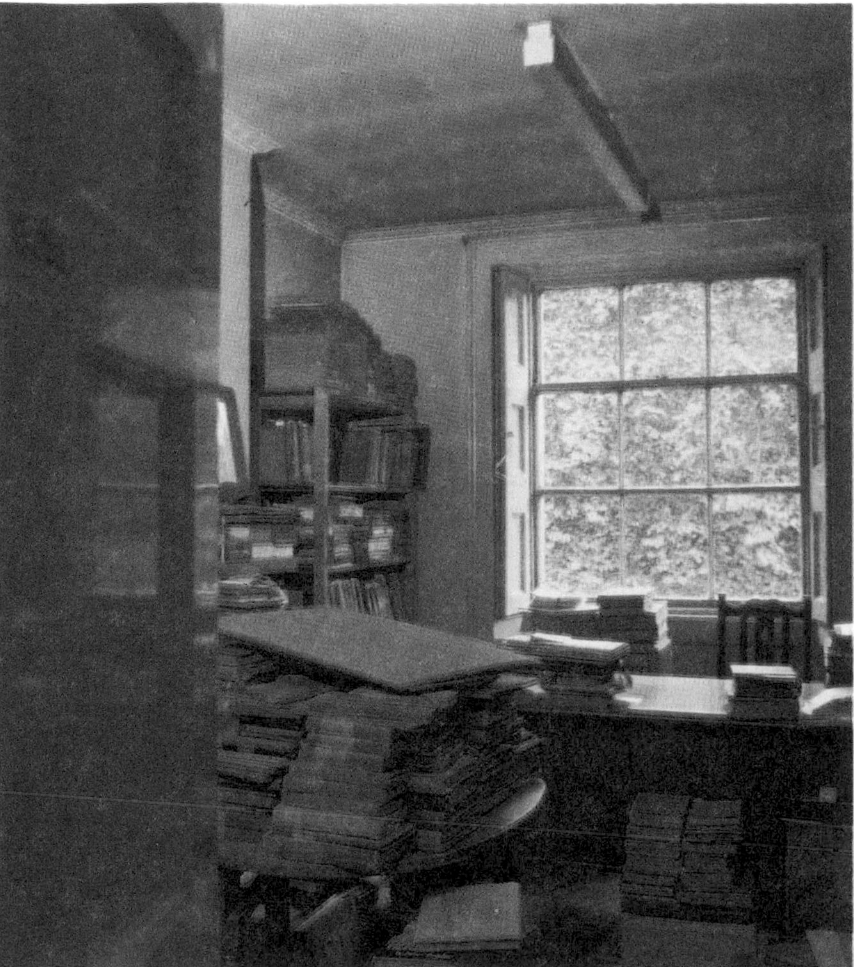

Above: reputedly the seat of all the disturbances – the haunted room at No 50, now quiet and tranquil as part of a modern office

Left: George Canning, sometime Prime Minister, who owned – but apparently did not return to haunt – the house in Berkeley Square

If Mrs Balfour had not, many people had, and stories about No 50 Berkeley Square continue to circulate even today. In the early years of the Second World War the house was taken over by antiquarian book sellers Maggs Brothers Ltd. According to a spokesman, in late 1981 they were still getting three or four calls a month from tourists seeking the ghosts: 'Unfortunately we can tell them nothing. The so-called "haunted room" is next to the accounts department; none of us has ever seen, or heard, or felt anything out of the ordinary there. During the war members of the staff used the room as a dormitory while firewatching without any discomfort apart from draughts. I can only regretfully suppose that the ghost was exorcised long before our arrival.'

The ghost and the gossips

The couple who took up lodgings at the home of Richard Parsons seemed ordinary enough. But with their arrival came a series of events that left Parsons fearing for his sanity – and his life

THE 18TH CENTURY, dubbed by the Victorians 'The Age of Reason', was in fact extravagantly credulous. In spite of – or perhaps because of – the influence of rationalists such as Rousseau and Voltaire, the great ruck of citizens, from high courtiers to low commoners, were obsessed with the supernatural, the unnatural and the downright bizarre.

Sir Isaac Newton, discoverer of gravity, President of the Royal Society and Master of the Royal Mint, spent the last quarter of a century before his death in 1727 in the study of alchemy. Ben Franklin, the writer John Wilkes and the satirical poet Charles Churchill donned monks' robes and cavorted at Sir Francis Dashwood's Hell Fire Club on the Thames, acting only half in jest. Nathanael St André, George I's resident anatomist, ruined his reputation by backing the claim of a woman named Mary Tofts, who swore that she had given birth to a litter of rabbits. And an oak tree in an inn yard near Winchester that groaned out prophecies attracted queues of stately carriages until a speaking tube was discovered leading from its trunk to the landlord's quarters.

More seriously, an 18-year-old servant girl named Elizabeth Canning disappeared for a month in 1753 and then reappeared to claim that she had been held captive in a brothel at Enfield, about 10 miles (15 kilometres) from her home in the City of London. She named her captive as Mother Wells, the 'madam', and her gypsy servant Mary Squires. They had, said Elizabeth, left her in a darkened room with only a loaf of dry bread and a jug of water for sustenance. Nevertheless 'angelic' intervention had kept her alive and fit enough to break out, at the end of the month, and walk home.

Despite the oddity of the story, the great Bow Street magistrate and novelist Henry Fielding believed it and sent Wells and Squires for trial at the Old Bailey. Wells was condemned to death, and Squires to branding and six months' hard labour. Fortunately, the Lord Major of London, Sir Crisp Gascoyne, had sufficient sense of the ridiculous to check the story further; he discovered incontrovertible evidence that the two accused had not been near Enfield at the time,

In the 18th century, it seems there were no limits to the extent of human credulity. For example, the claim made by Mary Tofts that she had given birth to a litter of rabbits (below) was apparently readily accepted by at least one eminent physician. And, in 1749, crowds of the curious crammed a London theatre to witness for themselves the amazing powers of the mysterious 'bottle conjurer', who – it was promised – would disappear into a wine bottle on stage and sing from inside it. He would also 'play' a common walking stick, reproducing the sound of any instrument then in use, and for an extra gratuity would raise the spirit of any historical character. The 'bottle conjurer' did indeed disappear, but before the performance – and along with the considerable box office takings

and they were released and pardoned – though not before pretty Mary Squires had been scarred with the branding iron.

The Canning affair had much in common with one of the greatest talking points of the century, the business of 'Scratching Fanny' – the ghost of Cock Lane. In both cases the credulous clamour of the mob put lives and reputations at stake on the flimsiest of evidence while eminent men looked on. Both cases promoted songs, poems, theatrical burlesques and controversy. But the hindsight of over two centuries and the light of modern psychical research suggest that something paranormal could have happened at Cock Lane, and that 18th-century mass hysteria may for once have clouded a real and striking case of poltergeist activity in the classic mould.

Cock Lane is a short, curving thoroughfare in the City of London on the fringes of Smithfield. In the mid 18th century it was a slightly run down, though respectable, area containing private houses, a tavern called the Wheat Sheaf, tradesmen's shops and a charity school. At what is now No 20 lived Richard Parsons, who drew a stipend as officiating clerk at the nearby church of St Sepulchre, Snow Hill, and had a wife and two young daughters, the eldest, Elizabeth, being about 11 years old when the Cock Lane mystery began.

Top: the modern Cock Lane, in the City of London. Situated on the outskirts of Smithfield (above), the street became the subject of gossip and scandal in the mid 18th century, for one of the houses was said to be haunted – by the ghost of a woman who seemed to be seeking revenge for her own untimely death

Today, Parsons would probably be considered a scandal to the church, for he was a heavy drinker with a tendency to run into debt, particularly with his accommodating friend James Franzen, landlord of the Wheat Sheaf. In 1759, however, his drinking habits were no better and no worse than those of many another minor cleric, and he kept himself solvent by taking in lodgers.

In October of that year, Parsons met a genteel looking couple who introduced themselves as Mr and Mrs William Kent, newly up from Norfolk and looking for lodgings until their house in Clerkenwell was ready for them. Parsons was happy to take them in, particularly because William Kent, after paying his rent in advance, lent Parsons 12 guineas, to be paid back at a guinea a month.

Soon landlord and lodger were on sufficiently friendly terms for William to let Parsons in on his secret: he and his 'wife' Frances, known as Fanny, were not married. Two years previously, William had kept an inn and a post office at the village of Stoke Ferry, Norfolk, and had married Elizabeth Lynes, the daughter of a well-to-do grocer. Unfortunately, Elizabeth was not strong and had a difficult pregnancy, during which her sister Fanny moved in with the Kents to look after her. Elizabeth died in childbirth, and her offspring died a month later. After going through this double tragedy together, William and Fanny had grown very close, but the law at the time forbade marriage between bereaved brothers- and sisters-in-law, so the pair had decided to live in sin. Coming up to London in the summer of 1759 they decided to prove their mutual love and trust by making wills in each other's favour. Fanny had the advantage here, for though, according to later testimony, she had 'a bare hundred pounds', William had 'a considerable fortune'. Apart from half a crown to each of her two brothers and four surviving sisters, Fanny left everything 'she had or might expect' to William 'at his absolute disposal'.

A disturbed relationship

The first intimation that something was odd about the house in Cock Lane came that autumn. Kent was out of town on business, and Fanny's maid, Esther Carlisle, a redhead nicknamed 'Carrots', had been given leave. Fanny was nervous about sleeping alone and asked Richard Parsons's elder daughter Elizabeth to share her four poster bed. During the few nights the pair slept together, both were awakened by a rapping noise, seemingly coming from the wainscot of the bedroom. Elizabeth asked her mother about the noise, and was told that it was probably made by the shoemaker next door, who was in the habit of working late. When the noise began on a Sunday night, however, the family became seriously alarmed, for the cobbler was absent; Parsons, the two women and Elizabeth all heard it.

The noise 'like knuckles rapping' went on night after night, and as the comfort of the household was disturbed, so was the relationship between William Kent and Richard Parsons. Parsons had failed to keep his agreement to repay a guinea a month to his lodger, and Kent, who by now was ready to move into his own house in Clerkenwell, put the matter into the hands of his attorney. The drunken Parsons rather spitefully reacted by broadcasting the news about the Kents' marital status, or lack of it, to all and sundry.

In January the Kents moved to Clerkenwell, but the pleasure of setting up home together was marred by the fact that Fanny,

The house in Cock Lane, home of the Parsons family, where every night strange rappings could be heard, apparently coming from the wooden panelling in one of the rooms. Despite investigation, no natural explanation of the sounds could be found – and Richard Parsons, the head of the household, began to fear that some supernatural agency was at work

six months pregnant, had become seriously ill. William hired a doctor and an apothecary to attend to her, and the doctor diagnosed 'a confluent smallpox of a very virulent nature'.

To the sanctimonious Parsons, Fanny's illness had been sent to 'punish her for her sins'. The knocking on his wainscot had not abated, and he was beginning to form a theory about that too: it was made by the ghost of Fanny's dead sister Elizabeth. His suspicions seemed confirmed when both he and James Franzen had a frightening experience towards the end of January.

Franzen had called at the house to see Parsons and, finding him out, had sat for a while with Mrs Parsons and her two daughters. The persistent knocking frightened him, however, and he got up to leave. As he reached the kitchen door 'he saw pass by him something in white, seemingly in a sheet, which shot by him and up stairs.' The vision gave off a radiance strong enough to illuminate the face of the clock in the charity school across the street.

Franzen, thoroughly alarmed, ran back to fortify himself with brandy at the Wheat Sheaf and had no sooner lifted the glass when he heard a thunderous knocking on his front door. When he had steeled himself to open it he found Parsons, white-faced and stammering on the doorstep.

'Give me the largest glass of brandy that you have,' demanded the cleric. 'Oh Franzen! As I was going into my house just now I saw the ghost.'

'And so did I!' replied the landlord. 'And have been greatly frightened ever since. Bless me! What can be the meaning of it? It is very unaccountable.'

Meanwhile there was alarm of a different kind in Clerkenwell, for Fanny Kent was dying. An acquaintance of William's, the Reverend Stephen Aldrich of St John's, Clerkenwell, and the doctor and apothecary sat with her night and day. In the last 50 hours of her life she could take nothing but a little liquid, prepared by the apothecary and administered by the doctor. On the evening of 2 February 1760, Fanny died.

William Kent was distraught with grief and ordered a decent coffin 'both lined and covered' but for fear of prosecution he asked the undertaker not to put a name plate on the lid; the risk was minimal, but nevertheless it was an offence to live together falsely as man and wife. Fanny was laid to rest in the 12th-century vaults of St John's, as her family fumed over the provisions in her will.

The rappings at Cock Lane continued; indeed, two new lodgers there, Catherine Friend and Joyce Weatheral, later testified that they had left the house rather than suffer them further. Frustrated and frightened, Parsons called in a carpenter, Bateman Griffiths, to strip away the wainscot to seek the cause of the trouble; nothing was found and the panelling was replaced. Then Parsons called in the Reverend John Moore, rector of St Bartholomew the Great, West Smithfield, to investigate the supernatural possibilities.

Poltergeist on trial

When investigators were called in to examine the 'ghost' of Cock Lane, they devised a test to establish once and for all who or what lay behind it. The revelations pointed to murder

Shops and taverns in the Cock Lane area did a roaring trade as a result of the activity at Richard Parsons's home, which daily drew crowds of sightseers to the street. Only the Parsons family, it seems, failed to profit from the phenomena

RICHARD PARSONS was becoming seriously alarmed by the mysterious noises at his home in Cock Lane. The strange rappings had continued for several months and no natural explanation could be found for them. Then, almost at his wits' end, Parsons asked the Reverend John Moore to investigate, to see if some paranormal agency were the cause.

Moore was a follower of John Wesley, who was himself no stranger to the supernatural. In 1715 Wesley's family home had been troubled by a 'knocking spirit', and his father, the Reverend Samuel Wesley, had 'communicated' with it by knocking back. Moore, told of Parsons's theories as to the origin of the phenomena – he now believed that the ghost of the newly dead Fanny Kent was responsible – began holding seances, using one knock for yes, and two for no, in order to find out the 'spirit's' wishes. The Wesley ghost had centred itself upon Hetty Wesley, John's younger sister, and the Cock Lane ghost now orientated itself upon the person of 11-year-old Elizabeth Parsons.

Moore's most productive sessions were held in Elizabeth's bedroom, after the girl had been put to bed. Sometimes the knocks came from the floorboards, sometimes from the bedstead or the walls. On the rare occasions when the 'spirit' appeared to be pleased, it made a noise like the fluttering of wings; when displeased it made a noise like 'a cat's claws scratching over a cane chair' – and it became known as 'Scratching Fanny'.

A demand for justice

Its message was brutally blunt. It was the ghost of Fanny Kent, murdered by William, who had poisoned her purl – a concoction of bitter herbs in ale popularly used as a restorative – about two hours before she died. Fanny wanted justice.

William Kent, slowly recovering from his bereavement, had set himself up as a stockbroker and busied himself in the City, and it was not until almost a year after Fanny's death, in January 1761, that he heard of the continuing saga of Cock Lane through a series of articles in the *Public Ledger* news sheet. Terrified by the 'ghost's' accusations – which were now, of course, public knowledge – he called on the Reverend Moore. Moore was impressed by Kent's manner and bearing, but assured him that 'there were very strange noises of knockings and scratchings every night, and that there was something behind darker than all the rest.'

As a result of their meeting, Kent went to Cock Lane to sit in on a seance himself. To his horror the knocks accused him personally of having killed Fanny with arsenic, and when he asked, at Moore's instigation, whether he would be hanged, the answer was a single knock.

'Thou art a lying spirit,' he shouted. 'Thou art not the ghost of my Fanny. She would never have said any such thing.'

By this time the ghost of 'Scratching

Fanny' had become a matter of enormous public interest, and crowds on foot and in carriages flocked to watch the comings and goings at the house. Horace Walpole wrote: 'Provisions are sent in like forage, and all the taverns and ale houses in the neighbourhood make fortunes.' To the credit of the Parsons family, however, none of them seems to have made any money from the phenomena.

As the year went on, so the seances continued. On one occasion, one of the sitters, William Legge, Earl of Dartmouth and himself a Methodist, decided to have Elizabeth Parsons moved to the house of a gentleman named Bray, just to see what would happen. The knockings accompanied her, seeming to show that she, and not the actual Cock Lane premises, was the catalyst. But the girl was watched closely, women attendants holding her hands and feet to rule out fraud, and still the noises went on.

The proceedings had taken on the atmosphere of a kangaroo court, with the doctor and apothecary who had attended Fanny Kent in her last illness denying that Kent could have poisoned her – she had drunk only their preparation in the 50 hours before her death – and the knocking contradicting them. The maid servant 'Carrots' Carlisle was implicated also, and indignantly shouted at the 'spirit': 'Then I am sure, Madam, you may be ashamed of yourself, for I never hurt you in my life.'

Elizabeth Parsons herself had begun to have epileptic fits. She claimed to have actually seen the ghost, 'in a shroud and without hands', but claimed that the only aspect of the matter that frightened her was 'what would become of her Daddy . . . if their matter should be supposed to be an imposture.'

William Kent was naturally anxious to clear up the matter; Moore, convinced that the ghost was telling the truth, was also eager for the authorities to act, but the only person in the City of London with the power to order a full investigation was the Lord Mayor, Sir Samuel Fludyer. He 'did not choose to stir much, for it was somewhat like Canning's affair', which had caused a great for his predecessor (see page 50), and he refused to order the arrest of either Kent – for suspected murder – or Parsons – for fraud. Instead, he insisted that an independent investigation should be held at the house of the Reverend Stephen Aldrich, vicar of St John's, Clerkenwell.

Above: Dr Samuel Johnson (left) with Oliver Goldsmith (centre). Johnson was one of the 'Committee of Gentlemen' formed by the vicar of St John's, Clerkenwell, and William Legge, Earl of Dartmouth (below), to investigate the Cock Lane affair and William Kent's role in it. The committee's findings – that no supernatural agency was involved – led to the publication of a pamphlet, generally believed to be the work of Oliver Goldsmith, which argued forcefully that Kent was innocent of all charges against him

Aldrich, to make sure that the investigation would be impartial, formed a committee with Lord Dartmouth. They chose Dr John Douglas, an amateur investigator who had exposed a number of frauds, Mrs Oakes, a hospital matron, Dr George Macaulay, a society physician, two or three gentlemen and Dr Samuel Johnson.

Johnson had long been fascinated by ghosts. The idea of total oblivion after death horrified him. He summed up his attitude to his biographer James Boswell: '. . . still it is undecided whether or not there has ever been an instance of the spirit of any person appearing after death. All argument is against it; but all belief is for it.'

But he undertook to assist in the investigation of 'Scratching Fanny' for a typically humanitarian reason. If the affair was a fraud, it was seriously damaging the reputation of William Kent, who seemed an honest and decent man.

The 'Committee of Gentlemen', as the newspapers termed it, decided on a new course of action. They arranged to test Elizabeth Parsons at Aldrich's house, and then, leaving her behind, they would descend to the vault of St John's, where the ghost would knock on Fanny Kent's coffin to 'prove' its objective existence. A preliminary seance was held, and the ghost agreed to these conditions.

The test begins

On the evening of 1 February 1762, Elizabeth was put to bed at Aldrich's house, attended by the matron, Mrs Oakes, and other women. According to Dr Johnson's report, the child said that she could feel the spirit 'like a mouse upon her back [but] no evidence of any preternatural power was exhibited'.

The committee then made its way to St John's, entered the vault, and called upon the spirit to keep its promise by knocking on the coffin. 'But nothing more than silence ensued. . . . It is therefore the opinion of the whole assembly that the child has some art of making or counterfeiting particular noises, and that there is no agency of a higher cause.'

One or two more seances followed, but the affair was nearing its end. On 3 February, a large gathering saw a curtain rod spin violently of its own volition, and heard a knocking of such violence, high up in the chimney, 'that they thought it would have broke it all to pieces'. Finally, Elizabeth was told that she had only one more night, 21 February, to prove her innocence, 'otherwise she and her

Above: St John's Church, Clerkenwell, where Fanny Kent was laid to rest in 1760. Although the investigating committee had, by implication, exonerated William Kent from the charge of Fanny's murder, the case was not closed. When the coffin was opened 90 years later, the corpse was found to be perfectly preserved – which, to modern forensic scientists, would suggest death by arsenic poisoning. So, was Fanny Kent murdered? And, if so, by whom? And why?

Left: John Wesley, whose family also experienced a 'knocking spirit', which centred on Wesley's younger sister – just as that at Cock Lane focused on 11-year-old Elizabeth Parsons. In the 18th century such disturbances were believed to be evil in nature; today they are recognised as classic symptoms of poltergeist activity

father and mother would all be sent to Newgate.'

This final session was held at the house of a gentleman named Missiter in Covent Garden and this time, perhaps not unexpectedly, there were positive results. The child was seen creeping from her bed to pick up a piece of wood with which she subsequently made knocking sounds. But Missiter and his companions agreed that this blatant piece of fraud produced sounds nothing like the ones heard previously: Elizabeth was, naturally, terrified for her freedom.

The tide had turned in Kent's favour. On 5 March a pamphlet entitled 'The mystery revealed', usually attributed to Oliver Goldsmith, put the case for his innocence with force. Later, Charles Churchill published a long poem, *The ghost*, which laughed at the affair – particularly Dr Johnson's part in it – and David Garrick turned the saga of 'Scratching Fanny' to good use by making it the centrepiece of a comic recitation, 'The Farmer's Return', at Drury Lane theatre.

On 9 February a new knocking ghost was advertised as 'likely to perform' in Broad Court, Covent Garden. The magistrate at nearby Bow Street was John Fielding, the half brother of Henry Fielding, and he sent the 'ghost' his compliments 'with an intimation that it would not meet with the lenity the Cock Lane spirit did, but that it should knock hemp in Bridewell. On which the ghost, very discreetly, omitted the intended exhibition.'

On 10 July, the 'conspirators' were brought for trial at the Court of King's Bench, Guildhall, before Lord Mansfield. The charge was that the Reverend John Moore, Richard Parsons, Mrs Parsons and others had conspired to 'take away the life of William Kent by charging him with the murder of Frances Lynes by giving her poison whereof she died'. James Franzen the landlord, 'Carrots' the servant, the doctor and the apothecary all gave evidence, while several people spoke up for Parsons.

After a trial lasting a day, the accused were found guilty. The Rev. Moore was heavily fined, Parsons was sentenced to two years' imprisonment and three sessions in the pillory, and his wife to one year's jail. Elizabeth Parsons did not stand trial, but was not, apparently, troubled by her 'ghost' again.

Even after leaving prison, Parsons protested his innocence, and his protests have a convincing ring to them. He had gained nothing from the Cock Lane affair but notoriety and punishment. He had had differences with Kent, it was true, but he was, drunkenness apart, a well-liked man of previous good character, with no wish to put another's life at stake. Furthermore hundreds of people – the Duke of York, Horace Walpole, and Lord Hertford included – had heard the knockings from the wainscot, a good distance from Elizabeth's bed.

A twist in the tale

And the manifestations themselves, centring on a young, prepubescent girl who had epileptic tendencies, closely echo modern cases held by parapsychologists to be 'genuine'. Perhaps the 'interpretation' of the Cock Lane rappings was the only fault of Parsons and Moore.

Or perhaps the 'ghost' had a point after all. The coffins were cleared from the vaults of St John's Church in 1860, but 10 years previously an illustrator, J. W. Archer, had visited them to produce illustrations for a book by Charles Mackay entitled *Memoirs of extraordinary popular delusions*, which featured the Cock Lane ghost. By the light of a lantern, the sexton's boy who accompanied Archer had opened the coffin said to be that of 'Scratching Fanny' and shown him the body within. The face was that of a once handsome woman, with a pronounced aquiline nose: 'an uncommon case,' wrote Archer, 'for the cartilage mostly gives way. The remains had become adipocere, and were perfectly preserved.'

There was no sign, as far as he could see, of the smallpox from which Fanny was said to have died. But the preservation of the features – the nose in particular – would unfailingly set a modern forensic scientist looking for traces of arsenic poisoning.

Burning with guilt

Left: Frendraught House, the family seat of the powerful Crichton clan for many years. Because of the tragedy that took place there in the 17th century, it is said to be haunted – and the wife of the present owner is one of the witnesses to the haunting

When a major feud between two great Scottish clans ended in a fire that killed several members of one faction, the local populace laid the blame on the lady of the manor. Today her guilt-ridden ghost still haunts the scene of the crime

ONE OF THE CLASSIC THEMES of supernatural lore is the unhappy ghost doomed to haunt the scene of its earthly wrongdoing until its sins are expiated. Is Frendraught House in Aberdeenshire just such a scene of a 'penitential' haunting? There are folklorists and witnesses who think that it is.

Frendraught House lies about 6 miles (9 kilometres) to the east of Huntly in the centre of the extensive Bognie estates. Its foundations date from 1203, though additions were made to it as recently as the 1840s. Its main bulk – containing inner walls up to 9 feet (2.7 metres) thick – was built between the 14th and 17th centuries when it was both home and fortress to the powerful Crichton family. During those three centuries the Crichtons, along with their cousins and neighbours the Gordons and Leslies, controlled the north-east of Scotland. They were often embroiled in bloody feuds.

In the spring of 1630 Frendraught was occupied by Sir James Crichton. He had made a good political marriage to Lady Elizabeth Gordon, eldest daughter of the Earl of Sutherland, and she took an active part in her husband's continual disputes. As one Victorian commentator put it, she played a role somewhere between that of Medusa and Lady Macbeth.

The 1630 dispute over boundary lands was between Sir James Crichton and Gordon, Laird of Rothiemay. Sir James settled it in typical fashion by shooting Gordon dead. The Marquis of Huntly, the local High Sheriff who was himself a Gordon closely related to both sides, fined Sir James heavily. This 'blood money' was paid to young John Gordon, the new Laird of Rothiemay, and honour seemed satisfied.

By midsummer, however, Sir James was fighting again, this time with Leslie of Pitcaple. Matters came to a head when a Crichton shot Leslie through the arm with an arrow. Again the Marquis of Huntly heard the case, this time ruling in favour of Sir James. The wounded Leslie rode off in a fury, openly swearing revenge on the house of Crichton. Sir James therefore took the precaution of assembling an armed party to escort him back to Frendraught. Surprisingly, it included young John Gordon of Rothiemay as well as the Marquis of Huntly's son, John Melgum Viscount Aboyne. The party arrived in the dusk of an October afternoon. Lady Crichton, perhaps relieved to see her husband home safe, pressed even the unloved Gordon kin to stay the night. The guests were put in the old tower.

Lord Melgum was given a room separated

Below: the scene of a modern-day haunting – part of the original old tower staircase at Frendraught. At the time of the fire, the rest of the tower staircases were wooden – and, burning fiercely, cut off the doomed guests

Right and below: Sir James and Lady Elizabeth Crichton. Their guests, among them some clan rivals, met death by fire at Frendraught House. Lady Crichton was known to be a strong support to Sir James in his many feuds, which may be why people thought her guilty of causing the fire

Below right: the Marquis of Huntly, the local High Sheriff, was closely involved in the events at Frendraught House – and not just as an official. His son, Lord Melgum, was one of those who burned to death in the old tower while trying to help the others

from the upper storeys by a wooden staircase. John Gordon of Rothiemay was on the second floor, and the other guests and servants above him. Spalding, a contemporary chronicler, tells what happened: 'About midnight that dolorous tower took fire in so sudden and furious a manner, and in ane clap, that the noble Viscount, the Laird of Rothiemay, English Will, Colonel Ivat and others, servants, were cruelly burned and tormented to death.'

Lord Melgum, it is said, ran to help the others, but the wooden stair caught fire and he was trapped with them. According to Spalding: 'They hurried to the window looking out into the close, piteously calling for help, but none was or could be rendered them.' Altogether about a dozen people lost their lives.

Death by design

An event of this magnitude cast shadows far beyond north-east Scotland, and the Privy Council in Edinburgh became involved, setting up a commission of bishops and neutral peers to investigate. The commission sat at Frendraught on 13 April 1631. The bishops merely declared that 'the fire could not have happened accidentally but designedly.' There the mystery of the fire rests, unsolved to this day. However, local opinion of the time laid the blame squarely on Lady Frendraught. An anonymous ballad written a few months after the event said of Rothiemay's final moments:

When he stood at the wire window
Most doleful to be seen
He did espy the Lady Frendraught
Who stood upon the green.
And mercy, mercy Lady Frendraught
Will ye not sink with sin
For first your husband kilt my father
And now ye burn his son.
Oh, then it spake Lady Frendraught
And loudly did she cry
It was great pity for good Lord John
But none for Rothiemay
But the keys are sunk in the deep draw well
Ye cannot get away.

To the Marquis of Huntly there was only one way to avenge his dead son. Laying aside his High Sheriff's impartiality, he recruited a small army of highlanders and raided Frendraught, carrying off 60 cattle and several dozen sheep.

Crichton appealed to Edinburgh, and the Privy Council came down in his favour. Huntly was fined and Sir James received damages.

Despite their vindication by the Privy Council, both Sir James and his Lady seemed changed by the terrible fire. Three years afterwards he gave a silver chalice, said to have been one of 11 brought north by Mary Queen of Scots, to the nearby kirk at Forgue. Today the chalice, the oldest known

piece of hallmarked silver in Scotland, lies in a bank vault in Huntly.

Lady Frendraught took her three daughters and went to live as a recluse at Kinnairdy on the River Deveron. Born a Catholic, she was excommunicated when she signed the Solemn League and Covenant supporting Presbyterianism. Turning back to her old faith, she was rebuffed. 'I refused absolutely to see her,' wrote Father Blackhall, 'because

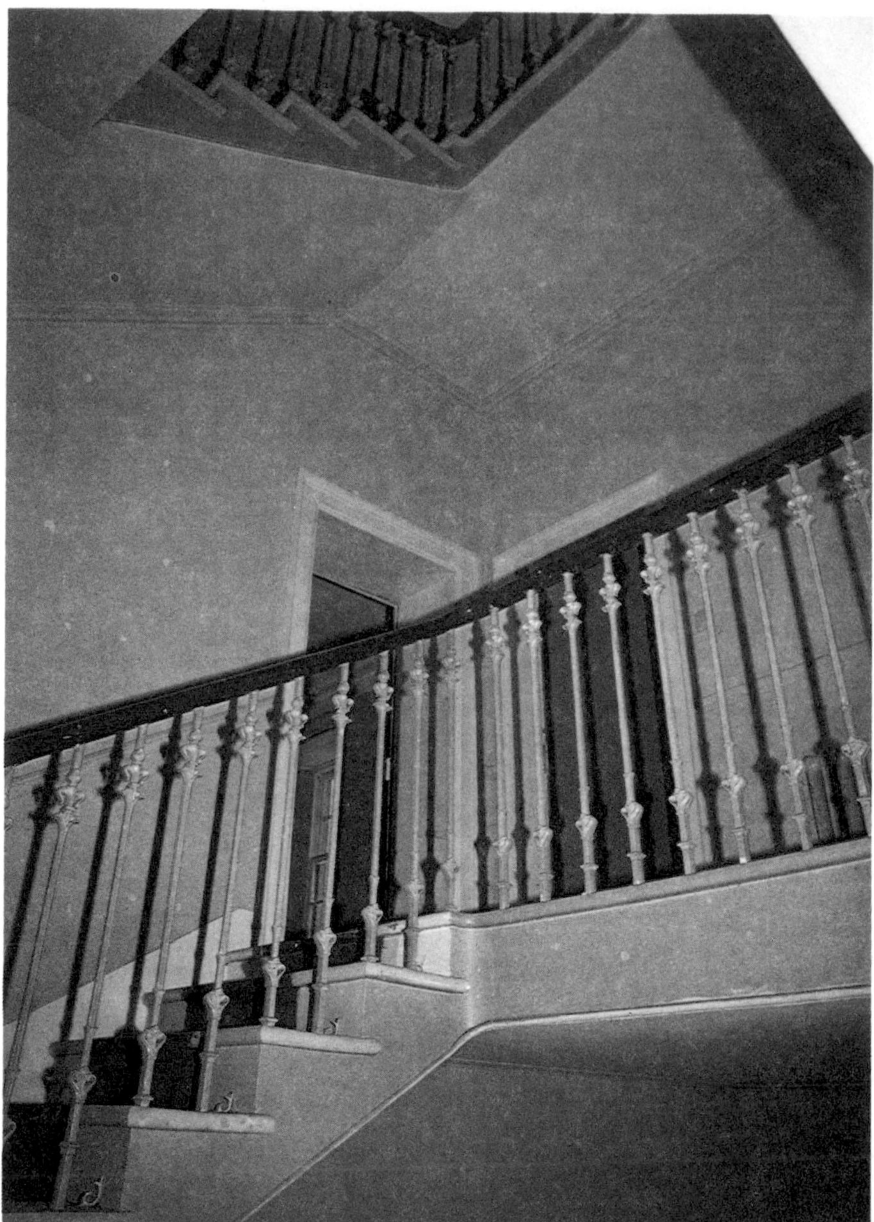

she was suspected to be guilty of the death of my Lord Aboyne. . . .' When she died, it was without benefit of clergy, on an unrecorded date. She was buried, like her husband, in an unmarked grave.

Sir James's eldest son was the last of his line. He was created Viscount Frendraught by his cousin Charles I for services rendered during the Civil War. After his death, his widow married George Morison of that Ilk, Chief of the Morison Clan and Laird of Bognie. His descendant, Alexander Gordon Morison, became Laird of Bognie and Mountblairy and owner of Frendraught House in 1942. He was born in Canada and inherited the chieftainship and family estates from his uncle. Immediately after the Second World War he and his young family lived at Frendraught House, but later moved to Mountblairy – not, he insists, for fear of ghosts, but for practical reasons. After several years of being leased, Frendraught House now stands empty.

'According to local opinion and the direct testimony of tenants, guests, and my wife,' says Mr Morison, 'Frendraught is haunted by Lady Elizabeth Crichton, who is bound there because of her guilt. I have never felt or seen anything myself, but according to legend the Laird never does anyway.' Mr Morison believes in Lady Crichton's guilt. He cites documents showing that, when the 'deep draw well' in the courtyard was cleaned out during alterations in the 1840s, massive keys were found. This supports the allegations of the old ballad.

The recorded sightings of a 'dark woman in a white dress' at Frendraught go back at least to the early 18th century when a Victorian clergyman-writer claimed that she was seen both in the house and among the great beeches around it. The first modern sighting on record occurred in 1938 when the house stood empty and locked. The late William Thomas, former manager of Glendronough Distillery on the borders of the Bognie estate, was in his early teens at the time. One autumn afternoon he was out shooting crows behind the house. Looking up, he saw a pale face surrounded by dark hair, watching him from a window overlooking the courtyard. He called a keeper who also saw the 'intruder'. Armed with their shotguns, the two broke in through a kitchen door and searched the house from top to bottom. There was nobody there, and no sign of forcible entry but their own.

Nearly 10 years later, Mrs Yvonne Morison encountered the ghost.

> It was 28 October. I remember the date because my husband had gone away with the Canadian Army reserve the day before. I was completely alone in the kitchens in the basement – the oldest part. Suddenly in the silence I heard footsteps coming down the staircase from the top of the house. I was

Opposite: the main staircase at Frendraught House. The ghost of Lady Frendraught in a white-and-gold dress has been seen here and on the back stairs, as well as in the grounds of the estate

Opposite below: the silver chalice presented to Forgue Kirk by Sir James three years after the fire. It is said to have been brought to Scotland by Mary Queen of Scots and is the oldest piece of hallmarked silver in the country. Did Sir James give it to the church to ease a guilty conscience?

> terrified, but something made me go to the bottom of the stairs where they eventually entered the kitchen. I peered up into the darkness and remember thinking very strongly – I may even have spoken aloud – 'Well, come on then. If you exist, show yourself.' Perhaps fortunately, the footfalls stopped at the top of the kitchen stairs, and I saw and heard nothing else.

The footsteps were too heavy and clear to be made by mice, she said, and rats had never been seen in the building. 'I knew all the "natural" creaks and groans of the old place. It was none of these.'

Above and left: the present owners of Frendraught House, Yvonne and Alexander Gordon Morison. The Morisons lived at Frendraught for a time after the Second World War, having inherited it in 1942. Mrs Morison had a personal encounter with the ghost of Lady Crichton – as did guests and later tenants

Twice the Morisons had guests who cut short their visits because of mysterious disturbances. On both occasions the guests were level-headed people. One was an old army colleague who had been in the thick of the fighting with Mr Morison during the Italian campaign. In both cases their stories matched in every detail, though they had never met. Mrs Morison explained:

> It was quite funny at first. They were a bit embarrassed and it became clear that they thought my husband and I had had a furious fight during the night. When we pointed out that the wall between our bedroom and theirs was 8 feet [2.4 metres] thick and totally soundproof, they became alarmed. They said that they had heard the most dreadful cries for help, with the sound of crashing, like heavy furniture being thrown about, and screams. They had been too terrified to investigate.

Curse of the chalice

Several guests and subsequent tenants at Frendraught had described seeing a dark lady in a white dress edged and decorated in gold. She was usually standing or walking on the main staircase or the back stairs.

Mr Cryle Shand, genealogist, lawyer, and tenant of Yonder Bognie Farm, has an open mind on the subject of the ghost, but feels that Lady Crichton was more to be pitied than blamed. According to his own theory, she may have been impelled to whatever action she took by a curse – the curse of the chalice that Sir James gave to Forgue Kirk three years after the fire.

> From my research I am almost certain that the cup was one of those brought north by Mary Queen of Scots in the middle of the 16th century: although it is hallmarked 1663 its base is typically pre-Reformation. The Bible says that 'he that eateth and drinketh unworthily, eateth and drinketh damnation unto himself.' Although the Crichtons were nominally a Catholic family, they were a fairly ungodly lot. I believe that Sir James used the sacred chalice for profane purposes – probably for drinking his dram out of – and that the troubles of his family and that of the Gordons who were so closely related to them were brought about by that Biblical damnation. That is why Crichton so piously repented and gave the cup back to the church. That is why it is treated with such respect by the elders of Forgue Kirk to this day. And that is why Dr Arthur Johnson, an 18th-century Scottish Latinist, describes Frendraught as *Tristis et infelix et semper inhospita turris* ('O sad and unhappy and ever inhospitable tower').

There are skulls that create supernatural disturbances because they want to stay in a favourite place. Can such tales be true? This chapter looks at the strange behaviour of the screaming skulls that won't stay buried

The skulls that screamed

IN THE QUIET VILLAGE CHURCHYARD of Chilton Cantelo in Somerset, England, picturesque in both name and setting, a lichen-covered tombstone dated 1670 marks the last resting place of one Theophilius Broome – or at least the resting place of most of him. For over 300 years his skull, polished like old ivory, has lain in a cupboard at his former home, Chilton Cantelo Manor. This fulfils a deathbed wish that his head should remain in residence. Not unnaturally, his heirs were uneasy about the idea. But they quickly discovered that attempts to bury the skull with the rest of the body only created problems for everyone.

According to the inscription on Theophilius's tombstone, 'horrid noises, portentive of sad displeasure' were heard throughout the village when attempts were made to rebury his head. These ceased only when the bony relic was disinterred and once more returned to its comfortable cupboard.

Right: the polished skull of Theophilius Broome in its permanent resting place at Chilton Cantelo Manor in Somerset. The skull made 'horrid noises' when anyone tried to bury it

Another skull, kept at Wardley Hall near Manchester, is said to be that of a Roman Catholic priest executed for treason in 1641. After being displayed on the tower of a Manchester church, it was recovered by a Catholic family and taken to Wardley. Like its Somerset equivalent, it made noises when removed from the premises. More, it was said to have caused violent thunderstorms. Besides all that, it refused to remain buried. In the chilling words of ghost hunter Eric Maple, it 'always managed to find its own way back [to the house] again'.

Burton Agnes Hall, a beautifully restored Elizabethan mansion in Humberside, contains the skull of Anne Griffith. She was the daughter of Sir Henry Griffith, who built the residence in 1590. Like Theophilius Broome, Anne made the deathbed request that her head be cut off after she died and kept in the house, and the wish was granted. The skull, known locally as 'Owd Nance', was removed on several occasions. Each time it screamed horrifyingly until it was returned to the house. To prevent any further outbreak of such supernatural annoyances, 'Owd Nance' was bricked into the walls of the house itself in 1900 – and Burton Agnes has been mercifully tranquil ever since.

'Screaming skull' legends form a small but curious part of the British folklore tradition. One suggestion is that such stories have their roots in the Romano-British practice of making 'foundation sacrifices' – burying a human or animal victim in the foundations of a house to ensure luck and propitiate the gods. It was perhaps with some knowledge of such practices in mind that Anne Griffith and

Below: the screaming skull of Bettiscombe Manor in Dorset. As recently as the early 1900s, the skull is said to have taken revenge on someone who tossed it out of the house it loved. Family tradition has it that the relic is the head of a black slave

Theophilius Broome made their strange requests. Another theory suggests that the stories arose from the rumoured custom of walling up monks and nuns as punishment for breaches of their chastity vows, though in fact such 'executions' were probably rare indeed. A third source could be the Celts. They revered the head in their religion and often preserved severed heads as family treasures or offerings to the gods in sanctuaries. Celtic cult heads of stone have been found in many places in Britain. Whatever their origins, 'screaming skulls' show a uniform objection to being moved from their chosen niches.

One of these 'guardian' skulls has a modern history coming down to the present day. It resides in Bettiscombe Manor near Sherborne in Dorset. Bettiscombe, a fine building of mellow brick and white stone, dates principally from the early 17th century. Parts of it are much older, however, and the land on which it stands has been inhabited since prehistory. The house was built by the Pinney family, who still farm the rich countryside around. Michael Pinney, a noted archaeologist and historian, lives in the manor house itself. His son, Charlie, breeds shire horses for use in film and television work. Both the professional Pinney and his practical son treat their guardian skull with deep respect.

Above: Burton Agnes Hall in Humberside, home of the head of Anne Griffith after her death in the 17th century. The skull was bricked into the walls in 1900 to prevent its ever being touched again – because it screamed terribly when it was moved

Left: Wardley Hall near Manchester. Its resident skull, supposedly that of a Catholic priest, not only screamed but also caused wild thunderstorms when removed from the premises

The earliest written accounts of the skull date from the early 18th century, but the story itself starts in 1685. At that time Azariah Pinney, the squire of Bettiscombe, took part in the Monmouth rebellion. Being on the losing side, he was exiled to the West Indies. As it turned out, his family flourished there, and his grandson, John Frederick Pinney, was able to return to Dorset in style and move back onto the lands of his ancestors. With him came a black slave who became part of the household and was soon a familiar sight in the village. The Negro had been promised that, on his death, his body would be returned by his master to Africa, from where he had been taken by slavers as a child.

But Pinney died first. When the slave died shortly afterwards, no one kept the promise to him and his body was buried in the local churchyard near that of his master. It did not rest content and a mournful wailing seemed to emanate from the grave. Crop failure, cattle disease and storms accompanied the months of moaning. Finally the body was disinterred and the skull taken back to its adopted home in the manor house. There it has remained. In recent years it has nested in a shoe box in Michael Pinney's study, fulfilling the double role of family heirloom and harbinger of doom to any that remove it. According to Pinney:

> It is said to scream and cause agricultural disaster if taken out of the house, and also causes the death, within a year,

> of the person who commits the deed. A photographer once carried it as far as the open doorway to take pictures of it, but my wife snatched it back indoors again without anything untoward occurring.

Local lore has it that the last time the skull was 'interfered with', it took its vengeance just as the legend says it would. At the beginning of the 20th century, a tenant who had leased Bettiscombe prior to moving to Australia had a boisterous Christmas party at the manor. During the party he took the skull and hurled it into a horse pond that lay at the side of the house. The following morning the skull was found not in the pond but on the doorstep. How did it get there, when it had to go up a flight of stairs and across a paved patio? One theory, said Michael Pinney, was that

> it had been blown there by the wind, but it must have been a very strange and powerful wind. In the Thirties, however, I had an unannounced visit from three young Australians. One of them said that he was the son of the former tenant. His father had indeed died suddenly in Australia within a year of the incident, and his mother had always told him that the skull had brought a curse on them.

Kept like an animal

Until alterations were made to the attics of Bettiscombe after the Second World War, the guardian skull had traditionally been kept in a small attic room. The remains of this room can be seen today among the chimney stacks and thick oak rafters under the roof. There is an alternative tale to the black slave legend connected with the attic. This version says that a young girl had been kept prisoner there, bedded on straw like an animal and fed through a grille in the door. Although there is no historical evidence for this story, as there is for John Frederick and his slave, there is a strong family tradition that the skull's 'place' for many years was under the rafters. In the early 1960s, on the track of the Bettiscombe skull, Eric Maple interviewed an old farm worker who claimed to remember 'hearing the skull screaming like a trapped rat in the attic'. Other locals claimed that during thunderstorms there was a rattling sometimes heard in the upper rooms – a rattling made by 'them' playing ninepins with the ancient relic. Exactly who 'they' were was left to the imagination.

Other snippets of lore about the skull seem to have been added on over the years.

Above: skulls placed in the niches of a French Celtic sanctuary as offerings to the gods. Celtic cult heads have been found in many places in Britain and may be a source for the stories of skulls that scream

A grisly exhibit

Jeremy Bentham, philosopher and political theorist whose reforming zeal helped improve 19th-century life in Britain, shared with the screaming skulls a desire to remain in a favourite place after his death. And he went to elaborate lengths to do so.

Bentham arranged that, when he died, a surgeon friend was to embalm his head and place it upon his skeleton – after the body had been dissected for the teaching of medical students. The skeleton, according to the fun-loving sage's instructions, was dressed in the clothes he had liked best. It was then seated in a glass-fronted upright mahogany box. This was placed in University College,

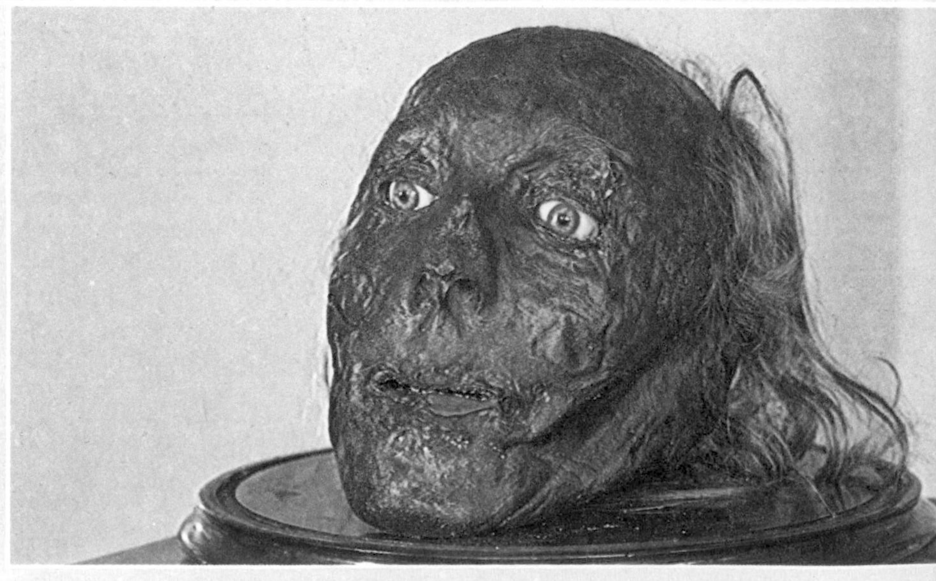

Michael Pinney and his wife were rather startled when a visitor asked if the skull had 'sweated blood in 1939 before the outbreak of the war, as it had in 1914'.

In fact, the 'screaming skull' of Bettiscombe Manor is probably not that of either the slave or the girl of the legend. In the 1950s, at Pinney's request, it was examined by Professor Gilbert Causey of the Royal College of Surgeons. He pronounced it to be much older than anyone had suspected. It was, he said, the skull of a prehistoric woman, a young girl with delicate features who died between 3000 and 4000 years ago.

So how did it come to be kept at Bettiscombe Manor, and why did such weird legends gather around it?

Death by the sword

There is some evidence of a Romano-British settlement on the site, which points back to the idea of a foundation sacrifice. But if Professor Causey's estimate is correct, the skull pre-dates any house that could have been in the settlement by several hundred years. An interesting parallel can be drawn with the screaming *ghosts* of Reculver in Kent. For many years a legend had persisted that screams and cries heard in woodland around this site of an early Roman settlement were made by the ghosts of children who had been murdered there. In 1964 important archaeological excavations were begun, during the course of which a number of children's skulls and bones were unearthed. One of these bore marks indicating that it had died by the sword. The pathetic skeletons were rather older than the Roman site, some dating from between 1000 and 500 BC.

Pinney himself has come up with a plausible if unusual explanation of the skull's arrival at Bettiscombe Manor: it made its own way there.

Behind the manor, the steep slopes of wooded Pilsdon Pen stretch up far beyond the house's tall chimneys. The tor shows signs of prehistoric fortifications dating from about the same period as Maiden Castle, the great earthworks fortress that lies some miles away to the south-east. Besides containing the remnants of hut circles, the tor is also studded with small burial mounds and cairns. Pinney has excavated some of them through professional interest as an archaeologist. Down from the hilltop trickles a clear stream that travels in an ancient culvert through an outhouse attached to the Bettiscombe kitchens. As Pinney explains:

> I can't prove it, of course, but I rather suspect that the skull was worked loose from the soil at the top of the hill, tumbled into the stream and rolled down the sloping bed of the brook and down into the outhouse here. Such a find would have been traumatic to say the least in a superstitious age. The finder may well have tried to get rid of it, only to feel uneasy about the event – perhaps odd things did occur which convinced him that the skull wished to stay where it had landed. Then the stories began to grow as news of the skull's arrival spread.

The story of the skull at Bettiscombe might easily have reached the ears of old Theophilius Broome at Chilton Cantelo in the adjoining county of Somerset. Perhaps it influenced his decision to arrange that his own head should stay above ground. Whether or not the same idea came to Anne Griffith in what was then Yorkshire from the Bettiscombe tales is anyone's guess.

For their part, Michael Pinney and his family have prospered despite the bizarre relic in the shoe box. So far, however, he has refused to allow the family 'heirloom' to be taken outside the walls of the old manor. 'I'm not superstitious,' he explains with a smile, 'but why risk it?'

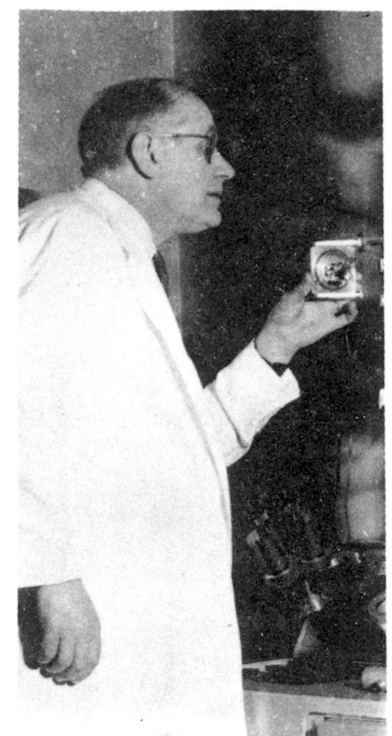

Top: Professor Gilbert Causey of the Royal College of Surgeons, who was called in to give an expert opinion on the Bettiscombe skull. He said it was that of a young prehistoric woman – a far cry from the slave of the traditional story

Above: the ruins of Reculver church in Kent, which is connected with local legends about children's ghosts that scream pitifully. Skulls dug up on the site proved to be from an earlier time than the stories indicated – suggesting that 'screaming skull' stories have their origins deep in ancient tradition

London, of which Bentham was a founder and constant supporter. It has remained on a landing of this building near the Gower Street entrance ever since Bentham's death in 1832.

A wax model has replaced the deteriorated head, but the figure still wears the genial philosopher's straw hat and holds his trusty walking stick. A number of witnesses have said that Bentham's ghost, tapping the stone flags with the cane, often walks the corridors near his curious coffin. According to Bill Grundy, the television producer who made a film of Bentham, the ghost 'seems to appear most in times of trouble' – during the 1940 blitz, for example. It is as though the philosopher had appointed himself the 'guardian of University College'.

A short history of hauntings

Above: Nathaniel Hawthorne (1804–1864), the American novelist and short-story writer. His account of the ghost of Dr Harris, which haunted the reading room of Boston's Athenaeum Library (left), is remarkable for its straightforward presentation of the facts

Ghosts seem to take many different forms, appear in the most unlikely places, and haunt all kinds of people. But what exactly are these apparitions? And what causes them? Frank Smyth searches for the answers and surveys some famous phantoms from the past

BEFORE HIS NOVEL *The scarlet letter* made him famous, the American novelist and short-story writer Nathaniel Hawthorne was an official at the Boston Customs House. At this time, in the 1830s, he went every day to the Athenaeum Library to research and write for a few hours. One of the other regulars there was the Reverend Doctor Harris, an octogenarian clergyman who for years had sat in 'his' chair by the fireplace, reading the *Boston Post*.

Hawthorne had never spoken to him, as conversation was strictly forbidden in the reading room, but Dr Harris was almost a fitment of the place, so that Hawthorne felt sure he would have missed him if Dr Harris had not been there. The novelist was, therefore, surprised one evening when a friend told him the old man had died some time previously. He was even more amazed when, the following day, he found the clergyman in his normal chair, reading the newspaper. For weeks Hawthorne continued to see Dr Harris, looking perfectly solid and lifelike.

One of the things that puzzled Hawthorne was the fact that many of the other regulars had been close friends of Dr Harris, though Hawthorne had not. So why did they not see him? Or *did* they see him, but suffer from the same reluctance as Hawthorne to acknowledge his 'presence'? Another factor that puzzled Hawthorne in retrospect was his own unwillingness to touch the figure, or perhaps snatch the newspaper from its hands: 'Perhaps I was loth to destroy the illusion, and to rob myself of so good a ghost story, which might have been explained in some very commonplace way.'

After a while the old gentleman appeared to be watching Hawthorne as if expecting him to 'fall into conversation'.

> But, if so, the ghost had shown the bad judgement common among the spiritual brotherhood, both as regarding the place of interview and the person whom he had selected as recipient of his communications. In the reading room of the Athenaeum, conversation is strictly forbidden, and I couldn't have addressed the apparition without

drawing the instant notice and indignant frowns of the slumberous old gentlemen around me. And what an absurd figure I would have made, solemnly . . . addressing what must have appeared in the eyes of all the rest of the company an empty chair.

'Besides,' concluded Hawthorne in a last appeal to the social proprieties, 'I had never been introduced to Dr Harris.' After some months, Hawthorne entered the Athenaeum to find the haunted chair empty, and he never saw Dr Harris again.

The only drawback to this story as a piece of psychical evidence is that it rests on the testimony of an author who wrote many short stories concerning the supernatural. Hawthorne was a friend of Edgar Allan Poe and Herman Melville, both of whom dealt with the realms of the unknown. On the other hand, he became interested in ghostly phenomena after moving into a house in Massachusetts reputed for years to be haunted. Of this place he wrote: 'I have often, while sitting in the parlour in the daytime, had a perception that somebody was passing the windows – but on looking towards them, nobody is there.'

First class evidence

In neither case – that of his house nor that of Dr Harris – does he appear to have tried to embellish the facts at all, and yet he is acknowledged as a great story writer, accustomed to giving his tales a beginning and a satisfactory end. As a ghost story of fiction, the Dr Harris tale is flat and relatively uninteresting; but as a piece of evidence for an apparition it is first class.

So what was it that Hawthorne saw? To many people the ready answer would be that he saw the earthbound spirit of Dr Harris, somehow trapped in the place that he had been accustomed to 'haunt' in life. Others would say that the ghost was a projection of Hawthorne's memory of the old man, echoing Hamlet's mother's comments on her son's visions: 'This is the very coinage of your brain.' More recently, psychical researchers would suggest that the apparently solid person by the fire was a sort of spiritual 'recording', left by the dead man on his environment, which was somehow received by Hawthorne's mind in much the same way as a television set receives a transmission.

One thing is certain: Nathaniel Hawthorne was far from being alone in seeing a 'ghost' – or what serious parapsychologists and psychical researchers prefer to term an 'apparition'. Since earliest times all civilisations have recorded 'ghosts' – some as a mere generality, a part of folklore, while others have produced specific instances. The difficulty, for the modern observer, is sifting the likely from the less likely instances.

About 500 years earlier, at the beginning of what are loosely known as the 'Dark Ages', a Benedictine monk named Brother John Goby took on a case of psychical research and recorded all the facts with commendable care. Again, although to modern eyes the incident seems bizarre enough at first to be dismissed out of hand, the Goby case was so rare for its time to be worthy of study.

Below: Edgar Allan Poe (1809–1849), master writer of the macabre short story. He was a friend of Nathaniel Hawthorne, and it is possible that he could have participated in the 'creation' of the ghost of Dr Harris at the Athenaeum Library

Below: 'Marley's ghost appears to Scrooge' from Dickens's *A Christmas carol*. Doomed to walk the earth to atone for his ill-spent life, 'Marley' warns that Scrooge too will be condemned unless he mends his ways

In December 1323, a merchant of Alais, in the south of France, died. His name was Guy de Torno, and within days of his death he was reputed to have returned to haunt his widow in the form of a 'spirit voice'. News of this persistent 'ghost' spread to the town of Avignon, 40 miles (65 kilometres) away, where Pope John XXII then had his residence. (This was during the Great Schism, when two popes, one in Avignon and one in Rome, vied for power.) Pope John was impressed, and appointed Brother John Goby, Prior of the Benedictine Abbey of Alais, to investigate.

Accompanied by three of his fellow Benedictines and about 100 of the town's most respected citizens, Brother John went to the widow's house on Christmas Day and began his investigations. First he examined the house and gardens for any hidden tricks or freak sound effects. Then he posted a guard around the premises to keep out sightseers. The focus of the ghostly manifestations was the bedroom. Goby asked the widow to lie on the bed, along with a 'worthy and elderly woman' while the four monks sat at each corner.

The monks then recited the Office for the Dead, and soon became aware of a sweeping sound in the air, like the brushing of a stiff

broom. The widow cried out in terror. Goby asked aloud if the noise was made by the dead man, and a thin voice answered: 'Yes, I am he.'

At this point some of the townspeople were admitted to the room as witnesses, and stood in a circle round the bed. The voice assured them that it was not an emissary of the Devil – the usual assumption in medieval times – but the earthbound ghost of Guy de Torno, condemned to haunt its old home because of the sins it had committed there. It said that it had every hope of getting to heaven once its period of purgatory was over. It also told Brother John that it knew he was carrying the Sacrament in a pyx – a silver box in which the Host is carried – concealed under his robes. This was a fact known only to Goby. The spirit added that its prime sin had been adultery, which carried the penalty of excommunication from the Sacrament in those days. The spirit then 'sighed and departed'.

Brother John wrote out his report and despatched it to the Pope at Avignon. The incident's abiding interest to psychical research lies in the objectivity with which the investigation was carried out. Of course it was not perfect and does leave a number of questions unanswered. The 'sweeping' noise and the 'sigh' might well have been a result of the Mistral, the mournful wind that blows across that part of France in the winter. The 'voice' itself may have been produced by ventriloquism on the part of the widow –

Above: Pope John XXII, who directed a Benedictine prior, Brother John Goby, to investigate the 'ghost of Alais' in 1323

Below: Prince Rupert leads his cavalry into the first major battle of the English Civil War at Edgehill in 1642. For months afterwards, people claimed to have seen a ghostly re-enactment of the battle; among those reported to have taken part was Prince Rupert himself – but he was still alive

consciously or unconsciously – particularly if she suspected her husband of infidelity and wanted to discredit his memory. Against this, however, has to be weighed the fact that, had she been discovered in such trickery, she stood a very real chance of being accused of witchcraft and suffering death at the stake.

Another impressive investigation, this time of a 'mass apparition', was conducted in 1644 by a number of level-headed army officers and remains an enigma: either they were all lying, or something untoward did indeed happen. On 23 October 1642, Royalist troops under Prince Rupert of the Rhine, nephew of King Charles I, and Parliamentarians under Robert Devereux, third Earl of Essex fought the first serious battle of the English Civil War at Edgehill, Warwickshire. After the indecisive clash the bodies of some 2000 men lay on the unseasonably frozen slopes of Edgehill.

A month after the battle, a number of local shepherds saw what they at first thought was another fight at the same spot: the thundering cavalry, rolling gunsmoke, flashing steel. And they also heard the neighing of horses, the screams of the wounded and the steady beat of drums. It was only when the whole tableau suddenly vanished that they took fright and ran to tell the authorities in the nearby town. On Christmas Eve the phantom battle was enacted again, and was so convincing that a London printer, Thomas Jackson, interviewed several witnesses and published an acount of the phenomenon in pamphlet form on 4 January 1643.

This was drawn to the attention of the King, who was so intrigued that despite his hard-pressed military position he appointed half a dozen army officers to investigate on his behalf. They were led by Colonel Sir Lewis Kirk, former governor of the garrison at Oxford, and a young cavalry captain named Dudley who had ridden at Edgehill.

On their return the officers brought detailed confirmation of the news. Not only had they interviewed the shepherds and recorded their accounts, but on two occasions they had seen the battle themselves, recognising not only a number of the men who had died on the field, but also Prince Rupert, who was still very much alive. Whether or not anyone took notice of it at the time, this last fact carried with it the intriguing suggestion that the phenomenon was a sort of action replay rather than haunting by revenant spirits.

Although Sir Lewis and his colleagues were justifiably startled, they drew no conclusions, merely reporting the facts of what they had seen. There was no obvious reason for them to lie: their evidence might have pleased the King or upset him. As it chanced he took the incident as a good omen – wrongly, as it turned out, for six years later he was beheaded.

The ghostly man in grey

A recent example of an apparition witnessed on innumerable occasions by literally dozens of people is that provided by the so-called 'man in grey' who is recorded as appearing at the Theatre Royal in Drury Lane, London, from the early 18th century until the late 1970s. The accounts are remarkably consistent, although the 'stagey' look of the ghost and the fact that it appears in a theatre has convinced more than one witness that they were seeing an actor dressed for a part.

The figure is that of a man of above average height with a strong, handsome face. He wears a three-cornered hat, powdered wig, long grey cloak, sword and riding boots, and emerges from a wall on the left hand side of the upper circle, walks around behind the seats, and vanishes into the opposite wall. He has never been known to speak or pay any attention to witnesses, and although he seems perfectly solid, if his way is barred by a living person he dissolves and then reappears on the other side of them.

The identity of the 'man in grey' has never been satisfactorily proven, but a possible clue turned up in the late 1840s, when workmen were making alterations to the wall from which he appears. In a bricked-up alcove they found the seated skeleton of a man, with a rusty dagger between his ribs. A few tattered remnants of cloth clung to the figure but crumbled to dust when touched. At the obligatory inquest it was suggested that the man may have been a victim of Christopher Ricks, the 'bad man of old Drury' who had managed the theatre in the time of Queen Anne and was notorious for his violence. Ricks made constant alterations to the theatre's structure, and could easily have disposed of a body without too much difficulty. However, there was no solid evidence, and after an open verdict was returned the body was given a pauper's funeral at a nearby graveyard.

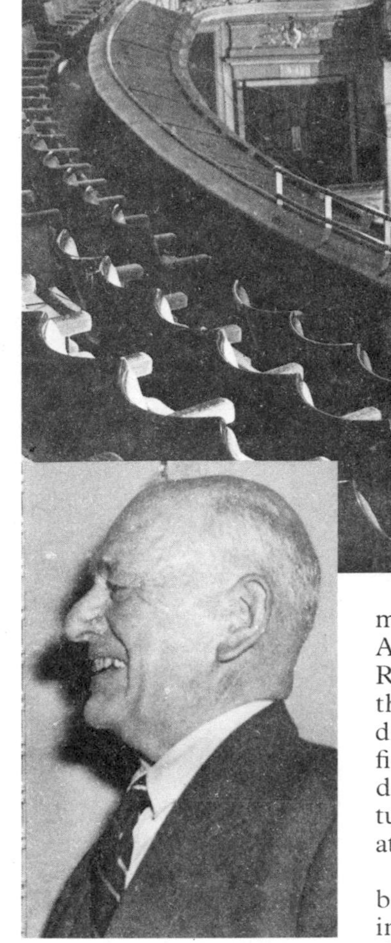

Top: this is not, as it may seem, final evidence for the existence of ghosts, but a carefully staged visitation photographed for the British Tourist Authority at London's Theatre Royal, Drury Lane. The ghostly apparition is the so-called 'man in grey', a spectre said to have haunted the theatre for over 200 years. Even in reality it obligingly appeared for the critic and historian W. J. McQueen Pope (above) when he was conducting sightseers round the theatre

However, the 'man in grey' continued to be seen throughout the Victorian era and on into the 20th century. W. J. McQueen Pope, theatre critic and historian, saw the ghost many times and made ardent but fruitless attempts to establish its identity. An interesting point was that the ghost appeared regularly in the period between the mid 1930s and Pope's death in 1960, while he was conducting sightseers around the Theatre Royal. On every occasion, the visitors saw the ghost too, many of them signing testimonials to this effect.

This fact raises a salient question in the minds of psychical researchers: did Pope serve as an unconscious catalyst for the apparition? We know that people differ in their ability both to perceive psychic phenomena and to project apparitions to others. If Pope was gifted in both respects, was the vision of his visitors somehow stimulated by him? Did he, in some way, summon up the 'man in grey'?

Certainly he did not invent the ghost, and its last recorded sighting, by an American who thought he was seeing an actor during an afternoon matinée, took place in 1977, 17 years after Pope's death. But it is certain that the spectre appeared most frequently during Pope's association with the Theatre Royal.

The Pope puzzle presents just one more baffling aspect of the complex phenomenon known to parapsychology as 'apparitions'..

Ghosts without souls?

If ghosts are spirits of the dead, as many believe, how can we account for the 'soulless' apparitions – such as those of animals, buses and other inanimate objects – that have been seen?

IN THE MIDDLE of the 1930s a large red London bus bearing a number 7 route number harassed motorists in the North Kensington area of London. The junction of St Mark's Road and Cambridge Gardens in that area had long been considered a dangerous corner – it was 'blind' from both roads – and had caused numerous accidents.

The decision of the local authority to straighten out the bend was partially influenced by the testimony of late night motorists, who claimed that they had crashed at the junction while swerving to avoid a speeding double decker bus that hurtled down St Mark's Road in the small hours, long after regular buses ceased service.

A typical report to the Kensington police read: 'I was turning the corner and saw a bus tearing towards me. The lights of the top and bottom decks and the headlights were full on but I could see no sign of crew or passengers. I yanked my steering wheel hard over, and mounted the pavement, scraping the roadside wall. The bus just vanished.'

After one fatal accident, during which a driver had swerved and hit the wall head on, an eyewitness told the coroner's inquest that he had seen the mystery bus hurtling towards the car seconds before the driver spun off the road. When the coroner expressed what was perhaps natural cynicism, dozens of local residents wrote to his office and to the local newspapers offering to testify that they had seen the 'ghost bus'. Among the most impressive of these witnesses was a local transport official who claimed that he had seen the vehicle draw up to the bus depot in the early hours of the morning, stand with engine purring for a moment, and then disappear.

Right: the tale of this phantom ship was reported by the American minister and author Dr Cotton Mather in his book *Wonders of the invisible world* (1702). The ship set sail from America but never reached its destination in England, and nothing was ever heard of it again. Some months later, however, spectators at the port from which it sailed saw what seemed to be the selfsame ship appear in a cloud; then it keeled over and simply disappeared

Below: the junction of St Mark's Road and Cambridge Gardens in Kensington, London, became renowned in the 1930s for the mysterious double decker bus that travelled at great speed in that area in the middle of the night – when no buses were in service

The mystery was never solved, but it is perhaps significant that the 'ghost' bus was not seen after the danger of the sharp corner was removed, and it was suggested that the vision was 'projected' onto the spot to dramatise the inherent danger of the intersection. If so, by whom? And if, as was also suggested, it was in the minds of the motorists themselves – a sort of natural projection of their fears at the corner – how did they manage to superimpose it on the vision of the passers-by, not to mention that of the bus depot official who saw it from an entirely different angle?

In fact, the phantom motor bus of Kensington epitomises a problem that for centuries has faced those who believe that ghosts

are revenant spirits. If a ghost is the 'soul' of a dead person returned to earth, how do we account for phantom buses – and of course their lineal ancestors phantom coaches, which feature so heavily in folklore?

Come to that, why do returning spirits not appear in the nude – for with very few reliably recorded exceptions, none do? As Lyall Watson succinctly puts it in his book *Supernature*: 'While I am prepared in principle to concede the possibility of an astral body, I cannot bring myself to believe in astral shoes and shirts and hats.'

'Ghostly' lore is strewn with stories of inanimate objects suddenly becoming apparent to the sense of observers, from the 'phantom' accordion accredited to Daniel Dunglas Home, the 19th-century Spiritualist, to Macbeth's dagger. In the latter case William Shakespeare, writing in an age steeped in superstition, seems to have been as aware of the anomaly of 'spirit objects' as he was of almost every other field of human experience: '. . . art thou, O fateful dagger, sensible to feeling as to sight, or art thou but a dagger of the mind, a false creation, proceeding from the heat oppressed brain?'

In his book *Supernature* Lyall Watson (below) suggests that the fact that ghosts appear as people remember them indicates that apparitions are part of a mental process rather than a supernatural one. Certainly most ghosts do appear fully clothed or are dressed in a shroudlike garment, as was the ghost that terrorised the residents of Hammersmith, London, in the early 1800s (bottom)

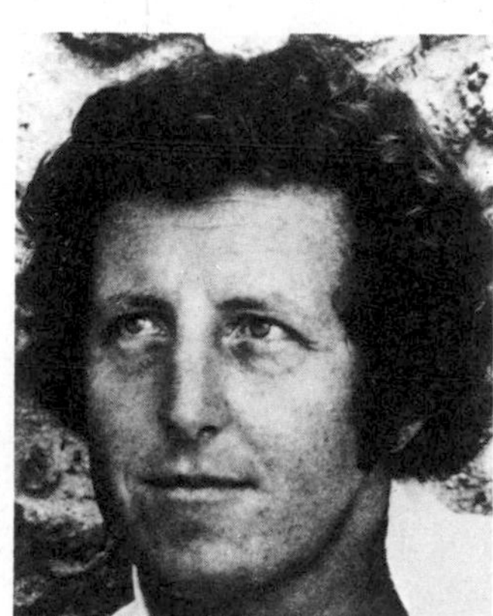

One of the most convincing stories of totally 'soulless' apparitions is recorded in the day book of the Tower of London – a place that according to popular belief is saturated with ghosts. The man who made the entry was Edmund Lenthal Swifte, who in 1814 was appointed Keeper of the Crown Jewels and continued in the office until 1842, a total of 28 years. The account of what he saw on a Sunday evening in October 1817 is best left to him.

> I was at supper with my wife, our little boy, and my wife's sister in the sitting room of the Jewel House, which is said to have been the 'doleful prison' of Anne Boleyn and of the ten bishops whom Oliver Cromwell piously accommodated there. The doors were all closed, heavy and dark curtains were let down over the windows, and the only light in the room was that of two candles on the table. I sat at the foot of the table, my son on my right, my wife fronting the chimney piece, and her sister on the opposite side. I had offered a glass of wine and water to my wife, when on putting it to her lips she paused, and exclaimed, 'Good God! what is that?'
>
> I looked up, and saw a cylindrical figure, like a glass tube, something about the thickness of my arm, and hovering between the ceiling and table; its contents appeared to be a dense fluid, white and pale azure . . . incessantly rolling and mingling within the cylinder. This lasted about two minutes, when it began to move before my sister-in-law, following the oblong shape of the table, before my son and myself. Passing behind my wife it paused for a moment over her right shoulder (observe there was no mirror opposite in which she could then behold it.) Instantly she crouched down, and with both hands covering her shoulder, shrieked out, 'Oh Christ! It has seized me!'
>
> Even now as I write I feel the horror of that moment. I caught up my chair striking at the 'appearance' with a blow that hit the wainscot behind her. It then crossed the upper end of the table and disappeared in the recess of the opposite window.

There was no recurrence of this curious manifestation, but some years later it did help Swifte's judgement of a soldier in the Tower who actually died from fright of what he had seen outside Swifte's 'front door'.

The soldier had been on sentry-go outside the Jewel House when, at around midnight, he had heard a guttural snarl behind him and turned to see a huge black bear, reared up on its hind legs, fangs bared, eyes red with rage, and talons groping towards him. The soldier rammed his bayonet into the belly of the animal, but the weapon passed clean through and the apparition disappeared.

A patrol found the soldier a few moments later, senseless. The bayonet, with a heavy 'Tower issue' musket attached, was embedded in the solid wood of the door. The soldier was taken, still insensible, to the guardroom, where a doctor pronounced that he was neither drunk nor asleep, and the following morning Swifte interviewed him; over and over the soldier repeated his bizarre tale until, three days later, he died.

For about 300 years, until the middle of the 17th century, the Tower housed a royal menagerie, and among the animals recorded as having been kept were a number of bears. Although no account of an autopsy on the soldier survives, the fact that he died three days after his experience could indicate that he was ill without knowing it, and that the apparition was an hallucination caused by his illness. On the other hand, animal ghosts make more sense as 'revenant spirits' than their human counterparts, for the reason already given; they at least 'appear' exactly as in life. The fact that Man has lost most of his 'primitive' instincts while animals retain theirs may also have an as-yet unexplained bearing on their 'paranormal' role.

A phantom pig

Stories of phantom dogs are common to the United States, Europe, and many parts of Africa. Ghostly horses, cattle, and even sheep have their part in folklore, and although, like all folk tales, the accounts of their appearances have undoubtedly become distorted in the telling over centuries, some are eerily convincing. In 1908 the British Society for Psychical Research (SPR) made exhaustive enquiries into the appearance of what appeared to be a phantom pig in the

Above: the Jewel House in the Tower of London where Edmund Swifte and his family were troubled by a cylindrical form filled with blue and white fluid

Below: phantom horses, complete with riders, are a common form of haunting, and are usually associated with a particular place. Possibly they are a kind of recording of a highly emotional or dramatic event, which is 'replayed' in certain circumstances

village of Hoe Benham, near Newbury, Berkshire.

On 2 November 1907, two young men named Oswald Pittman and Reginald Waud were painting in the garden of their house, Laburnum Villa. At 10 a.m. Pittman got up to speak to the milkman and saw his friend Miss Clarissa Miles coming up the lane; she was due to join the men for a painting session. Accompanying her like a pet dog was a large white pig with an unusually long snout. When Pittman told Waud about it, Waud asked him to tell Miss Miles to keep the animal outside and close the garden gate securely – Waud was a keen gardener and did not want it among his plants. However, when Miss Miles arrived she was alone, and denied all knowledge of the animal. If it had been following her, she pointed out, she would surely have heard it grunting and pattering. However, she and Pittman went back up the lane and asked several children if they had seen a pig that day; none of them had done so. The following morning the milkman, pressed by a bewildered Pittman, signed a statement to the effect that he had not seen a pig, and he pointed out that in any case the area was under a swine fever curfew, and any stray animal would be destroyed.

Pittman and Waud went to London for a few months and while there reported the odd incident to a member of the SPR. When they returned to Hoe Benham in February, however, the story of Pittman's apparition had become widespread, and shedding their natural reserve the villagers inundated them with stories of previous 'phantoms'. Local theory had it that they all stemmed from the suicide of a farmer named Tommy King whose farm, which was demolished in 1892, had bordered the lane. Investigation of the parish records showed there had been two Tommy Kings, one dying in 1741 and the other in 1753, but there was no indication of which one was the suicide. An old man named John Barrett testified that when he was a boy in 1850 he had been returning with seven or eight men in a hay cart along the lane when 'a white thing' appeared in the air. All the men had seen it, and the horses obviously had too, for they went wild.

'This thing kept a-bobbin' and a-bobbin' and the horses kept a-snortin' and a-snortin'' until the wagon reached the neighbourhood of King's Farm, when the shape vanished. In 1873, at the same spot, Barrett had seen a creature 'like a sheep' pawing the ground in the lane. He took a blow at it with his stick, but it disappeared before the stick landed.

Another man, Albert Thorne, said that in the autumn of 1904 he heard 'a noise like a whizzin' of leaves, and saw summat like a calf knuckled down' about 2½ feet (75 centimetres) high and 5 feet (1.5 metres) long, with glowing eyes. As he watched, it faded away. Yet another witness, unnamed, said that, in bright moonlight in January 1905, he had

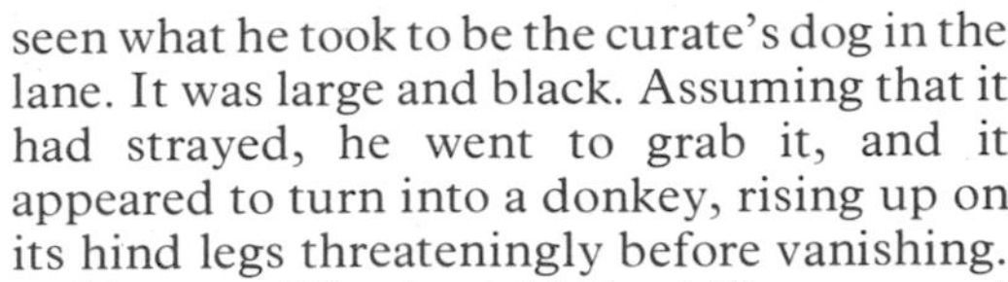

seen what he took to be the curate's dog in the lane. It was large and black. Assuming that it had strayed, he went to grab it, and it appeared to turn into a donkey, rising up on its hind legs threateningly before vanishing.

Pittman, Waud, and Miss Miles reported one more experience. While walking in the lane, Miss Miles was suddenly overcome by an irrational fear, and told her companions that she felt the presence of an evil being, charged with malice towards them. She also felt that she was suffocating. As they reached the spot where Pittman had seen the pig, all three heard an 'unearthly scream', although no one else was about. Waud, who had been sceptical from the beginning, was finally convinced that the ghostly animal existed by this cry from nowhere.

Animal investigators

The sensitivity of animals, particularly cats and dogs, to paranormal phenomena is almost a truism. Dr Robert Morris of Kentucky, a parapsychologist who used animals as 'controls' in his experiments in the 1960s, reported his investigation of a haunted house in one room of which a tragedy had occurred. He used a dog, cat, rat, and rattlesnake.

> The dog upon being taken about two or three feet [less than a metre] into the room immediately snarled at its owner and backed out of the door. No amount of cajoling could prevent the dog from struggling to get out and it refused to re-enter. The cat was brought into the room carried in its owner's arms. When the cat got a similar distance into the room, it immediately leaped upon the owner's shoulders, dug in, then leaped to the ground, orienting itself towards a chair. It spent several minutes hissing and spitting and staring at the unoccupied chair in a corner of the room until it was finally removed . . .
>
> [The rattlesnake] immediately assumed an attack posture focusing on the same chair that had been of interest to the cat. After a couple of minutes it slowly moved its head toward a window, then moved back and then receded into its alert posture about five minutes later . . .

The rat was the only creature not to react at all, but all four animals were tested in a separate room some time later, and there behaved normally.

In the misty world of apparitions, no one, not even the most dedicated psychical researcher, knows quite what is the motivation behind them. What we do know is that they are not confined to human beings; the 'ghosts' of both animals and inanimate objects have been lucidly recorded over the years, even including the 'soul' of a London Transport bus.

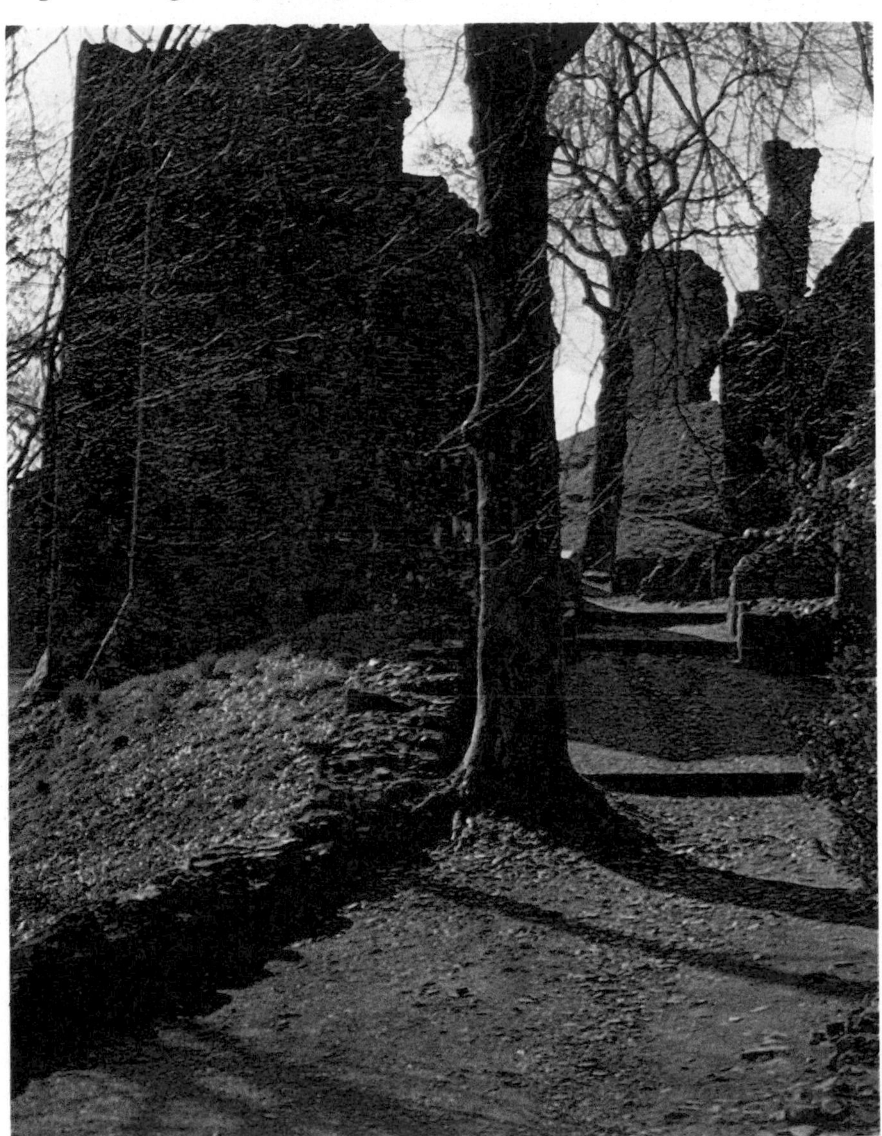

Okehampton Castle in Devon, England. A 17th-century phantom coach, constructed of the bones of the four husbands of the 'Wicked Lady Howard' – all of whom she is said to have murdered – travels the road that runs across the moor from Tavistock to Okehampton. The ashen, sheeted spectre of Lady Howard rides inside the coach and a skeleton hound runs before it. According to legend, each night the hound must pick a blade of grass from Okehampton Park to take back to Lady Howard's family home at Tavistock – a penance that must be endured until every blade of grass is picked

Understanding ghosts

The troubled spirits of the dead, phantom animals, spectral coaches – all these have been called 'ghosts'. But are they all the same? We can learn a great deal from what hauntings have in common – and how they differ

THE PERENNIAL QUESTION as to whether ghosts exist must, in view of various surveys carried out by such bodies as the British Society for Psychical Research (SPR) over the last 100 years or so, be answered in the affirmative. To reject the testimony of the many hundreds of respectable people who claim to have experienced apparitions as wishful thinking, self-delusion or downright lying would be sheer wilfulness.

The question facing modern parapsychologists and psychophysical researchers is: *how* do ghosts exist? Are they revenant spirits? Are they the result of telepathy? Are they produced by mass hallucination or self-hypnosis? Advances in psychology over the last few decades have brought us nearer to understanding some aspects of apparitions, but the definitive truth still eludes us.

The most common form of 'ghost' appears to be the 'crisis apparition', which occurs when a person under great stress – sometimes on the point of death – appears to someone close to them as a 'vision' or, occasionally, as a disembodied voice.

The majority of crisis apparition cases have tragic overtones. For instance, soldiers have appeared to their mothers or wives at the exact time of their own deaths on far-away battlefields. But not all do so.

Victoria Branden, in her book *Understanding ghosts*, quotes the case of a friend who was evacuated from England to Canada during the Second World War because of a health problem, leaving her husband behind in the Services. One evening, the children were busy with their homework, while their mother was ironing in what she admitted to Mrs Branden was 'a rather dreamlike state'.

Suddenly she saw the door of the room open, and her uniformed husband came in. Before she could recover from her astonishment, he vanished. She put down the iron and sat, near to fainting, in a chair. The children clustered around her anxiously and when she told them what had happened they said that they had not seen anything and the door certainly had not opened. The mother and the elder child had, however, read of crisis apparitions and became convinced that the vision meant that the husband had been killed or injured. They made a note of the time and circumstances, but agonisingly, that was all they could do.

Some days later, to what must have been their enormous relief, news came: the husband had been unexpectedly chosen to go on a training programme to Canada, at a camp very near to his family. This meant, of course, that he could live with them while abroad. When the couple were finally re-united the husband said that the news had come as a happy shock. He could not remember consciously 'projecting' any thought to his wife, but they worked out that he had probably opened his commanding officer's door after hearing the news at about the same time as the wife had 'seen' her door open.

An interesting point about this incident is that the wife was 'rather dreamlike' at the time, with her mind in an open and receptive state. The children, who saw nothing, were concentrating hard on their homework.

Exactly how telepathic information is communicated remains a mystery, particularly so in the case where an apparition

This photograph of the library at Combermere Abbey in Cheshire was taken on 5 December 1891 by Sybell Corbet, who had been staying at the house. When she developed the plate, she was startled to see the shape of an elderly gentleman sitting in a chair on the left of the picture. The figure was later identified as that of Lord Combermere himself: but at the time the photograph was taken, he was being buried a few miles away appears solid and living. However, scientists point out that perception is a much more complex business than at first appears: vivid dreams, for instance, often appear perfectly solid and physical, and in such cases the percipient is not receiving information through his eyes. A hypnotist may tell a subject that when he or she awakes only the hypnotist will be in the room – even though other people may be present. When the subject comes around he will not see the others present until the hypnotist removes the suggestion. Something like this may happen in cases of telepathy, although it seems remarkable that the agent – or person 'sending' the hallucination – can achieve at a distance, and in many cases while he is unconscious, what the hypnotist can only manage by giving specific instructions.

Evidence points to the fact that the agent's mind plays a smaller part in crisis apparitions than does that of the percipient. If we look at recorded cases it becomes apparent that the agent rarely appears as he is at the moment of 'transmission' – the percipient does not see a mangled body in a motor car, or a dying wounded soldier in a trench, but what appears to be a normal image of the agent that, moreover, relates to the percipient's surroundings.

This point is stressed by G. N. M. Tyrrell in his book *Apparitions*. He points out that apparitions in crisis cases have been guilty of such unghostlike phenomena as casting shadows or appearing reflected in a mirror.

> [They] adapt themselves almost miraculously to the physical conditions of the percipient's surroundings, of which the agent as a rule can know little or nothing. These facts reveal the apparition to be a piece of stage machinery which the percipient must have a large hand in creating and some of the details for which he must supply – that is to say, an apparition cannot be merely a direct expression of the agent's *idea*; it must be a drama worked out with that idea as its *motif*.

But telepathy can only partly explain cases of collective apparitions, where a group of people witness the same thing. And it is hard to see how it could play any part in the case of, for instance, the phantom London Transport bus (see page 68) for by definition the telepathic agent must be a sentient being. One of the most famous cases of a collective apparition was reported to the SPR in the late 19th century by Charles Lett, the son-in-law of a Captain Towns of Sydney. One day at about 9 p.m. some six weeks after the Captain's death, his daughter, Mrs Lett, and a Miss Berthon entered a bedroom at his home. The gas light was burning:

> And they were amazed to see, reflected in the polished surface of the wardrobe, the image of Captain Towns. It was . . . like an ordinary medallion portrait, but life-size. The face appeared wan and pale . . . and he wore a kind of grey flannel jacket, in which he had been accustomed to sleep. Surprised and half alarmed at what they saw, their first idea was that a portrait had been hung in the room and that what they saw was its reflection – but there was no picture of the kind. Whilst they were looking and wondering, my wife's sister, Miss Towns, came into the room and before any of the others had time to speak she exclaimed: 'Good gracious! Do you see Papa!'

Below: cases of crisis apparitions are most common in times of war, when a mother may see her son at the moment of his death on a battlefield. It seems that the shock of death causes some kind of telepathic communication between son and mother. But rarely does the mother have a vision of a dying soldier; in most cases she sees her son as he appeared in normal, everyday life

Left: when Mr Bootman, a bank manager pursuing his hobby of photographing church architecture, took this picture at Eastry, Kent, in 1956, his wife and a cleaning woman were the only other people present. But the ghostly form of a vicar somehow appeared on the film. Some years later Mr Bootman showed the photograph to a Women's Institute group and was told that a similar phantom had been seen in the same church in the 1940s. This may well be an example of what is called a 'place-centred' ghost: the vicar's strong attachment to the church could have led to a 'record' of his image being imprinted upon it

One of the housemaids passing by was called into the room. Immediately she cried: 'Oh miss! The Master!' The captain's own servant, the butler, and the nurse were also called in and immediately recognised him. Finally Mrs Towns was sent for and, seeing the apparition, she advanced towards it with her arm extended as if to touch it, and as she passed her hand over the panel of the wardrobe the figure gradually faded away, and never again appeared.

Those parapsychologists who lean to the telepathic origin of all apparitions would probably say that the vision was seen first by either Mrs Letts or Miss Berthon, who then passed it on by thought transference to each arrival. But the question remains: where did the vision come from in the first place?

One of the early SPR pioneers, F. W. H. Myers, author of the book *Human personality and its survival of bodily death*, suggested that it was the revenant spirit or 'essence' of Captain Towns taking a last look at his old home six weeks after death. Myers said that an apparition 'may be a manifestation of persistent personal energy' and quoted several cases to illustrate his point.

In one a travelling salesman, Mr F.G., arrived at a hotel in Boston, Massachusetts,

The ghost that grew and grew

One of the main problems facing the objective psychical researcher is that of sheer human gullibility. People like a good ghost story and tend to embellish the narrative, so that after a few re-tellings the stark facts of the case become wrapped up in a cocoon of invention.

In the summer of 1970 the author of this series, Frank Smyth, who was at that time an associate editor of the magazine *Man, Myth and Magic*, tried an experiment to examine the form taken by this gullibility. He *invented* a ghost, complete with location, background and 'witnesses' and published the story in the magazine.

The invention was completely random. One Sunday morning Smyth had gone down to London's dockland to meet John Philby, son of super-spy 'Kim' Philby. Philby's building company was renovating a site at Ratcliffe Wharf, and Smyth decided that the deserted dock was sufficiently eerie to provide a location for his ghost. Hard by Ratcliffe Wharf is the semi-derelict church of St Anne, and this, plus the fact that it was a Sunday morning, decided Smyth to make his 'ghost' that of a clergyman. Alongside the wharf runs Ratcliffe Highway, once – at least until the late 19th century – a thoroughfare of brothels, grog shops, and cheap boarding houses. The proximity of this old road suggested to Smyth that his vicar had been the owner of a sailor's rooming house, and that he had robbed 'homeward-bounders' (seamen newly paid off from ships in the Thames), had killed them in their lodgings, and disposed of their bodies in the river. Thus the background was set up.

Philby, himself a former war correspondent, and Smyth then decided that witnesses were important. They and one of Philby's employees lent their names to the fiction that they had seen the ghost – the figure of an old white haired man with a walking stick. They also agreed that if anyone, either researcher or interested enquirer, asked about the 'phenomenon' they would immediately confess that it was invented.

Smyth then wrote the story as a 'factual' article in *Man, Myth and Magic*. No one ever queried the credentials of the 'Phantom Vicar of Ratcliffe Wharf' but over the next twelve months or so eight books purporting to tell the stories of genuine ghosts appeared, each featuring the phantom vicar. Only one, by a London *Sunday Times* feature writer, treated the subject with some scepticism; the others not only recounted the tale without comment but one, by a well-known writer on the supernatural, actually embellished it.

In 1973 Smyth wrote an article telling of his experiment for the *Sunday Times*, and subsequently appeared in a BBC-2 film produced from Bristol entitled *A leap in the dark*. This film, too, told the story of the invention, but it also featured a number of people who claimed actually to have *seen* the phantom vicar. One man said that he had witnessed an old man in 18th-century clerical garb walking in the roadway outside the 'Town of Ramsgate' pub, near St Katherine's Dock – a good half mile from Ratcliffe Wharf. The writer Jilly Cooper told of interviewing a police superintendent who, on retirement from the River Branch of the Metropolitan force, had said that as a young man he had been unwilling to enter Ratcliffe Wharf for fear of the ghostly priest. A Thames waterman claimed that he had seen the shadowy form of the vicar standing on Ratcliffe Wharf some months before the story appeared in the magazine. After the television programme many other letters were sent to the BBC's Bristol office, most of them apparently sincere, telling of sightings.

There is absolutely no foundation for the Ratcliffe Wharf story. Nowhere in the record of Wapping – or indeed any other part of London's dockland – does there feature any tale of a ghostly cleric. One psychical researcher suggested that Smyth's ghost may have existed, and somehow made itself felt to him. The fact is that apparently reasonable people still claim to see the apparition in the area – despite its widespread refutation.

one afternoon and sat working in his room. He suddenly became aware of a presence and looked up to see his sister, who had died nine years previously. As he sprang delightedly to his feet and called her name she vanished, and yet he had time to take in every detail. 'She appeared as if alive,' he said, but added that there was a small red scratch on her right cheek.

Disturbed, Mr F.G. made an unscheduled stop at his parents' home and told them of his experience. When he mentioned the scratch, his mother was overcome with emotion, and said that she had made the scratch on the dead body of her daughter accidentally, as she was preparing it for burial. Two weeks later, the mother died.

Myers wrote that the figure was 'not the corpse with the dull mark on which the mother's regretful thoughts might dwell, but . . . the girl in health and happiness, with the symbolic *red* mark worn simply as a test of identity.' He suggested that the apparition was the spirit of the dead girl inducing her brother to go home and see their mother before she died.

Where an apparition persistently 'haunts' a place or a house – or sometimes even a person – believers in an afterlife assert that the spirit is trapped in its earthly environment, perhaps because of some unfulfilled task, or for the purpose of punishment. Unfortunately, unlike the ghosts of well-rounded fiction, these 'haunting' apparitions do not seem to make much sense in their actions; like Nathaniel Hawthorne's Dr Harris (see page 64), they carry on in a mundane fashion, either wandering about or simply staring out of windows.

By and large parapsychologists as a whole, however, tend to theorise that in certain cases a kind of psychic record may be imprinted on a location, perhaps because of some violence or strong emotion generated there. In these cases, the apparition would not be a sentient spirit, a 'mind', but merely a projection like a cinema film. This certainly seems to be the most likely explanation of, for instance, the Edgehill haunting (see page 64). It also ties in with the telepathy theories; if a person can send an image of himself telepathically to a percipient, may he not also be able to send a sort of 'free floating' image that hangs, as it were, in the atmosphere to be picked up by anyone sensitive enough to receive it?

Such a concept would also explain the occasionally convincing 'photographs' of apparitions; in such cases the photographic film may be more sensitive to the surroundings than its operator; conversely, where a photographer sees a ghost and his camera fails to do so, he may be hypersensitive.

If such phantom recordings are possible, it may be that they are not necessarily fixed for ever. Andrew Green, in his book *Ghost hunting*, quotes an interesting case of a woman in red shoes, red dress and a black head-dress reported to haunt a mansion in 18th-century England. In the early 19th century it was reported that the apparition was that of a lady in pink shoes, pink dress, and a grey head-dress. She was not witnessed again until the mid 19th century, when the figure had dwindled down to 'a lady in a white gown and with grey hair'. Just before the Second World War, all that was reported was 'the sound of a woman walking along the corridor and the swish of her dress'. In 1971, shortly before the demolition of the property involved, workmen felt 'a presence in one of the old corridors'.

All these explanations may account for the mysterious sightings of apparently solid, living beings where no such beings should be. Or perhaps none of them do. Modern scientific research – into, for instance, the baffling field of quantum physics – constantly produces new slants on old phenomena. Ghosts – whether human or non-human – may yet prove to belong to a sphere of reality so far undreamed of in our philosophy.

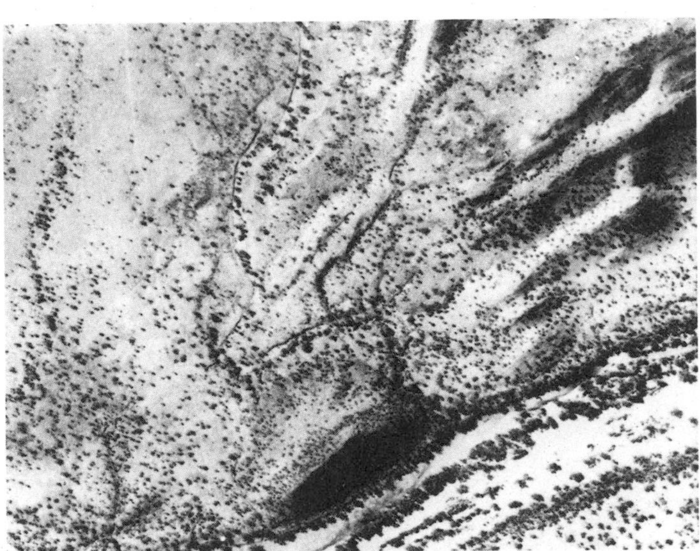

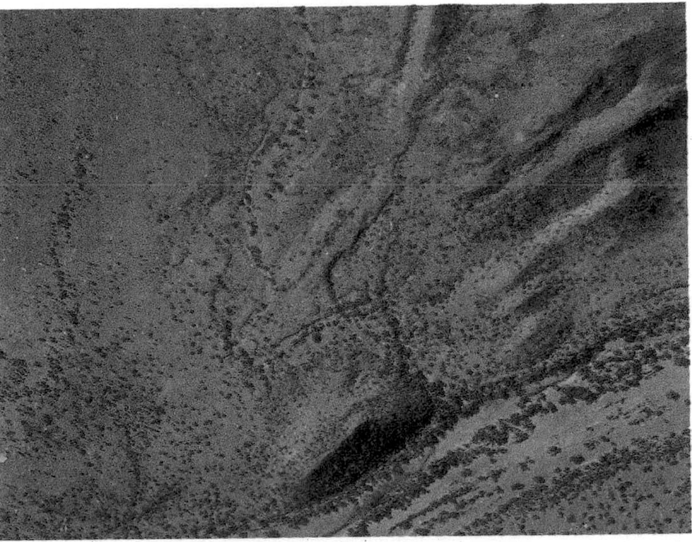

Ghost photographs often show images unseen by the human eye, as film is inherently more sensitive to certain light frequencies. The difference is rather like that between a picture shot with a standard film (left) and one taken with infra-red equipment (right). The infra-red photograph shows this tract of Australian desert more clearly and with much sharper detail, and provides information not otherwise available

In search of apparitions

No two ghosts are alike – and a good ghost hunter will approach each haunting differently. Serious researchers have developed special techniques for gathering and documenting the kind of evidence they seek

'FEAR CAME UPON ME, and trembling, which made all my bones to shake. Then a spirit passed before my face; the hair of my flesh stood up. It stood still, but I could not discern the form thereof.'

This is how the experience of seeing a ghost is described in the Book of Job 4: 14–16. The word 'ghost' comes from an ancient root meaning 'to be scared', and to many, including Job, encounters with ghosts have been literally hair-raising. Fortunately, some people, far from being frightened, are willing to seek out ghosts and actively investigate them.

The existence of ghosts has been accepted without question in almost all cultures throughout history. Only with the growth of the scientific outlook in the West in the last few centuries have their existence and nature been disputed. But serious attempts to find out what they are and to study their behaviour are surprisingly few. And many people still respond to the idea of ghosts with an irrational blend of fear, ridicule and laughter. We reject what we do not understand, rather than face the possibility that there are indeed more things in heaven and earth than are dreamed of, let alone taken seriously, by the scientific establishment.

Ghosts are even rejected by people who have seen them. 'I saw it, but I still don't believe it!' is a commonly reported reaction, for the human mind instinctively rejects information it cannot assimilate and interpret. Clearly, better evidence, and more of it, is needed before the ghost can find its way into the physics and biology textbooks.

What, to begin with, is a ghost? Dictionaries define it as the supposed disembodied spirit, or soul, of a dead person. This

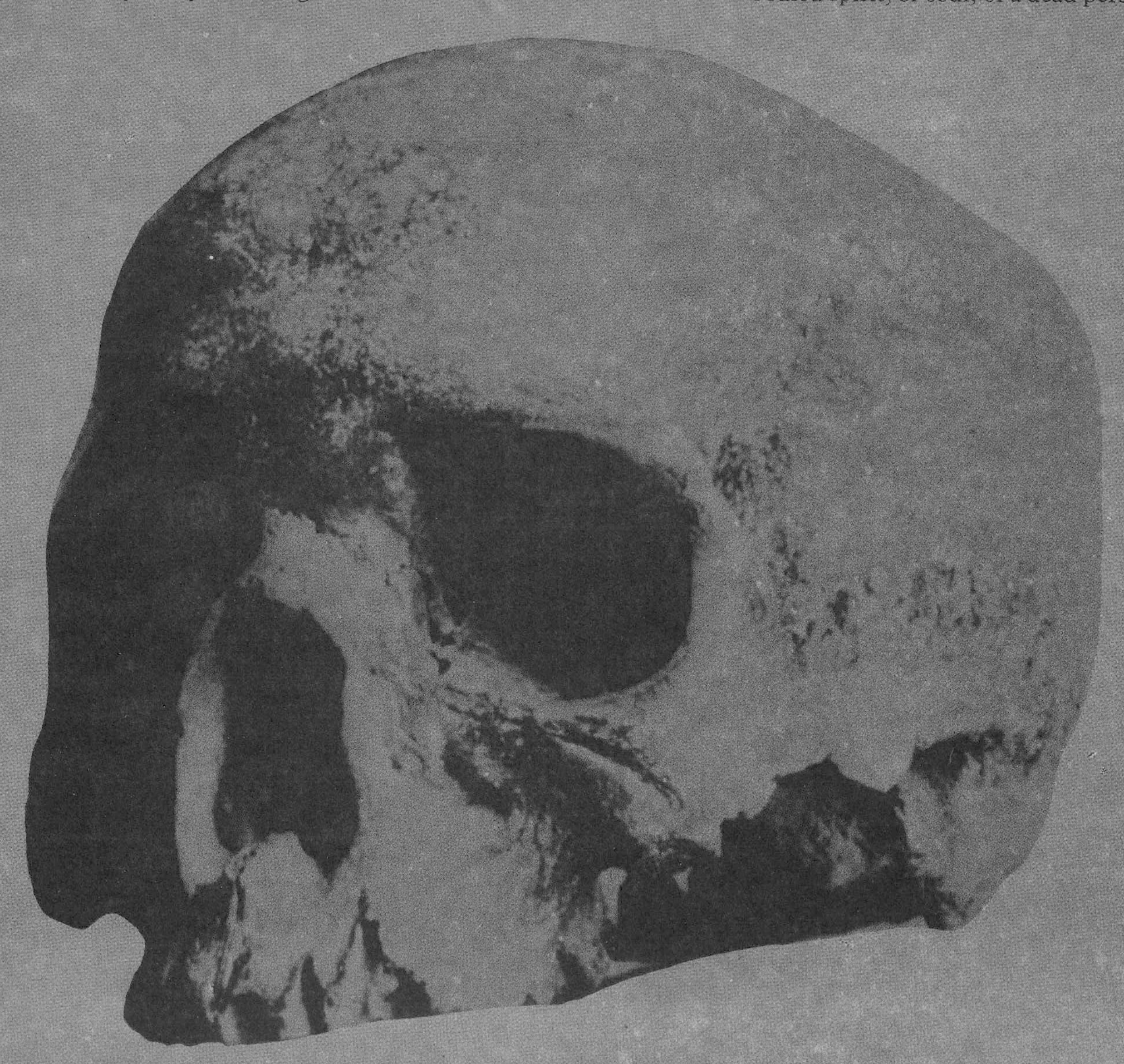

The screaming skull of Bettiscombe Manor in Dorset is said to be that of a West Indian slave who swore his spirit would not rest until he was buried in his African homeland

explanation of the nature of ghosts will not be assumed here, however, for apparitions of living people are frequent. The word 'ghost' has also acquired the sense of a vestige of something, as in 'the ghost of a smile'. Frederic W. H. Myers, a leader of Victorian psychical research, echoed this meaning in his characterisation of a ghost as 'a manifestation of persistent personal energy' – a conclusion he had reached after careful study of a mass of evidence.

A great deal of evidence is available, for seeing or hearing ghostly presences is a very common experience. In 1889 the British Society for Psychical Research, of which Myers was a founder member, embarked upon a large-scale survey of experiences of apparitions, asking the question:

> Have you ever, when believing yourself to be completely awake, had a vivid impression of seeing or being touched by a living being or inanimate object, or of hearing a voice; which impression, so far as you could discover, was not due to any external physical cause?

Almost 10 per cent of the 17,000 people who replied said 'yes'. Later surveys in several other countries confirm this picture.

Isolated appearances of a ghost may be undramatic, but when repeated over a long period become worthy of study. An example is the ghost reported in 1892 by a medical student, Miss R. C. Morton. She wrote:

> I saw the figure of a tall lady dressed in black, standing at the head of the stairs. After a few moments she descended the stairs, and I followed for a short distance, feeling curious what it could be. I had only a small piece of candle, and it suddenly burnt itself out; and being unable to see more, I went to my room.

This ghost lent itself to study. Over the following seven years six people besides Miss Morton saw the ghost, which closely resembled a known former occupant of the house, while about 20 people heard sounds apparently made by it. Sightings followed a regular pattern: the figure would walk downstairs (the resourceful Miss Morton sometimes tied threads across them, but they remained unbroken), enter the drawing-room and stand in the window. Then it would leave the room by the door, walk along the passage and disappear.

Cornering a phantom

Miss Morton, who must have been an exceptionally courageous young woman, made frequent attempts to converse with the ghost, but although it seemed aware of her presence, it never replied. She also tried to touch it, but it always got out of the way. 'On cornering her, as I did once or twice,' she wrote, 'she disappeared.' Miss Morton even tried to 'pounce on it', with the same result.

Once she saw the figure at the usual window and asked her father if he too could

Above: the Brown Lady of Raynham Hall in Norfolk. This ill-defined form was seen by the photographer as well as captured on film

Right: the form of a kneeling monk is said to appear in this picture, taken by a local solicitor in St Nicholas's Church, Arundel, in 1940

The amazing Gladys Hayter

While Gladys Hayter sits in trance, a phantom hand appears, unseen in the darkness but captured in this infra-red photograph

An East London psychic, Gladys Hayter, apparently has the ability to cause phantoms to materialise and living people and inanimate objects to dematerialise and change position, under the gaze of the camera. In 1970 Mrs Hayter, who already practised psychic healing, began photographing strange phenomena with a simple Instamatic camera. Glowing streaks of 'ectoplasm' often appear, emerging from her body. Sometimes her image does not appear in the picture, even though, as she insists, she has not moved. In fact, she claims she is unable to move when in trance during one of these sessions. The picture shown here is one of a number taken by a local photographer, using infra-red film in the near-darkness. The camera on the tripod is Mrs Hayter's.

see it, but he could not. When he walked to the window, the phantom promptly walked round him.

The family's cat took no notice at all of the ghost. The dogs, however, frequently reacted as if they had seen somebody. One would run to the foot of the stairs, wag its tail and jump up as if waiting to be patted, but then back away with its tail between its legs and hide under a sofa. Another dog was often found 'in a state of terror' for no obvious reason. This sensitivity of some animals to supernatural presences has prompted their use as 'ghost-detectors' (see page 68).

In any investigation, it helps to know something of the likely course of events. While the nature of ghosts is still mysterious, their behaviour has been studied in great detail. G. N. M. Tyrell, in his book *Apparitions*, published in 1943, identified four main groups by their pattern of activity.

Below: the kneeling figure in this photograph of the altar of St Mary's Church Woodford, was not seen by the photographer at the time the picture was taken

The first of Tyrrell's groups consists of apparitions that haunt certain places. These, of which Miss Morton's ghost is a typical example, are what are now termed 'place-centred', rather than 'person-centred'. On the whole they do not arouse fear and they sometimes come to be treated as part of the family. They rarely do any harm.

The second category consists of post-mortem apparitions, taking place some time after the death of the person seen, and not related to any particular place or event.

Thirdly, there are crisis cases, in which the apparition is of someone who is undergoing some profound experience at the time (often unknown to the percipient), such as an accident or illness or, of course, death.

Experimental apparitions

The last of Tyrrell's categories is the least-known type of apparition, but perhaps the most intriguing of all – the experimentally induced apparition. The ghost in these cases is not of a dead or dying person but of someone alive and well who has deliberately attempted to make his or her image visible to someone else. Tyrrell found records of 16 successful attempts of this type, and wondered why such an evidently repeatable experiment had been ignored by researchers. It remains a neglected area of study and, although there has been considerable recent study of 'out-of-the-body' experiences, reports of self-induced visibility at a distance remain very rare.

Those ghosts for which evidence is most compelling, and that critical researchers have concluded are genuine, usually show a number of features. Such a ghost obeys the laws of perspective, looking different to different observers; it appears solid; it is visible when viewed in a mirror; and it makes sounds appropriate to its movements – footsteps can be heard, for example. It generally gives the impression of being as real as a

Right: two ghostly forms appear behind the figure of an English lady, Miss Townsend, in the Basilica at Domrémy, in France. The apparitions were unseen by Miss Townsend's companion, Lady Palmer, when she took this photograph during a visit in 1925

Below: another haunting of a holy place. The church in this case is at Newby, in North Yorkshire. Its vicar, the Reverend K. F. Lord, was amazed to find this form on his developed photograph of the altar

living person, if only for a limited period. A sensation of sudden cold may be felt.

The feeling of coldness is also a commonly reported feature of poltergeist cases, but poltergeists are unlike conventional ghosts: they cause physical objects to move, yet they are not seen doing so. Apparitions have been reported in association with poltergeist activity, but we have yet to see one pick up an object and throw it.

When a ghost is seen by only one person, the suspicion arises of hallucination, error or deception – whether practised by the percipient or someone else. But ghosts are often seen by more than one person at the same time, though not necessarily by everybody present. This is often sufficient to rule out the possibility of deception or mistake, but the true nature of the apparition remains unknown. It is not necessarily a disembodied spirit – it could be an 'intersubjective' phenomenon, the joint creation of the percipients' minds.

An apparition may provide some plain evidence of its non-physical nature. It may pass through walls; sometimes it appears and disappears through phantom doors that open and close while 'real' doors stay closed; it may become transparent and fade away.

Nevertheless, these elusive wraiths can apparently be recorded on photographic film. There are many alleged photographs of ghosts, but few are convincing. Fraud has been so prevalent in the field of psychic photography that attention has been diverted

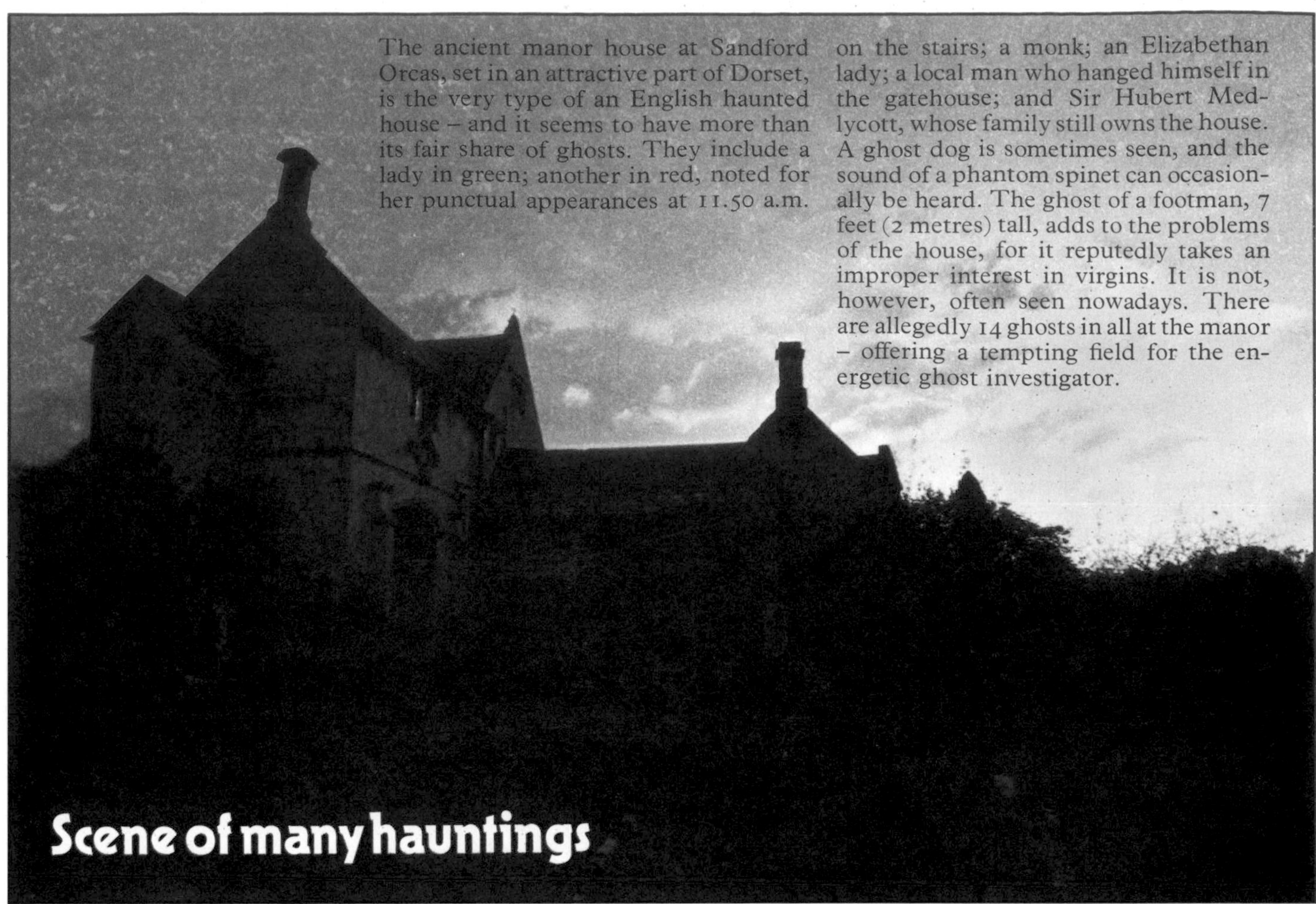

Scene of many hauntings

The ancient manor house at Sandford Orcas, set in an attractive part of Dorset, is the very type of an English haunted house – and it seems to have more than its fair share of ghosts. They include a lady in green; another in red, noted for her punctual appearances at 11.50 a.m. on the stairs; a monk; an Elizabethan lady; a local man who hanged himself in the gatehouse; and Sir Hubert Medlycott, whose family still owns the house. A ghost dog is sometimes seen, and the sound of a phantom spinet can occasionally be heard. The ghost of a footman, 7 feet (2 metres) tall, adds to the problems of the house, for it reputedly takes an improper interest in virgins. It is not, however, often seen nowadays. There are allegedly 14 ghosts in all at the manor – offering a tempting field for the energetic ghost investigator.

from the rare examples that may well be the real thing. One impressive case took place at Raynham Hall, Norfolk, home of the Marquis of Townshend, in 1936. A professional photographer and his assistant were taking photographs of the house. While photographing the staircase, the assistant reported seeing a ghostly figure coming down the stairs. The picture taken at that time, which has been pronounced genuine by photographic experts, does indeed show a misty form. The house has a long history of haunting by a lady in brown, who was seen simultaneously by two witnesses in 1835. Later she was seen by the author Captain Marryat, who ungallantly fired a shotgun at her. Despite this unwelcoming action, she was seen again in 1926 by Lord Townshend and two other witnesses.

Ghostly worshippers

Convincing pictures of ghosts have been taken in churches. In 1940, a local solicitor snapped an unmistakably human form in front of the altar of St Nicholas's church, in Arundel, Sussex. More solid in appearance than the brown lady of Raynham Hall, it was still partly transparent. Some have interpreted it as the figure of a kneeling priest. A similar figure appeared in a photo taken in St Mary's, Woodford, in Northamptonshire, by Gordon Carroll in 1966. Two ghostly priests turned up in the picture of Lady Palmer taken by her friend Miss Townsend in the Basilica of Domrémy, in France.

The prize for technical quality in a ghost photograph must go to the Reverend K. F. Lord of Newby, in Yorkshire, who recorded the presence of a very clear, if somewhat stagey, hollow-eyed spook before his altar.

These are examples of 'place-centred' ghosts. Photographic evidence for 'person-centred' apparitions is more ample. The family photograph albums of the London medium Gladys Hayter contain dozens of colour pictures of inexplicable lights, shadows and – apparently – partly dematerialised living human beings. In 1979 she took a shot of a child in a car, a picture that seems entirely normal except for the fact that, as she has testified, no child was in the car when the picture was taken.

There are no photographs, however, as persuasive as the best eyewitness accounts. Cumulatively, the weight of evidence, of all kinds, suggests that ghosts exist. But, despite a century of intensive research, what they are, and the conditions under which they manifest themselves, are questions that are still awaiting definitive answers. Ghost hunters still face mysteries in plenty.

A serious ghost investigation is long and arduous, and some publicity-conscious authors find it profitable not to be too critical of the cases they retail. What distinguishes a good ghost-hunter from a bad one?

'THE MOST HAUNTED HOUSE in England' was a local inhabitant's description of Borley Rectory, on the Essex-Suffolk border, when he gave directions to a motorist in 1929. The driver was Harry Price, self-styled ghost-hunter and the most energetic and controversial psychical researcher of the century. He found his way to Borley, where he found – or claimed to have found – the ingredients for a series of books, radio broadcasts and newspaper articles that he was to produce for the rest of his life. The case apparently had everything: ringing bells, strange lights, footsteps, flying stones, a skull wrapped in brown paper, mysterious writing on walls, and, of course, a ghost. Local legend had it that the rectory was built on the site of a monastery, from which a monk had unsuccessfully tried to elope with a young lady from a nearby nunnery. Both had been caught and executed, but the nun and the monk (minus his head) and the coach they used were said to be still around. Borley Rectory, Harry Price claimed, was 'the best-authenticated case of haunting in the annals of psychical research.'

This would be welcome news indeed, for surprisingly, although ghosts have been seen over the centuries, very few have ever been investigated thoroughly in order to learn their true nature. But had Price authenticated the Borley hauntings?

Not in the opinion of a team of members of the Society for Psychical Research (SPR), who tore the case to pieces in a devastating report published in 1956. Not only, they claimed, was there no proper evidence for any paranormal occurrences at Borley, but some of the reported phenomena had very probably been caused by Price himself. They quoted one outright accusation of fraud, made by a *Daily Mail* reporter, Charles Sutton, after Price's death:

> Many things happened the night I spent in the famous Borley Rectory with Harry Price and one of his colleagues, including one uncomfortable moment when a large pebble hit me on the head.
>
> After much noisy 'phenomena' I seized Harry and found his pockets full of bricks and pebbles. This was one 'phenomenon' he could not explain, so I rushed to the nearest village to 'phone the *Daily Mail* with my story, but after a conference with the lawyer my story was killed.

Even some of Price's fellow investigators concluded that he was more interested in a good story than in the truth of the case. A

Ghosts true and false

A brick flung through the air at the site of the ruined Borley Rectory is captured on film by a *Life* magazine photographer. Harry Price, who was present at the time, later cited this picture as photographic evidence of poltergeist activity at Borley – without mentioning the workman who was demolishing a nearby wall when the picture was taken typical example of this was given by a *Life* magazine reporter, Cynthia Ledsham, who visited Borley with Price and a photographer in 1944. The rectory, which had burned down in 1939, was being demolished. The photographer took a distant shot of the ruins, which showed a brick flying through the air. Price later claimed that this could be 'the first photograph ever taken of a poltergeist projectile in flight'. However, the reporter later admitted to the SPR investigators that while the picture was being taken a workman was dismantling a wall nearby, throwing bricks at regular intervals. She accused Price of 'the most bare-faced hocus pocus'.

Price's account of the haunting was demolished as surely as the building itself. The rectory had not been built on the site of a monastery after all. The 'nun' who had been spotted by a newspaper reporter 'flitting about in the gloom' was in fact the maid, a lively girl who later admitted to having carried out a spot of poltergeist activity herself. One former occupant of the rectory declared it to have been haunted by no more than 'rats and local superstition'. Another, the source of a great deal of the anecdotal material (which Price himself privately admitted to not believing), turned out to have lived previously near Amherst in Nova Scotia, scene of a well-publicised 19th-century haunting with many remarkable similarities to the alleged happenings at Borley. And so the indictment continues through 180 pages of a special issue of the SPR's *Proceedings* wholly devoted to an exposé of Price's bold claims.

In Trevor H. Hall's *Search for Harry Price* (1948), the 'ghost-hunter extraordinary' is depicted as a publicity-seeking charlatan and an unscrupulous liar. Although argument was still raging in 1980 in the pages of the SPR's *Journal* over both the facts of the Borley case and the integrity of its investigator-publicist, it cannot be claimed that Price made any useful contribution at all to our understanding of ghosts, or that there is any reason to believe a word of what he wrote about Borley.

Shock, horror, thrills

One moral of this lamentable episode seems to be that it is all too easy, and profitable, to offer the public what it wants – shock, horror and occult thrills. It is much more difficult and costly to do the painstaking work of a good investigator. The late Jay Anson, who scripted the film based on the novel *The exorcist*, made an estimated £3 million from his book *The Amityville horror*, but he had no first-hand experience of this case whatsoever. A researcher who followed up the case, Dr Stephen Kaplan, dismissed the book as 'mostly fiction'. Another writer who investigated the story, Melvin Harris, has written that 'there is plenty of evidence which shows unambiguously that the Amityville story is a gross fabrication'.

How, then, should ghosts be hunted? In an ideal world, funds, personnel and equipment would be available for an enquiry as thoroughly conducted as a police murder

Right: wreckage scattered over Florida swampland after the crash of Eastern Airlines' flight 401 on 29 December 1972, with two of the crew who died. The ghosts of the pilot, Bob Loft (centre), and the second officer, Don Repo (below), were later seen on other Eastern Airlines Tri-Star flights (inset)

A television special

In 1964 Anglia Television filmed a documentary at an allegedly haunted 16th-century manor house, Morley Old Hall in Norfolk. Anthony D. Cornell (below left) demonstrated how a ghost-hunter worked. After a night's investigation, he was interviewed in the room where the ghost was said to have appeared. He concluded there was little evidence for the haunting.

Five people contacted the television company to say that they had seen a 'hooded monk' standing between Cornell and the interviewer, Michael Robson. Although Robson could see nothing when he re-ran the film, he decided to broadcast it again. Viewers were asked to write in if they saw anything odd.

Twenty-seven viewers wrote in. Fifteen said they had seen a monk or priest; one said it was a lady in a mantilla; one said it was a hooded skull.

When some of the relevant frames were enlarged, certain markings were at last seen that corresponded with drawings sent in by viewers. They proved to be due to dampness on the stonework.

As Anthony Cornell commented, the case was of interest to psychical researchers. The dim lighting of the television screen and the 'atmosphere' engendered by the rest of the film favoured 'spectral' appearances. Secondly, an impressive number of witnesses sited the 'figure' exactly at the spot where a physical cause was later found. Lastly, although the markings were vague, many of the witnesses were in substantial agreement about the 'figure' they saw.

hunt, or as research into subatomic particles or the mating habits of cockroaches. But they are not available, and the work is left to individual investigators, many of whom understandably make a living by writing about their experiences. The best to be hoped for is that such individuals will record as much first-hand evidence as they can, as soon as possible after the event.

While the perfect ghost investigation has yet to be recorded, at least two cases of the 1970s were researched and written up in considerable detail. One consisted of a series of apparitions on board several jumbo jets of an American airline.

Airborne apparitions

An Eastern Airlines Tri-Star, flight 401, crashed in December 1972 in a Florida swamp, killing 101 people. The ghosts of the pilot, Bob Loft, and his flight engineer, Don Repo, were seen on more than twenty occasions by crew members of other Eastern Tri-Stars, especially those that had been fitted with salvaged parts of the crashed plane. The apparitions were invariably described as wholly lifelike. They were reported both by men and women who had known Loft and Repo and by others who had not, but who recognised them later from photographs. The haunting became well-known among people in the airline community, and an account of it even appeared in the newsletter of the US Flight Safety Foundation, in 1974.

An author, John G. Fuller, made thorough investigations of the case with the help of several airline personnel. They produced a mass of compelling testimony, including claims that log books recording apparitions had been withdrawn and crew members reporting them had been threatened with a visit to the company psychiatrist. Moreover, a seance was eventually held in the presence of Repo's widow at which evidence was produced that satisfied her of her husband's continuing existence. This would be a near-perfect case if the airline had co-operated but, perhaps understandably, it did not.

It is to be hoped that future ghosts will be as visible and informative as Loft and Repo, and that future hunters will be as determined as the investigators of this famous case. Ghost-hunting, says Andrew Green, himself an expert in the art, 'enlarges the field of knowledge, which is in itself a valid reason for any pursuit.' But for the dedicated ghost-hunter, the sheer fascination of the chase is a sufficient spur.

A ghost hunter's guide

Resourcefulness and skill are required to carry out an investigation of ghostly apparitions. This chapter describes how a good ghost hunter tests the authenticity of a haunting

FINDING A GHOST worthy of investigation is not too difficult. It is rather like looking for a flat: just as home hunters can go to an agency, look in the papers, and 'ask around', so ghost hunters can seek information from official organisations, from the specialised press and from friends and work-mates.

The first step for the would-be ghost hunter is to join a parapsychological organisation which exist in most countries. In Britain there is the Society for Psychical Research (SPR). It was founded in 1882 'to examine without prejudice or prepossession and in a scientific spirit those faculties of man, real or supposed, which appear to be inexplicable on any generally recognised hypothesis.' The SPR *Journal* is published regularly; its *Proceedings*, containing full reports and more technical articles, appears irregularly. It holds regular meetings and annual international conferences; and it offers its members, of which there are more than a thousand, the use of its unique library. It holds no corporate views, and its membership includes men and women with or without qualifications or religious convictions. Although ghosts are only one of many areas of research that come within its scope, the majority of Britain's serious ghost hunters have been, or are, members.

Above: the ghost hunter's dream come true – a meeting face-to-face with an apparition. However, this eminent investigator, the physicist Sir William Crookes, is generally thought to have been duped. The medium responsible for the 'materialisation' – Florence Cook, here apparently recumbent on the floor – bore a remarkable physical resemblance to the 'spirit', Katie King

The British weekly *Psychic News* is also an excellent source of new case material. Any good public library will have a number of books by such experienced ghost hunters as Andrew Green, Peter Underwood, Joan Forman and Andrew Mackenzie, many of which give the addresses of places with a well-established history of haunting. *Ghost-hunting, a practical guide* (1973) by Andrew Green is a particularly clear and concise work for beginners seeking a general introduction to the subject. The SPR's *Notes for investigators of spontaneous cases* are also recommended.

Finally, one can attempt to find a case by word-of-mouth contact. Since about one person in ten has had some kind of paranormal experience, it is more than likely that in an average office or factory there is somebody who has seen a ghost or knows someone who has.

Preliminary assessment

When a case has been found, the first thing to do is to make sure that there is enough firm evidence to make it worth investigating. The criteria for assessing evidence are much the same as in a criminal enquiry, and a study of police methods is useful to the ghost hunter. The following notes may sound somewhat obvious, but it is amazing how often research has been hampered because they have not been observed in the past.

Witnesses' descriptions must be recorded, in writing or, preferably, on tape. The place and date, both of the incident described and of the statement, should be included. Written statements should be signed.

Second-hand accounts are almost never of value. First-hand accounts of a single event by a single witness are virtually impossible to verify and, though they are worth recording, they are seldom worth following up, since further occurrences are unlikely.

If there are several witnesses, they should be interviewed separately. Questioning should be deferred until the statements have been obtained, in order not to put ideas into the witnesses' heads. Questioning will almost certainly be necessary, however, to make up deficiencies in the statements. The aim should be to arrive at as full an account as possible of the circumstances of the incident:

Above: Joan Forman has written valuable guides to the haunted places of East Anglia and southern England

Above right: the Society for Psychical Research plots cases of hauntings on this map, and maintains copious files concerning them

Below right: photographic evidence of a haunting, obtained by a budding ghost hunter. Andrew Green, then a 15-year-old boy, walked around this empty and reputedly haunted house in 1944. When he left, he took this photograph. When it was developed he was amazed to see the figure at the upper window. A murder and no fewer than 20 suicides took place here. It has been suggested that the figure is an apparition of Ann Hinchfield, who jumped from the tower in 1886, when she was 12 years old

Below: Andrew Green, today a noted researcher and author on parapsychology

time and place, the witnesses' activities and states of mind immediately before and during it, the physical layout of the scene, the positions of other people, independent confirming evidence – broken or displaced objects, for example – and any similar experiences that the witnesses may have had.

The occasional trick question can be useful. For example: 'Mrs Smith says the ghost was wearing a green hat. Are you *sure* it was bare-headed?' If the witness suddenly 'remembers' the green hat (which Mrs Smith did not mention) the hunter is dealing with an unreliable witness.

The witnesses should be interviewed on more than one occasion. Their stories may develop from one telling to the next; if so, it is necessary to judge whether this is really due to an increased recall, or to continuing inventiveness.

On the basis of these preliminary enquiries, which should be routine for any ghost report, the ghost hunter must judge whether a serious follow-up investigation is justified. Ideally, detailed and consistent reports will be provided by several witnesses, of good local reputations and no apparent motives for deceit (such as a council tenant's desire for a better house).

If more thorough research is undertaken, possible natural causes for the reported incident must first be sought. Ghostly noises are often made by such everyday agencies as the wind, water pipes, windows or ornaments vibrating in resonance with passing traffic, animals and so on. In one case a family was haunted by no more than rats, pushing apples stored in a loft down a cavity wall.

A superficial search for such a cause has a good chance of finding such a mundane explanation, but the variety of possible misleading occurrences is so great that little can

usefully be said here as guidance. The investigator must be sceptical of the easy paranormal explanations that suggest themselves, and imaginative in devising commonplace (but possibly far from obvious) causes that can be tested; he or she must aim to be a Sherlock Holmes of psychic detection, in fact.

A thorough investigation of the phenomena needs equipment (see box), patience and an acceptance of the likelihood of disappointment. If the occurrences are person-centred, there are great difficulties. It is rarely practicable to keep someone under continuous observation for long periods – let alone restrain their movements while apparent ghost activity is under way. There is

The well-equipped investigator

If the frequency of appearances is sufficient to justify lying in wait for a ghost, there is no end of material that might be useful to the investigator. The area being observed can be sealed off from human access by putting masking tape along the edges of doors and windows. Threads stretched across the ghost's route and scattered chalk powder will reveal a human presence. Fluorescent powder can also be scattered in suitable places – if it is picked up on the person of some occupant of the house, it will reveal itself when ultra-violet light is shone on it. Capacitance switches can be purchased, which will actuate cameras and tape recorders at the approach of a human being or animal. Tape recordings should be made in stereo if possible, and if an area can be surveyed with more than one tripod-mounted camera, so much the better. The 'fastest' (most sensitive) films available are black and white, and these can also be 'pushed' considerably in developing, in order to bring out more detail. If, however, it is planned to use flash, there is no reason why colour film should not be used. Since the space to be covered is usually confined, a short-focus (wide-angle) lens is valuable. A motor-drive attachment permits a sequence of photographs to be taken rapidly. Such obvious items as notebooks, pens, torch, luminous watch and a simple tool-kit should also not be omitted from the equipment list.

also the problem that people's feelings will be ruffled if they come to believe that they are being suspected of fraud.

On the other hand, ghostly phenomena, like some other paranormal events, may happen more predictably in the presence of certain people, and offer the opportunity of detailed study. Many mediums have claimed that it is possible to materialise a spirit. Past studies of such events, such as those carried out by the eminent physicist William Crookes in 1874, are still surrounded by controversy. Yet there remains a substantial body of evidence that certain mediums, such as the late Alec Harris, are able to cause such phenomena. It is a sad fact of the history of ghost hunting that few people have ever made a serious attempt to examine this subject properly. There are great opportunities for the ghost hunter here.

Setting up a team

Establishing the genuineness of a case is very much a matter of personal judgement, and since this is highly fallible, it is always a good idea for more than one person to study a given case. Unless the investigator is a qualified psychologist, physicist and chartered surveyor combined, he will need help from specialists. Furthermore, if an investigation team can be set up, it may be possible to keep the site under constant observation.

Ghost hunters will naturally want to see reported apparitions for themselves. They will almost certainly be disappointed. Perhaps ghosts will appear to order when we know more about the conditions they require; in the meantime, the more evidence that can be recorded about such conditions, the better for paranormal research.

Whatever the results of an investigation – whether it is called off at an early stage, ends inconclusively, or ends in a finding of fraud, misinterpretation or the genuinely paranormal – a report should be filed with the ASPR. In addition to its intrinsic interest it may gain significance in the future should it be studied in relation to other cases, or should developments take place in the same case.

The late Alec Harris, one of those mediums who can reputedly materialise spirits – an ability that may be related to some 'ordinary' hauntings

Where ghostly activities genuinely seem to be taking place, the question of getting rid of them may arise. If the ghost is not doing any harm, there is no need to do anything. In fact, it can be very good for trade in a pub or hotel (one of the motives for deceit that the ghost hunter must bear in mind).

But not all ghosts are harmless. The witnesses can be extremely frightened, and the phenomena can disrupt family life – or even, as in some recent cases, factory and office life. How can they be got rid of? There is no easy answer, but certain methods have been tried, with uneven success.

The best-known of these is exorcism. At the risk of oversimplifying this emotive and controversial subject, it can be said that it may be effective if the victim believes it will be. But it can also have dangerous side-effects, and in at least four well-reported cases of the 1970s, involving both Roman Catholics and Protestants, its use resulted in death.

A somewhat safer and less sensational way to combat an invisible agency is prayer. Canon J. D. Pearce-Higgins, former Vice-Provost of Southwark Cathedral, claims to have 'cleared' more than a hundred houses of 'unwanted visitors', by first identifying the entities with the help of a medium, and then persuading them to depart.

Ghosts will doubtless continue to provide entertainment in the newspapers and on the screen, and ghost hunters will continue to be regarded by some as harmless cranks. Yet the subject is a serious one, of tremendous potential significance. Once fully understood, it will vastly extend our knowledge both of the human mind and of matter. But it will not be understood unless far more people take it more seriously and investigate it more thoroughly. And the more amateur ghost hunters there are, collecting more and better evidence and forcing it upon the attention of scientists, the sooner this will happen.

Old soldiers never die

Phantoms are not always the lonely beings of the traditional ghost story; sometimes, especially in damp weather, they appear in large numbers, re-enacting old battles

THE BATTLE OF NASEBY, in Northamptonshire, England, was fought on 14 June 1645. One of the major engagements of the English Civil War, it ended in the rout of the Royalist forces by the Parliamentary armies. But it seems to have been fought not once, but repeatedly – to have been 'replayed' annually for about a century afterwards. Local villagers would congregate on a nearby hill to witness the re-enactment of the fight. The watchers heard cannonfire and saw men fighting and falling, banners flying and cavalry charging; they even heard the screams and groans of the wounded. Yet all this was enacted in the sky above the battlefield.

We are accustomed to think of ghosts as single apparitions, appearing one at a time to one or two observers. But some records exist of large-scale hauntings – of phantoms appearing *en masse*, engaged in collective activity. They are often refighting some historic battle, as in the case above.

Another important engagement of the Civil War, the battle of Marston Moor, near York, is re-enacted from time to time, according to a local legend. The most favourable weather for the occurrence of the apparition is said to be fog, even though the original battle of 1644 was fought in midsummer.

Yet another Civil War battle fought over again by phantoms was the battle of Edgehill (1642). Only a few days after the battle, there were reports of apparitions of soldiers, cavalry and phantom scenery – all appearing in the sky over the battlefield. King Charles sent a number of army officers from Oxford to the site – and they witnessed the events, swearing statements to that effect (see page 66).

Writer Joan Forman experienced the terror of a long-past battle herself, when travelling in Scotland some years ago. She had chosen to stay in Selkirk, because it is a good centre for touring and because she was interested in the career of James Graham, the first

An army sleeps on the eve of battle, while phantom warfare rages in the skies above. The apparition may be an anticipation of the bloodshed to come, or a re-enactment of some past engagement. Stories of 'armies in the sky' seen over battlefields are numerous – suggesting that the strenuous exertion and intense emotion of combat are somehow favourable to psychic phenomena

Marquis of Montrose. This great cavalier leader had been Charles I's chief supporter in Scotland – his Captain-General. He had fought the Covenanting forces, which sided with the English Parliament. He had spectacular gifts as a soldier, and in 1644 led his armies in some brilliant forced marches across the mountains to achieve equally extraordinary victories over the King's enemies.

But towards the end of that year Montrose found that his luck began to run out. In attempting to lead his small army away from a much larger force of the enemy, led by General David Leslie, Montrose headed for Philiphaugh, a small plateau near Selkirk, where the Glen of Yarrow meets that of Ettrick, and camped there.

But Leslie was almost upon them. Leslie's army of 6000 men fell on Montrose's force of 700. The Royalists were driven from one end of the valley to the other before they were penned in and cut down. The *annus mirabilis* of Montrose ended in the massacre of his men.

Local tradition has it that the Royalists were pinned down on the side of the valley that lies beneath Minchmoor. On the opposite side of the valley lay a castle known as Newark, perched on an escarpment above the battlefield. It was also said that, although General Leslie offered quarter to those Royalists who surrendered, many of the men and their camp followers were slaughtered after the battle.

Forman already knew of the battle, but not its details, and so she was glad when a knowledgeable Selkirk historian offered to guide her around the site. They found the ruins of the old Newark keep, isolated in its wild and beautiful valley, and entered the remains of the old courtyard. The guide began to describe the battle to her: how Leslie had caught Montrose's small force in a pincer movement and, in spite of heroic charges by the Royalist leader and his cavalry, had slowly driven them back until they were pinned beneath the mass of Minchmoor.

At this point in the narrative, Forman looked over the edge of the Newark courtyard and without warning was engulfed in a feeling of frantic misery and desperation. There was a sensation of turmoil, of many people struggling to escape and being forced back – not against the far side of the valley but right underneath the walls of the castle itself. She stood there for a few minutes, but the sense of furious and desperate fighting was unbearable. She moved away.

As she did so, she said that she believed Montrose's men had been massacred on this side of the valley and not on the other. The guide shook his head. 'Oh, no,' he said, 'I'm sure you're wrong. It is acknowledged that they died on the farther side.' She did not pursue the matter.

Then, as they walked away from that miserable place above the escarpment, Forman

Top: a crucial battle of the English Civil War is marked by this monument at Naseby, Northamptonshire. Local people saw phantom re-enactments of it during the following 100 years

Above: Oliver Cromwell at the battle of Marston Moor, in Yorkshire. Apparitions of this battle are alleged to occur even today

Right: James Graham, first Marquis of Montrose, led a small Royalist force that was massacred at Philiphaugh, Scotland. Over 300 years later, the terror of the event was apparently experienced by the author while visiting the site was again immersed in a wave of terror and anguish, now coming from the courtyard itself. This time the feeling of fear and wretched despair were overwhelming: for a few seconds she was unable to move. The air seemed filled with cries of anguish, though she knew she was hearing nothing with the ear.

'It's here,' she said. 'They killed them here in this very courtyard. Where I am standing, and over there by the wall. They must have executed a whole lot of people in this very place.'

The Selkirk man was silent, visibly upset. Finally he said: 'There were people killed later, I think. Leslie went back on his promise; some of the non-combatants – women and boys – were killed, and afterwards some of the men. But I don't think that it was here.'

She said no more, but the misery of the place was heavy and she was glad to go from it.

The kindly historian telephoned the following day and said that the curious episode had so impressed him that he had further investigated the local records. 'It seems you may be right and tradition wrong,' he said. 'There's a contemporary record that refers to the castle side of the valley as being the scene of the final massacre, and that would make it right under the place where we stood. What's more, there seems to be some justification for thinking executions did take place in the castle bailey after the battle.'

Some of Forman's ancestors belonged to the Graham clan and may have fought at Philiphaugh with their chief, Graham of Montrose. Could this fact have helped to make her a particularly sensitive 'receiver' for this strange experience?

Sounds of clashing metal

A further example of 'participation' in a past battle occurred in Windsor in the early 1970s. A house owned by Mr and Mrs Wakefield-Smith was apparently haunted by a man in a dark cloak, and they felt the atmosphere of the place to be unhappy. The garden, however, proved to be an equally interesting site. On one occasion when the owners had walked to the end of it, they suddenly seemed to be in an area of great heat and noise. Both husband and wife felt they were in the middle of a battle, for all around them were the sounds of clashing metal, like swords striking armour. There was a sensation of frenzied activity on all sides. Yet as suddenly as it began the phenomenon ended, and the garden was its usual tranquil self.

Although the Wakefield-Smiths' description of the ghosts suggests the Civil War period, the only battle referred to by local tradition was of a much earlier date, and was fought between Romans and Britons. It seems likely that this is what the couple encountered.

The great heat associated with the occurrence is interesting. Hauntings are generally associated with a fall in temperature, and this did indeed accompany the appearances of the ghost in the house. Was the experience of the battle a haunting, then, or some quite different phenomenon?

Not all large-scale manifestations relate to battles. The night-time activity seen by Dr and Mrs White at the beginning of January, 1969 on the Isle of Wight did not seem to have anything to do with war. Miss Edith Olivier, a Wiltshire author, was involved in a similar event during the First World War. She was driving towards the great Avebury Ring of standing stones as dusk was falling. As she came within sight of the circle she saw what she thought was an entire fair erected around and among the stones; she could hear music and see the lights of the booths. But as she drew level she found that the circle was empty, and there was no sound but that of the wind sighing among the great monoliths. Later Miss Olivier's enquiries revealed that fairs had been held at this spot in the past, but it had been at least 50 years since the last.

Frequently, communities that have lived

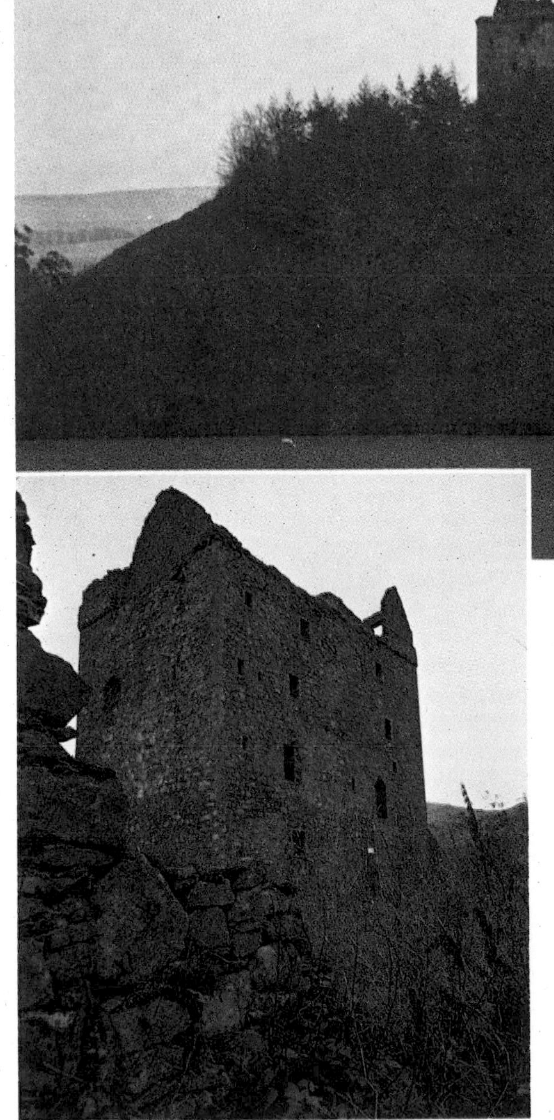

Above: Newark Castle, seen across the valley that was the scene of James Graham's defeat. The conventional opinion of historians is that Graham's men were trapped on the opposite side of the valley – behind the camera's viewpoint. But Joan Forman's experience while visiting the castle – apparently a 'replay' of the emotions of the battle – convinced her that the battle ended beneath the castle walls

Left: the keep of Newark Castle, from the courtyard. Here Forman experienced, for the second time, the sensation of being engulfed in the anguish of many people. Her belief that the massacre that followed the battle had taken place in the courtyard proved to be supported by independent historical evidence – as did her intuition about the battle itself by an inflexible timetable reappear regularly in apparitional form for many years after their earthly disappearance. Thus groups of monks and nuns, accustomed to process and attend prayer at set times of the day and night, may be seen and heard repeating the same pattern centuries later. Such stories are numerous throughout Britain. At Hinxworth Place, near Baldock in Hertfordshire, processions of monks have been seen to come through a wall, apparently on their way to or from their worship through a doorway long bricked up.

Occasionally an entire church congregation is seen, as at Dallington, Northamptonshire, in 1907. Two schoolgirls visited a country church at the end of a walk. One, a local girl, entered the church first but came out again in a great hurry. Her companion, a visitor to the area, was intrigued and went into the building. The place seemed full of kneeling people, though they appeared, she afterwards said, 'to be made of a substance similar to soap bubbles'. There seem to be no other reports of similar apparitions at this site, and there is no indication of the period to which the ghostly worshippers belonged.

Yet another instance of a group apparition was reported from Wiltshire, where a detachment of Roman soldiers was said to march along the old road beyond Oldbury Camp. A shepherd who sighted the band on one occasion gave this description of them: 'Men with beards, wearing skirts and big helmets with hair on the top. And a girt bird on a pole a' front on 'em.' A fair, if somewhat rustic, description of a Roman column, carrying its eagle insignia at its head.

Soldiers, in small groups or whole armies, in war or peace, seem to supply the bulk of mass-phantom phenomena. One of the most interesting cases is that of Major A. D. McDonagh, an officer serving in the Indian Army on the North-West Frontier.

Above: Hinxworth Place, in Hertfordshire, is one of the many places in England where a ghostly religious ritual is said to occur: a procession of monks appears through a wall

Below: a typically English church, at Dallington, in Northamptonshire. The ghostly congregation seen briefly in 1907 was more insubstantial – seemingly made of 'soap bubbles'

On one occasion the Major rode along a range of hills close to the River Indus. He eventually reached a ridge from which he could see across a wide horseshoe-shaped valley, which was heavily wooded. As he gazed down onto it, he abruptly found himself in a large group of soldiers, apparently from ancient Greek times, busy with the usual duties of a military encampment. He saw three altars, and noticed a group of men beyond them, at the head of the valley, gathered around some object. McDonagh could not see what was holding their attention until he walked across. Then he perceived a dressed stone slab with a newly cut inscription. The language was Greek, of which in ordinary life he had no knowledge. However, he found himself able to read and understand what was written here: the inscription seemed to relate to the death of one of the generals of Alexander the Great. He felt, too, a marked sensation of sorrow among the men with whom he stood.

Evidence in stone

Abruptly, the experience ended. Major McDonagh found himself back on the ridge, looking down into the valley, vividly aware of what he had just experienced.

Later he returned with Indian labourers to explore the area thoroughly. He found the place heavily overgrown with jungle vegetation and the men had to hack their way through to the head of the valley in which he had seen the inscribed rock. When eventually they reached it and cleared away the vegetation, they found a partially dressed rock surface with some traces of Greek lettering upon it, though the inscription was

Left: Oldbury Camp, an Iron Age earthwork in Wiltshire, apparently occupied by the Romans when they subdued Britain. A detachment of Roman soldiers is said still to march along the line of the old Roman road nearby

Below: Alexander the Great, (in a crown) before a Hindu idol, following his crossing of the Indus river in 326 BC. The painting is from a 15th-century Persian manuscript. A British officer, Major McDonagh, who had been riding near the river, suddenly found himself in the midst of this army. For an extended period he watched the men, apparently in mourning for one of their generals

badly eroded and defaced. McDonagh had no doubt, however, that this was the memorial he had seen earlier. The valley proved to be the site of one of the camps of Alexander before he forded the Indus in 326 BC.

This account is a particularly interesting example of a mass-phantom appearance. The distance in time between the original episode and its modern 'repeat' was over 2000 years – an exceptional period in these cases. Furthermore, the subject of the experience participated in the events he witnessed – moving around to get a view of the things he wanted to see, and finding himself able to understand a language normally unknown to him.

The idea of reincarnation suggests itself in cases like these. Was Major McDonagh a solider in Alexander's army in some former life? Or did he merely 'pick up' the sensations of the troop who had stood by the rock with its inscription to the dead general?

Occurrences of this nature are too rare to provide much evidence. However, appearances of phantoms *en masse* are not. There are at least two possible explanations of these. They may involve the *reproduction* of the sights and sounds of the original event – possibly because information stored by the physical surroundings is, in favourable conditions, 'retransmitted' to create the impression in the minds of certain specially sensitive witnesses that they are actually observing the original events. Alternatively, they may be true timeslips, in which past and present, or present and future, coexist temporarily. However, this process too might be triggered by the mind of the witness, interacting with information registered by the physical surroundings.

Ghosts on the march

Sometimes crowds of phantom figures appear, acting out events long past – or, occasionally, in the future. But why are so many mass phantom cases usually linked with emotional happenings?

THE OCCASIONAL SIGHTINGS of mass apparitions fall into a shadowy area in which it is difficult to distinguish timeslips from hauntings. The large-scale noise and activity, involving many phantom individuals at one time, and the sense of being overwhelmed by associated emotions, suggest that the subject has been plunged into events in some other era. On the other hand, the co-presence of familiar features of the everyday world suggests that it is the phantoms who have strayed into the wrong time.

A high proportion of mass phantom appearances relate to military activity. If they are a 'recording' of historical events, and if such recording is especially likely to occur in the presence of increased mental and emotional stress – and the evidence points in this direction – then it is not surprising that battles should figure so strongly among apparitions.

Weather conditions also seem to be important. Grey, overcast skies, mist or fog seem to be conducive to paranormal effects. One such case was reported by Mrs E. W. Reeves, of Holme Hale, Norfolk, England.

Mrs Reeves and her husband visited friends some miles away on the evening in question and returned home at about 2.30 a.m. The Moon was shining and there were patches of mist when Mrs Reeves got out of the car to open the garage doors for her husband. She heard shouting in the near distance and she drew her husband's attention to it, saying that she thought someone might be in need of help. Mr Reeves, however, who had not yet heard any sound, considered 2.30 in the morning to be an unlikely time for anyone to be needing assistance.

In the next moment the shouting was taken up by other voices, and now Mr Reeves also heard it. The clamour was accompanied by the sound of many running feet. Mr Reeves remarked that the sound seemed to be coming from the far side of a bridge a few hundred yards away. Disturbed and curious, the couple moved into the roadway for a better view. Nothing was to be seen, but the noises continued, presently augmented by the sounds of galloping horses.

The thought that anything paranormal was happening did not occur to the couple. They assumed that the horses they could hear belonged to a neighbouring farmer and they were concerned about stopping their flight. The galloping and shouting drew nearer, but the village street remained as empty of anything visible as when they had first left the car.

The sounds were now so loud that whatever was causing them appeared to be all around the couple, 'milling around us and

Above: a battle in the sky over Verviers, Belgium, in June 1815 – within a month of the battle of Waterloo, some 70 miles (110 kilometres) away. It was explained away as a mirage – yet mirages occur simultaneously with the events that cause them

Left: the rebellion of Robert Ket in 1549 may have been 'witnessed' over 400 years later. After the defeat of Ket – here seen denouncing a landowner – some of the rebels fled through the village of Holme Hale, where a phantom battle was heard in the 20th century

around the Red Lion forecourt opposite our house'. There were further sounds, 'of sticks hitting swords. It was like listening to a Robin Hood film fight.'

By now both husband and wife were bewildered, and shrank against the wall of their house, trying to evade whatever it was that was crashing around them. Presently the commotion shifted away from where they stood, into a field located next to the inn. Finally the noises moved up the hill beyond and faded into the distance. After that, according to Mrs Reeves, all the dogs in the village began to howl simultaneously, and continued to do so for several minutes.

The BBC later investigated this incident for a television programme called *Timeslips*. Their research revealed that, although no pitched battle in the neighbourhood of Holme Hale was on record, there were several likely candidates for the disturbance experienced by Mr and Mrs Reeves. The district was twice pillaged by the Danes in the 11th century; a series of riots against the enclosure of common lands occurred in the 1530s; there was further rioting during Ket's Rebellion in 1549, in which some of the rebels fled from Castle Rising to Watton, pursuing a line of retreat passing directly through Holme Hale. Certainly the rebel forces had a camp at Hingham, a short distance away, which was attacked by the troops of Sir Edmund Knyvett. The battle appears to have been fought with staves on one side and swords on the other, suggesting peasants facing organised troops. Ket's rising would appear to fit the facts of the case.

A well-documented sighting was reported by Dr James McHarg in the *Journal* of the Society for Psychical Research for December 1978. The incident concerned a Miss Smith, to whom the experience occurred in January 1950. She was walking home to the village of Letham in Angus, Scotland, after spending the evening at a friend's house. She had been driving back but her car had skidded on the icy road and into a ditch. She had therefore decided to walk the remaining 8 miles (13 kilometres).

She was about half a mile (800 metres) from her home village when the apparition began. It continued until she reached the houses, the whole experience lasting about 12 minutes. She must have been exceedingly

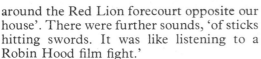

Below: Viking raiders may have been involved in the event that was acted out in the Holme Hale apparition. Vikings occupied large areas of Britain from the 8th to the 11th century. It was towards the end of this period that Holme Hale was twice pillaged by Danish marauders

'dark tights' and 'a sort of overall with a roll-collar'. There was a roll at the bottom of the tunic. The headgear seemed to be a flattish rolled cap, 'excellent for carrying things on the head with'. The torches were very long and made of a bright red material.

Dr McHarg obtained these details directly from Miss Smith in September 1971 and thoroughly investigated the background to her experience. He found that torches in Scotland were once made from the resinous roots of the Scots fir, which are reddish in colour, and would have been notable for their length. The costume description, too, is borne out by the dress of a figure of a Pictish warrior incised in stone at Golspie.

All in all, this is an impressive apparition. It has marked parallels with that experienced by Dr and Mrs White on the Isle of Wight in the winter of 1969. Both experiences occurred in January, though the weather was different: on the Isle of Wight it was cold, with brilliant moonlight and towering cloud masses, while at Nechtanesmere it was cold and wet after a snowfall that had been followed by rain. In each case the onset of the

tired at this time, for she had been carrying her small dog for the last part of the journey.

The experience began as she crested a rise that in daylight would have given her a view of Dunnichen Hill. Now, with the time nearing 2 a.m., she saw moving torches in the distance ahead of her. As she continued her journey, she followed a left-hand turning that brought the torches onto her right. Still farther down the road on her right, she saw other figures carrying torches. There were figures even closer to her, however, in a field about 50 yards (45 metres) distant. Miss Smith felt that she had stumbled upon some activity that was already in progress when she arrived.

The area that Miss Smith was traversing was the site of an ancient and now vanished loch, known as Nechtanesmere, a name given to it by the English rather than the Scots. It had been the scene of a battle in May 685. The Northumbrians, captained by their king, Egfrith, were defeated here by the Picts under their king Brude mac Beli, and the Northumbrian chief was killed. After falling into an ambush Egfrith's army was apparently routed, and the most desperate fighting seems to have taken place near the shores of the old loch.

This was the area crossed by Miss Smith, and although the loch waters had long been replaced by dry land, she apparently knew that a lake had once existed there, for her account referred to figures 'quite obviously skirting the mere'. She concluded that they were searching for their dead, for she noticed one person in particular turning over body after body and scrutinising each. The corpses also must therefore have been visible.

Miss Smith gave an excellent description of the dress worn by the figures. She saw

Above: the area bordering the site of a vanished loch, Nechtanesmere, which was traversed by phantom figures on a January night in 1950. Miss E.F. Smith watched them for about 12 minutes as the torch-carrying men apparently searched among corpses for their own dead, slain in battle. The battle of Nechtanesmere, fought in 685, resulted in the defeat of Egfrith, king of the Northumbrians, by the Pictish king Brude mac Beli

Right: a Pictish warrior, carved on a stone among animals and fish. His dress resembles that of the figures seen by Miss Smith: a tunic with a rolled hem and collar, and tights

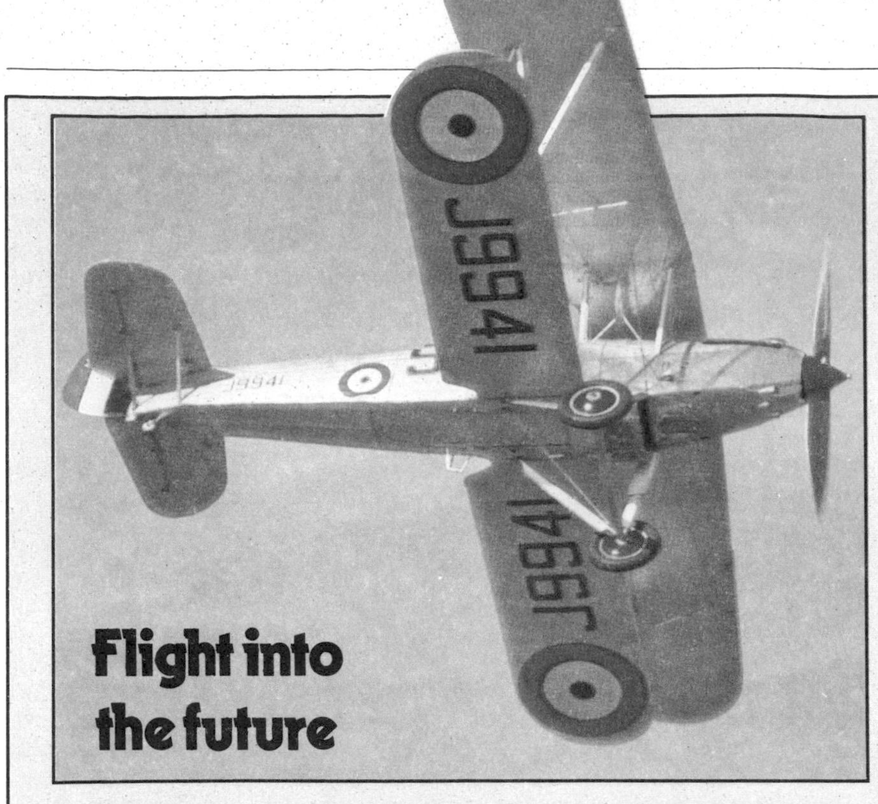

Flight into the future

Phantoms *en masse* are frequently seen in the air – but in one notable case an apparition on the ground was viewed from the air. Air Marshal Sir Victor Goddard told how in 1934 he had been flying a Hawker Hart bomber (left) over Scotland in mist and rain. He flew lower, looking for an abandoned airfield, Drem, as a landmark. He found it – apparently bathed in sunlight, and fully operational. Yellow aircraft were on the tarmac, being serviced by technicians in blue overalls. No one paid any attention to Goddard as he flew low overhead and then resumed his journey. It was only several years later that the meaning of what he had seen became clear to him. In 1938 Drem was put back into service as a flight training station. Trainer aircraft were for the first time painted yellow and ground crew were issued with a new style of uniform – coloured blue. Goddard believed he had glimpsed Drem airfield as it was to be.

vision took place as the parties crested a hill. Both apparitions featured the same type of scene: searching figures carrying lighted torches. It seems likely that they were engaged on the same mission in both cases – a search for the dead after a battle, in order to bury them. The differences in costume in the two cases are explicable by the differences in locality and, presumably, in the dates of the original events.

Action replay

For there seems little doubt that what was seen was in both cases some historical event – a record of a large-scale undertaking in the distant past. The most likely 'source' event is a battle, and the details of the battle of Nechtanesmere are sufficiently well-known to make its correspondence with Miss Smith's vision apparent. The reality behind the Whites' experience must remain speculative, for the Isle of Wight endured many military forays by a series of invaders. Only intensive research could reveal the 'template' for this experience.

What mechanism could cause this 'replay' of past events? Dr McHarg suggested that memories storied in what C. G. Jung called the collective unconscious are responsible. But if this is so, something in the physical setting must trigger the recollection, must 'press the button' that causes the brain to respond with its stored knowledge of the place.

It is just as likely that the physical surroundings themselves store the record of the event, the pattern of activity being printed indelibly on the place by the intense emotion generated by mass activity and a temporary unification of purpose. The subsequent presence in the neighbourhood of a person whose electrical brain patterns happen to 'resonate' in some way with those of the 'record' might result in a translation of the record into audio-visual experiences.

Perhaps in the future observers with correctly trained and 'tuned' mental equipment will be able to pick up the signals given out by large-scale present-day gatherings. For any crowd gathered together with a common purpose generates a high emotional charge (possibly an enhanced electrical potential) – whether they be football crowds or political demonstrators, carnival celebrators or spectators at royal weddings. Perhaps the global events we record today on videotape will in the future be replayed psychically.

Football supporters exult as their team scores a goal. The emotions aroused by the mock battle on the field can be almost as intense as those of a real battle. Will gatherings such as this – a phenomenon of the 20th century – provide material for collective apparitions in the future?

PART 3
THE OCCULT CONNECTION

THE OCCULT CONNECTION

Contents

Introduction

FACED WITH PESTILENCE, hunger, debt, grief, corruption, banditry, fire, flood and all the misfortune and misery that fate can bestow on humanity, people everywhere and in all ages have tried to discover a secret consistency underlying the inconstancy of existence. Most societies are cemented, at least in part, by the fact that they agree largely on the clues that may lead to the revelation of this redeeming, stable ground of being. In the West, we have subscribed for nearly 2000 years to the ethics and metaphysics of Christianity. But there have always been individuals who the generally accepted ideas have failed to console or satisfy: dissidents, intellectual buccaneers and adventurers — heretics or madmen to many of their contemporaries. A few of these souls (depraved as they must often have seemed) managed to convince some of their peers that there was wisdom in their quaint ideas; and, in time, those who inherited their beliefs saw them displace the prevailing wisdom and become the new form of orthodoxy. This was the story of the early Church: first persecuted without mercy by the Roman empire, it was at last proclaimed the official religion.

Yet there are some traditions that have never achieved this kind of ascendancy over the dominant beliefs of any age or society. They have existed for hundreds — in some cases for thousands — of years like a sort of intellectual and emotional undergrowth by the highway of conventional thought. They have been neither wholly tolerated nor entirely damned by the priesthood or the body politic. Astrology, once it had broken loose from its origins as the scientific forerunner of astronomy, became a system of arcane belief that attempted to give some order to our inscrutable destiny, and it has managed to survive with little enough harassment in widely different societies for centuries. Likewise, it seems reasonable to predict that another belief, that humanity will soon be relieved of responsibility for its own affairs by the advent of benign Space Beings (who are already watching over us), will probably persist in one form or another as long as we continue to probe the stars with elaborate forms of hardware.

But if these beliefs or systems of thought are so tenacious, why have they not dislodged the great religions, which are still so powerful in the affairs of men?

One part of the answer, I would suggest, is that they are not really in competition with the world's religions. It is true that both the religious outlook and the occult have in common a desire to decipher a meaning from the multifarious and confusing ways of the world. But each does so in its own distinct fashion, confronting different, if not entirely separate, mysteries. A religion tends to console its adherents, to counsel resignation to the outrages of fortune, and to provide a moral code whose observance, despite the manifest injustices of this life, will be rewarded hereafter. To that extent, a sense of religion is a sense of ultimate things; it is wrestling with the problem of life's meaning in the face of inevitable death. The occult systems, on the other hand, while also attempting to discern order amid the chaos (and in some cases suggesting that there are moral bases to their insights) are at once the more difficult and the more self-centred paths to 'enlightenment'. What has given the occult systems their extraordinary longevity is, as much as anything, their implicit claim to provide *the power to beat the system*. They offer not simply a means to withstand the pressures and problems of the world, but a way of getting out from under. One can control one's own fate, by foreseeing the future, by acquiring riches beyond the dreams of avarice, by entering the exclusive ranks of those chosen for salvation, by using occult 'powers' to achieve political mastery. Where religion is essentially passive, fatalistic and communal, the occult is active, individualistic, and self-serving.

One of the greatest explorations of this distinction between religion and the occult is the legend of Dr Faustus, most especially in the tragic treatment given it by Christopher Marlowe. Faustus allows his relentless curiosity and his desire for power to overcome him, and he loses his soul to the Devil, having gained a world that proves illusory. Faustus may have travelled in time, gained riches, fame, and the company of beautiful women, but he cannot in the end defy death. And therein may lie the one single reason why the occult has co-existed for so long with religion without really displacing it: for the occult offers no answer, finally, with which to deflect the attentions of the Great Reaper.

There is not, of course, any shortage of voices insisting that religion has no answers either, but is merely a distraction designed to keep the masses where they belong – oppressed, powerless, and afraid. A less ideological objection is that the consolations of religion are not based on demonstrable fact but on faith – a kind of cosmic wager that life's trials will all have been worthwhile. This is fair enough as far as it goes, but much the same argument can be raised against occult systems. It should, however, be easier for us to discover whether or not they work.

Certainly incautious predictions made by the UFO cults, such as the arrival of aid from the stars and the end of the world, have been embarrassingly inaccurate. Hitler's devotion to the musings of his astrologers did not prevent the onslaught of the Allied armies. No one has succeeded in transmuting lead into gold, not least because the instructions for doing so left by the alchemists of old are almost impenetrably obscure – they may even have been describing a spiritual rather than a material process.

At the same time it is fascinating to discover the astrological characteristics of one's best friends. As a Pisces with Sagittarius rising, I wonder if it is merely chance that the majority of my closest friends are Sagittarians? And are my capacities as a writer and editor somehow the result of being born under that most literary of signs, Pisces? Or what about the time I impertinently asked the same question of the *I Ching* three times, and it instructed me to be less frivolous, since I had asked the question twice before? The trouble is that most of the 'evidence' concerning divination systems is of this kind – anecdotal, impressionistic and unsatisfactory, because it lacks all statistical validity. And we all know people who have lost their sense of proportion when it comes to such systems, who can scarcely bring themselves to speak to anyone born under their opposing sign, or who cannot face the day if they do not first check it out with the *I Ching*. None of this improves the reputation of the system itself, even though such behaviour is scarcely the system's fault. In the following pages, at least, you will find a balanced assessment of the 'occult' – its origins, its significance and what it can (and cannot) do.

PETER BROOKESMITH

Saviours from the stars

Will the answers to humanity's problems come from the skies? Thousands of devoted believers in UFOs think they will. KEVIN McCLURE examines the 'flying saucer' cults and the contactees who are their prophets

OPINIONS ON THE true nature of UFOs vary widely, from the theory that they are as yet unexplained natural phenomena to the belief that they are illusions conjured up by demons to seduce mankind away from Christianity. If we bear in mind that such varying conclusions are all said to have been drawn from the same evidence and that such evidence is notoriously unreliable, then it appears that evidence and reason play a less important role in UFO belief than faith.

When faced with the unknown, the frightening, or the inexplicable, mankind tends to try to make it into a part of his religion: worships it, or damns it. UFO experience is no exception. Erich von Däniken believes that our religious history is actually one of UFO visitation and its misinterpretation. Arthur Shuttlewood, the chronicler of the mysterious events at Warminster in the southern county of Wiltshire, England believes that UFOs are 'the giants of past ages in modern guise, ever reminding us that mankind faces many challenges before he completes his final life-cycle at the very hub of our wonder-filled universe'. Lord Clancarty, who writes under the name Brinsley le Poer Trench, believes in the 'Sky People', who left Earth after the sinking of Atlantis, and who are occupied now in helping us raise ourselves to a better state of life in the next millennium. There may well be a common source and stimulus for reported UFO, spiritist, ghostly and religious events, and this source is likely to be identified one day, with a resulting dramatic effect upon the world's beliefs and religious philosophies. But one can no more prove that one is right in these suspicions than can von Däniken, Shuttlewood or Trench. It is all assumption, guesswork, and a certain amount of faith or wishful thinking.

This type of belief about UFOs, while not capable of proof, seems justifiable and necessary; without it there would be little experimentation, few advances in understanding. So long as the believers remain

Members of the Aetherius Society charge a 'prayer battery' with spiritual energy on Wimbledon Common in London. They believe that the energy, when released under the direction of the Interplanetary Parliament, can assist troubled parts of the globe to struggle against spiritual danger

flexible and open-minded, there is no harm to come of it. But there is another form of UFO belief for which there is much less to be said, where reason seems to be wholly suspended, and where detailed and inflexible beliefs about UFOs – their origin, nature, occupants, and purpose – become an overwhelming form of religious faith or personal philosophy and outlook. The belief itself becomes a preoccupation, and a justification for all sorts of actions.

Such beliefs take a variety of forms. Some groups see ufonauts as seeking to co-operate with certain chosen individuals on the Earth, for the improvement or continuation of the quality of our life here. According to the teachings of such groups, the UFO people do not wish or promise to take their followers away. Two American 'contactee cults' are quite typical of many others.

The One World Family, founded by Allen-Michael Noonan, is a California-based cult that has attracted some following. Many of its features recur in numerous other groups. In Noonan's case, it is said that he was working on a billboard when he was suddenly transported to another planet. He found himself surrounded by angelic creatures, seated around a fluorescent throne. A voice boomed: 'Will you agree to be the Saviour of the world?' Noonan agreed. He has since remained in contact with an extra-terrestrial known as Ashtar, has made trips to an inhabited Venus, and regards himself as the Messiah. He is writing a massive reinterpretation of the Bible, the 'Everlasting Gospel', which his followers help him produce. He believes that he is the only mouthpiece for communications from Ashtar. Hallucinogenic drugs and the exercise of psychic abilities feature in the cult.

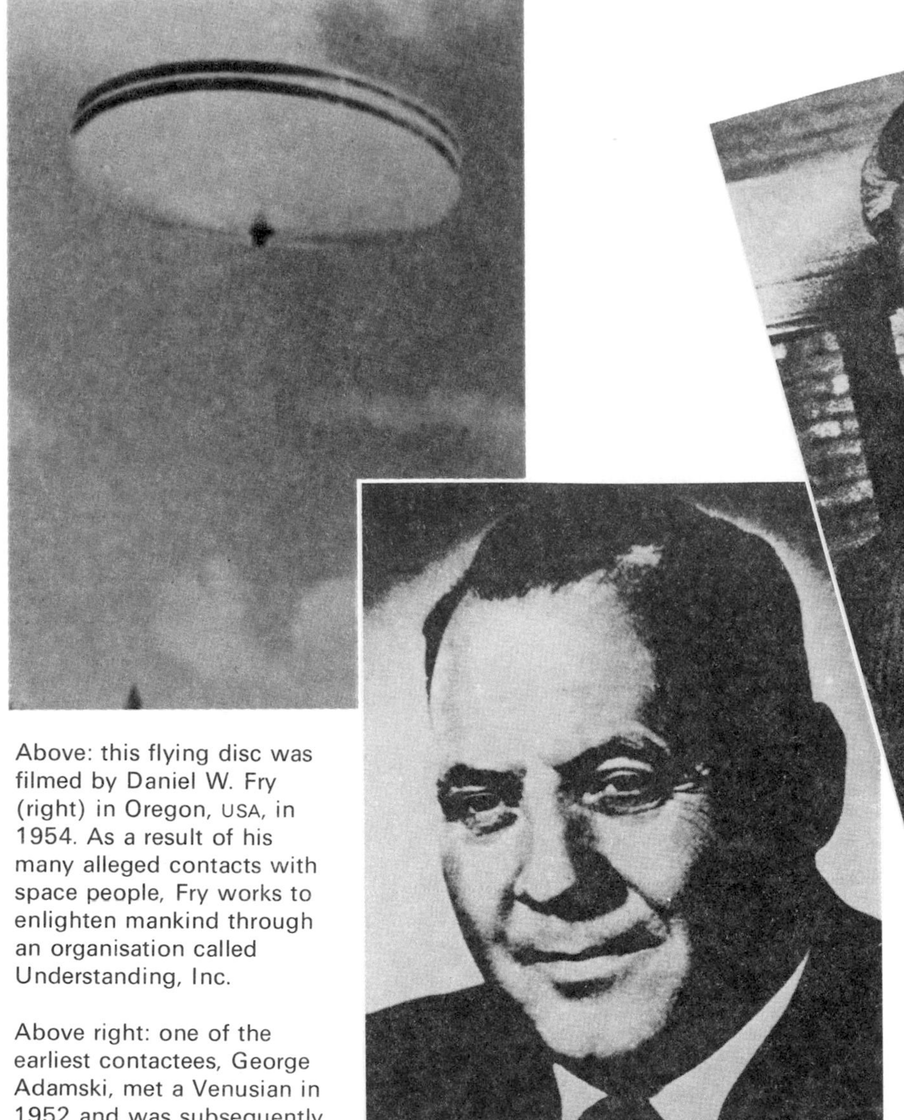

Above: this flying disc was filmed by Daniel W. Fry (right) in Oregon, USA, in 1954. As a result of his many alleged contacts with space people, Fry works to enlighten mankind through an organisation called Understanding, Inc.

Above right: one of the earliest contactees, George Adamski, met a Venusian in 1952 and was subsequently instructed in the Cosmic Philosophy

A new Messiah

Noonan also claims that, with the practical help of the aliens, the One World Family will eventually take over the government of the USA and the running of the United Nations; but only after all professing Christians have been, as they ambiguously phrase it, 'eliminated'. Allen-Michael Noonan is one of the least wholesome characters to have founded a UFO cult and it is impossible to tell whether or not he believes his own claims. But there is no doubt that his followers believe in both the claims and the individual, and try to act accordingly.

A less sinister, but none the less remarkable, cult group was the Institute for Cosmic Research, founded in Michigan, USA, in 1967 by a young man known as 'Gordon'. This group was developed around the supposed construction of a flying saucer that would actually fly – the *Bluebird* – and the group lasted as long as its members had faith in the unique achievement that would climax its slow and painstaking creation. Gordon claimed that his birth was supernatural: he arrived in his mother's arms, clad in white muslin, while a UFO hovered over the house. He was, he said, one of the seven Great White Brothers (a common type of claim in pseudo-Eastern movements). He also affirmed that he, and he alone, was in contact with extra-terrestrial entities from Io, one of the moons of Jupiter. There, he said, he had represented Earth at meetings of the 'Intergalactic Council'.

He told his followers that the Space Brothers had warned him that 'Earth's vortex is about to break because of an excess amount of hatred on this planet.' However, the Space Brothers had a plan: in order to change the ways of mankind they had chosen 'to provide Gordon with the technology to build a small flying saucer.' Potential members of the institute were told that only highly developed souls could be involved in work on it. They were to build the saucer and fly it into the skies. They would be joined by saucers from other planets and together would circle Earth for three days, darkening the sky. People would look up and wonder

why – and then would fall on their knees and start practising 'universal law'.

In Gordon's cosmology, the Sun was cold, and the stars, all of them, were inhabited planets. Despite all this, which surely must have been hard to believe, it is clear that Gordon had considerable charisma. The group lasted seven years before the basic untruth of the claims dawned on his adherents. Even then, many of the group members were unwilling to accept the fact. It is desperately hard to admit that you have been *so* wrong, for *so* long. The group had expended time, money, energy and faith: in some ways it was easier to go on believing than to have to cope with reality.

The great majority of UFO contactee cults come from the USA and British ufology is largely free of such extreme beliefs. But the most famous and long-lived contactee cult of all was started in Britain in about 1955. The Aetherius Society, which now has its headquarters in the London suburb of Fulham, has established itself in several of the world's major cities and has members in over 40 countries. Hundreds of devoted members attend the society's activities in Britain and the USA.

The story of the Aetherius Society and its development is very much that of its founder, George King. He built the society from nothing and now is held in the highest esteem by its members. It is worth considering, in a field where cults and belief groups are mostly transient and ephemeral, why the Aetherius Society has achieved a relatively wide appeal and has lasted so long. The key elements of the society's doctrine are very similar to those of the One World Family and the Institute for Cosmic Research. It offered its adherents a cosmology that was then beyond scientific disproof. (It asserted that most of the solar system was inhabited.) It provided an explanation for a mystery that held a widespread fascination: the flying saucers being seen all over the world. Many of them, it was said, represented a benign and concerned force – the Interplanetary Parliament. The doctrine imposed a task on the society's members: to store up, in conjunction with the extra-terrestrial entities, 'spiritual energy' in 'spiritual batteries'

Above left: Allen Noonan, founder of the One World Family, based in California. He receives communications from an extra-terrestrial called Ashtar and regards himself as the Messiah

Left: Frank E. Stranges, president of International Evangelism Crusades, Inc., received guidance from a Venusian called Val Thor, who had come to 'help mankind return to the Lord'

Far left: a well-known New York broadcaster, Long John Nebel (holding photographs), with George W. van Tassel, who founded the Ministry of Universal Wisdom to pass on teachings gleaned from regular UFO contacts

located in high places all over the world. This energy could then be discharged to prevent hardship, disease and disaster around the world. Lastly, the society possessed a priest: a go-between or communicator who alone had the ear of the Interplanetary Parliament, who would pass on the messages of the extra-terrestrials, and in turn would represent his followers to the mightier powers beyond. That communicator was, of course, George King.

The roots of the Aetherius Society lie in King's fascination, prior to 1954, with yoga and Eastern philosophy and metaphysics. His early life is not well-known, but he was born in Shropshire in 1919 and at various times worked as a fire service employee and a hire-car driver, and ran a healing sanctuary.

The publicity material has it that one day in May 1954, when King was alone in his flat in west London, he heard a voice say: 'Prepare yourself! You are to become the voice of Interplanetary Parliament.' Eight days later 'an Indian Swami of world renown [who] had obviously walked straight through' the locked door gave him information and instruction that dramatically changed his life and led to the founding of the society. In *You are responsible* King, not known for his humility, explains that he had to forsake his metaphysical studies, even though

> we believed that we were on the verge of discovering a new method of cancer treatment which could cure certain forms of this malignant scourge. Nevertheless, this command came out of the blue in such a way that no receiver could do anything else but listen and obey . . . . Quite soon after the deliverance of the Command, I was able to tune in and receive, telepathically, information which was relayed over millions of miles of etheric space. A message from Venus was recorded on our tape recorder. . . .

To be a little sceptical, it might have been better for the world if George King had persisted with his work on cancer, for much of the information he said he had received and the experiences he claimed to have had, implausible enough at the time, have since been rendered utterly absurd by the discoveries of space exploration. King wrote of his travels to Venus and Mars, and stated that Mercury was the only uninhabited planet. He detailed a battle he fought on a massive flying saucer of an interplanetary space fleet, 40 million miles (64 million kilometres) from Earth. In public meetings he gave trance messages from entities such as Mars Sector 6, the Master Aetherius and even the Master Jesus, who was apparently living on or near Venus. Without this last claim, the society might have been taken a little more seriously.

However, in spite of the utter lack of verifiable evidence for any of King's claims,

Above: Jupiter's innermost moon, Io. According to one 'Gordon', who founded the Institute for Cosmic Research in 1967, this world, slightly larger than our Moon, was the meeting place of the Intergalactic Council. If so, they chose a singularly inhospitable place. Space probes have discovered a world in violent turmoil, coloured reddish by sulphur spewed out by volcanoes larger than any on Earth

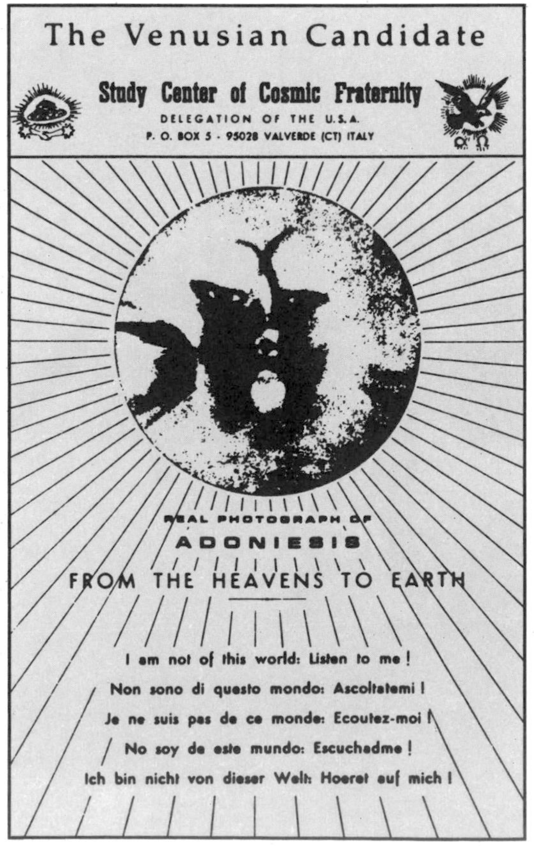

Right: publicity material of an Italian UFO contactee group, with a photograph allegedly showing their extra-terrestrial master. In 1976 this group wrote to US President Jimmy Carter, whose UFO sighting of a few years earlier had been widely reported. They told him that the authority he enjoyed had been 'granted from above'

his meetings grew larger. A regular journal, the *Cosmic Voice*, was launched soon after the society's inception. The messages relayed by King in an apparent trance state were taken seriously and acted upon though, like this example from Mars Sector 6, they were not always very clear: 'Take those M-ions inside of yourself, then your brain cells will release an opposite female magnetic energy. This will counteract the hurricane-force.'

That the society still thrives may seem surprising, but members, who seem often to be selfless and determined, concentrate much of their efforts on the 'task' previously mentioned. They have made pilgrimages, often in difficult and dangerous conditions, to a number of the world's mountains to fulfil the aims of plans bearing such names as Operation Sunbeam, Operation Bluewater and Operation Starlight. They have charged the spiritual energy batteries in such places as Ben Macdhui in Scotland, Mount Kilimanjaro in Tanzania and the Madrigerfluh in Switzerland. On the night of 27 June 1981, for instance, batteries E-1 and E-3 were charged at Holdstone Down, in south-west England. The 160 members of the society who were present stored a total of 219 hours and 28 minutes of prayer energy in battery E-1. Meanwhile, the extra-terrestrials put 1100 hours into battery E-3. On the same weekend, as part of Operation Sunbeam, 6000 prayer hours of energy were sent from Jupiter to the Psychic Centre in Scotland.

It is easy to make fun of such behaviour. But if there is any element of truth in what the society believes, then its members deserve credit for their selfless efforts. In a recent *Cosmic Voice* it was reported that a discharge under Operation Prayer Power was sent to Poland on 23 April 1981. It was intended to help prevent a Russian invasion.

The mechanics of the discharge were complex. The Los Angeles battery had to be substituted for the inadequate Detroit one because: 'the Prayer Energies were not being picked up by Adepts 002 and 003 [extra-terrestrials] in position in their (invisible) Space Craft above the central base of operations in Los Angeles.' George King reported during the operation that 'the Great White Brotherhood Retreat in Kilimanjaro, East Africa, had now joined in the release pattern.' At the end of the operation, Mars Sector 6 informed King that 'there was a heavy resonance of Spiritual Energies over the whole of Poland.' Perhaps the society is mistaken in trying to explain the mechanics of how prayer works. Older, possibly wiser, faiths keep the whole matter as vague and obscure as they can.

Though good will and a sense of common purpose hold the Aetherius Society together, one feature seems sure to limit severely the number of those who take it seriously. From being plain George King in 1954, the leader of the Aetherius Society had by the end of 1981 become the holder of such titles as Knight Commander, Doctor of Philosophy, Doctor of Divinity, Doctor of Sacred Humanities, Metropolitan Archbishop of the Aetherius Churches and Count de Florina. Some of these titles are conferred by the Aetherius Society, others are awarded by what are said to be ancient chivalric orders. Similarly, the society is deep in Knights, Ladies, Reverends and Doctors. Even this, the most respectable of the UFO cults, seems unable to understand what impression such excesses make on outsiders.

Below: George W. van Tassel, himself in regular contact with space beings, played host to UFO enthusiasts and other contactees at his Giant Rock Space Conventions, where participants watched for signals from UFOs – and sometimes saw them

Bottom: Mount Kilimanjaro, in East Africa, is a site of 'prayer energy' – thanks to the efforts of the Aetherius Society

Apocalypse now?

Messianic UFO contactees often give detailed warnings of impending disasters. But the cults invariably insist that only their own chosen few will be saved – a promise that attracts hopeful devotees

MOST UFO CULTS have appeared in the United States, long the home of countless eccentric religious and near-religious groups. The story of one of these cults is told in full by a trio of sociologists, Leon Festinger, Henry Riecken and Stanley Schachter. They 'planted' observers in a developing group centred on a UFO 'communicator' in 'Lake City', Utah. (The authors used fictitious names throughout, in order to protect their subjects.) The communicator was 'Marian Keech', who believed she had received the initial message from her late father. She sat quietly and regularly thereafter, waiting to produce automatic writing. She was soon contacted by 'higher forces': first by 'the Elder Brother', and then by entities from the planets Clarion and Cerus (neither of which is known to conventional astronomy). She received communications especially from one Sananda of Clarion, who claimed to have been Jesus in an earlier time.

Mrs Keech did not publicise her messages enthusiastically, but others from existing UFO groups and mystical or occult groups soon showed an interest, and in August 1954 a press release was issued. This summarised not only the more philosophical part of the communications, in which the media took little interest, but also predictions regarding a coming physical disaster of vast proportions. The nature of the event, as reported by Mrs Keech, varied at times, but as interest in the group grew its details became more firmly fixed. At the end of September the *Lake City Herald* published this typical report:

> Lake City will be destroyed by a flood from Great Lake just before dawn, December 21st, according to a suburban housewife. Mrs Marian Keech of 847 West School Street says the prophecy is not her own. It is the purport of many messages she has received by automatic writing, she says . . . . The messages, according to Mrs Keech, are sent to her by superior beings from a planet called 'Clarion'. These beings have been visiting the Earth, she says, in what we call 'Flying Saucers'. During their visits, she says, they have observed fault lines in the Earth's crust that foretoken the deluge. Mrs Keech reports she was told the flood will spread to form an inland sea stretching from the Arctic Circle to the Gulf of Mexico.

By now Marian Keech was referring to a group of communicators whom she called the 'Guardians', though Sananda remained the most important. Once the media had

Left: in a television science fiction play a throng of young people, controlled by armed police, gather at an ancient stone circle in the expectation that UFOs are about to take them to a new existence beyond the Earth. Invocations of 'space people' have taken place at pop festivals and UFO enthusiasts' gatherings – where badges such as these (inset) find a ready market. Many older and rather more staid people, however, have also expected to be contacted by UFOs and delivered from imminent cataclysm

started to publicise the group, Mrs Keech and her associates began to be afflicted by the problems that always beset UFO contactees. Increasing numbers of visitors called at her house, often when group members were present. She had explained to the group that if they did the right thing and were gathered together, ready, at the appointed time, they would not be drowned in the forthcoming flood but would be carried away in one or more flying saucers. The extra-terrestrials could come to make contact at any time and in any way: so Mrs Keech and her group had to decide whether or not visitors were extra-terrestrials and also whether they were good or evil extra-terrestrials.

The last days

The cult had now fallen into the classical pattern: it had a communicator, an explanation for the UFO mystery, a message of great importance, and a 'task' for its members – not so much to publicise the disaster as to prepare themselves to survive it. As the chosen date approached, the visitors became more frequent and more outlandish. Members of the group gave up jobs, possessions and relationships, and some took up unusual diets. All who could came together to await the fulfilment of their expectations. One condition of escape required by the Guardians was that all metal should be removed from the participants' persons. This led to some interesting arrangements for trousers and brassières, and a lively discussion about dental fillings.

The last few days before 21 December were traumatic for the group members, as their hopes were first raised and then dashed by increasingly strange messages and predictions, all proving to be inaccurate. The greatest shock came on the day itself, when no flood arrived, nor any spacecraft to save them from it. The group fell prey to disillusion and in due course dispersed.

Above: salvation from ageing and death was promised by George van Tassel, the 'Sage of Giant Rock'. On instructions from extra-terrestrials he built this structure, the 'Integratron', at Giant Rock Airport in California, USA. It was intended for research into 'the unseen truths of life', and to develop techniques of preventing and even reversing the processes of ageing in the human body. The structure, four storeys high, was made mostly of timber, and contained no metal

Another group that purveyed warnings of catastrophe transmitted from space beings called itself the 'Light Affiliates'. They were active in the late 1960s in Burnaby, British Columbia. Their launching statement read:

> We wish to notify all those interested that a phenomenon has occurred here in Vancouver. A young girl, age 22, suddenly began channeling on 23.10.69. Her source is a being identifying himself as Ox-Ho, who is relaying transmissions from a galaxy close to our own . . . . Her material is phenomenal in that she has been informed of the coming disasters, when to expect them, and what to do pertaining to the necessary evacuation of the danger areas and food supplies, etc, that will be needed.

The real name of the 'channel' was Robin McPherson, but she was renamed 'Estelle' by the 'being'. Her mother Aileen became 'Magdalene', her friend Sally became 'Celeste'. A young man involved in the early communications was given the evocative name 'Truman Merit'.

Ox-Ho explained that the day of judgement would begin during 22 November 1969. In these final hours Man would be 'given a last opportunity to repair his decadent house before the terminal series of disasters'. If mankind did not take the opportunity to change, 'the Space Brothers would remove the Chosen and return them to Earth after the planet had once again "crystallised", and been spiritually, as well as physically, restructured.' The 'restructuring' would involve the tilting of the Earth on its

axis and the disappearance beneath the sea of large land areas. The members of the Light Affiliates were exhorted to evangelise wherever possible.

Nothing seems to have happened on the predicted date to fulfil the expectations of the Light Affiliates. Robin McPherson ceased to communicate, but her mother continued the task. In an interview with the writer Brad Steiger in the mid 1970s, she explained where the predictions had gone wrong:

> We misinterpreted them, Brad, because it all happened so suddenly. The first visions I was given of destruction were very upsetting. I can see things now in a much broader perspective . . . . The thing is that it is the first ascension, and it is a *mental* ascension. The Brothers are trying to get as many people as possible into the Kingdom . . . . You know, I've been told by the Brotherhood that Earth is like an encounter therapy centre for the psychotics of the Universe . . . . I have been shown that the Earth is also wobbling very drastically on its axis.

It is sometimes less painful to find ways of showing that your beliefs are fundamentally correct by means of some elaborate reinterpretation than to concede that they are simply mistaken.

Claims that intelligent beings can visit us from the planets of the solar system have been made implausible by space exploration. Alien entities must come from distant star systems, even from other galaxies, of which science presently knows little. Some UFO cults – though by no means all – have adapted to the growth of knowledge by placing the source of their communications in suitably remote places.

The group that made the greatest impact during the 1970s was called HIM – Human Individual Metamorphosis. This group appeared in California in 1975 and appealed to some of those who had dabbled in the drug culture, personal spiritual development and 'New Age' mysticism. The movement was run by a middle-aged man and woman. They adopted names that were modest enough: Bo and Peep. Their teaching offered the advantages of life after death without the inconvenience of dying. Instead the adherents were to ascend physically. One of the cult's publicity posters read:

> UFOs – why they are here. Who they have come for. When they will land. Two individuals say they were sent from the level above human and will return to that level in a spaceship (UFO) within the next three months. This man and woman will discuss how the transition from the human level to the next level is accomplished, and when this may be done . . . . If you have ever entertained the idea that there might be a real PHYSICAL level in space beyond the Earth's confines, you will want to attend this meeting.

Above: Joan Culpepper tells reporters about her life with Human Individual Metamorphosis (HIM), the UFO cult run by the Two (below right). HIM offered its followers the prospect of being transported physically to a realm beyond the Earth's atmosphere. Joan Culpepper left the cult and set up a 'half-way house' to assist other disillusioned former adherents. Her two companions in this picture – still believing members of the cult – had taken the names 'Levi' and 'Moriah'. The Two called themselves Bo and Peep – but at the time the photograph was taken they bore their original names: Marshall Huff Applewhite and Bonnie Lu Trusdale Nettles. At the time they were under arrest by Texas police on charges of car theft and credit card fraud

More than human

Bo and Peep – formerly known as M.H. Applewhite and Bonnie Nettles – had convinced themselves that they were more than human, and had the strength of will and personality to maintain that impression; converts were clearly quite overwhelmed by them. At first they claimed that they would

one day be assassinated and then would be resurrected – after three days. Later these claims were set aside. As in other such groups, members were expected to make sacrifices: to give up their names and possessions, abandon the use of drugs, alcohol, radio and television, and not to indulge in sex – or even read books. The members generally lived in semi-permanent camps. The words of Bo and Peep in an interview recounted by Brad Steiger make their attitude to the family and other personal relationships clear:

> Husband and wife can take the trip at the same time – but not together. It would be impossible to become an individual if you went together on the trip . . . . In order to leave this Earth's atmosphere, you must go alone and overcome whatever needs you have for any other individual or thing of this Earth. Anything for which you depend on another human being or any thing on this Earth must be overcome.

Being a member of HIM was more like being a Moonie than participating in a traditional religion or even a traditional UFO cult. But the structure of the group was like that of other groups already described: there was a communicator, a message, a task.

No one has yet ascended to another physical realm above the atmosphere. Not many people seem to have got their money back, either. It turned out that Bo and Peep had met each other in a psychiatric hospital, where she was a nurse and he was a patient. Yet plenty of people remained willing to believe them and to accept their discipline. Like so many fringe religions, it seems to have met spiritual needs shared by many people at the present time.

Let us look, finally, at one further vision of salvation by UFOs – one that has been experienced in dreams by Sue and John Day, an English couple. They claim to have been taken on board an alien spacecraft near the village of Aveley in Essex, England. In their dreams they saw a deep red Sun and a dark sphere hanging in a blood-coloured sky. Columns of weary men, women and children made their way through a devastated landscape towards the summit of a high hill.

> There they waited for perhaps days, until their eyes caught the first glinting reflections from a formation of shining UFO-like craft appearing over the murky horizon, heading slowly in their direction. As they drew nearer a number of these craft broke away and descended over the hilltop, then began to lower ramps. The people seemed to know that at last 'they' had come. Come at last to take them away, away from the devastated planet Earth.

The Days identified the area in the dream as Dragon Hill, near Uffington. It seemed to them to be a presentiment of a possible, but avoidable, future – a future holding disaster, but also salvation for a fortunate few through the intervention of UFOs.

Dragon Hill, near Uffington in Oxfordshire, is one of England's most mysterious ancient sites. It was recognised by two contactees, John and Sue Day, as the scene of dreams they had that seemed to foreshadow some future disaster for the world. UFOs figured in the dreams as saving a disease-ravaged remnant of the human race

Reaching for the sky

Flying saucer cults may be no more than a haven for cranks – but is their interpretation of UFOs much odder than those of certain experts? This chapter compares some of the more exotic ideas entertained by ufologists

CULTS BASED ON UFO CONTACTEES have much in common – in their activities, in the way their leaders receive communications, and in the general tenor of those communications. But the specific claims made in the messages from 'space people' differ wildly from each other. The extra-terrestrials who guide them rarely even come from the same planet. However well-intentioned or warm-hearted the members of the groups may be, the divergences in their claims must lead the outsider to conclude that there is little reason to take them seriously. Whether or not the religious impulse that inspires them is authentic, the scientific trappings that they often don are distortions of valid science.

Yet the claims made by the cults are, if anything, less fantastic and disturbing than some of the theories that have been put forward by respected ufologists who have *not* surrounded themselves with followers and made claims to infallibility.

For example, although some of Brad Steiger's books should not be regarded as expressing his own opinions, the material in which his own attitude *can* be discerned seems to indicate a strong belief in the idea of

Above: UFOs descended on a French village in 1974 – but left no clue to their origin

Below: popular science writer Brad Steiger, who seems to believe that many historical figures were in touch with space beings

'Space Brothers' or 'Star People'. In one of his books the final chapter is contributed by his wife and is entitled 'How to contact multidimensional beings'. It states that 'Socrates, Napoleon, George Washington, Joan of Arc and Bernadette of Lourdes had contact with these beings.' Steiger himself has said:

> I am . . . convinced that there is a subtle kind of symbiotic relationship which exists between mankind and the UFO intelligences. I think that in some way, which we have yet to determine, they need us as much as we need them.

This begins to hint that mankind does not have control over its own destiny, but Steiger nevertheless believes that the higher beings with whom we are in contact are benevolent. Other writers have more frightening ideas. They believe that alien powers can control the experiences we have and the way we respond to them. Hypotheses of this kind are known as the 'control system theory', which is generally associated with Jacques Vallée:

> UFOs are the means through which man's concepts are being arranged. All we can do is to trace their effects on humans. . . . I suggest that it is human belief that is being controlled.

That is what Vallée wrote in *The invisible college*. He went further in *Messengers of deception*:

> I believe there is a machinery of mass

Above: D. Scott Rogo, whose account of UFOs includes the notion that the intelligence behind the phenomenon knows what humanity is thinking, and that contactees are 'the tools of a global plan'

manipulation behind the UFO phenomenon . . . UFO contactees are the tools of a global plan. These silent agents are walking among us unseen, placing social time bombs at strategic spiritual locations. Some fine morning we may wake up from our 'scientific' complacency to find strangers walking through the ruins of our Establishments.

Jerry Clark and D. Scott Rogo are a little plainer in their account:

> Let's begin by supposing that somewhere in the universe there is an intelligence or force – we'll call it the Phenomenon for want of a better word – that's beaming projections of various kinds into our world. . . . Whatever its nature, it has some deep sense of what human beings are thinking, and it provides us with visions that reflect the concerns of the human mind.

Writing on his own account, Rogo has stated:

> UFO abductions are physically real events. But they are dramas materialised into three-dimensional space for us by the Phenomenon. They are dreams that the Phenomenon made come to life in very frightening vividness. . . . Once someone has entered into psychic contact with the Phenomenon the link may become permanent, and reactivate periodically.

This is heady stuff, coming from figures of such stature and influence in the UFO field. But even Dr J. Allen Hynek, who has done so much to help make ufology respectable and acceptable on both sides of the Atlantic, has commented:

> There are people who've had UFO experiences who've claimed to have developed psychic ability. There have been reported cases of healings in close encounters, and there have been reported cases of precognition, where people had foreknowledge or forewarning that they were going to see something. There has been a change of outlook, a change of philosophy in persons' lives. Now, you see, these are rather tricky things to talk about, but it's there.
>
> Many people, like Jacques Vallée and I, to some extent, feel that it might be a conditioning process.

No hiding place

The control system theorists are not writing about occasional isolated incidents but about the worldwide evidence of a system to which mankind is bound and from which it cannot escape – a system that, they claim, existed before humanity appeared and will in turn outlive it.

John Keel's theories are perhaps the most terrifying of all. For him the control system, which he calls the Eighth Tower, is no longer running the show intelligently, but instead

The last days of the world

In *Messengers of deception* Jacques Vallée suggests that the UFO contactee cults are part of a sinister plan to undermine the power of rational thought for political ends. While the desire to change the world is plain enough in the 'teachings' of contactees like Claude Vorilhon (left and, below, his book), will many people act on them?

Vorilhon claims to have been chosen by extra-terrestrials because he is French, from 'the country where democracy was born', but in order to survive the 'last days' of the present age we must 'eliminate elections and votes' and disband the military everywhere. The 'Elohim' – a Hebrew word meaning 'the gods' – will then return and give us the benefit of their wisdom.

The space people also gave him a new name and his peculiar insignia – a swastika set within the star of David. As if this were not enough, Vorilhon (now 'Rael') naïvely recounts other benefits of his position such as his romp in a bathtub with no less than five singularly lovely extra-terrestrial female robots! All this is told in the course of appealing for funds to build a mansion to house the Elohim when they return.

Do Vorilhon's simplistic and contradictory notions hold any political dangers? Probably not – but this century *has* seen far more irrational ideas turn into hideous reality.

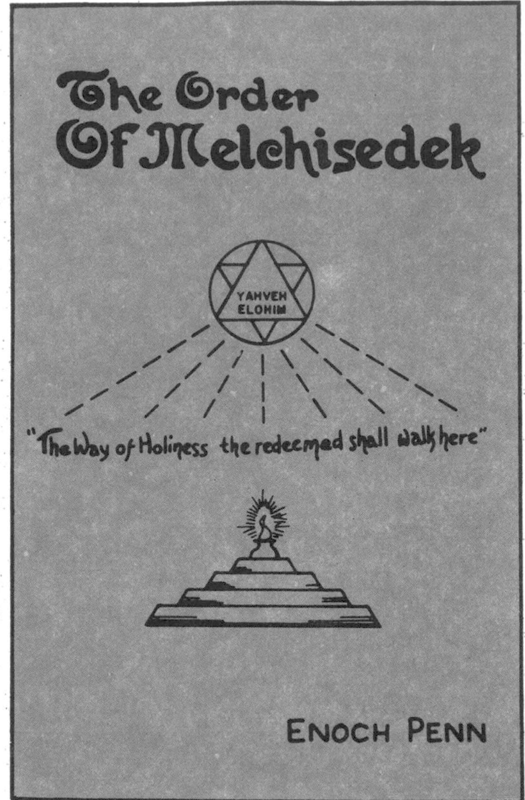

Left: the cover of a book by Enoch Penn, a member of the now-defunct American religious sect, the Order of Melchisedek. From its writings it is clear that the group expected to gain earthly power, though the means to gain that power (among other things members were enjoined to refrain from orgasm, for example) were not calculated to gain it much popularity. Some of the ideas as well as the name of the sect have been taken over by contactee cults in the USA and elsewhere. The pentacle (below) was given to author Jacques Vallée by the French Melchisedek group

Below: Brad and Francie Steiger's book *Star people*, in which they discuss the presence of aliens on Earth and their plans for humanity

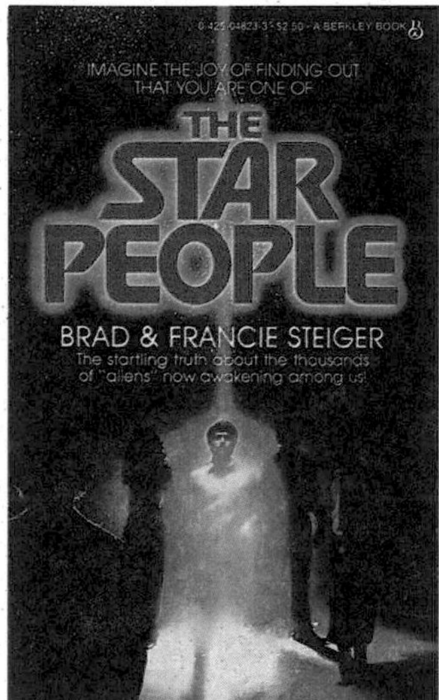

has gone out of control and is blindly following some preordained plan:

> The human race has always been aware that it was serving as a pawn in some cosmic game. . . . We have been programmed well, but the Eighth Tower is dying of old age. The manifestations around us are not the work of the gods, but of a senile machine playing out the end game.

This implies that humanity has only the illusion of free will in the conduct of its affairs – a view more pessimistic than all but some extremely Calvinistic forms of traditional religion.

Certain Christian groups, particularly among the evangelical movements, have viewed the UFOs as sinister, though not as controlling human activity. The respected *Journal* of the Spiritual Counterfeits Project devoted an issue to UFOs and concluded thus:

> Current UFO phenomena, insofar as they complete the patterns of fallen human speculation discussed earlier, while playing to that ignorant dynamism which drives us to the stars (to the neglect of our souls) cannot but be suspected of having their origin with Satan and his companions in spoilage and deceit. Add to this both the theological and statistical improbability that an extra-terrestrial race ever would (or could) visit Earth, and the odds lean greatly in favour of the possibility that UFOs *do* represent a visitation, but of extra*dimensionals* – demonic spirits which have gained the power to actually perform materialisations in the physical realm.

Setting Satan's stage

John Weldon and Zola Levitt, authors of a number of books on the paranormal written from a Christian viewpoint, have said:

> Quite simply we think the demons are preparing the coming of the Antichrist. . . . To properly set the stage for the Antichrist, who really is a supernatural personality, the world has to be made ready to think in terms of the new and the strange. . . .

Meanwhile, an English clergyman, the Reverend Eric Inglesby, comments:

> As psychic phenomena (which many UFOs are) the subject is interesting and potentially dangerous; in their spiritual aspect, involving the destiny of immortal souls, whether by false belief, or by spirit possession, or even by abduction, UFOs are not just dangerous – they are deadly. In some respects they are visible manifestations, to those who actually see them, of those principalities and powers which St Paul clearly identified as evil, not good.

Are UFOs as damaging as this mass of diverse opinion suggests? There is no convincing evidence to support the contention that they are physically or psychologically dangerous in a *direct* way: they cannot control our minds. But we can *make* UFOs dangerous to ourselves by bringing our own desires and fears to bear on the mass of recorded UFO data. Any of us can find material in that enormous accumulation to support our own personal opinions. The people who have created UFO contactee cults have built their own elaborate superstructures of belief.

We must regard the over-speculative interpretation of UFO data as a kind of temptation from which even the most intelligent, experienced and knowledgeable of commentators are not immune. The information we possess about UFOs makes a whole that is self-contradictory, confusing, outlandish and, often, incredible. We need to keep that simple fact in mind before building up our speculations on some selected part of the evidence.

The pattern of the future

How does one distinguish between prediction and prophecy? Can the concept of free will accommodate predestination? BRIAN INNES takes a look at the principal methods of divination, and begins with the ancient, but still flourishing, art of geomancy

'How now, you secret, black, and midnight hags!' Macbeth and Banquo encounter the Weird Sisters on a heath near Forres. The witches' prophecies were to change Macbeth's life, but they predicted nothing that did not remain in his control

THROUGHOUT THE HISTORY of mankind, those who were concerned about what the future held for them have sought guidance from 'wise' men and women. From the Azande tribesman who offers a chicken to the witch doctor in return for a prognostication of next month's weather, to the investor consulting his astrologer for assistance in forecasting future movements of the stock market, the motives, the means and the advice have always been very similar. But for all those prepared to *prophesy*, few would be prepared to say that they could *predict*.

The dangers inherent in placing too exact an interpretation on prophecy are exemplified very neatly in Shakespeare's *Macbeth*. Macbeth has – as the historian A.L. Rowse very rightly puts it – 'a flawed and ruined nobility – he is the victim of the Weird Sisters' prophecies; or, rather, of the promptings to which their "prophecies" gave confirmation.' In other words, Macbeth is given information that he interprets in one way; but subsequent events show that an entirely different, and equally plausible, interpretation could have been made.

When Macbeth first meets the witches, they hail him as thane of Cawdor, and as 'Macbeth, that shalt be king hereafter'. They also greet Banquo:

> *First Witch:* Lesser than Macbeth, and greater.
> *Second Witch:* Not so happy, yet much happier.
> *Third Witch:* Thou shalt get kings, though thou be none. . . .

Within minutes, Macbeth is named thane of Cawdor, and so, driven by ambition and the conviction that the witches have foretold his future, he murders King Duncan and himself becomes king of Scotland. Then, fearing that the rest of the witches' prophecy will also come true, he engineers the murder of Banquo – but Banquo's son Fleance escapes, and will sire a line of later kings.

But Macbeth must have more:

> I will tomorrow,
> And betimes I will, to the weird sisters:
> More shall they speak; for now I am bent to know,
> By the worst means, the worst.

The witches are only too happy to give Macbeth what he asks. They conjure up a succession of apparitions, who advise:

1. Beware Macduff.
2. None of woman born shall harm Macbeth.
3. Macbeth shall never be vanquished until Birnam wood comes to Dunsinane.
4. A line of kings shall follow Banquo's death.

Since he can do nothing about the last

prophecy, Macbeth determines to deal with the first. Learning that Macduff has already fled to England, he puts Lady Macduff and all her family to the sword. But he is greatly heartened by the other two prophecies, for they seem to imply clearly that no one shall harm him, and that he shall not be vanquished.

In the last scenes of the play, however, he discovers that the witches' words have another meaning. Birnam wood does indeed come to Dunsinane, for Malcolm's army wears its leafy branches as camouflage; and Macduff, who finally kills Macbeth, was not *born* of woman, but 'from his mother's womb untimely ripp'd' – that is, he was born by Caesarean section.

An inescapable fate?

Prophecy is the outcome of divination, and the example of Macbeth, and the advice given him by the witches, should serve to make clear the difference between divination and prediction. What the witches foretold was *not* predetermined: if Malcolm's men had not hidden behind leafy branches from Birnam wood, if Macduff had not returned from England to avenge the murder of his family, then Macbeth might well have lived out his reign and died in his own bed.

Indeed, Macbeth failed principally because of the psychological effect of the prophecies upon his self-confidence. The weird sisters did not make any specific predictions: they made only negative statements: 'None of woman born shall harm Macbeth. . .' and 'Macbeth shall never vanquished be until. . .'. They did not say that someone who was not born of woman *would* harm Macbeth; but the effect of their prophecy was that Macbeth's confidence was raised so high that, when he discovered that Macduff was not 'of woman born', he was immediately destroyed by his own guilt and superstitious fear.

If, then, divination is not prediction and is not concerned with predetermined events, what use is it? Why go to a fortune-teller with your problems, if a newspaper 'agony aunt' or even a close friend can provide you with a wealth of good advice? The reason, quite simply, is that the diviner does not make use of information that he or she consciously possesses about the person making the consultation: by the use of some means – whether it is the entrails of a freshly killed animal, arbitrarily chosen objects, a crystal ball, the astrological birth-chart of the subject or certain marks, such as moles, upon his person – the diviner is put in touch with information that is obtainable only by transcendental methods.

To those for whom a belief in the free will of the individual is paramount, the idea of a predetermined future is totally unacceptable. But look at it in this way. Someone's birth can be compared to the launching of a space vehicle. At the moment of 'lift-off', all the conditions are known and understood by mission control: the rocket will follow a predetermined trajectory, and at a known time the vehicle will be detached and will follow a predetermined course. The astronaut need do nothing thereafter; he can leave the future manoeuvring of the vehicle to those on Earth. But he is also provided with manual controls that he can use himself; he may become bored and start tinkering with fine adjustments in flight that produce results he did not expect; or, in a fit of rage – or other show of temperament – he may throw himself about the capsule and disturb its equilibrium. Whatever he does, *of his own free will*, will be recorded by mission control; and they can immediately inform him what will be the outcome of his actions, however unplanned.

They can, however, only advise. If he persists in what he is doing he may miss his target and disappear for ever in the depths of space, and nothing that anybody on Earth can do will help him.

This is how divination works. The diviner can give advice on the basis of information that is not available to his subject; he can predict the outcome of a particular course of action and suggest an alternative; but he cannot state that any future event will definitely occur.

All divination, by whatever method, follows the same sequence:

First, a question is formulated. This may range from something very specific – such as 'Will I win today's lottery?' or 'Should I marry this man?' – to general enquiries of the form 'What will my future life be like?' Obviously, the more specific the question, the more specific the answer is likely to be – and, therefore, the more trustworthy it is for the enquirer. Generalised questions usually attract answers that are susceptible of many different interpretations.

Next, some physical means is employed to

Below: a geomancer practises his art. Reading meaning into randomly generated patterns remains popular. In the West, tea leaves are read, in other cultures the throwing of inscribed tablets – similar to the throwing of dice – is a common method of divination (divining tablets from Mashonaland, Zimbabwe, right). The belief persists that a specially gifted person – shaman, witch doctor or fortune teller (a Vietnamese stick thrower, below right) – is needed to practise divination, but it seems that almost anyone can

Left: the life of an individual can be compared to a space mission. Its purpose is known to mission control, who can – and do – manoeuvre the spacecraft from the Earth. Yet the crew could depart from the prearranged programme. Mission control could advise the crew not to, and they could still take no notice. Similarly, *we* have free will; divination can only advise us; it does not actually determine the future of our lives

provide a link between the enquirer and the diviner. The enquirer may be asked to provide an intimate possession, to touch something belonging to the diviner, or to make an arbitrary choice of cards from a pack, objects thrown to the ground, or any random arrangement of things from which he does not make a conscious selection. Or the diviner may employ some device, such as a crystal ball or a pendulum, on which he can concentrate so intensely that consciousness of his surroundings recedes to a point where he is effectively in a trance. Drugs may also be used for this purpose.

Skill – or cunning?

Then, avoiding any temptation to make use of knowledge he may consciously possess about the enquirer, or to reason logically from one premise to another, the diviner *intuitively* produces his 'message'. Depending upon his skill – or cunning – this message may be straightforward advice of a practical nature, or a succession of cryptic statements that only the enquirer can interpret for himself. Frequently, as innumerable tales throughout history have told us, this advice can appear so obscure that the enquirer despairs of it; on occasion, diviners have been killed by their clients in an agony of frustration.

The methods of divination have their own archaic names, from abacomancy – divination from patterns of dust – to zoomancy – the observation of the behaviour of animals. There are, however, five methods of divination that have particularly attracted the attention of practitioners over the centuries, and that have therefore gathered about them a vast amount of literature and working tradition. These are astrology (see page 36), cartomancy, cheiromancy, geomancy, and the Chinese method of divination known as the *I Ching*.

Although astrology has claimed to be the oldest of these, there is little doubt that geomancy is as old – and it is certainly the simplest. In this context, geomancy got its name from the practice of making a pattern of holes in the earth, and should not be confused with the Chinese practice of *feng-shui*, which is concerned with finding propitious places on which to erect tombs, build houses or found cities.

Geomancy, in fact, may be the surviving ancestor of the *I Ching*: the divinatory figures of geomancy are made up of four lines, and those of the *I Ching* of six. Since each line can take one of two forms, the total number of combinations in geomancy is only 16, compared with the 64 of the *I Ching*.

The lines may be marked in the dust or earth – which is how the art of geomancy got its name; or they may be made up of kernels or stones; or they may of course be marked on paper.

The art is said to have originated in Persia, but it is widespread over the whole of the Mediterranean region, the near East and much of Africa, and since its spread over this area followed the spread of Islam it is at least possible that Arab traders had brought it from China. In Malagasy, geomancy is known as *sikidi*; on the west coast of Africa as *djabe* or *fa*. In Europe, the first full description occurs in the second book of the *Occult philosophy* of Cornelius Agrippa (1531).

The right lines

The 'lines' from which the geomantic figure is derived can be obtained in a wide variety of ways. They may be straight horizontal lines traced – randomly and without conscious direction – in the dust, which are distinguished as short or long lines; or they may be either straight or wavy. These two classes of line are then identified as 'odd' or 'even', and are represented conventionally by either one or two stones, palm kernels or dots. Or the lines may be made up of a random succession of dots, the oddness or evenness being determined by the number of dots. In

fa, a handful of 18 palm kernels is passed from the left to the right hand, and the number of kernels remaining in the left hand is counted as either odd or even.

To make a geomantic figure, four lines are required. If, for instance, the first and third are even, and the second and fourth odd, the resultant figure will be:

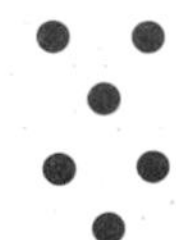

Altogether, there are 16 of these figures, each with its own name and significance, as detailed in the accompanying table.

Below: how the geomantic figures are traditionally interpreted in the four main methods – the European, which uses Latin designations; the two West African systems of *fa* and *djabe*; and the *sikidi* of Malagasy

The meaning of the figures

Figure	Latin name	Fa	Djabe	Sikidi
• • • • •	**Puer** Yellow; rash, inconsiderate	**Lete** Abscess	**Kaoussadji** Long Life	**Alakarabo** Leads to danger
• • • • • •	**Amissio** Loss	**Tche** Pearl	**Marili** Sickness	**Adalo** Tears; protection against enemies
• • • • • • •	**Albus** White; wisdom	**Touloukpin** Unripe papaya fruit	**Baiala** Family	**Alohomora** Favourable to thieves
• • • • • • • •	**Populus** The crowd	**Yekou** Spirits of the dead	**Djamaha** The crowd	**Asombola** Plenty
• • • • • •	**Fortuna major** Good luck	**Houolin** Pointed shell	**Adouhi** Victory over an enemy	**Adabaray** Fire
• • • • • •	**Conjunctio** Joining together	**Holi** Removal of an obstacle	**Dam'hi** Success	**Alatsimay** Protects thieves and enemies
• • • • •	**Puella** Girl; pretty face	**Toula** A firing gun	**Nagiha** Soon	**Alikisy** Good fortune in love; riches
• • • • • • •	**Rubeus** Red; passion, vice	**Ka** Canoe	**Oumra** Marriage	**Alabiavo** Riches, jewels
• • • • • •	**Aquisitio** Success, gains, good fortune	**Fou** Blowing the fire	**Kali** Good fortune on the right; bad on the left	**Alihotsy** Lightness of spirit
• • • • • •	**Carcer** Prison, delay, confinement	**Di** Resistance	**Sikaf** Law, command	**Akikola** Protects vagabonds
• • • • • • •	**Tristitia** Sorrow, melancholy	**Aklan** Porous stone	**Mankuss** Death	**Betsivongo** Obsession, tears
• • • • • • •	**Laetitia** Joy, health, beauty	**Abla** Connection	**Laila** Riches	**Alahijana** Strength; happy marriage
• • • • •	**Cauda Draconis** Exit, lower kingdom	**Gouda** Evil gods	**Sahili or Haridja** Serious intentions	**Karija** Fate
• • • • •	**Caput Draconis** Entrance, upper kingdom	**Sa** Between the thighs	**Raia** Health	**Alakaosy** Evil fate, disputes, war
• • • • • •	**Fortuna Minor** Less good fortune; external aid	**Losso** Riven tree	**Sapari** Journeys	**Soralahy** Pride, domination
• • • •	**Via** The way, journeys	**Gbe** Language	**Dariki** Children	**Taraiky** Loneliness; death

In Africa, these figures are interpreted singly, or in pairs. In the European tradition, the procedure is more complicated. In the first operation 16 lines are produced, and these are used to generate four 'Mother' figures. Suppose for example that the four following Mothers are produced:

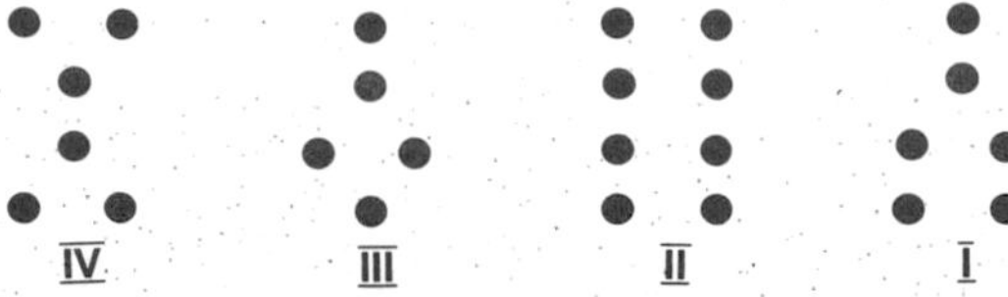

These are respectively: Fortuna Minor, Populus, Puer and Conjunctio.

From these four Mothers four Daughters are produced, by adding the four lines horizontally, from right to left:

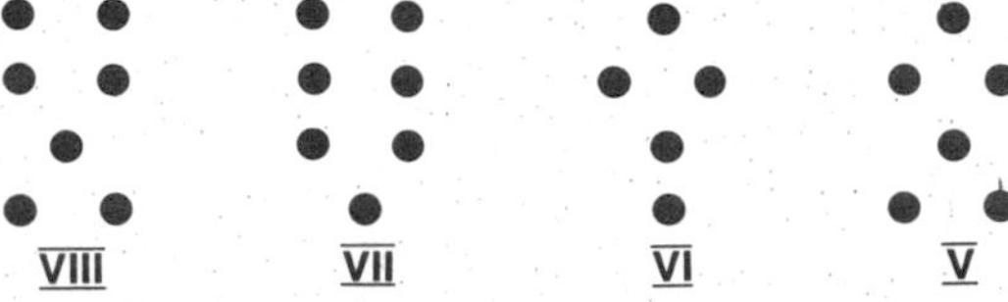

These are, respectively, Amissio, Puella, Tristitia and Albus.

Now four Nephews must be produced. The first Nephew is obtained by adding *together* the first and second Mothers, and marking the sum as before, with one dot for odd and two dots for even. So, from the first two Mothers, we get:

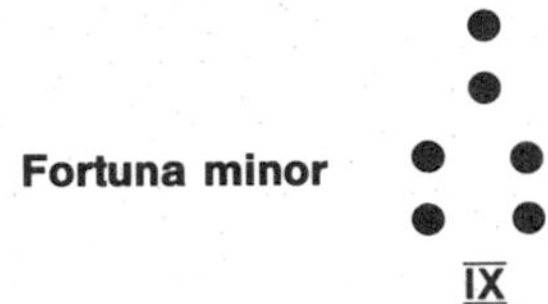

And from the second two Mothers:

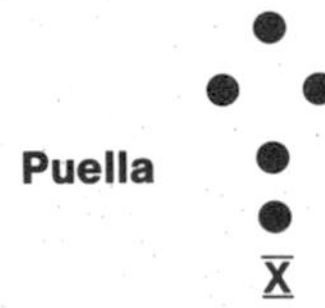

Similarly the third and fourth Nephews are formed by adding together the first and second, and the third and fourth, Daughters:

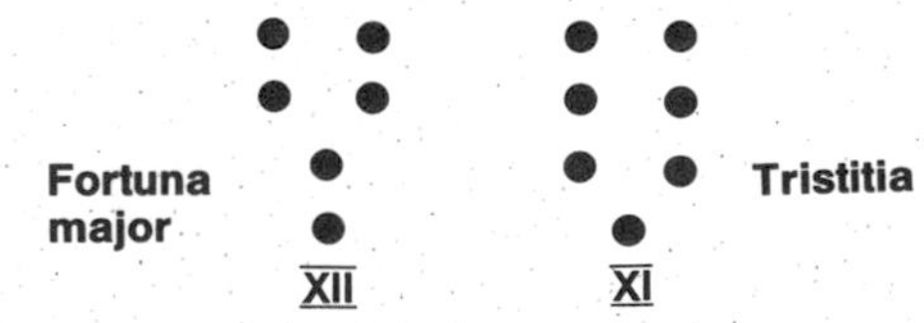

From the Nephews, two Witnesses are obtained by the same process of adding together:

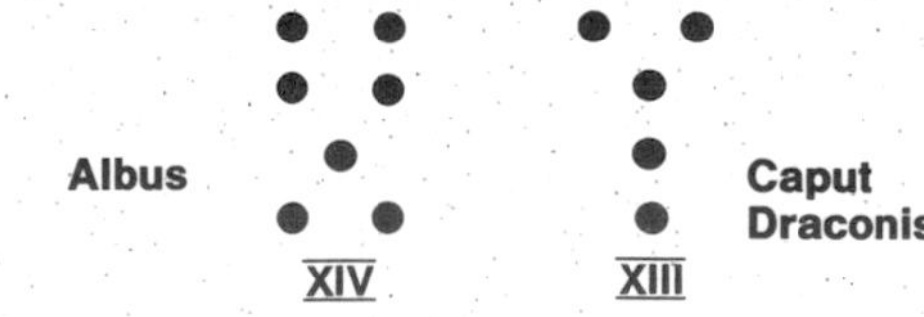

And finally, a Judge is obtained by adding together the lines of the two Witnesses:

The final pattern of 15 geomantic figures will provide the answer to one of 16 questions:

1. Will he have a long life?
2. Will he become rich?
3. Should he undertake the project?
4. How will the undertaking end?
5. Is the expected child a boy or a girl?
6. Are the servants honest?
7. Will the patient soon recover?
8. Will the lover be successful?
9. Will the inheritance be obtained?
10. Will the lawsuit be won?
11. Will he obtain employment?
12. How will he die?
13. Will the expected letter arrive?
14. Will the journey be successful?
15. Will good news arrive soon?
16. Will the adversary be overcome?

It can be seen that these questions cover most common preoccupations; with experience, the analysis of the geomantic pattern can be applied to other, rather more specific questions.

How are the figures interpreted, and how is the question answered? Let us suppose that the example above was obtained in answer to the question 'Will the lawsuit be won?'

In this case the Judge is Acquisitio, which signifies success, and the two Witnesses are Caput Draconis and Albus. These are all fortunate omens, and the implication is that wisdom will prevail and the lawsuit will be won with honour. We can investigate the progress of the lawsuit by considering the pattern of figures from the beginning. The outcome of the suit depends upon others (Fortuna Minor), whom we may suppose are the jury (Populus), likely to behave capriciously (Puer), but finally reaching a common verdict (Conjunctio). Perhaps the possibility of losing the suit (Amissio) is concerned with a girl (Puella), who can be the cause of sorrow (Tristitia) unless wisdom (Albus) prevails. The representative (Fortuna Minor) of the girl (Puella) could be a danger (Tristitia), but good fortune (Fortuna Major) will be the final outcome.

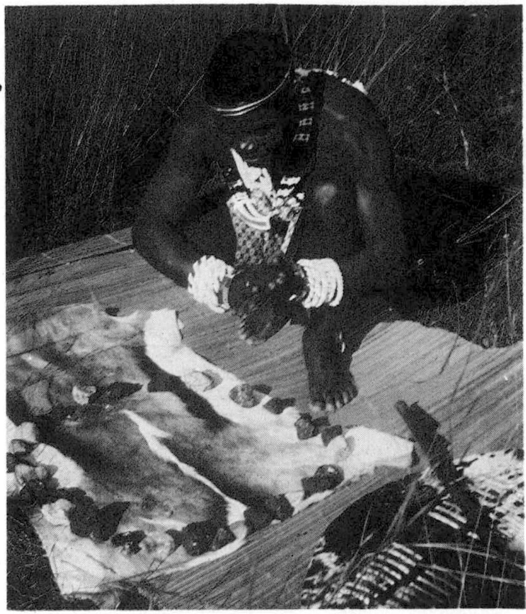

Right: a South African witch doctor casts and reads the 'wise stones'

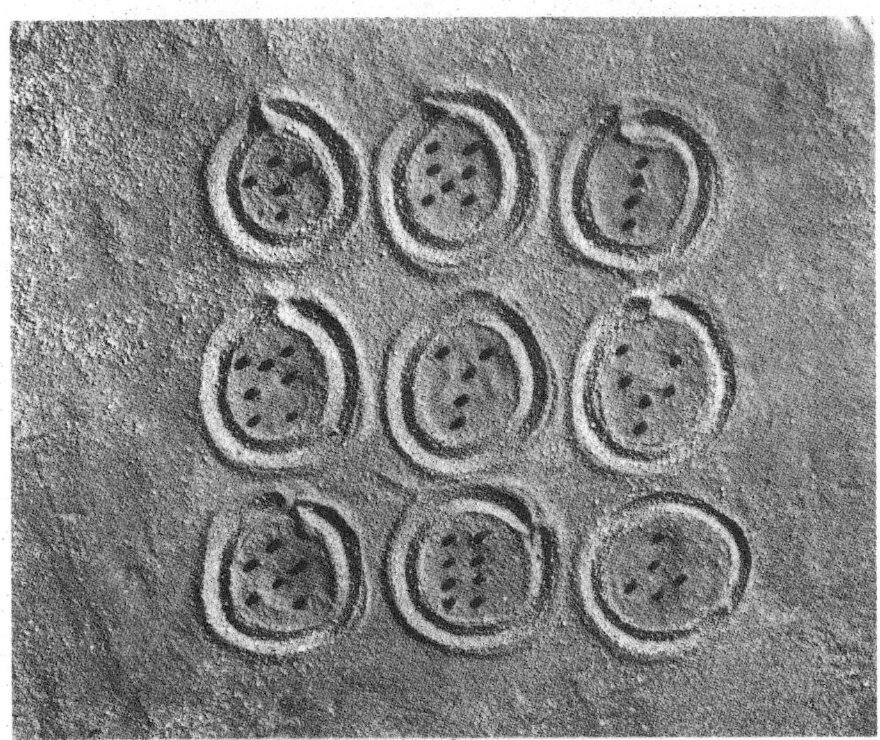

Below: on the west coast of Africa, in the geomantic method known as *fa*, palm kernels are passed from hand to hand for a few moments. Those that end up in the left hand are counted and the geomantic figures are then formed from them

Open to interpretation

Geomancy is the most primitive of all the methods of divination, but this example shows clearly how adaptable it is as a means of interpretation. Because of the sequence of operations by which the Judges and Witnesses are obtained, there are only eight possible Judges – Acquisitio, Amissio, Fortuna Major, Fortuna Minor, Populus, Via, Conjunctio, Carcer – and each of these Judges has a possible eight combinations of Witness, this figure being doubled due to the fact that each Witness may stand on either right or left of the Judge. Altogether, therefore, there are 128 possible configurations of Judge and Witnesses, each of which can be an answer to one of 16 questions.

Methods of divination to be considered in succeeding chapters are far more complex. In the *I Ching*, for example, there are 64 basic figures; while in the use of the Tarot cards there are a minimum of 22 cards, which may be disposed in an almost infinite variety of ways.

I Ching: enquire within

One of the oldest and most flexible of divinatory methods is also the most fascinating. This chapter continues our discussion of divination with a brief look at the Chinese Book of Change

CONFUCIUS SAID: 'If some years were added to my life, I would give 50 to the study of the *I Ching*, and might then escape falling into great error.' That was in 481 BC, when he was already nearly 70 years old, and had written a series of commentaries on the text of the book the Chinese call *I Ching*, which means 'the Book of Change'.

The *I Ching* is one of the oldest and most respected oracle books in the world. In its present form it can be traced back at least 3000 years – and even at that time it was already considered venerable, being based upon more primitive forms of oracle.

The Book of Change draws its basic philosophy from the ancient Chinese faith known as Tao. The word 'tao' is most usefully translated as 'way' – as in the Christian expression 'I am the Way, the Truth, the Life' – but no English word provides a really satisfactory equivalent, and even in Chinese it is susceptible of a variety of meanings. Indeed, as one Chinese inscription puts it: 'the Tao that can be put into words is not Everlasting Tao.'

Far right: K'ung Fu-tzu, the great Chinese philosopher known to us as Confucius

Below: a romanticised Western view of the ceremony involved in consulting the *I Ching*: the sticks are being passed through the smoke from an incense burner, while the enquirer makes his kowtows before them

Taoist writings are full, in fact, of negative definitions: 'power and learning is adding more and more to oneself, Tao is subtracting day by day; rigour is death, yielding is life; as laws increase, crimes increase.'

To the Taoist sage the world is not made up of discrete particles of time and space: everything is part of everything else, and reality consists of ceaseless change. The river that one paddled in yesterday is not the river one swims in today; and so the Universe is seen as a moving pattern in which nothing is permanent. So the *I Ching* is different from other oracle books: it does not regard the past, the present and the future as fixed; instead, it treats time and fate as dynamic and flowing, never the same from one moment to the next. The advice that one obtains by consulting the *I Ching*, therefore, is of possibilities: if you act in a particular way it is likely to result in such-and-such an outcome.

As a tool of divination, the *I Ching* is very similar to geomancy in principle (see page 19); but the divinatory figures that are generated are composed of six lines instead of four, and therefore there are a possible 64, rather than 16, figures. Moreover, where the

Below: the philosophy of Tao contains a strong sexual element, and intercourse is regarded as the interchange of yin and yang between the two partners. The cup represents Autumn Days, the last of the Thirty Heaven and Earth postures: 'The lord Yang lies on his back, his hand at the back of his head, and lady Yin sits on his stomach, but turning her face to his feet'

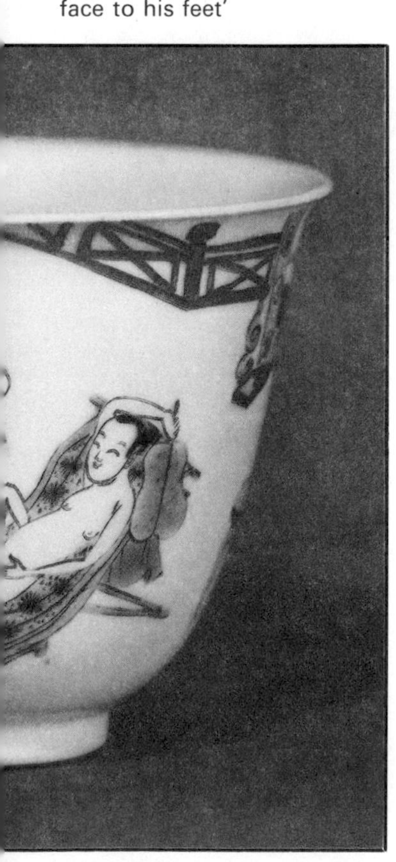

Witness-Judge procedure of geomancy results in only 128 different interpretations, each of the *I Ching* figures contains within itself 64 possible variations, and can generate at least one further figure: the total number of interpretations, therefore, is:

$$64 \times 64 + 64 = 4160.$$

Taoist philosophy classifies all the energies of the Universe under two headings, yin and yang. Yin is passive, watery, pertaining to the Moon, essentially female; yang is active, fiery, pertaining to the Sun, essentially male. The lines that make up the divinatory figures are described as either yin or yang lines; a broken line represents yin, a continuous line yang.

The six-line figures are known as hexagrams. Each can be regarded as made up of two three-line figures called trigrams. Since each line of each trigram can be either continuous or broken, the number of trigrams is $2 \times 2 \times 2 = 8$. And since each hexagram is made up of two trigrams, the number of hexagrams is $8 \times 8 = 64$.

The traditional way in which these figures are generated is long and complicated. A bundle of 50 dried yarrow stalks is required; yarrow was used because it had a certain holy significance to the Chinese. One of the stalks is set aside, and is not used in obtaining the hexagram; there is some dispute among Western writers as to whether the fiftieth stalk plays any part in the tradition of the *I Ching* or not.

The remaining 49 stalks are then separated into two piles. After this, the procedure is as follows:

1. One stalk from the right-hand pile is placed between the little finger and ring finger of the left hand.
2. Stalks are removed four at a time from the left-hand pile until four or less are left. These stalks are placed between the ring finger and the middle finger of the left hand.
3. Stalks are removed four at a time from the right-hand pile until four or less are left. These stalks are placed between the middle finger and the index finger of the left hand.

The stalks held between the fingers of the left hand will now total either 5 or 9:

$$1+1+3=5$$
$$\text{or } 1+3+1=5$$
$$\text{or } 1+2+2=5$$
$$\text{or } 1+4+4=9$$

These stalks are then put aside, and the process is repeated with the remaining 40 or 44 stalks. At the end, the stalks held between the fingers will total either 4 or 8:

$$1+1+2=4$$
$$\text{or } 1+2+1=4$$
$$\text{or } 1+4+3=8$$
$$\text{or } 1+3+4=8$$

This pile is also set aside, and the process repeated with the remaining stalks. Once more, the stalks held in the left hand will total either 4 or 8.

There are now three little piles: the first contains 5 or 9 stalks, the second and third each contain 4 or 8. There are therefore eight possible combinations of these three quantities. These provide a yin or yang line:

5+4+4	——o——	Old yang line
9+8+8	——x——	Old yin line
5+8+8 9+8+4 9+4+8	————	Young yang line
5+4+8 5+8+4 9+4+4	—— ——	Young yin line

The 'old' lines are also known as 'moving' lines: an Old yang line is seen to be changing into a Young yin line, and an Old yin line into a Young yang line. Each of the four types of line is also given a 'ritual number':

Old yin line	6
Young yang line	7
Young yin line	8
Old yang line	9

So far, only a single line has been generated. This is drawn as the bottom line of the hexagram, and then the procedure must be repeated five times more, the lines being drawn in ascending order.

Producing a single hexagram, therefore, can take five minutes or more. Those who let the *I Ching* govern their lives have developed a simpler and quicker method that requires only three coins. Chinese coins traditionally had an inscribed face and a blank or 'reverse' face – the side of a modern coin that gives the value is considered the inscribed side: if the blank face is given the value 3, and the inscribed face the value 2, tossing the three coins will provide a total of 6, 7, 8 or 9 – and so, taking this as the ritual number, the first line is obtained. It is possible, in this way, to obtain the hexagram in less than a minute.

What follows the obtaining of the hexagram? The texts of the *I Ching* are of several different periods and different kinds. First comes a description of the hexagram itself, in terms of the two trigrams of which it is composed; then comes the Judgement, which is said to have been composed by King Wen, the founder of the Chou dynasty (*c.* 1100 BC). This is a rather brief analysis of the hexagram as a whole.

'The superior man'

The next text, the Commentary, is traditionally attributed to Confucius, although it is improbable that he himself wrote it. This is generally longer than the Judgement, and takes note of the significance of the individual lines making up the whole hexagram. The third text, the Image, is succinct; it describes the kind of action that the sensible person – referred to usually as 'the superior man' – should take. This text has also been attributed to Confucius.

The final group of texts were composed by King Wen's son, the Duke of Chou, who destroyed the Shang dynasty in 1027 BC. These were written about 40 years after Wen's text: they are brief and rather cryptic, and they deal with the occurrence of Old yang and yin lines within the hexagram.

One or two specific examples will illustrate the nature of these different texts, and the way in which they are interpreted.

In hexagram 63, Chi Chi – Climax and After – the upper trigram is K'an, which symbolises dangerous deep water, the Moon, the winter season, the north, the middle son, an ear, the 'element' wood and the colour red; the lower trigram is Li, representing fire, the Sun, summer, the south, the middle daughter, the eye, and the colour yellow.

The text of *I Ching* describes Chi Chi as being an evolutionary phase of hexagram 11, T'ai, which means Peace. Hexagrams are read from the bottom, and the 'strong' positions are considered to be lines 1, 3 and 5. In T'ai, lines 1, 2 and 3 are occupied by yang lines, while lines 4, 5 and 6 are yin; in Chi Chi, the yang lines have migrated upward to their appropriate positions, displacing the yin lines to position 2, 4 and 6. Thus, says the text, everything is in its proper place. But although this is a very favourable hexagram, it still gives grounds for caution: for it is when equilibrium has been reached that any sudden displacement may cause order to revert to disorder.

The Judgement on Chi Chi reads: 'After the climax there is success in small matters. Righteous persistence brings its reward. Good fortune in the beginning, but disorder in the end.'

Now comes the Commentary. 'Chi Chi indicates progress in small matters. The proper position of the yang and yin lines shows that righteous persistence will be rewarded; the weak line at the centre of the lower trigram indicates good fortune in the beginning, but the way peters out, efforts come to an end, and disorder returns.' This is one of a number of cases in which the Commentary seems to add very little to the Judgement, but in other cases it can be of considerable value in elucidating the often obscure phrases of the Judgement.

The verses of the Duke of Chou refer to the occurrence of 'moving' lines, the Old yang and Old yin lines. The bottom line of Chi Chi is a yang line: if it is an Old yang line, with a ritual number 9, then the verse for that line should also be read.

These Old lines are also moving into Young lines. Suppose, for instance, that the hexagram Chi Chi was obtained as follows:

```
——— ———
———————
———x———
———————
——— ———
———o———
```

When the old lines have changed into their opposites, the hexagram will be:

```
——— ———
———————
———————
———————
——— ———
——— ———
```

This is a very different hexagram. It is 62,

Above right: how the sticks are held between the fingers of the left hand

Above far right: in this porcelain dish the shepherdess, a yin symbol, is surrounded by two male and one female sheep: these sheep represent the trigram Tui, or Joy

Right: an example of an English translation of the text of the *I Ching*, giving the Judgement, the Commentary and the typically cryptic verses written on the individual lines

63 Chi Chi Climax and After

The trigrams:
above: K'an dangerous deep water
below: Li fire, brightness

This hexagram represents an evolutionary phase of hexagram 11, T'ai, Peace. The strong yang lines have moved upward into their appropriately strong positions, displacing the yin lines into their proper weak positions. Everything is in its proper place. But although this is a very favourable hexagram, it still gives grounds for caution: for it is when equilibrium has been reached that any sudden movement may cause order to revert to disorder.

The Judgement
After the climax there is a success in small matters. Righteous persistence brings its reward. Good fortune in the beginning, but disorder in the end.

Commentary
Chi Chi indicates progress in small matters. The proper position of the yang and yin lines shows that righteous persistence will be rewarded; the weak line at the centre of the lower trigram indicates good fortune in the beginning, but the way peters out, efforts come to an end, and disorder returns.

The Image
Water over the fire, the image of Chi Chi. The superior man, accordingly, gives due thought to the misfortunes to come, and takes precautions in advance.

The Lines
In the bottom line, NINE signifies:
Like a driver who brakes his chariot,
Or a fox with a wet tail.
No blame.

In the second line, SIX signifies:
She loses her carriage curtain.
Do not run after it.
For in seven days it will be recovered.

In the third line, NINE signifies:
The Illustrious Ancestor
The emperor Wu Ting
Attacked the country of devils.
Three years he took in subduing it.
Small men are not fit for such enterprises.

In the fourth line, SIX signifies:
The finest clothes turn to rags.
Be careful all day long.

In the fifth line, NINE signifies:
The neighbour in the east sacrifices an ox:
But it is the neighbour in the west,
With his small spring sacrifice,
Who is blessed for his sincerity.

In the sixth line, SIX signifies:
His head is in the water.
Misfortune.

Hsiao Kuo. The Judgement, Commentary and Image for this second figure should also be read for interpretation, but since the lines have now moved the verses of the Duke of Chou are not significant.

One can go further: if the lines are moving independently of one another, there are two possible intermediate hexagrams between Chi Chi and Hsiao Kuo. These are:

or

The first is 49, Ko; the second is 39, Cheng. Reading the texts for these two hexagrams, but remembering that only one can be the true intermediate, may help in the interpretation.

One has to be very careful in trying to present an imaginary worked example of the use of the *I Ching*: too often, indeed, one finds that the hexagram obtained is Meng:

> I do not seek out the inexperienced; he comes to find me. When he first asks my advice, I instruct him. But if he comes a second or a third time, that is troublesome, and I do not advise the troublesome. . . .

As an experiment, I asked the *I Ching* 'whether it would be wise for me to finish this chapter tonight'. The hexagram I obtained was 20, Kuan:

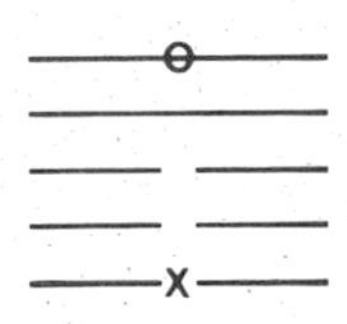

Kuan signifies contemplation: 'the worshipper who has washed his hands, but not yet made the offering'. The upper trigram of Kuan is Sun, representing wind and gentleness; the lower trigram is K'un, the Earth, the passive. The Image of Kuan is the wind moving over the Earth. 'So did the kings of old visit all parts of their kingdom, to see their people and give them instruction.'

There is an Old yin line in the second line, which signifies:

> Contemplation through the crack of the door
> Is sufficient only for a housewife

and the Old yang line in the sixth line signifies:

> Contemplating himself
> The superior man is without reproach.

It seems that *I Ching* is advising me not to continue with the chapter until I have had time to think about it some more; it also suggests that my time would be better occupied in assertaining whether the editorial staff have any problems.

Now the moving lines must be allowed to develop, and the resultant hexagram is 29, K'an:

This is one of only eight hexagrams in which the trigram is doubled. In each trigram a strong yang line has plunged into the deep between two yin lines, as water lies in a deep ravine. The Judgement reads: 'Abyss upon abyss, danger piled on danger. But if you are sincere there is success locked up within.' The Commentary continues the theme, and the Image of K'an is: 'The water flows on and on to its destination; the image of the abyss upon the abyss. So the superior man walks in eternal virtue, instructing others in the conduct of their affairs.'

The last part of this text clearly relates to the advice given above – although the warnings of danger seem unnecessarily strong in such a minor matter. Can the intermediate hexagrams throw any light on the matter?

The two possible intermediates are:

These are, respectively, 59, Huan, and 8, Pi.

Huan signifies dispersal, and the advantageousness of travel. In the sixth line, the Old yang line signifies:

> He disperses bloodiness
> Keeping evil at a distance
> Departing without blame.

Pi, on the other hand, is the image of holding together; it signifies those who follow the lead of the superior man.

It was only a light-hearted question, and it deserves a light-hearted answer. The *I Ching* has told me that it is time for me, and my staff, to stop work and go home!

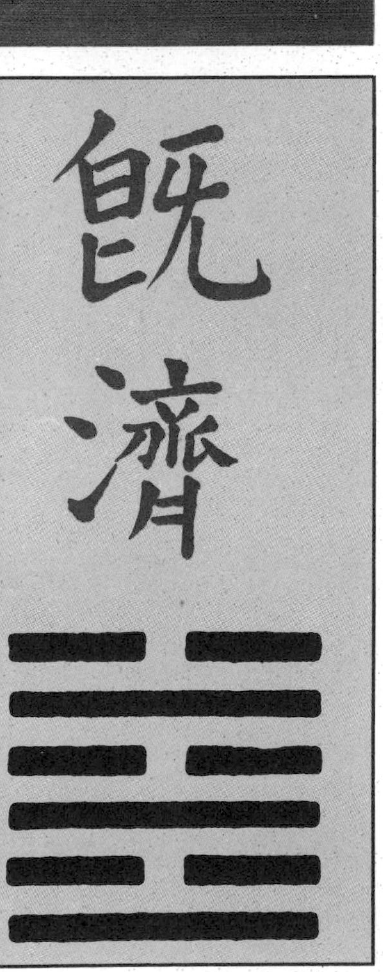

Is it possible to read an individual's future from a pack of Tarot cards? This chapter describes the most popular method of divination, explaining how the cards are consulted and how the significance of each one can be interpreted

The first mention of playing cards occurs in records for the years 1377 to 1379; by the end of the 15th century (above) they were widespread in Europe

Coming up trumps

THE DIVINATORY methods so far considered are aleatory – that is, they are based upon what seems to be a random selection of identical elements. The word 'aleatory' comes from the Latin for dice-player, and of course one of the simplest of divinatory methods consists in the throwing of one or two dice.

However, numerous experiments in psychokinesis have suggested that an experienced dice-thrower can influence the results of his play; and it may well be that the subconscious mind, or some transcendental aspect of it, is able to calculate the implications of the number of geomantic marks being made, or, as in the *I Ching*, yarrow stalks selected, before the hand has completed its movements.

It is certainly worth postulating that the mind, being in some kind of telepathic awareness of all the interpretations available, in some way selects the most suitable answer to the question that has been posed, and then subconsciously causes the appropriate figure to be generated.

Some process of this kind seems to be at work in divination by means of the Tarot pack, which is probably nowadays the most popular of all methods.

The use of a pack of cards for divination is definitely not aleatory, since each of the elements selected is distinct, and has a particular significance all its own. There are a number of packs of specially designed cards available for divination – the French firm of Grimaud, for example, market such sets as the cards of 'Mademoiselle Le Normand', or 'The Parlour Sybil' – but most diviners are able to make do with an ordinary pack of playing cards. And in this respect it is important to remember that the Tarot pack is also an *ordinary pack of playing cards*. Although some of the images of the Tarot pack may appear bizarre to north-western Europeans familiar only with the standard 52-card bridge and whist pack, they do not embody an intrinsic occult significance. For 500 years, the Tarot cards have been the standard pack for a variety of common card games that go under the generic name of *tarok* or *tarocchi*.

There are very many ways of 'consulting the cards', and there is no reason to suppose that any one way is more correct or successful than any other. All that is important is that the practitioner should be completely confident about his or her method and the way in which the cards are to be interpreted. The easier methods make use only of the 22 trumps, which have been given by occultists the impressive title of Greater Arcana; the distinctive images of these cards are of great help in attaching significance to each, and in remembering what that significance is.

More complicated methods employ all 78 cards; but here even experienced practitioners find it necessary to resort to textbooks to remind them of the accepted significance of the numbered suit cards.

Ideally, to make consulting the Tarot a true divinatory method, each practitioner should decide exactly what meaning to attach to each card – even if this departs widely from what is commonly held to be the meaning, it should not affect the process of divination in any way. In practice, it is common to consult a textbook on the subject; although this may provide a rather stilted, formalised interpretation, it makes divination by Tarot very much easier.

The same kind of divinatory process can of course be carried out with a pack devoid of

Opposite: stages in the development of the images of two representative Tarot cards, Strength (above) and The Fool (below). The packs represented are, respectively: one attributed to Bonifacio Bembo, executed about 1480 (left); the 'Swiss' pack published by Müller since the late 18th century (centre top); a modern Italian pack of traditional design published by Modiano (centre); the Grimaud 'Marseilles' pack, from a 17th-century design (centre bottom); pack designed by the occultist Oswald Wirth, late 19th century (top right); a Spanish pack of early 20th century design (centre right); and pack designed by another occultist, A.E. Waite, and published at the turn of the century (bottom right)

Tarot trumps, such as a common 52 or 56 card pack, but in this case the interpretation is commensurately more difficult.

The ways in which the cards are used in divination are of two kinds: either a select number of cards is chosen for interpretation, or the complete pack is disposed according to a formula, producing a pattern of distribution in which the position of the card determines its part in the divinatory process.

As in all other methods of divination, the process comprises a questioner, who asks for advice by proposing a particular question, and the diviner, who interprets the answer. The cards may be dealt out either by the questioner or by the diviner – no two authorities agree on this, and it may also depend upon the particular method employed – but it is essential that both should concentrate fully upon the question. As with the *I Ching*, a frivolous question, or one that is idly put, will provoke an answer that may be equally facetious or, possibly, quite frightening in its implications.

One example must suffice to show how the Tarot cards are laid out in a pattern, and how they are then used for divination.

The questioner in this case is a mature but

still young woman, who has been married for several years; she has a full-time professional job. Due partly to the tastes and partly to the particular ambitions of her husband, she finds herself compelled to live in a district that she finds unpleasant. Should she endeavour to make her present home as pleasant as possible, or should she try to persuade her husband to move elsewhere?

The particular arrangement of cards used is one known as the 'Celtic cross'; only the 22 Tarot trumps are required for this.

1. A card is chosen to represent the question; this is known as the significator. In this particular case The Star, representing 'new beginning; pleasure; salvation', was the card selected.

2. The questioner shuffles the remaining cards, cuts them, and places them in a pile some way to the left of the significator.

3. The top card of the pile is turned over from left to right (so that it remains as it was in the pile, either upright or reversed) and placed directly on top of the significator. This card represents the present conditions in which the questioner lives or works. The card is The World. In spite of the nature of the question asked, it therefore would appear that the questioner is on the whole satisfied

change; it brings knowledge of the future and new understanding of the past; it advises the questioner to face up to whatever change may come.

These first six cards drawn have presented a picture of the questioner and her problem, as well as revealing some small details that she did not provide. The final four cards, which are placed one above the other to the right of the table, supply the divinatory advice.

1. The first card represents the present position of the questioner, and may answer the question directly. It is Death – not to be taken literally, for this card represents change by transformation.

2. The second card represents people and factors that may have an influence upon the answer. It is the Wheel of Fortune which, though it also signifies change, counsels prudence.

3. The third card reveals the inner feelings of the questioner, which she may well have kept hidden. It is the Moon, reversed; this suggests very strongly that the questioner does not really want to make the change that she has said she is considering.

4. The final card represents the end result of everything indicated by the preceding cards. The Pope is the representative of the firm foundations of our lives, the concepts of natural law and justice. This card, appearing in this position, suggests that the questioner and her husband have a mutual sympathy and understanding; their marriage appears to be a successful one; and it would be dangerous to threaten its stability by pursuing the change that was the subject of the question.

The account book of the treasurer to Charles VI of France records a payment in the year 1392 to the painter Jacquemin Gringonneur for three packs of cards 'in gold and various colours, of several designs, for the amusement of the said King'. The three cards illustrated here – Death (left), The Sun (right) and The Fool (below right) – are from 17 that survive in the Bibliothèque Nationale in Paris and that were long believed to be the original Gringonneur cards. They are now, however, thought to be from the 15th century and of Italian origin

with her lot, and feels a sense of achievement in her work, and perhaps also in her home.

4. The second card is placed across the first, to represent any immediate influences that may affect the interests of the questioner. The card is Temperance: whatever decision is reached, it is likely to be controlled by reason.

5. The third card is placed above the first group of cards, to represent the ultimate aim of the questioner. This is the Fool, reversed, which confirms the previous card. And since it is reversed, it signifies the opposite of luck or fate, and implies a rational outcome.

6. The fourth card is placed below the first group to represent the influences from the past that have affected the questioner and the question she asks. The Empress tells us that she is a woman of considerable understanding and intuition.

7. The fifth card is placed to the right of the central group to represent the recent past. The Hermit suggests that the passage of time has brought wisdom and further understanding.

8. The sixth card is placed to the left of the central group to represent influences that may come into play in the near future. The Hanged Man represents adaptability and

A brief summary of the symbolic significance of the Tarot trumps

Trump	Significance
1 Magician	Man in search of knowledge; the answer he seeks
2 Woman Pope	Intuition, inspiration; subconscious memory, lack of foresight
3 Empress	Human understanding, femininity, sensuality, beauty and happiness
4 Emperor	Masculinity, independence, creativity, action
5 Pope	Advice; justice; healing
6 Lovers	Choice, decision
7 Chariot	Achievement, success; danger of defeat
8 Justice	Caution in taking advice; control of one's fate
9 Hermit	Time; wisdom; withdrawal
10 Wheel of Fortune	Change; prudence; the eternal return
11 Fortitude	Strength of purpose, coming danger
12 Hanged Man	Adaptability; desire to learn; violent change and sacrifice
13 Death	Change by transformation, rebirth
14 Temperance	Moderation, mercy; modification
15 Devil	The adversary; caution
16 The Tower	Punishment; pride; divine inspiration
17 The Star	New beginning; pleasure; salvation
18 The Moon	Uncertainty; changeability
19 The Sun	Splendour, health, wealth, affection; treachery
20 Judgement	Punishment or reward; final achievement
21 The World	Fulfilment, completion on a material level
0 The Fool	Fate; luck; the end

Above: how the Tarot cards are laid out in the spread known as the 'Celtic cross'. The significator card is The Star; laid on top of this is The World, representing the present condition of the questioner, and Temperance lies across both. Subsequent interpretation is explained in the text

A pattern of Tarot cards, however many have been laid out, is obviously very different from the pattern of dots obtained in geomancy (see page 19), or the pattern of lines in the *I Ching* (see page 24). Each of the cards has its own significance, and the position of each in the pattern also has a particular meaning. The Tarot cards must be read like the pages of a book: if we consider only the 22 trumps, there are over a thousand million million million different sequences. Add to this the incalculable number of groups of two, three, four or more and you will see that a combination can be obtained that will represent every conceivable situation – and that still leaves another 56 cards that can be used in interpretation

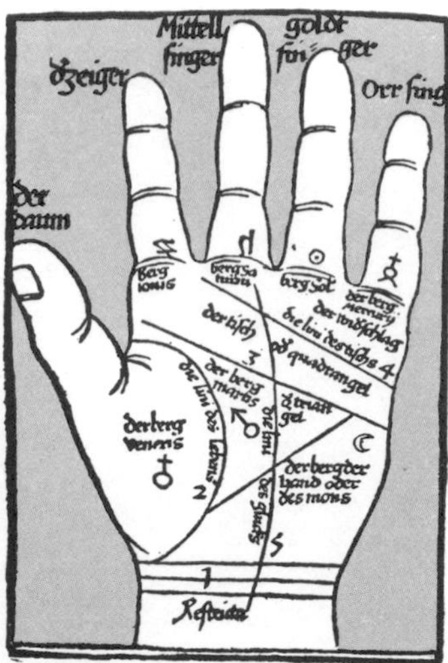

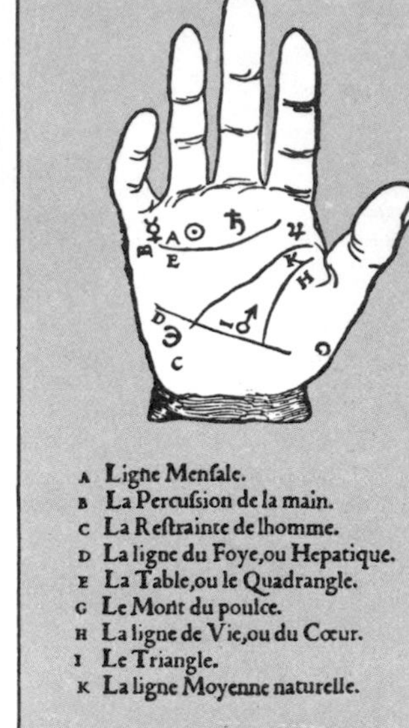

Above left: palmistry has a long and venerable history – and remains popular today

Top: a diagram from Bartolomeo Cocle and (above) from Jean d'Indagine illustrating the ancient association between parts of the hand and the planets

On the other hand...

The lines of the hand are as individual as personality – but is there a connection between them? And can a diviner trace a person's destiny in his or her palm? This chapter examines the practice of palmistry, still widely popular as a form of divination

DIVINATION IS a means of answering questions and giving advice on what future action should be undertaken by the questioner. It works best with intense concentration of both practitioner and questioner, apparently by providing some kind of telepathic insight into the nature of the problem, the personality of the questioner, and the probable outcome of any given action.

To obtain the necessary concentration, almost all practitioners require some object on which they can focus their conscious faculties, in order to give the subconscious a free rein. Certain practitioners make use of something like a crystal ball, or a pendulum; but greater success seems to be achieved if the object on which attention is focused has some direct physical relationship with the questioner: playing cards that have been shuffled and cut by him or her, or some other kind of object that has been handled.

So far, all the methods of divination described in these chapters – geomancy (see page 19), the *I Ching* (see page 24) and the Tarot (see page 28) – have required a personal involvement on the part of the questioner, but the means of divination has always been physically divorced from him or her. There remains one major divinatory method that requires the closest co-operation of the questioner, because the object being consulted is part of the human body itself. This method is cheiromancy, more popularly known as palmistry.

There are many who would not regard palmistry as a divinatory method at all. Since the law recognises the uniqueness of the human fingerprint, there is every reason to suppose that the palmprint is just as individual. We recognise a particular dog or cat

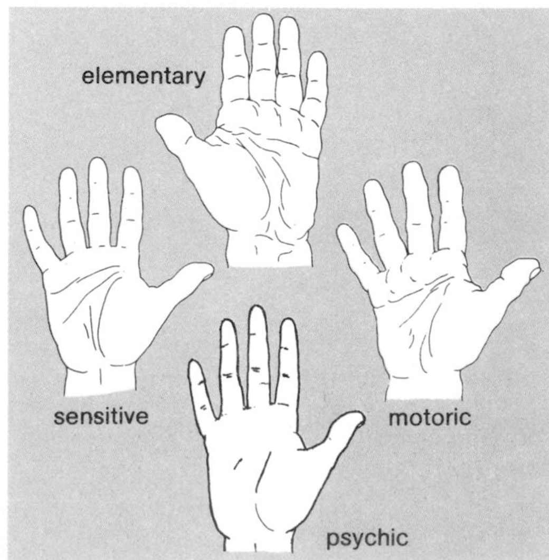

Left: the four basic shapes of the hand according to Carl Carus. The 'elementary' hand is typical of the manual worker; the 'motoric' is large and strong but flexible, and is found among businessmen and craftsmen; the 'sensitive' hand, typical of writers and artists, is not as strong as the 'motoric' but is full of energy; and the 'psychic' is long and soft, indicating a personality that is sensitive and intuitive

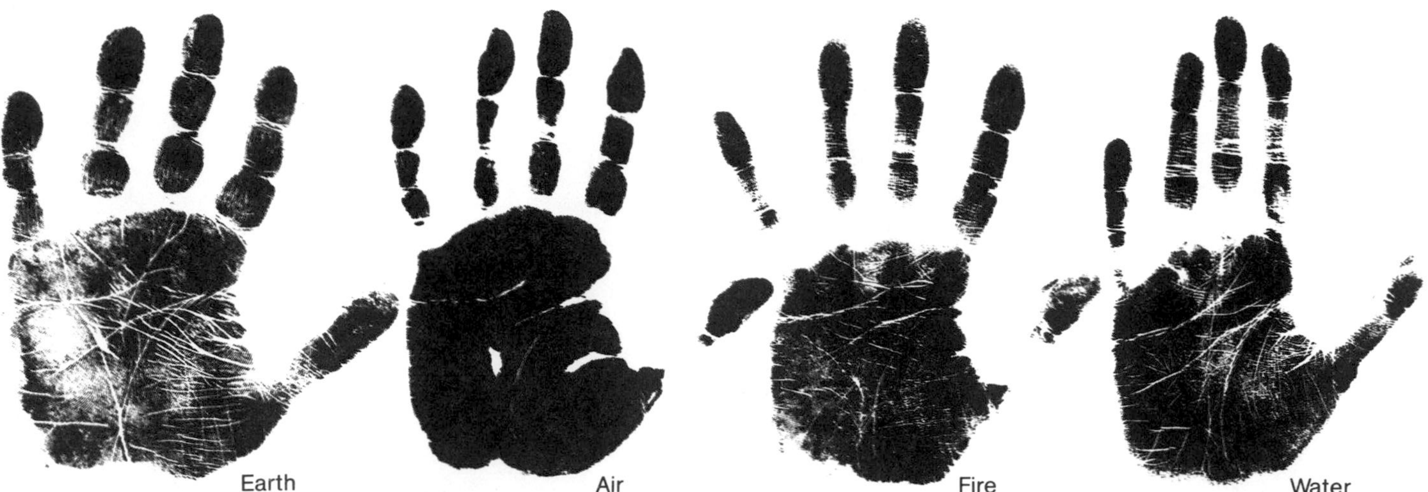

by the distinctive pattern of its coat, and we could similarly recognise a person by the pattern of their palmprint. Since it is well-known that animal coat patterns are affected by many factors – the climate, the time of year, the health and genetic background of the individual – it is at least arguable that the human palmprint similarly has something to tell us about the individual.

One palmist, in fact, has claimed that he read a young man's hand, saw that there was a strong indication that he might commit suicide, and suggested to him that he should have psychiatric help – and that six months later the lines of the young man's hand had changed out of all recognition.

There is some scientific evidence that the occurrence of abnormal lines on the hands may be related to certain hereditary diseases, such as heart defects or those related to chromosome deficiencies. In traditional palmistry the so-called 'simian' line – in which the Head line and the Heart line run as one – is held to be an indicator of 'degeneracy'; now a group of doctors in New York has reported that this line often occurs in mongoloid children or in those whose mother suffered an attack of rubella (German measles) during pregnancy.

Above: the 'Earth' hand is square, with short strong fingers and few lines; the 'Air' hand has longer fingers and finer lines; the fingers of the 'Fire' hand are short with many lines; and the 'Water' hand is narrow and delicate, with a mesh of fine lines

Below: the 'elementary' hand is typical of primitive people; the 'square' hand indicates a practical nature; the 'spatulative' hand denotes excitability; the 'philosophic' hand is self-explanatory; the 'conic' hand indicates someone who prefers pleasure to work; the 'psychic' hand speaks for itself. But most hands fall into the 'mixed' category

Right: the mounts and fingers

Whether or not there is any validity in this suggestion of a direct connection between the human metabolism and the lines of the hand, there is no doubt that the commonly accepted significance of the lines and parts of the hand must be based upon many centuries of empirical observation. Cheiromancy is recognised in the Bible, as in Proverbs 3:16: 'Long life is given in her right hand. In her left are riches and honour.' Or in Job 37:7: 'He seals up the hand of every man, that all men may know his work.'

Indeed, in this second verse, we can detect the old magical element in cheiromancy, the belief 'as above, so below'. It is quite possible that the first palmists believed the lines of the hand to be some sort of map of celestial motion, rather as if the subject's horoscope had been printed there.

But whatever credence we may give to the interpretations placed upon individual lines

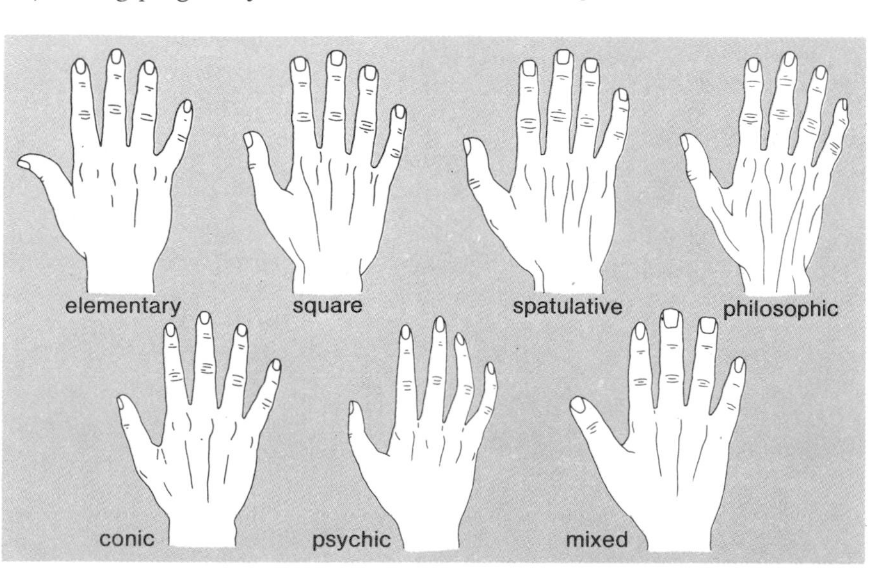

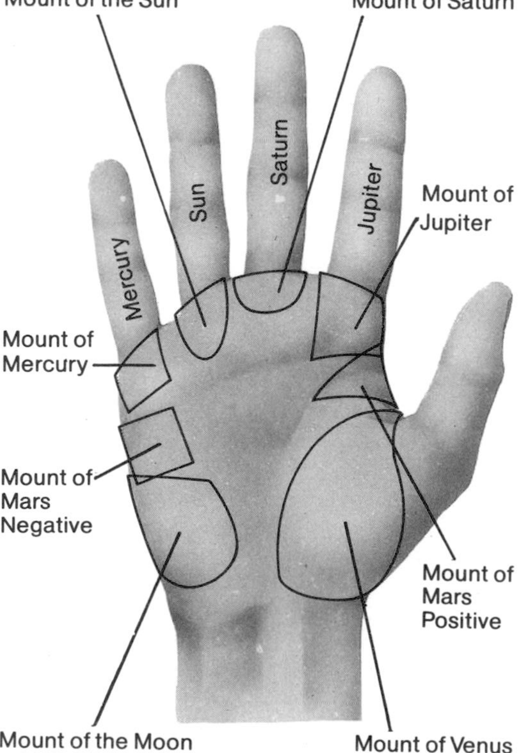

of the hand, there are other tenets of palmistry that are borne out by both popular and medical belief. Palmists place great importance on the form of the whole hand: its shape, its moistness or dryness, its relative fleshiness, the length and shape of the fingers, and the relationship of the thumb and fingers to the palm. And isn't this just what we all do – even subliminally – when we judge an individual's personality, and even the state of their health, from the touch of their hands?

There are a number of different methods of classification of the basic shape of the hand. The German Carl Carus proposed four types, which he named 'elementary', 'motoric', 'sensitive' and 'psychic'; the Frenchman Casimir d'Arpentigny increased this to seven, the 'elementary', 'square' (or 'useful'), 'spatulative' (or 'necessary'), 'philosophic', 'conic', (or 'artistic'), 'psychic and 'mixed' hands.

Under the pseudonym of le Comte de St Germain, a late-19th-century writer expanded these to 14, including such oddities as the Congenital Idiot's hand and the Brutal Murderer's hand. In the 20th century, however, the tendency has been to reduce the number of shapes once more to four; a popular classification has been into Earth, Air, Fire and Water hands.

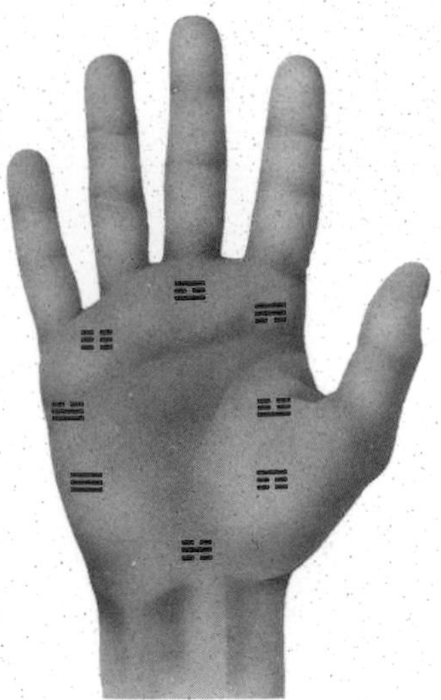

Above: the eight 'Palaces' of the hand in the Chinese system. Clockwise from the Mount of the Moon, these are: Ch'ien, for spiritual force; Tui, for sexual delight; K'un, for passivity; Li, for social and financial standing; Sun, for mental capacity; Chen, for energy and vitality; Ken, for obstinacy; and K'an, for difficulties to be faced

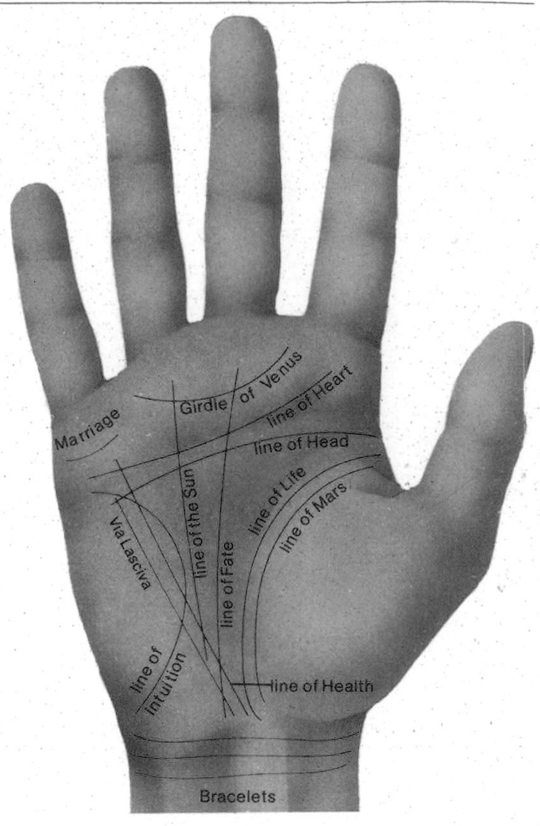

Above right: lines of the hand according to present-day practice

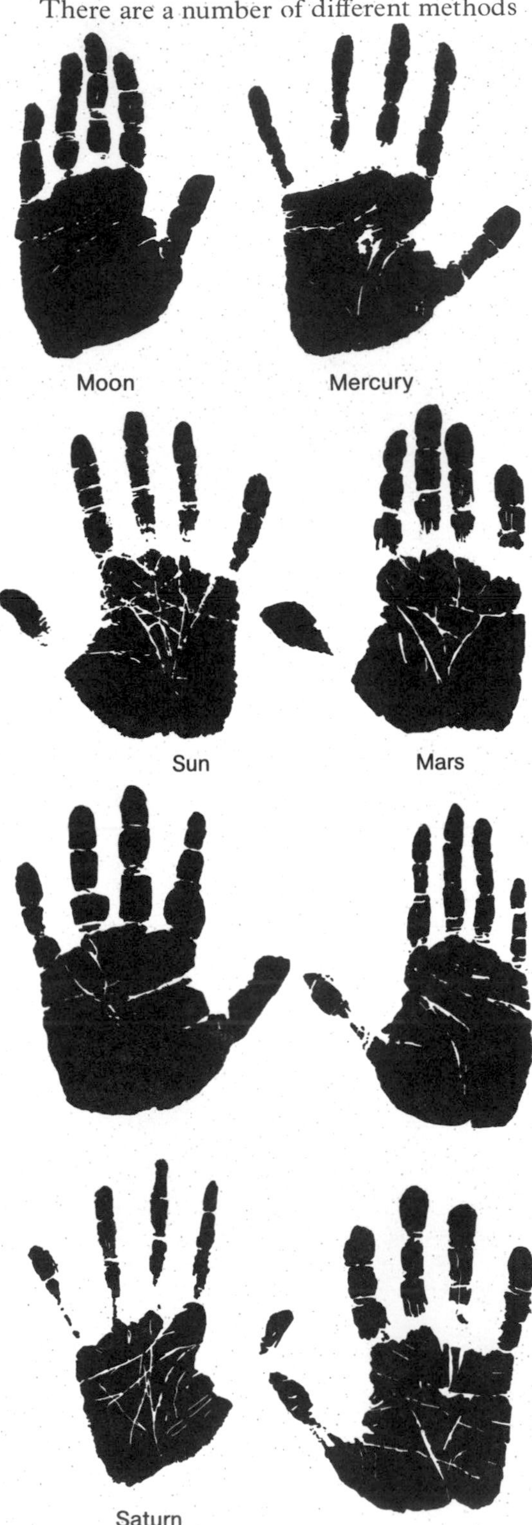

Left: classification of hand shapes on astrological principles. The Lunar hand is soft, with many lines: it indicates a restless but easygoing nature. The Mercurial hand, with its long finger of Mercury, denotes intellectual ability and quick wits. The Solar hand, with strong, short fingers, indicates ambition and trustworthiness. The Venusian hand, with its prominent Mount of Venus, is a sign of a cheerful and extrovert personality. The Martial hand has a very developed thumb and denotes courage and energy. The Jupiterian hand, with its thick and heavy fingers, is a sign of even temper and generosity. A long finger of Saturn characterises the Saturnine hand, indicating patience and shrewdness. The Earth hand is thick and firm, denoting a generous, slow but sure personality – and a loyal friend

Astrological magic

Classifications of this kind have a certain natural logic to them; it is when we come to the fingers and the 'mounts' of the hand that astrological magic begins to take over. The mounts are the fleshy areas of the hand around the central palm, and each, with its related finger, is associated with one of the planets.

It is interesting to note that the fourth finger, which is associated with Apollo or the Sun, was long believed to have a vein running through it that connected directly to the heart, and it is for this reason that wedding rings are always placed upon this finger.

And so we come to the very complicated markings that appear all over the palm, the wrist and the fingers, and that no two people possess identically. There has been a great deal of argument among palmists as to the relative significance of the lines on left and right hands respectively, which can differ quite markedly. The commonest (and perhaps the most sensible) theory is that, in a right-handed person whose lines will obviously be affected by the work they do throughout their lives, the lines of the left hand represent the destiny to which they were born, and the lines of the right hand represent what they have made of their life.

The lines of the palm are divided into principal and subsidiary lines. The 15th-century writer Jean d'Indagine recognised only four principal lines: the mensal, or line of Fortune; the line of Life, or line of Heart; the Middle line, which represented the subject's career; and the line of Liver, or Health line.

Indagine's near-contemporary, Bartolomeo Cocle, added a further line, the line of Fate, running from the wrist direct to the finger of Saturn; and later 17th-century writers identified more lines according to our modern nomenclature.

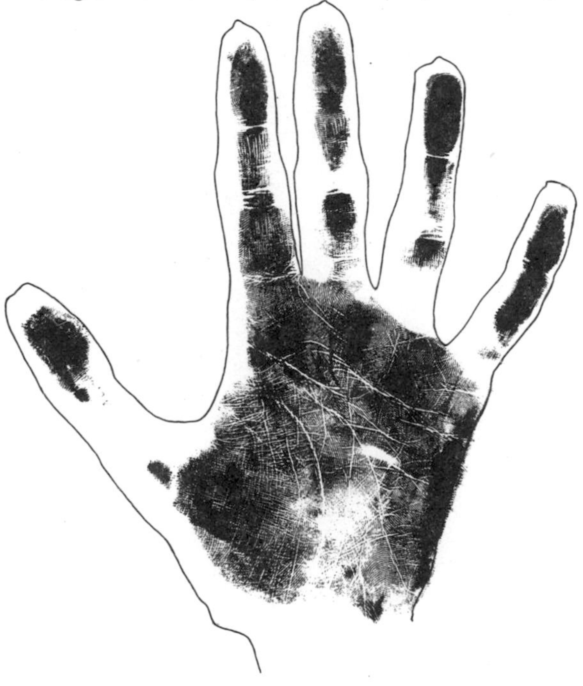

Below left: a female hand that is both 'psychic' and a typical 'Water' hand, with lunar characteristics. This is a sensitive, changeable person, but the well-developed finger of Jupiter suggests good judgement. The line of Life is strong and well-marked. Although the line of Heart begins quite strongly from below the Mount of Jupiter it breaks before ending, chained, below the Mount of Mercury. It seems as if this person had no one on whom to direct her affection until later life; there is only one 'line of Marriage'. The line of Head begins strongly on the Mount of Jupiter, indicating an ambitious character, but it breaks, revealing inner conflict. The line of Fate begins strongly at the wrist but stops on the line of Heart, perhaps indicating that emotional problems will interfere with her career

Below: hand of a young man before and after psychiatry. The deep line on the Mount of the Moon has almost vanished and the many lines under the finger of Apollo have become one strong line

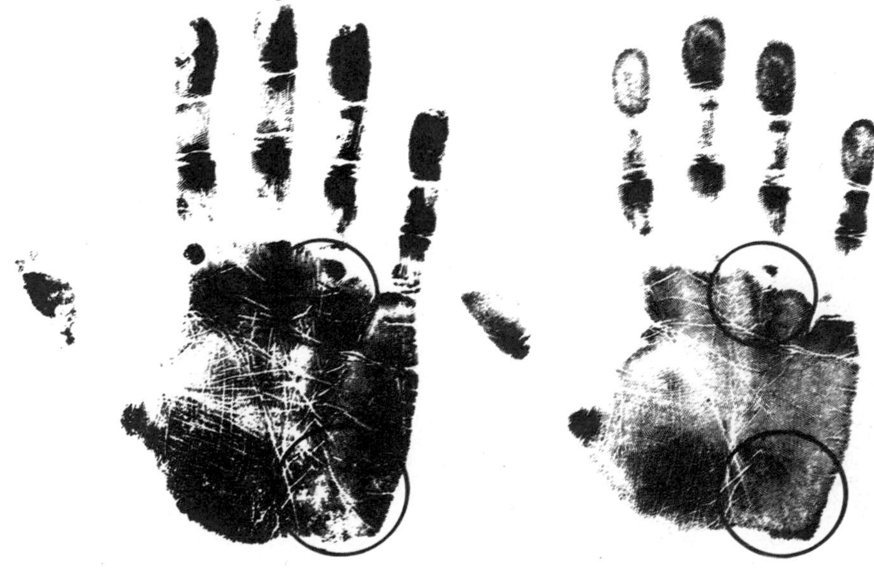

The subsidiary lines, which do not appear on every hand, are the Girdle of Venus, which runs from between the third and fourth fingers to between the first and second fingers; the line of the Sun, which runs from near the wrist to the finger of the Sun; the line of Mars, which runs round the Mount of Venus within the line of Life; the Via Lasciva, which runs parallel to the line of Health further toward the outside of the hand; the line of Intuition, which curves round the Mount of the Moon; and the line of Marriage, which curves across the Mount of Mercury. The Bracelets, which run across the wrist, are taken as indications of the constitution of the subject.

When the palmist has considered the form of the subject's hand, the relative size of the fingers, and the implications of the various lines, he will turn his attention to the many smaller marks that can be found on the palm surface and on the fingers. He will look particularly for marks in the form of a star, a cross, a square, a circle, a triangle, a tripod or a spearhead. 'Islands' or spots that break up the lines also have their significance.

Palmistry, like astrology and geomancy, is also practised in China; although it is interpreted very differently, the readings obtained nevertheless correlate very closely with those arrived at by Western methods.

Chinese palmistry divides the palm into eight 'Palaces', which are designated by the eight trigrams of the *I Ching* (see page 24). The procedures of Chinese palmistry are thus quite closely related to the initial stages of Western palmistry, in which particular attention is paid to the shape of the hand; considerably less attention is devoted to the significance of the individual lines, which are seen as defining the areas occupied by the eight Palaces.

With this brief description of the techniques of cheiromancy, we come to the end of our consideration of the principal methods of divination practised throughout the world. But there remain perhaps hundreds of minor methods, either peculiar to a particular region, or of such inscrutable complexity that they are understood only by their practitioners.

There are hundreds of textbooks from which the eager enquirer can learn the practice of divination by horoscope, geomancy, the *I Ching*, Tarot cards or palmistry. Those with developed clairvoyant faculties may try 'scrying' with a mirror, a bowl of water or a crystal ball. The businessman who wants advice on his investments, or the general who has hopes of becoming the ruler of his country, no longer expects the diviner to:

Pour in sow's blood that hath eaten
Her nine farrow; grease that sweaten
From the murderer's gibbet throw
Into the flame.

'As above, so below'

Although astrology has always been regarded as a mysterious and occult art, recent research has suggested it is scientifically valid. In the first part of this series, BRIAN INNES asks: what is a horoscope – and is it possible to use it to predict future events?

EVERY DAY, MANY MILLIONS of people turn to a section of the newspaper with a heading such as 'Your Horoscope for Today', and more than 60 per cent believe what they read there. At parties, guests greet one another: 'What are you?' 'I'm a Libran.' 'Oh good, we should get on together, I'm an Aquarian.'

This is the stuff of the common understanding of astrology, and it is arrant nonsense. A horoscope is a map – a rather simple, stylised map – showing the positions of the planets (a term that, in astrology, includes the Sun and Moon) in relation to each other and to Earth; at any given moment, the horoscope is exactly the same for everybody. And to say 'I'm a Libran' is to say no more than 'I was born between 24 September and 23 October'. Yet if you told your fellow guest at a party 'I was born on 10 October', it would sound rather ludicrous for him to reply 'Oh good, I was born on 15 February'; he is far more likely to say 'That means you're a Libran' in a significant tone, as if that implied a lot more.

People who understand astrology, and who take at least some part of it seriously, know that it is a subject far divorced from this popular mumbo-jumbo. They know that it is not a matter of 'What your stars foretell' – and, indeed, the stars themselves do not enter into any astrological calculations. Yet most criticisms by scientists against astrology are directed at just such misunderstandings – the former Astronomer Royal, Dr Harold Spencer Jones, could write, for instance: 'It is significant that I do not know of any astrologer who is an observer of the stars, nor do I know of any serious observer of the stars who is an astrologer.' It seems, in fact, that most of those who dismiss astrology as pure superstition have never bothered to find out what it is and how it is practised. This dismissive attitude is as intellectually shortsighted as the gullible belief in 'Your Horoscope for Today'.

Above: 'Mars rules in Scorpio by day, and in Aries by night. He exerts his influence in all manly pursuits: fencing and athletics and the arts of war.' An illumination from the 15th-century treatise on astrology, *De sphaera*

Left: the great circular 'calendar stone' that once stood halfway up the pyramid of Tenochtitlan in Mexico. The two circular 'zodiacs' represent all the days of the Mayan year

A science for love and war

Astrology is one of the oldest of the sciences, and for more than 2000 years it was synonymous with astronomy. It was established in Babylonian times, flourished in Egypt, was practised by the Greeks and Romans, and kept alive – like most other sciences – by the Arabs. And as a science it was similarly studied in China, in India, and in central America.

The principle behind the practice of astrology is very pithily expressed in a phrase that was believed to have been coined by

Left: this wooden mummy-case, now in the British Museum, is from west Thebes and once held the body of Sheik Abdu'l-Qurna. It shows the goddess Nut surrounded by signs of the zodiac

Below: how the Sun appears to be in the different constellations of the zodiac. The Earth moves round the Sun, taking 12 months to complete its orbit; and, if it were possible to see the star background to the Sun during daylight, it would appear that the Sun was in a particular constellation throughout each month. It is easy to work out that the constellation due south at midnight is diametrically opposite to the constellation in which the Sun is to be found

the Egyptian magician Hermes Trismegistos ('thrice-great Hermes'): 'As above, so below.' In other words, events on Earth reflect those in the heavens. The astrologers saw the planets – the word means 'wanderers' in Greek – moving purposefully or erratically against the background of the starry skies; and they supposed that the actions and experiences of these distant gods would be reflected in human affairs. When Mars, the god of war, burnt angrily in the night sky it was a time for quarrels and martial pursuits; when Venus glowed brightly as night fell, it was a time for love.

Circle of animals

The astrologers soon observed that the planets stayed within quite a narrow band of the sky, never moving far away from the path of the Sun – the ecliptic. This band was marked by particular constellations and, since there were 12 months (moon cycles) in the year that it took the Sun to return to its original position, they identified 12 constellations as marking the months. At some time very early in the history of astrology in Babylonia, these constellations were given the names of mythic animals or persons, and the word zodiac means 'circle of animals' in Greek.

In fact, the 12 constellations do not divide the year equally between them, and few of them even vaguely resemble the animal they are named for. Worse than that: when we say (for instance) that Mars is in Aries – that is, apparently making a statement that Mars in the night sky can be seen against a background of the constellation Aries – this is just not true. Some 3000 to 4000 years ago, however, it was true.

As we now know, the Sun and the other planets do not move round the Earth; it is the Earth that moves, like the other planets,

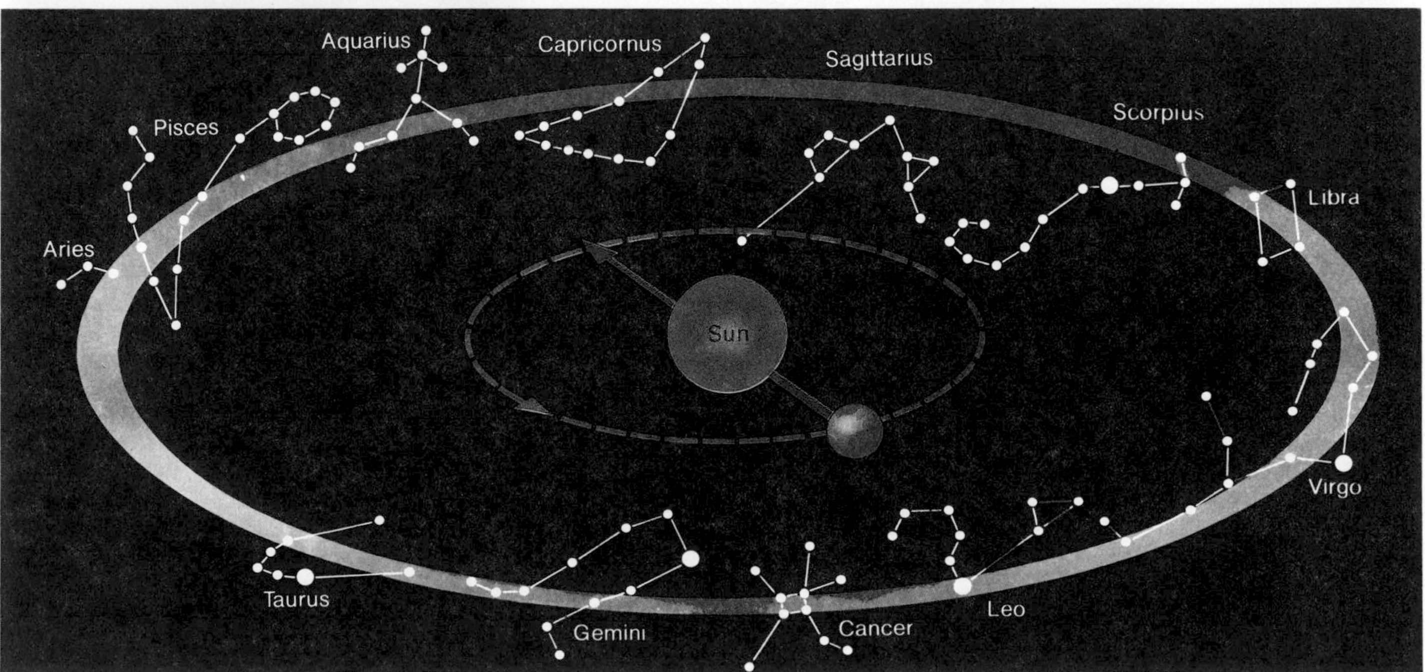

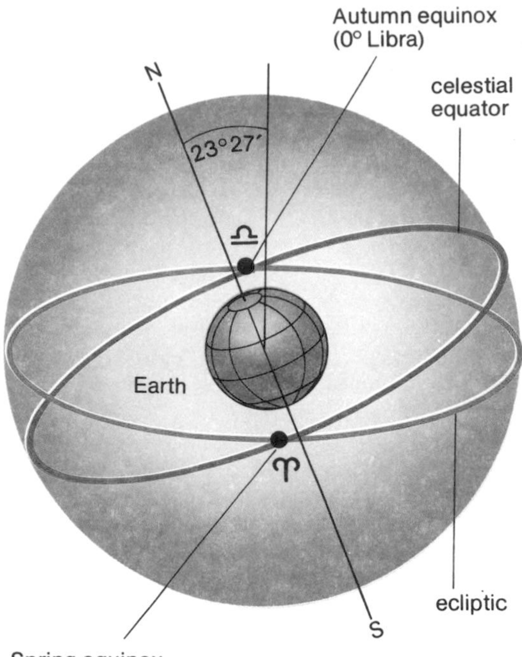

Left: in all simple astronomical and navigational calculations, the Earth is envisaged at the centre of the celestial sphere, which revolves along the line of the Earth's equator, while the apparent path of the Sun, the ecliptic, is at an angle to it. The equinoxes are the two points at which the ecliptic intersects with the celestial equator, and are defined as 0° Aries in spring, and 0° Libra in autumn

round the Sun, so that the Sun is against a different part of the background zodiac every day, and against a different constellation every month. In fact, of course, the Sun is so bright by day that we cannot see its star background; but during the night we can see the parts of the zodiac that are opposite the Sun by 12 hours, and so easily work out which constellation the Sun is 'in'.

However, the Earth, as it goes round the Sun, leans its axis of rotation by 23°27′ to the side. When the northern pole is leaning toward the Sun it is summer in the northern hemisphere, and the days are long; in winter the northern pole is leaning away from the Sun, and days are short. There are only two days every year on which the 24 hours are equally divided between night and day; these are the spring and autumn equinoxes, which occur usually on 20 or 21 March, and 22 or 23 September.

Four thousand years ago, when astrology was young, the Sun was in the constellation of Aries – or, more accurately, that twelfth of the zodiac in which Aries is situated – at the spring equinox. About 2000 years ago, the point on the zodiac circle marking the Sun's 'entering' at the spring equinox was therefore designated 0° Aries, the autumn equinox being 0° Libra.

Night and day

But the Earth is not just leaning to one side as it circles the Sun; it is also wobbling very slowly like a spinning top that is beginning to slow down. As a result, the direction in which it leans gradually changes. This gives rise to a phenomenon known as the 'precession of the equinoxes', which was discovered by the Greek astronomer Hipparchus about 120 BC; the result of the wobbling is that the position of the spring equinox constantly moves: in

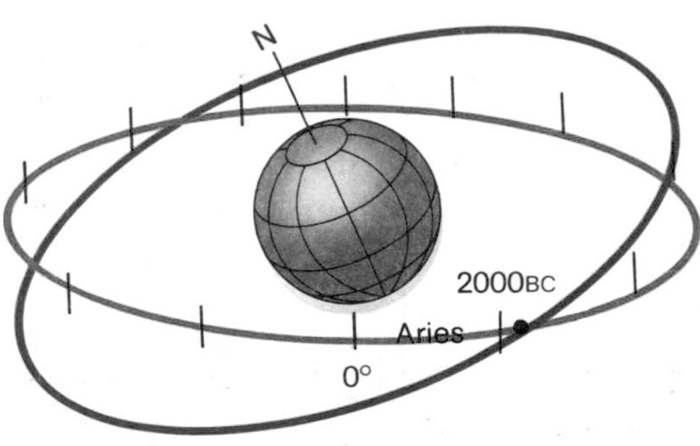

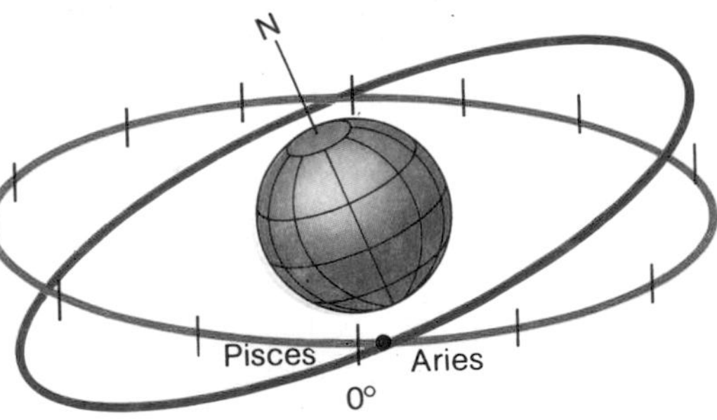

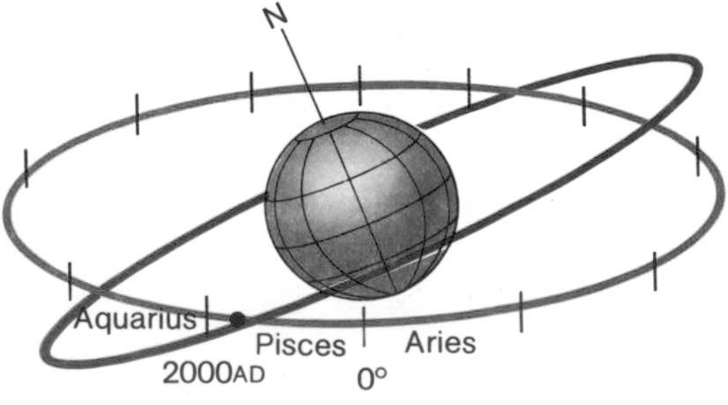

Right: a diagram of the phenomenon known as the precession of the equinoxes. The spring and autumn equinoxes are those two days in the year when day and night are of equal length; and because the Earth is slowly wobbling on its axis, the Sun appears in a different place in the zodiac each year at the equinox. About 4000 years ago the Sun was moving into Aries at the spring equinox (top); it gradually appeared to move backward through Aries, so that after about 2000 years it was at 0° Aries, and about to move into Pisces (middle). The position of the Sun at the spring equinox was then named 0° Aries, and this has defined the zodiac circle ever since. The equinox has now moved most of the way through Pisces, and within some 20 years will 'enter' Aquarius (bottom) – but the spring equinox will still be 0° Aries

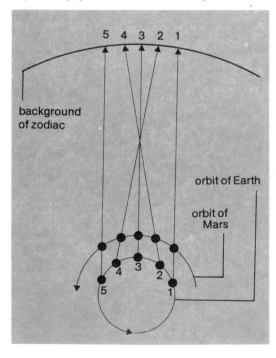

5 4 3 2 1
background of zodiac
orbit of Earth
orbit of Mars

Left: the word planet means 'wanderer', and many of the planets appear to move erratically about the sky, sometimes apparently going back on their tracks for days or weeks. In the diagram, it is clear how Mars appears to move backward between positions 2 and 4

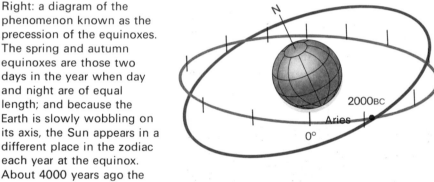

2000 years it moved right through 30° of Aries, and it is now most of the way through Pisces. As we near the end of the 20th century, the spring equinox is moving out of Pisces and into Aquarius. This is what is meant by 'the dawning of the Age of Aquarius'. In another 20,000 years the equinox will once more be at 0°Aries. But, for navigational, astronomical and astrological purposes, the spring equinox is always designated 0°Aries.

This, then, is one of the reasons why popular talk about 'sun signs' has so little significance. Three thousand years ago, when we said of somebody's birth that the Sun was in Scorpio, we meant just that; 1000 years ago it was in Libra; soon it will be in Virgo. But we still say of someone born in November that they are a Scorpian.

It is, in fact, the movements of the planets themselves that we are concerned with, not the star background against which they can be seen. They are like the many hands of a giant astronomical clock, and in recording their exact positions we are identifying a precise moment. This is what the horoscope does: it pinpoints the positions of the planets in the zodiac, as seen from Earth, and also their positions in relation to one another.

To the ancient astrologers the argument was transparently obvious. Since events in heaven were reflected by events on Earth, and since it was possible to predict the future positions of the gods (the planets) months or years in advance, then from knowledge of those positions it should be easy to predict events upon Earth.

Above: 'May', from the 15th-century codex *Les très riches heures du Duc de Berry*. The month, as the portion of the zodiac above the illustration shows, is divided between Taurus and Gemini

Planets are not gods . . .

Modern critics of astrology, who know that the planets are not gods and that heavenly phenomena are not reflected in earthly happenings, find it easy to dismiss the whole matter. There is no way in which some remote pieces of rock (or balls of gas) can affect human nature and destiny, they claim. And they are perhaps right.

However, this argument does not rule out the possibility of prediction. Suppose you receive a letter from your uncle, saying that he will be leaving his country home at about 10.15 a.m. and asking you to meet his train. A glance at the timetable will tell you that the only train he could possibly catch will arrive at the terminus at 1.05 p.m. An enquiry at the station will tell you that the train normally arrives at platform three. If you have a contact in the railway offices, you can probably discover the name of the driver of the train, the colour of the engine and its head code, and possibly all sorts of related facts.

If you take a friend with you to the station, you can tell him a surprising amount about future events. Pointing to the station clock, you tell him that when the two hands are together – in astrological terms this would be described as 'in conjunction' – a number of

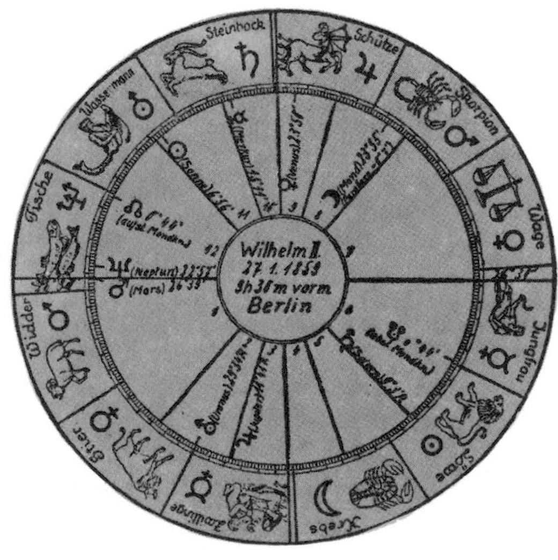

Left: a conventional horoscope drawn for Kaiser Wilhelm II. The horoscope is divided into 12 'houses' that do not correspond with the 12 signs of the zodiac; while the positions of the planets are indicated as degrees of angle within each zodiac division

things will happen: a blue engine (and you may even know its name and number), with the head code 06 and driven by a man named Harry Grimshaw, will arrive at platform three, and that a middle-aged man with glasses, walking with a stick, will get down from it. Your friend will be amazed: how could all these events have been caused by the influence of two hands on a clock?

The astrologer works with something very like a railway timetable. It is called an *ephemeris*, and it gives the positions of the various planets in the heavens at any particular time. Astronomers use very similar tables, and so do all sea and air navigators – in fact it is possible to draw up a horoscope perfectly satisfactorily from a 'nautical almanac'.

Astronomical aspects

It has been objected that the discovery of the planets Uranus, Neptune, and Pluto, which were unknown to the ancient astrologers, must have invalidated everything that went before. However these distant planets are relatively slow-moving, like hands on a clock that tell the century, the decade and the year. Uranus, for instance, remained in Libra from 1968 until December 1974; Neptune entered Sagittarius in 1970 and leaves it in 1984; Pluto takes from 1971 to 1983 to pass through Libra. So the 'influence' of these planets in the horoscope is equally slow-moving; of far greater significance to the modern astrologer is the relation of the position of one planet to another, something which is called its 'aspect'.

Astrological interpretation, in fact, falls into two distinct parts. First comes the drawing up of a horoscope. This need not be drawn up for the moment of a person's birth; it can just as well be for an event like a wedding or the issue of some new company stock. However, the Moon and Mercury move very rapidly through the horoscope, resulting in quickly changing aspects, and so the moment for which the horoscope is drawn should be defined as accurately as possible. It is mainly for this reason that the horoscopes most commonly drawn are natal horoscopes.

Left: a horoscope for the birth of John Milton, drawn up by the English astrologer John Gadbury. It is drawn in typical 17th-century style – the 12 triangular divisions surrounding the central square each represent one of the 12 'houses'

From a natal horoscope an astrologer claims to be able to make a detailed description of the physical attributes and spiritual nature of its subject, based upon 4000 years of experience. Working from such a deep understanding of the subject, it is then possible to make predictions of the way in which he or she will behave and develop in the future. Few present-day astrologers, even the most famous and successful, go much beyond this point. They may suggest, after calculating the future positions of the planets, the most favourable time for some enterprise, but not many are prepared to make detailed predictions of future events.

The truly predictive part of astrology, in fact, is a complex and time-consuming operation. It is necessary to draw up the horoscopes for various precisely defined times in the future, and then to relate these to the natal horoscope of the person whose fate is being considered. It is here that astrology begins to lose its credibility, for astrologers – in order to cut down the time involved in going through a succession of constantly changing horoscopes – have introduced the concept of 'secondary directions'. By this means the subject's horoscope is 'progressed' by periods of a day from the moment of birth, each day's changes in the positions of the planets being taken to represent a year, or a month, or a week in the subject's life – whichever the astrologer prefers. Whatever justification there may be for believing that the accurately drawn horoscope does contain useful information, there is none whatsoever for this artificial principle of progression.

Right: a set of horoscopes cast by the English astrologer (but drawn up after the event) for the birth, coronation and death of Louis XVI of France and his queen Marie-Antoinette

How to cast a horoscope

Millions of people scan their 'stars' in the newspapers every day. But a horoscope prepared for an individual would read very differently. This chapter explains how such a detailed chart of the heavens is drawn up

A HOROSCOPE IS A MAP – a map of the zodiac circle, with the Earth at its centre, and all the planets in the positions in which they can be seen from Earth. Some of the planets move relatively fast – the Moon, for instance, moves through more than one third of one 'sign' of the zodiac in the course of 24 hours – so the appearance of this map changes from minute to minute.

The basis of the horoscope has changed very little in 5000 years. The ancient Babylonians recognised that the stars were on a sphere that revolved once about the Earth every day, but that shifted very slightly in each revolution so that it did not return to its original orientation until the year had passed. Within this sphere the planets circled the Earth: the Sun went round the Earth once a day, the Moon rather faster, so that it passed through all the constellations of the zodiac in the time it took the Sun to pass through one. The other planets moved at different speeds, sometimes moving fast in one direction, then hesitating and going back on their tracks before moving forward again. This picture of the Universe is still employed in all navigational calculations and in many everyday astronomical ones.

Of course, we cannot see the stars in the daytime, nor can we see what is below the Earth's rim at night, but it does not require much observation to be able to work out that

An illustration from the 17th-century atlas *Harmonia macrocosmica* by Andreas Cellarius. Viewed from the southern hemisphere, the constellations of the zodiac run in reverse order, from Taurus, here seen as the ascendant sign, through Aries, Pisces, Aquarius and Capricorn, to Sagittarius disappearing below the western horizon the stars remain fixed in their positions on the heavenly sphere, so we know exactly where they are in relation to the Earth, even when they cannot be seen.

Stand facing due south on a clear night at about midnight. To make things easily understandable, the winter solstice, just before the end of December, is a good time to choose for this example; and, for convenience, assume you are in the northern hemisphere. At that time of year the Sun is said to be moving from Sagittarius into Capricorn but, because of the precession of the equinoxes, it is actually in Scorpio. Since it is

midnight, the constellation of Scorpius will be directly beneath your feet, and the constellation of Taurus will be visible in the southern sky. Eastward from Taurus, the constellations will be Gemini, Cancer, and Leo; westward they will be Aries and Pisces.

That is what you will actually see in the sky; but all astronomical and navigational tables are based on the assumption that the spring equinox is still at 0° Aries, as it was nearly 2000 years ago. So we must now imagine an entirely artificial zodiac circle, in which the Sun is just entering Capricorn, with Cancer just coming to the mid-heaven in the southern sky at midnight; then, eastward, the zodiac signs will be Leo and Virgo, with Libra just appearing over the eastern horizon; and westward will be Gemini and Taurus, with Aries disappearing below the western horizon.

The zodiac in the heavens

We begin to draw our horoscope, therefore, as a circle, divided into 12 equal parts to represent the 12 parts of the zodiac, which approximate to the 12 months. The top of the circle represents the mid-heaven, the highest point of the Sun's daily travel, and to the left and right are the eastern and western horizons. As the Earth revolves (from right to left, as it were), Libra will gradually rise in the east; at midnight of the winter solstice it is the ascendant sign. At dawn the ascendant sign will be Capricorn; and at midday the ascendant sign will be Aries.

At midnight, the Sun will be in the lowest part of our circular map, and so we mark it there. On the night of 22 December 1980, it was at 1° Capricorn. Mercury and Venus always remain fairly close to the Sun, and so they will not be visible in the midnight sky. In fact, on the night we have chosen, only the Moon is visible, almost due south and high in the sky; Mars, Jupiter and Saturn are below the horizon. From a set of tables known as an *ephemeris* we can get the figures for their positions: Mercury at 26° Sagittarius, Venus at 6° Sagittarius, Mars at 23° Capricorn, Jupiter at 9° Libra, Saturn at 9° Libra (in what is called a conjunction between Jupiter and Saturn).

There are also, of course, the planets that we cannot see, and that were only discovered within the last 200 years. Uranus is at 28° Scorpio, Neptune at 23° Sagittarius, and Pluto at 24° Libra. We can see from these figures that later in the night, before sunrise, first Jupiter and Saturn will rise, then (if we could only see it) Pluto, then Uranus, then Venus, Neptune and Mercury (the morning star) in that order. Mars will not be visible because the Sun will rise before it, and once the Sun has risen the stars and planets cannot be seen.

To draw up an accurate horoscope, so as to get the ascendant and the mid-heaven in exactly the right orientation, clock time is not

Left: this third-century Roman mosaic shows the close relationship between Ea, the Babylonian god of the oceans, and Poseidon, the Greek and Roman god. As *suhumarshu*, the fish-goat, Ea gave his name to the constellation we now call Capricorn

Below: the sky as it appeared in the northern hemisphere at midnight on 22 December 1980, together with the portion of sky containing the other half of the ecliptic that cannot be seen at night (bottom), and the equivalent horoscope for that hour (below right). In the sky, Taurus is in mid-heaven, and the Sun is 'in' the constellation Scorpius. In the horoscope, which makes no allowance for the precession of the equinoxes, the Sun is in Capricorn

Far right: in traditional astrology, each sign of the zodiac is associated with a particular part of the body

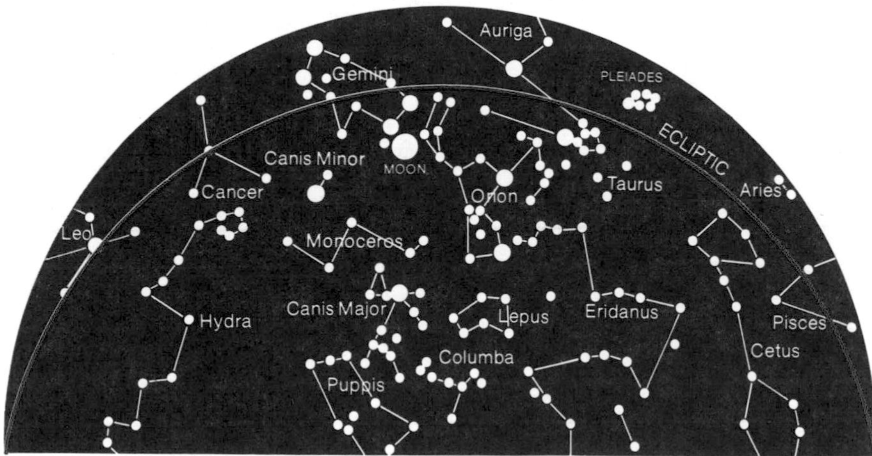

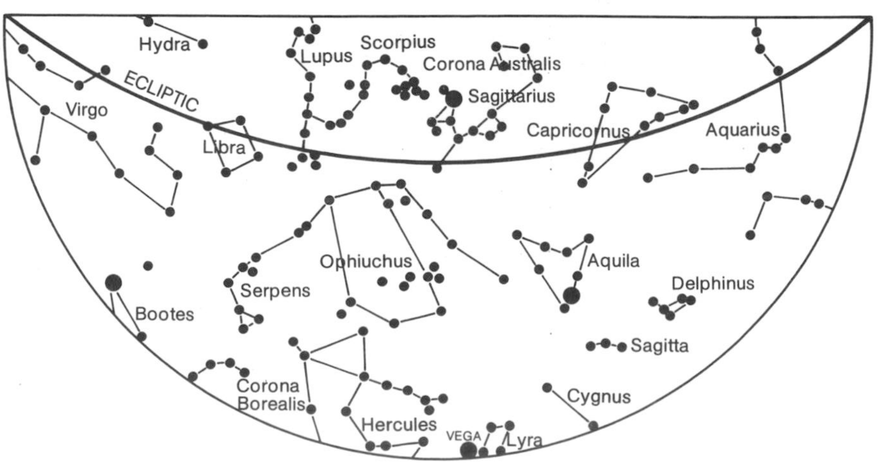

sufficiently accurate. Clock time is derived from Greenwich Mean Time; that is, from a calculation of the average length of a day, and the establishment of the average time at which the Sun is due south and at its zenith – because of small variations in the movement of the Earth, midday by Sun time can be as much as 20 minutes out. Astrologers therefore use star time, or 'sidereal time', which is similarly measured from the equinox; astronomers also use sidereal time to calculate at which part of the sky to point their telescopes, so that they can observe a particular star at a particular time.

Casting a horoscope

It is also necessary to make corrections for local clock time. When it is midnight in Britain, on or near the Greenwich meridian, it is midday in the central Pacific, with the Sun blazing high in the sky, and the sign of Aries just rising on the eastern horizon. Fortunately the calculations to change local time to GMT and then to sidereal time are very simple; once they are done it is a matter of minutes to look up the planetary positions in the *ephemeris* and draw up the horoscope.

This, then, is a horoscope: a map showing the positions of the planets relative to one another, and their orientation within the zodiac circle. Earth is the small dot at the centre of the circle, and all the way down the Greenwich meridian to the equator the horoscope remains essentially the same. Below the equator, where the Sun appears not in the southern sky but the northern sky, the map, or horoscope, is simply inverted.

The interpretation of the horoscope is based upon certain long-established rules. The Sun represents the real self, the fundamental ego; the ascendant represents the physical characteristics, the outward appearance; and the Moon denotes the soul, the subconscious psychological nature. In the horoscope we have drawn up the Sun is unequivocally in Capricorn, and will remain there for nearly four weeks; the Moon is in Cancer for two days before moving into Leo; and the ascendant sign is Libra.

In popular magazine astrology, it is only the position of the Sun that is considered: someone born in late December or the first three weeks of January is a Capricornian, and

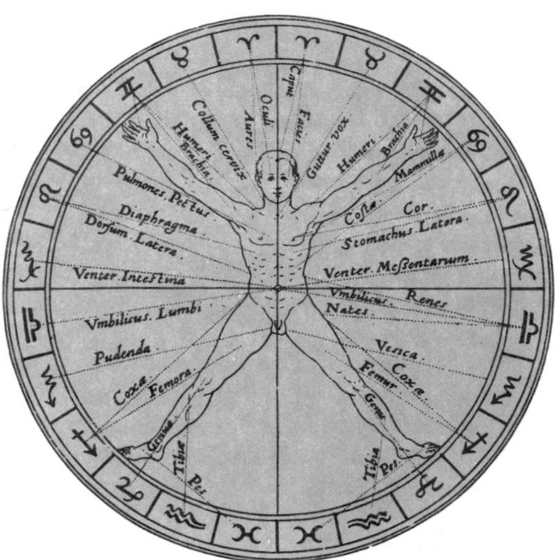

that is all that need be said. Capricornians, say the astrological textbooks, are strong-willed but self-centred, suspicious of others, clever in argument but likely to lose control of the situation by a sudden outbreak of irresponsibility. But Moon in Cancer denotes someone who is emotionally committed to domestic security and a stable marriage; while the ascendant Libra suggests someone of average height, well-formed and good-looking, with long blond hair, blue eyes and a healthy complexion.

Conjunctions and characters

This is just the beginning of astrological interpretation. Venus in Sagittarius is supposed to indicate a frank and open person, but one who values religious conformity; while Mercury and Neptune in conjunction in Sagittarius would be interpreted as revealing someone who could gain a reputation as a prophet. Mars in Capricorn denotes the attainment of material success and social standing; Jupiter and Saturn conjunct in Libra suggest someone who will apply experience to the settling of all kinds of problems, and probably become wealthy thereby.

There is no doubt that this kind of analysis already begins to give us a picture of a certain kind of person; whether any of those born at midnight on 22 December 1980 really

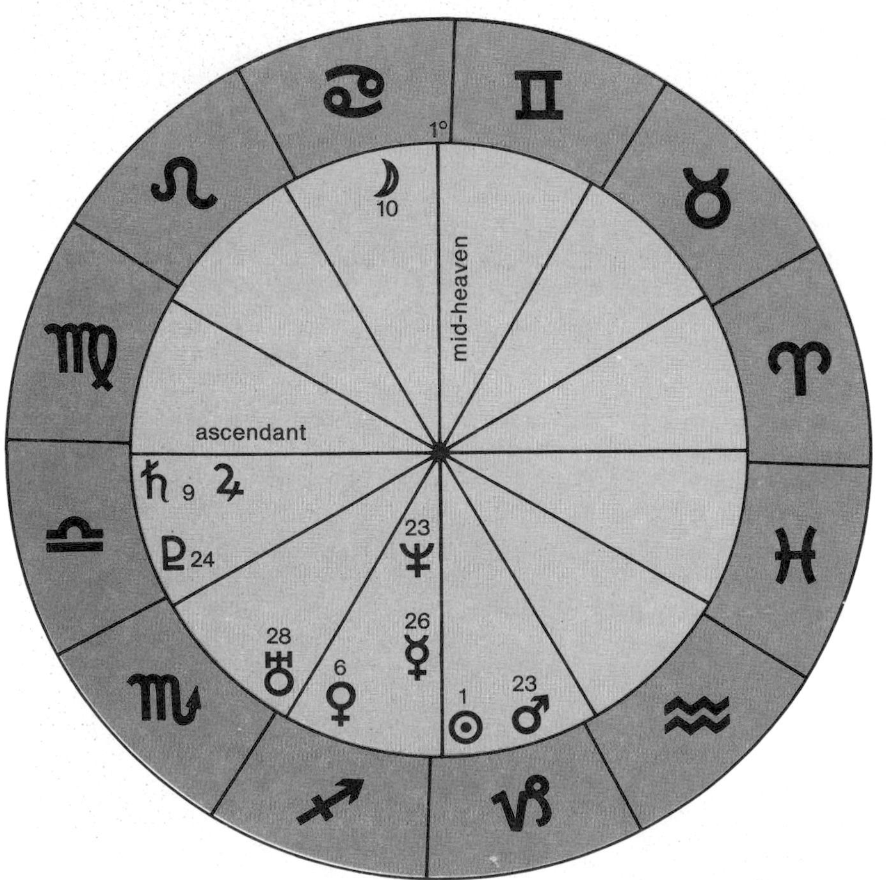

Right: in India, as in all other developed cultures of the world, astrology was long established as a science. This border design, from the early 17th-century *Jahangir's album*, reveals that the working tools of the astrologer have hardly changed in the course of many hundreds of years

develop in this way remains to be seen. Traditional astrology goes further; and it is particularly in these further refinements that modern scientific research has shown some correlation with the traditional beliefs.

Planetary aspects

In the more detailed analysis, the 'aspects' become of particular importance. These are the positions of the planets relative to one another in the sky. We all know, for instance, that when the Sun and Moon are in conjunction, or when they are opposed, as in the horoscope under discussion, the aggregate gravitational pull produces the phenomenon known as spring tides; while when the two are at right angles to one another – square, as it is known in astrology – the height of tides is at a minimum and we get neap tides. A similar kind of gravitational effect can be envisaged as being produced by the smaller or more distant planets: two planets conjunct or opposed reinforce each other's effect; two planets square to one another – separated by 90° or three zodiac signs – reduce each other's effect; and planets 'trine' to one another – that is, making up the points of an equilateral triangle, and separated one from the other by 120° or four signs of the zodiac – are balanced when there are planets at all three points of the triangle, but otherwise 'drag', as it were, the planetary effect to one side when there are only two.

One other element of astrological interpretation needs to be considered before the significance of the horoscope is fully understood. The ancient Babylonians saw the planets wandering about the sky like travellers in the desert; and they imagined that every so often they returned to their own houses, which they ruled like the master or mistress of a household. The Sun, obviously, was at the height of his powers in midsummer: he ruled in the house of Leo. The Moon, the queen of the planets, sat at the Sun's left hand: she ruled in Cancer. The other five planets, who roamed through day and night, each had two houses: one for daytime, and one for night-time. Thus Mercury ruled in the day house of Virgo, and in the night house of Gemini; Saturn ruled in Capricorn as his day house, and in Aquarius at night; and so on. When the planets were in their houses, their influence was believed to be particularly strong.

A rather different concept of houses was subsequently introduced: in due course some

Right: an Arabic model of the celestial sphere, made in the 18th century

Far right: a diagrammatic representation of the celestial sphere. The stars should be imagined painted on the inside surface of the sphere, with the Earth as a tiny point at the centre. The thick horizontal ring represents the horizon, so that the part of the heavens visible at any time is the interior surface of the sphere above the horizon. The celestial equator is the projection of the Earth's equator onto the sphere, and the ecliptic represents the apparent path of the Sun. The zodiac constellations lie in a band along the ecliptic. The sphere is envisaged divided into 12 'houses', each house being the home of one of the planets

astrologers began to define the mid-heaven as the dividing line between two houses. If this is so, and we then divide the horoscope into 12 houses of equal size, that to the east of the zenith will contain 29° of the sign at the zenith and 1° of the next sign west, and so on all round the circle. The great astronomer and astrologer Ptolemy, who practised in Alexandria in the second century AD, employed this method of house division, which is known as the 'equal house' method.

Arabian wisdom

In later centuries the Arabs, who had gained possession of all the ancient manuscripts from the library at Alexandria, became fascinated with mathematics, and introduced all sorts of complicated methods of calculating house divisions. The equal house system of Ptolemy divides the ecliptic – the apparent path of the Sun through the zodiac – into 12 equal houses. The system of the Arab mathematician Ibn Ezra – known in Europe as the Regiomontanus system – divides the celestial equator into 12 equal houses. This is all very well for astrologers near the Earth's equator, for there the difference is negligible, but in the high latitudes as much as 50° of the zodiac must be crammed within 30° of the horoscope for certain signs, while other signs must be stretched so that only 15° occupy one twelfth of the horoscope. There are other systems, based on different principles, but the most ridiculous of all is the system of Placidus. This is based upon the *time* taken by any degree of the zodiac to rise from the lowest part of the horoscope circle to the mid-heaven. Since above the Arctic Circle many degrees of the zodiac remain always above the horizon, these parts of the zodiac do not appear in a Placidean horoscope at all. The only reason why this extraordinary system has survived is that the most readily available *ephemeris* is Raphael's, which contains tables of houses according to Placidus.

Each house of the horoscope is also credited with controlling some part of the subject's destiny, from servants, conditions of employment, illness and recovery (house 6) to secrecy, the psychic faculties and places of concealment (house 12); but astrologers have never been able to agree on whether the division of the horoscope into 12 equal houses should be made from the ascendant, or the mid-heaven, or whether the ascendant or the mid-heaven should fall in the middle of its respective house. Houses are considered very important by many modern astrologers – they are held to represent, in a unique way, the fate of the individual. But the confusion about house division means the significance of the various planets relative to their houses has always been a little obscure.

This has been a very brief survey of the beliefs involved in the interpretation of a drawn-up horoscope; but some understanding of the principles involved is necessary in order to appreciate the remarkable discoveries that have been made in the past decade, discoveries that suggest there may be some justification in the age-old beliefs of astrology.

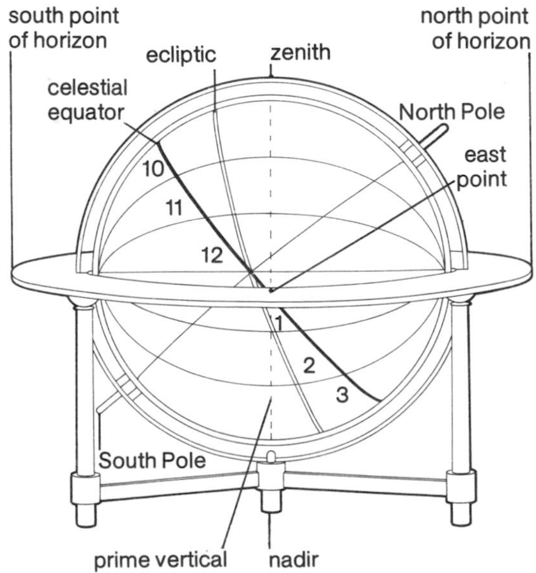

Above: another illustration from the 15th-century manuscript *De sphaera*. The Sun rules only by day, and his house is in Leo. The human occupations over which he exerts a particularly strong influence are concerned with power and domination over other people

Out of the cosmic s

Astrologers have always held that the planets influence our lives in quite specific ways. This chapter describes how – and reviews some modern research that may back up the astrologers' claims

ASTROLOGY IS A VERY ANCIENT SCIENCE: its tenets and principles have come down to us over thousands of years, so that now it is impossible to separate the original beliefs from those that have accrued to them over so many generations. Yet much of what is today considered traditional in astrology comes from no farther back than the end of the 19th century – a time when the study of astrology was suddenly revived in both England and France. The association of astrology with the Tarot cards, for instance, dates from this period; there is no historical connection whatsoever between the two, except insofar as the 22 Tarot trumps are the remnants of a much larger set of some 50 cards that at one time included 12 that represented the signs of the zodiac, with another seven to represent the planets.

Some measure of the confusion created by the 19th-century occultists can be obtained from the so-called 'tables of correspondences' published in 1909 in *Liber 777* by Aleister Crowley. There are altogether 194 tables, which provide the equivalents of the letters of the Hebrew alphabet to the planets, the spheres and the elements; to colours, Tarot cards, Egyptian, Roman and Hindu gods and goddesses, plants, precious stones, drugs, perfumes, and all sorts of concepts.

Magic and number symbolism

Crowley made much of this up for himself; parts he got from English occultists of the 1880s and 1890s such as L. Macgregor Mathers; some can be traced back to medieval magical writers such as Cornelius Agrippa; and a few scraps can be attributed to Roman astrology and to the beliefs associated with the Jewish *qabalah*. This system of 'correspondences' is very clearly a development of the 'as above, so below' principle designed to cover every contingency. Although it is completely artificial, this sort of thing is frequently made an essential part of what is taught in contemporary courses in astrology.

The sceptic may be forgiven for finding some of the fundamental principles of astrology equally questionable. When one reads, for instance, that the typical Pisces native has unusually prominent eyes and a fleshy body, with some kind of peculiarity about the feet, and that he or she is likely to be a good swimmer, one is justified in suspecting that the description is tailored to result in something that is essentially fish-like. This apparent anthropomorphism turns up throughout astrology: the Cancerian, for example is said to walk with a peculiar sideways gait; the Sagittarian has a long face with prominent front teeth, and female Sagittarians may wear their hair in a pony-tail; the Taurean is obstinate, with a broad face and thick-set body, and a thick muscular throat.

The characters supposed to be exhibited by the different planets seem to suffer from the same kind of identification. Waite's *Compendium of natal astrology* lists the following 'personal characteristics shown by the planets':

Sun: pride, generosity, egotism, honour, loyalty, ardour, vitality
Moon: sensitivity, sentiment, maternal instinct, femininity, changeableness
Mercury: quickness, sharpness, braininess, ready wit, flow of words
Venus: beauty, grace, charm, artistic tastes, affection, sociability
Mars: virility, energy, courage, initiative, impulsiveness, passion, aggression
Jupiter: optimism, cheer, generosity, joviality, sport, strength, nobility, ceremoniousness

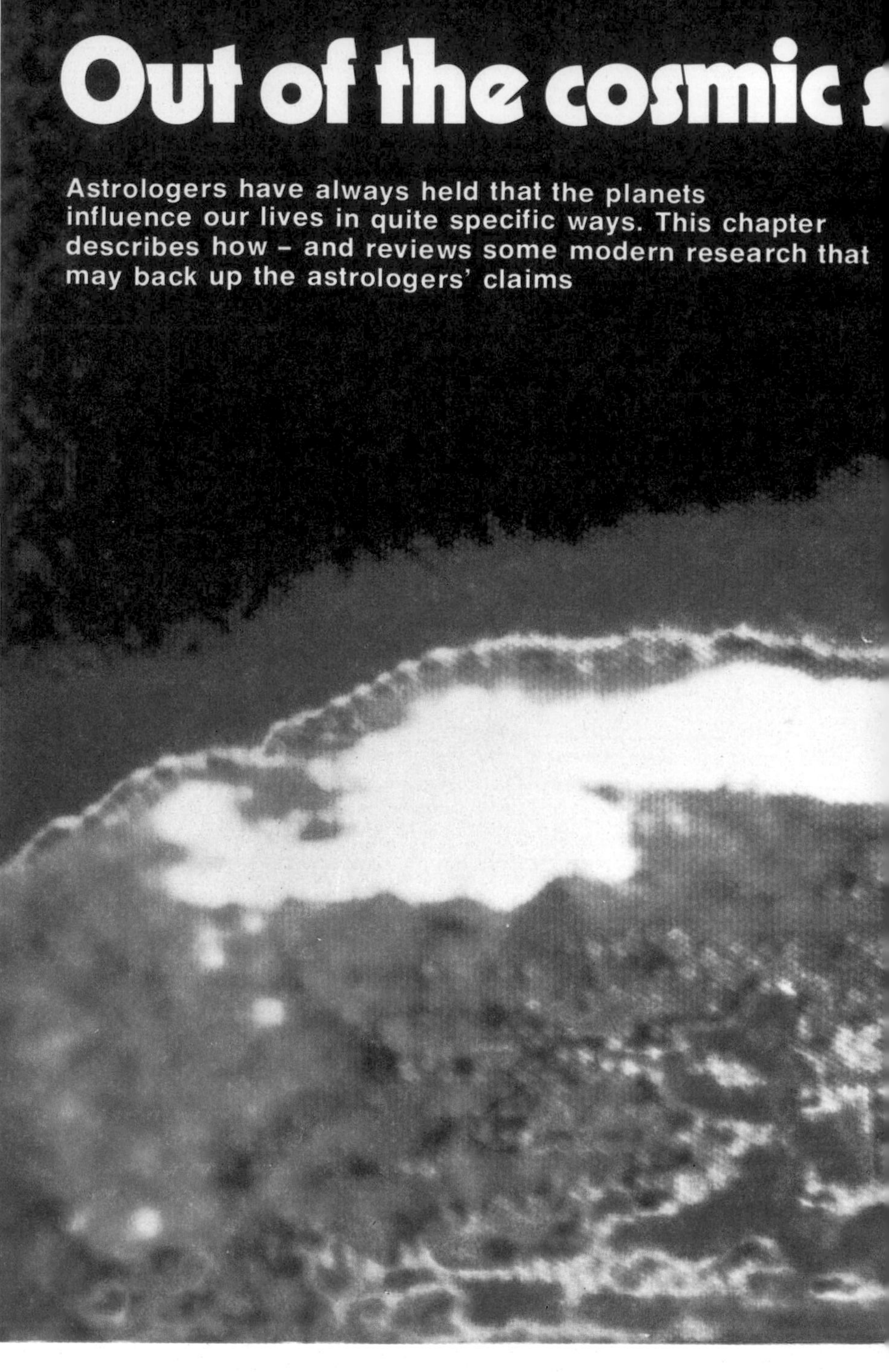

A giant solar flare, perhaps as much as 100,000 miles in length. The Sun plays such a major part in the lives of everyone on Earth that it is hard to believe that it has no effect upon the destiny of those born at different stages of its annual cycle. The observations made by John Nelson suggest that the relative positions of the planets affect activities on the surface of the Sun and, therefore, the amount of cosmic radiation falling upon the Earth

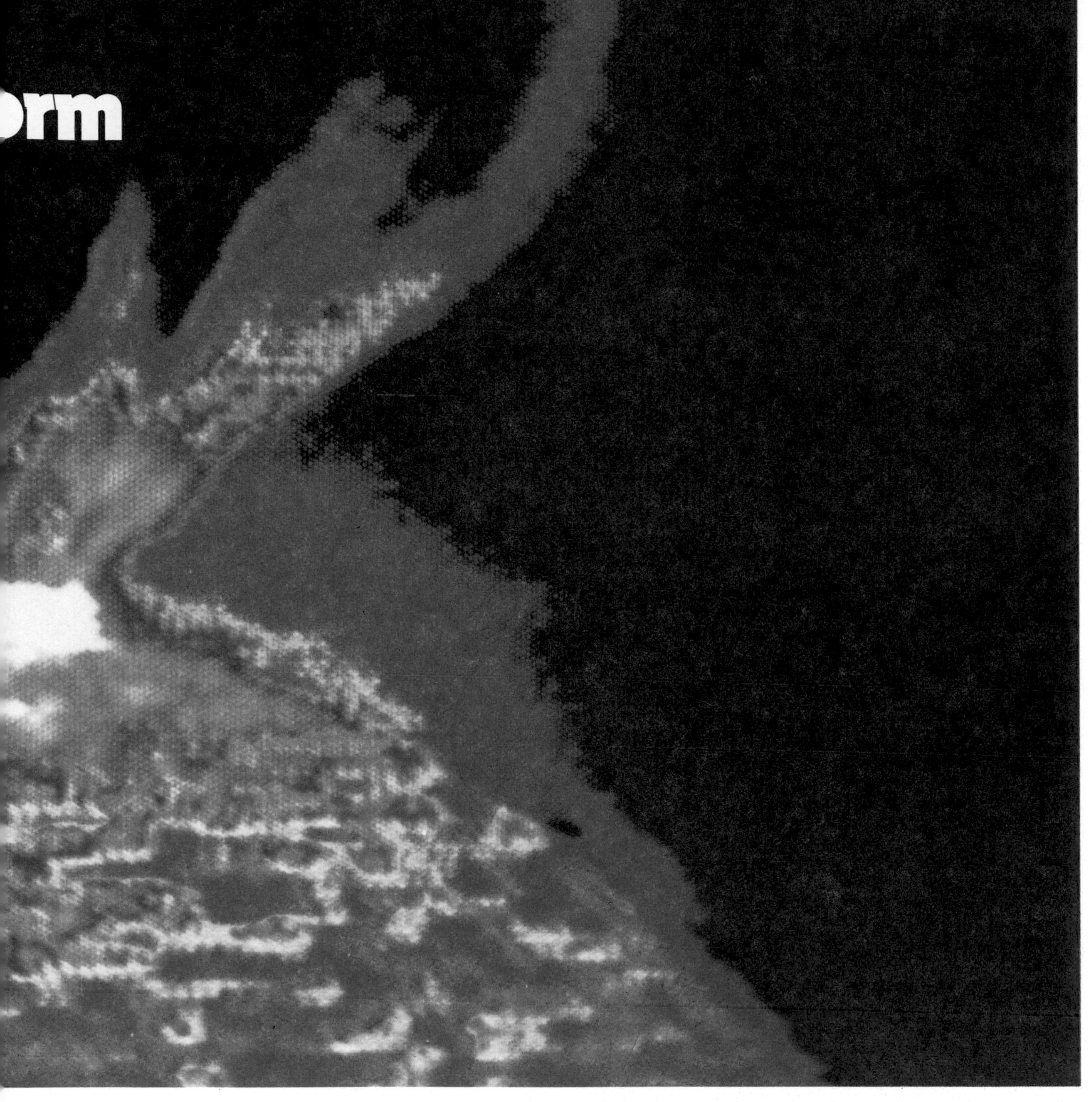

Saturn: caution, taciturnity, pessimism, self-restraint, profundity, steadfastness

(There are also characteristics given for Uranus, Neptune and Pluto, but they are less important and need not concern us here.)

These are, of course, the characteristics that one would expect the various gods to possess – but why has any particular god's name been given to any particular planet? Mars, of course, by its red coloration, can be identified with the god of war and so with what are generally considered essentially masculine traits; but why should one small, bright, quickly moving planet be identified with ready wit and braininess, while the other is identified with beauty and charm; why should one distant and slow-moving body represent optimism and generosity, while another represents caution and pessimism?

It is when we come to look at the Sun that a possible explanation begins to emerge. Nobody would object to a statement of the following general kind: that children born at midday in high summer tend to be very different in personality from those born at midnight in winter. Many people who would not subscribe to any of astrology's beliefs remain convinced that the season, the time of day and the weather prevailing at the moment a child is born can affect its nature and the way in which it will behave.

Following this line of argument, it is not

difficult to develop the statement above. Consider the following:

> Recent investigations by a well-known market research bureau have revealed that a high proportion of children born at or near midday during the first two weeks of August are healthier than the national average, generally strong and tall, and frequently blond. As they develop they show good qualities of leadership, being both practical and kind-hearted.

True or not, this is a plausible statement, and would be given due consideration by even the most sceptical scientists; however, had it begun 'Leos tend to be . . .' it would be likely to evoke cries of 'Nonsense!' and 'Superstition!' from the most broad-minded of astronomers and other members of the scientific establishment, so nervous are they of the subject of astrology.

And yet, as has already been pointed out, to say that the Sun is in Leo is to say no more than that the date is somewhere between 22 July and 21 August. Could it be, in fact, that the part of the zodiac in which the Sun is found at this time of year has been named Leo *because* the experience of centuries showed that those born in what we call August tended to exhibit leonine characteristics? After all, the shape of the constellation itself bears little if any resemblance to a lion – and indeed, the precession of the equinoxes means that during August the Sun is now really in Cancer.

It is possible, then, that all the constellations of the zodiac have been named for the characteristics exhibited by those born at that particular time of year. We are dealing with a mass of information gathered over nearly 2000 years by the astrologers of Babylon and their successors – far more detailed than the statistics assembled by the mythical market research bureau invoked above. And it is possible that the names of the planets equally indicate the temperaments of

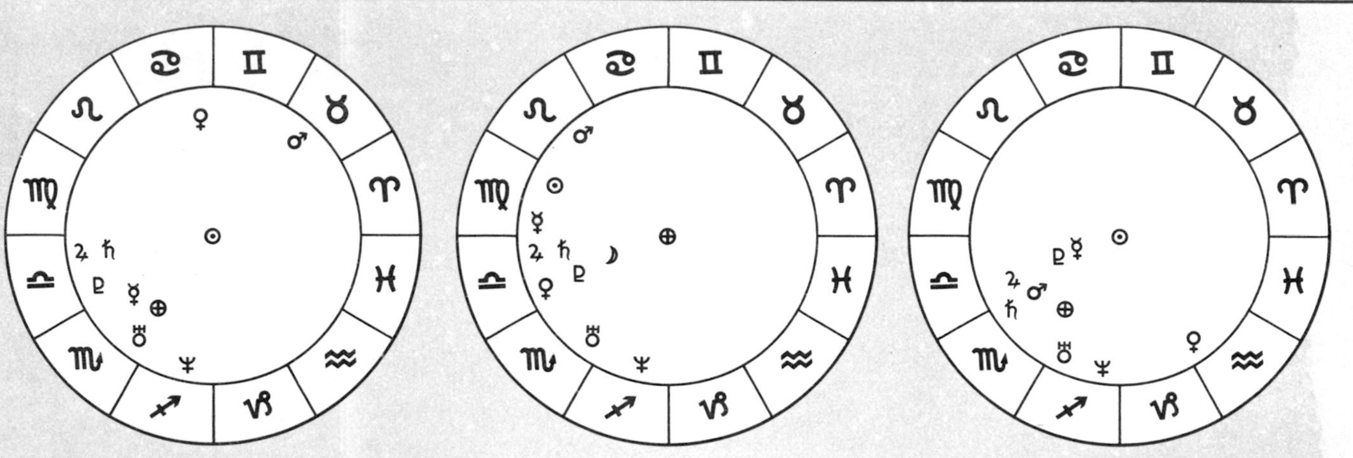

The Jupiter effect

Much has been made of the so-called 'Jupiter effect'. Jupiter and Saturn, the two largest planets, come into conjunction, or within a degree or two of one another, every 20 years or so. Such an event occurred in 1980–1981. Seen from the Earth, Saturn and Jupiter were in conjunction from November 1980 to March 1981, and again in August; seen from the Sun, they were in conjunction in May 1981. In 1974, in the first edition of their book *The Jupiter effect*, John Gribbin and S. Plagemann suggested that this conjunction would be accompanied by the lining up of most of the other planets – and Arthur Prieditis, an American writer, predicted 'world-shattering upheavals of the first magnitude'.

As seen from the Earth, the nearest to a lining up of planets occurred in early September 1981, when Saturn and Jupiter were respectively in 12° and 9° Libra, Pluto was in 22°, and Venus passed through Libra in the course of about three weeks, while the Moon was in Libra from 31 August to 2 September. The Sun did not enter Libra until nearly the end of the month. Throughout this month, Mercury was in Virgo and Mars in Leo, while Uranus was in Scorpio and Neptune in Sagittarius.

We now know, of course, that the cataclysmic events described by Prieditis failed to happen. Gribbin, indeed, withdrew much of the substance of his forecast before the dates concerned.

The closest grouping of planets relative to the Sun occurred about 20 May, when Saturn, Jupiter, Pluto, Mars and Mercury were all within about 17°; at this time the Earth was in mid Scorpio, Venus in Aquarius, Uranus and Neptune in Sagittarius. But again, we now know that nothing of momentous significance happened in May – nothing, for example, to compare with the British victory in the Falkland Islands or the Israeli invasion of the Lebanon, both of which occurred in *June* 1982.

Jupiter and Saturn were in conjunction relative to the Sun in May 1981 (left); all planets were together on one side of the Earth in September 1981 (centre); and the closest grouping relative to the Sun occurred in May 1982 (right). Below: John Gribbin

those born when the particular planet was dominant in the horoscope.

As we have seen, the horoscope is a time-map of a particular moment. For a person born at that moment, it gives their 'Sun-sign' – it tells us in which twelfth of the year the birth takes place; it gives us the time of day, in terms both of the position of the Sun in the horoscope circle and of the sign ascendant on the eastern horizon; and it also provides us with the relative positions in the heavens of up to nine other 'markers'.

The most important of these is the Moon, which moves right through each of the signs of the zodiac in less than three days. We accept that Sun and Moon exert a very great influence upon human lives: the Sun because it provides light and heat, and is essential for the production of food and the two together because they combine or oppose their gravitational forces to produce the tides. This is not the place to pursue the argument that mankind has evolved from an essentially aquatic animal, and that there is no reason to suppose that we do not remain as sensitive to tidal forces as present-day fish and plankton. Let us accept it as a possibility, and consider the way in which the movement of the planets can affect the nature of the gravitational and magnetic fields within the solar system.

The solar connection

In the mid 1940s, an engineer with RCA Communications Inc. named John Nelson set up a telescope on the roof of the company's office building in central Manhattan, and began to study the Sun. Nelson knew that unusual sunspot activity was accompanied by serious interruption of radio communications, and his job was to find some way of predicting the occurrence of these 'cosmic storms'. He knew little of astronomy and nothing of astrology, but in due course he discovered that there was a direct connection between intense solar disturbance and the relative positions of the planets – their astrological aspects.

By 1967, Nelson could claim a success rate of 93 per cent in his predictions of severe cosmic storms, out of a total of 1460 specific forecasts. For a severe storm, one of the four inner planets (Mercury, Venus, Earth or Mars) must be at an angle of 0°, 90° or 180° with another planet further from the Sun – relative to the Sun as centre. In addition, at least two other planets must be in an 'angular harmonic' relationship with the first pair, the principal harmonics employed by Nelson being the subdivisions by 2, 3, 4, 5 or 6 of 360° – that is, 180°, 120°, 90°, 72° and 60°. Could it possibly be that it is no more than a happy coincidence that Mercury – traditionally associated with communication by all astrologers – appeared to be the most significant planet in Nelson's investigations?

As Guy Lyon Playfair and Scott Hill put it in their book *The cycles of heaven*, 'Nelson's work is an example of what astrology may once have been and still could be: the study of the celestial motions and the *correct* interpretation of their terrestrial effects.' The nature of these terrestrial effects is so far undetermined; it may be no more than some kind of gravitational tide, or it may be the flood of cosmic radiation that accompanies a solar eruption. Many biologists certainly believe that violent cosmic storms can have the most marked effects upon evolution, and meteorologists understand only too well their effect upon the weather. As for the cause of the solar eruptions, it is hardly far-fetched to suggest that they could be the outcome of some kind of solar tidal surge due to the positions of the planets in relation to the Sun.

There are, then, at least two lines of enquiry to be followed. First: since Nelson's work has established a close connection between the positions of the planets relative to the Sun and the outbreak of unusual sunspot activity, is it possible to establish any similar kind of relationship between the aspects of the planets to the Earth and the birth of babies with particular kinds of personality? Second: if this kind of relationship could be proved – which would amount virtually to a proof of some of the most fundamental beliefs of astrology – was the influence upon the development of personality due to gravitational effects, or to the occurrence of different intensities of cosmic shower?

Not long after Nelson had erected his telescope on the roof of the RCA building, and well before the results of his research became public, a young French statistician named Michel Gauquelin, with a sceptical interest in astrology, set out to answer the first question – with unexpected results.

Right: Jupiter, from *De sphaera*. He signifies physical well-being and material success

Below: three of John Nelson's charts, showing planetary positions relative to the Sun when severe magnetic storms took place. Between 23 and 27 March 1940 (top), seven planets were either square or in opposition. From 12 to 16 November 1960 (centre) occurred the worst storm in 20 years, as predicted by Nelson. The greatest ever recorded cosmic shower was on 23 February 1956 (bottom)

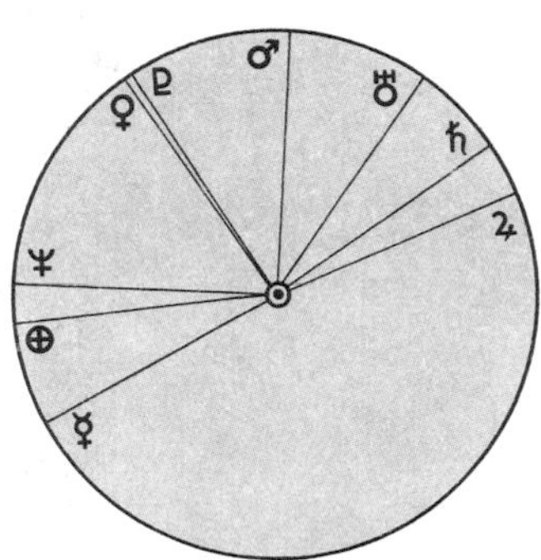

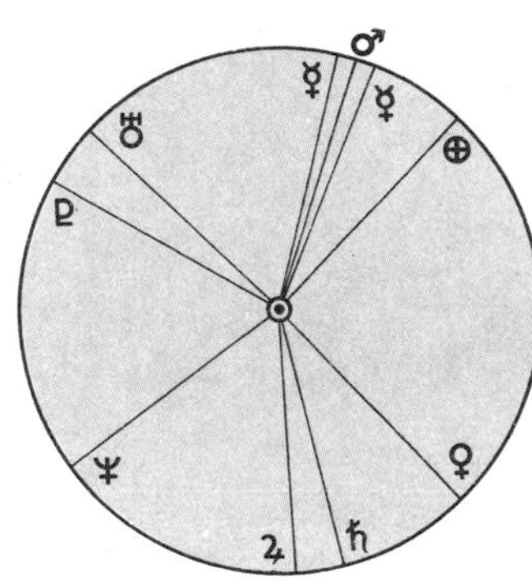

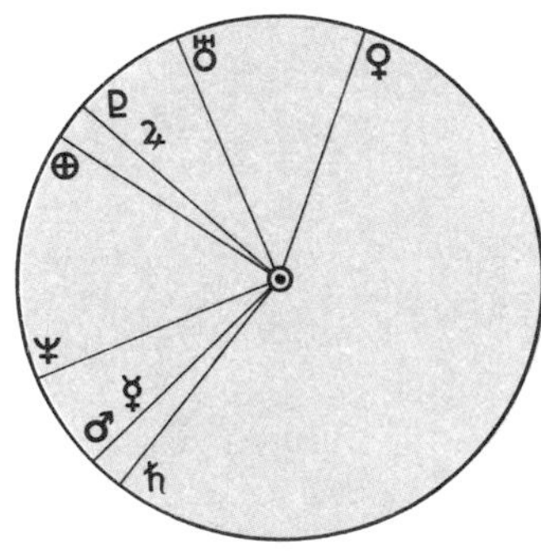

In the past 20 years, researchers have produced some startling evidence that appears to back up traditional astrological beliefs. This chapter investigates their findings

The signs of success

WHEN THE YOUNG FRENCH STATISTICIAN Michel Gauquelin began his investigations in 1950, it was his intention to prove that there was no connection between planetary positions at a person's birth and his future development. He had some previous examples before him: a rather superficial investigation by the famous psychologist C. G. Jung into the astrological relationships of married couples, which he had abandoned as the results became progressively more inconclusive, a vast accumulation of data by K. E. Krafft, the Swiss who was rumoured to have been Hitler's private astrologer, and a statistical analysis by the French astrologer Paul Choisnard, who claimed significant results in such relationships as Sun-Mars in cases of premature death, Mercury-Moon in the nativities of philosophers, Sun-Moon in those of celebrities, and the aspects of Mars in the birth charts of soldiers.

Gauquelin began by comparing the horoscopes of some 25,000 subjects; in France and other countries where it is legally required to register the time of birth of a child, it is possible to calculate accurate horoscopes from birth certificates without the necessity of approaching the individuals concerned. He was soon able to state with confidence that there were no grounds for the wild claims made by Krafft and Choisnard. There was, however, a lesser piece of research carried out by another French astrologer, Leon Lasson, who had found a significant correlation between Mars and its aspects with the ascendants or descendants of 134 politicians, between Venus and its aspects with the ascendants of 190 artists, and between Mercury and the ascendants or descendants of 209 actors and writers.

Putting his data to this test, Gauquelin was surprised to discover that he obtained the same kind of correlation. Taking a sample of no less than 576 eminent professors of medicine, he found that an unexpectedly high proportion were born just after Mars or Saturn had risen or passed the midheaven. In a second group of 508 leading doctors, he obtained a comparable correlation, and he calculated that the odds against this being a matter of pure chance were of the order of 1 million to one.

Fortunately for us – though less happily for himself, for he subsequently became the

Above: traditionally Saturn, seen here in an illustration from the 15th-century codex *De sphaera*, exerts his influence over activities that require mature judgement. The French statistician Michel Gauquelin found the position of Saturn to be particularly significant in the horoscopes of scientists and doctors

Right: Karl Ernst Krafft, a Swiss astrologer, who moved to Germany in 1939. He correctly predicted that Hitler's life would be in danger between 7 and 10 November; in the event, Hitler made a narrow escape when a bomb exploded in a Munich beer cellar

target of much bitter criticism from the scientific establishment – Gauquelin decided to pursue this line of investigation further. From all over France he collected birth data for groups of eminent soldiers, politicians, writers, sportsmen and clerics. In every case, they showed a distinct correlation between the position of certain planets at birth with the subsequent career of the subject. Great soldiers, for instance, tended to have Mars or Jupiter just past the ascendant or the mid-heaven in their horoscopes. Gauquelin calculated that the probability that this was due to chance was as high as one in five million in certain groups.

Statistics and pulp romance

Even more remarkably, Gauquelin discovered that these significant results applied only to those who were truly successful. For instance, in a group of 1458 scientists who had never won a prize, made any important discovery or published more than run-of-the-mill research papers, there was no suggestion of significance in the position of Mars, Jupiter or Saturn at the time of birth.

Gauquelin's results provoked a great deal of interest in the French popular press, but for a long time the scientific community could not be persuaded to comment. At length Jean Porte, administrator of the Institute of Statistics, replied that the figures applied only to France: they revealed some kind of national characteristic that had nothing to do with astrology, and the same methods, applied to other countries, would produce quite different results. (Astrologers have pointed out the flaw in Porte's argument: if a different set of correlations for another country were discovered, it would only strengthen their belief that *all* planetary positions are significant in the horoscope.)

Above: the French statistician Michel Gauquelin, who set out to disprove the standard beliefs of astrology. His research led him to a number of unexpected discoveries

A committee of Belgian scientists had been set up in 1953 expressly to study paranormal phenomena; a member of this committee, Marcel Boll, commented:

> Your conclusions are nothing but pulp-romances, the worst sort of proof, and the issue is without hope; for if you undertook the same inquiry in Great Britain, Germany, the USA or Russia you would come out with nothing but national idiosyncracies.

Challenged, Gauquelin and his wife set out on long journeys through Germany, Italy, Holland and Belgium to collect data from registers of birth. The results obtained after submission of the data to statistical analysis were substantially the same, with some interesting sidelights. It was found, for example, that Mars appeared in the significant positions for Italian soldiers far more frequently than for their German colleagues. Gauquelin pointed out that one would expect Germans, *as a nation*, to be far more warlike than Italians; so that successful German soldiers were far less in need of a powerful Martian influence in their horoscopes, while the Italians would require (as it were) an overdose of militarism.

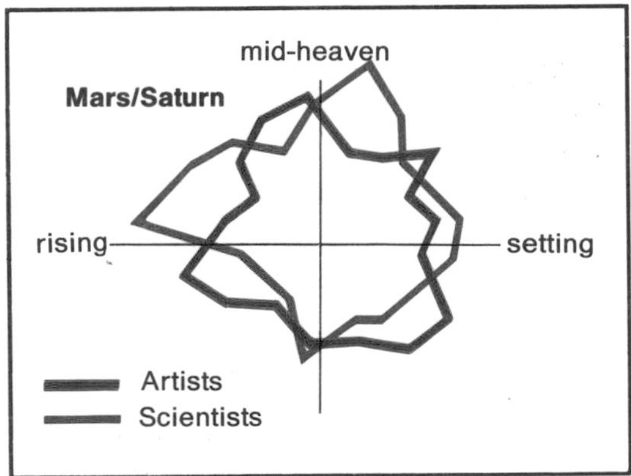

Right: graphs showing the positions of Mars and Saturn, combined as a single line, in the horoscopes of 3305 scientists and 2048 musicians and painters. The graph for scientists is well above average at rising and at mid-heaven, whereas the graph for musicians and painters is significantly below average in these positions

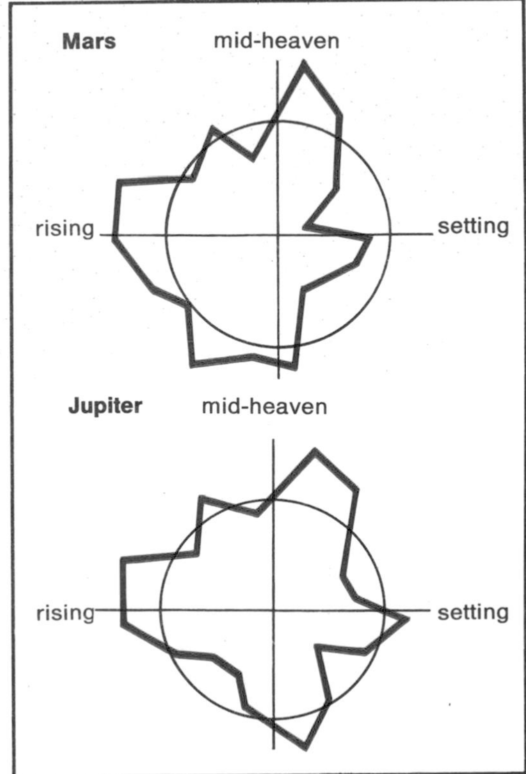

Left: graphs showing the positions of Mars and Jupiter in the horoscopes of 3142 military leaders. The circle represents the average distribution that would be expected in such a large sample, and the solid line indicates the number of people with either planet at a particular angle in their horoscope. Significantly high departures from the average can be seen for planetary positions just above the horizon and just past mid-heaven

Science and the stars

Gauquelin and his wife collected birth data for more than 25,000 people. In the charts of 3305 scientists, Mars was found in one or other of the significant positions 666 times, where chance would have predicted 551 – the odds against this were computed at 500,000 to one. In the charts of 3142 military leaders, Mars was associated with the ascendant or the mid-heaven (with an additional small increase at the nadir, the point opposite the mid-heaven) in 634 cases, where chance indicated 524 – the odds being 1 million to one. In the same charts, Jupiter appeared significantly close to the two angles 644 times. And for 1485 athletes, Mars appeared at the significant angles 327 times, against a chance level of 248.

A number of control experiments were carried out to give a base with which to compare Gauquelin's findings. Groups of horoscopes selected at random gave the results expected according to chance; and further examination of the horoscopes of men in subordinate positions continued to reveal little divergence from the norm. It was only those who were successful in their professions who showed the significant planetary positions in their charts.

Analysing the survey results again, Gauquelin spotted the occurrence of significantly low figures for planetary positions among certain specific groups. The table (above) summarises his analysis of his observations.

Rising or setting	Significant high frequency	Average frequency	Significant low frequency
Mars	scientists doctors athletes executives	politicians actors journalists	writers painters musicians
Jupiter	team athletes soldiers politicians actors journalists playwrights	painters musicians writers	solo athletes scientists doctors
Saturn	scientists doctors	politicians soldiers	actors painters journalists writers
Moon	politicians writers	scientists doctors painters musicians journalists	athletes soldiers

While he was pursuing these enquiries, Gauquelin was also looking out for any correlation with the position of the Sun – in other words, for some proof that the sign of the zodiac under which a person is born also affects their future development. He reported that he could find nothing of any statistical significance – but researchers in the USA and in Great Britain pursued this particular line of enquiry and obtained some interesting results. Because birth times are not generally recorded in these two countries, it was possible to work only with dates of birth, in which case the positions of the planets in the zodiac are known, but not their positions in relation to the ascendant or the mid-heaven.

Astrology and the professionals

In the USA, Edmund van Deusen processed 163,953 birth-dates for individuals born in the States and in Canada. In Great Britain, sociologist Joe Cooper, working with Dr Alan Smithers of the University of Bradford, studied some 35,000 birth-dates. Combining the results obtained by these researchers, we get the following generalisations:

Soldiers: From 16,000 British army officers and 12,000 Americans, it was discovered that a significantly high proportion were born in late summer and early autumn, with peaks appearing in Leo and Scorpio.

Doctors: 6412 British and American doctors show above average figures for birth-dates in summer and autumn; and medical officers in the British army show a marked peaking in Scorpio.

Musicians: From 8932 British and American musicians and composers, an above average proportion were born in Sagittarius, Capricorn, Aquarius and Pisces.

Lawyers: 6677 American lawyers show a peak in Gemini.

Bankers: From 2696 bankers, a significant proportion have birth dates in Virgo.

Politicians: British politicians show a disproportionate tendency to be born in Aries.

Advertising executives and diplomats: The sample was from 7118 advertising agency men and 1834 diplomats. Both showed Gemini as the favoured sign of the zodiac.

Teachers: Van Deusen found that, of 5056 American school-teachers, a significant proportion were born in Leo or Virgo.

Librarians: 5111 American and Canadian librarians showed a marked trend toward Libra.

Authors: From a sample of 3927 British and American writers, a remarkably high proportion were born in Virgo.

Comedians: Cooper and Smithers found a marked tendency for comedians' birthdays to fall in Aquarius, Pisces, Aries, Taurus or Gemini.

It is important to remember that these statements represent statistical analysis of quite large samples. They are not to be explained away by the fact that the graph of births tends to show a peak in February and a trough in December; this kind of variation is allowed for in the calculations.

At about the same time that these findings were published, three British doctors made

Below: Dr Alan Smithers (left) and Joe Cooper studied data compiled from some 35,000 birth-dates, and obtained some remarkable findings

an analysis of some 28,000 cases of patients born between 1921 and 1955 who were admitted to psychiatric wards in 1970 and 1971. They found that 9 per cent more schizophrenics and 7 per cent more manic depressives had been born during the first three months of the year.

From this plethora of statistical information it begins to emerge that there may be more than a little truth in the suggestion advanced earlier, that a person's future development may (at the very least) be affected by the time of year in which he or she is born. Taken in conjunction with Gauquelin's work, it seems to lend strong support to the belief that the traditional tenets of astrology are founded in some kind of empirical data.

Emotional and neurotic

In 1977 a professional astrologer, Jeff Mayo, and one of Britain's most eminent psychologists, Professor Hans Eysenck, got together to investigate another of astrology's claims: that persons born in Cancer, Scorpio or Pisces tend to be unduly emotional and neurotic. Using a standard personality test that had been introduced by Eysenck in 1964, they found a definite correlation between the odd-numbered birth signs (Aries, Gemini, Leo, Libra, Sagittarius and Aquarius) and a tendency to extrovert behaviour; while the even-numbered signs (Taurus, Cancer, Virgo, Scorpio, Capricorn and Pisces) were associated with introversion. Furthermore, they showed that Cancer, Scorpio and Pisces – and, to Jeff Mayo's considerable surprise, Aries – were statistically linked with emotional and neurotic personalities.

Above: Professor Hans Eysenck, of the Institute of Psychiatry in the University of London, who has publicly declared his growing belief in astrology

The most recent research seems to have gone even further toward popular beliefs about astrology than professional astrologers themselves would allow. It was pointed out in the first chapter in this series that astrologers did not accept the idea of 'compatibility' between those born in particular signs. But one of Eysenck's colleagues, Beverley Steffert, has been investigating the connection between Sun signs and happy marriages; and she believes that she has found that such marriages result when the couple involved were both born in either an even-numbered or an odd-numbered sign.

And there, for the moment, the case rests. Astrology is no longer merely a subject for popular columns in cheap newspapers, or for courses run by members of the mystic fringe for idle housewives. It is considered a suitable subject of study for medical men, statisticians and psychologists. Whether the movements of the planets provoke changes in the gravitational or magnetic fields of the solar system, or induce showers of cosmic radiation, and whether one or more of these influences has a profound (and predictable) effect upon the personality of those about to be born, only a great deal more research will reveal. But it seems true that we have underestimated the knowledge of the ancients: the magicians of Babylon knew rather more about the forces of destiny than we have, until now, given them credit for.

Astrological twins

When one looks at those who have achieved some degree of eminence in their professions, it is remarkable how many of them have related birth dates. Albert Einstein and Otto Hahn (below) were both born on 14 March 1879; operatic tenors Beniamino Gigli and Lauritz Melchior (far right) were both born on 20 March 1890. There are many other examples; Hermann Göring and Alfred Rosenberg, two prominent members of the Nazi party, were born on the same day and died in the same prison on the same day. Even those whose birthdays fall on the same day, but are separated by a year or two, such as Vincent Price and Peter Cushing (centre) have remarkably similar careers.

Hitler and the holy lance

The holy lance, which pierced Christ's side at his crucifixion, became a talisman for the Teutonic warlords of Europe. In the 20th century it was plundered by Adolf Hitler, who knew its mystical significance all too well. FRANK SMYTH tells how the would-be conqueror of the world linked his destiny with the lance

IN THE STREETS OF VIENNA in 1913, a down-and-out former art student vainly tried to make a living by selling postcard-sized watercolours. Occasionally, driven off the streets by cold, he would wander through the corridors of the Hofburg Museum. Here he was particularly fascinated by a number of valuable pieces known as the Habsburg regalia. And among these the unprepossessing young vagrant, Adolf Hitler, paid special attention to the Holy Lance – reputed to be the spear that pierced Christ's side when he had given up the ghost on the cross.

The legend of the Holy Lance takes its origin from John 19:33–37:

> But when they came to Jesus, and saw that he was dead already, they brake not his legs: But one of the soldiers with a spear pierced his side, and forthwith came there out blood and water. And he that saw it bare record, and his record is true: and he knoweth that he saith true, that ye might believe. For these things were done that the scripture should be fulfilled, A bone of him shall not be broken. And again another scripture saith, They shall look on him whom they pierced.

The verse following this tells how Joseph of Arimathaea gained permission to take the body of Jesus and, helped by Nicodemus, laid it in a tomb on the night of Good Friday.

Other oral and written traditions, beginning with the earliest Christians and continuing to the Middle Ages, depict the rich Jewish philanthropist as obsessed with the artefacts associated with the dead Christ. He is said to have preserved the cross itself, the nails, the crown of thorns, and the shroud from which Christ rose on the third day. Through clues left by Joseph, Helena, mother of the first Christian emperor, Constantine, was able to rediscover these relics.

But even before Christ's death, according to the same traditions, Joseph had begun collecting: after the last supper he took charge of the cup in which Jesus had consecrated the bread and wine. After the resurrection, Joseph kept this cup alongside the spear of John's Gospel: the Holy Grail and the Holy Lance.

Joseph's subsequent travels with the Grail

Far left: the blade of the Habsburg spear, reputed to be the lance that pierced Christ's side while he was on the cross. Because it was a holy relic, the iron blade has been extensively repaired with gold and silver during its long history. It is now bound together with wire and an inscribed 'sleeve'

Left: a Roman soldier confirms that Christ is dead by plunging a spear into him, in a painting by Rubens. According to tradition, it was revealed to the soldier at this moment that Christ was truly the Son of God, and the spear acquired enduring magical potency

Right: just one face in the crowds of Germans who exulted at the outbreak of the First World War: Adolf Hitler, poverty-stricken and obscure, but dreaming already of leading the Nordic 'master race' to supremacy

Below: by selling watercolours like this, Hitler scratched a living in Vienna in 1913

and the Lance are the subject of folk tales and legends in almost every country in Europe. In Britain he is said to have hidden the Grail at Glastonbury. Afterwards he thrust his staff into the ground, where it sprouted to become the still-surviving Glastonbury Thorn, which blooms only at Christmas.

Romantic writers, beginning with the French poet Chrétien de Troyes in about 1180, bound up the fate of the Holy Grail and the Holy Lance with the adventures of King Arthur and the Knights of the Round Table, notably with Lancelot, Gawain and Perceval.

Alongside these stories – themselves based on Celtic tradition and scraps of historical fact – there ran a thin thread of evidence that the Lance, at least, had survived the centuries, passed down sometimes through good hands, sometimes through

unworthy ones. With its ownership came power, to be used for great good or for terrible evil.

At least four 'Holy Lances' existed in Europe during the early part of the present century. Perhaps the best-known was in the keeping of the Vatican, although the Roman Catholic Church seems to have regarded it as no more than a curio. Certainly no preternatural powers were claimed for it by the papal authorities.

A second lance was kept in Paris, where it had been taken by St Louis in the 13th century, after his return from the crusades in Palestine.

Another lance, preserved in Cracow, Poland, was merely a copy of the Habsburg lance. The latter probably had the best pedigree of them all. It had been discovered at Antioch in 1098, during the first crusade, but mystery – and possibly imagination – obscured the manner of its finding. Crusaders had mounted a successful siege of the city and had taken control, when a more heavily armed band of Saracens rode up and turned the tables, shutting up the crusaders within the walls in their turn. After three weeks water and food were running low and surrender seemed the only course. Then a priest claimed to have had a miraculous vision of the Holy Lance, buried in the church of St Peter. When excavations at the spot revealed the iron spearhead, the crusaders were filled with a new zeal and rode out to rout their attackers.

Germanic tradition, somewhat at odds with these dates, claimed the Habsburg lance had in fact been carried as a talisman in the ninth century by Charlemagne through 47 victorious campaigns. It had also endowed him with clairvoyant powers. Only when he accidentally dropped it did Charlemagne die.

The lance later passed into the possession of Heinrich the Fowler, who founded the royal house of the Saxons and drove the Poles eastwards – a foreshadowing, Hitler may have thought in later years, of his own destiny. After passing through the hands of five Saxon monarchs, it fell into the possession of the succeeding Hohenstauffens of Swabia. One of the most outstanding of this line was Frederick Barbarossa, born in 1123. Before his death 67 years later Barbarossa had conquered Italy and driven the Pope himself into exile; again, Hitler may well have admired the brutal harshness coupled with charismatic personality that drove Barbarossa to success. Like Charlemagne, however, Barbarossa made the mistake of dropping the lance as he waded a stream in Sicily. He died within minutes of this event.

The fascination of the spear

This was the legend of the weapon now among the Habsburg regalia, which so fascinated the young Hitler. He spent his first visit to the lance studying its every detail. It was just over a foot (30 centimetres) long, tapering to a slender, leaf-shaped point, and at some time the blade had been grooved to admit a nail – allegedly one of those used in the crucifixion. This had been bound into place with gold wire. The spear had been broken, and the two halves were joined by a sheath of silver, while two gold crosses had been inlaid into the base, near the haft.

The evidence of Hitler's personal fascination with the Habsburg lance rests on the testimony of Dr Walter Johannes Stein, a mathematician, economist and occultist who claimed to have met the future Führer just before the First World War. Stein, a native of Vienna, was born in 1891, the son of a rich barrister. He was to be a polymath and an intellectual adventurer until his death in 1957. He took a first degree in science and a doctorate in psychophysical research at the University of Vienna. He became expert in archaeology, early Byzantine art and medieval history; in the First World War, as an officer in the Austrian Army, he was decorated for gallantry.

In 1928 he published an eccentric pamphlet, *World history in the light of the Holy Grail*, which was circulated in Germany, Holland and Britain. Just five years after that Reichsführer Heinrich Himmler ordered that he be pressed into service with the Nazi 'Occult Bureau', but Stein escaped to Britain.

The Second World War found him in the guise of British intelligence agent. After helping to obtain the plans for 'Operation Sealion' – Hitler's projected invasion of Britain – he acted as adviser to Winston Churchill on the German leader's occult involvements.

Stein never published his own memoirs, but before his death he befriended an ex-Sandhurst commando officer, then a journalist, Trevor Ravenscroft. Using Stein's notes and conversations, Ravenscroft published a book, *Spear of destiny*, in 1972, which first brought Hitler's fascination with the Habsburg spear to public attention.

What hold could the Holy Lance, a Christian symbol, have on the violently anti-Christian ex-Roman Catholic Adolf Hitler? Already he was given to violent anti-Semitic rantings, and already he was a devout student of Friedrich Nietzsche's *Anti-Christ*, with its condemnation of Christianity as 'the ultimate Jewish consequence'.

Part of the answer lay in a medieval occult tradition regarding the history of the Holy Lance. As the Gospel of John describes, the Roman soldier who pierced Christ had unwittingly fulfilled the Old Testament prophecies (that Christ's bones would not be broken). Had he not done as he did, the destiny of mankind would have been different. According to both Matthew and Mark the true nature of Christ was revealed to the soldier, said to be named Gaius Cassius Longinus, at that moment: 'And when the centurion, which stood over against him, saw that he so cried out, and gave up the ghost, he said, Truly this man was the Son of God.' (Mark 15:39.)

Above: Charlemagne, King of the Franks, became Holy Roman Emperor in AD 800. One of the legends that have grown up around him says that he owed his success in war to the Holy Lance

Below: the triumphal entry of Hitler into Vienna in March 1938. One of the Führer's first acts was to order the removal to Germany of the Habsburg treasure, which included the Holy Lance

To the mind of the occultist, an instrument used for such momentous purpose would itself become the focus of magical power. And as Richard Cavendish succinctly puts it, speaking of the Grail and the Lance in his book *King Arthur and the Grail*:

> A thing is not sacred because it is good. It is sacred because it contains mysterious and awesome power. It is as potent for good or evil as a huge charge of electricity. If it is tampered with, however compelling and understandable the motive, the consequences may be catastrophic for entirely innocent people.

According to Stein, Hitler was fully aware of this concept as early as 1912: indeed it was through Hitler's obsession with the legend of the lance and its power as a 'magic wand' that the two men met. In the summer of 1912 Dr Stein purchased an edition of *Parsival*, a Grail romance by the 13th-century German poet Wolfram von Eschenbach, from an occult bookseller in Vienna. It was full of scribbled marginal commentaries displaying a combination of occult learning and pathological racism. On the flyleaf its previous owner had signed his name: Adolf Hitler. Through the bookseller Stein traced Hitler and spent many hours with him, appalled but fascinated. Although it was to be years before the poverty-stricken postcard painter took his first steps on the road to power, there was already an evil charisma about the man. Through all the tortuous windings of his discourse one obsession stood out clearly: he had a mystic destiny to fulfil and, according to Stein, the lance held the key.

Hitler described to Stein how the spear had acquired a special significance for him:

> I slowly became aware of a mighty presence around it, the same awesome presence which I had experienced inwardly on those rare occasions in my life when I had sensed that a great destiny awaited me... a window in the future was opened up to me through which I saw in a single flash of illumination a future event by which I knew beyond contradiction that the blood in my veins would one day become the vessel of the Folk-Spirit of my people.

Hitler never revealed the nature of his 'vision'; but Stein believed that he had seen himself a quarter of a century later, in the Heldenplatz outside the Hofburg Museum, addressing Austrian Nazis and ordinary, bewildered Viennese. There, on 14 March 1938, the German Führer was to announce his annexation of Austria into the German Reich – and to give the order to carry the Habsburg regalia off to Nuremberg, spiritual home of the Nazi movement.

A curious priority

Taking possession of the treasure was a curious priority in view of the fact that Hitler despised the house of Habsburg as traitors to the Germanic race. Nevertheless on 13 October the spear and the other items of the regalia were loaded onto an armoured train with an SS guard and taken across the German border. They were lodged in the hall of St Catherine's Church, where Hitler proposed to set up a Nazi war museum. Stein believed that when Hitler had the lance in his possession, his latent ambitions for world conquest began to grow and flourish.

If Hitler's knowledge of the Habsburg spear's history was as extensive as Stein claimed, he must have been aware of the legends concerning the fate of Charlemagne, Barbarossa and others who had wielded it as a weapon, only to perish when it fell from their grasp. The legend seemed to be confirmed by a chilling coincidence that marked the end of his connection with the Lance.

After heavy Allied bombing in October 1944, during which Nuremberg suffered extensive damage, Hitler ordered the spear, along with the rest of the Habsburg regalia, to be buried in a specially constructed vault.

Left: the closing scene of *Parsifal*, Wagner's last opera. Hitler was fascinated by the legend on which the opera is based. Here the enchantress Kundry, redeemed from a life of evil, dies as Parsifal takes the Holy Grail from its shrine. He holds the Holy Lance, which, having been used to work evil by the black magician Klingsor, is an instrument of blessing in the hands of the virtuous Parsifal

Below: the Luitpold Arena in Nuremberg, scene of the Nazis' most spectacular prewar rallies, saw an informal 'march past' by victorious US soldiers in April 1945 (inset). In the ruins of the shattered city the Holy Lance, with other war booty, was found in a bombproof vault

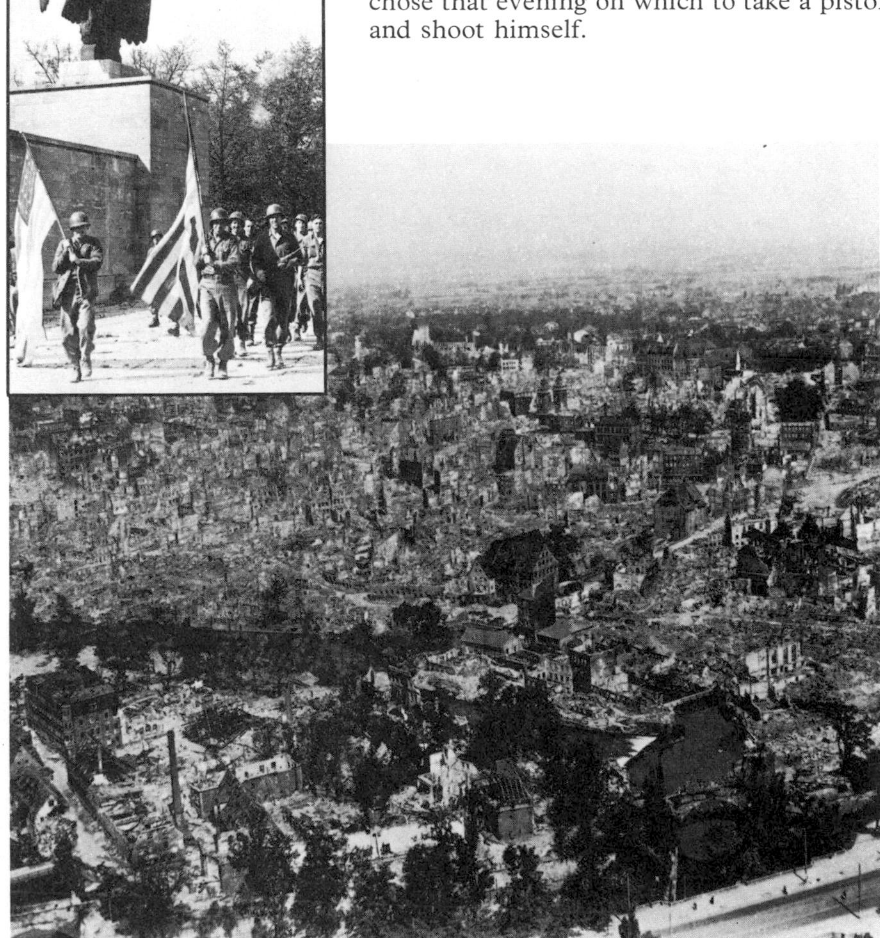

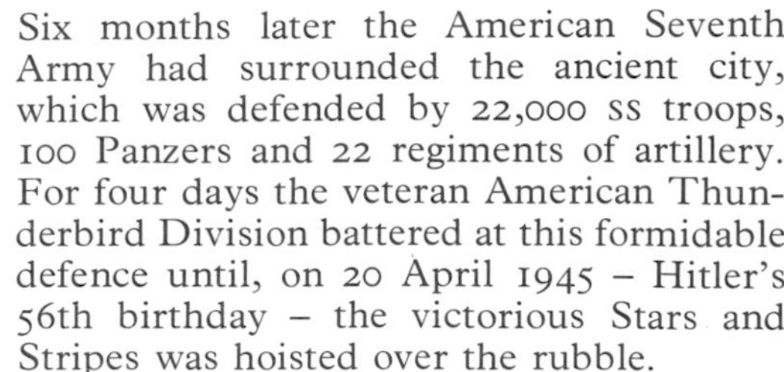

Six months later the American Seventh Army had surrounded the ancient city, which was defended by 22,000 SS troops, 100 Panzers and 22 regiments of artillery. For four days the veteran American Thunderbird Division battered at this formidable defence until, on 20 April 1945 – Hitler's 56th birthday – the victorious Stars and Stripes was hoisted over the rubble.

During the next few days, while American troops rounded up Nazi survivors and began the long process of interrogating them, Company C of the US Army's Third Military Government Regiment, under their commander Lieutenant William Horn, were detailed to search for the Habsburg treasure. By chance a shell had made their task easier by blowing away brickwork and revealing the entrance to the vault. After some difficulty with the vault's steel doors, Lieutenant Horn entered the underground chamber and peered through the dusty gloom. There, lying on a bed of faded red velvet, was the fabled spear of Longinus. Lieutenant Horn reached out and took possession of the spear on behalf of the United States government. It was the afternoon of 30 April 1945. That much is recorded history.

And however sceptical may be the critics – about Walter Stein, the occult in general and the Holy Lance legends in particular – it is also historical fact that a few hundred miles away in a bunker in Berlin, Adolf Hitler chose that evening on which to take a pistol and shoot himself.

Legions of hell

The Nazi Party's rise to power has been attributed to occult practice. And Adolf Hitler himself was undoubtedly fascinated by the 'black arts'. This chapter explains how and why this bizarre association developed

IN THE LATE SUMMER of 1940, as the battle of Britain was drawing to its close, Toby O'Brien, then press secretary to Winston Churchill, had an inspiration. He was sitting in his bath one morning when the words of a coarse comic song began to form 'unbidden' in his mind. He repeated his composition over lunch later that day to a group of high-ranking British officers in Whitehall. They were convulsed with mirth. Some of them wrote it down, while others memorised it. Within weeks it had filtered through the ranks and was on the lips of squadron leaders and squaddies, admirals and artificers. Sung to the tune of 'Colonel Bogey' it went:

Hitler, he only had one ball;
Göring had two but very small.
Himmler was very similar,
But poor old Goebbels
Had no balls at all.

Toby O'Brien certainly did not believe his composition was accurate: precious little was known about the sexual endowments or habits of the Führer. But when Russian military surgeons examined Hitler's charred remains in the Berlin bunker in May 1945, they discovered that Hitler was indeed monorchid: he possessed but one testicle. It was a bizarre and extreme coincidence.

But Hitler's defect may have had a profound significance for the development of his occult ideas. According to Dr Walter Stein,

The swastika became the official insignia of the Nazi Party (below: banners at a rally at Nuremberg in 1933) in the 1920s. Sitting on a white disc with a red background, it was a striking symbol, which to Adolf Hitler (right) represented all the ideals of the nationalist movement. Many have seen Hitler's decision to reverse the symbol – to use a 'left-handed' swastika rather than the traditional 'right-handed' one – as an indication of his sinister leanings. And, once a symbol of good fortune, the swastika is now seen as the embodiment of evil itself

Below: Toby O'Brien who, in 1940, penned an unwittingly accurate lampoon against Adolf Hitler

whose observations on his personal conversations with Hitler in Vienna formed the basis of Trevor Ravenscroft's *The spear of destiny*, Hitler had, as early as 1912, formed a passion for the music of Richard Wagner – particularly for *Parsifal*, which praised Teutonic knighthood and exalted the Aryan race. Soon Hitler discovered Wagner's source: the medieval poetry of Wolfram von Eschenbach. In fact it was through buying a copy of Eschenbach's *Parsival* that had once belonged to Hitler that Dr Stein met him. Dr Stein was impressed by the meticulousness of the marginal notes, though simultaneously appalled by the pathological race hatred that they showed. Among them appeared numerous references to the character Klingsor, whom Hitler apparently identified with the notorious ninth-century tyrant Landulph II of Capua.

Landulph's avaricious grasping for power had led him to study the black arts, and it was for these practices that he was excommunicated in AD 875. But one other fact must have given Hitler a sense of identity with the ninth-century 'Führer'. Landulph seems to have been either partly or totally castrated: Eschenbach described him as 'the man who was smooth between the legs'.

We know that Hitler was easily influenced as a youth, avidly soaking up the ideas of those – Wagner and Nietzsche, for instance – who impressed him. Landulph's power mania and his unfortunate anatomical similarity to himself must have struck the young Adolf, and there is reason to suspect that Landulph's black magic did so too. Another source gives us a very clear indication that Hitler was impressed by magical symbolism from the beginning of his political career.

Long before Guido von List (below) adopted the swastika as the emblem of his neo-pagan movement in Germany in the late 19th century, the 'crooked cross' was a widespread symbol of good luck, of life and of energy. The swastikas on this figure (right), on the handle of a bucket found in the 9th-century ship-burial at Oseberg, Norway, represent the hammers of Thor, god of thunder and of war. Those on the plinth of this statue of Kali (above right), the hideous aspect of the Hindu Goddess, signify a life-giving regenerating force

Throughout the latter half of the 19th century, German pseudo-intellectual circles had been obsessed with a movement compounded of pagan ritual and notions of Nordic purity invented by a man named Guido von List. Born in 1848, the son of a rich trader in leather goods and top boots – pointers, perhaps, to things to come – von List had renounced his Catholicism when he was 14 with a solemn oath that he would one day build a temple to Woden (also called Odin), war god of Scandinavian mythology.

By the 1870s von List had a sizeable group of followers, dedicated to observing 'pagan' feasts at the solstices and equinoxes. In 1875 they attracted attention to themselves by worshipping the Sun as Baldur, the Nordic god, slain in battle, who rose from the dead. The rite was held on a hilltop near Vienna, and concluded with von List burying eight wine bottles carefully laid out in the shape of a swastika.

The swastika had been a widespread symbol of good fortune from earliest times and among all nations; it had been found on Chinese, Mongolian and American Indian artefacts, was used by the ancient Greeks as a pottery decoration, and by medieval architects as a border design for stained glass windows. Its name in Middle English, *fylfot*, is said to mean 'fill foot', since it was a device used for 'filling the foot' of windows. 'Swastika' stems from the Sanskrit *Su asti*, which means, literally translated, 'Good, he is.' In fact the swastika, with its arms 'trailing' as if the whole pattern were spinning clockwise, symbolised the Sun, the powers of light.

In the 1920s, when the National Socialist movement was in its infancy, Hitler asked for designs to be submitted for an easily recognisable symbol, akin to the hammer and sickle of the Russian communists. Friedrich

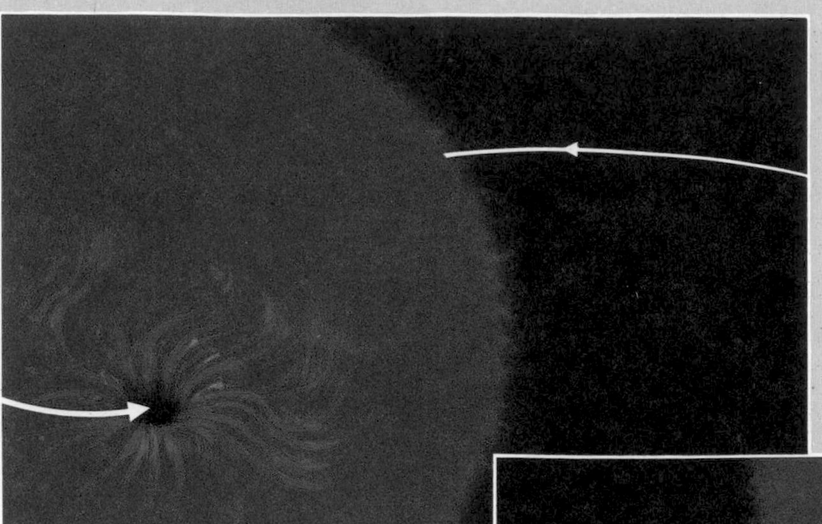

A world of ice

How did the cosmological theories of a blacksmith-turned-engineer become a mainstay of the Nazi world view?

The man in question was one Hanns Hörbiger (far right), who believed that, among the 'cosmic building stuff' that makes up the Universe, there exists water in its 'cosmic form' – ice. This ice forms itself into large blocks that orbit young stars. Ignoring Kepler's laws of motion, which state that orbiting bodies travel in ellipses, Hörbiger argued that these blocks of ice follow a spiral path, so that they eventually collide with the star (above), causing an enormous explosion. The star ejects a molten mass of rotating matter (above right), which forms a new solar system (right).

Hörbiger's belief that planets follow a spiral path led him to suggest that there were originally four moons orbiting the Earth, of which our present Moon is the only remaining one. The last collision of a moon with the Earth, some 13,000 years ago, he claimed, caused the disappearance of Atlantis – the continent that, the Nazis believed, was the original home of the Aryan race.

Himmler was particularly impressed with Hörbiger's theories, and a treatise on the cosmic ice theory was published as one of a series of handbooks for the SA (the paramilitary wing of the Nazi Party). And Hitler himself declared that he would build an observatory in his home town of Linz, dedicated to the three great cosmologists: Copernicus, Kepler – and Hanns Hörbiger.

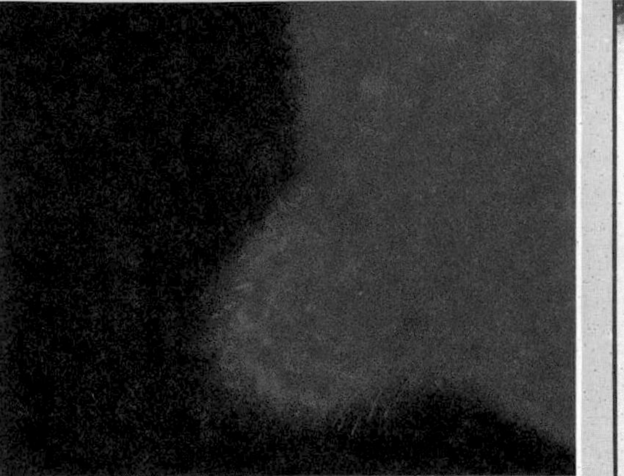

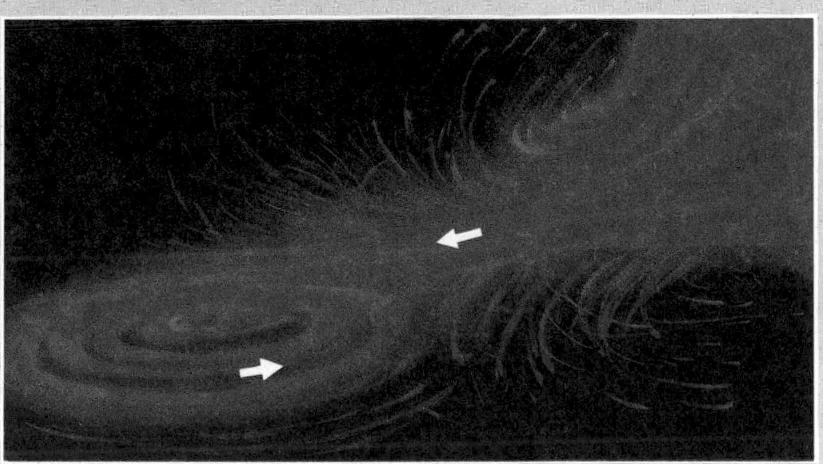

Krohn, a Sternberg dentist who was also an occultist, suggested a swastika on a white disc with a red background – red for blood and the social ideal, white for nationalism and purity of race, and the swastika for 'the struggle for victory of Aryan man'.

Hitler was delighted but for one detail – the traditional 'right-handed' swastika was to be reversed to form what the writer Francis King terms 'an evocation of evil, spiritual devolution and black magic'.

Dr Krohn fully realised Hitler's intention in changing the ancient sign, for he was a member of the *Germanenorden* – German Order – which, with the Thule Society, had taken over where von List's rather amateurish organisation had left off in the years before the First World War. Both societies – which eventually became almost interchangeable in ideas and even membership – were originally composed of the German officer class and professions, who were convinced of a massive international Jewish conspiracy backed up by occult practices. To counter this they established their own Nordic occult-based freemasonry, complete with elaborate rituals and robes, Viking helmets and swords. More importantly, the Thule Society – which took its name from the fabled land of Ultima Thule, a sort of paradise on Earth – began to recruit new members from the lower classes and disseminated anti-Semitic material in its various newspapers, one of which, the

Völkischer Beobachter, eventually became the official journal of the Nazi Party.

There is no doubt that Hitler, both in his down-and-out days in Vienna and later, as leader of the rising Nazi Party in the 1920s and 1930s, was constantly fascinated by 'fringe' occult theories. One of these was the lunatic 'World Ice Theory', a complicated set of ideas propagated by an Austrian engineer named Hanns Hörbiger (1860–1931). He claimed that the planets had been created by the collision of stars such as the Sun with huge chunks of ice. Hörbiger claimed that his system enabled him to forecast the weather accurately. Some occult writers, notably Pauwels and Bergier in their *Dawn of magic*, have suggested that Hörbiger's forecasts influenced Hitler's disastrous Russian campaign.

Latterly, Hitler became obsessed with map dowsing – swinging a pendulum over a map to find hidden objects. The topic was brought to the attention of Hitler's aides by an architect named Ludwig Straniak, yet another amateur occultist. Straniak demonstrated to German naval officers his apparent ability to pinpoint the whereabouts of their ships at sea, simply by dangling a pendulum over an admiralty chart. They were particularly impressed when he located the pocket battleship *Prinz Eugen*, at that time on a secret mission.

The 'black magicians'

Hitler's involvement with astrology, and prediction in general, has been much debated. It has even been claimed that he had powers of precognition, which allowed him to foresee the lack of opposition to his invasions of Austria and Czechoslovakia. But Hitler's real talent was as a masterly judge of the European political mood – and even this intuition deserted him when he decided to invade Poland in 1939.

Josef Goebbels, propaganda minister, used astrology cleverly but cynically – quoting Nostradamus, for instance, in support of Nazi domination. Hitler and, in particular, SS chief Himmler took astrology seriously.

In view of this varied preoccupation with the occult, many have suggested that, among high-ranking Nazis, Hitler and Himmler at least were in a real sense 'black magicians'. However, one great question confronts those who claim this. Why, when the Nazis rose to power, were occult writings and practices so rigorously stamped upon – for so they were?

In 1934 the first move was made when the Berlin police issued a ban on all forms of fortune-telling, from fairground palmists to society astrologers. That the orders came from central headquarters is certain, for the police officers who carried out the orders were extremely confused as to the intention behind them. They both impounded 'innocent' books and let go books of magic spells and similar works.

Next came a general suppression of all occult groups, even – to the chagrin and surprise of members – the German Order and the Thule Society. Both these contained many Nazis, of course, but even for these there was no exemption. For instance, Jörg Lanz von Liebenfels, whose writings inspired much of the German racial mystique, and who boasted that by introducing Hitler to occult groups he had been his 'guru', was told that he must not publish occult works in future.

Top: the German pocket battleship *Prinz Eugen*, which occultist Ludwig Straniak located simply by swinging a pendulum over a map. After hearing of Straniak's impressive demonstrations, Hitler himself became interested in – then obsessed with – map dowsing

Above: Josef Goebbels, Hitler's minister for propaganda and enlightenment. Although no believer in the occult, he recognised Hitler's fascination for the subject and skilfully used it as a psychological weapon to further the Nazi cause among the German people

With the sole exceptions of 'inner party members', such as certain of Himmler's personal SS aides, occultists of all shades had been done away with or driven underground in German-occupied countries by 1940.

The answer to the enigma has been pointed out by such writers as Francis King and J. H. Brennan. They argue that in regimes that in some ways are analogous with Hitler's – Mao's China, for instance, and Stalin's Russia – there was no such systematic weeding out of occultists. True, Stalin pounced on freemasons, cabalists, and the like, but only because they were 'secret societies' *per se*, not because of their 'magical' activities. In China, even after the Cultural Revolution, seers and astrologers were frowned upon as superstitious, but nothing desperate was done against them. They were more mocked at than persecuted. Authoritarian regimes do not seem to fear magical practices as such.

But Nazi Germany had to trample down 'freelance' occultists, because it was in effect trampling down its own rivals – in much the same way that Trotskyites suffered under Stalin.

There was only one occult movement permissible under the Third Reich, and it was hidden deep in its coils. It was led by the supreme magus, Adolf Hitler, and his acolyte, Heinrich Himmler: both of them powerful black magicians.

Was Hitler a black magician?

Adolf Hitler had an extraordinary ability to influence others. But was his charisma due to sheer strength of personality, to hypnotic skills – or to diabolical magic? Could he literally bewitch people?

THE GOAL OF EVERY MAGICIAN is power over natural forces. He aims to seize the infinite forces of the cosmos and wield them like a sword in his own service. A magician who seeks this power for his own ends, without the wish to serve any higher good, is a 'black' magician. According to most magical schools of thought he pays a high price in the end for his pride. Often he becomes possessed by the spirits he calls upon and is destroyed by them. In the view of several occultists, Adolf Hitler was a powerful black magician.

According to one of Hitler's few friends from his early years in Linz, his personal power had developed by the time he was 15 years old, and very startling it was. On one occasion:

> Adolf Hitler stood in front of me and gripped my hands and held them tight. . . . The words did not come smoothly from his mouth as they usually did, but rather erupted, hoarse and raucous. . . . It was as if another being spoke out of his body and moved him as much as it moved me. It was not at all a case of a speaker carried away by his own words. On the contrary; I rather felt as though he himself listened with astonishment and emotion to what burst forth from him with elemental force. . . .

The writer of this excerpt was August Kubizek. He was describing a midnight walk in 1904 with the 15-year-old Hitler following a performance of Wagner's opera *Rienzi*, which tells the story of the meteoric rise and fall of a Roman tribune. Hitler's inspired speech concerned the future of Germany and 'a mandate which, one day, he would receive from the people to lead them from servitude. . . .'

According to Kubizek, Hitler spent a great deal of time studying oriental mysticism, astrology, hypnotism, Germanic mythology and other aspects of occultism. By 1909 he had made contact with Dr Jörg Lanz von Liebenfels, a former Cistercian monk who, two years previously, had opened a temple of the 'Order of New Templars' at the tumbledown Werfenstein Castle on the banks of the Danube.

Von Liebenfels had assumed his

Below: Karl Dönitz, commander of the U-boat fleet, met Hitler as infrequently as possible, because he felt the Führer's 'powers of suggestion' impaired his judgement

aristocratic-sounding name: he was born plain Adolf Lanz and came of solid bourgeois stock. His following was small but wealthy. A disciple of Guido von List (see page 58), he flew a swastika flag from his battlements, performed ritual magic and ran a magazine entitled *Ostara*, a propaganda journal of occultism and race mysticism, to which the young Hitler became an avid subscriber. In 1932 Von Liebenfels wrote to a colleague:

> Hitler is one of our pupils . . . you will one day experience that he, and through him we, will one day be victorious and develop a movement that will make the world tremble.

The Italian dictator Benito Mussolini visited Hitler in Germany in 1943, mentally exhausted and deeply depressed. Yet Hitler's influence and the force of his personality were so strong that, according to Josef Goebbels, after only four days in his company Mussolini underwent a complete transformation

One of this ex-monk's pronouncements was that human breeding farms should be set up 'in order to eradicate Slavic and Alpine elements from Germanic heredity', prefiguring Himmler's idea of an SS stud farm by over 20 years.

By the onset of the First World War, Hitler seems to have developed an unshakable conviction of his own high destiny: as a messenger at the front he took enormous risks as if he knew that fate would not allow him to die just yet. By the time the war ended he had developed that curious, impersonal power over those around him that was to stand him in such good stead until late in his career.

Again and again the idea that Hitler was 'possessed' was echoed in the writings of those who knew him. His uncanny hold over individuals was a bugbear to those in the highest echelons of the state. Once, for example, Dr Hjalmar Schacht, Hitler's financial wizard, asked Hermann Göring to speak to Hitler about a minor point of economic policy. But in Hitler's presence Göring found himself unable to raise the matter. He told Schacht: 'I often make up my mind to say something to him, but when I meet him face to face my heart sinks. . . .'

Grand Admiral Karl Dönitz was so conscious of the Führer's influence that he avoided his company so as to leave his own judgement unimpaired:

> I purposely went very seldom to his headquarters, for I had the feeling that I would best preserve my power of initiative and also because, after several days at headquarters, I always had the feeling that I had to disengage myself from his powers of suggestion. . . . I was doubtless more fortunate than his staff, who were constantly exposed to his power and personality.

In his diary for 7 April 1943 Josef Goebbels recorded a remarkable instance of Hitler's use of the force of his personality. The Italian dictator Mussolini had visited Germany in a state of deep depression and mental exhaustion:

> By putting every ounce of nervous energy into the effort he [Hitler] succeeded in pushing Mussolini back onto the rails. In those four days the Duce underwent a complete change. When he got out of the train on his arrival the Führer thought he looked like a broken old man. When he left again he was in high fettle, ready for anything.

In March 1936 Hitler made a statement that precisely summed up the impressions of those who knew him best: 'I am going the way Providence dictates,' he said, 'with the assurance of a sleepwalker.' It was as if something else – not his own mind and soul – was in charge of his every action.

This ruling spirit, if such it was, was not always kind to its host. Hitler's frantic, screaming rages, when he would literally froth at the mouth and fall to the floor, are well-documented. Even more frightening is the account given by his confidant Hermann Rauschning in his book *Hitler speaks*:

> He wakes up in the night, screaming and in convulsions. He calls for help, and appears to be half paralysed. He is seized with panic that makes him tremble until the bed shakes. He utters confused and unintelligible sounds, gasping as if on the point of suffocation. . . .

Hitler was not certain at all times of his

Above: children born in the Steinhöring *Lebensborn*, one of many SS breeding farms set up by Heinrich Himmler to ensure the production of a Nordic 'super race'

Left: Hitler's ability to mesmerise individuals and groups, as at this informal gathering of his followers in Munich in the mid 1930s, led many to believe that he had supernatural powers

Left: Hitler laying the foundation stone of the House of German Art in Munich in 1933. The hammer used in the ceremony shattered; Hitler saw this as an ill omen and he was despondent for months. In January 1934 the architect of the building, Paul Ludwig Troost (below), died and Hitler's fears were allayed – he saw the incident as nothing but a warning of Troost's death

Bottom: the Externstein rocks in Lower Saxony, West Germany, which became a centre for Nazi neo-paganism in the 1930s

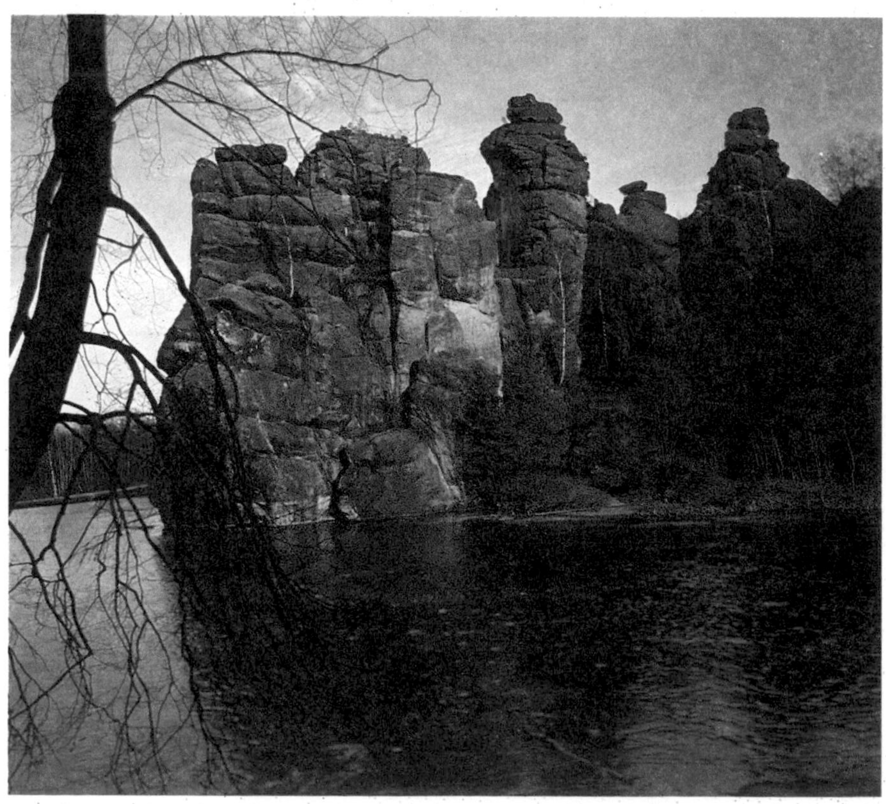

'guiding spirit's' intentions. He suffered from a horror of ill omens. Albert Speer, who became Hitler's personal architect and finally Germany's minister of war production, recounted an incident in October 1933 that shook Hitler's confidence more than anything up to that point had been able to do. He was laying the foundation stone of the House of German Art in Munich, which had been designed by his friend Paul Ludwig Troost and which Hitler felt embodied the highest ideals of Teutonic architecture. As he tapped the stone with a silver hammer, the instrument shattered to fragments in his hand. For almost three months Hitler was wrapped in morbid gloom; then on 21 January 1934 Troost died. Hitler's relief was immediate. He told Speer: 'When that hammer shattered I knew at once it was an evil omen. Something is going to happen, I thought. Now we know why the hammer broke. The architect was destined to die.'

Sorcerer's apprentice

Josef Goebbels pretended to an interest in the occult and in astrology in order to please the Führer – even going so far as to gain proficiency in drawing up a horoscope. Rudolf Hess may have dabbled in occult matters. But there was only one true 'sorcerer's apprentice' in Hitler's inner circle.

Heinrich Himmler was born of middle-class parents in Munich in 1900. A weak, pale and characterless youth, whose defective eyesight compelled him to wear thick-lensed spectacles, Himmler became a fervent Nazi in the early 1920s and was appointed secretary to the Nazi Party propaganda office in Lower Bavaria. There in his little office he sat and talked to a portrait of Hitler on the wall, long before he met the man himself. Although he had indubitable organising ability, Himmler's appearance made him something of a laughing stock, and it was almost jocularly that Hitler appointed him Deputy Reichsführer of the SS – the *Schutzstaffel*, or protective force, a body of about 300 men dedicated to bodyguard duties.

But by 1933 Himmler had built up the SS to such a strength that he was confident enough to purge it – retaining only men of the finest 'Germanic' physical characteristics and insisting that its officers should be able to show a non-Jewish ancestry going back to 1750. After a lengthy quasi-mystical novitiate, recruits were given a ceremonial dagger and permission to wear the full black uniform of the SS, complete with silver death's head. Thereafter they were obliged to attend what Francis King, author of *Satan and the swastika*, describes as 'neo-pagan ceremonies of a specifically SS religion devised by Himmler and clearly derived from his interest in occultism and the worship of Woden.'

Himmler had abandoned his Catholic faith for spiritualism, astrology and mesmerism in his late teens. He was convinced that he was the reincarnation of Heinrich the Fowler, founder of the Saxon royal house, who died in 936. All these elements were incorporated into his SS 'religion'.

Himmler devised new festivals to take the place of such Christian events as Christmas and Easter, he wrote out baptism and marriage ceremonies – though he believed polygamy would best serve the interests of the SS élite – and he even issued instructions on the correct manner of committing suicide.

The centre of the SS 'cult' became the castle of Wewelsburg in Westphalia, which Himmler bought as a ruin in 1934 and rebuilt over the next 11 years at a cost of 13 million marks. The central banqueting hall contained a vast round table with 13 throne-like seats to accommodate Himmler and 12 of his closest 'apostles' – making, as some occult writers have pointed out, a coven of 13. Beneath this hall was a 'Hall of the Dead', where plinths stood around a stone table. As each member of the inner circle of the SS died, his coat of arms would be burned and, together with his ashes, placed in an urn on one of these plinths for veneration.

In this slightly ludicrous atmosphere of theatricality, Himmler instigated the systematic genocide carried out by the Third Reich in its last years. Millions of Jews, gypsies, homosexuals and others who did not conform to the ideas of the Führer and of himself were slaughtered. Many of the atrocities were prompted by Himmler's bizarre theories. For example, his belief in the power of 'animal heat' led to experiments in which victims were exposed in freezing cold water and then revived – if they were fortunate – by being placed between the naked bodies of prostitutes. On another occasion, he decided that statistics should be collected of the measurements of Jewish skulls; but only the skulls of the newly dead would be suitable, so hundreds of people were decapitated.

Above: the castle of Wewelsburg in north-west Germany was bought by Heinrich Himmler (top) in 1934 and became the temple of his SS cult. The presence of the gypsy caravan so close to the Nazi shrine would not be tolerated for long, for gypsies were among the millions of non-Aryans exterminated by Himmler in his attempt to 'purify' the Germanic race

Less horrific but equally insane were SS researches into the Rosicrucian movement, the symbolism of the suppression of the Irish harp in Ulster, the occult significance of Gothic towers and the Eton top hat, and the magical power of the bells of Oxford, which, Himmler decided, had put a charm on the Luftwaffe, preventing it inflicting serious damage on the city.

The occult writer J. H. Brennan has gone so far as to suggest that Himmler was a 'non-person', a zombie without mind or soul of its own, drawing power from Hitler like a psychic leech. Francis King has pointed out that the huge Nuremberg rallies, presided over by Hitler at his most 'possessed', fulfil the conditions necessary for what some witch cults describe as a 'cone of power': searchlights pierced the night sky in a conical pattern above vast crowds, which generated a giant surge of emotion centred on the strutting figure of Hitler.

But if Himmler could be magically influenced for evil he could also be influenced for good in the same way. The unlikely instrument of this good was a plump blond masseur and occultist named Felix Kersten. He had been trained in osteopathy and allied skills by a mysterious Chinese doctor named Ko. Dr Ko was also an occultist and mystic, who apparently developed latent psychic powers in Kersten. Success and fame came to Kersten, and he was ordered to attend Himmler, who suffered from chronic stomach cramps, in 1938. Thereafter the SS chief was almost totally dependent on Kersten, who was able on a number of occasions to save hundreds of Jewish lives by his hold on Himmler's mind. A postwar investigating commission concluded that Kersten's service to mankind and to the cause of peace was 'so outstanding that no comparable precedent could be found for it in history.'

Awesome power

By what appears to have been sheer force of will, for instance, Kersten persuaded Himmler on more than one occasion to defer the extermination of concentration camp prisoners. Kersten would 'worry away like a terrier' until Himmler dropped the whole business. The masseur also managed, with at least partial success, to influence Himmler through deliberate misinterpretation of horoscopes – in which Himmler believed more fervently, perhaps, than Hitler himself.

From the middle of 1942 Kersten was busy sowing in Himmler's mind the notion that he should try to make a separate peace with the Western Allies; though he drew the Reichsführer to the brink on several occasions, he was unable to counteract the awesome power wielded by Hitler himself.

As Francis King has pointed out, Hitler's policies as Germany approached its collapse tallied exactly with what could be expected of a black magician's pact with evil powers. The essence of such a pact lies in sacrifice: an orgy of blood and destruction.

'Losses,' Hitler told Field Marshal Walther von Reichenau, 'can never be too high. They sow the seeds of future greatness.' And the historian Hugh Trevor-Roper said: 'Like an ancient hero, Hitler wished to be sent with human sacrifices to the grave.'

Hitler, although he knew all hope had gone, waited in his bunker until 30 April 1945 before shooting himself, with Eva Braun, whom he had just married. The date was too significant to occultists to be a coincidence. It was the day that ends in Walpurgis night – the high feast of the powers of darkness.

The sum of human knowledge

The ancient art of interpreting numbers answers to a deep-seated human need to find meaning in even the most commonplace things and events. HILDI HAWKINS explains the procedures and theories of the numerologists

The 'Hebrew' numerological system

1	2	3	4	5	6	7	8
A	B	C	D	E	U	O	F
I	K	G	M	H	V	Z	P
Q	R	L	T	N	W		
J		S			X		
Y							

Left: the table most generally used by numerologists to calculate the number corresponding to a particular name or word

Below: a magic square – a number array in which rows, columns and diagonals add up to the same total – is shown behind the gloomy figure in Dürer's engraving *Melencolia I* (1514). Such squares, epitomising the mystical properties of numbers, have often been used as magic talismans

CAN NUMBERS REVEAL the future? Or show the hidden aspects of a person's character? Practitioners of the ancient art of numerology believe they can.

Numerology is a method of making names, dates or events correspond to numbers – generally between one and nine, although sometimes 11 and 22 are included in the system. Each number has a certain significance: William Shakespeare corresponds to five, the number of versatility and resourcefulness.

The correspondence is established by a very simple identification of the letters of the alphabet with numbers according to the 'Hebrew system', as numerologists call it (see table).

To find your number, simply write down the number corresponding to each letter of your name, and add them together. If the resulting number is over nine, add up its digits and keep doing this until the result is less than 10. For instance, the letters of the name Charlotte Brontë add to five. (Charlotte = 3+5+1+2+3+7+4+4+5 = 34; Brontë = 2+2+7+5+4+5 = 25; 34+25 = 59; 5+9 = 14; 1+4 = 5.)

If the digits corresponding to your name add up to one, you are probably a dominant kind of person, a leader. 'Ones' are pioneers, inventors, designers – but they often put their plans into practice with little regard for the way they will affect the people most directly involved. They tend to dominate everyone they meet, they rarely have close friends and are sometimes, despite their confident appearance, very lonely people.

Two is interpreted by modern numerologists as the number of passive, receptive people. 'Twos' are quiet, unambitious, gentle, kind, tidy and conscientious. They often get their own way, however, by gentle persuasion rather than force. They are inclined to be hesitant, to make problems for themselves by putting off decisions for no good reason, and this quality can lead them into difficult situations.

Three is one of the most extrovert numbers, belonging to intelligent, creative and witty people, who generally make friends easily and seem to succeed at anything to which they turn their hands. They are proud, ambitious and pleasure-loving, but their great weakness lies in their inability to take anything – ideas or people – seriously for very long.

Four, like two, is a number corresponding to dependable, down-to-earth people. They are born organisers. They lack the volatility of 'ones' and 'threes', but they make up for this by their fairness and meticulous attention to detail. They may be subject to sudden

People whose names correspond to five are said to be clever and fast-moving, though feckless. Numerologists find confirmation in eminent people as diverse as Shakespeare (left), whom Coleridge called 'our myriad-minded Shakespeare', and Charlotte Brontë (below), who has been described as presenting the condition of women in early 19th-century England with an unprecedented 'frankness and ardour'

irrational rages or depressions that seem extraordinary in people who are usually models of calmness. Four has traditionally been regarded by numerologists as the number of ill-luck; people whose number is four often seem to pay dearly for any success they achieve in life.

Five is the number of bright, fast-moving, clever, impatient people. They live on their nerves, and love meeting people and seeking out new experiences. They are often physically attractive but rather feckless, hating to be tied down. Five is the number that represents sex (the digits of which also add up to five), and people whose number is five often have varied and exciting love-lives, often problematic. Sometimes the sexual side of their nature shows itself in excesses or perversions.

People whose number is six are among the happiest of the whole numerological system. They are happy, tranquil, well-balanced and home-loving. They are affectionate, loyal, sincere and conscientious. They are not uncreative; many of them are successful in the performing arts. The negative aspect of their character is their tendency to be rather fussy, conceited and self-satisfied.

Seven is the number of the loner, the introspective scholar, philosopher, mystic or occultist. These people tend to stand aside from the mainstream of life, content to observe it. They are dignified, self-controlled and reserved. They tend to be indifferent to worldly wealth but, while they may seem aloof and stand-offish, make loyal friends. Despite their powerful intellects, they are often surprisingly bad at putting their thoughts into words, and may even dislike discussing them if they feel their ideas are being challenged.

Below: the skyline of Manhattan at dusk. New York's number is three – representing pride, ambition and love of pleasure, but an inability to take ideas and people seriously for long. An apt description of the glittering capital of American finance and fashion?

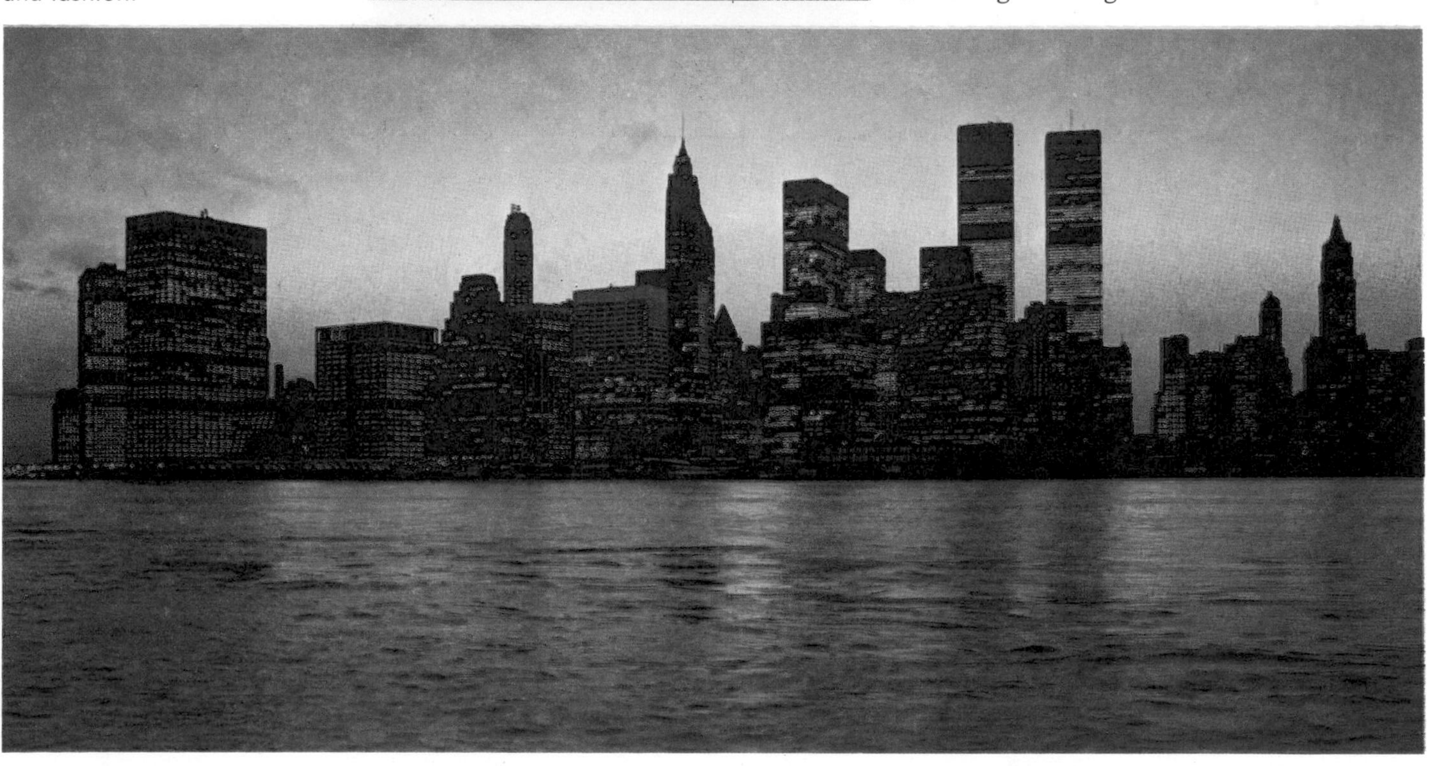

Eight represents worldly success, and people who have this number often make successful businessmen, politicians or lawyers. Their success is, however, often built on a great deal of hard work, which is often done at considerable expense to their warmer, more human qualities. They often seem to be hard, egocentric and grasping; but there can be, behind the unsympathetic exterior, a whimsical streak that endears them to other people.

Nine stands for the height of intellectual and spiritual achievement. People whose number is nine are the idealists, the romantics, the visionaries – poets, missionaries, doctors, religious teachers, brilliant scientists. Their great qualities are their unselfishness, their self-discipline and their determination. Their idealism is concerned with mankind as a whole – in their everyday lives they may be inclined to seek the limelight, and to be fickle friends or lovers.

Above: King's College, Cambridge. Seven is the number of the city – and of philosophers and scholars

Eleven is the number of those with a strong sense of vocation – from leaders such as Churchill (left) to reformers such as Florence Nightingale (far left). Human relationships mean less to them than their ideas: Einstein (below left) called himself a 'lone traveller'. What Picasso (below) was told by his mother could be said of any of them: 'If you become a soldier you'll be a general. If you become a monk you'll end up as the Pope'

Some numerologists also employ the numbers 11 and 22. They believe that these numbers represent a higher plane of experience than the numbers one to nine. Eleven is the number of those who experience revelations and suffer martyrdom; those with names that add up to this number are often people with a strong vocation for their work – preachers, doctors, nurses or teachers. They tend to prefer ideas to real people.

Twenty-two is the 'master' number: people whose names add to 22 combine the best qualities of all the other numbers.

Apply this procedure to the name you were given at birth and you will find, numerologists claim, the characteristics you were born with and that will underlie your personality throughout your life; apply it to the name you apply to yourself, or would like to have, and you will discover how your experiences in the world have moulded your

regarded as indicating a general type, not a detailed description. But that people whose names add to the same number share certain personality traits can be supported with numerous examples: the letters of the names Winston S. Churchill, Einstein, Pablo Picasso and Florence Nightingale, for instance, all add to 11 – the number of those with strong vocations.

The same technique can be applied to the names of cities, and many of the results seem to confirm the beliefs of numerologists. London adds up to five, indicating many-sidedness and resilience; New York to three, indicating brilliance and glitter. The ancient cities of Oxford and Cambridge both have the number seven – the number of the aloof, inward-turned scholar.

The 1920s (top), the third decade of the century, had the number three – the number of the pleasure-loving and fickle. The 1930s (centre) corresponded to four, representing unstable moods and ill-luck; the decade began with the Depression (a Christmas Day dole queue is shown here) and ended with the Second World War. After VE Day (above), the 1940s saw the return of prosperity and renewed experiment in fashions and life-styles – in character with the decade's number, five ('bright, clever, impatient')

personality. Using a nickname, you will be able to ascertain what your friends think of you. Comparing her maiden and married names, a married woman can find out how married life has changed her.

The total of vowel numbers in your name is your heart number, which shows your inner character; the total of consonants is your personality number, which indicates your outward personality, or the impression you make on the people around you. (This distinction is derived from Hebrew, in which only the consonants of any word are actually written down; the vowels are therefore 'hidden', and represent the aspects of the personality that are not outwardly apparent.)

Like the character types suggested by the sign of the zodiac you were born under, the traits indicated by these numbers are to be

But the ridiculous extremes to which numerology can be taken are indicated by the prediction of an American numerologist that, since Oakland, California, shares the number nine with Chicago, it will one day suffer a great fire, as did Chicago in 1871.

Numerology extends to the character of a year, a decade or a century. The present century carries the number one ($1+9+0+0=10$; $1+0=1$) and, according to numerologists, should be an ebullient time of invention and discovery, dominance and subjugation. All of this could be said to be true, although (here lies the weakness of the loose collection of attributes associated with each number) it could be regarded as equally true of the 19th century.

The year 1979 was characterised by the number eight ($1+9+7+9=26$; $2+6=8$). According to numerologists, it should have been a year when financial and political matters went exceptionally well. The 1980s are the ninth decade and should be characterised by nine, with great achievements in the arts and the world of learning.

Past decades are depicted by numerologists as confirming their theories: the brilliant 1920s, a 3-decade, followed by the more subdued 1930s, overshadowed in its latter half by the threat of war; the recovery of confidence of the 1940s and the self-assurance of the 6-decade of the 1950s; the

dreaming withdrawal into mysticism of the 1960s, characterised by the number seven, and the hardening up of attitudes in the money-conscious 1970s, reflected in its number, eight. But this appropriateness is in the eye of the beholder: for example, some might view the 1950s, which saw the appearance of the H-bomb and rock'n'roll, and the intensification of the cold war, as badly represented by six (happy, tranquil, balanced).

Numerologists believe that numbers can be used to suggest beneficial courses of action. If your number is seven, for example, you should take care to make difficult decisions or perform important tasks on days of the month that add up to seven: the seventh, the 16th and the 25th. People whose names add up to eight should eat plenty of oranges, since the word 'oranges' adds up to eight – but presumably never a single orange at a time! Certain years, too, can be good or bad for an individual; to find your year-number, add your month and date of birth to the *current* year: 1981, for instance, is a 9-year for someone born on 24 Februarty 1956 (24+2+1981=2007; 2+0+0+7=9), indicating it is a year of high spiritual and intellectual achievement.

The 1950s (top) seem poorly characterised by their number, six (happy and well-balanced). But seven (the mystic and occult) seems appropriate to the 1960s, the hippy decade (above). And eight, the number of businessmen, politicians and lawyers, seems to suit the 1970s, the decade of oil crises (below)

Why should the numerological system work? Numerologists are quick to point out instances that seem to show the importance of number, such as the career of Louis XIV of France. He came to the throne in 1643, which adds up to 14; he died in 1715, which adds up to 14, at the age of 77 – which adds up to 14. But is this any more than coincidence?

Numerologists counter this question by claiming that there is no such thing as coincidence. They believe the Universe is like a vast harp with countless strings, each vibrating at a certain rate, characterised by a number. Number, they believe, is at the root of all things and they point out that science has found that light, sound, atomic structure and many other things are dependent on frequency, or number. But what of the objection that, even if this view of the Universe is correct, basing the system on a person's name must be wrong, since the naming of a child is largely a matter of the personal tastes and whims of the parents? The numerologists have their answers ready; as Florence Campbell, an American, explains:

> The Soul has taken many journeys in the past and *knows* its present needs. The Soul wants progress upwards on the Great Spiral and *chooses* for the incarnating ego the vowels whose total shall accomplish this purpose. . . . There is a long 'Dark Cycle' before the child is born, and during this Dark Cycle the vibrations that are to label the new life are so impressed upon the subconscious minds of the parents that they are compelled to carry out the plan.

In other words, the numerologist believes that the name each person carries is no accident, and that it tells something significant about its bearer, in a code to which the numerologist has the key.

The thought that counts

Ancient philosophers were enthralled by the mathematical relationships they found in nature, and believed that numbers underlay every aspect of reality. This chapter explains how certain numbers then acquired their own symbolic 'personality'

THE MOST FUNDAMENTAL arithmetical operation is tallying: the matching, one for one, of one set of objects with another – or with marks in the dust, or pebbles, or knots in a string – in order to compare quantities. The next step is to give names to numbers and to match objects against *these* in sequence – that is, to count. Some peoples, such as certain New Guineans and Brazilian Indians, have no names for numbers beyond three. And the number words that do exist may vary according to the type of object being counted. (This survives in modern English: we speak of a brace of gamebirds, pistols or dogs, but of nothing else.) It must have been a magical moment when the abstract nature of number was realised: the idea that three trees, three people, or even a collection of three different things all had one thing in common: their 'threeness'.

The power of this abstract idea must have been apparent very early. Number seemed somehow to underlie reality: all collections of three objects were united by their 'threeness'. At a very deep level, perhaps they were the *same*. It is small wonder that the mysterious power of the concept of number inspired a powerful tradition of mystical thought that still colours the way we think about numbers. The tradition comes to us from the medieval Christian Church, which in turn drew its inspiration from two major intellectual traditions, Greek Pythagoreanism and Hebrew *gematria*.

The school of Pythagoras was a religious community founded by the semi-legendary figure of Pythagoras in the Greek colony of Croton, in southern Italy, around 530 BC. It was dedicated to the study of geometry, mathematics and astronomy, and to experimentation in music. The Pythagorean school studied the variations in pitch produced by vibrating strings of varying lengths, and is credited with the discovery that musical intervals may be represented in terms of simple ratios of whole numbers.

It may have been the discovery of the mathematical nature of musical intervals that gave the Pythagoreans their idea that number was the key to the Universe. Whatever the origin of the belief, they clung to it fervently and bequeathed it to the West.

Above: the Beast from the sea described in chapter 13 of the book of Revelation, as portrayed in a German altarpiece of about 1400. The meaning of the Beast's 7 heads, 10 horns and 10 crowns, and of its number, 666, has been the subject of much speculation by number mystics. They have variously interpreted the Beast as representing Rome, the emperor Nero, and even Napoleon Bonaparte

Left: Pythagoras and a disciple experiment with musical tones. The size of a bell or the amount of water in a cup determines the pitch of the note each produces. The discovery by Pythagoras that simple numerical ratios between these quantities correspond to harmony or discord between notes fed his belief that 'all is number'

Like all Greeks, they thought of number geometrically. One was a point, two a line, three a triangle, the first plane figure, and four a tetrahedron (which resembles a pyramid, but has a triangular base), the first solid figure. These four numbers between them thus describe the whole of space. The Pythagoreans venerated them in a symmetrical pattern called the *tetractys*, and believed it was 'eternal nature's fountain spring'.

Number pervaded the Pythagoreans' entire cosmology. Creation was seen as the division of primordial unity into parts. Each number had a certain significance attached to it; broadly, the Pythagoreans believed that the world was composed of a series of ten pairs of opposites corresponding to oddness or evenness in numbers – limited/unlimited, right/left, male/female, and so on.

In Hebrew, as in Greek, numbers were represented by letters of the alphabet, and this may well have stimulated *gematria*, the Jewish art of turning names into numbers. This was done simply by totalling the numbers that the letters stood for. The central idea of *gematria* was that things referred to by words whose letters added up to the same number were somehow the same; number expressed their true essence.

This technique was applied, for example, to the story told in Genesis 18: Abraham was sitting at the door of his tent in the plains of Mamre 'and lo, three men stood by him'. The Hebrew for 'and lo, three men' adds, by *gematria*, to 701 – and so do the words 'these are Michael, Gabriel and Raphael'. The obvious conclusion was that the three 'men' were actually archangels.

It was natural for early Christians to take up the numerological ideas of the two dominant intellectual traditions – Greek and Jewish – that surrounded them. The early symbol of the dove for Christ, for example, was probably adopted because the Greek letters alpha and omega – 'I am Alpha and Omega, the beginning and the ending, saith the Lord' (Revelation 1:8) – add to 801, the number of *peristera*, the Greek for 'dove'.

For the Christians, as for the Pythagoreans, goodness and maleness were associated with the odd numbers. One stands for perfection, unity, God. Two, as the first number to break away from that perfection, represents the Devil. And since odd numbers dominate in addition (odd + even = odd), and addition represents sexual union, odd numbers must represent the male sex.

The Bible, early Christian theologians believed, provided confirmation of the evil associated with two. For in the account of the Creation, did not God neglect on the second day to find that his work was good? And before the Flood, the unclean animals went into Noah's ark two by two, whereas the clean animals went in by sevens.

Modern numerologists are more generous to the number two, preferring to emphasise its positive qualities, but it nonetheless remains the least favoured of the numbers (see page 66).

Three is the first male number. One by itself, although perfect, is barren; two introduces a discord that can only be resolved by adding the two numbers together to make three. It is this symbolism that is behind the Christian doctrine of the Trinity; as the 19th-century French magician Eliphas Levi put it:

> Were God only one, He would never be creator or father. Were He two, there would be antagonism or division in the infinite, which would mean the division also, or death, of all possible things. He is therefore three for the creation by Himself and in His image of the infinite multitude of beings and numbers.

The number of ill-luck

Four is the Pythagorean number of solid earth, being the number of points required to define a tetrahedron. It may be solid and uninspiring, but as Plutarch put it, writing around the turn of the first century AD, 'Those who exalt Four teach us a lesson that is not without value, that by reason of this number all solids came into being.' But four is also the number of evil and ill-luck, being made up of two twos, in two different ways ($4 = 2 + 2 = 2 \times 2$).

Five, on the other hand, is the number of male sexuality: it is made up of two and three: the first feminine number added to the first masculine number. Thus, in love, woman is given to man – and man 'naturally' dominates.

Six is the first 'perfect' number – it is the sum of its factors (numbers that divide it without remainder). Thus $6 = 1 + 2 + 3$. Perfect numbers were venerated for their tranquillity and harmoniousness. In ancient times only the first four perfect numbers were known: 6, 28, 496 and 8128. The next one – 33,550,336 – was apparently not discovered until the mid 15th century.

Seven is a number rich in biblical associations. There are seven deadly sins, seven Christian virtues, seven petitions in the Lord's prayer; on the seventh day of the siege of Jericho, Joshua marched seven times

Top: to the Greeks, the number one corresponded to a point, and two to a line; three points defined a triangle, the simplest plane figure; four points defined a tetrahedron, the simplest space-occupying form. The Pythagorean *tetractys* (above) was composed of one, two, three and four dots arranged in rows

Below: in Hebrew, numbers are represented by letters. To write 456 the letters for 400, 50 and 6 would be written together

Hebrew numerals

1	2	3	4	5	6	7	8	9
א	ב	ג	ד	ה	ו	ז	ח	ט
10	20	30	40	50	60	70	80	90
י	כ	ל	מ	נ	ס	ע	פ	צ
100	200	300	400	500	600	700	800	900
ק	ר	ש	ת	ך	ם	ן	ף	ץ

Pyramids and prophecies

One of the more eccentric manifestations of mankind's fascination with number symbolism is pyramidology. One pyramidologist in particular, an American named Worth Smith, claimed that the Grand Gallery of the Great Pyramid of Cheops (right) enshrined a complete history of the Christian Church, with particular emphasis on Britain's history. (He believed the pyramid was built by ancestors of the British.)

He believed that the point at which the Grand Gallery begins represents Christ's birth on 6 October in the year 4 BC. Each inch (2.5 centimetres) represents a year. For the first 400 inches (10 metres) the stones are smooth; then they suddenly become scarred and broken. This, Smith claimed, represented the first 400 years of the Church's existence, a reasonably peaceful period that ended with the invasion by the Visigoths.

The prophetic insight of the Egyptian builders – or their lack of engineering

skill – is demonstrated by another badly surfaced stretch: this, according to Smith, represents the rise of Islam from 622 (Mohammed's flight from Mecca) to an important defeat in Europe in 732.

At the point supposedly corresponding to 1844 the gallery ends in the Great Step, which is 3 feet (1 metre) high. This should represent some kind of improvement in the fortunes of Christendom, but Smith is forced to admit that there was no great advance in 1844. He theorises rather lamely that 'almost the whole lot of the discoveries and inventions in common usage have come into existence since the year 1844.'

According to Smith the scale now changes so that one inch represents a month. A new tunnel, the Low Passage, supposedly begins on 4 August 1914, the date of Britain's entry into the First World War, and ends on 9 November, date of the Kaiser's abdication. Smith expected the current year – 1936 – to see the dethronement of Satan himself.

Right: the Devil tempts Jesus, in a 12th-century painting from the ceiling of a Swiss church. The time that Jesus spent in the wilderness being tempted by the Devil was 40 days and 40 nights – a period that occurs often in the myth and folklore of all countries

Left: the Trinity, painted by El Greco in about 1600. God the Father cradles Jesus, his son, while the Holy Spirit, in the form of a dove, hovers above. The difficult notion of the three-in-one God is not explicitly stated in the Bible, but was formulated by theologians to reconcile various conceptions of God scattered through the Old and New Testaments. To numerologists, God could not be single, since he would then be uncreative; nor twofold, since this is the nature of antagonism and conflict

round the walls of the city and flattened them with a blast from seven trumpets; and Pharaoh's dream, which Joseph interpreted, involved seven fat and seven lean cows, seven plump ears of corn and seven blighted ones. In folklore, too, mystery attaches to the number seven; magical properties are attributed to seventh sons and seventh sons of seventh sons. The power of the number seven stretches far back in time: around 2500 BC the great Sumerian king Lugulannemund built a temple in the city of Adab to the goddess Nintu, with seven gates and seven doors, purified with the sacrifice of seven times seven fatted oxen and sheep. One can only guess at the significance of this frequent use of the number – but it seems that it is linked with the phases of the Moon, which take about 28 ($=4\times7$) days to go through a complete cycle. The ancients believed that the cycles of birth and death, growth and decay, depend on the waxing and waning of the Moon.

The symbolism of the numbers eight and

nine is connected with human procreation: a woman's body has eight orifices, the eighth being the one through which new life enters the world. Eight is thus the number of worldly success. Nine is the number of completeness because a human child is conceived, formed and born in nine months.

A few numbers greater than nine were regarded as having a special significance. Twelve, for instance, is a number of completeness: there are 12 months in the year, 12 signs of the zodiac, 12 tribes of Israel and, of course, 12 disciples. Thirteen is a number of excess – it goes one beyond a number of completeness. The fact that there were 13 people at the Last Supper strengthens the uneasiness many people still feel about the number. This feeling is so strong that, for instance, when Queen Elizabeth II visited West Germany in 1965, the number of the platform at Duisburg station from which her train left was changed from 13 to 12a.

One more number with ancient sacred and mystical connections is 40. The rain that caused the Flood in Genesis continued for 40 days and 40 nights; this is also the time that Moses spent on Mount Sinai, speaking with God. The children of Israel walked 40 years in the wilderness, and Jesus was tempted by the Devil for 40 days and 40 nights. Forty has been sacred since ancient Babylonian times, when it was known as *kissatum*, 'the excellent quality'. The Greek poet Hesiod, writing in the eighth century BC, explains that 40 days is the period for which the star cluster called the Pleiades disappears. These stars are of widespread importance: ancient authors state that autumn sowing should be performed when the Pleiades set at dawn, and some peoples use them to mark the passage of a year. The 40-day disappearance of the Pleiades may also have started the habit of measuring periods of time of agricultural significance in 40-day periods – as in the belief that a fine St Swithin's day (15 July) will be followed by 40 days of good weather, while a rainy one presages 40 days of rain.

Armed with these interpretations of numbers, the Christian theologian had at his fingertips a powerful tool for unravelling the

Below: 13 people are present at the Last Supper: Jesus and the 12 disciples, of whom one, Judas Iscariot, turns away in shame. This scene, familiar to all Christians, strengthened the superstitions that surrounded the number 13

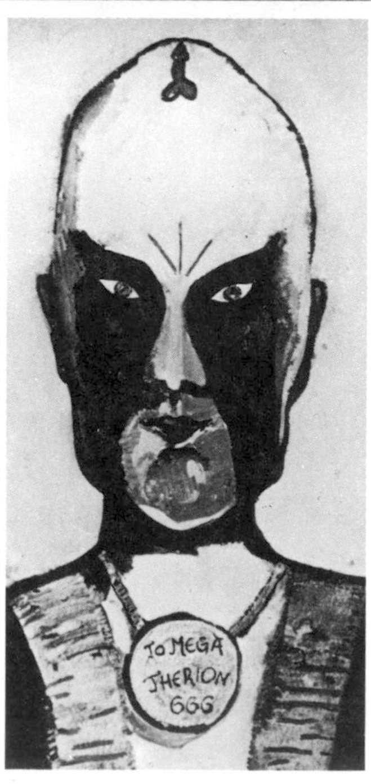

Bottom: 'The Great Beast' is the inscription in Greek on the medallion worn by the magician Aleister Crowley in this self-portrait. Crowley adopted the mysterious number ascribed to the Beast in the book of Revelation: 'six hundred threescore and six'

hidden meaning of any biblical text. The crowning glory of biblical number symbolism is the book of Revelation. Written in 22 chapters – the 'master' number, the number of things traditionally supposed to have been created by God, the number of letters in the Hebrew alphabet – it is full of numerological puzzles. The greatest and most famous of these is the puzzle of the number of the Beast, 666:

> And I stood upon the sand of the sea, and saw a beast rise up out of the sea, having seven heads and ten horns, and upon his horns ten crowns, and upon his heads the name of blasphemy. . . . And I saw one of his heads as it were wounded to death; and his deadly wound was healed: and all the world wondered after the beast. . . . Let him that hath understanding count the number of the beast: for it is the number of a man; and his number is Six hundred threescore and six.

The identity of the Beast

There have been many conjectures as to the identity of the Beast. It is now generally accepted that the Beast is meant to stand for the Roman empire, and the seven heads for seven emperors. The head wounded to death and then healed could represent Nero; he was murdered in AD 68, but there were persistent rumours that he lived on. Nero, in Hebrew, adds up to 666 – but only if spelt with an extra N. Otherwise it adds up to 616 – and some early manuscripts do, indeed, give the number of the Beast as 616. The 'image of the Beast' of chapter 15 may represent Caligula, who in AD 30 had set up a statue of himself in the Holy of Holies in Jerusalem, and gave the order that the Jews were to worship it (although he died before the command could be enforced). Gaius Caligula Caesar in Hebrew adds to 616, as does Gaios Kaisar in Greek.

Numerologists, however, have not been content with these simple explanations, and speculations as to the Beast's identity have ranged far and wide. In the early 19th century there was an attempt to make Napoleon into the Beast. Thomas Macaulay, the English statesman, refused to accept this hypothesis; with typically mordant wit, he announced that the House of Commons was obviously the Beast: it had 658 members, three clerks, a serjeant and a deputy, a doorkeeper, a chaplain and a librarian – making 666 in all. The magician Aleister Crowley believed *himself* to be the Beast; he had, he claimed, discovered his true identity while still a boy, with 'a passionately ecstatic sense of identity'. He signed himself 'The Beast 666' – or sometimes *To mega therion*, which means 'the great Beast' in Greek. Its number is 666.

Numbered among the great

Left: a rare instance of a painting deliberately designed using the golden section: *The parade,* by Seurat. The ratios of the dimensions indicated are all approximately 1.618:1

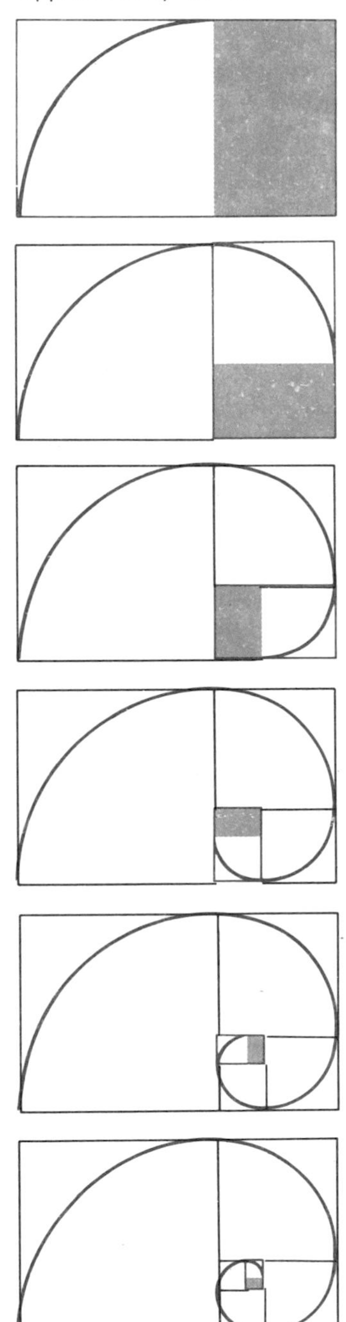

Above: cutting a square from a rectangle with sides in the ratio of the golden section (1.618) leaves a smaller 'golden' rectangle.

Number lies behind scientific theory, ideas of artistic proportion and rules of musical harmony. Many great thinkers have been convinced that number is therefore the very essence of the world. This chapter explains how artists and scientists have seen meaning in number, and how patterns of numbers have guided them in their creative work

THE BELIEF THAT NUMBER is the key to the secrets of the Universe – a belief verging on the mystical – lay at the heart of many arts and branches of learning up to, and even after, the scientific revolution of the 17th century. It was the inspiration for some of their most spectacular achievements. Diverse disciplines were brought together by the common language of number: music, astronomy, architecture, poetry and theology reflected the *harmonia mundi*, the harmony of the world, by means of number.

Number was in everything; a typical expression of this idea is St Augustine's remark on dancing:

> Ask what delights you in dancing and number will reply, 'Lo, here am I!' Examine the beauty of bodily form, and you will find that everything is in its place by number. Examine the beauty of bodily motion, and you will find everything in its due time by number.

Number was the essence of the *harmonia mundi*. And so the way to create a perfect work of art was to use number in the correct way. This belief can be traced to Plato, who states in his philosophical dialogue *Philebus*: 'The qualities of measure and proportion invariably . . . constitute beauty and elegance.' The architect Leon Battista Alberti, writing in the mid 15th century, echoes the idea:

> Nature is sure to act consistently, and with a constant Analogy in all her operations: from whence I conclude, that the same Numbers, by means of which the Agreement of Sounds affects our ears with delight, are the very same which please our eyes and minds.

The large number of handbooks on architectural proportion that appeared during the Renaissance are testimony to the seriousness with which this idea was regarded. And in the 20th century a major attempt at constructing a harmonious system of design by proportion was made by the great architect Le Corbusier.

Golden proportions

Called the Modulor, Corbusier's system was based on the golden section, a ratio regarded since ancient times as especially pleasing. If a line is divided into unequal parts in such a way that the ratio of the whole to the longer part equals the ratio of the longer part to the shorter, the line is said to be divided in golden section. This ratio is called by the Greek letter 'phi'. It is approximately equal to 1.618. If this number is repeatedly multiplied by itself, a series of numbers is formed, every member of which (after the first two) is equal to the sum of the proceding two numbers.

A simpler example of such a series – they are called Fibonacci series after Leonardo Fibonacci, a mathematician who worked in Pisa about 1200 – is the sequence: 1, 2, 3, 5, 8. . . . Fibonacci series are found in the proportions and ratios of many natural patterns: the pads on a cat's foot, the arrangement of leaves on a plant, the spirals of a snail's shell.

Building by numbers

Corbusier claimed that the proportions of ideal human figures embodied the golden section, and that buildings designed in accordance with it would be both beautiful and well-adapted to human needs. He designed several buildings using the Fibonacci series, based on the figure of a man 6 feet (1.8 metres) tall. He even believed that his system had reconciled the metric and imperial systems of units. The buildings based on the Modulor include the chapel at Ronchamp, in France, blocks of flats in many famous cities, and the administrative centre at Chandigarh, in the Punjab.

Are these buildings more beautiful than others not constructed on any particular system of proportion? The question is almost impossible to answer, since the buildings named are the work of a great architect and, as such, are likely to be better than those of an indifferent architect, whether designed according to a system or not.

It is even doubtful that the golden section leads to more beautiful proportions than any other ratio. A rectangle with length and breadth in the ratio of the golden section has long been regarded as in some sense ideal. Yet as long ago as 1876 it was found by experiment that, although subjects preferred golden-section rectangles in the laboratory (35 per cent chose them when offered a choice of 10 rectangles), a much shorter rectangle was preferred for pictures in a

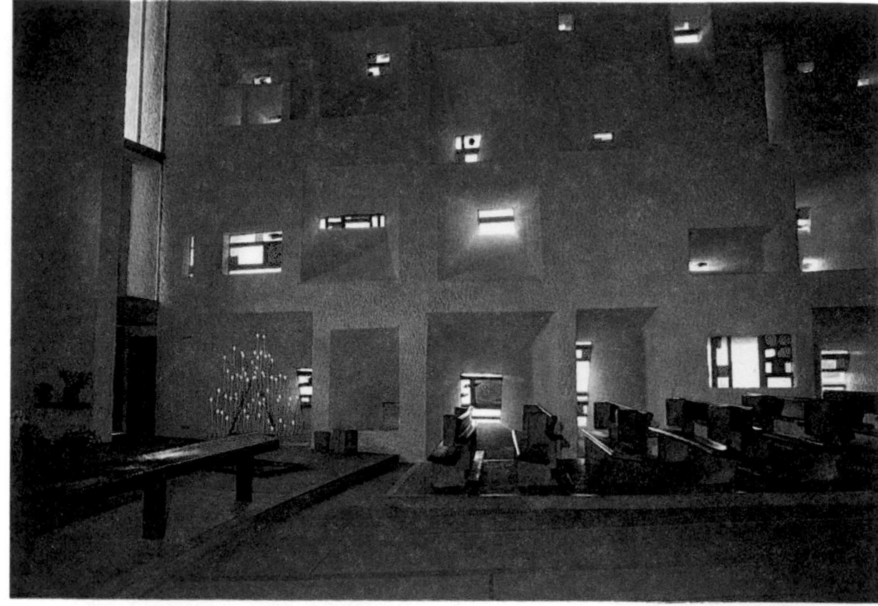

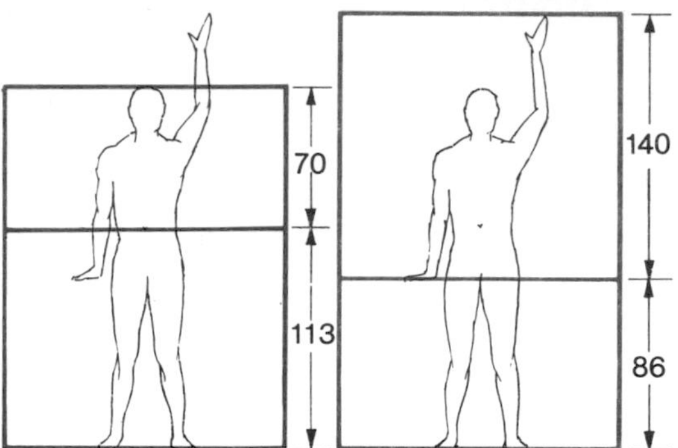

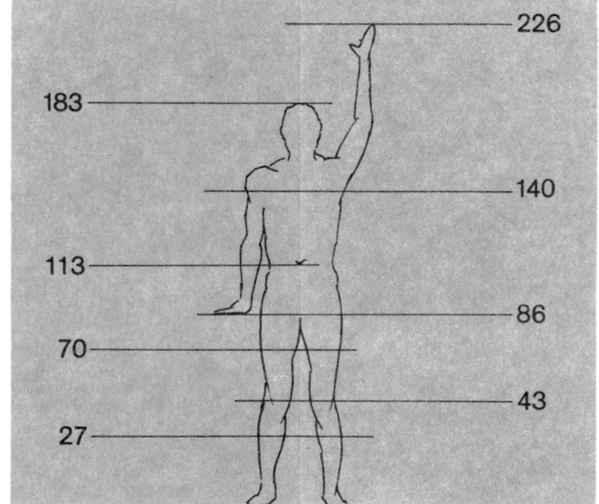

The golden section, which fascinated Le Corbusier, occurs repeatedly in the windows and recesses of his chapel at Ronchamp (above). His Modulor system was based on a man 6 feet (183 centimetres) tall. In the 'red' series this height is divided in golden section by the height of the navel. The 'blue' series is based on the height of the raised hand, above the ground and above the groin. Dividing these distances (shown here in centimetres) by the golden section extends the two series (right), which are related to basic human postures (below)

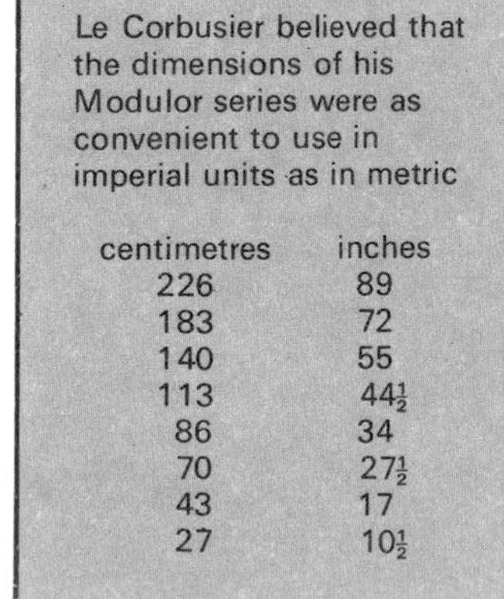

Le Corbusier believed that the dimensions of his Modulor series were as convenient to use in imperial units as in metric

centimetres	inches
226	89
183	72
140	55
113	44½
86	34
70	27½
43	17
27	10½

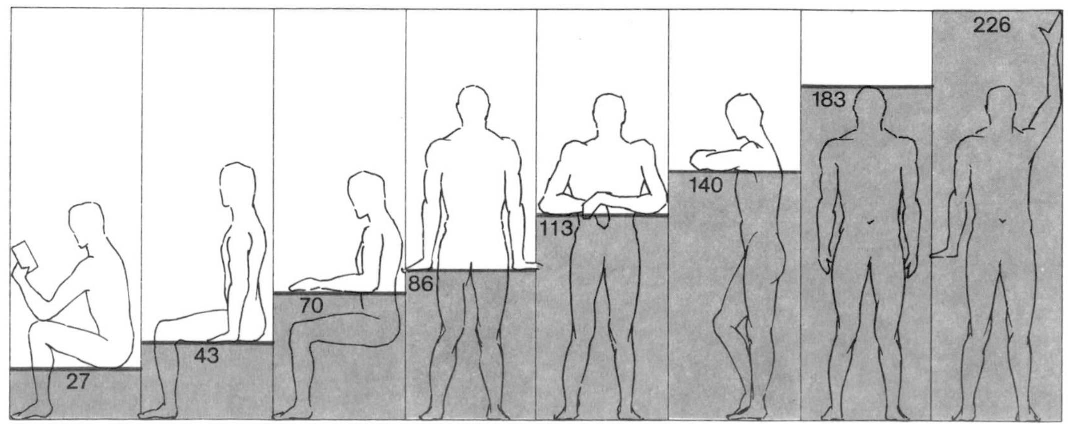

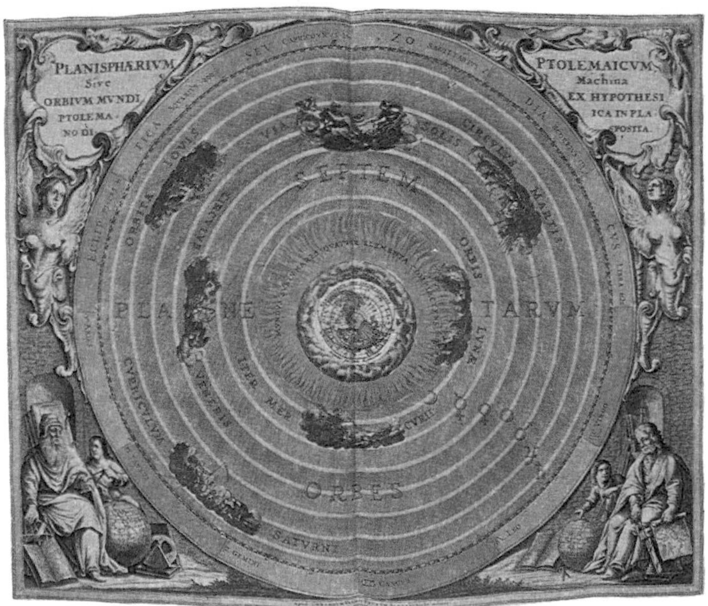

gallery – 5:4 for upright shapes, 4:3 for horizontal. If it were the case that certain proportions were preferred, then, as the architectural writer P. H. Scholfield points out:

> One would expect the same types of relationships to have appeared spontaneously in all periods of good design. In fact, this is not the case, and the sorts of mathematical relationships which occur are closely related to the mathematical knowledge of the period.

What role is played by number relationships in science? The idea that there was an underlying numerical harmony in the world made it natural for the ancients to seek scientific explanations in terms of number. Reasoning of this sort led them to think that God must have made the world in six days because six is the first 'perfect' number – a number equal to the sum of its factors (see page 71).

Today it seems that such an argument has no validity whatever. Yet it is undeniable that important discoveries have been made when numerical patterns have been noticed in natural phenomena, even if explanations for those patterns were still unknown.

An example is the Titius-Bode 'law', which led to the discovery of the asteroids. It was noticed that the relative distances of the planets from the Sun fall roughly into a sequence of numbers generated by a simple mathematical rule. But there is a gap in the series, between Mars and Jupiter. It was argued that there should be a planet at the corresponding position. A search was made, and an object was indeed found there. It was not a planet but the first known asteroid – a small rocky body, one of thousands that are now known.

Another example of scientific discovery guided by numerical patterns comes from chemistry. In the 19th century the Russian chemist Dmitri Mendeleev noticed that when the elements are listed in order of their atomic weights (which are, literally, the relative weights of their atoms), patterns emerge: the list can be arranged in rows and columns so that the chemical properties change systematically along the rows and down the columns. To make this system work, it was sometimes necessary to revise the atomic weights assigned to certain elements, or to suppose that there were gaps, corresponding to as yet undiscovered elements. Subsequent discoveries vindicated Mendeleev's ideas triumphantly. All known elements fit neatly into this 'periodic' table, and modern knowledge of atomic structure explains why these patterns should exist.

Above: the transition from an Earth-centred view of the Universe (left) to a Sun-centred view (right) was made largely on grounds of mathematical elegance and harmony. The ancient system worked well (despite the dejected appearance of the ancient astronomers depicted at the foot of this map, drawn in 1660). Yet many of the most able scientists accepted the arguments of Copernicus for the mathematically simpler Sun-centred system, even before telescopic evidence supported the theory

Below: Dmitri Mendeleev, the Russian chemist whose classification of the elements on the basis of their atomic weights underlies modern chemistry

The modern view

The modern attitude to such numerical relationships among phenomena, empirically found, is very different from that which was prevalent as late as the 18th century. We see them as the inevitable product of relatively simple physical laws: ancient philosophers and scientists, not knowing their explanations, saw every such instance of regularity as another proof of the harmonious and beautiful design of the world.

The desire to see the world as a place ruled by harmony and governed by number may seem naïve today, but it is an expression of the perennial tendency – and desire – of human beings to see order and pattern in everything around them. Number may not be everything, but the unprovable assumption that nature is rational and intelligible is the basis of science – and of the practical reasoning of everyday life.

A radical attempt to account for this intelligibility of the Universe was made by the German philosopher Immanuel Kant in the 18th century. He saw the source of the orderliness of the world as being the human mind itself, and the concepts with which it does its thinking. He went so far as to say: 'Our intellect does not draw its laws from nature . . . but imposes them on nature.'

Cause and effect, time and space, the laws of mathematics and logic, are the result of the constitution of our minds.

Sir Arthur Eddington, an English astronomer, pushed a form of this idea even further in the early 20th century. He believed that many highly detailed facts about the Universe – namely, the value of certain numerical constants – could be calculated without any appeal to experiment or observation, but by pure mathematics alone.

But very few scientists and philosophers have accepted this view. The specific features of the Universe are not to be explained by reference to the structure of the human mind: and only experience can show which theories are actually true of the world. It is therefore highly remarkable that the Universe should prove to obey laws that are in fact simple, and harmonious.

Even more remarkable: nature has (so far) proved to be not only intelligible by rational laws but intelligible in a way that is frequently elegant and even beautiful. When Copernicus put forward his idea that the Earth revolved around the Sun, rather than vice versa, it was not so much the experimental evidence as the theory's elegance, or aesthetic appeal, that was persuasive to contemporary thinkers.

Similarly, Einstein developed the theory of relativity on the premise that 'absolute' motion does not exist; that is, there can be no justification for saying that, of two scientific observers moving relatively to each other, one is 'really' at rest and the other is not. There is no absolute standard of rest in the Universe. Einstein was very little influenced by the problems raised by such experiments as that of American physicists Michelson and Morley. The grace and inherent power of the theory played a large part in the theory's quick acceptance and the conviction of scientists that it *must* be true.

Above: Immanuel Kant believed the mathematical regularities of the world to be, in some sense, created by the human mind

That the laws of nature should be not only rational but elegant seems almost too much to expect. Yet this astonishing metaphysical hypothesis is constantly being borne out by science. Time and again physical reality is found to coincide with the speculations of scientists, evolved from a few basic facts and couched in the subtle language of mathematics. The existence of many subatomic particles has been suggested by 'gaps' in mathematical patterns somewhat analogous to Mendeleev's table of the elements. The branch of mathematics responsible for these achievements, called 'group theory', was evolved between the World Wars as a part of purely abstract algebra; yet it seemed tailor-made for the understanding of particles that were to be discovered decades later.

In view of these amazing anticipations of experimental results by the mathematical speculations of theoretical physicists, how does modern science differ from numerology? It differs in that it makes no assumptions about the symbolic meaning of numbers: numbers do not give insight into some divine master plan of the Universe. But the assumption on which science rests – that nature is regular and comprehensible by human reason – is every bit as mystical as the idea that 'number is all'.

Music of the spheres

The work of the great astronomer Johannes Kepler (1571–1630) shows a curious fusion of numerological and scientific thought. It was Kepler who formulated the extraordinarily elegant laws that govern planetary motion. This man, one of the first great modern scientists, was also a profound mystic.

Like Pythagoras and Plato, Kepler believed that the world was ruled by number. He tried hard to prove that the distances of the planets from the Sun were given by an arrangement of Euclid's five regular solids (left); by doing so, he believed, he could demonstrate something of the order of the mind of God. But his faith in number went further: he believed that musical harmony, mathematically expressed, and the harmony of the spheres were one and the same thing: 'I affirm and demonstrate that the movements [of the planets] are modulated according to harmonic proportions.'

Kepler could not resist pushing his theory further. Each planet, he believed, sings a characteristic tune – and, by a calculation involving the angle it describes in a day, as seen from the Sun, he was able to work out what the tune for each planet was. The Earth sings a simple little ditty – mi fa mi – indicating, Kepler asserted, that 'in this our domicile *mi*sery and *fa*mine obtain.'

The search for the Philosopher's Stone

The dream of finding a substance that could transform base metals into gold has lured alchemists for thousands of years. Although now generally derided as no more than misguided mystics, these passionate researchers actually contributed much to scientific knowledge. And some reliable witnesses have claimed that, for a select few alchemists, the dream came true. BRIAN INNES narrates the history of this ancient occult science

TWO DAYS AFTER CHRISTMAS in 1666, an unprepossessing stranger visited Johann Friedrich Schweitzer, physician to the Prince of Orange. He was

> of a mean stature, a little long face, with a few small pock holes, and most black hair, not at all curled, a beardless chin, about three or four and forty years of age (as I guessed), and born in North Holland.

It is clear that Schweitzer – the author of one or two books on medical and botanical matters – was a careful and objective observer.

After some idle conversation, the stranger asked Schweitzer whether he would recognise the 'Philosopher's Stone' if he saw it. This was an astounding question. The Philosopher's Stone was the goal of the alchemists – a fabled substance that could transmute metals into gold, banish all illness and bestow long and vigorous life.

The visitor produced from his pocket a small ivory box that held 'three ponderous pieces or small lumps . . . each about the bigness of a small walnut, transparent, of a pale brimstone colour'. This, he said, was the substance that men had sought so long. Schweitzer took one of the pieces greedily, and begged the man to give him just a small piece. When he was refused, he contrived to scrape a speck beneath his fingernail.

When the visitor had left, promising to return in three weeks and show him 'some curious arts in the fire', Schweitzer hurried to his laboratory for a crucible. He melted some lead in it, and then added the tiny piece of stone. But the metal did not change into gold: 'Almost the whole mass of lead flew away, and the remainder turned into a mere glassy earth.'

Impatiently, the physician awaited the return of the stranger, half believing that he would not come again; but in exactly three weeks his mysterious visitor was once more at the door. For a long time the stranger refused to let Schweitzer take another look at the marvellous stone, but at last 'he gave me a crumb as big as a rape or turnip seed, saying, receive this small parcel of the greatest treasure of the world, which truly few kings or princes have ever known or seen.'

Most ungratefully, Schweitzer protested that this was not sufficient to transmute as much as four grains of lead into gold; whereupon the stranger took it back, cut it in half, and flung one part in the fire, exclaiming: 'It is yet sufficient for thee!'

Schweitzer then confessed his former theft, and described his lack of success. The stranger laughed and said:

> Thou art more dextrous to commit theft than to apply thy medicine; for if thou hadst only wrapped up thy stolen prey in yellow wax, to preserve it from the arising fumes of lead, it would have penetrated to the bottom of the lead, and transmuted it to gold.

Above: carrying out their investigations blindly, with little understanding of scientific method or the design of experiments, the alchemists nevertheless laid the basis of modern chemical research. Although the alchemical laboratory frequently looked more like a blacksmith's forge, as in this satirical woodcut, the more sophisticated apparatus changed hardly at all in a thousand years

Previous page: the moment at which the First Matter distils over into the receiving flask is caught wonderfully in this painting by the 18th-century artist Joseph Wright of Derby

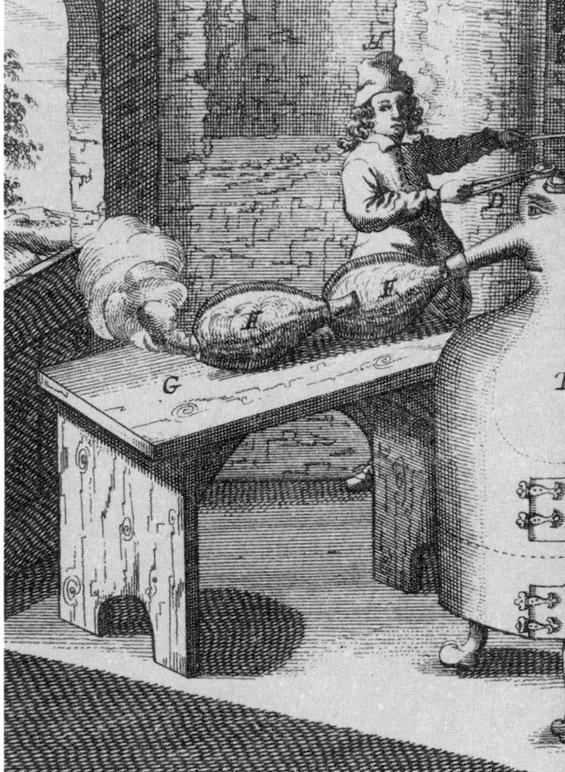

He promised to return at nine the next morning and show Schweitzer the correct method.

> But the next day he came not, nor ever since. Only he sent an excuse at half an hour past nine that morning, by reason of his great business, and promised to come at three in the afternoon, but never came, nor have I heard of him since; whereupon I began to doubt of the whole matter. Nevertheless late that night my wife . . . came soliciting and vexing me to make experiment . . . saying to me, unless this be done, I shall have no rest nor sleep all this night. . . . She being so earnest, I commanded a fire to be made – thinking, alas, now is this man (though so divine

in discourse) found guilty of falsehood. . . . My wife wrapped the said matter in wax, and I cut half an ounce or six drams of old lead, and put [it] into a crucible in the fire, which being melted, my wife put in the said Medicine made up in a small pill or button, which presently made such a hissing and bubbling in its perfect operation, that within a quarter of an hour all the mass of lead was transmuted into the . . . finest gold . . . .

The philosopher Spinoza, who lived not far away, came the next day to examine the gold, and was convinced that Schweitzer was telling the truth. The Assay Master of the province, a certain Mr Porelius, tested the metal and pronounced it genuine; and Mr Buectel, the silversmith, subjected it to further tests that confirmed that it was gold.

There is nothing in Schweitzer's account itself to inspire doubt; he was a reputable medical man and a trained scientific observer, and not given to fraud or practical jokes. And yet, knowing what we do now about the nature of matter, and in particular about the properties of metals, it is impossible to believe that such a transmutation could have taken place.

Schweitzer was certainly not the only scientist, however, to be convinced by practical demonstration that the Philosopher's Stone truly existed, and that it would effect the transmutation of base metals into gold. Another was Jan Baptista van Helmont, a respected chemical experimenter. He had been responsible for a number of important discoveries and was the first man to realise that there were other gases than air; indeed, the word 'gas' was his invention. He had written, some 20 years before Schweitzer's meeting with the mysterious stranger:

For truly I have divers times seen it [the Philosopher's Stone] and handled it with my hands, but it was of colour, such as is in Saffron in its powder, yet weighty, and shining like unto powdered glass. There was once given unto me one fourth part of one grain [16 milligrams]. . . . I projected [it] upon eight ounces [227 grams] of quicksilver [mercury] made hot in a crucible; and straightaway all the quicksilver, with a certain degree of noise, stood still from flowing, and being congealed, settled like unto a yellow lump; but after pouring it out, the bellows blowing, there were found eight ounces and a little less than eleven grains of the purest gold.

A fatal blow?

Van Helmont was so impressed with this result that he christened his son Mercurius. Another 17th-century scientist, Rudolf Glauber, the German physician and chemist, believed that he had found one of the ingredients of the Philosopher's Stone in the waters of a spa where he had gone to take a cure. What he found was in fact sodium sulphate, which to this day we know as Glauber's salt – an effective laxative, but not capable of producing gold. No less a thinker than Sir Isaac Newton remained convinced of the possibility of transmutation; so did Descartes, the great French philosopher; and Leibniz, the great philosopher and mathematician. Even Robert Boyle, whose book, *The sceptical chymist*, is generally believed to have struck a fatal blow to any serious belief in alchemy, remained certain to the end of his days that transmutation was possible.

Why were all these scientists convinced that it was possible to change metals into gold? The concept is a very ancient one, which seems to answer to deep human motivations. It came to medieval Europe by way of the Arabs. When they invaded Egypt, which they called Khem, in the seventh century, the Arabs discovered that the

Below: a chemical laboratory of the 17th century, that of Rudolf Glauber. The furnace, A, contains a flask, B. Above the flask a 'pelican', D – a crude distillation device – delivers vapour into a series of vessels known as 'udels', F

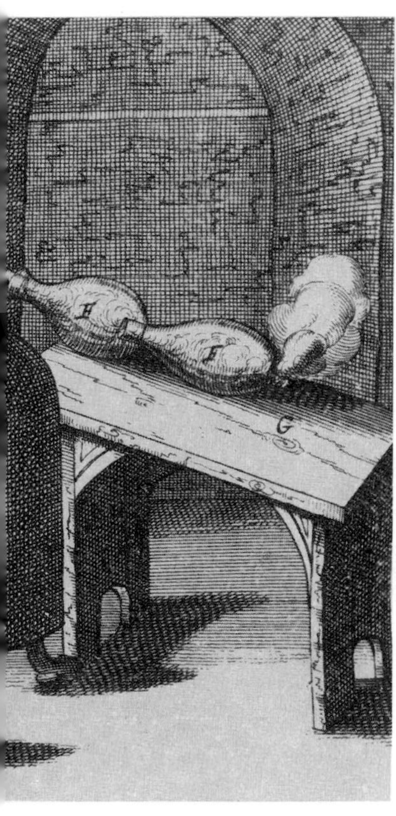

Right: an Egyptian wall painting of 1300 BC shows goldsmiths (at the left of the two rows of figures), together with joiners. The smiths could make cheap alloys resembling gold and may have possessed the art of electroplating

Far left: Johann Friedrich Schweitzer, known frequently by the Latinised form of his name, Helvetius, was one of the many scientists who believed they had seen the production of gold from base metals

Egyptians were masters of the art of working in gold. They called gold-working *al-kimiya* – 'the art of the land of Khem' – and so, according to one account, the word 'alchemy' was born.

In the great library of Alexandria the Arabs discovered all the writings of the Greek philosophers – in particular those of Aristotle, who lived in the fourth century BC and who can truly be called the first great scientist. The Arabs had the manuscripts copied and translated into Arabic and they found their way all over the Arab world.

Aristotle believed that the material world was made from 'prime matter', which in itself lacked all physical properties, but on which different 'forms' could be impressed. Form was not merely physical shape, but every specific property of a body or a substance. Among these were four 'qualities': wetness, dryness, heat and cold. These qualities gave rise to four 'elements', or simple substances: fire, which was hot and dry; air (for example, steam) which was hot and wet; water, which was cold and wet; earth, which was cold and dry.

From this scheme of things it was very easy to progress to the idea that every substance was composed of all four elements in various proportions. For instance, consider a piece of green wood heated over a fire. First, water appears in droplets at the end of the wood; then steam and vapour are given off; then the wood burns, apparently releasing fire; and finally ash, or earth, is left. To change one substance into another, therefore, it was only necessary to change the proportions of elements in them by addition or subtraction.

Advances in alchemy

Faced with the impressive skills of the Egyptian metal workers, who knew how to colour cheaper metals to make them look like gold, the Arabs naturally supposed that their secret lay in the application of Aristotle's theories. For hundreds of years Arab scientists experimented in their laboratories. They made many important chemical discoveries and they invented most of the apparatus that is still used by chemists today. But they did not discover how to turn base metal into gold. However, one of the earliest Arab philosophers, Jabir ibn Hayyan, made an important contribution to the development of alchemical theory.

Aristotle had regarded the smoke produced in burning as earthy, and contrasted it with the watery vapour produced when water boils. Stones and minerals that were unchanged by the fire supposedly consisted mainly of this earthy smoke, while metals, which became liquid, were formed from the watery vapour.

Jabir suggested that the vapour produced by boiling water was an intermediate stage in its transformation into air. The vapour could be transformed into a material he called mercury, though this was not the familiar metal, but an ideal substance combining the qualities of lustre and liquidity. Earthy smoke was likewise earth in the process of becoming air, and it could be turned into 'sulphur', which combined the qualities of earthiness and combustibility. The various metals and minerals were formed in the earth from combinations of mercury and sulphur.

Jabir investigated what happened when he distilled a wide variety of organic materials – that is, substances derived from living things. In every case he obtained a liquid, which he identified as the element water since it was cold and wet; an 'oil', which, being hot and wet, must be air; a coloured substance – a tincture – that burned, which he thought to be the element fire; and a dry black residue, which he identified as the element earth. He had thus, he believed, isolated the four elements of Aristotle.

He then set out to purify these elements

Good as gold

Mankind recognised very early that gold, being virtually indestructible, non-rusting, yet highly malleable, was an ideal medium of exchange. The economy of the major powers is still based on it. Gold almost always appears in the metallic state, commonly in seams or nuggets. Alluvial gold is found deposited in the beds of rivers that have been carrying gold-bearing rocks away for millions of years. Pyrites, or 'fool's gold', is often found close by.

The assaying, or testing, of gold has always been a matter of high importance. Gold jewellery, which must not be damaged, can be weighed and its volume can be measured in order to determine its density: alloys are generally less dense than gold of high purity. In addition, the metal is 'touched' to a touchstone, such as a piece of black jasper, a variety of quartz. The colour of the mark made by gold is different from that made by gilt, brass or copper alloys.

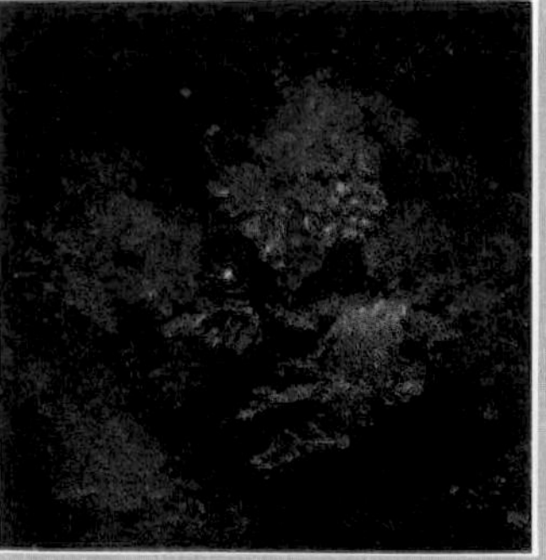

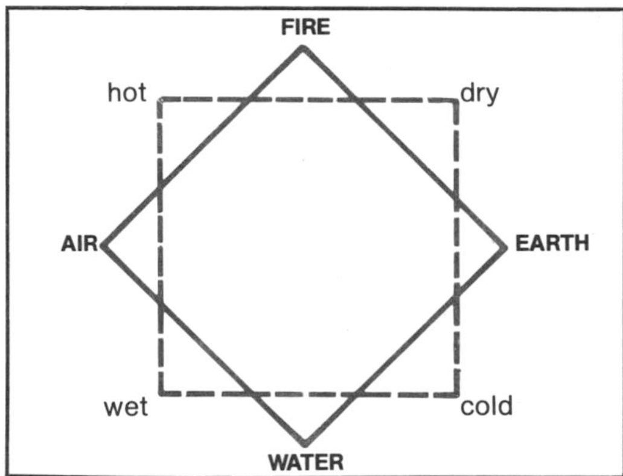

Right: Aristotle's scheme of the four elements. Each possesses the two neighbouring 'qualities'. The earth, water, air and fire with which we are familiar are more or less impure approximations to these ideal substances

Below: the scientist Jan Baptista van Helmont added his voice in support of the reality of transmutation

If a piece of gold-bearing ore is to be assayed, the gold is first extracted. The ground ore is heated in a fireclay crucible with lead oxide and charcoal; molten lead settles at the bottom of the crucible as an alloy with any gold and silver present in the ore. The other mineral contents form a floating liquid slag.

The lead 'button' is then heated gently in a small 'cupel', a vessel made of bone ash. The lead turns back into lead oxide, which is absorbed into the cupel, leaving a bead of gold and silver – together, perhaps, with a small amount of platinum. The silver is 'parted' from the gold by being dissolved in hot dilute nitric acid.

Medieval alchemists discovered that gold would not dissolve in nitric, sulphuric or hydrochloric acids – but that it would dissolve in aqua regia, a mixture of nitric and hydrochloric acids. This led to serious misapprehension, since it was often assumed that anything that dissolved in aqua regia (and a great many substances will do so) was thus proved to be gold.

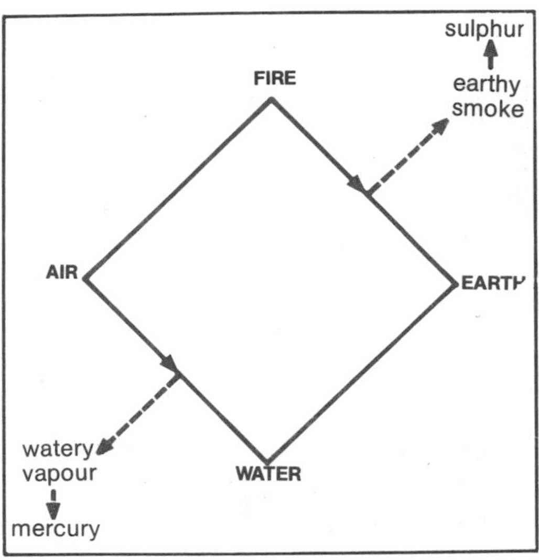

Right: how Jabir ibn Hayyan modified the theory of Aristotle. Like the original four elements, his 'mercury' and 'sulphur' are idealised substances. They combine, respectively, the qualities of lustre and liquidity, and earthiness and combustibility

Below: the Arab alchemist Jabir, in a fanciful European representation of the 17th century

Right: title page from the 1603 edition of the works of Paracelsus. The author himself is portrayed at the head of the page, and the figure on the right is a representation of Hermes Trismegistos, whose principle 'as above, so below' was the basis of all medieval magical experimentation

and isolate each *quality*. By distilling water 700 times, he wrote, he had obtained a brilliant white substance, which crystallised like salt. This, he said, was the purified quality of coldness. He supposed that he would be able to prepare pure moistness from his 'oil', pure dryness from his 'earth', and pure heat from his 'tincture'. He described the last as a transparent substance, brilliant, lustrous and red. This was the substance that the European alchemists named the Philosopher's Stone.

The philosophy of the Greeks returned to Europe, together with all the additions made by the Arabs, when Moslem rule was ended in Toledo, in central Spain, towards the end of the 11th century, and Christian scholars were able to translate the Arabic manuscripts in the library there. Soon after, many Europeans began to experiment with alchemy: they included Albrecht, a churchman and philosopher who became known as 'Albertus Magnus' and was renowned for the breadth and profundity of his learning; Roger Bacon, the learned doctor of Oxford University; and Philippus Aureolus Theophrastus Bombastus von Hohenheim.

This arrogant, boastful, colourful character has given his name to all the languages of Europe, for we now describe such a man as 'bombastic'. But he preferred to call himself Paracelsus, implying that he was greater than Celsus, the first-century writer who had been regarded as the greatest authority on medical matters. It was Paracelsus, writing in an extraordinary mixture of Latin, German and invented words, who took the Arabic word for black eye-paint, *al-kohl*, and gave it to spirits of wine, which has borne the name 'alcohol' ever since. From the German *all-Geist* he made up the word 'alkahest', denoting a supposed universal solvent that would convert all bodies into their prime matter. And from Jabir's theory of elemental sulphur and mercury he developed an alchemical principle that seems to reveal some kind of intuitive understanding of 20th-century physics (see page 92). His influence was to be a crucial stimulus to the slow development of modern chemistry. But the pursuit of the Philosopher's Stone and the Elixir of Life was still very far from over.

The Elixir of Life

One of the aims of the alchemist's work was the discovery of the Philosopher's Stone and the Elixir of Life. This chapter describes one alchemist who was rumoured to have succeeded

Above: alchemists grew old and decrepit in their quest for the Elixir of Life. Yet stories persist that some fortunate practitioners found some way to survive beyond their natural span

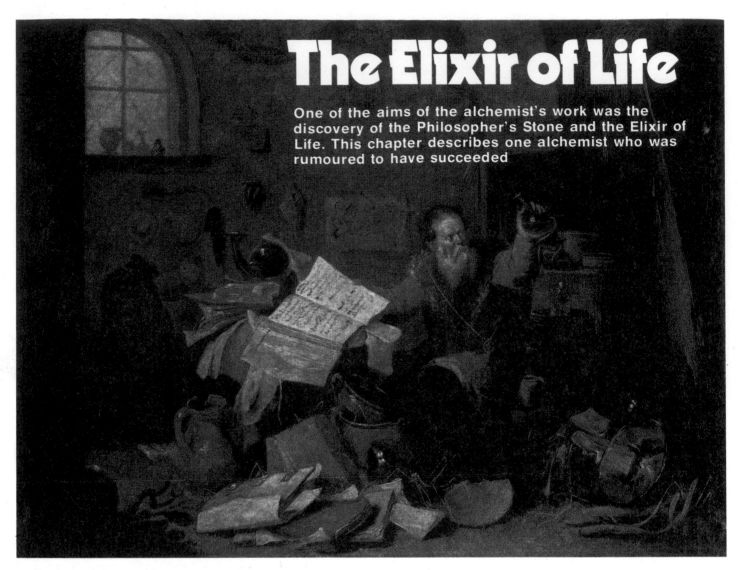

'ALWAYS DRUNK AND ALWAYS LUCID' was how a biographer described Theophrastus Bombastus von Hohenheim, who gave himself the name 'Paracelsus'. His career included the study of magic under Hans von Trittenheim at Würzburg in Germany, working for a year at the mining school of Sigismund Fugger, travelling through Germany, Italy, France, the Netherlands, England, Scandinavia and Russia, serving as an army surgeon in Italy and taking a medical degree at the University of Ferrara. He was appointed city physician of Basel, in Switzerland, in 1526, and he celebrated his appointment with a remarkable tirade in the city square.

In one hand he held a brass pan full of glowing coals. Into the fire he thrust the works of Avicenna, the 11th-century Arab philosopher, and of Galen, the second-century Greek medical authority. He sprinkled sulphur and saltpetre over them so that they were consumed in spectacular flames, and spoke:

> If your physicians only knew that their prince Galen – they call none like him – was sticking in Hell, from whence he has sent letters to me, they would make the sign of the cross upon themselves with a fox's tail. In the same way your Avicenna sits in the vestibule of the Infernal portal; and I have disputed with him about his . . . Tincture of the Philosophers, his Quintessence, and Philosopher's Stone . . . and all the rest. O you hypocrites, who despise the truths taught you by a great physician [he meant himself]. . . . Come then, and listen, impostors who prevail only by the authority of your high positions! After my death, my disciples will burst forth and drag you to the light, and shall expose your dirty drugs, wherewith up to this time you have compassed the death of princes. . . .

In spite of his overweening, egotistical style, Paracelsus was an important influence in the development of the science of pharmacy. He was among the first to recognise that the processes of alchemy were the same as those of baking and cooking – he even dignified the man who lit and tended the fires with the title of 'alchemist'. And he replaced the four elements of Aristotle (see page 82) by three 'hypostatical principles': mercury, sulphur and salt. The term 'hypostatical' meant that

Below: Theophrastus Bombastus von Hohenheim, city physician of Basel, contributed much to alchemical theory, as well as to pharmacy

these were not the ordinary substances: they were, rather, three ideal substances, which a 17th-century text described in these terms:

> *Mercury* is that sharp, permeating, ethereal and very pure fluid to which all nutrition, sense, motion, power, colours and retardation of age are due. It is derived from air and water; it is the food of life. . . .
>
> *Sulphur* is that sweet, oleaginous and viscid [glutinous] balsam conserving the natural heat of the parts, instrument of all vegetation [unconscious activity of plants or animals, such as assimilating food], increase and transmutation, and the fountain and origin of all colours. It is inflammable, yet has great power of conglutinating [sticking together] extreme contraries.
>
> *Salt* is that dry saline body preserving mixtures from putrefaction, having wonderful powers of dissolving, coagulating, cleansing, evacuating, conferring solidity, consistency, taste and the like. It resembles earth, not as being cold and dry, but as being firm and fixed.

Paracelsus saw these three principles in terms of spirit (mercury), soul (sulphur) and body (salt). As he himself put it in one of his alchemical writings:

> But as there are many kinds of fruit, so there are many kinds of sulphur, salt and mercury. A different sulphur is in gold, another in silver, another in lead, another in iron, tin, etc. Also a different one in sapphire, another in the emerald, another in the ruby, chrysolite, amethyst, magnets, etc. Also another in stones, flint, salts, spring-waters, etc. . . .

Two targets of the wrath of Paracelsus: the Greek writer Galen (above), an authority on drugs, and the Arab ibn Sina, known in Europe as Avicenna (below), author of *The canon of medicine*

This kind of thinking led Paracelsus to the search for the 'quintessence' of each material, the refined and purified extract that was the essential part of it. Supposedly he identified this with the 'mercury' specific to that substance. In his public speech in Basel he was contrasting the quintessences of various metals, which he had prepared by distillation, to common 'dirty drugs'.

An innovation in alchemy

The concept of hypostatic mercury, sulphur and salt gave a new impetus to alchemical enquiry; and Paracelsus achieved apparent success in medical treatment with some of his 'quintessences'. They were probably weak acid solutions, pepped up in some instances with alcohol.

The ideas of Paracelsus also encouraged the search for the Elixir of Life. This remarkable substance, which supposedly conferred longevity or even immortality, had reputedly been discovered already. It was important in Chinese alchemy, the story of which will be told later (see page 88). In Europe alchemists were rumoured at various times to have gained immortality. One was Nicolas Flamel.

Flamel was a thrifty and industrious scrivener (a scribe and copyist) in 14th-century Paris. In 1357 he bought a very old and large illuminated book:

> The cover of it was of brass, well bound, all engraven with letters or strange figures. . . . This I know that I could not read them nor were they either Latin or French letters. . . . As to

What was the Philosopher's Stone?

Early philosophers were convinced that by lengthy processes of purification it must be possible to extract from minerals the natural 'principle' that supposedly caused gold to 'grow' in the earth. The anonymous 17th-century book *The sophic hydrolith* tells us that the Philosopher's Stone is prepared from a mineral by first 'purging it of all that is thick, nebulous, opaque and dark', yielding mercurial water or 'water of the Sun', which has a pleasant penetrating smell and is very volatile.

Part of this liquid is put on one side, and the rest mixed with one twelfth its weight of 'the divinely endowed body of gold' – ordinary gold being useless because it is defiled by daily use. The mixture forms a solid amalgam, which is then heated gently for a week. It is then dissolved in some of the mercurial water in an egg-shaped phial.

Then the remaining mercurial water is added gradually, in seven portions; the phial is sealed, and kept at such a temperature as will hatch an egg. After 40 days, the phial's contents will be as black as a raven's head; after seven more days small grainy bodies like fish-eyes appear.

Gold had to be added to the Philosopher's Stone to make further gold. This is symbolised here by the lion devouring the serpent in order to transform it

The Philosopher's Stone begins to make its appearance: first reddish in colour; then white, green and yellow like a peacock's tail; then a dazzling white; and later a deep glowing red. Finally, 'the revivified body is quickened, perfected and glorified' and appears of a most beautiful purple colour.

Gradually, over the centuries, alchemists came to identify the Philosopher's Stone with the Elixir, the substance that would confer eternal life.

As for the mineral from which the Stone was to be prepared, *Gloria mundi* (1526) says it is 'familiar to all men, both young and old, is found in the country, in the village, in the town. . . . No-one prizes it, though, next to the human soul, it is the most beautiful and most precious thing upon earth. . . .'

> the matter that was written within, it was engraved (as I suppose) with an iron pencil or graver upon . . . bark leaves, and curiously coloured. . . .

On the first page was written in golden letters: 'Abraham the Jew, Priest, Prince, Levite, Astrologer and Philosopher, to the Nation of the Jews dispersed by the Wrath of God in France, wisheth Health'. Flamel subsequently referred to this manuscript as 'the book of Abraham the Jew'. The dedication was followed by execrations against anyone who was neither priest nor scribe and who might read the book. As Flamel was a scribe, he was emboldened to read further.

The author intended to give the dispersed Jews assistance in paying their taxes to the Roman authorities by teaching them how to transmute base metals into gold. The instructions were clear and easy to follow, but unfortunately they referred only to the later stages of the process. The only guidance to the earlier stages was said to be in the illustrations given on the fourth and fifth leaves of the book. To his great disappointment, Flamel found that, although these pictures were well painted,

> yet by that could no man ever have been able to understand it without being well skilled in their Qabalah, which is a series of old traditions, and also to have been well studied in their books.

For 21 years Flamel tried without success to find someone who could explain these pictures to him. At last his wife Perrenelle suggested that he should travel to Spain to seek out some learned Jew who could shed light on the matter. Flamel decided to make the famous pilgrimage to the shrine of St James at Compostela; and so, with his pilgrim's staff and broad-brimmed hat, and carrying carefully made copies of the mysterious illustrations, he set out on foot.

When he had made his devotions at the shrine, he travelled on to the city of León, in northern Spain, where by chance he made the acquaintance of a certain Master Canches, a learned Jewish physician. When he saw the pictures, he was 'ravished with great astonishment and joy', recognising them as parts of a book that he had long believed lost. He made up his mind at once to return with Flamel to France. But at Orléans, wearied and old, he died. Flamel, having seen him buried, returned alone to Paris.

> I had now the *prima materia*, the first principles, yet not their first preparation, which is a thing most difficult, above all things in the world. . . . Finally, I found that which I desired, which I also knew by the strong scent and odour thereof. Having this, I easily accomplished the Mastery. . . . The first time that I made projection [accomplished transmutation] was upon Mercury, whereof I turned half a pound [227 grams], or thereabouts,

Left and above left: two pages from an early copy of 'The book of Abraham the Jew' in Paris. The lower picture shows those who seek for gold in the garden; the figure at bottom right, if we may believe Ninian Bres, is Nicolas Flamel himself. In the upper picture, titled 'the three colours of the work', the rider mounted on a black lion represents gold in maceration; the second, on a red lion, represents the inner ferment; and the crowned rider on a white lion symbolises success

Left: a supposed portrait of Nicolas Flamel, from an early 19th-century work

Right: another picture from 'The book of Abraham the Jew'. This has been called 'the fair flower on the mountain'. The red and white flowers stand for stages in the Great Work, the dragons for sophic (that is, 'ideal') mercury, and the griffins for a combination of the lion (the fixed principle) and the eagle (the volatile principle)

Above: an 18th-century engraving of the frescoes that were painted for Flamel in the churchyard of the Holy Innocents in Paris, and which had survived for 400 years. A pair of small figures below the centre represent Flamel and his wife Perrenelle, while the panels at the top show seven of the illustrations from 'The book of Abraham the Jew'. Numerous copies of these pictures were made over the centuries, and it is now very difficult to determine what was in the original

> into pure silver, better than that of the Mine, as I myself assayed, and made others assay many times. This was upon a Monday, the 17th of January about noon, in my home, Perrenelle only being present, in the year of the restoring of mankind 1382.

Three months later Flamel made his first transmutation into gold. He and Perrenelle put their new-found wealth to good use: they endowed

> fourteen hospitals, three chapels and seven churches, in the city of Paris, all which we had new built from the ground, and enriched with great gifts and revenues, with many reparations in their churchyards. We also have done at Boulogne about as much as we have done at Paris, not to speak of the charitable acts which we both did to particular poor people, principally to widows and orphans. . . .

After Flamel's death in 1419 the rumours began. Hoping that the Philosopher's Stone might still be hidden in one of his houses, people searched through them again and again, until one was reduced to a pile of rubble. There were stories that both Perrenelle and Nicolas were still alive; that she had gone to live in Switzerland while he buried a log in her grave, and that later he did the same at his own 'funeral'.

In the centuries since, legends have persisted that the wealthy alchemist had defeated death. The 17th-century traveller Paul Lucas, while travelling in Asia Minor, met a distinguished Turkish philosopher. He was told that

> true philosophers had had the secret of prolonging life for anything up to a thousand years. . . . At last I took the liberty of naming the celebrated Flamel, who, it was said, possessed the Philosopher's Stone, yet was certainly dead. He smiled at my simplicity, and asked with an air of mirth: Do you really believe this? No, no, my friend, Flamel is still living; neither he nor his wife has yet tasted death. It is not above three years since I left both . . . in India; he is one of my best friends.

A couple who cheated death

In 1761 Flamel and his wife were said to have attended the opera in Paris. Still later there were stories very reminiscent of those concerning the Count St Germain, who was also supposed to have discovered the secret of the Elixir of Life. What are we to make of that almost unknown work *Le corbeau menteur* (*The lying raven*) by the 19th-century writer Ninian Bres?

> He was a little less than middle height, stooping somewhat with the weight of years, but still with a firm step and a clear eye, and with a complexion strangely smooth and transparent, like fine alabaster. Both he and the woman with him – clearly his wife, although she appeared almost imperceptibly the older and more decisive of the two – were dressed in a style that seemed only a few years out of fashion and yet had an indefinable air of antiquity about it. I stood, half-concealed in a little archway toward the end of the Boulevard du Temple: my hands were stained with acid, and my topcoat stank of the furnace. As the couple came abreast of the spot where I stood, Flamel turned toward me and seemed about to speak, but Perrenelle drew him quickly on, and they were almost at once lost in the crowd. You ask how I am so confident that this was Nicolas Flamel? I tell you that I have spent many hours in the Bibliothèque Nationale, poring over the book of Abraham the Jew: look carefully at the first side of the fifth leaf and there, in the lower right-hand corner of the representation of those who seek for gold in the garden, you will see the face that searched mine that evening on the Boulevard du Temple, and that has haunted my dreams ever since. . . .

Alchemy in both East and West was concerned with the purification of the soul as much as with the transmutation of metals. This chapter relates the two traditions to each other and to primitive magic

ALCHEMY GATHERED into its literature a whole bestiary of symbols: the black crow; the white pelican, its breast spotted red with its own blood, on which, by popular belief, its young fed; the phoenix; the dove; the peacock, with its tail of wonderful colours; red and green lions; dragons of all hues. There were human symbols as well: the red man and the white woman, sometimes twined together in sexual union; the king murdered by his own son; and above all the androgyne, or hermaphrodite, which represented the combination of opposites that produced the Philosopher's Stone.

The symbols are so striking and so numerous that they caught the attention of the psychologist Carl Jung, who devoted a whole book to them. Throughout his life, Jung had studied the way in which the same kind of symbols appear to have the same kind of meaning in communities and cultures widely separated in time or place. It was, Jung thought, as if these symbols were a part of mankind's fundamental make-up.

One of Jung's predecessors was Herbert Silberer. In his book *Problems of mysticism and its symbolism* he attaches great importance to the work of one of the first alchemists to set his thoughts down in writing, Zosimos of Panopolis, in Egypt. Zosimos, who lived about AD 300, wrote down some of the secrets of alchemy in terms of a strange vision:

> I asked him who he was and in a feeble voice he answered me: I am he-who-is, the priest of the sanctuary, and I am overwhelmed by another's strength. For at break of day came a deputy who

Alchemy: sex and symbolism

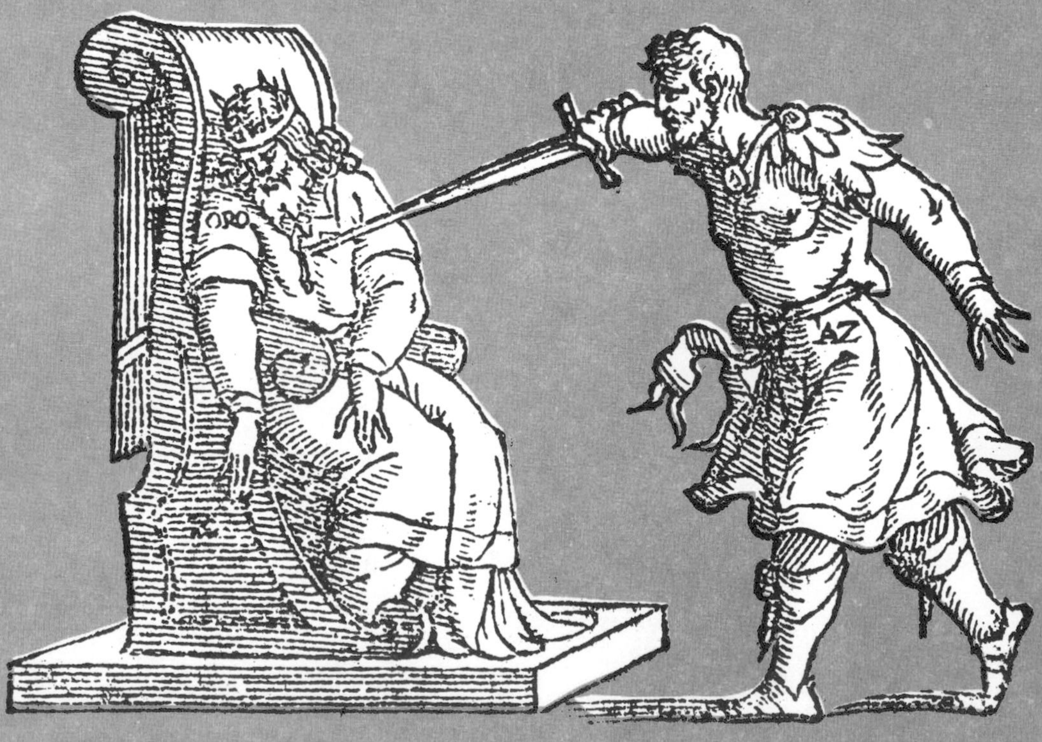

Above: when lead is kept molten in a basin over a furnace, it will form an encrustation of bright yellow crystals of lead oxide, or litharge. Here the aged Saturn symbolises lead, while the gold-crested white dove is the 'sublime' spirit of the lead, its quintessence. That, at least, is one interpretation of this illustration from the 16th-century manuscript *Splendor solis*, but several other equally plausible explanations have been proposed

Right: in this woodcut from *The new pearl of great price* (1546), the crowned king is gold, killed by his son Mercury. After many vicissitudes he rises again

> swiftly seized me, cleaving me with a sword and dividing me in pieces; and after flaying all the skin from my head he mixed my bones with my flesh and burned them in the fire. . . .

When we look at the illustrations from alchemical works written some 1200 years later, or read the descriptions of the Great Work, it is not really surprising to find the same kind of imagery employed, for in this instance it is easy to trace a direct line of descent. But what is remarkable is to compare the vision of Zosimos with the visions of the shamans, the priests of the nomadic tribes of Siberia and North America.

As adolescents, future shamans were suddenly seized by a 'sickness', a kind of divine madness that was the first sign of their priestly vocation. During this phase they saw extraordinary visions. One future shaman, for instance, described how he saw himself enter a mountain, where a naked man was working a bellows to keep a cauldron heating on a fire. The man seized the shaman with a great pair of tongs, cut off his head and sliced up his body, and threw everything into the cauldron, where it cooked for three years. There were three anvils in the cave, and on one of them the man forged the shaman's head; then he rescued the bones, joined them together, and covered them with flesh.

The mystique of the metalworker

Many of the initiation visions seen by the shamans took similar forms to this, and the famous anthropologist Mercia Eliade has shown that they are closely related to the high priestly standing enjoyed by metalworkers among primitive peoples.

In some very early mythologies, the Sun was seen as plunging every evening into the womb of Earth, sowing the 'seed' of the metals. It was supposed that the metals gradually developed, passing through various stages, until the final result was gold. (We have seen how even the scientist Aristotle believed that the Earth somehow 'bred' metals – see page 84.)

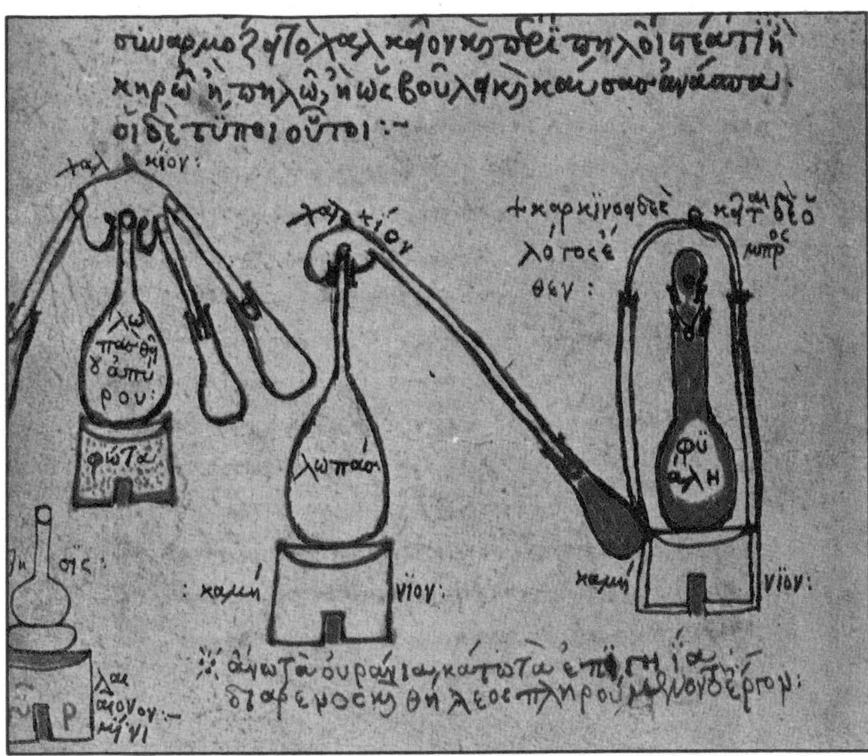

Top: a 15th-century copy of an alchemical treatise by Zosimos of Panopolis

Above: a travelling Tuareg silversmith from Niger. These artisans are often outcasts, regarded with fear and awe

Left: another tantalising illustration from *Splendor solis*. A fair white woman offers a scarlet cloak to a man emerging from primeval blackness into a ruddy form that is reminiscent in some ways of a new-born child

Metalworkers, who knew how to take mineral ores and, by smelting them in a womb-shaped furnace, to produce metals, and who further understood how to shape the metal produced, were thus performing much the same kind of marvel as the Sun-god himself. They were venerated as priests who stood closer than ordinary men to the god.

It was natural to suppose that, if a man could make himself truly god-like, he would gain the power to transform baser metals into gold, by exactly the same processes that they underwent in the Earth. This belief was expressed on the Emerald Tablet, a record said to have been inscribed by the god Thoth, who was supposed to have taught the ancient Egyptians the sciences and the art of writing. (The Greeks identified Thoth with one form of their god Hermes – Hermes Trismegistos, the 'thrice-great'. Hence the term 'hermetic art' for alchemy.)

The principle of the Emerald Tablet can be expressed in a phrase widely used by alchemists: 'as above, so below'. The tablet appears to have carried a set of mystical instructions for the manufacture of gold by transmutation – the 'operation of Sol'. The seventh of these precepts reads: 'Separate the earth from the fire, the subtle from the gross, acting prudently and with judgement.' The eighth reads: 'Ascend with the greatest sagacity from the Earth to heaven, and then again descend to the Earth, and unite together the powers of things superior and things inferior. . . .' These can be read as straightforward metaphors for separating and recombining elements. The 'ascent' and 'descent' could refer to the circulatory action of a kerotakis, a type of still.

But on another level these same precepts

could be, and were, taken as referring to a spiritual work of self-purification – a long and arduous liberation of the divine part of the alchemist's nature from the grossness of his body and senses.

All these various strands came together: the primitive belief that the search for a way to transmute base metals into gold involved a succession of god-like actions developed into the belief that an important part of alchemy was the attempt to become like God – 'as above, so below'. From this, no doubt, stems the conviction that the final result of the alchemical quest was to achieve eternal life.

It is striking that, although there is no evidence of any connection between the alchemy of the Arabs (as it was later transmitted to medieval Europe) and that of the Far East, the Chinese alchemists were also concerned with the attainment of immortality. They were undoubtedly very interested in the production of gold, but principally for its value as an elixir. The substance with which they attempted to prolong life was cinnabar, a bright-red compound of two of the vital substances of western alchemy: mercury and sulphur.

Above: the Emerald Tablet, as it was imagined by Heinrich Khunrath in his *Amphitheatrum sapientiae aeternae* (*Amphitheatre of eternal wisdom*), which was first published in 1609. Below the Latin text, Khunrath provides a translation into German

The ancient philosophy of Tao is concerned with the delicate blending of two fundamental energies: *yin*, the feminine principle, and *yang*, the masculine. The careful commingling of *yin* and *yang* was believed to be a means of prolonging life.

At the lower levels of Taoist practice, the mixing of *yin* and *yang* could be achieved by controlled sexual intercourse; the more advanced mystics practised various meditative procedures, designed to bring about a kind of 'distillation' of *yang* within the body. These practices were commonly known as 'sexual alchemy'.

The body was seen as a tier of three crucibles (*tan-t'ien*) on a central column. The lowest, the cauldron or three-footed furnace, was in the belly below the solar plexus; the second was behind the solar plexus; the third between the eyes.

The 'prime substance' of this inner alchemy was the primitive sexual energy, *ching*, residing in the lowest crucible. It was one of three forces, the others being *ch'i*, the moving vitality, in the middle crucible and *shen*, the luminous personal spirit, in the upper crucible. Meditation began with rhythmical deep breathing: the 'heavenly fire of the heart' began to circulate and was impelled – as if by a bellows – down to the furnace in the belly. Gradually, as energy rose up the 'distillation column' of the spine, the content of *yang* increased; then, as it

An experiment with immortality

The Tao master Wei Po-Yang went into the mountains one day, accompanied by three disciples and his white dog. The master had concocted a certain 'gold medicine', reputed to be the Elixir of Immortality. He fed a little of the medicine to his dog, which promptly died. Wei Po-Yang said to his disciples: 'To live without taking the medicine would be just the same as to die of the medicine. I must take it.' He did so and, like the dog, expired.

Two of the grief-stricken disciples immediately set off to find implements with which to bury their late master. But the third, Yü by name, was more thoughtful; it seemed to him that Wei Po-Yang must have known what he was

doing. Yü therefore took some of the medicine himself, and also died.

A short while later, Wei Po-Yang revived, for his medicine had contained only enough impurity to cause temporary death. He put a little more of the medicine into the mouths of the dog and of Yü, both of whom also recovered after a few moments. Together, the three strolled off into immortality.

Wei Po-Yang lived in the second century AD, and he is credited with the authorship of the treatise *Ts'an-t'ung-ch'i (The three ways unified and harmonised)*, a work that made Taoism into a coherent system. Among other things it deals with the 'pills of immortality', which, says Wei, are 'extremely efficacious, although their individual size is so small that they occupy only the point of a knife or the edge of a spatula.'

condensed at the top of the head and descended again, *yin* replaced *yang*. Eventually, the heat of the furnace was sufficient to drive the *ching*, transformed, up to the second crucible, where it combined with the *ch'i*. As in the alchemist's vessel known as a pelican, the two were continuously recycled, rising up the central column and then dropping back into the furnace for further purification. As the furnace was fanned to greater heat, the combined *ching* and *ch'i* eventually reached the *shen* in the upper crucible; and suddenly the 'inner copulation of the dragon and the tiger' took place. Su Tung P'o put it this way in AD 1110:

> The dragon is mercury. It is the semen and the blood. He issues from the kidneys and is stored in the liver. The tiger is lead. He is breath and bodily strength. He issues from the mind and the lungs bear him. When the mind is moved, breath and strength act with it. When the kidneys are flushed, then semen and blood flow. . . .

When the *ching-ch'i-shen* was rising and descending like liquid in a briskly bubbling still, it progressively purified until it was one with the energies of the cosmos. Then a special ambrosial fluid flowed like saliva in the mouth. Two lights, gold and silver, slowly descended into the furnace; the body's breathing ceased, to be replaced by the breathing of a foetus formed from the impregnation of the ambrosia by the gold and silver lights. Slowly, the foetus grew into a homunculus, a 'crystal child'; it rose slowly to the crown of the head, and was there born as an immortal.

The alchemy of Tantra

Taoist inner alchemy possesses a striking resemblance to the basic beliefs of Tantra, which is claimed to be the oldest religion of India. The Tantric meditator begins by visualising the inner central column of his spine, the *sushumna*, as the axis of the cosmos. Up the *sushumna* are strung a series of 'wheels', or *chakras*; there are usually six, with a seventh in the top of the skull. The lowest *chakra* is at the base of the pelvis, and here sleeps the serpent Kundalini, coiled around an inner phallus (*lingam*), with its tip in her mouth. By means of various yoga exercises Kundalini is awakened, straightens herself, and enters the bottom of the *sushumna*. The ultimate intention is that Kundalini shall ascend permanently to the top of the skull, where a transcendental sexual union takes place.

The postures that awaken Kundalini are frequently sexual, and even the Tantric ascetic will imagine an ideal girl as Kundalini ascends. The Tantric obtains his energy through sexual intercourse, and the woman is regarded as the possessor of particularly important power.

The Tantric yogi is credited with many abilities, of which one is the transmutation of base metals into gold; even his urine and faeces may bring about transmutation. He recognises the importance of mercury and sulphur. As an ancient treatise puts it:

> When quicksilver is killed with an equal weight of sulphur it cures leprosy; when killed with thrice its weight of sulphur it cures mental languor; when it is killed with four times its weight of sulphur it removes grey hair and wrinkles; when it is killed by five times its weight of sulphur it cures consumption; when it is killed with six times its weight of sulphur it becomes a panacea for all the ills. . . .

The close similarity of the imagery – and the substances used – in alchemy in all these very different cultures is striking. A major difference is equally striking: that medieval European alchemy does not seem to have had any explicit sexual basis. It was not until ancient Taoist and Tantric manuscripts became available in translation toward the end of the 19th century that sex entered western alchemy. The magical society called the Golden Dawn taught some kind of esoteric link between the two; Karl Kellner, who founded the Ordo Templi Orientis (OTO) in 1906 was more explicit. And Aleister Crowley, who was a member of both secret societies, seized upon the connection with enthusiasm, and developed his own brand of sexual magic. And then the psychologists who found the symbolism of alchemy so fascinating were to teach that sex is at the heart of all human action.

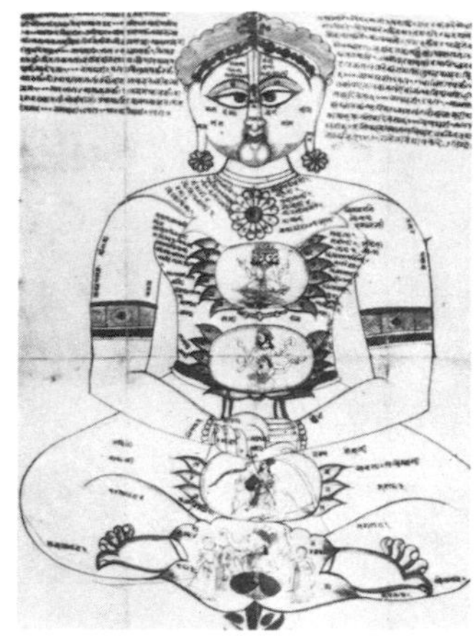

Above: in this Indian drawing from the 18th century, the 'subtle body' is represented as a plant growing from the ground. The *chakras*, or centres of energy positioned along the spinal *sushumna*, are shown symbolically by human and animal figures

Above and top right: the close symbolic relationship between Western alchemy and Tantric 'sexual alchemy' is clearly shown in these two pictures, one an Indian popular print of the early 19th century, the other a 16th-century European woodcut. In the upper illustration, the goddess Kali has beheaded herself, and her blood sprays onto the tongues of her attendants, while a couple make love in a lotus flower at her feet. The lower illustration shows the hermetic androgyne, a being formed when the son of Hermes and Aphrodite became united with the nymph Salmacis – a symbol of the union of opposites in chemical reactions

Alchemy's hidden truth

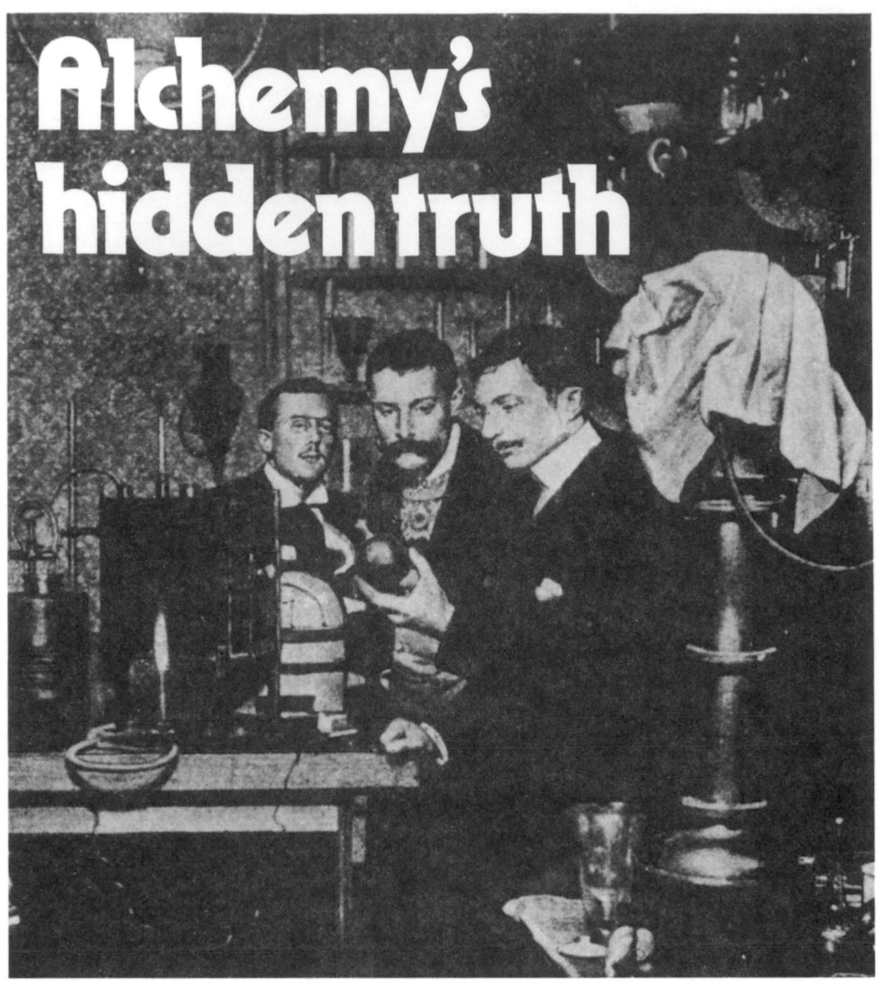

In the 20th century science has achieved the alchemical dream of transmuting the elements. But modern alchemists still use traditional methods in pursuit of their quest.

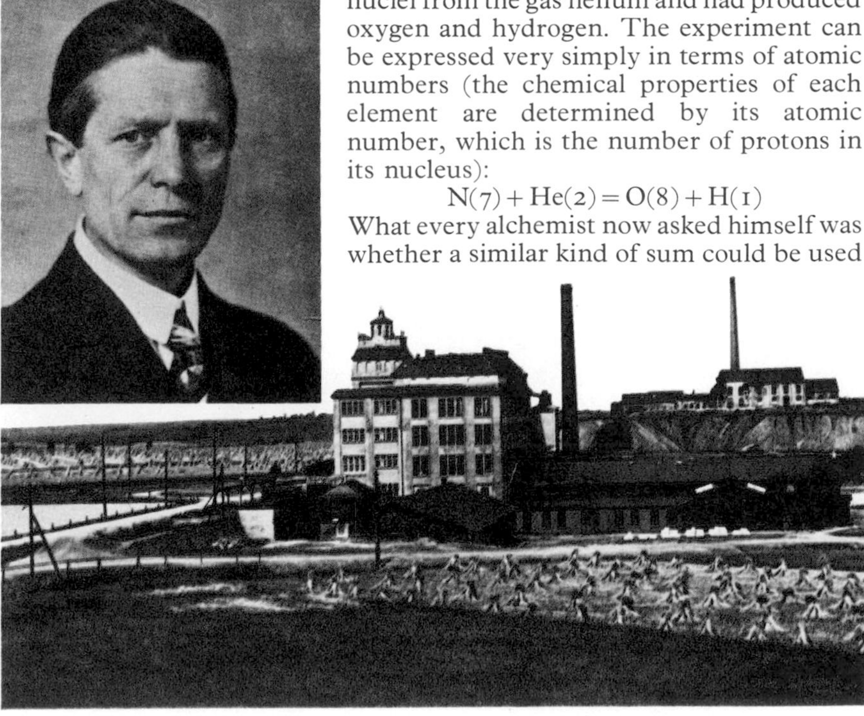

THE GROWTH OF experimental science during the 18th and 19th centuries; the work of chemists such as Lavoisier, Priestley and Davy; the establishment of Dalton's atomic theory; and the subsequent discoveries of a host of scientists in all aspects of chemistry and physics – such developments should have sounded the death knell of alchemy. And yet they did not.

During the 19th and early 20th centuries, it is true, alchemists retreated into the mystical, spiritual aspects of their study. They were drawn into the Rosicrucianist occultism of societies such as the Golden Dawn and the Ordo Templi Orientis (OTO), which contrived to combine ill-digested snippets of oriental philosophy with the western European magical tradition.

Then, in 1919, the British physicist Ernest Rutherford announced that he had successfully achieved the transmutation of one element into another.

He had, in fact, changed nitrogen into oxygen. Admittedly, the amount of oxygen produced, some 20 parts per million, was minute, and the technique used, involving high-energy radiation, did not resemble in the slightest the procedures of the alchemists. But the experiment refuted the insistence of most scientists that transmutation was impossible, and all aspiring alchemists took heart.

It was in fact already known that transmutation took place in nature. The radioactive elements gradually 'decay', giving off radiation and producing further radioactive 'daughter' elements, which in turn decay. After a series of decays the end product, lead, is formed.

What Rutherford had done was to reverse the process. He had bombarded nitrogen gas with radiation consisting of fast-moving nuclei from the gas helium and had produced oxygen and hydrogen. The experiment can be expressed very simply in terms of atomic numbers (the chemical properties of each element are determined by its atomic number, which is the number of protons in its nucleus):

$$N(7) + He(2) = O(8) + H(1)$$

What every alchemist now asked himself was whether a similar kind of sum could be used

Opposite, top: the directors of the *Société Alchimique et Astrologique de France* in their laboratory in 1903. Despite the discoveries of 19th-century chemistry and physics, alchemy refused to die. The magazine that featured this picture said: 'To turn astrology into a true science, in which there is no room for fantasy – this is what they preach in their journal, *Rosa Alchemica*'

Opposite, below: the young Adolf Hitler (far left), with his patron, Erich Ludendorff. In association with Franz Tausend (centre), Ludendorff formed Company 164 to 'manufacture' gold. As a result they were able to divert 400,000 marks into Nazi Party funds. Tausend set up his gold-production laboratory at a quarry near Munich (right)

as a guide to the conversion of lead (82) into gold (79). Or perhaps another element might be a better starting point?

One of those who took renewed inspiration from the results of this experiment was a 36-year-old chemical worker in Munich, Franz Tausend. He had a theory about the structure of the elements that was a peculiar blend of the beliefs of Pythagoras, who had regarded the Universe as a combination of musical harmonies, and the discoveries of modern chemistry.

Tausend had published a pamphlet called *180 elements, their atomic weight, and their incorporation in a system of harmonic periods.* He believed that every atom had a frequency of vibration characteristic of that element, related to the weight of the atom's nucleus and to the grouping of electrons in orbital rings around it. Later research showed that this part, at least, of his theory was basically true. Tausend went on, however, to suggest that matter could be 'orchestrated': by adding the right substance to an element, it should be possible to change its vibration frequency into that of another element.

In 1924 Adolf Hitler was sent to prison for attempting to organise an armed uprising; one of his fellow conspirators, General Erich Ludendorff, was acquitted and in the following year stood for election as President of the German Republic. After being resoundingly defeated by the national hero Hindenburg, he turned his attention to raising funds for the infant Nazi Party. There were rumours in government circles that a certain Tausend had succeeded in making gold by transmutation, and Ludendorff got together a group of industrialists and businessmen to investigate the matter.

On Tausend's instructions one of the group, the merchant Stremmel, purchased the necessary materials – mainly iron oxide and quartz. They were melted together in a crucible, which Stremmel then took to his hotel bedroom for the night so that it could not be tampered with. In the morning, Tausend heated the crucible again in his electric furnace, in the presence of his visitors, and then added a small quantity of white powder to the molten mass. When the crucible had cooled it was broken open, and a gold nugget weighing a quarter of an ounce (7 grams) was found inside.

Financing the Nazis

Ludendorff was overjoyed and immediately set about forming a company, which he called 'Company 164' – a number that, intriguingly, is twice the atomic number of lead. Ludendorff was to receive 75 per cent of the profits and Tausend 5 per cent. Investment money poured in and within a year the General had managed to divert some 400,000 marks into Nazi Party funds. Then, in December 1926, he resigned, leaving Tausend to handle all the debts. Nevertheless, Tausend contrived to continue raising money and on 16 June 1928 allegedly made 25 ounces (723 grams) of gold in a single

Atomic alchemy

Rutherford's work strengthened the conviction of orthodox scientists that the methods of the alchemists could never lead to the transmutation of elements. It was found that the atom has a central nucleus consisting of particles called protons, with positive electrical charge, and an equal or greater number of neutrons, lacking charge. Relatively light negatively charged electrons orbit the nucleus and fix the atom's chemical properties. The number of electrons is equal to the number of protons in the nucleus, so that the atom's positive and negative electrical charges balance.

So to change one element into another it is necessary to change the number of protons in the nucleus of each atom. The nucleus must be bombarded with fast-moving particles – either to force in additional protons or to disrupt the atom so that it loses protons. Today physicists use particles artificially accelerated by 'atom-smashing' machines. And they insist that chemical processes affect only the outer electrons, not the atom's deep interior.

Above: a modern particle-accelerating device

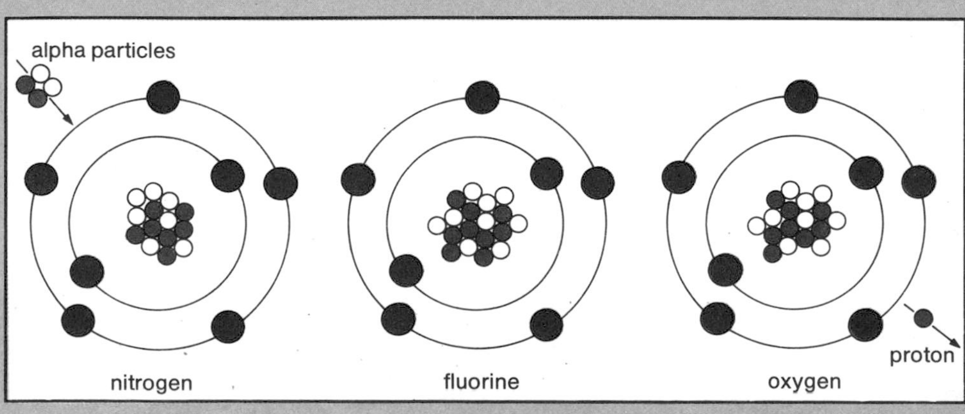

Left: Rutherford bombarded nitrogen atoms (seven protons, seven neutrons) with alpha particles (two protons bound to two neutrons), forming fluorine atoms (nine protons, nine neutrons). These lost a proton, forming a type of oxygen (eight protons, nine neutrons)

operation. On the strength of this he was able to issue a series of share certificates, each to the value of 22 pounds (10 kilograms) of gold.

But when, a year or so later, no more gold had been produced, Tausend was arrested for fraud; and on 5 February 1931, after a sensational trial, he was found guilty and sentenced to four years' imprisonment. While awaiting trial he had succeeded in producing gold under strict supervision in the Munich Mint – but the evidence was contested in court and did not save him.

The same fate was to befall a Polish engineer named Dunikovski who, in the same year that Tausend was convicted, announced in Paris that he had discovered a new kind of radiation – 'z-rays' – which would transmute quartz into gold. The mineral, spread on copper plates, was melted by an electric discharge at 110,000 volts, and was then irradiated with the z-rays.

The world was becoming accustomed to new types of radiation with remarkable properties. X-rays had been discovered a few decades before. Three kinds of radiation – alpha, beta and gamma – had been identified in the emissions from radioactive substances. Intense 'cosmic' radiations had been discovered bombarding the Earth from space.

Rays with miraculous properties were a staple of futuristic fiction. The public was ready to believe that gold-creating rays could exist – even if their nature was rather inadequately explained by Dunikovski. Investors poured some two million francs into his process.

But within a few months, when no gold was forthcoming, he also was tried and found guilty of fraud. After two years in prison his lawyer succeeded in obtaining his release, and Dunikovski went with his family to San Remo in Italy, where he resumed his experiments.

Soon there were rumours that he was supporting himself by the occasional sale of lumps of gold. His lawyer, accompanied by the eminent chemist Albert Bonn, set out for San Remo to see for himself.

It was found that the quartz being used by Dunikovski already contained minute amounts of gold; but whereas the usual methods of extraction produced gold in quantities of only 10 parts per million, Dunikovski's methods yielded almost one hundred times as much. Each experiment, however, involved only minute quantities of quartz, so the quantity of gold produced was very small.

In October 1936 Dunikovski demonstrated his process before an invited group of scientists. He was very secretive about his apparatus, but gave a theoretical explanation that is reminiscent of the primitive origins of alchemy. He proposed that all minerals contained 'embryonic atoms' undergoing a transformation that in nature took many thousands of years to complete. He claimed that his process merely accelerated the natural growth of embryonic gold in quartz.

Making gold from sand

The demonstration attracted considerable attention and an Anglo-French syndicate was formed, which was to bring sand from Africa and treat it in a big new laboratory on the south coast of England. But the Second World War broke out and little more was heard of Dunikovski. There were rumours that he had established a factory on the Swiss-French border, and there were stories that when the Germans occupied France they manufactured gold to bolster their failing economy – but there is no proof.

There have been, and still are, many more practitioners of alchemy in the 20th century. One was Archibald Cockren, who was killed when a bomb struck his tiny laboratory during the blitz on London. He was a respected osteopath who practised gold therapy. He began his investigations with the metal antimony, then turned his attention to iron, copper, silver, mercury and gold. Then:

> I entered upon a new course of experiment, with a metal . . .with which I had had no previous experience. This metal, after being reduced to its salts

Above: an engraving from the 17th-century alchemical work *Atalanta fugiens*, illustrating the ubiquitous nature of the Philosopher's Stone. It may be of significance that the form of the Stone shown here could represent crystals of salt or sand

Left: the Polish engineer Dunikovski, escorted by police officers, leaves the Paris polytechnic where he had been demonstrating his alchemical process while awaiting trial for fraud

Above right: wringing out canvas sheets that have been spread to collect the morning dew. This illustration is from the alchemical treatise called *Mutus liber*

Right: Armand Barbault followed the directions of *Mutus liber* in his 20th-century alchemical work

and undergoing special preparation and distillation, delivered up the Mercury of the Philosophers, the Aqua Benedicta, the Aqua Coelestis, the Water of Paradise. The first intimation I had of this triumph was a violent hissing, jets of vapour pouring from the retort and into the receiver, like sharp bursts from a machine gun, and then a violent explosion, whilst a very potent and subtle odour filled the laboratory and its surroundings. . . .

Whatever Cockren's true achievement, nearly all his discoveries were lost in the bomb blast that killed him. A liquid that he called 'oil of gold' was used in later years, however, for medical purposes.

Postwar alchemy

Since the Second World War, much of the publicly known activity in alchemy has been centred in France. Apart from Eugène Canseliet, who claimed to have been a pupil of the mysterious Fulcanelli, and who has been seen on television at work in his laboratory, there were others such as the writer Roger Caro and the painter Louis Cattiaux.

But undoubtedly the most notorious was Armand Barbault. An essential part of the Barbault process was the gathering of dew in canvas sheets every morning between 21 March and 24 June. This is not a new idea: it is shown in the wordless book of engravings known as the *Mutus liber* ('silent book'), and it is recommended by Salmon in his *Polygraphica*: 'If you are indeed an Artist, you may by this turn all metals into their first matter.' Barbault described his first matter as a 'germ', which grew in black earth.

It is time to ask whether there might be any truth in the tales of the alchemists. Did competent scientists such as van Helmont, Schweitzer and Boyle really witness the transmutation of a base metal into gold? Did Archibald Cockren isolate the ideal 'mercury' and 'sulphur' sought by the alchemists? And did Tausend and Dunikovski really succeed in producing gold from quartz?

Although the ancient alchemists could not possibly have had access to sources of energy sufficient to perform Rutherford's transmutation, perhaps they had some kind of intuitive understanding of what could happen. We wrote Rutherford's experiment as:

$$N(7) + He(2) = O(8) + H(1)$$

Now look at the three alchemical essentials postulated by Paracelsus: sulphur (symbol S, atomic number 16), mercury (symbol Hg, atomic number 80) and salt (sodium chloride, symbol NaCl – the atomic numbers of sodium and chlorine are 11 and 17, respectively). We can write a hypothetical reaction among these three as follows:

$$NaCl(28) + S(16) = NaS(27) + Cl(17)$$
$$NaS(27) + Hg(80) = Au(79) + NaCl(28)$$

Salt and sulphur are added together; chlorine gas is given off (to the alchemists this would simply have been 'air'); when mercury is added, the result is the original salt – and gold (Au).

The atomic numbers balance impressively. However, this is not the sort of reaction that ordinarily takes place in the chemical laboratory, where everything is either solid, liquid or gaseous. But there is a fourth state of matter, called plasma, in which atoms lose or gain electrons and can take part in chemical reactions that are impossible for them in their normal state. One of the easiest ways to produce a stream of plasma is to burn salt in the flame of the mundane Bunsen burner. Could this give a hint as to how the alchemists might have succeeded in bringing about 'impossible' reactions?

In our present state of knowledge, these are mere games with numbers. But they may bear further examination. Cockren began his research with antimony (Sb), but achieved his successes with 'a metal . . . with which I had had no previous experience.' He might have been referring to silicon (Si), which is not, in fact, a metal but a metalloid, belonging in a group of elements comprising carbon, germanium, tin and lead. It is the essential component of quartz, which is an almost pure compound of silicon and oxygen, silicon dioxide. We can easily write another 'Rutherford equation':

$$Si(14) + Si(14) + Sb(51) = Au(79)$$

A chance relationship among these atomic numbers? Or a guide to a possible gold-producing process involving silicon and antimony?

It seems improbable, despite the testimony that has accumulated over the centuries, that physical transmutation of a base metal into gold was ever achieved by any alchemist. But did those alchemists, striving to make themselves one with God, perhaps gain some intuitive understanding of the structure of matter? And when they described the Philosopher's Stone as 'the vilest and meanest of things . . . cast away and rejected by all', were they speaking of silicon dioxide – known to us as ordinary sand?

PART 4

UFOs: WHERE DO THEY COME FROM?

PART 4

UFOs: WHERE DO THEY COME FROM?

Contents

Introduction

THE TITLES ON ANY SHELF of UFO books – *Flying saucers from outer space*, *Spacecraft from beyond the sun*, *Flying saucers from the moon*, *UFO contact from the Pleiades* – bear witness to the generally held belief that if UFOs exist at all, they come from somewhere beyond our Earth. Moreover, the hypotheses of their speculative authors are supported by people who claim to have spoken with the creatures who fly the UFOs; though surprisingly human-like in appearance and behaviour, they invariably identify themselves as coming from one of the other planets of our solar system or some more exotic part of the universe.

Unfortunately, everything we learn about UFOs on the one hand, and our universe on the other, tends to make these claims more suspect. Early accounts often designated the moon as their place of origin, and George Adamski was taken on a flight during which he saw the cities and fauna of the hidden face of our satellite. Today, now that our own spacecraft have landed there, his story seems even less credible than it did at the time. True, there exists a school of thought which insists that we never went to the moon. And there are others who, though prepared to admit that we probably did get there, point out that we have visited only a minute fraction of its surface, and have no more valid a right to describe conditions there than would a traveller from space whose only visit to Earth had been a landing in the Sahara Desert. But if UFOs do not come from other worlds – as many have claimed – what other explanations are there?

In the first years of the UFO era, it was naturally assumed by the two leading participants in the Cold War that the UFOs represented some dramatic technological breakthrough on the part of their potential foe. It was well known that German scientists had been working on some very advanced, if not always very realistic, devices towards the end of the Second World War, and the Americans and Russians were eager to see if there was anything of value in these experiments. So when in June 1952 an extraordinary UFO sighting was reported in the Soviet zone of Germany, it was natural for Antony Terry, Berlin correspondent for Kemsley Newspapers, to inquire in his headline, 'Are the flying saucers Russian owned?'

It soon became clear that the answer was no. Neither of the big powers had the resources to produce devices of such capability, nor in such numbers as were now being reported from all over the globe. Perhaps the most impressive hypothesis was that of Italian writer Renato Vesco who, in three deeply-researched volumes, argued that the source of the UFOs was neither America nor Russia, but 'the great absentee of the space race', Britain, who had developed the devices and was testing them in the vast and largely inaccessible Canadian wastelands. Vesco offered a wealth of fascinating detail which suggested a great deal of clandestine activity of a very intriguing nature; what he failed to demonstrate was why, if Britain *was* the source, so many UFOs should be seen in the airspace of rival nations, where a forced landing would put priceless information into the captor's hands.

No more convincing are the theories of those who have proposed that UFOs are operating from secret bases here on Earth – from the mountains of Tibet, the ocean floor or Antarctica. One of ufology's most beguiling tales is that of Albert Bender, a prominent flying saucer buff, who in 1953 was running a large UFO organisation when he came to believe he had discovered 'the secret of the saucers'. He sent his ideas by mail to a colleague; next thing he knew, three strange entities materialised in his room and told him that, yes, he had indeed stumbled on their secret, but he must keep his finding quiet, withdraw from ufology and disband his organisation. All of this he obediently did, and was rewarded by being taken to the secret UFO bases in Antarctica.

Others have claimed to locate UFO bases nearer home. At the time of the 1977 Welsh flap (period showing a high incidence of UFO sighting reports), author Peter Paget suggested that Stack Rock, off the Dyfed coast, was a UFO base; however, though he was only a few kilometres from the greatest news story of all time, he managed to stifle his curiosity and never visited the island to check his claim.

The fact that many UFOs have been reported as emerging from the sea has suggested to some speculators that there are subterranean UFO bases. This proposal is frequently linked with the Bermuda Triangle: French author Jean Prachan, in his *Le Triangle des Bermudes – base secrète des OVNIs*, makes out a plausible if ultimately unconvincing case. However, the idea is intrinsically less improbable than that which proposes that flying saucers are from the Earth's interior, linking UFOs to that splendid old theory, the hollow Earth.

Most such suggestions are made in a more or less scientific spirit, their authors trying valiantly to parade solid evidence for their hypotheses. There is, however, another class of UFO theorists who rely on simple assertion, with little or no factual back-up. This class ascribes the UFOs to divine or diabolic sources. Billy Graham is just one of those who have wondered if UFOs are 'God's chariots' with crews of angels. This school of thought is far outnumbered by those who believe they are piloted by demonic beings, helping to prepare Earth for the coming of the Antichrist. Such ideas are particularly popular in that home of far-out beliefs, California: *UFOs – satanic terror* is one of many titles supporting this view.

The failure of these authors to produce anything in the way of solid evidence to support their assertions has persuaded many theorists to swing to the opposite extreme. The champions of 'the new ufology' tend to adopt one variant or another of the 'psycho-social hypothesis' which can be loosely summarised as holding that UFOs exist only in the mind – though in the mind of society as a whole as much as that of the individual. This is not of course to dismiss the UFOs altogether, for if it should be shown that hallucination is indeed taking place on this astonishing scale, then it constitutes a sociological phenomenon of the most alarming significance. The most daring proponent of these ideas is probably French ufologist Jacques Vallée, who has offered us the suggestion that the entire UFO phenomenon is a psycho-social artefact, deliberately engineered by some machiavellian power for a sinister purpose which we lesser beings can only guess at.

Even if we are reluctant to go along with such dramatic conspiracy theories, we can hardly deny that there is a substantial psychological element in many UFO sightings; many witnesses give indications of mental instability, which makes it reasonable to suppose that though they may be sincere in their beliefs about what happened, nevertheless the UFOs they 'saw' emanated from their own minds.

The same is no doubt often true of cases where the

An artist's impression of the surface of Venus, based on television pictures connection takes us beyond psychology into parapsychology, where the witnesses are troubled by poltergeist phenomena or have strange premonitions. Once again, it is not the sincerity of the witnesses which is in doubt, but their ability to interpret what they have seen. Consequently, today's researchers are learning to check the psychological and psychical characteristics of witnesses when evaluating their reports.

Nevertheless, there is no question of 'explaining away' UFO reports, except on the part of the most determined sceptics. One consideration is that there have been too many UFOs which have resulted in physical effects such as radiation burns. Only by invoking the hypothesis of psychosomatic origin – that the mind of the witness somehow causes burns to appear on his body, just as the stigmata (wounds corresponding to those of Christ) found on the bodies of religious visionaries are attributed by some to hysteria – can one avoid the conclusion that the UFOs are physical objects capable of causing physical effects. Such an alternative explanation, though feasible, does not account for cases where there have been multiple sightings of the offending UFO. In the Cash-Landrum case of December 1980, for example, three witnesses were hospitalised as a consequence of their encounter with an object which was certainly flying and just as certainly not identified. It has been suggested that no extra-terrestrial spacecraft was involved, but a secret device in the course of testing by the American government which was malfunctioning at the time of the sighting. On the face of it, it seems highly improbable that the American government would dare to test a highly dangerous device in a public area, but the assertion is supported by the fact that the object was last seen being escorted away from the area by a fleet of helicopters, similar in design to those used by the U.S. Air Force, though the Air Force has denied involvement.

Could it have been a device of terrestrial origin? There are strong arguments against the suggestion, yet it is well known that the American government – and perhaps others – has been less than open with the public. Long ago, the FBI denied that it had ever taken any interest in UFOs, but documents recently released under the Freedom of Information Act show this to have been a downright lie. Again, the researches of Bill Moore and Stanton Friedman, for Charles Berlitz' book *The Roswell Incident*, turned up sufficient hard evidence to demonstrate that if it wasn't a crashed saucer that landed near the Mexican border in July 1947, then it was certainly *something* that the U.S. authorities were anxious to keep quiet. Perhaps the current lawsuit by the victims of the Cash-Landrum encounter, claiming damages for personal injuries from the U.S. government, will show that Renato Vesco's ideas weren't so wide of the mark after all.

Even if it should be shown that some UFOs can be attributed to truly down-to-earth sources, this is unlikely to be a valid explanation for more than a tiny percentage of reports. There are two categories in particular which defy the psycho-social explanations of the 'new ufologists' on the one hand, and the allegations of the 'conspiracy buffs' on the other.

One of these comprises those objects seen, and often photographed, in circumstances where no such explanation is plausible. In the barren wastes of Hessdalen in the almost uninhabited Norwegian uplands, enormous luminous objects have been seen moving, at so low an altitude above the ground that the neighbouring hills can be seen behind them, enabling distance and therefore size to be roughly estimated. These objects move slowly and often stand completely still – which is very helpful for the photographer: they are completely silent, and they have been seen covering a distance of many kilometres of the roughest ground in a matter of minutes. No man-made object could behave in this way, yet the fact that they have been photographed on many occasions proves that they cannot be illusions.

Probably the most reasonable explanation for UFOs of this kind lies in the area of geophysical effects. It is known that forces operating at or beneath the earth's surface can cause surprising side-effects. Some of these are purely physical, such as earthquake lights which are clearly related in some way to earthquakes, but whose nature is still unknown; and indeed, their very existence was generally denied until recently. Other effects are physiological, and lead to further, psychological, effects. Such is the 'ion-effect', whereby geophysical events may cause a dramatic increase or decrease in the number of electrically charged particles in the atmosphere, which can lead to our experiencing a variety of unusual conditions.

Perhaps, compared with alien spaceships, a geophysical explanation of this kind may seem depressingly humdrum; in fact, it would mean an exciting breakthrough in our knowledge of the universe, indicating forces as yet unrecognised by science. This is one of the reasons why ufologists believe their work to be something more than an enjoyable pastime! Moreover, a geophysical origin does not rule out effects which may seem paranormal. One Norwegian investigator of the Hessdalen lights, who has spent countless nights observing the phenomenon, is convinced that the lights not only register his presence but respond to it. Critics pooh-pooh such claims as fancies induced by over-indulgence in sky-watching, but similar claims have been made by too great a number of UFO witnesses to be lightly dismissed. If they are indeed fancies, they are fancies of a very sophisticated kind which certainly merit scientific investigation.

Finally, there remains a hard core of cases which challenge every possible effort on the part of the debunkers;those in which a number of independent witnesses see, more or less simultaneously, an object whose appearance and behaviour are far beyond anything we know, as when four persons, strangers to one another, saw an illuminated object the size of a football field gliding silently through the sky over Manchester at 6 p.m. one winter evening; or when two experienced engineers watched for twenty minutes while two silver objects manoeuvred this way and that in a cloudless sky at midday. Sightings such as these defy any explanation in terms of natural phenomena, or psycho-social illusion; the UFOs' capability shows them to be far beyond anything that human technology can achieve, yet at the same time there is nothing to indicate that they are being operated either by God's angels or by Satan's demons.

In asking of any UFO, 'Where does it come from?', we should first ask ourselves, 'Does it come from *anywhere* at all?' Could it be imaginary, a hallucination created by the witness himself in consequence of a personal emotion or a current cultural trend? If this can be ruled out and the object clearly evinces physical existence, then we should question whether the explanation of it as man-made is plausible; whether the witness saw some kind of exotic device of human origin. Alternatively, we must consider the possibility of some hitherto unknown natural phenomenon, either geophysical in origin, something like ball lightning, or organic, some undiscovered creature of the atmosphere.

If the reported object fails to fit any of these categories, then it may be that we have no alternative but to take seriously the possibility that the extra-terrestrial hypothesis, held by so many, may, despite its improbability and many contradictions, be the only acceptable explanation – that UFOs do indeed come from somewhere beyond our Earth.

HILARY EVANS

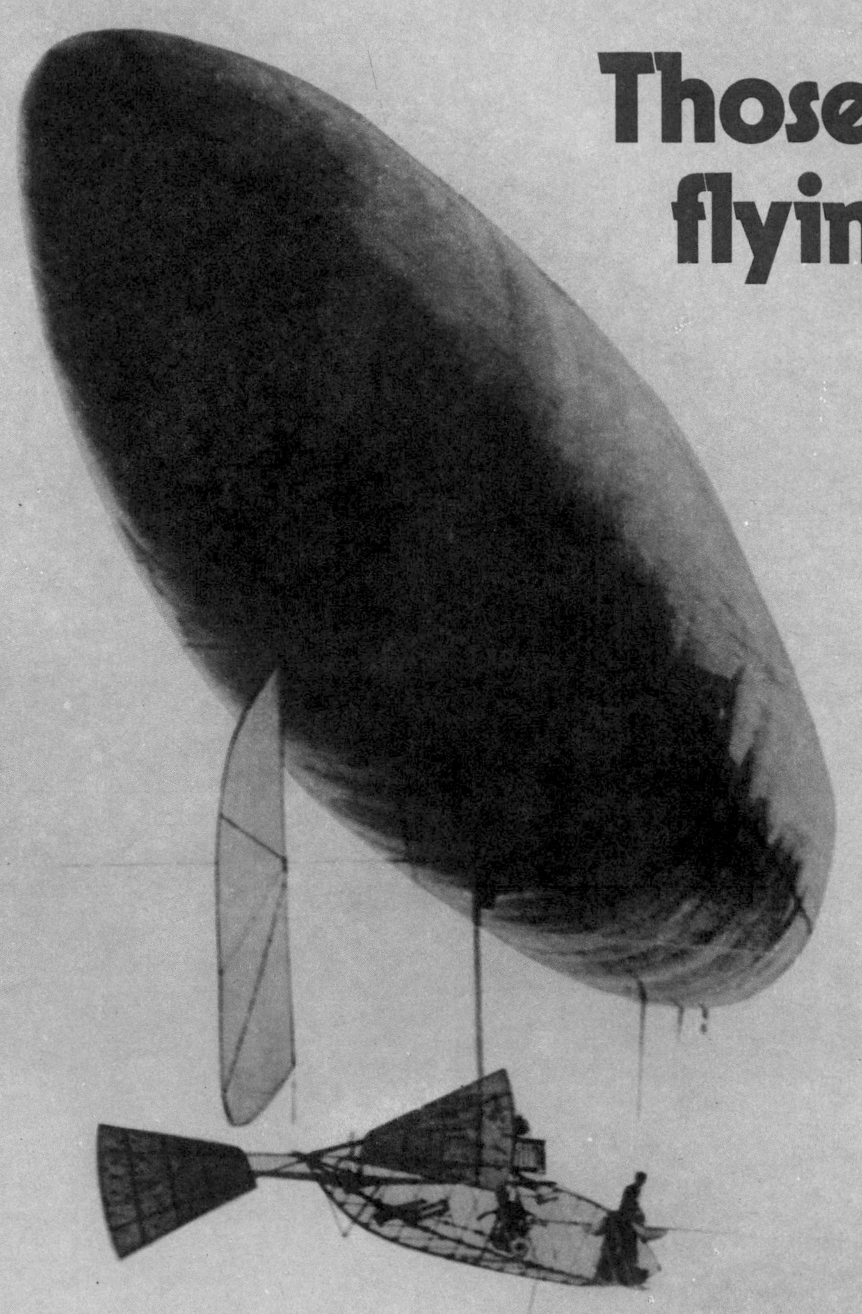

Those mysterious flying machines

The predecessors of today's unidentified flying objects were mysterious 'airships', sighted in huge numbers in the 1890s. W. A. HARBINSON suggests that they – and some later UFOs – are the creations of human engineers, working in secret at the far frontiers of aviation science

THE EXPLANATIONS OFFERED for unidentified flying objects have been numerous and varied. In past ages they have been regarded as supernatural visitants or omens, divine or demonic. In our own technological age, they are surmised to be visitors from distant civilisations in space, time-travellers, or emissaries of dwellers inside the Earth. Those who despair of finding evidence for such conjectures speculate that UFOs might be thought forms created by those who perceive them, or that they are the results of governmental manipulation of mass psychology. Scientific debunkers insist that they are misinterpreted natural phenomena or conventional aircraft. But when military spokesmen comment, they always exclude the possibility that they might be *accurately* perceived aircraft – aircraft of remarkable capabilities, intended to remain hidden from the eyes of the public.

Above: a non-rigid airship built by Santos-Dumont of France at the turn of the century. Nothing as advanced as this was publicly known in the USA, where mysterious airships were then being sighted

Right: an aerial object seen over California in 1896, as portrayed in a local newspaper. Witnesses saw a dark body above a brilliant light, apparently descending

The UFO sightings of much earlier times might have been natural phenomena of a kind that would have baffled and frightened people less technically developed than ourselves: phenomena such as sun dogs, comets, meteors, noctilucent clouds, ball lightning, mirages, and so forth. But there is considerable evidence to support the suggestion that the modern wave of 'flying saucer' sightings may be based on a new factor: flying machines constructed *here on Earth*.

The first 'modern' UFO sightings were the 'mystery airships' that were seen by thousands of people all over the United States between November 1896 and May 1897. At that time, European inventors were far ahead of their American counterparts in airship experimentation, but neither the French nor the Germans had managed to design an airship that could do much more than hover helplessly. Not until 1904 was the first dirigible – Thomas Baldwin's *California Arrow* – flown, in Oakland, California. Consequently, the mystery airships of 1896 and 1897 were then as inexplicable and frightening as are the UFOs today.

Significantly, the mystery airships were invariably reported as being cylindrical or cigar shaped, and driven by a motor attached

to a propeller – in short, they were exactly like the forthcoming airships. They were manned by human beings, not by creatures from another world. In fact, their occupants were often reported to have talked to the witnesses, usually asking them for water for their machine. Perhaps the most intriguing of all such cases were those involving a man who called himself Wilson.

Top: in 1900 the world's conception of air travel was still dominated by the image of the airship. Here an artist imagines an aerial ironclad of the year 2000, suspended from a somewhat vulnerable gasbag and battling with aeroplanes and ships

Above: one of Samuel Pierpont Langley's designs for a pilotless aeroplane, powered by a light petrol engine. Some of his small aircraft were successful, but in 1903 two of his full-scale planes crashed. The discouraged Langley died a few years later, the butt of the nation's newspapers

Landing in a pasture

The Houston *Post* of 21 April 1897 carried an account of the first Wilson incident. It had occurred in Beaumont, Texas, two days before, when J. B. Ligon, the local agent for Magnolia Brewery, and his son noticed lights in a neighbour's pasture a few hundred yards away. They went to investigate and came upon four men standing beside a 'large, dark object', which neither of the witnesses could see clearly. One of the men asked Ligon for a bucket of water. Ligon gave it to him and the man gave his name as Mr Wilson. He then told Ligon that he and his friends were travelling in a flying machine, that they had taken a trip 'out of the Gulf' and that they were returning to the 'quiet Iowa town' where the airship and four others like it had been constructed. When asked, Wilson explained that the wings of the airship were powered by electricity. Then he and his friends got back into the passenger car at the bottom of the airship and Ligon and his son watched it ascend and fly away.

The next day, 20 April, Sheriff H. W. Baylor of Uvalde, also in Texas, went to investigate a strange light and voices behind his house. He encountered an airship and three men – and one of the men gave his name as Wilson, from Goshen, New York. Wilson then enquired about one C. C. Akers, former Sheriff of Zavalia County, saying that he had met him in Fort Worth in 1877 and now wanted to see him again. Sheriff Baylor, surprised, replied that Akers was now at Eagle Pass and Wilson, apparently disappointed, asked to be remembered to him the next time Sheriff Baylor visited him. The men from the airship asked for water and requested that their visit be kept a secret from the townspeople. Then they climbed into the passenger car of the airship, and 'its great wings and fans were set in motion and it sped away northward in the direction of San Angelo.' The county clerk also claimed to have seen the airship as it left the area.

Two days later, in Josserand, Texas, a 'whirring sound' awakened a farmer, Frank Nichols, who looked out of his window and saw 'brilliant lights streaming from a ponderous vessel of strange proportions' in his cornfield. Nichols went outside to investigate, but before he reached the object two men walked up to him and asked if they could have water from his well. Nichols agreed, and the men then invited him to view the airship. He noticed that there were six to eight crew members. One of these told him that the ship's motive power was 'highly condensed electricity' and that it was one of five that had been constructed 'in a small town in Iowa' with the backing of a large company in New York.

The next day, 23 April, witnesses described by the *Post* as 'two responsible men' reported that an airship had descended where they lived in Kountze, Texas, and that two of the occupants had given their names as Jackson and . . . Wilson.

On 27 April the Galveston *Daily News* printed a letter from C. C. Akers, who claimed that he had indeed known a man in Fort Worth named Wilson, that Wilson was from New York, and that he was 'of a mechanical turn of mind and was then working on aerial navigation and something that would astonish the world.'

The German engineer Otto Lilienthal flying one of his biplane gliders. Lilienthal was the first inventor to build and fly successful controllable aircraft. He steered by shifting his dangling body and legs from side to side. He was killed in a flying accident in 1896, soon after this flight. His successes inspired other pioneers, including the Wright brothers

Sighting at Deadwood

Subsequently, the Houston *Post* reported that in Deadwood, Texas, a farmer called H. C. Lagrone had heard his horse bucking as if about to run amok. Going outside he saw a bright white light circling around the fields nearby and illuminating the entire area before descending and landing in one of the fields. Walking to the landing spot, Lagrone found a crew of five men, three of whom talked to him while the others collected water in rubber bags. The men informed Lagrone that their airship was one of five that had been flying around the country recently, that theirs was the same vessel that had landed in Beaumont in the first incident, and that all the ships had been constructed in 'an interior town in Illinois' (which borders Iowa). They were reluctant to say anything more because they had not yet taken out any patents on their machine.

By May, the mysterious airship sightings had stopped. What lay behind them? Could such airships have been financed by a powerful company in New York and constructed secretly in the wilds of Iowa or Illinois?

That is certainly a possibility. In the late 1890s numerous inventors in the United States obtained patents for planned airships. But since most of them worried constantly about the possible theft or plagiarism of their designs, they also kept many of their ideas secret. Knowing this, many Americans came to believe that Wilson and his friends had indeed invented successful airships.

Experimentation in aerodynamics was highly advanced by the 1890s, particularly in Massachusetts (an area having numerous

Other mystery airships

The American mystery airship wave began in November 1896, when citizens of Sacramento, California, watched a light moving through the night sky. Further sightings came in from all parts of California throughout the month, with a few from farther north, in Washington state and Canada. A dark shape supporting the light could sometimes be glimpsed: it was shaped like a cigar, a barrel or an egg. The airship's motion was invariably slow, and often undulating, suggesting a wind-blown craft. Some newspapers named the inventors who, they speculated, could be responsible. Others floated the idea that the 'airships' were visitors from Mars. Occasionally airships were seen on the ground: in one such case two Methodist ministers saw a 'fiery object' taking off as they approached. Three strange beings, very tall and with bald heads, allegedly attempted to kidnap two men on a country road, and then fled in a cigar-shaped craft.

After a two-month lull the sightings again came thick and fast from all over the United States and Canada. At one point, each day saw a score of reports coming in. A citizen of Michigan reported that a voice from above the clouds asked him for four dozen egg sandwiches and a pot of coffee – which were duly hauled up to the unseen craft in a scoop. The main 'flap' was over by mid 1897. But later in the year there were isolated sightings from other parts of the world, including Sweden, Norway and Russia.

mystery airship sightings) and New York, reportedly Wilson's home city. At the Massachusetts Institute of Technology (MIT) there were plenty of informal courses on propulsion and the behaviour of fluids, which is relevant to aerodynamics. By 1896, instructors and students at MIT had built a wind tunnel and were experimenting with it to get practical knowledge of aerodynamics. A man such as Wilson could have attended those courses and then gone on to Cornell University in Ithica, New York, where by the mid 1890s it was possible to obtain a bachelor's degree in aeronautics.

Pioneers in the public eye

Cornell University was noted for its courses in aerodynamics. One of the men who gave a series of lectures at the college in 1897 and 1898 was Octave Chanute, the world-famous engineer. In 1896 he had emulated the successful manned hang glider experiments of the German engineer Otto Lilienthal. The courses included experimental engineering, mechanical and electrical engineering, and machine design and construction. Aeronautical texts would have included the Smithsonian Institute's *Experiments in aerodynamics* (1891), Sir Hiram Maxim's reports on his experiments with engines, propellers and aircraft designs (1893), and the *Aeronautical Annual*, which contained highly innovative contributions from most of the leading aeronautical scientists.

By 1896 the first successful flights of S.P. Langley's flying machines took place in Washington, DC. By the following year numerous patents for other flying machines had been registered.

The scientific advances of the last decade of the 19th century were of staggering magnitude, and laid the ground work for advanced aeronautical experimentation. If a particularly dedicated team of scientists were working on an airship project in secrecy, it

Above: the *Flyer*, built by the Wright brothers, takes off on its first brief journey and inaugurates a new age. Four flights were made on that day, 17 December 1903. They were the first sustained, powered and controlled flights known to history. But could other inventors working in secret have anticipated the Wrights and been responsible for the earlier 'airship' sightings?

Right: Louis Blériot's Number XI flying machine above the cliffs of Dover at the end of the prize-winning cross-Channel flight on 25 July 1909

becomes possible that the sightings all over the country during that period were of man-made flying machines.

No more was heard of the mysterious Mr Wilson. But the following years saw an extraordinarily fast advance in aeronautics. By 1901 Santos-Dumont had flown an airship from St-Cloud to the Eiffel Tower and back in less than 30 minutes; two years later, at Kitty Hawk, North Carolina, the Wright brothers made the first known heavier-than-air manned flight; and by 1906 the American Robert Goddard had begun his experiments in rocketry. On the last day of December 1908, Wilbur Smith flew 77 miles (123 kilometres) in two hours and thirty minutes. Seven months later, the French aviator Louis Blériot flew across the English Channel from Calais to Dover.

Since these were all highly publicised achievements, is it possible that even greater advances were being made away from the public gaze? The numerous UFO sightings of the early 20th century, and the rapid pace of technological development suggest that this may have been so. In 1904, US Navy Lieutenant Frank H. Schofield – later to be Commander in Chief of the US Pacific Fleet – officially reported seeing, from the deck of his ship, three bright lights that were travelling in echelon, remained above the clouds, and *ascended* before disappearing. In 1909 numerous unidentified aircraft were reported over Massachusetts. On 30 August 1919, at about 9 p.m., a long black object flew low over Madison Square, New York city, and was witnessed by hundreds of people. The nature and origin of this object was also never determined.

Scandinavian ghost planes

In 1933 and 1934 what would now be called a UFO 'flap' occurred over Scandinavia. 'Ghost planes' were reported on scores of occasions. They frequently appeared, or were heard, flying overhead in 'impossible' conditions for the aircraft of that time. They were described as monoplanes, usually grey in colour. Sometimes their crews could be glimpsed. Often their engines would cut out, and the aircraft would glide for long periods before their power was turned on again – an unlikely feat for conventional aircraft. Sometimes brilliant searchlights would be directed from them onto the ground below.

In 1934 the Swedish Air Force began a thorough search of the remote areas from which the ghost plane reports were emanating. Twenty-four aircraft took part in the search, and two of them crashed during it. No traces were found of the bases that would be required to support the activities of the intruders. In April 1934 a high-ranking Swedish military officer stated to the press:

> Comparison of these reports shows that there can be no doubt about illegal air traffic over our secret military areas. . . . In every case the same remark has been noted: no insignias or identifying marks were visible on the machine. . . . It is impossible to explain away the whole thing as imagination. The question is: Who are they? And why have they been invading our air territory?

The same questions were being asked in Norway and Finland, where similar sightings were occurring. But they were never satisfactorily answered.

The 'aeronautical age' outgrew its infancy in a few brief decades. Aeronautics advanced from its first crude experiments with wind tunnels in Massachusetts to the highly complex rocket research at Peenemünde that led to the V-2. On the principle that all scientific research remembles an iceberg – nine-tenths hidden from public view – the possibility arises that secret research in America, Europe, or both, had led to the construction of machines much more powerful and unorthodox in design than those that were officially put into use. Certainly it is a fact that from the First World War onward, more and more technological research was being financed and controlled by governments interested mainly in the military applications of such research.

Is it possible that citizens of the United States and some European countries had witnessed the clandestine aeronautical experiments of their own leaders?

The pace of aviation development accelerated during the Second World War. Jet aircraft, radar navigation and detection, ballistic missiles and bombers of unprecedented size appeared in response to the desperate necessities of the combatants. And sightings of mysterious 'aircraft' entered a new phase, in the skies over embattled Germany.

Only 40 years after the Wright brothers' first flight, air warfare had advanced to the point where the first rocket propelled, long range ballistic missiles were being readied for use against cities. Here three experimental V-2 rockets stand on their trailers at the Nazis' Peenemünde research centre

The UFO goes to war

Flying discs were built by the Nazis and later by the victorious powers. This chapter describes these unconventional craft and asks whether, despite military denials, man-made saucers are behind many UFO reports

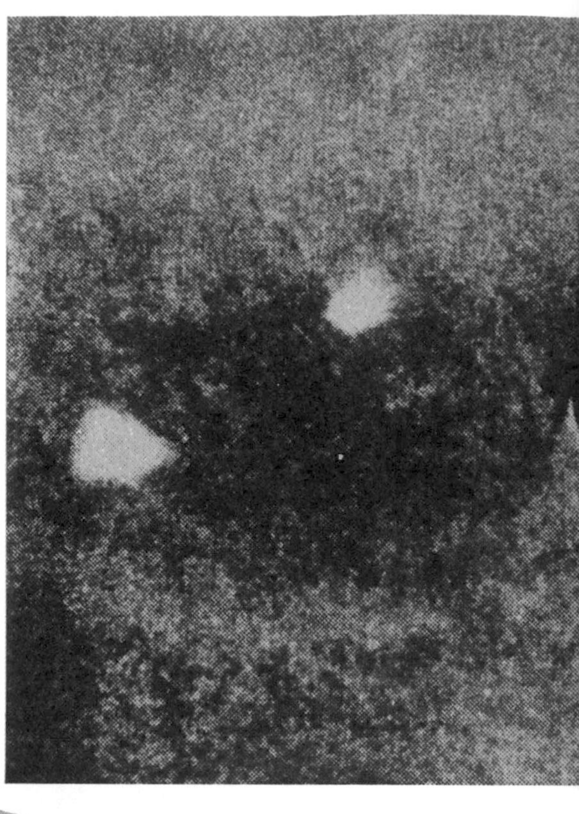

'THE NAZIS HAVE THROWN something new into the night skies over Germany. It is the weird, mysterious "foo fighter" balls which race alongside the wings of Beaufighters flying intruder missions over Germany. Pilots have been encountering this eerie weapon for more than a month in their night flights. No one apparently knows what this sky weapon is. The "balls of fire" appear suddenly and accompany the planes for miles. They seem to be radio-controlled from the ground. . . .' The sightings referred to in this news story showed remarkable

similarities. Lieutenant Schlueter of the 415th US Night Fighter Squadron reported being harassed by 'ten small balls of reddish fire' on the night of 23 November 1944 when flying over the Rhine. Pilots Henry Giblin and Walter Cleary reported that on the night of 27 September 1944 they had been harassed in the vicinity of Speyer by 'an enormous burning light' that was flying above their aircraft at about 250 miles per hour (400 km/h). The mass of UFO reports agreed on two major points: the foo fighters invariably appeared to *ascend* towards the aircraft from the ground; and they usually caused the aircraft's ignition systems to malfunction. Other reports, unconfirmed by the Allied forces, suggested that the malfunctioning of the ignition systems had actually caused some aircraft to crash.

At first the Allies thought that the foo fighters were static electricity charges. This theory disproven, they then began to think that they were either German or Japanese secret weapons designed to foul the ignition systems of the bombers. Another theory was that the objects had been designed purely as psychological warfare weapons, sent aloft to confuse and unnerve Allied pilots. Finally, both the RAF and the US Eighth Army, unable to solve the mystery, concluded officially that the foo fighters were the product of 'mass hallucination'. However, the cause was never discovered – officially, at any rate.

The foo fighters disappeared from the skies a few weeks before the end of the war. The next wave of UFO sightings occurred in Western Europe and Scandinavia, where from 1946 to 1948 many people, including airline pilots and radar operatives, reported seeing strange cigar- or disc-shaped objects in the skies. On 21 June 1947 Harold Dahl reported seeing saucer-shaped objects flying towards the Canadian border. Three days later Kenneth Arnold made his more famous sighting of saucer-shaped objects over the Cascades, also flying towards the Canadian border. There was much speculation that both the Soviets and the Americans, utilising the men and material captured in the secret research plants of Nazi Germany, were developing advanced disc-shaped aircraft.

Speculation that there might be a connection between Nazi secret weapons and the flying saucers increased when various West German newspapers and magazines began publishing articles during the mid 1950s about one *Flugkapitän* Rudolf Schriever. According to these reports this former Luftwaffe aeronautical engineer had designed, in the spring of 1941, the prototype for a 'flying top', which was test-flown in June 1942. With his colleagues Habermohl, Miethe and Bellonzo, he constructed a larger version of the original 'flying disc' in the summer of 1944. At the BMW plant near Prague they then redesigned the larger model, replacing its former engines with advanced jets.

A brief description of *Projekt Saucer* and the aborted flying saucer is given in Major Rudolf Lusar's important book *German secret weapons of the Second World War*:

> Habermohl and Schriever chose a wide-surface ring which rotated round a fixed, cupola-shaped cockpit. The ring consisted of adjustable wing-discs which could be brought into appropriate position for the take-off or horizontal flight, respectively. Miethe developed a discus-shaped plate of a diameter of 42 metres [138 feet], in which adjustable jets were inserted.

Other reports, which sometimes conflict in their details of the overall project, agree on the flying saucer's diameter, and that it had a height from base to canopy of 105 feet (32 metres), reached an altitude of approximately 40,000 feet (12,000 metres) and attained a horizontal flight speed of 1250 miles per hour (2000 km/h).

Rudolf Schriever himself claimed in the late 1950s that he had indeed worked on a wartime research programme called *Projekt*

Above: a rare photograph of foo fighters in company with Allied planes during the Second World War. Some aircrew described the mysterious spheres as being like silver Christmas tree decorations. The nickname came from the 'Smokey Stover' comic strip, popular at the time, in which the phrase 'where there's foo, there's fire' was often used

Right: the Chance-Vought Flying Flapjack, also known as the Navy Flounder. Although it could take off nearly vertically and fly as slowly as 35 miles per hour (55 km/h), it was reported also to be capable of speeds greater than 400 miles per hour (640 km/h)

Left: the Avro Car, built for the US Air Force and US Army by the Avro-Canada company. It was designed by an English engineer, John Frost. Officially, work on it was dropped in 1960 – despite the early claim that the machine would reach twice the speed of sound

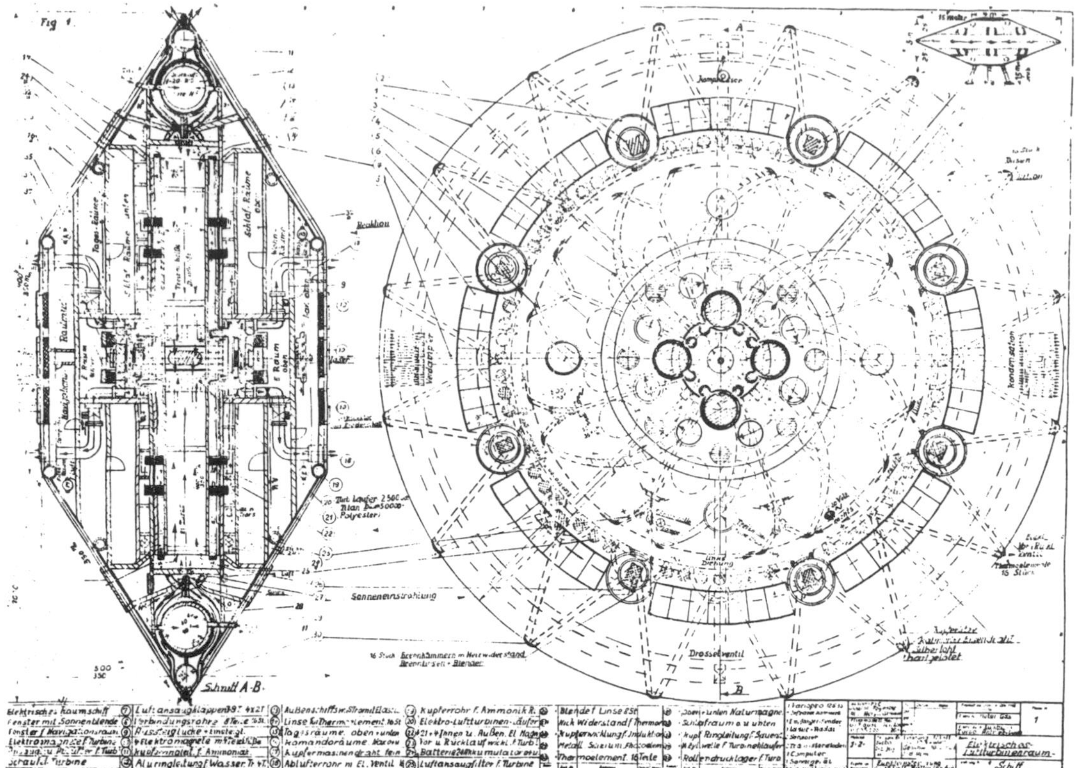

Left: blueprints for a flying saucer. According to the obscure single-issue publication *Brisant*, in which these diagrams appeared in 1978, they are plans for a disc-shaped spaceship, modified by the West German government to make them 'safe' for publication. Although 'electromagnetic turbines', 'laser-radar' and computers are indicated, the design is not a practical one. The diagrams appear in an article on Rudolf Schriever's Second World War designs, and may have been inspired by them

Saucer. His 'flying disc' had been ready for testing in early 1945, but with the advance of the Allies into Germany, the test had been cancelled, the machine destroyed, and his complete papers mislaid or stolen in the chaos of the Nazi retreat.

Schriever died not long after these revelations, convinced to the end that the UFO sightings since the end of the war were proof that his original ideas had been taken further with successful results.

But what were the foo fighters? An identification was proposed by an Italian author, Renato Vesco, in a book first published in 1968. According to him the foo fighter was actually the German *Feuerball* (Fireball), first constructed at an aeronautical establishment at Wiener Neustadt. The craft was a flat, circular flying machine, powered by a turbojet. It was used during the closing stages of the war both as an anti-radar device and as a psychological weapon designed to disturb Allied pilots. Vesco says:

> The fiery halo around its perimeter – caused by a very rich fuel mixture – and the chemical additives that interrupted the flow of electricity by overionising the atmosphere in the vicinity of the plane, generally around the wing tips or tail surfaces, subjected the H_2S radar on the plane to the action of powerful electrostatic fields and electromagnetic impulses.

Vesco also claims that the basic principles of the *Feuerball* were later applied to a much larger 'symmetrical circular aircraft' known as the *Kugelblitz* (Ball Lightning), which could rise vertically by 'jet lift'.

Since neither the British, the Americans nor the Russians are ever likely to reveal what, precisely, was discovered in the secret factories of Nazi Germany, it is worth noting that in 1945 Sir Roy Feddon, leader of a technical mission to Germany for the British Ministry of Aircraft Production, reported:

> I have seen enough of their designs and production plans to realise that if they had managed to prolong the war some months longer, we would have been confronted with a set of entirely new and deadly developments in air warfare.

In 1956, Captain Edward J. Ruppelt, then head of the US Air Force Project Blue Book, was able to state:

> When World War II ended, the Germans had several radical types of aircraft and guided missiles under development. The majority of these were in the most preliminary stages, but they were the only known craft that could even approach the performances of the objects reported by UFO observers.

Post-war saucer projects

The first concrete evidence for post-war flying saucer construction projects came in 1954. The Canadian government announced that the enormous UFO seen over Albuquerque, New Mexico, in 1951 was similar to one they had tried to build shortly after the war. Owing to their lack of adequate technology, they had eventually passed the design over to the United States.

Further evidence for United States involvement with saucer-shaped aircraft projects was to be found in the US Navy's Flying

Above: a US soldier guards a V-2 rocket, still lacking its outer skin. This vast underground factory at Nordhausen in Germany was top secret during the war, along with many others whose secrets may still not have been revealed by the Allied governments

Above right: Wernher von Braun, creator of the V-2, with senior military staff at the Peenemünde range

Flapjack. The Flapjack, also known as the Navy Flounder, was a circular aircraft, the design of which was begun during the Second World War. At that time what the Navy desperately needed was an aeroplane that could rise almost vertically so that it could take off from carriers, and could fly at as little as 35 miles per hour (55 km/h).

Little was known about that machine until early 1950, shortly after the US Air Force had ended its UFO investigation programme, Project Grudge (the forerunner to Project Blue Book). As part of an attempt to show that UFOs did not merit further investigation, the Air Force released photographs and vague information about the Flying Flapjack.

Apparently, because the aircraft was wingless, the reduced stability had presented problems. A later model, reportedly designated the XF-5-U-1, solved that problem and was rumoured to be over 100 feet (30 metres) in diameter, and to have jet nozzles – resembling the 'glowing windows' seen on so many UFOs – arranged round its rim. It was built in three layers, the central layer being slightly larger than the other two. Since the saucer's velocity and manoeuvring abilities were controlled by the power and tilt of the separate jet nozzles, there were no ailerons, rudders or other protruding surfaces. The machine was remarkably similar to those reported by UFO witnesses.

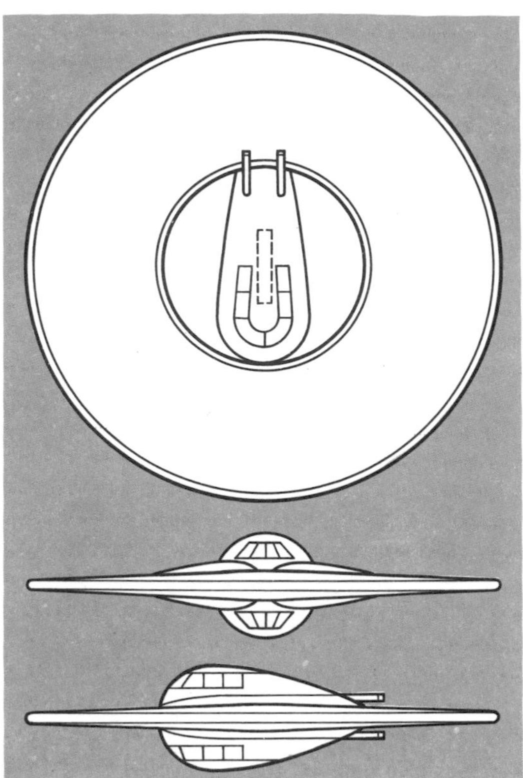

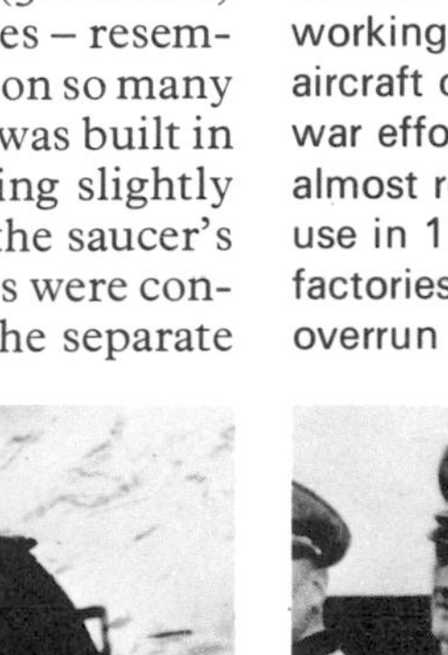

Right: a flying disc designed by Dr Miethe, one of the team of brilliant engineers working on unconventional aircraft designs for the Nazi war effort. This 'saucer' was almost ready for operational use in 1945, when the factories in Prague were overrun by the Allies

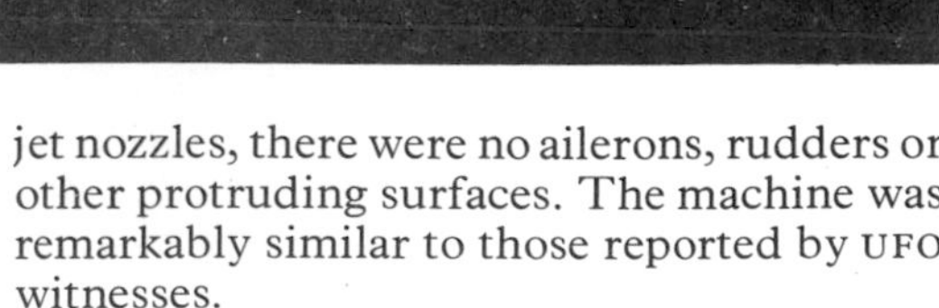

Research on saucer-shaped aircraft did not stop with the XF-5-U-1. On 11 February 1953 the Toronto *Star* reported that a new flying saucer was being developed at the Avro-Canada plant in Malton, Ontario. On 16 February the Minister for Defence Production informed the Canadian House of Commons that Avro-Canada was working on a 'mock-up model' of a flying saucer, capable of flying at 1500 miles per hour (2400 km/h) and climbing vertically. Then the president of Avro-Canada wrote in *Avro News* that the prototype being built was so revolutionary that it would make all other forms of supersonic aircraft obsolete. The craft's official name was the Avro Car.

But by 1960 it was being officially claimed that the project had been dropped. The prototype of the Avro flying saucer is now in the US Air Force Museum in Fort Eustis, Virginia. The Canadian and US governments have insisted that they are no longer involved with flying saucer construction projects.

Yet is this necessarily true? The possibility remains that the Canadian, United States or Soviet governments could have continued to work on highly advanced, saucer-shaped, supersonic aircraft. The people directly involved in the projects, understanding the impossibility of testing the machines in complete secrecy, may have opted for creating a smokescreen of confusion, rumour and systematic humiliation of UFO observers, thereby ensuring that they can fly their machines with impunity.

But could man-made machines have such remarkable performance?

We have only to think of the extraordinary innovations of contemporary science and technology – jet aircraft, space rockets, reconnaissance satellites, pulse beam weapons – and then remember that such miracles are merely the tip of the iceberg, and that what goes on behind the guarded fences of our top-secret military and scientific establishments is probably decades ahead of these. Then it becomes easier to answer 'yes'.

Secret weapons and cyborgs

Top secret research aircraft often outrage normal ideas of how an aeroplane should look and perform. Could these bizarre man-made aircraft be responsible for a large proportion of UFO sightings?

COULD AN EXTRAORDINARY research project to build flying saucers have been kept wrapped in secrecy since the Second World War? And could our present technology possibly account for the advanced capabilities ascribed to UFOs?

It is entirely possible that the necessary research establishments could have been hidden well away from the gaze of the public or media. The underground research factories of Nazi Germany were gigantic feats of construction, containing wind tunnels, machine shops, assembly plants, rocket launching pads, supply dumps and accommodation for the thousands who worked there; yet very few outsiders knew that they existed. Likewise, the Cheyenne Complex in Colorado Springs, operated by the US Aerospace Defense Command, is virtually an underground city in the heart of a mountain. It rests on giant shock absorbers to counteract the blast of nuclear attack, it is webbed with miles of underground tunnels, it is completely sealed off from the outer world, and invisible from the air – and very few people, other than those who have worked there (all of whom are sworn to secrecy), know what goes on inside the establishment.

Equally large and complex establishments for the construction of highly advanced disc-shaped aircraft could, therefore, exist in other desolate parts of the world, such as the wildernesses of Russia and North America, the Arctic or the Antarctic.

While secrecy might prevail during the construction of the machines, it could not be reliably maintained once the machines were test-flown or actually used for reconnaissance or other purposes. It is therefore possible that the relevant authorities simply decided to fly them openly while simultaneously creating an international smokescreen of confusion and incredulity. The systematic harassment and humiliation of UFO observers and the deliberate inefficiency of official UFO investigations could have been their chosen methods of obscuring the issues.

This theory would also go a long way towards explaining such suppressive measures as a US Joint Chiefs of Staff directive of December 1953, which made the unauthorised release of information on UFO sightings a crime under the Espionage Act, punishable by a prison term of 1 to 10 years

Above: this remotely piloted research aircraft (RPRA), designed by NASA, would certainly have confused non-expert witnesses to its flights. Its cigar-shaped wing could be swung to as much as 45° from its normal angle to optimise performance at varying speeds

Right: NASA's 'lifting body' craft lacked wings, since its whole upper surface generated lift. It was launched from a bomber at high altitude

Right: an unmanned probe – not from space but from Westland, a British helicopter manufacturer. This remotely controlled helicopter had rotors 5 feet (1.5 metres) wide, and a body 2 feet (60 centimetres) wide, which could carry a variety of surveillance equipment. The 'feet' could leave marks similar to the circular depressions in the ground often described in cases of UFO landings

Right: first prototype of the British Flying Wing, one of several post-war designs that dispensed with the heavy fuselage of conventional aeroplanes. The resulting crescent shape is reminiscent of many UFO reports, including, interestingly, Kenneth Arnold's sighting of 1947 that began the modern UFO wave

or a fine of $10,000. It might also explain what happened to the only scientifically sound attempts to determine the size and capability of UFOs and whether or not they were intelligently controlled (see box).

Nonetheless, assuming that the saucer-shaped machines are man-made, we are still faced with the second major question: could modern technology achieve the extraordinary capabilities reported by UFO observers and the equally extraordinary physical appearance that some reported UFO crew members display?

In his important book *Ufology*, James M. McCampbell employs his training in engineering and physics to examine in great detail the physical properties that UFOs must possess to be capable of their reported speeds and manoeuvres. According to McCampbell, UFOs probably use some advanced means of propulsion that at present exists only on designers' drawing boards. They might employ ion rockets, in which the exhaust stream consists of ions (electrically charged particles) accelerated to high speeds by extremely strong electrical fields. Or thrust might be provided by a nuclear fusion pulse rocket, in which a continuous sequence of H-bomb explosions pushes the craft along. Or it might be that the craft uses anti-gravity shields – perhaps in combination with one of these forms of propulsion.

Ionisation of the air, with accompanying electrical discharges, could account for the glow that so fascinates UFO witnesses. The anti-gravity shield would account for the lack of turbulence and sonic booms associated with the passing of a UFO, and also for the crews' apparent ability to withstand extraordinary changes of speed and direction.

Shielded from gravity

McCampbell claims that the lift-off of a typical UFO would require as much energy as the detonation of an atomic bomb, would cause the body of the machine to heat up to about 155,000°F (85,000°C) and would cause intense radioactivity in the ground and atmosphere – unless an anti-gravity shield is used. In this case a virtually massless body would result and it would require only modest force for the UFO to achieve enormously high accelerations. This would account for the ability of UFOs to disappear in the blinking of an eye, to come to a very abrupt stop, hover in the air and make seemingly impossible right-angle turns.

In this context, it is to be noted that as far back as 1965 at least 46 unclassified projects concerned with gravity were being undertaken in the United States alone – by the Air Force, the Navy, the Army, NASA, the Atomic Energy Commission and the National Science Foundation. Since these were only the *un*classified projects, it is reasonable to assume that even more advanced projects – both in anti-gravity and the forms of propulsion mentioned above – are still being conducted in numerous top-secret establishments.

Another mysterious aspect of the UFO phenomenon is the frequency with which UFOs have materialised on photographs taken abducted by them, frequently describe how they felt 'drawn towards' the aliens and were 'compelled' to obey them – even when the aliens apparently did not speak. The common factor in such stories is a feeling of remoteness, unreality and divorce from the self. The contactees invariably behave like programmed zombies. Usually, after their initial terror, they are 'pacified' or 'hypnotised' by various means – a beam of light, a metallic object pressed against the neck, the 'laying on' of an alien's hands, a mere wave of an alien's hand, or strange, frequently indescribable sounds. None of this is necessarily extraordinary in the light of present-day knowledge.

Numerous brain wave experiments have

by people who did not see such an object through the viewfinder. This, combined with the fact that the UFOs have never been seen by reconnaissance satellites (at least as far as we know from official sources), has led some scientists to speculate that the UFOs may have the ability to make themselves invisible to human eyes.

Civilian and military establishments may have been experimenting along these lines for years – and it has long been claimed that the famous 'Philadelphia experiment' of 1943 (in which a US Navy ship was said to have dematerialised and then materialised elsewhere) was part of just such a project. However, doubts surround this sensational case and have helped to confuse the issue of government activity in these fields.

So much for the capabilities of UFOs as seen by observers at a distance. What of the evidence provided by witnesses who claim to have had close contact with the craft and their occupants?

A bizarre yet common aspect of contactee stories is the apparent lack of will, or resistance, on the part of the person involved. People claiming to have been in close contact with the occupants of flying saucers, or even

Above left: the Dornier Kiebitz, a tethered experimental helicopter. This robot craft's rotors span 26 feet (8 metres). The craft is designed to relay communications and reconnoitre battlefields. Its airframe is shaped to minimise radar reflections. Invisibility to radar is a prime goal of military research – and an attribute that UFOs often display

Above: the skeleton of another robot Dornier craft, the Aerodyne. The turbine-driven propeller, providing direct lift, is housed in the shroud at the left. Some of the airstream from the propeller is led along the boom to provide guidance. This weirdly shaped assembly was designed to be housed in a wingless robot aircraft

UFOs under wraps

The US Air Force was responsible for the investigation of UFO reports in the United States from 1948 to 1969, during which period the number of cases on file grew to over 12,600. Of these 701, or more than 5 per cent, were classified as unexplained. Critics claimed that Project Blue Book, as the investigation came to be called, lacked staff of the necessary technical and scientific calibre. One of Blue Book's own consultants, Dr Allen Hynek, made vehement accusations of obstruction and incompetence against the Air Force.

One of Blue Book's more vigorous heads, Captain Edward J. Ruppelt, proposed that a number of radar stations be equipped with photographic equipment to make a permanent record of radar screens during the tracking of UFOs. This scheme was aborted by his superiors. Another officer, Major Dewey Fournet, carried out a detailed statistical study of shown that light and sound can have disturbing mental and physical effects on perfectly normal people. For instance, a light flickering at between 8 and 12 cycles per second, close to the frequency of the brain's alpha waves, can cause extremely violent reactions in the person exposed to it, including jerking of the limbs, faintness, lightness in the head, or unconsciousness. It is therefore possible that the 'beam of light' described by so many contactees flickers on and off at the particular rate that affects the brain's basic rhythmic patterns and encourages hypnosis, hallucination, or both.

It is also a fact that infrasounds, which are just below the frequency limit of human hearing (thus the contactees' confusion as to whether they 'heard' or 'felt' something), can affect human beings in the same way as flickering lights. Indeed, certain low frequency sounds can lead not only to a change in the brain's rhythmic patterns but to actual physical changes, including severe migraine (a common contactee complaint) and temporary paralysis of the limbs.

Deprivation of will

Time and again a contactee reports that the alien pressed the side of his neck with its hand or with a 'metal object' and thereby rendered him unconscious or temporarily without will. This could simply be a standard form of hypnosis known as the 'instantaneous technique', or the 'carotid procedure', in which pressure is applied to a blood vessel near the ear, thus interfering with the circulation of blood to the brain and rendering the subject confused and susceptible to hypnotic suggestion. Hallucination, shock, or deliberate confusion through hypnosis are likely causes of such accounts.

It is not stretching credibility too far to suggest that the known advances made in prosthetics, cybernetic anthropomorphous machine systems (CAMS, or humanoid robots) and genetic and cybernetic engineering in general are excelled by an even more frightening secret achievement: highly advanced, disc-shaped machines operated by programmed or remotely controlled 'cyborgs' – half-men, half-machines.

Far-fetched? Not at all. Among projects relating to extended space flight and the exploration of the Moon and Mars, the writer David Rorvik lists a proposed cyborg that would be considerably more agile and certainly far more effective than our present-day astronauts. Since the envisaged cyborg's lungs would be partially collapsed and the blood in them artificially cooled, the cyborg's mouth and nose would be superfluous and hence sealed and totally non-functioning. Chemicals and concentrated foods would be constantly recycled through the cyborg's bloodstream to nourish and protect him, wastes would be recycled to make new foods, and communications would be carried out by radio, the signals originating directly in the cyborg's vocal cords.

If such an experiment has already been completed in any one of our top-secret research establishments, then the frighteningly persuasive close encounters of the third kind could represent contact not with extraterrestrials but with cybernetically modified fellow human beings.

How far this kind of work has progressed we do not know; however, we *do* know that as long ago as 1967, Professor Robert White of the Cleveland Metropolitan General Hospital was able to state categorically to the eminent journalist Oriana Fallaci: 'We can transfer the head of a man on to the trunk of another man . . . It can be accomplished now with existing techniques.'

Above: a starship driven by the power of the hydrogen bomb. Project Daedalus is a detailed scheme by the British Interplanetary Society for an unmanned interstellar expedition. Fuel pellets from the globular tanks would be 'burned' in a series of H-bomb explosions, driving the ship at an appreciable fraction of the speed of light. This concept exists only on the drawing board – as far as is publicly known

the reports to determine the manoeuvring abilities of UFOs. The Air Force was later to deny its very existence.

The celebrated Condon Report of 1966 was the climax of a two-year study carried out by a team from the University of Colorado under contract from the Air Force. In the body of the report at least 20 per cent of the sightings discussed were unexplained. Several individual case discussions virtually conceded the reality of UFOs, or spoke of rare and poorly understood natural phenomena. Yet the conclusions of the study, personally written by Dr Edward U. Condon, the head of the investigation, said: 'Nothing has come from the study of UFOs in the past 21 years that has added to scientific knowledge. . . .' In December 1969 the US Air Force closed down Project Blue Book and officially ended its UFO investigations, yet many of its findings remain secret to this day. In the eyes of ufologists the official US studies of UFOs over the years had been botched – from incompetence or by the design.

The creatures described in close encounter reports come in a confusing variety of shapes and sizes. What are we to make of them? ALVIN LAWSON analyses the reports – and comes up with a startling new theory about the origin of alien beings

THE CLASSIC PICTURE of an alien being is of a small, spindly creature with a large head and bulbous eyes, but often no other visible facial features, dressed in a one-piece grey suit without buttons or zips. The startling similarity of descriptions of aliens in many close encounter reports has led to speculation that all UFOs originate in one place. But for every report of these foetus-like aliens, there is one of creatures of a completely different kind – sometimes stiffly moving, like robots, sometimes indistinguishable from human beings, sometimes green and gnome-like.

What can ufology make of this fascinating but bewildering array of descriptions of supposed alien life forms? Are we to suppose that the Earth is being bombarded with spacecraft from many alien cultures, all conducting reconnaissance missions, or do the pilots of the alien craft have some obscure purpose in disguising themselves now in one form, now in another? Or will we be forced to make a more radical hypothesis?

Let us begin by creating a tool for analysing the wealth of reports of close encounters of the third kind – those UFO reports that involve aliens. Some kind of classification system will be useful; let us start with those aliens that take the same basic form as human beings, and are immediately identified as such by the witnesses. They are generally dressed in one-piece suits, and move and speak normally. Their average height, in all the reports, is between 5 and 7 feet (1.5 and 2.1 metres). These are 'human entities'.

Perhaps the most commonly reported aliens are the humanoids. They resemble humans, but witnesses report clear anatomical differences. They often have disproportionately large heads, pallid skins, underdeveloped facial features, and hairless bodies – giving them an appearance reminiscent of human foetuses. The single feature most often reported is their exceptionally large eyes, sometimes described as unblinking, or having vertical pupils. They are small, with an average height of between 3 and 5½ feet (90 centimetres and 1.7 metres). Unlike human entities, they generally communicate not through normal speech, but telepathically; but like them, humanoid entities are generally dressed in one-piece, close-fitting suits, usually of silver or grey, although space-suits are also sometimes reported.

Somewhat rarer are 'animal entities'. They are characterised by distinctly mammalian, reptilian, fishlike or other features, including fur, claws, a tail, scales or similarly strange skin texture, pointed ears, a snout, enlarged teeth, and non-human eyes. Their heights range from 6 to 8 feet (1.8 to 2.4 metres). Most are ape-like in appearance, and walk on two legs. Their method of communication ranges from animal cries to telepathy.

Another form of alien is the 'robot entity'. Robots seem to be made of metallic or other artificial body materials, and often move in a jerky, stiff or otherwise unnatural manner. Glowing eyes are often reported; so is the robots' ability to float, or to make witnesses float. Their shape varies from bipedal to huge machines; their height can be anything between 6 inches and 20 feet (15 centimetres and 6 metres). They often wear padded space-suits with bubble-dome headgear. Their method of communication varies from a flat metallic voice to telepathy.

Other types of alien exhibit a variety of strange characteristics – they are the 'exotic

The good, the bad and the ugly

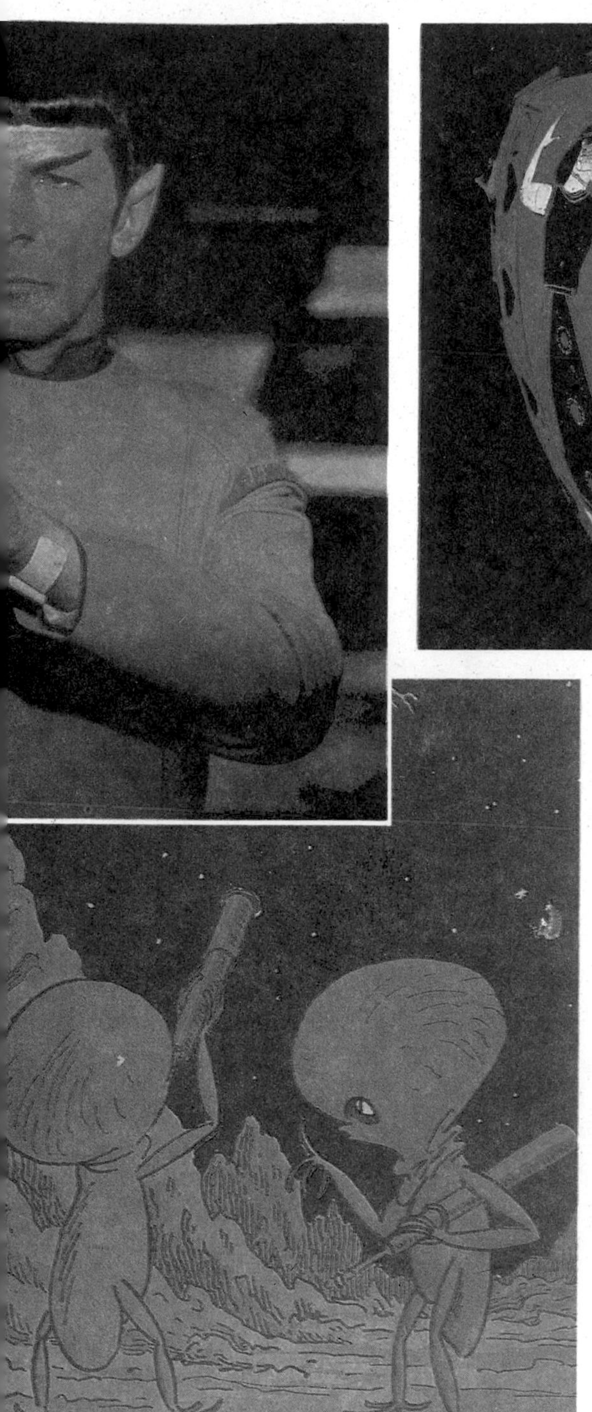

Alvin Lawson has proposed a sixfold classification of alien beings reported in close encounter cases. Mr Spock (above left), from the planet Vulcan, is an example of the 'human entity' category familiar from television's *Star Trek*. The classification can also be applied to creatures from before the start of the modern UFO era in 1947. In this illustration from a 1918 issue of the French magazine *La Baionnette* (left) lunar entities – evidently belonging to Lawson's humanoid class – conjecture that Earth wars are a device to prevent the planet cooling. The Cyclops of Greek legend (far left) – in a painting by Odilon Redon (1840–1916) – is a member of Lawson's 'exotic class'; and the Greek river god Achelous (above) – seen here with Herakles – is an example of the 'apparitional entity'; he could change his shape at will

entities'. They may have grotesquely exaggerated animal or human features; they may combine human characteristics with non-animal ones – humans with robot arms, for instance. Most exotic entities are bipeds; but some of them combine the characteristics of two or more of the other categories. They range in height from 1 to 10 feet (30 centimetres to 3 metres). They may move like humans or animals, or like robots, or float; they often communicate telepathically, rather than by ordinary means..

The final category is also the most puzzling. It consists of 'apparitional entities' – aliens that share many of the characteristics of ghosts. They may materialise or dematerialise, change form, manifest themselves selectively to witnesses, or move matter, including people, about at will. Their average height is 5 to 6 feet (1.5 to 1.8 metres); they often float rather than walk, and they generally communicate by telepathy. Here again, they most often appear dressed in one-piece suits.

Let us use this system of classification to analyse the close encounter cases described in Webb's *1973 – year of the humanoids*. Of a total of 66 cases, 16 were humanoids, 12 robots, 10 human, 8 animal, 7 exotic, 5 apparitional – and 8 were impossible to categorise because the descriptions were so vague.

It seems we have a working classification system. But is there an additional significance in the fact that *all* reported aliens appear to fall into one of six well-defined groups?

'Intelligent scum'

Some scientists have speculated about the existence of alien creatures that are so unusual that it would be impossible to classify them under the six-category system. For example, in his novel *The black cloud*, astronomer Sir Fred Hoyle describes a vast, intelligent cloud that 'lives' in interstellar space, complete with molecular heart system, brain and other necessary organs. It feeds on raw energy and its central nervous system functions via radio waves. And Ronald Bracewell writes of an 'intelligent scum', an enormous living civilisation that controls its environment through evolutionary specialisation. But in fact, such creatures are rarely, if ever, described in genuine close encounter reports.

Can the six-class categorisation be applied to any other phenomena, real or imaginary? The most well-established single pattern in the groups described above has to do with entity clothing, typically a seamless, one-piece outfit that covers the body except for the head. This is distinctly similar to the clothing generally worn by brownies, traditional folklore figures. Another interesting parallel is provided by the many reports of instrument-carrying aliens and similar reports of elves from folk tradition. And a close examination of folk tradition shows that folk creatures fit the six-class categorisation neatly. Giants, for example, are human entities; pookas, gnomes and pixies are humanoid; kelpies are animal; stocks, wooden dolls substituted by fairies for kidnapped babies, are robotic; the fachan, a bizarre creature with one eye, one hand emerging from his chest, and one leg, is exotic; and fairies, like demons and divinities, are 'shape shifters', or apparitional.

The images of traditional Christianity fall into the same categories. At the centre is the human Christ. The cherubim and seraphim, ageless, sexless beings, are humanoid. The key symbol of the Garden of Eden is the serpent – an animal entity. Adam is the father of all 'robots' – inert matter infused by God with life, consciousness and sensibility. Devils and tempters show horrific bodily distortion – and fall into the exotic class; and angels, with their capacity for abruptly appearing and disappearing, are apparitional. And so on. The classification can be extended to the Greek gods, demonology, science fiction, many of the works of Shakespeare and Lewis Carroll – and even the characters of the *Wizard of Oz*.

It seems that our system of classification is perhaps more than merely a useful tool for analysis – could it be that it is actually a set of archetypes, deeply rooted in the subconscious, on which the mind draws when it is subjected to unusual stimuli?

Evidence that this may be the correct interpretation comes from a series of hypnosis experiments conducted by Dr W.C. McCall, John DeHerrerra and the author at Anaheim Memorial Hospital, near Los Angeles, California, in 1977. In these experiments, a number of subjects were hypnotised and asked questions about an imaginary UFO 'abduction'. The results were compared with 'real' cases – and, startlingly, the descriptions, in particular of the aliens involved, were closely similar. Here is part of an 'imaginary' description of an abduction:

> They [the aliens] seem to be humanoid in form. They have round heads that are much larger than . . . humans. . . . They don't really have fingers. They seem to be kind of webbed. . . . I can't see any legs, or feet, because they're . . . what looks like possibly a . . . an article of clothing goes right to the floor. . . . Costume is . . . more purplish than blue in color. Seems to be all one . . . all made in one piece. There don't seem to be any seams on the costume. . . . They stand about four feet, two inches [1.2 metres] tall. Maybe a little taller . . . .

It is a typical description of the humanoid type. This seems to be powerful evidence that the imagery of close encounters of the third kind is stored in the collective unconscious – that it is, in the terms of Carl Gustav Jung, archetypal.

An analysis of hallucinations and the images remembered from near-death experiences shows similar parallels with reports of close encounters of the third kind. Do all these similarities prove that close encounter cases are illusory? Not necessarily,

Below left: a detail of a chained devil from a stained glass window in the St Lawrence chapel of Strasbourg Cathedral, France. With its goatish beard, cow's horns, ass's ears and bird's talons, this devil exhibits the characteristics of Lawson's 'exotic' category. Interestingly, other aspects of Christian imagery show equally striking parallels with reports of alien creatures

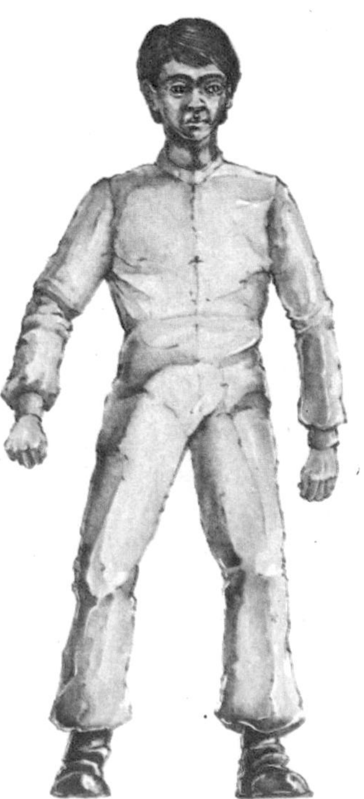

for four reasons. First, many abduction and other close encounter reports involve multiple witnesses, and it seems unlikely that multiple hallucinations lasting for several hours occur with significant frequency; second, there are reported physiological, psychological and physical effects associated with abduction experiences that - where authenticated – suggest that *something* happened. Third, hallucinating patients and those who have gone through near-death experiences are generally convinced only by extremely vivid experiences; but most close encounter witnesses are convinced very early of the 'reality' of the event – however unlikely they know it to be. Fourth, while the triggering mechanism or stimulus for hallucinations and near-death experiences can apparently be determined with some accuracy, the stimulus for 'real' close encounter experiences continues to be one of the major unknowns of ufology. No one knows what it is that makes a particular person, at a particular place and time, likely to experience a close encounter.

Although none of these arguments in itself provides positive proof, taken together they make it seem likely that close encounter reports are elicited by a real stimulus; but, as the French ufologist Claud Rifat has speculated,

> UFO reports . . . do not give us any indication of the true stimulus which elicited the report; they give us only what the subject fancies about the nature of a UFO . . . CE IIIs [close encounters of the third kind] are LSD-like experiences in which a subject perceives a mixture of the real world and of her/his inner unconscious one.

I myself feel certain that accounts given by witnesses reflect what their senses have reported – that is, they do actually perceive humanoids, exotics, and so on. But if the six entity-types are indeed already in the collective unconscious, they are perhaps, therefore, already in some sense in the mind of the witness before his close encounter. If so, while perceptions of alien entities may well be stimulated in the witnesses by what can only be loosely called the UFO phenomenon, they only indicate that some kind of stimulus is present – they tell us nothing at all about the nature of that stimulus.

Above: *The scream*, by the Norwegian artist Edvard Munch (1863–1944), which, according to the painter, represents the 'primal scream of nature'. On another level, however, Munch has unconsciously reproduced the archetype of the typical humanoid of Lawson's categorisation. This 16th-century stained glass window (right) shows Adam and Eve – whom Lawson sees as examples of 'robots'

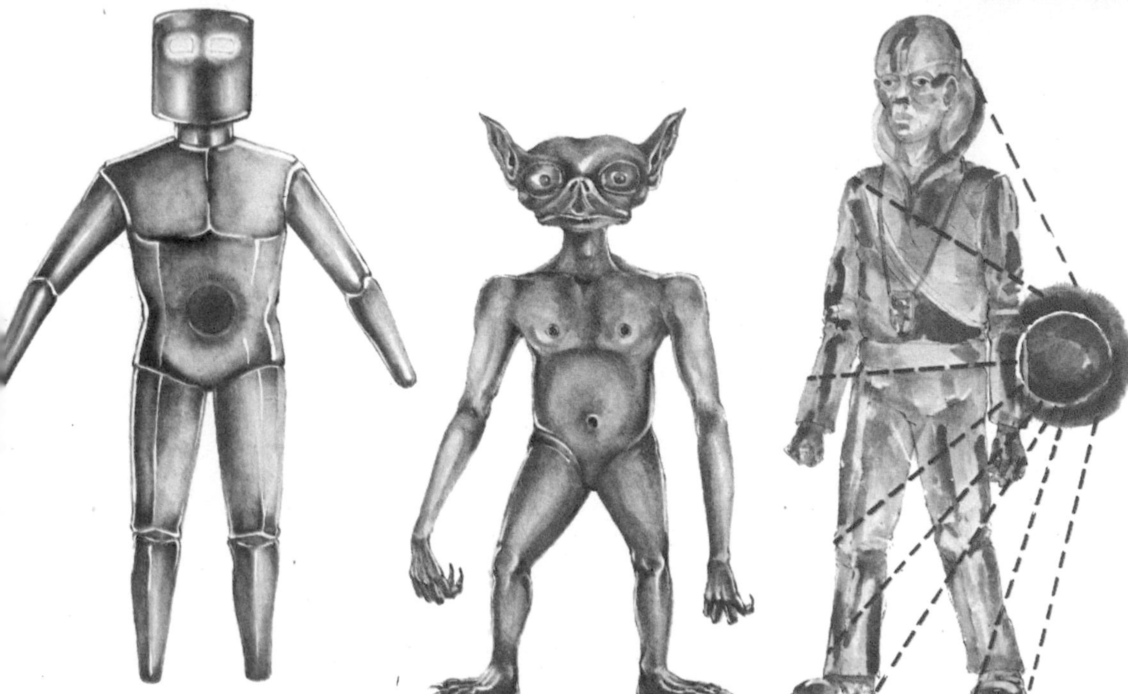

Left: artist's impressions of each of Alvin Lawson's six categories of alien. They are, from left to right, human, humanoid, animal, robot, exotic and apparitional. Lawson argues that these categories are actually archetypal: that they are somehow built into the human mind, awaiting only the right trigger to bring them to the conscious mind

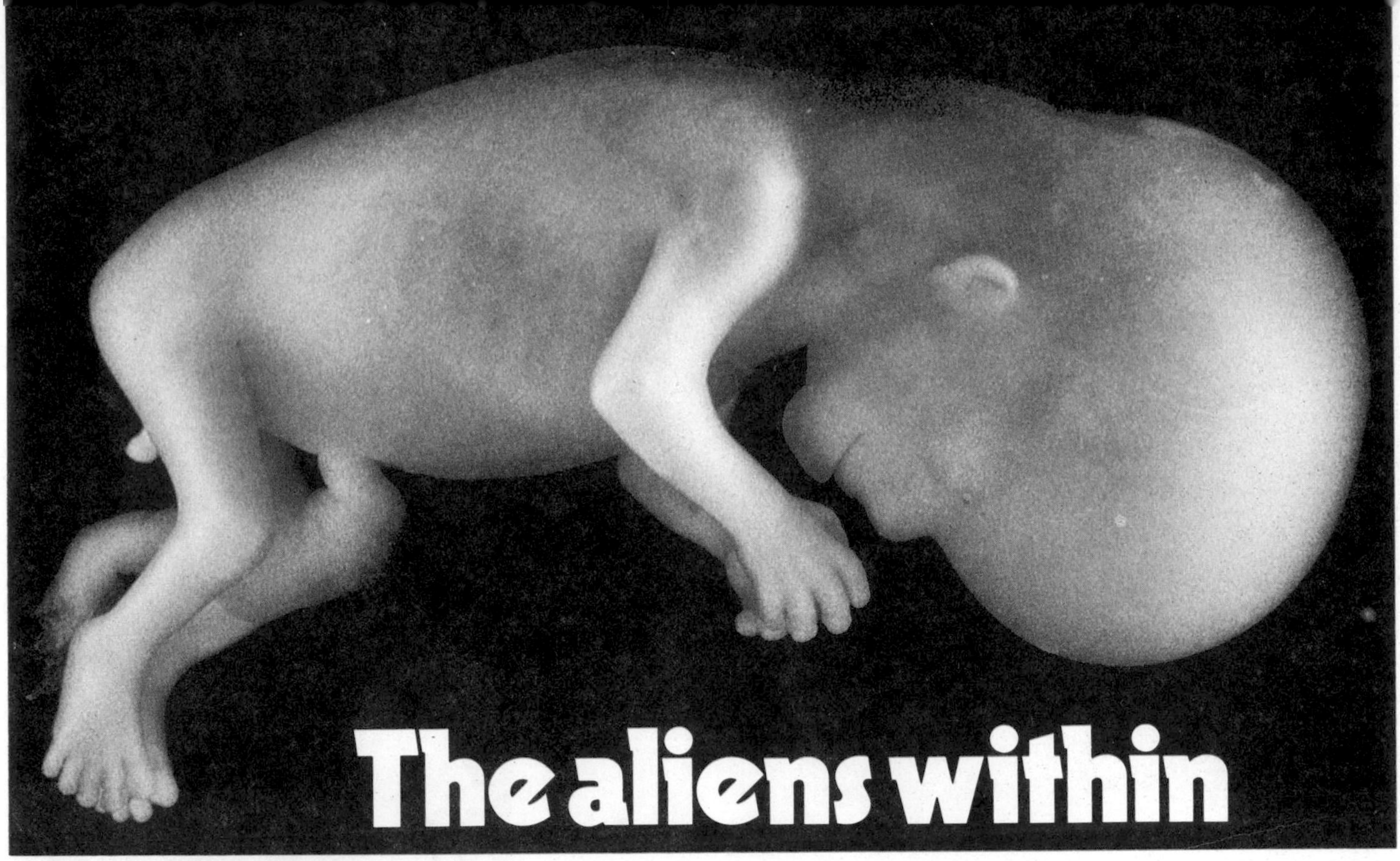

The aliens within

The startling parallels between abduction reports from all over the world suggest that these experiences are linked in some way. This chapter presents a new and original theory – that they all stem from the trauma of being born, which is common to everyone

OF ALL THE ALIENS reported by witnesses of close encounters of the third kind, by far the commonest are those of the humanoid type (see page 24). Fairly small, with disproportionately large heads and eyes, spindly-limbed, clad in one-piece, tight-fitting suits, they resemble nothing so much as a human foetus. Is this merely coincidence – or could there be more to it?

Let us analyse the similarities between a typical humanoid from a close encounter report, and an unborn baby. The first striking feature is the diminutive size of humanoids – on average 3 to $5\frac{1}{2}$ feet (90 centimetres to 1.7 metres); the human foetus is, of course, small throughout the gestation period and humanoids' bodies are generally reported to be frail-looking. Humanoid reports tell of creatures with disproportionately large heads and eyes: the foetal head size is disproportionately large from the fourth week onwards; the eye sockets are large, and after the eyes form during the fourth week they grow rapidly until at birth they are half the size of those of an adult – but in a body very much smaller. The bodily features of humanoids are generally reported to be rudimentary, or missing altogether. This is also true of the human foetus until very late in its development. The hands begin to form in the fifth week, and the feet in the sixth week; both fingers and toes remain webbed until around the eighth week. The underdeveloped ears, nose, mouth and shape of the face mean that the developing baby does not have a recognisably 'human' face until the tenth week – it is, instead, very similar to what we understand as 'humanoid'. Humanoids are in most cases reported as having no evident genitalia; the genitalia of the foetus remain ambiguous or underdeveloped until the twelfth week.

The arms of humanoids are often described as longer than the legs; the arms of the foetus are longer than its legs until the fourth month. Humanoids walk clumsily, as if unaccustomed to such movements; the human foetus does not make perceptible movements until the fifth month. Humanoids' skin is generally either pallid – grey or white – or reddish; foetal skin colour is pallid until the sixth month, and reddish in the seventh. Humanoids have wrinkled skins and hairless bodies; the human foetus has a wrinkled skin in the seventh month, and hair does not appear until the eighth month. Humanoids are often reported as having no eyebrows, and sometimes – when their skin is not wrinkled – it is said to be unnaturally smooth; eyebrows become visible in the unborn baby in the eighth month, and the skin becomes waxy and smooth just before birth, in the eighth and ninth months.

These striking similarities suggest that the unborn child – particularly in the period of the first eight weeks from conception – may be the model for the humanoids reported in many close encounter cases.

The similarities between humanoids reported in close encounter cases and those

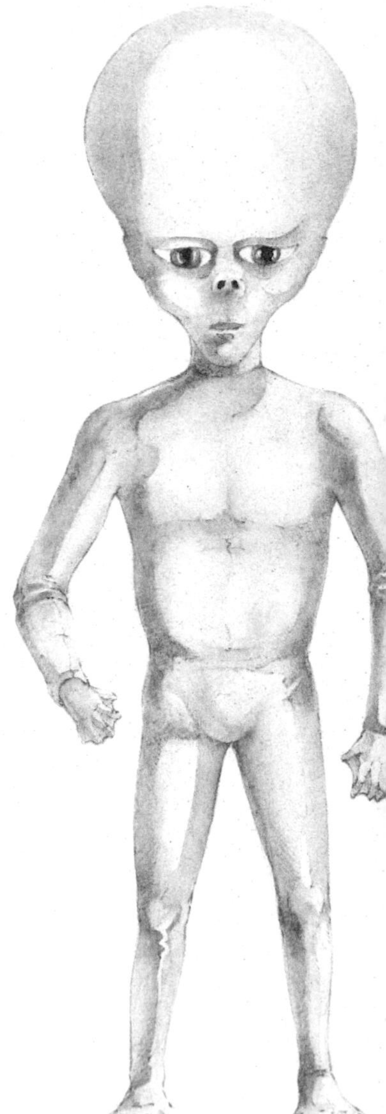

described in a hypnosis experiment in which subjects were asked to describe an *imaginary* close encounter and imagery from LSD-induced 'trips', suggest that our early prenatal experiences may provide a rich store of imagery that can become conscious when somehow triggered.

Psychiatrist Stanislav Grof, who has years of experience in the therapeutic use of LSD, believes that many of his patients relive their own birth trauma during LSD sessions:

> In a way that is not quite clear at the present stage of research, the [subjects'] experiences seem to be related to the circumstances of the biological birth. LSD subjects frequently refer to them quite explicitly as reliving their own birth trauma. [Others] quite regularly show the cluster of physical symptoms . . . that can best be interpreted as a derivative of the biological birth. They also assume postures and move in complex sequences that bear a striking similarity to those of a child during the various stages of delivery.

Grof also describes experiences in which LSD patients seem to 'tune in' to the 'consciousness' of a particular organ or tissue of their own body, and even regress, apparently, into a cellular or subcellular consciousness. Grof says it is 'commonly reported' by such subjects that they even identify with the sperm and ovum at the time of conception, and sometimes describe an accelerated process of foetal development.

One cellular component not mentioned in Grof's data is potentially stunning in its implications for ufology. When the fertilised human ovum is six days old and attaches itself to the wall of the uterus, the distinctly embryonic tissue inside the ovum assumes an intriguing shape: it resembles a flattened, circular plate – the basic UFO pattern – and is known as the *embryonic disc.* This stage of prenatal life is the first in which the fertilised tissues can be thought of as something integral, whole, or individual.

Left: a 10-week-old human embryo – and an artist's impression of one of the humanoids allegedly seen by Travis Walton during his five-day abduction from Heber, Arizona, USA, on 5 November 1975 (below left). The similarity between human foetuses and humanoids from a wide range of close encounter cases is striking: is this merely coincidence, or is there more to it?

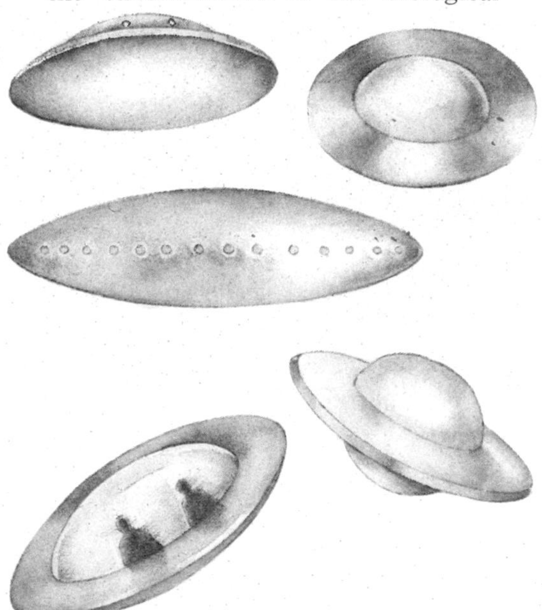

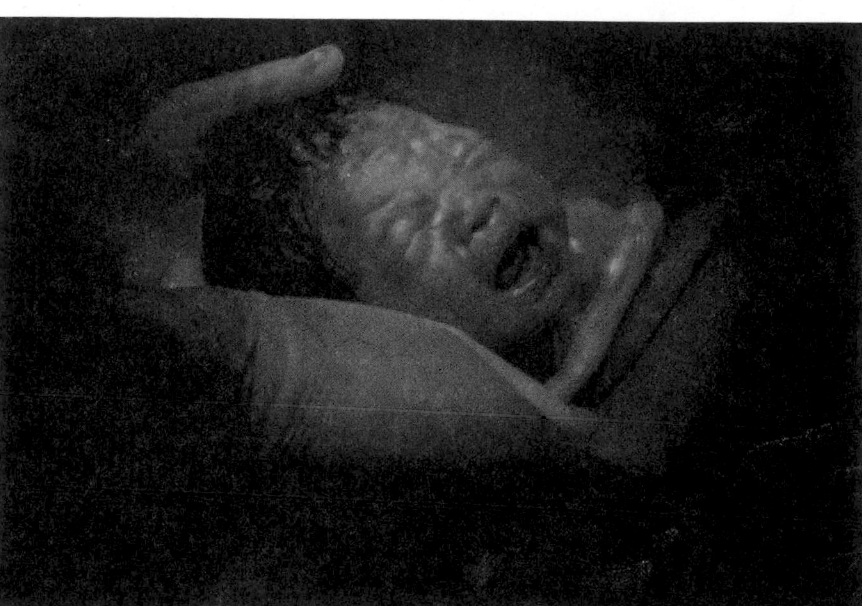

Above: a baby emerges from its mother's womb into the outside world. Alvin Lawson suggests that the travel through tunnels frequently described in abduction reports may represent the baby's passage down the birth canal

Above left: an artist's impression of a number of typical 'flying saucers' from assorted UFO sightings. Six days after conception, the fertilised human egg assumes the form of a flattened, circular shape. Could this be the origin of the familiar form of the flying saucer?

The psychologist Carl Gustav Jung found an analogy between the shapes of 'flying saucers' and 'mandalas', which he defined as archetypal symbols of unity, wholeness, and individuation. If Grof's work is true, it could be interpreted as providing a physiological basis for Jung's theories about archetypal imagery and his related speculations on the collective unconscious. At the very least, it is somewhat startling to realise that every human being who ever lived was – for a few hours – shaped very like a flying saucer. With that in mind one can speculate: perhaps the embryonic disc does manifest itself as a Jungian mandala or saucer archetype in everyone's sensibility during the embryonic stage; later it could emerge as part of a witness's UFO-related imagery. Thus UFO witnesses might be predisposed to perceive saucer-shaped 'somethings' in the presence of whatever psycho-physical stimulus triggers off the UFO phenomenon – though what the witnesses perceive may be an archetypal echo of their own prenatal experiences.

One of the most difficult problems for ufology is the study of abduction cases. Often seemingly totally unsupported by fact, reports of abduction cases often seem pointless or even ridiculous; but they nevertheless present a coherent body of evidence that deserves to be taken seriously. How do abduction reports fare under an analysis of the subject's own prenatal experiences?

Stanislav Grof presents a useful breakdown of the birth process into four stages, each of which, he believes, has major implications for later personality development and behaviour. Stage one is of primal union with the mother, characterised for the foetus by nothing more than what Grof terms 'good' and 'bad' womb experiences – periods of disturbed or undisturbed life in the womb. Then, with the onset of the birth process, come contractions within the closed system of the womb – stage two. And next, in stage three, the foetus works together with the mother in its propulsion down the birth canal. And finally there is stage four, separation from the mother – the termination of the foetus's union with its mother and the formation of a new relationship both with her and with the external world: birth itself.

Traces of all these elements may be found in abductee reports. Grof finds that many of his LSD patients relive their 'bad' womb experiences of foetal distress in feelings of sickness, nausea and mild paranoia, which may be traceable to any of several causes such as the mother's physical or emotional health, her ingestion of noxious substances, or attempted abortion. Reliving 'good' womb experiences manifests itself in visions of pre-birth bliss including feelings of cosmic unity, transcendence of space and time, visions of paradise, 'oceanic' emotions, and other parallels with mystical or ecstatic experiences. Abduction reports are full of similar elements – cosmic vistas, feelings of harmony and peaceful self-awareness, intuitive insights into the nature of the Universe; and reports of nausea after the event, discomfort, unpleasant tastes and odours.

Below: a Buddhist painting showing a Buddha inside a mandala surrounded by demons. Alvin Lawson suggests that the mandala may represent the womb – safe and secure within, but surrounded by all kinds of unknown dangers. And the famous psychologist Carl Gustav Jung believed that flying saucers were a form of mandala – a fact that ties in very neatly with Professor Lawson's contention that flying saucers can be regarded as representations of the womb

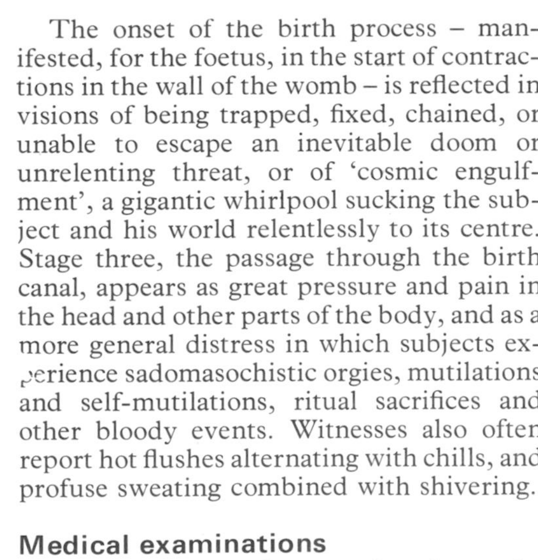

The onset of the birth process – manifested, for the foetus, in the start of contractions in the wall of the womb – is reflected in visions of being trapped, fixed, chained, or unable to escape an inevitable doom or unrelenting threat, or of 'cosmic engulfment', a gigantic whirlpool sucking the subject and his world relentlessly to its centre. Stage three, the passage through the birth canal, appears as great pressure and pain in the head and other parts of the body, and as a more general distress in which subjects experience sadomasochistic orgies, mutilations and self-mutilations, ritual sacrifices and other bloody events. Witnesses also often report hot flushes alternating with chills, and profuse sweating combined with shivering.

Medical examinations

The final stage, of separation from the mother and confrontation of a new world, is mirrored in the breathing difficulties that many witnesses report, and the severe pain in the umbilical region, often spreading to the pelvic region. There may also be a feeling that the victim's body is being cut open and his heart or other organs removed 'for medical examination'; their eventual replacement brings a sense of rebirth and renewal.

It is easy to see how the immediate surroundings of the unborn foetus become reflected in 'close encounter' reports. Tubes and tunnels are frequent elements of these reports – witnesses are often 'sucked up' a tube, apparently made of light or a luminous material, into the UFO. These may well be memories of the baby's passage down the

birth canal – a theory that was reinforced by a study of eight subjects who had been born by Caesarian section, of whom seven used no tube or tunnel imagery in their accounts of how they boarded or left the UFO. The exception had been treated as a normal birth until her mother had a haemorrhage and a Caesarian operation became necessary – by which time the subject had experienced an hour or two in the birth canal, perhaps long enough to establish the tunnel and tube imagery in her mind.

Above: at around 10 p.m. on 27 October 1974 the Day family, driving towards Aveley in Essex, England, suddenly ran into a mysterious bank of green mist. When hypnotically regressed, John Day described being drawn up a beam of white light into an alien craft. Alvin Lawson sees the light beam, a recurrent motif in close encounter reports, as a representation of the umbilical cord. He also points out that the golden beam traditionally used to represent the impregnation of the Virgin Mary by the Holy Spirit – as in this painting of the annunciation (above left) by Carlo Crivelli (*c.*1430–*c.*1495) – may have the same origin

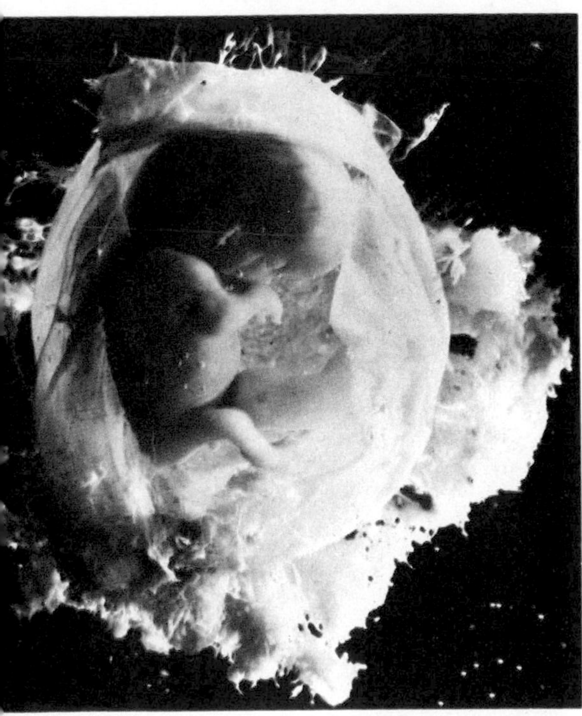

Left: a foetus, attached to the placenta. Alvin Lawson suggests that the placenta may emerge in abduction accounts as a UFO shape or as the rucksacks often reportedly worn by aliens like this one (right), seen at Vilvorde, Belgium, in December 1973. The helmet may represent the amniotic sac

Images of doors or passageways are nearly as plentiful in abduction reports as tubes. Most witnesses describe unorthodox doors that appear suddenly in walls or on an object's exterior, disappearing without a trace soon afterwards. Such doors tend to open from the centre rather than on pivots, or have sliding panels. Some reports tell of doors that disintegrate or 'explode' just before witnesses pass through them. All these unusual doorways and passages can be interpreted as suggesting another birth trauma event – the opening of the cervix. Supporting this idea is the fact that a control subject, a normal birth, responded to a suggested situation of cervical dilation with the comment, 'It's like a door opening.' Surely the birth process is a more likely explanation of the many doors and tubes or tunnels in close encounter narratives than any attempt to make these descriptions plausible as realistic accounts of the interior design of alien spacecraft?

The placenta may emerge in abduction narratives as a UFO shape and also as the rucksack often allegedly worn by aliens. The umbilical cord suggests the tube leading from the rucksack, and it may also take the form of the retracting light beam. The amniotic sac may have an analogue in the various 'bubbledome' headgear on reported aliens, as well as in the transparent UFOs that feature in many reports of close encounters of the third kind.

Such extraordinary parallels suggest that abductions may indeed be relivings of the birth trauma – an event that has been experienced by all human beings, whatever their race or culture.

Is the UFO phenomenon rooted in the experience of human birth? Analysing the famous Andreasson case, this chapter concludes that it is – and stresses the importance of this testable hypothesis for ufology

AMERINDIAN SHAMANS, like Black Elk of the Oglala Sioux, believed that they could travel from Earth to other worlds via a 'cosmic pillar', often symbolised by a pole or a tree. Black Elk often chose a spot beside a tree to begin his trances. Shortly a spirit guide in the form of a bird would lead him upwards through a tunnel-like aperture and further upwards into a 'flaming rainbow tepee' where Black Elk met and communicated with a group of 'grandfathers'. At this point in many accounts, the shaman is forced to undergo painful bodily dismemberment – a demon removes every organ, bone and even blood cell in his body! But everything is then replaced, after being cleansed and purified – and the shaman is spiritually and physically reborn, ready to return to his people with renewed spiritual energies. Sometimes Black Elk was returned on a 'little cloud'. Clearly, 'abduction' stories such as these, extraordinarily similar to UFO abduction narratives with their echoes of the events that accompany birth – the perinatal events – have been around for a very long time.

Those people who believe that UFO abductions relate to alien beings, parallel universes or other exotic origins will eventually have to explain – along with the lack of unambiguous physical evidence – why the incidents and images reported by abductees are so similar to those reported in a variety of obviously psychological processes, including drug-induced hallucinations, near-death experiences, religious and metaphysical ecstasies and shamans' trances – like Black Elk's.

Every one of us has undergone a birth trauma. The universal phenomenon of birth is free from ordinary cultural influences – for we experience it before we have undergone any kind of cultural conditioning – and is, as far as we know, one of the first significant events consciously experienced by human beings. Although it is important to note that the causal link between specific events of biological birth and particular images has yet to be established, it seems that in the birth trauma we have a powerful experience that

Below: an American Indian medicine man goes into a trance. American Indian folklore tells how shamans – as recent as Black Elk of the Oglala Sioux, photographed here in 1947 (left) – regularly underwent experiences closely similar to UFO abduction reports

Abductions: the inside story

Left: when Betty Andreasson was abducted from her home in South Ashburnham, Massachusetts, on 25 January 1967, she found herself sitting in a clear plastic chair with a fitted cover filled with a grey liquid. Closing her eyes, she felt pleasant vibrations and was fed some sweet fluid through a tube in her mouth. She felt relaxed and happy. The whole experience, Alvin Lawson points out, is a classic reflection of good experiences in the womb

could serve as the source of much imagery – among it that reported by alleged victims of abductions by alien creatures. The fact that the experience of birth is similar for everyone accounts for the similarity of abduction reports from all over the world, while the fact that no two births are identical accounts for the differences between them.

Let us examine one of ufology's classic abduction cases in the light of the birth trauma hypothesis.

At about 7 p.m. on 25 January 1967 Mrs Betty Andreasson, of South Ashburnham, Massachusetts, USA, was allegedly abducted from her living room by a group of alien beings. Her abduction began with a bright light that flashed outside her house, shortly after which a group of 4-foot (1.2-metre) beings appeared. They communicated with Betty, then floated her outside and into a waiting craft where she was examined, immersed in a liquid, and then apparently taken for a journey into alien realms. At the climax of her adventure she witnessed a huge bird that spoke to her and then, phoenix-like, was consumed in flames – an event that Betty, a devout fundamentalist Christian, interpreted in religious terms. She heard a voice that she thought was God's saying, 'I have chosen to show you the world,' apparently because of her sincere faith. After this, Betty's captors returned her safely home. The alleged abduction had lasted about 3 hours and 40 minutes.

The Andreasson case is useful because it has been extensively investigated by a group of dedicated ufologists, the main witness is considered reliable, and the case details are representative of abduction narratives as a whole. Further, Betty is a competent artist and was able to provide many sketches of her adventure. In short, the Andreasson close encounter of the third kind is about as reliable and detailed as any abduction case we are likely to find. At the same time, it has significant implications for UFO abduction research, for it contains a wealth of perinatal images and events that support a non-physical or psychological interpretation of this case and of the UFO abduction mystery in general.

The Andreasson case presents several clear birth trauma images. For example, Betty's humanoids were of the classic foetus variety – greyish skin, oversized heads, huge eyes, and underdeveloped features like noses, ears and mouths (see page 26) – although they behaved like apparitions in passing through solid doors and materialising at will. The leader seemed to change his facial features so that he became yet more foetus-like in his final meeting with Betty.

Pleasant vibrations

The event most obviously linked with perinatal imagery occurred in what Betty described as the cylindrical room, where she was enclosed in a clear plastic chair with a fitted cover, which her captors filled with a grey fluid. She breathed through clear tubes that fitted into her nostrils and mouth. A telepathic voice told her to close her eyes. Suddenly she felt pleasant vibrations, the fluid whirled, she was fed some sweet substance through the tube in her mouth, and she was relaxed and happy. Floating and tranquil, she became one with the 'undulating fluid'. After a time the fluid was drained, she was taken out, and she realised that her head hurt.

The scene can obviously be interpreted as

Below: *The garden of delights* by Hieronymus Bosch (*c*.1450–*c*.1516). This picture of a kind of paradise shares with many abduction cases the imagery of what Alvin Lawson calls 'good' womb experiences – a pleasant state of suspension within a transparent sac (left), for example, and the ocean as a symbol of prenatal well-being (top)

Three Kentucky women were allegedly abducted by aliens on 7 January 1976. Sketches they later produced while under hypnosis show clear birth trauma imagery. They saw a woman on an observation table or bed, apparently being examined by humanoids (top) – an obvious parallel with a baby's first moments outside the womb; and a huge eye (above), a symbol of the universal consciousness often associated in other abduction reports with tranquil periods of the foetus's life within the womb

a return to the womb: the cylindrical room is itself only one of several womb analogues in Betty's narrative; the transparent chair suggests the amniotic sac in which Betty floated in a foetal position; the grey liquid is the amniotic fluid; the breathing and feeding tubes are the umbilical cord. The tranquillising undulations and vibrations suggest a reversion to 'good' womb experiences (see page 28). Betty's headache may be a manifestation of the onset of another part of the remembered birth process.

Betty spent much of her time on board the UFO 'floating' from one womblike room to another, through tunnels and on elevators or other counterparts of the birth canal. Betty's tunnels varied in length but typically ended with doorways into brightly lit, dome-shaped rooms, where she was undressed, examined or 'cleansed'. The doorways suggest the cervical openings: usually a bare wall seemed to separate with a soft 'whoosh' on approach and unite again afterwards, leaving no trace; other openings Betty described included a circular membrane and some mirror-like doors through which she crashed harmlessly.

Alien probes

During the medical examination that Betty alleges she underwent – in a big, bright room – the aliens inserted needle-tipped tubes into her nasal cavities and into her navel. In a hypnotic session conducted later by investigators, Betty remembered this experience:

> I can feel them moving that thing . . . he's going to put it in my navel! O-h-h. I don't like this . . . I can feel them moving that thing around in my stomach or my body . . . Oh! He's pushing that again . . . around, feeling things . . . . Feels like he's going right around my stuff inside – feeling it, or something with that needle.

Betty was told by the aliens that the navel probe was a test for 'procreation', and afterwards she was told that there were 'some parts missing'. Betty had had an hysterectomy, and was evidently reliving her own medical history; but the navel also commonly appears as an analogue of the umbilical cord in abduction reports. The aliens said they were 'awakening' something with their probing – an element of death and rebirth that was articulated in Betty's case more clearly by the phoenix.

In Betty's vision, a worm emerged from the ashes of the phoenix. At the same time two things seemed to be happening to her, both well-established perinatal events: she felt an intense, shivering chill come over her, when only a moment before she had been complaining of intense heat, and 'the worst thing I've ever experienced'.

It seems that the birth trauma hypothesis 'fits' – but is it correct to say that all abduction narratives are relivings of the witness's birth trauma? Even if this is the case, of course, it does not invalidate the experience or prove that abduction experiences are all in the mind. What it means is that the UFO phenomenon stimulates a certain kind of hallucination in the human mind. The nature of the phenomenon itself remains obscure.

The importance to ufology of the birth trauma hypothesis lies in the fact that it is one of the very few testable theories ever to have been proposed in this most sensational area of the UFO phenomenon. If ufology is ever to become a truly scientific discipline, viable hypotheses will have to be offered – and also tested. In this instance, serious and objective investigators should make a thorough study of perinatal events and investigate the medical and birth history of the abductee before proceeding to an analysis of the abduction case. For, until the abduction witness's psychology is made the main focus of investigation in close encounters of the third kind, and fantastic theories such as the extra-terrestrial hypothesis are allowed to await whatever extraordinary proofs they may demand, abduction researchers will not attract – neither will they deserve – serious and widespread scientific attention.

UFOs: the case for a cover up

The US government has long denied any interest in UFOs, yet keeps thousands of UFO documents on the secret list. When UFO researchers unmasked this secrecy, they revealed a bizarre CIA plot to mislead the public

UFO RESEARCHERS HAVE long maintained that their governments know more about the UFO phenomenon than they officially admit. One reason for thinking this has been the unfailingly sceptical attitude taken by government officials when questioned about any particular sighting – even the best-documented reports are greeted with cries of 'weather balloons' or 'the planet Venus seen under unusual conditions'. Another cause for suspicion has been the peculiar interest that UFOs take in military establishments from time to time. Some, at least, of the frightening and infamous men in black may have been genuine government agents, and the thought may linger in many ufologists' minds that the MIB's elusive nature is only the smoke of folklore behind which lurks the sinister fire of clandestine operations. In the United States the idea of a deliberate government attack on ufology was confirmed for many by the publication in 1969 of the Condon Report, widely regarded as at best complacent or at worst wilfully ignorant.

An unidentified flying object skims over the desert outside Phoenix, Arizona, on 12 September 1972. Checked by computerised enhancement techniques, the photograph has been declared genuine by Ground Saucer Watch. Despite evidence like this, secret government agencies like the CIA (inset: the agency's official seal) deny the existence of UFOs

Documents obtained by Ground Saucer Watch (GSW) from the United States government under the Freedom of Information Act now confirm that there has indeed been a cover up – right from the start of the modern UFO era in the late 1940s. But what is revealed by the documents is not that there is a worldwide plot to hide the true nature of UFOs – involving secret contact with extraterrestrials or some gruesome conspiracy against humanity, or some other outlandish suggestion. What is indicated, rather, is that the US government wishes to maintain a certain public *attitude* toward UFOs.

This atmosphere of doubt and derision has been created in a number of ways. Anyone can offer more or less plausible explanations for a UFO sighting: bright planets, unusual atmospheric conditions, meteorites, aircraft and so on. This approach

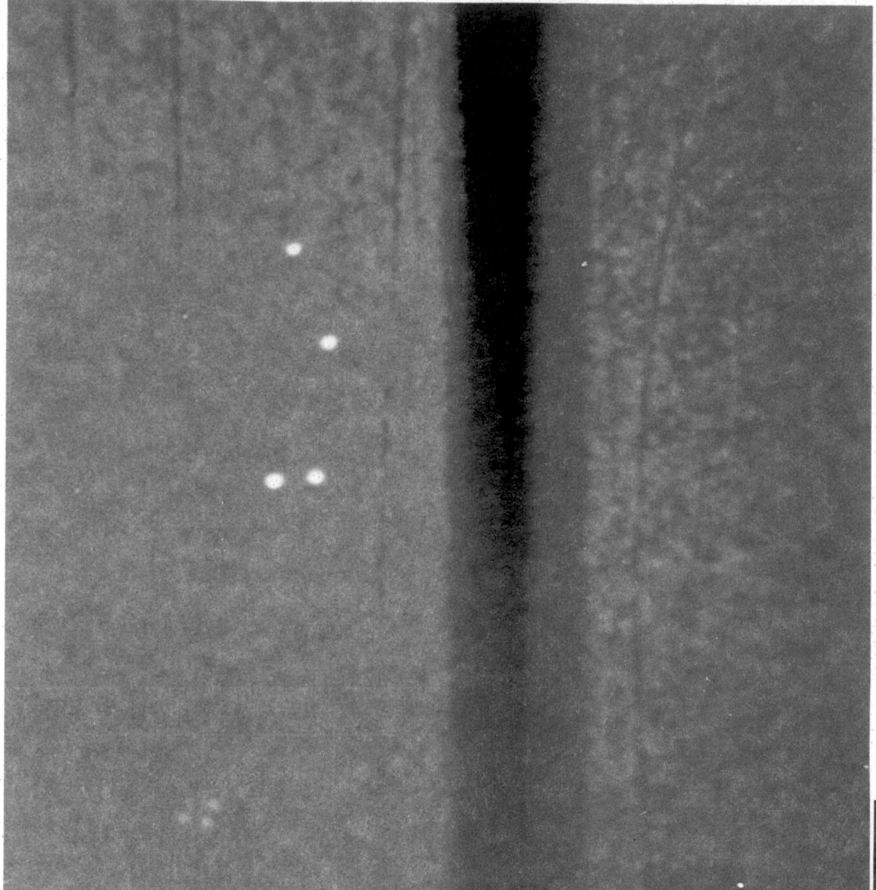

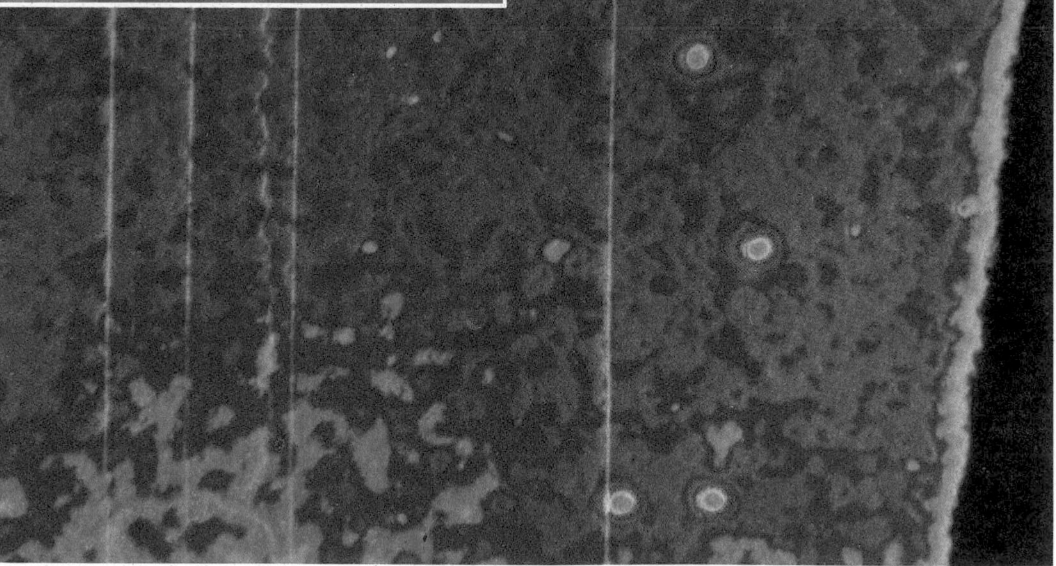

Above: a still from the film shot by Delbert C. Newhouse on 2 July 1952, 7 miles (11 kilometres) north of Tremonton, Utah, USA. Newhouse saw 'gunmetal-coloured objects shaped like two saucers, one inverted on top of the other' near the eastern horizon. Mystified, he shot some 16-millimetre film of them. A few frames have been released to the public, but many more remain in CIA hands. Ground Saucer Watch analysed the available frames with a range of techniques that included colour contrasting (right) – which demonstrated that the objects were indeed solid. Sceptics have claimed the UFOs were birds or planes, but computerised images of these at comparable distances (centre right: a bird; far right: a plane) show quite different characteristics of shape, reflectivity and density. GSW concluded that the images represented craft about 50 feet (15 metres) in diameter and 5 to 7 miles (8 to 11 kilometres) distant

cannot help but be successful, since as many as 95 per cent of alleged UFOs are indeed misinterpretations of known objects. Some sceptical investigators maintain that if these statistics are valid, then *all* UFO reports must represent objects that could be identified, were sufficient information on each sighting available. How can the man in the street argue with logic like that?

The debunking campaign has been successful too because well-known military or government figures have weighed in against the UFO. Most people have an automatic respect for public figures, whose statements are easily accepted. The few researchers who believed that they saw through the screen of official denials were easily dismissed as mavericks or cranks. There was, according to the official line, nothing to research. The government knew about everything there was to be seen in the sky.

But perhaps the cover up was so successful because no one could prove it was going on. There was no hard evidence to back the claim that the government was not being completely honest with the public.

And if the government knows so much, why haven't ex-employees come forward with their stories – revelations far more explosive, potentially, than any political scandal. Yet fewer than a dozen such individuals have come forward.

Despite all this, one's suspicions remain. Over the years GSW has encountered numerous incidents that showed every sign of direct or indirect government interference. Photographs went missing. Ground markings were ploughed under. Occasional witnesses talked about visits from military or intelligence officers who wanted to suppress the story of their UFO encounter. Too many cases came to an abrupt halt because some of the evidence was missing, making it impossible to reach a firm conclusion.

Largely at the insistence of Todd Zechel, GSW's director of research (and himself an ex-member of the intelligence community), it was decided to attack the issue head on – and approach the government directly. In the first place, GSW questioned the US Air Force – with predictable results. Typical replies were that 'the phenomenon does not represent any advanced technology beyond our present capability and . . . poses no direct threat to the United States.' And that 'there is no evidence indicating that sightings categorized as "unidentified" are extraterrestrial vehicles.' This was no more than expected; the next step was to confront the CIA – the agency most likely to be involved in suppressing UFO material. The CIA's reply – in a letter to GSW dated 26 March 1976 – is intriguing in the light of later events:

> In order that you may be aware of the true facts concerning the involvement of the CIA in the investigation of UFO phenomena, let me give you the following brief history. Late in 1952, the National Security Council levied upon the CIA the requirement to determine if the existence of UFOs would create a danger to the security of the United States. The Office of Scientific Intelligence established the Intelligence Advisory Committee to study the matter. That committee made the recommendations [in] the *Robertson Panel Report*. At no time prior to the formation of the Robertson Panel and subsequent to this issuance of the panel's report [in January 1953], has the CIA engaged in the study of UFO phenomena. The *Robertson Panel Report* is the summation of the Agency's interest and involvement in this matter.

Above: research director Todd Zechel (left) and director William H. Spaulding (right) of Ground Saucer Watch, discussing the UFO problem

The Robertson Panel's conclusions – after an intensive briefing by top airmen, astronomers and several CIA men – were simple. There was no cause for alarm militarily or scientifically, but – significantly for our case – the panel concluded that 'the continued emphasis on the reporting of these phenomena does, in these perilous times, result in a threat to the orderly functioning of the protective organs of the body politic.' Their recommendations were framed accordingly – debunk UFOs and educate people to recognise aerial phenomena.

In fact, the CIA did not let the matter drop there and then in 1953. Searches through the National Archives had shown that many reports were missing from the files. Dozens more letters to other agencies and even to the White House simply elicited the same official response – essentially, that UFOs did not exist. Why, then, the missing documents? When GSW made specific requests under the Freedom of Information Act a few papers were released – and so highly 'sanitised' that only a mind reader could have made sense of some of them. GSW then decided to attack in the courts. After 14 months of gruelling legal action the government released, on 15 December 1978, close to 1000 pages of documents. It was a major victory for GSW and ufology in general. What do the papers show?

First, that CIA involvement in UFOs actually pre-dates the National Security Council directive to set up what became the Robertson Panel – indeed it was the CIA that urged an investigation on the Council! Second, the implications for psychological warfare attract considerable attention. As one memo puts it, 'a fair proportion of our population is mentally conditioned to the acceptance of the incredible. In this fact lies the potential for the touching-off of mass hysteria and panic.' The third concern is with the vulnerability of US air defences: 'At any moment of attack . . . we cannot . . . distinguish hardware from phantom. . . .' The use of the word 'phantom' is interesting here. For another memo, from the Deputy Director for Intelligence, CIA, dated November 1952, says bluntly:

> Sightings of unexplained objects at great altitudes and traveling at high speeds in the vicinity of major US defense installations are of such a nature that they are not attributable to natural phenomena or known types of aerial vehicles.

In the light of that it is not surprising that when Edward Tauss, then Acting Chief of the Weapons and Equipment Division of the Office of Scientific Intelligence, recommended that the CIA 'continue' (*not* 'begin') coverage of the subject in August 1952, he should add:

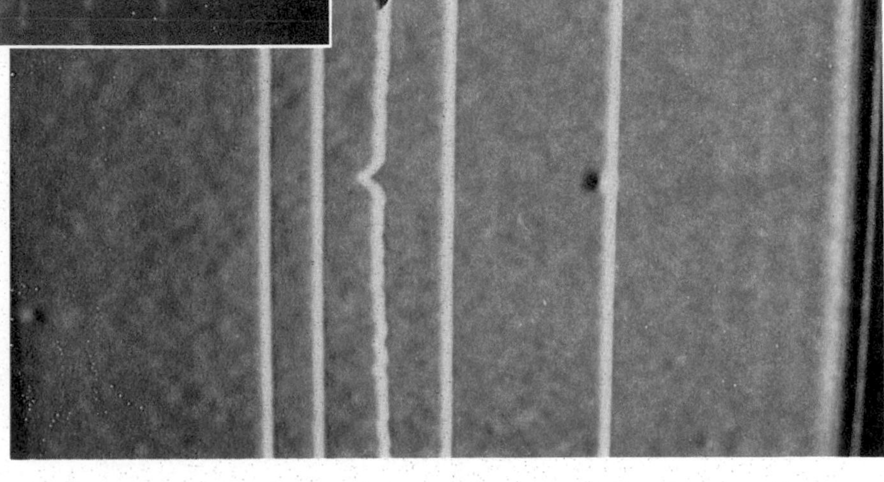

> It is strongly urged, however, that no indication of CIA interest or concern reach the press or public, in view of their probably alarmist tendencies to accept such interest as 'confirmatory' of the soundness of 'unpublished facts in the hands of the US government'.

It is clear then that the government – or the CIA at least – believed in the reality of the UFO phenomenon. It was also alarmed by it. And it was determined to keep what it did know to itself.

Nor was the report of the Robertson Panel the last word, though the CIA pretended to accept its findings. The US Air Force, after all, maintained Project Blue Book until 1969, after the Condon Committee published its findings – though whether Blue Book was ever told the whole truth either by the USAF itself or by other defence agencies remains in

Right: the last members of Project Blue Book, the US Air Force's full-time UFO investigation unit, disbanded in 1969 while under the leadership of Major Hector Quintanilla (seated). The project's tiny staff was unable to deal in any depth with the thousands of UFO reports it received every year, suggesting that the USAF was dragging its feet over the UFO question. But the more likely explanation is that the real research was being done in secret by the CIA, leaving Blue Book as a public relations front

The marine, the CIA and the UFO

One of the oddest UFO cases on record is the 1952 sighting by US Marine Ralph Mayher (top). It is odd not because of the sighting itself, which was as 'normal' as any UFO event, but because of what happened afterward to Mayher and the film he managed to take.

Ralph Mayher had heard that on the night of 28 July 1952 a couple named Goldstein had seen a flying saucer near their home. He was an experienced movie photographer and was interested in UFOs, so he arranged to meet the Goldsteins the next day and rented a camera – he had a theory that saucers sometimes appear on consecutive nights. At 9.30 p.m. on 29 July Mayher heard a woman across the street shout that a UFO was in view. The Goldsteins and another neighbour, Herman Stern, also saw the object, which remained visible over the ocean for about three minutes. Mayher managed to shoot only some 40 frames of film because his view was obscured by trees and buildings. The object was travelling horizontally toward the witnesses then 'turned' and shot away.

Mayher had his film processed at once and, as his unit commander had no objections, released some frames to the Miami press (centre) and even recorded a radio interview. But within 48 hours, USAF investigators were on the scene and threw a security blanket over the case. Mayher was visited by a number of men with CIA credentials, who apparently told him to keep quiet about the event. On enquiry Mayher was also told that the USAF thought the 'pinpoints of light' (*sic*) too small to analyse properly. But the film was never returned.

Perhaps the strangest part of the story is that while well-informed UFO investigators like Major Donald Keyhoe heard nothing of the film, ace debunker Dr Donald Menzel soon became familiar with it. With surreal inventiveness, Menzel said it showed a cobweb. GSW's computer analysis (bottom) indicates that the object is solid, 50 feet (15 metres) in diameter, and travelling at 2500 miles per hour (4000 km/h).

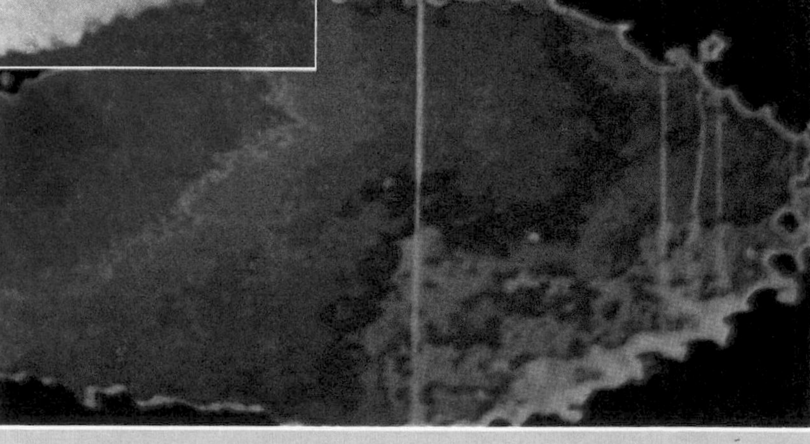

some doubt. The probable fate of the film taken by US Navy Warrant Officer Delbert C. Newhouse in 1952 – the 'Tremonton movie' that was shown to the Robertson Panel – is one indication of the CIA's true reaction to the evidence.

This film has been subject to several attempts at debunking. According to the witness, it shows a number of unusual craft travelling at enormous speed some 10 miles (16 kilometres) from the camera. Newhouse's report of the incident (he was a trained Navy photographer) is confirmed by GSW's computerised tests on the film – as it was by the USAF photo laboratory at Wright-Patterson AFB, who first analysed it. The film was then handed to the Naval Photographic Interpretation Center (NavPIC) at Anacostia, Maryland, and subjected to over 1000 man-hours of study. The Navy had no explanation for the objects but said they appeared to be 'self-luminous' spheres travelling at up to 7560 miles per hour (12,096 km/h). The Robertson Panel argued over the film for about two hours. They were also shown film of seagulls giving intense reflections of light in bright sunshine. The panel duly reported that 'the objects were considered strongly to represent birds.'

Who laid on that film of seagulls? Was it the CIA, experienced hands as they were at manipulation and suggestion? What they did not do was stop studying films of UFOs. As soon as the Robertson Panel had reported, NavPIC was dissolved. Some of its members, however, were moved to the CIA to form the National Photographic Interpretation Center (NPIC). Material dating from at least 1950 is kept there. Says GSW's Todd Zechel: 'There is a direct link between NavPIC's work on the Tremonton analysis and the decision of the CIA to place the analysis programme under its direct authority. In other words, rather than thinking the Tremonton analysis was in error, as has been purported, the CIA was impressed enough to immediately transfer the project to its headquarters.'

A cover for the CIA

Small wonder, then, that the USAF's Project Blue Book got such short shrift. According to Todd Zechel, Blue Book was 'in reality . . . no more than a PR front, primarily covering for the secret research being conducted by the CIA. . . . to give Blue Book full support would have been a waste, since it would have been duplicating research already being conducted by the CIA. Therefore, and for the most part unwittingly, Blue Book's façade enabled the CIA to pull off the greatest propaganda fraud in history.'

The documents obtained by GSW support the view that the CIA has persisted in UFO research. Among them are numerous reports, dutifully filed by US embassies abroad, of UFO sightings: 25 cases from Spain alone in one nine-month period between 1973 and 1974, a case from Portugal, multiple events in Tunisia in 1976 with many witnesses, radar tracking and police reports. 'A very concerned Chief of Military Security, General Balma' wanted to know if the US Sixth Fleet could 'shed any light on who or what they might be'. Not only was this – and innumerable other cases – being reported in 1976, seven years after the US government had supposedly given up its interest in UFOs in the wake of the Condon Report, but all UFO reports from the embassies are sent to the CIA – and the even more shadowy Defense Intelligence Agency, the National Security Council, the Secretary of Defense and the Secretary of State.

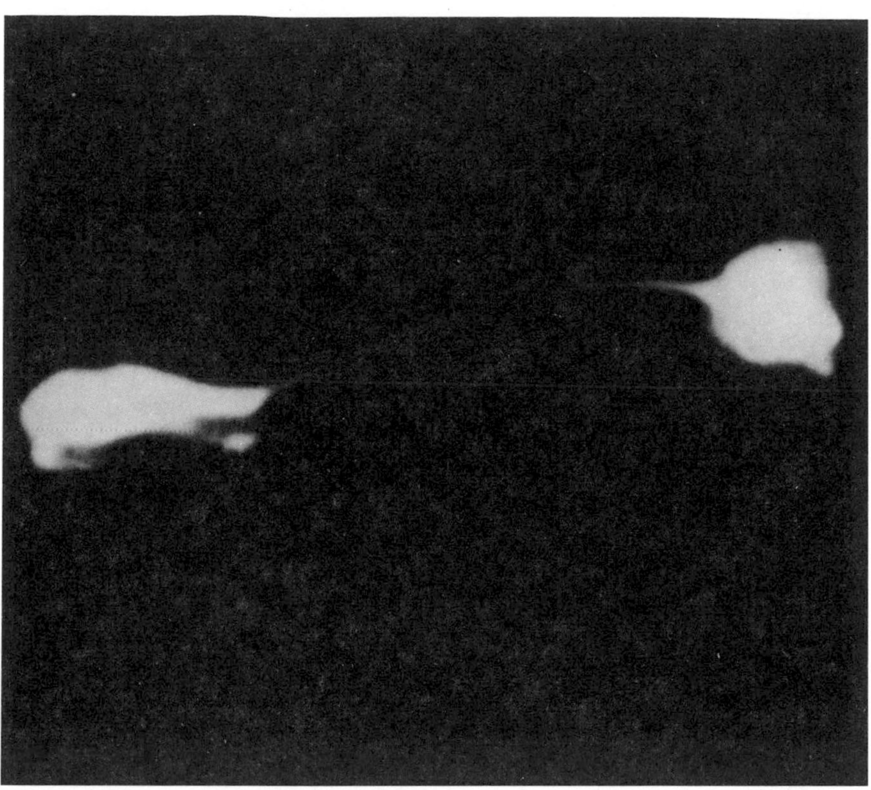

An unexplained mass of light seen over Ibiza in May 1974, which remained stationary for a brief period before rapidly climbing to a high altitude and vanishing. Reports such as this have been collected by the CIA from all over the world. Despite official claims that the agency ceased to have an interest in UFOs in 1953, documents have been obtained from CIA archives detailing sightings as late as 1976

Of course it is in the government's interests to pretend that it can identify everything in the sky: the security of the Western Alliance depends on that assumption. But the evidence indicates that the cover up does not stop at a desire to prevent alarm and despondency from spreading among the people. Just the opposite, if you happen to be a witness to a UFO: agents from the CIA Directorate of Operations (Clandestine Services) and Domestic Operations Division (sometimes called the 'Contact Division') have been known to harass, intimidate and silence people (see box).

Further to this, a more sinister game is perhaps being played out. For while the intelligence services attempt to deflate the UFO controversy, it would seem that they are also helping to feed it. It is to this aspect of the cover up, and the possible reasons for it, that we turn next.

Agents of confusion

For decades ufology has been in a state of confusion and disarray, struggling to research a phenomenon for which there is only slender evidence. Could the reason be that secret government agencies have been manipulating the evidence and the witnesses?

WHAT CONCLUSIONS can we draw from the documents that GSW has drawn from the CIA and the State Department? To answer that question, we first have to look objectively at some salient facts about the state of ufology. For that is the raw material that the CIA has used to its advantage over the years in its campaign of debunking, disinformation and calculated manipulation.

In the first place, most information about UFOs is based on the (usually unsupported) word of the witnesses. In many instances, this type of report is labelled 'authentic' by the pro-UFO community after an investigation that usually amounts to little more than a conversation with the participants. The ability of witnesses to 'identify' unusual aerial phenomena is notoriously unreliable: take for example the numerous cases of dome-shaped, spinning, saucer-like craft that perform extraordinary manoeuvres and display unusual lighting configurations reported by numerous reliable individuals – and then turn out to be aircraft towing advertising material. Lack of time, money and effective research techniques all contribute to the large element of foul-up in ufology.

On the other hand not all UFO events can be categorised as 'identifiable'. There is a small residue of events that seem to be caused by real objects (or what appear to be real objects). Blue Book estimated these at some 3 per cent of the total; civilian investigators put the figure at about 8 per cent. Probably the true figure is somewhere in between. But relatively little can be done to investigate these cases scientifically: there are few physical traces to take into the laboratory. What does seem certain is that no event represents a visitation from outer space. The mathematical odds are simply too remote for the extraterrestrial hypothesis to be taken seriously. Whatever true UFOs are, they would appear

The Goodyear blimp broadcasts its message to the world. But at some angles, could it be taken for a UFO? On 29 April 1978, Mr and Mrs S of Aurora, Illinois, reported a brilliantly lit, saucer-shaped craft 'as big as a football field' that was also seen by numerous other witnesses. With lights 'twirling round it', it followed the couple's car and allegedly caused power failures in the locality. But Allan Hendry, then investigator for the Center for UFO Studies, identified the 'saucer' as an aircraft owned by Ad Airlines of Chicago. This 'classic' UFO – and its mundane explanation – is a perfect example of the suggestibility of people. Anyone wishing to exploit such credulousness would have an easy task

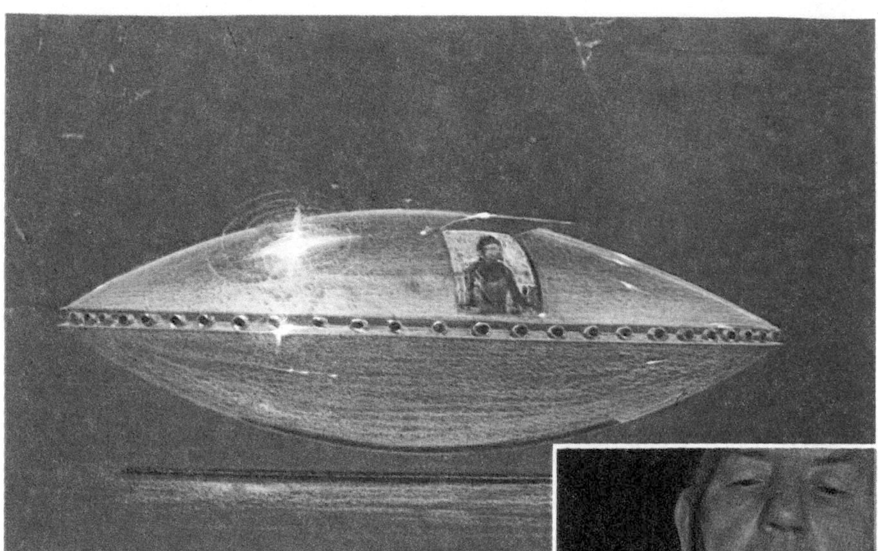

to have a distinctly earthly origin.

Even so, the transparent ineffectiveness of the official investigations, the ineptitude of the special commissions, and the constant stonewalling of the government led many civilian researchers to believe that a massive conspiracy was at work to cover up the government's knowledge of contact from outer space. In the 1940s, rumours of crashed saucers and dead aliens were rife. In the 1970s there were contactee and abduction stories galore. Not only that, but odd leaks and whispers of information came the way of the research groups from seemingly well-placed military and intelligence sources. What other conclusion was there to draw? Who else but aliens could be behind these tantalising stories?

Undoubtedly the government – as embodied in the CIA – has been involved in a cover up, as we have seen in the previous article. But what we are about to suggest is that while the CIA was collecting UFO information from around the globe (though claiming to be doing nothing of the kind), it was also manufacturing the rumour that the government knew more than it was prepared to admit. This tactic was employed partly to distract ufologists' attention from what the government was actually up to, and partly to add to the disarray of ufology.

Top: artist's impression of the 'spacecraft' seen by Joe Simonton in 1961, one of whose occupants gave him a pancake (above). Was he hoaxed by a secret government agency such as the DIA or NSA (below: their official seals)? And to what extent has the US government connived at rumours of 'captured aliens'? This picture (right) almost certainly shows a monkey used in rocket tests, not (as alleged) a space visitor

Behind the smokescreen of confusion and ignorance that it created, the CIA could proceed with its own outlandish experiments, whose real nature would be further disguised by the fact that they seemed no weirder than the rest of the whole bizarre phenomenon. And such activity would be just as intractable to scientific investigation, whether by the USAF or by civilians. In this it was fundamental that the USAF's investigations, for example, should be kept secret.

Clues to what really came to fascinate the CIA about the UFO question are scattered throughout the documents obtained by GSW. Of course, the government's conspirators of silence may not be from the CIA: they may be from the Defense Intelligence Agency, the National Security Agency, or the super-secret National Reconnaissance Organisation, or some clandestine group within any of these. Though the evidence to hand points to the CIA, the precise identity of the culprits is unimportant as long as the principles on which they seem to be working remain obscure.

From the first the CIA was intrigued by the psychological implications of the flying saucer mystery. Says part of one memorandum from 1952:

> With world-wide sightings reported, it was found that, up to the time of this investigation, there had been in the Soviet press no report or comment on flying saucers. With a state-controlled press, this could only result from an official policy decision. The question, therefore, arises as to whether or not these sightings: 1) could be controlled, 2) could be predicted, and 3) could be used from a psychological warfare

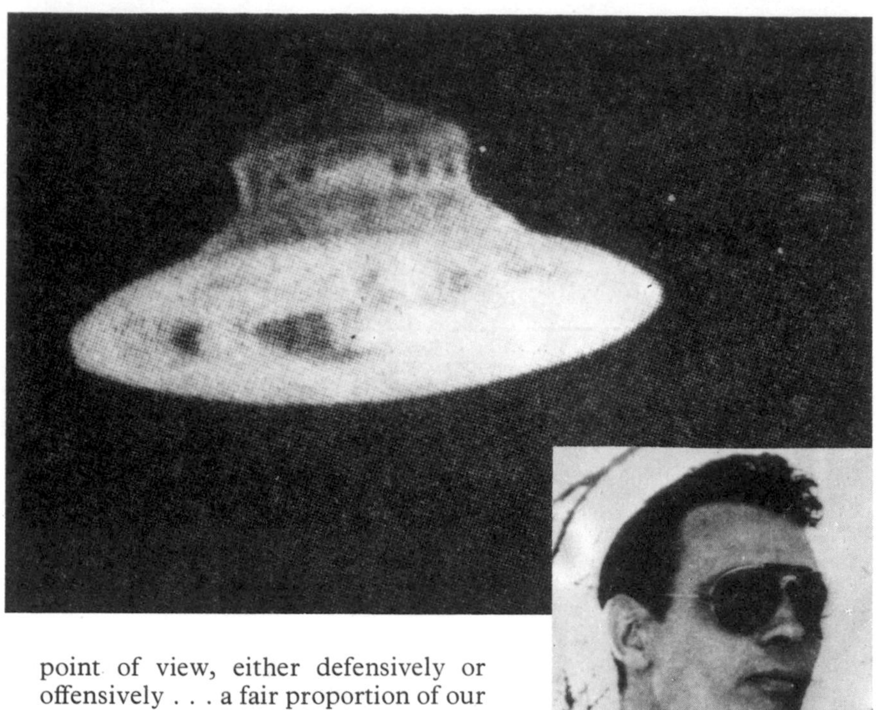

point of view, either defensively or offensively . . . a fair proportion of our population is mentally conditioned to the acceptance of the incredible.

These concerns were echoed in the secret report of the Robertson Panel in 1953, after which the CIA took over the real business of UFO investigation. At this time, the documents show, the CIA's Office of Scientific Intelligence was privately convinced that UFOs were extra-terrestrial craft. While awaiting proof of this, a debunking campaign was designed to defuse any potential public hysteria. Everyone expected that UFOs, like any other fad, would thus be helped to evaporate from the public consciousness.

The 'spaceship' (top) that was photographed by Howard Menger (above). The ship is suspiciously similar to that seen by Adamski, and its occupants imparted a similar, banal, wisdom. Who hoaxed whom?

But at some point – perhaps when the extra-terrestrial hypothesis was discarded, or perhaps when it became indisputable that UFOs were not simply a passing craze, or perhaps with the growth of secret high-technology research – the Agency realised that it could conduct experiments in psychological warfare of its own. If the Soviets were not behind the sightings in an attempt to manipulate the populace, there was no reason why the CIA should not get behind them instead. The benefits would be manifold: the military could get on with its secret aerial projects in comfort, since anyone coming unwittingly in contact with them would fall foul of the CIA's disinformation service and public debunking routine; and the CIA would discover just how far public attitudes could be manipulated, how individuals reacted to bizarre and unprecedented events, and how the information was disseminated and what reactions it generated.

This paradoxical programme of simultaneous encouragement and discouragement of the UFO controversy would work on several fronts. The idea of a cover up would be nurtured through leaks of classified information to civilian investigators, while a number of events could, quite simply, be staged. A number of agents infiltrating the research organisations would then be able to feed disinformation to the UFO groups and at the same time monitor their awareness of secret military hardware. Friends in the press would dutifully play up UFO material whether it were hoax, misidentification or staged event.

This programme is what GSW calls the

Anonymity guaranteed

At a UFO conference held at Fort Smith, Arkansas, in 1974 the research group APRO announced that henceforth it was intending to concentrate solely on contactee and abduction cases. Whether this was out of boredom with run-of-the-mill UFO sightings or because APRO hoped to gain publicity is not known. Some of the cases APRO has espoused are highly questionable – the famous Walton abduction case being but one instance. Here is another.

In February 1981 Ground Saucer Watch received from APRO an anonymous letter purporting to come from a US airman. It described a UFO landing near Kirtland Air Force Base, New Mexico. An individual in a metallic suit got out, got in again, and the craft flew away. A Civil Air Patrol Cadet, one Craig R. Weitzel, apparently took photographs of the landing. Later, he was (the letter said) visited by men in black, which Weitzel reported to the USAF security police, who in turn notified the Kirtland AFB Office of Special Investigations. A Mr Dody then looked into the matter, though the letter-writer claimed that Dody later disavowed all knowledge of the incident. The letter-writer also claimed that his commanding officer, one Colonel Bruce Purvine, had admitted to him that OSI was investigating UFO sightings – in the greatest secrecy. Mention was also made of crashed saucers, some of which are supposedly kept in the Sandia area of Kirtland AFB.

Ground Saucer Watch did what it could to check this report, which confirmed the existence of the Sandia area and of Mr Dody of the OSI. Colonel Purvine expressed some astonishment that he should be reported as discussing classified information with enlisted men, and denied discussing UFOs at all with anyone. He also pointed out that the 'airman' had got the name of Col. Purvine's command quite wrong.

Who led APRO up the garden path?

Coral Lorenzen, founder of APRO, which concentrates on UFO contacts and abductions. Mrs Lorenzen has said that such cases show 'a careful, methodical and in-depth study of Earth and its inhabitants is underway'

'Federal hypothesis'. It would not require especially large resources to be effective, since only a small number – no more than the unexplained 5 per cent – of events need to be created. The network of enthusiasts would do the rest. As the ripples spread out from ufologists a segment of the public would respond with psychic experiences, fantasies, a smattering of hoaxes and numerous 'induced' misinterpretations of aircraft, birds and planets. Another flap would be under way. And a similar pattern of manipulation could be used to cover up mishaps with military equipment or explain away occasional instances of its illegal testing. Once the technique was established there would be no reason not to use it to distract public attention from political embarrassment at home or abroad.

How far can we prove the Federal hypothesis? The documents obtained under the Freedom of Information Act reveal the CIA's persistent interest in psychological warfare. Is it coincidence that several members of the board of Governors of the National Investigations Committee on Aerial Phenomena (NICAP) are former members of the CIA? One, Colonel Joseph Bryan III, USAF (Ret.), is actually reputed to have been the founder of the CIA's psychological warfare section; another NICAP officer, Nicholas de Rochefort, had come to the CIA through its predecessor, the Office of Strategic Services – and was also an expert in psychological warfare. No less telling in GSW's view is the decision by the Aerial Phenomena Research Organisation in 1974 to concentrate solely on contact and abduction cases, which may have led them straight into the hands of the manipulators (see box). How many other UFO organisations have been infiltrated? How many other publications have been fed stories?

There is evidence that Generso Pope, owner of the *National Enquirer*, is an ex-CIA member and is still an associate of the Covert Action Staff (Disinformation and Propaganda) of the CIA's Operations Directorate (Clandestine Services). And who has paid the highest sums for the most exotic and sensational UFO stories – and so helped shape American popular opinion – but the *National Enquirer*? Such a technique is standard with the CIA: in December 1977 the *New York Times* reported that in the mid 1960s the CIA 'owned, subsidised or otherwise influenced . . . more than 800 news and public information organisations and individuals'.

It is also significant that UFO stories undergo reincarnation: the crashed saucer tales of the 1940s are emerging once again in the 1980s, while the fashion for contactee experiences of the early 1950s recurred in the 1970s. In a more sinister vein, what kind of psychological manipulation may be involved in close encounter cases? How many times have we all heard a baffled researcher say in all honesty that the event was 'real in the mind of the witness', despite a total lack of supporting evidence? It is at such specific instances of the UFO phenomenon, and its manipulation, that we must look next.

Above: a ground marking allegedly left by a UFO near Tully in Queensland, Australia, in 1966. Hard evidence like this is rare – and is rarely investigated by qualified scientists

In its attempts to get to the truth about the UFO phenomenon, GSW made an approach to President Jimmy Carter (above), who, while campaigning for the presidency, had announced his intention to pursue the mystery and had himself filed a UFO report (left). But NASA denied Carter's request to review UFO data, and the President himself was unable to further GSW's suit against the CIA. Said GSW: 'The guests in the White House come and go every four to eight years, but the CIA goes on for ever'

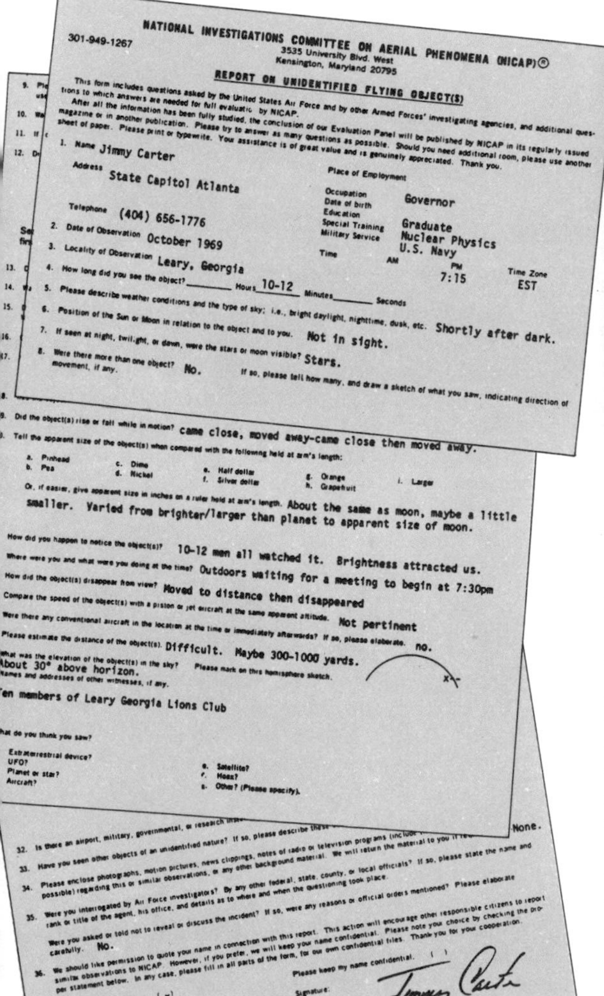

301-949-1267

NATIONAL INVESTIGATIONS COMMITTEE ON AERIAL PHENOMENA (NICAP)®
3535 University Blvd. West
Kensington, Maryland 20795

REPORT ON UNIDENTIFIED FLYING OBJECT(S)

This form includes questions asked by the United States Air Force and by other Armed Forces' investigating agencies, and additional questions to which answers are needed for full evaluation by NICAP.
After all the information has been fully studied, the conclusion of our Evaluation Panel will be published by NICAP in its regularly issued magazine or in another publication. Please try to answer as many questions as possible. Should you need additional room, please use another sheet of paper. Please print or typewrite. Your assistance is of great value and is genuinely appreciated. Thank you.

1. Name Jimmy Carter — Place of Employment
Address State Capitol Atlanta — Occupation Governor
Date of birth
Education Graduate
Telephone (404) 656-1776 — Special Training Nuclear Physics
Military Service U.S. Navy
2. Date of Observation October 1969 — Time AM PM 7:15 Time Zone EST
3. Locality of Observation Leary, Georgia
4. How long did you see the object? ______ Hours 10-12 Minutes ______ Seconds
5. Please describe weather conditions and the type of sky; i.e., bright daylight, nighttime, dusk, etc. Shortly after dark.
6. Position of the Sun or Moon in relation to the object and to you. Not in sight.
7. If seen at night, twilight, or dawn, were the stars or moon visible? Stars.
8. Were there more than one object? No. If so, please tell how many, and draw a sketch of what you saw, indicating direction of movement, if any.

9. Did the object(s) rise or fall while in motion? came close, moved away-came close then moved away.
10. Tell the apparent size of the object(s) when compared with the following held at arm's length:
a. Pinhead b. Pea c. Dime d. Nickel e. Half dollar f. Silver dollar g. Orange h. Grapefruit i. Larger
Or, if easier, give apparent size in inches on a ruler held at arm's length. About the same as moon, maybe a little smaller. Varied from brighter/larger than planet to apparent size of moon.

How did you happen to notice the object(s)? 10-12 men all watched it. Brightness attracted us.
Where were you and what were you doing at the time? Outdoors waiting for a meeting to begin at 7:30pm
How did the object(s) disappear from view? Moved to distance then disappeared
Compare the speed of the object(s) with a piston or jet aircraft at the same apparent altitude. Not pertinent
Were there any conventional aircraft in the location at the time or immediately afterwards? If so, please elaborate. no.
Please estimate the distance of the object(s). Difficult. Maybe 300-1000 yards.
What was the elevation of the object(s) in the sky? Please mark on this hemisphere sketch. About 30° above horizon.
Names and addresses of other witnesses, if any. Ten members of Leary Georgia Lions Club

What do you think you saw?
Extraterrestrial device? UFO? Planet or star? Aircraft? e. Satellite? f. Hoax? g. Other? (Please specify).

32. Is there an airport, military, governmental, or research ... None.
33. Have you seen other objects of an unidentified nature? If so, please describe these ...
34. Please enclose photographs, motion pictures, news clippings, notes of radio or television programs (include ... possible) regarding this or similar observations, or any other background material. We will return the material to you if ...
35. Were you interrogated by Air Force investigators? By any other federal, state, county, or local officials? If so, please state the name and rank or title of the agent, his office, and details as to where and when the questioning took place.
Were you asked or told not to reveal or discuss the incident? If so, were any reasons or official orders mentioned? Please elaborate carefully. No.
36. We should like permission to quote your name in connection with this report. This action will encourage other responsible citizens to report similar observations to NICAP. However, if you prefer, we will keep your name confidential. Please note your choice by checking the proper statement below. In any case, please fill in all parts of the form, for our own confidential files. Thank you for your cooperation.
You may use my name. (x) — Please keep my name confidential. ( )
Signature: Jimmy Carter
37. Date of filling out this report 9-18-73

UFOs: a Federal case

Is a government conspiracy really at the root of the UFO mystery? Having studied the documents obtained by Ground Saucer Watch, PETER BROOKESMITH suggests why the CIA and the US military might indeed embark on such a programme of deception

'I SUGGEST THAT we discuss at an early board meeting the possible offensive or defensive utilization of these phenomena for psychological warfare purposes.'

The subject of the secret memorandum in which this sentence appeared was 'Flying Saucers'. It was written in the early 1950s by Walter B. Smith, Director of the CIA, to the Director of the Psychological Strategy Board. And it would appear that in the intervening years the CIA – or possibly some other clandestine agency – has indeed been using the UFO phenomenon in a form of psychological warfare. And the objects of the CIA's attention have been the citizens of the United States.

This is, to say the least, a disturbing proposition, but there are several reasons why the US government might want to encourage a belief in UFOs, and then manipulate that belief among the populace at large. By looking at specific aspects of the UFO phenomenon as we now understand it, these reasons become clear.

In the first place the United States has a massive investment in military technology, especially in the field of airborne weapons. And while the armed services have literally thousands of square miles of desert and scrub in which to test craft such as the radar-defeating 'Stealth' aeroplane, remotely piloted vehicles, unusual aerofoil configurations and even biochemical weapons, there are occasions when these need to be tested in unrestricted areas. The advantage of a general willingness to 'believe in UFOs' is inestimable in such a case.

Take the Stealth aircraft, for instance. Development work on an aeroplane that can make itself virtually invisible to radar has been going on since at least 1966. The project was classified in 1977, but pictures released by Boeing show a small, oddly shaped bomber resembling nothing so much as a paper dart, unusual enough, perhaps, to be taken for a UFO even in daylight.

But in 1975 a mobile radar unit of the United States Air Force in California picked up a target flying at 460 miles per hour (740 km/h) from Edwards Air Force Base. Then it turned – and in one sweep of the radar had vanished. This was taken to mean that it had accelerated instantly to over 2000 miles per

Above: a Teledyne Ryan 262 remotely controlled drone on a test flight. The craft is designed to be virtually invisible to radar and infra-red detection, and is nearly soundless. Its purpose: surveillance and electronic warfare. Pilotless craft are a new growth area for military technology – and perhaps for ufology too

Right: Boeing's version of a Stealth aircraft prototype

Roswell and after

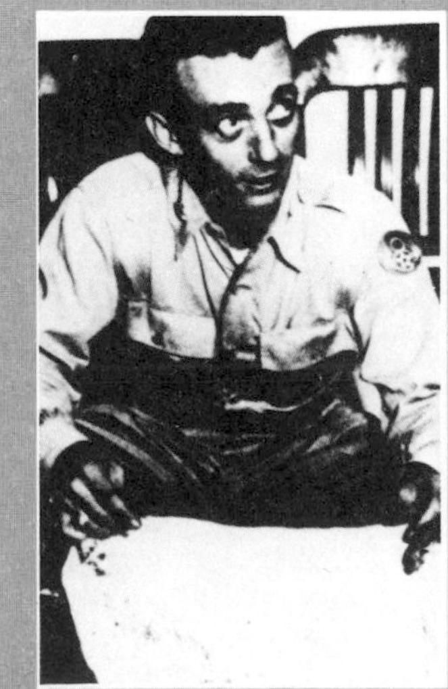

'The many rumours regarding the flying disc became a reality yesterday when the intelligence office of the 509th Bomb Group of the Eighth Air Force, Roswell Army Air Field, was fortunate enough to gain possession of a disc through the co-operation of one of the local ranchers and the sheriff's office of Chaves County.'

Thus began the press release issued by Lieutenant Walter Haut of the US Army Air Force on 8 July 1947 – and so the legend of the Roswell Incident was born. In fact, what was found was wreckage of a rather unusual type – so unusual, according to Major (later Lieutenant Colonel) Jesse A. Marcel, that it was rapidly substituted with the remains of a weather balloon, which he then presented to the press (left) as the material he had found in the New Mexico desert.

The case for a flying disc or some extra-terrestrial craft being involved is flimsy to say the least, and based largely on second-hand accounts to boot, while hour (3200 km/h) – typical UFO behaviour! In fact, the target was a Stealth aircraft on test, and had switched to its 'invisible' mode just after it came on screen. Officially it was logged as 'unidentified' – one part of the USAF seeing no need for another part to know what it was doing. The foundations of the UFO myth were made a little stronger – and the secret aircraft remained secret.

The presence of 'moles' from the intelligence community within UFO organisations will further ensure that no really vital information can leak to the outside world without being first carefully distorted. In much the same way, what looks like an over-enthusiastic and ill-informed reaction on the part of a press officer in the US Army Air Force has been kept alive as 'evidence' of an alien saucer that supposedly crashed in New Mexico in July 1947 – just days after the first polyethylene research balloons were launched from the nearby White Sands proving ground (see box).

More sinister are the unexplained cases of cattle mutilation associated with UFO sightings, reported from the USA. The 'operations' on these animals are always said to have been done with unnerving neatness. It is possible – and if one accepts the notion of a government UFO conspiracy it is probable – that this 'surgery' is performed on animals that have been exposed to biochemical weapons. On this theory the government is deliberately reinforcing the belief in the incredible or paranormal origin of the mutilations. It may be doing this to camouflage its tests of biochemical weapons and of the extent to which their use is detectable by experienced farmers and veterinary surgeons. Or it may be using the UFO mythology to disguise gruesome incompetence by the military – the unintentional injury of cattle by its toxic materials.

Snippy the horse, owned by Mrs Berle Lewis (centre) of Alamosa, Colorado, USA, is tested for radiation after dying 'in mysterious circumstances'. Radiation was indeed detected – so was the damage to the animal caused by predators, or was there some more human agency at work? Those who prefer a paranormal explanation or who offer ufonauts as the culprits may be unwittingly aiding a cover up of tests of biochemical weapons

A more direct form of experiment in aggressive psychology may lie behind the murky history of the 'men in black'. It is altogether likely that the CIA has actually staged a number of UFO events, especially contact and abduction cases. The recurrent claim of MIB victims that no one but they knew of the sighting would then be a delusion, 'MIBs' having in fact set it up.

It would serve the interests of psychological warfare to know how people react to empty threats: the MIBs, after all, never seem to follow through their promises to maim or silence their unwilling hosts.

Similarly, the MIB technique could be used to evaluate responses to bizarre (not to say unearthly) behaviour. Hence the stream of surreal comments, inane questions and asocial activity that MIBs like to indulge in. Techniques of surveillance are now so subtle that agents would not have to follow through the visit, which could simply be recorded remotely. And any leakage only adds to the mass of incoherent absurdities that make up most of ufology.

This absurdity is deliberate. A phenomenon with no logic, yet that undeniably exists, serves to keep investigators occupied in the hopeless attempt to *create* a logic, a theory, that will tie all the loose ends together. In turn a very large public will apply its energies to ufology, energies that cannot reach a conclusion. This serves government purposes – *any* government's purposes. It was apparent very early on that the public was not going to get tired of the UFO question (even the sceptical Robertson Panel gloomily predicted an increase in sightings). The clever solution was then to direct this interest and control it – and hope that a large number of otherwise troublesome people would be kept occupied with an insoluble problem,

members of a University of Pennsylvania archaeology team who helped gather the wreckage have apparently not been contacted by researchers.

So what did crash? On 3 July 1947, the approximate date of the crash, the White Sands Missile Range launched both a V-2 rocket and (for the US Army Air Force) the first polyethylene balloons. Either of these, impacting off the range, may have been responsible for the wreckage found in the desert – and would have caused the embarrassed 'cover up' that followed the ill-advised press notice issued by Lieutenant Haut. Likewise, the accounts of the material as light but very tough and distinctly unfamiliar would be explained.

The significance of the incident for ufologists may lie in White Sands' own admission that some 7 per cent of their firings go awry, including heavyweight tactical missiles like the Pershing (right): one crashed in 1967 in Van Horn, Texas, 250 miles (400 kilometres) away.

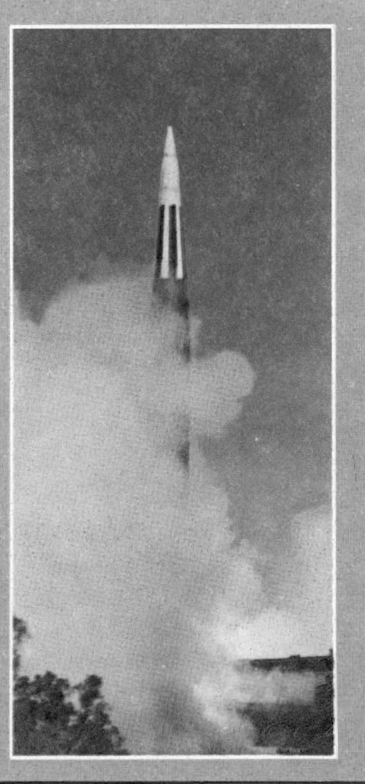

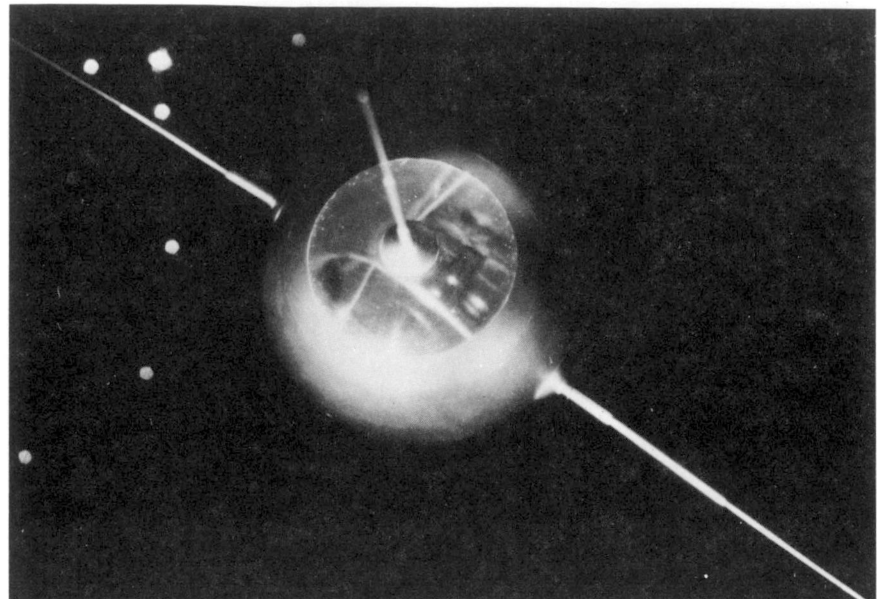

thus removing some sources of political challenge. A persistent harping on the (actually untenable) extra-terrestrial hypothesis has undoubtedly led to the creation of several pseudo-religions. The adherents of these saucer cults will certainly not berate the government for its mishandling of the economy or foreign policy, since the Galactic Brotherhood will see us right in the end.

Public dissatisfaction with the US government's performance was certainly diverted by a UFO event in 1957 – an indication of both how quickly and how soon the operation was mounted. At that time the United States suffered several humiliations as attempt after attempt to launch its first space vehicle, the Vanguard rocket, ended in disaster. Then in November 1957 the USSR succeeded in putting a *second* satellite into orbit, a mere 30 days after the epoch-making *Sputnik*. Within hours UFOs appeared over Texas and New Mexico – and elbowed the Soviet achievement out of the headlines. With so much interest in space, the extra-terrestrial obsession was given another nudge forward, and national embarrassment was temporarily forgotten.

Even abduction cases can serve a dual – or even triple – purpose. It is not difficult to stage a UFO encounter or abduction that is 'real in the mind of the witness', provided one can get at the victim with drugs, hypnosis – or both. Other special effects would scarcely stretch the resources or ingenuity of a banana republic, let alone the US government. And so the experimenters could add to the UFO myth; test their psychological or hallucinogenic techniques; note whether the victim succumbs entirely; observe how the information is treated by the media, by ufologists and by the public; and, having generated another outrageous story, keep serious scientists away from the UFO scene. The subjective reality of the experience for the witness will also strengthen 'saucer' enthusiasts in their belief that sceptics are ignoring the issue of the century while government and scientists are covering up the truth. As they are, but not quite in the way that ufologists first thought.

Above: *Sputnik I*, whose launch in October 1957 shocked Americans by its demonstration of Soviet technological superiority. It may be no accident that when the USSR launched a second satellite only a month later, a sudden wave of UFO reports from Texas and New Mexico flooded the press to divert the public's attention

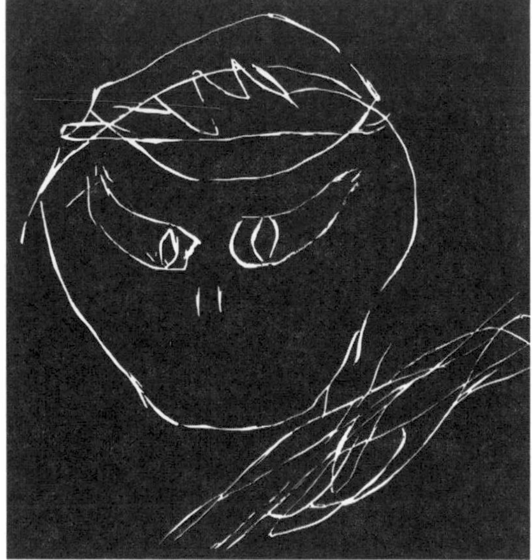

Right: the ufonaut, drawn by Betty Hill (below), that allegedly abducted her and her husband Barney. Were they the victims of a bizarre experiment in mind-bending by CIA psychologists?

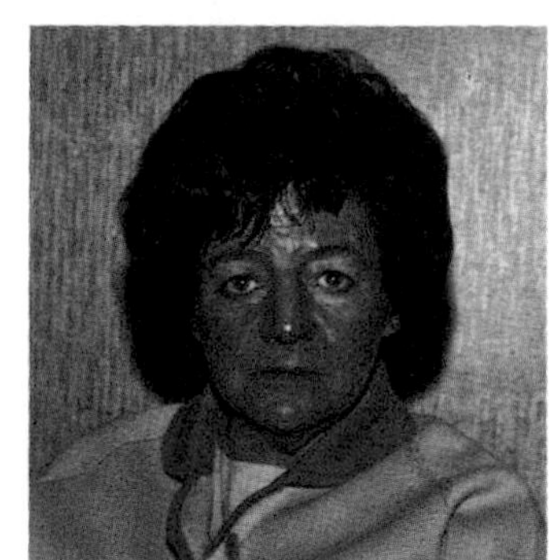

This conspiracy theory will probably be offensive to many ufologists. But one further fact supports it: and that is the total lack of progress that has been made on the question of what true UFOs really are. If researchers could answer that question, the concern with abductions and contact cases (which consumes so much more energy among researchers) would have some purpose.

The present state of publicly available knowledge is ably summarised by William H. Spaulding, who first raised the 'Federal hypothesis' to account for the elusiveness of the phenomenon:

> What new, startling breakthroughs have emerged from the pro-saucer movement? The past 30 years have been wasted attempting to research something that wasn't there in the first place. . . . The fact that the saucer belief system has survived so long with so little logical and evidential support is a testimony to the tenacity of human credulity. The audacity and creativity of the CIA and other researchers in this subject have created three generations of enthusiasts and have captured the imagination of the public. . . . What makes the saucer saga so interesting and significant is that it is a genuine psycho-social movement that has been born and is still growing in our own time.

A world-famous authority on UFOs once expressed his private belief that the phenomenon was controlled by some kind of intelligence – though whose it was he was not prepared to say.

The answer seems to be that UFOs, in the USA at least, are controlled not so much by an intelligence as by an intelligence *agency*.

In the summer of 1980 the crew of the *Caioba-Seahorse* tugboat saw a mysterious object floating on the water off the coast of Brazil. It seemed to be signalling by turning on various coloured lights – and soon after a UFO descended. Slowly the two objects linked up and then, as one, rose and swept out to sea. Did the crew witness a rescue operation of a USO by a UFO?

An unfathomable mystery

Everyone has heard of unidentified flying objects, but what about unidentified submarine objects? A growing number of reports about USOs has led JANET and COLIN BORD to investigate this phenomenon

ON THE EVENING of 30 July 1967 Jorge Montoya was officer on duty on the Argentinian ship *Naviero* as it steamed in the South Atlantic 120 miles (190 kilometres) from the Brazilian coast. The off-duty officers and crew were below having their evening meal and all was calm and as it should be. Glancing over to the starboard side, Montoya was suddenly startled to see a strange cigar-shaped craft gliding silently through the water 50 feet (15 metres) away. He stared in amazement for a moment and then alerted the captain on the intercom. When Captain Julián Ardanza arrived on deck the mysterious vessel was still running alongside his ship. The two men studied it for some 15 minutes as it held its position. The mystery vessel glowed with a brilliant bluish-white light and left no wake. They estimated its length as about 105 to 110 feet (32 to 33.5 metres).

Then, without any warning, the unidentified vessel turned towards the merchant ship and, glowing brilliantly as it accelerated, it dived beneath the ship and rapidly disappeared into the ocean depths. The officers and crew of the *Naviero* had just witnessed one of the enigmatic unidentified submarine objects (USOs). In a subsequent press interview the captain said that it was certainly no conventional submarine nor a whale, and during 20 years at sea he had never seen anything like it.

The number of UFO sightings recorded since the late 1940s runs into tens of thousands, and the reports that have been collected suggest that USOs are almost as numerous in the waters of this planet as are UFOs in the skies. More than 70 per cent of the Earth's surface is covered with water. The average depth of the seas and oceans is 2 miles (3 kilometres), and Man has barely begun to explore the vast area that lies beneath the surface. Here technologically advanced beings would find an ideal place in which to pursue their activities well away from the sight of men.

Just as diligent researchers have unearthed reports of UFOs that pre-date the 1947 sightings – believed by many to be the first – so there are also reports of USOs from the past century. On the night of 24 February 1885 in the North Pacific the crew of the ship *Innerwich* watched as a huge object, glowing with a brilliant red light, dived into the sea, throwing up a large volume of water as it sank below the waves. On 12 November 1887 near Cape Race, Newfoundland, Captain Moore of the British ship *Siberian* watched for five minutes as 'a large ball of fire' rose from the ocean to a height of 50 feet (15 metres). It moved towards his ship and against the prevailing wind before it departed. These and many other reports suggest that USOs can sometimes become UFOs, and vice versa.

One of the most dramatic cases in the USO files occurred on the night of 26 July 1980.

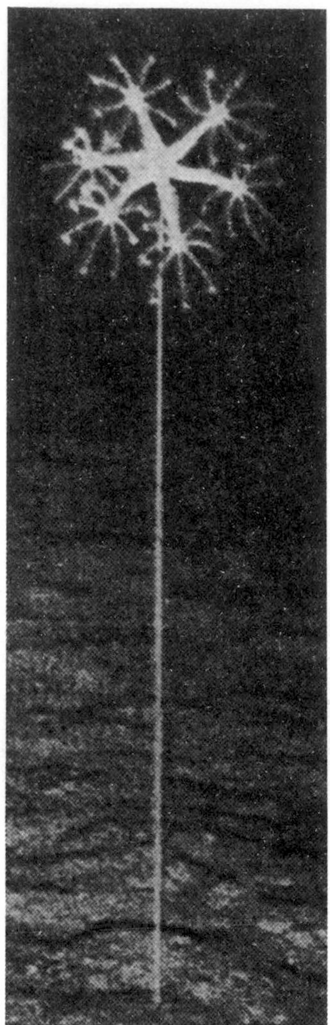

The object on the left was photographed in the ocean west of the Cape of Good Hope in 1964 and has puzzled marine biologists ever since. It looks as if it was built, and the cross-arms are suggestive of some kind of antenna. But is it anything other than a marine animal? Could it in fact be one of the tall polyps (above) that live in the same waters?

The tugboat *Caioba-Seahorse* was on a routine journey when, 60 miles (95 kilometres) from the Brazilian coast near Natal, the first mate was suddenly aware of a grey object 30 feet (10 metres) in diameter floating on the surface straight ahead. At the same time a bright light could be seen over the sea rapidly approaching them. The first mate quickly changed direction to avoid a collision with the floating object, which then turned on various coloured lights – yellow, red, green and blue. The bright light had now reached them and could be seen as a glowing oval body hovering silently about 200 feet (60 metres) above the floating USO. The tugboat's engines had stopped and the crew watched with fear and fascination as the UFO slowly descended onto the floating USO. A link-up took place, the USO lights went out, and the two bodies rose together. After hovering for some minutes in the area the UFO with its load swept rapidly out to sea. This event naturally prompted a high-level investigation by the naval authorities, and much speculation from the Brazilian civilian ufologists. Did the tugboat crew witness a rescue operation of one UFO by another? Or was it more of a routine pick-up, at a prearranged location? No conclusion could be reached, but whatever the naval authorities found out they kept to themselves.

A green glow at sea

USOs have also been sighted off the North American coast, one witness being 19-year-old Wesley Gruman who was driving to Oak Bluff, Massachusetts, on the evening of 27 March 1979. Noticing a green glow over the top of some sand dunes, he looked towards the sea as soon as his view of it was unobstructed. Some 200 feet (60 metres) offshore a 30-foot (9-metre) long luminous cylinder was floating on the water. Gruman stopped his car as the USO silently rose from the surface and he got out to watch its ascent. He decided to get his powerful hand lamp from the car, but found he could move only his head. This paralysis lasted until the USO had flown out of sight, and Gruman also reported two other odd effects. The first was a low frequency hum that his AM car radio had emitted during the sighting, and the second was the behaviour of his wristwatch. This hand-wound calendar model had been three days ahead with its date before his experience, but the next day it was showing the correct date and has done since then.

At Newport, Rhode Island, John Gallagher observed during daylight hours something unidentified that was lifted or propelled from the sea. In April 1961 he was working on a house by the beach and noticed a red sphere bobbing on the waves. Intrigued, he went to the second floor for a better view, and he could then see that it was about 200 yards (180 metres) offshore and drifting seawards. Suddenly, it rose steadily to a height of about 60 feet (18 metres), stopped, and then, accelerating to about 100 miles per hour (160 km/h), moved with an undeviating flight out to sea. Gallagher was sure he had not seen a balloon, for its movements and speed had not been those of an object being blown by the wind, but of one under intelligent control.

Unidentified submarine objects also extend their activities to inland waters. There are reports of them seen entering and leaving lakes and rivers, harbours, creeks and fjords. There was a mass sighting on the Araguari River in Brazil in November 1980 when more than 70 people who were waiting for a ferry saw a solid object 15 feet (5 metres) in diameter rise from under the water. For some four minutes it hovered at a height of 650 feet (200 metres), and then slowly moved out to sea. At one point it moved to within 100 feet (30 metres) of the bank.

The man who saw 'a typical flying saucer' rise from the Thompson River near Kamloops, British Columbia, Canada, wished to remain anonymous, but he is known as a reliable individual to Dr J. Allen Hynek, world renowned UFO authority. On the sunny afternoon of 16 May 1981, the witness was quietly fishing when, with a noise 'like water being poured into a hot frying pan', the strange craft emerged from the frothing water about 100 yards (90 metres) offshore. Then, with a rapid acceleration, it zoomed up over his head and quickly flew away. As it did so there was a pattering sound as pellets of something from the object rained down around him. He collected some of this material, which was taken for analysis by the Center for UFO Studies in Illinois, USA. At the end of 1981 the results were still to be announced.

The driver and passengers of a London bus had a front-seat view when a silver cigar-shaped USO dived into the River Lea after cutting through telephone wires and gouging a scar in the concrete bank. Bob Fall was driving his number 123 bus towards Tottenham on 13 April 1964 when the USO dived across the road in front of him and landed in the river. The police, who found nothing when they dragged the 6-foot (2-metre) deep river, suggested that the witnesses may have seen a flight of ducks – but that still does not explain broken wires and damaged concrete.

Another 'impossible' USO was observed in the St Lawrence River near the city of Quebec, Canada, in March 1965. For four or five minutes Captain Claude Laurin of Quebecair and his co-pilot could see the 'submarine' lying below the surface over 200 miles (320 kilometres) from the open sea, a situation that would be extremely hazardous for any ordinary submersible. On 23 May 1969 three eyewitnesses watched 'a round shining object with flashing red lights' dive into the St Lawrence. A police search 'found nothing'.

The possibility that some UFOs, after a supersonic flight through the atmosphere, need to cool their overheated structures is persuasively supported by the following report. In the summer of 1967 a cub master and his assistant were camping with their cub pack on the shore of a quiet lake 20 miles (32 kilometres) from St John, New Brunswick,

Titicus reservoir in New York state, USA. This body of water was the scene of a USO sighting by a couple called Bordes in 1955. They were followed by the lights of a floating object for a time, but came to no harm. Reports indicate that reservoirs seem to be of special interest to USOs

Canada. The boys were asleep and the two men had walked down to the lake to fetch water. Down through the dusk came a UFO shaped like two saucers – or plates placed face to face – with lights flashing red, orange, green and blue around its edge. As it touched the water and sank there was a sizzling noise, reminiscent of the sound reported by the man who saw a UFO rise from the Kamloops River in 1981. The lake contained clear, cold water and was fed by mountain snows, but when the men looked at it the next morning it was quite muddy and felt lukewarm.

Not many people spend their nights outdoors on lakes, but those who do may see strange sights, as did Mr and Mrs Bordes who, on the night of 16 September 1955, were fishing on the Titicus reservoir in New York state. By 1.30 a.m. they had had no luck. Then Mrs Bordes saw a pink luminous sphere rise from the water and splash back in again. A short while later, back on shore, they both saw a dark shape out on the water. It had two white horizontal streaks of light at its base and a pale yellow revolving light above. Mr Bordes, more curious than afraid, rowed towards the lights, and they retreated at a faster rate. Then they came towards him and he in turn rowed away. His wife did not like the situation at all, so they rowed a mile (1.6 kilometres) to the mooring stage, the lights following at a distance. As they drove off in their car the lights were still visible on the reservoir. Reservoirs seem to be of particular interest to UFOs and USOs, and there are many reports of their activity over and in such waters. Speculation among researchers runs the gamut from the suggestion that they are monitoring the pollution to which humanity subjects itself, to the belief that they are

Lake Siljan in Sweden in the green lush of summer (above) and as it looked in the icy winter of 1976 when a USO ploughed across it (below). Three witnesses saw a big grey object cut a channel through the thick ice of the lake – an incident that has remained a mystery to this day. The way the ice was broken suggests that something extremely powerful may have pushed up from below rather than fallen from the sky

Opposite: newspaper stories speculate about the mystery objects falling into Swedish lakes and about the 'ghost rockets' seen in Swedish skies. One theory was that the UFOs were V2 rockets (far right) being tested by the Russians. But the known facts about V2s do not bear this out

systematically doping our drinking water for reasons best known to themselves.

The power of these enigmatic machines, if machines they are, seems to be immense, as the following reports from the ice-clad waters of Sweden indicate. On 30 April 1976 between 5.15 and 5.30 p.m. three witnesses watched as a 30-foot (9-metre) long, dark grey object ploughed across Lake Siljan in central Sweden, cutting a channel through the 8-inch (20-centimetre) thick ice. The channel was 10 to 12 feet (3 to 3.6 metres) wide and ran across the lake for more than half a mile (800 metres). As the USO ripped through the ice at about 60 miles per hour (95 km/h), ice blocks and water cascaded up on either side. Eight years earlier, on 5 April 1968, *The Times* reported that 'something "incredibly powerful" has smashed a huge hole through the ice covering a lake in Central Sweden, but scientists and military experts are uncertain about what it was.' Two local people had found the hole, which was 700 square yards (585 square metres) in area, near Malung. Leading the investigation was Colonel Curt Hermansson, who said that an aircraft crash was out of the question as there were no traces around the hole, 'only big blocks of ice which have been thrown up, indicating that whatever went into the lake was incredibly powerful'. The fact that the 3-foot (1-metre) thick ice had been thrown *up* suggests that, in view of the USO activity that has been logged, something 'incredibly powerful' may have come *up* from below – but who can be certain? Divers who went down could find nothing on the muddy lake bottom to explain the mystery. A few days later another large hole was discovered in the ice covering a lake at Serna, and that too remained a mystery.

It is not surprising that the authorities assumed that the holes had been made by objects falling into the water. For years the Scandinavians have been plagued by unidentified objects falling from the skies into their lakes. A great many of these occurred in 1946 and were at first dubbed meteors by the press, but when reports of silver torpedo-shaped projectiles emitting trails of smoke continued to be made, very often several reports each day, they were termed 'ghost rockets'. The first assumption was that these were captured German V2 rockets being tested by the Russians, but these speculations were not borne out by the facts. Although the German Peenemünde rocket development complex had been occupied by the Russians in May 1945, the German scientists had already surrendered to the American forces, leaving the testing facilities completely wrecked. It would not have been possible for Russian scientists to start assembling and firing V1s or V2s in the time available, let alone develop and build hundreds of new rockets with flight characteristics quite different from those of the V2.

A typical 'ghost rocket' report was made on 19 July 1946 by a family group who reported that, with a noise 'like a mighty wind', two rockets, 7 feet (2 metres) long and with stubby 3-foot (1-metre) wings halfway down their bodies, swept overhead and dived into Lake Mjøsa 60 miles (96 kilometres) north of Oslo in Norway. A crater could be seen at the bottom of the lake, but dredging by the military authorities found nothing. The ghost rockets were tracked on radar as they made abrupt changes of direction, but they were rarely seen to crash. But when they did they always crashed into a lake – yet no traces of wreckage were ever found, despite intensive searches by troops.

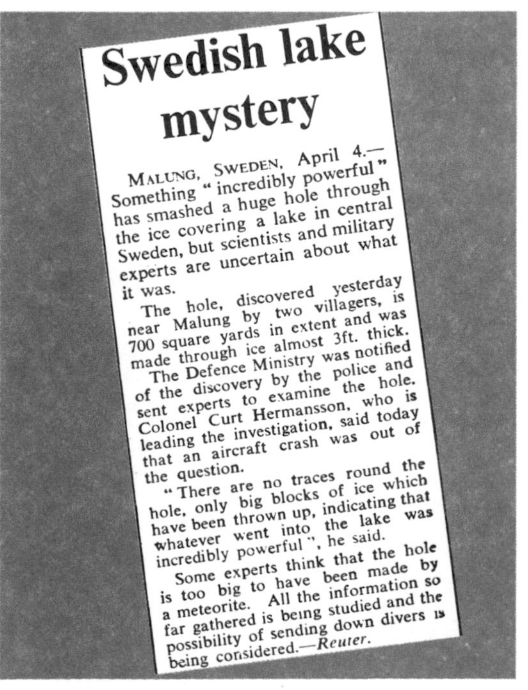

Swedish lake mystery

MALUNG, SWEDEN, April 4.—Something "incredibly powerful" has smashed a huge hole through the ice covering a lake in central Sweden, but scientists and military experts are uncertain about what it was.

The hole, discovered yesterday near Malung by two villagers, is 700 square yards in extent and was made through ice almost 3ft. thick.

The Defence Ministry was notified of the discovery by the police and sent experts to examine the hole. Colonel Curt Hermansson, who is leading the investigation, said today that an aircraft crash was out of the question.

"There are no traces round the hole, only big blocks of ice which have been thrown up, indicating that whatever went into the lake was incredibly powerful", he said.

Some experts think that the hole is too big to have been made by a meteorite. All the information so far gathered is being studied and the possibility of sending down divers is being considered.—*Reuter.*

MYSTERY ROCKETS OVER SWEDEN "FOR PRACTICE"

SWEDISH military officials, who have been investigating about 300 reports of "fireballs" which they received from various parts of Sweden between 9 July and 12 July, are no longer in doubt that the country is being used for regular practice with steered rockets.

The authorities have promised a communique when their researches are complete.

Some reports indicate that the projectiles are furnished

This photograph, just received from Stockholm, shows one of the many rockets which have been seen flying over Sweden.

with a self-destruction device, since explosions have apparently occurred in the air.

The longest line of flight over Swedish territory mapped by military experts covered about 625 miles. The first German V-2's made flights of only 175 to 235 miles.—A.P.

The alien fleet

From the vast expanses of the world's oceans come reports of mysterious underwater entities that are as intriguing as UFOs. And, like UFOs, they seem to appear regularly in specific regions of the Earth

SINCE THE END of the Second World War the navies of the world have frequently tracked large submarine craft whose performance is greatly superior to anything that they themselves possess. In common with unidentified submarine objects (USOs), these mystery craft seem to congregate in particular areas of this planet, two of the most notable being the Scandinavian waters and off the eastern coast of South America.

When we mention submarines and Scandinavian offshore waters, many readers' minds will immediately jump to the incident of autumn 1981 when a Russian captain ran his submarine ashore at Karlskrona, Sweden, due to 'faulty navigation'. Undoubtedly the Russians like to keep themselves informed about the navies of other nations and to keep track of their exercises and activity, and some of the unidentified submarines that have been located have doubtless been Russian. But, just as the Russians were originally blamed for the Swedish 'ghost rockets' of 1946 (see page 49), so may they equally unjustifiably have been blamed for many of the mystery submarines reported since the 1950s.

The performance and behaviour of some of these USOs exceed those of conventional naval craft in the same way that Earth's aircraft are outperformed by UFOs. The maximum speed that the latest submarine can achieve is about 45 knots or 50 miles per hour (80 km/h), but these mystery submarines have been detected travelling underwater at over three times that speed. When on manoeuvres in the North Atlantic in 1963 the United States aircraft carrier *Wasp* and 12 other vessels detected a huge underwater craft travelling at 150 knots or 175 miles per hour (280 km/h). It stayed with them for four days, manoeuvring around them and diving to depths of 27,000 feet (8200 metres). The record depth for a dive by a known submarine is 6250 feet (1900 metres). During July 1972 an unidentified submarine cruised off the coast of Chile, usually at a depth of 3300 feet (1000 metres), far deeper than conventional submarines dive, for at this depth the tremendous pressure presents a very real danger.

Was it a Russian spy submarine that penetrated some 90 miles (150 kilometres) into the Norwegian fjords during November 1972? For three weeks the Norwegian Navy, assisted by NATO ships and aircraft, hunted the mysterious intruder, which was repeatedly tracked underwater and lost again in the Sogne fjord. Several dozen ships plus helicopters took part in the hunt and depth charges were systematically used, but the strange vessel could not be made to surface. On 23 November a large dark object was seen moving below the surface in the Luster fjord,

When naval forces detect unidentified submarine objects their first fear is that conventional enemies are intruding in national waters. In this case, in November 1981, the fears proved justified: Swedish forces trapped a Soviet submarine, which had a highly unconvincing excuse for being there. But perhaps, in the back of the naval commanders' minds, were memories of the occasions when USOs have been more baffling – resembling no vessel of human construction and displaying 'impossible' manoeuvrability

a branch of the main fjord, while at about the same time in the Aurlands fjord, another branch, a warship tracked a submarine with sonar. That night Martin Nielson saw six red rockets fired into the sky from below the surface, while nearby on an inaccessible peak overlooking the Aurlands fjord red and green lights were seen flashing. On 24 November the combined forces made a concerted attack with depth charges. The only result was that a very powerful – but unknown – jamming source opened up, completely disrupting all communications and rendering all radar and sonar inoperative. On 27 November the Norwegian authorities stated that the mystery submarine had left, still unseen and unidentified. Similar incidents have occurred in other Norwegian fjords, in Swedish coastal waters and around the coast of Greenland, usually in areas apparently devoid of military significance, but no vessels have ever been trapped, damaged or positively identified.

Machines or monsters?

USOs are also seen in the lakes of Sweden. An object with what appeared to be a clear perspex dome was seen in Bullaren Lake, Bohuslan. There were repeated sightings in Lake Rasvalen of an object more than 50 feet (15 metres) long, and from Stensjön Lake in Ostergötland a USO with a conning tower was reported. We have reports from several other lakes of large dark bodies seen below the surface. Whether these are machines, or monsters of the Loch Ness type, is a matter for conjecture.

Another USO hunt similar to the Norwegian one took place in February 1960 in the Nuevo Gulf when for two weeks the Argentinian Navy chased two mystery submarines originally assumed to be Russian, but their speed and manoeuvrability must have caused the authorities to think again. Due to the continual UFO and USO activity along this coastline, the locals were openly speaking of 'the Martians' who, they believed, operated from underwater bases. Eight months earlier in Buenos Aires harbour the naval authorities had been having trouble with a large, fast and very manoeuvrable USO that was shaped like a fish and was silver in colour. Its distinctive feature was a large vertical tail fin such as might be seen on an airliner. They knew what it looked like because they were able to send down divers to examine the craft, but they were not able to identify it.

During 1978 there was a tremendous wave of UFO activity over Italy; more than 500 reports were made and after all the errors and hoaxes had been eliminated the figures still indicated that a tremendous amount of activity had taken place, which had risen to a peak in the last three months of the year. Along the Adriatic coastline the unexplained phenomena included columns of water rising from calm seas to a height of 100 feet (30 metres), red and white lights following fishing boats at night, USOs seen on or below the surface, emerging and diving into the sea, and electrical interference on radar, radio and television equipment. Fishermen refused to go to sea without naval protection. On the evening of 9 November Nello di Valentino, captain of an Italian naval boat sent to patrol the coast, saw, with two of his men, a brilliant red light emerge from the sea 1100 yards (1000 metres) away. It rose to a height of 1000 to 1300 feet (300 to 400 metres) and then flew quickly away to the east. While this was happening, radio communication with the shore was disrupted. Many of the population spent the night hours watching for UFOs and USOs, and inevitably some normal occurrences were

Above: a Hawker-Siddeley Nimrod, one of the most powerful anti-submarine aircraft in operation. The ceaseless reconnaissance carried out by the major powers in the search for hostile missile-carrying submarines may well be yielding large numbers of USO reports from military personnel

Below: a three-week USO search in Sogne fjord, Norway, ended fruitlessly with a depth charge attack

thought to be of extra-terrestrial origin. In the dawn light of 7 December in the Gulf of Venice near Cáorle, hundreds of people who had been watching lights at sea during the night saw with alarm strange craft and entities emerging from the water. This turned out to be a combined air/naval exercise with amphibious craft and troops.

Not so easily explained is the experience of three French fishermen from the Mediterranean port of Le Brusc who, at 11 p.m. on 1 August 1962, were out in their boats on a clear, calm night. About 330 yards (300 metres) away a long metallic craft appeared, moving slowly on the surface. The men discussed it among themselves and agreed that it must be a submarine, though not of a type they could identify. The water next to the craft became disturbed and a dozen frogmen emerged from the water and climbed onto the strange submarine. The Frenchmen hailed them across the water with a friendly greeting, but the strangers took no notice as they climbed inside the vessel, until the last one was about to descend. Before doing so he turned towards the fishermen and raised his right arm in acknowledgement. Then he too disappeared into the craft. The amazed fishermen watched the strange object rise into the air and hang just above the waves. Red and green lights flashed, and it slowly started to revolve from left to right. As it did so, the body glowed with an orange light and, describing a graceful arc above the sea, it accelerated rapidly into the sky until the glowing dot could no longer be distinguished.

Similar night activities have been recorded elsewhere: only a month earlier in the Gulf of Catalina, south of Los Angeles, a chartered fishing boat skipper and his mate studied a strange vessel through their night glasses from 440 yards (400 metres) away. It appeared to be a submarine low in the water, steel-grey and without markings. It carried an odd after-structure around which five figures could be seen moving, apparently working on something. After a time the mystery submarine started to move and the fishing boat skipper had to take evasive action in order to avoid being run down. The strange vessel swept by them at high speed. It was noiseless and left no wake, but made a big swell in the water as it headed towards the open sea. The naval authorities were interested in the men's report, and during an interview showed them silhouettes of foreign submarines in an attempt at identification.

Artefacts from the ocean

The origin of these mysterious USOs and their amphibious crews remains unknown, but a clue to the purpose of their nocturnal activities might possibly be gained from some of the elusive artefacts that they may have left on the sea bed in some locations. One example is the shiny metal cylinder 23 feet (7 metres) long and 10 feet (3 metres) in diameter that a Spanish aqualung diver found on the sea bed on the Spanish Mediterranean coast in July 1970. The smooth rivetless walls of the cylinder had no apparent opening and as it was so clean it could hardly have been underwater for long. The next morning he returned to have another look, but the object was gone. He searched the area but could not find it. A similar object may have been found by Martin Meylach, a treasure hunter, on the coast of Miami, Florida, in September 1966. Meylach returned with two naval divers. Whether the object was salvaged or disappeared like the Spanish object, we do not know. Air Force officials denied that it could have been a missile dropped by an aircraft. In April 1967 two Danish boys saw a UFO drop several objects into the Kattegat Strait near Sjaellands Odde, 50 miles (80 kilometres) north-east of Copenhagen. Matter that was later recovered included 'lime and inorganic [*sic*] coal, combined in a manner completely unknown'. Lorentz Johnson watched

Left: the USO that attracted the attention of the authorities in Buenos Aires harbour in 1959 was unusual in having a fin resembling an aircraft's. Though it was fast and manoeuvrable, it stayed still long enough to permit divers to examine it. The numerous USO reports in the area led local people to joke about underwater 'Martians'

as a glowing cigar dropped two long objects into the waters of Namsen fjord in December 1959. Some while later, UFO investigators using sonar found an object 20 feet (6 metres) long by 7 feet (2.1 metres) high, but at a depth of 300 feet (90 metres) it was too difficult for divers to reach. They did report that they could see wheel tracks on the bottom, leading out to sea. Unidentified tracks 3 feet (1 metre) wide, seemingly ploughed by something resembling a globe, were found on a beach in Venezuela in August 1967. Two days later two American scientists arrived to study the tracks and apparently found them of great interest. The UFO that was seen to land and take off from the sea at Rio de Janeiro, Brazil, in June 1970 left a red cylinder in the water, which was later collected by an official police launch. It would seem that the governments of the world take a greater interest in these underwater activities than they wish to admit, but how much they have learned from the artefacts they have salvaged is unknown.

The French port of Le Brusc (below) was the scene of an extraordinary USO sighting in August 1962. Three fishermen watched as a submarine-like craft took a dozen 'frogmen' on board – then flew away (bottom)

In 1970 Ivan T. Sanderson, biologist and founder of the Society for the Investigation of the Unexplained (SITU), published his book *Invisible residents* in which he presents some of the material that we have been examining. In it he suggests that beneath the oceans could live a far older race than human kind, possibly descended from the life that did not leave the primeval seas to develop on land but remained to develop more rapidly underwater. Being many millions of years ahead of humanity, they avoid direct contact with the primitive life – mankind – on the planet's surface and have developed their technology to the point that they can now easily make interstellar journeys in their craft, which we know as UFOs and USOs.

UFO researcher John Keel suggests that 'someone is operating a clandestine air force and navy on this planet', and theorises that underwater bases may be in the regions above the Arctic Circle. The founders of the Aerial Phenomena Research Organisation (APRO), Jim and Coral Lorenzen, suggest that USO phenomena are a result of the mapping and mining operations carried out by extra-terrestrials who have arrived in UFOs from other planets. In 1973 the Argentine Society for the Investigation of Unusual Phenomena stated that following years of investigation and research they now have no doubt that machines from another world have established undersea bases in the Gulfs of San Matias and San Jorge on the Patagonian coast; while in Venezuela so many UFOs have been seen diving into and emerging from the Caribbean Sea that many people believe undersea bases exist, though opinions vary on whether these are in the ocean depths, the coastal shallows, or in great 'mother ships' lying on the sea bed. The value of undersea bases for a technologically advanced but secretive civilisation that might share our planet is obvious. But the underwater world is still a largely unknown environment and, as in so much of ufology, the proof continues to elude investigators.

When dreams come true

Tales of close encounters often seem to describe some kind of psychic, rather than 'nuts and bolts', experience. JENNY RANDLES discusses some cases where the paranormal and ufology appear to overlap

MANY REPORTS of encounters with UFOs and ghosts contain curiously similar or even identical elements, which suggest to the objective researcher that both kinds of experience may be psychic phenomena that originate in the mind. All such experiences are strongly subjective and often defy scientific explanation. Frequently entities of one kind or another appear to a single person, while others also present notice nothing. Physical effects are noticed by witnesses: tingling sensations and humming noises are linked with UFO sightings, while a marked drop in temperature is often said to accompany the appearance of ghosts. And the vast majority of such encounters occur at night, often when the witness is alone or in some way 'vulnerable'. The two types of experience may be very different but, as the following examples show, the similarities give cause for reflection.

In 1960 a well-to-do businessman of Manchester, England, was spending the night with a girlfriend when he felt the bedroom invaded by a curious tingling sensation. The air was full of an electromagnetic humming. Worried, he glanced around the room; he noted the time, just after 3 a.m. Then a figure appeared, standing by the bedside and blocking out the light that filtered through the window. It was a woman, only inches away from him and as plain and solid as the mattress on which he lay. His mind absorbed her features and her dress. Then he cried out. Quickly, the image melted into the blackness of night and he sheepishly awoke his sleeping companion to tell her of the ordeal. She knew what he had seen, for it was not the first time such a phantasm had appeared. The description perfectly matched the girl's dead mother.

It was not long after 3 a.m. on 9 March 1977. Brian Grimshawe and a fellow night shift factory worker were driving to the factory through the almost deserted streets of Nelson in Lancashire, England. Suddenly, a light appeared over Pendle Hill, famous for its long association with witchcraft. A dark cigar shape, flashing different colours, floated through the sky towards them. As it approached, both the engine and lights of the car cut out. The men became frightened.

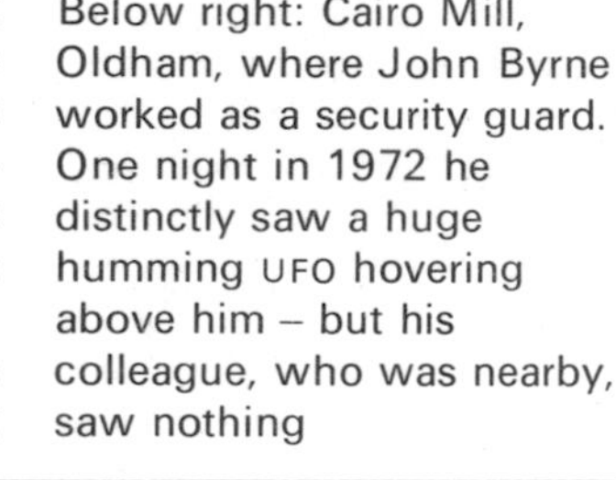

Below: Pendle Hill, traditional meeting place for witches, near Nelson in Lancashire. On 9 March 1977 Brian Grimshawe and a friend saw a dark, cigar-shaped UFO with flashing lights appear over the hill. It approached them, then drifted away

Right: a 'doughnut-shaped' UFO pursued 15-year-old Frank Earp and two friends at Wollaton, near Nottingham in 1966. Then a huge, furry creature with 'legs that faded away into nothingness' appeared – but only two of the boys saw it

Below right: Cairo Mill, Oldham, where John Byrne worked as a security guard. One night in 1972 he distinctly saw a huge humming UFO hovering above him – but his colleague, who was nearby, saw nothing

that they were looking for UFOs. As darkness came, a mist began to rise from the water-course. This was not unusual. But then a cloud, the size of a fairground dodgem car, detached itself in the shape of a doughnut (without a central hole). It drifted towards them. Becoming disturbed they set off for home, quickly breaking into a trot as the apparently intelligent 'cloud' pursued them. They could all see it, glowing inside with a strange luminescence.

Friend, foe – or fiend?

As they approached the edge of the village they decided to stop. Frank was delegated to confront the intruder for they were now close enough to home and could escape, should anything go wrong. Frank turned, to find the cloud just 20 feet (6 metres) away. He tried to ask if it was friend or foe, but his words were cut short by one of his friends, clearly terrified, tapping his shoulder and urging, 'When I say run – *run*!' He looked ahead into the gloom and understood the reason for this fear. For there stood a 6-foot (1.8-metre) furry figure, silhouetted in front of the glowing object. In claw-like hands it gripped two red 'pencils', and its legs faded into nothingness. The third boy stood only inches from the creature. As the other two fled he called after them, bemused. It later transpired that although he was almost touching the figure he had not seen it. But he had seen the cloud.

These experiences pose a difficult question. Just where is the dividing line between different types of paranormal event? Does a dividing line even exist? Was the figure met by Ken Edwards of Risley, Lancs., England, a UFO entity or a ghost? Did the boys at Wollaton chance upon a boggart (a furry figure), a ghost or a 'sasquatch'? There are no easy answers. For once again there are features that are common to them all.

At Cairo Mill, Oldham, England, on 8 October 1972, John Byrne, a security guard

They felt a strange tingling sensation, and an electromagnetic hum filled their ears. They tried desperately to escape the hovering UFO, but the car was dead. Then, just as suddenly as it had come, the UFO drifted away southwards. The car's lights and engine jerked back to life and the oppressive sensations disappeared. The two men sped back to the factory and soon developed pounding headaches as a result of their terrifying experience.

The materialisation of a ghost and the sighting of a UFO . . . is that what these two events were? Perhaps, but the similarities between them are most intriguing and they are duplicated time and again in other strange encounters.

Witness Frank Earp gives a graphic account of his own encounter in 1966 at Wollaton, near Nottingham, England, in the February 1981 issue of *Northern Earth Mysteries*. He was 15 at the time and playing with two friends beside a disused canal. He admits

at the Ferranti engineering works, saw a massive UFO hovering above him. It emitted a strange blue light and a high-pitched humming whine, but his fellow guard, just yards away, saw and heard absolutely nothing – just as Frank Earp's friend did not see the furry creature.

At Machynlleth, Wales, in July 1975 a terrified teenager saw a landed disc and undulating jelly-like entities. The experience so shocked him he suffered from persistent hysterical blindness for a long time afterwards. The disc became transparent in parts and blended into the surroundings before vanishing entirely – just like the Wollaton boggart or the traditional ghost, which it is claimed one can see through.

Ordeal for animals

Another common factor in stories about ghosts is the manner with which animals allegedly react, even before the presence is confirmed by a human observer. A family in Gorton, Greater Manchester, were plagued by a poltergeist in June 1981. The invisible force upturned settees, threw planks of wood around the living room and scrawled messages in toothpaste on household mirrors. Before these outbursts, the family's Alsatian dog had become disturbed, running about, barking madly, and leaping into the air as if to attack an unseen adversary.

A dog plays a part in the following case, but this time there was no apparent ghost or poltergeist. Instead there was a very peculiar figure, wearing a spacesuit.

The witness was an Army NCO, stationed at Dakelia barracks, Cyprus, in September 1968. At 3 a.m. his dog, a fierce Turkish wolfhound, suddenly sat up and began growling, its fur standing on end. Fearing a possible terrorist attack the soldier went to the door, then a high pitched humming filled his skull. The dog was by now under the bed, whimpering and cowering. Out on the landing the soldier saw to his horror the head and shoulders of a creature floating up the wooden stairs. It was humanoid and clad in a light blue suit. It had an eerie face that glowed orange, huge round eyes and a tousled shock of red hair. It could swivel its head 180°.

The soldier rushed back to the sanctuary of his room. He sat on the edge of his bed, shaking uncontrollably, as the whining outside rose to a crescendo. Now he could hear a sliding sound as if the creature were approaching the door. He snatched up his underwater speargun, loaded it and aimed it at the door; the sliding noise faded away. An hour or so later, the soldier was found, still sitting on his bed and trembling with fear. And overnight the dog turned into a quivering wreck.

A woman called Mary was driving her car near Norwalk, Connecticut, USA, in the summer of 1973 when the radio was suddenly filled with strange static interference. She heard a man's voice inside her head and found herself within a huge 'spacecraft'. How she got there she has no idea. Standing before her was a tall entity with fair hair and dressed in a silver one-piece suit. It conversed with her by telepathy, or directly from mind to mind. She was greeted with the strange words, 'Welcome my friend, Mary Angel.' During the time the witness spent on board this 'craft', before being returned

At Dakelia barracks, Cyprus (above), an NCO and his dog – a fierce Irish wolfhound – were reduced to nervous wrecks by the sudden appearance of a ghostly creature that floated up the stairs after them (below). Yet this 'ghost' seemed to be wearing a spacesuit

mysteriously to her car, the 'alien' gave her a tour of his UFO. It was supposedly peopled by no fewer than 200 crew, who came from what they called 'the galaxy of Guentatori-Elfi'. The aliens prophesied specific floods that would occur in the USA. In due course the prediction came true.

But the aliens do not always display such insight. A woman in Belfast, Northern Ireland, was taken on board a UFO in 1976. She was told that Princess Anne would have twins and that Canada was about to join the European Common Market. Needless to say, several years later these extremely unlikely events have still not come to pass.

Yet, perhaps it is a relief that these aliens can be remarkably human in their fallibility, for some of their prophecies are not so amusing.

Two men in their late twenties were returning from a night at a friend's house in Palos Verdes, southern California, during a summer in the early 1970s. As they were about to drive off, their headlights illuminated two weird shapes on the road. They were the size of basketballs and looked not unlike giant human brains. After observing them for a few seconds they manoeuvred the car around them and hurried on their way. After taking his friend home (a five-minute journey) the driver continued on to his destination (another five minutes), only to discover that two and a half hours had gone by instead of the expected 10 minutes.

One night in the early 1970s two young men saw 'giant human brains' on a Californian road (above). Later, under hypnotic regression, one witness recalled humanoids with 'webbed features' (below)

The man, whom investigator Ann Druffel calls John Hodges, was put under regressive hypnosis in 1976 to try to restore his detailed memory of the event. He was anxious to find out what had happened to him. In this condition he described how, when alone in his car, he was taken into a room and conversed telepathically with one of the brains. 'The voice comes within me . . . but it sounds like you are talking to me,' Hodges said. Some grey-skinned humanoid creatures with 'webbed' features were also present, apparently acting as crewmen. The giant brain showed Hodges 'advanced three-dimensional holograms' depicting nuclear explosions, and explained that atomic power was being misused on Earth. Hodges later 'remembered' that the humanoids were in fact the real controllers and the brains simply acted as translation devices (alive, and yet not quite alive). A miniaturised 'translator cell' was implanted in Hodges's brain on the night of the contact, which would allow information to flow freely in the future. Eventually he was returned to his car, but his memory was blocked and he felt a curious 'buzzing and tingling' all over his body.

A third world war

Since 1976 John Hodges has received numerous messages via his 'translator'. These include detailed information about a world war that will erupt in the Middle East and then spread to Europe between 1982 and 1984. Nuclear weapons will be used. After the war ends and a world government is created, the aliens will land in 1987 and trigger the thousands of people who, like Hodges, have been implanted with 'translators' without their conscious knowledge.

Such a story sounds utter nonsense, yet so do most of the other alien contact incidents that are reported. At the very least, however, they demand a reasonable hearing.

There is a considerable problem in trying to trace a common source of these incredible events for they are presented in many different contexts. They involve ghost-like beings, weird monsters, spirit entities, and a veritable menagerie of aliens from all over the Universe. Yet all of them share an underlying theme and many consistent internal characteristics. Are intelligent extraterrestrial beings contacting us and behaving like skilled impressionists? Or could these experiences stem from a source that is somewhat closer to home – namely ourselves?

Consider this statement by John Hodges. 'The words . . . actually come from within the mind . . . loud, clear, crisp. The voice sounded male, but it's odd. It sounded as if it was the same voice I have to myself, when I *think*.'

Variations on a theme

A woman described being abducted by a UFO as it was happening – but no one else saw it. How many other close encounters take place in the mind, 'real' only in a subjective sense?

CAROL AND STEVE W. are a young married couple from Gateshead in north-east England. In August 1979 they had cause to become very worried when their home was suddenly invaded. This was no ordinary plague of mice or rats disturbing the normality of their lives; instead it involved tiny UFOs and strange alien beings.

It began on 17 August. Carol was alone in the house with her three-year-old daughter as her husband was working on the night shift. She was unable to sleep because of a searing toothache; the time was about 2 a.m. She went downstairs, made a cup of tea and sipped it while sitting on her bed. A red light shone in through the curtains. Puzzled, she got up and drew them apart – and was amazed to see a cymbal-shaped object above the rooftops opposite. The UFO hovered for a while, displaying multicoloured lights, and then spiralled upwards into the sky.

Back in bed, Carol became distressed when a low rumble announced the return of what looked to be the same object – this time in miniature – appearing *on* the curtains and flying *into* the room. In its wake was a trail of glittering specks. She felt a tingle on her body and heard a buzzing as the swarm of lights fell towards her. The specks then returned to the 18-inch (45-centimetre) disc and left the room through the open door.

The mini-UFO reappeared to Carol 13 nights later when she went into her daughter's bedroom to settle her back to sleep. The tingling returned and she screamed to her husband. He arrived just in time to see a flash of light outside the window. The disc had flown out through the window, although it was shut and remained undamaged.

Four nights later Carol decided that her husband's next night shift could not be tolerated alone so she went to stay with her mother, who lived nearby. At 4 a.m. she was again paralysed by the buzzing and tingling as the mini-UFO entered the room. This time it was accompanied by 12 weird human-like creatures, 2 feet 6 inches (76 centimetres) tall. They wore white suits and had pale, feminine features. Their hair looked unreal and reminded Carol of an Action Man doll. Some of the beings approached the bed, showed interest in her eyes, and conversed in clicking sounds.

The invasion continued for over two months. Carol's family felt the tingle and paralysis at least once, and the dog was sent into a frenzy whenever the buzzing noises enveloped the house. Then, just as suddenly as they had begun, the experiences mysteriously stopped.

This is an amazing story, which one must

Opposite: at 2 a.m. on 17 August 1979 Carol W. from Gateshead, England, was drinking a cup of tea to help her sleep when she became aware of a mysterious red light shining through her bedroom curtains. Drawing them back to investigate, she was startled to see a cymbal-shaped UFO hovering over the rooftops (top). It flashed many-coloured lights before spiralling upwards and disappearing from sight. Back in bed, the witness was alarmed to see what appeared to be the same UFO *but in miniature* coming into her room through the curtains, trailing brilliant 'specks' behind it (bottom). She tingled all over her body and heard a buzzing sound as the tiny lights turned towards her. The specks then retreated into the disc, which left through the closed window. Four nights later, although Carol was in a different house, the UFO visited her again – and this time brought along its crew as well

Above: on 5 July 1952 a huge blue UFO hovered over Mrs Maureen Puddy's car near Frankston in Victoria, Australia. Twenty days later it returned as she was driving past almost the same spot; this time it stopped the car. She heard a voice in her head that urged her to make her story public and assured her that 'we mean no harm'. Six months passed, then Mrs Puddy heard the voice again; it told her to visit the scene of the sighting once more. Two investigators, Judith Magee and Paul Norman, accompanied her there, where she described a UFO, its crew – and an attempted abduction. Yet the others saw nothing, and Maureen Puddy remained in the car all the time. Was something or someone projecting images into her mind, trying to control it?

either accept or reject. There is no reason why the family should have willingly placed themselves under so much strain, and they continually asked for no publicity. But the events pose many questions. Just how could a UFO appear inside a bedroom? How could a dozen figures 2 foot 6 inches (76 centimetres) tall come from a disc only 18 inches (45 centimetres) in diameter? How could it fly through a closed window? The most obvious solution is that no object was ever physically present. What Carol observed was perhaps a projection, akin to a moving hologram or three-dimensional image, shone into the room from some unknown projector.

All too often in UFO encounters the unbending physical laws of nature are shattered beyond recognition. Solids cannot pass through solids without trace. Objects do not travel faster than sound without creating sonic booms. Yet these things, and many more, are described in UFO reports with a regularity that is remarkable. But if the UFO or entity were in fact just a film show, projected into our natural environment, then most of these 'problems' would not arise. Think of the movie we all star in at night, with its screen inside our heads. Dreams have no need to follow the laws of physics. Anything is possible provided our subconscious is capable of imagining it.

On 5 July 1972, 27-year-old Maureen Puddy saw a UFO on the Mooraduc Road near Frankston, in Victoria, Australia. The object was a huge blue disc, which hovered above her car as she returned from visiting her son in hospital. Twenty days later, at almost the same spot, it returned. This time it seemed to drain power from the car, causing it to stop; indeed, the car appeared to steer itself to the roadside. A voice in her head told her, 'All your tests will be negative.' It then said: 'Tell media, do not panic. We mean no harm.'

Judith Magee, a respected researcher, investigated the case and about six months later received a telephone call from Mrs Puddy asking for an urgent meeting. She said that a voice had called her name and told her to return to Mooraduc Road. Judith Magee went with fellow investigator Paul Norman to meet Mrs Puddy at the scene of the sighting. Mrs Puddy said that on her way to meet the ufologists a figure in a golden suit had materialised in the car beside her.

As the investigators sat talking to the woman at the site, she claimed that the entity had returned and was standing in front of the car headlights. Neither researcher could see anything. Mrs Puddy began to describe the scene inside a UFO that she claimed was nearby. Over the next few minutes she kept alternating between being 'here' (in the car) and 'there' (inside the UFO), although all the time she was physically present with the investigators. Maureen Puddy claimed the being wanted her to go with it, which she violently opposed. The researchers sensed the battle going on within her and saw her tears as the situation got too much. Yet, if the testimony of the investigators is anything to go by, although Mrs Puddy felt she was 'inside' a UFO and 'observing an entity', this experience had no reality outside her mind.

Just how many other UFO abductions occur at this same subjective level?

The story of the Sunderland family from Oakenholt, North Wales, is a complex and incredible one. It provides a neat encapsulation of the many difficulties in trying to suggest how such experiences occur.

Every member of the family (both parents and all five children) has claimed involvement in at least one paranormal event, during the period 1976 to 1981. On occasions more than one person witnessed the same event but most often it was a solitary experience. These events took many forms, most importantly UFO sightings but also mild poltergeist outbreaks and a vast assortment of associated anomalies. Three of the children claim to have had independent contact with different alien races, including ground landings, communication and even actual trips to other realms of being.

The principal focus has been the eldest girl, Gaynor, who has experienced direct contact, has visited an alien zoo, been taken for a ride on board a disc-like UFO, taken a guided tour of an alien city, suffered time dislocations and even produced apparently paranormal effects on photographic film.

Below: the Sunderland family of Oakenholt, North Wales. Every member claims to have had some psychic experience between 1976 and 1981 and three of the children, especially Gaynor (standing at the back), say they have met 'aliens' and have been taken by them to visit other realms of being. Author and UFO investigator Jenny Randles (centre left) believes that people with a psychic background are likely to see UFOs and report close encounters

Bottom: an alleged alien footprint, photographed in Florida, USA, by Ron Whritenour in 1966. If the print is authentic then some extra-terrestrial beings are real enough to leave physical traces and, therefore, cannot be 'all in the mind'

What is particularly interesting is that Gaynor says she has always been 'psychic'. Since a baby she has seen what might be called UFOs or ghosts. She claims to see the aura round the human body. At first she assumed all these things were normal; she had no cause to suspect she was different. Gaynor has been observed in the middle of one of her 'trips' to an alien world. Her mother saw her at the time and says she was in bed in a strange, trance-like sleep.

It does seem that the alien contacts experienced by the Sunderlands have a direct relation with the other paranormal events. It is reinforced by the fact that in an amazingly high percentage of UFO contacts the central percipient has a history of claimed psychic experience, which continues after the events that they initially report.

A form of expression

There seem to be two broad possibilities: either something external is trying to get in (perhaps aliens, who find psychic people the easiest channel of communication), or something internal is trying to get out.

John Hodges in California (see page 57) would have us believe the first answer is correct. So would most of those who say they have seen aliens, for that is what the aliens tell them. George Adamski (see page 89) was advised in the 1950s that they 'come from Venus', and in 1964 a Bolton woman met 'aliens from Pluto'. But now science has ruled out these planets as abodes of advanced forms of life and modern contactees have reported different origins for their aliens. All this sounds very suspicious. If there is no reason to trust the aliens when they tell us where they come from, what reason is there to trust them when they tell us they are aliens? Since all belief in ufonauts as interstellar voyagers stems from this one source, there is little justification for accepting such an explanation.

An internal origin for these contacts, however, would explain the puzzling relationship between paranormal phenomena. All of them would be essentially a similar

Right: diagram explaining the theory of subconscious projection. This relies on the idea that everyone possesses a store of subconscious archetypes that change only in context. For example, in the past these probably included angels and demons, whereas today they are replaced by benign or malevolent humanoids. According to this theory, something triggers off a projection of a paranormal encounter, peopled by archetypes and experienced as objective reality by the subject. This fits in well with the ideas of author and researcher Hilary Evans who believes that paranormal experiences can be located on a continuous spectrum with dreams at one end and solid, everyday reality at the other

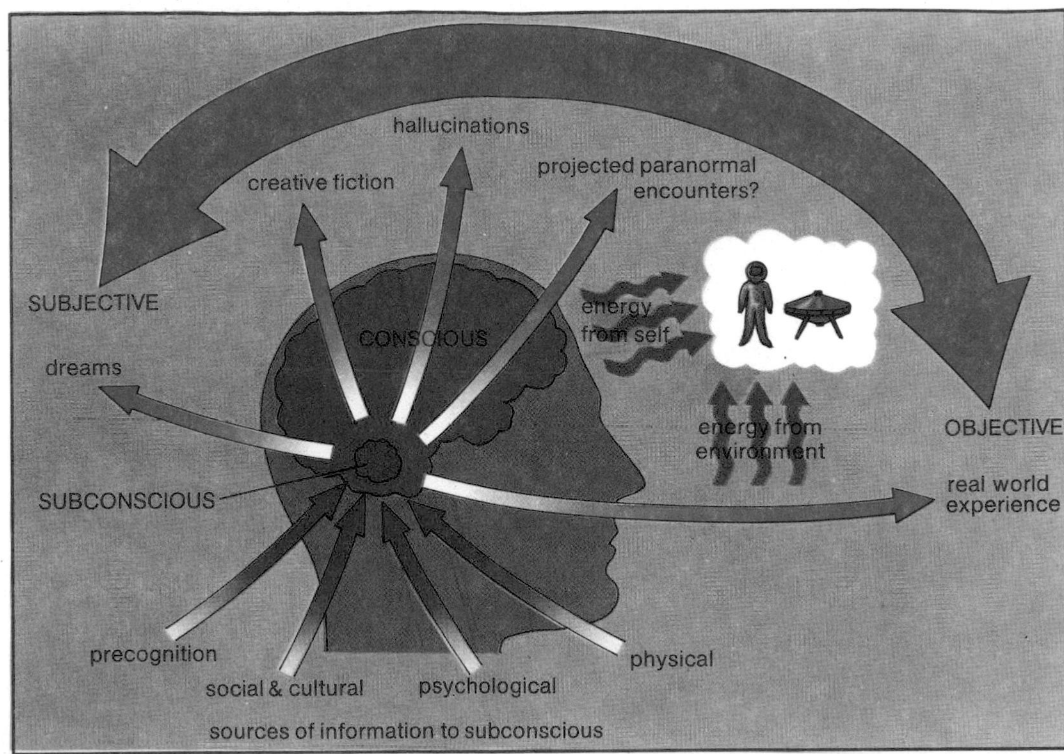

Above: George King and his wife in London in October 1957. King, who founded the Aetherius Society in 1956, claimed to have been called 'to become the voice of the Interplanetary Parliament'. The voice he heard was not psychic, he stressed, but was 'completely physical'. It told him that spiritually advanced 'masters' live on other planets and are concerned about the welfare of mankind. King is seen here with the tape recorder he used to record the messages from the 'masters'

process, clothed in terms to suit the personal beliefs and imagination of the witness. If he wants aliens from zeta Reticuli, then he gets them. If he is more inclined to believe in ghosts, then he gets them instead (or nowadays perhaps both things together). Such a concept would explain why these contacts vary so widely from case to case, and yet remain within a basic pattern. It would give us a means to understand how a ghost can be created by rumour, and endowed with substance by those who perceive it, as in the case of a deliberately invented phantom vicar of Ratcliffe Wharf. It would also provide a reason for the obvious subjectivity of most of the contacts (real to Maureen Puddy, but not to those with her).

There are many comparisons between alien contacts, out-of-the-body experiences (known as OOBES), and the deep hallucinations known to occur on the threshold of sleep and wakefulness. For example, time lapses, jumps from scene to scene, and certain internal features are found in all of these. And there is also the peaking of experiences at 2 or 3 a.m., when the mind is most relaxed and brainwave patterns most receptive, a time when normally we dream our deepest dreams.

For this possibility to be accepted two strong objections need to be overcome. What about the occasional physical evidence of UFOs, such as the stopping of car engines or marks on the ground? If we are willing to accept psychokinesis (the moving of objects without visible or known force) and we believe that the American Ted Serios and others can mentally impress images on to photographic film, then it is possible that the effects found in some UFO contact cases could be caused in a similar way, perhaps by psychic people when their brainwaves are most receptive. The source of these productions could be deep and uncontrollable.

Dreams emerge from the depths of our subconscious, translated into images that have symbolic meaning to us personally. There seems justification for a belief that UFO contacts may work in a similar manner, and that dreams, hallucinations, and possibly something just a little beyond that are all portions of a continual spectrum emerging from ourselves and our internal or collective needs. It may be that UFOs are images in our minds, not travellers from space. In some cases these images may become so powerful that they are projected by the mind and seen as semi-material entities.

What is the purpose behind the UFO phenomenon? Some people are convinced that UFOs are essentially evil – that they may actually be emissaries of the Devil. HILARY EVANS investigates this bizarre notion

'UFOS ARE HERE TO POSSESS YOUR SOUL!' Headlines such as this – from the American magazine *Official UFO* – are generally dismissed as coming from the lunatic fringe of ufology. The theory that UFOs are controlled by demonic forces seeking to delude or destroy mankind is often derided as just another crackpot suggestion, to be taken no more seriously than the idea that there is a UFO base in Dyfed near the Welsh coast. But by no means all those who support the theory of the demonic origin of UFOs are eccentrics: among the nonsense are a number of realistic ideas that may point to a viable interpretation of the UFO mystery.

What is it that makes a ufologist turn to theories of this sort? Is it merely that nothing else seems to fit – or is there solid evidence that really seems to point in that direction? Some commentators have suspected the former; in their book *Flying saucers are hostile* (1967), American authors Brad Steiger and Joan Whritenour observed:

> Certain saucer cultists, who have been expecting space brethren to bring along some pie in the sky, continue to deliver saucer-inspired sermons on the theme that the saucers come to bring starry salvation to a troubled world. The self-appointed ministers who preach this extraordinary brand of evangelism ignore the fact that not all 'saucers' can be considered friendly. Many give evidence of hostile actions. There is a wealth of well-documented evidence that UFOs have been responsible for murders, assaults, burning with direct-ray focus, radiation sickness, kidnappings, pursuits of automobiles, attacks on homes, disruption of power sources, paralysis, mysterious cremations, and destructions of aircraft. Dozens of reputable eye-witnesses claim to have seen alien personnel loading their space vehicles with specimens from earth, including animals, soil and rocks, water, and struggling human beings.

Commenting in *True's New Report* on this

The typical UFO is frightening, or even menacing – as in this artist's impression of a demonic-looking flying saucer. Can it be, as many writers have suggested, that UFOs are representatives of an evil power?

Saucers of Satan

horrifying catalogue, science-fiction author Frederick Pohl riposted:

> It's as false as false can be; there not only is not a 'wealth' of such evidence, there isn't *any*. The absolute best you can say in support of that claim is that there are many people who *think* such things happen, and a mass of circumstantial bits and pieces of events. There is no evidence at all for the assumption that the saucers are almost certainly hostile.

It is perhaps significant that even Steiger himself seems to have backed down from his former position. *Flying saucers are hostile* was just one of the books he wrote in the 1960s; others were entitled *Flying saucer invasion – target Earth*, and *The flying saucer menace*. But his *Gods of Aquarius* of 1976 is subtitled 'UFOs and the transformation of Man', and expresses the belief that 'the UFO will serve as the spiritual midwife that will bring about mankind's starbirth into the universe.' Cynics might suggest that Steiger, having milked the UFO-scare theme for all it can give, is now finding the positive approach more profitable; but perhaps he has genuinely changed his mind.

However, there is no lack of continuing support for the demonic theory. But the crude business of rape and murder is not for the new demonists: what they fear is a more subtle take-over aimed at men's minds or, for those whose beliefs include such a thing, their souls.

In the Baptist Church at Warminster on 28 January 1979 Arthur Eedle, physicist and astronomer, delivered a public address in which he told of his own personal encounters with demonic UFOs:

What are the aliens after? According to many UFO experts, it's not our technology, our wealth, or even the planet itself, but — literally! — our very souls which are at stake!
©1977 RAOUL F. VEZINA

Above: an illustration showing UFO witnesses being brainwashed, from the American magazine *Official UFO* of March 1978. Supporters of the hypothesis that UFOs are demonic in origin cite in its favour evidence of physical and mental illness suffered by UFO witnesses after sightings. There is, however, an equally strong group of ufologists, among them Frederick Pohl (left), who believe that the evidence is too slight to prove the evil origin of UFOs

> In the summer of 1967 I was out watching for UFOs with a teenager by the name of Philip. As we waited in the dark we became conscious that something was hovering silently overhead and quite near. I began to feel cold, more cold than seemed appropriate for the time of year. But Philip reacted badly to this thing, which incidentally we were only just able to make out, so low was its luminescence. He started to shake uncontrollably, and I realised that he was in some kind of danger. I bundled him into my car and took him home. We sat by the kitchen boiler and tried to warm up, but Philip could not recover from the shakes. The effect was no longer due to the cold, but to some induced effect from the UFO. I said, 'Philip, do you believe in God?' 'I don't know,' he answered, 'I have never given it any thought.' I laid my hands upon his head and said, 'In the name of Jesus Christ I command this influence to leave Philip at once.' The result was quite dramatic. Philip explained that a cold sensation travelled upwards

through his body and out through my hands and away. Within a few seconds all the shaking had stopped. Feeling a lot better, he looked at me and said that he now believed in God AND the Devil!

A short time later Philip contracted the shakes all over again. I sensed that he was possessed of an evil spirit. Commanding this spirit to manifest itself, an old cracked voice spoke through Philip's mouth saying that his name was Satan. I commanded it to leave in the name of the Lord Jesus, and it did so.

Taking away men's minds

Evidently, for Arthur Eedle the Devil is very much a living reality. Further confirmation came from another UFO-related incident in the course of which he had a dramatic encounter with three fallen angels. They told him of their plan to take away men's minds and reduce them to 'a zombie-like state'. Identifying themselves as coming from the planet Martarus, they said they aimed to bring peace to the world by eliminating Man's destructive urges – which involved removing his soul entirely.

But this, Eedle claims, is a pack of lies. 'They lie about their origin, saying they are from outer space; they lie about their purpose, saying they have come to help mankind; and they lie about their identity, saying they are extraterrestrials.' In fact, Eedle insists, they are the fallen angels, based here on Earth where they are preparing for a final take-over that has been prophesied throughout history and is now imminent. He continues:

> The present UFO activity points to the fact that these prophecies are on the point of fulfilment. People are already being brainwashed, and those many humans who are possessed of evil spirits have been prepared for the day of their coming. And it is clear that some of them are here already. The basic purpose behind all UFO phenomena today is to prepare for the coming of the Antichrist, and the setting up of World domination under the Devil.

This is all very well – but, before people can be brought to appreciate the mortal danger they are in, they must first be convinced that devils themselves are a reality. For most of us today, devils no longer form part of our system of belief; evil is seen as resulting from distorted impulses in people's minds, rather than from some tangible external source. So the first concern of believers like Arthur Eedle is to reawaken the public to the fact that the Devil is real.

In a privately-printed booklet entitled *Who pilots the flying saucers?* Gordon Cove insisted that, by refusing to believe in devils, people were laying themselves open to

Terrifying aliens with huge, cabbage-like heads, from the 1950s movie *Invasion of the hell creatures.* Such movies have done a great deal to fuel the idea that UFOs are hostile

attack. In 1954, when the booklet was published, the majority of ufologists were inclined to interpret UFOs as physically real spacecraft, piloted by aliens from elsewhere in the Universe. Cove goes along with this view – but gives it his own interpretation:

> What we are suggesting is the possibility that Satan has seized one of the planets as his base of operations to attack the earth. This thought . . . may seem fantastic: but upon cool meditation, does it seem so absurd? The first thing a military general seeks, when war is declared, is a convenient headquarters. Satan is the cleverest military genius ever known. Is it feasible that Satan, along with his principalities and powers, his wicked angels and demons, would continue to float airily around in the atmosphere for thousands of years, when there are literally millions of planets which would be well adapted for a headquarters?
>
> Satan is partially powerless unless he can get some willing instruments to work through. Therefore, if Satan wanted to manufacture some flying saucers in order to facilitate the flight of his evil hosts throughout the vast universe, it would also be to his great advantage to get a race of beings under his control who would manufacture them for him. Could he not inspire the Venusians, if such exist, with supernatural cunning and wisdom to make a fleet of flying saucers, and also show them how to pilot these supernatural machines?

So, Cove concludes, the beings that have contacted people with terrible warnings may have been 'demon-possessed Venusians or Martians' whose seeming benevolence was a sham, designed to deceive.

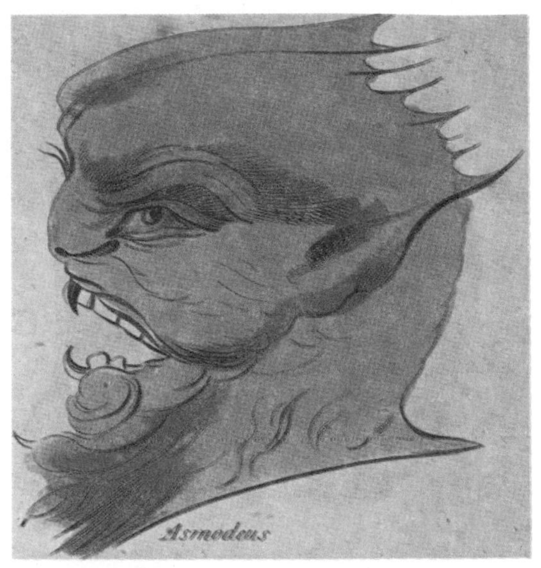

An illustration from Francis Barrett's *The magus*, showing the demon Asmodeus who, in one of the stories of the Apocrypha, is conquered by the archangel Raphael. The face shows a marked similarity to those described by present-day witnesses of humanoids; it has been suggested by some writers that 'evil' humanoids are merely a kind of updated version of medieval demons

However, he does not rule out altogether the possibility that some of the UFOs may be piloted by benevolent beings. The striking increase in UFO activity of recent years, he argues, must surely indicate that a full-scale attack by the satanic forces is imminent; and the forces of good must be aware of this. So some, at least, of the flying saucers may contain angels, sent by God to report on the state of the Earth:

> The question arises, what are the angels reporting to God after their tour of inspection? They cannot have failed to observe the awful tide of corruption and sin that is fast engulfing both the USA and Great Britain. Our sins rise up to the heavens like giant mountain peaks and literally scream to God to pour out his vials of wrath upon us!

However, we may draw some comfort from

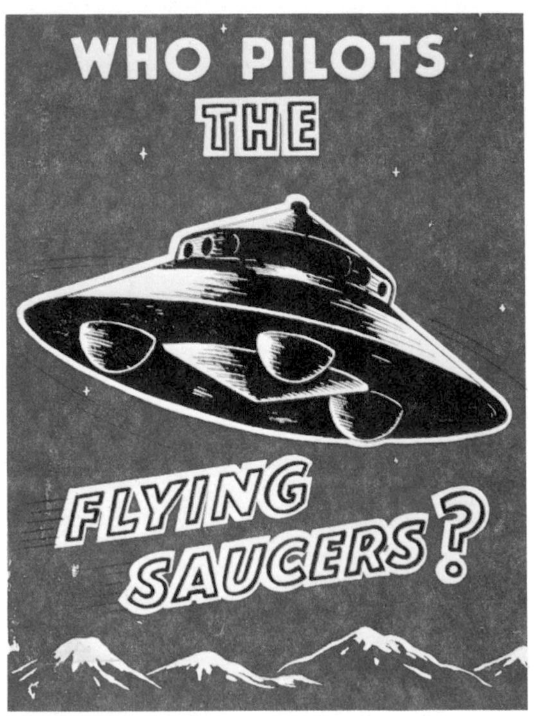

Sensationalist books such as these testify to the belief that UFOs are sinister, bent on doing harm to mankind

Right: an illustration by Doré of the fall of Satan after his expulsion from heaven, as it is described in Milton's epic poem *Paradise lost*: 'From Morn/To noon he fell, from noon to dewy eve.' Could it be, as ufologist Gordon Cove has suggested, that Satan, 'once a member of God's astronauts', has now enlisted the support of inhabitants of other planets in his fight against goodness?

the fact that he quotes a prophet named Hehr, to whom it was revealed as long ago as 1903 that 'a Third World War may wipe out our civilisation, and that an older race on Venus is taking measures to re-establish a new and better order in the shortest possible time. When the atomic bombs fall, these extra-terrestrial aeroforms may be used to salvage what is good in our civilisation, either persons or things.' And when is all this to happen? Hehr's target date for the start of the Third World War was 1960, and peace was to be re-established, after five years of chaos and total anarchy, in 1965!

However, even though we managed to escape that particular calamity, it doesn't do to be complacent: there are plenty more prophets with plenty more warnings of doom. Bob Geyer, of the Church of Jesus the Saucerian in Los Angeles, told the writer Eric Norman in 1970, 'Our conversations on the religious aspects of UFOs brought forth the conclusion that they herald the Second Coming of Christ.' But whereas Gordon Cove asserts that the UFOs are piloted by devils masquerading as alien visitors from space, Geyer takes an opposite view. For him, the UFO pilots really are extra-terrestrials. It is we, here on Earth, who have labelled them as devils – not realising that Satan himself is an alien, who has persuaded other aliens to join him:

> Satan, the old prince of darkness, and his legions of demons, are also beings from other worlds. They came down from another planet. Once, Satan was a member of God's astronauts. He became too greedy and too ambitious. He may have exploited the inhabitants of earth, or other planets. He may have tricked people into slavery.

The interpretations may vary, but the demonists are agreed on the main issues. Whatever the UFOs may be, they represent a menace to us on Earth; and the scale of their activity shows that menace to be imminent. But just what danger is it that they threaten?

Ufologists have noted close parallels between the devils that, in the medieval period, were believed to be real, and modern UFOs. But does this really mean that UFOs are essentially evil?

Heralds of the Antichrist?

ON 18 MARCH 1978 Bill Herrmann, a 30-year-old truck driver of Charleston, South Carolina, was watching a 'slick metal disc, about sixty feet [20 metres] in diameter', as it manoeuvred in the sky near his home. Abruptly, it dropped towards him: 'Suddenly it was right in front of me. I fell backward. The next thing I knew, there was light all around me, green and blue, and I felt myself being tugged upward.'

In what seemed to him only a moment, Herrmann found himself sitting miles away in an open field, in a diminishing circle of orange light, as the spacecraft skittered away in a triangular flight pattern that, he was told later, was designed to avoid damage from Earth radar sources. 'I couldn't remember anything. I didn't know where I was. A terrible fear came over me, and I stood there weeping for what seemed a long time. I felt dirty. I felt like . . . I can't describe it. I felt like I had been around something I shouldn't have been around.'

Below: demons torture their victims in hell, in a 16th-century illustration from a French manuscript. UFO expert Jacques Vallée has pointed out the similarity between some medieval accounts of demonic torture and the 'medical examinations' that many victims of close encounters of the third kind allege they are forced by their kidnappers to undergo. Other ufologists have been quick to name the power they believe inspires such events: the fallen angel Satan

Later, under hypnosis, Herrmann recalled an examining table, flashing lights, and creatures resembling human foetuses, with over-large heads and eyes, spongy white skin, and wearing rust-coloured jumpsuits. They were about $4\frac{1}{2}$ feet (150 centimetres) high. For Herrmann, there was no question but that his experience was a 'Satanic delusion'. Since then, whenever he sees a UFO – and he has had several more encounters – he renounces it in God's name. This apparently works very effectively.

It is important to note that Herrmann is a fundamentalist Baptist by persuasion. Clearly his experiences are in some way related to his beliefs; what is less clear is whether his beliefs caused his experience, or whether they simply caused him to interpret it in a particular way. As a matter of historical fact, the majority of UFO reports have come from countries with a Christian culture, so it is not surprising that most metaphysical explanations for them have a Christian slant and set the UFO in a Christian context.

There is, of course, no rigid Christian dogma in UFO matters; but a concept that has been held by many Christians, from the foundation of their religion, is that of an Antichrist. Briefly, the Antichrist is a false Messiah, the exact opposite of Jesus, possessing many of his miraculous powers and offering – or seeming to offer – many of the same benefits. In fact, the origins of the idea of such a being antedate Christianity by many centuries: the notion is simply a personification of the dualism of good and evil that seems to have been one of Man's conceptions since he became capable of thinking.

Over the centuries a tradition has gradually been formulated that the Antichrist is destined to enjoy a temporary success, gaining control of Earth for a short while before a final conflict in which – it is confidently predicted – he will be worsted by Christ, who will then take over the reins of world government and inaugurate a golden age of everlasting peace. If we mere Earthlings know this, then presumably the omniscient Antichrist must know it too, but the prospect of inevitable defeat does not seem to deter him.

Certainly the demonic theorists have no doubt of his determination to continue the struggle, and in the turbulence of the present age with its violence, its sexual permissiveness, its decline of faith, they see indications that the coming of Antichrist is at hand: and the UFOs are the tangible signs that herald that coming. Two American theorists who take this view literally are John Weldon and Zola Levitt. In their book *UFOs – what on Earth is happening?*, published in 1975, they state:

UFOs are a manifestation of demon activity. They are here to misguide the multitudes and they are doing pretty well. They have judiciously utilised their powers through selected people to fascinate the masses, and they have widely promulgated their doctrines. They do not march through Times Square, of course, because this would reveal too much of the spiritual world. This might make people reconsider, as well, the existence of God, and the nether forces would have advertised for their enemy.

Just how 'real' are the UFOs – solid objects or subtle delusions?

Are the flying machines really up there? Maybe so; it's not that important. If the demons wish them to be there, they are there, and if they wish people to imagine they're there, then they are imagined to be there.

But there is no such ambiguity about the demons who pilot them:

Are they just ideas of ours? No, not the way the Bible characterises them. They have motives and they take action. We are by no means making them happen or just dreaming up their activities. We believe demons can induce a whole series of experiences that, in fact, never really happened, similar to the experiences psychic Uri Geller and Dr Andrija Puharich found were induced by their extraterrestrial contacts. They can also, however, through various means produce 'real' UFOs which are visible to anyone. With the powers we know demons have, they could theoretically transform a large chunk of rock into a UFO, assume human form inside of it, and land openly, thus 'proving' the existence of advanced intergalactic civilisations.

However, the authors doubt if this is often done: 'more likely, the standard UFO sighting is either a projection into our atmosphere, or the self-transformation of whatever material the demons themselves are composed of.' As for their purpose, there can be no doubt about that:

Quite simply, we think the demons are preparing the coming of the Antichrist. The Antichrist is not your run-of-the-mill world dictator. He is, in fact, something we have never contended with before; a political leader of great acumen – virtually a sorcerer, engaging and appealing – a kind of inverse Messiah.

In what way do the UFOs herald the Antichrist? They are a form of cultural conditioning. 'To properly set the stage for the Antichrist, who really is a supernatural personality, the world has to be made ready to think in terms of the new and the strange. Here's where we think the UFOs come in.'

Dan Lloyd is another demonist who does not underestimate the cunning of his enemy. No less than the fundamentalist Christians, Lloyd contemplates with misgivings the UFO-inspired cult followers who look towards 'benign visitors from outer space, visitors who will one day land on Earth and take over the reins from a humanity gone sadly astray and unable to solve its global problems'. He asks, 'Could it be that Antichrist will manifest in a guise that will fulfill

Top: the begetting of the Antichrist, with attendant demons, from a 15th-century woodcut. The existence of the Antichrist – a figure opposite to Christ in every respect – was widely believed in from the early medieval period onwards.

Above: Bill Herrmann, a truck driver from South Carolina, USA, who experienced a terrifying close encounter of the third kind in March 1978. His conclusion was that he had been the victim of a 'Satanic delusion'

all the expectations of these sky watchers with their distorted religious longings?'

Lloyd quotes with approval the theory put forward by the eminent French ufologist Jacques Vallée in his 'control-system' hypothesis:

> I believe there is a system around us that transcends time as it transcends space. The system may well be able to locate itself in outer space, but its manifestations are not spacecraft in the ordinary 'nuts and bolts' sense. The UFOs are physical manifestations that cannot be understood apart from their psychic and symbolic reality. What we see in effect here is not an alien invasion. It is a control system which acts on humans and uses humans.

What evidence does Vallée have for such a system? He points to the continuity of reported happenings, which shows that today's UFO reports are only yesterday's folklore in an updated form. One of the cases he cites is the alleged abduction of Barney and Betty Hill:

> While she was in the craft, Betty was submitted to a simulated medical test. Under hypnosis, she reported that a long needle was inserted into her navel, that she felt pain, and that the pain stopped when the leader made a certain gesture. . . . A fifteenth-century French calendar, the *Kalendrier des bergiers*, shows the tortures inflicted by demons on the people they have taken: the demons are depicted piercing their victims' abdomens with long needles.

Above: a detail from a 14th-century interpretation of the events described in the book of Revelation. Among these is a struggle between the forces of good and evil. Believers in the demonic origin of UFOs see the powers behind the UFO phenomenon as the latest contenders in the age-old battle between good and evil

To explain such parallels, Vallée claims, they must be seen as part of a larger pattern; and that pattern implies a pattern-maker. But who that pattern-maker may be, who is operating the control-system, and for what purpose, Vallée cannot or will not say.

But many of those who, like Dan Lloyd, believe in supernatural beings of one sort or another, do not share Vallée's hesitation:

> Vallée is unable to point a finger at the group in question, but it should not be difficult for Anthroposophists to be alert to the fact that behind whatever human group may be active in this area, there hovers the invisible presence of the Being who acts as their inspirer . . . the cosmic being who has been known since ancient Persian times as Ahriman. In the Bible he is known as Satan.

Like Weldon and Levitt, Lloyd credits the Ahrimanic beings with the capability to create UFOs spontaneously to serve their purposes:

> It is not from some hypothetical 'fourth dimension' that what we call UFOs are manifesting. It would be truer to say that they are deliberately distorted etheric effects, and it should surprise no one to learn that such effects can influence physical matter and create, in turn, physical effects.

Another group that welcomes UFOs as grist to its mill is that of the occultists – though perhaps 'welcome' is an inappropriate word, for occultists, too, see them as a menace to be taken very seriously. Anthony Roberts and Geoff Gilbertson see UFOs as the latest manifestation of a centuries-old conspiracy of evil forces – gods, demons, spirits, fairies – who seek to manipulate human credulity for their own ends:

> The reason this activity is today manifesting itself in such a strictly scientific manner (spacecraft, men in silver suits, green aliens, weird technological gadgetry, and so on) is simply that this is a highly technological age and the phenomenon has merely adjusted accordingly. It knows how to put up a good front.

The authors cite a number of cases in which, they suggest, 'the observant reader will notice some darker ambiguities hovering round them'. Ambiguities certainly hovered round the first case they quote, the sighting at Dyfed, West Wales in the spring of 1977, though not perhaps of the kind that Roberts and Gilbertson had in mind; nor is their final case very convincing. Roberts describes how he was driving along the Kingston bypass, outside London, one evening, when both his wife and he saw an object variously described as 'huge' and as 'the size of a very large grapefruit' – does he mean the size of a grapefruit held at arm's length? This so impressed them that they stopped and watched it for 20 minutes as it manoeuvred above them. Now, they were there and we were not; nevertheless, anyone familiar with the traffic conditions on the Kingston bypass must be sceptical of an account that involves a car pulling to the side of that very busy road, and an astonishing aerial display overhead lasting 20 minutes, apparently seen by no one else.

Alien monster?

It remains the case that UFO experiences are undoubtedly a matter of sober fact, whatever their interpretation. There is certainly a case to be answered. But when so improbable a hypothesis as a cosmic conspiracy is being put forward, the evidence needs to be of the very best. The case of Albert Bender, allegedly visited by three men in black, is another instance of the conspiracy that Robert and Gilbertson claim to have unearthed; but, as many investigations have already clearly shown, the Bender case is, to put it kindly, dubious. Nor is 'the observant reader' likely to accept readily the authors' version of the Loch Ness mystery: seemingly ready to detect sinister forces in every anomalous phenomenon, they endorse the dramatic adventure of American contactee Ted Owens who claims he acts as an Earth-based agent for the Space Intelligences:

> They sent me on a mission and Loch Ness was one of the places I was to visit. It was the dark of night, just after midnight, when I stood on the shores of the lake. That's when the monster came up out of the depths and surfaced. . . . It stared at me and in the moonlight I could see a long neck, about eight inches [20 centimetres] in diameter, and a small head. I communicated with the creature. It is from another dimension and has a link with the Space Intelligences.

Above: Jacques Vallée, a ufologist who has pointed out the parallels between UFOs and the ancient belief in devils. Vallée himself does not go as far as to conclude that UFOs are demonic in origin – but a number of ufologists have been less cautious

In the course of their thesis, Roberts and Gilbertson point the finger at any number of forces who, they imply, are either servants of or unwitting agents for the Dark Gods. The CIA, the Mafia, the KGB, the Theosophists and the magicians, the House of Rothschild and the Rosicrucians – all are playing their part in a conspiracy of which the UFOs are merely the outward sign. When they add 'and can we not add the MIB [men in black] for good measure?' the reader may begin to suspect it's all a gigantic spoof. Unfortunately, the authors show not a glimmer of a sense of humour. It seems they are in deadly earnest when they speak of 'a cosmic battleground' where there is to be fought a battle between forces that are (here they quote the American author H. P. Lovecraft) 'coterminous with all space and coexistent with all time'. But this is rather more than most human imaginations are able to cope with; and for most demonists, the cosmic war is a much more here-and-now affair.

Everlasting conflict

If a good God created everything in the world, how can evil have come into being? This has been one of the besetting problems for theologians of all religions for thousands of years. There have been many suggested solutions; most involve the dualistic notion of the opposition of the two independent powers of good and evil, God and the Devil – as exemplified in this medieval illustration of the kingdoms of heaven and hell (left).

One of the most extreme – and the most influential – forms of dualism was the doctrine preached by a third-century Babylonian prince named Mani, which spread to the West through heretical Christian sects like the Cathars. Mani claimed that an angel had revealed to him that the world was governed by two spirits, one good and one evil. Man was created by the evil spirit – but God, the good spirit, has given us the knowledge of good and the power, if we wish, to attain it. Thus the world is in constant conflict, with the forces of good and evil continually trying to enlist the support of mankind – all in all, a state of affairs that seems strangely close to what the demonic ufologists believe to be the case.

Sign of the times

Some ufologists believe that the powers behind the UFO phenomenon intend to take over men's minds and turn humankind into a race of robot-slaves. But how strong is the evidence for this claim?

'COULD I REALLY BE SURE the people I was then talking with were representatives of the real space brotherhood who wished humankind well?' This was the dilemma facing Howard Menger, who in 1956 allegedly met a group of 'space people' who not only introduced him to space music and the space potato (with five times as much protein as the Earth-grown variety) but revealed that he himself was Venusian, as was his second wife. They themselves claimed variously that they came from Venus, Mars, Jupiter and Saturn – and, as though that were not sufficiently confusing, they also informed him that there were bad spacepersons as well as good. Since the bad ones pretended to be good, how could a mere Earthling know whom to trust?

> The man looked at me sadly. 'My friend, this earth is the battlefield of Armageddon, and the battle is for men's minds and souls. Prayer, good thoughts and caution are your best insulation.' I shouldn't have doubted these people for a moment, but I was quite ill at ease. I had been sheltered from the knowledge that all of the space people's work on this planet is not sweetness and light. The others I had contacted must have been on the 'right side', for what I had seen convinced me they were a good people. Then the young lady spoke; 'You don't know, Howard, that there is a very powerful group on this planet, which possesses tremendous knowledge of technology, psychology, and most unfortunate of all, advanced brain therapy. They are using certain key people in the governments of your world. This group is anti-God, and might be termed instruments of your mythical "Satan". They are using the credulity and simple faith of many people to attain their own ends.' For the first time there was anger and frustration in her voice.

Above: Howard Menger who, in an encounter with 'space people' in 1956, was informed that he was a Venusian

Below: *The great day of his wrath*, by John Martin. Many people believe that UFOs presage Armageddon

The gathering swarms of UFOs are an indication of approaching crisis. Eric Norman, in his *Gods, demons and UFOs*, cites the opinion of an unnamed research physicist at Stanford Research Institute, California:

> The mounting evidence leads me to believe that UFOs are extraterrestrial in origin, piloted by intelligent beings. Their appearance in recent years is probably in some way associated with the imminent second coming of Jesus Christ.

Many Christians believe in the imminence of such a second coming; but the traditional teachings are clear that Satan isn't going to let Christ walk in and take over the Earth without putting up a fight. The belief in a 'final battle' is a key element in every scenario for 'the last days', however they differ in other respects. What's more, it is going to be

Left: a photograph taken by Howard Menger of an alleged space woman with a shining 'gadget' on her belt. The space woman gave Menger an explicit warning that a powerful group on Earth was using advanced brain therapy techniques to further the aims of Satan

Below: one of the 'mystery planes' seen over Sweden during the 1930s. The French theorist Jean Robin has suggested that these were an early manifestation of the UFO phenomenon which, he has noted, seems to stay always one step ahead of Man's technological achievement. The aim, he believes, is 'the projection of a false belief system, just beyond existing beliefs'

a real war, fought by real people with real weapons. Dr Clifford Wilson, of New Zealand, has no doubt that the battle of Armageddon is scheduled for the very near future, and points out that the satanic forces will need all the people who can be pressed into service. Consequently, he suggests, men and women are being brainwashed, even possessed, 'so that when the signal is given they will be ready to give total allegiance to these beings who will then show themselves as their masters':

> Even the act of taking over humans is to be taken literally: It seems that when these beings enter the solid state which is necessary for humans to observe them, they utilise atoms from the world in which we live. They do actually take blood and other physical matter from human beings and animals alike. In this way they are able to adapt themselves so that we limited human beings will understand them, and ultimately be programmed by them.

The French theorist Jean Robin takes a subtler view. For him, UFOs are only the latest manifestation in a long tradition of strange reports; and what strikes him most forcibly about these reports is that they seem to be imitating – or perhaps mocking – human ideas. In 1886, he points out, Jules Verne wrote his famous *Robur le conquerant* which features a massive airborne 'clipper of the clouds'; a decade later, in America, there was a wave of UFO sightings in the form of airships, which at that date were purely experimental and to be seen only over France.

The subtitle of Robin's book is 'The great parody': every manifestation of the UFO phenomenon – the American airships of the 1880s, the Scandinavian 'mystery planes' of the 1930s, the Swedish rockets of 1946, the UFOs of today's space age – has been just one step ahead of human achievement. 'The heart of the problem,' he insists, 'is the projection of a false belief system, just beyond existing beliefs.'

And what is the point of this exercise? For some, it's a sign that the millennium is at hand, the advent of the brave new world brought by a new Messiah. But Robin is less optimistic. We are in for 'a cursed time when there will reign beings who are almost totally dehumanised, robots or golems artificially and temporarily animated by the satanic spirit'. And he adds, 'while it is certainly not our intention to forecast the precise form which the reign of Antichrist will take, it's not too far-fetched to imagine him descending from a flying saucer.'

Many ufologists, whose thinking disagrees in other respects, agree that whatever else is going on, humanity is certainly being conned. Too many UFO sightings have a 'staged' quality, as though someone is putting on a show; too many contact encounters,

author of *UFOs and the Christian*, declared that 'Flying Saucers and Nazism are simply aspects of the same thing', and declared, 'UFOs are not just dangerous – they are deadly. It is a sphere in which the Christian (and indeed everyone else) is warned to KEEP OUT.'

Welsh UFO investigator Randall Jones Pugh echoed Inglesby when, in a 1979 letter to the *BUFORA Journal*, he wrote:

> I feel we must accept, for want of a better description, the potential and probable presence of entities (as human beings) whose sole purpose is to destroy straightforward belief in Jesus Christ. . . . I would add a note of warning to all those concerned with the investigation of the paranormal, however innocent it may be – if you wish to delve deeply into what the UFO represents, then you should indeed work with Christ, because the search for ufological knowledge can be extremely dangerous.

Less than 18 months later, Pugh renounced the subject altogether. In a newspaper interview he declared that:

> UFOs are dangerous and their aim is to disorientate, bemuse and eventually destroy the mind of mankind. . . . My first warning that I was into something very dangerous came from a friend of mine who became involved with UFOs from a scientific point of view after a sighting. After just 14 months he came to the conclusion that UFOs were involved with the occult, and decided to burn his books. He built a bonfire in the garden, but when he threw the books on it gave off an incredible heat. The

with their phoney medical examinations and absurd 'messages', simply fail to ring true. John Keel asserts that 'The ufonauts are the liars, not the contactees. And they are lying deliberately as part of the bewildering smoke-screen which they have established to cover their real origin, purpose, and motivation.'

The ufonauts' purpose, he feels sure, is sinister and menacing, and for that reason he insists 'This is not a subject for teen-agers and wild-eyed believers. I strongly recommend that parents forbid their children from becoming involved.' Others share this feeling. Ivar Mackay, one-time Chairman of BUFORA, Britain's largest UFO organisation, claimed that 'some Intelligence or Energy is ready to invade our minds', and indeed had already started 'as has been only too apparent among some researchers in recent years'. He believed that many years' intensive training in the occult was necessary before seeking to tackle the UFO problem. Another BUFORA chairman, Roger Stanway, declared in November 1976 that he was now convinced that UFOs were of satanic origin, and that he was abandoning ufology. Eric Inglesby, the

Above: an illustration of the 'Clipper of the Clouds' from Jules Verne's *Robur le conquerant*, published in 1886. A decade later there was a wave of airship sightings over the USA, at a time when such machines were to be seen only over France – an example that seems to lend support to the contention that UFOs anticipate the technological advances of mankind

Right: a hideous 8-foot (2.4-metre) furry, webbed-footed creature warns UFO enthusiasts John Stuart and Barbara Turner to discontinue their UFO research. They declined to do so – with horrific results

> smoke billowed up in the form of a human being, and two hands began to reach out. He was scared out of his wits, and later pleaded with me to destroy my documents, but warned me not to burn them. I took his advice, but when it came to my collection of slides, I stupidly threw them in the living room fire. Immediately there were loud cracks like explosions, and the heat was fantastic. I thought the chimney breast was going to split. It was a terrible experience, and I'm convinced the slides were satanically blessed.

The force of the Devil

Just how dangerous it can be to play with demonic forces was well-illustrated by what is said to have happened in 1954 to John Stuart and Barbara Turner of Flying Saucer Investigators of New Zealand. John and Barbara met every night (seemingly with his wife's approval) to discuss UFO theories and their implications. They took the demonic theory very seriously: 'There had to be some connection with Satan. But what?' As they got deeper into the subject, a change started to come over 'sweet, kind, innocent Barbara'. She, who seemingly took no interest in boys, suddenly interrupted their UFO-chat to say 'Gee, I'm glad I'm a girl. I like to be kissed. I like to tease boys, with a partly open shirt, brief shorts, all that.' Her smile turned more sensual, and she whispered in a very suggestive manner, 'I'd like to sit here naked. Like me to?'

Stuart concluded that this was 'some sort of evil possession'. However, the two UFO enthusiasts refused to abandon their studies despite many warnings, including one from a hideous 8-foot (2.4-metre) creature with a furry body and webbed feet. So it came about that, one night, 13 entities came to Barbara's bedroom, and while 10 of them watched, the other three raped her for three hours, marking her all over with scratches that she showed Stuart the following morning. This seems to have convinced her that UFO investigation was too risky, and Stuart himself was menaced by a creature that was male above the waist and female below one moment, vice versa the next – whereupon he too deserted ufology. History does not record what happened to Barbara or, for that matter, Stuart's long-suffering wife.

Such accounts seem to place the demonic theory of UFOs definitely within the lunatic fringe, but it is as well to remember that similar theories are taken seriously by some leading UFO specialists. Few researchers in Britain have contributed more to ufology than Gordon Creighton, yet he wholeheartedly concurs with William James's observation that 'the Demonic Theory will come into its own again one day':

> Time is running out fast. All the indications are that before the close of this century, cataclysmic and apocalyptic events will rend the planet. As the waves of senseless, irrational violence rise higher and higher on the Earth, and as the signs of moral and spiritual decay multiply, who can doubt that certain of the 'UFO entities' have a hand in the wrecking, and in the stirring of the nauseating brew?

Does the UFO evidence really support the demonists, or are they guilty of interpreting the phenomena to suit their personal beliefs? We shall each of us have our own opinion on that score, but one thing is clear: in the minds of many people, Satan is alive and well and piloting a UFO.

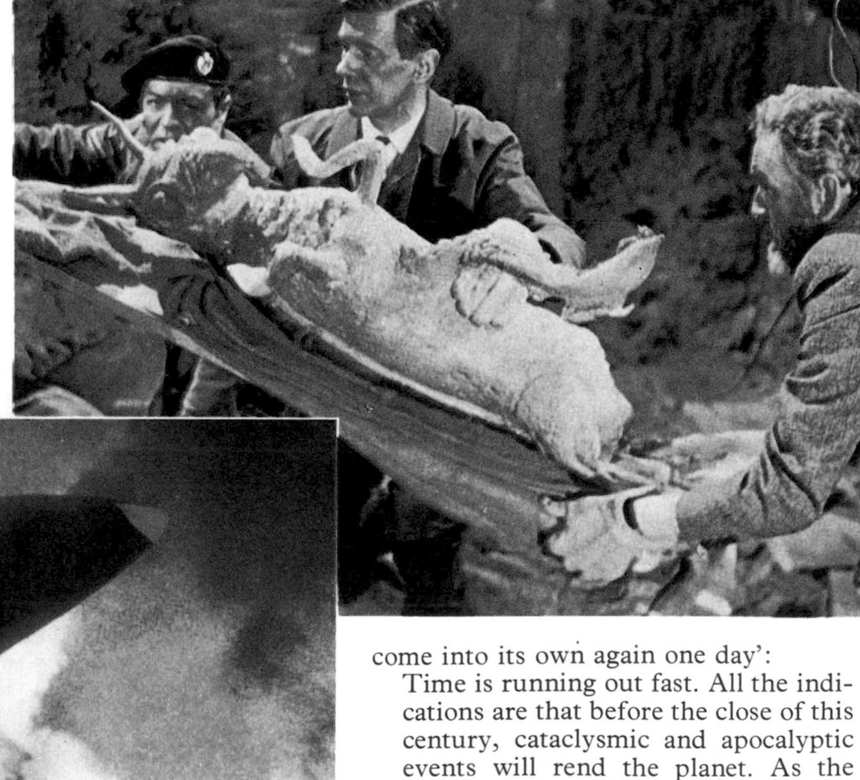

Images of hostile aliens: the discovery of a dead Martian in *Quatermass and the pit* (below), and urban destruction by a UFO in *War of the worlds* (bottom)

Reach for the stars

Space probes and manned space flight have brought us closer to the stars, but still we have not contacted any extra-terrestrial intelligences. RON HYAMS looks at the problems we face in our continuing search for proof that we are not alone in the Universe

Main picture: Mars – the 'red planet' as photographed by the approaching Viking I space probe in 1976

Inset: a close up of the surface of Mars with the Viking scoop in the foreground. Laboratory analysis of Martian soil showed it to be devoid of organic life

Left: American astronomer Dr Carl Sagan pictured with a replica of a Viking space probe. Dr Sagan believes that there may be as many as a billion Earth-like planets in our Galaxy alone

IS MAN ALONE in this Galaxy? Some astronomers believed that they had the answer at the turn of the century. They trained their telescopes on Mars and thought that they could make out signs that a dying race was fighting a dramatic battle against the planet's parched deserts.

Although most observers failed to detect these signs, the astronomers claimed to be able to see 'canals' on Mars – gigantic irrigation channels designed to carry water from the polar caps to the equator. For the first time there appeared to be evidence to support the hypothesis of extra-terrestrial intelligence (ETI), and the imagination of the public was fired.

As popular interest in ETI grew, the scientific establishment began to invest large sums of money in the search for intelligent life on other planets. The launching of the Mariner 4 spacecraft in 1965 was the first important step. To quote a National Aeronautics and Space Administration (NASA) spokesman: 'It is one of the major thrusts of our program . . . the search for life on other planets.'

Mariner 4's cameras were trained on the planet Mars, and the pictures were radioed back to Earth. They revealed something unexpected and disappointing: a cratered surface that looked more like that of the Moon than that of Earth. Of the 'canals' – and of life – there was no sign.

A full photographic survey of Mars was not undertaken until 1971, when Mariner 9 was launched. The pictures that the spacecraft transmitted to Earth revealed one particularly interesting feature: wiggly lines that looked like rivers. Could it be that Mars had water? And if so, could the planet provide a suitable environment for life after all?

Above: the Viking space 'laboratory' which carried out 'instant' tests on soil and other samples retrieved by the crab-like scoop of the Viking probe

In 1975 the landing on Mars of the United States' Viking 1 space probe marked the most difficult technical achievement in the history of the Space Age. A NASA spokesman pointed out the potential significance of this: 'The Viking landings on Mars should have a stimulating effect on public interest in astronautics. This will be especially true if evidence is found of life on Mars.'

Viking 1 carried a miniature laboratory

Below: Dr Stanley L. Miller, Professor of Chemistry at the University of California, whose chemical experiments in 1953 proved that it is relatively simple to create amino acids – the basis of all life

equipped to analyse Martian soil that was to be collected by a sampling arm operated by remote control. Tests had shown that the equipment was sensitive enough to detect organic matter even in the barren soil of the Antarctic. Scientists hoped that the incubation of Martian soil might permit them to isolate living organisms. Yet the results of all the tests conducted on the soil retrieved by Viking I were negative. We must conclude that if there is any life at all on Mars, it must be very primitive. As far as the search for intelligent life is concerned, NASA will have to look elsewhere.

The failure of the mission to find life on Mars shook the belief of some people in the idea of ETI. The search for life on other planets may be pointless, they began to think; perhaps we are alone after all, and there is something so special about Earth that it alone can support life. Perhaps . . . but an experiment carried out first by Stanley Miller in 1953 suggests that this surmise may be unfounded.

In Dr Miller's experiment electrical discharges – artificial lightning – were passed through a mixture of water, ammonia, methane and hydrogen, the substances that were then believed to have formed the primitive atmosphere of the Earth. At the end of a week, two of the simplest amino acids – essential for life – had been formed. The latest findings of modern research suggest that the early atmosphere of the Earth was actually made up of carbon dioxide and water vapour. But, when Dr Miller's experiment was repeated using carbon dioxide, water and small traces of compounds of nitrogen, similar results were obtained – again, simple amino acids were formed. The inevitable conclusion was that, provided certain simple conditions exist, these complex molecules will always be formed. In other words, no magic ingredient is required to initiate the process that leads to the emergence of living organisms – and there is no reason at all why life should not emerge spontaneously on any Earth-like planet.

Furthermore, some biologists believe that intelligence confers such advantages that evolutionary pressures will always tend to promote the development of intelligent species – and that an intelligent species is likely to develop a technology that will enable it to reach out and make contact with beings on other planets.

All this seems to imply that the Universe is teeming with intelligent life. Unfortunately, that may not be the case.

American astronomer Dr Carl Sagan, one

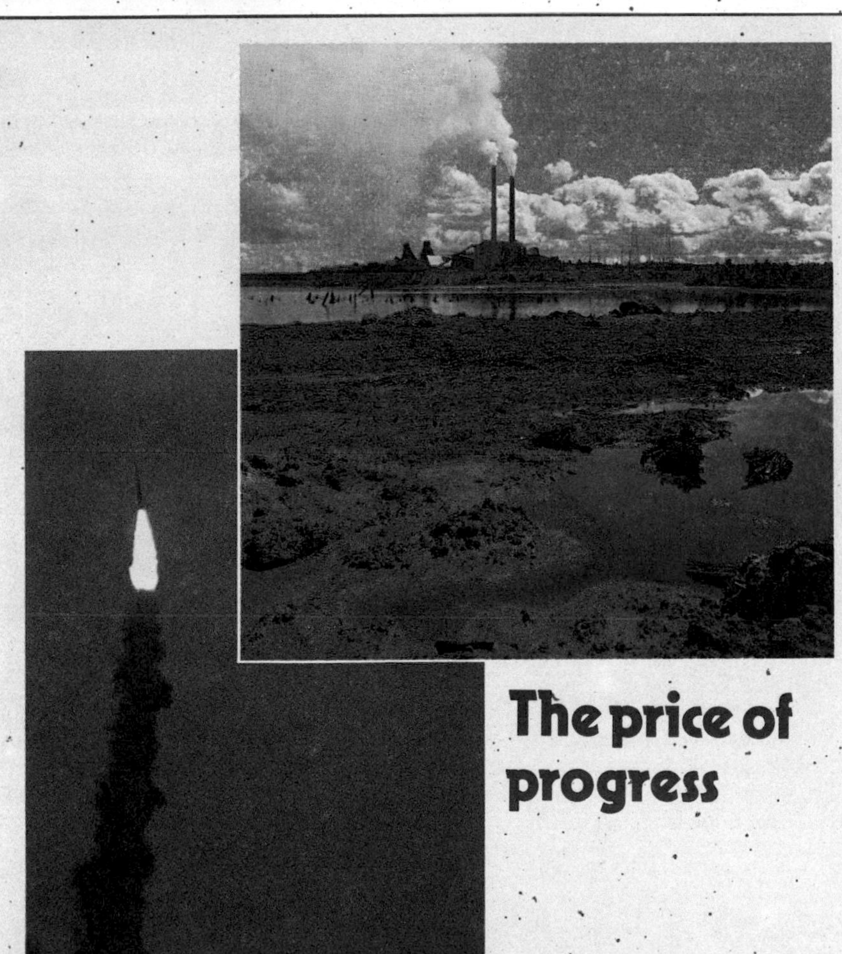

The price of progress

Perhaps there is some evolutionary flaw that makes all intelligent species seek self-destruction. The very basis of evolutionary advance is competition, the struggle for survival, but to an intelligent being competition is more than a battle for the next scrap of food; it is also a fight for long-term advantage, which inevitably provokes confrontation. The advance of technology cannot help but lead increasingly to *fatal* confrontation. Of course, not all technology is geared to killing, but the products of almost any sophisticated technology can be modified to kill if the motives of anger or fear are present.

Homo sapiens has already reached the point at which a full-scale nuclear war could end Earth's civilisation – perhaps for ever. And even if such a war does not take place, he stands a good chance of poisoning his planet with industrial or chemical waste, of releasing a new plague created in the genetic engineering laboratories, or simply of succumbing to the strain of a fruitless attempt to meet the needs of an increasing population.

Man evolved on this planet over 50,000 years ago, but only in the last decade or so has his technology advanced to the point at which he can communicate with the stars. Time will tell if his faltering technological civilisation will destroy itself or allow him to live out his full time on Earth.

of the leading investigators in the field, has suggested that there may be as many as a billion Earth-like (and therefore habitable) planets in our Galaxy. Yet the chain that links the formation of molecules with the emergence of actual life is extremely complex and depends on the unpredictable conjunction of many favourable circumstances. For this reason biologists have traditionally assumed that out of 10 planets on which suitable conditions exist, life might develop on only one. Even this cautious assumption may be an overestimate. Our search for a planet that harbours intelligent life may be a long and exacting one.

Theorists have raised another issue – an even more daunting one: even if it could be assumed with confidence that there were intelligent beings on other planets, we do not know how long the civilisations created by these beings might endure.

This is an important point. It would be reasonable to suppose that each civilisation lasts for a short time only. (We do not have to look far for a justification for this assumption. We find it hard to co-operate in our search for solutions to problems on Earth: local quarrels often appear to generate more concern than does our survival as a planet.) If civilisations on other planets are short-lived, most are either still growing or have already died. As intelligence is unlikely to reach an advanced stage on two planets at the same time, it could be argued that we are not likely to encounter another civilisation at the brief moment of its full flowering. It is possible that technologically skilled civilisations from different planets may never meet.

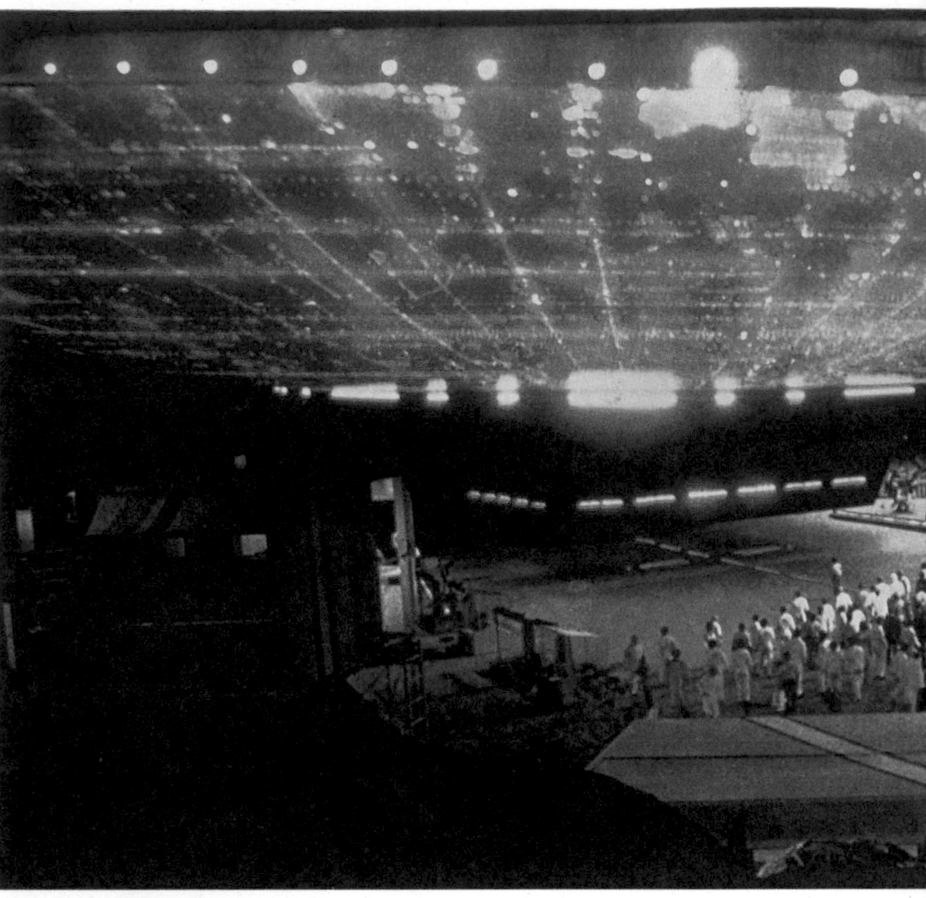

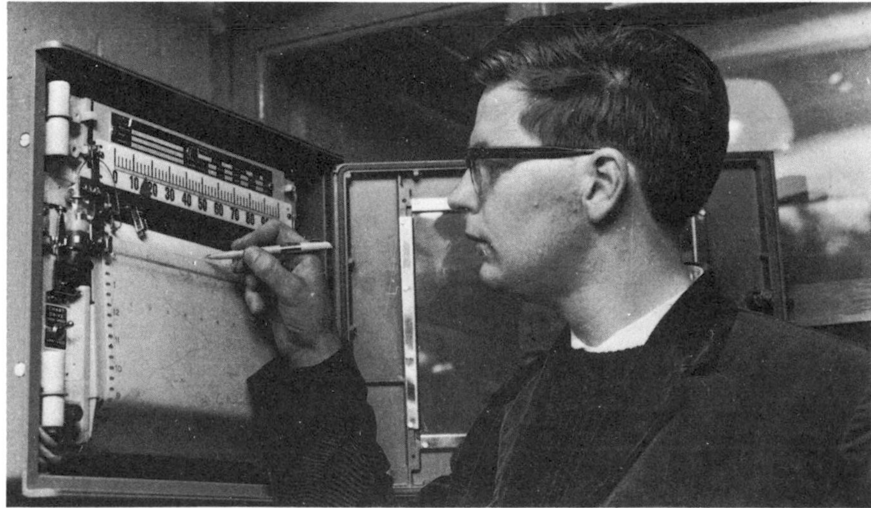

Above: Gerrit Verschuur, a top radio astronomy research engineer attached to the Fiske Planetarium in Boulder, Colorado, USA. He estimates that there are only 10 or 20 civilisations comparable to our own in the Galaxy

The implications of the estimated lifetime of advanced civilisations have been considered by Gerrit Verschuur of the Fiske Planetarium in Boulder, Colorado, USA. If civilisations really last only a few centuries, he calculates that there are at present no more than 10 or 20 scattered throughout the whole Galaxy. The law of averages would suggest therefore that the nearest is at least 2000 light-years distant from Earth and virtually impossible to reach. If we assume a short lifetime, he says, 'we are effectively alone in the Galaxy.' Even assuming a much longer lifetime of, say, 10 million years, communicative societies would still be about 100 light-years distant. Verschuur is not at all hopeful that contact would be possible even then.

But all this is mere speculation. The only way to find out whether intelligent life exists on other planets is to watch out for signs of intelligence from space. This point was made in 1959 by physicists Philip Morrison and Guiseppe Cocconi, in a paper that was the first openly to suggest a search by radio astronomers for interstellar messages; and the point remains as cogent today as ever.

Of course, there is an increasingly widespread view that we already are in contact with ETI, that Earth is being visited now. Such a view is based on sightings of UFOs, objects that no one can identify and that are said to be interstellar spaceships. There are thousands of UFO reports each year. Many are hoaxes; many are genuine but easily explained. There is no doubt whatever that some sightings are genuine and entirely mysterious. There is, however, no reason to suppose that any object cited in a UFO report is an extra-terrestrial spaceship. Such a craft is not inconceivable, to be sure, but at present there is no conclusive evidence that an interstellar spaceship has been identified.

Why is belief in extra-terrestrials so widespread? Professor Menzel of Harvard University sees it as a modern myth devised to

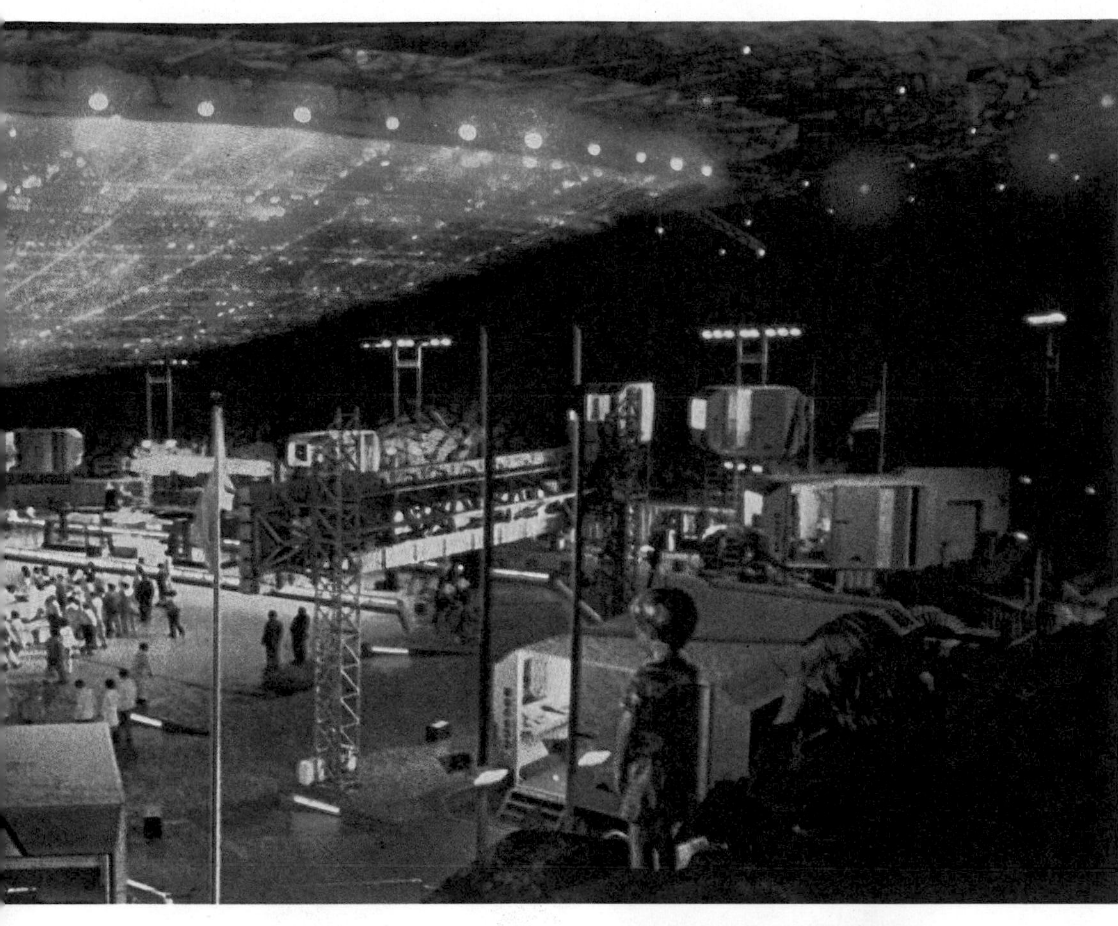

Left: the climax of the highly successful film *Close encounters of the third kind*. The subtitle – 'we are not alone' – accurately pinpoints the hopes of many people: that there is 'somebody out there' who watches over us

explain what we can't understand. 'People see some queer, luminous formation in the sky. They are frightened because they don't know what causes the apparition. They attempt, therefore, to interpret it in terms of whatever ideas are in vogue at the time.'

When flying saucers came into the news with the first 'sighting' in 1947 there was a ready-made tradition waiting for them. The writer Charles Fort devoted his life to collecting oddities in the news. He suggested that strange natural phenomena (such as falls of stone, fish or frogs) were the result of beings from some extra-terrestrial civilisation 'fishing for us'. The idea of flying saucers caught on and spread worldwide. The time was ripe for the concept: Man was already contemplating space exploration, so why not space travel in reverse? The view seized upon by dozens of writers – some not too scrupulous about the facts – inflamed a credulous public with stories that were largely baseless about flying saucers from outer space. So began the UFO cult.

The UFO mystery may have a basis in fact, but undoubtedly it also contains a large subjective element. Perhaps the tendency to interpret UFOs as the craft of extra-terrestrials reflects Man's need for a belief in the magical and wonderful. Our scientific age has destroyed much of the mystical, non-rational element of belief; it is possible that the extra-terrestrial hypothesis has arisen to fill the vacuum. Lester Grinspoon, Professor of Psychiatry at Harvard University, has

Above: Professor Philip Morrison who, together with fellow physicist Guiseppe Cocconi, suggested in 1959 that we actively attract interstellar messages by transmitting our own

expanded on this theme:

> The extraordinary effect generated by the UFO controversy derives from the unconscious conflicts displaced on to it concerning the problem of death and immortality. Our guess is that for some of those who vehemently defend the extraterrestrial hypothesis it symbolically represents a denial of the finite nature of life. Those that deny their anxiety may, on the other hand, be led to attack the hypothesis with considerable passion. . . . clearly this degree of subjective involvement is an obstacle to solving the UFO puzzle.

Given the emotional energy that has been released by the debate, clearly reaction to the discovery of ETI (if it ever happens) will be pronounced. As yet we do not know whether there are beings superior to us anywhere in the Universe; thus we tend to regard ourselves as the pinnacle of creation.

Perhaps we will become wiser as a result of the mere search for ETI. The thought of civilisations more advanced than our own may prompt us to acknowledge the pettiness of our own differences and may shame us into more serious attempts at co-operation. And even if all our searches fail and we suspect that we are alone in the Galaxy, may we not discover that our small planet is a precious jewel, too rare to risk in childish squabbles?

Is there anybody out there?

Astronomers have made several attempts to contact alien intelligences. But even if anyone is listening, will they understand our messages, considering the difficulties of interplanetary communication?

MANKIND'S FIRST radio message to the stars was transmitted at 5 p.m. on 16 November 1974 by the world's largest radio telescope, a disc 1000 feet (300 metres) in diameter, situated in Arecibo, Puerto Rico. The message was a three-minute signal sent out across the vastness of space towards a group of stars 24,000 light years away; it is believed to be the strongest signal yet radiated by mankind. In the words of the Arecibo staff, it was intended to be 'a concrete demonstration that terrestrial radio astronomy has now reached a level of advance entirely adequate for interstellar radio communication over immense distances'.

The Arecibo transmission was a statement of faith by the scientific community; it bore witness to the confidence of scientists in the fact that intelligent extra-terrestrial beings exist and are 'out there', listening. In fact, many would argue that it would be very surprising if Man were alone in the Galaxy in which he lives – more surprising still if there were no other beings to share the huge Universe. It has been suggested that there are millions of Earth-like planets among the billions of planets in the Galaxy, and that the conditions essential to the emergence of life must have been present on such planets on innumerable occasions. If that is the case, it is likely not only that extra-terrestrial intelligence (ETI) exists, but also that in many cases the technology of civilisations on other planets must have developed to a stage as advanced as, or even much more advanced than, our own.

Above: the Arecibo observatory in Puerto Rico

Above right: the control room at Arecibo

Below: Charles Cros (1842–1888) who suggested sending a coded message to Mars using flashing lights

The impulse to attempt to make contact with beings on other planets is clearly very strong in Man. In the mid 19th century – a hundred years before sophisticated technology made such ambitions realistic – many people took it more or less for granted that there were civilisations on the Moon and on other planets that could be reached with the aid of science. Various methods of communicating with these civilisations were proposed.

The French inventor Charles Cros (1842–88), for example, suggested the construction of a vast mirror that could be used to reflect sunlight from Earth to Mars. It could be tilted, he thought, to flash out a form of code. (The idea was ingenious, but it raised an insurmountable problem: there was no guarantee that a Martian civilisation would recognise, or would be able to respond to, such a code.)

Interest in establishing communication with extra-terrestrial beings grew to fever pitch. In Paris in 1900 a prize of 100,000 francs was offered to the first person who managed to make contact with ETI. The competition excluded communication with Mars, however – that was thought too easy a feat to be worth the money!

The enthusiastic experiments of 19th-century scientists proved fruitless. It is doubtful whether the crude techniques that were suggested could have served the purpose of initiating contact with extra-terrestrial civilisations, and it has since been established that there is no ETI on the Moon, on Venus or on Mars. Yet the search for intelligent life on other planets continues; and, ironically enough, in the 20th century we have transmitted spectacular messages to the stars with no special effort.

Right: the tiny human outline to the right of the picture is an artist's idea of what an illuminated figure would look like from Mars. The shape – which was to be formed by illuminating 'several square miles' of snow with electric lamps – was proposed in 1893 as a means of communicating with other planets

Below: another late-Victorian proposal – a cross of powerful electric lights to be strung across Lake Michigan. The lights would flash on for 10 minutes and off for 10 – an artificial phasing that, it was hoped, would attract interstellar attention

Since the 1940s powerful microwave beams from radar and TV transmitters have been leaking out into space. This radio noise is already washing over the stars nearest to Earth like a tide of electromagnetic flotsam, and although its intensity is minute, a sufficiently sensitive receiver could pick up the signal up to 40 light years away.

What would an extra-terrestrial astronomer make of this swelling tide of radio noise? If he had sustained his observations over a long period of time, he would have made an interesting discovery: today Earth is emitting radiation at the frequency of radio waves that is a million times more intense than it was a few decades ago. And if he used his radio telescope to measure the radio power emerging from this small planet at metre wavelengths, he would make an even more astounding discovery: Earth is emitting almost as much radiation as the Sun at a time of low sunspot activity. In fact in the radio spectrum our planet is as bright as a star!

Above: Dr Edward Mills Purcell, the physicist whose experimental results paved the way for radio astronomers to establish a channel between ourselves and aliens

Extra-terrestrial scientists would perhaps attempt to formulate a 'natural' explanation for the phenomenon, but any such attempt would eventually prove unsatisfactory. They would be forced to acknowledge that the radio emission could not be explained by the action of natural forces: it could only be produced by artificial means. However, scientists on other planets might not regard such weak signals as incontrovertible proof of the existence of a civilisation somewhere near our Sun, and even if they concluded that a civilisation did exist, they would probably find it impossible to make sense of the complicated mix of signals.

One solution to this dilemma is for us to indicate our presence unambiguously by transmitting a constant and deliberate message via a powerful radio beam aimed at the stars. Existing radio telescopes provide us with the technological means to do this, and the idea that interstellar communication may be possible is now widely accepted.

If we are trying to contact civilisations that may exist on other planets, it is conceivable that such civilisations may be attempting to communicate with Earth – perhaps some are transmitting messages now. Our radio telescopes would be sensitive enough to pick up their signals, but for two problems: we know neither where their transmissions might come from, nor which wavelength we should tune into.

To appreciate the difficulties facing radio astronomers, imagine a transistor radio that is unable to pick up a radio station unless its aerial is pointed directly at the transmitter. The search for a particular station would involve not only exhaustive research to identify the direction of the transmitter, but also tuning through all the wavebands to find the right channel. Radio astronomers face just this problem, except that they are obliged to search through a vastly greater frequency band, and there is the added disadvantage that they may need to listen for several minutes on each wavelength in order to detect any faint signal against the background noise.

Radio telescopes can be tuned to receive a specific wavelength, but if a message were being transmitted on another wavelength, it would be missed. It would clearly be impracticable to construct radio telescopes tuned to every possible wavelength in the hope of picking up signals from other planets: is there some way in which the task could be simplified? Is it possible to determine which wavelengths might be chosen for the transmission of messages from other planets?

During the Second World War the Dutch astronomer Hendrick Christoffel van den Hulst calculated that hydrogen atoms might sometimes change from one energy state to another and, in so doing, might emit a photon (a quantity of electromagnetic radiation energy) with a frequency corresponding to a radio wavelength of 21 centimetres. Individual hydrogen atoms, he postulated, would undergo this transition very rarely; however, because hydrogen is the predominant element in the Universe, he predicted that the microwave 'notes' emitted by vast quantities of hydrogen atoms should build up to a level detectable by super-sensitive equipment. In 1951 the American physicist Edward Mills Purcell made some observations that confirmed Van den Hulst's prediction.

Above: Dr Frank Drake, whose Project Ozma represented the first intensive search for messages from outer space. His team listened for 150 hours for an intelligible signal – but heard nothing that could be construed as a message

Below: the radio telescope at the National Radio Astronomy Observatory in Green Bank, West Virginia, used in Project Ozma

Since hydrogen is the most abundant substance in the Universe, it is reasonable to assume that any civilisation with an advanced technology would discover this property of hydrogen atoms and would conclude, as radio astronomers on Earth have done, that the 21-centimetre wavelength is one on which signals could be transmitted and received anywhere in the Universe, given sophisticated technology.

The idea of listening for interstellar communications transmitted on the 21-centimetre wavelength was first suggested in 1959 by physicists Giuseppe Cocconi and Philip Morrison, and has been widely adopted by subsequent signal searchers.

Another suggestion on the same lines is to make use of hydroxyl, the two-atom combination of hydrogen and oxygen that, next to hydrogen itself, is the most widespread emitter of microwaves in space. Its microwave emission has a wavelength of 17 centimetres. Since hydrogen and hydroxyl together make water, the wave band from 17 to 21 centimetres is sometimes called the 'waterhole'. This region of the radio spectrum happens to have the least interference from background radiation and thus makes an ideal, naturally defined search band for interstellar communication. Its name is particularly apt, because the hope is that different civilisations will send and receive messages in this band in the same way as different species of animals come to drink at waterholes on Earth.

In 1960 the first serious attempt was made to listen to the 21-centimetre wavelength in the hope of detecting messages from the stars. It was Frank Drake's Project Ozma. The listening began at 4 a.m. on 8 April 1960 with no publicity, as the astronomers feared ridicule. For 150 hours they listened for signs of an intelligible signal, but they found absolutely nothing.

Since Ozma the most comprehensive search undertaken to date was completed in 1976, at Green Bank Observatory, by Benjamin Zuckerman and Patrick Palmer. They took four years to survey the 659 stars most likely to harbour life between 6 and 76 light years away from the Sun. Although their equipment was very much more sensitive than that used in Ozma, they drew a blank.

Perhaps the lack of results indicates that we are on the wrong trail. Up to this point we have considered only interstellar radio contact among civilisations at, or just beyond, our own state of technical advance. Yet the bulk of technical civilisations may be immensely more advanced than ours. Perhaps we should consider how these technologies might communicate with us.

The Soviet astronomer Kardashev has suggested that civilisations might exist at three levels. A Level I civilisation might be regarded as Earth-like, able to exploit only a portion of the energy resources available to it; a Level II civilisation might tap the entire energy of its star, thus harnessing energies 100 trillion times those of Level I civilisations; and a Level III civilisation might tap entire galaxies, thus disposing of energies 100 billion times greater than those of Level II civilisations. If Kardashev's theory is sound, a Level II civilisation should easily be detectable throughout its galaxy, and a Level III civilisation throughout the Universe.

Thus we might be tempted to dismiss the possibility of the existence of such civilisations on the grounds that we can detect no signs of them anywhere. But are we listening in the right way? Are we deaf to a signal that we are receiving loud and clear?

In 1965 Soviet radio astronomer Scholomitski studied the radio source CTA 102 and announced that it was varying significantly in intensity, with an apparent period of 100 days, and transmitting at a wavelength near 18 centimetres that had previously been proposed for interstellar communication. It was speculated that the oscillation might serve as a beacon calling attention to CTA 102, and that on a much shorter timescale than 100 days the individual words of an interstellar communication channel might be deciphered. In the Soviet press some astronomers openly speculated that CTA 102 bore all the signs of an artificial source.

CTA 102 was later identified as a quasar – a natural source. But even so, might it not be under the control of a Level II or Level III civilisation? And might not the same be true of pulsars, stars that also send out regular pulses of radiation?

To be sure, the variations in intensity seem to be quite irregular in the case of quasars and quite regular in the case of pulsars; in neither case do we appear to be receiving information from an intelligent source. But could the signals be messages from beings so intelligent that we cannot understand them because our mental capacity is limited? Perhaps – but it seems unlikely because any advanced civilisation would no doubt appreciate the problems of interstellar discourse and would use the simplest possible method for establishing contact.

A more serious problem might be raised, however, by contact with less advanced civilisations than our own. How would we communicate with beings as dull-witted, say, as cows, or as primitive as Stone Age man – even supposing that we were to discover such communities? And if we could devise some means of communication, we might wish to preserve their culture and way of life by leaving them undisturbed. (Of course, super-advanced extra-terrestrial civilisations may regard human beings as fumbling incompetents and may be taking exactly this 'conservationist' attitude towards us.)

But whether our neighbours in the Universe are super-brains or savages, much bigger projects will have to be set up if the search for ETI is to be carried on with any hope of success. The most famous such proposal is the National Aeronautics and Space Administration (NASA) Cyclops project, which would involve 1000 or more radio telescopes, each the size of a football pitch, steered in unison by a computerised electronic system. Their combined performance would be equivalent to that of a single disc 6.2 miles (10 kilometres) in diameter, which would be impossible to construct because it would collapse under its own weight.

This array of radio telescopes would be able to detect radiation as weak as Earth's inadvertent leakage of microwaves even from a distance of 100 light years, while a message from another civilisation could be detected at a distance of at least 1000 light years.

Project Cyclops would not be easy or cheap to construct, though it is perfectly feasible using existing technology. It has been estimated that it would cost between 10 and 50 billion dollars to build and run, so that the project would represent a considerable commitment to the search for ETI.

Our technology is capable of mounting a very effective search for extra-terrestrial signals. But is the search worthwhile? Our biggest hurdle is the fact that we cannot guarantee success.

Artist's impressions of the proposed NASA scheme, Project Cyclops, designed to achieve optimum efficiency in detecting radio signals from other intelligences

Below: a densely-packed array of radio telescopes as they would look on the Moon's surface. The lunar Cyclops project is, at present, very much a scientist's dream

Below right: the Cyclops telescopes as they would appear in the pilot scheme, based on Earth

Where do the aliens live?

We know which stars may support life. But have aliens already recognised that there is life on Earth – and have they already started to investigate our planet?

THE BELIEF THAT mankind is not the sole representative of intelligent life in the Universe is very old. And it is more than a belief: as the philosopher Metrodorus put it in the third century BC, 'to consider the Earth the only populated world in infinite space is as absurd as to assert that in an entire field sown with millet, only one grain will grow.' There is indeed a high mathematical chance that Man is not the only intelligent creature in the vastness of space, but there remain a number of problems to be overcome before we can be sure of actually making contact with another civilisation.

One of them, as we have seen, is the question of whether an advanced technological civilisation will survive long enough to receive any signal from Earth. By the same logic, *we* may have destroyed ourselves in the time it takes for the signal to be picked up and answered. Another is the matter of *where* we should direct our signals – and even if our messages are received, how can we be sure that they will be understood?

If we take an optimistic view of our own chance of survival on Earth, and assume equally long lives for extra-terrestrial civilisations, the next step is to deduce where another intelligence may have arisen.

The conditions for life

We are assuming, in looking for such a place, that the life that we may find there is the same, biologically speaking, as life on Earth: that is, one based on carbon and water. There is some logic in this notion, for though in theory life could emerge at temperatures ranging from those on the surface of a star to those experienced on a cold planet, such a form of life is unlikely to be composed of the same materials, or even resemble that on Earth. Besides, terrestrial biology makes use of material – carbon, nitrogen, hydrogen and oxygen – that exists in very large quantities in space, while the conditions on Earth are peculiarly suitable for life based on them to emerge. It makes sense that life arises from substances that are abundant, as Metrodorus instinctively recognised. And it certainly makes sense for Man to look for life forms that, because they should be biologically similar, he can recognise as such – and that in turn will recognise *him*.

In effect, this means starting the search by looking for stars similar to our own Sun. The Sun is, as stars go, neither particularly large nor especially small – and it is this moderateness that is crucial to the development of life. A heavy star burns bright and burns fast: one only twice as massive will be twice as hot, but will last only a tenth of the Sun's predicted lifetime – a thousand million years as against 10,000 million. Not only that, but it will be pumping out huge amounts of deadly shortwave radiation, in the face of which no life of any kind could gain a foothold.

A relatively lightweight star, on the other hand, will last a very long time. But it will not

Above: an artist's impression of a binary star system as it would be seen from the surface of a nearby planet. The 'small', bright blue star – actually about three times larger than our Sun – orbits an enormous red supergiant. This is so large that if it took the place of our Sun, Earth and its orbit would be trapped inside it

Left: animal life on Earth depends on the oxygen given off by plants – could life on other planets be similarly organised?

produce sufficient light to support life, despite the comparatively harmless radiation it generates. For the earliest and most primitive forms of life – plants – depend on sunlight to break down the carbon dioxide in the atmosphere, using the carbon as 'food' and releasing oxygen.

Our Sun is a happy compromise between the extremes of heat and cold, and there are some 5000 million stars like it in our Galaxy.

However, the mere existence of Sun-like stars does not mean that life is – or may be – stirring nearby. Any biological process needs the protection of a planet – a place that is shielded by its atmosphere from ultra-violet radiation, and that forms a meeting place for the chemical constituents of life. Finding the right kind of star is, for a modern astronomer, easy enough. Finding one with a planetary system is a little more complicated.

The results of an investigation into the nature of planet-bearing stars, published in 1976 by Helmut Abt and Saul Levy, are crucial in this respect. Abt and Levy observed that double-star systems (or binary stars) fall into two categories: those that take 100 years or more to orbit each other, and those, with the stars closer together, that orbit much more quickly. They reasoned that the closer, short-period binary systems came into being when the spinning blob of gas from which stars form split in two. As the rotation of the blob increased, so did its density, and the proto-star became unstable, eventually breaking up to form a double star. By calculating the amount of energy in these systems they further concluded that *all* condensing proto-stars split in this way. However, a third of the stars that Abt and Levy studied had no companion suns. The conclusion they reached was that planets, rather than stars, had been formed instead.

Astronomers reckon that stars that are one-and-a-half times the mass of our Sun or smaller will produce sufficient light and will last long enough for life to emerge on their planets. It follows from Abt and Levy's work that stars of this size, and those that are not part of a close binary system, should have planets. And those planets could support life – and if life, why not civilisation?

It is possible to detect the existence of planets around a star by looking for variations in its movement through space. The movement results from the rotation of our entire Galaxy; the variation is a 'wobble' produced by the gravitational effect of any satellites the star may have. And in 1963, Peter van de Kamp, an astronomer at Sproul Observatory in Pennsylvania, USA, announced that the red dwarf known as Barnard's star – the second nearest star to our Sun – seemed to have a planetary system. By 1978 some dozen stars with planets as big or bigger than our own giant planet Jupiter had been detected: but every one of them was a red dwarf. None could support life.

Other astronomers are, however, looking at more promising stars, using the much more sensitive method of spectroscopy. This measures the changes in wavelength of the light emitted by stars that are caused by the planets orbiting about them. Another method is speckle interferometry, which cuts out much of the effect of the Earth's atmosphere and allows precise measurement of star behaviour. But the work is long and delicate, and will take years to produce results.

And once planets are discovered, what then? Radio signals still seem the best method of making contact, and then it will be only technologically advanced civilisations that could reply. Probes equipped with cameras would produce little evidence of life that was not highly developed, since the cameras would need extremely high resolution, with the ability to distinguish fine details only a few metres apart.

On the other hand, while astronauts have not set foot beyond the Moon, automatic probes have already landed on Mars and Venus and travelled beyond Mercury and Jupiter. Our first exploration of the stars might then be by stellar probes rather than by astronaut. On the same logic it is possible that if aliens tried to visit us, they would do so at first not in person but by sending probes that would pass through our solar system and

Below: Helmut Abt who, with Saul Levy, made important discoveries about the nature of planet-bearing stars and conditions necessary for life

Below right: Barnard's star (marked with an arrow) is a red dwarf and the second nearest star to our Sun. Although it has a large planetary system, all its known planets are lifeless

Left: spectroscopic analysis of the wavelength of starlight

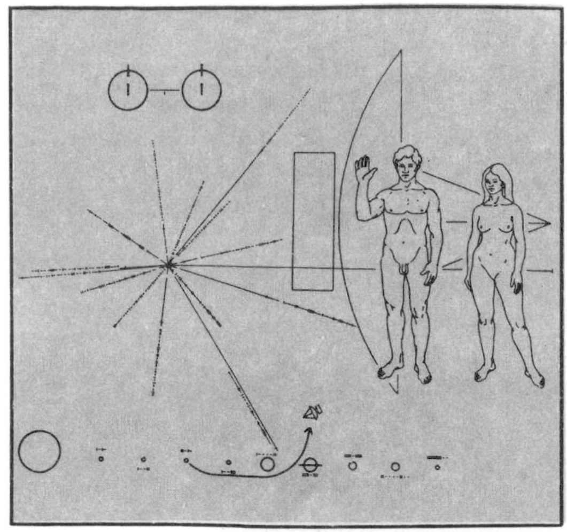

Right: the pictorial plaque that was attached to NASA's Pioneer 10 spacecraft, launched in 1972. It was intended to convey to any 'scientifically educated' aliens complex information about the position of our planet, our Solar system and ourselves. The man's raised hand, intended as a gesture of goodwill, could, some critics point out, be interpreted as a sign of aggression. But by the time it is intercepted mankind could have died out

send messages back about life on Earth.

We ourselves have sent probes not just to signal back information but to carry a message from Earth to other beings in space. On 3 March 1972 the Jupiter probe Pioneer 10 was launched. Attached to its antenna was a small plaque etched into a gold-anodised aluminium plate 6 inches by 9 inches (15 centimetres by 22.5 centimetres).

Etched on the plate is a code message that was composed by the American astronomers Carl Sagan and Frank Donald Drake. It is written in the binary code used by computers and locates the Earth by reference to nearby pulsars, which should be recognisable 'land marks' for any technologically advanced civilisation. Another part of the engraving shows the positions of the planets of the solar system with the path followed by Pioneer 10 marked on it. But the most controversial item on the plaque is a diagram showing Pioneer 10, and in front of it, to scale, representations of a naked man and woman. Much debate has been aroused by the fact that the man's arm is lifted in what, it is hoped, will be interpreted as a gesture of peace. Science writer Ian Ridpath, however, reports that on raising his arm to a cageful of Rhesus monkeys, which are quite closely related to man, they attacked him.

What will other beings make of this? Presumably any civilisation sufficiently advanced to pick up the probe will have the scientific knowledge to understand the purely technical symbols. Sagan points out, though, that the pictures of humans may well puzzle them, since they may not resemble any life form they have ever encountered – they may not even recognise us as life forms at all.

But what if an alien probe has already passed by Earth? Would they take an interest in us? Would they actually bother to try and visit us in person? Do we offer anything that might interest them? We are just beginning to show that we can send rockets from our own planet to other worlds. We've also amply demonstrated a remarkable inability to live in peace and solve the problems of our own planet. But now that we are able to propel ourselves and our problems out to the stars we may suddenly be of great interest to the inhabitants of other worlds. Any Galactic federation concerned for its own survival and the peace of the Galaxy would no doubt want to watch us very carefully indeed.

In fact might it not be that extra-terrestrials are already living among us? If we were interested in studying a primitive culture, we would try to be as unobtrusive as possible. Similarly, a good alien scientist would rather observe us humans without himself being observed. And if the aliens really wanted to understand us, they would probably want to mingle with us. What better way would they have than to disguise themselves in human form so as to mix unnoticed amongst us? So perhaps we are already being watched, and perhaps aliens are much closer than we dare imagine.

Sounds of human life

The strangest, and possibly the most important, long-playing record ever made on Earth was despatched into deepest space on board the two *Voyager* spacecraft, launched in August 1977. This 12-inch (30-centimetre) copper disc, designed to be played at $16\frac{2}{3}$ revolutions per minute, plays for two hours. A selection of 116 pictures, recorded in electronic form, shows 20th-century life on Earth including 'pictures' of a foetus, a mother and baby, a family, people of different races and a variety of animal life and plants. Buildings and a rocket launching are chosen to represent Man's technology. There are also oral greetings in 55 languages and other sounds of Earth – natural ones including wind, surf, frogs and whales, and man-made sounds such as a tractor engine, and the Saturn 5 lift-off. The inventor of *Sounds of Earth*, Dr Carl Sagan, describes it as 'a bottle cast into the cosmic ocean'. But will it ever be found – and if so how will the aliens understand it?

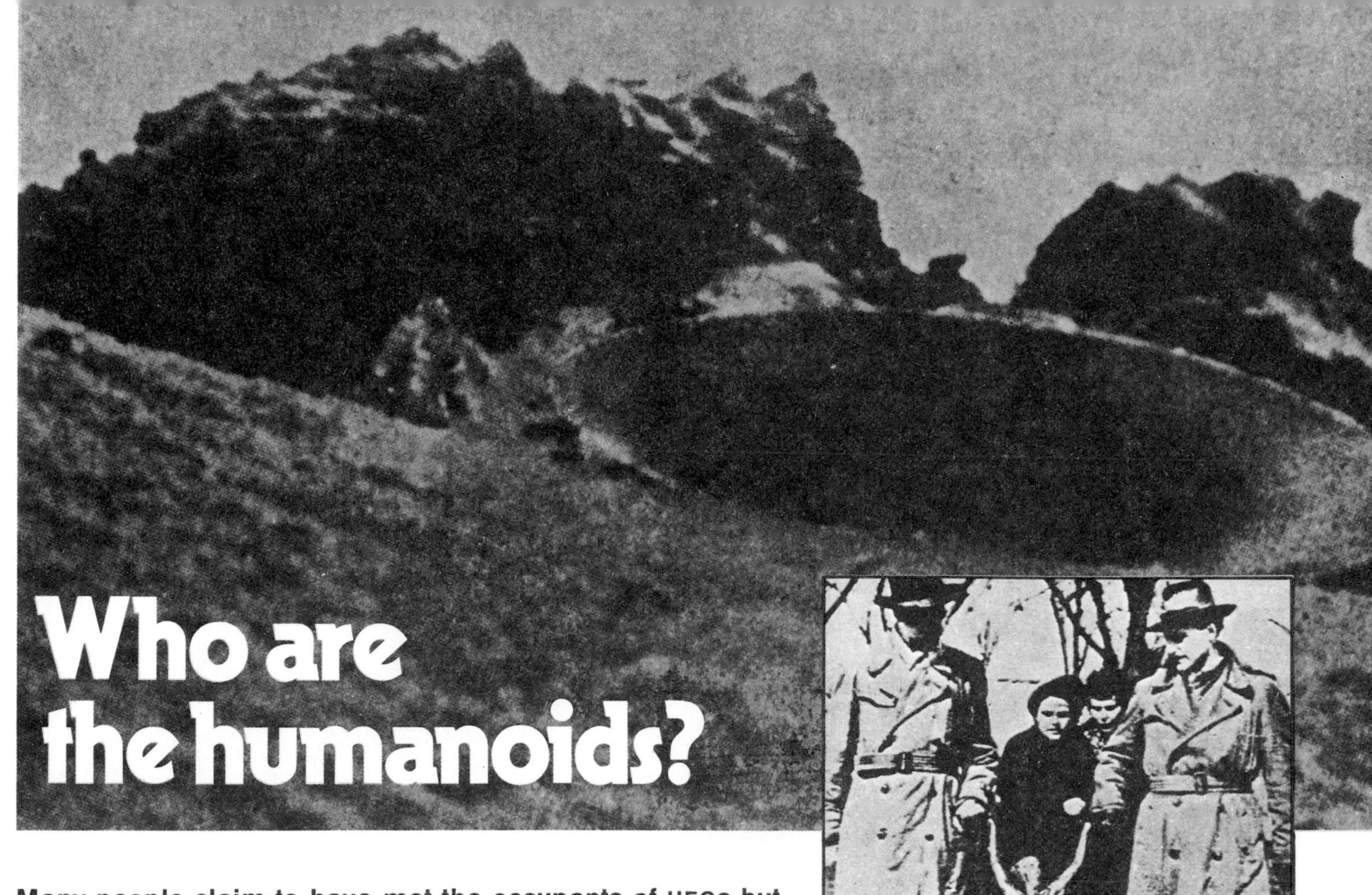

Who are the humanoids?

Many people claim to have met the occupants of UFOs but accounts of the humanoids' behaviour seem strangely inconsistent. CHARLES BOWEN begins an examination of these bizarre encounters

THE SIGHTING of nine unusual flying craft in Washington State, USA, by American airman Kenneth Arnold in June 1947, marked the advent of modern publicity for the 'flying saucer' or UFO phenomenon. The frequently reported ultra-high speeds and breathtaking manoeuvrability of the objects inevitably led to speculation by observers, newsmen and the public that what was being witnessed were intrusions into our airspace by extra-terrestrial visitors – beings from outer space. And, as the behaviour of these objects seemed to indicate superior technology and its fluent control, then the big question was: control by whom, or by what?

Those questions were not quickly resolved for, although the phenomenon was so persistent that the US Air Force set up an investigatory unit, Project Blue Book, officialdom did not appear to want to know the answers. By 1952 many accounts of sightings and even landings had been filed with the Project, but in his book *The report on* UFOs, Blue Book's commanding officer, Captain Edward Ruppelt, stated he was plagued by reports of landings and that his team conscientiously ignored them.

However, there are always those whose sense of wonder overcomes official intransigence. Groups of doggedly inquisitive civilian researchers drifted together and, to the limits of their slender resources, gathered and recorded information from around the world. They included people like Aimé Michel and Jacques Vallée from France (Vallée now lives and works in the USA), Coral and Jim Lorenzen and their Aerial Phenomena Research Organisation (APRO) in Arizona, Len Stringfield in Ohio, Major Donald Keyhoe's National Investigations Committee on Aerial Phenomena (NICAP) in Washington DC (who, like Ruppelt, were at first none too happy about the landing reports) and, in Britain, the supporters of the *Flying Saucer Review*.

Above: a purported humanoid stands to the left of an alleged grounded UFO in the Bernina Mountains, Italy, on 31 July 1952

Inset: this controversial picture is said to show a dead crew member from a crashed UFO found near Mexico City in the 1950s. The creature was apparently taken to Germany for examination – never to be heard of again

From the impressive body of evidence collected by these veterans, and others, it is quite obvious now that there is a phenomenon within the UFO phenomenon – that of their occupants. The shapes, sizes, appearance and behaviour of the 'pilots', as reported by their alleged observers, are often quite extraordinary. Out of the thousands of reported sightings no coherent picture emerges of their nature and intentions. Their actions seldom seem to be related to any kind of organised surveillance of our planet. And sometimes these aliens are even reported without the apparent presence of a UFO.

From 1947 to 1952, while the reality of

UFOs and their occupants was often the subject of heated debate, allegedly *hominid* (man-like) creatures had already been seen close to, or in, UFOs in widely separated parts of the world.

For instance, at Baurú, in the state of São Paulo, Brazil, on 23 July 1947 – less than a month after Kenneth Arnold's aerial encounter near Mount Rainier – a survey worker named José Higgins, and several of his fellow workers, saw a large metallic disc come to earth and settle down on curved legs.

Higgins stood his ground while his colleagues fled, and found himself face to face with three 7 foot (2.1 metre) tall beings, all wearing transparent overalls with metal boxes on their backs. One entity pointed a tube at him and moved as though to apprehend him. But Señor Higgins dodged the creature and observed that it was shy of following him into the sunlight.

The creatures had large bald heads, big round eyes, no eyebrows or beards and long legs. They leapt and gambolled, picking up and tossing huge boulders about. They also made holes in the ground, perhaps trying to indicate what could have been the positions of planets around the sun, and pointing particularly to the seventh hole from the centre – could that seventh 'planet' be Uranus? The creatures then re-entered their craft, which took off with a great whistling noise. Higgins's subsequent account appeared in two Brazilian newspapers.

Three weeks later, far away in north-eastern Italy, a Professor Johannis was on a mountain walk on 14 August 1947, near Villa Santina, Carni, in the province of Friuli. He suddenly saw a red metallic disc in a rocky cleft and emerged from trees to look at it. He then noticed that two dwarf-like creatures were following him, moving with tiny strides, hands perfectly motionless at their sides and heads still. As they came nearer Johannis' strength failed him; he seemed paralysed.

Top: Captain Edward J. Ruppelt, the commanding officer of the highly criticised Project Blue Book

Centre: Aimé Michel, the famous French UFO investigator

Above: Major Donald E. Keyhoe, the head of the National Investigations Committee on Aerial Phenomena (NICAP), based in Washington DC, USA

Left and top right: artist's impressions of the humanoids reported by José Higgins in Brazil and Professor Johannis in Italy in 1947

The little beings – less than 3 feet (1 metre) tall – wore translucent blue coveralls, with red collars and belts. The witness could detect no hair, but he described their facial skin colour as 'earthy green'. He also noted straight noses, slits for mouths that opened and closed like fishes' mouths, and large, round protruding eyes.

Johannis says he shouted to them on an impulse and waved his alpine pick, whereupon one dwarf raised a hand to his belt, the centre of which apparently emitted a puff of smoke. The pick flew out of Johannis' hand, and he fell flat on his back. One entity then retrieved the pick, and the pair retreated to the disc, which soon shot up, hovered briefly over the panic-stricken professor, then suddenly seemed to shrink and vanish.

On 19 August 1949, in Death Valley, California, two prospectors saw the apparent crash-landing of a disc. Two small beings emerged and were chased by the prospectors until the aliens were lost among sand dunes. When the two men returned to their site the disc-shaped object had gone.

Again, on 18 March 1950, Argentine rancher Wilfredo Arévalo saw one 'aluminium' disc land while another hovered over it. The object that landed was surrounded by a greenish blue vapour, and in its centre was a transparent cabin in which Arévalo saw 'four tall, well-shaped men dressed in Cellophane-like clothing'. They shone a beam of light at the rancher, the disc glowed a brighter blue, flames shot from the base, and it rose from the ground. The two objects disappeared swiftly towards the Chilean border.

Right: this is said to be a 'Venusian scout ship' photographed by George Adamski on 13 December 1952 at Palomar Gardens, California, USA

Below: Adamski's picture of an 'interplanetary carrier' and six 'scouts'

Bottom: George Adamski with the 6 inch (15 centimetre) telescope through which he took his controversial UFO photographs

While such reports seemed to promise interesting material for future investigation, they did not appear to indicate a serious threat of alien ('take me to your leader') invasion. Perhaps the official reluctance even to consider landing reports, which were said to be flooding in, was due simply to a fear of being swamped with crazy stories of 'little green men', which did become ready targets for ridicule in the media. Serious researchers eventually coined the name humanoids.

Back in 1953, however, something happened that shocked most serious-minded investigators, for it was in that year that a certain Mr George Adamski broke in on the UFO scene with a book co-authored with Desmond Leslie – *Flying saucers have landed*. In this controversial book Adamski claimed to have conversed with a being from a flying saucer and to have taken photographs of the craft. The book rapidly became a bestseller and was a boon to those early serious researchers – although they would never admit

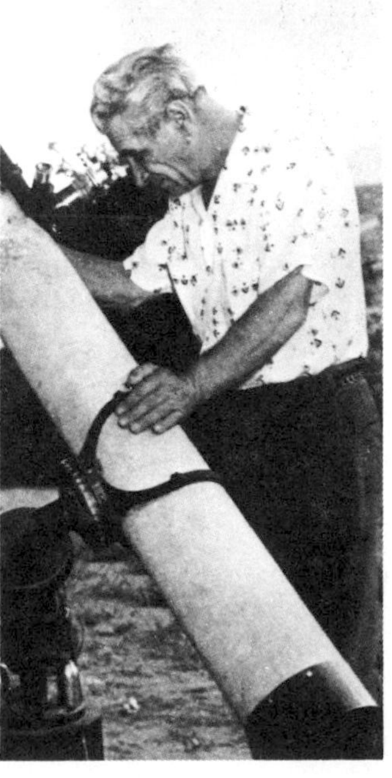

it – in that it brought to thousands of casual readers an interest in ufology.

George Adamski (1891–1965) was an amateur astronomer who operated his Newtonian reflector telescopes from his home at Palomar Gardens, California. He developed an obsessive interest in flying saucer reports, frequently claimed to have seen the objects and to have photographed them telescopically, as on 5 March 1951, when he captured on film a giant cigar-shaped object surrounded by emerging scout craft, and on 1 May 1952, when he took a picture of another giant cigar-shaped 'mother ship'. Then, on 20 November 1952, with a small party of friends, Adamski was driven out to a place just off the road to Parker, in Arizona. The purpose of the trip was to look for, and photograph, UFOs.

Adamski and the Venusian

A 6 inch (15 centimetre) portable telescope was set up at a convenient place and Adamski settled down to wait while his companions retreated to watch from a distance. Before long, he said, he was rewarded with the sight of an object landing among the hills before him, and he photographed it at long range before it disappeared.

A 'person' then appeared and approached him. The stranger, about 5 feet 6 inches (1.7 metres) tall, wore ski-suit style clothing and had long hair down to his shoulders. There was an aura of friendliness about him, and Adamski said that they were able to communicate telepathically about many things, the visitor specifically indicating that he came from Venus.

The stranger's 'scout craft' then turned up and, refusing Adamski's request for a ride, the 'Venusian' departed, taking one of Adamski's film plate-holders with him. The ufonaut left footprints in the sand and a member of the party obligingly produced plaster of Paris to make casts of the imprints.

On 13 December 1952, the Venusian returned to Earth, bringing back the plate-holder, and it was then, so Adamski claims, that he took close-up pictures of the craft.

In his second book, *Inside the space ships*, Adamski stated that he had finally made that trip – round the Moon – and that a space companion pointed out the *rivers* and *lakes* on the unseen far side.

All of this seems to indicate that Adamski was not telling the truth, or that he had been deliberately misled by some entities that had a vested interest in spreading a little confusion on Earth. Perhaps the story Adamski told was real to him; that he chose to elaborate on it and embroider it here and there is another matter. Meanwhile, reports of visitations by humanoid occupants of UFOs have continued to increase over the years and provide some fascinating information.

Close encounters of the third kind

'Close encounters of the third kind' refers to the experience of coming face to face with a humanoid, or occupant of a UFO. Reports of such incidents are increasing, but who or what are these creatures and how 'real' are they?

AS MORE AND more UFO reports were collected throughout the Fifties and Sixties, an interesting pattern soon became apparent: their dates revealed marked peaking of UFO activity. This came to be known as the 'wave' or 'flap' phenomenon and, invariably, at or around the crests of the waves came reports of humanoid occupants of the UFOs – a phenomenon within a phenomenon.

Perhaps the most intense of all, so far, was that of 1954 in north-west Europe, particularly France – other great waves since then include those of 1957–58 (the Americas and Australasia), 1962–63 (South America), 1964 (USA), 1965 (worldwide), 1977–78 (Britain and Italy). The 1954 wave was very complex with one main and several secondary peaks, and then came reports of widespread humanoid encounters.

The Quarouble case of 10 September 1954, with its grotesque dwarves in diving suits and their craft with its immobilising beam, have been described in a previous volume. Shortly after that there was another report from France, near Cénon, where, at 10.30 p.m. on 17 September 1954, a farmer on his bicycle suddenly started to itch all over. He dismounted and slowly became immobilised (he described it as being 'paralysed') as he observed a 'machine' on the road ahead of him. A little creature, apparently clad in a diving suit, came towards him, uttered strange sounds, and touched the farmer's shoulder before moving off to enter the object, which glowed green and took off like lightning. As it went the farmer regained his mobility.

Creatures of terror

Next, an account with a hint of menace. At 8.30 p.m. on 27 September 1954 four French farmer's children playing in their father's barn at Prémanon, high up in the Jura Mountains, heard their dog barking. The eldest boy went to investigate and encountered a rectangular creature 'like a sugar lump' standing on end and split at the bottom. The boy threw pebbles and shot a toy arrow at it. He then moved as if to touch the thing, only to be flung to the ground by an invisible force. He screamed, jumped up, and ran terrified into the yard and saw the 'being' waddling off towards a meadow.

The children then ran to the house and, on the way, saw a glowing red sphere wobbling over the meadow grass 165 yards (150 metres) away. Next day gendarmes discovered a 13 foot (4 metre) diameter circle of flattened grass.

At 7 p.m. on 9 October 1954 a labourer cycling at Lavoux, near Poitiers in France, met a weird 4 foot (1.3 metre) tall creature, again apparently in a diver's suit, and what could be seen of its head looked like a mass of hair with big eyes shining through. The creature shuffled along the road for a minute, then disappeared into the adjacent trees.

Not surprisingly this story was the subject of hilarious jokes in the French national press. What the journalists did not know was that on 10 October in north-eastern France at Pournoy-la-Chétive (in the Moselle area), at about 6.30 p.m., a 'shiny machine' was seen to land by three children who were out roller skating. A 'kind of man', just under 4 feet (1.2 metres) tall, emerged dressed in a 'black sack' like a priest's cassock. They later described him as 'a ghost'. His face was very hairy and he had big eyes. He held a flashlight that dazzled the children, and uttered words they did not understand. Frightened, they beat a hasty retreat, then, looking back, saw the machine climb rapidly into the sky.

Far left: an artist's impression of the black, headless creature that terrified some young people in Kent, England, in 1963

Left: dressed in a cassock-like robe, with a mass of hair for a face and described as 'a ghost', this humanoid was witnessed by three French children in 1954

Below: an encounter in Finland in 1971 – a forestry worker was burnt when he touched a humanoid

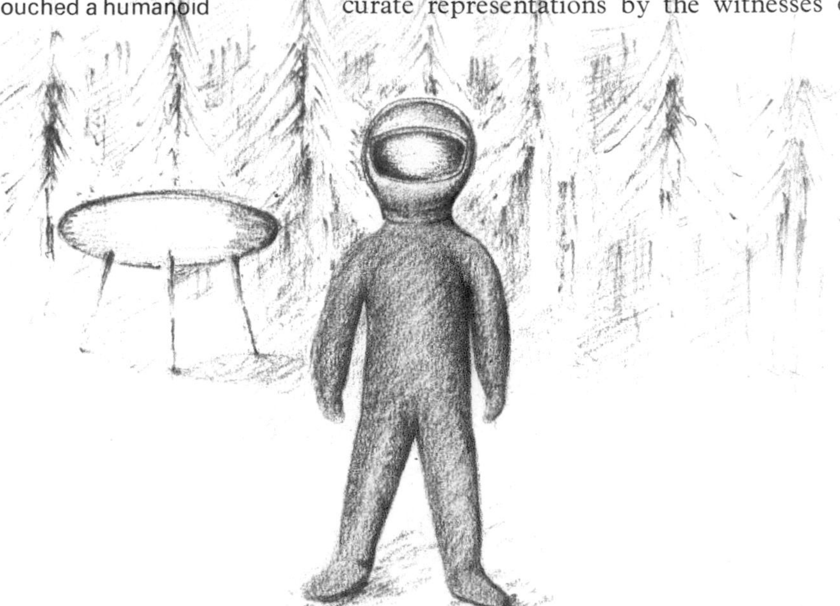

Next day, three men from Bordeaux were driving at Tapignac, near Royan on the Atlantic coast of France, when they saw a red glow lighting up the fields and sky; it was about 7.30 p.m. They stopped, got out, and saw a disc-shaped object with a red-orange dome about 275 yards (250 metres) away, hovering about 35 feet (10 metres) above the ground. After a few seconds it moved away among trees where its light was still visible. The men took a torch and walked towards the light when, some 450 yards (400 metres) away, they came upon the object, now landed and with four 3 foot (1 metre) high beings busy at some task under the craft. The little creatures then disappeared inside the disc, which, after undergoing rapid colour changes, took off at great speed.

The diversity and variety of reported humanoid behaviour is immediately apparent, even from this small sample of case histories. Entities who were tall, gawky and gambolling wearing transparent suits; tall and well-shaped beings apparently dressed in Cellophane; armless midgets shuffling along in garb similar to divers' suits with massive helmets; waddling, rectangular creatures like sugar lumps who pack a hidden punch; hirsute, pop-eyed monsters in black, sack-like clothing. Also reported were entities tapping shoulders or brushing coldly past; entities hurling boulders, or playing hide-and-seek, or seen tinkering beneath their craft. Some aimed beams of light, or rays, at human witnesses, several of whom complained of temporary 'paralysis'. All this is far removed from the style and behaviour of the long-haired, gentle 'Venusian' who allegedly held a polite telepathic discussion with George Adamski.

What of the eyewitnesses who experience such 'close encounters of the third kind'? (The phrase was first used by Dr J. Allen Hynek in his book *The UFO experience* – borrowed spectacularly by the film-makers.) They have included surveyors, prospectors, a rancher, businessmen, children, a farmer, a labourer and a professor. And if, for example, the doctors, police officers, servicemen, housewives, scientists, factory workers and airmen, all of whom have had a variety of similar experiences, and who help to make up a very fair cross-section of the public, are added to the list, strikingly consistent patterns of behaviour emerge.

The contactees are deeply disturbed, amazed or frightened, and feel an obsessive obligation to discuss the incident with friends, or are strongly motivated to report it to the authorities – often, however, followed by a wish that they had kept it to themselves.

Very few of the thousands of witnesses of this kind actively seek publicity, go off on lecture tours, or write books about their encounters. Yet the very nature of contact with humanoids: the strangeness, the dreamlike quality of many of the reports, the inconclusiveness and pointlessness of many of the reported activities of the creatures, militate in favour of the stories being accurate representations by the witnesses of what they saw. Hoaxers might well feel compelled to give their stories a neater shape and a definite message.

The flow of humanoid reports continues unabated. At about 3 p.m. on 5 February 1971 two forestry workers at Kinnula, Finland, saw a UFO that landed on stilt-like legs in the clearing where they were working. A creature less than 3 feet (1 metre) high, clad in a green one-piece suit, including a helmet equipped with a lens, emerged from an aperture and glided towards them. The creature's hands appeared rounded, with no fingers visible.

One worker went forwards with his hand-held chain saw running; the being retreated and floated up towards the craft in which other entities could now be seen. The worker grabbed at the creature's foot, only to have his hand burned. The alien entered the craft, which then promptly took off.

A year earlier, on 7 January 1970, two Finns who were resting during a cross-country ski run in a forest glade near Imjärvi, Heinola, saw a mist-enshrouded domed disc appear overhead from which a beam of light was emitted vertically to the ground. Sparks danced where the beam hit the snow, and a small being suddenly appeared in the beam.

The creature had thin arms and legs, a hooked nose, green overalls and boots, a shining conical helmet, and was less than 3 feet (1 metre) tall. It aimed a 'box' at one of the men, Aarne Heinonen, and then both beam and entity faded upwards into the 'saucer' that, suddenly, was gone. Heinonen was ill for months after the incident.

Is seeing believing?

In the early hours of 12 October 1963, truck driver Eugenio Douglas was dazzled by a bright light on the road ahead of him near Monte Maíz, Córdoba, in Argentina. The truck ran into a ditch and Douglas climbed out to see a huge metallic object astride the road. Three robot-like beings, of an estimated height of about 13 feet (4 metres), emerged from a door. They had helmets, and suits that 'stuck to their bodies'. Douglas fired several shots at them, then fled. He was 'buzzed' by the UFO, which subjected him to prickling-sensation 'rays' as he ran.

In October 1963 a woman living on Whidby Island, Washington, USA, saw three occupants in a cylindrical UFO. One emerged *through* the side of the craft and approached her. It wore grey overalls with an aperture for eyes, but no eyes were visible. The being later returned to the craft in the same disconcerting manner.

One month later, on 16 November 1963, two young men from Kent, England, were walking with their girlfriends near Sandling Park in Saltwood, when they saw a bright 'star' descend, hover, and move among trees 80 yards (73 metres) away from them. The golden oval-shaped UFO stopped and, instantly, a human-sized figure emerged and came shambling towards them. When they saw it was completely black, headless and had wings like a bat, panic seized the four and they fled.

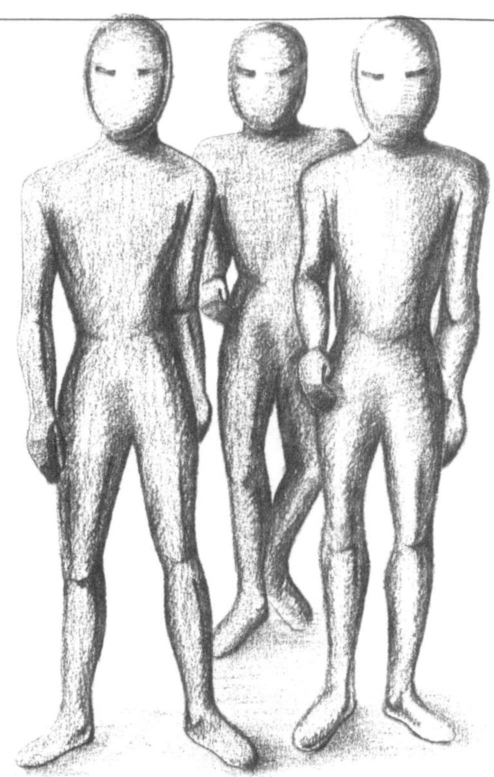

Right: an encounter too close for comfort. Eugenio Douglas shot at these robot-like creatures; they then fled into a UFO and disappeared

Below: the entity that confronted Aarne Heinonen in 1970, making the reluctant witness ill for months

In many of these cases both UFOs and their occupants use beams of light and rays, or some kind of invisible force. Moreover, the instant appearances and instant retreats; the ghostlike walking through walls; and the floating up and down beams seem to indicate that in many cases the witnesses were seeing images projected from intelligences within the craft. Later on came evidence to support the idea that the UFO occupants were selecting clairvoyants and potentially deep-trance subjects as their contacts.

In a brilliant series of articles, which appeared in the *Flying Saucer Review* entitled 'A long cool look at alien intelligence', the author, C. Maxwell Cade, a radiation medicine specialist, suggested that UFO occupants could monitor witnesses' fears ('My God, a flying saucer . . . is there a hairy monster in it?'). Such emanation, amplified, could be relayed back to the mind of the witness and – lo and behold . . . a hairy monster appears!

Maxwell Cade points out that there are many ways of inducing hallucinations, from simple overdoses of alcohol, hypnotic suggestion and drugs (such as LSD) to irradiating the brain with high-frequency waves: all of which are more or less dangerous to the subject. If such techniques are within our grasp, then who can tell what mind-bending methods could be employed by superior intelligences?

Behind the humanoid mask

Hundreds of ordinary people have reported 'close encounters', but even more startling are the reports of people who claim to have experienced abductions by humanoids

ARE THE HUMANOID OCCUPANTS of the UFOS – and even the UFOS themselves – nothing more than images projected for responsive witnesses to see or sense? Perhaps these projections are intended to test the reactions of selected witnesses to hypnotic control: and perhaps only the less successful – or 'shallow trance' – subjects ever report their 'close encounters'. So those who are not responsive to hypnotic control in any way could well have no encounter to report.

But for those who are susceptible to hypnosis – 'deep trance' subjects – it could be a very different story. Many witnesses of UFOS or their humanoid occupants have suffered inexplicable 'time lapses'. In recent years testimonies have been obtained by regressing deep trance subjects. Under hypnosis they frequently reveal that their minds had been manipulated by whatever controls the UFOS even to the extent of being mentally 'abducted' – for experimental purposes perhaps.

Physical or mental abduction by UFOS is now referred to as a 'close encounter of the fourth kind' (CE4), although it was not part of Dr J. A. Hynek's original classification of close encounters. The connection between CE3 (or 'contactee' reports) and the sinister CE4 cases can be clearly seen in the following cases.

At 11.30 p.m. on 17 March 1978 service engineer Ken Edwards, who was returning home after a union meeting at Sale, Greater Manchester, took the Risley exit from the M62 motorway. The exit (Drayton Road) is bounded by embankments, has open ground and an atomic energy plant with a 10-foot (3-metre) high security fence surmounting the embankment. In his headlights, Ken picked up a 7-foot (2-metre) tall figure descending the slope. It leaned forward as it walked, with its arms held out in the same direction (how on earth could it maintain balance?). Furthermore the arms seemed to be rooted in the creature's chest, and not at its shoulders. The being was clad in silvery overalls and a helmet through which the witness could only make out two round eyes.

Ken drew the van into the side of the road. He watched, alarmed, as the figure stopped in the middle of the road and, from about 15 feet (4.5 metres) away, swivelled its head in the van's direction. Then two pencil-thin beams of light projected from the being's eyes and struck him. After a minute of this it continued its progress to the left-hand side of the road, walked up the embankment, *straight through* a security fence – and disappeared from sight in 'dead ground'.

Ken stated later that he felt a 'kind of paralysis' while the beams were directed at him. He added – when interviewed by Jenny Randles of UFO Investigators' Network (UFOIN) – that the whole encounter lasted about four to five minutes and that he took a further five minutes to drive home. Yet his wife was adamant that he arrived home at about 12.30 a.m. and not 11.40 p.m. as might have been expected. Here then was an unaccounted-for time lapse. In this instance there was no mention of a UFO, but experience suggests there may well have been one around somewhere.

Another frightening 'close encounter' happened in Belo Horizonte, Brazil. At 7.30 p.m. on 28 August 1963 three boys were in

Below: an artist's impression of the humanoid that reportedly terrorised Ken Edwards on 17 March 1978 at Sale, in Greater Manchester. It is said to have emitted 'pencil-thin' beams of light from its eyes, which had a paralysing effect on the reluctant witness

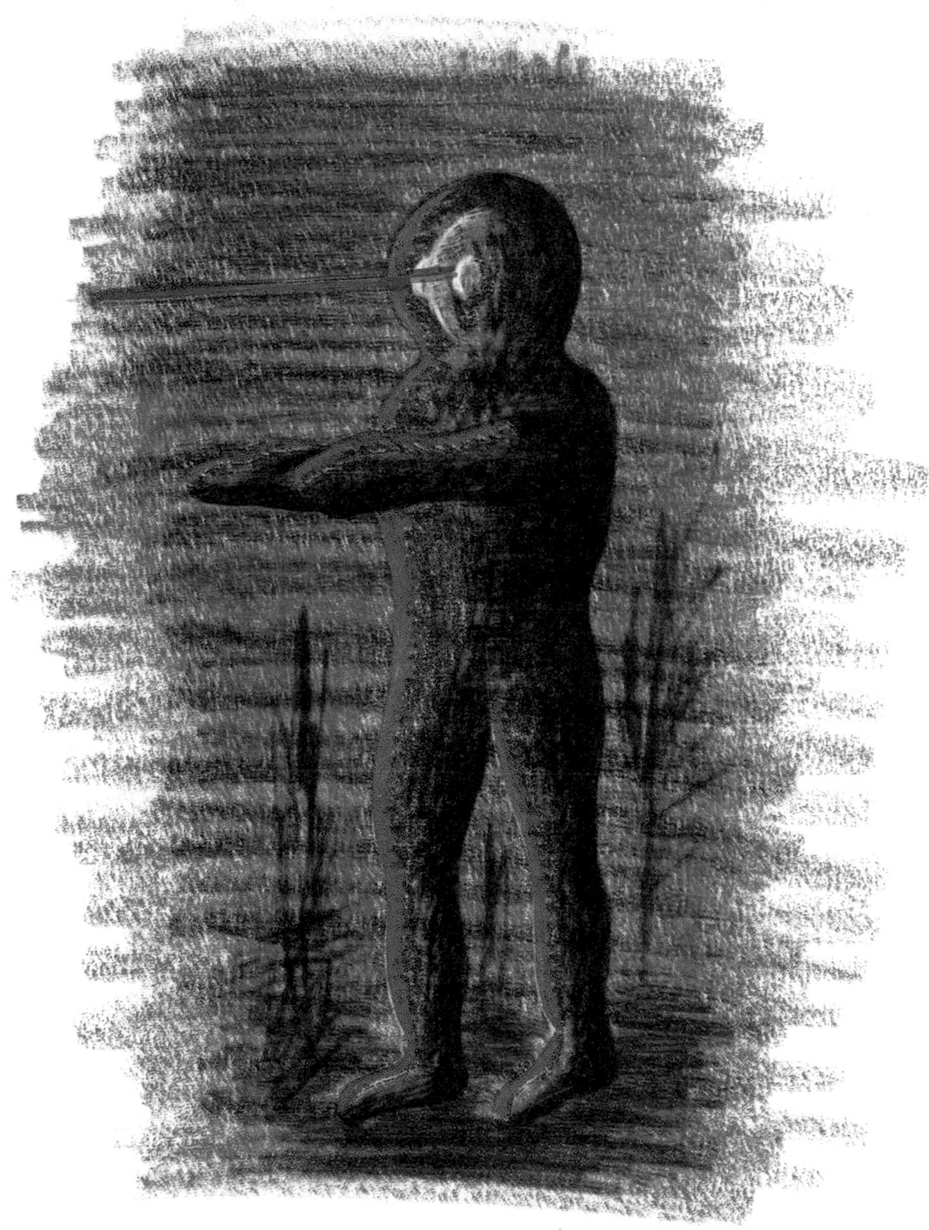

their garden washing out a coffee percolator at the well after supper. They saw a spherical object floating in the air about 5 yards (5 metres) above the garden. It was transparent and illuminated within so that they could see the four occupants sitting on stools inside. One seemed to be busy at a panel of instruments and they all wore a kind of diver's suit.

One of them came out through the underside of the craft and descended, motionless and upright, between two shafts of yellow light. With deliberate steps and swinging arms the entity moved toward the well. It fixed them with its one eye, made gestures with its hands and uttered strange sounds, then sat on the wall round the well.

One boy struggled against the 'paralysis' felt in the creature's presence and managed to pick up a brick. Instantly the entity shone a beam of light at him, extending from its middle, and the brick fell from his fingers. After more gesticulations the creature moved away and floated up the beam of light into the craft – whereupon there was a great brightness and the sphere rose in the dark sky. Suddenly freed from their bizarre restraint, the boys ran indoors yelling for their mother.

Humanoid or hologram?

At about 8.40 p.m. on 7 January 1974 a Belgian businessman was driving near Warneton on the Franco-Belgian frontier when his headlights were abruptly extinguished, his car's engine cut out, and the radio went dead. He hand-braked to a halt and saw in a field, about 165 yards (150 metres) away, an object like a 'British Tommy's steel helmet' standing on three legs. Then, with growing fear, he became aware of two weird figures approaching him. The smaller – who was very like the 'Michelin man' – had a round helmet, marble-like eyes and a slit for a mouth. The taller wore a kind of uniform with a Sam Browne belt and a cube-shaped helmet. They seemed to have identical faces.

The taller being opened its mouth and the alarmed businessman felt a shock at the back of his head and heard a modulated sound. At this point another car came over the distant horizon. The two entities turned as one and walked stiffly but briskly with identical movements – and with no signs of difficulty despite the heavy mud – to their craft where they joined a third similar creature. They all disappeared up into the object; the legs of the machine disappeared from view, it rose into the air and vanished completely just as the second car drew up.

If these different and detailed reports involved cases of projection then how is it done? In an article in *Flying Saucer Review* in February 1980 J. G. Adams reviewed some features of other humanoid reports where the beings were only partly visible – to which can be added the case of Oscar Iriart in Argentina who was puzzled to see that the entities he met in 1968 had transparent legs only.

Mr Adams lists entities who have been observed 'standing' in mid-air; others who glide across the ground; those surrounded by a glow and those who fade or disappear abruptly from sight. All these phenomena, he says, are features typical of holograms.

Technologically we have the ability 'to project into open space a *visually* solid object' using a beam of light – especially a laser beam – and a transparent plate which 'contains the image and which need not be as large as the image produced' . . . Anomalies such as partial images could occur where the beam is obscured.

Are the humanoids so often reported produced by variations on the holographic theme, with the superior facility of penetrating the human mind?

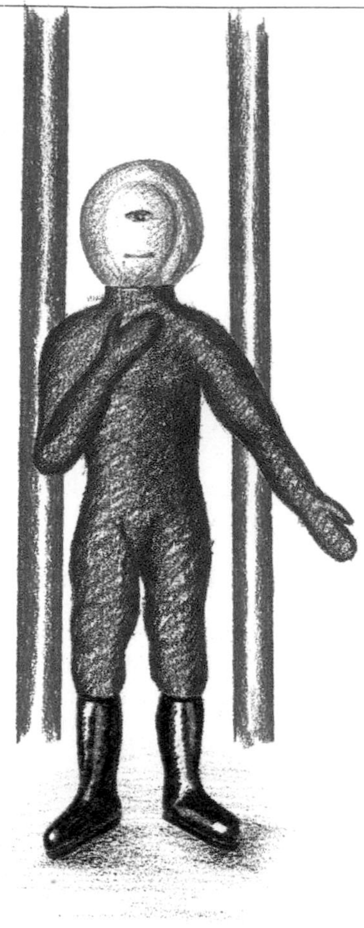

Above: a drawing from the descriptions given by three boys in Brazil, 1963, of a one-eyed humanoid who terrified them. Its very presence caused the boys to feel paralysed

Below: one of M. Masse's 'little men' – whom he discovered furtively picking lavender on 1 July 1965 at Valensole, France

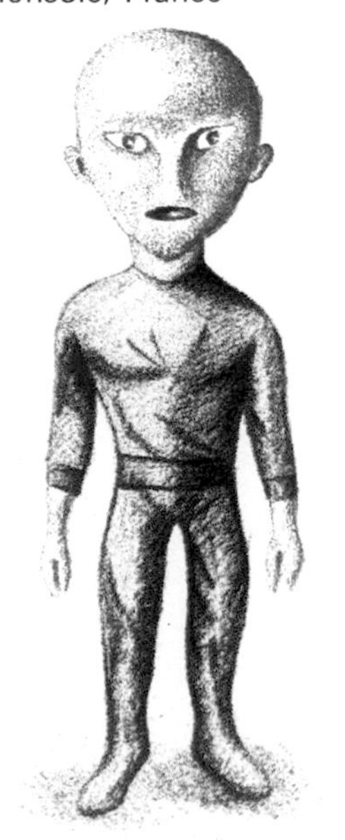

Abductions by the aliens

On the morning of 1 July 1965 farmer Maurice Masse was walking through a vineyard next to one of his lavender fields at Valensole in the Basses Alpes, France, when he saw a landed object in the shape of a rugby football and the size of a Dauphine car. Nearby were two small beings (described 'as of the height and build of a child of about eight') who were picking lavender shoots. Masse advanced on them stealthily but was seen by one of the entities who pointed a 'stick' at him – whereupon he froze on the spot, 'paralysed'. When the creatures finally returned to their craft they did so by 'bubbling up a beam of light'. The immobilised farmer could see them still observing him through the transparent walls of their machine. There was a thump, the legs of the craft whirled round, the object floated away and vanished at 22 yards (20 metres).

Maurice Masse has never disclosed what happened to him while he was in the presence of the little 'men' with their big pumpkin heads, almond-shaped eyes, slit mouths and very pointed chins. Was he 'abducted'? If so, for what purpose?

Significantly, the facial characteristics of the Valensole creatures were similar to those of the entities involved in a classic CE4 case – that of the abduction of Betty and Barney Hill in New Hampshire in 1961, allegedly for 'medical examination', and those who are said to have abducted Antonio Villas Boas in Minas Gerais, Brazil, in 1957 for medical examination and sexual experiment.

As more and more reports are gathered into the net fascinating similarities and patterns of humanoid behaviour have begun to emerge, even when individual witnesses could have no possible knowledge of other contactee stories around the world.

In *The Tujunga Canyon contacts*, published in the USA in 1980 a witness was reported as being hypnotically regressed and questioned by a doctor. In a trance state she revealed that she had been abducted and 'floated' up a beam of light into the craft.

And now to a final case that may give us some clues as to what may be going on . . .

In the early hours of 31 May 1974 a young couple, Peter and Frances, were driving from Salisbury (in what was then Rhodesia) to Durban in South Africa by way of Beit Bridge. Their car, a Peugeot 404, was escorted by a glowing object from close by Umvuma to just short of Fort Victoria. The lights all went out apart from a strange glow around the outside of the car – which seemed to have been taken from the driver's control; it became very cold; the radio continued to play a Lourenço Marques programme far beyond the end of its normal range. At Fort Victoria when they stopped to refill the petrol tank the UFO rose high in the sky and temporarily disappeared. They set off again at 5.30 a.m. but this time they were escorted by two UFOs. One took up station directly overhead.

Above: the humanoids reminiscent of a 'Michelin man' (left) and a 'British Tommy with a Sam Browne belt and a cube-shaped head' (right) as described by a Belgian businessman who is said to have encountered them near the Franco-Belgian border on 7 January 1974. They met a third humanoid and then all disappeared from view in a UFO

The familiar dry terrain suddenly changed to one of lush vegetation and swamps and the road straightened out. Peter was in a semi-comatose state – something else was controlling the car. Frances went to sleep at 6.15 a.m. She awoke at about 7 a.m. when they were a mile or so from Beit Bridge. Again the UFOs rose high in the sky above their car, as if at a signal.

The border officials were amused to find the couple wrapped in woollens and blankets on a fine warm morning. When they drove over the bridge and went to buy cheaper petrol in South Africa they found – to their amazement – that the tank was still full. The car used nothing during the 174 mile (280 kilometre) journey!

That was all Peter and Frances could remember of their strange journey. But six months later, still disturbed by their experience, they approached the *Natal Mercury* in Durban after reading an article sympathetic to witnesses of UFOs in that paper. Researcher Carl van Vlierden was called in, and sensing that theirs had been a time lapse experience, he arranged for a doctor to regress and question Peter under hypnosis. The result was a much more detailed account of the extraordinary encounter.

It seemed that after they left Fort Victoria the UFO above them sent down beams of light to the car; using these and the radio they took control of the car. They set up screens around it and projected lush country scenes onto them. The car was teleported high above the road. Peter felt he knew this was going to happen and put up a mental struggle against the 'take over'. He added that he and Frances were programmed inside the car and that his wife was put to sleep by the voice of 'them' speaking through their radio.

Frances, it seems, is not a deep trance subject but Peter is and is also psychic: under hypnosis he said that this was discovered by 'them in seven seconds flat'.

More questions than answers

A being came down the beam of light and sat beside the sleeping Frances; it could assume any shape the beholder wished. Peter said he was then shown the interior of the UFO *through the beam that linked it to the car.* He was also given many facts about the aliens – a great number of whom allegedly live among us on Earth. They never directly intervene in our affairs, it was claimed. Instead they are the schemers, the influencers, the persuaders.

The rest of the message seems to be the usual gobbledygook about the aliens coming from 'outer galaxies' – and later in the interrogation – from 'twelve planets of the Milky Way'.

In his normal, conscious state, Peter (on the tapes) sounds a businesslike and down-to-earth young man who would have no truck with such nonsense. But the fact remains that under hypnosis the story he has to tell is an extraordinary one of abduction by aliens. Was he selected by something somewhere because he is a deep trance subject?

Are the humanoids simply projections from alien minds or are images already in the witnesses' subconscious minds being tapped and returned to them in a more fearsome guise by some unknown agency, as suggested by C. Maxwell Cade? Perhaps the witnesses are their own agency – their subconscious minds creating incredibly real images for their conscious minds to register as close encounters?

And who knows, perhaps the much maligned George Adamski was a deep trance subject whose mind had been manipulated and implanted with fantastic images which he took to be 'real'? Could he have been set up just to be knocked down? Do 'they' have a vested interest in creating ufological martyrs?

If something, somewhere, is programming the brains of selected witnesses so that the stories they tell can be confirmed and elaborated on even under hypnosis, then who is it and why is there this organised manipulation? Perhaps these alien creatures really are – in their own words – 'the schemers, the influencers, the persuaders' . . .

PART 5

WHEN THE IMPOSSIBLE HAPPENS

WHEN THE IMPOSSIBLE HAPPENS

Contents

Introduction

THERE WAS A TIME when people who witnessed unlikely events or who held unorthodox opinions ran the risk of torture or death at the hands of the Church. In later centuries the danger of meeting an unpleasant end for failing to conform in this way has receded; the poet and painter William Blake was merely given a sound thrashing by his father for saying he had seen some angels sitting in a tree, for instance. But that was in the 18th century, when a spirit of tolerance was deemed a natural outcome of taking a logical and rational view of the world. It was, however, tolerance that went only so far, as the youthful poet's tingling skin doubtless reminded him.

The guardians of truth today are not priests but scientists, and their weapons are not the thumbscrew and the rack (though one sometimes wonders if they did not wish it otherwise) but silence, derision, wilful ignorance and sometimes outright abuse. The intrepid researcher into the bizarre and anomalous risks all of these should he so much as whisper his interest to one of our white-coated witch doctors. For to science such events as spontaneous human combustion, levitation, impossible explosions and unnatural coincidences *can't happen*. They don't fit the rules that science recognises; there is no *known* means by which fish can flop to earth out of a clear sky – and for many scientists, what is not known is simply not possible – it just does not happen.

But such things, apparently, do happen. Furthermore, the unknown and unexpected persist in happening in science itself, much to the dismay of those rash enough to have said otherwise. Meteors and ball lightning are famous cases of phenomena long rejected by science as impossible. Greater embarrassment can be induced by various unkind reminders of the prophecies of scientists: Sir Ernest Rutherford, who first discovered how to split the atom, was convinced that the energy produced by doing so would be 'a very poor kind of thing' – a prediction for which the people of Hiroshima were, in due course of time, properly grateful. Simon Newcomb, a celebrated astronomer, declared the aeroplane 'utterly impossible' in 1902. Thomas J. Watson of IBM, no less, once calculated that there would be a world market for 'about five computers'. And so it goes on.

To anyone with an open mind, it is surely obvious that the 'impossible' happens all the time, which is another way of saying that science can examine and account for only a part – if a large and important part – of what we recognise as reality. So it is that science is sensibly silent about some of the wonders that we all take – perhaps too easily – for granted: the creative force that produces a great painting, a poem or a magnificently moving piece of music, the spirit that moves men to be heroes or the worst of villains, the enormous power of our feelings when we fall in love. Such things don't fit into the materialistic, predictable scheme of things that science can handle. There *are* those biologists and behaviourists who insist that consciousness – thought and feeling – is only an illusion produced by the brain's electrical activity and that 'ideas don't move muscles', but that is of a different order from the incapacity to accept that even the most seemingly obvious of rules can be broken.

It is matters such as these that are dealt with in this book. By their very nature they are almost impossible for science to investigate adequately; you cannot examine an event like spontaneous human combustion since it is impossible to reproduce it in the laboratory. And the great collector of reports of such peculiar occurrences, Charles Fort, may have put his finger on the key to the mystery with his notion of a 'cosmic joker' at work in the Universe.

After all, if we can play pranks upon one another, why shouldn't the Universe, of which we are but a part, laugh at itself from time to time? And, like a good magician, refuse to tell how the trick is done?

The cosmic joker will, therefore, play most merrily with reality – and with our all-too-human tendency to expect consistency in the world. He will on one occasion appeal to our own sense of humour – causing a truck laden with carrots to collide with another carrying olive oil to make the biggest carrot salad in the world, for instance, or inexorably drawing a man called Phang into a career in dentistry. He will, on the other hand, mock the scepticism of science by dropping an enormous lump of ice out of a blue sky to land at the feet of a distinguished meteorologist, forcing him to accept the unexplicable. No less outrageously, the cosmic joker presents sea monsters and UFOs to photographers, and then causes their cameras to jam for the first and last time.

But the jokes may be more subtle than that. What, for example, is one to make of the notorious photographs of fairies taken at Cottingley, England, earlier this century? Many critics have remarked how like scissors-and-paste jobs they look. Others may feel that such a trick is typical of the cosmic joker, who would, of course, make absolutely certain that the best evidence for such other-dimensional beings *should* seem so suspect. That is all part of the prank of tantalising innocent humans with a glimpse of such creatures in the first place. And if humanity insists on taking itself and its ideas so seriously, doesn't it *deserve* to be teased?

Welcome, then, to the games that reality can play.

PETER BROOKESMITH

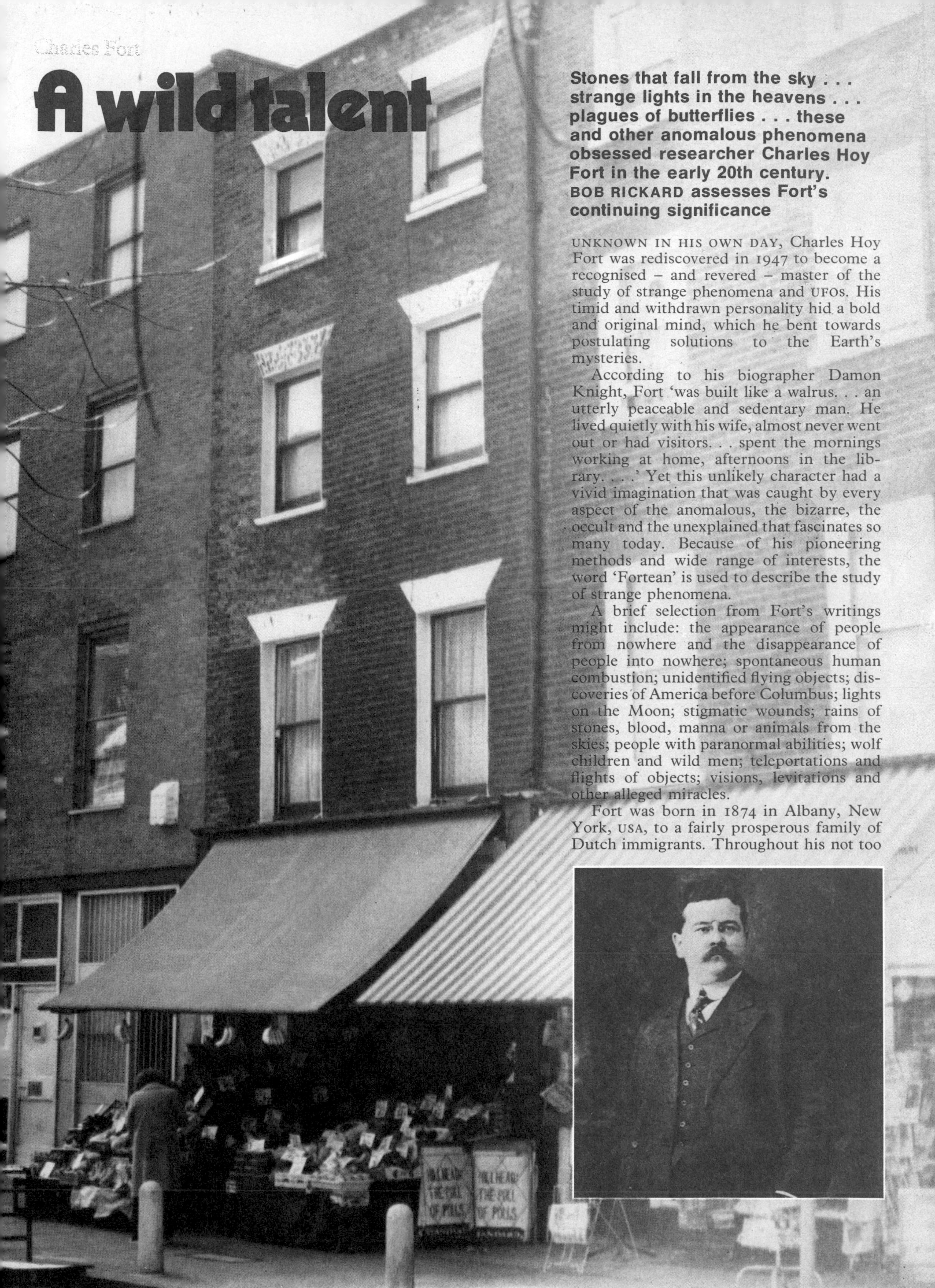

A wild talent

Stones that fall from the sky . . . strange lights in the heavens . . . plagues of butterflies . . . these and other anomalous phenomena obsessed researcher Charles Hoy Fort in the early 20th century. BOB RICKARD assesses Fort's continuing significance

UNKNOWN IN HIS OWN DAY, Charles Hoy Fort was rediscovered in 1947 to become a recognised – and revered – master of the study of strange phenomena and UFOs. His timid and withdrawn personality hid a bold and original mind, which he bent towards postulating solutions to the Earth's mysteries.

According to his biographer Damon Knight, Fort 'was built like a walrus. . . an utterly peaceable and sedentary man. He lived quietly with his wife, almost never went out or had visitors. . . spent the mornings working at home, afternoons in the library. . . .' Yet this unlikely character had a vivid imagination that was caught by every aspect of the anomalous, the bizarre, the occult and the unexplained that fascinates so many today. Because of his pioneering methods and wide range of interests, the word 'Fortean' is used to describe the study of strange phenomena.

A brief selection from Fort's writings might include: the appearance of people from nowhere and the disappearance of people into nowhere; spontaneous human combustion; unidentified flying objects; discoveries of America before Columbus; lights on the Moon; stigmatic wounds; rains of stones, blood, manna or animals from the skies; people with paranormal abilities; wolf children and wild men; teleportations and flights of objects; visions, levitations and other alleged miracles.

Fort was born in 1874 in Albany, New York, USA, to a fairly prosperous family of Dutch immigrants. Throughout his not too

In his quest for stories of anomalous phenomena, Charles Fort (previous page) spent several years in the 1920s among the archives of the British Library (right) at the British Museum in London. During his 'London period' he lived in Marchmont Street (previous page), then a run-down area, close to the British Museum. He unearthed thousands of reports of extraordinary happenings, including cases of spontaneous human combustion, inexplicable flash floods and falls of red rain. Fort offered a characteristic non-explanation for such phenomena saying, 'we are being played with'

happy childhood, Fort suffered much physical punishment at his father's hands, which made him hate authority. His rebellions prepared him for a life questioning authority and dogma. When he was 18 he left home to hitch-hike around the world in order, as he saw it, to put some 'capital into the bank of experience'. One day Fort boasted to a bedridden neighbour of his travels, but the man was not impressed. He too had travelled when he was younger, but it was only when he was confined to his room, he said, that he began to extract lasting values from his experiences. This impressed Fort very much and he later wrote: 'I [realised] that one should not scatter one's self upon all life, but center upon some one kind of life and know it thoroughly.' And that is what he did for the remaining 35 years of his life.

Fort's 'grand tour'

In 1897, at the age of 23, Fort read every scientific book and journal he could find and, within a few years, had amassed 25,000 notes on the infallible public face of authoritarian science. He burned them because 'they were not what I wanted.' He resumed what he called his 'grand tour', reading through the world's major newspapers and scientific journals and taking notes on small squares of paper in a cramped shorthand of his own invention. By 1915 he had several tens of thousands of notes, and he began writing two books. One was called *X* and explored the idea that life on Earth has been controlled by events or beings on Mars. The other was called *Y*. In this Fort presented evidence indicating that a sinister civilisation existed at the South Pole. In writing to his friend Theodore Dreiser, the influential American novelist, he commented: 'You have at least one thing to be thankful for – I might have begun with *A*.'

Then Fort's luck turned – an uncle died leaving him just enough income to relieve him from the worry of earning his daily bread. Dissatisfied with the lack of publishing interest in his unusual books, Fort burned the manuscripts of *X* and *Y* and promptly began a third gleaned from his fabulous collection of notes. Dreiser was taken with the new work, *The book of the damned*, and persuaded his publisher to issue it.

When it appeared in 1919, most critics did not know what to make of it. It obviously presented a radical critique of contemporary science but it was fragmented, choppy and hard to follow. Eminently quotable, by turns compassionate, violent, poetic, ironic and deceptively wise, it was written in a difficult stream-of-consciousness style.

Fort was a cynic about scientific explanations. He observed how scientists argued for and against various theories, facts and kinds of phenomena according to their own beliefs rather than the rules of evidence. He was particularly appalled at the way in which any datum that did not fit one scientist's view, or the collective view, was ignored, suppressed, discredited or explained away. Fort called such rejected data 'the damned' because they were 'excommunicated' by science, which acted like a religion.

Fort did not like to be told what to think and expected his readers to think for themselves as well. His favourite technique was to state the bald facts flatly and then criticise them according to their validity and usefulness. Then he would present some 'expert's'

According to Fort almost anything can, and sometimes does, fall from the sky, to heap knee-deep around the bewildered onlooker. Among the many eyewitness accounts are descriptions of the classic 'fire from heaven' (below) and rains of various artefacts, such as the steel ingots that fell on the citizens of Basel, Switzerland, in the late 15th century (right)

case or explanation, and put in opposition to it a few, often fantastic, theories of his own based on precisely the same evidence. Whether the results gripped the readers' belief or sense of humour, he left up to them. For example, throughout his writings he expressed doubts about the Darwinian theory of evolution. Again, in *The book of the damned* he anticipated the von Däniken premise of 'ancient astronauts' by over 40 years. In thinking aloud about the strange vitrified forts of Scotland, he imagined that they had been destroyed in some ancient space war. 'I think we're property,' he wrote, and elaborated his meaning: 'That once upon a time, this Earth was No-Man's-Land, that other worlds explored and colonised here, and fought among themselves for possession, but now it's owned by something, all others warned off.' In *Wild talents* he elaborated:

> I now have a theory that, of themselves, men never did evolve from lower animals: but that, in early and plastic times, a human being from somewhere else appeared upon this Earth, and that many kinds of animals took him for a model, and rudely and grotesquely imitated his appearance, so that today, though gorillas of the Congo, and of Chicago, are only caricatures, some of the rest of us are somewhat passable imitations of human beings.

Travels of a prophet

The year after the publication of *The book of the damned*, Fort fell into a depression. He again burned his notes – which numbered 40,000 – and set sail for London. He could hardly contain his joy at the masses of material in the British Museum. In the next eight years he undertook his 'grand tour' several more times, at each pass widening his horizons to new subjects and new correlations. During this period, his belief in the eventuality of space travel developed, and he was sometimes to be heard giving forth on the subject to an uncomprehending crowd at Speaker's Corner in Hyde Park.

At this time Fort wrote *New lands*, the least successful and most cranky of his books. It was largely a satirical attack upon the pomposity of astronomers, who, he said, were 'led by a cloud of rubbish by day and a pillar of bosh by night . . . .' In 1929, Fort and his wife returned to New York and he began to work on *Lo!* He completed his last book, *Wild talents*, which dealt with the occult or psychic abilities of humans, in 1932, during progressive blindness and weakness. A few weeks later, on 3 May 1932, he was admitted to hospital; he died within a few hours. He took notes almost to the end; the last one said simply: 'Difficulty shaving. Gaunt places in face.'

In 1931, the year before Fort's death, Dreiser and another novelist, Tiffany Thayer, organised a meeting to launch the Fortean Society. Fort was not altogether

A monstrous regiment

Long before the term 'psychic warfare' was coined, Charles Hoy Fort came up with the startling idea of harnessing psychic powers to conquer the enemy. He envisioned a fighting unit of 'poltergeist girls' on the battlefield.

This passage on such poltergeist activity from his last book (*Wild talents*, 1932) illustrates his typical style of throwing out his thoughts.

'. . . A squad of poltergeist girls – and they pick a fleet out of the sea, or out of the sky – if, as far back as the year 1923, something picked French airplanes out of the sky – arguing that some nations that renounced fleets as obsolete would go on building them just the same.

'Girls at the front – and they are discussing their usual not very profound subjects. Command to the poltergeist girls to concentrate – and under their chairs they stick their wads of chewing gum.

'A regiment bursts into flames, and the soldiers are torches. Horses snort smoke from the combustion of their entrails. Re-inforcements are smashed under cliffs that are teleported from the Rocky mountains. The snatch of Niagara falls – it pours upon the battlefield. The little poltergeist girls reach for their wads of chewing gum.'

Such a regiment would surely be the ultimate in deterrent weaponry.

surprised, but declined the presidency. He had actually put his objection to such an organisation several years before. In 1926 in a reply to the science fiction writer Edmund Hamilton's discussion of the growing number of people who had read Fort and wished to pursue his ideas, Fort wrote:

> That we shall ever organise does not seem likely to me . . . . The great trouble is that the majority of persons who are attracted are the ones we do not want; Spiritualists, Fundamentalists, persons who are revolting against science, not in the least because they are affronted by the myth-stuff of the sciences, but because scientists either oppose or do not encourage them.

Nevertheless, Thayer founded the Fortean Society and it enjoyed much success in its early years. But because Thayer championed ever more cranky ideas – a flat Earth, for example – the society, and its journal *Doubt*, petered out with his death in 1959.

Method in his madness?

Today we can appreciate the method in Fort's madness as we see some of his wildest data in a wider context. For example, we acknowledge him as one of the main influences upon the developing study of UFOs, not least because such writers as Eric Frank Russell and Vincent H. Gaddis were originally members of the Fortean Society. Gaddis was already contributing articles on mysterious crafts and lights in the skies before the famous sighting by Kenneth Arnold at Mount Ranier, Washington, USA, in 1947, when the term 'flying saucers' was coined. Thirty years previously Fort had begun to collect notes on lights and dark objects seen dancing, speeding and hovering in the skies over many countries. He wondered then if they were the aerial transports of alien visitors – 'super-constructions' as he called them. He also conjectured that some of them might be little-known forms of natural phenomena.

Fort must also be credited with the discovery that UFO sightings come in 'flaps', as exemplified by the series of sightings of mystery airships across America (1896–1897), and Britain (1904–1905 and 1908–1909). At those times, no known airship could match the mystery crafts' speeds, design or powerful lights. It was this groundwork that prepared the early ufologists for the study of the wave of 'missile-like meteors', later called 'ghost rockets', that were sighted throughout northern and western Europe in 1946. If there were aliens with technologies in advance of ours, Fort mused in *New lands*, they might be able to project images of themselves onto Earth. Or, they might have appeared on Earth in person in earlier times and been taken for apparitions or demons. So that if we consider the history of apparitional phenomena, could not, as Fort asked, many of the 'appearances [be] beings and objects that visited this Earth, not from a spiritual existence, but from outer space'? Although Fort was being deliberately provocative, this passage does anticipate the psychological, psychical and paraphysical dimensions of close encounter experiences of the 'contactees' of today.

Another fundamental contribution by Fort to contemporary theorising is his notion of teleportation as a primary force for distribution of matter, objects and life forms throughout the Universe. From his acquaintance with the literature of Spiritualism, he was aware of the phenomenon of

Top: a sea monster, one of the many 'impossible' creatures listed by Fort as having been reported by sober, reliable witnesses – and dismissed totally by equally 'reliable' scientists

Above: Theodore Dreiser (1871–1945), the American writer who was passionately concerned with projecting Fort as an immensely readable and worthwhile researcher. As he wrote in his review of Fort's *Lo!* (right): 'Charles Fort is the most fascinating literary figure since Poe.' But unlike Poe's works, Fort's were non-fiction – or were they?

Left: the 'airship' that was seen over Peterborough, Cambridgeshire, on 23 March 1909, and which featured in *Lo!* Two constables, going about their duties at 5.10 a.m., saw and described the object as being 'somewhat oblong and narrow in shape, carrying a powerful light'. It also sounded like a powerful motor ticking over. Fort reported that several accounts of other strange aerial phenomena were received by sensationalist newspapers – but were not used by them. Fort suggested that the reason for this was that 'unaccountable lights and objects in the sky are not supposed to have sex'

'apports' – objects that materialise in the seance room. He felt that apports had an affinity to the appearances and disappearances of people, things and animals, the mysterious transportations and flight of objects usually, but not necessarily, during 'hauntings', and the phenomena of things and animals that fall in the open air in improbable circumstances. Fort coined the word 'teleportation' to describe such phenomena when he was writing *The book of the damned*. He saw teleportation as one of the basic forces of nature. It not only distributed life forms among the planets, but actually shifted materials of which they were built and shaped their environment. In the early days, wrote Fort, this force would have been extremely active. But as life and matter became more equally distributed among the inhabitable worlds, and became better established in their new homes, the need for the force would lessen. Eventually, he said, it would become vestigial, functioning erratically: 'The crash of falling islands – the humps of piling continents – and then the cosmic humour of it all – that the force that once heaped the peaks of the Rocky Mountains now slings pebbles at a couple of farmers near Trenton, New Jersey.'

It was the operation of this force of teleportation within the sphere of living creatures that most fascinated Fort. He could explain falling fishes or frogs in terms of the animals being whisked away from wherever they were abundant to some point in a distant sky, from which they then proceeded to fall. This could account for the sudden appearance of animals far from their usual habitats, or the appearance of fish in a freshly dug pond in spring, 1921. The teleportive force might even come under human control from time to time: poltergeist phenomena, levitation, bilocation or psychokinesis could occur consciously. Many of these ideas were eagerly seized upon by such American science fiction and fantasy writers as Robert Heinlein, Theodore Sturgeon, James Blish, Charles Harness, August Derleth and Philip Jose Farmer, some of whom were also members of the Fortean Society.

Over a two-year period when he was in his early fifties, Fort wrote a series of four letters to the *New York Times* in which he maintained that aliens were patrolling the skies. They were regarded as crank letters. When he died, the same dignified newspaper called him a 'foe of science' in its obituary on him. Fort would probably have expected such an epithet from people who had never tried to understand him. But his reputation has leaped over the *Times*'s opinion. Today some people regard Charles Hoy Fort as a prophet and visionary – and few who have studied him are prepared to dismiss him entirely.

Below: part of the vitrified fort near Strathpeffer, Ross and Cromarty, in the Highland region of Scotland. Fort was ahead of his time in ascribing the vitrification to intense heat from the fires of battle

A wise fool

Did Charles Fort stumble onto some cosmic understanding as a result of collecting anomalous phenomena ignored by scientists?

THE PUBLICATION OF *The book of the damned* by Charles Hoy Fort in 1919 changed the standard of reporting of anomalous phenomena in American newspapers for the better. Nonetheless, there was a sting in the tail. For whenever journalists reported a sighting of a sea serpent, or a home disrupted by a poltergeist, or a shower of frogs, they would comment to the effect that 'here is another datum for the archenemy of science, Charles Fort.'

This unfortunate reputation of Fort as an enemy of science lingers. Anyone who has read his books, however, must disagree. Fort was extremely well-versed and up to date in nearly all branches of science in his day and understood the scientific method, the rules of evidence and proper scholarship. Fort had looked closely at the great and impressive edifice of science and found it full of cracks. He found scientists who made pontifical pronouncements without bothering with the facts of the case, who substituted dogma for true scientific enquiry, who suppressed, ignored or explained away embarrassing data. He felt that anomalies held significance for science and should be studied. To understand that significance, it is necessary to look briefly at how science develops and changes.

Above: a UFO photograph of 1965, listed in the Condon Report as a possible fake. Fort's interest in and notes on UFOs helped set the stage for the development of present-day ufology

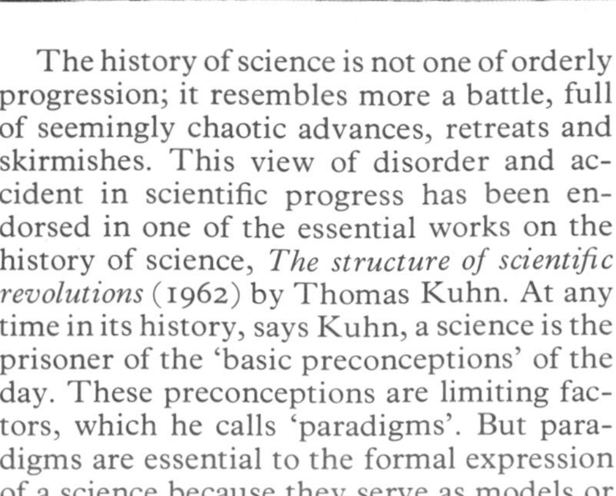

Right: Galileo demonstrates his telescope to Florentine nobles. The first person to use a telescope for the study of the skies, Galileo made a series of important findings in the early 17th century – but his work was rejected by hide-bound scholars and the then all-powerful Church because it went against accepted ideas

The history of science is not one of orderly progression; it resembles more a battle, full of seemingly chaotic advances, retreats and skirmishes. This view of disorder and accident in scientific progress has been endorsed in one of the essential works on the history of science, *The structure of scientific revolutions* (1962) by Thomas Kuhn. At any time in its history, says Kuhn, a science is the prisoner of the 'basic preconceptions' of the day. These preconceptions are limiting factors, which he calls 'paradigms'. But paradigms are essential to the formal expression of a science because they serve as models or structures with which to organise whole areas of knowledge and to provide the context for explanations.

Kuhn shows that the rise of a new paradigm in science, and the demise of the outdated one, is not the'graceful surrender' by fair-minded individuals that science propagandists would have us believe. It is often as painful and protracted as any religious or political revolution, and for much the same reason. Scientists are human beings with all the weaknesses and worries of human beings. They have a great deal invested in their job, their status and their credibility – factors of more value to their security than the ideal of an open mind. Above all, they tend to be loyal to the familiar paradigm.

The classic example of reluctance to accept something new is that of the group of Italian scientists who refused to look through Galileo's telescope lest they, like the Jesuit Clavius, be tempted to abandon their comfortable view of a geocentric Universe on seeing Jupiter's satellites through the instrument. Indeed, the revolutions of moons about Jupiter, the model for the new idea of the solar system, remained in contention for

Above: this illustration from Marco Polo's account of his Asian travels in the 13th century shows the fantastic creatures that, he had heard, lived in India. Such travellers' tales are still part of the data base of anomalous phenomena

many years after Galileo proposed the idea.

A new paradigm, or the data that leads to it, can seem threatening, even sinister. So the body of orthodox science behaves like an invaded organism and closes ranks against the 'infectious' data. Eventually the anomalies mount up and there comes a time when they can no longer be ignored. There ensues a crisis period during which whole fields of science are broken apart and the pieces reassembled incorporating the new data. What was once anomalous is now accepted or explained as a self-evident fact. Recurrent crisis is not only typical of scientific progress,

Below: Antoine Lavoisier, the 'father of modern chemistry'. Despite his distinction as a scientist, he dismissed out of hand the existence of meteors – and helped prevent their being studied by science for decades

Kuhn says, it is essential to it. In *Lo!*, Fort called science 'the conventionalization of alleged knowledge', explaining: 'it acts to maintain itself against further enlightenment, but when giving in, there is not surrender but partnership, and something that had been bitterly fought then becomes another factor in its prestige.'

The main aim of orthodox science is to consolidate the field of knowledge, not to seek out oddities of fact or theory. Repeatability and regularity are preferred to anomalousness.

Age-old oddities

The study of strange phenomena is clearly not in the same stage of development as mainstream science. In the field of 'anomalistics', as some American scholars call it, collections of oddities have long abounded, however. Many of the works of the Greek philosophers such as Pliny, Pausanias and Athenaeus are rich in Forteana. So are the writings of travellers such as Ibn Batutah and Marco Polo and of the compilers of early bestiaries and natural histories such as Olaus Magnus and Edward Topsell. Their work forms a vast data base on the subjects currently lumped under the heading of 'the unexplained'.

If this data base corresponds roughly to what Kuhn calls the 'morass' of data at the early point of a science, then we are only awaiting the coming of that organising paradigm to begin our transformation into scientists. Once again Fort points the direction, giving us a particularly useful expression. He says that orthodox science is, by its own definition, 'exclusionist'. A scientific experiment, for example, is an attempt to isolate something from the rest of the Universe. The flaw of orthodoxy lies in its attempts to put things into units or categories. Yet anyone who has seriously investigated strange data knows that they defy categorisation. Exclusionist science functions well enough but bases its criteria on arbitrary decisions. As science progresses, such distinctions become obsolete and collapse. Thus in the early 19th century many biologists still regarded living things as essentially different from non-living things: for these 'vitalists' there was an unbridgeable gap between the animate and inanimate worlds. But from 1828 onwards, as chemists learned to synthesise organic compounds (compounds such as urea or acetic acid, which are produced by living organisms), the distinction between the animate and the inanimate lost its fundamental importance for chemists, and to present-day scientists seems little short of superstition. They tend to forget that many of the dividing lines drawn by today's science – such as that between mind and matter, for example – may be redrawn or abandoned; and they slavishly accept or reject data by criteria that are, at best, transient. It is clear that this arbitrary structure predetermines how we interrogate the Universe – and how we interpret its answers. The German physicist Werner K. Heisenberg wrote: 'What we observe is not nature itself, but nature exposed to our method of questioning.' So light will behave like a wave or a particle according to the context in which it is investigated. Or, as the duck said with peculiar logic in *Alice in Wonderland*: 'When *I* find a thing, it's usually a frog or a worm.'

Left: Werner Heisenberg, a Nobel prize-winner for his work in nuclear physics. The quantum theory, to which he made a great contribution, was not taught at one of Britain's ancient universities for 30 years after its formulation – a striking example of how scientists will sometimes resist new ideas from even their most distinguished colleagues

The barriers between the acceptable and unacceptable in science are changing all the time. What is magic or superstition to one era may become the science of the next. The great French chemist Antoine Lavoisier told the Academy of Sciences in 1769 that only peasants could believe stones could fall from the sky, because 'there *are* no stones in the sky.' His influence prevented scientific study of meteorites – the 'stones from the sky' – until 1803.

But some barriers are breaking down. Today's life sciences contain much rehabilitated folklore: old herbals have been used for new pharmaceuticals and the practices of shamans have been adapted for new treatments. Apparitional phenomena, once the preserve of theologians and demonologists, are now the subject of psychical research and psychology. A number of Fort's special correlations – strange lights on the Moon, curious aerial lights and sounds that accompany or precede earthquakes, lunar periodicities in biological processes and behaviour, lake monsters and UFOs – are all matters of serious academic study today.

In answer to how strange phenomena could relate to the main body of science, Fort suggested that it was science that would make the move to assimilate anomalous phenomena by adopting a more radical, inclusive approach. Inclusionists would 'substitute acceptance for belief', he said, but only temporarily until better data or theories arose. This is exactly what true scientists do, of course, because for them enquiring after the truth is more important than being right or first. Inclusionism would recognise a state of existence in which all things, creatures, ideas and phenomena were interrelated and so 'of an underlying oneness'. From his thousands of notes, Fort came to the realisation that the Universe functioned more like an organism than a machine and that, while

Below: a prism creates a colour spectrum when light passes through it – a fact that led to the theory that light was made up of waves, although Newton, who first performed this experiment, believed that light was composed of particles. Today light is considered to behave as a wave form *or* as a stream of particles (photons), depending on the experimental circumstances. This progression in the way that scientists explain light shows how a paradigm can change

Left: Charles Hoy Fort at his super checkerboard. He invented a game called super checkers (draughts), which was so complicated that it usually took all night to play it to the end

general principles applied universally, eccentricities, deviations and anomalies were the inevitable result of local expression of those principles. This almost mystical view anticipates C.G. Jung's notion of the collective unconscious and similar beliefs that appear in the cosmologies of primitive and animistic religions. Yet another theory in which the world is seen as functioning more like an organism than a machine emerged in 1981 – Dr Rupert Sheldrake's revolutionary principle of formative causation. This appears to offer philosophical tools for exploring continuity and synchronicity by postulating a resonance between forms of similar structure, whether living or not, that operates outside time and space.

Portents of change

In earlier times, most cultures had an appreciation of anomalies that we have lost. They also had some framework in which to study them, usually as omens or portents of social change, as C. G. Jung suggested UFOs might be. Priests in rural Scandinavia in the late medieval period were obliged to report to their bishops anything contrary to the 'natural order'. Their chronicles that survive are treasure troves of sea serpent sightings, falls of mice and fish, animal battles and other strange phenomena.

Today such stories are absent from the scientific journals, where Fort found them, and are used as small filler paragraphs in the newspapers, written inaccurately and for laughs. Apart from a few excellent specialist magazines, the only regular journals devoted to the reporting and discussion of Fortean phenomena are two American publications, the *Journal* of the International Fortean Organisation and *Pursuit*, published by the Society for the Investigation of the Unexplained (SITU), and Britain's independent *Fortean Times*. The only scientific body concerned with anomalous phenomena is the Center for the Study of Short-Lived Phenomena, formerly part of the Smithsonian Institution in Washington DC, USA. It is now a successful self-funding venture. The establishment in London in 1981 of the Association for the Scientific Study of Anomalous Phenomena (ASSAP) may be a sign of hope for interdisciplinary studies of all sorts in the future.

One day, when orthodox science widens its circle of attention, the task of assimilating Fortean phenomena will have been made easier by the dedicated collectors of obscure and weird data. Their true function, in relation to mainstream science, is elegantly stated in a line from Enid Elsford's book on the medieval fool: 'The Fool does not lead a revolt against the Law; he lures us into a region of the spirit, where . . . the writ does not run.'

For the present author at least, Charles Hoy Fort was science's fool.

Below: a medieval fool. The jester poked holes in the customs and beliefs of his society – a role Fort played in ridiculing the scientific establishment of his day

Right: the simply marked grave of Fort at Albany, New York, where he was born

The great Siberian f

In 1908 a vast area of Siberia was devastated by the explosion of a huge fireball. Trees were scorched and felled, and the skins of many animals broke out in scabs. Could this have been a nuclear explosion? IAN RIDPATH analyses the facts

ON THE MORNING OF 30 JUNE 1908, farmer S. B. Semenov was sitting on his porch in the isolated Siberian trading station of Vanavara, 500 miles (750 kilometres) north-west of Lake Baykal. It was still only 7.15 a.m., but the day was already well under way; the Sun rises early in midsummer this far north. Nearby, Semenov's neighbour P. P. Kosalopov was pulling nails out of a window frame with pincers. Neither man could have had an inkling of the drama they were about to witness.

Suddenly, Semenov was startled to see, towards the north-west, a brilliant fireball that 'covered an enormous part of the sky'. Semenov twisted in pain, for the fireball's heat felt as though it were burning his shirt. Next door, Kosalopov dropped his pincers and clasped his hands to his ears, which felt as though they were burning. He first glanced at his roof, suspecting it to be on fire, then turned to Semenov. 'Did you see anything?' Kosalopov asked. 'How could one help but see it?' replied the frightened Semenov, still stinging from his burns.

A few seconds later, the blinding, bright blue, fireball, trailing a column of dust, exploded 40 miles (65 kilometres) from Vanavara with a force that knocked Semenov off his porch, where he lay unconscious for a few seconds. On coming to, he felt ground tremors that shook the entire house, broke the barn door, and shattered windows. In the house of Kosalopov, earth fell from the ceiling and a door flew off the stove. Sounds like thunder rumbled in the air.

The great Siberian fireball of 1908 was an event so exceptional that it excited a controversy that continues to this day. Explanations for it range into the realm of the bizarre, including the remarkable hypothesis that it was caused by nothing less than the emergency landing of a nuclear spacecraft,

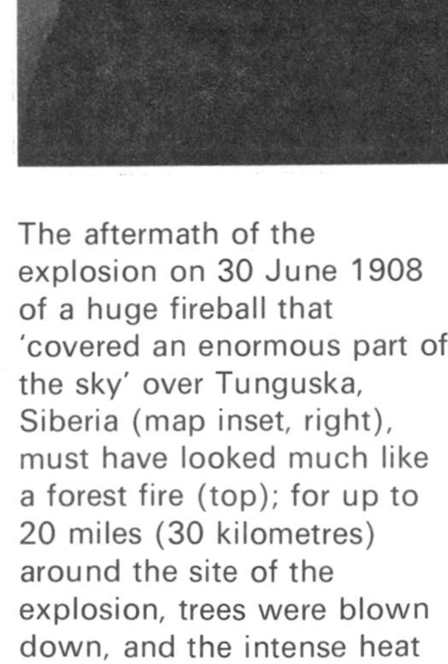

The aftermath of the explosion on 30 June 1908 of a huge fireball that 'covered an enormous part of the sky' over Tunguska, Siberia (map inset, right), must have looked much like a forest fire (top); for up to 20 miles (30 kilometres) around the site of the explosion, trees were blown down, and the intense heat of the blast set the forest alight

Thirteen years after the Tunguska explosion, Soviet mineralogist Leonid Kulik (above) led an expedition to the site, travelling by horse-drawn sled and boat (right). His route is shown in the map (above right). Kulik found dramatic evidence of the blast – whole forests of scorched and uprooted trees (left)

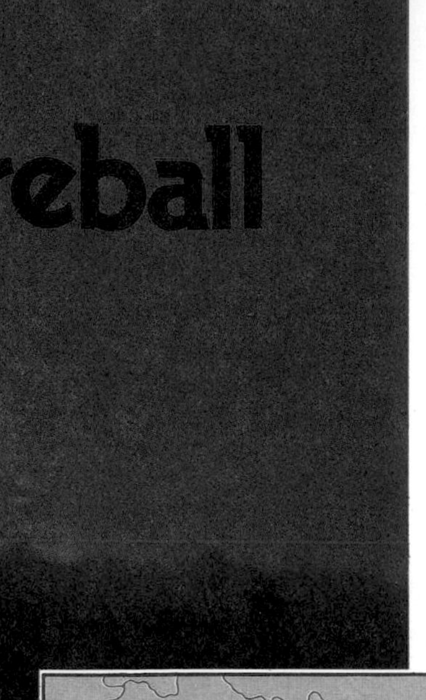

perhaps even of extra-terrestrial origin.

The area on which the object fell, in the valley of the Stony Tunguska river, was sparsely inhabited by the Tungus, a nomadic, Mongol-like people who herded reindeer. Near the centre of the fall, north of Vanavara, several Tungus were thrown into the air by the explosion, and their tents were carried away in a violent wind. Around them, the forest began to blaze.

As the dazed Tungus cautiously inspected the site of the blast, they found scenes of terrifying devastation. Trees were felled like matchsticks for up to 20 miles (30 kilometres) around. The intense heat from the explosion had melted metal objects, destroyed storehouses, and burned reindeer to death. No living animals were left in the area but, miraculously, no humans were killed by the blast. There were also reports that a mysterious 'black rain' had fallen in the area.

The effects of the Tunguska blast were seen and felt for 600 miles (1000 kilometres) around. Reports from the district of Kansk, 400 miles (600 kilometres) from the blast, described boatmen being thrown into the river and horses being knocked over by shock waves, while houses shook and crockery crashed off shelves. The driver of the Trans-Siberian express stopped his train for fear of a derailment when the carriages and rails began to shake.

Other effects were noted around the world, but their cause remained a puzzle for a long time, as news of the fireball and explosion did not become widely known for many years. Seismic waves like those from an earthquake were recorded throughout Europe, as well as disturbances of the Earth's magnetic field. Meteorologists later found from microbarograph records that atmospheric shock waves from the blast had circled the Earth twice.

Echoes of distant Siberia

A woman in Huntingdon, England, wrote to *The Times* to report that the night skies were so bright that shortly after midnight on 1 July 'it was possible to read large print indoors. . . . At about 1.30 a.m. the room was quite light, as if it had been day. It would be interesting if anyone would explain the cause of so unusual a sight.' But, at that time, no one *could* explain.

Similar eerie night-time effects were noted over much of Europe and western Asia after the fall. Reports from this area record nights up to 100 times brighter than normal and crimson hues in the sky, like the glare from fires towards the north. The strange lights did not flicker or form arches like the *aurora borealis*; they were like effects that followed the outburst of Krakatoa, which injected vast clouds of dust into the atmosphere.

At the time of the Tunguska fall, Russia was entering a period of major political upheaval and the national press did not give any coverage to what it saw as a minor event in a remote part of the empire. Despite the exceptional nature of the Tunguska event, news about it remained buried in local Siberian newspapers until 13 years later, when word of it reached a Soviet mineralogist, Leonid Kulik.

Kulik had a particular interest in fallen meteorites, not least because of the rich source of iron they could provide for industry. He became convinced that the object that had fallen on 30 June 1908 in the valley of the Stony Tunguska river was an iron meteorite even larger than that which formed the vast Barringer crater in Arizona 25,000 years or so ago.

After years of planning, Kulik set out in 1927 on an expedition to reach the site of the

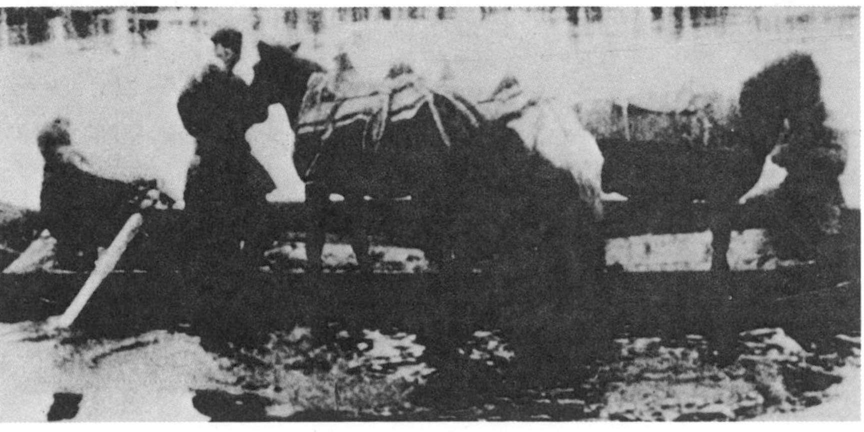

Above: members of the Tungus tribe, who were the most directly affected by the Tunguska explosion. They reported that, after the blast, many of their reindeer broke out in scabs – a fact that has led some scientists, assuming that the scabs were evidence of radiation sickness, to suggest that a nuclear explosion had occurred

Tunguska fall. From the railway town of Taishet, Kulik and his team crossed 400 miles (600 kilometres) of frozen *taiga* by horse-drawn sled until they reached Vanavara. There, they heard the remarkable stories of the inhabitants, convincing Kulik more than ever that he was on the track of a truly enormous meteorite.

A sudden snowfall held up progress for over a week. On 8 April, Kulik, a colleague, and a local guide set out on horseback on the final leg of the journey. They marched northwards through scenes of increasing devastation: birch and pine trees lay on the ground where they had been uprooted by the force of the shock wave 19 years before. Many of the trees had been scorched or even set alight by the same intense heat that farmer Semenov had felt in Vanavara.

Surveying the blast area from a ridge, Kulik wrote:

> From our observation point no sign of forest can be seen, for everything has been devastated and burned, and around the edge of this dead area the young twenty-year-old forest growth has moved forward furiously, seeking sunshine and life. One has an uncanny feeling when one sees 20- to 30-inch [50- to 75-centimetre] thick giant trees snapped across like twigs, and their tops hurled many metres away to the south.

Visit of the god of fire

Kulik wanted to press on the remaining few miles to the centre of the blast, but the Tungus guides were superstitious, for their legends said the area had been visited by the god of fire, and they would go no further. Kulik had to return to Vanavara to recruit new guides, and another month passed before he arrived again at the devastated area and finally reached the centre of the fall – to discover the great riddle of Tunguska.

Of the giant crater he had expected there was not a sign. Instead, he found a frozen swamp and a curious stand of trees which, despite being at the centre of the explosion, had escaped the effects of the blast that had levelled everything around them. Whatever object caused the explosion, it had never reached the ground. Although he returned to the area with bigger expeditions in subsequent years, Kulik never found any fragments of meteoric iron.

So if the Tunguska blast was not caused by the impact of an iron meteorite, what *was* the cause? In 1930, the English meteorologist Francis J. W. Whipple, assistant director of the Meteorological Office, proposed that the event had been caused by the collision of the Earth with a small comet, a suggestion supported by the Soviet astronomer A. S. Astapovich.

The popular view of a comet is a giant glowing ball of dust and gas trailing streamers for millions of miles, as with the spectacular Halley's Comet in 1910. But such brilliant comets are the exception rather than the rule. A dozen or more comets may be tracked by astronomers each year, but few or none of them ever become visible to the naked eye. Most comets are smaller and fainter than those illustrated in astronomy books; some comets, particularly old ones, may show no tail at all.

According to the most popular theory, a comet resembles a dirty snowball of frozen gas and dust. Old comets run out of gas to become nothing more than loose 'bags' of low-density rocks. Such an object would indeed cause a blazing fireball as it burned up by friction after plunging at high speed into the Earth's atmosphere, eventually shattering explosively as the forces of deceleration overcame its own strength. The mid-air blast of such an object would explain why there was no crater or meteorite fragments at

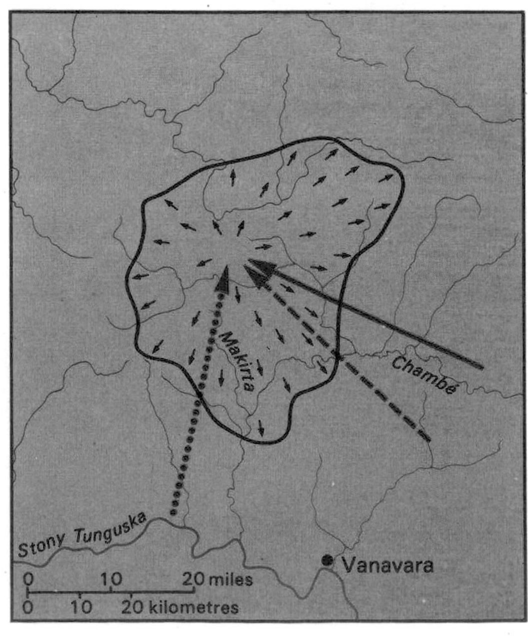

Right: The area of devastation in Tunguska, showing the centre of the explosion and the direction of the fallen trees, together with three different suggestions of the path taken by the fireball. The path indicated by the solid red arrow was proposed by scientists K. P. Florensky and V. G. Konenkin, and is now generally considered to be the correct one

Right: the flight path of the Tunguska fireball in the area immediately surrounding the impact point, as reconstructed by Soviet ufologist Felix Zigel from the study of the damage created by the atmospheric shock wave, and the evidence given in a number of eyewitness accounts. The arrows through towns indicate the direction in which the object appeared to be travelling

Below: some of the evidence of large-scale destruction found by Kulik and his team 13 years after the blast: scorched trees, knocked flat by the force of the explosion or, where they were still standing, of stunted and scrubby growth

Tunguska. But critics of the comet theory argued that no comet had been seen in the sky before the Tunguska blast.

There has been a host of alternative explanations, including a bizarre suggestion that a mini black hole blasted into Siberia. According to astronomical theory, mini black holes, with the mass of an asteroid packed into the size of an atomic particle, could have been formed in the maelstrom following the Big Bang explosion that is believed to have marked the origin of the Universe. The passage of a mini black hole through the Earth would, according to University of Texas physicists A. A. Jackson and Michael Ryan, have all the observed effects of the Tunguska fireball – except that the mini black hole should have carried right on through the Earth and emerged in the north Atlantic, producing similar spectacular effects as it departed. Unfortunately for the theory, no such effects occurred.

Spacecraft from Mars?

Of all the theories for the Tunguska blast, the most controversial was put forward in 1946 by the Soviet science-fiction writer Alexander Kazantsev. Disguising his theory as a fictional story, Kazantsev proposed that the explosion over Siberia had been caused by the burn-up of a nuclear-powered spacecraft, perhaps from Mars. Kazantsev speculated that the aliens had come to collect water from Lake Baykal, the largest volume of fresh water on Earth. As the craft plummeted into the atmosphere it heated up by friction until the engines erupted in a mid-air blast like the Hiroshima bomb.

Soviet ufologists Felix Zigel and Alexei Zolotov have supported the exploding nuclear spacecraft idea. Zigel even proposed that the craft performed a crazy zig-zag as it desperately attempted to land, although none of the eyewitnesses actually reported seeing the fireball change course.

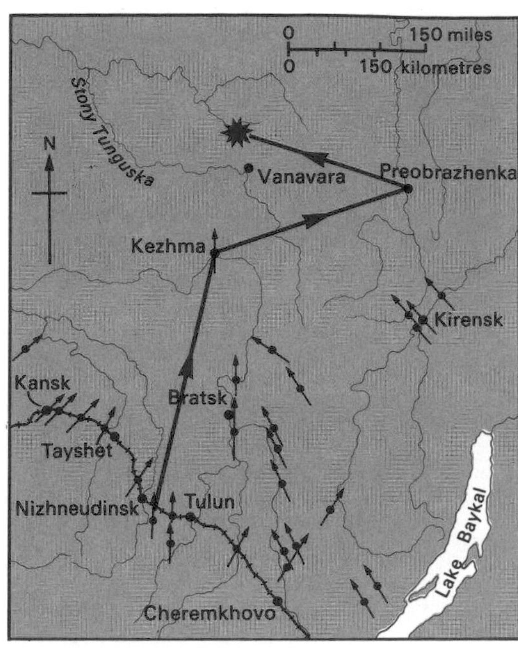

Another science-fiction writer, John Baxter, in his book *The fire came by*, published in 1976, followed Kazantsev in comparing the effects of the Tunguska explosion with those of the Hiroshima bomb – the strong thermal flash, the updraught of heated air that caused a 'fiery pillar', and the characteristic clump of trees that remained standing at the centre of the Tunguska devastation, as they had under the explosion point of the Hiroshima bomb.

There was even talk of deadly radiation at the site. One of the characters in Alexander Kazantsev's story speaks of a man who, shortly after examining the Tunguska blast area, died in terrible pain as if from an invisible fire. 'It could be nothing other than radioactivity,' explains the fictional character. In fact, there is no record that anyone died from the Tunguska blast – but the Tungus people reported that reindeer in the area broke out in scabs, which modern writers such as Baxter have attributed to radiation burns.

Expeditions to the area noted an accelerated growth of vegetation around the blast site, again attributed by some to genetic damage from radiation. There were reports in popular writings that radioactivity had been detected in the wood from the area, and an analysis of radiocarbon from tree rings in the United States by Nobel prize-winner Willard Libby showed an increase in radiocarbon following 1908. All of which seemed to indicate that the Tunguska explosion could have been nuclear.

This theory raises some alarming questions – for the Tunguska explosion occurred a good 30 years before the first nuclear tests. Who, or what, could have caused a blast of such proportions?

The Tunguska explosion was the disastrous end of a visitor from space. But was that visitor a spacecraft or a fragment of a comet?

What really happened at Tunguska?

SIBERIA, 30 JUNE 1908: a brilliant fireball blazed through the Earth's atmosphere, exploding at a height of 5 miles (8 kilometres) above the valley of the Stony Tunguska river with the force of a 12½-megatonne nuclear bomb. According to one popular theory, the Tunguska explosion really was a nuclear blast, caused by the burn-up of a nuclear-powered alien spacecraft. But another leading theory says the Tunguska object was the head of a small comet. What evidence is there to back up these rival theories?

Important clues to the nature of the Tunguska explosion were obtained on three expeditions to the site, in 1958, 1961 and 1962, led by Soviet geochemist Kirill Florensky. His 1962 expedition used a helicopter to chart the disaster area. Instead of looking for large meteoritic fragments, as Leonid Kulik had done in the late 1920s, Florensky's team sifted the soil for microscopic particles that would have been scattered by the burn-up and disintegration of the Tunguska object. Their search proved fruitful. The scientists traced a narrow tongue of cosmic dust stretching for 150 miles (250 kilometres) north-west of the site, composed of magnetite (magnetic iron oxide) and glassy droplets of fused rock. The expedition found thousands of examples of metal and silicate particles fused together, indicating that the Tunguska object had not been of uniform composition. A low-density stony composition containing flecks of iron is believed to be typical of interplanetary debris, particularly meteors ('shooting stars'), which are themselves composed of dust from comets. The particles spread north-west of the Tunguska blast were apparently the vaporised remains of a comet's head.

Below: Willard F. Libby, one of a team who thought they had found an increase in atmospheric radioactive carbon-14 following the Tunguska explosion

Bottom: within a year of the explosion, Tunguska looked like this: fresh green growth pushing through the dead timber

These actual samples of the Tunguska object should have been enough to settle the controversy once and for all. Florensky wrote about his expeditions in a 1963 article in the magazine *Sky & Telescope*. The article was entitled, 'Did a comet collide with the Earth in 1908?' Among astronomers, the comet theory has always been the front runner. In his article, Florensky said that this viewpoint 'was now confirmed'.

Radiation check

Florensky's expedition carefully checked for the existence of radiation at the site. He reported that the only radioactivity in the trees from the Tunguska area was fallout from atomic tests, which had been absorbed into the wood. Florensky's party also looked in detail at the acceleration of forest growth in the devastated area, which some had put down to genetic damage from radiation. Biologists concluded that only the normal acceleration of growth after a fire, a well-known phenomenon, had taken place.

But what of the 'scabs' reported to have broken out on reindeer after the blast? In the absence of any veterinary report one can only speculate, but most likely these were not caused by atomic radiation but simply by the great flash of heat given out by the blast, which also set fire to the trees. Humans near enough to have felt the heat of the fireball showed no signs of radiation sickness, and remained alive and healthy when Leonid Kulik visited the site over a dozen years later.

Believers in the nuclear explosion theory quote investigations in 1965 by three American physicists, Clyde Cowan, C.R. Atluri, and Willard Libby, who reported a 1 per cent increase in radiocarbon in tree rings following the Tunguska blast. A nuclear explosion releases a burst of neutrons, which turn atmospheric nitrogen into radioactive carbon-14 that is taken up by plants along with ordinary carbon during their normal photosynthesis. If the Tunguska blast were nuclear, excess radiocarbon would be expected in the plants growing at the time.

To test this prediction, the American scientists examined tree rings from a 300-year-old Douglas fir from the Catalina Mountains near Tucson, Arizona, and also from an ancient oak tree near Los Angeles. They found that the level of radiocarbon in the rings of both trees had jumped by 1 per cent from 1908 to 1909. The picture is confused by erratic fluctuations of up to 2 per cent that exist in the levels of radiocarbon measured in the tree rings from year to year. Therefore a 1 per cent radiocarbon increase is not outside the range of normal fluctuations caused by natural effects. An important double-check was made by three Dutch scientists on a tree from Trondheim, Norway – much nearer the blast, where the radiocarbon effects would be expected to be more noticeable. Instead of a radiocarbon rise in 1909, they found a steady decrease around that time. Therefore the increase in American trees found by Cowan, Atluri and Libby must be due to local effects – and not to the Tunguska blast.

Pattern of destruction

Lastly, what about the clump of trees left standing at the centre of the Tunguska blast area, as were trees under the explosion point of the Hiroshima bomb, and the 'fiery pillar' seen after the explosion? In fact, these effects are not unique to a nuclear blast. Any explosion is followed by an updraught of heated air and a puff of smoke. Brilliant exploding fireballs happen frequently as chunks of solar system debris plunge into the atmosphere; fortunately for us, most of them are far smaller than the Tunguska object.

The clump of standing trees would be left behind by an aerial explosion of any kind, as shown by the scale-model experiments of Igor Zotkin and Mikhail Tsikulin of the Soviet Academy of Sciences' meteorite committee. They set off small explosions over a field of model trees, and found they were able to reproduce the pattern of felled trees including the central standing clump.

Therefore it seems that all the 'evidence' adduced for a nuclear explosion at Tunguska is either misinterpretation or mischievous distortion.

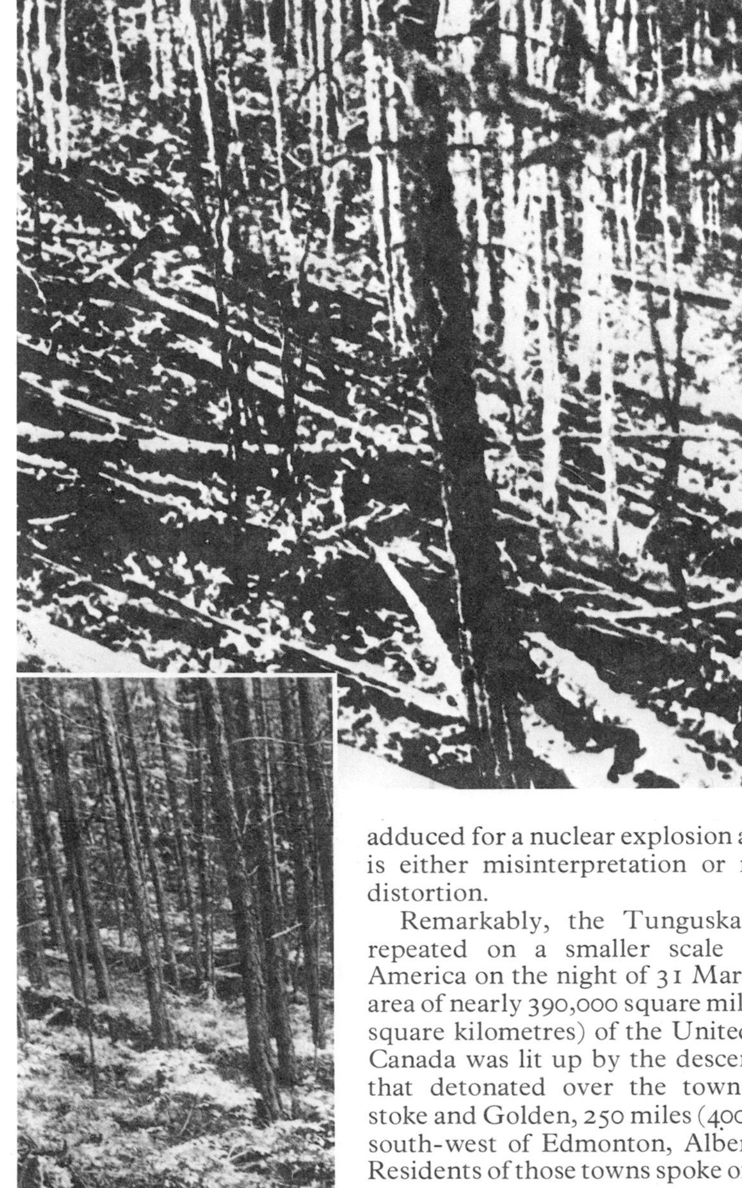

The healing processes of the Siberian forest have not yet obliterated the scars of the 1908 explosion. Within a few years saplings had grown between the trunks strewn on the ground (top). But even today the fallen trees are still evident beneath a covering of moss and foliage (above)

Remarkably, the Tunguska event was repeated on a smaller scale over North America on the night of 31 March 1965. An area of nearly 390,000 square miles (1 million square kilometres) of the United States and Canada was lit up by the descent of a body that detonated over the towns of Revelstoke and Golden, 250 miles (400 kilometres) south-west of Edmonton, Alberta, Canada. Residents of those towns spoke of a 'thunderous roar' that rattled and broke windows. The energy released was equal to several kilotonnes of TNT.

Scientists predicted the meteorite's point of impact and set out to look for a crater, much as Leonid Kulik had done in Siberia half a century before. Like him, they were unsuccessful. Scanning the snow-covered ground from the air, the scientists were unable to find traces of the meteorite, or of a crater. Only when investigators went into the area on foot did they find that a strange black dust coated the snow for miles around. Samples of this dirt were scraped up, and proved to have the composition of a particularly fragile type of stony meteorite known to scientists as a carbonaceous chondrite. The 1965 object fragmented in mid-air, raining thousands of tonnes of crumbly black dust upon the snow. Significantly, witnesses to the Tunguska blast described just such a 'black rain'.

Clinching evidence for the cometary nature of the Tunguska object comes from the results of the latest Soviet expeditions to the site, reported in 1977. Microscopic rocky particles found in the 1908 peat layers have the same composition as cosmic particles collected from the upper atmosphere by rockets. Thousands of tonnes of this material are estimated to be scattered around the fall area. Along with these particles of rock from space were jagged particles of meteoric iron. The Soviet researchers concluded that the Tunguska object was a comet of carbonaceous chondrite composition. This comes as no surprise, for astronomers are finding that a carbonaceous chondrite composition is typical of interplanetary debris.

But if it was a comet, why was it not seen in the sky prior to impact? Firstly, it always stayed close to the Sun so that it was lost in glare; and secondly, it was too small to have ever become bright enough to see even in a dark sky. Astronomers now believe that the Tunguska object was actually a fragment broken several thousand years ago from Comet Encke, an old and faint comet with the shortest known orbit of any comet around the Sun. A Czech astronomer, Lubor Kresak, pointed out in 1976 that the orbit of the Tunguska object, deduced from the direction and angle at which it struck the Earth, is remarkably similar to that of Encke's comet. Dr Kresak estimates that the body had a diameter of only about 100 yards (100 metres) when in space, and a mass of up to a million tonnes. Dust from its disintegration in the atmosphere caused the bright nights observed in the northern hemisphere in the period following the Tunguska event.

'The identification of the Tunguska object as an extinct cometary fragment appears to be the only plausible explanation of the event; and a common origin with Comet Encke appears very probable,' concludes Dr Kresak.

What is more, an event like Tunguska can happen again. Astronomers have found a number of small asteroids whose orbits cross the path of the Earth. For instance, in 1976 a direct repetition of the Tunguska event was avoided by hours as a previously unknown asteroid with a diameter of a few hundred yards swept past the Earth at a distance of 750,000 miles (1.2 million kilometres). Astronomers estimate that an object the size of the Tunguska comet hits the Earth once in about 2000 years on average. So it is only a matter of time before we are hit again – and next time it could do a lot of damage.

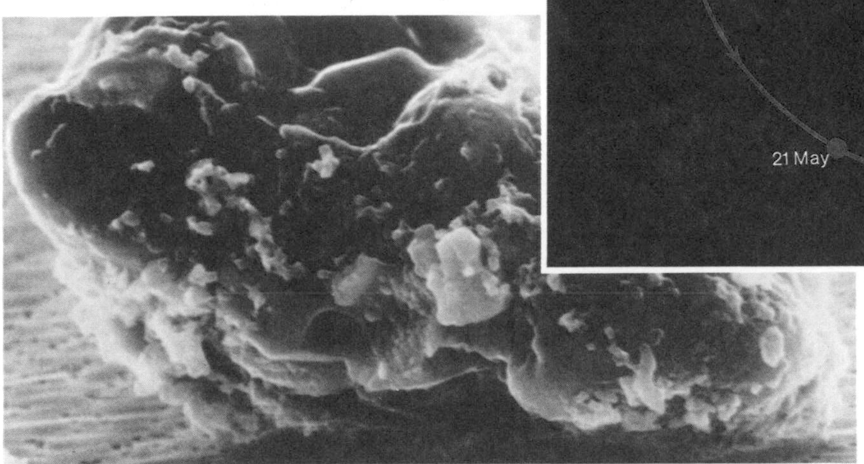

Top: how the Tunguska explosion may have happened. The comet Encke could have shed a rock fragment that was captured by the Earth

Above: this dust grain, magnified 10,000 times, was collected in the stratosphere. It is thought to have come from a comet

Left: the rings of recent Tunguska trees (top) are thicker than those of trees killed in the disaster (bottom). Some scientists claim that radioactivity from the explosion caused a spurt in plant growth

The strange world of twins

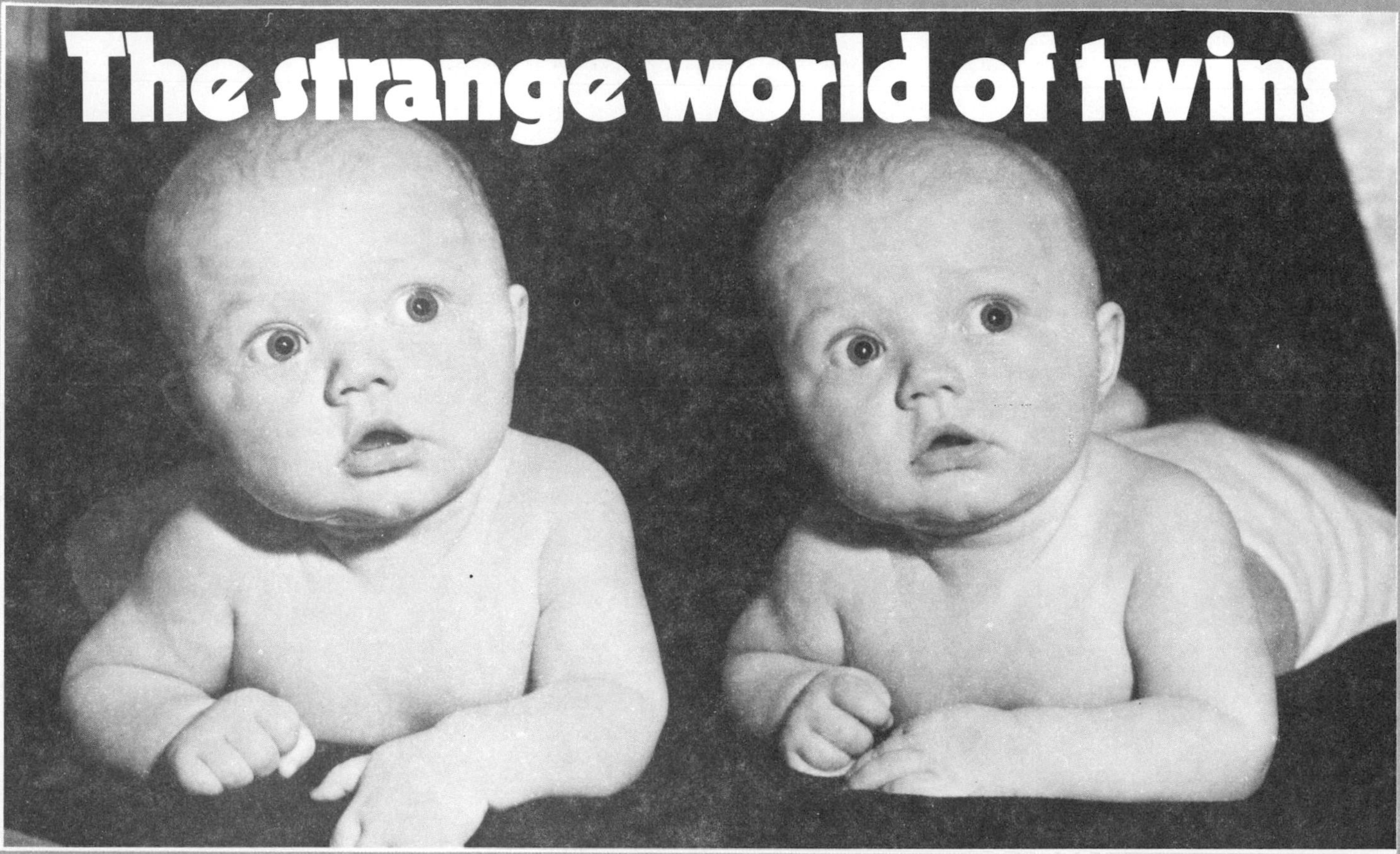

Identical twins who are brought up together are expected not only to look alike, but also to exhibit similarities of behaviour. Yet, as PAUL SIEVEKING shows, even twins who are separated at birth and reared apart still lead lives with astonishing parallels

OF THE HUNDRED MILLION or so twins in the world, about a third are *monozygotic*. This means that the babies have come from a single fertilised egg, which then divides into two in the womb. Such twins have identical sets of genes, and are alike in every detail – even down to their fingerprints – meaning that any differences between them must be exclusively non-genetic.

Those that have been brought up together naturally influence each other, so it is almost impossible to pinpoint to what extent their genetic blueprints shape their destinies. But there are on record about 80 pairs of twins who have, for one reason or another, been brought up separately, completely unaware of each other. A study of these twins offers fascinating clues to the relative significance of nature and nurture, heredity and environment. By studying such cases, we can gain some insight into how much of one's character is determined biologically, how much by upbringing and education – and discover how much is simply beyond our present understanding.

For example, identical twins Jacqueline and Sheila Lewis were adopted at birth by different families, and neither even knew the other existed. In June 1976, 26 years later, they were admitted to Southmead Hospital in Bristol, England, on the same day with the same rare hereditary skin disease. They were, by sheer chance, also put in the same treatment room. They soon discovered they were identical twins, even down to tiny details such as moles on their left knees, birthmarks on their necks and double-jointed little fingers. Both had suffered from pain in their left legs for several years and both had also had kidney trouble. Sheila's

Identical twins come in all shapes and sizes, from the appealing American babies (above) to the unwieldy brothers attending the greatest ever 'get together' of twins at Barvaux, Belgium, in 1966 (below). The 24-year-old heavyweights pose with year-old identical twins, whose individual identities have not yet had time to develop. However, it seems likely that their parents will follow the tradition of dressing them similarly – at least until the twins reach adolescence, the time when more assertive twins tend to stress their individuality

and hated spelling; and as boys both owned dogs called Troy. Both had married women called Linda, divorced and then married 'Bettys'. Their first sons were named, respectively, James Alan and James Allan. Both families had taken their holidays for years at the same small beach in St Petersburg, Florida – driving there in Chevrolets. Both men had worked as attendants at filling stations, for the same hamburger chain, and part-time as deputy sheriffs. They had both taken up carpentry and technical drawing as hobbies. They were compulsive nail-biters; shared the same sleeping problems, smoking and drinking habits, and used the same slang words. Each is 6 feet (1.8 metres) tall and weighs 180 pounds (80 kilograms). After they met, their families noted similarities in speech patterns, mannerisms and posture.

At the age of 18, both the Jim twins started having tension headaches, which always began in the afternoon then turned into migraines. (They later used almost identical words to describe the pain.) Both stopped having them at the same age, then they started again for a time before stopping finally. It had never been thought that such a complicated migraine pattern could be 'programmed' by heredity. Moreover, both men have had confirmed or suspected heart attacks, had developed haemorrhoids, and both put on 10 pounds (4.5 kilograms) at the same time in their lives, and then lost it again.

In fact, synchronisation of ailments does seem to be a common feature between most twins, separated or not. Peter and Barry Ilott had their tonsils out together and both subsequently caught colds. 'It always follows the

husband had died on the same day that Jackie had divorced her husband.

1979 was a bumper year for the reunion of identical twins. It began with the 'Jim twins'. In August 1939 in Piqua, Ohio, USA, five-week-old identical twin boys were adopted by different families. One set of adoptive parents, Jess and Lucille Lewis, lived in Lima, while Ernest and Sarah Springer lived in Dayton 80 miles (130 kilometres) away. Both couples were told that the other twin had died; but Mrs Lewis learned the truth by accident six years later when she returned to probate court to complete adoption procedures. When she said that she had called the child James Edward, the court official said: 'You can't do that. They named the other little boy James.' The secret was out. But James he remained.

James Springer grew up believing his twin was dead, while James Lewis had no idea where his twin was, and hesitated for many years before tracing him painstakingly through the bureaucratic processes of the adoption courts. They were 39 when they finally met in February 1979. The level of synchronicity between them was quite astonishing. Both grew up with adopted brothers called Larry; at school both liked maths

Above: Jim Springer and Jim Lewis – the 'Jim twins' – with Lewis's adoptive mother. Separated at birth and reared by different families in Ohio, USA, they reunited at the age of 39 in 1979, and discovered an astonishing range of identical behaviour, such as calling their dogs Troy and having the same jobs in the same order. More incredible was the fact that both their adopted brothers had the same name. And both 'Jims' had married twice: the first time to a 'Linda' and the second to a 'Betty'. The odds against such coincidences happening through chance alone are overwhelming

same pattern,' said their mother. 'Barry is first to get the symptoms and within hours Peter has the same trouble.' Harold and Gerald Weitz also had their tonsils out together. In middle age, Harold had a heart attack, and Gerald followed suit a year later. Their doctor commented that their conditions were so similar that he could swear he was operating on the same person.

There have been several studies of separated twins, the largest being by the doyen of IQ testing, Sir Cyril Burt, who published the results of 45 years of research in 1966. He

Above: 300 pairs of identical twins take part in the *Frost Programme* on 17 January 1968 in London. At first glance each pair seems literally identical; they are – through habit or by request – wearing the same clothes and hairstyles, and seem to share the same physical mannerisms, such as the way they cross their legs or position their hands. However, a closer inspection reveals slight differences, enough, in most cases, to be able to tell the twins apart. But the big mystery about identical twins is not their appearance but the extraordinary degree of synchronicity in their lives

Left: Jeanette Hamilton and identical twin Irene Reid at their first meeting in 1981, 35 years after their adoption at birth. Uncannily they shared many experiences and even discovered they both had the same phobias – about water and heights

claimed to have studied 53 pairs of separated monozygotic twins. However, his reports were ambiguously phrased, giving no indication of the nature of the tests involved, and his IQ correlations were suspiciously uniform. His results were, it seems, 'cooked'. Burt's twin data was gathered between 1913 and 1939, and the bulk of his research papers was lost when a German bomb destroyed the basement records office of University College, London. His claim to have studied a further 32 cases between 1955 and 1964 is almost certainly untrue: much of his 1966 study appears to be a reconstruction of his pre-war work presented as post-war research. His assistants 'Miss Howard' and 'Miss Conway' simply never existed. In short, the father of British educational psychology was highly unscrupulous and his research on twins very suspect.

The other major studies of separated twins also suffer from grave defects, and lay the researchers involved open to the charge of 'hereditarian bias', that is, in their IQ studies they were prejudiced in favour of genetic rather than environmental influences. The 19 cases studied by Newman, Freeman and Holzinger in Chicago in 1937 were all apparently selected because they were very much like each other to begin with. Of the 37 allegedly 'separated' twins studied by Dr James Shields in London in 1962, many were actually looked after by different members of the same family, often living in the same town. The sample of N. Juel-Nielsen in Denmark in 1965 – 12 cases in all – was too small for scientifically valid conclusions to be drawn.

News of the Jim twins prompted psychologist Thomas Bouchard of the University of Minnesota, USA, to instigate a much more detailed study of separated twins than had previously been attempted. As a result of publicity, more than 30 cases of identical twins, separated in the first few months of their lives and not reunited until adulthood, have come to light, and each pair has been intensively studied for a week at Minnesota. (In mid 1981 the research was still being evaluated.)

A sample of this size offers a golden opportunity that may not arise again. This is because the likelihood of twins being separated at birth is diminishing as the stigma attached to illegitimacy disappears and fewer babies are 'put up' for adoption.

A surprising Sunday

One day in August 1979 Jeanette Hamilton opened the *Sunday Post* at her home in Paisley, Scotland, and saw her mirror image. The face staring up at her belonged to Irene Reid, who lived 300 miles (480 kilometres) away in Market Harborough, Leicestershire, and was looking for her long-lost twin. Jeanette and Irene spent the next three hours on the telephone making up for lost time.

Their unmarried mother had put them up for adoption in 1944. They discovered that they were both terrified of heights, had at one time led scout packs and worked part-time for the same cosmetics firm. They get a pain in the same spot on the right leg in wet weather. Both have such an aversion to water that when they go to the beach they tend to sit with their backs to the sea. They are compulsive calculators: if they see a lorry they will count the wheels on it. They suffer from claustrophobia, and hated having to enter one of the small testing rooms at Minnesota. Both have an extremely high rate of blinking, much higher than anyone else in the survey, but exactly the same as each other.

Sir Cyril Burt (1883–1971), a distinguished British psychologist whose development of IQ testing led him to investigate the IQs of identical twins. His work implied there was, in almost every case, a perfect correlation. Unfortunately most of his records were destroyed in the blitz. Later, evidence came to light that undermined the validity of Burt's findings and seemed to prove that he had deliberately 'cooked' his results. Despite this, twins may indeed have very similar IQs

Also in 1979 Mrs Bridget Harrison of Leicester and Mrs Dorothy Lowe of Burnley, Lancashire, discovered they were twins. They had been apart since their birth in Lancashire in 1943. They had both married within a year of each other. One had called her son Richard Andrew, and the other called hers Andrew Richard. Bridget's daughter is Catherine Louise, Dorothy's is Karen Louise (and even then she was only called Karen to please a relative – Dorothy had really wanted to call her Katherine). Both had studied piano to the same grade, then stopped playing altogether after taking examinations at the same level. Both had had meningitis. Both collect soft toys, have cats called Tiger and wore almost identical wedding dresses. They leave their bedroom doors ajar; they wear the same perfume. They both kept a diary for just one year – 1960 – and the diaries they bought were the same make and design. The entries they made matched, day for day. Their mannerisms are identical, especially when they laugh. When they are nervous they cover their mouths with the same hand, and when talking they both put a hand on the back of their neck or pick at their nails. When Bouchard picked them up at Minneapolis airport in December 1979 he was astonished to see that both were wearing seven rings on one wrist, and, on the other, a bracelet and a watch. The Minneapolis study showed striking similarities between them in all areas, including their IQs, although, interestingly, the twin who had been raised in the more modest household did slightly better.

Bouchard and his team deny an hereditarian bias themselves, being more interested in environmental influences and individual differences, but admit that the scores on many tests were incredibly close.

Sharing the same fate

On 27 July 1939 Helena Jacobsson, an unmarried Finnish student, gave birth to twin girls in Hammersmith Hospital, London. They were christened Dagmar (or Daphne) Margaret – who was the elder by just 12 minutes – and Gerda (Barbara). Both were adopted, Barbara growing up in London, and Daphne in Luton. They were 39 when they met in May 1979. It had taken Barbara five years' research to find her twin.

Barbara Herbert and her family live in southern England, while Daphne Goodship and her family live in the north. Both their adoptive mothers died when they were children. Both girls had fallen downstairs when they were 15, leaving them with weak ankles. Both met their future husbands at town hall dances when they were 16 and were married in their early twenties in big autumn weddings, complete with choir. Both miscarried their first babies, then each had two boys followed by a girl – though Daphne had two more children later.

Daphne and Barbara with Professor Bouchard

They like carving, though Barbara uses wood and Daphne soap. They have crooked little fingers and a habit of pushing up their noses, which they both call 'squidging'. They hate heights and are squeamish about blood. Both women giggle a lot. They enjoy novels by Alistair Maclean and Catherine Cookson, and both used to read the women's magazine *My Weekly* but stopped. Each has a minimal heart murmur and a slightly enlarged thyroid gland. Neither had ever voted – feeling too ill-informed about the political issues involved – except once when they were actually employed as polling clerks. At their reunion they were both wearing beige dresses, brown velvet jackets and identical white petticoats, and had tinted their greying hair almost the same shade of auburn. One difference was their weights: Daphne had been dieting and was 20 pounds (9 kilograms) lighter.

The only striking exception was of twins, one of whom was a fisherman in Florida, the other a CIA electronics expert. The fisherman was raised by an uneducated manual labourer, his twin by a highly educated man. Although both were great raconteurs, the difference in their IQs was considerable – about 20 points. It seems that the differences in background have to be very drastic before affecting the grown twins' IQs significantly.

Phobias were often shared – as we have seen in the case of Jeanette and Irene – which seems to disprove the conventional belief that these are the result of specific individual traumas. On the other hand, tests showed that most twins do not share the same allergies, so these seem unlikely to be genetic in origin. Smoking, too, seems to be an individual addiction. In several cases, one twin was a smoker and the other a non-smoker, but even so, the state of the lungs of the twins was very similar.

The astonishing similarity of names is one of the most unexplained of all the 'coincidences' involved, but the correspondence of children's names seems to be twice as mysterious because presumably the twin's husband or wife also had had a say in the matter. As for choosing wives with the same name (and in the case of the Jim twins not just once but twice) it would almost seem as if some kind of cosmic joker were responsible.

Then there is the odd phenomenon of *astro-twins* – people of the same sex born at the same time, *but not related* – who have led remarkably parallel lives. These cases offset some of the bizarre synchronicities of biological twins. For example: Goran Lundberg of Sweden was born on the same day as another Goran Lundberg. Both won scholarships to study in the USA in 1966. And both chose to attend Bethany College in Lingsborg, Kansas, where they met. Jacqueline Luscher and Elizabeth Boxxhard, born on the same day in the same town in Switzerland, married on the same day and also moved to Los Angeles simultaneously. Both had baby girls in the same hospital on the same day, attended by the same doctor.

Above: identical twins Oscar Stohr and Jack Yufe, who were reunited in 1979. Theirs must be the most ironical of all separated-twin stories: Oscar had been reared as a fanatical Nazi – and Jack as a Jew

Below: English twins Bridget Harrison of Leicester and Dorothy Lowe from Burnley, Lancashire, who took part in Professor Bouchard's twin study. Aged 36 when they met for the first time, it almost seemed as if the same person had been living in two places at once, so strong were the similarities between them

But the most striking case of highly-synchronised, separated twins must be that of Oscar Stohr and Jack Yufe. They were born in Trinidad in 1933 and separated shortly afterwards when their parents quarrelled. Oscar was taken to Germany by his mother, where he became an ardent Nazi. With profound irony, Jack was reared in Trinidad by his father, a Jewish merchant. He attended the synagogue and became a King's Scout.

Identical: Nazi and Jew

In 1979, Jack read about the Jim twins and wrote to Bouchard suggesting that the scientists arrange a meeting between Oscar and himself to study them. When they met at the airport, they were both wearing wire-rimmed, rectangular spectacles and blue shirts with epaulettes, and both had short clipped moustaches.

The study revealed they had identical habits: they both flush the lavatory before and after using it; store rubber bands on their wrists; and prefer to dine alone in restaurants because they like to read over meals. Before eating, they clear the tables of all extraneous items. They both dip buttered toast into their coffee; read magazines from back to front; and like to scare people in lifts by sneezing very loudly. They have the same gait and way of sitting, and they speak with the same rhythms, even though Oscar speaks only German and Jack only English. So Nazi and Jew were brothers. However much scientists talk of 'hereditarian bias' and genetic versus environmental influences, one cannot help feeling that fate had a hand in this.

Double trouble

Some identical twins behave so similarly that, to a casual observer, they seem to share one identity, one personality.

INCREDIBLE THOUGH IT MAY SEEM, identical twins who are reared completely apart often exhibit more similarities of behaviour than those who grow up together. But when they reach their early teens most twins begin to develop a desire to be individuals, even if this is expressed only by dressing differently. Some, however, fail to do this, and grow up as if they were one person.

One of the most striking examples of this phenomenon became known in 1980 when the 38-year-old Chaplin twins, Greta and Freda, were brought before magistrates in York, England, charged with behaving in a manner likely to cause a breach of the peace.

Freda and Greta Chaplin of York, England, twins who exhibit 'mirror-imaging' to an uncanny degree. They seem to dress identically, but there are differences; for example, if Greta loses a shoelace from her left shoe than Freda will pull out her right shoelace. Similarly, when given two differently coloured bars of soap they suffered real distress until they cut the bars in half and shared them

They had, it was asserted, been harassing Mr Ken Iveson, once a neighbour of theirs, for 15 years: following him about, waiting for him outside the glassworks where he was employed as a lorry driver, shouting abuse at him and even hitting him with their handbags. This extraordinary fixation, however, was not the reason that psychiatrists, social workers and journalists were so fascinated by the case – for the twins spoke in what appeared to be *precise synchronisation.*

They exhibit other signs that seem to indicate that they are effectively one person. They are so alike in the way they think, speak, move and dress that children, believing them to be witches, have thrown stones at them in the street and adults have spat in their faces. They are a familiar sight in York – and are generally given a wide berth.

They wear identical grey coats, but as one originally came with green buttons and one with grey, they cut off two buttons each, and now both coats have two green and two grey. When given two different pairs of gloves they simply took one from each pair. Similarly a gift of two different coloured bars of soap caused them real anguish. They burst into tears, then solved the problem by cutting the bars in half and sharing them. When Greta got a prescription for bronchitis, Freda demanded the same medicine.

Speaking as one

The twins eat in unison, slowly raising forks and spoons together, finishing up one item of food before starting on the next. But most uncannily, they speak the same words at the same time, especially when excited or under stress; careful listening, however, reveals that the words of one come out a split second later than those of the other.

They also exhibit 'mirror-imaging', which is characteristically found in monozygotic or single-egg twins. In typical cases one twin is right-handed, the other left-handed; the whorls of the hair grow clockwise in one and anti-clockwise in the other; the left thumbprint of one almost matches the right thumbprint of the other, or similar wrinkles appear on opposite ears. Photographs of twins are most similar if one negative is flipped to produce a reversed image.

The Chaplins dress in mirror image of each other, although a casual observer would say they dress identically, and eccentrically, in their long skirts, clashing colours and headscarves. When Greta wears a bracelet on her left wrist, Freda wears one on her right, and if one breaks a shoelace, the other pulls a lace out of her opposite shoe.

Although the twins are difficult and unpredictable to interview, some journalists have managed to talk to them. Sue Heal from *Woman's Own* elicited this telling statement from them: 'We're so close that we're really one person. We know exactly what each other is thinking because we're just one brain.' Sue Heal remarked, 'You go gently for fear they'll disappear and leave you thinking you dreamed them up, like something from *Alice in Wonderland*.' She must have gained their confidence, however, because she did find out that they wear different underclothes.

And they do argue, sometimes hitting each other lightly with their identical handbags, then sitting sulking together for hours. If they believe they are the same person then how can an argument happen?

A closer examination of their history shows that their extraordinary togetherness was actively fostered by their parents, especially by their mother, who dressed them identically and allowed them no friends. They were not mentally abnormal and attended a secondary school near their York home. Teachers and fellow pupils remember them as neat, clean and quiet – and although among the slowest students they could read and write as well as the others in their class. The deputy headmaster of the school has no doubts about what turned them into the disturbed adults they are today: 'It was clear that they had a doting mother who never allowed them any separate identity. . . . The other kids just saw them as a bit quaint. I don't think they were acutely isolated then or maladjusted.' They had not, at that point, begun to speak simultaneously.

Clearly their mother's attitude towards them had triggered off a pattern of abnormal behaviour, perhaps aided by their biological affinity. Both parents seem to have been uncommunicative and friendless and Mrs Chaplin is said to be obsessively houseproud. This emphasis on cleanliness may explain why the twins' only apparent pleasure is bathing together, grooming each other, washing each other's long hair. They are said to use an average of 14 bars of soap and three large bottles of shampoo each week.

The unfortunate Ken Iveson had grown up next door to the Chaplins; he married when the twins were two years old, but continued to live at his parents' home with his wife and children. Neither he nor his parents had ever set foot inside their neighbours' house; they were never asked in and never saw anyone else pay social calls. Iveson would pass the time of day with the girls, who, isolated from the outside world, obviously took this as some kind of romantic encouragement. They rapidly became a nuisance and eventually, after 15 years, Iveson could take no more of it. Their case came to court.

The Chaplins first achieved national notoriety in 1980 when they were brought before the York magistrates charged with persistently hounding Mr Ken Iveson (right) for 15 years. Their fixation with him became intolerable: they would lie in wait for him and shout abuse or hit him – this, it seemed, was their way of showing affection. It was their appearance in court that revealed the extent of their simultaneous behaviour (below), making them the focus for many newspaper and magazine articles, and the centre of a medical controversy

The twins' parents had, it transpired, forced them to leave home. When asked about this, Freda and Greta reply as one: 'Something must have happened. Yes yes yes. Something strange. Must have happened.'

Mr and Mrs Chaplin refuse to talk to the press, and exactly why the twins left is not known. They now live in a hostel for the mentally handicapped.

Curiously, the local psychiatrists, called in by the court as expert witnesses, were baffled by the twins' case, describing it vaguely as 'a personality disorder'. Yet their behaviour towards Mr Iveson matches the textbook symptoms of *erotomania*, a form of schizophrenia that has been recognised as a clinical condition since the mid 1960s. Dr Morgan Enoch, of the Maudsley mental hospital in south London, has discovered that if one identical twin is schizophrenic then the other is also likely to suffer from the disease.

But does erotomania – or any form of schizophrenia – entirely explain the Chaplins' behaviour, especially their strange way of speaking? In their case there seem to be many highly influential factors – genetic, environmental, social – that have made them the objects of sympathy and derision that they are today.

Perhaps the Chaplins' peculiarity of speech is just one aspect of the way twins communicate with one another. Better

'Snap aduk, Cabenga, chase die-dipana' – at this mysterious command from one of the Kennedy twins, they both began to play with the doll's house. Grace and Virginia were believed to be mentally retarded until it was discovered that they had developed a language of their own, complete with extensive vocabulary and syntax. 'Poto' and 'Cabenga', as they called themselves, were investigated by speech therapist Anne Koenecke at the Children's Hospital in San Diego, California; she finally coaxed them into speaking a little English. Their curious, private language was an example of ideoglossia, which is developed most often by identical twins apparently to exclude the outside world

known is *ideoglossia*, the phenomenon in which two individuals, most often twin children, develop between them a unique and private language complete with highly original vocabulary and syntax.

It is, however, commonly confused with a sub-category, *twin speech* – a private collection of distorted words and idioms used, it is estimated, by 40 per cent of all twins because they feel isolated, or secretive, or both. Most twins tend to give it up at the age of three, although twin Robert A. Nelson wrote to the *New York Times* in 1932 that 'It is a matter of record in my family that when my brother and I first started to talk, and until we were well past six, we conversed with each other in a strange tongue of our own.' The only other person who could understand their particular speech was their brother, who was eight years older.

Identical twins Grace and Virginia were born in 1970 in Columbus, Georgia, USA, to Tom Kennedy and his German-born wife Christine. The day after the girls were born, Grace suddenly raised her head and stared at her father. Virginia did the same thing the next day. These strangely precocious acts, labelled 'convulsive seizures' by doctors, continued periodically for six months, in spite of treatment. At 17 months they apparently developed ideoglossia, beginning to speak rapidly in a language of their own – their only concession to English being 'mommy' and 'daddy'. They called each other Poto and Cabenga.

When the twins were two years old, the family moved to California, but there were very few other children in the neighbourhood for Grace and Virginia to play with. They were left to themselves or entrusted to their maternal grandmother, Paula Kunert, a stern disciplinarian who still spoke only her native German.

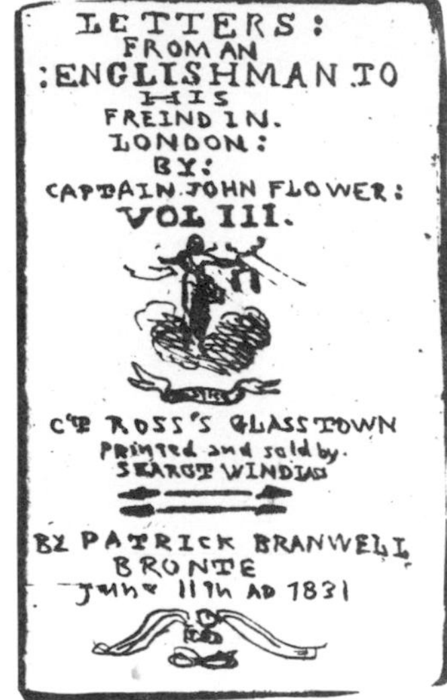

LETTERS:
FROM AN
:ENGLISHMAN TO
HIS
FREIND IN.
LONDON:
BY:
CAPTAIN JOHN FLOWER:
VOL III.

CP ROSS'S GLASSTOWN
Printed and sold by.
SEARGT WINDIAS

BY PATRICK BRANWELL
BRONTE
June 11th AD 1831

Not all children who share an intensely private world are twins. This tiny book (above) – so small that it can be read only with the aid of a magnifying glass – was one of the 'books' written by the children of the Brontë family. They created imaginary lands, Angria, Gondal and Glasstown, peopled with vivid characters and spoken of only in secret. Two of the children were particularly close: Charlotte (who later wrote *Jane Eyre*) and her brother Patrick Branwell. At least once they shared a strong telepathic experience when they were many miles apart

In 1977 the speech therapists at the Children's Hospital in San Diego, California, began to study the twins, taping their conversation in the hope of learning something about the mysteries of developing language. Is it, they wondered, predominantly a product of genetic programming or a learned response to the world around them? A typical conversation between the girls would run:

'Genebene manita.'
'Nomemee.'
'Eebedeebeda. Dis din qui naba.'
'Neveda. Ca Baedabada.'

When the study began, the twins spoke no English, but gradually the therapists coaxed some out of them – which they spoke with a curious high-speed delivery. Anne Koenecke even tried to talk to them in their own language, but they just looked at her as if she were crazy.

'Snap aduk, Cabenga, chase die-dipana,' said 'Poto' masterfully. Having apparently issued a command she and 'Cabenga' instantly began to play with a doll's house.

Analysis of the tapes showed that their communication was something less than true ideoglossia. Many of the apparently new words turned out to be mispronounced words and phrases from German and English jammed together and said at high speed. However, a few words, such as 'nunukid' and 'pulana', remain unidentified. As the twins grew older they suddenly began to speak English – but they remain silent about the meaning of their once private language.

There are such strong links between some twins that they suffer simultaneous injuries – although miles apart – even dying at the same moment.

One in life and death

SINCE 1953, Professor Luigi Gedda of the Gregor Mendel Institute in Rome has studied more than 15,000 pairs of twins, and has elaborated a 'clock of life' hypothesis to account for the extraordinary correspondences in the lives of twins, which he describes in his book *Chronogenetics* (1978). There seems to be a whole range of major and minor manifestations of the mental bonds that link twins, from fairly commonplace telepathy – such as a simultaneous impulse to contact each other – to the actual transmission of pain and even physical wounds. Beyond these mental bonds are the even more astonishing cases of 'carbon-copy' accidents, which stubbornly defy rational or scientific explanation.

The 45 sets of twins of Haverhill, Suffolk – all were under the age of 20 in January 1980. This strange clustering of double births was particularly noticeable in a population of just 17,500, and naturally led to much speculation about the cause. One mother of twins said, 'I'm convinced it's the water. All my neighbours and friends have had twins.' Here the parents of the newest additions to the group tempt fate by toasting the camera – in water

In *The Corsican brothers* by Alexandre Dumas, Louis de Franchi is fatally wounded in a duel. At the moment he is shot his identical twin Lucien, 500 miles (800 kilometres) away, is struck with agonising pain. He feels as if a bullet has penetrated above his sixth rib and emerged just above his hip – exactly where Louis has been shot. This was fiction; but such strange bonds between twins have been reported many times in real life.

At 4.35 on a Saturday afternoon in July 1948 Alice Lambe, a 20-year-old typist, sat reading in the parlour of her family home outside Springfield, Illinois, USA. Suddenly, she felt an enormous jolt on the left side of her body, followed by a sharp stabbing pain and a feeling of shock. The impact of the unseen blow was enough to knock her off her chair. Before passing out, she cried out to her father 'Something's happened to Dianne!'

Dianne was her identical twin who had spent the day in St Louis, 70 miles (110

Professor Luigi Gedda with a colleague and twins at Gregor Mendel Institute in Rome. Gedda's researches into the curious correspondences in the lives of twins led him to postulate the existence of a 'clock of life' that, as it were, ticks in perfect synchronisation for both twins

kilometres) away. At 4.35 p.m. the train on which she was returning was derailed and Dianne was thrown across the carriage, landing on her left side. The next thing she knew was waking up in hospital. She had suffered two fractured ribs and severe concussion. She was off work for three weeks – but then so was Alice, whose continual complaints of stabbing pain eventually led to her being X-rayed. It turned out that she had fractured the same two ribs in the same place as her sister.

On 21 July 1975 Nettie Porter was involved in a car crash in Roseville, California. At the same time her twin sister Nita Hust, at work in a hospital 400 miles (640 kilometres) away, felt severe pains down her left leg, rolled up her trousers and was amazed to see bruises working their way up the left side of her body. The matron at the hospital bore witness to the spontaneous development of her marks, which corresponded to Nettie's injuries.

Ted Wolner and Harvey Stein give the following case in *Parallels: a look at twins* (1978). A young woman had an identical twin with acute appendicitis. She said: 'When they came to tell me this, they found me on the floor in pain. When the doctors took her into surgery, I could tell the moment when they started cutting and when they sewed her up. I was in the waiting room with my mother who said, "The operation should be over by now," and I said, "No, mother, the doctor has just started." And, indeed, the doctor later verified that the operation had been delayed.'

Sometimes the transference of injury can be fatal. Mrs Joyce Crominski wrote to the Australian magazine *Truth* about her identical twin sisters Helen and Peg. At 11.15 one evening Helen awoke, white-faced and screaming, with a terrible pain in her chest. Her parents sent for an ambulance but she died on the way to hospital – as did Peg, who had been in a car accident at exactly the same time as Helen awoke. The steering wheel had penetrated her chest.

Silvia Landa, aged five, burnt herself on a hot iron, and her twin Marta felt the pain 12 miles (20 kilometres) away. Both developed a burn scar on their right hands. Jayne Wilkinson, also five, fell and broke her nose – and her twin sister Claire had a nosebleed. Helen Fry, 13, was out shopping with her grandmother when she began to stagger about quite dazed and had to be taken home, where she fell asleep on the settee. Her twin Lorraine was in hospital for a minor operation, and both twins had experienced the anaesthetic. Alan Richmond shattered his knee in several places and his identical twin Arthur suffered the pain in his knee. As Ann Matthews's pregnancy progressed, her twin Ruth Harvey put on weight and suffered early morning sickness; she also shared the labour pains.

Dizygotic – or non-identical – twins also experience pain transference, even though genetically they are no more alike than ordinary brothers and sisters. On two occasions when Yvonne Green had a baby, her twin brother Christopher Gool had labour pains 300 miles (480 kilometres) away. Another time when Christopher, who is a policeman, hurt his arm in a brawl, Yvonne fell over and had to go to hospital to have her arm injuries treated.

Martha Burke of California, USA, suffered

Twins in twins

The phenomenon of the 'vanishing twin' has been studied by Dr Lucien Schneider of the University of Paris. This refers to cases where only one twin develops in the womb, while the other is reabsorbed by the mother's body. Sometimes, however, this fails to happen and one twin is born inside the other, as Isla Sneddon (left) discovered in 1980.

This 18-year-old student nurse from Glasgow, Scotland, complained of a cyst on her chest and was duly X-rayed. It was discovered that the 'cyst' was in fact her embryo twin, which had grown as big as a tennis ball and was preventing the blood supply reaching her right lung. If it had not been removed it would almost certainly have killed her. Isla said, 'I have always wanted a twin. It was a strange feeling. Perhaps I subconsciously knew.' Vanishing twins are, however, rare. From 1900 to 1979 there were only 11 similar cases reported throughout Britain.

from burning pains in her chest and stomach as her non-identical twin was burned to death in the Canary Island aeroplane crash of 1977, which claimed 582 lives. She sued the airlines for damages; not surprisingly her claim was unsuccessful. Mrs Sheargold went to hospital with a leg injury and her twin brother was kept awake by the pain. Later he cracked a rib, and *she* felt *his* pains.

Twins frequently give birth together. Jacky and Geraldine (née Herz) had babies within days of each other on 12 occasions. Many other twins have managed this feat at least once, often with greater synchronisation. In June 1970 Vera and Anita, twin daughters of Otto Heise of Einbeck, West Germany, who were quite unlike each other in looks, character and ways of life, were both taken to the same clinic and delivered of babies at the same moment. Jennifer Vickers and Patricia Harlow gave birth 'within hours' in 1974, and the following year Maureen Smith and Yvonne Gale gave birth within 23 minutes at Kingston Hospital, Surrey, England.

Death, too, can strike at the same time. Twins John and Arthur Mowforth, aged 66, were seized with chest pains on the same evening, 22 May 1975; they were rushed to hospitals in Bristol and Windsor respectively, and died of heart attacks in the evening. Twins Ida Torrey and Freda Palmer were born in Geronimo, Texas, in 1905. They died the same day in 1979, 350 miles (560 kilometres) apart. The same year, Frederick and Mary Ward of Portland, Maine, had fatal heart attacks at the age of 71, only 12 minutes apart. And in 1981, Margaret Cox and Florence Parrish of Georgia, born exactly two hours apart in 1894, died exactly two hours apart. Margaret, who had been born first, also died first.

Identical twins Maureen Smith and Yvonne Gale gave birth to sons within 23 minutes of each other in Kingston Hospital, Surrey, on 15 January 1975. Does Professor Gedda's 'clock of life' account for such startling correspondences in the lives of twins?

Dr David Lykken and his colleague Dr Thomas J. Bouchard of the University of Minnesota, USA. Their extensive investigation of identical twins suggests that many possess a strong telepathic link

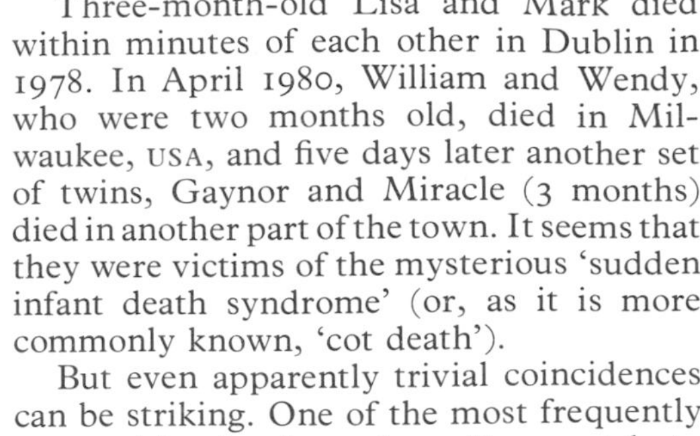

Three-month-old Lisa and Mark died within minutes of each other in Dublin in 1978. In April 1980, William and Wendy, who were two months old, died in Milwaukee, USA, and five days later another set of twins, Gaynor and Miracle (3 months) died in another part of the town. It seems that they were victims of the mysterious 'sudden infant death syndrome' (or, as it is more commonly known, 'cot death').

But even apparently trivial coincidences can be striking. One of the most frequently reported is of twins going off separately to buy dresses for a party and turning up in exactly the same outfits. This happened to Nettie and Nita in California: 'Both of us showed up wearing a yellow silk-screen print dress with a flared skirt, exactly identical; even our . . . shoes were the same.'

Another, perhaps even more frequent event, is twins thinking of each other at the same time. Dr David Lykken of the University of Minnesota notes that when Nettie or Nita concentrates on her twin, the other soon telephones. This telepathic link is widely known but difficult to test by controlled experiment. Results are never quite conclusive. Thus we see from an undated clipping from the *Journal* of the American Association for the Advancement of Science that Doctors Duane and Behrendt wired up a pair of identical twins in separate rooms to record their brain waves, and found that a stimulus administered to the brain of one twin was simultaneously received by the other. Yet of 16 other pairs of twins later tested by the doctors only one pair responded similarly.

Twin telepathy is sometimes strikingly demonstrated by examination results. Twins Nancy and Ruth Schneider were born in Virginia, USA, in 1927. Sitting for college entrance exams in opposite corners of the room, they chose the same essay subject and wrote 'word for word' the same story, according to one of the invigilators, Dr Sara Roody.

In 1979, twins Elaine and Linda Beveridge graduated in social policy and administration at Leeds University. They sat for eight papers, getting identical marks on five. On one paper there was a difference of one mark, and on two papers and their dissertations, there was a difference of two marks. It had been the same with their 'O' and 'A' level examination results: exactly the same or different by only a few marks. Duncan and Alistair Dissett of Somerset got identical marks in all the eight 'O' level papers they took in 1980.

In January 1974 twins Frank and Jack Clatworthy, also from Somerset, were in adjoining hospital beds after being injured within an hour of each other in separate accidents 3 miles (5 kilometres) apart on the same road outside Taunton, returning from the same party. Frank's car overturned, and Jack's went into a hedge (according to *The Times*), or overturned as well (according to the *Daily Mail*).

Norris and Ross McWhirter, creators of *The Guinness book of records*. Both sub-lieutenants in the Royal Navy during the Second World War, they were detailed to separate minesweepers – which then collided with each other at Malta

On 27 December 1972 the Jay twins, Helen and Catherine, had their handbags stolen in different BBC offices in London within five minutes of each other. They telephoned their bank simultaneously to cancel their stolen credit cards.

In 1973 Wendy Styles, 13, fell in the school gym and broke her left leg. She was waiting outside for the doctor when, a couple of minutes later, her twin sister Denise was also carried out, having broken her right leg.

The McWhirter twins, who created the *Guinness book of records*, were both sub-lieutenants in the Royal Navy in the Second World War. Norris was detailed to a minesweeper in Singapore, Ross to one in the Mediterranean. The vessels made their separate ways to Valletta, Malta, where they collided. Similarly, twins George and Stephen Youngblood went off on motorbikes in October 1980, in opposite directions, to joyride along the backroads of Missouri, USA. Stephen died and George was injured when they met in a head-on collision.

Most of these incidents could be dismissed as the results of blind chance. Coincidences in general have the curious quality of seeming to be tremendously important, yet the nature of their significance remains frustratingly elusive.

Consider, finally, the story of Peet and Daan Snyman, identical twins from Pretoria in South Africa.

The Snymans, born in 1945, had appendicitis within a few days of each other and then meningitis at almost the same time. At the age of seven both were badly bitten in the leg by different dogs. They grew up to take such incidents for granted. In December 1964 Peet lost two fingers on his left hand while attempting to adjust the fan belt in his car. Two weeks later his twin lost the same fingers on his right hand in a car accident. This was particularly disastrous because by this time they were both professional guitarists. During the next 14 years both married and their lives diverged. Peet's wife had two children while Daan's remained childless.

But the pattern began again in February 1978 when Peet lost his right eye in a car accident. Eight months later Daan lost his left eye in another accident. Then, while Peet was out fishing, his line snapped and the lead sinker hit him in his good eye, making him totally blind. In 1980 his wife started divorce proceedings, saying she could not live with a blind man. In the circumstances, Daan began looking after his right eye very carefully, and wondered if his marriage would last much longer . . .

Right: Denise and Wendy Styles of Brading, Isle of Wight. In December 1973 the 13-year-old twins both fell and broke a leg in the school gymnasium within minutes of each other. Denise broke her right leg and Wendy her left: is this an example of 'mirror-imaging'?

Nothing but trouble

Curses have always been feared – with justice it seems, for disease, loss of loved ones and death have often befallen the victims. But is this coincidence or, asks PAUL SIEVEKING, could it be the direct result of knowing that one is cursed?

A Mycenaean funeral mask representing Agamemnon – one of the many sufferers from the ancient curse on the House of Atreus by Hermes. Agamemnon, the grandson of Atreus, was killed by his wife and her lover as a direct result

A CURSE IS AN INVOCATION of destruction or evil, part of the accustomed armoury of the priest, magician, shaman or ill-wisher. But do curses work and, if so, how? Swearing at someone gives vent to pent-up feelings; most psychologists would say that ritual curses do nothing more, *unless the victim is expecting trouble.* Sandford Cohen, a psychologist at Boston University, USA, is convinced from field research that curses can be lethal, because of the feeling of utter helplessness they can inspire. He sees a striking similarity between western Man dying from a fear of some disease generally believed to be fatal, and primitive Man dying from a witch doctor's curse.

Another explanation involves the 'tape recording' theory – that a thought can imprint itself on an object or person, and can be transferred to others. If the thought is malevolent, so is the effect. There do seem to be numerous cases of curse victims being totally sceptical of supernatural 'mumbo-jumbo', which nevertheless does nothing to save them from the effects.

Take the case of Robert Heinl junior, a retired colonel in the US Marine Corps. From 1958 to 1963 he served on Haiti as chief of the US naval mission, while his wife studied the voodoo religion. Afterwards, back in the United States, they wrote *Written in blood*, a history of Haiti that was openly critical of the ruling dynasty of François 'Papa Doc' Duvalier. Then they learned from a newspaper published by Haitian exiles that a curse had been placed on the book, probably after Papa Doc's death in 1971 by his widow, Simone.

At first, the Heinls were flattered that their book was thought to be worth cursing, but amusement soon turned to fear. First, the manuscript was lost on the way to the publishers, then it turned up four months later in a room the publishers never used. Meanwhile, the Heinls prepared another copy of the manuscript and sent it off for binding and stitching. The machine immediately broke down. A *Washington Post* reporter who was preparing to interview the authors was struck down with acute appendicitis. The colonel fell through a stage when he was delivering a speech, injuring his leg. And while walking near his home he was suddenly – and severely – bitten by a dog.

The omens continued, two involving the number 22, which Papa Doc considered a magic number. Finally, on 5 May 1979, the Heinls were on holiday on St Barthelemy Island, near Haiti, when the colonel dropped dead from a heart attack. His widow mused: 'There is a belief that the closer you get to Haiti, the more powerful the magic becomes.'

In Royal David's city

Curses, precisely laid down in many rituals, are still cast by priests in the major religions. In September 1981 Rabbi Moshe Hirsch, leader of the Neturei Karta, an orthodox Jewish sect, was threatening to invoke the 'Rod of Light' against the Israeli archaeologist Yigal Shilo if he persisted in excavating the biblical city of David, which the rabbi maintained involved desecrating a medieval Jewish cemetery. The archaeologists denied the existence of such a cemetery.

The Rod of Light ceremony involves the reading of a text based on *qabalistic* writings. The participants burn black candles, sound a ram's horn and invoke the name of the cursed man's mother. 'This ceremony is an absolute last resort,' said the rabbi. 'It has only been invoked twice in the last 30 years, both times with horrible consequences. There are many ways of dying, some less pleasant than others.' But unfortunately the

Left: Robert and Nancy Heinl, who fell foul of the Haitian dictator François 'Papa Doc' Duvalier and his wife Simone (below) while researching their book *Written in blood* – which was openly critical of Duvalier's regime – in the 1960s. The Heinls discovered that Simone Duvalier had cursed them and an extraordinary chain of events, culminating in the sudden death of Robert Heinl, followed. Coincidence? Nancy Heinl was in no doubt that the curse was responsible for their bad luck

rabbi claims he failed to discover Shilo's mother's name.

Even in the calm glade of the Church of England, spiritual contracts are occasionally put out on church thieves. Since the 1970s in Gloucestershire alone, two vicars have performed the commination service: the Reverend Harold Cheales of Wych Rissington in 1973, and the Reverend Robert Nesham of Down Ampney in 1981. The commination service contains 12 curses and leaves room for extemporisation. It first appeared in the 1662 Book of Common Prayer, but in the 1928 revision 'curse' was replaced by 'God's anger and judgement'. It was traditionally used against enemies of the Church on the first day of Lent, or whenever a church or churchyard had been desecrated. Christian curses seem to be, on occasion, just as effective as demonic ones: the old abbeys that Henry VIII seized from the monks after the dissolution of the monasteries in the early 16th century often bedevilled their new owners over generations with the curses laid by angry monks (see box).

There is a widespread ancient belief that no good will come from disturbing old stones or buried treasure – folklore worldwide is full of such tales. We can see the theme continuing in the enduring popularity of the idea of a mummy's curse in newspapers and films. Some researchers believe that such deep-seated and widespread beliefs, as part of the collective unconscious, can exert a material influence, thus bringing myths to life – and perpetually reinforcing them.

A heart of stone

The old castle of Syrie in Aberdeenshire, Scotland, has a legendary curse on it. A group of stones in the river there is known as the Weeping Stones, one of which is missing. It is said that no heir to Syrie will ever succeed until the missing stone is found.

In 1944 a 2-tonne 'Witch's Stone' was shifted from a crossroads at Scrapfaggot Green, Great Leighs, Essex, England, to widen the road. Psychic havoc broke out. A great boulder was found outside the local pub, chickens were found locked up in rabbit hutches, rabbits were loose in the garden, the church bells chimed irregularly, 30 sheep and two horses were found dead in a field, and a village builder found his scaffold poles tumbled about 'like matchsticks'. The 'Witch's Stone' was replaced and peace was restored.

In 1980 a 30-tonne boulder was removed from the Devil's Marbles to a park in Tennant Creek, an isolated copper mining town in the Australian outback. Aborigines of the Warramungu tribe believe the Marbles are a relic from the 'Dream Time' – when ancestral spirits created the world – and any interference with such relics will lead to sickness and death. After the boulder's removal, a number of Aboriginal children fell ill

By fire and water

Battle Abbey in Sussex (below) was the scene of a grim curse laid on the descendants of Sir Anthony Browne, 'Esquire to the Body of Henry VIII, Master of the Horse and Justice in Eyre', in 1538.

with sores on their legs, and a tribal elder, Mick Taylor, warned that 'someone would get killed' if the stone were not returned. In March 1981 Mick Taylor died from meningitis at the age of 50. The town then agreed to return the boulder.

In late 1981 councillors in King's Lynn, Norfolk, England, refused to move an 18th-century obelisk that was in danger from vandals. A Latin inscription reads: 'Whoever shall remove or have removed this monument let him die the last of his line.'

Rocks of wrath

During the summer of 1977 airline vice-president Ralph Loffert, of Buffalo, New York state, USA, his wife and four children visited the Hawaiian volcano Mauna Loa. While there they collected some stones from the volcano despite a warning from the locals that this would anger the volcano goddess, Pele. Some claim to have seen Pele, who traditionally appears to warn of imminent eruptions. Shortly after they returned home, Mauna Loa erupted. Within a few months one of the Loffert boys, Todd, developed appendicitis, had knee surgery and broke his wrist; another son, Mark, sprained an ankle and broke his arm; another son, Dan, caught an eye infection and had to wear glasses; and the daughter, Rebecca, lost two front teeth in a fall. In July 1978, the Lofferts sent the stones to a friend in Hawaii who was asked to return them to the volcano. But the disasters continued – Mark hurt his knee, Rebecca broke three more teeth, Dan fractured a hand bone, while Todd dislocated an elbow and fractured his wrist again. Mark then confessed that he still had three stones. They were returned – and the trouble ceased.

Mrs Allison Raymond of Ontario, Canada, and her family also took some stones away from the volcano. She told reporters:

Above: a 788-year-old curse is ritually lifted by the Chief Rabbi at the consecration of Clifford's Tower in York on 31 October 1978. On the night of 16 March 1190, 150 Jews fled to the tower where they died by their own hand rather than fall into a mob's hands. The last to die was the Chief Rabbi, whose final act was to curse the city of York. Until well into the 20th century York was avoided by Jews – even though nearby Leeds has always had a thriving Jewish community

Right: 'The curse has come upon me, cried the Lady of Shallott' – Tennyson's doomed heroine prepares to meet her fate

According to tradition, Sir Anthony was cursed at the feast held to celebrate his ownership of the abbey by a monk who was angry at the seizure of Church lands during the Reformation.

The curse was specific: the family would die 'by fire or water'. It seems, however, that the curse went awry: Sir Anthony's other property, Cowdray Park – which he had inherited from his half-cousin, the Earl of Southampton – was burned down; but this was much later, in 1793, after the property had passed into the hands of another family.

Antony Hippisley Coxe, compiler of *Haunted Britain* (1974), records that the curse came unstuck yet again, in 1907, when the Duchess of Cleveland – who had rented Battle Abbey briefly – drowned in its grounds on her way to church, but her daughter, who was with her, survived.

Above: the Devil's Marbles, Australia, a sacred Aboriginal site. In 1980 one of the boulders was removed; Mick Taylor, a tribal elder, warned that the removal would lead to sickness and death. Several children fell ill – and he died the next year, at the age of 50

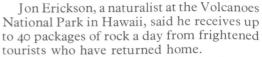

> My husband was killed in a head-on car crash and my mother died of cancer. My younger son was rushed to hospital with a pancreas condition that's slowly getting worse. Then he broke his leg. My daughter's marriage nearly broke up and it was only when I posted the rocks back that our luck improved.

Despite warnings, Nixon Morris, a hardwood dealer from El Paso, Texas, took a Mauna Loa stone home in 1979. After returning home he fell off his roof, lightning struck an aerial and ruined several home appliances, and his wife fell ill with a mysterious infection that left her knee swollen.

Then Morris broke a hip and thigh when he fought with a burglar in their house. The family cat was sleeping under the bonnet of his wife's car when she started the engine and was stripped of its fur down one side. Then Morris's grand-daughter fell and broke her arm in two places.

Morris said he had broken the rock in two and given a piece to a friend, adding: 'He brought the rock back to me after he wrecked four cars in less than two years, and he'd never before had a wreck in his life.' In March 1981 Morris sent the rocks back.

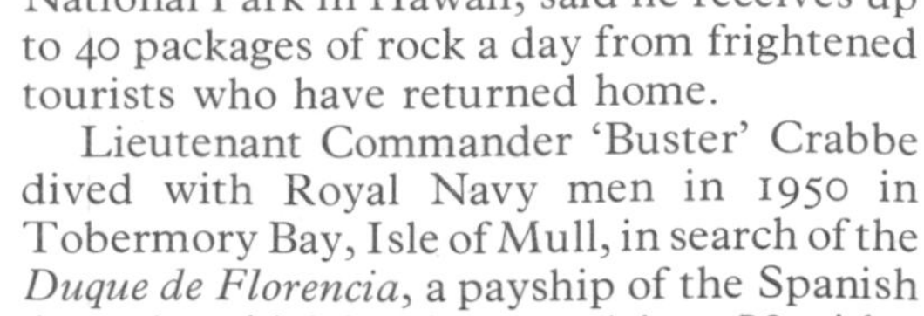

Jon Erickson, a naturalist at the Volcanoes National Park in Hawaii, said he receives up to 40 packages of rock a day from frightened tourists who have returned home.

Lieutenant Commander 'Buster' Crabbe dived with Royal Navy men in 1950 in Tobermory Bay, Isle of Mull, in search of the *Duque de Florencia*, a payship of the Spanish Armada, which had been sunk in 1588 with a reputed 30 million pounds of gold on board. One of the trophies with which he surfaced was a skull that medical experts said had belonged to a North African woman. Crabbe disappeared, some maintain mysteriously, while on an underwater mission near Russian warships in Portsmouth harbour in 1956. The following year a coroner decided that the headless body of a frogman washed up at Chichester, Sussex, was that of Crabbe.

The skull that had been found on the

wreck was kept in the Western Isles Hotel, Tobermory, Scotland, where one day the barman accidentally caused it to fall and break. The same day he crashed his motor scooter and cracked *his* skull. He never returned to the island. The hotel owner, Donald Maclean, stored the skull away in a cupboard. In 1970 Richard Forrester, the new English owner of the hotel, drilled a hole in the skull so that he could hang it up in his cocktail bar:

> I was using an ordinary electric drill. The first odd thing that happened was that the metal bit of the drill, after piercing the bone, bent inside at an angle of 45 degrees. I found this surprising but thought nothing more about it. Two hours later I was struck

Below: the Mauna Loa volcano of Hawaii. In 1977 the Loffert family, on holiday from the USA, picked up some stones from the volcano – despite a warning that this would anger the local deity, the goddess Pele. A series of disasters struck the family, ceasing only when the last stone had been sent back to Hawaii. Other tourists have reported similar runs of bad luck after taking stones away

The curse of the Pharoahs

Archaeologists can be said to be modern grave robbers – and as such seem to have paid the price, for many ancient Egyptian tombs apparently carry curses for any who dare to desecrate them.

According to the American journalist Webb Garrison, Professor S. Resden opened an Egyptian tomb in the 1890s that was thus inscribed: 'Whosoever desecrates the tomb of Prince Sennar will be overtaken by the sands and destroyed.' Resden knew he was doomed, it is said. He left Egypt by ship – and died on board, a victim of suffocation with no discernible cause. Small amounts of sand were found clutched in his hands.

The poetic neatness of this story is, it must be said, rather suspicious and should perhaps be taken with a pinch of salt – or sand.

But the 'curse of the pharaoh' continues. In September 1979, George LaBrash had a stroke while guarding the Tutankhamun mask (left) in San Francisco. In January 1982 he sued the city authorities for disability pay, claiming that the stroke was a job-related injury caused by the alleged curse on the tomb's desecration. The case was dismissed. Was this in itself a refinement of the curse? Has the curse of the boy king moved into legal circles?

Above: the appalling crash that killed film star Jayne Mansfield on 29 June 1967. This was widely rumoured as being no *accident* – Jayne had been cursed by her former friend, Anton la Vey, head of the Church of Satan

Above right: Lance Sieveking, broadcaster and father of author Paul Sieveking. He demonstrated an unusual immunity to a curse laid by black magician Aleister Crowley by living 30 years longer than the curse allowed

> by excruciating pain in the back of the head. I was completely incapacitated for two days. Since then I have been taking prescribed pills but the searing pain continues and never leaves.

And the only other person to handle the skull since the drilling had also experienced searing headaches.

The notion of a curse affecting a whole family is at least as old as civilisation. The ancient Greeks were firm believers in the efficacy of curses – the most celebrated curse affecting the house of Atreus: Atreus killed the son of the god Hermes in a love contest, and Hermes put a curse on the murderer 'and all his house'. Atreus killed his own son by mistake; his grandson, the Homeric hero Agamemnon, was killed by his wife and her lover; and she in turn was murdered by her son and daughter.

In Moorish Spain, a curse was believed to hang over the great Abencerrage family – 'the Flower of Granada'. Many died in war and vendettas before the whole family was wiped out by King Muley Hassan on one of the patios of the Alhambra palace during the 15th century.

Relatively speaking

In Britain, several aristocratic families are believed to be afflicted by family curses. In the 18th century the Scottish Earl of Breadaulbin moved a graveyard to build the castle of Taynmouth. According to tradition a lady whose grave was disturbed laid a curse on the family whereby no two earls of the same line would succeed each other. The prophecy apparently came true.

Even writing about curses might be considered a hazardous business, but this author draws a certain comfort from the apparent immunity of his father. In 1928 the magician Aleister Crowley ('The Beast'), recently expelled from Sicily, met the young radio producer Lance Sieveking in Cassis on the French Riviera. They spent many hours in conversation, and Crowley subsequently cast Sieveking's horoscope. It contained a number of predictions that were later fulfilled. One, however, was not. Crowley wrote: 'By the way, you will oblige me personally by dying at the age of forty-five.' Sieveking was then 32 but he disobligingly lived to be 75.

Crowley's curses, however, often successfully claimed their victims. The last to go was young Dr William Brown Thompson, who withheld the addicted Beast's supply of morphia. In a rage, Crowley put a curse on him, saying that when he died he would take the doctor with him. And so it came to pass. Crowley died on 1 December 1947, aged 72. Thompson was dead within 24 hours.

EXTRA! BUFFALO EVENING NEWS. EXTRA!

VOL. XLII—NO. 132. BUFFALO, N. Y., FRIDAY, SEPTEMBER 13, 1901. PRICE ONE CENT.

EXTRA! | EXTRA! | EXTRA! | EXTRA!

PRESIDENT DEAD!

William McKinley Passed Away at the Milburn Home From Effects of Cowardly Assassin's Bullet.

No hiding place

Bad luck appears to attach itself to some people with a single-mindedness that seems to imply an organising intelligence.

WHILE A CURSE is a conscious invocation of misfortune against others, a jinx is merely a bringer of bad luck – why it starts is anybody's guess. Jinxes may be curses in disguise, unknown to the victims. It could even be that someone who suffers a series of inexplicable misfortunes comes to believe himself to be jinxed – and so unconsciously brings about further disasters.

For 400 years the Haanappel family of Doesburg in Holland have had the palms of their hands turn black six months after they are born. Doctors say this is the result of a gene mutation, but local folklore maintains that a Haanappel saved a church from fire by ringing the bells, burning his hands as he slid down the bell rope. The Devil, in his anger, cursed him and his heirs forever.

No one has come up with an explanation for the misfortunes of the Guinness brewery family. In 1978 they suffered four deaths in as many months: in May Lady Henrietta Guinness plunged to her death from an aqueduct in Spoleto, Italy; in June another Guinness heiress drowned in a bath while trying to inject herself with heroin. Also in June, Major Dennys Guinness was found dead in Hampshire with an empty pill bottle by his side. In August, John Guinness, then an aide to British Prime Minister James Callaghan, survived a head-on collision in Norfolk, but his four-year-old son was killed and another son seriously injured. Lady Henrietta's cousin, Tara Browne, had died in a car crash in Chelsea in 1966.

Jinxes can perform to the most exacting timetables. The Milli family, from a lonely mountain village in central Italy, seem to

Below: the death of 21-year old Tara Browne – heir to the Guinness family fortune – in 1966 was only one tragedy in the long history of the family jinx. Fatal crashes and inexplicable suicides, death plunges and drug accidents have bedevilled the Guinness family

have such a jinx. On 17 January 1949 a woman in the family died, as happened on the same day in 1959 and 1969. On 17 January 1978, misfortune struck a year early when Giuseppina Milli, aged 72, died of a heart attack. On 17 January 1989 the remaining family members plan to stay in hospital, taking no chances.

Black Tuesday

This patterning effect sometimes emerges around specific days of the week as well. The Marquis of Chaumont hated Tuesday so much that he had the word cut out of all his books and papers. He was ill every Tuesday for 79 years and died on a Tuesday in 1780.

One famous periodical jinx hangs over the American presidency. Since 1840 no president elected in a year ending with a zero has survived his term of office. Pneumonia took off William H. Harrison (elected in 1840). Lincoln (1860), Garfield (1880), McKinley (whose second term began in 1900) and Kennedy (1960) were all assassinated while still in office. Harding (1920) had a heart attack; Roosevelt (1940) died of polio. And there has already been one assassination attempt on Reagan (1980).

There is a jinxed aria in Halévy's opera *Charles VI*, which was premiered at the Opéra Comique in Paris in 1852. As the celebrated tenor Maffiani sang 'Oh God, smash him', meaning the traitorous villain, he lifted his eyes to the ceiling. One of the stage hands immediately toppled to his death from a perch aloft. Maffiani was inconsolable, and the following morning the newspapers were calling it the 'Curse Aria'. On the next night when he sang it he fixed his eyes on an empty box. Suddenly, the curtains of the box parted and a man taking his seat swayed and toppled to his death. On the third night the tenor sang the aria staring at the floor, but a musician in the orchestra pit played off-key. Maffiani glared at him and he died of a heart attack.

One of the most famous periodical jinxes hangs over American presidents who are elected in years ending with a zero. Abraham Lincoln (left, centre), who came to office in 1860, McKinley (left), who was elected in 1900 for the second time, Roosevelt (bottom centre), whose third term as president began in 1940, and John F. Kennedy (below), who was elected in 1960, all died during their terms of office. And there has already been one attempt on the life of Ronald Reagan (bottom), who was elected in 1980

Further performances were cancelled, but in 1858 Napoleon III asked Halévy to stage *Charles VI* for him. On the night before the performance Napoleon and Eugénie narrowly escaped bombs hurled by Italian revolutionaries. The opera was cancelled and has never been staged since.

Various stretches of railway and road appear to have jinxes on them. The railway line between Acklington and Belford in Northumberland, a distance of 21 miles (34 kilometres), has been dubbed the 'hoodoo line'. Passengers just fall out of 'secure' doors on London to Edinburgh expresses. Two lives were lost within 18 days in August 1980, exactly a year after an identical death fall. A young sailor had also died on the same stretch in 1978. British Rail remain mystified.

A 100-yard (90-metre) section of the M4 motorway between Swindon and Chippenham in Wiltshire claimed four lives within a week in the spring of 1979. Traffic experts could find no obvious cause. Equally baffling were a string of fatal 'carbon-copy' accidents at night on a stretch of the Sevenoaks bypass between Gracious Lane Bridge and Chipstead flyover in Kent. In each case the driver swerved inexplicably across the grass verge separating the two carriageways.

In the first crash in November 1977, three people lost their lives. Then in May 1978 three young men died 100 yards (90 metres away. In the following August another young man in a car swerved to his death, and in February 1979 a mother and her son heading for Tonbridge were killed when another car left the northbound carriageway and hit them head-on.

Road to dusty death

A possible clue lies in the unnerving experience of Mrs Babs Davidson, an employee of British Telecom. She was driving home in winter moonlight along the jinxed road around the time of the last-mentioned crash. She knew the road well, but suddenly the way ahead was no longer familiar. Part of it was blacked out and a road she had never seen before forked mistily away to her right. 'I felt a tremendous compulsion to take it,' she recalled, 'but forced myself to go on. I was very relieved when I found I had done the right thing and was still heading north on the carriageway.' The appearance of a ghost road could easily be dismissed as an hallucination due to fatigue, but Mrs Davidson claims to have seen it on two subsequent occasions, although she is unable to identify the spot exactly. And usually her claims have been taken seriously by Department of Transport investigators looking for the cause of the crashes.

Many jinxes seem to be analogous to an outbreak of disease that infects a few victims and then peters out. Behavioural syndromes

Left: the jinxed stretch of the Sevenoaks bypass in Kent, between Gracious Lane Bridge and Chipstead flyover, where several fatal 'carbon copy' accidents took place in the late 1970s. One driver who avoided disaster was Mrs Babs Davidson who, on three occasions, claims to have seen a 'ghost' road branching off the main carriageway. She felt an overwhelming urge to follow it, but managed to continue on her route. Had the other drivers succumbed and taken the ghost road – to their deaths?

such as mass faintings and the spread of rumours and panic also seem to fit this pattern.

Films about the occult often seem to engender such an outbreak, their productions plagued with accidents, illness and death. *The omen I* was typical. Star Gregory Peck's aeroplane was struck by lightning, as was one carrying author David Seltzer and Robert Munger, who devised the film. Director Richard Donner had a rough flight too and was later hit by a car. Lightning struck the building next to his Rome hotel. Special effects man John Richardson was in a car accident with a lorry in Holland, and his passenger was killed. When he regained consciousness, he saw a milestone for the town of Ommen. A pack of dogs ran amok and injured two stuntmen, and a zoo keeper was killed by a tiger the day the film crew left the zoo.

Casualties of curses?

We all know, or have read about, accident-prone people. Whether they suffer from some elusive behavioural 'infection' or had a curse put on them at an early age by some ill-disposed person, it is impossible to say. Perhaps someone (or something) 'up there' (or wherever) is trying to get a message through to the hapless victims.

Brian Challender, a bricklayer from Bournemouth, Dorset, was born on a Friday the 13th, which he believes accounts for his run of misfortune. As a boy he had a bad bicycle accident, was knocked out by a golf club and attacked by a man with an axe. He was stabbed at a fairground, pinned down by a 55-tonne motorway earth mover, trapped under a garage door, stunned by falling metal on a building site (he had removed his hard hat in the heat to cool down), scarred for life by steam and rammed by a rowing boat off Bournemouth pier. His last recorded disaster was when he was bending down to pick up a pin for good luck – he was knocked unconscious by a falling brick.

Besides the accident-prone, there are the 'Jonahs', those people who always seem to be around to witness the misfortune of others. A certain Mrs Murray was a passenger on the final journeys of three doomed ships: the *Titanic*, the *Lusitania* and the *Celtic*, which was rammed by the *Anaconda* in 1927. It happens on land too. Dr Max Benis, a specialist in allergies, has been on hand at least 19 times to help people in distress. Wherever he goes people touch live wires, choke on their food, begin to drown or fall off high rocks. Said the *Daily Mail* of 6 December 1977, 'not many of the victims seem particularly grateful to Dr Max.'

Also within this category are people who seem to trigger illness in others in some unfathomable way. The classic example is 'Typhoid Mary', a cook in New York in 1906. Several people contracted typhoid and she was detained in hospital for three years, even though she was not suffering from typhoid herself. After her release she returned to work as a cook under various aliases. About five years later, 25 people in the Sloane Maternity Hospital, New York, went down with the disease and two died. Mary was cooking at the hospital and was detained again.

Below: the *Lusitania*, which sank in 1915. A certain Mrs Murray survived not only the wreck of this ship but also that of the *Titanic*, in 1912, and that of the *Celtic*, in 1927. Jinx, curse – or some kind of *good* luck?

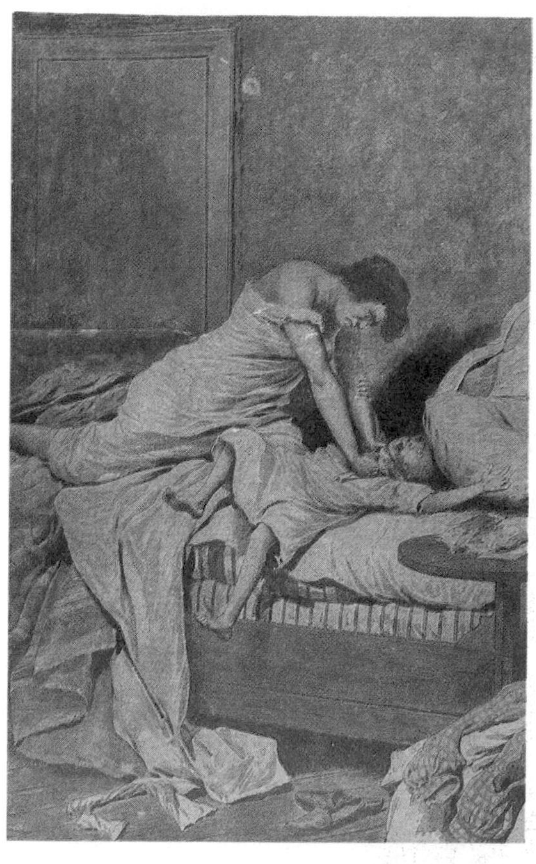

Left: the popular view of the 'crimes' of the Frenchwoman Jeanne Weber, known as 'the Ogress'. Accused of murdering several children in the early 1900s, she was finally acquitted – for it seemed that she was one of those unfortunate people whose mere presence causes the sudden, inexplicable death of others

Below: Wesley MacIntire is carried from the wreck of the Sunshine Skyway Bridge in Florida, USA, which was rammed by a freighter in May 1980 (bottom). He was the sole survivor of this disaster and has emerged unscathed from many others. He devoutly hopes that his life is not being preserved by Providence just for one final accident

The case of Jeanne Weber, known throughout France as 'the Ogress', is featured in this author's book *Man bites man* (1981). In 1906 she was accused of murdering two of her children and two of her nephews. The children had died after being alone with her, but the deaths were proved to be natural and she was acquitted. The following year she was staying in the house of a woodcutter when a small child died of convulsions while sitting on her knee. After two further trials she was acquitted.

More recently, four children died and three narrowly escaped death while being watched over by an 18-year-old epileptic, Christine Fallings of Blountstown, Florida, USA. In February 1980, the first died of encephalitis, an inflammation of the brain. A few days later, another nearly died of meningitis. In February 1981, after Christine had moved to Lakeland, Florida, two young brothers in her care went into convulsions, but recovered after emergency treatment. A few days later, on 23 February, Christine was looking after another boy when he died of myocarditis, an inflammation of the heart muscle. Three days later, the same disease killed another of her charges. Finally, on 14 July 1981, a little girl died in her arms after being inoculated against diphtheria, whooping cough and tetanus. Extensive medical tests showed that Christine was not carrying any communicable diseases. She told the Florida newspaper *Sentinel Star*: 'Sometimes I wonder if I don't have some kind of spell over me when I get around young'uns.'

Another category of jinxed folk are those who constantly emerge unscathed from accidents. The life story of Wesley MacIntire illustrates this rather well. On 9 May 1980 a freighter rammed the Sunshine Skyway Bridge in Florida, USA. Thirty-five people were killed, and the sole survivor was MacIntire, who swam to the surface when his pick-up truck plunged into the river.

During the Second World War when he was in the navy he had dived off the side of his

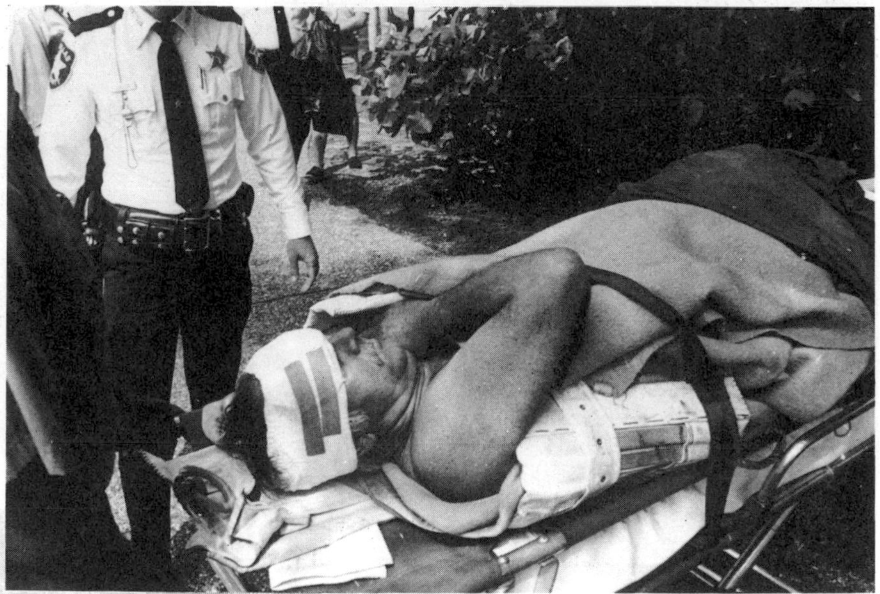

ship seconds before it was bombed. Later, as a lorry driver, he drove a 20-tonne load of gravel $1\frac{1}{2}$ miles (2.5 kilometres) down a mountainside after his brakes failed, and managed to spin the lorry round and round in a parking lot until it stopped. In 1959 he crashed a container lorry loaded with explosive gases. It did not explode. Then an air tank in another lorry he was driving did explode, but MacIntire was saved by his mattress. There were many other accidents that he managed to survive. 'The only thing I can think of,' he said, 'is that the Good Lord must really be saving me up for something. I hope it's not another accident.'

Coincidences and connections

Below: the German philosopher Arthur Schopenhauer (1788–1860), who believed that coincidences were a reflection of the 'wonderful pre-established harmony' of the Universe

Every one of us has, at some time, experienced a coincidence. Mathematicians explain them away as mere chance events – but there are those who seek deeper reasons. PERROTT PHILLIPS investigates

ON THE EVENING OF 28 JULY 1900, King Umberto I of Italy dined with his aide in a restaurant in Monza, where he was due to attend an athletics meeting the next day. With astonishment, he noticed that the proprietor looked exactly like him and, speaking to him, he discovered that there were other similarities.

The restaurateur was also called Umberto; like the King, he had been born in Turin – and on the same day; and he had married a girl called Margherita on the day the King married his Queen Margherita. And he had opened his restaurant on the day that Umberto I was crowned King of Italy.

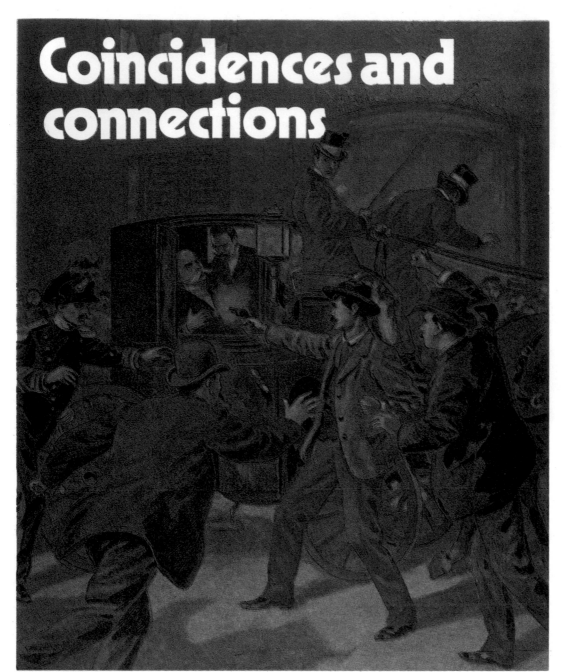

Above: the assassination of King Umberto I of Italy by the anarchist Bresci on 29 July 1900. His death and important events in his life were astonishingly closely paralleled by the life of another Umberto – a restaurant proprietor in a small town in northern Italy

The King was intrigued, and invited his double to attend the athletics meeting with him. But next day at the stadium the King's aide informed him that the restaurateur had died that morning in a mysterious shooting accident. And even as the King expressed his regret, he himself was shot dead by an anarchist in the crowd.

Another strange coincidence connected with a death occurred much more recently. On Sunday 6 August 1978 the little alarm clock that Pope Paul VI had bought in 1923 – and that for 55 years had woken him at six every morning – rang suddenly and shrilly. But it was not six o'clock: the time was 9.40 p.m. and, for no explicable reason, the clock started ringing as the Pope lay dying. Later, Father Romeo Panciroli, a Vatican spokesman, commented, 'It was most strange. The

The Renaissance philosopher Pico della Mirandola, one of a long line of thinkers, starting with Hippocrates, the 'father of medicine', who believed that the world was governed by a principle of wholeness – and that coincidences could be explained as like events seeking each other out

These foolish things...

The most striking coincidences often involve the most commonplace of objects or occasions, like the bizarre experience related by the Chicago newspaper columnist Irv Kupcinet (left):

'I had just checked into the Savoy Hotel in London. Opening a drawer in my room, I found, to my astonishment, that it contained some personal things belonging to a friend of mine, Harry Hannin, then with the Harlem Globetrotters basketball team.

'Two days later, I received a letter from Harry, posted in the Hotel Meurice, in Paris, which began "You'll never believe this." Apparently, Harry had opened a drawer in *his* room and found a tie with my name on it. It was a room I had stayed in a few months earlier.'

Pope was very fond of the clock. He bought it in Poland and always took it with him on his trips.'

Every one of us has experienced a coincidence – however trivial – at some time or other. But some of the extreme examples seem to defy all logic, luck or reason.

Powers of the Universe

It is not surprising, therefore, that the 'theory of coincidence' has excited scientists, philosophers and mathematicians for more than 2000 years. Running like a thread through all their theories and speculations is one theme: what are coincidences about? Do they have a hidden message for us? What unknown force do they represent? Only in this century have any real answers been suggested, answers that strike at the very roots of established science and prompt the question: are there powers in the Universe of which we are still only dimly aware?

Early cosmologists believed that the world was held together by a kind of principle of wholeness. Hippocrates, known as the father of medicine, who lived at some time between 460 and 375 BC, believed the Universe was joined together by 'hidden affinities' and wrote: 'There is one common flow, one common breathing, all things are in sympathy.' According to this theory, coincidence could be explained by 'sympathetic' elements seeking each other out.

The Renaissance philosopher Pico della Mirandola wrote in 1557: 'Firstly, there is a unity in things whereby each thing is at one with itself. Secondly, there is the unity whereby one creature is united with the others and all parts of the world constitute one world.'

This belief has continued, in a barely altered form, in much more modern times. The philosopher Arthur Schopenhauer (1788–1860) defined coincidence as 'the simultaneous occurrence of causally unconnected events.' He went on to suggest that simultaneous events ran in parallel lines and the selfsame event, although a link in

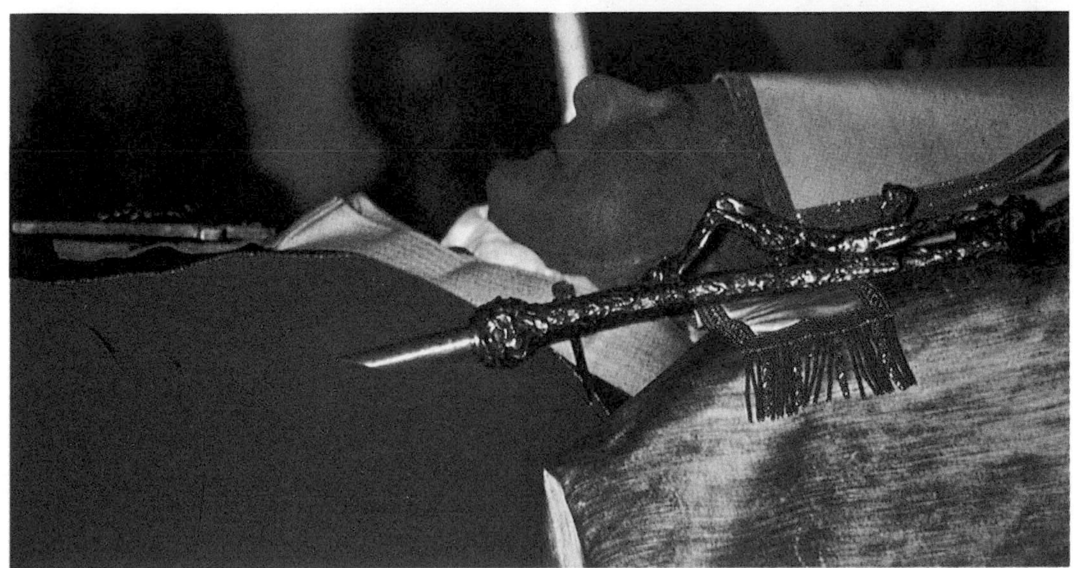

The lying-in-state of Pope Paul VI. At 9.40 p.m. on 6 August 1978, as the Pope lay dying, his bedside alarm clock – set for six in the morning – inexplicably began to ring

totally different chains, nevertheless falls into place in both, so that the fate of one individual invariably fits the fate of another, and each is the hero of his own drama while simultaneously figuring in a drama foreign to him. This is something that surpasses our powers of comprehension and can only be conceived as possible by the virtue of the most wonderful pre-established harmony. Everyone must participate in it. Thus everything is interrelated and mutually attuned.

Probing the future

The idea of a 'collective unconscious' – an underground storehouse of memories through which minds can communicate – has been debated by several thinkers. One of the more extreme theories to explain coincidence was put forward by the British mathematician Adrian Dobbs in the 1960s. He coined the word 'psitron' to describe an unknown force that probed, like radar, a second time dimension that was probabilistic rather than deterministic. The psitron absorbed future probabilities and relayed them back to the present, bypassing the normal human senses and somehow conveying the information directly to the brain.

The first person to study the laws of coincidence scientifically was Dr Paul Kammerer, Director of the Institute of Experimental Biology in Vienna. From the age of 20, he started to keep a 'logbook' of coincidences. Many were essentially trivial: people's names that kept cropping up in separate conversations, successive concert or cloakroom tickets with the same number, a phrase in a book that kept recurring in real life. For hours, Kammerer sat on park

Dr Paul Kammerer who, in 1919, published the first systematic study of coincidence

benches recording the people who wandered past, noting their sex, age, dress, whether they carried walking sticks or umbrellas. After making the necessary allowances for things like rush-hour, weather and time of year, he found the results broke down into 'clusters of numbers' of a kind familiar to statisticians, gamblers, insurance companies and opinion pollsters.

Kammerer called the phenomenon 'seriality', and in 1919 he published his conclusions in a book called *Das Gesetz der Serie* (The law of seriality). Coincidences, he claimed, came in series – or 'a recurrence or clustering in time or space whereby the individual numbers in the sequence are not connected by the same active cause.'

Coincidence, suggested Kammerer, was merely the tip of an iceberg in a larger cosmic principle that mankind, as yet, hardly recognises.

Like gravity, it is a mystery; but unlike gravity, it acts selectively to bring together in space and time things that possess some affinity. 'We thus arrive,' he concluded, 'at the image of a world mosaic or cosmic kaleidoscope, which, in spite of constant shufflings and rearrangements, also takes care of bringing like and like together.'

The great leap forward happened 50 years later, when two of Europe's most brilliant minds collaborated to produce the most searching book on the powers of coincidence – one that was to provoke both controversy and attack from rival theorists.

The two men were Wolfgang Pauli – whose daringly conceived exclusion principle earned him the Nobel Prize for Physics – and the Swiss psychologist-philosopher, Professor Carl Gustav Jung. Their treatise bore the unexciting title: *Synchronicity, an*

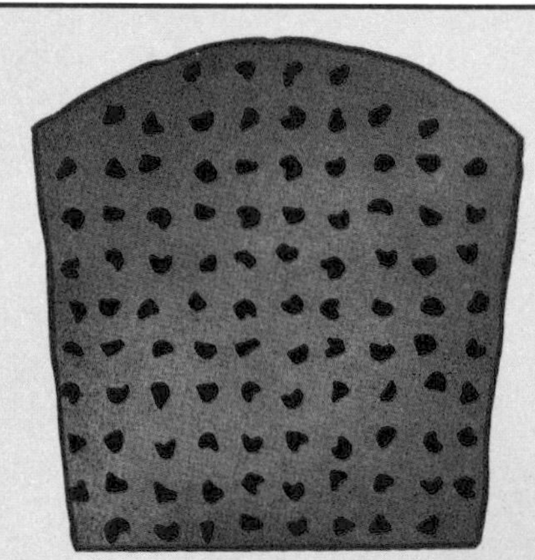

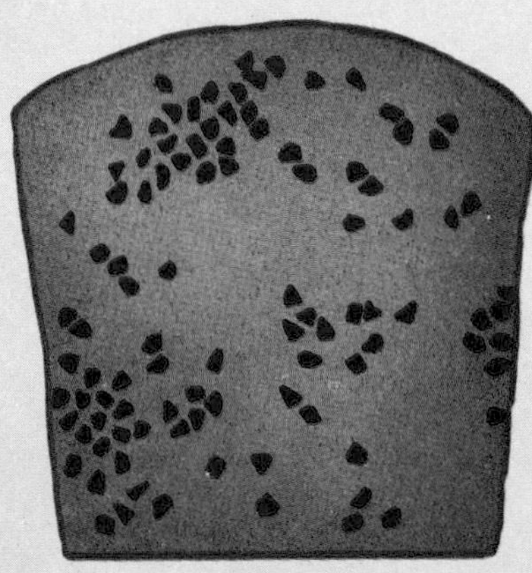

In his book *Homo Faber* Max Frisch tells the extraordinary story of a man who, through a series of coincidences, meets the daughter he never knew he had, falls in love with her and sets in motion a train of events that results in her death. But Faber, a rational man, refuses to see anything more than the laws of chance in his story:

'I don't deny that it was more than a coincidence which made things turn out as they did, it was a whole series of coincidences. . . . The occasional occurrence of the improbable does not imply the intervention of a higher power. . . . The term probability includes improbability at the extreme limits of probability, and when the improbable does occur this is no cause for surprise, bewilderment or mystification.'

Few people could be so matter-of-fact in the face of the events Frisch describes – but Faber may be right. Every mathematician knows that a random distribution of events produces – surprisingly – a clustering effect, just as cherries randomly distributed in a cake will tend to be found in groups (left) rather than in the orderly arrangement one might expect (far left). The mathematician is not surprised by coincidences, or clusters of random events – but neither can he predict them!

Above: Wolfgang Pauli (1900–1958), the Nobel prize-winning physicist who, together with the eminent psychologist C.G. Jung, introduced the concept of *synchronicity* to help explain the occurrence of coincidences

Right: the decorated dome of the mosque of Madresh, Isfahan, Iran. The pattern represents the eternal pilgrimage of the soul – it unrolls in a continuous thread like the breath of the Universe, by which all things are connected. Modern physics suggests that this idea of 'interconnectedness' may be of use in providing non-causal explanations of events that are now dismissed as coincidence

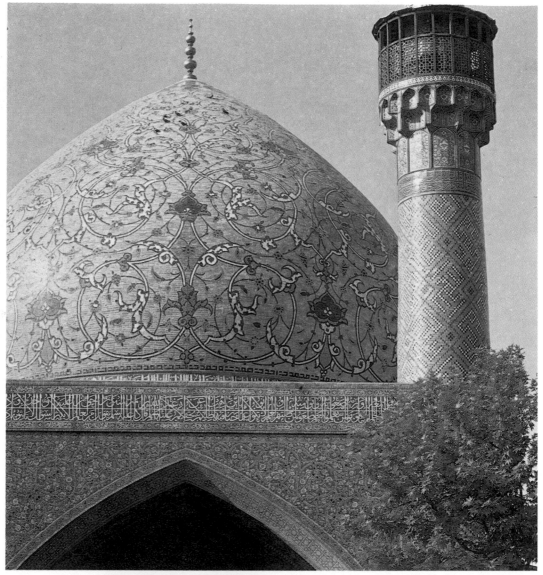

acausal connecting principle. Described by one American reviewer as 'the paranormal equivalent of a nuclear explosion', it used the term 'synchronicity' to extend Kammerer's theory of seriality.

Order out of chaos

According to Pauli, coincidences were 'the visible traces of untraceable principles'. Coincidences, elaborated Jung, whether they come singly or in series, are manifestations of a barely understood universal principle that operates quite independently of the known laws of physics. Interpreters of the Pauli-Jung theory have concluded that telepathy, precognition and coincidences themselves are all manifestations of a single mysterious force at work in the Universe that is trying to impose its own kind of discipline on the utter confusion of human life.

Of all contemporary thinkers, none has written more extensively about the theory of coincidence than Arthur Koestler, who sums up the phenomenon in the vivid phrase 'puns of destiny'.

One particularly striking 'pun' was related to Koestler by a 12-year-old English schoolboy named Nigel Parker:

Above: Arthur Koestler, a science journalist who has written extensively about the search for a scientific explanation of coincidence – and its philosophical implications. It was he who coined the apt phrase 'puns of destiny' to describe the phenomenon

> Many years ago, the American horror-story writer, Edgar Allan Poe, wrote a book called *The narrative of Arthur Gordon Pym.* In it, Mr Pym was travelling in a ship that wrecked. The four survivors were in an open boat for many days before they decided to kill and eat the cabin boy whose name was Richard Parker.
>
> Some years *later*, in the summer of 1884, my great-grandfather's cousin was cabin boy in the yawl *Mignonette* when she foundered, and the four survivors were in an open boat for many days. Eventually, the three senior members of the crew killed and ate the cabin boy. His name was Richard Parker.

Such strange and seemingly meaningful incidents abound – can there really be no more to them than mere coincidence?

Against all the odds

It is a curious fact that the most striking coincidences often involve the most trivial of events. If, as many people believe, coincidences have some inner meaning, why are they apparently so pointless?

THE BRITISH ACTOR Anthony Hopkins was delighted to hear he had landed a leading role in a film based on the book *The girl from Petrovka* by George Feifer. A few days after signing the contract, Hopkins travelled to London to buy a copy of the book. He tried several bookshops, but there wasn't one to be had. Waiting at Leicester Square underground station for his train home, he noticed a book lying apparently discarded on a bench. Incredibly, it was *The girl from Petrovka*. That in itself would have been coincidence enough, but in fact it was merely the beginning of an extraordinary chain of events. Two years later, in the middle of filming in Vienna, Hopkins was visited by George Feifer, the author. Feifer mentioned that he did not have a copy of his own book. He had lent the last one – containing his own annotations – to a friend who had lost it somewhere in London. With mounting astonishment, Hopkins handed Feifer the book he had found. 'Is this the one?' he asked, 'with the notes scribbled in the margins?' It was the same book.

Dr Paul Kammerer, the former Director of the Institute of Experimental Biology in Vienna – and one of the first men to try to define the 'laws of coincidence' – would have relished that example. He was particularly fond of literary coincidences, and there are several in his book *Das Gesetz der Serie* ('The law of seriality'), published in 1919, which introduced the theory of 'seriality'.

Kammerer's work was also too early to include another literary coincidence, which was experienced by Dame Rebecca West, the novelist and historian. She found herself at a dead end when she went to the Royal Institute of International Affairs to research a specific episode in the Nuremberg trials:

> I looked up the Trials in the library and was horrified to find they were published in a form almost useless to the researcher. After hours of search, I went along the line of shelves to an assistant librarian and said, 'I can't find it, there's no clue, it could be *any* of these volumes.' I put my hand on one volume on a shelf, took it out and carelessly looked at it. It was not only the right volume out of hundreds, but it had fallen open at the right page.

British actor Anthony Hopkins (right) found himself caught up in an extraordinary sequence of events when he picked up a book in an underground station in London. Amazingly, it was *The girl from Petrovka* by George Feifer (below), whose film version he was to star in – and it was Feifer's own copy

Bottom: Dame Rebecca West, who experienced a classic case of both 'literary' and 'helpful' coincidence when she had come to a dead end in her research

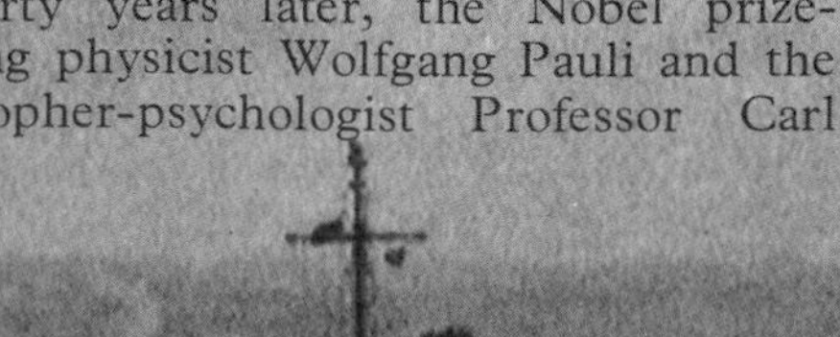

Kammerer – who committed suicide in 1926 – suggested that coincidences occurred in series or clusters and defined 'seriality' as 'a recurrence of the same or similar things or events in time or space.' Seriality, he concluded, 'is ubiquitous and continuous in life, nature and cosmos. It is the umbilical cord that connects thought, feeling, science and art with the womb of the universe which gave birth to them.'

Thirty years later, the Nobel prize-winning physicist Wolfgang Pauli and the philosopher-psychologist Professor Carl

Gustav Jung extended Kammerer's work with their theory of 'synchronicity'. Jung defined the word as 'the simultaneous occurrence of two meaningful but not causally connected events . . . a coincidence in time of two or more causally unrelated events which have the same or similar meaning.'

Although approaching the theory of coincidences from different directions, all three men hinted at a mysterious and barely understood force at work in the Universe, a force that was trying to impose its own kind of order on the chaos of human life.

If this seems fanciful, one of the most prolific of all contemporary thinkers on the subject, Arthur Koestler, points out that current biological – as well as physical – research strongly suggests a basic tendency of nature to create order out of disorder.

Not surprisingly, sceptics reject these theories. They explain coincidence in terms of the laws of probability: if something *can* happen then, however small the probability of the event, you should not be too surprised if it eventually *does* happen. A classic example is that a monkey at a typewriter, pressing the keys at random, will eventually – 'as time tends to infinity', as the mathematicians say – type out the entire works of Shakespeare. As science writer Martin Gardner puts it, 'Trillions of events, large and trivial, happen to billions of human beings every day. Therefore, it is inevitable that surprising things occur now and again.'

Another example is the unlikely chance of a bridge player being dealt all 13 cards of one suit. The odds are something like 635 billion to one. Yet, according to probability theory, if enough bridge hands are dealt, it will eventually happen. And indeed it did. Vera Nettick, of Princeton, New Jersey, found herself holding all 13 diamonds. She bid a grand slam and had the memorable experience of being able to lay her incredible hand down on the table.

The followers of seriality and synchronicity – and their later developments – think otherwise. Dealing cards and spinning coins are one thing, they claim. But bizarre coincidences that throw together people or events represent an entirely different force at work.

In his early researches, Kammerer classified coincidences – and he had collected hundreds of examples, often quite trivial, to support his theories – into various types. These mainly depended on the order in which they occurred, the number of parallel coincidences, whether they related to names numbers or situations, and the elements they had in common.

Modern research now divides coincidences into two main categories, the trivial – like the incredible bridge hand – and the significant. Significant coincidences are subdivided into clearly recognisable types: the literary coincidence (like Dame Rebecca West's experience in the library), warning coincidences, useful coincidences (where the right thing happens at the right time), it's-a-small-world coincidences (bringing people together when least expected) and conjuring coincidences, incidents that are like examples of psychic sleight-of-hand.

Nazis in Fleet Street?

There are classic examples in each category, but the quintessential literary coincidence happened just before the Allied invasion of Europe in 1944.

Every aspect of the huge campaign – to drive out the Nazis and end the Second World War – was top secret and referred to only by codewords. The operation itself was known as OVERLORD. The naval spearhead was disguised by the name NEPTUNE. The two French beaches where the landing was to take place were coded UTAH and OMAHA. And the artificial harbours to be used to supply the troops at the beach-head were known as MULBERRY.

Incredibly, in the 33 days before D-Day, 6 June, each of these secret words appeared as the answer to a clue in the London *Daily*

Left: by an amazing coincidence, many of the key code-words used in the strategic planning of the Allied invasion of Europe in 1944 – OVERLORD, NEPTUNE, MULBERRY, UTAH, OMAHA – appeared as solutions to *Daily Telegraph* crossword clues in the weeks before D-Day. Security men quickly checked the *Telegraph* offices – but found no Nazi spy, only schoolmaster Leonard Dawe, who had been compiling the crossword for 20 years

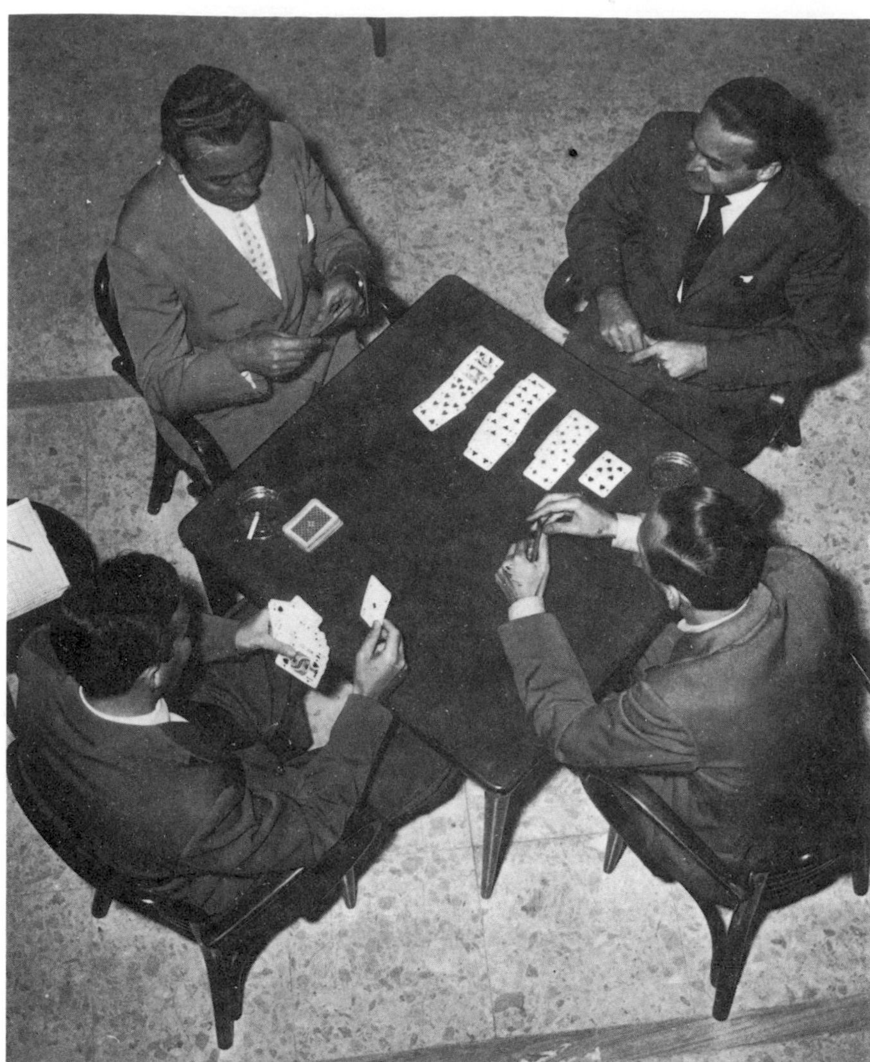

Telegraph crossword. The key word OVERLORD appeared only four days before the landing.

Security men immediately descended on the Fleet Street offices of the *Telegraph*, expecting to bag a Nazi spy. Instead, they found schoolmaster Leonard Dawe, who had been harmlessly compiling the paper's crossword for 20 years. Dawe was flabbergasted, and took a long time to convince them that he had been totally ignorant of the significance of the words.

The clairvoyant photograph

For an extraordinary conjuring coincidence, however, one can do no better than listen to the curious, and strangely inconsequential, experience of Mrs Eileen Bithell, of Portsmouth, Hampshire.

'For more than 20 years, a framed sign saying Closed on Wednesdays hung in the window of my parents' grocery shop. A few days before my brother's wedding, the sign was taken down to be altered. When we removed it from the frame, we discovered to our surprise that the sign had been painted on the back of a photograph. There was an even bigger surprise. The picture showed my brother's bride-to-be as a small girl, in the arms of his future father-in-law.

'Nobody knows how this particular photograph came to be used as the shop sign. For none of the people were known to my family at the time the sign was put up. Yet now, 20 years later, our two families were to be joined in marriage.'

Coincidences like these support the view of Sir James Jeans, the British scientist who died in 1946, who once commented, 'the stream of knowledge is heading towards a non-mechanical reality; the universe begins to look more like a great thought than a great machine' – or, as Eddington put it, 'The stuff of the world is mind-stuff.'

Top: a game of bridge in progress. Card games provide the opportunity for the most spectacular, if trivial, of coincidences

Above: Sir James Jeans (1877–1946), the eminent physicist who remarked that science shows that the Universe looks more like 'a great thought than a great machine'

The rational and the occult

In his book *The challenge of chance*, Arthur Koestler suggested that coincidences 'can at least serve as pointers towards a single major mystery – the spontaneous emergence of order out of randomness, and the philosophical challenge implied in that concept. And if that sounds too rational or too occult, collecting coincidences still remains an amusing parlour game.'

Some coincidences start slowly and seem to gain momentum as one improbability follows another. One to cap any 'parlour game' was recounted by a former Fleet Street editor, now a distinguished author. For reasons that will become obvious, all the names have been changed; here is the story:

'Around 12 years ago, when I was editor of a weekly magazine in London, I met and fell in love with a Fleet Street woman journalist named Jackie. Some time afterwards, I parted company with the magazine after a difference of opinion and immediately went, with Jackie, on a Press trip to Capri. What I *didn't* know was that, in the meantime, the girl had met someone else. She had joined a Press party aboard a Swedish ship and had fallen in love with Egon, the shipping line's PRO [public relations officer].

'Six years elapsed in which everyone changed places. Jackie and I split up. She married Egon. He eventually broke with the shipping line. They got a new PRO, a girl named Jan. And Harry was appointed editor of the magazine.

'Then, like some supernatural "action replay", it all started happening again. Harry had an almost identical difference of opinion with the management and left. He immediately went on a previously-arranged Press facility trip . . . to Capri. Who should be on the same trip – again – but Jackie. The man in charge of the visit was her husband, Egon. Meanwhile, I was on the same Swedish ship on which Jackie and Egon had first met and had been introduced to his successor, Jan, who was completely unaware of the earlier relationships. We are now married. And all five of us live in the same area.'

Strange tricks of fate

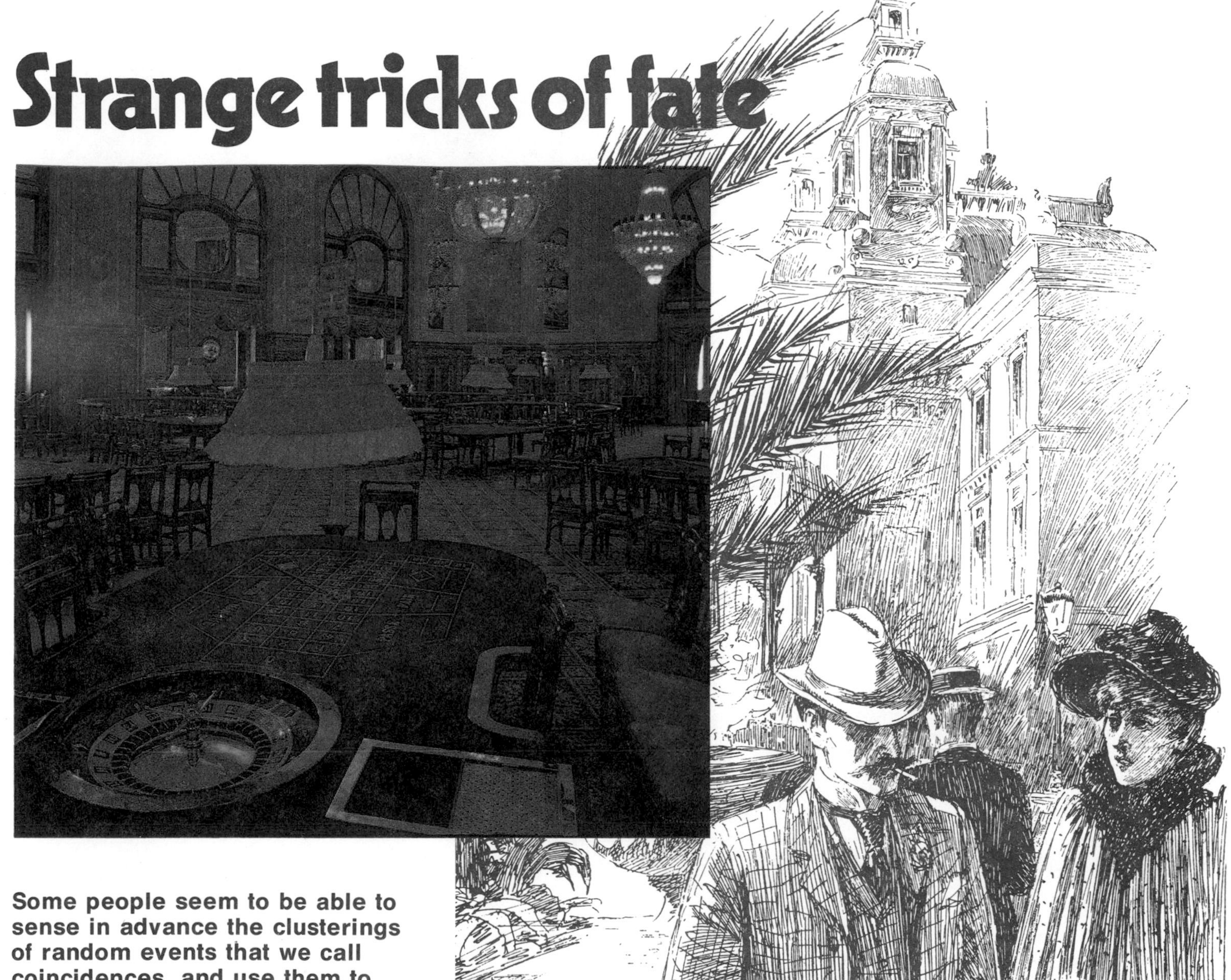

Some people seem to be able to sense in advance the clusterings of random events that we call coincidences, and use them to their advantage.

IT WAS ONLY WHEN his train steamed into Louisville station that George D. Bryson decided to break his trip to New York and visit the historic Kentucky town. He had never been there before and he had to ask where to find the best hotel. Nobody knew he was in Louisville, and, as a joke, he asked the desk clerk at the Brown Hotel, 'Any mail for me?' He was astonished when the clerk handed over a letter addressed to him and bearing his room number. The previous occupant of Room 307 had been another, and entirely different, George D. Bryson.

A remarkable coincidence, by any standards, but made particularly piquant by the fact that the man who tells it most frequently is Dr Warren Weaver, the American mathematician and expert on probabilities, who believes in the theory that coincidences are governed by the laws of chance, and rejects any suggestion of the uncanny or paranormal in coincidences.

On the opposite side of the fence are those who follow the 'seriality' or 'synchronicity' theories of Dr Paul Kammerer, Wolfgang Pauli, and Carl Gustav Jung.

Although the three men approached the theory of coincidences from different directions, their conclusions all hinted at a mysterious and barely understood force at work in the Universe, a force that was trying to impose its own kind of order on the chaos of our world. Modern scientific research, particularly in the fields of biology and physics, also seems to suggest a basic tendency of nature to create order out of chaos.

The sceptics, however, stand firm. When events are happening at random, they argue, you are bound to encounter the clusterings we call 'coincidence'. It is even possible to predict such clusterings or, at least, to predict the frequency with which they are likely to happen.

If you toss a coin many times, the laws of probability dictate that you will end up with an almost equal number of heads and tails. However, the heads and tails will not alternate. There will be runs of one and runs of

In 1891 an unknown Englishman named Charles Wells became an overnight sensation as *The man that broke the bank at Monte Carlo*, as a music-hall song later called him. Using no apparent system, he three times 'broke' the 100,000-franc 'bank' allocated to his roulette table at the famous Monte Carlo casino (seen as it is today, above left; in a contemporary drawing from the *Illustrated London News*, above right). Can coincidence explain how Wells was somehow able to sense the winning numbers? We shall never know; after winning for the third time, Wells disappeared, taking his secret with him. He was never seen again the other. Dr Weaver calculates that, if you toss a coin 1024 times, for instance, it is likely that there will be one run of eight tails in a row, two of seven in a row, four of six in a row and eight runs of five in a row.

The same is true of roulette. 'Evens' once came up 28 times in succession at Monte Carlo casino. The odds against this happening are around 268 million to one. Yet the randomness experts claim that, as it *could* happen, it did happen – and will happen again somewhere in the world if enough roulette wheels keep spinning long enough.

Mathematicians use this law, for example, to explain the fantastic series of winning numbers that earned Charles Wells the title – in song – of *The man that broke the bank at Monte Carlo*.

Wells – a fat and slightly sinister Englishman – became the subject of the popular music-hall ditty in 1891, when he broke the bank at the Monte Carlo casino three times. He used no apparent system, but put even money bets on red and black, winning nearly every time until he finally exceeded the 100,000 francs 'bank' allocated to each table. On each occasion, attendants lugubriously covered the table with a black 'mourning' cloth and closed it for the rest of the day. The third and last time Wells appeared at the casino, he placed his opening bet on number five, at odds of 35 to 1. He won. He left his original bet and added his winnings to it. Five came up again. This happened five times in succession. Out came the black cloth. And out went Wells with his winnings, never to be seen there again.

Above: Dr Warren Weaver, the American mathematician and probability expert whose study of coincidence has led him to oppose any suggestion that a paranormal force is involved

When a commuter train plunged from an open drawbridge into Newark Bay in New York (below), over 30 people lost their lives. By an ironic coincidence, this tragic incident won many New Yorkers large sums of money. A newspaper picture of the accident (left) showed the number 932 on the rear coach of the train, and many people, sensing some meaning in the number, put their money on it in the Manhattan numbers game – and won

The seriality and synchronicity theorists – and those who have extended the work of Kammerer, Pauli and Jung – accept the idea of 'clusters' of numbers. But they see 'luck' and 'coincidence' as two sides of the same coin. The classic paranormal concepts of ESP, telepathy and precognition – recurring elements in coincidences – might offer an alternative explanation of why some people are 'luckier' than others.

Modern research breaks coincidences down into two distinct types: trivial (like spinning coins, runs of numbers and amazing hands of cards) and significant. Significant coincidences are those that shuffle together people, events, space and time – past, present and future – in a manner that seems to cross the delicate borderline into the doubtful region of the paranormal.

Macabre significance

Sometimes a coincidence occurs that seems to link, almost capriciously, the rival theories. After a New York commuter train plunged into Newark Bay – killing many passengers – work started on recovering the coaches from the water. One front-page newspaper picture showed the rear coach being winched up, with the number 932 clearly visible on its side. That day, the number 932 came up in the Manhattan numbers game, winning hundreds of thousands of dollars for the hordes of people who – sensing an occult significance in the number – had put their money on it.

Modern researchers now divide significant coincidences into several categories. One is the warning coincidence, with its presentiment of danger or disaster.

Warning coincidences often have an extraordinarily long reach, which is why many

Coincidence links the fates of the *Titanian* (above) and the famous *Titanic*. Both hit icebergs in the same waters; but the *Titanian* survived

are ignored or go unrecognised. That was certainly the case with three ships, the *Titan*, the *Titanic* and the *Titanian*. In 1898, the American writer Morgan Robertson published a novel about a giant liner, the *Titan*, which sank one freezing April night in the Atlantic after hitting an iceberg on her maiden voyage.

Fourteen years later – in one of the world's worst sea disasters – the *Titanic* sank on a freezing April night in the Atlantic after hitting an iceberg on *her* maiden voyage.

The coincidences did not end there. The ships, both fact and fiction, were around the same tonnage and both disasters occurred in the same stretch of the ocean. Both liners were regarded as 'unsinkable', and neither carried sufficient lifeboats.

Coincidence and premonition

With the extraordinary story of the *Titanian*, the *Titan-Titanic* coincidences begin to defy human belief. On watch one night in April 1935 – during the *Titanian's* coal-run from the Tyne to Canada – crewman William Reeves began to feel a strong sense of foreboding. By the time the *Titanian* reached the spot where the two other ships had gone down, the feeling was overpowering. Could Reeves stop the ship merely because of a premonition? One thing – a *further* coincidence – made the decision for him. He had been born on the day of the *Titanic* disaster. 'Danger ahead!' he bellowed to the bridge. The words were barely out of his mouth when an iceberg loomed out of the darkness. The ship avoided it just in time.

Another category is the 'it's-a-small-world coincidence', which brings together people and places when least expected – a phenomenon vouched for by Arthur Butterworth, of Skipton, Yorkshire.

During the Second World War, while serving in the army, he ordered a secondhand book on music from a London bookseller. The book eventually reached him at his camp – disguised by the usual military postcode – in the grounds of Taverham Hall, near Norwich. Standing at the window of his army hut, he opened the parcel and, as he did so, a picture postcard – presumably used as a bookmark – fell out. The writing on one side showed the postcard had been written on 4 August 1913. To his astonishment, when he turned it over, the picture showed 'the exact view I had from my hut window at that very moment . . . Taverham Hall.'

If coincidence can reach so easily across time and space in its quest for 'order out of chaos', it is not surprising that it can stretch beyond the grave, too.

Below: Charles Coghlan, whose dead body made an immense sea journey before being cast up on the shore of his home town

While on a tour of Texas in 1899, the Canadian actor Charles Francis Coghlan was taken ill in Galveston and died. It was too far to return his remains to his home on Prince Edward Island, in the Gulf of St Lawrence – more than 3500 miles (5600 kilometres) away by the sea-route – and he was buried in a lead coffin inside a granite vault. His bones had rested less than a year when the great hurricane of September 1900 hit Galveston Island, flooding the cemetery. The vault was shattered and Coghlan's coffin floated out into the Gulf of Mexico. Slowly, it drifted along the Florida coastline and into the Atlantic, where the Gulf Stream picked it up and carried it northwards.

Eight years passed. Then, one day in October 1908, some fishermen on Prince Edward Island spotted a long, weather-scarred box floating near the shore. Coghlan's body had come home. With respect mingled with awe, his fellow islanders buried the actor in the nearby church where he had been christened as a baby.

Chance? Destiny? A mere trick of 'randomness'? Or that strange and powerful force, striving to make sense of the Universe, that some call coincidence?

The meaning of coincidence

Are coincidences merely random events, as mathematicians would have us believe – or is there much more to them? DOUGLAS HILL explores the extraordinary theory developed by the famous psychologist C.G. Jung

'COINCIDENCE' IS A WORD that is often levelled by rationalists at anyone who presumes to suggest that evidence exists for paranormal phenomena. But in recent years defenders of the paranormal have found their own weapon in the concept of 'synchronicity' developed by the great psychologist and philosopher Carl Gustav Jung.

For Jung, a tireless champion of open-mindedness, calling an event 'coincidence' did not automatically shut the door on any further examination of the facts. Coincidences happen – fact. Further and more important, coincidences often seem to have *meaning* to the percipients – also an established fact. Jung pointed out that there can be few people who have not had some experience in their lives that they recognise as 'meaningful coincidence'. Many of us may be reluctant to try to explain or evaluate these events for fear of being accused of credulity or superstition. But at the same time we often feel that there is more to them than mere chance.

In his essay on synchronicity, subtitled *An acausal connecting principle*, Jung bravely ventures into this unexplored area (which he describes as 'dark, dubious and hedged about with prejudice'). He reminds us that the natural laws by which we live are based on the principle of *causality*: if this happens, that follows. Empirical observation and experiment prove that this is so, every time. But, Jung insists, there are *facts* that the old principle of causality cannot explain.

Below: Professor J. B. Rhine, the American pioneer ESP researcher whose work was cited by Jung as objective evidence for the existence of an active force behind coincidence

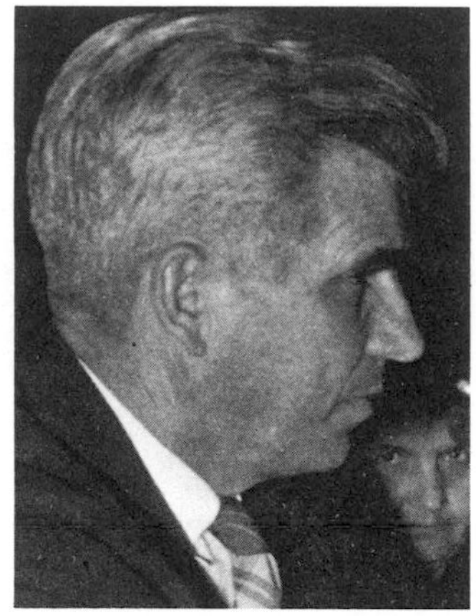

Jung's study of coincidence was stimulated by his own experiences. One extraordinary case involved a golden scarab (below), Egyptian symbol of rebirth, and its European relative, the rose scarab (right)

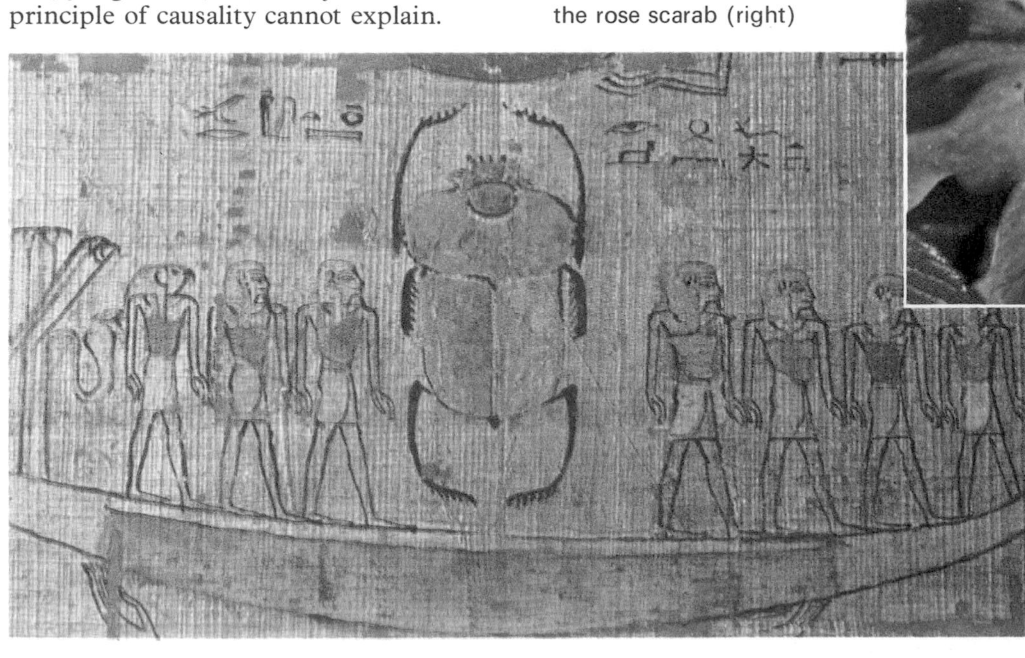

He cites evidence from the many well-authenticated phenomena gathered by psychical researchers – material on ESP collected by Dr J.B. Rhine, verified cases of precognitive or clairvoyant dreams, and the 'meaningful coincidences' chronicled by researchers such as Dr Paul Kammerer.

Jung was drawn to this mass of material by an intriguing sense that it might contribute in a major way to a greater understanding of the human psyche. In his pioneering essay on synchronicity he is concerned to 'open the field', in the hope that a more thorough and comprehensive tilling will come later. And he is doubtless right to think that his work will inspire later researchers – his preliminary thoughts are breathtaking, for anyone who can overcome prejudice.

Jung is at pains to emphasise what he sees as the true significance of many synchronistic events (his term for meaningful coincidences or 'symbolic parallels'), in which he sees a stirring or 'constellating' of *archetypes* – those immensely powerful motifs that seem to underlie human consciousness. He offers several examples of constellation from his own experience, including the case of a patient whose rationalist preconceptions had set up rigid barriers against the progress of her analysis. She was relating a dream to Jung that involved a golden scarab – a particularly potent symbol of regeneration,

especially in ancient Egypt. As she spoke, an insect flew in at the window – and, with astonishment Jung identified it as one of a species that is the closest thing to a scarab beetle that can be found in Europe. Since 'rebirth' is one way of expressing the transformation that is the goal of Jungian psychotherapy – and since this oddly resonant reinforcing of the rebirth archetype led to a breakthrough for Jung's patient – it is clear how important meaningful coincidence can be.

But isolated phenomena, however remarkable, do not help to build up a workable hypothesis, and Jung went looking for empirical material. He was well aware that he was looking in areas where the scientific establishment said such material did not exist – but then, he points out wryly, so was Galileo. In fact, he chose to examine a body of traditional processes where the idea of synchronicity is taken for granted – that is, the forms of divination that are essentially techniques designed to interpret the meanings of coincidence.

Chinese horoscopes

First he examined the *I Ching*, that ancient Chinese means of summoning our 'intuitive' faculties to aid, or even supplant, our reason in making judgements. From there he turned to traditional astrology, where he put aside the dubious and subjective 'analysis' of character traits and focused instead on a 'harder' connection: the planetary aspects,

The promising Hollywood actor James Dean (right) was killed in a tragic motoring accident in September 1955. Afterwards when the wreck (above) was towed to a garage, the engine slipped and fell onto a mechanic, breaking both his legs. The engine was bought by a doctor, who put it into a racing car and was killed shortly afterwards. In the same race, another driver was killed in a car with the drive shaft from Dean's car. Dean's car was later repaired – and a fire broke out at the garage. It was displayed in Sacramento, and fell of its mount, breaking a teenager's hip. Then, in Oregon, the truck on which the car was mounted slipped and smashed into a shop front. Finally, in 1959, it broke into 11 pieces while sitting on stationary steel supports

Below: a diagram invented by Jung and Pauli to explain their idea that acausility may be a ruling principle of the Universe

indestructible energy

constant connection through effect (causality)

inconstant connection through contingency, equivalence, or 'meaning' (synchronicity)

space-time continuum

especially conjunction of Sun and Moon, long associated by astrologers with marriage. And his empirical search turned up an interestingly high percentage of married couples whose horoscopes *did* show the aspects in question.

Jung would have been very interested in the recent work of the young French statistician Michel Gauquelin, who has sought – and found – correlations between people's professions and the presence in their horoscopes of certain astrological elements.

Perhaps inevitably, however, this aspect of Jung's research has been the one that has attracted the most censure from those who wish to discredit him. People – mostly journalists – who have never read a word of Jung's own voluminous writings are now firmly convinced that he was a credulous crank, or a charlatan, because he 'believed' in astrology, alchemy and other weird subjects. But in fact Jung's own conclusions were that, while he accepted that the results of his experiment were not statistically valid – and that, even if they were, they would not prove the validity of astrology – they did provide him with a set of data concerning the phenomenon of synchronicity.

From his observations Jung draws some conclusions about synchronicity

and the crucial role that the human psyche plays in it. Coincidences may be purely random events but, as Jung points out, as soon as they seem to carry some symbolic meaning they cease to be random as far as the person involved is concerned. He even considers the idea that the psyche may somehow be operating on external reality to 'cause' coincidences – or that, as in precognitive dreams, the external phenomena are somehow 'transmitted' to the psyche. But he quickly concludes that, because such ideas involve a suspension of our known 'laws' of space and time, we are not capable of ascertaining whether these hypotheses are relevant. And so he comes back to his own theory of an 'acausal' connecting principle governing certain chains of events.

In the face of a meaningful coincidence, Jung says, we can respond in any one of three ways. We can call it 'mere random chance', and turn away with our minds clamped shut; we can call it magic – or telepathy or telekinesis – which is not a great deal more helpful or informative. Or we can postulate the existence of a principle of acausality, and use this idea to investigate the phenomenon more thoroughly.

In the course of doing this Jung puts forward the unsettling thought that space and time may have no real objective existence. They may be only concepts created by the psyche in the course of empirical science's attempts to make rational, measurable sense of the Universe. It is certainly true that these concepts have little true meaning in the systems of thought of many primitive tribes. And, as many leading Jungians have pointed out, a great deal of damage has been done to conventional ideas of space and time by post-Einsteinian advances in particle physics, where so often causality vanishes and probability rules. So, if space and time are merely mental concepts, it is quite reasonable to suppose that they will be capable of being 'conditioned' by the psyche.

A 19th-century Chinese porcelain dish showing the eight trigrams, or symbols of the primary subdivisions of creation; the symbol in the middle represents the positive and negative forces in life, *yang* and *yin*. These concepts were central to the *I Ching*, a Chinese method of divination studied by Jung in his research into coincidences

Using this hypothesis, Jung goes on to pose a fascinating question. He assumes that, when a meaningful coincidence happens, an image – perhaps from the unconscious – comes into consciousness, and an 'outer' objective phenomenon coincides with it. The psyche perceives meaning in this juxtaposition of events. But what if the meaning could also exist *outside* the psyche? What if meaning exists within the phenomenon itself – just as causality exists, demonstrably, within objective cause-and-effect phenomena?

Rationalising the absurd

To put it another way, for clarity: we perceive causality with our minds – so, in a way, it can be regarded as a psychic event. Experiment proves that causality always obtains in 'outer', objective events so we know that it, too, has an objective existence. But equally, we perceive acausal connections (meaningful coincidences) with our minds, so we know that acausality is a mental – or psychic – phenomenon. Could it also be that it actually happens in the outer world, and so has an objective existence of its own?

In short, might it not be that acausality is a cardinal structural principle of connection that lies at the very foundation of outer reality, a fourth to join the great triad of space, time and causality?

The implications of the idea are almost too difficult to imagine – in part, as Jung was the first to appreciate, because to pursue the possibilities further involves the extraordinary task of setting the psyche to investigate the deeper reaches of itself. But this is, of course, the central purpose of depth psychology. And the rewards for attempting such a piece of research could be immense – Jung's idea of synchronicity does, at the very least, indicate vast frontiers, philosophical as well as psychological, that await exploration.

Jung made his pioneering steps untroubled by his awareness that he would have to travel along some paths in the 'dark and dubious' areas that orthodox science is inclined to dismiss as superstition – mankind's ancient and still thriving traditions of divination, magic and the paranormal. We may still hope that a time will come when fear, prejudice and mental laziness will no longer prevent other people from setting out to determine whether Jung's idea of synchronicity may indeed lead to new ways of perceiving the nature of mind, the nature of matter – and the nature of Nature itself.

Above: a sharpened version of the first photograph (right), which shows Frances Griffiths behind a group of dancing fairies. Photographic experts examined the negative and the print but could find no trace of trickery

The case of the Cottingley fairies

All of us, when we were children, believed in fairies. Here, JOE COOPER tells the extraordinary story of two little girls who not only believed in fairies, but made friends with them – and even captured them on film

IN THE WEEK BEFORE the end of the First World War, 11-year-old Frances Griffiths sent a letter to a friend in South Africa, where she had lived most of her life. Dated 9 November 1918, it ran:

> Dear Joe [Johanna],
>
> I hope you are quite well. I wrote a letter before, only I lost it or it got mislaid. Do you play with Elsie and Nora Biddles? I am learning French, Geometry, Cookery and Algebra at school now. Dad came home from France the other week after being there ten months, and we all think the war will be over in a few days. We are going to get our flags to hang upstairs in our bedroom. I am sending two photos, both of me, one of me in a bathing costume in our back yard, Uncle Arthur took that, while the other is me with some fairies up the beck, Elsie took that one. Rosebud is as fat as ever and I have made her some new clothes. How are Teddy and dolly?

An ordinary and matter-of-fact letter from a schoolgirl to her friend, one might say, apart from the rather startling reference to fairies. But, as both Frances and her cousin Elsie Wright have since pointed out (they are now grandmothers), they were not particularly surprised by seeing fairies; they seemed a natural part of the rural countryside around the 'beck' (stream) at the bottom of the long garden in Cottingley, near Bradford, in West Yorkshire.

The photograph enclosed by Frances – the famous one, which has since been reproduced thousands of times around the world, albeit in an improved and sharpened version – showed a little girl staring firmly at a camera, since fairies were frequently to be seen, but she herself was photographed not so often! On the back of the snap was scrawled in untidy schoolgirl writing:

> Elsie and I are very friendly with the beck Fairies. It is funny I never used to see thém in Africa. It must be too hot for them there.

Elsie had borrowed her father's camera – a Midg quarter-plate – one Saturday afternoon in July 1917 in order to take Frances's photo and cheer her up (for her cousin had fallen in the beck and been scolded for wetting her clothes). They were away for about half an hour and Mr Wright developed the plate later in the afternoon. He was surprised to see strange white shapes coming up, imagining them to be first birds and then sandwich papers left lying around; in vain Elsie behind him in the dark-room said they were fairies.

In August it was Frances who had the camera, when she and Elsie scaled the sides of the beck and went up to the old oaks. There she took a photograph of Elsie with a gnome. The print was under-exposed and unclear, as might be expected when taken by a young lady rising 10 years old. The plate was again developed by Elsie's father, Arthur, who suspected that the girls had been playing tricks and refused to lend his camera to them any more.

Parents turn sleuth

Both Arthur and his wife, Polly, searched the girls' bedroom and waste-paper basket for any scraps of pictures or cut-outs, and also went down to the beck in search of evidence of fakery. They found nothing, and the girls stuck to their story – that they had seen fairies and photographed them. Prints of the pictures were circulated among friends and neighbours, but then interest in the odd affair gradually petered out.

The matter first became public in the summer of 1919 when Polly Wright went to a meeting at the Theosophical Society in Bradford. She was interested in the occult, having had some experiences of astral projection and memories of past lives herself. The lecture that night was on 'fairy life', and Polly mentioned to the person sitting next to her that fairy prints had been taken by her daughter and niece. The result of this conversation was that two 'rough prints' (as they were later called) came to the notice of Theosophists at the Harrogate conference in the autumn, and thence to a leading Theosophist, Edward Gardner, by early 1920.

Mr Gardner was a precise, particular man. Even a look at his photograph conveys this precision, which is also suggested by the neat copies he kept of his letters. Gardner's immediate impulse after seeing the fairy pictures was to clarify the prints and, in a letter to a photographic expert, Fred Barlow, he describes the instructions he gave to his assistants:

> Then I told them to make new negatives (from the positives of the originals) and do the very best with them short of altering anything mechanically. The result was that they turned out two first class negatives which . . . are the same in every respect as the originals except that they are sharp cut and clear and far finer for printing purposes . . .

Above: Sir Arthur Conan Doyle, who used sharpened prints of the first two Cottingley photographs to illustrate his article on fairies, which was published in the Christmas 1920 issue of the *Strand Magazine*

It seems incredible to us today that he could be so naïve, not anticipating the inevitable questions from critics as to shutter speed, figure definition, the suspicious resemblance of the fairies' clothes and hairstyles to the latest fashions . . . But Gardner only wanted the clearest pictures – as a Theosophist he had been studying fairy lore for years and had heard many accounts of fairy sightings, so the possible reactions of sceptics never entered his head.

By a striking coincidence, Sir Arthur Conan Doyle (creator of Sherlock Holmes and fanatical Spiritualist) had been commissioned by the *Strand Magazine* to write an article on fairies for their Christmas issue, to be published at the end of November 1920. He was preparing this in June when he heard of the two fairy prints in circulation and eventually made contact with Gardner and borrowed copies.

Above: Elsie Wright and her cousin Frances (above right). The girls were close companions and spent hours playing together near the beck where the fairy photographs were taken

Below: Polly Wright, Elsie's mother, began to take the photographs seriously after she had attended a Theosophical Society lecture on 'fairy life'

From the beginning, contrary to the impression the public later gained of him, Conan Doyle was on his guard. He showed the prints to Sir Oliver Lodge, a pioneer psychical researcher, who thought them fakes – perhaps involving a troupe of dancers masquerading as fairies. One fairy authority told him that the hairstyles of the sprites were too 'Parisienne' for his liking. Lodge also passed them on to a clairvoyant for psychometric impressions – Gardner's photoprinter, Mr Snelling (who had prepared the second batch of prints from the originals) was described accurately.

What seems rather mysterious to us today is that no one was over-anxious to examine the original photographs, but seemed content to analyse prints. Snelling (of whom it had been said 'What Snelling doesn't know about faked photography isn't worth knowing') said in his first report to Gardner on the

Above: a sharpened print of 'Elsie and the gnome', the second fairy photograph, which was taken by Frances in August 1917. The original was examined by experts in the same way as the first – again no evidence of fakery could be found

Below: Arthur Wright, Elsie's father, whose camera – a Midg quarter-plate – was used to take the photographs

'rough' print that he could detect movement in all the fairy figures. Kodak, by contrast, stated that an experienced photographer may have been involved – which suggests that the prints that they had been examining may have been sharpened ones.

A possible explanation is that Conan Doyle and Gardner may have wished to avoid any mention of improving the originals at that stage; perhaps they did not consider the matter important. What was vital to them was the propagation of Theosophical and Spiritualist doctrines. As far as they were concerned, clear prints showing recognisable fairies and a gnome would provide the long-sought firm evidence for 'dwellers at the border' (as Conan Doyle was later to term nature spirits).

Conan Doyle despatched his 'Watson' – in this real-life case, Gardner – to Cottingley in July. Gardner reported that the whole Wright family seemed honest and totally respectable. Conan Doyle and Gardner decided that if further fairy photographs were taken then the matter would be put firmly beyond question. Gardner journeyed north in August with cameras and 20 photographic plates to leave with Elsie and Frances hoping to persuade them to take more photographs. Only in this way, he felt, could it be proved that the fairies were genuine.

Meanwhile, the *Strand* article was completed, featuring the two sharpened prints, and Conan Doyle sailed for Australia and a lecture tour to spread the gospel of Spiritualism. He left his colleagues to face the public reactions to the fairy business.

Newspaper sensation

That issue of the *Strand* sold out within days of publication at the end of November. Reaction was vigorous – especially from critics. The leading voice among them was that of one Major Hall-Edwards, a radium expert. He declared:

> On the evidence I have no hesitation in saying that these photographs could have been 'faked'. I criticise the attitude of those who declared there is something supernatural in the circumstances attending to the taking of these pictures because, as a medical man, I believe that the inculcation of such absurd ideas into the minds of children will result in later life in manifestations and nervous disorder and mental disturbances . . .

Newspaper comments were varied. On 5 January 1921 *Truth* declared: 'For the true explanation of these fairy photographs what is wanted is not a knowledge of occult phenomena but a knowledge of children.' On the other hand the *South Wales Argus* of 27 November 1920 took a more whimsical and tolerant view: 'The day we kill our Santa Claus with our statistics we shall have plunged a glorious world into deepest darkness'. The Day's Thought underneath was a Welsh proverb: ''Tis true as the fairy tales told in books.' *City News*, on 29 January, said straightforwardly: 'It seems at this point that we must either believe in the almost incredible mystery of the fairy or in the almost incredible wonders of faked photographs.'

The *Westminster Gazette* broke the aliases used by Conan Doyle to protect Frances and Elsie – and a reporter went north. However, nothing sensational, or even new, was added to the story by his investigation. He found out that Elsie had borrowed her father's camera to take the first picture, and that Frances had taken a picture of Elsie and a gnome. In fact there was nothing he could add to the facts listed by Conan Doyle in his article 'Fairies photographed – an epoch-making event'. The reporter considered Polly and Arthur Wright to be honest enough folk – and he returned a verdict of 'unexplained' to his paper in London.

The case might well have faded away with the coming of spring in 1921, had not the unexpected happened: Elsie and Frances took three more fairy photographs.

The reappearance of the fairies

The Cottingley 'fairy' pictures provoked heated argument. To Sir Arthur Conan Doyle they were the long-awaited proof of the existence of spirits – but to many people they were just clever fakes.

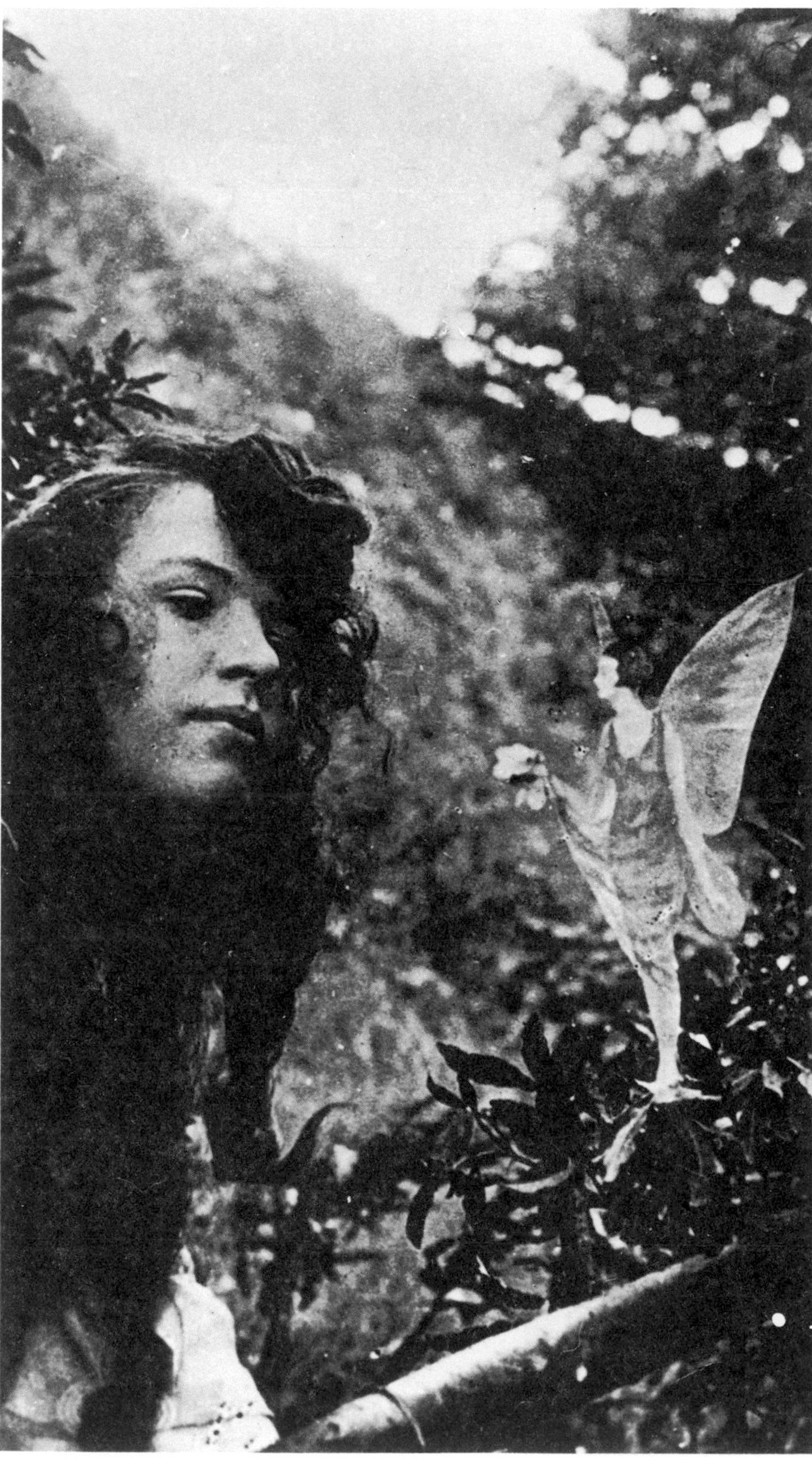

IN THE SCHOOL HOLIDAYS of August 1920, Frances Griffiths was asked to come by train to Cottingley from Scarborough, where she had gone to live with her mother and father after the First World War. Aunt Polly had written to say that Edward Gardner would be travelling up from London, with new cameras, so that the cousins might have further opportunities of taking fairy photographs to add to the two they took in 1917.

Frances was a month away from her 14th birthday and had won a scholarship to go to grammar school, being both industrious and intelligent. Elsie, by contrast, had thankfully left school at the age of 13.

Edward Gardner came from London to Bradford by train and took the tram out to Cottingley Bar, three miles (5 kilometres) away. He had brought with him two cameras and two dozen secretly marked photographic plates. He described the briefing of the girls thus in his book *Fairies: a book of real fairies* published in 1945:

> I went off, too, to Cottingley again, taking the two cameras and plates from London, and met the family and explained to the two girls the simple working of the cameras, giving one each to keep. The cameras were loaded, and my final advice was that they need go up to the glen only on fine days as they had been accustomed to do before and tice the fairies, as they called their way of attracting them, and see what they could get. I suggested only the most obvious and easy precautions about lighting and distance, for I knew it was essential they should feel free and unhampered and have no burden of responsibility. If nothing came of it all, I told them, they were not to mind a bit.

Only two more fairies

One might imagine the scene in the parlour of the Wright household. Beautiful Polly, listening intently, gangly 19-year-old Elsie with her auburn gold hair and gentle blue eyes, and sharp Frances, her energies suppressed for the occasion. ('Pity anyone with corns who is around when Frances gets excited,' Polly had written wryly on one occasion.) And solemn Edward Gardner, bearded and perhaps sporting a bow tie as usual, eager to engender some sort of scientific atmosphere but, in his heart, really not hoping for very much, in spite of the new cameras and carefully marked plates. So he returned to London, hoping for fine weather at least.

Alas, it rained for two weeks. They had little opportunity of adding anything to fairy history, and the first record of anything happening is in a letter to Gardner from

Left: a fairy offering flowers to Elsie, 1920. Elsie Wright said that the flowers were tiny harebells, and that the colours of the fairy's dress were pastel shades of mauve and yellow. This particular Cottingley photograph prompted widespread criticism: the fairy has a suspiciously contemporary appearance, with its bobbed hair and fashionable dress

Polly, which is truly astounding in its modesty. She wrote about the events of Thursday, 19 August 1920:

> The morning was dull and misty so they did not take any photos until after dinner when the mist had cleared away and it was sunny. I went to my sister's for tea and left them to it. When I got back they had only managed two with fairies, I was disappointed.

and about those of two days after:

> They went up again on Saturday afternoon and took several photos but there was only one with anything on and it's a queer one, we can't make it out. Elsie put the plates in this time and Arthur developed them next day.

and what must rank as one of the most charming postscripts ever: 'P.S. She did not take one flying after all.'

So the plates were returned to London. Elsie remembers the care with which they were packed in cotton wool by her father, who was puzzled – about the whole affair. He never understood it until the end of his days (he died in 1926) and Conan Doyle went down in his estimation. Before the great man had shown an interest in fairies, Arthur held him in high regard; afterwards he found it hard to believe that so intelligent a man could be bamboozled 'by our Elsie, and her at the bottom of the class!' But whereas Arthur could not bring himself to believe in fairies, Polly, as the tone of her letter suggests, supported her daughter and acknowledged the existence of nature spirits.

Gardner was elated to receive the secretly marked plates which bore such intriguing fairy photographs and telegrams were sent off to Conan Doyle who was on his Australian lecture tour, currently in Melbourne. Conan Doyle wrote back:

> My heart was gladdened when out here in far Australia I had your note and the

Above: Frances and the leaping fairy, taken by Elsie from a distance of about 3 feet (1 metre). The fairy was said to be leaping, not flying, as it appears to be. It bounded up in the air four times before Elsie took the picture. The fifth leap was so vigorous that Frances thought it was jumping at her face and flung her head back; the movement can be seen in the print

three wonderful pictures which are confirmatory of our published results. When our fairies are admitted other psychic phenomena will find a more ready acceptance . . . we have had continued messages at seances for some time that a visible sign was coming through . . .

Both Conan Doyle and Edward Gardner were primarily interested in spreading their own ideas of the infinite to what they considered to be a far from receptive public. Conan Doyle saw the Cottingley fairies incident as (perhaps literally) a gift from the gods, paving the way for more profound truths that may gradually become acceptable to a materialistic world. He used the last three photographs to illustrate a second article in the *Strand Magazine* in 1921. It described other accounts of alleged fairy sightings and served as the foundation for his later book entitled *The coming of the fairies*, published in 1922.

Reactions to the new fairy photographs were, as before, varied. The most common criticism was that the fairies looked suspiciously like the traditional fairies of nursery tales and that they had very fashionable hairstyles. It was also pointed out that the pictures were particularly sharply-defined, as if some improvement had been made by an expert photographer.

However, some public figures were sympathetic – sometimes embarrassingly so. Margaret McMillan, the educational and social reformer (who, among other reforms, brought the benefits of public baths to the slum children of Bradford), waxed fulsome about the Cottingley incidents: 'How wonderful that to these dear children such a wonderful gift has been vouchsafed.'

Above: the 'fairy bower' long believed by some fairylorists to exist, but, as Conan Doyle exclaimed, 'Never before, or other where [*sic*], has a fairy's bower been photographed!' The cocoon-like structure is said to be used by fairies to bathe in after long spells of dull and misty weather

Below: Cottingley as it was in the 1920s

Another eminent personality of the day, the novelist Henry de Vere Stacpoole, decided to take the fairy photographs – and the girls – at face value. He accepted intuitively that both girls and pictures were genuine. In a letter to Gardner he said:

> Look at Alice's face. Look at Iris's face. There is an extraordinary thing called TRUTH which has 10 million faces and forms – it is God's currency and the cleverest coiner or forger can't imitate it . . .

(The aliases 'Alice' and 'Iris' first used by Conan Doyle to protect the anonymity of the girls were deliberately preserved by Stacpoole.)

'Fed up with fairies!'

The fifth, and last, fairy photograph is often believed to be the most striking. Nobody has ever been able to give a satisfactory explanation as to what seems to be happening in the picture. However, Conan Doyle, in his *The coming of the fairies* advances a detailed, if somewhat over-elaborate, view of the pictured proceedings:

> Seated on the upper left hand edge with wing well displayed is an undraped fairy apparently considering whether it is time to get up. An earlier riser of more mature age is seen on the right possessing abundant hair and wonderful wings. Her slightly denser body can be glimpsed within her fairy dress.

This piece of whimsy from the creator of that most unsentimental and coldly logical character in English fiction – Sherlock Holmes – provided the 'Conan Doyle's going soft' school with formidable ammunition. It is perhaps unfortunate that his ardent interest in Spiritualism should coincide with his

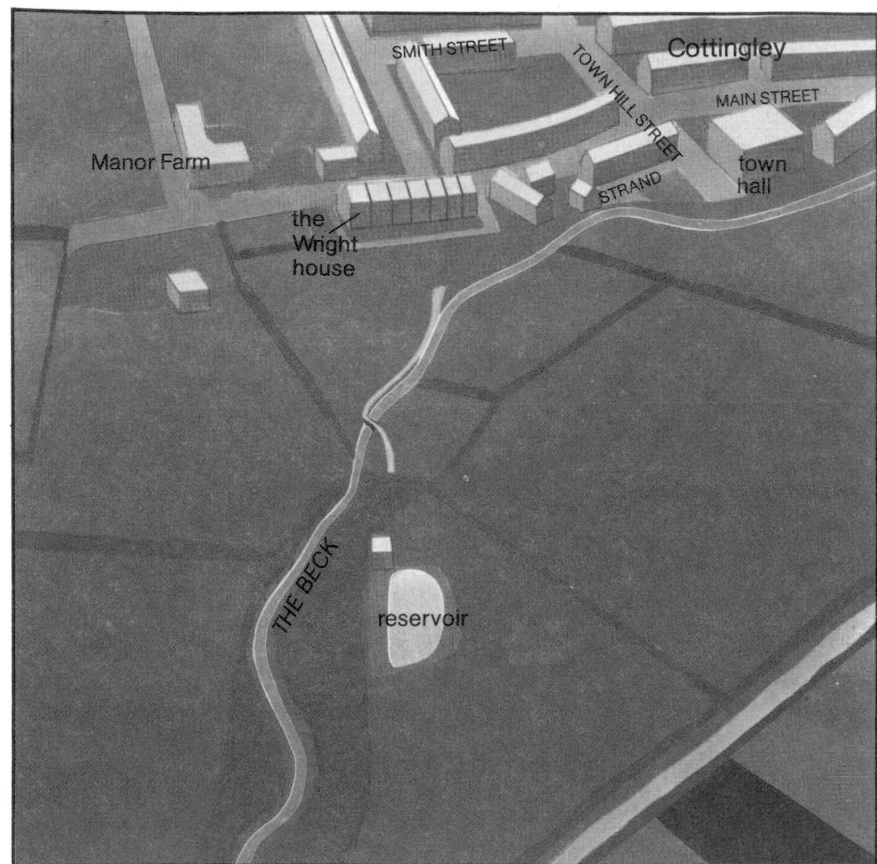

later years, especially in an age when anyone in his or her sixties was very much considered 'past their best'. His championship of the Cottingley fairies did little to dispel the growing image of him as a gullible old man. However, he was by no means the only believer in elemental spirits.

As can be seen from a map of Cottingley, it is virtually on the outskirts of populous Bradford, and is not, as many imagine, an isolated village. There is a reservoir and an old water bridge over the 'beck' – key markers for the fairy photographs. Traditionally nature spirits inhabit wooded and watery places and there are many stories of nature spirits being observed in such secluded spots. Also, the oak, ash and thorn are traditionally associated with fairies and these varieties of tree are found around the beck.

In August 1921, a last expedition was made to Cottingley – this time the clairvoyant, Geoffrey Hodson, was brought along to verify any fairy sightings. (The feeling being that if anyone, apart from the girls, could see the fairies, Hodson could.) Alas, the fairies refused to be photographed – although they were seen both by Hodson and by Elsie.

But by then both Elsie and Frances were tired of the whole fairy business. Many years later, Elsie looked at a photograph of herself and Frances taken with Hodson and said: 'Look at that – fed up with fairies!' Both Elsie and Frances have since agreed that they humoured Hodson to a sometimes ludicrous extent. This naïve admission played right into the hands of their critics. Quite apart from 'playing Mr Hodson along' there were still the allegations of faking the whole fairy business in the first place and when more fairy photographs were not forthcoming, the 'Cottingley incident' seemed all set to be relegated to the dusty gallery of 'famous fakes'. Yet the episode is not closed. . . .

Above left: a map of the Cottingley area, showing the 'beck' where Elsie and Frances claimed to have photographed the fairies

Above: Geoffrey Hodson, a clairvoyant recommended by Sir Arthur Conan Doyle, pictured here with Elsie, aged 20, and Frances, 14, in 1921. He had personal experience of fairies and gnomes and was to publish his *Fairies at work and play* in 1922

Left: Bernard Partridge's famous caricature of the aging Conan Doyle. Though still chained by public opinion to his great fictional character Sherlock Holmes, he is seen with his head in the clouds of Spiritualism

The Cottingley fairies revisited

Ever since two young girls took 'fairy photographs' in the 1920s controversy has raged over their authenticity.

THE FIRST PHOTOGRAPH of fairies taken by Elsie Wright of Cottingley, near Bradford, in 1917 has threatened to become overexposed in the occult-conscious late 20th century, for the photograph of the sprites pictured in front of a pleasant-faced Frances has been reproduced so often that it is in danger of becoming a sort of visual cliché. It is especially irritating to those who find the whole fairy business distasteful, even fraudulent; they object, shrilly at times, to the strangely artificial look of the fairy dancers – although they are less vocal on the other four photographs that were subsequently taken. The believers, as always, believe, and speak of 'more things in Heaven and Earth . . .'

The position of critics on the one hand and champions on the other may be summed up thus:

The 'prosecution' points out that Elsie painted and drew well, that she had always seemed immersed in drawing fairies, had been fascinated by the art of photography and had worked at a photographer's, and seemed suspiciously evasive in the 1971 BBC-TV *Nationwide* interview. Both Elsie and her cousin Frances admit to a strong sense of humour; both admit to having deceived the medium Geoffrey Hodson during the 1921 investigation (in terms of giving overgenerous endorsements to his descriptions of teeming fairy life in and around the beck). No third party was ever present when the five photographs were taken. The girls spent hours together playing down at the beck, which was well away from the house and concealed, by 40-foot (12-metre) banks, from public view. They shared a fair-sized attic bedroom in which they could have hatched their plots. In 1978 the 'Amazing Randi' (a professional American stage illusionist and self-appointed debunker of all paranormal phenomena) and a team from *New Scientist* subjected the photographs to 'enhancement' – a process used to bring out greater detail from Moon photographs – and thought they could see strings attached to some figures. Randi also pointed out that the figures in the first photograph bore a resemblance to those in an illustration in *Princess Mary's gift book*, published in 1914.

The 'defence' asserts that Elsie's job at the photographer's lasted only six months and amounted to running errands and cleaning up prints. She drew fairies because she saw

Above: the young Elsie Wright's watercolour *Fairies flying over a cottage*. She often painted fairies, because, she said, she often saw them

Left: an illustration from *Princess Mary's gift book*, which was very popular in 1914. These fairies bear some resemblance to those allegedly seen and photographed at Cottingley

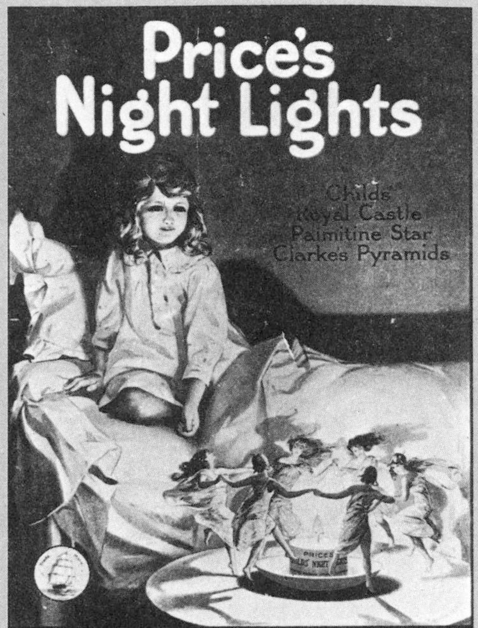

Most people do not believe in fairies and therefore, to them, any alleged fairy photographs must be fakes. To sceptics there is no question about it: the Cottingley fairies were cut out of a children's book and superimposed, very cleverly (for no one has conclusively proved that they were faked), on photographs of the cousins, Elsie and Frances.

There was no shortage of material had they wanted to search for fairy 'models'. Fairies were common enough in children's books around the turn of the century. Most girls of their age, living at that time, could have described a fairy, for most illustrations reflected a similar, traditional fairy image.

In fact, Elsie and Frances's fairies were, if anything, slightly more fashion-conscious than, say, those pictured in the popular *Princess Mary's gift book* of 1914. The Cottingley fairies had up-to-the-minute bobbed hair and beaded Charleston dresses (although Elsie's gnome remained traditionally grotesque).

When psychical researcher E.L. Gardner visited Cottingley in the 1920s he claimed mediumistic powers for both girls, but especially for Frances. He believed that the elemental spirits – fairies – used loosely-knit ectoplasm emanating from the girls with which to form visible bodies, visible, that is, only to the girls and the eye of the camera. The exact form they took was, he hazarded, 'chosen' by the subconscious minds of the girls, hence the strange mixture of traditional and contemporary. But, for whatever reason, both girls stopped seeing fairies after 1921.

Several critics pointed out that the Cottingley fairies looked suspiciously similar to those featured in the advertisement for Price's night lights (above right). One sceptic, William Marriott, produced this deliberate fake (above left) by superimposing the 'night light' fairies on a picture of Sir Arthur Conan Doyle

Some fairies of the era:
Left: fairies dancing, by E. Gertrude Thomson from William Allingham's *The fairies* (1886)

Above: a ring of fairies from Florence Harrison's *In the fairy ring* (1910)

Above right: a girl with fairies, from *Princess Mary's gift book* (1914)

them often and, anyway, her drawings were no better than might be expected from a fairly talented 16-year-old. As for the *Gift book* illustrations – fairies dancing around are bound to resemble each other and the ones in the Christmas 1914 publication lack wings. The string in the report in *New Scientist* of 3 August 1978 may be printing streaks, and even real figures would not stay absolutely motionless in the breeze that usually blew gently down the beck; and where might they be hung from? And what variety of invisible 'string' was used at the time? By the time Hodson came they were bored and nodded confirmation for the sake of peace and quiet. Elsie prevaricated because she wanted the matter to be forgotten. They did not have the motivation, materials, time, privacy, or expertise to fake the photographs. And, most significantly, they have always maintained they saw fairies and photographed them.

Newspapers, magazines and television companies have become increasingly interested in Elsie and Frances since Peter Chambers of the *Daily Express* discovered where Elsie lived in 1966. He quotes Elsie as saying that the fairies might have been 'figments of

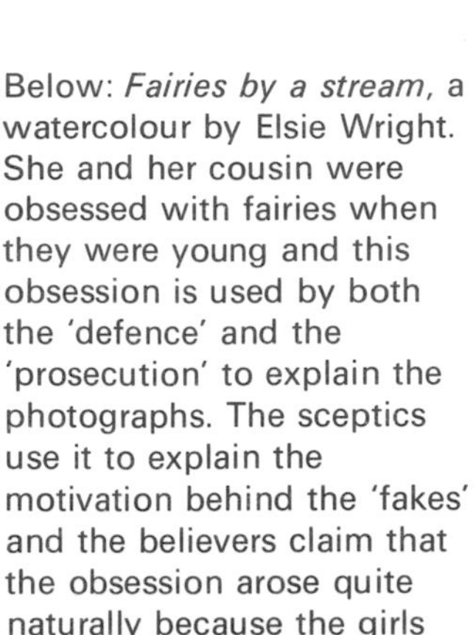

Below: *Fairies by a stream*, a watercolour by Elsie Wright. She and her cousin were obsessed with fairies when they were young and this obsession is used by both the 'defence' and the 'prosecution' to explain the photographs. The sceptics use it to explain the motivation behind the 'fakes' and the believers claim that the obsession arose quite naturally because the girls saw fairies all the time

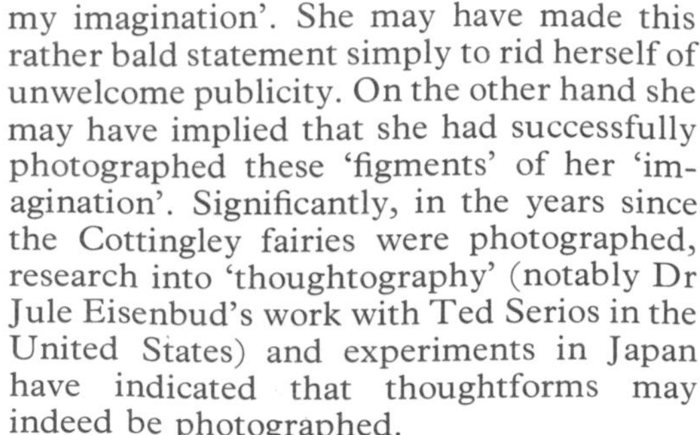

my imagination'. She may have made this rather bald statement simply to rid herself of unwelcome publicity. On the other hand she may have implied that she had successfully photographed these 'figments' of her 'imagination'. Significantly, in the years since the Cottingley fairies were photographed, research into 'thoughtography' (notably Dr Jule Eisenbud's work with Ted Serios in the United States) and experiments in Japan have indicated that thoughtforms may indeed be photographed.

Elsie and Frances interrogated

For five years Elsie managed to avoid publicity; then, in 1971, BBC-TV's *Nationwide* programme took up the case. For 10 days she was interrogated, taken back to Cottingley and subjected to this sort of thing:

(The interviewer points out that, since the original fairy investigator, E. L. Gardner, died the year before, Elsie might wish to be more explicit.)

Elsie: I didn't want to upset Mr Gardner . . . I don't mind talking now . . .

(It is then suggested that Elsie's father had a hand in matters.)

Elsie: I would swear on the Bible father didn't know what was going on.

Interviewer: Could you equally swear on the Bible you didn't play any tricks?

Elsie (after a pause): I took the photographs . . . I took two of them . . . no, three . . . Frances took two . . .

Interviewer: Are they trick photographs? Could you swear on the Bible about that?

Elsie (after a pause): I'd rather leave that open if you don't mind . . . but my father had nothing to do with it I can promise you that . . .

Interviewer: Have you had your fun with the world for 50 years? Have you been kidding us for 10 days?

(Elsie laughs.)

Elsie (gently): I think we'll close on that if you don't mind.

More objective was Austin Mitchell's interview for Yorkshire Television in September 1976. On the spot where the photographs had allegedly been taken, the following dialogue took place:

Mitchell: A rational person doesn't see fairies. If people say they see fairies, then one's bound to be critical.

Frances: Yes.

Mitchell: Now, if you say you saw them, at the time the photograph was taken, that means that if there's a confidence trick, then you're both part of it.

Frances: Yes – that's fair enough – yes.

Mitchell: So are you?

Frances: No.

Elsie: No.

Frances: Of course not.

Mitchell: Did you, in any way, fabricate those photographs?

Frances: Of course not. You tell us how she could do it – remember she was 16 and I was

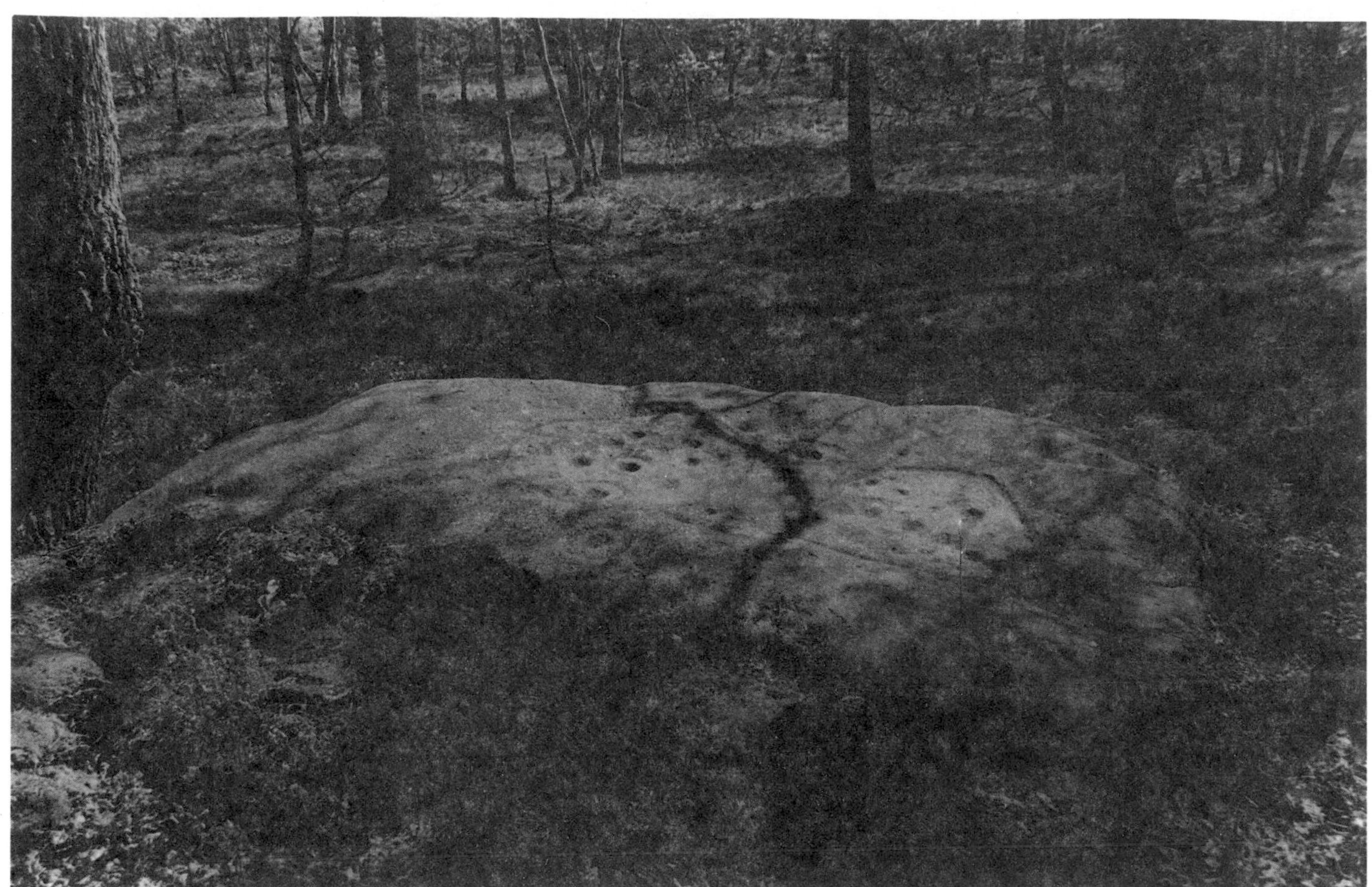

Above: a rare 'cup and ring' stone, found in Cottingley Glen, close to the beck. Such strangely marked stones are traditionally associated with supernatural activities and have often been linked with fairy sightings

10. Now then, as a child of 10, can you go through life and keep a secret?

The Yorkshire Television team, however, believed the 'cardboard cutout' theory. Austin Mitchell duly appeared on the screen, personable as ever, with a row of fairy figures before him set against a background of greenery. He flicked them around a little (perhaps to reassure viewers that elementals had not invaded the prosaic surroundings of Kirkstall Road, Leeds).

'Simple cardboard cutouts,' he commented on the live magazine programme. 'Done by our photographic department and mounted on wire frames. They discovered that you really need wire to make them stand up – paper figures droop, of course. That's how it could have been done.'

But quite apart from the pronouncements of critics and champions, tapes, letters and newspaper cuttings are now available for anyone who would delve deeper into the fairy photographs. Understandably, Elsie and Frances would rather people kept away and respected their privacy after the passage of so many years.

The critics – Lewis of *Nationwide*, Austin Mitchell of Yorkshire TV, Randi, and Stewart Sanderson and Katherine Briggs of the Folklore Society – all these are fair-minded individuals interested in balancing probability on the available evidence. This extremely delicate balance did seem to have shifted in favour of the ladies' honesty during the 1970s but, obviously, many points could still be elucidated by further research.

Austin Mitchell said 'a rational person doesn't see fairies', and there are some sociologists who would say that rationality might be socially constructed. One's 'rationality' mostly depends on one's personal experiences and one's reading. There are, believe it or not, hundreds of instances of people claiming to have seen fairies. A perusal of Conan Doyle's book *The coming of the fairies*, or *Visions or beliefs* by Lady Gregory and the poet W. B. Yeats, should prove that more than a handful of such claims have been made.

The author has now met seven people who claim to have seen nature spirits. One of them, an ex-wrestler of powerful build – an unlikely figure to consort with sprites – is adamant in his assertions. It is interesting to note how many are prepared to listen to him with an unusual degree of tolerance.

It is usually possible to demolish individual accounts; taken collectively, however, some patterns begin to emerge. F. W. Holiday in his book *The dragon and the disc* likens the appearance of the Cottingley gnome to that of Icelandic Bronze Age figures, and William Riley, the Yorkshire author, puts the five fairy pictures into perhaps the most relevant context: 'I have many times come across several people who have seen pixies at certain favoured spots in Upper Airedale and Wharfedale.'

Defying the law of gravity

The power to overcome the force of gravity may be the product of long training, or may occur spontaneously, amazing levitator and onlookers alike. LYNN PICKNETT surveys some famous cases of this extraordinary talent

THREE NOTABLE MEMBERS of London society witnessed, on 16 December 1868, an incident so extraordinary that it is still the focus of controversy. Viscount Adare, the Master of Lindsay and Captain Wynne saw the famous medium Daniel Dunglas Home rise into the air and float out of one window in a large house in fashionable London and then float in at another – over 80 feet (24 metres) from the ground it is claimed. D. D. Home became known primarily for his levitations, of himself and of objects – on one occasion a grand piano – but he was not alone in having this 'impossible' ability to defy the law of gravity.

St Joseph of Copertino (1603–1663) flew into the air every time he was emotionally excited. Being of an excitable nature, he often made levitations, and they were well witnessed. A simple peasant – some say he was actually feeble-minded – this boy from Apulia, Italy, spent his youth trying to achieve religious ecstasy by such means as self-flagellation, starvation and wearing hair-shirts. He became a Franciscan at the age of 22, and then his religious fervour 'took off' quite literally.

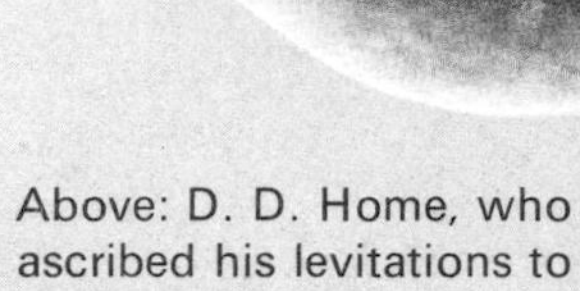

Above: D. D. Home, who ascribed his levitations to the work of spirits

Above right: Home floats into the air with no visible means of support

Below: St Joseph of Copertino owed his canonisation to his ability to levitate

St Joseph and his 'giddiness'

Joseph became something of an embarrassment to his superiors. During Mass one Sunday he rose into the air and flew onto the altar in the midst of the candles; he was quite badly burned as a result.

For 35 years Joseph was excluded from all public services because of his disconcerting habits, but still tales of his levitations spread. While walking with a Benedictine monk in the monastery gardens he suddenly flew up into an olive tree. Unfortunately he couldn't fly back down, so his fellow-monks had to fetch a ladder.

A surgeon, at least two cardinals and one Pope (Urban VIII), among many others, witnessed Joseph's extraordinary spells of weightlessness – which he called 'my giddinesses'. He spent his entire life in a state of prayer, and the Church concluded the levitations must be the work of God.

Another levitating saint was St Teresa of Avila, who died in 1582. This remarkable mystic experienced the same feelings as many people feel during the common 'flying dreams'. She described how she felt about her levitations:

> It seemed to me, when I tried to make some resistance, as if a great force

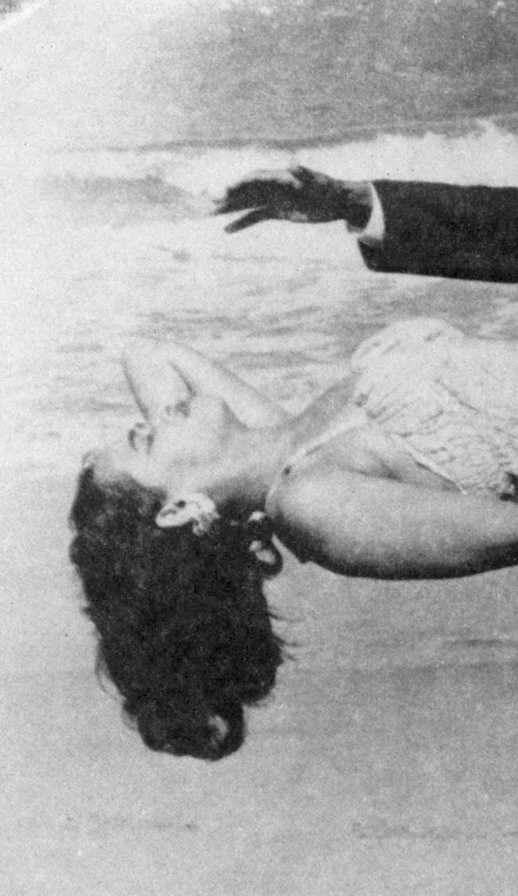

> beneath my feet lifted me up. . . . I confess that it threw me into great fear, very great indeed at first; for in seeing one's body thus lifted up from the earth, though the spirit draws it upwards after itself (and that with great sweetness, if unresisted) the senses are not lost; at least I was so much myself as able to see that I was being lifted up. After the rapture was over, I have to say my body seemed frequently to be buoyant, as if all weight had departed from it, so much so that now and then I scarce knew my feet touched the ground.

So insistent were her levitations that she begged the sisters to hold her down when she felt an 'attack' coming on, but often there was no time for preventive measures – she simply rose off the floor until the weightlessness passed.

Most levitators are believers in one particular system, be it Christianity, Hindu mysticism, ancient Egyptian mysteries or Spiritualism. It was to this last category that D. D. Home belonged.

Born in Scotland and brought up in America, Home was a puny, artistic child. At the age of 13 he had a vision of a friend, Edwin. Home announced to his aunt's family that it must mean that Edwin had been dead for three days. This was proved to be true. Home's career as a medium had begun – but it was not until he was 19 that he was to defy the law of gravity.

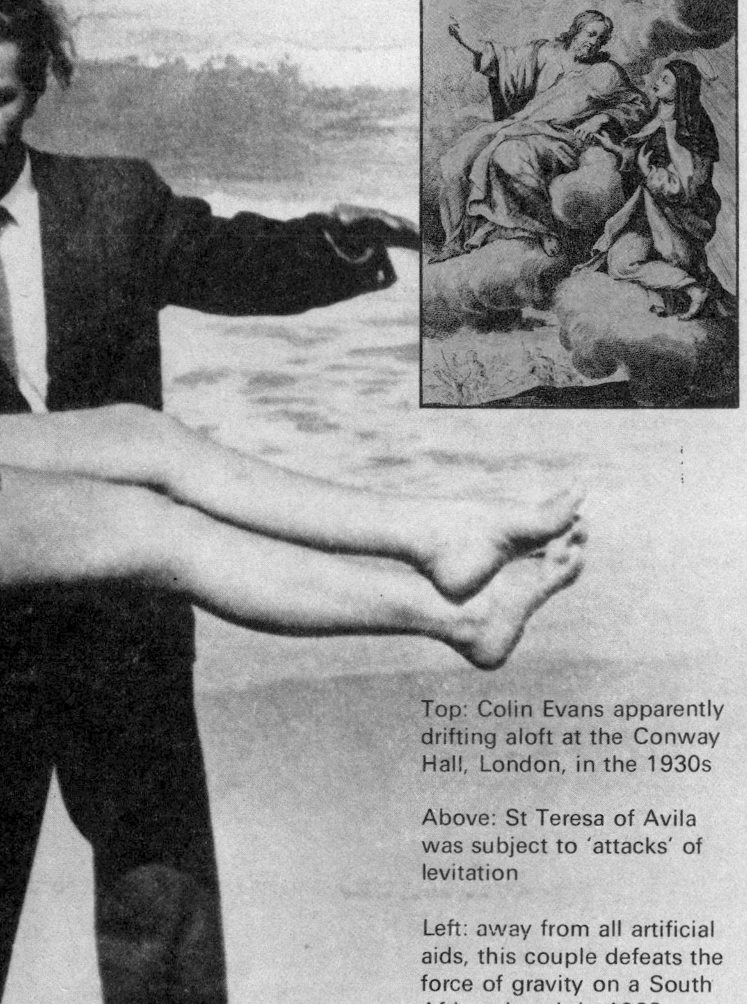

Top: Colin Evans apparently drifting aloft at the Conway Hall, London, in the 1930s

Above: St Teresa of Avila was subject to 'attacks' of levitation

Left: away from all artificial aids, this couple defeats the force of gravity on a South African beach in 1962

Ward Cheney, a prosperous silk-manufacturer, held a seance at his home in Connecticut in August 1852. D. D. Home was there to provide the usual 'spiritualist' manifestations – table-turning, rappings, floating trumpets and mysterious lights.

Home was quite capable of keeping the guests entertained in this fashion but something happened, completely unannounced, that made his name overnight. He floated up into the air until his head was touching the ceiling. Among the guests was the sceptical reporter, F. L. Burr, editor of the *Hartford Times.* He wrote of this bizarre and unexpected incident:

> Suddenly, without any expectation on the part of the company, Home was taken up into the air. I had hold of his hand at the time and I felt his feet – they were lifted a foot [30 centimetres] from the floor. He palpitated from head to foot with the contending emotions of joy and fear which choked his utterances. Again and again he was taken from the floor, and the third time he was carried to the ceiling of the apartment, with which his hands and feet came into gentle contact.

Home's career advanced rapidly; he was lionised in seance parlour and royal court alike. He came back to Europe to inspire adoration and scepticism (Robert Browning's

satirical poem 'Mr Sludge' was based on his own biased view of the medium). Wherever he went there were bizarre phenomena – winds howled in still rooms, apports of fresh flowers fell from the ceiling, doors opened and shut, fireballs zigzagged around the room – and Home levitated.

The famous occasion already mentioned when he floated out of one window and in through another, is still the subject of heated debate, particularly since the incident was documented by respectable witnesses. One of them, the Master of Lindsay (later the Earl of Crawford) wrote:

> I was sitting with Mr Home and Lord Adare and a cousin of his [Captain Wynne]. During the sitting Mr Home went into a trance and in that state was carried out of the window in the room next to where we were, and was brought in at our window. The distance between the windows was about seven feet six inches [2.3 metres], and there was not the slightest foothold between them, nor was there more than a 12-inch [30-centimetre] projection to each window, which served as a ledge to put flowers on. We heard the window in the next room lift up, and almost immediately after we saw Home floating in the air outside our window. The moon was shining full into the room; my back was to the light, and I saw the shadow on the wall of the windowsill, and Home's feet about six inches [15 centimetres] above it. He remained in this position for a few seconds, then raised the window and glided into the room feet foremost and sat down.

Sceptics such as Frank Podmore or, more recently, John Sladek, have tried to disprove this levitation, although neither of them was among the witnesses. Sladek attempts to discredit the three who were present by comparing the details of their stories – such as how high the balconies were from the street, or indeed, whether there were any balconies at all.

Podmore, on the other hand, is more subtle in his sceptism. He mentions the fact that a few days before the levitation, and in front of the same witnesses, Home had opened the window and stood on the ledge outside. He had pointedly drawn their attention to himself standing on the narrow ledge some considerable distance from the ground. Podmore remarked drily 'the medium had thus, as it were, furnished a rough sketch of the picture which he aimed at producing.' On another occasion Home suddenly announced 'I'm rising, I'm rising', before proceeding to levitate in front of several witnesses.

Podmore implied that Home's levitations were nothing more than hallucinations produced by his hypnotic suggestion, rather in the same manner that the Indian rope trick is said to be a mass hallucination, the secret being in the magician's patter.

But even in the face of extreme hostility, Home remained a successful levitator for over 40 years. Among his witnesses were Emperor Napoleon III, John Ruskin and Bulwer Lytton – and many hundreds more, not all of whom were as inconsistent in their testimonies as Adare, Wynne and Lindsay. Moreover during that long span of time and mostly in broad daylight, Home was never proved to be a fraud. And despite Podmore's accusations Home never went out of his way to build up an atmosphere heavy with suggestibility. In fact, he was one of the few

Top: the classic stage levitation. The girl, Marva Ganzel, is first hypnotised into a cataleptic trance while balanced on two swords. When one is taken away, she somehow remains suspended in mid-air

Above: Frank Podmore, who suggested that D. D. Home's most famous levitation was merely an hallucination

Right: accounts of levitation and other manifestations of the seance room did not impress *Punch*, which in 1863 published this lampoon, showing that some surprises, at least, could be administered by all too explicable means

Ridicule has long been poured on the notion that people can free themselves from the force of gravity: this cartoon (left), entitled 'The Day's Folly', was published by Sergent in 1783. But Alexandra David-Neel (below) came back from 14 years in Tibet with no doubt that adepts could achieve weightlessness

mediums who actively eschewed 'atmosphere' – he preferred a normal or bright light to darkness and encouraged the sitters to chat normally rather than 'hold hands and concentrate'.

Although in his mature years Home could levitate at will, he apparently also levitated without being aware of it. On one occasion, when his host drew his attention to the fact that he was hovering above the cushions of his armchair, Home seemed most surprised.

Stage illusionists frequently pride themselves on their *pièce de résistance*; putting their assistant into a 'trance', balancing her on the points of two swords – then removing the swords so that she hangs in the air without apparent support. Sometimes she is 'hypnotised' and seen to rise further into the air – still without visible means of support. One of two things must be happening: either she does not rise into the air at all (that is, we all suffer a mass hallucination) or she rises aided by machinery invisible to us.

Of course, Home and other spiritualists would also attribute their feats of apportation or levitation to 'machinery invisible to us' – but in their case the machinery would be the agency of spirits. To the end of his life, Home maintained that he could only fly through the air because he was lifted up by the spirits, who thus demonstrated their existence. But he described a typical levitation as follows:

> I feel no hands supporting me, and, since the first time, I have never felt fear; though, should I have fallen from the ceiling of some rooms in which I have been raised, I could not have escaped serious injury. I am generally lifted up perpendicularly; my arms frequently become rigid, and are drawn above my head, as if I were grasping the unseen power which slowly raises me from the floor.

The gravity enigma

And yet we do not refer in this spiritualistic way to the 'unseen power' that keeps us *on* the floor. Every schoolboy knows about Newton and his discovery of the law of gravity. But psychical research points to the relative ease with which certain sensitives can turn this law on its head.

In her book *Mystère et magique en Tibet* (1931), Madame Alexandra David-Neel, the French explorer who spent 14 years in and around Tibet, told how she came upon a naked man, weighed down with heavy chains. His companion explained to her that his mystical training had made his body so light that, unless he wore iron chains, he would float away.

It would seem that gravity does not necessarily have the hold on us we have been taught it has. Sir William Crookes, the renowned scientist and psychical researcher, had this to say about D. D. Home:

> The phenomena I am prepared to attest are so extraordinary, and so directly oppose the most firmly-rooted articles of scientific belief – amongst others, the ubiquity and invariable action of the force of gravitation – that, even now, on recalling the details of what I have witnessed, there is an antagonism in my mind between *reason*, which pronounces it to be scientifically impossible, and the consciousness that my senses, both of touch and sight, are not lying witnesses.

So we conclude that in some *special* cases – such as saints or particularly gifted mediums – levitation exists. But there is a growing body of thought that puts forward the idea that anyone can do it, providing he or she has the right training – students of transcendental meditation claim to do it all the time.

The art of levitation

It is claimed that many ancient peoples knew the secrets of levitation. But it is not, apparently, a lost art: some people today claim to be able to attain weightlessness by an effort of will

A UNIQUE SERIES of photographs appeared in the magazine *Illustrated London News* on 6 June 1936. They showed the successive stages in the levitation of an Indian *yogi*, Subbayah Pullavar – thus proving that, whatever else it was, this phenomenon was not a hypnotic illusion.

A European witness of the event, P. Y. Plunkett, sets the scene:

> The time was about 12.30 p.m. and the sun directly above us so that shadows played no part in the performance. . . . Standing quietly by was Subbayah Pullavar, the performer, with long hair, a drooping moustache and a wild look in his eye. He salaamed to us and stood chatting for a while. He had been practising this particular branch of yoga for nearly 20 years (as had past generations of his family). We asked permission to take photographs of the performance and he gave it willingly. . . .

Plunkett gathered together about 150 witnesses while the performer began his ritual preparations. Water was poured around the tent in which the act of levitation was to take place; leather-soled shoes were banned inside the circle, and the performer entered the tent alone. Some minutes later helpers removed the tent and there, inside the circle, was the fakir, floating on the air.

Plunkett and another witness came forward to investigate: the fakir was suspended in the air about a yard from the ground. Although he held on to a cloth-covered stick, this seemed to be for purposes of balance only – not for support. Plunkett and his friend examined the space around and under Subbayah Pullavar, and found it innocent of any strings or other 'invisible' apparatus. The yogi was in a trance and many witnesses believed that he had indisputably levitated,

Photographs taken of a levitation performance carried out by an Indian yogi, Subbayah Pullavar, before a large number of witnesses. The photographs were taken by the Englishman P. Y. Plunkett and a friend, and published in the *Illustrated London News* of 6 June 1936. The first photograph (below) shows the yogi before levitation, lying inside a tent. He is grasping a cloth-wrapped stick, which he continues to hold throughout the performance. The tent is then closed (right) for some minutes during the mysterious act of levitation itself

As the levitation performance continues, the curtains of the tent are drawn back and the yogi appears, floating in mid-air (top). Plunkett and his friend examined the space beneath and around the yogi, but were unable to find any evidence of strings or other supporting apparatus. Although some sceptics have claimed that the yogi was, in fact, not levitating but merely in a cataleptic trance, the relaxed position of the hand on the post suggests that the body of the yogi was indeed very nearly weightless during the performance. After levitation (above right) the yogi's body was so stiff that five men could not bend his limbs

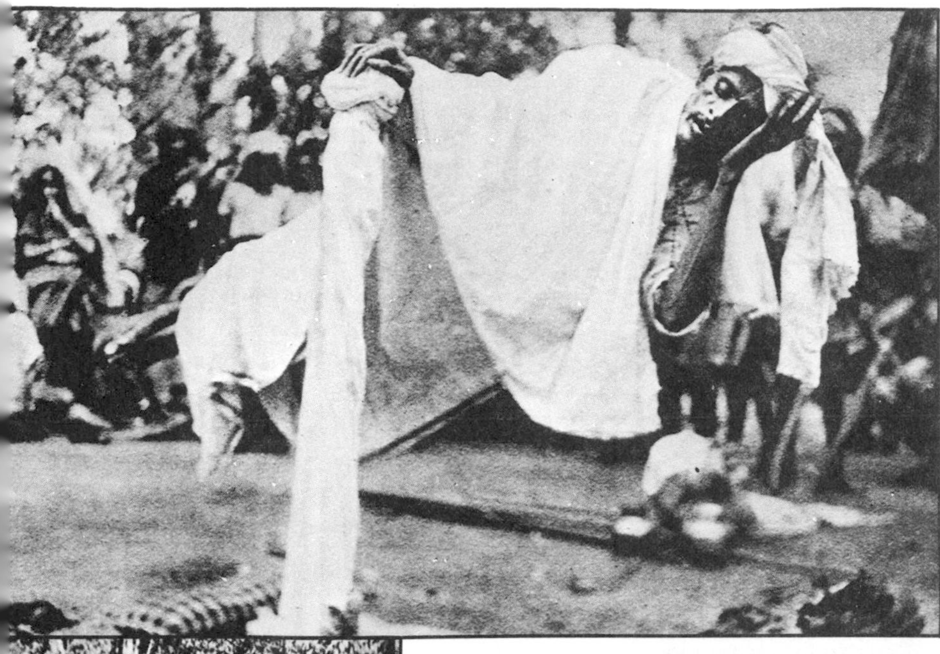

although it has been suggested that he had, in fact, merely passed into a cataleptic trance. The famous photographs were taken from various angles during the four minutes of the performance, and then the tent was re-erected around the fakir. Evidently the 'descent' was something very private, but Plunkett managed to witness it through the thin tent walls:

> After about a minute he appeared to sway and then very slowly began to descend, still in a horizontal position. He took about five minutes to move from the top of the stick to the ground, a distance of about three feet [1 metre] . . . When Subbayah was back on the ground his assistants carried him over to where we were sitting and asked if we would try to bend his limbs. Even with assistance we were unable to do so.

The yogi was rubbed and splashed with cold water for a further five minutes before he came out of his trance and regained full use of his limbs.

The swaying motion and horizontal position that Plunkett witnessed seem to be essential to true levitation. Students of transcendental meditation (TM) are taught, under the supervision of the Maharishi Mahesh Yogi at his headquarters in Switzerland, to levitate. One student described this 'impossible' achievement:

> People would rock gently, then more and more, and then start lifting off in to the air. You should really be in a lotus position to do it – you can hurt yourself landing if you've got a dangling undercarriage. To begin with it's like the Wright brothers' first flight – you come down with a bump. That's why we have to sit on foam rubber cushions. Then you learn to control it better, and it becomes totally exhilarating.

So can *anyone* induce levitation? The TM

Right: the Transcendental Meditation movement claims that this photograph shows students levitating. It is alleged that, under the supervision of tutors, the students achieve weightlessness through meditation

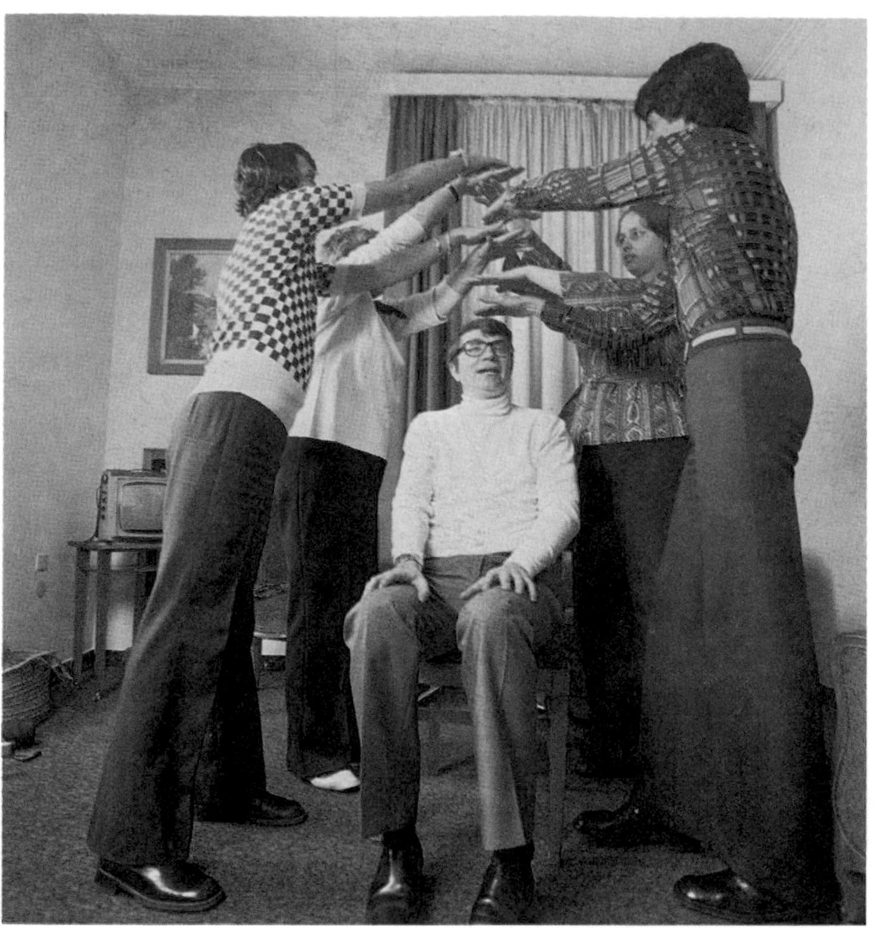

students believe they can, after a stringent mental training; the disciplines, both spiritual and physical, of the yogis seem to prepare them to defy gravity. It is fairly easy to induce a state of semi-weightlessness, as this account of a fat publican – a perfectly ordinary person – being raised in the air as a party trick shows.

The fat man sat on a chair and four people, including his small daughter, demonstrated the impossibility of lifting him with their index fingers only, placed in his armpits and the crooks of his knees. They then removed their fingers and put their hands in a pile on top of his head, taking care to interleave their hands so that no one person's two hands were touching. The four concentrated deeply for about 15 seconds; then someone gave a signal, and quickly they replaced their fingers in armpits and knees – and the fat publican floated into the air.

Sceptics might point to the intervention of non-spiritual spirits, bearing in mind the location of the event, but the phenomenon has been witnessed hundreds of times in pubs, homes, and school-yards. If it works – and one must assume it does – then how is it possible?

The sudden burst of concentration of four people with a single, 'impossible' target could, some people believe, unlock the hidden magic of the human will. Or it has been suggested that a little-known natural force, perhaps the same one that guides the dowser's rod, intervenes to achieve the miracle of nullifying the force of gravity.

It seems that religious fervour may have something to do with the phenomenon; there are many reports of levitation by both Christian and Buddhist monks. In 1902 Aleister Crowley met his compatriot Alan Bennett, who had become a Buddhist monk, at his monastery in Burma in 1902; he, too, had become so weightless that he was 'blown about like a leaf'.

Alexandra David-Neel, the French explorer of the early 20th century, describes witnessing an extraordinary kind of long-distance running by a Tibetan lama: 'The man did not run. He seemed to lift himself from the ground proceeding by leaps. It looked as if he had been endowed with the elasticity of a ball and rebounded each time his feet touched the ground. His steps had the regularity of a pendulum.' The lama is said to have run hundreds of miles using this strange form of locomotion, keeping his eyes fixed on some far-distant goal.

The famous Russian ballet dancer Nijinsky, too, had the extraordinary ability of appearing to be almost weightless. He would jump up high and fall as lightly – and slowly – as thistledown in what was known as the 'slow vault'.

Like many inexplicable phenomena, levitation seems to be singularly useless. The distance covered is rarely more than a few

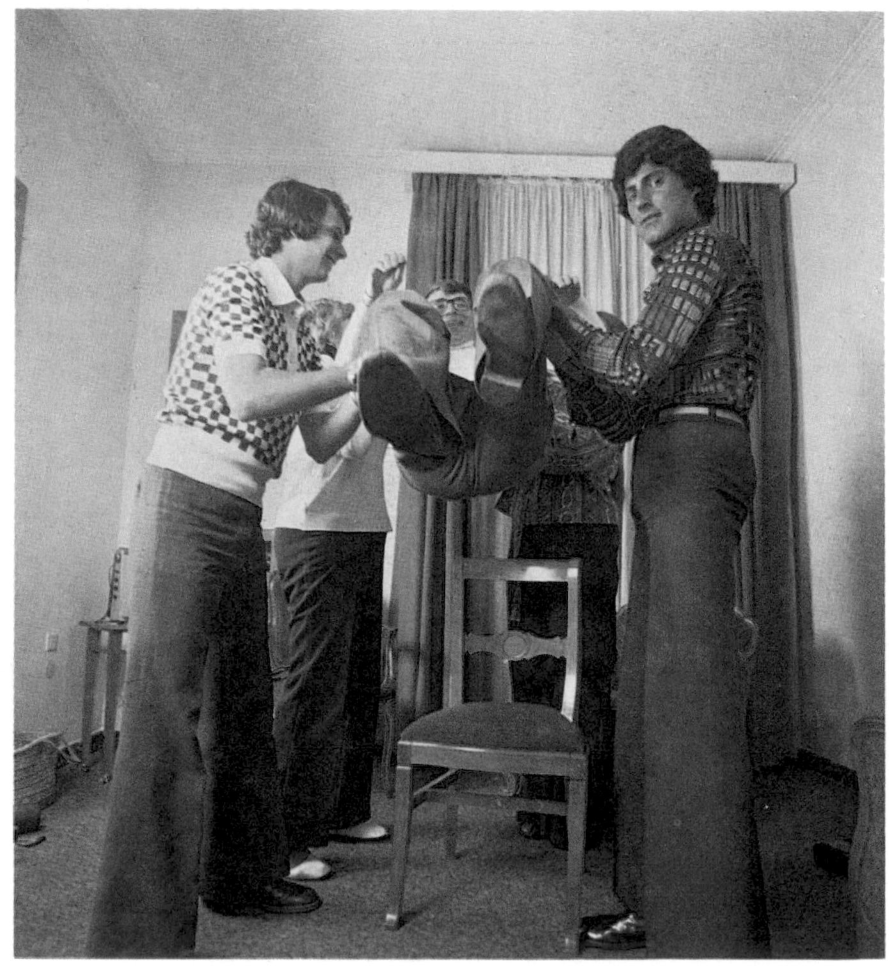

Left: an aerial view of the white horse at Uffington in Oxfordshire. The terrain on which it is carved is so hilly that its true shape can only really be appreciated from the air – a fact that has led some to speculate that the people who carved it were able to levitate and inspect their work from above

Opposite page: Uri Geller and some friends conduct a levitation session with Colin Wilson as subject. First (top) the experimenters place their hands on top of the subject's head, in such a way that no one person's two hands are touching. Then, on a command from Geller, they remove their hands from the subject's head and place their index fingers under his arms and knees. The subject immediately rises into the air (bottom)

feet or, at the most, the height of a room – useful only for dusting or decorating the home. But some people believe that the ancients could levitate quite easily, and did so to design certain enormous earthworks that can be appreciated only from the air, such as some of the white horses of the chalk downland in England and the desert patterns in Peru.

The limitations of modern levitation need not have applied to the ancients – perhaps they had developed the art to a high degree and could soar into the sky at will. Like other psychic faculties, it appears that levitation is an art, once almost lost, that is now being re-learned by determined students. Perhaps one day, modern levitators will be able to 'fly' as the ancient Druids supposedly could.

The reported 'flights' of the ancients suggest to some researchers that they were a type of out-of-the-body experience or astral travel rather than actual flesh-and-blood transportation. Certainly, many accounts of levitation or flying read like lucid dreams – and dreams of flying are very common experiences. Some dreamers wake up convinced they *can* fly; fortunately, the sights and sounds of the real world generally bring them to their senses before they can experiment.

With a few exceptions, it seems that one can levitate only after long periods of training and discipline: in this way, the body is mysteriously 'given permission' to defy the law of gravity. Perhaps there is a law of levitation with a secret formula – an 'Open, Sesame' – which the initiate uses before rising off the ground.

This theory would explain the unusual cases of spontaneous or random levitation that fascinated Charles Fort. One such case was 12-year-old Henry Jones from Shepton Mallet who, during the year 1657, was observed on several occasions to rise into the air. Once he was able to put his hands flat against the ceiling, and on another occasion he took off and sailed 30 yards (27 metres) over the garden wall. The phenomenon lasted only a year – but this was long enough for the rumour to spread that he was 'bewitched'.

Certainly levitation is a rare phenomenon, but when considered with other accounts of equally rare and bizarre human attributes, such as incombustibility, elongation and superhuman strength, it must be taken seriously. Mothers who lift cars off their trapped children, firewalkers and eaters and the sleepwalkers who perform 'impossible' feats pose profound questions about the nature of Man's physical and psychical potential. Perhaps we are intended to be able to defy gravity at will. Until we understand the nature of the phenomenon it must remain one of Man's mysterious hidden powers.

D.D. Home: flight from reality?

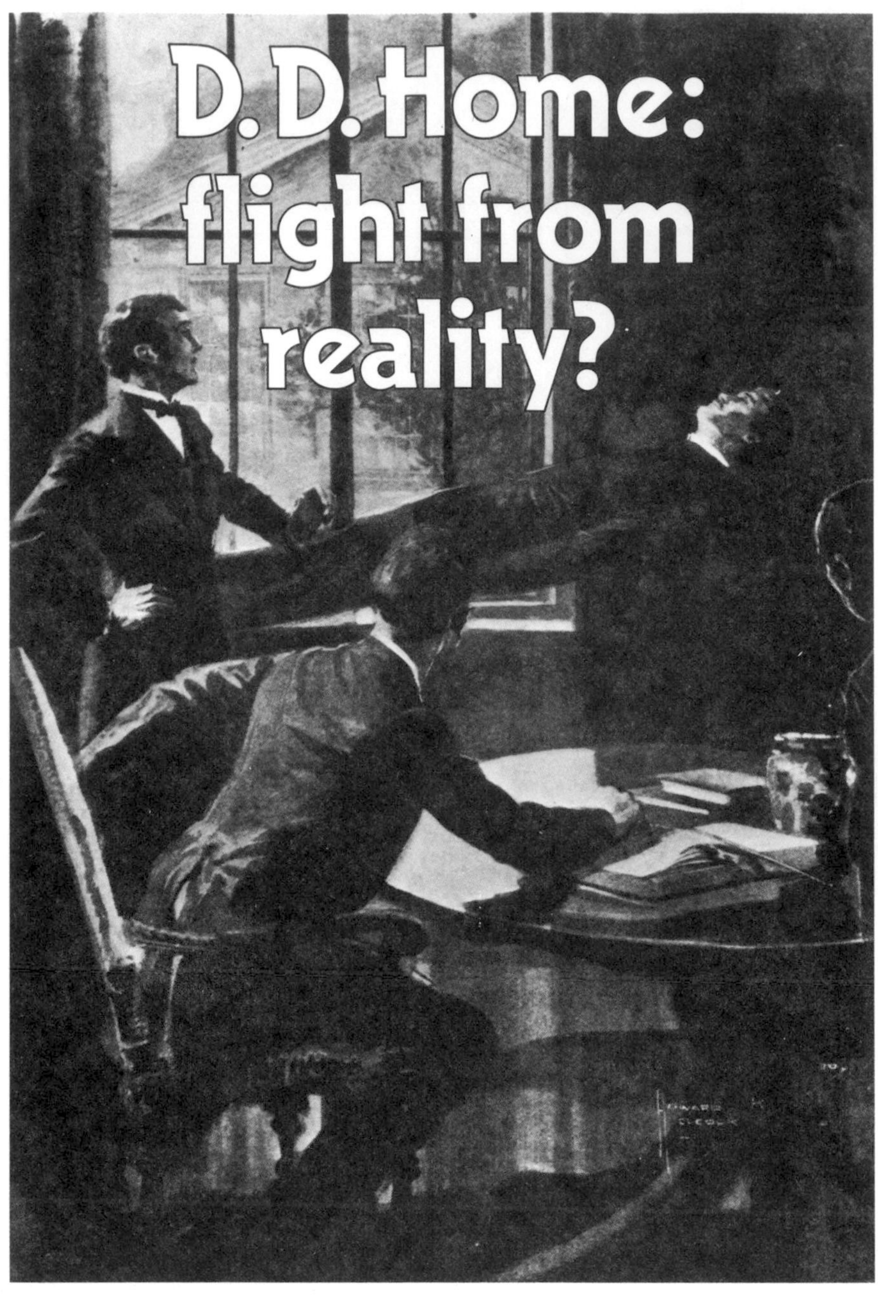

The pinnacle of D.D. Home's career came when he was seen to float out of one window and in through another

Above: an artist's impression of Home levitating. Although his psychic talents included incombustibility, bodily elongation and the manifestation of apports, he was primarily famous for his spectacular levitations

ONE OF THE MOST controversial events in the history of paranormal phenomena involved the most famous Victorian medium, Daniel Dunglas Home, who had never been detected in fraudulent activity during any of his 1500 recorded seances. This particular event, so special yet to many so suspicious, was Home's alleged levitation out of one window – some considerable distance from the ground – and back in through another. There were three witnesses to this bizarre incident: Lord Adare, his cousin Captain Charles Wynne, and the Master of Lindsay – all prominent and reputable members of London society. Yet the curious thing is that those are the only details about this event that are known with any certainty. The classic – some would say credulous – account has already been given. The results of more penetrating and objective modern research are given space here.

On 13 December 1868 those three gentlemen met for a seance with Home in an apartment in the central London area. Even their accounts of where the incident took place differed. Lord Adare said 5 Buckingham Gate, Kensington; he also said in another account that it took place at Ashley Place, Westminster. Lindsay, however, favoured Victoria Street, Westminster.

Author, sceptic and debunker of the paranormal John Sladek lists other discrepancies among the witnesses' various statements in his book *The New Apocrypha*:

> There was a ledge 4 inches [10 centimetres] wide below the windows (Adare); a ledge $1\frac{1}{2}$ inches [4 centimetres] wide (Lindsay); no foothold at all (Lindsay); balconies 7 feet [2 metres] apart (Adare); no balconies at all (Lindsay). The windows were 85 feet [25 metres] from the street (Lindsay); 70 feet [21 metres] (Lindsay); 80 feet [24 metres] (Home); on the third floor (Adare); on the first floor (Adare). It was dark (Adare); there was bright moonlight (Lindsay). Home was asleep in one room and the witnesses went into the next (Adare); Home left the witnesses in one room and went himself into the next (Adare).

In the footsteps of D.D. Home

Significantly, Captain Wynne's only recorded statement on the matter simply says: 'Home went out of one window and came in at another.' The word 'levitation' is conspicuous by its absence.

However, discrediting the witnesses by quoting the discrepancies in their statements does not necessarily imply the incident never took place. Nor have the conflicting addresses given proved too much of an obstacle in tracing the scene of the phenomenon. Archie Jarman, in his meticulously researched article published in *Alpha* magazine in October 1980, described how he managed to track down the house in question, using as his first reference *one* letter – written to Sir Francis Burnand by Lord Adare.

In this letter Adare states that the event took place at Ashley House, but gave it the wrong address, saying it was in Victoria Street. Archie Jarman noted:

> The two rooms at Ashley House were connected by folding doors . . . The sash-windows opened onto stone balconies about 15 inches [38 centimetres] wide and running the width of the windows. Lord Lindsay later recorded that the balconies were 7 feet 5 inches [2 metres 13 centimetres] apart and it was this gap that Home was supposed

to have crossed by means of levitation. An important clue given by Adare was that there was a 6-inch [15-centimetre] recess in the main wall of the building between the windows.

Jarman walked the length of Victoria Street hoping to find a faded inscription on one of the older buildings that would reveal the real 'Ashley House', but he found nothing helpful and no one who knew of its existence. But he did find an 'Ashley Place' close to the precincts of Westminster Cathedral and one of its few remaining older buildings looked promising. This was 1–10 Ashley Place. The caretaker told Jarman of the building's chequered history since its construction in 1845; of the minor repairs carried out after a bomb had exploded close to it in 1944, and that the suites – residential in Home's time – were now offices. But more significant was the fact that it used to be called 'Ashley House' before the GPO changed it to 'Ashley Place' in 1930 for some reason of their own.

Teetering on the ledge

As Jarman says, 'seeing as Home had been flying high' he took the lift to the top floor, now occupied by a firm of architects. Rather surprisingly, perhaps, Mr Perry, one of the executives of the firm, did not think Mr Jarman a crank in his search for the suite where D. D. Home 'flew'. Indeed, he was most helpful. He showed Jarman that two of his rooms were, in fact, connected by folding doors as described in Adare's account.

Mr Perry and Archie Jarman measured the distance between the balconies – 7 feet 5 inches (2 metres 13 centimetres), confirming Lindsay's description and the 6-inch (15-centimetre) recess mentioned by Adare was also present. The drop to the ground was 45 feet (13.5 metres) – not quite the 80 feet (24 metres) claimed by Home, but still a long way to fall.

Jarman noticed an architectural feature not mentioned in any of the witnesses' accounts – a flat cornice, or ledge, about 5 inches (13 centimetres) wide, ran just below the balconies. Perhaps, after all, the irreproachable Home had edged his way along this narrow foothold from window to window, simply fulfilling Captain Wynne's baldly descriptive statement.

However, Mr Jarman was nothing if not courageous. With some help from the caretaker, and taking sensible precautions, he tried to make his own way along the ledge but soon gave up. It was impossible to cross between the balconies on that ledge.

Another explanation that occurred to Archie Jarman was that Home had perhaps walked a tightrope between the balconies, having previously strung a rope or cord between them and attached it to the old-fashioned pivot-bolt of the blinds, which would have protruded beyond the windows. Intrepidly, Jarman proposed to try this death-defying feat himself but the landlords refused to sanction such a dangerous 'reconstruction'. However, it seems likely that Home could have faked his *pièce de résistance* by some artificial means such as tightrope-walking, or even swinging, Tarzan-like, between balconies.

Right: Daniel Dunglas Home (1833–1886) was undoubtedly the most famous medium of all time. He claimed to be the love-child of a Scottish peer but was brought up modestly in the United States by an aunt

Above: Home was often the butt of cartoonists. His spectacular feats brought him wealth and fame; but critics accused him of being a fraud and a gold-digger and his close friendship with Lord Adare was whispered to be 'unnatural'. The press made the most of Home's legal adoption by a rich old lady, and the fact that he fled from her when her attentions became more than motherly

Jarman's suspicions had been aroused by two unusual conditions surrounding the 'levitation' on the evening of 13 December 1868. One was Home's insistence that he *would* 'levitate' out of a specific window and back in through another. Yet this was the very medium who often remarked that he had no control over the 'spirits' who, he believed, raised him up. So why put them to the test with 45 feet (13.5 metres) of thin air and a stony pavement beneath him?

Jarman draws our attention to a second suspicious factor. Before his exit from the window Home made the three witnesses promise not to move from their chairs until he re-emerged. When he reappeared he thanked them for their co-operation in this matter. But if they had rushed to the window what would they have seen, what would their presence have ruined? The powers of the spirits? Home's concentration as he walked the tightrope or swung from balcony to balcony? Home's entire reputation once and for all? We shall never know, for like the noble English gentlemen they were, they kept their promise and remained seated, well away from the window. They saw him go out of one window and come in through another. That is all they saw.

And yet hundreds of people had witnessed Home levitate in drawing rooms in America and all over Europe. There was no doubt in their minds that the levitations they witnessed were totally genuine, inexplicable phenomena. It would be very sad if Home's only deliberate cheating was on the occasion of his most famous 'triumph'.

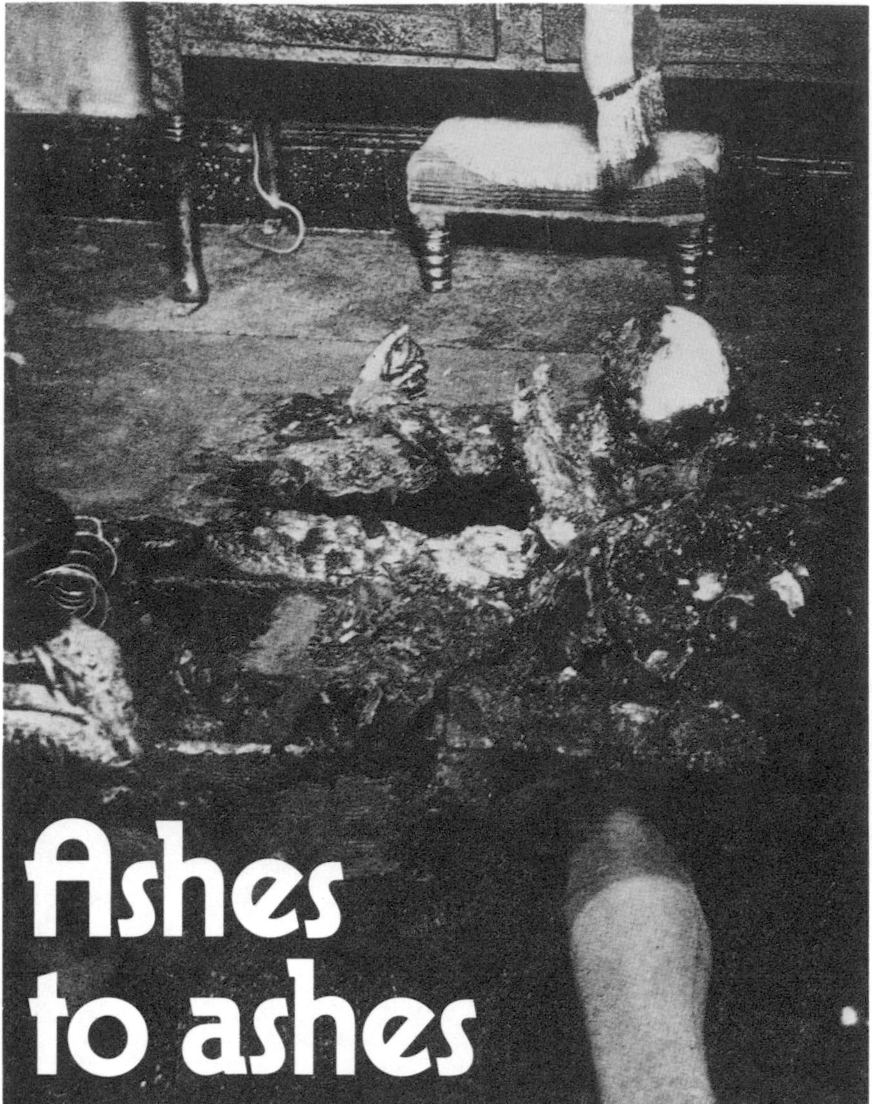

Ashes to ashes

Of all the strange and inexplicable fates that may befall a person, perhaps the most bizarre is to burst into flames without warning and without apparent cause. BOB RICKARD describes cases that still defy science

PEOPLE HAVE LONG BELIEVED that in certain circumstances the human body can burst into flames of its own accord. Flames, furthermore, of such ferocity that within minutes the victim is reduced to a heap of carbonised ashes. This idea – some call it a superstition – has been around for centuries, smouldering in the belief in divine retribution. 'By the blast of God they perish,' says the author of *Job*, 'and by the breath of his nostrils are they consumed.'

This Gothic horror was hugely popular in the 18th and 19th centuries, and its literary use is still extensively discussed in the pages of *The Dickensian*, stimulated by Charles Dickens' own fascination with the subject. Dickens had examined the case for spontaneous human combustion (SHC) 'as a Judge might have done', and knew most of the early authorities and collections of cases. He probably based his description of Krook's death in *Bleak House* (1852–3), upon the cases of Countess Bandi and Grace Pett.

The aftermath of spontaneous human combustion. The fire has reduced most of the body to ashes, leaving only parts of the lower legs, the left hand and portions of the skull, and was intense enough to burn a hole in the floor. Enormously high temperatures must have been involved, yet for some mysterious reason the fire has been contained, causing little further damage to the surroundings

The death of the 62-year-old Countess Cornelia Bandi, near Verona, is perhaps one of the first of the more reliable reports of SHC. According to a statement by Bianchini, a prebendary of Verona, dated 4 April 1731, the Countess had been put to bed after supper, and fell asleep after several hours' conversation with her maid. In the morning the maid returned to wake her and found a grisly scene. As the *Gentlemen's Magazine* reported: 'The floor of the chamber was thick-smear'd with a gluish moisture, not easily got off . . . and from the lower part of the window trickl'd down a greasy, loathsome, yellowish liquor with an unusual stink.'

Specks of soot hung in the air and covered all the surfaces in the room, and the smell had penetrated adjoining rooms. The bed was undamaged, the sheets turned back, indicating the Countess had got out of bed.

> Four feet [1.3 metres] from the bed was a heap of ashes, two legs untouch'd, stockings on, between which lay the head, the brains, half of the back-part of the skull and the whole chin burn'd to ashes, among which were found three fingers blacken'd. All the rest was ashes which had this quality, that they left in the hand a greasy and stinking moisture.

A hole burnt in the floor

Bianchini could have been describing some of our modern cases. The diligent researches of Larry E. Arnold unearthed the fate of Dr J. Irving Bentley, a 93-year-old retired physician of Coudersport, Pennsylvania. Gas company worker Don Gosnell discovered the remains after smelling a 'light-blue smoke of unusual odor'. The fire had been so intense that it almost totally consumed the old man. John Dec the deputy coroner said: 'All I found was a knee joint atop a post in the basement, the lower leg from the knee down, and the now-scattered ashes 6 feet [2 metres] below.' And yet the fire had, mysteriously, been contained; firemen testified to the existence of a few embers around the hole, and a slight scorching on the bathtub about a foot (30 centimetres) away was the only other sign of this fiercely fatal fire. The burns on the bath were still visible when Arnold investigated nine years later.

It was suggested that Bentley was a careless smoker – small burns riddled his everyday clothes and the bedroom floor – and that he had wakened to find himself on fire, struggled to the bathroom in search of water, and there collapsed and died. Arnold, in his report on the case in the journal *Pursuit*, 1976, points out that there are several inconsistencies in this account, though it was accepted by the local newspaper and the coroner.

Bentley's pipe had been 'carefully placed' on its stand by his chair; not the action of a man on fire. A broken hip six years before had left him with no feeling in his left leg, and he walked with difficulty – his 'walker' can be seen fallen across the hole. He was enough of a doctor to realise that his only chance of survival, had his clothes been on fire, would be to take them off there and then, rather than risk the precarious trip to the bathroom.

It is more likely that whatever happened to Bentley occurred when he visited the bathroom for some other reason, and that he was beginning to burn before he took off his robe, setting fire to it in the process – it was found smouldering in the bathtub. The autopsy was a mere formality, yet despite having so little to go on – just half a leg; the ashes were never analysed – the coroner decided that Dr Bentley had died of *asphyxiation*, probably because that is the usual cause of death during fires.

Primarily due to the efforts of Charles Fort, the pioneer collector of accounts of strange phenomena, and the small number of people and journals who continue his work, we have accumulated a respectable number of records, from newspapers and medical journals, of SHC right up to the present. Very few of the accounts mention SHC, because officially there is no such phenomenon, and coroners and their advisers have the unenviable task of dealing with evidence that seems to contradict accepted physical laws and medical opinion. Inevitably, suppositions are made about knocked over heaters, flying sparks, careless smoking, and in the case of child victims, playing with matches. Faced with the alternative – a nightmare out of the Dark Ages – it is not surprising that they are accepted.

There are occasional exceptions, which are far more useful to those who truly wish to solve the enigma, like the report in *Lloyds Weekly News* of 5 February 1905. A woman asleep by a fireplace woke to find herself in flames and later died. The honest coroner said he could not understand: the woman had gone to sleep facing the fire, so any cinder that shot out from the grate would ignite the front of her clothes. Yet it was her back that bore the severe burns.

Fear of the truth

At worst, a story may be rejected out of fear or disbelief, as in the case of the elderly spinster, Wilhelmina Dewar, who combusted near midnight on 22 March 1908, in the Northumberland town of Whitley Bay. Wilhelmina was found by her sister Margaret who, in a shocked state, managed to summon her neighbours. In the house they found the severely charred body of Wilhelmina in an upstairs bed. The bedclothes were unscorched and there was no sign of fire anywhere else in the house.

When Margaret told this story at the inquest, the coroner thought it preposterous and asked her to think again. Repeatedly she said she was telling the truth and could not change her story – even after a policeman testified that Margaret was so drunk she couldn't have known what she was saying. As Fort points out, the policeman 'was not called upon to state how he distinguished between signs of excitement and terror, and intoxication.' The coroner adjourned the inquest to give her more time to think. When it was reconvened a few days later it was obvious that a great deal of pressure had been placed upon poor Margaret.

Both sisters were retired school teachers and, up until then, lived respectably. Now the coroner was calling her a liar, the papers called her a drunk, and friends and neighbours turned away, leaving her to face a

A villain meets his end

In chapter 32 of *Bleak House*, Charles Dickens' characters, William Guppy and Tony Weevle, discover that the evil Krook has been mysteriously burned to a few charred lumps and ashes, filling the room with 'hateful soot' and objects coated with an offensive 'thick yellow liquor'. 'Call the death by any name . . . attribute it to whom you will, or say it might have been prevented how you will, it is the same death eternally – inborn, inbred, engendered in the corrupt humours of the vicious body itself, and that only – Spontaneous Combustion, and none other of all the deaths that can be died.'

hostile court. Not surprisingly, she said she had been inaccurate. This time she told a story of finding her sister burned, but alive, in a lower part of the house. Then she helped her upstairs to bed, where she died.

This sounded superficially more plausible, was accepted, and the proceedings promptly closed. The court was not interested in how Wilhelmina was transformed from someone who could be helped upstairs into the cindered corpse with charred abdomen and legs; or how, if she continued to smoulder after being helped into bed, there was no mark of fire in the house. 'But the coroner was satisfied,' wrote Fort sarcastically. 'The proper testimony had been recorded.'

Yet it was medico-legal interest that kept alive the notion of SHC, with pathologists endorsing the phenomenon, than rejecting it in favour of 'preternatural combustibility'. In addition, there was the perennial possibility that a murderer may simulate SHC to hide his crime. One of the earliest test cases occurred in Rheims in 1725 when an innkeeper, Jean Millet, was accused of having an affair with a pretty servant girl and killing his wife. The wife, who was often drunk, was found one morning about a foot (30 centimetres) away from the hearth.

'A part of the head only, with a portion of the lower extremities, and a few of the vertebrae, had escaped combustion. A foot and a half (45 centimetres) of the flooring under the body had been consumed, but a kneading-trough and a powdering tub very near the body sustained no injury.' A young assistant doctor, named Le Cat, was staying at the inn and managed to convince the court that this was no ordinary fire death but a 'visitation of God' upon the drunken woman, and an obvious result of soaking one's innards with spirits. Millet was vindicated, and Le Cat went on to qualify with distinction, and publish a memoir on SHC.

Spontaneous human combustion received its severest criticism from the great pioneer chemist, Baron Justus von Liebig, who wrote a spirited refutation of both spontaneous and preternatural combustion, on the grounds that no one had seen it happen. As a scientist he saw the historical evidence as an unsupported record of the *belief* in SHC, rather than actual proof of spontaneous burning deaths. Further, he lamented the lack of expert witnesses, and dismissed the accounts generally because they 'proceed from ignorant persons, unpractised in observation, and bear in themselves the stamp of untrustworthiness.'

Despite Liebig's assertion, however, there is plenty of evidence from both medical and police sources. Many of these bear witness to the ferocity of the phenomenon, as in the case investigated by Merille, a surgeon in Caen, recorded in Trotter's *Essay on drunkenness* (1804). On 3 June 1782, Merille was asked by 'the king's officers' in the city to report on the death of Mademoiselle Thaurs, a lady of over 60 who had been observed, that day, to have drunk three bottles of wine and one of brandy. Merille wrote:

> The body lay with the crown of the head resting against one of the handirons . . . 18 inches [45 centimetres] from the fire, the remainder of the body was placed obliquely before the chimney, the whole being nothing but a mass of ashes. Even the most solid bones had lost their form and consistence. The right foot was found entire and scorched at its upper junction; the left was more burnt. The day was cold but there was nothing in the grate except two or three bits of wood about an inch in diameter, burnt in the middle.

Dr Wilton Krogman, who investigated a famous case of SHC, and experimented with

Left: the great chemist Baron Justus von Liebig. He rejected tales of spontaneous human combustion because of the lack of expert witnesses – and because his attempts to make flesh burn with the same intensity as SHC were, without exception, a dismal failure

Below: an anonymous victim of SHC lies with its apparently unburnt head resting in a grate. An electric fire is also visible – but how did the body burn so thoroughly without setting fire to the rest of the room?

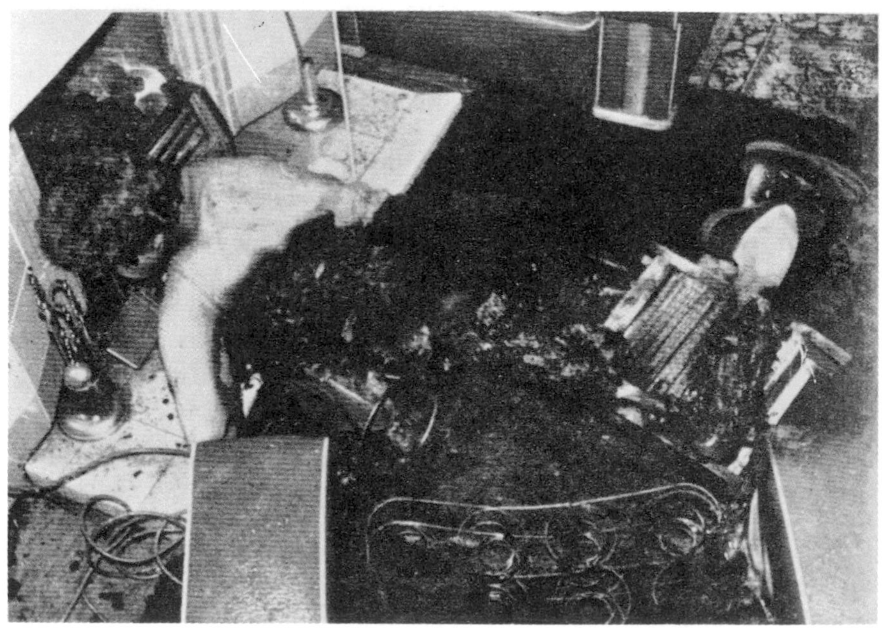

The burning of Dr Bentley

Dr J. Irving Bentley, a retired physician, lived on the ground floor of an apartment building in Coudersport, northern Pennsylvania. On the cold morning of 5 December 1966, Don Gosnell entered the building's basement to read the meter for the North Pen Gas Company. In the basement a 'light-blue smoke of unusual odor' hung in the air. Scattering an unfamiliar heap in the corner with his boot, Gosnell found it was ashes. There had been no answer to his greeting on the way in, so he decided to look in on the old man. There was more strange smoke in the bedroom but no sign of Bentley. Gosnell peered into the bathroom and was confronted with a sight he will never forget. A large hole had burned through the floor to the basement, exposing the joists and pipework below. On the edge of the hole he saw '. . . a brown leg from the knee down, like that of a mannequin. I didn't look further!' Gosnell fled from the building.

sophisticated crematorium equipment, said: 'Only at 3000°F (1500°C) plus have I seen bone fuse or melt so that it ran and became volatile.' Such a heat would certainly char everything within a considerable radius and set the house ablaze, yet the meticulous Merille writes:

> None of the furniture in the apartment was damaged. The chair on which she was sitting was found at the distance of a foot from her, and absolutely untouched . . . the consumption of the body had taken place in less than 7 hours, though according to appearance, nothing around the body was burnt but the clothes.

Reluctant admissions

Modern researchers into SHC readily quash the idea that the phenomenon is as rare as some commentators suggest. Similarly, there is a growing number of cases testified to by doctors and pathologists, and this number would probably increase if the fear of ridicule could be completely removed. A Dr B. H. Hartwell reported to the Massachusetts Medico-Legal Society an unusual case of SHC that he witnessed while driving through Ayer, Massachusetts, on 12 May 1890.

He was stopped and called into a wood where he saw a horrible sight. In a clearing a woman was crouching 'in flames at the shoulders, both sides of the abdomen, and both legs.' Neither he nor the other witnesses could find an obvious cause for the fire.

This doctor's experience was not unique. Support for the suspicion that many a doctor would be able to tell of an encounter with mysterious and fatal fires comes in a coincidental and roundabout way. Maxwell Cade and Delphine Davis, authors of the imaginative study of ball lightning *Taming of the thunderbolts* (1969), confessed they themselves would not have put much faith in the above story, or in the existence of SHC, 'if a doctor friend had not told us of a lecture which he attended at the Massachusetts Medico-Legal Society, where several such cases were discussed. When we expressed cautious doubts, the doctor assured us that he had been called to a similar case himself as recently as the autumn of 1959.'

When Dr D. J. Gee of the University of Leeds delivered his well-known paper on 'A case of spontaneous combustion' he was surprised by the candid discussion that followed. He is quoted as saying:

> Dr George Manning described his experience of several similar cases, and indicated that the phenomenon was certainly not as rare as might be supposed from the literature. This view was supported by Dr David Price, who said that he met with this phenomenon approximately once in every four years.

A strange unnatural fire

The idea that human beings can burst into flames of their own accord is odd enough. But, as BOB RICKARD shows, everything about spontaneous human combustion is bizarre

Spontaneous human combustion strikes with astonishing speed, yet the heat generated is sufficient to char even the bones of the victim. In contrast, a body can take hours to burn away in the sustained fire of a crematorium – and even then only the flesh is thoroughly destroyed

PERHAPS THE MOST common characteristic of SHC is the sheer speed with which it strikes. Many victims were seen alive only a few moments before the fire struck from nowhere. An Italian surgeon called Battaglio reported the death of a priest, named Bertholi, in the town of Filetto, in 1789. Lodging with his brother-in-law, he had been left alone in his room reading a prayerbook. A few minutes later he screamed. People came running to find him on the floor surrounded by a pale flame, which receded as they approached.

Bertholi wore a sackcloth under his clothes, next to his skin, and it was immediately apparent that the outer clothes had burned away leaving the sackcloth intact. Under the sackcloth the skin on the man's trunk was not burned, but detached from the flesh and hung in shreds.

Some writers deduce that the fire develops with particular rapidity, from the fact that the victims are often discovered still sitting calmly, as though nothing had happened.

A dramatic example is given in Ron Willis's article on SHC in *INFO Journal* 8 (1972). In 1960, five charred bodies were found in a burned-out car near Pikeville, Kentucky. The coroner commented: 'They were sitting there as though they'd just gotten into the car. With all that heat it seems there'd be some sort of struggle to escape. But there hadn't been.'

Another almost universal characteristic of SHC is the extreme intensity of heat that is involved. Under normal circumstances the human body is very hard to set alight, especially if still alive, and people who die in fires usually sustain only partial or superficial damage to the body. Reduction to a pile of calcined ashes, experts all agree, demands a fierce heat which needs to be externally fuelled and maintained for hours, and even so crematoria still have to grind up the bones that remain afterward.

The death of Mrs Reeser (see box) was investigated by Dr Wilton M. Krogman, a renowned forensic anthropologist from the University of Pennsylvania School of Medicine, who has researched and experimented the causes and effects of deaths by and during fires. He said he has watched bodies in a crematorium burn for over 8 hours at 2000°F (1110°C) without any sign of the bones becoming ashes or powder; and that it takes a heat of about 3000°F (1650°C) to make bone melt and become volatile. Willis mentions the case of Leon Eveille, aged 40, found burnt to a crisp in his locked car at Arcis-sur-Aube, France, on 17 June 1971. The heat had melted the windows. It was estimated that a burning car normally reaches about 1300°F (700°C), but to melt glass the temperature must have been over 1800°F (1000°C).

Time and again in cases of SHC, we encounter a further strange effect: the confinement of the heat. Charred bodies are found lying in unscorched beds, sitting on slightly singed chairs, or with their clothing intact.

In 1905 the *British Medical Journal* reported the death of 'an elderly woman of intemperate habits'. Authorities broke into a house from which smoke was issuing to find

> a small pyramidal heap of broken calcinated human bones, on the top of

Dr Wilton Krogman, an expert on the effects of fire on the human body. He was astonished by the state of Mrs Reeser's corpse, and constructed an elaborate theory to account for it

which was a skull, on the floor in front of a chair. All the bones were completely bleached and brittle; every particle of soft tissue had been consumed, and yet a tablecloth within three feet of the remains was not even scorched. . . .

Curiously, the ceiling was scorched, as if the woman had become a pillar of fire.

Fort, in his *Complete books* (1941) gives two startling cases. The first, from the *Daily News* of 17 December 1904, describes how Mrs Thomas Cochrane, of Falkirk, was found in a bedroom burned to death 'beyond recognition'. There had been no outcry, and little else burned, with no fire in the grate. Her charred corpse was found 'sitting in a chair, surrounded by pillows and cushions'. The second is from the *Madras Mail* of 13 May 1907 concerning a woman in the village of Manner, near Dinapore. Flames had consumed her body, but not her clothes. Two constables had found the corpse in a room in which nothing else showed signs of fire, and had carried the smouldering body to the District Magistrate.

In 1841 the *British Medical Journal* reported an address by Dr F. S. Reynolds to the Manchester Pathological Society on the subject of SHC. Although rejecting the idea of 'spontaneous' combustion, he admitted there were baffling cases, and gave an instance from his experience of a woman of 40 who fell near a hearth. She was found next morning still burning. What astonished him was the damage to the legs: inside unharmed stockings her femora were carbonised and knee-joints opened.

Some chroniclers of SHC have drawn attention to the lack of outcry and struggle by victims. 'In their grim submission,' Fort wrote, 'it is almost as if they had been lulled by the wings of a vampire.' There is more to it than being overcome by drink and fumes – some psychic or psychological component of the phenomenon prefaces or accompanies the burning, and this may explain the lack of escape, and the inability of surviving victims to tell what happened to them.

For example, the *Hull Daily Mail* of 6 January 1905 describes how an elderly

The destruction of Mary Reeser

Workmen are seen here clearing away the remains of the chair in which Mrs Mary Reeser, a widow of 67, of St Petersburg, Florida, departed this life on a pillar of fire, during the night of 1 July 1951. Damage to the surroundings was minimal. The overstuffed chair was burned down to its springs, there was a patch of soot on the ceiling above and a small circle of carpet was charred around the chair, but a pile of papers nearby was unscorched. Dr Wilton Krogman, a forensic scientist who specialised in fire deaths, was visiting in the area and joined the investigation. He said:

> I cannot conceive of such complete cremation without more burning of the apartment itself. In fact the apartment and everything in it should have been consumed. Never have I seen a human skull shrunk by intense heat. The opposite has always been true; the skulls have been either abnormally swollen or have virtually exploded into hundreds of pieces . . . I regard it as the most amazing thing I have ever seen. As I review it, the short hairs on my neck bristle with vague fear. Were I living in the Middle Ages, I'd mutter something about black magic.

Police considered every likely theory, and a few unasked-for ideas from cranky members of the public: suicide by petrol, ignition of methane gas in her body, murder by flame-thrower, 'atomic pill' (whatever that meant), magnesium, phosphorus and napalm substances . . . and even a 'ball of fire' which one anonymous letter-writer claimed to see. In the end the coroner accepted the FBI theory, that she had fallen asleep while smoking and set her clothes alight.

Dr Krogman himself proffered the idea that Mrs Reeser had been burned elsewhere by someone with access to crematorium-type equipment or materials, then was carried back to the apartment, where the mystery assailant had added the finishing touches, like heat-buckled plastic objects, and a doorknob that was still hot in the morning. A year later, the police confessed the case was still open.

woman, Elizabeth Clark, was found in the morning with fatal burns, while her bed, in the Trinity Almshouse, Hull, was unmarked by fire. There had been no outcry or sounds of struggle through the thin partitions. She was 'unable to give an articulate account' of her accident, and later died. Of course that could mean that the authorities – not for the first time – simply didn't believe her account.

In *Lo!* (1930), Fort describes the complex fires that plagued Binbrook Farm, near Grimsby, in the winter of 1904–5. One incident involved a young servant girl who was burning without her knowledge, and might have been another SHC statistic had not her employer roused her from her day-dreaming (or trance). According to a local newspaper, the farmer said:

> Our servant girl, whom we had taken from the workhouse . . . was sweeping the kitchen. There was a very small fire in the grate; there was a guard there so that no one can come within 2 feet [0.6 metres] or more of the fire, and she was at the other end of the room, and had not been near. I suddenly came into the kitchen and there she was, sweeping away while the back of her dress was on fire. She looked around as I shouted, and seeing the flames, rushed through the door. She tripped and I smothered the fire out with wet sacks.

The girl had obviously been on fire for some time and was 'terribly burned'.

As we have seen in the Pikeville car case, several people have combusted together, but such cases are extremely rare. Baron Liebig thought that the occurrence of multiple SHC cases disproved the 'disease' theory (see box), since in his experience a disease has never run the same course in two or more people, detail for detail, culminating in their simultaneous death. Certainly none of the 'diseases' that are suggested by the theory's apologists has done so.

Willis describes the case of the Rooneys who lived in a farmhouse near Seneca, Illinois:

> On Christmas Eve 1885, Patrick Rooney and his wife and their hired man, John Larson, were drinking whiskey in the kitchen. Larson went to bed and woke up Christmas morning feeling sick. Downstairs in the kitchen he found everything covered with an oily film, and on the floor, Patrick Rooney dead. Larson rode to get help from Rooney's son John, who lived nearby. Back at the farm the two men noticed that there was a charred hole next to the kitchen table. Looking into the hole they found, on the earth under the kitchen floor, a calcined skull, a few charred bones and a pile of ashes. Mrs Rooney had been obliterated by a fantastically hot fire that had not spread beyond her immediate area.

The coroner soon found that Patrick had been suffocated by the smoke of the burning body of his wife.

Charles Fort, who spent a lifetime collecting reports of SHC and other inexplicable occurrences. Fort wondered if SHC might be connected with demonology: 'I think our data relate not to "spontaneous combustion of human bodies" but to things or beings, that with a flaming process consume men and women, but like werewolves or alleged werewolves, mostly pick women.'

Fuelling the human fireball

Among the early pathologists the theory arose that in certain circumstances the body may produce gases that combust on exposure to quantities of oxygen. The distinguished scientist Baron Karl von Reichenbach wrote of the 'miasma of putrefaction' of human bodies, for instance. But Liebig could find no evidence of such a gas, 'in health, in disease, nay not even in the putrefaction of dead bodies.'

Dixon Mann and W. A. Brend, in their *Forensic medicine and toxicology* (1914) give the case of a fat man who died two hours after admission to Guy's Hospital, London, in 1885. The following day his corpse was found bloated, the skin distended all over and filled with gas, although there was no sign of decomposition. 'When punctures were made in the skin, the gas escaped and burnt with a flame like that of carburetted hydrogen; as many as a dozen flames were burning at the same time.' Had the man died at home near a fire, another case of 'spontaneous combustion' would have been reported to confuse researchers further.

However, gases within the body tissues of the sort suggested would be fatally toxic, and the victim would have been gravely ill or dead. And generally there are no such symptoms: victims have often been seen alive shortly before their flaming. Nor does this theory account for the observed fact of clothes that are left unburnt on a charred corpse.

As an alternative to the disease theory, we might consider organic or mechanical malfunctions of normal processes within the body. Ivan Sanderson and, before him, Vincent Gaddis, speculated about the build-up of phosphagens in muscle tissue, particularly the vitamin B10, vital to normal energy supplies. A technical paper in *Applied Trophology* (December 1957) included this relevant paragraph:

> Phosphagen is a compound like nitro-glycerine, of endothermic formation. It is no doubt so highly developed in certain sedentary persons as to make their bodies actually combustible, subject to ignition, burning like wet gun-powder under some circumstances.

This may explain the readiness of some bodies to blaze, but we still have to identify the source of ignition.

An unmistakable case of simultaneous SHC is summarised by Fort, of an elderly couple named Kiley, who lived near Southampton. On the morning of 26 February 1905, neighbours heard a curious 'scratching' and went next door to investigate. They entered the house and found it in flames inside. Kiley was found burned to death on the floor. Mrs Kiley, burned to death, was sitting in a chair in the same room, 'badly charred but recognisable'. Both bodies were fully dressed,

> judging by the fragments of clothes, indicating they had been burned before their time for going to bed . . . the mystery was that two persons, neither of whom had cried for help, presumably not asleep in any ordinary sense, should have been burned to death in a fire that did not manifest as a general fire until hours later.

There are on record two cases of SHC which coincided with suicide attempts, the implication of which is obscure unless one presupposes some form of the 'psychic suicide' theory in which victims combust because they have given up on life.

On 13 December 1959, 27-year-old Billy Peterson, of Pontiac, Michigan, said goodbye to his mother and drove to his garage where he hooked a pipe from the car's exhaust into the car itself. Only 40 minutes after Billy had left his mother, a passing motorist saw the smoke and investigated. Inside the car Billy was dead from carbon monoxide poisoning, but it was the condition of his body that puzzled pathologists. His back, arms and legs were covered in third-degree burns, and some parts of him were charred to a crisp. Despite all this, his clothes and underclothes were quite unharmed.

On 18 September 1952, Glen Denney, 46, a foundry worker in Louisiana, cut the arteries in his left arm and both wrists and ankles, but he had died from inhaling smoke. When found, he was a 'mass of flames' with nothing else in the room ablaze. The coroner guessed that he had poured kerosene over himself and lit a match, though no container was found, and just how he could hold, let alone light, a match with arterial blood pumping over his hands at about 4 per cent of body volume per second was not explained. The investigator, Otto Burma, wrote: 'There is no doubt in my mind that Denney did in fact attempt suicide. But while in the process of carrying out this act his body caught fire due to some unknown cause.'

Many other aspects of SHC would reward investigation. There are, for instance, demonstrable connections with poltergeist phenomena, which frequently involve mysterious spontaneous fires. Then there are people who are fire-prone, in whose presence fires repeatedly break out. Examining these and other facts that surround SHC may lead us nearer to understanding the phenomenon – and perhaps to identifying its causes.

The end of an old soldier

On 19 February 1888, Dr J. Mackenzie Booth, a lecturer at Aberdeen University, was called to the loft of a stable in Constitution Street, where he found the charred corpse of a 65-year-old pensioner. There was considerable damage to the body: most of the fleshy parts had burned away exposing the calcined ends of bones. The floor around the man had burnt through so that the corpse rested on a charred beam. The heat had also burned the roofing slats above him, causing some slates to fall onto his chest and damage his brittle form further. He was last seen going into the loft with a bottle and lamp the previous evening.

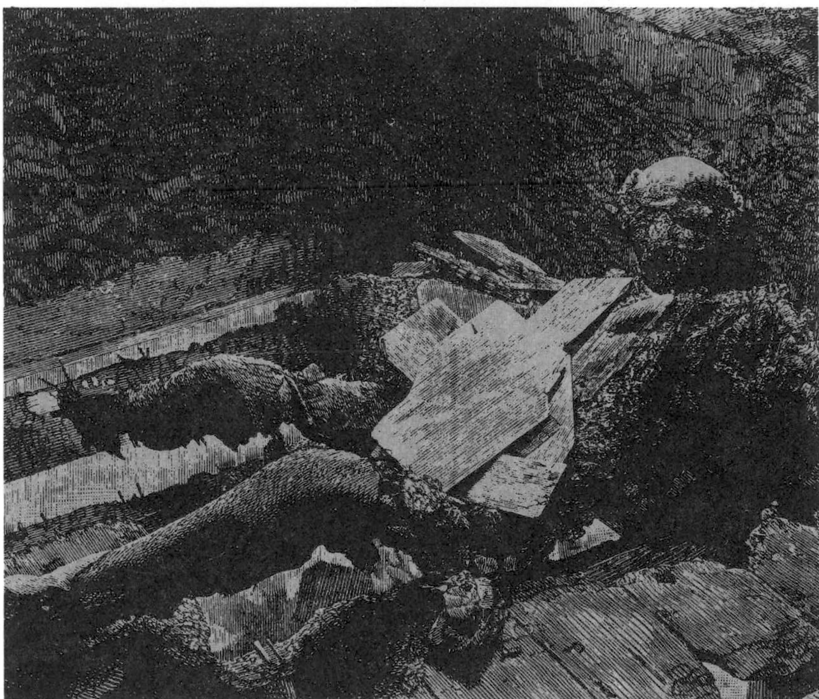

It was thought that he had knocked the lamp over and then been overcome by drink and smoke. (Booth's report describes the 'old soldier' as being 'of inebriate habits'.) But the lamp had been seen to go out shortly after he went into the loft, and no fire was seen during the night. Furthermore, it is clear from this engraving (from the *British Medical Journal* of 21 April 1888, and based directly on a photograph of the scene) that the bales of hay surrounding the man did not catch fire. The carbonised face retained recognisable features, from which, and from 'the comfortably recumbent attitude of the body' Booth noted that 'it was evident that there had been no death struggle.'

Mysteries of the human bonfire

Medical men and scientists have long doubted that spontaneous human combustion actually occurs. But the facts stubbornly refuse to fit their conventional explanations

DEATHS THAT APPEAR to have been caused by spontaneous human combustion (SHC) have always been an embarrassment to the medical profession. The refusal to believe in SHC is not the result of a deliberate conspiracy to suppress the evidence, however. Rather there has been a turning away, a wish not to think about such an outrage of accepted medical and scentific knowledge.

If SHC is mentioned at all, it is only to be dismissed as a belief mistakenly held by the uninformed, or as a superstition lingering from less enlightened times. J. L. Casper, for example, in his *Handbook of the practice of forensic medicine*, complained: 'It is sad to think that in an earnest scientific work, in this year of grace 1861, we must still treat of the fable of "spontaneous combustion".' And opinion today is hardly less compromising. Dr Gavin Thurston, the coroner for Inner West London, has said that 'no such phenomenon as spontaneous combustion exists, or has ever occurred'.

At the same time, those scientists and doctors who have examined the effects closely, acknowledge that there have been cases of death by burning that are genuinely inexplicable. But since SHC officially does not exist, some other reason has had to be found for the same effects. And so the notion of 'preternatural combustibility' was born.

The next step was to identify the causes of such a combustibility – and, in any given case, to discover its source of ignition. So, in the middle of the 19th century, a typical SHC victim was thought to be almost certainly a drinker and a smoker; most likely an elderly, solitary, corpulent woman of sedentary habits. Alcohol was both the physical and the moral cause of conflagration. Horrific tales circulated about divine punishment for inebriation, in which the lambent and inextinguishable flames were but a foretaste of the everlasting hellfire to come. Boineau, a French priest, reported the 1749 case of an 80-year-old woman reduced to a carbonised skeleton as she sat sipping brandy. As Baron Justus von Liebig noted sarcastically, 'The chair, which of course had not sinned, did not burn.'

Liebig, in fact, sceptical of SHC though he was, utterly discredited the notion that there was any connection between the phenomenon and drinking. Liebig showed conclusively that alcohol-saturated flesh will burn only until the alcohol is used up; and fatty tissue behaves in the same way – when it can be set alight.

In his 1965 article in *Medicine, science and the law*, Dr D. J. Gee, a lecturer in forensic

Top: Only the legs remain of Mrs E.M., a widow who died on 29 January 1958. Was she burnt by the fire in the grate, or did she combust of her own accord?

Above: Dr Gavin Thurston, who has firmly stated that SHC has never taken place medicine at Leeds University, described his own experiments following his examination of a charred corpse in 1963. Dr Gee successfully, set light to small quantities of fat, but the burning could be sustained only by placing the sample in a strong draught. Even this resulted in no more than a slow smouldering, not the spectacular blaze typical of SHC. However, this has only made it necessary for investigators of what would otherwise be admitted as cases of SHC to look for the 'explanatory' sustaining draught, and prompted some writers to highlight victims who were found in or near a fireplace, where there would be such an updraught.

The readiness with which coroners have adopted these suggestions seems to indicate a strong desire to terminate the proceedings as quickly, conveniently and 'reasonably' as possible, rather than admit a bizarre and frightening mystery. Some verdicts are far from satisfactory. Consider the case of Grace Pett, a fishwife of Ipswich, who was found on the morning of 10 April 1744, lying on the floor near the grate, and burning 'like a block of wood . . . with a glowing fire without flame'. After the fire was put out, Grace was seen to be 'like a heap of charcoal covered with white ashes'. That Grace was a regular smoker, and had the previous evening 'drunk plentifully of gin' in welcoming a daughter home from Gibraltar, were sufficient for the advocates of temperance and preternatural combustibility.

There are several details in this case, however, that afford these apologists no comfort. According to the account in Sir David Brewster's *Natural magic* (1842) there had been no fire at all in the grate, and a candle, in use that fateful evening, had burnt down safely overnight in its candlestick. And worse: 'The clothes of a child on one side of her, and a paper screen on the other were untouched', and the wooden floor beneath her burning body 'was neither singed nor discoloured'.

Can we, in the 20th century, offer an alternative explanation for SHC besides 'preternatural combustibility'? The savants of the 19th century can be forgiven for thinking only in terms of conventional fire. But since the admirable Liebig's day the physical and medical sciences have made enormous progress. Today we know of many forms of death that can penetrate a man's body silently and invisibly. Military research into 'radiation weapons' has supplemented nuclear radiation with beamed ultrasound, X-ray lasers, microwave projectors and other horrors, all of which can cook a man inside his clothes. But the spirit of Liebig exhorts us to be rigorous: even if we credit the idea of an

Sir David Brewster, whose account of one fire death bears all the marks of a case of SHC. The coroner, however, thought otherwise

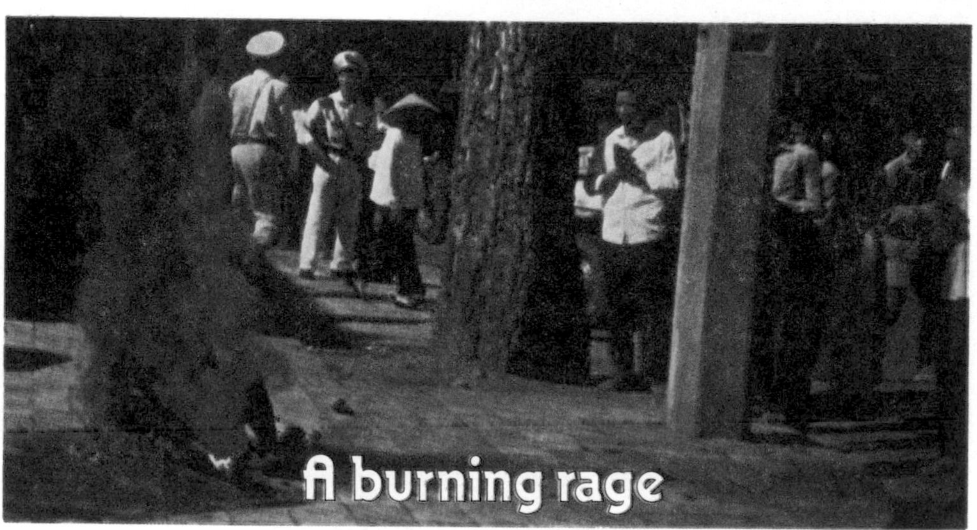

A burning rage

Reviewing the cases of SHC in his book *Mysterious fires and lights* (1967), veteran Fortean Vincent Gaddis noted that a high proportion of victims had apparently given up on life. 'Some were alcoholics, and alcoholism is a form of escape from reality . . . Most were elderly with lowered resistance and perhaps tired of life. Many were invalids or poverty-stricken, dying in rest homes or almshouses. Many led idle, sedentary lives.' Charles Fort and his successors have also observed a significant number of 'no-hopers' among SHC victims. In *Fire from heaven* Michael Harrison suggests that there are several kinds of SHC, one of which is self-induced by people who are depressed, lonely, deprived, frightened and perhaps resentful. Harrison wonders if normally controlled reserves of physical and psychical energy are not suddenly released in a fatal conflagration, as a kind of 'psychic suicide'.

Suicide by fire has always had symbolic overtones, and has been used to make a political gesture. That a massive build-up of rage or despair may result in a spontaneous blaze is appealing, but it is highly conjectural. Besides, it would account for only some cases.

ubiquitous madman recently on the loose with a death ray, we still have to account for the instances from the past.

There are in fact a number of theories that might account for SHC, though not all are equally attractive. Among the least likely are the 'psychic suicide' theory (see box), and the proposition that people whose clothes are set alight catch fire themselves.

This was the suggestion in the case of Phyllis Newcombe. At midnight on 27 August 1938 she and her fiancé were leaving the dance floor of a Chelmsford ballroom, when she suddenly screamed. Her crinoline dress had become a mass of flames. It was put out with some difficulty – and too late, for Phyllis died in hospital a few hours later. At the inquest it was suggested that a discarded cigarette had set the dress alight. The material flamed when a lighter was put to it, but failed to catch fire when lit cigarettes were thrown at it. The coroner expressed his puzzlement and gave a verdict of accidental death. Puzzled he might have been, since in any case external fires cannot produce burns as extensive as those in SHC cases unless large quantities of fuel and oxygen are supplied over a considerable period of time. Even when these conditions are met, the body is burnt from the outside *in*. But there are many cases of SHC in which the burning takes place *within* the flesh, and the clothes or surroundings remain unharmed.

Another somewhat unsatisfactory thesis is the 'corrosive liquid' theory, and it likewise attempts to explain *away* certain cases of death by fire. Nevertheless this was the reason suggested for the death of Madge Knight. At about 3.30 a.m. on 19 November 1943 she was asleep alone in the spare room of her house in Aldingbourne, Sussex. She awoke feeling as if she were on fire. Her screams brought her husband and others who were sharing the house.

The scorching of a slim lady

Photographic evidence of bizarre burning deaths is very rare and not readily accessible even to the dedicated and bona fide researcher. The charred remains shown here are of 'a slim lady, 85 years old, who was in good health' when she was consumed by flames in November 1963. The case was investigated by Dr D. J. Gee. Because of extensive damage to the body (but to little else) it was assumed that the victim had been in a state of unusual combustibility, and was set alight by an ember or a spark – a theory that would accord with the results of Dr Gee's experiments and the theory of preternatural combustibility.

Conflagration of a clergyman

While away from his parish in Stockcross, Newbury, England, the Reverend Mr Adams burned to death in a hotel room in New York, in 1876, apparently as a result of spontaneous combustion. In *Fire from heaven*, Michael Harrison remarks that 'ecclesiastics, as a class' seem strangely vulnerable to SHC and other paranormal heat phenomena.

Madge was naked under the bedclothes, but she was in agony because extensive burning had removed most of the skin from her back. A doctor administered morphine, and, bemused, called in a Harley Street specialist. The specialist later told the coroner that he thought the burns must have been caused by a corrosive liquid because there was no sign of fire on the sheets or anywhere else in the room, and no smell of burning. Madge was repeatedly questioned but could not, or would not, say what had happened before she died in hospital in Chichester, on 6 December.

The lack of any sign of fire in many cases has led some researchers to theorise about substances that can burn without flame. In Madge Knight's case, no trace of any corrosive chemical could be found, nor any possible container for it. The notion that Madge hid the evidence before crawling into bed is too absurd to contemplate.

Perhaps the most fruitful clue to the

nature of the phenomenon came in 1975, with Livingstone Gearhart's article in the Fortean journal *Pursuit*. He had discovered that a significant number of SHC cases took place on or near a peak in the geomagnetic flux. The strength of the Earth's magnetic field rises and falls quite dramatically in relation to solar activity. Global averages of the daily figures are gathered for astronomers and geophysicists, and these show a distinct correlation between the incidence of SHC and high geomagnetic readings. This seems to indicate that SHC may be the result of a very complex chain of events, in which there is an interaction between certain astronomical conditions and the state of an individual's body. These in turn form the preconditions for the 'ball lightning' theory.

Ball lightning has been offered as one possible culprit for Mrs Reeser's demise. And hers is not the only case. According to an article in *Fate* (April 1961) by the Reverend Winogene Savage, a friend's brother awoke one morning to his wife's screams. Rushing to their living room he found her on the floor, ablaze, with a strange fireball hovering over her blackened form. With the help of neighbours and several buckets of water the flames were put out; but the lady later died, and her husband suffered burns from his ministrations. Witnesses noted that although the wife's clothes had been burnt off, there was no scorching on the rug where she had collapsed, and no other sign of fire damage in the room.

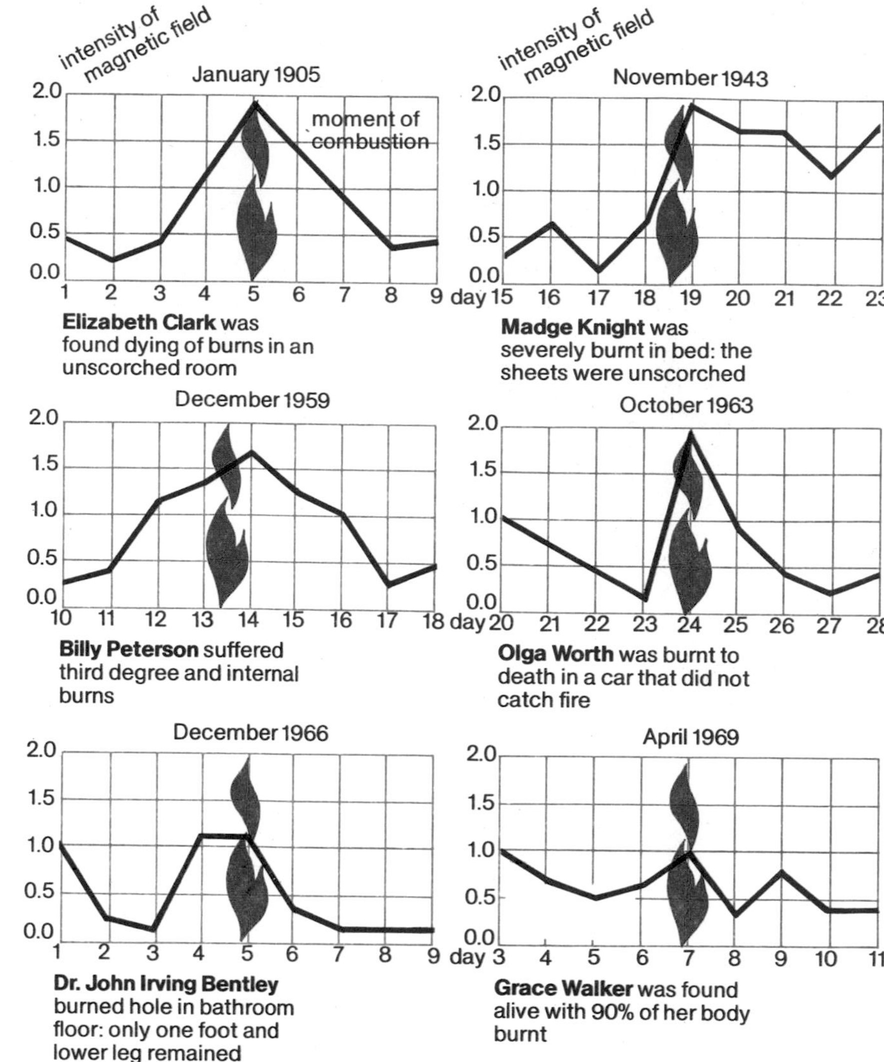

Death from natural causes

Maxwell Cade and Delphine Davis include this account in their 1969 study of ball lightning, *Taming of the thunderbolts*, and note its similarity to the records of spontaneous human combustion. They review the theories of several physicists who suggest that the huge energies of ball lightning could, in certain circumstances, manifest short radio waves of the kind used in microwave ovens. And they speculate:

> If this theory is correct . . . it is possible for victims to be burned to death, not merely within their clothes, but even within their skin, either by the proximity of a lightning ball or by having a ball form within their body, or just by the action of the intense radio-frequency field which, in the absence of their body, would have formed a lightning ball at that place.

As it is a natural phenomenon, and because ball lightning is notoriously capricious, it is the best candidate so far for the cause of SHC cases, whether ancient or modern. It would also account for the victims being fried from the inside out. Microwave diathermy can heat different materials at different rates, and this may explain the curious phenomenon of selective burning that is associated with SHC.

Not one of these theories can account by itself for the bizarre varieties of burning that have been authoritatively recorded. The fact that SHC occurs infrequently (if not so rarely as some writers claim) also suggests that it requires special circumstances to come about, and depends on the correct conjunction of many necessary factors. Some we can guess at; others remain unknown. But we can at least offer the following synthesis.

Age and sex seem less important than the victim's psychic and physiological state. We may imagine a lonely, sedentary person, incapacitated by illness or injury, or psychically by despair, fear, depression and perhaps resentment. This incapacity may psychosomatically affect the body and its metabolism, causing an imbalance of phosphagens and erratic behaviour in the body's heat-regulating mechanisms. Normally, this state would pass unnoticed. But imagine that it should happen a few days after intense sunspot activity, with a magnetic storm pushing up the value of the geomagnetic field to abnormal heights for the victim's locality. Now all that is needed is a trigger: a cosmic ray, a natural burst of low-frequency energy, or a lightning ball. And then we have a human bonfire.

The force of the Earth's magnetism is surprisingly uneven. It is unequally distributed around the globe, and fluctuates in intensity (measured in gausses). These six charts show the curious relationship between a high reading on the geomagnetic scale and the incidence of SHC

When fish pour down l

For centuries there have been incidents of fish falling from the sky, the latest as recently as 1975. BOB RICKARD discusses this strange phenomenon, one of the least explicable quirks of nature

ON 16 FEBRUARY 1861 a violent earthquake shook the island of Singapore. For the following six days, rain fell in torrents. Then, on the morning of the 22nd, after a last furious downpour, it stopped. François de Castelnau, a French naturalist staying on the island, reported what happened next to the Academy of Sciences in Paris, later that year.

> At 10 a.m. the sun lifted, and from my window I saw a large number of Malays and Chinese filling baskets with fishes which they picked up in the pools of water which covered the ground. On being asked where the fishes came from they answered that they had fallen from the sky. Three days afterwards, when the pools had dried up, we found many dead fishes.

Although de Castelnau did not see the rain of fish himself, he was convinced that they had fallen from the sky. Dr A. D. Bajkov, an American marine scientist, was luckier. On 23 October 1947 he was having breakfast with his wife in a café in Marksville, Louisiana, USA, when shortly after a sudden shower of rain, he noticed fish lying in the streets: 'sunfish, goggle-eyed minnows and black bass up to 9 inches [23 centimetres] long.' More fish were found on rooftops, cold

Right: despite the fact that the phenomenon of fish falling from the sky has been the subject of discussion and eyewitness reports for centuries, no 'natural' explanation has yet been found. This illustration of falling fish comes from a book by Claus Magnus, *Historia de gentibus septentrionalibus* (1555), in which the author discusses falls of fish, frogs and other animals

Far right: one of the most reliably recorded incidents in Britain involved a timber yard worker, John Lewis, of Mountain Ash, Glamorganshire. On 9 February 1859 he was hit by falling fish, as illustrated in Charles Tomlinson's *Raincloud and snowstorm* (1864)

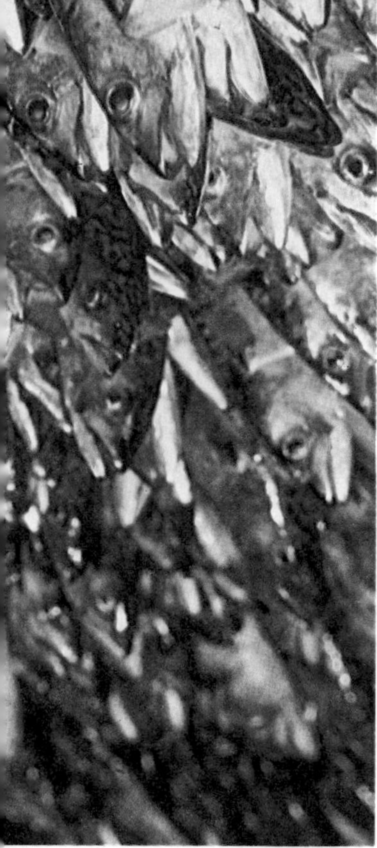

ke rain

and dead, but nevertheless still fit to eat.

On their own, such accounts are not much to go on. Much of the evidence for fish falling from the sky is circumstantial – fish being found, usually after heavy rain, in places and on surfaces where no fish were before. But there are some eyewitness accounts.

One of the best attested cases to have occurred in Britain was at Mountain Ash, Glamorganshire, Wales, in 1859. In a paper published in the *Fortean Times* of Autumn 1979, Robert Schadwald established on the evidence of eyewitness accounts published at the time that it had happened on 9 February 1859. John Lewis, working in a timber yard at Mountain Ash, was startled at 11 a.m. by being suddenly struck by small objects falling out of the sky. One of the objects fell down the back of his neck.

> On putting my hand down my neck I was surprised to find they were small fish. By this time I saw that the whole ground was covered with them. I took off my hat, the brim of which was full of them. They were jumping all about . . . The shed [pointing to a large workshop] was covered with them, and the shoots were quite full of them. My mates and I might have gathered bucketsful of them, scraping with our hands . . . There were two showers . . . It was not blowing very hard, but uncommon wet . . . They came down in the rain in 'a body like'.

A similar experience happened some 85 years later to Ron Spencer of Lancashire, while serving with the RAF at Kamilla, India, near the Burmese border. Speaking on BBC Radio 4 in April 1975, after another listener had described his experience of a fish fall, Ron said that he had loved going out into the monsoon rains to wash himself. On one occasion he was standing naked in the middle of this ritual when

> Things started to hit me, and looking round, I could see myriads of small wriggling shapes on the ground and thousands being swept off the roofs, along channels and into the paddy fields. They were small sardine-sized fish. Needless to say, very shortly after the heavy storm none were left. Scavengers had gobbled them up.

No one has yet discovered how often fish falls occur. The records are widely scattered and there is not a full study available that has collected *all* known cases. But it seems that only falls of frogs and toads are more abundant. For example, Dr E. W. Gudger, of the US Museum of Natural History, collected accounts for 40 years, and found only 78 reports spanning 2350 years. Seventeen of these occurred in the USA; 13 in India; 11 in Germany; 9 in Scotland; 7 in Australia; and 5 in England and Canada. But Gilbert Whitley, working from the records in the Australian Museum, lists over 50 fish falls in Australasia alone between 1879 and 1971.

One of the earliest references to a fish fall is to be found in the ancient Greek text the *Deipnosophistai*, compiled at the end of the second century AD by Athenaeus. These fragments, drawn from the records of nearly 800 writers, contain the report:

> I know also that it rained fishes. At all events Phoenias, in the second book of his *Eresian magistrates*, says that in the Chersonesus it once rained fishes uninterruptedly for three days and Phylarchus in his fourth book says that the people had often seen it raining fish.

The earliest known case in England happened in Kent in 1666, and was reported in the *Philosophical Transactions* of 1698.

But despite the wealth of authenticated and reliable reports that fish falls have occurred, no one has yet produced a convincing account of *why* they happen. One of the most plausible explanations is that they are caused by tornadoes, waterspouts or whirlwinds lifting water containing fish high up into a cloud mass and carrying them inland.

Other explanations include the suggestion that the phenomenon is caused by fish 'migrating overland'; that fish-eating birds regurgitate or drop their food; that fish are left behind by ponds and streams overflowing; and that fish hibernating in mud are brought to life again by rain. But these do not account for the variety of eyewitness reports, the assortment of species found in the same place, the variety of terrain where fish have been found and the sheer number of fish involved in some cases. And even though there are well-documented cases of whirlwinds and waterspouts transporting fish, this explanation is inadequate to cover *all* cases.

Whirlwinds, tornadoes and waterspouts are very messy. They tend to pick up anything in their way and scatter it in every direction. This conflicts dramatically with the great majority of cases of fish falls. In the

Above: one popular theory as to how fish could be transported overland and then 'dropped' from the sky is that water containing quantities of fish is gathered up by tornadoes. This tornado was photographed in Nebraska

Mountain Ash case, for example, the fall was restricted to an area 80 yards by 12 yards (73 metres by 11 metres). In the Kent case of 1666 it was claimed that the fish were dumped in one particular field and not in any of the surrounding ones. Most falls, in fact, seem to follow this localised pattern. Perhaps the most extreme example of this orderly fall of fish took place south of Calcutta on 20 September 1839. An eyewitness said: 'The most strange thing which ever struck me was that the fish did not fall helter-skelter . . . but in a straight line not more than one cubit [an ancient measurement deriving from the length of the forearm] in breadth.'

Whirlwinds move continuously. There is considerable evidence that fish falls have lasted much longer than the time possible for them to have been caused by a whirlwind. The torrent of many hundreds of sand eels on Hendon, a suburb of Sunderland, north-east England, on 24 August 1918 is a case in point. A. Meek, a marine biologist, reported seeing a fall, that lasted a full 10 minutes and was confined to one small area.

Even if whirlwinds do retrace their path, some fish falls have occurred in such a rapid succession that they could not have been caused by one whirlwind. John Lewis of Mountain Ash, for example, witnessed 'two showers, with an interval of ten minutes [between them] and each shower lasted about two minutes, or thereabouts.'

The length of time during which fish have been transported through the air seems, according to the evidence, to vary considerably. In many accounts, the fish are alive and thrashing when found on the ground; in other cases they have been found dead, but fresh and edible. It is difficult to believe that fish could be hurled against the ground and not be killed, but the evidence suggests that even those found dead were not killed by their fall. In his *History of Ceylon*, Sir James Tennant describes fish that were not injured by their fall onto gravel.

More puzzling still are the falls of dead fish. On two occasions in India, at Futtepoor in 1833 and at Allahabad in 1836, the fish that fell from the sky were not only dead, but dried. In the former case, the number of fish that fell was estimated to be between 3000 and 4000, all of one species. It is difficult to imagine how a whirlwind could keep so many fish in the air long enough for them to have dried out. But, despite widespread publicity in the Indian press at the time, no one came forward to report that a whirlwind *had* snatched up a valuable heap of dried fish! Perhaps even more extraordinary is the case from Essen, Germany, in 1896, where a Crucian carp fell out of the sky during a storm, encased in ice. Here, the fish must have been kept aloft by vertical currents long enough to become the nucleus of an egg-sized hailstone.

Sticklebacks from the sky

In the falls of other animals and insects there is a tendency for only one species to descend at any one time. But the evidence available concerning fish falls shows that they can be equally divided between falls of a single species and mixed falls. Up to six different species have been identified in a single fall, lending support to the idea that the phenomenon is caused by a waterspout scooping randomly from seas and lakes.

Falls of single species present many problems. The Mountain Ash fall in Glamorganshire, for example, was found to contain mostly sticklebacks with just a few minnows. Sticklebacks live in freshwater streams and do not congregate in shoals. How was it possible for a whirlwind to have scooped out such a vast quantity of sticklebacks together from a single source and deposit them all in one place? Similar questions apply to other cases of fish falls involving just one species. Another curious feature is the absence of all accompanying debris.

Objects caught up in the currents of a whirlwind might be expected to be hurled out at different times and distances according to their mass, size or shape. Contrary to this expectation, however, fish falls often involve many different sizes of fish. At Feridpoor,

India, for example, two species of fish fell in 1830, one larger and heavier than the other. Similarly, fish ranging in length from 6 to 12 inches (15 to 30 centimetres) fell in several gardens in Harlow, Essex, on 12 August 1968, according to next day's newspapers.

Charles Fort, who spent a lifetime collecting accounts of strange phenomena, suggested that fish falls are the result of what he called 'teleportation', a force that can transport objects from place to place without traversing the intervening distance. Such a force, Fort claimed, was once more active than it is now, and survives today as an erratic and feeble semblance of its former self. Through this agency fish are snatched away from a place of abundance to a point in the sky, from which they fall. Sometimes this point is not very high off the ground, which would account for the fact that the fish are often found alive. At other times the point is *very* close to the ground, accounting for the many observations of fish that seem to have appeared on the ground during a rainstorm.

Fort further suggested that fish falls might be the result of a new pond 'vibrating with its need for fish'. There is the case of Major Cox, for example, a well–known writer in England after the First World War. In an article published in the *Daily Mail* on 6 October 1921, Cox reported that the pond at his Sussex home had been drained and scraped of mud. The pond was then left dry for five months before refilling with water in November 1920. The following May, Cox was astonished to find it teeming with tench.

In 1941 the *American Journal of Science* published a story of a farm in Cambridge, Maryland, USA, where work on a new system of drains was halted because of rain. When work resumed, the ditch was found to be full of rainwater and hundreds of perch, of two different species, measuring between 4 and 7 inches (10 to 18 centimetres).

In neither case, however, was there time for aestivation. Overflows and migrating fish were ruled out because of the distance of both sites from any surrounding water. Fort also ruled out the possibility that the fish fell from the sky since they were found only in the new water. If they had fallen from the sky one would expect there to be some dead fish lying around. But none was found.

Most fish falls occur during heavy rains, so the whirlwind theory seems to be partially acceptable. A look at the range of reported cases, however, shows that a number of falls have occurred in cloudless skies and quite independently of any accompanying strong wind. But if teleportation seems too far-fetched – and it is difficult to believe that fish can disappear from one place and reappear in mid-air – what other explanation is there? At present the only rational explanation in terms of known causes seems to be the whirlwind theory. But this, as we have seen, cannot account for all cases. The fish fall remains one of the oddest, and least explicable, quirks of nature – if, indeed, it *is* nature, as we understand it, at work here.

Left: another drawing from Claus Magnus' *Historia de gentibus septentrionalibus* (1555) showing fish falling from the sky onto a town

Below: this woodcut showing a man struggling through a torrential shower of rain and fish was based on an 18th century incident in Transylvania

The great escape

When his parachute went up in flames 18,000 feet above Berlin, Flight Sergeant Nicholas Alkemade decided to jump rather than burn to death. The miracle was, as BEALE McIVER reveals, that he survived to tell the tale

FLIGHT SERGEANT Nicholas Alkemade was a little nervous at the thought that this was to be his thirteenth bombing mission over Germany. Just 21 years old, he had the loneliest, most dangerous job in RAF Bomber Command: tail-gunner in a Lancaster. Still, he and the crew of *S for Sugar* had survived so far.

Besides the danger, being tail-gunner in a Lancaster was uncomfortable. There was room enough in that tiny perspex bubble for the gunner, his ammunition and four Browning machine guns. And that was all. Even the parachute had to be stowed outside the turret. At 20,000 feet (6000 metres) it could get very cold indeed – and 24 March 1944 was a chilly spring night.

Little bothered the flight from 115 Squadron as they droned over the German mainland. A little flak above Frankfurt, then Berlin – already lit up by Pathfinder flares and the sharp beams of searchlights trying to ensnare the 300 Allied bombers that had come to pound the beleaguered enemy capital that night. At last, Alkemade heard the magic words: 'Bombs away!' Two tonnes of high explosive and nearly three of incendiaries dropped away. At once the pilot, Jack Newman, turned the big plane toward home and safety.

There was one massive explosion. Then cannon shells tearing down the fuselage towards Alkemade. Two ripped through his turret, shattering the perspex. Splinters dug into him. Then he saw the attacker: a lone Junkers 88, closing in now to finish off the wounded bomber. Alkemade aimed and fired, his tracer arcing toward the enemy, now only 50 yards (45 metres) distant. The Junker's port engine exploded and it dipped away, doomed. Alkemade was elated.

Top left: an Avro Lancaster bomber. Capable in some versions of carrying 10 tonnes of bombs, it was used against German industry as well as in incendiary raids on enemy cities – like the one Sgt Alkemade flew in March 1944

Top right: the versatile Junkers 88 was adapted to many combat roles. A night fighter version crippled Alkemade's *S for Sugar* – and brought about a miracle

Above: Nicholas Alkemade, alive and well despite several close encounters with death

Not for long. Flames were already leaping past the remains of his turret. In a moment Jack Newman's voice came over the intercom: 'You'll have to jump for it. Bail out. Bail out.' Unfortunately, that, for Alkemade, meant retrieving his parachute from its rack behind him – somewhere amid those tongues of fire. He shoved open the doors into the fuselage momentarily and gaped at the blaze within. But this was his only hope. He tried again, spotted the parachute – then watched in horror as it disintegrated in flames.

'My stomach seemed to drop out of my body,' he said. 'I now knew that I was going to die. I said to myself, "You've had your lot."'

But not, he decided, by being burnt to death. 'Better a quick, clean death than frying.' Nicholas Alkemade was going to jump. Tearing off his already melting oxygen mask, he managed to manoeuvre the turret so that the hole faced toward the rear again. Then he somersaulted backwards into space.

Sheer relief at once replaced the terror. Alkemade felt perfectly calm. As he later put it: 'It was perfectly quiet and cool, like resting on a cloud . . . as though I was lowered onto a super-soft mattress. There was no sensation of falling. . . . I thought, well, if this is dying, it's not so bad.'

Indeed he felt so peaceful that he was able to calculate that from 18,000 feet (5500 metres) it would take him 90 seconds to hit the ground. And he had been looking forward to his next leave in a week's time. Now he wouldn't be seeing his girlfriend Pearl. Lying on his back in the air, he gazed at the

stars and thought how foolish Man's struggles seemed. Then he passed out.

Alkemade couldn't understand why he felt so cold. He was supposed to be dead. He opened an eye. A star shone through the fir trees above him. He dug out his cigarette case and lighter, suddenly desperate for a smoke, then checked the time. It was 3.10 a.m. and he had been unconscious for three hours. 'Jesus Christ,' he said out loud. 'I'm alive.'

Somehow, the trees had broken his fall. Eighteen inches (45 centimetres) of snow made a final cushion. He had dropped over 3 miles (5 kilometres) out of the sky and lived to tell the tale. Not only that – he was hardly damaged at all. Some burns, a badly twisted right knee, but everything else seemed to work. He couldn't walk, and then began to worry about exposure. 'The prospect of being a POW didn't seem so bad. I wanted to be found.'

Members of the local *Volkssturm* heard the blasts from his regulation whistle, and found him still smoking his cigarette. When they picked him up he fainted. And then the problems began.

He was taken to hospital, and tried to explain what had happened to a doctor. 'Nix parachute,' he announced. The doctor smiled mirthlessly and tapped his head gently. Obviously Alkemade was mad. At Dalag Luft POW camp near Frankfurt it was no better. Alkemade suffered three interrogations and solitary confinement for sticking to his unbelievable story. He was clearly lying, and just as clearly he was really a spy.

But Alkemade heard that a Lancaster had been reported crashing on the night of 24 March near where he was found. Perhaps it was *S for Sugar*. And perhaps the remains of his parachute could be found in the wreck. Leutnant Hans Feidal of the Luftwaffe was eventually persuaded to look into the story. Sure enough, the harness of the tail-gunner's parachute was there, and was brought back. Alkemade tried it on. The snaphooks and lift webbing were still tied down with thread – and would have broken had the parachute been opened. Then the Germans found the scorched handle of the ripcord in the wreckage. The camp commandant could only pronounce Alkemade's escape a miracle.

His fellow prisoners later presented him with the flyleaf of a Bible. On it was written:

> DALAG LUFT
> It has been investigated and corroborated by the German authorities that the claim made by Sergeant Alkemade 1431537 RAF, is true in all respects, namely that he made a descent from 18,000 feet without parachute and made a safe landing without injury, his parachute having been on fire in the aircraft. He landed in deep snow among fir trees.
> Corroboration witnessed by:
> Flt Lt H.J. Moore, Senior British Officer.
> Flt Sgt R.R. Lamb 1339582.
> Flt Sgt T.A. Jones 411 Senior British NCO. Date 25.4.44.

Nicholas Alkemade survived his thirteenth bombing mission, against all the odds. And he continued to live a charmed life. He worked in a chemical factory in his home town of Loughborough after the war. Once a 224-pound (100-kilogram) steel girder fell on him. He was hauled out for dead, but walked away with a bruised scalp. On another occasion he was drenched with sulphuric acid. He had an electric shock that threw him into a hole where he lay breathing chlorine gas for a quarter of an hour, and lived to tell that tale as well. Someone, somewhere, is looking after Nicholas Alkemade.

Below: the cramped quarters of a Lancaster's tail gun bubble. A rear gunner was known in the RAF as 'arse-end Charlie' – an attempt at humour that failed to disguise the high mortality rate that went with the job

Below right: the airman's view of an incendiary raid on a sleeping German city. These attacks were intended to demoralise the civilian population. Though very destructive, they failed in their psychological objective

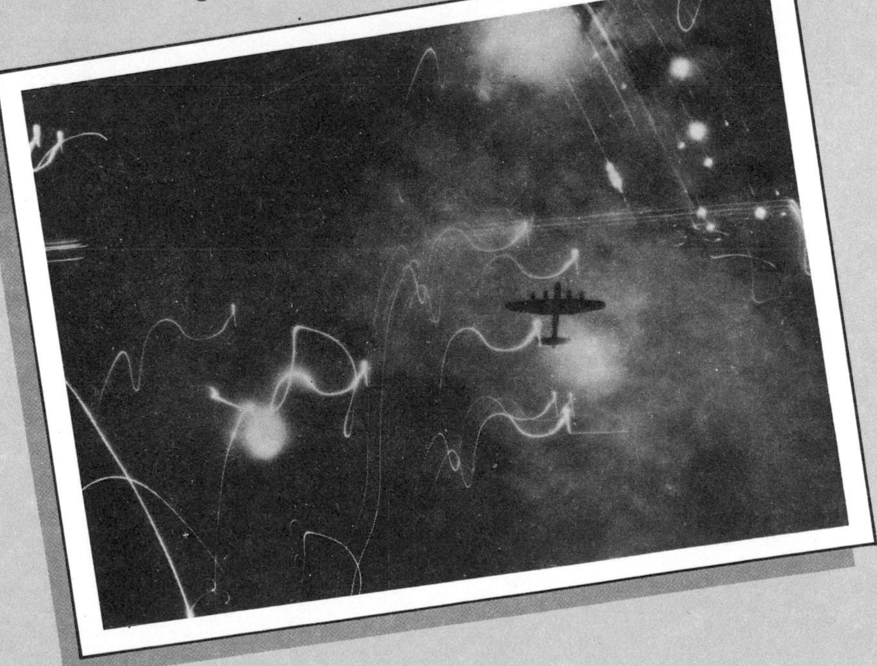

Index

Page numbers for illustrations are given in italic